INDIANA SOURCE BOOK

Genealogical Material from THE HOOSIER GENEALOGIST, 1973-1979

Volume Three

**Edited by
Willard Heiss**

The Family History Section

**Indiana Historical Society
1982**

**315 West Ohio Street
Indianapolis, Indiana 46202**

PREFACE

This volume completes the projected trilogy of the best from *The Hoosier Genealogist*. Indiana vital records and other valued genealogical data have been culled form eighteen years of publication. Queries, announcements, and other items of a transient nature have not been reproduced.

The Hoosier Genealogist is nationally recognized for the dissemination of original source material. This is the result of first-rate editors: Alameda McCollough, Nell Reeser, and Dorothy Riker. During her many years of service Dorothy Riker has "made this a quarterly of paragon importance..." Rebah M. Fraustein is presently the editor and is carrying forward the same standards set by predecessors.

As these lines are typed, the monumental task to compile an every-name index for these three volumes has begun. It is estimated that there will be 168,000 to 175,000 names in this index.

I must say that it is with some satisfaction that I lay this torch aside and hope that years hence it will be picked up to begin another series of "source books."

-W.H.

CONTENTS
County Records

General Records

Family Records

TWO LETTERS CONCERNING THE BOONE FAMILY

Typed copies of the two following letters concerning one branch of the Boone family were sent to Willard Heiss, chairman of the Indiana Historical Society's Genealogy Committee, by way of the *Tri-State Trader*, by Jesse H. Boone of East Moline, Illinois, with permission to publish them. The original letters are in the possession of a relative of Mr. Boone. They were written in 1858 by Andrew J. Boone, of Lebanon, Indiana, to Nathan R. Boone, grandfather of Jesse H. Boone, living in Illinois. Andrew and Nathan had a common grandfather, Daniel Boone. The information given by the writer of the letters does not entirely agree with that given in the sketch of Andrew J. Boone which appears in Crist's *History of Boone County*, nor does it agree with an article on Nelson Boon(e) which appeared in the centennial edition of the Richmond *Palladium*, January 1, 1931.

The original wording of the letters has been preserved, but punctuation and paragraphs have been used for the sake of readability. Ellipses indicate the omission of portions that were not pertinent. Information supplied by Jesse H. Boone or by the editor is in brackets.

Andrew J. Boone, Lebanon, Indiana, to Nathan R. Boone, April 12, 1858.

Yours of last month come to hand short time since & I have delayed an answer until now having been engaged in court most of the time since I received your letter. . . .

We have had a very moderate winter for the most part & grass and other crops are as much or more advanced now than they were on the first of May last year. The waters are now very high here and still raining. Stock is very low & money scarce. I am trying to start a little farm east of town & want 40 or 50 head of cattle to put on it. Have bought some for less than half what they would have sold for a year ago, cows $10 & 12, yearlings 5 & 6$, corn 25 cents per bushel, wheat 50 cents, flour $4 per barrel.

I am not able to give you a very definite history of our family but will do the best I can. Your grandfather Daniel Boon knew but little about the history beyond himself. He wrote the name Boon but it should be Boone. Our grandfather Daniel Boone was the son of Jacob Boone, who from the best information I can get was brother to Daniel Boone who first settled Kentucky. Jacob Boone was killed by the Indians when grandfather was small and he had no recollection of his father but recollects having seen his mother, who died a short time, probably a year after the father was killed. The children, Daniel, John, one other brother and a sister whose names I do not now recollect, were raised by their mother's people, some ninety miles from where the Boones lived in North Carolina. Daniel married a woman by the name of Fall and moved to Kentucky in 1790 and then to Ohio in 1795, crossing the Ohio at Cincinnati and settling in the territory which afterward became Preble County. There he lived until 1848 when he moved to Boone County, Indiana, where he lived until 1854 when he moved to Buchanan County, Iowa, where he died in 1856. [Daniel was age 75 in 1850, so he was born about 1775]. Daniel's wife, our grandmother I believe died in 1838 in Preble County, Ohio. The children by this marriage are as follows:

Benjamin, now living in Boone County, Indiana;

Charity, married William Shisher and died in Ohio;

George, died in Iowa;

William D., died in Iowa 1856;

Lewis, your father [married Julia Ann Page in 1824 in Preble Co., Ohio; settled in McHenry Co., Ill., in 1837. Nathan, their first child, born in Dayton in 1826 ;]

John, now in Iowa;

Elizabeth, married ——Witt and died in Boone County, 1857;

Nelson, died at Centerville, Indiana 1834;

Martin F., now in Iowa.

Nelson Boone was a printer, a man of some learning and literary taste and was generally respected for his manner and skill in his profession. The others were all respectable farmers and mechanics.

My father, Benjamin Boone, married Charlotte Poyner in Preble County, Ohio, in 1819. The children of this marriage were: myself, [Andrew J.], born 17 July 1820 Preble County, Ohio; Wilson T., born 1821 Ohio, died near Knoxville, Tenn., 6 Dec. 1854; Daniel F., born 1823 Ohio, died 1834 in Rush County, Ind.; Elizabeth, born 1825 Ohio and now living in Boone County, and single; Nancy P., born 1826 in Indiana and died in Boone County in 1855; Michael O., born 1828 Indiana and died in Boone County in 1854; Julia A., born 1831 and died 1834 in Rush County; Mary A., married and living in Thorntown; Sarah, born Rush County 1838, married and living in Boone County. . . . None of the two families I have enumerated have, with the exception of myself and Wilson Boone, engaged in any of the business professions. He chose Medicine and was a respectable practicing physician for some years before his death. I chose the law. . . .

Andrew J. Boone, Lebanon, to Nathan R. Boone, November 6, 1858.

In turning some papers in a file in my desk this evening, I turned up a letter written last April in answer to yours of that month, which I thought had been forwarded long ago. I see that you desired a history of our family as far as I could give it. I do not know that any of the older ones ever held public office, except a military office. Grandfather was captain of the militia in Preble County, Ohio, before and after the War of 1812 but was not in the service in that war. Your Uncle Ben was a representative in the Indiana legislature from Rush County, 1837-38, and from Boone County, 1843-44. I do not know that any of of the other brothers ever held public stations of any notoriety. They all began in the world with little or no property, but by industry acquired a competence and a few became wealthy. They were universally companionable and would generally be classed as clever, fond of jokes, wit, and occasionally a little mischievous. A few of them were mimics of sharp cost and could turn in fine style many characters bordering on the ridiculous. They were ingenious in the use of tools, inventive and full of expedients. While young your father was regarded as a very stout man and a good mechanic. Some of the men were under 5 feet 10 inches tall, bony and straight, fond of active sports and rather inclined to travel.

Your Uncle Nelson, my brothers Wilson and Michael, and myself were perhaps the most inclined to literary habits so far as my knowledge goes. The former when a boy spent much of his idle time in reading books and after he went into the printing business was considered a fair newspaper writer, was easy in company, and conversed readily and intelligently on subjects generally. During his life he established two newspapers [the Richmond *Palladium* and Centerville *Western Times*] and had purchased a third just before he died. He left a widow and one child, Arminta; the latter has grown up and is now married and living in Preble County, Ohio. [According to Preble County marriage records, Nelson Boone married Phebe Morgan and after his death she married Henry H. Carr.]

So far as our own experience goes we have found that much of this life is doomed to disappointment, and those cares and losses which wear away our frames, shatter the mind, and destroy the energy of our race are sure to come sooner or later. My father in my youth had much property and carried on a heavy business for a number of years; the family, or at least that portion approaching manhood, very naturally expected a reasonable outfit on arriving at age. But we were in that as in other things doomed to disappointment. In 1840 he broke and we gave up our little property to assist in paying debts. Property sold under the hammer at less than one third its actual cost to us. Having a more distinct recollection of my own outfit, I can state this with certainty: it consisted of fifty cents in money, some clothes, one hat, and a pair of boots. Having the misfortune to get my ankle out of place, I could wear but one of the boots. I spent the money for a certificate from the school examiners to teach a country school. This business I pursued with satisfaction to my patrons at the same house for the space of six months for which I received the sum of $90. I was then elected Auditor of Boone County and came to Lebanon to live the 22d of August 1841. I filled that station two years and one quarter, and read law and history at nights and Sundays as I could only walk on crutches. . . . Before I came to this town I procured books at the county library which I carried home seven miles and read at idle times; this I managed to keep up without in any way interfering with my daily business, even during the time I was teaching.

On the 6th of December 1843, I resigned the office of auditor with a determination to go to college, for the purpose of adding to my small fund of knowledge. . . . Another cause of my resignation was that the legislature had reduced my salary to $150 a year, which I deemed too poor pay for my services. . . . I went to the University at Bloomington where I remained two years and having spent all my money was compelled to quit and turn my attention to some business to recruit my means. Teaching was considered the most proper and being offered $20 per month at the seminary at Leavenworth [Kansas], I repaired there and pursued that avocation with success, pursuing at the same time my classic studies; I was afterwards employed at $50 per month in the county clerk's office.

My health becoming poor I returned to Boone County and taught in country and town for near two years; I then commenced acting as the deputy in various county offices, having pursued the study of law ever since I left college. In 1848 I spent most of my time in the study of law and in 1849 part of my time. In 1849-50 I served as clerk of the House of Representatives for which I received $4.00 per day. I again served in that office in 1850-51 and in 1852, while still devoting time to the law. By this time I was able to put out my shingle and since 1852 have steadily pursued the practice of law. In April 1851 I married [Mary Eliza McLaughlin]. . . .

More than once I spent the last red cent on hand in board and lodging while attending school or pursuing my studies. At other times I have made money rapidly but my business and associations compelled me to spend it rapidly. I boarded for twelve years in succession at all prices from 65 cents per week to $1.50 per day. I have some acquaintance with all the public and business men of the state and drank deep in public life for one of my age and circumstances and have learned that he who serves the public must, if he does

his duty, to some extent neglect his own affairs, neglect his children, and become a kind of lackey for every one to order about. You must attend personally, no odds how unwell you are, nor what condition your family or friends are in, you must be present in court or in your office.

If you have boys raise them to be farmers or mechanics, give them fair common education if possible and train them to habits of industry and honesty, and you will have prepared them for more independence, more happiness, and longer lives, than is allotted to active men in this profession. Drones anywhere are of no use except when there is an over crop of vegetation; there influence is bad and they disgrace any business or profession they engage in unless it is to whittle store boxes or some fancy work of that kind. .

The season here has been over wet and the wheat and corn crop almost a failure. It is now raining and disagreeable and I am informed that corn is rotting considerably on the stalk. I have some 40 or 50 head of cattle to winter but shall expect them to live on hay principally; the same with my neighbors. Jacob Witt was in the office this afternoon, said they were all well. We are tolerably, only our youngest now 3 months old is not well; Frank goes to school and Wilson does about as he pleases; is sometimes at the office and sometimes at home. I had a letter a few days ago from our cousin Florrida Boone [the remainder of the letter lost] . [Andrew J. Boone died in 1875.]

JOHNSON COUNTY WILLS, 1827-1845

Compiled from microfilm of Johnson County Will Records, Vol. A, 1857-1851, in Genealogy Division, Indiana State Library.

ABLE, JOHN. Will dated Aug. 22, 1844; probated Aug. 31, 1844. Heirs: widow, 2 infant children, and son, William D. Executor: Elijah Harrell. Witnesses: Josiah H. Bass, Garrett Brewer, Berry Carder, Will Record A, pp. 84-86.

ALEXANDER, THOMAS. Will dated Sep. 9, 1834; probated Oct. 7, 1834. Heirs: wife, Mary; sons, Stephen, Joseph, John, and others (names not given). Executor: sons Stephen and Joseph. Witnesses: Thomas Henderson, William Magill. pp. 26-27.

BANTA, PETER D. Will dated Aug. 24, 1844; probated Sep. 25, 1844. Heirs: wife, Joanna, and children (names not given). Executor: John and Peter Vorris. Witnesses: Thomas Henderson, John Terhune. pp. 89-91.

BARNES, THOMAS. Will dated May 5, 1832; probated Aug. 14, 1832. Heirs: wife, Jane; sons, Eaton, Jesse, Turner. Executors: wife, son Eaton, son-in-law John Decoursey. Witnesses: James G. Crocker, Samuel Fleaner. pp. 15-16.

BARNETT, JOHN, SR. Will dated Oct. 2, 1827; codicil added July 3, 1828. Probated Oct. 20, 1828. Heirs: wife, Elizabeth; children, James, William, Spencer, George, Lucy Townsend, Thomas, John, Jr., Ambrose, Elizabeth Ahn Records. Executor: son, William. Witnesses: William G. Springer, William Shaffer, James Fite. pp. 4-5.

BOWLING, ELIJAH. Will dated Apr. 23, 1836; probated June 3, 1836. Heirs: wife, Lucy. Executor: wife. Witnesses: Hiram T. Craig, Benet Jacobs. p. 36.

BRYCE, WILLIAM. Will dated March 31, 1832; probated May 14, 1832. Heirs: wife, Hannah; children, William, Samuel, Cyrena Bryce. Mentions his saddler's shop. Wants executors to erect comfortable home on lot 34 in Franklin for wife and children. Executors: George W. King, John Herriott. Witnesses: William G. Shilledy, William Shaffer. pp. 13-15.

CAMPBELL, JOHN. Will dated April 25, 1829; probated Sep. 8, 1829. Heirs: wife, Ruth; children, Daniel (oldest son) and others, names not given; to Moses Threlkeld, the two lots he now occupies. Executors: wife and son, Daniel. Witnesses: John Lewis, Hiram Smith. pp. 8-9.

CARROL, BARTHOLOMEW. Will dated Jan. 13, 1825; probated March 18, 1828. Heirs: wife, Katharine, and children (names not given). Executor: wife. Witnesses: Thomas Jones, John Carrol, Thomas Davis. pp. 2-3.

CHRISTIAN, WILLIAM. Will dated Oct. 26, 1838; probated Nov. 12, 1838. Heirs: wife, Prudence; Nathaniel Poor's son William; Nancy Wirick, daughter of William Poor; Nathaniel Poor to have one half of the estate due from brother Benjamin's estate. Executor: Austin Jacobs. Witnesses: Austin Jacobs, Jesse Staton, Martha Poor. pp. 44-45.

CLARK, ELISHA. Will dated Feb. 25, 1842; probate record not found. Heirs: son, William M., children of son Allen W.; children of daughter, Minty Figg, deceased. Executor: son Allen W. Witnesses: Asa B. Nay, J. R. Callahan, Henry Branch. p. 78.

CLEM, ADAM. Will dated July 12, 1841; probated July 27, 1844. Heirs: wife, Nancy; daughters, America, Martha, Elizabeth; sons, James, Henry, Julian (?), Thomas. Executor: Allen D. Graham. Witnesses: William and Isaac Clem. pp. 80-82.

COX, ROBERTSON, of White River Twp. Will dated Sep. 19, 1839; probated Oct. 26, 1839. Heirs: wife, Nancy; William and Samuel Cox (relationship not given). Witnesses: Henry Conner, John Surface, Jr. pp. 46-47.

EDDY, WILLIAM. Will dated Aug. 10, 1833; probated Nov. 11, 1833. Heirs: wife, Jane; sons, Gideon, Alexander, James, William, Hiram, Preston; daughters, Malinda Blake, Julia McBride; grandchildren, William Blake, Retta Jane Mc Bride. Executors: Col. John Wishard, son Alexander. Witnesses: Robert C. Wishard, Archibald Glenn. pp. 22-23.

GODSON, DECIMUS. Will dated Dec. 4, 1835; probated Dec. 21, 1835. Heirs: Drury Abbot, Nathaniel Wilson. Owned land in Hamilton Co., Ind. Witnesses: Pierson Murphy, Nicholas C. Shaffer. pp. 33-34.

GROSECLOSE, JOHN. Will dated Sep. 25, 1837; probate record not found. Heirs: wife, Sarah; children, Peter, Jeremiah (?), Sarah, John, Jacob, Katharine, Elizabeth, William, Molly. Executors: William Smith, Thomas Lowe. Witnesses: Abraham Lowe, William Byram, George Cakely (?). pp. 42-43.

HAMNER, JOHN. Will dated Aug. 7, 1836; probated Nov. 14, 1836. Heirs: wife, Mary; sons, John and George; daughters, Rebecca, Sally, Elizabeth, Mary; children of daughter, Nancy Noel. Executor: sons, James, John, George. Witnesses: William C. Adams, William Chambers. pp. 38-39.

HARDIN, CATHARINE. Will dated June 5, 1840; probated April 10, 1841. Heirs: sons, Thomas and Benjamin; daughters, Hannah Hardin, Rachel Weddle. Witnesses: William Paddock. pp. 55-56.

HARDIN, ELIHU. Will dated Sep. 2, 1833; probated Nov. 11, 1833. Heirs: mother, and others (relationship not given), Mahlon Seybold, Franklin Hardin, Robert Burns. Owned land in Illinois. Executor: Archibald Glenn. Witnesses: John Todd, Archibald Glenn. pp. 23-24.

HARDIN, ELIZABETH. Will dated Sep. 1, 1833; died that same day. Probated Oct. 6, 1833. Heirs: mother, Catharine Hardin; others (relationship not given), Elizabeth Ann Seybold, Mahlon Seybold, Franklin Hardin, Robert Burns. Witnesses: Tabitha Sanders, Elizabeth Sweney (?). pp. 24-25.

HARGAN, JOHN. Will dated Mar. 14, 1836; probated Apr. 6, 1836. Heirs: wife and son William. Executor: George Hargan, Arthur Robison. Witnesses: Caleb Day, James S. Shields. pp. 34-35.

HINKLEY, A. R. Will dated Sep. 23, 1841; probated Oct. 18, 1841. Heirs: wife, Louisa. Executor: Henry Banta. Witnesses: Robert W. McKinney, William N. Stinson. pp. 62-63.

JAMISON, ALEXANDER. Will dated Aug. 8, 1845; probated Sep. 13, 1845. Heirs: wife, and children, James, Charles, Richard, Ellen, Manda C., Louisy, Lucinda, America Ann, Margaret Jane, Mary Emily, Susan Frances. Executor: Richard Foster. Witnesses: Richardson Hensley, William Coons. pp. 103-105.

JOHNSTON, SAMUEL. Will dated June 24, 1834; probated Aug. 16, 1834 in Marion Co.; 1841 in Johnson Co. Heirs: wife, Susannah and minor children (names not given). Owned land in Marion & Johnson cos. Executors: John G. Brown, Caleb Scudder of Indianapolis. Witnesses: Archibald C. Reed, John Campbell, James Morrison. pp. 64-65.

KEGLEY, CHRISTOPHER. Will dated May 6, 1838; probated May 31, 1838. Heirs: wife, Charlotte, and children (names not given). Executors: James Gillcrease (?) of Morgan Co.; William L. Woolford of Johnson Co. Witnesses: William Dresslar, Christian Kegley. pp. 43-44.

KELLY, HENRY H. Will dated May 15, 1844; probated Aug. 5, 1844. Heirs: brother, Jefferson, "my share of father's estate for taking care of me in my illness"; personal property to be divided between brothers and sisters including children of deceased brother James and Joseph Stewart's wife. Witnesses: Daniel McLean, Samuel Tetrick. pp. 82-83.

KNAPP, JOSHUA. Will dated July 11, 1840; probated Aug. 10, 1840. Heirs: children, Liticia, Milton, Eliza, John, George Washington; Rebecca Ann Dehart (no relative) "one bed and bedding for the respect I have for her." Witnesses: John Knapp, Sylvanus Bills. p. 52.

LOWE, ABSALOM. Will dated Feb. 6, 1827; probated March 5, 1827. Heirs: brothers and sisters, Kesiah Lowe, Elizabeth Groseclose, Tabitha Sanders, Charity Mullinex, Thomas, Abraham, and Jefferson Lowe. Executors: Samuel Herriot, Abraham Lowe. Witnesses: Henry Brown, Peter Doty. pp. 1-2.

LYONS, JOHN. Will dated July 20, 1839; probated April 15, 1842. Died April 11, 1842. Heirs: wife, Elizabeth, and children (names not given except for Mary, the youngest, and Joseph). Witnesses: Thomas J. Todd, John H. McGee. pp. 66-67.

McCASLIN, DAVID W. Will dated June 17, 1830; probated July 9, 1830. Heirs: wife, Jane; son, George Franklin, and unborn child, should it live; $5.00 toward building of Presbyterian meeting house. Executors: wife and Newton McCaslin, George W. King, Hezekiah L. McKinney. Witnesses: Thomas Williams, Hervey McCaslin. pp. 11-12.

McCASLIN, WILLIAM R. Will dated March 1, 1842; probated Aug. 1, 1842. Heirs: wife, Eliza, and children, William S. (youngest), Wesley White, Thomas Ludlow, George, Elizabeth McCaslin. Witnesses: Allen D. Graham, John S. Brown. pp. 68-69.

McCAULLY, ROBERT. Will dated July 13, 1841; probated Sep. 14, 1842. Heirs: wife, Margaret, and daughters, Mariah and Rachel. Executors: Peter and John P. Banta, Samuel VanNuys. Witnesses: Thomas Henderson, Madison J. Alexander. pp. 70-71.

McCOOL, JOHN. Will not dated; probated Oct. 10, 1840. Heirs: wife, Rachel, children of brothers and sisters, $4.00 each. Executors: Robert and Harvey S. Lyons. Witnesses: John and Samuel Alexander, Levi Todd. p. 53.

McGAUGHEY, DAVID R. Will dated Feb. 19, 1845; probated March 14, 1845. Heirs: wife, and children (names not given). Executors: J. B. Dobson, John McGaughey, and wife. Witnesses: Henry McAlpin, David Parr. pp. 92-93.

MAZE, SAMUEL, of Edinburg. Will dated Aug. 4, 1845; probated Sep. 12, 1845. Heir: daughter, Mariah T. Had an interest in Shelby Co. land owned by his mother and had shop in Edinburg. Executor and guardian of Mariah: Alfred C. Thompson. Witnesses: William Irwin, Isaac White. pp. 100-102.

MESSERSMITH, PETER. Will dated Feb. 10, 1837; probated Sep. 2, 1844. Heirs: wife, Doraty; children John, Peter, Anthony, Andrew, Barnabas, George, Catharine Robe, Fanny Grossclose, Margaret Brown, Doraty Byram, Mary Ritcherson (?). Executors: Thomas Lowe, John Grossclose. Witnesses: Abraham Lowe, Thomas Lowe, John Grossclose. pp. 86-89.

MULLINIX, PRIMENTER. Will dated Feb. , 1834; probated Mar. 6, 1834. Died Feb. 15, 1834. Heirs: wife, Charity, and children (names not given). Witnessed by: Robert C. Wishard, Isaac Sutton, Nathaniel St. John on Feb. 8, 1834. pp. 25-26.

NANCE, JAMES. Will dated Aug. 21, 1842; probated Sep. 21, 1842. Heirs: wife, Jane, and children (names not given). Executor: Amos Compton. Witnesses: L. C. Persons, George C. Comstock. pp. 72-73.

PITCHER, WILLIAM, of Nineveh Twp. Will dated Oct. 13, 1831; probated Nov. 18, 1835. Heirs: sons, Morgan, Franklin W., William, Benjamin; daughters, Susannah Swingle, Margaret McAbee (?). Executor: Thomas Lowry (?). Witnesses: Jacob Maxey, Henry Gaines, Edwin J. Beall. pp. 29-30.

PREWIT, SAMUEL. Will dated Aug. 19, 1839; probated Nov. 15, 1839. Heirs: wife, Mary, and at her death property to be equally divided between children, taking into account the fact that some have already received their share. Lists children, whom they married, and the amount each has already received. Married children listed: Elizabeth, m. Whitnul (?) Stephens; John m. Mary Fleener; Rachel m. Stephen Weddle; Nathan left home 3-4-1835, age 33; Susanah m. John Coots; Polly m. Hiram Weddle. Other children: Phebe, Elisha, Nancy, Catharine, and Hugh Prewit. Sons Samuel and John to be guardians of minor children. Witnesses: John Lowe, John Wollard. pp. 49-52.

RIVERS, ANDREW. Will dated Oct. 19, 1843; probate record not found. Heirs: father, mother, brothers: Thomas, Richard, John Washington. Witnesses: Charles Dyer, John Rivers, William Harris. p. 79.

RUNNENBERG, HENRY A. Will dated Feb. 14, 1845; probated March 25, 1845. Heir: wife, Henrietta Asinath; daughter, Albortha Susanna, all the estate due me in Germany and property in Edinburg. Executor: Albert Lang of Terre Haute. Witnesses: Josiah M. Norris, John Russell, Samuel Maze. pp. 94-95.

ST. JOHN, JACOB. Will dated May 19, 1845; probated June 17, 1845. Heirs: wife (name not given); daughters, Mary Crawford, Nancy Robe, Charity Hughs, Jane St. John; sons, Jacob M., Lewis W., Lyman Beecher St. John. Witnesses: Gideon Drake, Nicholas Selch, Jacob Bromwell. pp. 96-98.

SCHRUM, JOHN. Will dated July 31, 1832; probated Sep. 5, 1832. Heirs: wife, Eleanor; son, David; grandson, John David. Executor: wife and son. Witnesses: John Woollard, James McNutt. pp. 17-18.

SHILLEDY, DOUGLAS B. Will dated Aug. 26, 1833; probated Nov. 11, 1833. Heirs: wife, Elizabeth; sons, James, William G., Samuel Watson, and Henry Baker Shilledy; daughters, Betsy Jane and Sarah Amanda Shilledy. Executors: wife and son, William G. Latter also guardian of minor children. Witnesses:

Zebulon Wallace, Samuel McKinney. pp. 20-21.

SHILLEDY, WILLIAM G. Will dated March 24, 1837; probated May 17, 1837. Heirs: wife, Eliza Jane; sons, Leander Douglass, James Allen. Wife and brother, Samuel Watson Shilledy, to be guardians of children. Executors: Ephraim Herriott, Fabius M. Finch. Witnesses: James D. Shilledy, Abram Bergen. pp. 41-42.

SHOEMAKER, ADAM. Will dated Dec. 16, 1842; probated Jan. 12, 1843. Heirs: sons, Adam and Washington. Executor: David Durbin. Witnesses: James L. Shields, James H. Mitchell, Lewis Prichard. pp. 74-75.

SMILEY, JOHN. Will dated Dec. 20, 1842; probated Jan. 27, 1843. Heirs: wife, Eliza, and son, William; daughters, Mary Ann, Rachel, Nancy. Executor: Meshach —— (?). Witnesses: John Smiley, Sr., Samuel Smiley. p. 76.

SMITH, SAMUEL. Will dated Sep. 18, 1833; probated March 3, 1834. Heirs: wife, Mary; sons, Washington, Robert, John, Samuel; daughters, Elizabeth Ann Smith, Eleanor Stalcup, Aby Dean, Rebecca Wishard. Samuel Smith to be guardian of Washington and Elizabeth Ann. Executors: John Smith, Phillip Dea— (?). Witnesses: Samuel and John Alexander. pp. 18-19.

SMOCK, HENRY. Will dated Aug. 29, 1831 (?); probated Sep. 28, 1835. Heirs: wife, Polly; brother, Isaac; nephew and niece, John R. and Jane Smock, children of James, deceased. $5.00 to go to erection of meeting house for Cranfield (?) church in our settlement. Executor: brother, Isaac. Witnesses: James Morrison, Joseph Lyon, John McGee, Samuel W. Richey. pp. 30-32.

SMOCK, MARY. Will dated Aug. 30. 1836; probated Sep. 10, 1836. Heirs: neice, Nancy Rickenbaugh (?), Cornelius Smock, Polly Smock, wife of John D., brother, Robert McKamay; sister, Nancy McAfee; Society for Foreign Missions, $50. Executor: Daniel Bouser, Sr. Witnesses: Henry H. Hunter, George S. Noble.

STEPHENS, JOHN. Will dated Feb. 3, 1841; probated March 15, 1841. Heirs: wife, Sarah; daughters, Polly Dixon, Nancy Graham, Elizabeth Barns; son, Gideon, and his daughter Polly by his first wife; heirs of son David. Witnesses: Jesse Wells, Alexander Jamison. pp. 54, 58-59.

TAYLOR, DANIEL. Will dated April 7, 1830; probated May 3, 1830. Heirs: wife, Elizabeth, and minor children, Richard Allen, Gabriel Allen. His brother Caleb W. Taylor and friend Samuel Allen of Cincinnati to take two sons and raise them. Executors: Pierson Murphy, Samuel Herriott. Witnesses: Abner Taylor, Thomas Williams. pp. 10-11.

TAYLOR, JOHN. Will dated Feb. 6, 1841; probated May 11, 1841. Heirs: wife, Mary, and children (names not given). Executor: wife. Witnesses: John Adams, Samuel Smiley. pp. 56-57.

TEETER, JONATHAN. Will dated June 23, 1834; probated Aug. 25, 1834. Heirs: wife (name not given); sons, Robert, James Thomas, Samuel Martin, William Harvey; daughters (names not given). Witnesses: Andrew Shell, Thomas Teeter. pp. 27-28.

THOMPSON, JAMES. Will dated April 1, 1836; probate record not found. Heirs: wife, Abigail, and children (names not given). Executor: wife. Witnesses: James R. Alexander, John Adams. p. 35.

THOMPSON, WILLIAM. Will dated Dec. 14, 1836; probated Feb. 6, 1837. Heirs: wife, Susannah, and children (names not given). Executors: James A. Alexander, Samuel Herriott. Witnesses: John Foster, John Thompson. pp. 40-41.

TRACY, JAMES. Will dated Feb. 14, 1833; probated March 12, 1833. Heirs: wife, Mary; children, Margaret, James, Josiah H., Elizabeth, Mary Jane, Mathew (the six youngest), Nathaniel, Cisiah, Elenor, Thomas, John. Executors: John and Mary Tracy, Allen D. Graham. Witnesses: Allen D. Graham, Isaac Clem, Richard H. Crittenden. pp. 19-20.

TRESSLAR, PETER. Will dated Aug. 12, 1827; probated Oct. 21, 1828. Heirs: wife, Barbara; children, Jacob (youngest son), John, Catharine, Michael, Christina Dunn, Valentine, Henry. Had money owing to him in Virginia. Executor: wife and son, Valentine. Witnesses: Henry Brown, John McCord. pp. 5-8.

WALKER, SAMUEL. Will dated Aug. 15, 1841; probated Sep. 6, 1841. Heirs: wife, Emarine, and children (names not given); wife's sister, Miss Elizabeth Wilson, who is now living with us. Executor: Walker D. Prichard. Witnesses: James Ritchey, John Gore, David Wells. pp. 60-61.

WEBB, HARLOW. Will dated Dec. 28, 1844; probated Aug. 5, 1845. Heirs: brothers, Alexander and Clark Webb. Witnesses: Elizabeth Webb, John Mozingo. pp. 99-100.

WOLFE, ANDREW. Will dated April 10, 1833; probated March 14, 1835. Heirs: wife, Susannah, and children (names not given). Witnesses: Moses Parr, George Wolfe. p. 28.

YOUNG, LINCHFIELD. Will dated July 20, 1845; probated Oct. 11, 1845. Heirs: wife, Mary, and children, William, James, Martha, Richard Madison, Mary Ellen. Executor: wife. Witnesses: Lewis Shouse, Allen Clark, John Lowe. pp. 106-108.

PERRY COUNTY MARRIAGES, 1814-1830

Compiled from microfilm copy in Genealogy Division of Marriage Record at Cannelton; the original record had been recopied by local officials.

Abbitt, William - Deborah Parks	6-19-1825
Agnew, William - Elizabeth Davis	7-24-1825
Akins, William - Charlotte Noble	9-21-1819
Allen, David - Mary Hargis	1-12-1815
Allen, Granville - Ann Kyler	5-22-1823
Allen, Samuel - Eleanor Wisehart	9-29-1826
Alvey, John - Charlotte Alvey	9- 8-1826
Alvey, Thomas - Henrietta Alvey	lic. 3-13-1823
Ammons, William - Polly Carter	3-24-1820
Anderson, James E. - Electa Mallary	7- 8-1829
Anderson, Josiah - America Critchlow	6- 1-1828
Anderson, Samuel - Indiana Claycomb	8-13-1829
Artman, Elijah Thomas - Sarah Richards	lic. 1-10-1827
Artman, Elisha - Dolly Vanpelt	11-29-1827
Asbury, William - Melinda Roff	1- 3-1830
Askins, John - Rebeckah Fisher	7- 6-1816
Auskins, Jacob - Lydia Stark	5-14-1815
Austin, John S. - Catharine Shannon	8-15-1822
Baker, William - Katharine Dunn	7- 4-1825
Ball, Catesby ap Henry - Isabella Lamb	4-21-1829
Ballard, Burril - Lavina Taylor	12-3-1826
Barger, Samuel - Rachael Frakes	8-22-1829
Baysinger, Jacob - Polly Barns	lic. 4-29-1825
Beard, Bedant - Rachel Clayton	lic. 7- 7-1816
Beard, Samuel - Nancy Matison	8-29-1830
Bibb, Edward - Mary Laforce	lic.9- 7-1817
Black, John - Rachel Fort	8-21-1828
Blain, Daniel - Polly Johnson	lic. 2- 9-1825
Blain, James - Sarah Crash	lic. 2-21-1820
Blanchard, Dillis - Elizabeth Boultinghouse	3-10-1822
Blanchard, Ezra - Hannah Parks	5- 3-1830
Blanchard, Ira A. - Levina Critchlow	8-30-1825
Blanchard, Ira A. - Margaret Rutherford	5-16-1827
Blanchard, William - Sophia Shepard	lic. 1-11-1826
Boiles, Simon - Nancy Howard	12-17-1823
Boiles, see also Boyles	
Bolin, Christopher - Nancy Gibson	11-8-1819
Bolin, Ellet - Jenny Mercer	lic. 2-29-1820
Bollin, James - Rebecca Kinder	11-9-1820
Bolin, Thomas - Polly Manly	5- 3-1830
Boling, William - Charity Sandage	2-20-1819
Borer, James (or John) - Catharine Walker	8-14-1823
Borer, John - Nancy Richardson	lic. 2-21-1825
Boyd, Hiram - Anny Reed	2-26-1828
Boyd, Thomas - Levina Sparks	8-18-1820
Boyles, Samuel - Phebe Brown	lic. 12-5-1821
Boyles, Simon - Isabel Brown	12-13-1822
Boyles, see also Boiles	
Brashears, William - Polly Lasher	10-23-1828
Brightman, William - Ada Stapleton	9-28-1820
Briley, Absolom - Hannah Wheeler	8- 8-1822
Bristow, James - Polly Haddrights	3-10-1824
Brown, Anthony - Peggy Owens	3- 3-1820
Brown, James - Betsey Mattey	lic. 7-21-1818
Brown, Thomas - Eleanor Bristow	lic. 7- 1-1826
Burdett, Peyton - Anna E. Grant	4-15-1830
Burnet, John - Sally Vanpelt	5- 7-1829
Busely, Jesse - Caty Cambron	6-25-1817
Busely, Siles - Nancy Horn	6-25-1816
Butler, Abel - Milbourn Litherland	1-24-1816
Byrn, Solomen - Jemima Faith	6- 3-1819

Cambron, Edward - Margaret Cambron	lic. 10-10-1826
Cambron, Ezekiel - Eleanor Springer	lic. 5-30-1825
Canaday, Richard - Polly Artman	8-23-1821
Carlton, James - Philena Askins	lic. 9-14-1821
Carr, Absolem - Sally Claycomb	lic. 5-14-1825
Carr, Elijah - Jenny Connor	3-30-1820
Carr, Otho - Nancy Claycomb	10-9-1828
Cart, John, Jr. - Jane Gilleland	7-30-1829
Carter, George - Rhoda Dewitt	12-25-1821
Carter, Mason - Margaret Dewitt	lic. 12-25-1817
Carter, Mason - Margaret Artman	2-23-1827
Carter, Silas - Permilia Irwin	10-28-1828
Carter, William - Margaret Connor	2-15-1818
Cary, Benedict - Ann Allen	lic. 4- 5-1827
Cassidy, James - Nancy Hix	10-9-1828
Cavender, Anson - Tabitha Thrasher	3-30-1828
Cavender, Bardin - Nancy Davison	2-25-1830
Cavender, James - Sally Davidson	10-17-1827
Cavender, William - Charity Staunton	9- 8-1829
Chaffin, George - Rachel Maddock	7-11-1823
Champion, Philip - Cama Cunningham	9-12-1830
Chriswell, Robert - Margaret Moor	2-16-1820
Clark, David - Polly Underhill	1-15-1826
Clark, George - Lucinda Ballard	10-14-1817
Clark, Henry - Margaret Abbot	1-26-1826
Cockrill, William - Phebe Hyde	lic. 2- 4-1827
Coleman, Jefferson - Eliza Yocomb	2- 2-1829
Collins, James - Mary Lindsey	lic. 4- 4-1823
Comstock, Daniel - Betsey Lanman	1- 1-1828
Comstock, Nathan - Polly Sandage	9-14-1826
Comstock, Oliver - Ruth Wakefield	1- 8-1829
Conley, David - Susannah Howard	lic. 1-25-1825
Connor, Alfred - Nancy Lang	lic. 4-16-1823
Connor, John - Mary Sincleer	10-9-1816
Connor, John - Anna Main	10-27-1818
Connor, Samuel - Nancy Carr Hyde	12-14-1820
Connor, Samuel, Jr. - Margaret Groves	4- 1-1827
Connor, Tarrence - Merah Main	11-6-1814
Cooley, Colbert - Mary Hibbs	lic. 2- 4-1828
Cotton, Robert C. - Louisa Protsman	3- 4-1828
Cox, James - Frankey Decker	6- 7-1818
Cox, William - Melinda Hills	7- 6-1826
Crask, Joseph - Nancy Wilson	6-12-1821
Cummings, Eli - Polly Glen	12-27-1819
Cummings, James - Margaret Hoskinson	1-13-1825
Cummings, Thomas - Patsey Reed	1- 6-1819
Curle, William - Mahala Cunningham	9-10-1829
Dalton, David - Rosanah Basham	12-25-1829
Daniel, John - Elizabeth Wright	2- 4-1819
Daniel, Peter - Eliza Sigman	5-20-1821
Davidson, Peter - Rachel Deaver (?)	1- 6-1826
Davidson, William - Mary Hawley	10-17-1827
Davis, Jacob - Polly Elder	4-20-1817
Davis, John - Abigail Dunn	11-6-1822
Deen, Stephen - Susannah Sprinkle	8-10-1815
Degroodt, Samuel J. - Harriet Bates	6-24-1824
Dewitt, Abel - Nancy Miller	8-16-1822
Dewitt, Elijah - Lucy Barbre	lic. 1-28-1824
Dodson, Abisha - Nicey Walker	7-23-1822
Dodson, John - Eliza Stapleton	7-23-1829
Dodson, Jonathan - Rebeckah West	1-27-1825

Doling, William M. - Elizabeth Gibson	8- 3-1815	
Dougherty, Charles - Susannah Morgan	lic. 3-23-1825	
Dougherty, George - Katharine Henderson	2-16-1826	
Drinkwater, Joseph - Fanny Asbury	10-31-1816	
(widow of James T. Asbury)		
Drinkwater, Paul - Sally Boyd	8-3-1820	
Duncan, Warren - Sally Daniel	lic. 3-17-1819	
Dunn, John - Abigail Hedden	9-24-1818	
Edwards, Philip - Catharine Latimer	lic. 7-20-1824	
Elder, Andrew - Melina Faulkinborough	lic. 9-7-1830	
Elder, James - Dorotha Ann Johnson	lic. 8-27-1830	
Elder, John - Parthena Mitchell	9-23-1829	
Elzer, John - Lusy Tate	7-19-1821	
Enlow (?), David - Nancy Fitzjerald	3-28-1825	
Enlow, Samuel - Delila May	3-11-1824	
Ewing, Edward - Nancy Todd	11-9-1826	
Ewing, Samuel - Mariala Faulkinborough	8-21-1827	
Ewing, William G. - Mary Kellenbarger	lic. 7-16-1830	
Faith, William - Mary Bogart	4-15-1823	
Fall, Jeremiah - Susan Newton	9- 6-1825	
Farmer, Richard - Mary Gilleland	4-28-1827	
Farr, Archibald - Elizabeth Bogart	3-20-1824	
Farriss, Franklin - Betsey Niles	1- 1-1828	
Farriss, John, Jr. - Polly Niles	3- 1-1827	
Felix, Charles - Mary Sulinger	lic. 5- 4-1827	
Fenwick, Henry - Elizabeth Conradt	4-13-1817	
Figgins, Isaac - Rachel Hendrickson	lic. 5- 1-1826	
Figgins, William - Susannah Toothman	11- 7-1822	
Finch, Abraham - Milla Ashcroft	12-17-1816	
Finch, Philip - Elizabeth Claycomb	2- 4-1820	
Fitzgerald, Aaron - Rachel Comstock	11-24-1819	
Fortune, Benjamin - Mary Hoover	12-24-1828	
Fortune, John - Elizabeth Fuller	7-15-1827	
Fortune, Williamson - Rebecca Daviss	lic 1-21-1826	
Frakes, James - Sally Barger	lic. 4- 4-1829	
Frakes, Thompson - Betsey Barger	4-12-1829	
Frisbie, Samuel - Margaret Connor	lic. 3-15-1825	
Froman, John - Rachel Sapp	4-19-1827	
Fuller, Herman - Sarah Duggans	6-10-1824	
Fulton, James - Bebecca Boultinghouse	9-26-1830	
Galey, Benjamin - Susannah Figgins	1-23-1823	
Galey, Lewis - Elizabeth Frakes	1-28-1829	
Galey, Simon - Mary Freeman	4-16-1827	
Gardner, Robert - Eliza Connor	6-12-1828	
Gear, George - Jane Jarbo	8-27-1821	
Geer, Asa - Elva Lamar	1-15-1818	
Geddens (Gidings), Kinzie - Celia Morgan	1-11-1827	
Gilbert, Jacob - Elizabeth Blain	lic.11-29-1819	
Gilleland, John S. - Phebe Barns	lic. 2-13-1821	
Gilleland, Robert - Eleanor Frakes	lic. 12-3-1830	
Goble, Daniel - Letha Walker	11-26-1827	
Goble, William - Susannah Hill	lic. 6- 6-1820	
Goff, John - Nancy Steel	5-30-1820	
Goff, John W. - Melissa Wilson	7-20-1826	
Green, Anthony - Elizabeth Connor	12-14-1815	
Green, Joel - Mary Green	9- 1-1825	
Green, John - Matilda Durky	5-12-1825	
Green, Reuben - Sybil Graybill	9- 1-1825	
Green, William - Nancy Anderson	lic. 4- 3-1821	
Griffith, Thomas - Elizabeth Lindsey	lic. 5-26-1825	
Grimes, David D. Bathsheba Lamb	5-2-1816	
Groves, Jacob - Sally Hyde	7-18-1830	
Groves, John - Polly Cart	1- 5-1826	
Hagerman, Samuel - Nancy Stuck	12-22-1826	
Hale, James - Sarah Taylor	lic. 5-29-1830	
Hall, Presley - Nancy Anderson	5-28-1820	

Hall, Richard P. - Margaret Wilkinson	lic. 11-9-1830	
Hamilton, George - Elizabeth Bird	5-17-1829	
Hammack, Daniel - Mary Dodson	9- 2-1824	
Hammack, Ephraim - Cynthia Hix	4-10-1828	
Hampton, David - Elizabeth Smith	1-11-1824	
Hampton, Thomas - Milly Evans	lic. 2-25-1824	
Hardin, Mark - Lavina Lamb	4-23-1829	
Hardin, William - Catharine Shoemaker	1- 3-1830	
Hargis, John - Nancy Allen	4-15-1819	
Hargis, William - Elizabeth Kepler	11-6-1823	
Harlin, John - Polly Farmer	lic. 12-30-1824	
Harp, John - Tresy Medcalf	lic. 7- 1-1817	
Harp, John - Susan P. Harris	12-16-1830	
Harp, Joseph - Paulina Galey	12-4-1829	
Harris, James - Nancy Pollard	11-14-1830	
Haughee, James - Armina Little	lic. 7-12-1820	
Hauser, John G. - Mary Frederick	lic. 8-27-1820	
Hays, Joseph H. - Agnes Goodwin	6- 5-1816	
Hays, John - Agnes Coke	6-23-1830	
Henderson, Barnet - Betsey Galloway	lic. 7- 6-1830	
Hendrickson, Richard - Rebecca Thoothman	10-2-1829	
Hensley, Edward - Anne McGlothlin	8- 2-1824	
Hicks, Allen - Sally Noble	1-28-1830	
Hifil, Wilson - Jane West	lic. 9- 1-1825	
Hiley, Abraham, Jr. - Eda Hinton	3-21-1822	
Hills, Ishmael - Elizabeth Wright	8- 7-1826	
Hills, James - Phebe Shoemaker	10-27-1822	
Hills, Robert - Elizabeth Cox	6-24-1824	
Hix, James H. - Susannah Royal	1-31-1822	
Hix, John L. - Polly Cart	3-22-1827	
Hix, William - Lydia Crist	12-18-1828	
Hobbs, Hiram - Sabre Hifil	5-17-1823	
Holmes, Samuel - Jane Bratchell	11-5-1830	
Hornback, Abraham - Hannah Dewitt	lic. 11-20-1822	
Hornback, Benjamin - Elizabeth Edwards	lic. 10-13-1817	
Hoskinson, Wilford H. - Farreby Howard	4-12-1827	
Howel, Philip - Phebe Harding	10-20-1825	
Howel, Philip - Mary Sandage	5- 6-1830	
Huckeby, Joshua - Rebecca Lang (or Long)	4- 4-1824	
Huff, John W. - Maria N. Weatherholt	lic. 8-18-1829	
Hull, Homer C. D. Z. (?) - Sally Ailsworth	lic. 7- 7-1824	
Humphrey, Alexander H. - Henrietta Harris	7- 6-1829	
Humphrey, Hart - Frances Harris	11-28-1830	
Hyde, Samuel - Mary Kyler	4-23-1826	
Hyde, William - Margaret Critchlow	6-20-1824	
Jackson, John - Catharine Lamar	lic. 1-21-1821	
Jarbo, John - Elizabeth Robinson	lic. 3-15-1824	
Jarboe, Richard - Margaret Miller	11-3-1830	
Jarvis, John - Polly Ray	1-21-1830	
Jennings, Edmund - Sarah Pearce	lic. 3- 7-1818	
Jennings, James - Rosanna Gregory	lic. 1-22-1819	
Johnson, Ignatius - Ann McGlothlin	11-3-1830	
Jones, James G. - Lucretia Shepherd	10-1-1815	
Jones, William - Malinda Wire	8-20-1815	
Keins, Josiah - Jeny M. Harney	12-30-1819	
Keysucker, William - Elizabeth Bullock	8- 2-1827	
Kinder, David - Anna Richardson	6-15-1820	
Kinder, David - Elizabeth Fisher	lic. 2-17-1824	
Kinison, Samuel - Luana Crowe	6- 8-1825	
Kitterman, Christopher - Elizabeth Hifil	3-23-1827	
Kitterman, Elias - Sarah Archibald	lic. 3-18-1825	
Kitterman, George - Mary Fortune	3-26-1824	
Kitterman, Michael - Lydia Clark	lic. 10-2-1827	
Knox, Robert - Margaret Carter	lic. 3-19-1822	
Lacefield, Benjamin - Elizabeth Jarbo	4-11-1823	

Lacy, Jeremiah - Vina Lamar	9-14-1815
Laforce, Samuel - Mary Fulton	6-27-1816
Lake, Harris - Jane Branham	1-27-1822
Lake, Israel - Anna Long	3-17-1829
Lake, Jess - Polly Riddle	lic. 12-13-1820
Lake, William - Elizabeth Thompson	7- 7-1824
Lamar, Elijah - Polly Wright	lic. 11-24-1817
Lamar, John - Mourning Edwards	lic. 11-28-1816
Lamb, Dorastus - Elizabeth Miller	lic. 3- 6-1825
Lamb, John - Sarah Phillips	lic. 8-21-1817
Lamb, Rodolphus P. - Eleanor Anderson	5-14-1822
Lamb, William B. - Sophia Anderson	5-28-1820
Lang, John J. - Polly Connor	8-13-1829
Lanman, George - Polly Vanwinkle	lic. 10-25-1816
Lanman, James - Betsy Jarbo	10-29-1818
Lans, James - Elizabeth Springston	8- 7-1817
Lasher, George - Huldah Mallery	lic. 3-5 -1828
Lasher, Jacob - Betsey Comstock	8- 4-1819
Latimer, David - Susannah Vanpelt	10-7-1827
Latimer, Elisha - Catharine Litherland	lic. 6-14-1822
Latimer, Luther - Parthenia Huff	5-10-1822
Laurence, Robert - Sarah Rowe	4-19-1824
Lea, Jesse - Mirriam Morgan	5-18-1826
Leftridge, William - Esther Wheeler	10-21-1824
Linch, Dillings - Sophia Hanks	6-13-1827
Links, Elijah - Susan Huff	5-11-1827
Litherland, Jonathan - Lydia Litherland	6- 2-1830
Litherland, William - Catherine Donnely	10-9-1830
Little, James - Polly Frymire	6-28-1829
Little, John - Nancy Huff	lic. 7-16-1822
Logston, John - Margaret Hill	lic. 4- 3-1820
Logston, Vann - Charlotte Constant	4- 4-1822
Lowe, Benjamin - Mahala Westerfield	lic. 5- 3-1828
Lyon, Stephen - Sally Packinpaugh	4- 7-1818
McCall, Samuel - Elmirah Kennedy	7-13-1824
McCallister, Thomas - Sarah Cook	lic. 9-14-1817
McDaniel, Stephin - Betsey Williams	lic. 5-22-1816
McGrew, Willis - Sarah B. Beatty (?)	9-27-1830
McKim, John - Pamela Cummings	1-20-1822
McKim, Thomas - Sally Bird	lic. 3-30-1822
McKinney, H.D. Solomon - Rhoda Speer	2-17-1820
McMillan, Jonathan - Mary Lindsey	9-16-1824
Mahan, Gabriel - Rebecca Roff	1- 3-1830
Main, John - Olive Mallery	lic. 5-31-1817
Main, Riley - Patsey Walker	11-19-1818
Main, Samuel - Mary Miles (or Mills)	1-22-1818
Main, Samuel - Milly Springer	2-28-1828
Mallery, John - Cynthia M. Lamb	11-2-1819
Mallery, Lanson - Nancy Gordon	lic. 10-20-1822
Mallery, Lewis - Ada G. Stapleton Brightman	3-14-1824
Martin, Littleton - Lucretia Nicols	5-28-1816
Martin, Samuel - Elizabeth Hargis	3-18-1815
Mason, Dudley D. - Christena Bird	12-28-1820
Mason, John - Sally Webb	6-13-1826
Masterson, John - Eleanor Ewing	5- 4-1815
Matingly, Bartin - Elizabeth Cambron	1- 1-1817
Mattingly, Lewis - Barbary Trenary	10-10-1824
May, David - Rebecca Vanwinkle	6-16-1825
Meredith, Lewis - Ruth Spurnier	9-19-1824
Miles, Samuel - Lucretia Main	2-17-1820
Miller, Alfred H. - Gertrude E. Williams	lic. 9- 8-1823
Miller, Henry - Nancy Elder	lic. 4-14-1830
Miller, James - Sally Storms	12-2-1825
Miller, John - Michal McDaniel	lic. 10-19-1816
Miller, John W. - Lucy Carr	lic. 3- 9-1830
Miller, Joseph - Louisa Talbot	8-29-1823

Miller, Lewis - Elizabeth Wheatly	4-22-1824
Miller, Michael - Matilda E. Bell	lic. 4-30-1828
Miller, Robert - Elizabeth Evans	10-12-1825
Miller, Samuel - Polly Comstock	8-23-1821
Mills, Benjamin - Elizabeth Jenkins	6-16-1824
Mills, Ignatius - Elizabeth Cambron	5-31-1825
Minner, John - Nancy Litherland	lic. 5-21-1817
More, Peter - Elizabeth Goble	lic. 10-18-1825
Morgan, Joseph - Deborah Comstock	1- 1-1824
Morgin, Asa - Saly Reuby	5-18-1815
Mudd, James H. - Eliza Jones	7-11-1823
Murray, Joseph - Ally Lamar	11-9-1815
Myers, Isaac - Ruth Stephenson	11-26-1824
Nevill, Enoch - Hannah Reed	lic. 2-20-1827
Nicholls, William M. - Sally Bruner	lic. 3-15-1830
Niles, Chester - Sarah Lamb	lic. 4-30-1830
Niles, Ebenezer - Nancy Farris	11-2-1826
Niles, Stephen - Margaret Howard	lic. 8-10-1825
Noble, Robert - Nancy Devers	11-10-1823
Norton, Jeremiah, Jr. - Betsey Robinson	lic. 6-10-1830
Noyes, Jonathan - Amy Blanchard	lic. 10-17-1817
Noyes, Jonathan - Nancy Miller	lic. 3- 6-1825
Parkinson, William - Nancy Gregory	lic. 8- 1-1820
Parrot, John - Sally Masterson	lic. 12-31-1817
Phelps, Edwin - Jemima Catlin	12-18-1826
Phillips, David H. - Sally Fortune	10-4-1829
Phillips, Robert - Mary Jones	lic. 10-29-1819
Pitcher, Hiram - Matilda Anderson	2- 3-1824
Polke, Charles - Rebecca White	1-14-1819
Polke, Edmund - Polly Winchell	3-26-1818
Polke, Edmund - Fanny Thomas	12-30-1820
Polke, Edmund - Eliza Holt	lic. 2-22-1825
Polke, Edmund - Esther Tobin	lic. 6-29-1826
Polke, Greenville - Matilda Simms	12-5-1827
Polke, Thomas - Melvina Ryan	1-14-1827
Pool, Logston - Catharine Franks	11-15-1821
Pool, Sanford - Polly Critchelow	lic. 9-10-1821
Powell, John - Sally Collins	lic. 7-10-1820
Prather, Robert - Elizabeth Horton	1-23-1823
Prather, William G. - Mahala Vanmatre	1- 2-1826
Purcell, Solomon - Anna Ewing	12-9-1829
Quick, Barnet - Isabel Mahan	9-17-1829
Quick, James - Eleanor Hayden	9-26-1829
Ramsey, Alexander F. - Nancy Cummings	lic. 3- 2-1829
Ransom, Joseph - Eleanor Jarbo	lic. 3-29-1830
Ray, William - Nancy Stephenson	10-23-1817
Read, Armin - Dolly Phillips	2- 9-1824
Reed, David - Mahana Bolin	10-11-1827
Reed, Ephraim - Sally Bolin	10-19-1827
Reed, John - Catharine Vanpelt	lic. 1- 6-1830
Reed, Zebulon - Catharine Litherland	lic. 2-24-1822
Reynolds, Joseph - Mary Petty	9- 8-1827
Reynolds, Mason - Mary Edwards	1-19-1817
Reynolds, Reuben - Susanna Cannada	2- 8-1819
Reynolds, Waller - Marianna Barbre	9- 7-1828
Rice, Allen - Katharine Thompson	2- 3-1822
Richards, Elijah J. - Polly Dougherty	4- 2-1830
Richardson, Beriman - Polly Reed	2-16-1815
Richardson, James - Mary Webb	7-27-1815
Richardson, Larkin - Miranda Cummings	1-17-1820
Richardson, Thomas - Nancy Parsons	lic. 1-13-1819
Ricks, John W. - Louisa Stonements	6- 6-1830
Ricks, Thomas - Eliza Kyler	7-11-1819
Riddle, Jesse - Catharine Ballard	lic. 11-1-1820
Riley, John C. - Mary Horton	1- 3-1828
Roberts, Butler - Lucy Rice	10-1-1815

Robertson, George - Anna Witterman	lic. 12-3-1825	
Robinson, Stephen - Elizabeth Maxwell	10-4-1827	
Robinson, William - Harriet Wheeler	12-2-1827	
Rosecrantz, John - Nancy Cart	8-31-1820	
Rosecrantz, Richard - Fanny Gilliland	6- 5-1820	
Rowe, William - Fanny Lawrence	8-19-1824	
Rowland, William - Mary Miller	1- 1-1824	
Rusher, Charles - Rhody Clark	10-30-1830	
Ryan, Daniel - Lydia Tobin	1-11-1817	
Ryan, Nelson - Louisa Cockrell	7- 6-1829	
Sandage, Moses - Deborah Comstock	10-4-1826	
Sandage, Moses - Sally Harding	11-6-1828	
Sandage, Nathan - Nancy Quick	lic. 3-24-1825	
Sandage, Thomas - Mary Ann Gibson	2-21-1819	
Sandage, Thomas - Rachel Terry	4-18-1821	
Sandage, Thomas - Margaret Lasher	2- 1-1827	
Sanders, Eligha - Elizabeth Hagelon	3- 3-1822	
Sanders, Jordan (or Hardin) - Eliza A. Newton	11-28-1829	
Sapp, William L. - Nancy Rounder	6-19-1823	
Sawyer, Samuel - Permina Parrish	1- 2-1830	
Sebastian, Charles - Elizabeth Murray	lic. 3-14-1821	
Shoemaker, John - Sarah Donaghy	2-14-1819	
Shoemaker, John - Nancy Fortune	2-24-1825	
Shoemaker, Stephen - Elizabeth Taylor	7-28-1816	
Short, Stephen - Nancy Prunty	4- 4-1827	
Shroads, William - Mary Shroads	2- 4-1818	
Shurley, William - Nancy Froman	6- 4-1815	
Simms, George - Patsey Cummings	lic. 2-13-1825	
Simpson, Thomas - Charlotte Akins	lic. 2-20-1823	
Singleton, James G. - Lititia Richardson	8- 9-1829	
Sipes, William - Elizabeth Sipes	lic. 5- 1-1827	
Skaggs, John - Jane Byer	lic. 3-20-1823	
Skaggs, John - Elizabeth Howe	lic. 1-16-1830	
Skinner, Richard - Rebecca Connor	3-25-1820	
Slavey, Andrew - Anna Posey	lic. 4-12-1818	
Small, Matthew - Elizabeth Waide	lic. 8-28-1818	
Smiley, William - Sarah Springer	2- 5-1825	
Smith, Benjamin - Susanah Boultinghouse	9- 7-1815	
Spencer, Isaac - Polly Dever	lic. 11-22-1826	
Spencer, William - Sophia Claycomb	12-1-1825	
Spilman, Harvey - Mary Mason	12-19-1830	
Springer, Charles - Comfort Walker	6-13-1816	
Springer, George - Eleanor Mattingly	9- 2-1819	
Springer, John C. - Locicy Sapp	7-18-1822	
Sprinkle, Joseph - Milly Horton	3- 6-1828	
Sprinkle, Michael - Agnes Spears	2- 5-1825	
Sprinkle, Thomas - America Gailey	lic. 2-21-1829	
Sprinkle, William - Charlotte Horton	4-19-1827	
Stansel, William - Celia Barbre	11-26-1818	
Stapleton, Isom - Polly Taylor	10-27-1819	
Stapleton, John - Letha Hoskinson	1-22-1824	
Steel, John - Polly Wilson	7-14-1825	
Stephenson, Stephen - Nancy Neighbours	12-20-1818	
Stillwell, Hiram - Diana Barlow	4-20-1823	
Stilwell, Johnson - Maria Price	4-19-1830	
Stine, Isaac - Catharine Morgan	3- 5-1826	
Stuck, Isom - Catharine Artman	10-6-1827	
Stuck, Peter - Margaret Kepler	7-13-1820	
Summers, James, - Ezelima Gregory	lic. 3-12-1819	
Sumner, Jesse - Prudence Linch	10-2-1815	
Sumner, Seward - Elizabeth Cummings	7-19-1825	
Tate, David - Elizabeth Blain	12-6-1819	
Tate (Tait), James - Mary Miller	10-20-1815	

Taylor, Ebenezer - Ruth Maxwell	8-31-1830	
Taylor, Hiram - Hannah Claycomb	1- 8-1824	
Taylor, James - Appa McDaniel	7-27-1815	
Taylor, Lewis - Nancy Hyde	lic. 1-17-1829	
Taylor, Obadiah - Deborah Main	3-20-1820	
Taylor, Thomas - Elizabeth Mallery	7-27-1823	
Taylor, William - Eleanor Royal	12-16-1818	
Taylor, William - Mary Dewitt	4-17-1823	
Terry, Elias - Eleanor Sandage	lic. 9-28-1826	
Terry, Elisha - Sally Small	1- 7-1816	
Thomas, John L. - Fanny Cavender	6-14-1824	
Thomas, William - Rachel Ewing	10-7-1826	
Thompson, John - Eliza Hinton	3-29-1830	
Thompson, John L. - Polly Claycomb	lic. 11-16-1826	
Thrasher, Eli - Nancy Jordan	10-17-1827	
Thrasher, Elias - Catharine McConnell	1-27-1828	
Thrasher, John - Catherine Edwards	12-11-1828	
Thrasher, Thomas - Rhoda Spears	3-11-1822	
Thrasher, Thomas - Elizabeth Artman	7- 5-1830	
Thunler, William T. - Phebe Woods	5-27-1817	
Tindall, Hankins - Louisa Burnet	7- 6-1829	
Tindall, Isaac - Rebeckah Askins	5- 6-1816	
Tindall, John - Mareanne Edwards	12-27-1820	
Tobin, Joseph - Susannah Finch	8-27-1818	
Tobin, Thomas - Sarah Polke	2-16-1814	
Trenary, Benjamin - Elizabeth Miller	4- 7-1822	
Trigger, Solomon - Sally Allen	9-19-1830	
Vandever, James - Mary Howell	4- 7-1829	
Vanmeter, Henry - Elizabeth Truax	.7-24-1817	
Vanwinkle, Abraham - Permilla White	lic. 10-23-1821	
Vanwinkle, Alexander - Phebe Miller	1-28-1824	
Vanwinkle, Isaac - Sarah Cummings	2-20-1819	
Vanwinkle, James - Matilda Hinton	lic. 1-21-1823	
Vanwinkle, Simeon - Berlinda Hinton	6-20-1828	
Vaughan, Davis - Susannah Wells	5-19-1825	
Wakefield, William - Anny Comstock	2-15-1830	
Walker, Elijah - Nancy Shaver	1- 1-1818	
Walker, Milton - Anny Riley	4-15-1828	
Walker, Philip - Elizabeth E. Riley	lic. 12-22-1821	
Waller, William - Lydia Taylor	lic. 9-14-1828	
Ward, Samuel - Levina Davis	lic. 11-19-1821	
Weatherholt, Henry - Polly Simms	lic. 4-12-1818	
Weatherholt, William - Sally Waggoner	3-29-1821	
Wells, Henry - Sally Hawley	2-21-1828	
Welch, Edward - Polly Waller	lic. 3- 9-1825	
West, Fossat - Doranda Roff	4- 9-1829	
West, James - Mary McConnel	3-18-1827	
West, Nicholas - Elizabeth Bogard	5- 5-1828	
Wheatley, Arthur - Rebecca Taylor	2-22-1830	
Wheatley, George - Mary Ann Jarbo	lic. 3-17-1821	
Wheatley, Henry - Susan Farmer	lic. 6- 7-1828	
Wheatley, Thomas - Elizabeth Mitchell	7-10-1827	
Wheeler, James - Sarah Claycomb	10-10-1819	
Whelkel, Davis - Mary Irwin (?)	11-14-1823	
White, John - Esther Terry (?)	lic. 6-11-1818	
White, Joseph, Jr. - Polly Thomas	12-16-1824	
White, William - Elizabeth Thomas	11-18-1824	
Whitten, William - Rebecca Wooling (or Woolens)		
	lic. 6-24-1827	
Wilson, Adam - Eleanor Cambron	lic. 2-10-1824	
Wright, Levin - Mary Seargeant	lic. 9-12-1829	
York, Ezekiel - Elizabeth Litherland	6- 1-1827	
York, Jeremiah - Lititian Boyd	9-24-1827	
Young, Jacob - Cathey Bruner	11-5-1815	

10

BATTLE OF TIPPECANOE

How many know that 162 years ago, after a long cheerless night followed by the first light of morning of November 7, 1811, a small force of militia supported by a contingent of the Fourth U. S. Regiment, repelled a savage attack of the Indians of the Northwest? The latter were under the leadership of Tecumseh and his brother, the Prophet, although only the latter took part in the engagement. This battle was not great in numbers but mighty in its consequences. It was the most significant engagement ever fought on the soil of Indiana.

Participants in this event numbered scarcely more than nine hundred men under the command of General William Henry Harrison, then Governor of Indiana Territory. Encamped on a narrow ridge of dry land, in the midst of swamps into which it extended, were two hundred and fifty regulars, sixty Kentuckians, and six hundred Indiana pioneers—with the last named composing nearly two-thirds of the total force pitted against the enemy which had gathered at Prophetstown, a short distance to the east.

The incidents and adventures experienced on this occasion furnished the substance of fireside chats for many years thereafter. The descendants of these brave men are numerous throughout Indiana and elsewhere. Probably not more than a fourth of them know they had an ancestor in the Battle of Tippecanoe. Although a monument was dedicated in 1908 upon which appear the names of those gallant officers and thirty-seven privates who lost their lives defending this historic spot, it is important that the names of all participants be known before the Battle Ground Association executes its plan to enlarge the facilities of the park this summer.

To perpetuate the memory of those persons who fought at Tippecanoe during this second and last struggle for independence, there is membership in the General Society of the War of 1812 open to male descendants. For women, as well as children up to twenty-one years of age, there is the National Society, United States Daughters of 1812, organized in 1892. There are four chapters in Indiana—Tippecanoe in Greencastle, Major David Steele in South Bend, Phillip Schoff in Indianapolis, and Wabash Valley in Lafayette. Mrs. George E. Carroll, of South Bend, is the Indiana State president.

Eligibility to membership depends upon lineal descent from ancestors who rendered military, naval, or civil service to our country during the years 1784 through 1815 inclusive. Of particular interest to those with a Hoosier heritage, however, is the specific event of national significance which is claimed by many to have been "the first shot" in the War of 1812. Its decisive outcome insured the western frontiers with the opportunity for peaceful settlement.

ROLL OF THE ARMY COMMANDED BY WILLIAM HENRY HARRISON
FROM SEPTEMBER 6 TO NOVEMBER 24, 1811

Compiled from photostatic copies of the Pay Rolls in the Genealogy Division, Indiana State Library. Only the Indiana and Kentucky troops are listed, omitting those of the Fourth U. S. Regiment commanded by Col. John P. Boyd. Some names appear more than once due to promotions and transfers.

GENERAL STAFF

William McFarland, Col. & Adjt.
Nathl. F. Adams, Lieut. & Adjt. Belonged to Regular Army of U. S.
Henry Hurst & Waller Taylor, Majors & Aids-de-Camp to the Comr. in Chief
Abraham Owen, Col. Kentucky Militia, Aid-de-Camp, *killed in action*
Marston G. Clark, Brigade Inspector, promoted Sept. 20
Robert Buntin, Sr., Capt. & Qr. Master
Robert Buntin, Jr., 2d Lieut. & Forage Master

FIELD AND STAFF OFFICERS OF INDIANA MILITIA

Joseph Bartholomew, Lieut. Col., *wounded in action*
Rezin Redman, Major
Andrew P. Hay, Surgeon's Mate
Joseph Brown, Adjt. & Paymaster
Joseph Clarke, app'ted Sergt. Mate Oct. 29
Chapman Denslow, Sergt. Mate
James Curry, 2d Sergt.

FIELD AND STAFF OF INFANTRY

Luke Decker, Lieut. Col., *wounded in action*
Noah Purcell, Major

Daniel Sullivan, Lieut. Adjt.
William Ready, Sergt. Major
Benjamin V. Beckes, Qr. Master
William Gamble, Qr. M. Sergt., app'ted Sep. 25; previously in Walter Wilson's Company
Edward Scull, Asst. Surgeon, *wounded in action*
James Smith, Qr. Master, promoted to Capt. Nov. 9 of Jacob Warrick's Company

FIELD AND STAFF OF DRAGOONS

Joseph H. Daveiss, Major, *killed in action*
Benjamin Parke, Major, promoted Nov. 7
Davis Floyd, Adjt.
Charles Smith, Qr. M., sick; returned home Oct. 28
General W. Johnston, Qr. M., after Oct. 30
William Prince, Sergt. Major

TOUSSAINT DUBOIS' COMPANY OF SPIES AND GUIDES

Toussaint Dubois, Captain

Privates

Silas McCulloch
G. R. C. Sullivan
William Bruce
William Polk
Pierre Andre

Ephraim Jorden
William Shaw
    wounded badly
William Hogue
    discharged Oct. 4
David Wilkins
John Hollingsworth
Thomas Levins

Joseph Harpin
Abraham Decker
Samuel James
David Mills
Stewart Cunningham
Bocker Childers
Thomas Jurdan
    Last six men transferred
    to Capt. Robb's Company

CHARLES BEGGS' COMPANY OF LIGHT DRAGOONS [Clark County area]

Charles Beggs, Captain
John Thompson, Lieut., promoted Sep. 18
Henry Bottorff, Lieut., promoted Sep. 18
Mordecai Sweeney, Cornet, promoted Sep. 18
Davis Floyd, Sergt., promoted to Adjutant Sep. 23
Sergts.: John Carr, James Sage, James Fisler, Abraham Miller
Corpls.: George Rider, Sion Prather, Hugh Ross, Samuel Bottorff
Trumpeter, John Deats, not regularly mustered

Privates

Jacob Cressmore
    wounded
William Kelley
    killed in action
William Lewis
    not regularly mustered
James Ellison

Timothy R. Rayment
John Cowan
Jonathon Gibbons
William Perry
Edward Perry
John Goodwin
James Hay
John Newland
George Twilley

Milo Davis
Marston G. Clark
    promoted to Brigade
    Major Sep. 20
Samuel Carr
Jos. McCormack
Richard Ward
    died Nov. 12
John Farris
Charles F. Ross

THOMAS BERRY'S DETACHMENT OF MOUNTED RIFLEMEN [Harrison County area]

Thomas Berry, Lieut., *killed in action*
Zachary Linley, Sergt., *badly wounded*

Privates

John Briese
John Beck
Frederick Carns
    badly wounded
John Dougherty
Thomas Elliot
Griffith Edwards

Peter Hanks
    mortally wounded
David Hederick
Henry Hickey
    killed in action
Caleb Harrison
Anthony Taylor
William Lee
Jacob Lutes

Daniel McMickle
    killed in action
Henry Moore
Peter McMickle
    badly wounded
George Mahon
Fredk. Wyman
Saml. Lockhart
Joseph Edwards

JAMES BIGGER'S COMPANY OF RIFLEMEN [Clark County area]

James Bigger, Captain
John T. Chunn, Lieut.
Joseph Stilwell, Ensign
John Owens, Drummer
Jacob L. Stilwell, Fifer
Sergts.: John Drummond, Isaac Nailor, Rice G. McCoy, Thomas Nicholas (discharged Oct. 16), Josiah
    Thomas (promoted Oct. 6)
Corpls.: James B. McCullough, Jonathan Heartley, Thomas Chapple, David Bigger

Privates

James Robertson
Joseph Warnick
   killed in action
John Hutcherson
   killed in action
Danl. Peyton
Danl. Williams
James Garner
Amos Little
Hezekiah Robertson
   Henry Hucklebury sub-
   stituted in his place
Joseph Daniel
John Denney
James King
John Gibson, Jr.
   George Uland sub-
   stituted in his place
John Walker
Danl. Pettit
John Carr

William Nailor
Vinyard Pound
Andrew Holland
John Heartley
Danl. Kimberlain
Saml. Stockwell
David Owens, Jr.
Robert Robertson, Jr.
   deserted Sep. 25
Absalom Carr
Thomas Gibson
   wounded in action
James Robertson, Jr.
James Anderson
William Tissler
   killed in action
William Hutto
Thomas Burnett
Charles Mathews
John Covert
William Wright
John Finley

John Martin
Isaac Stark
John Kelley
Wilson Sargent
David Copple
William G. Gubrick
James Elliot
John Agins
Moses Stark
John Reed
George Reed
Benjn. Pool
James McDonald
Isaac D. Huffman
Alexr. Montgomery
William Hooker
   deserted Oct. 14
Leonard Houston
   wounded in action
James Mooney
Tobias Miller
Lucius Kibby
John Gibson, Sr.

WILLIAM HARGROVE'S COMPANY OF INFANTRY [Knox County area]

William Hargrove, Captain
Cary Ashley, Ensign, resigned Oct. 1811
Isaac Montgomery, Lieut.
Henry Hopkins, Ensign, promoted to Sergt.
Sergts.: Bolden Conner, James Evens, Daniel Miller, William Scales
Corpls.: David Johnson, Paten Whealer, William Taylor, David Brumfield

Privates

Samuel Anderson
John Braselton
Jer. Harrison
John Fleanor
Joseph Ladd
Pinkney Anderson
Thomas Archer
William Archer
James Lenn
Charles Collins
Joshua Day
   deserted Oct. 2
Charles Penelton
   deserted Oct. 16
William Person
John Mills
Robert Milborn
Jon'n Cochran
John Lout
Nathl. Wodrough
James Young
John Tucker

Arthur Meeks
   deserted Oct. 12
John Conner
Reuben Fitzgerald
   wounded slightly
Zachary Skelton
Jacob Skelton
Benjn. Scales
William Gordon
Laben Putman
Reding Putman
John Many
Johnson Fitzgerald
Thomas Arnett
James Skelton
Elias Barker
Saml. Whealor
Robert Whealor
William Mangoon
Coonrod Lancaster
   deserted Oct. 2
James McClure
Haz. Putman
Benj. Cannon

Joshua Stapleton
William Skelton
William Harrington
Randolph Owens
Isaac Twedle
James Crow
Richard M. Kirk
George Coningham
James Skidmore
Joseph Mixson
Samuel Gasten
Edwd. Whitacor
Charles Meeks
Robert Skelton
   badly wounded
David Laurence
   discharged Sep. 19
Joseph Inglish
   discharged Sep. 19
Robt. Montgomery
   discharged Sep. 19
Cabreen Merry
   discharged Sep. 19

JOHN NORRIS' COMPANY OF INFANTRY [Clark County area]

John Norris, Captain, *wounded in action*
John Harrod, Lieut.
Joseph Carr, Ensign
Elisha Carr, Drummer
Joseph Perry, Fifer
Sergts.: George Drummond, William Coombs, Bazil Prather, David Smith
Corpls.: Henry Ward, John Harman, Joel Combs, Robert Hombs, David Kelley (app'ted Sep. 30)

Privates

Robert McNight
William Stacey
Gasper Loots
Saml. Duke
Edward Norris
James Shipman
Henry Cresamore
Peter Sherwood
C. Fipps
George Ditsler
John Gray
John Kelly
Jacob Daily
David Cross
Thos. Clendennan
killed in action
Robt. Cunningham
Abraham Kelley
killed in action
Henry Jones
killed in action

James Curry
Saml. McClung
app'ted Qr. M. Sergt.
Sep. 27
James Smith
John Perry
Jeris Fordyce
Benoni Wood
James Kelly
Cornelius Kelly
wounded
Amos Goodwin
Em'l Wayman
William Harman
John Newland
John Tilfero
William Walker app'ted
substitute in his place
Micajah Peyton
Loyd Prather
Adam Peck
Saml. McClintick

Benjn. Thompson
John Weathers
William Eakin
Evan Arnold
John D. Jacob
Hugh Epsy
Robert Pippin
Townly Ruby
John McClintick
Wm. Rayson
Wm. Aston
Reubin Slead
Josiah Taylor
George Hoke
Danl. McCoy
Jacob Piersall
Henry Hope
Saml. Neal
Thomas Highfill
Robt. McClellan
James Taylor

BENJAMIN PARKE'S TROOP OF LIGHT DRAGOONS [Knox County area]

Benjamin Parke, Captain (promoted to Major)
Lieuts.: Thomas Emerson, George Wallace, Jr.
Sergts.: Christian Grater, William Harper, Henry Ruble, John McClure
Corpls.: W. H. Dunnica, Charles Allen, Reuben Sallinger, Levi Elliot
Cornet: John Bathis
Sadler: John Braden

Privates

Charles Smith
Peter Jones
Joshua Bond
Parmenas Beckes
William Prince
Jesse Slawson
Toussaint Dubois, Jr.
Thomas Randolph
killed in action
John McDonald
Miles Dolahan
John Dolahan
John Elliot
Mathias Rose, Jr.
Henry Dubois
Jesse Lucas
William Berry
discharged Oct. 28
William Purcell
John Crosby
William Mehan
killed in action
Leonard Crosby

Saml. Drake
Saml. Emerson
Nathl. Harness
Daniel Decker
Howson Seaton
John D. Hay
Hiram Decker
Ebenezer Welton
John I. Neely
John McBain
app'ted trumpeter
Sep. 29
Pierre Laplante
James Steen
Andrew Purcell
John Pea
Albert Badolett
Josiah L. Holmes
William W. Holmes
Thomas Coulter
Charles McClure
Jacque Andre
Thomas McClure
Thomas Palmer

General W. Johnston
William A. McClure
James McClure
Arch'd McClure
James Neal
John Wyant
Charles Scott
James S. Petty
Isaac White
killed in action
John McClure
Henry I. Mills
James Meed
George Croghhn
Abner Hynes
Benjn. Sanders
James Nabb
John O'Fallen
badly wounded
William Luckett
Landon Carter
Robert Buntin, Jr.
John I. Smith
Robert Sturgen
James Harper

DAVID ROBB'S COMPANY OF INFANTRY [Knox County area]

David Robb, Captain
Joseph Montgomery, Lieut.
John Waller, Ensign
Bryant Harper, Trumpeter
Sergts.: Elsberry Armstrong, Henry Reel, John Benson, William Maxidon
Corpls.: Ezekiel Kite, George Anthees (wounded), James Robb (badly wounded), William Johnson

Privates

Abm. Decker
James Tweedle
John Za Orton
Armstead Bennett
William Peters
Stewart Cunningham
Francis Hall
   died Nov. 2
Booker Shields
William Tweedle
John Slaven
James Langsdown
John Suverns
Thomas Sullivan
Jesse Music
Daniel Fisher
   mortally wounded;
   died Nov. 12
William Allsop
Joseph Garress
Thomas C. Vines
Edward Butner
   mortally wounded;
   died Nov. 8
Saml. James
Thomas Shouse
Frederick Reel
William Selvey

James Bass
George Leech, Jr.
David Mills
Thomas Gwins
John Black
   mortally wounded;
   died Nov. 13
Jonah Robinson
Isaac Rogers
   wounded in action
William Robinson
John Rogers
   badly wounded
William Carson
George Litton
David Knight
William Downing
Thomas Jordan
   transferred to Capt.
   Dubois' Company
James Banks
   wounded in action
William Bass
James Miner
Hugh Shaw
Peter Cutright
David Lilley
Thomas Garress
   badly wounded

James Asberry
   killed in action
Joseph Tobin
   slightly wounded
Robert Wilson
   wounded
John Riggs
John Christ
Theodorus Davis
Thomas Parker Vanpelt
John Crawford
Kader Powell
   killed in action
Thomas Dunn
Jacob Korter
William Askin
Jonathan Humphreys
Alexr. Mahen
   badly wounded
William Witherholt
Moses Sandridge
David Edwards
John Dragoo
Saml. Hamilton
Robert Tennesson
Richard Potts
Joseph Wright
George Robinson
Thomas West
   badly wounded

THOMAS SCOTT'S COMPANY OF INFANTRY [Knox County area]

Thomas Scott, Captain
Jonathon Purcell, Lieut.
Ensigns: John Scott, John Welton, Francis Mallet, Lanty Johnston (sick; sent home Sep. 29), Samuel
   Roquest
Corpls.: John Moore, Abm. Westfall (sick; sent home Oct. 2), Elick C. Dushane, Charles Bono

Privates

Jesse Willas
   sick; sent home
   Oct. 29
James McDonald
Jon'n Hornback
Alpheus Pickard
John McCoy
   killed in action
Zebulon Hogue
   sick; sent home
   Oct. 29
Andrew Westfall
William Watson
Walter Neil
William A. Clark
William Welton
   wounded badly
Henry Lain

Abraham Wood
   killed in action
John Collins
William Williams
Saml. Risley
William Collins
   badly wounded
Charles Fisher
Robert Johnston
Absolem Thorn
William Penny
William Young
William Jones
John Collins, Jr.
   sick; went home
William Bailey
Charles Mail
Richard Westrope
Thomas McClain
Joseph Ridley

Henry O'Niel
Joseph Alton
Baptist Topah
Antoine Gerome
Mitchel Rusherville
Charles Dudware
John Baptist Bono
Joseph Bushby
Henry Merceau
Augusta Lature
Louis Abair
Charles Soudriett
Ambrose Dashney
Francis Berbo
Francis Bonah
   killed in action
Semo Belonga
   died Nov. 18
Lewis Lovellett
Francis Boryeau

15

Thomas Scott's Company, *continued*

John Mominny
  discharged Oct. 8
Pierre Delurya, Sr.
Pierre Delurya, Jr.
Joseph Besaw
Louis Boyeaw

Dominic Pashy
Antoine Cornia
Antoine Ravellett
J. Baptist Cardinal
Jack Obah
  killed in action
Toussaint Deno (?)

Joseph Renno (?)
Eustace Sevanne
Nicholas Velmare
Joseph Sansusee
Francis Arpah
Antoine Shennett
Madan Cardinal
Louis Lonya

SPIER SPENCER'S COMPANY OF MOUNTED RIFLEMEN [Harrison County area]

Spier Spencer, Captain, *killed in action*
Richard McMahan, 1st Lieut., *killed in action*
George F. Pope, 2d Lieut., resigned Oct. 21
Samuel Flanagan, promoted from Ensign to 2d Lieut., & then to 1st Lieut.
John Tipton, promoted from Private to Ensign & then to Captain
Jacob Zenor, promoted from Private to 2d Lieut.
Philip Bell, promoted from Private to Ensign
Sergts.: Pearce Chamberlain, Henry Batman (*wounded*), Elijah Hurst, Benjamin Bogard
Corpls.: Robert Biggs (*badly wounded*), John Taylor, Benjamin Shields, William Bennington
Musicians: Daniel Cline, Isham Stroud (*wounded*)

Privates

John Arick
Ignatius Able
Enos Best
Alpheus Branham
Gadon Branham
  badly wounded
Daniel Bell
James Brown
Jesse Butler
Mason Carter
John Cline
Marshall Dunken
  killed in action
William Davis
  killed in action
Thomas Davidson

James Dyce [Dyer]
Henry Enlow
James Harbison
James Hubbourd
Beverly Hurst
William Hurst
William Hurst, Jr.
Robert Jones
James Kelley
Thomas McColley
Noah Mathena
William Nance
Thomas Owens
Samuel Pfrimer
Edward Ransdle
  slightly wounded
James Spencer
  slightly wounded
Christover Shucks

Joshua Shields
  badly wounded
Samuel Sand
  killed in action
George Spencer
  badly wounded
Jacob Snider
Jonathan Wright
James Wilson
  badly wounded
John Wheeler
  slightly wounded
James Watts
Isham Vest
George Zenor
P. McMickle
Sandford Ransdle
  slightly wounded

JACOB WARRICK'S COMPANY OF INFANTRY [Knox County area]

Jacob Warrick, Captain, *wounded in action;* died Nov. 9
James Smith, Jr., Captain, app'ted Nov. 9
William Calton, Lieut., discharged Sep. 27
James Duckworth, Ensign
Sergts.: Robert Montgomery, Robt McGary, Jeremiah Piercall, Isaac Woods
Corpls.: Benjn. Venables, Thomas Black, Robt Denney, Thos Montgomery, Jr. (promoted to Lieut. Sep. 30)

Privates

James Alsop
  sick; sent home
  Sep. 24
James Stewart
Jesse Key
  sick; discharged
  Sep. 27
Bennet Key
Jesse Brewer
Richard Davis
Asa Musick
Smith Mounce
  deserted Oct. 15

James Stapleton
Fielding Lucas
John McGary
Thomas Montgomery
  discharged Oct. 15
John Montgomery
James Weathers
  badly wounded
Ephraim Murphy
Langston Drew
William Gwins
  badly wounded
William Black

Joshua Capps
  sick; discharged
  Oct. 27
Andrew McFaddin
Lewis Sealy
James Bohannon
  deserted Sep. 27
Danl. Duff
  sick; discharged
Squire McFaddin
Wilson Jones
Jeremiah Robinson
Hugh Todd

Jacob Warrick's Company, *continued*

John Gwins
 wounded slightly
Martin Laughon
 badly wounded
William Todd
Burton Litton
George Linxwiler
Peter Whetstone
 deserted Oct. 15
William Stevens
 wounded slightly

Timothy Downy
John Colyer
 sick; discharged
 Sep. 24
Benjn. Stoker
 promoted to Corpl.
Thomas Aldmond
 badly wounded
Miles Armstrong

William Aldmond
William Young
Thomas Duckworth
Maxwell Jolly
John Robb
 wounded slightly
John Neel
Randolph Clarke
William Black

ANDREW WILKINS' COMPANY OF INFANTRY [Knox County area]

Andrew Wilkins, Captain, *slightly wounded*
Adam Lisman, Lieut.
Samuel McClure, Ensign
Sergts.: John Hadden, Thomas Black, Samuel Leman, Charles Booth
Corpls.: Daniel Carlin, John Edwards, Richard Engle, Abraham Bogard (Charles Landon app'ted substitute for Bogard Oct. 27)

Privates

John Johnston
Thomas Robins
Peter Johnston
John Mills
Abraham Johnston
James Mitchel
Robert Murphy
Jesse Cox
 John Curry app'ted as
 substitute Sep. 22
William Ashby
 Nathl. Robins appted
 as substitute Sep. 24
Loudwick Earnest
Edward Wilks
Rubin Moore
Thomas Anderson
Saml. Middleton
James Calleway
James Tims
Isaac Luzader
Saml. Carruthers
Asa McCord
Nathaniel Adams
 Stephen Terry app'ted
 as substitute Oct. 22

Robert Lilley
John Elliot
William Hollingsworth
William Francis
Obediah F. Patrick
Aaron Quick
 Nathan Check app'ted
 as substitute Oct. 22
John Murphy
Ebenezer Blackston
James Horrell
 app'ted corpl. Oct. 27
Sam. Culbertson
Robert Elsey
John Davis
Christopher Coleman
Henry Matney (or Many)
Robert Bratton
William Flint
 John Flint app'ted as
 substitute Oct. 13
John Rodarmel
John Culbertson
Joseph Hobbs
Albert Davis
Thomas Horrel
 discharged Sep. 26

Joseph Edwards
William Hill
 app'ted corpl. Oct. 18
John Engle
Henry Collins
John Meek
Thomas Johnston
Madison Collins
William Black
Luke Matson
 furloughed Sep. 22
John Harden
Edward Bowls
Robert Polke
Charles Ellison
George Gill
James Grayham
 furloughed Oct. 22
Joseph McRonnels
 William Brown app'ted
 as substitute Oct. 22
Jon'n Purrell
George Bright
Peter Lisman
William Arnet
Saml. Ledgerwood
Martin Palmore

WALTER WILSON'S COMPANY OF INFANTRY [Knox County area]

Walter Wilson, Captain
Benjamin Beckes, Lieut., app'ted Qr. Master Nov. 10
Sergts.: Thomas I. Withers, Thomas White (*badly wounded*), Isaac Minor, John Decker (sick; sent home
 Oct. 27)
Corpls.: Daniel Risley, William Shuck, John Grey, Peter Brinton (sick; sent home Oct. 11)
Ensign, Joseph Macomb

Privates

William Gamble
 app'ted Qr. M.
 Sergt., Sep. 25
William Brinton
 sick; sent home
 Oct. 27

Batest Chavalar
Asa Thorn
Thomas Chambers
Joseph Harbour
Adam Harness
James Jordan
John Chambers

John Anthis
Lewis Frederick
Lewis Reel
 died Oct. 13
Richard Greentree
Saml. Clutter
Jacob Anthis

Walter Wilson's Company, *continued*

James Walker
  sick; discharged
  Oct. 27
Nathan Baker
John Bargor
Sinicky Almy
Peter Bargor
Moses Decker
  badly wounded
Joseph Voodry
Woolsey Pride
Robert Brinton
  deserted Oct. 24

Abraham Pea
Thomas Milbourn
  deserted Oct. 24
William Pride
Benjn. Walker
Jacob Harbonson
  deserted Oct. 24
Sutton Coleman
  deserted Oct. 24
Joab Chappel
Robert McClure

John Risley
  deserted Oct. 24
Jon'n Walker
  deserted Oct. 24
Isaac Walker
David Knight
  sick; sent home
  Sep. 27
James Parcell
  sick; sent home
  Sep. 24

KENTUCKY TROOPS

Taken from the Report of the Adjutant General of Kentucky, 1891. Some Kentucky men served in Indiana companies.

Field and Staff of Battalion of Kentucky Light Dragoons

Samuel Wells, Major
James Hunter, Adjt.

PETER FUNK'S COMPANY

Peter Funk, Captain
Lewis Hite, Lieut,
Samuel Kelly, Cornet
Samuel Frederick, Farrier
William Cooper, trumpeter (app'ted Sep. 16)
Sergts.: Adam Mills, (*killed in action*), James Martin (*killed in action*), Henry Canning, Lee White (app'ted Sep. 24)
Corpl.: Elliot Wilson, app'ted Oct. 16

Privates

William Duberly
John Edlin
William Ferguson
Benjamin W. Gath
James Hite
Isaac Hollingsworth
Samuel U. Luckett

William M. Luckett
  transferred to Benj.
  Parke's Co. Sep. 23
Joseph Kennison
Enos Mackey
Thomas P. Majors
James Muckleroy
John Murphy

John Shaw
  transferred to
  spies, Sep. 23
Thomas Stafford
John Smith
William T. Tully
Moses Williamson
Samuel Wills (or Willis)

FREDERICK GEIGER'S COMPANY OF MOUNTED RIFLEMEN

Frederick Geiger, Captain, *wounded slightly*
Presley Ross, Lieut.   William Edwards, Ensign
Joseph Paxton, trumpeter
Sergts.: Robert McIntire, (*wounded*), Robert Edwards, Daniel McClellan, John Jackson
Corpls.: Stephen Mars (*killed in action*), John Hicks, John Nash, Henry Waltz

Privates

Martin Adams
Phillip Allen
Springer Augustus
Robert Barnaba
Joseph Barkshire
Charles Barkshire
  wounded
George Beck
Thomas Beeler
William Brown
James Ballard
Adam Burket
John Buskirk
  wounded
Charles L. Byrn
Temple C. Byrn
William Cline
John Dunbar

James M. Edwards
Richard Findley
Nicholas Fleener
  wounded
Joseph Funk
John Grimes
Isaac R. Gwathmey
Henry Hawkins
James Hanks
Zachariah Ingram
Joshua Jest
John Lock
Elijah Lane
Hudson Martin
John Maxwell
  wounded badly
Josh. (or John) Maxwell
Daniel Minor
John Ousley
  killed in action

Michael Plaster
Samuel Pound
Jonathan Pound
Peter Priest
Patrick Shields
John W. Slaughter
Joseph Smith
  killed in action
Thomas Speeks (or Spunks)
James Summerville
  killed in action
Edmond Ship
Wilson Taylor
Samuel Trigg
William Trigg
Abraham Walk
George W. Wells
Samuel W. White
Greenbury Wright

EXCERPTS FROM ACCOUNTS
OF WAYNE COUNTY OLD SETTLERS
MEETINGS, 1855-1856,
as reported in the *Richmond Palladium*

Henry Hoover spoke as follows: Towards the last of March, 1807, my father left Warren County, Ohio, and with his family, myself the oldest, landed in a snow storm on the last day of March, on the bluff a little north of Griffin Mendenhall's residence in what is now Richmond. The snow covered the ground until the 10th of April, when the process of grubbing and clearing land commenced in good earnest. . . . Until 1811 Dearborn County extended from the Ohio River up to Fort Recovery, but in that year Wayne County was formed and organized. I was a member of the first jury that tried a criminal case in this county. The court was one of Oyer and Terminer and was advertised to sit at the house of Richard Rue, Esq. Benjamin Parke was president judge and James Noble, prosecuting attorney. The court adjourned to the woods and there we the jury listened to the case of a certain boy who had stolen a Barlow knife, worth 25 cents, from the store of John Smith. . . .

The War of 1812 brought with it trouble and retarded the settlement of the county. The Presbyterian, the Baptist, the Methodist, the Newlight or Christian, and the Quaker had had up to that time no difficulties about creeds or baptism—they helped each other roll logs, raise barns and houses, postponing doctrinal differences until they became more independent of each other. The war hastened this independence for until then it was not known to our neighbors that we Quakers would not fight. I was drafted to perform an eight day tour on the frontiers, hunting for moccasin tracks. I refused and for this disobedience was fined sixteen sheep. The years 1812, '13, and '14 was a reign of terror on a small scale for Quakers—some were put in jail and some had their farming implements taken and sold. . . .

Thomas Bulla, being requested to give some incidents of his settlement in the county, said he was born in Randolph County, North Carolina, Aug. 2, 1780, and came to this county, then the Northwest Territory, about the middle of October, 1806. Mr. Foutz came in company with him, from Germantown, Ohio. There was no road, and they came through the woods, without any evidence of the correctness of their course, except their supposed location of the Whitewater country. They built a cabin 12 feet square, and went back to Ohio, brought out the family of Mr. Foutz, his mother-in-law, and returned for his own. He got them, with a few household articles in a wagon, which he drove himself as well as the cow. He came part of the way with Andrew Hoover, and part of his family, but the greater part of the way by himself, driving his horses and his cow and calf. His cabin had no door, no "chinking" between the logs, and the winter was very severe.

The cold Friday, which is remembered by all who lived at that day, occurred this winter, and he was kept busy through that and other days, making fires. He gave several other incidents which we do not now remember, and concluded by saying they had pretty hard times, but when he thought of the poor soil of the country he came from, and the dark rich soil upon which he then was, he was content, feeling that with health, prosperity would attend his labors. Although he had to go some 30 miles, to Twin Creek, to mill, and endured many other privations, he was as happy then as he had ever been since, and would be willing to be thrown again to the same situation in life.

He had a grateful recollection of the sincere friendship that characterized the conduct of the settlers of that day—their free and open hospitality, their ever-ready disposition to aid and assist each other. Then he was not uneasy about obtaining money, or the safety of investments. When they had meat, corn and milk, and the sympathy of a few neighbors, he was happy. His daughter Jane was, he supposed, the first white child that died in the county, which was in 1807. She was buried near Whiteheads. Old Mr. Crull was the first preacher he ever heard preach in the county. The first crop of corn raised in the county was much injured by the frost, and the squirrels took most of it at that.

John Peele said he was born in Wayne County, North Carolina, March 27, 1791, and came to this county in March, 1815. He was seven weeks on the road, and when he came to where Richmond now is, he found John Smith selling goods in a small building at the corner of Main and Front streets. He went up north and worked for Geo. Shuggart, for $10 per month. While there, in 1815, he traded pantaloons, with Thomas Woodward, and the pants he got, were the identical ones he now had on. They were made of cotton, which was picked from pods and seeds, carded, spun and wove by hand. This was before Whitney's cotton gin, the carding machine, and power loom came into general use. He had no money when he came here. Sold his wagon for a cow and some sheep. The dogs killed his sheep, his horse died, and his cow killed herself by drinking syrup from a sugar camp kettle, which had been left exposed. Notwithstanding this he was contented and happy. The first sermon he heard preached was by Wm. Holman.

Col. Smith Hunt being called upon read the following sketch of his emigration and settlement of this county.

About the first of March in the year 1806, my father, three brothers and myself, left Clermont County, Ohio, for the purpose of settling in the valley of Whitewater. We found an indistinct road as far as where Fairhaven is now situated; but the remainder of the way to Elkhorn we had to cut out a road for our teams. We arrived at Elkhorn on the 10th of the month. On the evening of our arrival we cut a board tree—the next day we cut the logs, hauled them, raised a cabin 16 by 18 feet, made the clap boards, covered our cabin, and moved into it that evening. We then went to work and cleared off five acres of land, and planted it in corn. This done we commenced building a mill, which was ready for cracking corn in the month of August. The difficulty then was, that there was but little corn to crack, until the growing corn ripened. A large proportion of the corn was so badly frost-bitten, the people could not think of eating it. It was so much injured that it smelled when being ground. However, some persons had to eat it and they looked well and were hearty. The hogs were fattened on beach mast.

There had some four or five families come out in advance of us, and those who had raised any corn had to pack it to the Great Miami or to Brookville, as there was no mill nearer, except hand mills, until we got ours into operation.

There was but a small strip of territory, about eight miles wide, between the old boundary line and the Ohio State line, running up to Fort Recovery, belonging to Dearborn County. In the fall we built a somewhat more comfortable cabin, when our father moved up the family, consisting of three sisters, two younger brothers, Charles and Stephen, and one nephew, James H. Andrews, leaving the three oldest brothers, Jonathan, James and Timothy in Ohio. The brothers who came with me were named George, John and William.

By this time quite a number of newcomers had landed in our neighborhood, and the small strip of territory was nearly all taken up—cabins were built all over the woods and wherever a cabin was put up, the string of the latch always hung on the outside.

Soon after General William Henry Harrison made the treaty of 1809, by which the Twelve Mile Purchase was secured, and even before it was surveyed, and offered for sale, the squatters moved onto it, and by the time of the War of 1812, there was quite a population on it. When the Indians commenced stealing horses, the people became much alarmed—some left for the settlements from whence they came and others moved into blockhouses.

After William Hull's surrender, General Harrison was appointed Commander in Chief of the Northwestern army. My brother George was Colonel of the 8th Regiment of militia; myself and James Brown were Majors General. Harrison ordered that our regiment should furnish one company to march to the north. We organized the company and marched as far as Piqua, but when the Indians commenced depredations upon our frontier, we petitioned Gen. Harrison that the company might be returned and stationed on the frontier, which petition was granted. I spent the entire summer of 1813, finding my own horse and provisions, in raising troops and ranging to protect the frontier, but not having been enrolled in the regular army, I cannot derive any pay under the pension laws. Major Brown died soon after this, whilst a member of the Legislature at Corydon.

Sometime before the war my three elder brothers moved into the neighborhood, so there were nine of us in the immediate settlement. Four of them died and were buried in the graveyard at Elkhorn; three removed to La Porte and have since died, so there are but two of the nine brothers remaining, Charles who resides in Iowa and myself.

The families who resided here before we came were Richard Rue, and our venerable old friend George Holman, who is still with us, Rev. Lazarus Whitehead, Andrew Endsley, and their families and perhaps others. Our neighborhood was called the Kentucky settlement, because Geo. Holman and Richard Rue, the two first settlers, had come from that state. There was a small settlement at the mouth of Hanna's creek, which was called the Carolina settlement, the emigration having been from South Carolina.

Names	Age	Date of Immigr't'n	Birth-place	Names	Age	Date of Immigr't'n	Birth-place
Albin, Moreland	62	1839	OH	Clark, D. J.	82	1834	VT
Albin, Mrs.	58	1838	PA	Cline, Jacob	57	1839	GER
Albright, Jonas	77	1837	NC	Coon, Mrs.	43	1833	IN
Bachelor, Daniel	71	1836	ME	Cooper, John A.	54	1839	OH
Bachelor, Mrs.	67	1835	OH	Corey, Rev. C.	80	1832	NY
Back, Mrs.	56	1833	OH	Cormary, Mrs.	63	1834	VA
Banta, Mrs. E.	62	1829	OH	Cornell, B. F.	65	1833	OH
Basher, Michael	70	1834	PA	Cornell, Mrs. B. F.	60	1835	NJ
Beane, Esler	70	1836	VA	Corpe, E. H.	43	1835	OH
Beane, W A.	51	1836	OH	Cowan, J. W.	57	1834	OH
Beard, Frederick	63	1831	OH	Cowan, Mrs.	54	1837	PA
Beardsley, Mrs. Dr.	73	1830	—	Crary, C. W.	49	1837	NY
Beck, Albert	65	1833	OH	Crary, James H.	—	----	—
Beck, Sr., James	76	1830	KY	Crary, John L	59	1834	OH
Beck, Mrs.	66	1830	ME	Crary, Mrs. J. L.	—	----	—
Beck, Noah	63	1834	MD	Cripe, B. C.	59	1830	OH
Beckner, Jacob	84	1834	VA	Cripe, Daniel T.	58	1830	OH
Benner, Benj	75	1834	PA	Cripe, J. M.	54	1830	OH
Benner, Mrs.	66	1834	NY	Darr, David	60	1830	OH
Bishop, D. C.	62	1837	NY	DeCamp, Silas	58	1834	IN
Bishop, Mrs.	58	1835	NY	DeCamp, Mrs.	53	1834	IN
Blue, Abner	60	1836	OH	Defrees, J. H.	67	1831	TN
Boomershire, S.	66	1838	OH	Defrees, Mrs.	58	1833	—
Bowser, Elijah	58	1832	OH	Dewey, Mrs. O. F.	48	1836	SC
Bowser, T.	50	1832	OH	Dodge, E. F.	45	1833	IN
Bowser, Wm.	62	1832	OH	Eby, David	60	1835	OH
Bowser, Mrs.	60	1831	OH	Eby, Samuel	72	1837	OH
Boyd, Thomas	66	1839	PA	Eisenbeis, Wm.	53	1834	MD
Braden, R. D.	70	1834	OH	Eisenbeis, Mrs.	54	1835	OH
Braden, Mrs.	65	1834	OH	Eldridge, David	—	1835	OH
Broderick, Mrs. N. F.	64	1835	—	Ellis, J. W.	54	1831	NY
Brown, Amos	62	1837	PA	Ellis, Joel	58	1830	NY
Brown, H. K.	82	1835	TN	Engle, Andrew	57	1832	OH
Brown, T. C.	55	1837	PA	Engle, Mrs.	60	1839	VA
Bunger, S.	53	1828	OH	Farber, C. S.	68	1835	VA
Bunger, Mrs.	49	1835	CAN	Fetters, Peter	73	1833	PA
Burns, Mrs. John	60	1832	OH	Foster, C. E.	50	1836	CT
Burns, Torrance	72	1834	KY	Funk, Joseph	57	1823	OH
Butler, T. P.	52	1831	OH	Gamberling, Geo.	50	1846	OH
Butler, W. H.	48	1831	IN	Gamberling, Mrs.	47	1835	VA
Caldwell, Robert	43	1836	IN	Ganger, Daniel	72	1829	PA
Carlton, Mrs.	57	1834	—	Ganger, Samuel	73	1836	PA
Carmien, W. H.	43	1836	IN	Garrison, A.	53	1838	NY
Carmien, Wm.	76	1831	MD	Garven, D.	60	1835	OH
Carpenter, Mrs. Elias	74	1829	VA	Gregory, E.	63	1837	CT
Case, B. V.	69	1836	NY	Grissamer, R.	55	1836	PA
Case, Ettie	42	1837	IN	Hahn, —	54	1830	—
Case, L. F.	73	1836	NY	Halstead, Elizabeth	53	1838	NY
Case, Mrs.	69	1836	NY	Hascall, C. S.	68	1837	NY
Cathcart, B. F.	61	1830	IN	Hascall, Mrs.	59	1835	NY
Chamberlain, Mrs. E. G.	60	1839	NY	Hawks, Cephas	67	1835	NY
Chamberlain, Mrs. P. A.	63	1837	NY	Hawks, Mrs.	61	1838	VT
Childs, Mrs. S.	67	1830	NY	Hawks, E.	61	1837	NY

Names	Age	Date of Immigr't'n	Birth-place
Hawks, J. P.	57	1837	NY
Hawks, Mrs.	55	1835	NY
Heaton, P.	70	1835	OH
Hendricks, W. C.	77	1839	CT
Henry, Mrs. Dr.	62	1840	—
Hess, B.	63	1829	OH
Hess, E.	68	1829	OH
Hess, Mrs.	62	1833	OH
Hess, I.	61	1829	OH
Hire, John	62	1832	OH
Hire, Mrs.	40	1839	IN
Hitchcock, H. H.	63	1837	NY
Hitchcock, Mrs.	54	1837	NY
Hively, Mrs.	53	1835	OH
Hixon, S. L.	73	1834	PA
Hockert, J.	55	1829	IN
Hockert, Mrs.	48	1836	OH
Hopkins, Mrs.	44	1835	OH
Howenstein, R.	60	1838	OH
Hubbell, A. L.	63	1834	OH
Irwin, E.	53	1832	PA
Irwin, R. D.	55	1832	PA
Irwin, Mrs.	47	1835	PA
Jackson, F.	65	1838	IRE
Jackson, Mrs.	58	1835	OH
Jackson, Ira	59	1829	OH
Jackson, Mrs. Ira	56	1838	NY
Jacobs, Mrs. Henry	—	—	—
Johnson, G C	56	1836	—
Juday, A.	54	1838	—
Juday, B.	42	1836	OH
Juday, J.	73	1830	—
Kellogg, Mrs.	73	1837	—
King, M. D.	68	1837	PA
King, Mrs.	53	1839	OH
Kinnison, A.	54	1837	OH
Kinnison, A.	58	1833	VA
Kitson, Mrs.	71	1838	NY
Knapp, D. J.	43	1836	IN
Knox, J. D.	72	1831	VA
Koonce, Wm.	60	1835	VA
Krupp, D. H.	43	1837	—
Lake, R. T.	64	1837	VA
Lake, Mrs.	57	1830	OH
Larimer, Brice	—	1835	OH
Latta, James M.	46	1834	IN
Linderman, J. A.	60	1832	GER
Linderman, John	63	1834	MD
Long, H.	52	1839	—
Longacre, J. W.	58	1829	IN
Longacre, T.	48	1831	IN
McBride, Mrs.	63	1831	IN
McCloud, James	69	1834	OH
McCullough, Andrew	76	1838	PA
McCullough, Mrs. Andrew	71	1838	PA
McCumsey, Luke	53	1835	OH
McCumsey, Mrs.	50	1839	—
McDowell, Mrs. S.	56	1835	WV
McKibben, J.	75	1838	IRE
McNutt, Joseph	71	1835	VA
McReynolds, Mrs. Jas.	—	—	—
Manning, A.	62	1834	OH
Manning, Mrs.	50	1835	PA
Martin, Ed.	71	1832	PA
Martin, Mrs.	63	1833	OH
Matthews, D.	59	1829	OH
Matthews, E.	60	1830	OH
Matthews, John	61	1831	OH
Mayfield, J. H.	59	1834	DC
Mayfield, Mrs.	55	1830	OH
Mercer, M.	59	1832	PA
Mercer, Mary	81	1839	VA
Messick, Mrs. P. C.	43	1836	IN
Miller, Henry	57	1839	PA
Miller, Rebecca	57	1831	IN
Miller, Sam R.	60	1835	PA
Mills, A. H.	76	1835	VA
Mills, J. W.	44	1836	IN
Mitchell, Mrs. E.	53	1839	OH
Mitchell, Elizabeth	—	1830	—
Moore, John	59	1835	NY
Moore, Thomas	47	1835	NY
Newell, George	40	1839	IN
Newell, Joseph	45	1835	NY
Newell, Mrs.	76	1831	MD
Newell, W. B.	50	1838	NH
Nihart, J.	54	1835	PA
Nihart, John	—	—	—
Norton, A. A.	76	1838	NY
Norton, Mrs.	75	1838	NY
Norton, W. H.	43	1838	NY
Pearman, B. F.	52	1829	IN
Pease, Warren	52	1830	OH
Pickerel, John	59	1835	OH
Poorbaugh, P.	63	1830	PA
Potter, Mrs.	58	1836	NY
Powell, J. L.	78	1839	VA
Powell, Mrs.	66	1837	NY
Price, M.	49	1831	OH
Prickett, Thomas	47	1833	IN
Purl, Mrs.	60	1833	MD
Purl, Mrs. Gabe	67	1835	VA

Names	Age	Date of Immigr't'n	Birth-place
Rippey, M.	76	1831	OH
Rohrer, John	53	1832	OH
Rohrer, Mrs.	52	1833	OH
Rohrer, Jos.	47	1832	OH
Rohrer, Mrs.	63	1831	OH
Roller, P. M.	77	1835	VA
Rosenberger, Nancy	53	1833	PA
Rowell, Geo. P.	—	1835	NH
Rowell, Mrs. Geo. P.	—	—	—
Rush, I.	51	1829	IN
Rush, R.	52	1828	OH
Rush, Mrs.	49	1836	NY
Scranage, Samuel	68	1836	VA
Shaefer, W.	53	1837	—
Sherwin, Leander	78	1837	NY
Shoup, Noah	54	1830	OH
Shrock, Mrs.	64	1834	VA
Shuey, J. H.	53	1837	OH
Shuey, Mrs.	43	1837	NY
Shuey, Mrs.	76	1837	—
Simonton, D. S.	61	1832	OH
Simonton, Mrs.	54	1834	NY
Smith, C. J.	65	1839	NJ
Smith, Mrs.	55	1835	MD
Smith, Con.	49	1838	NY
Smith, Mrs. Conrad	86	1838	NY
Smith, Mrs. N.	43	1836	OH
Smith, T.	67	1828	—
Snavely, Mrs. E.	44	1835	IN
Snyder, John	53	1835	OH
Sparklin, John	45	1834	IN
Sparklin, Mrs.	41	1838	IN
Stancliff, Mary	62	1830	IN
Starks, N.	47	1832	PA
Starks, Philo	73	1832	VT
Starks, Mrs.	71	1832	PA
Stauffer, Mrs. J.	57	1838	OH
Stauffer, Margaret	—	—	—
Stephenson, D. S.	48	1832	OH
Stephenson, Mrs.	45	1834	OH
Stetler, J. W.	40	1839	IN
Stetler, John	80	1838	PA
Stetler, Mrs.	73	1838	PA
Stevens, Mrs. B. F.	46	1834	NY
Stevens, Mrs. Ed.	47	1831	IN
Stillman, A. H.	49	1833	NY
Stillman, Mrs. Frances	62	1832-40	—
Stillman, Mrs. Rox	75	1837	—
Stiver, John	48	1836	OH
Stockdale, John N.	71	1834	OH
Stonder, Sam	50	1832	OH
Stotts, Mrs.	74	1831	OH
Strong, S. F.	62	1834	OH
Stroup, J.	50	1836	MI
Stroup, R.	74	1836	GER
Stump, A. D.	56	1838	—
Stutsman, Aaron	54	1839	PA
Stutsman, Sam	57	1832	OH
Stutz, Mrs.	54	1835	OH
Summey, Eli	61	1829	IN
Summey, Malinda	68	1832	OH
Swab, Wm	—	1833	OH
Swab, Wm, Mrs.	—	1832	IN
Terwilliger, R.	46	1837	NY
Thomas, C. M.	45	1838	PA
Thomas, W. A.	63	1828	VA
Thomas, W. A., Mrs.	46	1835	IN
Thompson, J. E.	51	1828	IN
Tibbetts, Mrs.	50	1832	OH
Unrue, Isaac	80	1836	VA
Vail, J. D.	65	1837	PA
Vail, Mrs.	51	1828	OH
Van Frank, C. P.	46	1835	NY
Van Frank, J.	76	1835	NY
Van Frank, Mrs. J.	71	1835	RI
Venamon, Harvey	75	1834	KY
Vinson, Irwin	63	1831	KY
Violett, Isaiah	44	1835	IN
Violett, John H.	50	1829	IN
Walburn, John	67	1838	OH
Walburn, Mrs.	65	1838	OH
Walker, E. W.	48	1835	OH
Walters, Geo.	74	1836	PA
Waugh, Wm	80	1831	DE
Weddell, J. E.	49	1831	PA
Weybright, D.	55	1830	OH
Weybright, M.	57	1830	OH
Weybright, Mrs.	56	1830	OH
Weyburn, Mrs. S. H.	53	1834	NY
Wilkinson, N.	52	1835	OH
Witmer, L. W.	48	1838	OH
Witmer, Mrs.	43	1837	NY
Yeoman, Mrs. S. P.	59	1837	OH
Zinn, Geo.	60	1837	OH
Zollinger, Jos.	56	1836	PA
Zollinger, Mrs.	54	1835	OH

JACKSON COUNTY MARRIAGES, 1816-1836

Compiled from microfilm copy in Genealogy Division of Jackson County Marriage Records, 1816-49, in courthouse at Brownstown. The original record books containing the marriages for these years were copied in 1899 and this copy made the official record. The names were checked with a typed compilation in the Genealogy Division made by the Daughters of the American Revolution.

Abel, Cudwith - Polly Conn	1- 3-1833
Abel, David - Milley Abel	lic. 10- 5-1833
Acton, Richard - Auvena Lorance	lic. 11-28-1835
Alexander, James - Fanny Maxwell	lic. 9-20-1836
Allen, James - Polly Goen	12-20-1832
Alloway, John - Anna Burns	lic. 3- 4-1831
Almes (or Alwes), John - Mary McBride	4- 1-1832
Alsup, Daniel - Elizabeth Reynolds	4- 9-1833
Alsup, Jesse - Selina Blackwood	lic. 11- 2-1836
Alsup, Leonard - Polly Brewer	lic. 7-23-1834
Anderson, James - Nancy Bryant	lic. 2- 1-1829
Applegate, Robert W. - Emily Johnson	lic. 8- 9-1836
Arnold, George - Cunnpendunk (?) Depurden	
	lic. 8-15-1835
Arthur, Joseph - Susanah Hurd	lic. 6-15-1831
Arthur, Ludwig - Anna David	lic. 4-24-1835
Bagwell, Elias - Lucy Chambers	lic 1-19-1822
Bagwell, Washington - Matilda Rogers	lic. 8-28-1829
Bagwell, William - Elvira S. Neff	lic. 12-22-1834
Baker, William - Anna Ellams	lic. 2- 3-1829
Baldwin, Jacob - Elizabeth Shields	lic. 7-13-1820
Baldwin, William - Peggy Henderson	lic. 6- 5-1824
Baldwin, William - Parmelia Brown	lic. 9-21-1829
Banks, Albert - Mehetabel Vermilya	lic. 7-24-1821
Banks, Samuel - Rhoda Coop	lic. 5-16-1836
Barnes, George - Abigail Taylor	lic. 7-14-1831
Barnes, John C. - Judith Taylor	lic 2-19-1831
Barnes, John C. - Angeline S. Dennison	
	lic. 12- 8-1834
Bates, James - Charity Sturgeon	10-21-1819
Bayright, Senecca - Lydia Ireland	12- 4-1817
Beckley, John - Rachel Burcham	8- 2-1817
Bedel, Calvin - Malinda McDonald	lic. 3-13-1830
Bedel, Samuel - Elizabeth A. Brooks	lic. 8-11-1834
Beem, Daniel S. - Malinda Richards	lic. 11-11-1834
Beem, Enoch - Phebe Richards	lic. 6-25-1824
Beem, Michael - Mary Lockman	3-11-1816
Beem, Neely - Leah Storm	1-26-1816
Beem, Richard - Rebecca Launcing	10-20-1817
Begsby, Nathaniel - Susanah Johnson	lic. 2-28-1829
Bell, James B. - Nancy Ann Collins	lic. 12- 8-1834
Bell, James H. - Nancy Richardson	lic. 3-23-1835
Bell, William D. - Elizabeth Thomas	lic. 3-20-1832
Benton, Henry - Sally Rose	lic. 4-10-1830
Benton, Norman - Hannah Wright	lic. 6-27-1830
Benton, Walter - Mehetabel Banks	lic. 3-30-1824
Berkey, Henry - Polly Iseminger	lic. 12-25-1819
Berkey, Jacob - Jane B. Graham	lic. 4-24-1830
Berkey, Michael - Eliza Burge	lic. 6-14-1834
Beyer, Henry - Nancy Smith	lic. 7-15-1835
Billings, Dennison S. - Clarissa Ann Morenn	
	6-10-1832
Black, Richard - Mary Ann Zollman	3-21-1833
Blair, Pryor S. - Eleanor Gouldy	7-20-1834
Bland, Meredith - Priscilla Burge	lic. 2-23-1835
Blevins, Jonathan - Elizabeth Tabor	3-22-1832
Blevins, Levi - Cynthia Mahuron	lic. 7- 1-1834
Bliss, James - Mary R. White	lic. 11-30-1820

Blunk, Moses - Catharine Abel	11-16-1834
Blunk, William - Lilly Ann Parker	lic. 1-10-1834
Bogard, Levi - Susannah Hoopingarner	lic. 8- 8-1820
Bough, Rufus - Mary Ann Zike	9- 6-1832
Boyatt, Jordan - Elizabeth Gregory	lic. 1- 2-1830
Boyles, David - Lydia Thompson	lic. 10-24-1820
Bramlett, William - Rebecca Livingston	lic. 5-15-1830
Brammer, Alexander - Elizabeth Morgan	1-19-1832
Branaman, Abraham - Barthena Wood	1-20-1832
Brandum, Lemuel - Patsey Mitchell	2-27-1834
Brannen, Thomas - Elizabeth Shelton	lic. 5-12-1836
Breadlove, John - Cyntha Mitchner	3-29-1832
Breadlove, Thomas - Elizabeth Mitchner	
	lic. 12- 9-1833
Brewer, Aaron - Bersheba West	lic. 4- 9-1835
Brewer, Mathew G. - Polly Redman	7-24-1832
Brewer, Samuel - Louisa Harrell	lic. 11-16-1836
Briner, Peter - Diadema Silence	lic. 1- 8-1834
Briner, William - Matilda Carl	lic. 11- 6-1826
Brockin, Joseph - Elizabeth Dowden	5-19-1817
Brooks, John - Sally Bedel	lic. 8-12-1834
Brown, Benjamin - Polly Chandler	lic. 4-17-1834
Brown, Isaac - Ruth Marshall	lic. 2- 9-1830
Brown, Isaiah - Gertrude Brammer	lic. 6- 3-1834
Brown, James - Polly Mooney	lic. 11-12-1821
Brown, John - Lovicy Jones	lic. 3-21-1830
Brown, John - Elizabeth Prather	lic. 10-12-1833
Brown, John B. - Elizabeth Abel	2-21-1833
Brown, Joseph - Anna Caldwell	lic. 12-19-1833
Brown, Thomas L. (or S.) - Catharine Sullivan	
	lic. 4-22-1834
Bryant, John - Nancy Burcham	lic. 3-14-1832
Buntin, Alfred - Lucinda Tinder	lic. 10-17-1836
Buntin, Tennessee - Elizabeth Shutters	7-25-1833
Burcham, William - Polly Speaks	lic. 4-13-1830
Burdsall, James - Margaret Winn	12-12-1833
Burge, Henry - Margaret Hecock	lic. 10-17-1830
Burgett, George - Esther Carr	lic. 8- 3-1836
Burrell, Bartholom - Mary Stephenson	
	lic. 9-29-1830
Burrell, Jesse - Martha Hanners	3-15-1821
Burton, David - Mary Ann Fentress	1-29-1833
Eutler, William - Lucinda Bierd	lic. 12-19-1835
Carr, John F. - Catharine Peck	lic. 3- 3-1832
Carr, Thomas - Jane Scantling	lic. 7- 9-1836
Carter, Benjamin M. - Margaret Naylor	7- 8-1832
Carter, Matthew - Allie Langley	lic. 2-25-1829
Carter, Robert - Anna Santland	9-25-1832
Carter, William E. - Thurza Johnson	lic. 1-25-1831
Cartright, John - Maria Link	lic. 12-24-1823
Cavendar, Robert - Isabel Boas	6- 9-1833
Chambers, Charles - Martha Jacobs	lic. 10-18-1836
Champion, Nathaniel - Hester Monroe	12- 1-1836
Chilcott, John - Rachel Robertson	7-29-1819
Clark, Asa - Mary Mathis	lic. 6-13-1833
Clark, David - Sallie Thomas	lic. 1-22-1822
Clark, Lewis - Phillis Murray	lic. 9-24-1829
Clark, Preston - Sarah Keller	lic. 8-27-1836

Clark, Samuel M. - Nancy Allison   9- 7-1820
Claypool, Reuben - Martha Russell   lic. 9- 7-1820
Clayton, Archibald - Lydia Dixon   lic. 5-12-1824
Coats, Stewart -   lic. 9- 7-1836
Coats, Stuart - Emily Perry   lic. 2-10-1832
Cochran, John - Sarah Johnson   11-23-1819
Cockerham, Daniel - Nancy Griffin   lic. 6-13-1829
Cockerham, Stephen - Rachel Osborn   lic. 6-22-1821
Cockerham, William - Elizabeth Winkler
                                     lic. 10- 6-1829
Cody, James - Millie Kindred   1-31-1833
Coffey, James H. - Ann E. Graham   lic. 11-14-1834
Coffin, Samuel - Sophia Fisler   lic. 6- 8-1830
Cole, Isaac - Sally Gill   7-22-1817
Collins, Thomas - Peggy Briner   7-27-1820
Collins, William - Rebecca Livingston lic. 9-11-1835
Combs, William - Eliza Wilkerson   lic 3-28-1834
Compton, Orsemus - Lavina England   lic. 11-12-1833
Condra, Henry - Deborah Littler   3-24-1832
Condra, Jacob - Matilda Ballinger   1-23-1831
Condra, Jacob - Matilda Graham   lic. 4-16-1836
Conn, Lorenzo Dow - Susan Moore   lic. 4- 1-1836
Cook, Willis - Sarah Hollowell   7-20-1822
Coop, David - Catharine Carmans   lic. 10-22-1834
Copeland, Hugh - Charlotte Alexander lic. 11-20-1820
Cosens, James - Tabitha Newby   lic. 12-27-1836
Cotney, Finney - Sarah Rogers   10-22-1817
Cotney, Rutherford - Sallie Shipman   12- 7-1819
Cotney, Woods - Nancy Shipman   lic. 5- -1819
Cox, Abner - Sarah Shewmaker   lic. 11-13-1834
Cox, Andrew - Clara Crossers   lic. 8- 7-1829
Cox, Benjamin - Elizabeth Curtis   lic. 7-26-1830
Cox, Frederick - Polly Rawson   lic. 8-12-1833
Cox, Herman - Nancy Cox   12-19-1817
Cox, John - Sarah Stanfield   8-12-1818
Cox, Jonathan - Sally Mahan   1-28-1834
Cox, Peter - Jane Rains   7-10-1820
Cox, Saint Clair - Hetty Helton   2-18-1834
Cox, Stephen - Sarah Hare   7- 3-1816
Cox, Solomon - Elizabeth Johnston   6-24-1819
Crabb, Edward - Eunice Douglass   12-30-1819
Crabb, James - Pauline Threlkild   lic. 1-10-1821
Crabb, Stephen S. - Julia Ann Miller   9-27-1832
Crabb, Thomas - Priscilla Young   lic. 1-14-1830
Crane, David - Harriett Crabb   9-22-1819
Crane, Isaac B. - Minerva Laraway   5- 4-1834
Crane, Jabez - Olive Olds   5- 5-1819
Crane, Jabez S. - Lora Shiney   lic. 6-30-1821
Crane, James - Sallie Mitchell   lic. 1-30-1830
Crane, Wickliffe K. - Effa Douglass   6- 5-1833
Crenshaw, William - Olive Crane   lic. 5-24-1830
Crenshaw, William - Elizabeth Woody   11- 8-1832
Crider, George - Elizabeth Fleetwood lic. 7-11-1832
Croucher, Andrew - Polly Wood   10- 3-1830
Crow, William - Eliza Adams   lic. 6-26-1836
Crum, Jonathan - Sallie Davis   3-20-1823
Cummins, Major - Polly Carothers   lic. 11-19-1833
Cunningham, Joseph - Betsey Mathews   9-12-1816
Curry, Elias W. - Lucinda Hamblen (Hamlin on lic.)
                                         6-30-1836
Curry, William H. - Mary Weddel   5-15-1830

Dailey, Eli W. - Polly Tuell   lic. 4-29-1836
Daniels, Ephraim - Hetty Weddle   lic. 1-21-1836
Daniels, Smith - Dilla Owens   4-25-1833

Davenport, William - Delilah Hensley   12-10-1819
David, Jeremiah - Susannah Prather   lic. 7-29-1824
Davis, Denny - Hannah Johnson   2-26-1831
Davis, John H. - Sarah Acton   9- 5-1833
Davis, Joseph - Catharine Brown   lic. 6-21-1836
Day, Jesse - Polly Brown   9- 5-1833
Day, Nathan - Phebe Day   lic. 3-14-1830
Day, William H. - Sarah Hamilton   5- 8-1834
Dee, Anderson - Polly Nelson   lic. 11- 7-1835
Dickison, Henry - Polly Findley   7-30-1820
Dixon, Jackson - Ann Dixon   lic. 11-25-1836
Dixon, Shaderick - Sarah Weddle   lic. 4-24-1836
Dixon, Thomas - Sallie Newkirk   lic. 12-19-1820
Dobson, William - Winnie Sumler   12- 8-1831
Dorser, Thomas - Nancy Collins   lic. 1-28-1822
Dotson, Hiram - Polly Wilson   9- 4-1821
Douglas, Martin - Malinda Wheden   4- 7-1818
Douglass, Ebenezer - Jane Findley   lic. 3-31-1830
Douglass, Homer - Eliza Fisler   lic. 1- 6-1835
Douglass, Martin - Anna Burns   3-27-1831
Douglass, Warner - Caroline Brooks   1- 3-1830
Dowden, Clemons - Rachel Carter   lic. 7-14-1834
Dowden, Zachariah - Catharine Herrod lic. 5-28-1817
Downs, Charles - Hannah Richards   lic. 8-11-1836
Draper, Jonathan - Polly Thomas   8-23-1833
Draper, Joseph - Polly Thomas   lic. 5-27-1833
Draper, Peter - Susannah Dudley   lic. 8-23-1820
Dudley, John - Diana Houston   lic. 5- 4-1830
Durham, Hannibal - Susan Henderlider   6-26-1834
Durland, Gilbert B. - Margaret Mooney lic. 10- 7-1834
Durland, Nelson C. - Elizabeth Stilwell
                                     lic. 12-12-1836
Durland, Phineas Y. - Elizabeth N. Dennison
                                     lic. 5-19-1835

East, Joseph - Olive Neff   lic. 11- 8-1834
Easton, Jacob - Patsy Ruddick   lic. 10-17-1836
Easton, James - Susanah Wiley   11-21-1833
Easton, Richard - Elizabeth Kindred   1- 1-1822
Edwards, Eli - Catharine Taylor   lic. 6- 9-1822
Edwards, Joel - Elizabeth Gregory   lic. 10-17-1832
Elkins, Jesse - Matilda Bagwell   lic. 6-19-1835
Elkins, Thomas - Rebecca Stogdill   lic. 6- 8-1831
Ellis, Seth - Mary Huffman   7- 1-1819
Elliott, John - Susan Woodmansee   9-21-1820
Elliott, Peter - Diana Newby   lic. 1- 7-1830
Empson, Azariah P. - Martha B. Holmes
                                     lic. 2-17-1831
Evans, Alexander - Wilma Jackson   lic. 8- 7-1824
Evans, Andrew - Jane Wray   lic. 1-26-1830
Ewing, Thomas - Elizabeth Hutsheson   6- 6-1818
Ewing, William H. - Lucinda Crenshaw   3-30-1820

Fentress, Jesse - Malinda Sweaney   lic. 3-24-1835
Ferguson, Andrew - Peggy Dugger   7-28-1817
Ferrell, Clemens G. - Elizabeth Thompson
                                     lic. 10-23-1833
Findley, Hugh D. - Rebecca Cordell   lic. 11-27-1821
Findley, Isaac - Mary Murphy   12- 4-1832
Findley, Thomas - Polly Combs   lic. 2-20-1830
Findley, William - Hannah Edwards   7-20-1820
Fisler, Jacob - Fanny Fortner   lic. 11-17-1830
Fleetwood, Hiram - Matilda Harden   lic. 4-22-1834
Fleetwood, Jesse - Cynthia Stuart   3-29-1834
Flinn, John - Mary Flinn   lic. 10-17-1816
Flinn, William Jr. - Sallie Houston lic. 10- 2-1819

Fortner, Alfred - Fanny Love   lic. 5-11-1822
Fountain, Thomas - Jincy Owens   lic. 4- 2-1831
Fox, Elijah - Nancy Asking   4- 2-1820
Francum, Simon - Sallie Johnston   6-24-1819
Frank, Jacob - Diadem Keith   lic. 5- 5-1821
Franklin, Anderson - Sarah Keller   lic. 4-19-1824
Fullbright, Joseph M. - Mary Ann Carter
                                      lic. 11-27-1830

Gallion, Gilbert - Milly Weddle   lic. 1- 2-1830
George, Enoch - Polly Nix   lic. 12-12-1834
Gilbert, Francis - Elizabeth Smith   lic. 8- 1-1835
Gilbert, Wells - Elizabeth Youtsey   lic. 8- 6-1834
Giles, George - Cicelia Arthur   3- 8-1832
Goodale, Jason - Sarah Chapman   lic. 12-14-1820
Goodson, Thomas - Jane Cameron   lic. 2-15-1830
Gossett, Stauker - Henrietta Wheeler lic. 10-21-1836
Gould, Austin - Jane Durland   lic. 6-22-1822
Graham, Jeremiah - Nancy Stephens   2-28-1818
Graham, John L. - Permelia Ann Puckett
                                      lic. 4-27-1836
Grant, Robert - Jane Lee   lic. 3- 1-1820
Gray, James - Sarah Stevens   lic. 12-23-1829
Gray, William - Maria Stephens   8-15-1829
Green, Francis W. - Catharine Hathorn   5-30-1833
Gregory, James - Martha Cox   lic. 1- 7-1834
Griffin, Benjamin - Milley Martin   lic. 4- 2-1834
Griffin, Elijah - Amanda Roberts   lic. 8- 3-1836
Griffin, Matthew - Jane Come (or Conce or Corne)
                                      lic. 11-30-1836
Griffin, William - Catharine Morrison   4-25-1833
Grissmore, Jonathan - Sarah Ann Harrell
                                      lic. 9-28-1836
Groce, John - Margaret Ambes   lic. 7-15-1835
Guthrie, Samuel - Thirza Weddle   lic. 3-21-1829
Guyer, Henry - Frances Brooks   1-27-1833

Hall, John L. - Rebecca Brosheres   lic. 8- 6-1835
Hamblin, Pleasant R. - Milly Weddle   11-22-1831
Hamilton, John R. - Esther Robertson lic. 11-16-1835
Hanna, Joseph - Elizabeth Nichols   6-28-1832
Hanner, John - Rebecca Burrell   7- 2-1818
Hardy, Spencer - Elender Brooks   lic. 3-27-1834
Harmon, Erastus - Ruby Coats   lic. 1-16-1821
Harmon, John - Polly Findley   12-18-1818
Harrell, Edmond - Sally Richards   10- 9-1831
Harrell, Isaac - Nancy Alsop   lic. 8-15-1831
Harrell, James - Elsie Herrod   lic. 8-10-1821
Harrell, John - Catharine Thompson   4- 2-1820
Harrell, Waller - Julia Ann Blackwood lic. 2- 4-1835
Heacock, Dunlap - Elizabeth Holmes   lic. 7-30-1831
Heacock, Ebenezer - Elizabeth Griffin lic. 4-25-1831
Hecock, Ebenezer - Elizabeth Bradley
                                      lic. 10-10-1821
Helton, Thomas - Margaret Dobson   lic. 10-24-1836
Henderlider, Martin - Rachel Peck   11-22-1832
Henderson, John - Delilah Turpin   10-31-1833
Henderson, Joseph - Phebe White   lic. 12- 5-1836
Henderson, Robert - Elizabeth Taggert lic. 3-22-1821
Henderson, William - Jemima Newkirk   12-31-1817
Hensley, James - Polly Burcham   lic. 7- 2-1822
Hill, John - Polly Kiziah   lic. 4-15-1831
Hill, John, Jr. - Elender Jane Prather   12- 2-1830
Hinkle, Seth T. - Esther T. Gray   lic. 6- 1-1835
Hinston, John - Elizabeth Owens   lic. 4-15-1831
Hodges, John - Rachel Shields   2-11-1818

Hogland, Isaac - Allie Ann Applegate lic. 12- 8-1830
Holeman, Daniel - Pressy Crabb   lic. 6- 7-1829
Holeman, John - Jane Threlkild   lic. 6-20-1835
Holeman, John C. - Rowena Laraway   7-14-1833
Hollen, Andrew B. - Rachel Richards   7-13-1818
Hollenback, John - Rhoda Henderson   9-22-1817
Holliday, John - Mary Jump   lic. 4-21-1830
Holmes, Benjamin - Elizabeth Lindsey   3-11-1819
Holmes, Peter L. - Catharine Berkey   lic. 7-23-1836
Holmes, Solomon - Elizabeth Thompson   6-22-1820
Holmes, William L. (or S.) - Elizabeth Iseminger
                                      lic. 10-21-1830
Hornady, Ezekiel D. - Nancy Tuell   lic. 11-11-1836
Hotchkiss, Peter - Rebecca M. Knight
                                      lic. 9-10-1821
Houston, William - Elizabeth Flinn   lic. 3-29-1819
Hubbard, David - Sarah Rice   lic. 2-16-1831
Hubble, Benjamin - Maria Wheden   4-24-1817
Huff, Morgan - Elizabeth Parsely   lic. 6- 8-1835
Humphreys, John - Susanah Rebecca Case
                                      lic. 1-26-1835
Huntsinger, Peter - Polly Pool   7-17-1831
Hunsucker, Isaac - Patsey Lockman   lic. 11-28-1835
Hydon, John - Elizabeth Craig   lic. 6-25-1824

Ingle, Fleming - Catharine Smith   lic. 7-19-1830
Ireland, Daniel - Susan Johnson   lic. 10-17-1836
Isaacs, John W. - Elizabeth McPherson
                                      lic. 7- 8-1834
Isaacs, William - Highly Reynolds   lic. 12-19-1833
Iseminger, Daniel - Susan Ribble   lic. 12- 2-1836
Iseminger, Jacob - Nancy Rogers   2- 2-1821

Jackson, Byron - Nancy Mitchner   8-19-1832
Jackson, Joel - Susannah Cordell   lic. 11-28-1829
Jackson, Jordan - Lavina Henderlider lic. 4-18-1836
Jasper, George F. - Harriet Sample   lic. 9-20-1836
Johnson, Alvin - Mahala Blair   4-17-1834
Johnson, Charles - Elizabeth Rudes   6- 7-1821
Johnson, David Jr. - Elizabeth Breadlove   3-23-1824
Johnson, Isaac - Lucy Conn   lic. 5- 4-1829
Johnson, Isaiah - Rachel Powell   6- 8-1834
Johnson, James - Gincy Brannen   lic. 12-15-1835
Johnson, William - Sarah Ann Cummins
                                      lic. 9-21-1829
Johnston, John - Betsey Jackson   12-11-1816
Jones, David L. - Cartha Osborn   lic. 10-15-1831
Jones, Gabriel - Mariah Sheets   4-10-1818
Jones, James - Louisa Lane   lic. 11- 7-1836
Jones, Major - Elizabeth H. Hinkley   3- 7-1833
Jones, William - Mary Magatha   1-31-1833
Judy, John J. - Fanny Berkey   lic. 2-22-1830
Judy, Isaac C. - Phebe Ann Stites   lic. 7-17-1836
Judy, Rezin S. - Theresa Blackwood   9-25-1832

Keller, Abraham - Nancy Ballinger   lic. 12-19-1820
Kelley, ———— - Minerva Bell   lic. 8- 1-1824
Kelley, David Jr. - Jane Smith   lic. 12-10-1835
Kelley, George - Jane Jackson   7-22-1817
Kelley, William - Sarah G. Weddle   lic. 7-21-1836
Kelley, Woodruff - Harriet Coates   lic. 9-28-1831
Kerby, Jesse - Nancy Summers   10-19-1829
Kesler, John - Elizabeth Johnson   lic. 3-26-1824
Kester, John J. - Nancy Smith   lic. 3-13-1830
Kester, Simeon B. - Lydia Scott   lic. 3-26-1831

Kindle, Henry - Polly Dowden	11-19-1816
Kindred, Thomas - Nancy Weddle	2-27-1834
King, ———— - Ann Lyster	lic. 3-19-1824
Kitchell, Asa - Abiah Olds	lic. 8-15-1821
Kiziah, John - Eliza Wilson	lic. 11-24-1834
Kiziah, John - Hannah Elkins	lic. 10- 8-1836
Knight, Israel - Rebecca M. Wells	6-26-1817
Kress, Christian - Nancy Lee	lic. 10-10-1836
Kress, Daniel - Amanda M.F. Bowren	lic. 2-16-1835
Kress, Jonas C. - Penelope Pearson	lic. 9-14-1831
Lamb, Adam - Sally Thomas	2- 2-1832
Lamb, Gilbert - Priscilla Partridge	lic. 11-26-1834
Lamb, Hiram - Nancy Dockery	lic. 1-21-1834
Lanier, Nicholas - Sarah Goss	1-12-1834
Lanning, Joseph - Mary Maxwell	lic. 8- 8-1836
Lanning, Joseph Jr. - Charlana Laraway	
	lic. 5-19-1831
Lee, John - Catharine Boas	lic. 10-12-1831
Leonard, David - Nancy Day	8- 1-1832
Linebarger, Lewis - Jane Henderson	lic. 2- 5-1822
Locke, Abraham - Sarah Skinner	lic. 6-20-1822
Lockhart, Andrew - Elizabeth Shutters	
	lic. 11-12-1836
Lockman, Vincent - Polly Hare	6-26-1817
Love, Beufort - Nancy Carter	lic. 3-26-1830
Love, Braxton - Martha I. Love	lic. 4-18-1834
Lutes, Jacob - Sarah Elkins	lic. 4-14-1835
Lux, William G. - Mary Ann Kelley	lic. 10- 1-1829
Lymbarger, Alfred - Lucinda Morrison	2- 9-1832
Lyster, Henry - Juliette Hagan	6- 5-1832
Lyster, Henry - Betsey Ann Woodmansee	
	lic. 12-21-1835
Lyster, John - Mary Summers	lic. 9-15-1836
Lyster, Peter - Lucy Harkinson	5-16-1822
McConnell, Thomas - Kiziah Morgan	7-25-1833
McConnell, William - Jane Potts	lic. 6- 9-1831
McCormick, James - Susannah Kongleton	6-24-1818
McCormick, John - Rebecca Findley	lic. 12-25-1823
McCormick, Thomas - Sylvia Stites	lic. 6- 3-1824
McCoy, Stephen - Sallie Lindsey	lic. 9-12-1820
McDaniel, John - Elizabeth Harris	1-19-1832
McGeary, William - Nancy Love	lic. 8-28-1835
McVey, James - Rachel Merryfield	lic. 1-28-1830
Maloney, Archibald - Sarah Lyster	6-30-1831
Maples, John - Eliza Jane Mahuron	lic. 8-31-1833
Marling, Elijah - Mary Ellenor Cox	lic. 3-19-1831
Marling, Hiram - Jane McDonald	lic. 2-23-1830
Maron, Ansalem - Alice Ann Shore	lic. 7-17-1821
Marquess, Wilson H. - Catharine Barnaby	
	lic. 1-31-1831
Marsh, Gravenor - Polly Weathers	lic. 3- 3-1831
Marsh, Robert - Mary Wilson	10-24-1819
Marshall, John - Amanda R. bertson	4-11-1833
Marshall, John H. - Margaret Kindle	1-22-1831
Matthias, ———— - ————Flinn	lic. 10-20-1820
Maxwell, John - Mahala Weddle	3- 8-1834
May, Ephraim - Eunice Mitchell	lic. 10-28-1830
Merrifield, Alexander - Elizabeth Cordell	1- 2-1834
Miller, Francis - Rachel Bunch	lic. 7-16-1834
Miller, Francis B. - Permelia Scott	lic. 9-12-1836
Miller, Thomas - Mary Harmon	lic. 4-27-1832
Minor, Reuben - Eleanor Findley	lic. 1- 8-1833
Mitchell, James - Mary Wheeler	lic. 10-29-1834

Mitchell, Philip - Polly Mitchell	lic. 5- 5-1821
Mitchell, Robert - Jane Harmon	1-28-1819
Mitchell, Thomas - Nancy Stuart	lic. 1-26-1830
Mitchell, William - Susanah Hensley	lic. 11-30-1821
Mitchner, William - Matilda Chandler	lic. 10-17-1836
Monroe, Hamilton - Elizabeth Champion	1-12-1832
Monroe, James - Sally Brown	3-28-1833
Montgomery, Richard - Jerusha Willis	lic. 8-19-1834
Mooney, John P. - Susanah Crenshaw	7-22-1832
Mooney, Lewis - Mary Rudes	6- 7-1821
Mooney, Samuel P. - Eliza McTaggart	10- 8-1833
Moore, Ezekiel - Betsey Ann Rooney	lic. 6-14-1835
Moore, Henry - Rebecca Marshall	lic. 11-19-1833
Moore, Henry - Jane Williams	lic. 6-10-1836
Moreland, Richard - Effa Mapes	1-27-1833
Morgan, William - Elsie Ann Hoagland	lic. 6-23-1836
Morris, Benjamin - Mary Lancaster	3-22-1834
	lic. 12-18-1833
Mulligan, Thomas C.P. - Nancy Taylor	12-30-1832
Murphy, James L. - Polly Ann Woody	7- 5-1832
Murphy, Lewis F. - Cyrene Congleton	12-27-1823
Murphy, Louis F. - Rachel Wells	lic. 12-12-1832
Murphy, Samuel J. - Elizabeth Warner	lic. 2- 8-1831
Naul, Adam - Anna Robertson	lic. 4- 9-1831
Naylor, Isaac - Margaret Langley	lic. 6-18-1834
Neel, Lewis - Milley Cox	10-20-1817
Neff, Daniel B. - Maria Thomas	1-15-1833
Nelson, Enoch - Rachel Elkins	lic. 7-14-1831
Nelson, William - Polly Miller	lic. 10- 1-1829
Newby, James - Zelpha Nixon	11-20-1831
Newby, Joseph - Malinda Bennett	lic. 2- 5-1835
Newby, Robert - Tabitha Pew	12- 9-1819
Newby, Willis - Millison Newby	12-29-1832
Newkirk, Henry - Polly Henderson	3-13-1819
Newkirk, Moses K. - Eleanor Fountain	8-29-1833
Newland, William - Susannah S. Herrold	3-25-1817
Nicholson, Cornelius - Polly Beem	lic. 12-21-1833
Noblet, Levi - Catharine Owley	lic. 1-21-1822
Nowland, Henry - Elizabeth Pitcher	lic. 1-31-1821
Olds, Briggs C. - Sarah Morrison	2- 9-1832
Owen, George W. - Sallie Mooney	lic. 1-31-1820
Owens, Albert - Elizabeth H. Thomas	lic. 9- 6-1831
Owens, Barnett - Nancy H. Thomas	12-27-1832
Owens, William - Sarah Cox	lic. 4-5--1831
Packwood, Elisha - Perline Prather	2- 9-1832
Packwood, John - Abigail Packwood	2-12-1832
Parker, David - Elizabeth Wilkerson	12- 2-1819
Parker, Enoch F. - Jane Ellen Sullivan	
	lic. 4- 8-1835
Parker, Woodsen D. - Abigail Mitchell	2-14-1817
Parsley, Edwin H. - Margaret Johnson	lic. 6- 1-1824
Partridge, James - Nancy Mitchell	lic. 2- 4-1835
Peck, William - Evaline Stites	lic. 2- 4-1832
Perry, David - Lorena Abbott	lic. 1-23-1834
Persise, James F. - Nancy C. Graham	1- 3-1833
Phegley, Leo - Leona Scott	4-10-1834
Phegley, John - Rachel Thompson	lic. 11-19-1833
Phelps, Ashbel - Margaret Stowers	7-17-1818
Phillips, Isaac - Lucy Weddle	lic. 12-30-1835
Potter, William - Matilda Carr	11-25-1832
Powell, Jesse - Polly House	lic. 10-15-1821
Pownall, Joseph - Sallie Arnold	10-12-1819
Prather, James - Josephine Haggert	lic. 2-20-1824

Prather, Thomas - Hannah Arthur   12-28-1831
Prather, Walter - Elizabeth Young   lic. 10-17-1836
Prather, William - Sarah C. Smith   10-25-1832
Preston, William - Malinda Hays   lic. 5-19-1830

Ramey, James - Sarah Woods   7- 5-1832
Randolph, David - Susanah Easter   11-18-1832
Randolph, Lott - Polly Champion   lic. 1-30-1830
Redman, Rezin A. - Elizabeth Stanley lic. 1-27-1830
Reemy, Benjamin - Nancy Agnes Holmes
                                     lic. 12-11-1833
Reemy, John - Margaret Potts   lic. 9- 2-1835
Reeve, Joseph - Sarah Ireland   lic. 10-10-1829
Reno, Wilkinson - Julia Ann Fryhoofer
                                     lic. 8- 4-1835
Reynolds, James - Allie Asking   lic. 7- 3-1821
Reynolds, Joseph L. - Martha Morrison
                                     lic. 4-16-1831
Rich, Joseph Jr. - Ann Sowder   10-21-1832
Richards, Benjamin M. - Martha Prow   7-25-1833
Robertson, Andrew - Esther Hamilton   2- 4-1819
Robertson, Blaze - Mary Robertson   lic. 11-23-1835
Robertson, Nelson - Harriet Henderson
                                     lic. 1- 9-1836
Robertson, James - Lillian Lawrence lic. 3- 8-1822
Robertson, William - Mary Hamilton   3- 9-1819
Rodenbarger, Madison - Ann Elizabeth Bearsth
                                     lic. 12-25-1833
Rogers, Acquilla - Rebecca Rogers   9- 1-1818
Rogers, Benjamin - Elizabeth Arnold   3- 4-1819
Rogers, James - Susannah Kindle   lic. 9-23-1816
Rogers, Lewis - Nancy Richards   7-30-1818
Rowland, David - Margaret Holmes   lic. 12-11-1821
Rucker, Nathan - Marther Garner   lic. 11-26-1823
Ruddick, Elisha - Betsy Findley   lic. 11- 8-1836
Ruddick, John - Rebecca Ann Jane Parker
                                     lic. 10-20-1834
Ruddick, Solomon - Elizabeth Keith   10-27-1818
Ruddick, Solomon - Margaret Fentress lic. 12-15-1829
Ruggles, William B. - Mary Benton   8-12-1819
Russell, John - Hannah Cameron   12-26-1832
Rust, John B. - Nancy McAffee   lic. 6-17-1835

Sanders, Daniel - Sally Sowder   lic. 5-18-1836
Scott, Allen - Janey Florney   10-13-1831
Scott, Almon - Polly Williams   lic. 5-28-1836
Scott, David - Holly Skinner   5-22-1818
Scott, Jacob - Polly Sutphin   lic. 7- 3-1824
Scott, John R. - Cynthia Dodds   lic. 12-17-1836
Scott, Rawley - Phebe Braman   3-25-1832
Scott, Samuel - Rebecca Tabor   10- 6-1818
Scott, William - Mary Wood   lic. 2-23-1835
Sender, Casper - Mary Brugman   lic. 7-18-1834
Shelton, Eli - Elizabeth Weathers   lic. 2- 6-1836
Shelton, Henly - Rachel Jarvis   lic. 7-15-1834
Shepherd, Eli - Elizabeth Springer   lic. 10-13-1831
Sherrill, William - Eliza Jones   7- 5-1832
Shields, James - Fanny Henderlider   lic. 10-24-1833
Shields, Meedy W. - Eliza Ewing   8-18-1833
Shiner, Erastus - Celia Carr   1- 2-1831
Shipman, John - Nancy Empson   lic. 3-27-1820
Shoebridge, Joseph B. - Mahala Grant   11-21-1831
Shortridge, Andrew - Hannah Davis   6-27-1833
Shortridge, Miles H. - Sarah O'Neal   8- 1-1833
Shutter, Mathias - Nancy Thomas   lic. 10-30-1833
Silence, Edmond - Elizabeth Morgan   1-23-1833

Simpson, John - Sarah Crabb   lic. 6-26-1822
Skinner, Zachariah - Nancy Skinner• lic. 10- 6-1821
Smith, Arthur J. - Julia Ann Day   lic. 5-21-1832
Smith, Ephraim - Rebecca Saint Clair lic. 6- 2-1823
Smith, Joseph - Rebecca Burge   lic. 9- 7-1829
Smith, William - Deborah Abel   lic. 6- 6-1834
Smith, William M. - Melissa Heacock   10-20-1833
Sparks, Benjamin - Amanda Boley   lic. 7-20-1836
Sparks, Martin - Sarah Reynolds   lic. 9-12-1836
Sparks, Richard A. - Julia Ann Cummins
                                     lic. 6-17-1830
Spear, Joseph - Priscilla Flinn   lic.• 12- 6-1819
Spears, John - Polly Flinn•   5-13-1817
Springer, John H. - Elizabeth Whitson   10- 9-1817
Spurling, Silas - Polly Berry   lic. 4-14-1836
Stanfield, Eli - Elizabeth White   lic. 5- 1-1834
Stanfield, Joel - Nancy Fentress   1- 3-1833
Stanfield, John - Catharine Cox   lic. 1-21-1821
Stanfield, Samuel - Lydia Cox   10-14-1819
Stanfield, Samuel - Kiziah Sweaney   7-12-1832
Stanfield, William - Susan Sweaney   lic. 3- 9-1830
Stanley, Samuel - Elizabeth Murphy   lic. 2- 4-1824
Stark, Aaron - Nancy Sowder   lic. 8- 9-1832
Stevens, Mathew - Agnes Banks   lic. 7- 3-1824
Stewart, Moses - Patsey Robbins   lic. 1-30-1832
Sturgeon, John - Susan W. Young   lic. 5-15-1834
Stryker, Aaron - Eliza Ireland   lic. 4-21-1832
Sullivan, Henry - Sarah Thomas   4-11-1819
Sullivan, John - Leah Marshall   6-13-1833
Sullivan, William - Anna Rogers   1- 1-1829
Summers, Price - Phebe Smith   lic. 9-11-1831
Summers, William - Elizabeth Kindle lic. 6-23-1817
Sutton, Richard - Patsey Bennet   lic. 5-14-1822
Sweaney, John Jr. - Electa Rawson   lic. 9-28-1831
Sweaney, Lewis - Julia Ann Youtsey   lic. 8-24-1833
Sweaney, Thomas - Lydia Cox   lic. 11-14-1829
Syers, William - Polly Hanners   12-13-1817

Tabor, Jesse - Theresa Skinner   5-30-1819
Tabor, Jesse - Nellie Allman   lic. 8- 7-1836
Tabor, Martin - Elizabeth Phillips   lic. 9- 2-1833
Tabor, Robert - Ruth Winkles   3-15-1832
Tabor, William - Sarah Whitson   11-21-1831
Taggert, James - Jane Weddle   1-10-1822
Talbott, Edward - Polly Lanning   2-11-1819
Taylor, Abner - Nancy M. Smith   10-28-1832
Terrill, William - Elizabeth White   2-21-1819
Thomas, John S. - Margaret Day   lic. 2-18-1830
Thomas, Lewis H. - Frances Owens   3- 1-1832
Thomas, Ward S. - Nancy Tadlock   7-18-1833
Thomas, William - Elizabeth Shirrer lic. 1-10-1834
Thompson, Alexander - Margaret McGee   4- 9-1821
Thompson, Cornelius - Lydia Dodson   12-17-1816
Thompson, James - Polly Ennis   lic. 7- 3-1822
Thompson, John - Elizabeth Boswell   lic. 2- 7-1832
Thompson, John - Elizabeth Langley   lic. 12-24-1835
Thompson, Richard - Lydia Ruddick   8-12-1819
Thompson, Thomas - Elizabeth Skinner
                                     lic. 12-25-1833
Thompson, William - Winnie Taylor   lic. 1-22-1822
Thompson, William - Elizabeth Grissmore   2-28-1833
Threlkild, Stephen - Martha James   lic. 8- 6-1835
Tilford, Jefferson - Matilda Mooney   9-17-1833
Tinder, William J. - ————— Youtsey   3- 1-1832
Todd, John - Anna Bailes   lic. 2- 1-1830
Trimble, Martin - Clara Ann Kissle   12- 5-1833

Tuell, Colby - Catharine Woodmansec		6-21-1833		
Turnbull, John - Sarah Sullivan	lic.	7-25-1821		
Turnbull, John C. - Rhoda Ann Crane	lic.	1- 9-1835		
Turner, John - Susannah Littell	lic.	3-29-1831		
Turpin, Aaron - Lucinda Miller	lic.	2-18-1832		

Van Swerenger, Thomas - Rebecca Riley lic. 9-30-1830
Vannoy, Nathaniel - Peggy Marr 2-21-1821
Vermilya, Jesse - Maria McTaggart lic. 7- 4-1832

Waddle, John - Sarah Ann Berry lic. 12-12-1836
Waggoner, David - Elizabeth Young lic. 8-26-1835
Weathers, Charles - Betsey Marsh lic. 12- 8-1830
Weathers, Thomas - Priscilla Sullander lic. 4- 9-1834
Weddel, John A. - Elizabeth Stephens 4- 1-1830
Weddle, Edward - Polly Kindred 12-16-1819
Weddle, Gabriel L. - Polly Henderlider 2- 8-1831
Weddle, Hiram C. - Sarah Henderson lic. 6-22-1829
Weddle, Isaac G. - Elizabeth Weddle lic. 11-26-1830
Weddle, John D. - Nancy Daniels lic. 12-14-1835
Wells, James - Malinda Owens 5- 5-1832
Wheadon, Alpha - Isabel Findley 12-31-1819
Wheadon, Samuel - Polly Lockman lic. 8- 3-1824
Wheden, Samuel - Sallie Connor 5-20-1818
Whedon, Marcena - Almina Williams lic. 3-14-1822
Wheeler, James - Julitha Cox lic. 9- 4-1831
Wheeler, Orrel - Betsey Love lic. 3- 3-1830
White, David - Sarah Sutherland lic. 5- 5-1821
White, Joseph - Delilah Henderson 8-24-1820
Whitson, Peter - Christina Champion lic. 7- 1-1835
Whitson, Thomas - Poily Woolery lic. 6-18-1830

Whittington, Francis - Patsey Reynolds lic. 9-12-1833
Williams, Isaac - Elizabeth Jackson lic. 12-23-1835
Williams, Martin - Mary Allen lic. 12-22-1835
Wills, John - Cinderilla Miller lic. 4-24-1834
Wilson, John A. - Sallie Lanning lic. 12-11-1823
Wilson, William - Elizabeth Kitchell 1-15-1817
Winkles, Edward - Luanna Scott 6- 5-1833
Winkles, Jeremiah - Lydia Sawyer lic. 1-12-1836
Winslow, Samuel - Rebecca Short lic. 5-16-1836
Wood, John - Polly Turpin lic. 7-13-1822
Wood, Laurence - Nancy Mooney lic. 8-20-1829
Wooden, Thomas - Kate Simmons 7-19-[1817]
Woodmansee, Asa - America L. Fisler lic. 4- 1-1835
Woodmansee, Asher - Frances E. Brown 6-27-1833
Woodmansee, Gabriel - Nancy Murphy lic. 1-21-1830
Woodmansee, Gabriel - Margaret Stites 1- 6-1833
Woodmansee, James - Anna Stevenson lic. 11-19-1829
Woodmansee, James W. --Rachel B. Hanner lic. 10-17-1835
Woolery, Richard - Sally Kinworthy lic. 6-18-1830
Woolery, Thomas - Mary Burrell lic. 4-25-1829
Wray, Anderson - Sarah Campbell 11-15-1832
Wray, Villorous - Amanda Sparks lic. 6-17-1836
Wright, Elijah - Polly Dukes lic. 5-26-1834

Young, Alexander - Polly Cody lic. 1-16-1832
Young, Joseph - Priscilla Johnston 8- 1-1816
Young, William Harrison - Rebecca Sturgeon lic. 6-10-1835
Youtsey, Adam - Eliza McCoy 3-11-1832

Zike, David - Milley Haggard lic. 10-21-1835

STEINMETZ FAMILY BIBLE RECORDS

Contributed by Mrs. Michael L. Cook, Evansville.

Marriages

Matilda, daughter of John and Elizabeth Wahl, to Barney, son of Henry and Oleva Steinmetz, at the home of her parents 10-7-1884 by Rev. Tanse

John H. Steinmetz to Myrtle Lewis, 11-23-1921
Laura B. Steinmetz to Carl Althoff, 9-27-1916
Albert A. Steinmetz to Mildred Norstrom, 2-23-1920
Florence Irene Steinmetz to William Walker, 11-28-1925
Frances Mildred Steinmetz to H. Andrew Wolf, Dec. 1924

Births

John H. Steinmetz 7-25-1929
Clara Lu Ella Steinmetz 7-18-1888
Laura Bell Steinmetz 1-20-1890
Albert H. Steinmetz 8-9-1892

Florence I. Steinmetz 10-28-1894
Frances M. Steinmetz 9-12-1902
Barney Steinmetz 1-15-1862
Matilda Steinmetz 1-29-1864

Deaths

Clara Lu Ella Steinmetz 3-27-1889
Barney Steinmetz 1-4-1951

Matilda Steinmetz 5-3-1949

Grandchildren

Lynn Stuart Steinmetz b. July 25, 1929

Andy Wolf Jr. b. March 9, 1939
Jacquline Joy Steinmetz b. December 18, 1921 to A.H.S.
John Henry Steinmetz Jr. b. September 23, 1922 to J.H.S.
Jean Evelyn Wolf b. April 16, 1925 to F.M.W.
Marilyn Helen Wolf b. December 10, 1926 to F.M.W.

Memoranda

September 18, 1921 - Matilda Steinmetz was baptised and joined the Church of the Seventh Day Advents; previous to this was a member of the M.E. Church at McCuthanville [McCutchanville]. Later transferred to the Wesley M.E. Church of which she was a member for 15 years.

FRANKLIN COUNTY MARRIAGES, 1811-1824

Compiled from the microfilm of Vols. I and II of Franklin County Marriage Records in the Courthouse at Brookville. Vol. I covering the years 1811-1819 is a copy made in 1927 of the original record book, which has since been lost. Some names were omitted in the copying and these have been picked up from the compilation made apparently from the original volume by the Brookville Chapter of the Daughters of the American Revolution.

Abbott, John - Jane Carson	6-10-1823
Abbott, Joshua - Elizabeth Parcus	1-12-1817
Abernathy, Richard - Rebecca Moore	
	lic. 2- 2-1820
Adair, Isaac - Jane Holland	1-18-1821
Adair, John - Lucy Trusler	5-21-1812
Adair, John - Susannah Thomas	10-26-1815
Adair, John - Sally Trusler	10- 2-1817
Adams, John - Sarah Harmmon	2-26-1819
Adams, Joseph - Lydia Baker	9-16-1813
Adams, Pattrick - Nancy Dickerson	12-25-1817
Adams, Thomas - Mary Deakens	3-18-1819
Adams, William - Elizabeth George	9-23-1815
Adams, William - Prudence Powers	2- 1-1820
Adams, Wilson - Elizabeth Fruit	10-28-1819
Alexander, Joseph - Catherine Kingery	
	10- 1-1818
Alexander, Ralph - Elizabeth Fields	2-27-1821
Alexander, Robert - Elizabeth Crist	4-25-1816
Allen, David E. - Maria Whetsel	5-29-1821
Allen, Eli - Elizabeth Shepherd	7-29-1818
Allen, Henry C. - Nancy Hammond	
	lic. 12-30-1814
Allen, Jacob - Betsey Harper	7-13-1823
Allen, John - Nancy Bridget	lic. 5-12-1820
Allen, Joseph S. - Mary Simes	3-21-1822
Alley, John, Jr. - Sarah Alley	lic. 3-30-1822
Alley, Sampson - Lucretia Hobbs	11-28-1819
Allington, William - Frances Bennet	4-15-1820
Allison, James - Mary Stubbs	5-29-1823
Allyea, Isaac - Keziah Smith	9-25-1817
Alsman, John - Elizabeth Crewsenbury	
	7-25-1824
Alyea, Gideon - Elizabeth Foster	11-28-1822
Ames, Simon - Elizabeth Hitt	9- 6-1821
Anthony, William - Margaret Eads	9-12-1812
Armstrong, Elijah - Letty Sailor	11-11-1821
Armstrong, Henry - Elizabeth Clayton	
	11-28-1816
Armstrong, James - Polly Lions	1-14-1819
Armstrong, Robert - Catherine Selfridge	
	2-13-1816
Arnett, Thomas - Mary Morrow	lic. 9- 3-1824
Arnett, William - Lucinda Eastes	lic. 5-31-1823
Arnold, Andrew - Elizabeth Williams	12-17-1818
Arnold, John - Sonna Cooper	lic. 7-30-1813
Arnold, John - Celia Dickerson	6-10-1819
Arnold, William - Mary Ann Toner	10-20-1820
Arrett, Thomas - Jane Cherry	7-31-1817
Asher, John - Isabel Manley	2- 2-1813
Askew, Drewry - Nancy Silvey	lic. 5-23-1817
Ayres, David - Mary Fruit	lic. 11-25-1816
Bail, Hugh M. - Mary Coy (widow)	9- 5-1824
Bailey, Ezekiel - Ruth Elliott	lic. 6- 8-1816
Baily, James - Elizabeth Johnson	
	lic. 6-23-1824

Bake, William - Mary Thurston	10-19-1820
Baker, Elijah - Sary Vance	7-15-1816
Baker, Peter - Febe Runnolds	lic. 5-20-1822
Baker, Stephen - Sarah Lemmon	1-28-1821
Ballanger, George - Ruthy Russel	7-23-1812
Banks, Charles - Mary Pyle	7- 4-1821
Banks, William - Sarah Bateman	2-17-1821
Barber, Simeon - Deborah Eels	3-31-1822
Barlow, John - Sally Fruit	lic. 10- 8-1822
Barney, John - Desdemonia Maker	11- 1-1820
Barrackman, Jacob - Janey Templeton	
	11- 2-1820
Bartlow, James - Phebe Fort	2-20-1822
Bartlow, John - Elizabeth Morgan	12-26-1815
Bassett, David - Susanna Haly	12-11-1823
Bassett, Nathaniel - Elizabeth Dubois	4-8-1819
Bastian, Henry - Matilda Street	3-13-1823
Bastian, Lawrence S. - Catharine Martin	
	2-19-1823
Bateman, Carleton - Sally Cooksey	4- 1-1819
Bates, Hervey - Sidney Sedwick	3- 7-1819
Bean, Levi - Sarah Morgan	lic. 4-12-1823
Bedwell, George - Rachel Stout	11-26-1819
Bell, William - Sally Henderson	7- 3-1813
Bennet, Thomas - Miranda Coffin	10-12-1820
Berkley, William - Rebecca Burbridge	
	lic. 5-2- 1818
Billings, Edmund - Charity Cline	8-11-1814
Billops, Robert - Sarah Huddleston	
	lic. 3- 9-1818
Bishop, Stephen - Margaret Adams	6-10-1819
Black, John - Margaret Petree	11- 6-1817
Blackburn, Nathaniel - Ellenor Snodgrass	
	8-11-1814
Blackman, Remember - Lois Tyler	9- 1-1814
Blair, Samuel - Elizabeth Fauch	9-29-1824
Blue, James - Mary Hergereder	10-19-1820
Blue, John - Margarete Mets	2-18-1816
Bonham, John - Mary Boutcher	10-18-1823
Bonner, Hugh - Susan Leeper	11- 8-1821
Boots, Samuel - Ruoh Lutes	6- ?-1819
Bourne, Samuel - Mary Smith	lic. 2-28-1815
Bowlesby, Lewis - Juliann Shannon	
	lic. 3-29-1820
Bown, Cornelius, Elizabeth Bennett	10-24-1819
Bowne, Cornelius - Elizabeth Hill	
	lic. 9-11-1819
Boyer, John - Elizabeth Wilson	lic. 1-27-1824
Brackenridge, Robert - Hannah Northup	
	7-27-1820
Brackney, Nimrod - Martha Seals	8-20-1812
Bradford, John - Sarah Blades	3-20-1817
Bradway, John - Eunis Burk	2-19-1818
Brannon, Moses - Keziah Davis	6-19-1818
Brewin, Wm. H. - Matilda Cambridge	9- 7-1817
Bridget, Jacob - Betsey Scott	7-29-1819
Brison, Hugh - Ruth (?)	11-14-1811

Broadwell, Jacob Jr. - Mary Magdalene Capp
         7-29-1824
Brooks, George - Ruth Ramey   8-22-1824
Brown, Henry - Susanna Witter   5- 2-1820
Brown, Isaac - Margaret Harrell   12- 9-1819
Brown, John - Margaret Shepherd   1- 1-1818
Brown, Mathew - Mary Ann Hanna   8-31-1813
Brown, Thomas - Sarah Lollar   12-24-1818
Brown, William - Sarah Brown   2- 5-1819
Brown, William - Phebe Westcott 11-29-1819
Bryson, Cornelius - Polly Hawkins   6- 3-1816
Buchanan, Robert - Mary Halberstadt 1- 9-1817
Buck, William - Mary Shannon   2-10-1819
Budd, Robert - Nancy Golden   12-19-1816
Burch, Joseph - Mary Ann Tullis   7- 3-1823

Caldwell, John - Martha McDill   11-19-1817
Cale, Solomon - Sally Ramy   4-29-1819
Campbell, Alexander - Mary (Elizabeth?) Davis
         3-21-1816
Cambridge, Littleton - Marval Bullock
         11-25-1819
Cambridge, William - Mary Cambridge 6- 5-1817
Cammel, John - Sarah Brown   lic. 12-23-1811
Campbell, John - Polly Lewis   11-29-1817
Campbell, Joseph - Mary Davis   3-24-1816
Cantrel, John - Sarah Redenour   7-29-1823
Carmicle, And. - Brunetia Rucker 12-12-1816
Carpenter, Abner - Rebecca McNair 3-28-1822
Carson, John - Elizabeth Baker   12-30-1813
Carter, Chapman - Jane McCausland 6- 5-1823
Carter, John - Elizabeth Glidewell 12-18-1817
Carter, John - Hanah Quick   lic. 5-20-1824
Carter, William - Margaret Dunn 12-20-1820
Cartwright, William - Nancy Waddell 9-14-1820
Cary, Isaac - Mary Miller   12-23-1819
Casady, Simon - Mima McCray   3-15-1818
Case, James - Nancy Moore   5-20-1813
Case, John - Hannah Wildridge   6-10-1813
Case, John, Jr. - Mary Wildridge 6- 9-1819
Cason, John - Fanny Burkhalter   3- 1-1821
Cate, Robert - Isabelle Carter   3-19-1818
Cates, Jewel Doige - Elizabeth Clifton
         6-10-1824
Cather, Robert M. - Mary Mosley 2- 7-1822
Cathers, Robert - Elizabeth Williams 4- 6-1823
Cay, Shuball - Clancy Kinsley   8-29-1819
Chance, Evens - Mary Jones   5-19-1817
Chance, William - Anne Gant   3- 5-1812
Chapman, Elisha - Mihilda Egans 11- 2-1820
Chapman, Enoch - Jane Trimmer (?)
  Consent to grant lic.   9- 4-1819
Chapman, Enoch - Mary Schoonover 2-12-1823
Chapman, Hared - Elizabeth Egans 7- 8-1821
Chapman, John - Nancy Price   1- 4-1816
Chapman, Thomas - Hester Johnson (widow)
         1- 9-1823
Chapman, William - Lydia Price   6-12-1818
Chatham, Josiah W. - Sally Jones 11- 2-1823
Cherry, William - Cinthy Jackson 8-10-1820
Christ, Daniel - Anna Mowry   1-16-1817
Christ, William - Mary McCoy   2- 6-1817
Clain, Peter - Isabel Gray   lic. 5-12-1813
Clancy, James - Ruthen Merridoth 4-18-1820
Clark, Elisha - Rebecca Williams 5- 1-1816

Clark, George - Mary McWhorter 4-11-1822
Clark, William - Jane McDonnald 8-11-1812
Clary, William - Elizabeth Brown 1-27-1820
Clearwater, Thomas - Susanna Anthony
         2- 5-1818
Clifton, Simon - Margaret Cantly 4-10-1821
Cline, John - Isabel Shannon   8- 5-1813
Cline, Peter Davis - Jemima Neal 1-18-1818
Coffman, John - Catherine Witter 4- 1-1819
Cole, William - Nancy Haymond 10- ?-1820
Collens, Zachariah - Polly Jacobs 9-23-1813
Collett, Charles - Sarah Quick   10- 5-1823
Collett, Williamson - Mary Hardy 11-25-1819
Collins, John - Ruth Russell   2-16-1811
Collins, John - Rebecca McCoy   12-24-1812
Colwell, James - Elenor Haymond 2-16-1814
Combs, William - Mary Ann Dubois
        lic. 11-18-1815
Compton, Henry - Mary Harthorn 5-29-1822
Comstock, Samuel - Rachel Story lic. 8-10-1816
Conn, John - Lucretia Clary   7-23-1818
Conner, John - Viney Winship   3-13-1813
Conner, William - Mary Clayton   6-29-1820
Conwell, Abraham - Betsey Sparks
        lic. 2-20-1821
Cook, Joseph - Mary Hollings   1-10-1819
Cooksey, Thomas - Lydia Spangueler 5- 9-1819
Cooksey, Zachariah - Mary Case   2- 8-1816
Cooley, John T. - Elizabeth Weir 9-14-1820
Cooly, John - Hannah Gant   10-14-1824
Cooper, Thomas - Sally McCoy   1- 6-1817
Cooper, Thomas - Margaret Mowery 8-22-1819
Cory, Elnathan - Nancy Whitacre 5- 8-1816
Cossairt, Henry - Mary Nailor lic. 12-12-1814
Cottrell, Bradbury - Mary Douglass 1-13-1820
Cox, John - Betsey Lockwood   10- 2-1823
Coy, George - Polly Meredith   2-11-1819
Cragan, Caleb - Sarah James   3- 9-1820
Cragun, Joshua - Sally Rader lic. 10- 5-1822
Craig, James - Christian Short lic. 1-29-1822
Craigg, Thomas - Sarah Eastes   7-14-1817
Craven, William - Jenny Selfridge
        lic. 12-31-1813
Creek, John - Rebecca Waddle lic. 6- 4-1811
Creek, Thomas - Isabella Glidewell 3-16-1820
Crist, John - Mary Smalley   10- 2-1822
Crist, William - Jane Harman lic. 5-10-1816
Croak, Richard - Amy Allen   7-17-1817
Cross, William - A. Smith   lic. 9-23-1816
Crouch, Nathan - Elizabeth Heward 9-16-1819
Cully, Joseph - Sarah Lewiston   9-24-1818
Cully, Simon - Elizabeth Seely   9-29-1816
Cummins, John - Ann Smalley   1- 8-1824
Cummins, William - Rachel Stout 8-21-1823
Curry, James - Ann Furgeson   11-26-1819
Curry, John - Lucy Williams   10- 1-1818

Daffron, George - Seney Tweedy 3-23-1818
Dale, Joseph - Mary Ann Bradburn 6- 9-1814
Dannelsbeck, Jacob - Mary Rusing 4- 8-1824
Darson, Garrison - Rebeccah Sutton 3-20-1817
Darter, Samuel - Lettica Parker 11-23-1815
Darton, Ephream - Mary Sater   8- 5-1819
Dates, Nathaniel - Peggy Schoonover 2-25-1819
Davidson, James - Patsey Griffin 7- 2-1820

Davidson, Robert - Sarah Rickman   1- 1-1824
Davis, David H. - Matilda Wakefield   1-18-1821
Davis, Elias - Ruey Loller   8-28-1814
Davis, Elisha - Elizabeth Shaffer   9-11-1817
Davis, James - Morrilla Hackleman   8- 5-1817
Davis, Joel - Nancy Holway   10-12-1820
Davis, John - Phebe Cutler   9-21-1819
Davis, John - Jane Harding   lic. 3-31-1822
Davis, Samuel - Dorcus Flint   12-18-1817
Davis, Stephen - Lydia Shafer   9-30-1817
Davis, Stephen - Anna Walden   2- 1-1823
Davis, William - Elizabeth Wakefield 2-29-1816
Davis, William - Polly Swords   10- 5-1817
Davis, William - Mary Cross   lic. 4- 2-1824
Dawson, William - Tabitha Simpson   3-26-1818
Dearmond, King - Febe Shaw   5-14-1821
Deford, Charles - Catherine Cavender 4-3-1815
Deford, Thomas - Elizabeth Wilson
                                lic. 8-10-1822
Defrees, Anthony - Betsy McKnight   10-23-1821
Denison, John - Jane Billings   7- 9-1816
Denson, Asha - Sarah Cantwell   1- 9-1816
Denson, Ezra - Sarah Cantwell   11-22-1815
Derham, Jeremiah - Sarah Cooly   5-31-1813
Deweese, William - Hannah Ross   11-19-1818
Dickerson, Alexander - Ann Arnold   10-15-1815
Dickerson, Daniel - Hanah Kiger   7-29-1823
Dickinson, William - Nancy Corn   10- 5-1815
Dixson, William - Nancy Wilson   4-11-1822
Dollar, James - Lavina Tharp   5-29-1816
Dorsey, John W. - Jane Conner   4-21-1811
Dotson, Levi - Letty Burbague   12-14-1820
Doty, James - Mary Manwaring   9- 2-1824
Doty, Joshua - Lydia Schoonover   2-21-1824
Doty, Silas - Judeth Whitney   1-19-1822
Drak, Nathaniel - Ann Dickerson   1- 9-1812
Drake, James - Elizabeth Dickerson   4-21-1811
Dubois, David - Elizabeth Elwell   3-19-1822
Duffee, John - Lydia McCay   8-13-1820
Duglass, Ebenezer - Mary Ward   10-26-1823
Duit, Squire - Maria Seward   3-13-1818
Dunham, Elisha - Frances Hunter   7- 3-1818
Dunkin, Peter - Rebeccah Ewing lic. 7-12-1823
Dunlap, John - Elizabeth Dunn   6- 4-1817
Dunlap, Oliver - Susan Backhouse   1-15-1823
Dunn, Nemiah - Rachel Deboun   2-27-1823
Durham, Silas - Polly Flood   6- 1-1815
Durr, Peter - Malindy Smith   3-29-1821

Eads, Elijah - Lucy Ann Hutchison   4-18-1813
Eckasen, Jacob - Elizabeth Gorville 11-12-1820
Eggers, Benoni - Lydia Dalton   7- 3-1819
Eggers, James - Sarah Rash   12-10-1811
Elston, Jesse - Phebe Caron   2-20-1816
Elwell, Abraham - Esther Combs lic. 1-10-1816
Emerson, Jesse - Anna Henry   3-12-1820
Erwin, Jacob P. - Easter Billings   6-13-1820
Estes, Philimon - Rachel Newlin   4-10-1817
Etter, William - Sally Haynes   9-25-1823
Ewing, George V. - Mahala Osbin   2-13-1823

Fairchild, Edward - Lucy Hubbill   9-20-1818
Fall, George - Polly Taylor   lic. 8-21-1813
Felphs, Reuben B. - Ruth Carson   10-23-1813
Ferguson, Moses - Elizabeth Williams 6-6-1815

Ferrel, Andrew - Susannah Colyear   8- 5-1813
Finch, Abraham - Charity Woodworth   4-28-1815
Finch, Benoni W. - Elizabeth Tyner   10-16-1816
Finch, Moses Jr. - Huldah Gardner   4-30-1820
Fisher, I. W. - Kate Ely   7-18-1811
Flack, John - Ann Sater   1-13-1820
Flint, Benjamin - Elizabeth White   5-29-1824
Flint, John - Charlott Gibbs   lic. 7-18-1812
Flint, Thomas - Anna Thirston   9-12-1822
Flood, Noah - Hannah Crist   3-10-1817
Forbes, Charles - Mary McCaw   10- 9-1823
Forbes, Joseph, of Butler Co. Ohio -
    Margaret Crooks   11- 7-1813
Foredyce, Isaac - Elenor Davis   4-24-1821
Fort, John - Margaret Wood   lic. 12-17-1821
Fosdick, Benjamin - Elizabeth Stanton
                                      6-24-1820
Fosdick, William - Gulielma Stanton 2-17-1819
Foster, John - Elizabeth Green   9-24-1820
Foster, Thornton - Sarah Wallace   2-24-1824
Fowler, William - Comfort L. Alley   11- 9-1820
Fred, John - Lydia Guthery   4-26-1812
Freels, James - Martha Osborn   2- 6-1816
Freels, John - Ruth Wilson   9- 1-1818
Freels, William - Rebecca Osburn   10-29-1812
Freemain, Thomas - Elizabeth Spear
                                lic. 6- 1-1816
French, Jonathan - Elizabeth Johnson 8-4-1820
Friley, Jonas - Sarah McNair   3-28-1822
Fruit, Martin - Sarah Updike   8- 5-1822
Fuget, Jesse B. - Nancy Ploughe   7-19-1821
Fullen, John - Jemima Harton   11- 6-1818
Fullin, Samuel - Anne Pogue   10- 2-1817
Furgeson, Joseph - Mary Gates   6-17-1817
Furnedge, John - Nancy Keeney   8-17-1815
Furtue, Martin - Susanna Sebley   3-30-1820

Gallihan, George - Elizabeth Adams 12-24-1812
Gallion, Nathan D. - Hannah Douglass
                                      3-19-1815
Gant, Briton - Mary Russell   1-16-1817
Gant, Giles - Nancy Smith   11-20-1817
Gant, John - Catharine Carter   lic. 11- 7-1822
Gant, John - Elizabeth Cooly   3-16-1823
Gardner, Archibald - Unice Shaw   12-24-1816
Gary, James - Anna Johnson   1- 9-1821
Gates, Brice - Sally Smith   9- 8-1815
Gates, Jacob - Mary Shaw   11-21-1811
Gates, John - Elizabeth Litteral   4-22-1817
Gates, Richard - Caty Litteral   6-17-1817
Gavin, John - Elizabeth Richardson   5- 1-1814
Gayle, Temple E. - Mary Ann Shipley 8-16-1821
Gearhart, Abraham - Polly Lennon   7-23-1812
George, Andrew - Nancy Adams   8- 8-1822
George, John - Rachel Webb   lic. 9-28-1822
George, Jonathan - Catharine Rudisel 9-25-1823
George, Solomon - Mille Deford   7- 6-1815
Giger, Jacob - Patsey Simes   7-23-1818
Gillan, John - B. Carwell   7- 7-1811
Gilmore, Robert - Sarah Stevens   9-22-1820
Gilmore, William - Mary Stinson lic. 3-27-1824
Girten, Jacob - Susanna Hansel   12-14-1821
Glenn, Thomas - Jane Smith   6-25-1821
Glidewell, Robert - Sarah Hansel   5- 1-1817
Glidewell, Robert - Jane Breese   2-10-1824
Glidewell, Thomas - Rachel Master   3- 6-1823

Glidewell, William - Nancy Butler
                              lic. 11-22-1814
Glidewell, Trash (?) - Anna Colman 11- 2-1814
Golden, Andrew - Catherine Bates   2-13-1817
Goodrich, Abner - Eunice Bush   5-20-1819
Goodwin, Benjamin - Lilley Hildreth 2-20-1823
Goodwin, Caleb - Polly Henry   5-17-1821
Goodwin, Reason - Matilda Stephenson5-5-1821
Gorgun, Thomas Will - Matildah Fordyce
                              5-21-1820
Gosset, Alex. - Sarah Jordan   1- 3-1817
Goudie, Joseph - Pamela Clarkson 3-20-1823
Goudie, Samuel - Rebecca Stout   12- 4-1821
Graves, Alven C. - Betsey Webb lic. 6-24-1816
Gray, Robert - Delila Golding .   8- 4-1819
Green, James - Mary Ewing   3- 4-1819
Gregg, Isreal - Maria May Mary Keen (or Green)
                              3- 3-1816
Griffen, Benjamin - Mary Caldwell
  Notice of consent to issue lic. 8-22-1815
Griffin, John (man of color) - Alesy Thewston
  (woman of color)   lic. 8-21-1821
Griffith, John - Rachel Porter lic. 7- 8-1812
Grist, Ebenezer - Elizabeth Belk   8-19-1824
Grist, John - Sarah Martin   7-24-1823

Hackleman, Jacob - Riller Robertson 6- 8-1817
Hackleman, James - Jane Blades   8-21-1817
Hackleman, Michael - Catey Webb   8-18-1814
Hackleman, Richard - Hannah W. Clune
                            1- 2-1817
Halberstadt, Thomas - Leanor Kentley
                           11-17-1814
Hall, Peter C. - Hannah Shoemaker 7- 4-1822
Hall, Stephen - Mary Ann Turpen   8- 5-1824
Halverstadt, John - Mary Guilbert 2-13-1816
Hamel, George - Elizabeth Watts   4- 2-1818
Hamilton, Adam - Nancy Lee   9-14-1815
Hamilton, George - Nancy Martin   1- 2-1812
Hamilton, William - Sarah Knapp   3-30-1824
Hammond, Henry - Fanna Herndon   3- 5-1812
Hand, Amos - Polly S. Todd   12-24-1822
Hand, Miller - Abigail Rouse   11- 4-1823
Hankins, Daniel - Sarah Mount   4- 1-1824
Hanna, David G. - Agnes Taylor   8-13-1812
Hanna, David G. - Mary McKenny   1-26-1815
Hanna, James - Polly Crafford lic. 6-12-1811
Hanna, James Craig - Ellender Crafford
                       lic. 3- ?-1813
Hanna, John - Sally Crawford   12-20-1821
Hanna, Robert - Sally Mowery   3-18-1813
Hanna, Robert E. - Nancy Adams
                    lic. 8-26-1822
Hanna, William - Phebe Crawford 6-24-1819
Hansel, David - Catharine Smith   3- 4-1824
Hansel, George - Hannah Howell 10- 8-1822
Hansel, John - Jane Dinogh   8-16-1823
Harden, John - Nancy Abrams   11-30-1815
Hardesty, Daniel - Barbary White   6-17-1816
Harding, Jesse - Mary Stevens   11- 9-1822
Hardy, William - Elizabeth Collet 8- 5-1819
Harlan, John - Catharine Harlan 10-13-1815
Harlan, Valentine - Sarah Hollingsworth
                         12-18-1814
Harley, John C. - Jane Lewis   10-28-1813

Harlin, Joshuaway - Elizabeth Hammer
                      11- 7-1816
Harman, James - Philadelphia Dickerson
                      2-18-1816
Harmon, William - Nancy Campbell 12-23-1814
Harper, Elijah - Sarah Hammer   3- 9-1815
Harrel, Moses - Rebecca Scott   11-13-1821
Harrell, William - Elizabeth Miles 2- 3-1822
Harris, Amos - Sarah Vanmeter   4- 4-1820
Harris, John - Ann Dubois   2- 3-1820
Harris, Samuel - Mary Sparks   4- 6-1824
Harris, William - Rebeccah Short lic. 5-12-1824
Hart, William - Nelly Tweedy   3-15-1818
Hartman, Henry - Alsy Tharp   5- 9-1819
Hartpence, James - Anna Jenkins 11-27-1823
Harvey, Charles - Sarah Osbourne 1-26-1812
Harvey, William - Jane Eastes   5- 1-1815
Harwood, John - Eliza Cavel (or Carrel)
                      9- 5-1824
Hasson, Charles - Jane Andrew 11-30-1820
Hawkins, James - Rhoda Davis lic. 1- 2-1817
Hawkins, John - Nancy Hackleman 9- 7-1815
Hawkins, Nathan - Elizabeth Glidewell
                      5- 8-1820
Hawkins, Reuben - Mary Lefforge 2-23-1823
Hawkins, Robert - Sarah Curry   7-25-1816
Haymond, Thomas - Hannah Stansbury
                      9-12-1822
Hays, William - Nancy Gambel lic. 11-16-1813
Heavenridge, William - Mary Maxwell
                      12-26-1816
Hedley, John - Elizabeth Carson 9-18-1817
Henderson, John - Nancy Orr   7-20-1813
Henderson, Nathan - Anna Sexton 9-27-1814
Henderson, William - Telphy Youngblood
                      4-14-1812
Hendrickson, John - Miranda Goble 9- 2-1824
Herndon, Carter - Sarah Davis   3-14-1816
Herndon, Ryleigh - Nancy Rucker 1-16-1817
Herndon, Wesley - Easter Halberstadt 5-26-1813
Hicks, James - Lydia Cragan   4-15-1819
Hicks, James - Mahala Fowler   11- 9-1820
Hiday, Henry - Mary Winn   3-18-1821
Higbee, Abel - Elizabeth Hadley 6-15-1820
Higgins, Martin - Jane Trimble 12-25-1812
Higgins, William - Patsey Loller 10- 9-1814
Hildreth, Joseph - Sally M. Finley 10- 4-1821
Hill, E. - Elizabeth Peterson lic. 10- 7-1815
Hill, Peter - Susannah Leach   10- 3-1818
Hinton, Elijah - — Miller, a woman of color
                      3-12-1816
Hobbs, Elisha - Elizabeth Rader   4- 5-1821
Hobbs, Robert - Rachel Alley   7-22-1824
Hodgson, Joseph - Polly Ramy   11-29-1821
Hollingsworth, Joel - Lydia Spriggs 12-22-1819
Hollingsworth, Jonathan - Elender Ramsey
                      4- 3-1817
Hollingsworth, Jonathan - Jane Baty 11-12-1820
Hoover, Daniel - Polly Patten   12-27-1817
Hornaday, Moses - Margaret Rardon 7-27-1815
Horner, Joseph - Miriam Hollingsworth
                      4- 6-1817
Howard, Hugh - Mary Lewis   lic. 8- 2-1824
Howe, Calven B. - Eliza Garrison 4-24-1817
Howe, Julin - Sarah Crist   lic. 7-30-1823

Howel, John - Nancy Flint   lic. 7-18-1812
Howell, Samuel - Phillis Flint   3-11-1824
Hubart, Samuel - Nancy Glidewell   11- 9-1821
Huddleston, Abel - Polly Ferrill   10- 2-1817
Hudson, William - Mary Gates   11-25-1819
Hufan, Aran - Catharine Williams   12-24-1815
Hughes, Matthew - Jane Logan   5-27-1824
Hurt, Shubal - Hannah Castor   lic. 3- 8-1817
Huston, John - Sarah Vansel   11-17-1817
Hutchen, Ebenezer - Getty Hoagland 3-21-1822
Hutchinson, John - Mary Oakes   1- 4-1821
Hutson, James - Charlotte Style   2-11-1817
Hutson, John - Sally Malilee   8-13-1818
Hydra, John - Rebeccke Snodgrass   2-26-1819

Ives, N. - Nancy Whitford   12- 2-1811

Jackman, Edward - Polly Brison   2-16-1815
Jacobs, John - Nancy Allison   1-23-1819
James, Elisha - Fanna Hammond   2-10-1823
Jenkins, Crocker - Mary Hussey Snow
                                     9-16-1821
Jenks, Jesse - Hannah Redpath   9- 3-1822
Jenks, William - Sarah Davidson   11-13-1823
Johnson, Chittenden - Marian Conner 1-27-1814
Johnson, David - Deliah Hall   11-25-1819
Johnson, Edward - Nancy Records   1-28-1824
Johnson, Jeremiah - Rach Raigen   9-23-1821
Johnson, Phineas I. - Clarissa Harlow Clark
                                     6-25-1818
Johnson, William - Hessey Price   1-16-1812
Johnston, James - Eliza Wasson   11- 2-1819
Jones, Abram - Susanna McGuire   8-10-1815
Jones, Isaac - Ginsey Osborn   10-22-1818
Jones, Jonathan - Sally Shaw   10-18-1820
Jones, Joshua - Mary Summers   1-23-1817
Jones, Thomas - Mary Ann Maple
                               lic. 11-21-1814
Jones, William C. - Elizabeth Stringer
                                     9-19-1822
Julin, George - Sarah Fullin   1- 7-1817
Julin, Jesse - Jane Reed   4-24-1817
Justice, James - Mary Egan   lic. 11-20-1815
Justice, Morton - Dorcas Eaton lic. 11- 4-1816

Kally, Nathaniel - Rebecca Hammon 10-12-1820
Keeler, Ira - Cyntha Stone   9-10-1823
Keen, William - Nancy Clark   6- ?-1820
Kelley, William - Margaret Gossett
                               lic. 3- 6-1823
Kenady, James - Susanna Burch   2-13-1820
Kennady, William - Jane Burch   8-23-1821
Kidwell, William - Mary Allen   6-11-1818
Kimble, George W. - Mary Campbell   5-16-1819
Kimble, Solon - Armarrella Perry   5-12-1823
Kincaid, Samuel - Polly Hansel   10- 5-1820
Kindle, James - Elizabeth Smith   11- 6-1823
Kindle, William - Mary Leviney Sanders
                                     2- 5-1824
King, Stevens - Elizabeth Scott   1- 7-1819
Kingery, Jacob - Elizabeth Kingery   1-18-1821
Kinsley, Apollos - Alice Curry   9-12-1822
Kiser, Christopher - Rachel Mansfield
                                    10-20-1813
Kitchel, John - Margaret Weire   6-29-1823

Klum, William - Sarah Rockafellar   1-18-1818
Knight, James - Cassandra Wingate   5- 2-1822

Lackey, Thomas - Mary Fort   4-21-1823
Lacky, Andrew - Sarah Todd   4- 5-1821
Lacy, Fielding - Martha Glover   8-30-1816
Ladd, John - Nancy Stafford   5-21-1818
Laine, Benjamin Franklin - Nancy Colwell
                                    12-24-1818
Laing (?), Benjamin F. - Nancy Caldwell
                                    12-24-1818
Lane, George W. - Nancy Reddick   5- 1-1823
Langston, James - Jane Cook   3-18-1819
Laning, Rich - Anna Wallace   8-16-1813
Large, Nathaniel - Else Odle   4-15-1813
Larmer, Jacob - Elenor Brant   11- 6-1823
Larrison, James - Elizabeth Merredith 1-13-1821
Lawpple (or Sawpple), Uriah - Martha Sering
                                     2- 3-1819
Lawson, James - Penima Sandiford   1-16-1817
League, Green B. - Nancy Dewessee 2-14-1819
Leforge, John - Sarah Lyons   8- 3-1815
Leonard, Abner - Nancy Dewitt   7-17-1817
Leonard, Abner - Hanah Baldwin   12-14-1823
Levi, Martin - Patsy Clevenger lic. 10-26-1823
Leviston, James - Nancy Templeton 10-20-1812
Leviston, James - Mary Cully   5-27-1819
Lewis, Abner - Elizabeth Timberman 9- 6-1821
Lewis, Avenent T. - Amy Wyeth   4-27-1823
Lewis, Daniel - Margaret Russel   12-20-1821
Lewis, John - Susanna Barber   1- 5-1817
Lewis, John Allen - Polly Churchill 4-16-1818
Lewis, Matthew - Isabel Davison   9- 3-1815
Lewis, Morgan - Susanna Pain   6-29-1820
Lewis, Nathan - Jane Trusler   9-30-1813
Lewis, Samuel - Catherine Wallace 12-10-1818
Lewis, Zimri - Rebecca Henderson   1-11-1817
Lines, Aaron - Jane Blair   lic. 12-17-1823
Lines, John - Dica Herndon   3-16-1820
Linn, George W. - Elizabeth Hadley 10-27-1822
Lions, Richard - Polly Baker   4- 9-1817
Lions, William - Jane Smith   12-28-1820
Lockwood, Hervey - Betsey Tharp   5-25-1818
Logan, Alexander - Jane Nugent   8-31-1820
Logan, John - Sarah Ewing   12-31-1812
Logan, Samuel - Susanna Duffer   6- 3-1813
Logan, William - Elizabeth McCarty 3-31-1814
Logan, William - Lightly Tharp   1-17-1822
Long, Henry - Polly Ronon (?)   1-21-1821
Loper, Oliver - Hatty Baxter   2-14-1822
Loyd, James - Anna Eli   7-27-1820
Lybrook, Phillip - Hannah Penticost 10-8-1818
Lyons, Isaac - Sally Higgs   9-12-1822

McArthur, James - Polly Brison   5- 4-1820
McCafferty, William - Elender Bennett
                               lic. 1- 8-1823
McCafferty, William - Edy Osborn
                               lic. 4-20-1824
McCain, Daniel - Thankful Runnels
  Note of consent to grant lic.   8- 7-1819
McCarty, Benjamin - Deido Walker   11-30-1815
McCarty, Isaac W. - Margaret Cooksey
                               lic. 5-20-1823
McCarty, James - Martha Hamilton   1-13-1814

34

McCarty, Jonathan - Desdemona Harrison
                        3-29-1818
McCarty, Michael - Mary McGuire   2-15-1821
McCarty, William - Thursey Alley
                   lic. 3-21-1812
McCausland, William - Nancy Bennett 4-5-1818
McClain, Matthew - Sophia Snell   2-24-1817
McClary, William - Eleanor Knight   6-11-1818
McCleland, William - Mary Murphy   11-13-1823
McClure, Alexander - Nancy Ramsey
     Note of consent to grant lic.   6-25-1819
McCombs, James - Elizabeth Skinner 4-27-1822
McCoy, John - Sally Dunkin   4-30-1818
McCoy, Moses - Nancy McClelland   6- 4-1818
McCoy, William - Hannah Jerrett lic. 5-11-1818
McCray, Aaron - Mary Williams   11-13-1817
McCray, Moses - Jane Sparks   2- 6-1817
McCullough, Samuel - Elizabeth Neal 1-22-1818
McCune, Samuel - Sally Gregg   1- 5-1815
McDaniel, Reuben - Rachael Beeks
                   lic. 6-23-1821
McDill, Thomas - Martha Bonner   11-12-1818
McDonald, William T. - R. Griggs   1- 8-1811
McDugle, Robert - Elizabeth Seward (?)
                   lic. 4-23-1813
McFarland, Garrison - Catherine Leonard
                   8- 5-1820
McFarland, Levin - Lydia Vannette 7-10-1823
McGee, William - Isabelle Sinclair lic. 2-2-1818
McGlaughin, John - Ann Vanneaton   1-23-1812
McGreer, Alexander - Jane Leviston 9- 6-1819
McGuire, John - Rebecca Kidwell   2-15-1821
McGuire, Michael - Mary Ann Feels   5-14-1814
McGuire, Samuel - Milly McCarty lic. 6- 5-1823
McKenny, James - Eddy Harrel   8- 4-1812
McKinny, John - Sarah Ray   7- 5-1818
McKnight, John - Sarah Telford   7- 4-1822
McNail, Adam - Alley Stevens   6- 5-1817
McQueston, James - Margaret McDill 8-23-1820
McQuoid, John - Mary Rouze (?)   9-22-1824
McWhorter, James - Louisa Williams 4- 1-1823
McWhorter, John - Mary Linn   7-31-1823

Major, William - Rebecca Clark   10- 5-1820
Manwaring, William S. - Rachel Williams
                   5-15-1823
Maple, Stephen - Sarah Cooper   10-15-1814
Marchant, Samuel - Peggy Cooper 10-13-1814
Martin, Giles - Linney Coffee   lic. 1-13-1822
Martin, Roger - Mary Davison   lic. 10-11-1816
Mason, Daniel - Deborah Allen   7-25-1816
Maze, David - Sally Pigman   9- ?-1817
Mead, Luke - Mary Timberman   6- 7-1821
Mead, Nathaniel - Hannah Crane   4- 8-1819
Meeks, Joseph - Lucinda Adair   11- 4-1821
Melhallance (or Milholland), Thomas -
    Susanah Wallace Richey   3-21-1821
Merrill, John - Elizabeth Alexander
                   lic. 6-26-1822
Meyer, Jesse - Nancy Metton   6-25-1818
Miers, Ephraim - Mary Lawson   9- 3-1816
Miller, Jacob - Ann Crawford   10-21-1819
Miller, Jacob F. - Rebecca Lewis   5- 2-1822
Miller, Jeremiah - Sally Mayhew   1-26-1820
Miller, John - Anna Heap   8-21-1823

Miller, Thomas - Elizabeth Armstrong
                   2-28-1813
Miller, William - Patsey Timberman 10- 2-1823
Miller, Willis B. - Mary McCarty   12- 7-1811
Mills, David - Elizabeth Snow   9-16-1821
Milner, William - Sarah Hackleman   3- 3-1814
Miner, Noah - Elizabeth Howren   6-12-1817
Mins (or Mina), William - Betsey Ann Cartwright
                   1-14-1819
Misner, Demarcus - Milly Haymond   7-20-1815
Misner, Lewis - Lucindia Posey   4- 4-1822
Moffitt, Joseph - Olive Parmelia Clark
                 12-20-1818
Monday, John - Rachel Ellis   1-26-1819

Monday, Samuel - Abitha Morris   8- 9-1816
Montgomery, John - Anne Heward   4-28-1823
Moore, Artimus- Jane Moore   9-18-1817
Moore, David - Polly Montacue (?)   4-16-1816
Moore, Ezra - Valentine Speer   2- 4-1816
Moore, Gardner - Peggy Lyons   5-25-1815
Moore, John - Lydia Foster   8-10-1815
Moore, John - Asenath Tuttle   lic. 3-31-1817
Moore, Joseph - Elizabeth Reed   2- 6-1822
Moore, Levi - Elizabeth Lions   8-28-1814
Moore, Morgan - Sarah Mead   2-12-1820
Morgan, John - Martha Sims (widow) 1-11-1824
Morrison, James - Lydia Lee   9-14-1815
Morrison, Joseph - Mary Ann Hamilton
                   5- 8-1811
Morrison, Steward - Delilah Remy   9-20-1824
Murphy, Thomas - Mary Rudman   lic. 4-12-1824
Myers, Isaac - Milberry Hix (?)   4-12-1819
Myers, Jacob - Millender Phillips   11-10-1813

Nailor, John - Jermima Williams   10-22-1816
Neal, Daniel - Elisabeth Bell   8-29-1815
Neal, Thomas - Louisa Sirman   2-23-1816
Neal, Thomas - Ann Boun   7-31-1817
Neal, Thomas - Mary Dunn   1-27-1822
Neely, Thomas - Catherine Brown   7-30-1817
Neff, Ebenezer - Margaret Douglas   2-15-1824
Nelson, John - Nancy Ward   1- 2-1821
Newbrough, David - Sarah Yancy   5- 1-1819
Newell, William - Charity Olive Fuller
                 10-31-1818
Newhouse, Samuel - Polly Sandaford 12-19-1811
Newlan, James - Hanna Hough   1-18-1815
Newland, John H. - Sarah Huff   9-26-1816
Newlin, Peter - Jane Master   4-17-1817
Newman, John - Elizabeth Skinner   11-30-1820
Newton, Charles - Labre Whitsel   1-18-1819
Nicholas, Henry - Patsey Giger   6-15-1820
Nicholas, Joseph - Phebe Hartford   1-18-1817
Nickels, Henry - Anna Ramsey   4-22-1819
Nickels, William - Elizabeth Nickels 11-9-1820
Nichols, James - Ellender Tailor   1-31-1813
Nickelson, William - Amy Marcum   5-22-1817
Noble, David - Rebecca Norris   5-20-1813
Noble, James - Elizabeth Mays   1- 4-1816
Noble, Thomas G. - Sarah J. Jacobs 3-13-1822
Norman, William - Sarah Shumate   3-12-1820
Norris, William - Rebecca Hollingsworth
                 11-17-1811
Norris, William - Nancy Isreal   3- 2-1820
Norton, Samuel - Hannah Caldwell   8- 4-1821

Odeor, William - Mary Henderson	4-11-1824
Odle, John - Dorothy Petree	11-27-1817
Ogden, Hezekiah - Lydia Hughes	1- 1-1824
O'Neal, John - Sarah Tiler	6-12-1817
O'Neal, Thomas - Sarah Brown lic.	8-20-1823
Osborn, Bennet - Catherine Osborn	8-26-1818
Osborn, James - Ruth Nelson	11- 9-1820
Osburn, James - Alesey Armstrong	5-18-1820
Osburn, John - Rachel Freels	2-16-1815
Owen, Harris - Susan Maker	7-23-1824
Owen, Samuel D. - Rachel Spear	
	lic. 11-13-1823
Owsley, Zachariah - Elizabeth Neal	
	lic. 2-14-1814
Page, John - Rebeccah Snell	4- 1-1824
Palmer, Benjamin - Sarah Fortner	4-19-1821
Palmer, Joshua - Mary Losey (?)	9- 8-1811
Parker, Archibald - Elizabeth Patton	5- 2-1816
Parker, Henry - Jane Blades	10-22-1812
Parker (Porter in index), Nathan -	
Nancy Rowland	9-26-1813
Parsel, David - Herssa Kellogg lic.	11-28-1821
Partlow, Jacob - Polly Abrams	9-13-1815
Patten, William - Rebecca Easley	6-10-1818
Patterson, Samuel - Catharine Fruit	3- 5-1822
Patton, Isaac - Jane Norris	11- 2-1815
Peak, John - Burnice Dubois	4-25-1819
Pelton, Michael - Catherine Gilyea	12-30-1813
Penticost, Andrew - Lydia Broomhall	
	11-28-1816
Penwell, Eli - Nancy Scott	10-26-1811
Penwell, George - Anna Tyner	6-18-1812
Penwell, Reuben - Sarah Winship	2- 4-1813
Perkins, Jesse - Charlotte Herndon	5-11-1820
Perkins, Robert - Malindy Lions lic.	3-18-1817
Perrin, Glover - Sally Smith	11- 8-1818
Persell, Benjamin - Rhoda Crump	10-26-1820
Pettit, Enoch - Anna Powell	4-23-1823
Phares, William - Jerisha Hutchinson	1-15-1818
Phelps, see Felphs	
Phillips, William - Catharine Stevens	5-23-1822
Phipps, Abraham - Ann Crist	6-14-1821
Phipps, John B. - Rebeccah Snell	3-12-1823
Pierson, John - Elizabeth Williams	4- 8-1819
Pigman, Adam - Mary Eli	11- 9-1815
Pippin, Richard - Elizabeth Hobbs	10-15-1819
Ploughe, Isaac - Polly Hobbs	11- 8-1821
Poe, Narban - Amy Coombs	3-25-1821
Pogue, Thomas - Sally Sailors lic.	1-25-1819
Pollard, John - Polly Porter	10-22-1818
Pollard, William - Nancy Curry	11-30-1820
Pond, Henry - Catharine Watson	1- 1-1824
Popenoe, William - Sarah Thomson	12-12-1821
Pounder, Johnson - Mary Owens	12-29-1814
Powell, Samuel - Nancy Pettit	5-14-1823
Powell, Wiley - Sarah Carter	5-16-1815
Powers (Powell in index), Arion -	
Nancy Tyler	8-13-1818
Powers, Ezekiel - Jane Simpson	1- 9-1816
Price, John - Nelly Webb	9-29-1813
Price, John - Leanna Chapman	8-10-1815
Price, Samuel - Sally Centley	3-23-1819
Priddy, Thomas - Elizabeth Wates	8-31-1820
Pritchard, John - Erreley (?) Hubart	6-17-1824
Pumphrey, Nicholas - Alde Goe	8-10-1817
Pyle, Jesse - Catherine Blades lic.	4-24-1822

Quick, Elijah - Mary Sailors	3- 1-1821
Quick, James - Elizabeth McClure	10-30-1823
Raab, Eleazer - Mary Shank	5-21-1823
Ramsey, Aaron - Elizabeth Barber	3-22-1818
Ramsey, Allen - Joycy Alley	12-25-1816
Ramsey, Aquilla - Jane Cumbens	8-19-1813
Ramsey, Tobias - Margret Shreve	7-23-1812
Ramey, John - Rachel R. Stansbury	12-16-1813
Rariden, James - Mary H. Test	9- 5-1824
Rash, Joseph - Mary Stevens	8- 2-1818
Rasnick, Lazarus - Elizabeth Holmes	
	10- 2-1823
Ray, David - Margaret Turner	1-17-1822
Ray, Robert - Hannah Fordyce	6-13-1820
Raymond, Lewis - Anna Rockafellar	12-25-1816
Reading, Andrew J. - Elizabeth Miles	
	lic. 12- 7-1822
Redd, Joseph - Elisabeth Mulkens	10-27-1814
Redman, Edward - Ann Shearwood	10-15-1820
Reed, Alexander - Elizabeth Dawson	
(or Lawson)	12-12-1816
Reed, Hugh - Axa Moore	5-29-1823
Reel, Henry - Susannah Simmons lic.	4- 1-1821
Remy, Joseph - Byes Nichols	4-22-1824
Richardson, Aron - Elizabeth Herndon	
	3- 5-1813
Richardson, William - Jane Cather	4- 7-1822
Rickets, Charles - Phebe Hughell	2-11-1821
Ridenour, Samuel - Barbary Miller	10-28-1819
Riggs, Isaac T. - Eleanor Killgore	6-19-1823
Riggs, John W. - Electa Wager (?)	1-10-1822
Riker, Artemas - Jane Schoonover	3-26-1818
Ring, William - Sarah Crews lic.	1- 6-1813
Roberts, Thomas - Leanner Lollar	8- 3-1823
Robertson, Henry - Elizabeth Lollar	
	lic. 4- 1-1823
Robertson, John - Mary Deford	2-17-1817
Robertson, John - Polly Lions	3-15-1818
Robison, Charles - Sarah Partelow	8- 4-1818
Robly, Henry - Elisa Spencer	3-21-1819
Rogers, John - Eliza Smith	2-27-1823
Ronan, Jonathan - Nancy Cooksey	3-16-1815
Rony (?), Charles - Isabel Hall	1- 8-1818
Roop, John - Mary Smith	6-15-1823
Roope, Morgan - Nancy Carson	3- 5-1818
Rose, John - Rachael Dickerson	6-27-1822
Rose, William - Rebecca Duboise	3-25-1819
Rose, William - Sarah Duboise	3-26-1822
Roseboom, John - Sarah Ezell lic.	10- 3-1822
Royster, Robert - Jane Johnson lic.	6-25-1814
Royster, Stanhope - Catherine Johnston	
	12-18-1813
Rucker, Benjamin - Mary Barlow lic.	1-19-1822
Rucker, Benjamin - Susan Shaw	10-23-1823
Rucker, Elliott - Sarah Barlow	6-22-1820
Rudicil, John - Sarah Stipp	4-15-1820
Rudman, Peter - Catharine Henry lic.	7-10-1824
Russel, David - Martha Moore lic.	12-21-1816
Russel, Jesse - Sally Moore lic.	11-10-1815
Russel, Jonathan - Susanna Buckler	
	lic. 8-22-1822
Russell, John - Laura Ann Spencer	10-25-1818
Russell, Enoch - E. Collins	1-22-1811
Russell, James - Margaret Williams	6- 3-1813
Russell, Robert - Franky Scott	4-11-1811

Russell, William - Elizabeth Davison 7-23-1812
Russell, William - Hannah Osborn   1- 5-1815
Rydenour, Jacob - Letitia Brown   2-15-1817
Ryley, Ralph - Martha Rockafellar   1- 6-1820
Rynehart, Martin - Elinor Gray   lic. 3-15-1819

Sailors, Hezekiah - Fanny Sailors   4-16-1818
Sailors, Reuben - Louisa Wythe   5-18-1821
St. John, Samuel - Sophia McClain (widow)
                                      2-19-1824
Salla, Lewis - Julianna Gordon   2-14-1822
Salyer, James - Elizabeth Arnett   5- 5-1821
Salyers, Charles - Peggy Watters   1-23-1817
Sanders, Amos - Polly Singhorse   6- 1-1815
Sanders, Joseph - Edye Brock   6- ?-1815
Sanders, William - Tobetha Hicks   4-10-1817
Sater, Henry - Martha Davis   1- 3-1814
Scofield, Isaac D. - Lydia Moore (widow)
                                 lic. 2-11-1823
Scott, Jesse - Sarah Collins   2-14-1811
Scott, Powell - Rachel Eastes   11- 6-1823
Scott, Samuel - Elenor Conner   4-11-1820
Scott, Thomas - Milky Osburn   3-20-1817
Scott, William - Jane Morley   2-27-1817
Seely, Benjamin - Juliane Ann Lott   7- 8-1824
Serring, David - Fanny Wallace   6-23-1812
Shearwood, James - Polly Upenhouse
                                 lic. 1- 9-1818
Shelby, David - Polly Abel   6-17-1818
Sherwood, Somon - Anna Doughty   2- ?-1817
Shideles, Daniel - Rebecca Landes   2-10-1820
Shanks, Thomas - Sarah Lafforge   10-15-1820
Sharp, Thomas - Elizabeth Haymond   12- 9-1818
Shepherd, Solomon - Elizabeth Allen   2-16-1815
Shirk, Andrew - Mary Stout   11-30-1815
Shirk, Samuel - Elizabeth Stout   8-29-1815
Short, Adam - Agness Moore   3-13-1822
Siers, Joseph - Nelly Dorson   1- 9-1813
Siers, William - Hannah Fitchjarrel
                                 lic. 1-18-1813
Silvey, Hilary - Patience Williams   11-27-1823
Simes, James - Martha Lyons   8- 5-1821
Simes, Stephen - Elizabeth McCarty
                                 lic. 9- 9-1813
Simpson, Nathan - Morning Ramsey   2- 6-1817
Sims, John - Irene Allen   lic. 6-27-1823
Sims, Richard - Polly Baker   4- 9-1817
Singhorse, William - Sarah Price   3-26-1812
Skinner, James - Mary Burtt   6-19-1823
Smith, Amos - Polly Metton   10-26-1816
Smith, Charles - Phebe Barlow   7- 4-1816
Smith, Gabriel - Phebe Hall   1 12 1823
Smith, James - Lucy Wheat   lic. 1 3 1816
Smith, John - Nancy McCarty   6-27-1811
Smith, John - Annis Hatley   7-17-1817
Smith, John - Hannah Moffet   10-28-1821
Smith, John - Susanna Lackey   lic. 4-13-1822
Smith, Jonathan I. - Leah Bilby   3-25-1822
Smith, Peter - Alley Smith   1- 4-1821
Smith, Richard - Patty Lyons   2-27-1821
Smith, Summor G. - Rachel Bulkley
                                 lic. 11-21-1822
Smith, Summors G. - Sally Bulkley
                                 lic. 1- 1-1824
Smith, Thomas M. - Martha Campbell 10-13-1822

Smith, William - Hannah Lackey   3- 1-1821
Smith, William - Sarah Jane Moody   9-30-1824
Snodgrass, James - Mabel Morley   2- 8-1813
Snow, Herculis - Polly Abbercombia   3-16-1817
Snowden, Peter - Catherine Brown   6-18-1818
Snowdon, William Allee - Mary Meserby
                                      4-19-1821
Spahr, John - Vashti Wright   8- 5-1819
Sparks, John - Mary Campbell   4-23-1823
Sparks, Joshua - Rachael McCray   4- 9-1818
Sparks, Lemuel - Nancy Bartelow   11-26-1818
Sparks, Thomas - Jeney Harwood   11-12-1818
Sparks, Zachariah - Elizabeth Carter 5-16-1815
Spear, Joseph - Amy McDonnald   8-26-1817
Spear, Robert - Lydia Mulkins   6-15-1814
Spears, Andrew - Edy Lions   9-10-1818
Speer, Andrew - Elizabeth Osborn
                                 lic. 4-13-1812
Speers, Andrew - Julian Craig   1-20-1821
Speers, Jacob - Nancy Hobbs   4- 4-1819
Spivey, Adam - Ann Morrison   10-23-1823
Spradling, Elisha - Dalla Moody   7-12-1821
Spradling, William - Jane Billings   10- 2-1823
Spriggs, Henry - Mary Hollingsworth   8-19-1819
Springer, James - Margarett Colwell   8- 4-1820
Stacy, George - Frances Alley   2- 4-1816
Stafford, Tyra - Susannah Lions   6-14-1818
Stalcup, John - Mary Peterson   9-26-1822
Stansbury, Henry - Catherine Ramey   8- 4-1814
Starkey, James - Sarah Taylor   11-13-1814
Stebbins, Horace - Lucinda Aaron   9- 3-1818
Steel, John - Elizabeth Glenn   4- 5-1821
Stephens, Eliot - Sarah Osborn   2-24-1820
Stephens, Isaac - Elizabeth Smith   1- 8-1818
Stephens, Joseph - Mary Anne Kidwell
                                      3-23-1815
Stephens, Lewis - Catherine Weeks   9-28-1820
Stevens, Francis - Mary Kidwell   8-25-1816
Stevens, John - Surrena Stevens   12-26-1822
Stevens, John - Amy Stevens   1- 5-1824
Stevens, Stephen C. - Jane Lee   7-23-1818
Stevens, Wells - Agnes Carewele   1- 6-1819
Steward, Archibald - Elizabeth Mongomery
                                      2-10-1822
Steward, James - Jane Leeper   lic. 9-19-1820
Stewart, Jacob - Sarah Brook   lic. 3- 5-1816
Stewart, Samuel - Ann Stewart   lic. 10-19-1815
Stinson, Samuel - Mary Pouner   lic. 9-16-1817
Stoop, Robert - Catharine Carter   11-10-1822
Stoops, John - Edy Martin   12-26-1822
Stoops, William - Elizabeth Martin   11- 9-1820
Stout, Abner - Malinda Tyner   12- 5-1822
Stout, David - Lucinda Keen   3-23-1824
Stout, Jonathan - Leah Warmsley lic. 1-20-1821
Stout, Nathaniel - Catharine Stout lic. 6-21-1821
Strainge, Moses - Milly Hampton lic. 1-14-1823
Stringer, William - Anna Blades   1-29-1824
Strong, Samuel - Amy Styles   10- 1-1818
Stroube, John - Mary McCune   lic. 3-14-1815
Sumpter, John - Nancy Calvin
    Note of consent to grant lic.   12-29-1819
Swanson, Edward J. - Mary Conn   6-18-1811
Swift, Noah - Sarah Manwaring   11- 9-1820
Swift, Thomas - Asenath Moore   12-18-1820
Swordes, Jonathan - Elizabeth McCoy 9-11-1817

Talles (?), Leonard - P. Hudson   10-15-1820
Tanner, Christopher - Polly Parker   3-26-1818
Tappen, Isaac - Elinor Olive Dunham 1-25-1821
Taylor, Richard - Jane McKinny   8-16-1820
Taylor, Silas - Susanna Chandlar   3-12-1811
Teagarden, Henry - Valarie Vanmeter 9-21-1812
                                    (or 1814)
Templeton, David - Jane Barrickman 6-30-1814
Templeton, Robert - Mary Adams   2-14-1811
Templeton, Robert A. - Margaret T. Moore
                              lic. 7-17-1823
Templeton, William - Mary Churchill 2- 8-1821
Terrel, Solomon - Hannah Snow   3-17-1816
Terry, Reuben - Patsey Higgans   11-13-1823
Terry, Robert - Elizabeth Lions   6- 2-1822
Tharp, John - Elizabeth Dollar   11- 8-1812
Thirston, Moses - Martha Willett   8-31-1823
Thirston, William - Mary Tilford   8-16-1822
Thomas, Esom - Susanna Webb   1-30-1822
Thomas, Thomas - Jane Harlin   11-13-1817
Thompson, Jeremiah - Rebeccah Sankey (?)
                              lic. 2-17-1821
Thompson, John - Jane Sanders   7-11-1816
Thompson, Robert - Susanna Sailors 8-13-1818
Thompson, Samuel - Anna Johnson   11-18-1819
Thorn (?), Henry - Polly Bouram   8-19-1824
Timberman, Samuel - Polly Wallace 11-12-1820
Todd, John - Elizabeth Lacky   8-12-1824
Townsend, William - Sarah McKee
                              lic. 3-22-1817
Trusler, Edmund - Permelia Moore   8- 1-1823
Trusler, James - Anna Martin   8-18-1813
Trusler, John - Elizabeth Priddy   12-31-1820
Tucker, Enoch M. - Elizabeth Frazee 8-27-1819
Tucker, Walter - Jane Kenedy   2-14-1821
Tucker, Walter - Jane Underwood (widow)
                                    9-28-1823
Tuttle, William - Mary Hart   3-25-1824
Tweedy, Robert - Patsey Norris   3-30-1820
Tyler, Herman D. - Mary Decker   3- 7-1822
Tyner, Elijah - Martha McCune   4- 7-1818
Tyner, Elijah - Mary Nelson   9- 8-1822
Tyner, Harris - Margaret Thompson 9-15-1814
Tyner, John - Nancy Sailors   9- 3-1818

Updike, Isaac - Ruth Dickeson lic. 10-24-1823
Updike, John - Margaret Armstrong 2-26-1821
Utter, Jimmie - Susan Winchell   12-25-1817
Vanblaricum, David L. - Mary Hadley 8-22-1819
Vanblaricum, Michael - Elizabeth Schoonover
                                    12- 7-1816
Vandolsem, Samuel - Judeth Arnold 3-18-1822
Vaneator, Joseph - Catherine Campbell
                                    1-20-1818
Vanmeter, Samuel - Cornelia Clark 6-19-1817
Vansickle, Winecup - Patsey Tweedy 12-21-1813
Vincent, Jeremiah - Nancy Hastings 1-20-1820
Vincent, John - Lydia Wilson   10-17-1815
Vincent, William - Nancy Stoops   6-27-1816
Viney, William - Jane Logan   4- 6-1816

Waddle, Elijah - Rebeckah Davis   10-20-1814
Wadell, David - Sally Eaton   2-11-1819
Wakefield, Abell - Sarah Stuckey   8-29-1814
Walden, Jesse - Elizabeth Miller   7-22-1817
Walker, Albert - Elizabeth Loan (?)
                              lic. 10- 8-1817

Walker, Robert - Elize Williams   8- 1-1816
Walker, William - Sarah Waddle   6-22-1816
Wallace, George - Mary Simmons   9-19-1820
Wallen, Isaac - Mary Murphy   5-18-1821
Ward, Luther - Judy Toler   4-27-1820
Ward, Samuel - Margery Douglas   10- 7-1819
Warmsley, Isaac - Elizabeth Carson 5-23-1819
Waters, James - Jane Priddy   5-22-1821
Watters, James - Elizabeth Wilson 5- 5-1814
Watton, John - Febe Foster   10-19-1821
Way, Isaac - Nancy Miller
    Notice of consent to grant lic. 9-19-1818
Webb, Brazella - Cynthia Scott   5-29-1823
Webb, David - Rebecca Conner lic. 11-25-1811
Webb, Ishorn - Mary Huston   3-30-1820
Webb, Jonathan - Fanny Stacy   4-13-1819
Webb, Joseph - Sarah Fuget   11-20-1819
Webber, Nicholas - Mary Barlow   7-13-1815
Webster, Rhueben - Mary Miller   9-26-1816
Weir, Robert - Sally Parker   3-16-1820
Welsey, Jeremiah - Sarah Patten   6-11-1820
West, Sephen B. - Isabel Rollf   6-29-1822
Weston, Benjamin - Margaret Wilson 2- 6-1823
Weston, John - Elender Lewis   9- 1-1819
Wheelair, Thaddius - Sarah Rose lic. 3- 2-1816
White, Benjamin - Mary McCray   7- 3-1818
White, Charles - Elizabeth McCray 12-10-1818
White, Lyman - Elizabeth Bake   10- 9-1819
Whitelock, William - Jane Cloak lic. 12- 3-1823
Whitlock, Joseph - Suzanna Tegarden 12-?-1819
Whitmore, Henry - Elizabeth Foster 6- 4-1820
Whitney, Jeremiah - Clarissa Tylar 3- 7-1822
Wickman, Nathan - Nancy Peterson 8-20-1821
Wier, Samuel - Sabra Chambers (widow)
                                    6-30-1822
Wildridge, James - Nancy Abercromby 9-19-1822
Wiley, Spencer - Nancy Backhouse   6-21-1818
Williams, Amer - Lethea Lollar   1-25-1821
Williams, Amer - Polly Robinson   2- 2-1824
Williams, Benjamin - Betsey Curry 11-11-1813
Williams, David - Hannah Mase   3- 8-1821
Williams, Elisha - Nancy Flack   2-19-1818
Williams, Jacob - Rebecca Carmichael
                                    9-10-1812
Williams, James - Anna Sims   9- 2-1819
Williams, John - Deidea Tharp   5-11-1820
Williams, Richard - Sarah Simes lic. 3-21-1812
Williams, Richard - Mary Curry   10-15-1812
Williams, Thomas - Adelila Carvel (or Carrel)
                                    8- 6-1818
Williams, Thomas - Catharine Winchell
                              lic. 2- 9-1822
Willis, John - Sarah Right (Bright?) 1-26-1815
Wilson, Aaron - Anna Washburn   4- 5-1821
Wilson, Andrew - Hanna Hardesty   4-11-1816
Wilson, Benjamin - Elizabeth Vardeman
                                    6-24-1813
Wilson, Daniel - Susan Luce   6-28-1822
Wilson, George - Mary Ann Hughell 8- 3-1824
Wilson, Isaac - Elizabeth Vincent 12-29-1814
Wilson, James P. - Elizabeth Cones (widow)
                                    7- 1-1824
Wilson, Joel - Mary Hasting   12-30-1821
Wilson, John - Polly Vincent   6-23-1811
Wilson, John - Polly Williams   1- 9-1812
Wilson, Joseph - Mary Deford   2-29-1816

Wilson, Joseph - Polly Freel	1-17-1818	Wood, Alonzo - Elizabeth Hervey	1- 6-1820
Wilson, Robert - W. Ward	11- 2-1820	Wood, Charles - Margaret Powers	8-27-1816
Wilson, Robert - Mary Hannah Thorn	11-13-1823	Wood, Edward - Polly Bartlow lic.	1- 8-1822
Wilson, Samuel - Diana Martin	5- 6-1824	Wood, John - Sarah Brooks	4- 7-1819
Wilson, William - Catherine Williams	12-23-1813	Wooley, Zachariah - Mary McGuire	8-10-1820
Wilson, William - Comfort Osborn	3-15-1819	Wooters, Richard - Martha Duboise	11-24-1812
Wilson, William - Nancy Spratt	1-20-1822	Worsham, Jeremiah - Nancy Fullen	5- 4-1813
Winchel, Peter - Elizabeth Ann Hanna	8-24-1814	Wright, Elisha - Anna Chambers	2-20-1817
Winchel, Robert - Catherine Utter	4- 5-1817	Wright, Enoch - Mary Eggers	4-24-1817
Winchell, Stephen - Janey Norris	9-19-1811	Wyatt, Thomas - Cynthanah Brown	3-19-1822
Winchell, Stephen - Seney Norris	11-18-1815	Wynn, Samuel - Sarah McGuire	10-18-1822
Winn, John - Rachel Goudie	5-20-1820		
Winn, Joseph - Margaret Armstrong	8- 8-1822	Young, James R. - Hannah Gregg	1- 4-1824
Winscott, Solomon - Sarah Robertson	3-13-1814	Young, Nathan - Mary Jones	4-24-1819
Winship, Joseph - Elizabeth Ross	9- 7-1818	Young, Robert - Catherine McCoy	4-16-1812
Witter, George - Fanny Kingery	1-25-1820	Youngblood, Peter - Sally Booe	11- 9-1815

GENEALOGICAL INFORMATION ON SOME INDIANA CIVIL WAR VETERANS
Contributed by Ruth Flack McKnight, Indianapolis

The information contained here has been extracted from pension and military records received from the National Archives in my family research. All of the surnames of veterans appear on my Ancestor Chart although they are not all direct ancestors.

Ayers, Nathaniel was age 49 on 12 Sep. 1888. Served as private in Co. H, 143d Regt., Ind. Vols. Was 5'8'' tall, had dark complexion, black hair, hazel eyes; occupation, farmer. Born in Tennessee or Indiana. Married Susan C. **Anderson** 13 June 1858, Jefferson Co., Ind. Died 3 Dec. 1889. Susan age 53 on 12 July 1890; was last paid $8.00 on 4 Feb. 1899 & was dropped for failure to claim for 3 yrs.

Beck, Nicholis Jackson served as Private & Corporal in Co. I, 97th Regt., Ind. Vols. Died Camp Sherman, Jackson, Miss., 23 Aug. 1863. Married Cassa Ann **Bedwell** 31 Oct. 1850, Sullivan Co., Ind. Children born Sullivan Co. between 1855 & 1863: Florence V., Charles A., Cephes L., John A., Denver J. (exact dates given in record). Nicholis was wounded 16 July 1863 on line of battle before Rebel works at Jackson, Miss. His arm was amputated 13 Aug. 1863 above elbow; died of complications of gangrene & typhoid fever.

Bedwell, John was born 1836 Sullivan Co., Ind. Served in Co. I, 97th Regt., Ind. Vols. Was 5'9'' tall, complexion dark, blue eyes; occupation, farmer. Residence after service was Stafford Twp., Greene Co., P.O. Pleasantville. Married for first time Susan S. **Wilson** in Greene Co., 29 Mar. 1888. One son, John, born 10 May 1889; John, Sr., died 23 May 1909. Susan died 10 Aug. 1934. John Bedwell was brother-in-law of Nicholis Jackson Beck.

Flack, David served in Co. B, 91st Regt., Ind. Vols. Discharged at Saulsberry, N.C. 26 June 1865; contracted disability of great toe on right foot in line of duty in July, 1864. Married Susan M. **Williams** 28 Jan. 1854 in Warrick Co., Ind. Children: Alice Ann, George C., William R., Simon (dates given in record). Lived Oakland City upon return from service. David died 3 Sep. 1903. Susan was age 90 on 9 Sep. 1903; last paid $8.00 on 4 Aug. 1905; dropped because of death. (Note: David said marriage was 28 Jan. 1864, but Susan declared on her pension application they were married 12 Jan. 1853)

Flack, Isadore A. was born 23 June 1846 in Dublin, Ireland. Died 29 Sep. 1932 in Springfield, Ohio. Enlisted at Evansville, Ind., although residence was Shawneetown, Ill. Was 5'9'' tall, blue eyes, fair complexion, grey hair; occupation, clerk for Morgan Reev Co., Wholesale Boots and Shoes. Served in Co. F, 136th Regt., Ind. Vols. Married (1) Elizabeth **Edwards** 14 June 1876 in Springfield, Ohio; following her death 25 Dec. 1888 at Douglaston, Long Island, N.Y., he married (2) Bertha Dickson **Falconer** 14 Jan. 1891 Clifton Springs, N.Y. She died 12 Nov. 1944. Children by 1st wife: Reginald Edwards, Eleanor Francis, Beatrice Veronica, Paul Howard, Roger Aldin; by 2d wife: Elizabeth, Gladys, Robert, Maxwell, (exact dates given in record).

The name Isadore **Flack** was an alias; he was born Alexander Isadore **McNally**, son of Robert and Frances (Morgan) McNally; his mother was from Wales. He went by the name of **Flack** until age 29 when he assumed his real name of McNally. Residences after his discharge were Cincinnati, 1866; New York City, 1867-1889; Springfield, Ohio, from 1889 to 1906.

Flack, John was born 9 March 1842 in Reinburg, Germany. Serviced as Private in Co. A, 151st Regt., Ind. Vols., enrolling from La Porte Co. 6 Feb. 1865. Was 5'8½" tall, dark complexion, grey eyes, black hair; occupation, farmer. After leaving service lived in New Durham Twp., La Porte Co. & Walkerton, St. Joseph Co. Married Ida **Malchow** 11 Oct. 1863 (marriage license gives her name as Freiderike Malchow). Children: John, Ella, Anna. John died 1 March 1921; Ida died 14 May 1925.

Flack, Simon served as a Private in Co. D, 44th Regt., Ind. Vols. He died in Warrick Co., Ind. 1 Feb. 1891. He married (1) Hannah **Nicholson** 17 Oct. 1867 in Warrick Co., & following her death 22 July 1884 he married (2) Mary E. **Franklin** 15 Nov. 1884. Children by 1st wife: Laura, Ella, Rosa. (Note: Sworn affadavits filed with pension record concerning his two wives differ from the above and should be checked with original records to avoid error.)

Flack, William C. was 66 years of age on 14 Jan. 1891 and a resident of Enterprise, Kansas when he filed for a pension. He served as a surgeon with the 50th Regt., Ind. Vols. He married M. Elizabeth **Reineking** at New Albany on 1 May 1856 with consent of C. A. Reineking, guardian. William died 21 Sep. 1902 and Elizabeth applied for pension on 3 Nov. 1902 at Morris Co., Kansas. Elizabeth died 28 April 1921 at Los Angeles; body was cremated & ashes sent to Council Grove, Kansas. Children living in 1898 were Cecelia **Moriarty**, Annie C. **Lower**, and J. B. **Flack**.

Franklin, Stephen A. married Mary E. **Attum** 11 Jan. 1876 in Boone Co., Ind. (Note: The marriage license of above veteran enclosed with pension records, probably by mistake.)

Hanna, Ambrose was born Jackson Co., Ind., occupation farmer. Served in Co. A, 31st Regt., Ind. Vols. At time of applying for pension on 21 Feb. 1864 he was 31, & totally disabled with paralysis of left side & loss of sight of left eye and loss of hearing in right ear. Married (1) Josephine **Carmichael** who died 11 Apr. 1860 in Greene Co.; (2) Arrina **Holiday** 4 Oct. 1860. Children by first wife: J. F. **Hanna**, b. 1856; by 2d wife: J. C., Levi S., A. M., Celia J., Stephen N., W. B., Martha E., Elizabeth (dates given in record).

Hanna, Levi was born 9 Jan. 1835 at Bedford, Ind. Served in Co. K, 51st Regt., Ind. Vols. Was captured at Rome, Ga. 3 May 1863 and paroled at City Point, Va. 15 May 1863. Died 6 June 1918 at Worthington. Married (1) Almira **Burcham** Dec. 1856 & following her death 23 March 1872, he married (2) Sarah A. **Nicholson**. Children by 1st wife: Jasper, Joseph, Levi, Alice, Scyuyler; by 2d wife: Timothy, Sarah Jane, Lucinda, Martha, Cornelius Aden (dates given in record).

Hanna, Levi M. enrolled in Co. C, 115th Regt., Ind. Vols. 10 July 1863 at age 20; died Greencastle 18 July 1908. Married (1) Ella C. **Ellis** 23 Mar. 1862; she died 13 July 1891 leaving son Robert abt age 16; (2) Missouri R—————— 7 Jan. 1897, no issue. She was 53 at time of applying for pension in 1908; died 10 Oct. 1933 in Burbank, Calif.

Humes, John S. enrolled 25 Nov. 1861 in Co. H, 49th Regt., Ind. Vols. at age of 49; discharged 29 Nov. 1864 in Indianapolis. Married (1) Nancy Eunice **Oze** 23 Dec. 1858 in Crawford Co., Ind.; she died 16 April 1881; married (2) Nancy Jane **Allman** 9 Aug. 1883 in Pike Co., Ind. She was daughter of Wm. & Elizabeth (Coto) Shewmaker; previously married to Samuel **Allman** who died 1873. Children by 1st wife: Joseph Coleman, James William, Michael Grant, Perry Allen, Oscar Dellman, Nora Allie; by 2d wife: John Samuel. Nancy Jane died 28 Nov. 1937 at Carmi, Ill., & is buried in Mt. Pleasant Cemetery, Burnt Prairie Twp., White Co., Ill. John died 16 Aug. 1908

McNally, Alexander Isadore, *see* Isadore **Flack**.

Pearson, William Allen was born Orange Co., Ind., served in Co. H, 17th Regt., Ind. Vols. Was age 47 on 19 June 1880, occupation farmer. Married Angeline **McPherson Nunley**, widow of Elijah **Nunley**, 16 June 1866 in Gibson Co. Children: Emma L., Ruth A., Joseph M. (birth dates given in records). William died 20 April 1885 Oakland City; Angeline died 27 Oct. 1929.

Skelton, Robert R. was born Warrick Co., enlisted 7 Aug. 1862 in Co. A, 58th Regt., age 23; occupation, miller & farmer. Residence after service in Moultrie Co., Ill. & Gibson Co., Ind. Died 21 Aug. 1887 in Gibson Co. Married (1) Nancy **Birchfield** who died 25 Feb. 1868; (2) Nancy J. **Montgomery** 10 June 1869, at Francisco, Gibson Co. Children of 2d marriage: Alice M., Arthur, Charles, Eda. Nancy died 30 Dec. 1918.

Stevenson, Stephen N. was born 6 Oct. 1832 at Huntington (Hunterdon?), N. J.; served in Co. G, 149th Regt., Ind. Vols., enlisting at Terre Haute; was 5'8" tall, fair complexion, blue eyes; occupation farmer. Residence after service in Greene & Sullivan cos. Died 18 June 1910. Married Elizabeth **Hanna**, sister of Ambrose & Levi **Hanna**, 6 Oct. 1857 in Greene Co.; she died 27 March 1919 at Sullivan.

JEFFERSON COUNTY MARRIAGES, 1811-1831

Compiled from microfilm copy of Volume I of the Jefferson County Marriage Records in the Genealogy Division, Indiana State Library. The names have been checked with the compilation made by the John Paul Chapter of the D.A.R. at Madison. The D.A.R. compilation covers the period 1811 to 1873. Some of the names were difficult to read on the microfilm.

Abot, John, Jr. - Sally M. Reynolds	12-25-1823		Barber, James H. - Sythe A. Lee	8-13-1826
Acre, Thomas - Elizabeth Gudgel	11- 5-1818		Barber, Timothy - Susannah Horton	5-14-1829
Adair, William - Betsy Hall	8- 5-1813		Bare, Jacob - Parmela Davis	5-29-1831
Adams, George - Mary Freeland	3- 4-1818		Barker, David - Mariah Comstock	12-26-1813
Adams, Leven - Martha Hood	8-10-1820		Barnes, John - Tabitha Wilkinson	2-10-1831
Adams, Martin - Jane Davis	8-18-1825		Barnet, Samuel - Hester Ann Rogers	2-20-1831
Agan, James - Ann Woodfill	11-22-1821		Barns, Leonard - Rebecca Bennett	9- 4-1819
Aikens, William H. - Polly Vaughn	3- 6-1828		Barnum, Daniel - Sarah Thorn	6-20-1830
Aikens, William H. - Nancy Shirk	10- 6-1831		Barr(?), William - Margaret Jamison	10-17-1822
Aimes, Aron H. - Fanny Maria Lanham	4-12-1826		Bartle, John - Jane Wesley	11-12-1820
Alcom, James N. - Sally Smith	11-13-1826		Barton, Robert - Mary Brown	1-21-1821
Alcom, William - Hannah Olmstead	11-25-1827		Basett, Desha - Elizabeth Foster	2- 2-1815
Alexander, James W. - Mary Pollard	4-10-1831		Bathrick, Napum - Eliza Hall	3- 9-1828
Allen, John - Betsy L. Woodfill	4-29-1819		Batterton, David - Eliza R. Maxwell	9-18-1828
Allen, Robert - Nancy Weatherspoon	7- 1-1828		Batterton, Peter - Matilda Maxwell	12-21-1820
Allen, Sampson - Naomi Owens	9-19-1830		Baugh, Joseph - Patsy Anderson	3-13-1813
Allen, William M. - Mary Wilkins	4-28-1825		Baulding, Coleman - Elizabeth Landrum	6-14-1830
Allison, James - Rachel Wilkins	6-15-1826		Baxter, Daniel - Susanna Wilson	12-25-1817
Allison, James - Elizabeth Woodfill	3-20-1829		Baxter, William - Jane Karr (?)	8-28-1828
Allison, John F. - Nancy Henning	2-23-1826		Bayless, Nathaniel - Mary Whedden	4-25-1824
Allison, William - Sarah Haman	4- 8-1830		Bear, Abner - Orpha Lewis	4-21-1825
Allison, William - Oser Grant	12-13-1830		Bear, Henry - Jane Jackson	8-12-1820
Allison, William - Nancy Rynearson	12-29-1830		Bear, Michael - Betsy Barrister	9-30-1827
Alphree, James - Nancy Holmes	12-16-1825		Beaird, Thomas - Polly McCaslen	12-27-1821
Alstott, William - Betsy Hillis	12-10-1825		Beebe, Timothy - Rachel Harris	12-21-1828
Ames, John - Eliza Turrell	7-25-1822		Bender, Samuel - Mary Ann Dow	4- 9-1820
Anderson, Abraham - Sarah Damer	1-23-1827		Benefiel, James C. - Elizabeth Taylor	2- ?-1829
Anderson, Alexander - Evelinah Stuart	6-22-1819		Benefiel, Robert - Amy Ryker	5-12-1831
Anderson, Dana - Leroy McCaslin	9-28-1824		Benefiel, Robert - Amy Ryker	6- ?-1831
Anderson, James C. - Susanna Monroe	11- 1-1820		Benefiel, Samuel - Nancy M. Taylor	2- ?-1829
Anderson, John - Susan Hogland	6-27-1821		Benefield, George - Ann Ryker	8-12-1816
Anderson, John - Catherine Brooks	12-28-1821		Benefield, Jesse - Sarah Ann Huckstep	4- 6-1824
Anderson, John - Eliza Cummins	12- 6-1827		Benefield, William B. - Phebe Conner	4-13-1815
Anderson, John - Frances C. Wilson	3- 2-1830		Bennett, Francis - Jane Denton	6-24-1829
Anderson, Mitchell M. - Margaret E. Monroe	4-10-1828		Bennett, John - Elizabeth Fowler	12-28-1818
Anderson, Robert H. - Jane Wood	2-21-1818		Bently, Bazil - Mary Ramsey	6- 7-1827
Anderson, Thomas - Livina Bailey	4-22-1823		Berry, James - Rebecca Jones	4-16-1814
Andrews, Stephen - Maria Atkinson	1-24-1821		Best, Samuel - Nancy Philips	10-16-1828
Arbuckle, James - Fannie Lawrence (?)	5-18-1815		Black, George - Matilda Stewart	9- 8-1824
Arbuckle, John - Sally Jones	4- 2-1817		Blackmore, Jonathan L. - Roxa Ingalls	2- 8-1821
Arbuckle, John - Elizabeth Smock	1-27-1828		Blankenship, Avery - Rhody Blankenship	1- 1-1818
Arbuckle, Nathan - Catherine Jennings	2-15-1812		Blankenship, Isom - Elizabeth Chitwood	5-29-1817
Arbuckle, Samuel - Mary Arbuckle	1-27-1831		Blankenship, Lewis - Hannah Thomas	10-27-1811
Arbuckle, William - Maria Wellington	8- 3-1831		Blankenship, William - Betsy Chambers	1-24-1811
Arrison, Matthew D. - Elizabeth Swope	6-12-1827		Blankenship, William - Polly Whitsitt	10-18-1820
Arthurn, Jethro - Jane Wagner	4-26-1827		Blunk, Daniel - Hannah Griggs	4- 4-1831
Ash, Evan - Mary Stradford	8- 2-1827		Blunk, David - Hannah Grigs	3- ?-1831
Athrean, William - Sarah Alling	6- 5-1823		Bolls, William - Elizabeth McClelehan	5-26-1815
Atkinson, William - Eliza Wilson	11-25-1825		Bolton, Nathaniel - Sarah Barrett	10-16-1831
Ayers, Francis - Amanda Weatherington	3-18-1830		Bondurant, Thomas - Elizabeth Woodfill	4-13-1830
			Boswell, John - Sally Milton	12-13-1817
Bacon, James E. - Eliza Brown	4-21-1822		Bowen, John H. - Polly Wilson	1- 8-1829
Badgely, John - Anna Spann	3-13-1818		Bowen, Stephen - Harriet Johnson	7-27-1831
Bain, Robert L. - Eliza Irvin	4-21-1829		Bowman, Abraham - Lucretia Stucker	4- 8-1830
Baird, David - Elizabeth Barnes	9-12-1824		Bowman, Jacob - Mary Gudgel	5-26-1831
Baker, Henry - Elenor Homer (?)	9-19-1830		Boyd, Jesse - Sally Staples	5-29-1828
Baker, Solomon - Lucy James	1-13-1820		Boyd, Lindsay - Deborah Hoard	4- 5-1829
Baker, Thomas - Mariah Burton	6-11-1826		Brady, Elisha - Mary Hyatt	6-25-1822
Banta, Cornelius - Rebecca Eccles	8- 8-1826		Braley, John - Polly Boswell	12-20-1819

Bramwell, John - Mary Underwood 3-30-1814
Brandon, John - Barsheba Thomas 2-18-1817
Branham, Thomas - Margaret Williams 7- 6-1815
Brawdy, Jonathan - Nancy Bolin 3-25-1831
Brazelton, John B. - Elizabeth Stephens 1- 3-1826
Brazelton, William B. - Eliza Brazelton 8-15-1825
Brazelton, William - Elizabeth Brazelton 10-15-1829
Brent, William - Frances Gillaspy 12-31-1829
Brewer, Enoch - Margaret Walton (?) 12-26-1816
Bridges, Benjamin - Eleanor Wilson 1-24-1828
Briggs, John - Lidda Whitas 7-10-1825
Brisben, James - Julia McClung 10-30-1821
Brisben, William A. - Sarah Wilson 11- 1-1827
Brody, Jonathan - Hannah Bolin 1- 1-1828
Brooks, Benjamin - Matilda Manville 4- 6-1815
Brooks, Humphrey - Ann Eliza Sheets 9-29-1831
Brooks, James - Sarah Mayberry 4- 3-1827
Brooks, John - Lucinda M. Hutchinson 5-16-1830
Brooks, Noah - Ann Burress 2-17-1818
Brown, George - Delilah C. Bishop 9-29-1831
Brown, John - Rachel Rogers 5- 2-1822
Brown, John Jr. - Elizabeth Jackson 5-13-1830
Brown, Robert - Elizabeth McClurg 6- 2-1825
Brown, Samuel - Martha Stites 10-27-1825
Brown, William P. - Alice L. Crafford 4- 9-1820
Brown, William - Judith Bennett 1-26-1823
Browning, Woodville - Julianna Strickland 11- 1-1826
Brunton, John - Mariah Wagner 2-26-1831
Brunton, John - Eliza S. West 3-17-1831
Brunston, Joseph - Sarah Layton 12-19-1820
Brushfield (?), Jeremiah - Jemima Johnston 2-20-1831
Bryan, Theophilus - Nancy Cox 4-14-1825
Bryant, William A. - Ruth Ann Wallace 5-14-1829
Buccles, John - Lavinia E. Hughes 1-31-1830
Buchanan, William - Edna Hankins 3-25-1824
Buckanan, William - Catherine Yount 10- 8-1813
Buckhalter, Charles - Lucy Cosby 1-28-1831
Buckhanan, John - Rachel Short 5-20-1813
Buckhanan, Wilson - Zelah Forester 1- 9-1817
Bulfin (?), John - Phebe Hall 5-30-1815
Bundy, John - Rachel Berger 5-21-1816
Burnham, Joshua - Hannah Aikens 6-15-1830
Burns, Maxa H. - Maria Vawter 12-16-1828
Burrows, Abel - Hermanda Brown 10- 1-1829
Burrows, Madison - Matilda Lanham 4-15-1830
Burton, George - Briton Casan 10-11-1831
Burton, Henry B. - Mary Alcorn 3-12-1823
Burton, John - Aurilla Scritchfield 7-22-1830
Burwell, Isham - Eliza Umpstead 7-24-1822
Byas, John - H. O'Loughlin 1-26-1831

Cain, Christopher - Margaret Wilkins 12-14-1824
Cain, David - Melissa Mitchell 3- 2-1830
Cain, Peter - Dolly Edwards 7- 8-1819
Callon, Patrick - Mary O'Keeff 1-11-1822
Camel, Joseph - Elizabeth Richey 6-16-1824
Campbell, Alexander - Lidia Ingram 2-25-1819
Campbell, John - Elizabeth Shepard 7-25-1824
Campbell, Joseph - June Holt 11-10-1821
Campbell, William - Sarah Cox 3- 2-1820
Campbell, William B. - Nancy Ingram 9- 2-1828
Caplinger, Samuel - Jane Ryker 9-18-1817
Caplinger, Solomon - Mary Nay 7-29-1830
Carpenter, George - Rebecca Hooker 10- 1-1824
Carpenter, John - Elizabeth Cattlehan 6-10-1813
Casey, Charles - Sally Morrison 9-17-1820

Caslin, William - Eliza White 10-27-1826
Causly, Henry - Lucy Turner 4-18-1824
Chamberlain, Isaac - Catharine Brown 10-15-1829
Chamberlain, Moses - Elizabeth Brown 11- 8-1830
Chamberlin, Uebeder - Phebe Reed 9-12-1822
Chambers, Anthony W. - Polly Roseberry 4-22-1823
Chambers, John - Nancy Anderson 12-21-1820
Chambers, Samuel - Lucinda Hughes 4-22-1824
Chambers, William - Sarah Blankenship 10-27-1811
Chambers, William - Catherine Blankenship 7- 4-1825
Chandler, John - Nancy Monroe 3-27-1823
Chapman, John - Zona Wolf 4- 3-1825
Chapman, John - Mary Ann McKim 9-17-1826
Chasteen, Isaac - Polly Robins 2-25-1819
Chasteen, Samuel - Margaret Johnson 9-28-1815
Chenowith, John P. - Ann Stout 8- 9-1831
Chenoweth, Joseph C. - Sophia Taylor 7-18-1830
Chevis, Malachi - Elizabeth Shelton 5-11-1831
Childs, Lorain - Charlotte Wiley 4-10-1831
Chinoth, James - Rachel Hill 1-27-1820
Clark, Barrabas - Eliza Rogers 8- 9-1821
Clay, Daniel G. - Harriet Smith 1- 5-1830
Clemons, John - Nancy Holt 1- 5-1815
Clifton, Nathan - Elizabeth Vaughn 11- 3-1826
Cline, Jacob - Catherine Hogland 11-16-1821
Cline, Jesse - Sarah Miner 12- 3-1822
Close, Samuel - Nancy Collier 4-11-1822
Close, William - Mahala Arbuckle 9- 2-1824
Cloud, William - Rebecca Hood 12-23-1813
Cochran, Alex - Margaret Anderson 3- 7-1822
Cochran, James - Harriett Richie (?) 11-12-1829
Coffey, Elijah - Sally Simmons 2-27-1820
Coghill, Nimrod - Rachel Littlejohn 3- 1-1831
Cokes, James - Eliza Hall 7- 3-1828
Cole, John - Elizabeth Peters 8-28-1814
Coleman, John - Jane Byrne 4-13-1821
Collier, Simeon - Elizabeth Barkshire 9-11-1827
Collins, Andrew - Nancy Roe 12-28-1823
Colman, Wiatt - Catherine Nicholson 4-23-1826
Combs, Asa - Frances Fore 8-23-1829
Compton, William - Sarah Woodburn 12- ?-1827
Comstock, Botsford - Margaret L. Bell 3- 3-1831
Comstock, Harmenius - Eliza Ann Bell 12-23-1830
Cook, John - Mahala Comly 10- 8-1823
Cooke, Capias D. - Mariah Meek 7- 4-1824
Cooly, Matthew - Nancy Smith 2-13-1823
Cooper, Murdock - Martha McClane 8- 3-1826
Cooper, Thomas - Hannah Burton 10- 8-1829
Cooperider, Henry - Catherine Howell 11- 3-1831
Cooperider, Jacob - Fanny Smith 1- 3-1832
Cope, Jonathan - Sarah Woodfield 11-10-1831
Cope, William - Margaret Littlejohn 10-28-1819
Copeland, James - Ann Skeene 1- 5-1821
Copeland, James - Polly Phillips 9-16-1824
Copeland, John - Sally Stewart 6- 7-1820
Copeland, Matton A. - Elizabeth Bondurant 12-10-1830
Coplen, Thomas - Sarah Hopper 8- 6-1818
Cosby, Charles - Synthia Depaw 12-13-1824
Cousley, Samuel - Mary Bowman 1-28-1830
Cowden, James H. - Margaret F. Wallace 10-21-1821
Cowdry, Caleb - Peggy Whitesides 11-13-1817
Cowen, John - Ann Maxwell 12-30-1819
Cox, Asa - Mary Spellar 3-29-1828
Cox, Christopher - Anna Littlejohn 4- 7-1816
Cox, David - Betsy Smith 10-12-1820
Cox, Harris - Nancy McClelland 8-19-1830

Cox, Jacob M. - Martha Hudson	10- 6-1831
Cox, Jonathan - Hannah Daniels	11-25-1818
Cox, Russel - Margaret Underwood	2- 3-1820
Coy, Conrad - Mary Robertson	10-16-1820
Crafton, John - Cynthia Crawford	4- 1-1823
Craig, Andrew R. - Sarah Brindle	12-26-1826
Craig, William - Eliza Martin	7- 2-1829
Cravens, Benjamin - Margaret F. Blackburn	6-27-1820
Cravens, Robert - Sarah G. Paul	5-26-1818
Crawford, David - Sally McNeeley	6-28-1820
Crawford, Thomas H. - Clementine Eloise Martin	
	5-31-1831
Crisman, John - Caroline Pelman	12-24-1825
Crocket, James - Cloe Law	7-30-1826
Crocket, James - Lear Meddock	5-11-1829
Crosby, Cyrus - Elizabeth H. Wiley	3-25-1829
Crothers, John - Jane Spears	12-22-1814
Cross, Samuel T. - Emily H. McIntire	12- 6-1821
Crusan, John - Louise Arbuckle	12- 9-1824
Culbertson, Charles - Maria Logan	7-21-1824
Cumings, Thomas - Sally Gabbard	3-20-1824
Cumming, Wesley - Hester W. Irvin	12-30-1830
Cunningham, David L. - Nancy McClain	1-27-1831
Currie, James - Jane Park	12- 4-1823
Curry, George - Margaret Patterson	11- 2-1826
Curry, Robert - Mary Patterson	9- 3-1820
Custer, Arnold - Leanah Moore	4-17-1831
Custer, Isaac - Peggy Nichols	5- 4-1829
Custer, James - Catherine Ross	2-26-1828
Custer, Jesse - Nancy Spurgin	4- 1-1830
Custer, William - Sally Downer	5- 4-1820
Cutler, Benjamin - Nancy Nicholson	7-30-1820
Daily, Eugene O. - Sarah Stephenson	1-19-1821
David, Atwell - Rebecca Conner	12- 3-1818
David, Daniel - Rhoda Cook	2-25-1830
Davidson, Andrew - Rebecca Duffy	6-14-1828
Davidson, James - Nancy Hensly	1- 1-1829
Davidson, James - Maria Tallen	2-17-1831
Davidson, Samuel - Jenny —	10-25-1819
Davis, Beaden - Elizabeth Sample	12-25-1823
Davis, Harvey H. - Mary Ann Jones	9-11-1831
Davis, I. D. - Fanny Jones	7-23-1823
Davis, James - Mary R. Dungan	12- 1-1825
Davis, James D. - Lucy Lawrence	8-27-1823
Davis, John - Eliza Davis	3- 8-1827
Davis, John W. - Polly Roberts	8-17-1831
Davis, Joshua - Nancy Barnum	7-12-1826
Davis, Noah - Nancy Mings	12-31-1829
Davis, Septimus - Elizabeth Davis	3-12-1828
Davis, Thomas - Mary Jane Sample	1-17-1828
Dejonneth, John F. - Elizabeth West	7- 1-1830
Delap, Robert - Nancy Fenton	7-14-1820
Delap, William - Phebe King	8-21-1816
Demaree, Daniel - Sarah Lee	6- 5-1817
Demaree, Jesse - Elizabeth Myers	11-23-1827
Demaree, John A. - Sarah Myers	3-12-1827
Dennis, Jesse - Julian Oliver	5- 9-1825
Dennis, Robert - Nancy Roseberry	8-29-1830
Denny, John - Elizabeth Custer	1- 7-1828
Deputy, Joshua - Polly Woods	4- 7-1817
Deringer, Jacob - Nancy Cook	7-16-1815
Dhor, Zerlem Hamber - Fanny Golay	2- 3-1814
Dickerson, Lambert W. - Margaret Snodgrass	
	12-28-1824
Dickson, Abraham - Elizabeth Hunt	7-19-1831

Dixon, Benjamin - Lucy Henderson	8-27-1813
Dixon, John - Jane Thompson	4-21-1822
Dixon, Patrick W. - Livinea Stafford	11-19-1818
Dixon, Samuel - Margaret Shileday	3-19-1824
Dodson, Richard H. - Sarah Wells	7-27-1829
Donner, John - Sally Lame	2-12-1818
Dorsey, Henry - Adeliade Hicks	11-25-1828
Dorsey, James - Cintha Hopper	12-22-1826
Doty, John - Nancy Wingate	8- 6-1818
Douglas, Ashel - Jane Kirkendall	1-25-1821
Douglas, Aurzi (or Amzi) - Mahala Kirkendall	1-9-1827
Douglas, Jeremiah - Catherione Reden	3-31-1825
Doyle, Thomas J. - Eliza G. McIntire	7-22-1830
Dryden, Thomas - Polly Anderson	5-10-1821
Duffy, John - Nancy Minroe (?)	2-25-1828
Duffy, John - Lavinia McCaslin	7-15-1828
Duffy, William R. - Melissa Cooper	7-26-1827
Dugan, Samuel - Nancy Melton	10-28-1819
Dugan, Samuel - Eleanor Laws	8-27-1829
Duncan, Frederic - Eliza R. McCormic	6-17-1831
Dungan, Samuel - Sarah Wining	7-25-1821
Dunn, Samuel - Ruth Lewis	3- 9-1819
Dunn, Samuel - Betsy Body	11-27-1827
Dunning, Festus - Caroline Nichols	6-17-1828
Dunning, Matthew A. - Elizabeth Law	11-12-1822
Dyer, Samuel - Angalina B. Sutter	3-16-1828
Earhart, Samuel - Jane Barnes	11- 2-1826
Eastman, Justus - Elen O'Keefe	12-20-1821
Easton, David - Nancy Griffin	1-13-1814
Eblin, Joshua - Mathilda Bennit	12- 8-1818
Eccles, Doctor - Sarah Yost	3- 8-1827
Eccles, Samuel - Nancy Hillis	11-23-1820
Eckton, Aron - Polly Woodfill	11- 5-1826
Eddeman, Samuel - Rachel Kelly	7-24-1828
Eddleman, Amos - Phebe Smith	11-10-1831
Edens, Elias - Nancy Bradshaw	9-13-1831
Edwards, Elijah - Charlotte Davison	5-31-1824
Edwards, James - Fanny Stribling	2-12-1827
Eliot, Robert - Eliza Spear	8-31-1823
Elliott, Anthony L. - Elizabeth J. Craig	3-21-1831
Elliott, Robert - Louisa Spear	8-31-1823
Elliott, William - Jane Marquis	5-21-1816
Elrod, Benjamin - Sarah Redinbough	9-10-1826
Elston, George - Nancy Stewart	10-15-1829
Elwell, David - Catherine Medock	10-15-1824
Elzey, John - Sarah McNew	2-10-1829
Emberson, Benjamin - Phebe Yates	9-20-1821
English, Elisha G. - Mahala Eastin	11- 9-1819
English, Loving - Mary Tucker	1- 9-1813(?)
English, Robert - Mary Brink	12-11-1814
Epperson, James - Hannah Smith	11- 9-1823
Eudaily, Isaac - Polly Briggs	7-26-1816
Evans, Lewis - Laura Woolford	2-11-1824
Evans, Whedon W. - Elizabeth J. Ward	11- 3-1829
Evans, William - Casandra Field	2-25-1829
Everhart, Charles - Mary B. Menser	8-26-1830
Everhart, William - Nancy Lowden	4-27-1821
Farley, Thomas - Polly Clark	8-29-1819
Faulkner, James - Rachel Brown	5-10-1815
Favour, Thomas - Sarah Buckhanan	9-30-1819
Field, Henry - Rachel Arbuckle	7-12-1820
Finnacle, Samuel - Harriett Ramsey	11- 6-1828
Fisher, Schuyler. - Sally Douglass	5-16-1826
Fisher, William - Susannah N. Johnson	11-23-1831

Fitzgerald, Joab H. - Sally W. Ward	6- 2-1831
Fitzpatrick, James - Jane Ansen	4-19-1820
Fix, Jacob - Polly Stucker	1-29-1818
Fix, Philip - Sintha Dorety	9-30-1824
Fix, Samuel - Nancy Mellinger	9-13-1827
Fix, William - Sally Cousley	2-20-1823
Fletcher, Eli - Mary McKay	6-24-1830
Ford, Achilles - Katherine Fuel (Tull)	10-11-1829
Ford, Washington - Mary Ann Miller	12-24-1829
Ford, William - Sarah Murphy	8-14-1815
Foster, Gabriel - Ann Clark	5-18-1829
Foster, Hiram - Polly Trumbo	12-24-1818
Foster, John M. - Lydia McMillin	11-27-1823
Foster, Zebulon - Catherine Mills	4-21-1825
Fowler, Benjamin - Emiline Aikins	11- 8-1825
Fowler, Joshua - Jane Midcap	12-27-1818
Francis, James - Mary Carr	3- 5-1828
Francis, John - Mary Brown	2-21-1822
Francis, Walter - Jane Brown	2- 7-1822
Franklin, George W. - Emily Ward	7- ?-1829
Freman, Peter - Letty Conley	9-14-1822
Frick, Frederick - Keziah Wagner	9- 1-1828
Fuel, John H. - Elizabeth Duffie	12- 4-1826
Fuel, William - Margaret Lichlighter	3- 4-1830
Fuell, James - Sally Sullivan	12-27-1829
Fullenwider, Samuel - Jane Houston	6-28-1827
Fuller, William - Anna Roberts	10-14-1813
Furgeson, Jack (or Joel) - Polly Brock	1- 6-1822
Furgusson, Washington - Patsy Hughes	4-12-1821
Gaddis, William - Mathilda Monroe	12-10-1830
Gageby, David - Malinda Woods	4- 6-1824
Gale, Elmon - Elizabeth Brown	1-10-1827
Gardner, William - Anna Woodfield	4- 7-1816
Garrison, Samuel G. - Margaret B. McNutt	11- 5-1829
Gayer, John Conrad - Almyra Sawyer	12-28-1820
Getty, Andrew - Ann Hayes	10-12-1827
Ghilchrist, James - Mary Anderson	8-13-1826
Gibbs, Spruce - Eliza Ann Fith	4- 1-1829
Gillam, James - Mima Falkner	6-21-1818
Gillum, Enoch - Elizabeth Eador	1-18-1830
Glover, James - Elizabeth Vawter	6-24-1813
Goar, Levi P. - Rebecca Sanders	5-31-1824
Gobens, Jesse R. - R. Minty Plunkett	12- 8-1829
Goode, Samuel M. - Sarah G. Cravens	5-23-1824
Goodlet, Ebenezer - Elizabeth Thompson	11- 3-1825
Goodnow, Samuel - Elizabeth Logan	10-19-1824
Gordon, James - Kezia Hillis	2-23-1820
Gordon, John - Sarah Scott	1- 1-1829
Gordon, Joseph - Margaret McClean	5- 4-1816
Gordon, William - Isabel Gordon	1-18-1820
Gore, Alisicen (?) - Catherine Doolittle	10-25-1819
Gow, Peter - Betsy Cotton	3-11-1830
Graber, John Christain Jacob - Mary Ann Bukber	
	5-12-1831
Graham, Samuel - Lucy Fuel	12-28-1829
Gray, Joseph - Melinda Jaquay	10-23-1831
Gray, Moses - Sarah Robinson	11- 3-1814
Gray, William - Nancy Freeman	6-30-1827
Gray, William - Doanna Lynch	4-21-1831
Green, David - Malinda Ryker	2-14-1822
Green, John - Cloe Lang (or Law)	5-20-1825
Gregg, Samuel - Susan Logan	3-27-1828
Griffin, Adam - Nelly Francis	3-11-1817
Griffin, Benjamin H. - Burilah Hankins	4-15-1830
Griffin, Ephraim - — Cassey	9-14-1826

Grinstead, John T. - Catherine Waggoner	4-20-1815
Griswold, Alexander - Clarissa Bowen	3-28-1825
Groscup, Benjamin - Jane Taylor	4- 4-1831
Grover, Nicholas D. - Elizabeth W. Brisben	6-20-1821
Gudgel, John - Jane Smith	9- 8-1824
Gudgel, Nathaniel - Rachael Chasteen	7-13-1818
Gudgil, Mahlon - Charlotte Snodgrass	6-15-1820
Guttery, John - Mathilda Ritchie	7-12-1816
Hadden (or Hudson), Peter B. -	
Mary Lyttle (or Suttle)	5-17-1825
Hall, Abner - Jane Roseberry	12-18-1816
Hall, David - Jane Crawford	1- 5-1814
Hall, Edward - Maria McCullough	9-17-1818
Hall, Henry - Rebecca Hankins	3-28-1822
Hall, Hezekiah - Judith Goule (?)	12-29-1825
Hall, John - Prudence Hall	7- 2-1824
Hall, John - Sarah Elwell	2-14-1826
Hall, Squire - Sally Loughridge	1-20-1830
Hall, William - Lucy McCartney	6-18-1827
Hall, Zachariah - Mary Hall	3-16-1815
Hamilton, James - Susanna Mitchell	11- 9-1819
Hamilton, James - Nancy Fullenwider	2-14-1822
Hamilton, Joseph D. - Charity Holden	12-25-1823
Hamilton, William - Margaret Byers	10-30-1821
Hamilton, William - Jemima Utt	7-22-1830
Hamilton, William D. - Jane Smith	4-10-1828
Hamlin, William - Rebecca West	12-25-1814
Hammond, George M. - Mary Eccles	3- 4-1830
Hammond, James - Julia Lard	3-22-1821
Haney, John - Patsy Kennedy	10-25-1821
Hankins, Absolom - Catherine McCarty	4- 5-1814
Hankins, John - Patsy Buchanan	1- 1-1824
Hanlain, William - Lidia McCarty	1-15-1811
Harbord, Joseph - Sarah Kempton	1-21-1829
Harbord, Robert - Rebecca Marshall	3- 2-1820
Harbough, Jacob - Ellen Beigler	4-18-1826
Harendon, John D. - Betsy Adams	4-18-1820
Harren, Isaac - Lydia Devore	8- 6-1823
Hart, Alexander - Hannah Badgely	9-30-1818
Hartwell, Alba - Calista Twaddle	1- 1-1826
Hartwell, John - Amelia Kenneday	8-19-1830
Hartwell, Lester - Sarah Mosley	5-19-1829
Hartwell, Lester - Polly Jones	10-13-1830
Hatfield, John - Elizabeth Magness	12-26-1819
Haughute, Leonard - Elizabeth Modly (?)	8-17-1824
Hays, James - Margaret McIlroy	8-14-1820
Hays (or Hoyt), James - Mary Jones	6- 7-1827
Hays, James - Martha Underwood	3- ?-1828
Hays, James - Sally Walton	1-18-1829
Hays, John - Elizabeth Spiller	12-27-1827
Hays, John - Frances Chandler	2-11-1830
Heath, Edwin - Sally Brooks	6-15-1830
Heath, William - Martha Rogers	6-15-1830
Helms, Abraham - Jemima Whitkill	5-13-1818
Helms, David - Nancy Hardigen	4- 4-1827
Helms, George - Nancy Ryker	9-13-1825
Helms, Isaac - Permelia Engles	12-30-1824
Henderson, John A. - Hannah Johnston	10- 2-1831
Hendricks, Adam R. - Rebecca Stephens	11- 4-1824
Hendricks, William - Ann P. Paul	5-19-1816
Henry, David A. - Caroline Stapp	5- 5-1831
Henry, Elisha - Judith Halley	8-25-1831
Henry, George - Martha Buchanan	7- 8-1819
Henry, James - Anna Berger	2-10-1831
Hensley, George W. - Julia Ann Hudson	9-10-1829

Hensley, William - Lucy West	5-12-1824	
Henthorn, Elijah - Matilda Burch	7- 5-1827	
Herigen, John - Jane Irwin	11-18-1820	
Herin, William - Barbary Bare	5-27-1831	
Herman, James - Elizabeth Woodard	3-25-1830	
Herod, Isaac - Sarah McCrory	2-24-1820	
Herring, Bartlett - Loiay Mill	3-11-1824	
Hicksten (?), William - Betsy Carrel	10-16-1817	
Hill, Abraham - Caroline Houston	3-29-1827	
Hill, Abraham - Nancy Lame	6- 5-1828	
Hill, Charles - Cinthia Bayer	4- 5-1824	
Hill, Joseph - Lany Busby	5-25-1830	
Hill, Wyllys - Mary Wildman	12- 6-1827	
Hillis, George - Margaret Hays	1- 3-1826	
Hillis, Hiram - Louisa Etherton	5-19-1831	
Hillis, William H. - Margaret Farmer	9-20-1828	
Hinton, Thomas - Jane Mitchell	9- 5-1822	
Hinton, Thomas - Polly Hill	4-23-1831	
Hite, F. A. - Kezia L. Talbott	10-18-1831	
Hoagland, John W. - Polly Monroe	12- 1-1831	
Hoagland, Moses - Nelly Hoagland	1- 2-1823	
Hoagland, William - Rachel Chambers	10-19-1820	
Hobbs, Thomas - Ellen Snodgrass	11-22-1830	
Hodges, Willis - Elizabeth Robinson	3- 4-1829	
Hogland, Henry - Jane Peters	8-28-1814	
Hogland, James - Mary Smith	4-17-1823	
Hoglin, William - Margaret Monroe	10- 5-1825	
Holden, John - Polly Thompson	6-12-1823	
Hollenback, Andrew - Milly Henderson	8-26-1819	
Hollenback, Henry - Peggy McFaddin	10- 5-1825	
Hollenbeck, Lawrence - Mary Harlan	12-16-1819	
Hollinsworth, Abraham - Eleanor Wilson	3- 1-1827	
Hollis, John P. - Nancy McMellan	3-16-1820	
Holt, John - Jane Ingram	2-12-1818	
Hood, John - Mary Holton	11- 9-1826	
Hood, William - Kitty Depbois	8- 9-1812	
Hood, William - Frances Ragan	10- 4-1827	
Hopkins, Jacob - Nancy Welch	4- 1-1820	
Hopper, Elijah - Deborough Cox	12-11-1826	
Hopper, Smallwood - Elizabeth Smith	8- 6-1818	
Hopper, William - Melinda Wilhite	3-14-1819	
Horton, Adam - Barbery Scott	10- 9-1817	
Horton, James - Elizabeth Minor	2-13-1823	
Horton, John - Jane Holcomb	12-11-1823	
Howard, Daniel - Mary Lee	2-25-1821	
Howard, Isaac - Lucy Manville	2-12-1818	
Howard, Osten - Rebecca Teen (?)	3-10-1823	
Howard, Thomas - Jaily Underwood	10-25-1827	
Hoyt, Ferdinand C. - Eliza Ewing	12-15-1827	
Hubbs, Benjamin - Sarah Ann Basnett	5- 4-1830	
Hubeck, Samuel - Susanah Thorn	3-11-1824	
Hudson, Cuthbird R. - Eliza Johnson	2- 1-1827	
Hudson, John - Sarah Spann	4-24-1828	
Hudson, Thomas - Polina Hensly	12-30-1830	
Hughes, David - Rebecca Long	3- 2-1826	
Hughes, James - Sally Johnston	2-15-1821	
Hughes, James - Jane Dunn	9-13-1831	
Hughes, John - Catherine Tatum	8-19-1827	
Hughes, William - Jane Robinson	2- 2-1815	
Hughes, William - Jane Robinson	12-18-1816	
Hughes, William - Mary King	12-26-1820	
Hukel, Henry - Rachel Copeland	1- ?-1823	
Hulbert, Lewis - Pamelia Foster	4-30-1820	
Huleck, Abraham - Elen Mills	1-17-1822	
Hull, Jesse L. - Nancy Hammond	3-22-1829	
Humphries, Love J. - Polly Ramsey	12- 6-1821	

Humphries, William H. - Elizabeth Cope	9-17-1829	
Hunt, John - Polly Wilson	4- 9-1814	
Hunter, Levi - Mary Ann Davis	3-22-1828	
Hutchinson, Abraham P. - Olive Whitson	8-27-1828	
Hutchinson, Ebenezer - Sophia Thompson	11-15-1822	
Hutchinson, John - Delilah Cox	6-15-1830	
Hutchison, William - Mary Ann Durall	7-18-1824	
Hutsell, Stephen - Mary Troutman	4-16-1828	
Hutton, Absolom - Elizabeth Wells	9- 9-1829	
Ingles, Chester - Pamelia Wells	9- 6-1818	
Irvin, John - Abigail Allison	11-12-1829	
Irwin, John - Sophia Bear	6- 4-1826	
Jackman, Henry - Elizabeth Colyet	8-28-1824	
Jackman, James C. - Ealy Matthews	1-28-1831	
Jackson, Aquilla - Mary Ann Logan	7-12-1827	
Jackson, George - Elizabeth Lott	12- 9-1824	
Jackson, Gideon - Rachel Custer	6-10-1819	
Jackson, Henry - Keziah Gordon	9- 8-1825	
Jackson, Hiram - Polly Ann Tool	9-16-1830	
Jackson, James - Polly Arbuckle	4- 3-1817	
Jackson, James - Martha Brown	2- 5-1829	
Jackson, Reuben - Sarah Ann Deger	2-10-1831	
Jackson, Samuel - Esther Clore	6- 6-1819	
Jackson, Samuel - Jane Hillis	4-22-1824	
Jackson, Willis - Polly McCormick	5-27-1831	
James, John - Polly Carrol	6- 7-1820	
James, Robert - Rebecca C. Spann	4-29-1830	
James, Thomas - Elizabeth Johns	4-14-1825	
Jameson, Robert - Polly Welch	4-20-1820	
Jameson, Samuel - Martha Wildman	6-10-1831	
Jennings, Aaron - Sarah Jennings	1- 8-1812	
Jennings, Sherod - Frevilla Reed	6-28-1821	
Jewell, John - Sarah Davidson	12-21-1819	
Johns, Jacob - Sarah Sconce	2-27-1822	
Johns, John - Polly Wilson	1-1-1823 (1824?)	
Johnson, Jack - Judah Provine	10-24-1812	
Johnson, Samuel - Susannah Cook	1- 3-1828	
Johnson, William - Polly Day	2-22-1821	
Johnston, Bartemus - Malinda Guthrie	2- 4-1823	
Johnston, Elisha - Priscilla O'Laughlin	4-28-1822	
Johnston, Isaac - Mary McKinley	3-18-1829	
Johnston, Samuel - Mary Ryker	3- ?-1830	
Johnston, William - Ann Snyder	10-28-1831	
Jones, Daniel L. - Sarah Suddath	6-10-1831	
Jones, David - Susanna Cline	5-18-1822	
Jones, Eli P. - Ann VanCleave	8-11-1831	
Jones, Isaac - Mary Mungs	12-11-1828	
Jonston, Harvey - Mary Young	5-27-1823	
Keeler, Heman - Lydia Green	12-20-1819	
Kelso, Charles H. - Sary Ann Adams	5- 9-1827	
Kenady, Alexander - Polly McNew	9- 2-1824	
Kenady, David - Ascy Read	5-15-1823	
Kendall, William - Matilda Cline	12-18-1827	
Kenedy, James C. - Nancy McNew	10- 6-1831	
Kennedy, Peter B. - Nancy M. Hillis	3-25-1830	
Kennedy, William - Elizabeth Glover	10-11-1827	
Kenney, Henry - Charlotte Ward	4-14-1825	
Kerns (or Hems), John - Edney Smith	10-21-1830	
Kersey, Meredith P. - Polly J. Pullian	1-24-1828	
Kertz(?), George - Susannah Free	11-22-1830	
King, George - Mary Guthrie	12-23-1819	
King, Jeremiah N. - Phebe Rector	7-27-1820	
King, John R. - Mary Witt	10-22-1829	

King, Robert - Nancy Hensley	2- 7-1823	Long, John - Lavinda Long	6- 9-1825
Kirkendall, Samuel - Louca Smith	11-11-1824	Long, John - Lovia McDonald	11-29-1825
Kirkham, Michael - Charity Whitson	12-29-1829	Long, John - Sarah McCartney	2- 9-1827
Kirtley, Abraham - Lidea Underwood	6-27-1816	Long, Lewis - Mary Hall	1- 7-1830
Kistler, Edmond - Minta Jones	12-23-1825	Loring, Richard - Cinthia Rector	9-16-1823
Knight, Andrew - Elizabeth Patton	9-26-1830	Lorridge, John - Mary Faboun	6-26-1816
Knight, Washington - Nancy Thomas	12- 8-1830	Lott, Elijah - Rebecca Berry	11-15-1821
Knowlton, Joshua - Eliza Holmes	3-13-1821	Lott, Jesse - Eleanor Kelly	12-30-1819
Knox (or Nocks), Samuel - Nancy Harvey	4- 5-1824	Lott, John - Phebe Lott	10-15-1818
Kyle, William - Sarah Hardwick	12-20-1828	Loudon, Thomas - Myrana Dixon	11- 5-1829
		Ludley, James - Lucy Cooper	3- 4-1824
Lador, Jesse - Ann Lewis	4-20-1831	Lund (Lunn?), John - Ann Conner	4-15-1830
Lafayette, Marcus D. - Eliza Gant	9-25-1824	Lunn, John - Elizabeth Laton	1-13-1825
Lamar, John - Caty Smith	9- 3-1817		
Lame, Abel - Frances Cox	2-16-1826	McAllister, Daniel - Hester Francis	4-25-1822
Lame, Caleb - Sarah Hill	1-27-1820	McCall, Thomas - Sally Pennick	2-15-1831
Lame, John - Cynthia Denny	5-25-1830	McCament, Thomas - Jane Fleming	2- 2-1813
Lame, Joseph - Polly Cope	1-29-1824	McCan, William - Jannet Park	5- 2-1822
Lame, Newton - Martha A. Woodford (?)	7-15-1831	McCartney, James - Mary Ann McCartney	4- 8-1830
Lanciscus, Jacob - America King	9-10-1829	McCartney, William - Providence Thompson	2-11-1827
Landrum, John - Polly McKinney	11- 7-1827	McCarty, Daniel - Polly Lott	9- 8-1825
Landrum, Thomas - Priscilla Bulden	7- 3-1830	McCarty, James - Mary Benefield	9-28-1815
Lanham, John - Lucy McCoy	1- 4-1825	McCarty, Nicholas - Nancy Smith	5-18-1815
Lanham, Warren - Rhoda Yates	4- 7-1831	McCasland, James H. - Jane Hood	4- 4-1831
Lanier, James F. D. - Elizabeth Gardener	12- 7-1819	McCasland, Robert - Rhoda McKinney	2-10-1828
Lathrop, Augustus - Luca Hillis	1-16-1825	McCaslen, William D. - Mary G. Cochran	4-22-1824
Lathrop, Lyman - Susan Wilson	2-15-1821	McCaslin, Andrew - Polly McCartney	12-21-1826
Latty, William R. - Mary Miner	2-22-1821	McCaslin, David - Rachel Sargent	12-21-1828
Law, Jesse - Jane Staples	5-26-1825	McCaslin, Richard - Ann Hemphill	6-16-1824
Law, John - Julia Carroll	9-12-1827	McClelland, James - Sarah McKinley	10- 5-1815
Law, Willis - Susanna Baur	12- 2-1814	McClerhan, Robert - Lucy Davis	9- 5-1815
Lawler, John - Barbary Wise	9-12-1827	McColough, James - Margaret Maxwell	8-18-1812
Lawler, Osborne - Elizabeth Westbrook	2-28-1830	McCord, David L. - Elizabeth Ann Grover	1-13-1824
Lawrence, Ephraim - Sarah Redenbaugh	3-23-1831	McCoy, Abram - Mary B. Piles	10-30-1828
Laws, Samuel G. - Mariah Jane Hannah	2-26-1829	McCoy, Daniel - Rachel Philips	10-17-1826
Lawson, William - Sarah Short	9- 1-1823	McCoy, George - Frances Hering	7- 2-1820
Layton, Gabriel - Elizabeth Miner	10-10-1825	McCoy, John - Nancy Henning	12-13-1827
Layton, Hiram - Ann Minor	2- 3-1831	McCrory, John - Polly Wilson	4- 3-1817
Layton, Washington - Polly Halley	8-25-1831	McCrory, Samuel L. - Mary Baily	12- 6-1827
Ledgerwood, William - Lucy Akins	2-18-1823	McCroskey, Alexander - Roxana M. Cady	7-20-1817
Lee, John - Susanna Best	1- 2-1820	McCullough, William D. - Margaret A. Henderson	
Lee, Lewis - Julia Ann Eddleman	11-25-1828		1-27-1820
Lee, Stephen - Hester Dickerson	10-11-1821	McCune, Joseph - Mariah Redenbaugh	2-24-1824
Leferry, George - Hannah Hunt	3-25-1822	McDaniel, Roderick - Sally Moncrief	5-19-1816
Leonard, George W. - Sarah T. Baker	4-18-1821	McDoale, Jonathan - Eliza M. Wilson	9-25-1823
Leonard, Linus R. - Julia Ann Baker	8-10-1819	McFarland, Richard - Sarah Houseright	6-16-1824
Levit, Benjamin C. - Susan Nichols	1-19-1823	McFetridge, Michael - Mahala Smith	3-19-1827
Levit, Joseph - Chola Lewis	10-18-1823	McGaughey, Daniel - Frances Hiker	10-21-1824
Lewis, Alexander - Anna Vawter	6-22-1815	McGee, William - Margaret Ann Large	4-20-1824
Lewis, Chancy - Jannet Rogers	11-10-1825	McGill, James - Hannah Stevens	8-31-1819
Lewis, Cosby - Uzilla Mayberry	9- 9-1827	McGill, William - Mary Stevens	12-31-1829
Lewis, William - Nancy Wilson	3-28-1815	McGlore, Lawrence - Margaret Ann Campbell	8-2-1820
Lindley, Alvin - Nancy Welch	4-25-1822	McGreggor, Alexander - Martha Ann Rogers	8-7-1827
Lindley, Francis S. - Rhoda Barber	10-30-1828	McGuire, John - Elenor Lee	9-25-1821
Little, Joseph - Matilda Barnes	5-15-1827	McGuire, William - Sarah Edy	5-28-1831
Littlejohn, Ira - Mary Bradshaw	1-29-1829	McIlroy, John - Mary Hamilton	6- 7-1827
Littlejohn, Lemuel - Alice Rice (?)	5-22-1825	McIntire, Alexander - Sarah Eastin	10-11-1818
Lloyd, Zepheniah (?) - Ann Larimore	10- 3-1824	McIntire, Edward - Rachel D. Brit	12-15-1824
Lockard, James - Rebecca Garrett	12- 8-1825	McKay, Enoch - Charlotte Barnes	11- 5-1829
Lockard, John - Delila Millis	2-21-1823	McKay, George - Elizabeth Francis	7-20-1830
Lockard, Joseph - Nancy Bear	7-15-1830	McKay, John - Mary Francis	6- 4-1828
Lockard, William - Sally Day	9-13-1829	McKay, Moses - Celia Jones	12-17-1818
Lodge, John - Susannah Arion	8- 7-1817	McKinley, James - Elizabeth Stucker	12-25-1815
Lodge, Nelson - Rebecca K. Lemon	6-27-1826	McKinley, William - Katherine Smock	7-28-1828
Lodge, William - Mary Lemon	12-23-1824	McKinney, Henry - Polly Landrean	4-21-1827
Logan, James - Mary Alexander	12-27-1829	McKinney, James - Lyda Landrum	11- 8-1827

McKinney, John - Patsy Walton	6-10-1825
McKinsey, Alexander - Lydia Glover	8- 1-1820
McKinstry, William - Elizabeth Rothbum	4-14-1825
McLane, John - Margaret Matthews	4-20-1821
McLean, Matthew - Emilia Ann Swincher	7-23-1829
McMillan, Andrew - Hannah Ramsey	1-11-1827
McMillen, John - Mary Shannon	4-26-1815
McNealy, John - Margaret Ware	8-24-1819
Madden, William - Louisa Bench	11-20-1824
Man, James - Sary Magness	9-27-1825
Manford, James - Sally Rutherford	3-29-1827
Manford, Jeremiah - Mary Gordon	12- 8-1828
Maning, Edward - Elizabeth Pearson (?)	12-14-1820
Manville, Butler - Elizabeth Washer	6-29-1823
Margason, James - Martha Bowen	3-18-1830
Margason, John - Mary Ann Evins	2-17-1829
Marguson, Joseph - Lucretia Tatum	5-28-1829
Marquis, David - Charlotte Ward	11-19-1827
Marquis, Ebenezer - Jane Underwood	10-16-1817
Marquis, George - Sarah Woodfill	12- 8-1816
Marquis, John - Rebecca Hillis	10-16-1817
Marsell (Marshall), Joshua - Mary Dunbar	3-15-1827
Marshall, Edward - Catherine Custer	1-18-1827
Marshall, John - Elizabeth Edwards	4- 6-1815
Marshall, Robert - Polly Blankenship	5- 1-1823
Marshall, Thomas - Sarah Kinnear	1- 8-1824
Martin, Caius M. - Eastin Ann Cutler	12- 1-1829
Martin, John - Matilda Allen	7-23-1826
Martin, Nelson - Mary Cooke	7-22-1830
Masters, James - Polly Gaddis	6- 5-1828
Matthews, John - Elizabeth Lee	5- 5-1831
Matthews, William - Mary Henry	5-28-1829
Maxwell, James L. - Martha G. Reed	8-19-1821
Maxwell, John - Elenor Marquis	11-22-1819
Maxwell, Samuel - Rebecca Marquis	8-24-1820
Maxwell, Samuel - Sally Stevens	9-16-1824
Maxwell, William - Rachel Stephens	10- 8-1812
May, Charles A. - Mary Ann Crump	4-15-1830
Means, James - Ann Hutchinson	11-11-1830
Means, Joseph - Sarah Brooks	8-16-1827
Means, William - Fanny Murmood	1-13-1831
Meek, Norval - Elizabeth N. Wallace	6- 6-1830
Melton, John - Elizabeth Denny	9-30-1824
Melton, Ward M. - Mary Denny	8-20-1829
Mezingo, William - Margaret Poland	2-10-1825
Midcalf, Uri - Polly Hutcherson	3-26-1826
Miles, Isaac - Elizabeth Miles	4-15-1828
Miles, James - Scynthia Whadon	11- 3-1831
Miles, John - Polly Kinder	7-11-1822
Miller, Abraham - Matilda Ellison	12-25-1826
Miller, James - Sarah Woods	4- 4-1826
Miller, John - Polly Whiteside	7- 1-1824
Miller, Jonathan - Rebecca Shannon	9- 6-1824
Miller, Samuel - Elizabeth Ash	2-11-1819
Millett, Alva - Lorilla Brown	11-22-1827
Millhouse, Henry - Betsy Whitesides	4- 8-1830
Mills, Elisha - Mary Hankins	8- 2-1812
Milton, Alen - Mary Smith	2-17-1825
Miner, James - Mary McLin	5-16-1825
Miner, Thomas - Barbary Lotts	10-10-1825
Miner, Thomas - Euphemia Woodfill	10- 2-1828
Minton, William - Charlotte Johnston	3-18-1819
Mitchell, Daniel K. - Polly Copeland	7-20-1823
Mitchell, William - Mary Frazier	3-27-1822

Mobly, Elias - Rachel Hill	9-19-1824
Moncrief, Abner - Ann Vawter	1-27-1820
Moncrief, Gideon - Hannah Williams	6-20-1822
Monfort, Henry - Susannah Samples	10-25-1828
Monroe, Bryan - Elizabeth McKinney	11-10-1830
Monroe, Campbell R. - Lucretia M. Woodward	4-26-1827
Monroe, George - Nancy Chambers	12- 4-1828
Monroe, James - Mary Wood	4- 6-1826
Monroe, Solomon D. - Mary Chambers	11-22-1823
Monroe, William - Jane Tilford	12-28-1825
Monroe, William - Martha Perkinson	6-11-1826
Montjan, Samuel - Sarah Hawkins	12-12-1821
Mooney, Isaac - Matilda Jackman	5-29-1827
Moore, George - Sarah Valely	12-27-1824
Moore, James G. - Sarah Ann McIntire	4-20-1831
Moore, John H. - Abigail Gray	1- 5-1824
Moore, Samuel - Mary S. Smock	3-17-1831
More, William - Amy Brumbarger	9- 9-1829
Morgan, Henry - Nancy Baxter	11- 9-1820
Morgan, Robert - Jane Jackson	8-20-1820
Morris, James - Matilda Jones	8-24-1826
Morrow, James - Margaret Fulton	1- 2-1823
Mosely, Peter - Nancy Hendricks	10-24-1812
Mounts, James - Mary Mounts	10-21-1823
Mounts, Providence - Elizabeth Griffin	2-11-1831
Mounts, Thomas - Malvin McDaniel	10-21-1823
Munson, Alanson - Rosanna Sage	1-20-1820
Murdock, Harvey - Nancy Melton	6-14-1827
Murdock, Eli - Jane Rolin	6-23-1825
Murphey, Peter - Rachel Ryker	6-20-1819
Neal, Daniel - Elizabeth Brooks	7-25-1816
Neal, Jesse - Nancy Brooks	8-20-1816
Neal, John - Margaret Hall	5- 9-1816
Neal, John - Nancy Elizabeth Howard	5-23-1822
Neal, John - Nancy Jackson	12-24-1822
Nelson, Hyram - Elizabeth Hutchinson	12- 8-1827
Neville, James - Elizabeth Martin	11-19-1829
Neville, Thomas - Eleanor Jones	5- 8-1831
New, Hickman - Lamira (?) Ann Fridly (?)	1- 2-1825
Nichols, Isaac - Katherine McAllister	12- 2-1830
Nichols, Jacob - Margaret Trousdail	1- 6-1831
Nicholson, Jesse C. - Ann Fallott	9-19-1824
Nicholson, William - Jemima Hill	6- 8-1824
Norris, Samuel - Ann Wheatly	12-30-1819
Norton, William - Sarah Harland	9-30-1819
Noulton, Jesse S. - Kitty M. Deputy	3-31-1825
Obousier, Lewis G. - Marianne Golay	1- 1-1812
Ogdon, John - Sarah Atkinson	12-12-1814
O'Laughtey, William - Hannah Bolin	3-18-1824
O'Laughlin, John - Decy Johnson	6-22-1817
Oliver, James - Jane Doney	9-24-1826
O'Neal, James - Maria Ogan	1-13-1820
Orrill, William - Lucinda Humphrey	9- 8-1831
Overton, Jason - Nancy Hudall	7-12-1831
Owen, Thomas - Elizabeth Lewis	8-30-1813
Pain, William - Jane Trow	12- 9-1824
Pancake, Isaiah - --Patton	4- 3-1823
Parkinson, Elisha - Polly Monroe	10-11-1821
Patterson (?), James - Lucy Ann Bowley	8-14-1821
Patterson, James - Ann Tuttle	6-28-1826
Patterson, John - Mary Blood	10-13-1818
Patton, Hezekiah E. - Ann Wilson	9-11-1817

Patton, James C. - Polly Hubbard	6- 5-1824
Paul, John Peter - Eliza Meek	2-17-1831
Payne, John - Polly Taff	12-27-1821
Payne, William H. - Sally Montgomery	9-20-1829
Pearson, Moses B. - Amanda Poor	9-21-1819
Peas (or Poe), Warren - Norma Sutton	10- 5-1822
Pender, Daniel - Margaret Varvel	7-23-1829
Penn, John W. - Hulda Christie	2-24-1831
Perry, William - Hester Cobb	8-25-1825
Petty, Francis - Delila Badgly	6-25-1827
Philips, John - Sally Wells	6-24-1824
Phillips, Amos - Patsy, a woman of color	6- 8-1823
Phillips, Amos - Sidney Hodges	11-23-1831
Phillips, Henry - Elizabeth Snyder	12- 9-1830
Phillips, Presley - Sarah Hall	8-25-1820
Pixley, John C. - Malinda Gray	3-25-1825
Platt, Richard E. - Susannah Brown	8-28-1828
Plunket, Jesse L. - Elizabeth Scantlin	2-17-1831
Plunkett, Jonathan - Letty Banta	1-13-1830
Pogue, William - Elenor P. Henderson	11-30-1825
Polk, Isaac - Lucky West	9-22-1814
Poston, Levi - Reny Matthews	2- 8-1827
Pouge, George - Mary Brent	11- 6-1829
Pouge, John - Grezul Park	8-19-1824
Powell, William - Nancy Mansfield	5-13-1826
Pringle, William - Margaret Mikle	7- 8-1814
Prothero, Evan - Margaret Caplinger	7- 4-1822
Prothero, William - Phebe Watts	8-18-1818
Pryor, Cloyer - Sarah Mudix (?)	1-11-1827
Pryor, John - Mary Cole	10-15-1815
Pullen, Robert - Elizabeth Skeene	2- ?-1819
Purse(?), Vincent - Catherine Magness	1-18-1827
Pursell, Enoch - Abigail Lane	9-22-1825
Ramsey, John P. - Mary F. Childs	11- 8-1831
Randall, John - Frances Glover	12-23-1819
Rankin, James - Eliza Fisher	1-13-1825
Rankin, Joseph - Lettitia Smith	6- 3-1824
Rankins, Reuben - Malvina Smith	12-20-1829
Rapp, Jonathan - Polly Field	3- 3-1825
Rayborn, Enoch - Mary Caplinger	5-30-1827
Rea, David - Patsy Rea	7-24-1827
Rea, Matthew F. - Rachel Hughey	9- 2-1819
Rea, Wright - Mary Armstrong	10-20-1829
Rector, Daniel - Ruth Delap	6-17-1819
Rector, Hezekiah P. - Mary Hughes	8-12-1816
Rector, John - Sally King	12- 9-1819
Rector, Nathaniel - Agnes Grimes	2-14-1828
Reddenbough, George - Margaret Stucker	5-25-1820
Redenbough, Philip - Fanny Arbuckle	3-31-1824
Redinbaugh, Henry - Mary Douglas	10-15-1823
Redman, Washington - Jane Baker	2-23-1817
Reece, Benjamin - Sarah Davis	9-21-1815
Reed, Abraham G.- Nancy Kyle	1-20-1820
Reed, George - Jane Shannon	12-15-1825
Reed, Joshua W. - Mary Fleming	12- 8-1819
Reed, Levin - Hannah Rarden	1-25-1827
Reed, Thomas - Rachel Banta	6-29-1820
Reed, William - Polly Payne	2- 8-1827
Reese, John - Elizabeth Simenton	10-10-1827
Reese, William - Polly McNew	3-12-1823
Rice, Stephen - Rhoda Condra	12-20-1821
Richman, Elijah - Nelly Douthett	7- 2-1818
Righthouse, John - Catherine Turner	11-10-1827
Ripley, Joseph - Laura Ann Sutton	7-22-1830
Ritchie, James - Nancy Moncrief	12- 4-1816

Ritchie, John - Sophie Branham	12-31-1829
Ritchie, Silas - Sarah Ann Taylor	5-25-1824
Roberts, Redin - Elizabeth Short	6- 5-1825
Roberts, Silvester - Libby Robins	4-15-1818
Roberts, William - Rebecca Roberts	10-23-1817
Robertson, Matthew - Sarah James	3- 7-1820
Robins, William - Bether(?) Furguson	5-28-1818
Robinson, Darius - Eleanor Wilson	5-21-1827
Robinson, George M. - Abigail Brooks	1-26-1831
Robinson, Hardy - Catharine Stucker	3-11-1823
Robinson, Russel - Mahala Trumbo	7-20-1820
Robinson, Simeon M. - Sarah Bull	10-27-1831
Robinson, William - Maria Gudgel	6-21-1827
Rodgers, John - Jemima Green	5-13-1818
Rogers, John - Eliza Culbertson	4-17-1827
Rollinson, Nathaniel - Jane Chambers	9-25-1818
Romine, Jacob B. - Susana Dyer	9-16-1829
Romine, Jacob B. - Betsy Johnston	12-24-1830
Roseberry, George - Peggy Anderson	3-23-1820
Ross, James - Sarah G. Reed	2-23-1817
Rowen, Ross- Eliza Trousdale	5-17-1827
Rowland, Isaac - Polly Wilson	11-18-1830
Runion, Isaac L. - Polly Ingram	3- 9-1820
Runyon, Kelso - Ann McClain	1- 4-1829
Rupert, John Jr. - Sally Roe	11-14-1821
Rutherford, Shelton - Sally Helms	1-10-1820
Rutledge, James - Rebecca Marguson	7-25-1829
Ryans, William - Rebecca Lee	8-24-1821
Ryker, Abraham - May Smith	9- 2-1824
Ryker, Gerardus - Jane Eaten	3-29-1825
Ryker, Jacob - Mary Bergen	6- 7-1821
Ryker, John - Nancy Ledgerwood	3- 2-1816
Ryker, John G. - Sarah Jones	3- 6-1814
Ryker, John J. - Polly McCleland	8-11-1824
Ryker, John S. - Polly McClelland	8-11-1825
Ryker, Peter - Sarah Lewis	1- 3-1826
Ryker, Peter W. - Nancy Conaway	10-26-1820
Ryker, Samuel - Margaret Holton	5- 4-1830
Ryker, Samuel S. - Eleanor Berger	9- 3-1818
Sage, Caleb - Hannah Jones	4-15-1827
Sage, James - Catherine McCartney	11-12-1822
Sage, John - Margaret McCartney	11- 4-1819
Sage, William - Sarah Lawler	12-25-1825
Sample, Robert - Susanna Lewis	9-28-1819
Sanders, John T. - Ann Elizabeth White	9- 9-1829
Sawyer, Levi - Mary Smith	7-20-1826
Sawyer, Moses - Lucy West	12-15-1822
Sawyer, Stephen - Catherine Rutledge	12-28-1820
Scaggs, Zachariah - Nancy Devons	1-27-1816
Scantling, Walter - Eveline Gentry	4- 4-1824
Scaum (Seamon?), — - — Haughrice	7-21-1824
Scott, James - Polly Marquis	12-31-1812
Scott, John - Rebecca Welch	9-30-1824
Scott, John H. - Melinda Austin	8-23-1827
Scott, John H. - Ann Minerva Higgenbottom	8- 9-1831
Scritchfield, John - Patsy Jackson	12- 9-1829
Seburn, John - Deborah Smock	9- 7-1830
Sering, John - Ruth Grover	11-26-1812
Sering, Mitchell D. - Elizabeth Radikin	6-23-1831
Settle, Henry - Elizabeth Thompson	8-27-1822
Shafer, John - Sarah Cook	7- 4-1819
Shannon, George - Elizabeth Gordon	4- 1-1831
Shannon, Thomas - Elizabeth Spears	4- 4-1822
Sharp, Ross - Margery McKay	8- ?-1822

Shed, Coburn - Pheby Shed	8-22-1822	Stone, Jacob - Mary Madden	10-12-1826
Sheets, Jonah S. - Ann Brooks	7-22-1830	Storm, John - Rachel Robins	5-10-1812
Shelton, George P. - Charlotte Heath	8-23-1826	Story, Thomas - Mary Ross	6-12-1818
Shelton, Peter - Anna Eblin	12- 6-1827	Story, Thomas J. - Elizabeth Spann	12-24-1822
Shepherd, Jesse - Rebecca Eblin	12-25-1827	Stribling, Willis C. - Achsa Stott	6- 9-1816
Shepherd, William - Jane McClelland(?)	1- 8-1818	Stuart, George - Ann Wilson	4-12-1825
Sherman, Alpheus - Almyra Lochard	11- 1-1828	Stucker, Andrew - Elizabeth Fix	2- 4-1823
Shildeday, Ephraim - Eliza D. Diven (?)	8-18-1829	Stucker, George - Sophia Davis	2-14-1828
Shirk, John - Nancy Stillwell	3-19-1823	Stucker, Henry - Betsy Mellinger	11- 8-1827
Short, Elisha - Mary Ward	2- 6-1819	Stucker, Jacob - Elizabeth Housewright	10-25-1817
Short, George - Mary McFarland	5- 3-1818	Stucker, Jeptha - Elizabeth Bowman	2-10-1829
Short, Isaac - Nancy Buckhanan	1- 7-1816	Stucker, John - Susannah Stucker	1-14-1819
Short, William - Francis Rogers	8-28-1825	Stucker, John - Margarite Snodgrass	11- 2-1821
Simpkins, Samuel C. - Lavinia Tannehill	6-19-1828	Stucker, Reason - Melissa Kinnear	5-13-1830
Skeene, Jonathan - Malinda Matthews	11-15-1821	Stucker, Samuel - Betsy Reddenbough	5- 6-1816
Slater, Philip - Nancy Law	6- 2-1819	Stucker, Stephen - Louisa Rhody (or Rhods)	3- 6-1828
Smith, Alexander - Emily Boyd	5-13-1830	Stull, Henry - Rebecca V. Hughes	3- 9-1819
Smith, Barney B. - Casandra Hopper	8- 6-1818	Sullender, Jacob - Jensy Needham	10-27-1831
Smith, Benjamin - Inda West	4-23-1822	Sullivan, Harrison - Maria Hall	10- 7-1830
Smith, James - Clausia Coldwater	10- 1-1824	Sullivan, James - Luezy Sullivan	3-10-1823
Smith, James H. - Susana Cogwell	7-15-1824	Sullivan, Jeremiah - Charlotte Cutler	7-23-1818
Smith, James S. - Elizabeth Davis	4-18-1822	Sullivan, John H. - Balinda Armstrong	10- 7-1830
Smith, John - Margaret Stevens	5-28-1812	Sullivan, William C. - Ann Barber	12-21-1819
Smith, John - Milly Humphreys	6-12-1814	Suttle, Henry - Elizabeth Good	5- 1-1828
Smith, John - Martha Mount	3-11-1824	Suttle, John - Martha K. Hudson	4-25-1828
Smith, John - Ann Holton	12-13-1827	Suttle, William B. - Martha Cosby	12- 4-1823
Smith, Joseph - Nancy Macklin	12-16-1830	Swann, Thomas - Jane Holden	3-20-1824
Smith, Nicholas - Hannah Foster	7-16-1818	Swincher, James - Polly Boys	6-20-1823
Smith, Samuel - Nancy Gardener	3-10-1824	Swincher, William - Rachel Kirke	1-31-1827
Smith, Samuel - Margaret Wils	9-29-1825		
Smith, Stephen - Cynthia Hall	2- 2-1812	Talbott, Daniel - Lucy M. Smith	9-15-1825
Smith, Strother - Elizabeth Toole	3-15-1818	Tatem, John - Drusilla Davidson	1-21-1830
Smith, William - Catherine Cogwell	4-21-1825	Tatum, Joseph - Polly Ann Smith	8-18-1831
Smith, William - Agnes Brody	12-11-1827	Tatum, William - Nancy Gow	8-26-1824
Smock, Jacob - Sally Aimes	3-15-1822	Taylor, Frederick - Isabella Milligan	4-28-1831
Smock, John - Elizabeth Tilford	1-22-1821	Taylor, James - Eveline Stratton	10-12-1831
Snediger, James - Polly Grimes	6- 8-1826	Taylor, James A. - Rebecca S. Driggs	3-16-1830
Snodgrass, James - Ann Jones	1-15-1829	Taylor, John - Elizabeth Taylor	11-16-1820
Snodgrass, Samuel - Semiramis Hardy	12- 7-1824	Taylor, John - Delila Hogarth	12-31-1828
Snodgrass, William D. - Hannah Byres	4-27-1820	Taylor, Larkin B. - Catherine Newman	7-28-1828
Snow, Ambrose - Nancy Madden	7-26-1821	Taylor, Robert - Ann Spear	3- 8-1827
Snyder, John - Salome Phillips	4- 7-1831	Taylor, William - Mary Jane Wallace	1-23-1827
Snyder, William - Jane Walker	7- 5-1827	Teague, Willet - Malinda Humphrey	5- 6-1830
Spaffin, Orlean - Jane Patton	4- 3-1822	Terrell, Enoch - Rebecca Roseberry	1-18-1829
Spann, Moses - Jane Furgusson	10-12-1820	Terrill, Andrew - Susana Thixton	8-14-1825
Spann, Moses - Matilda Smith	8-20-1822	Terrill, Edmon - Mary Monroe	12-13-1829
Spencer, Charles R. - Eleanor Minor	3- 4-1827	Thomas, Clinton - Sally Abbot	7-15-1822
Spurgin, William - Velinda Nicholson	1-27-1830	Thomas, Daniel - Jane Comly	3-11-1827
Stafford, Gib - Leah Woodford	10-25-1830	Thomas, Evan - Polly Hankins	7-18-1811
Stafford, Peter - Mildred Jackson	12-27-1827	Thomas, James - Jamima Cambers	12- 3-1814
Stafford, Stepney - Polly Wilson	12-15-1816	Thomas, James - Serene Kelly	12- 7-1821
Stafford, Thomas - Mariah Jones	9-20-1831	Thomas, Joseph - Elizabeth Cope	6-26-1825
Stapp, John - Ann Crawford	12- 6-1821	Thomas, William F. - Sarah A. Hurst	10-21-1822
Stapp, Silas - Jane Shannon	12-21-1824	Thompson, Elisha - Hannah Watson	5-30-1816
Starks, Amos - Sarah Dodge	6-24-1827	Thompson, George S. - Jane McKay	12- 7-1820
Steele, James - Jane Wilson	5-11-1826	Thompson, Richard - Lucinda R. Richardson	
Steele, Joseph - Polly Wilson	4- 1-1824		12-26-1827
Stephens, Amos - Jemima Wilson	5-18-1827	Thorn, Alexander C. - Elizabeth Taylor	1- 7-1824
Stevens, James - Polly Watts	4-20-1817	Tilford, William - Sally Monroe	12-12-1822
Stevens, Thomas - Elizabeth Matthews	5- 4-1828	Todd, Matthew - Lotte Taylor	12-24-1829
Stevens, Thomas J. - Betsey Hall	7-10-1827	Toler, Christopher - Mary Jewell	8- 3-1830
Stevenson, Benjamin C. - Sarah G. Goode	9-15-1831	Tool, Silas - Sarah Wilson	5-15-1828
Stewart, David - Catherine Troutman	12-24-1818	Tool, Silas - Delitha Wilson	11-18-1829
Stewart, Isaiah - Polly McCarty	3-24-1821	Totten, Archibald - Peggy Miller	12- 9-1819
Stewart, John - Anna(?) Penn	7-29-1825	Trousdail, Thomas - Margaret Patton	7-22-1831
Stiver, John - Betsy Mitchell	4-15-1824	Troutman, John S. - Margaret Troutman	2-22-1831

49

Troutman, Peter - Margaret Logan	3-29-1827
Troutman, William - Elizabeth Howell	11-10-1829
Truett(?), William - Permelia May	2-26-1830
Tull, James B. - Ann Monroe	8-28-1828
Tull, Joseph - Patience Blankenship	3-30-1826
Tull, Samuel - Lucretia Blankenship	8-11-1831
Tull, William - Eleanor Tull	2-13-1822
Turmount, John - Mary L. Trousdail	5-11-1831
Turner, Moses - Severy Howard	3-19-1822
Underwood, Benjamin - Lucy Tate	9-16-1824
Underwood, George - Sabina Reed	11- 9-1820
Underwood, Jacob - Fanny Davis	10-21-1819
Underwood, Nathan - Dorcas Johnston	7- 2-1826
Underwood, Zachariah - Lolly Jones	4-10-1823
Vail, Jacob Jennings - Mary Branham	9-30-1821
Van Cleave, Peter - Elizabeth Woodfield	7-25-1816
Vanorman, Hysam - Elizabeth Walden	12-27-1824
Vanosdol, Abraham - Mary Taylor	10-28-1830
Vanosdol, Simon - Betsy Kinder	7- ?-1828
Varvil, Abraham - Peggy Righthouse	3-28-1816
Vawter, Achilles - Martha Smith	8-16-1814
Vawter, Beverly - Betsy Crawford	3- 5-1812
Vawter, David - Lucinda Glover	4-27-1823
Viles, Joseph - Betsy Ellis	4- 3-1820
Waggoner, Jacob J. - Rebecca Van Cleave	5-18-1829
Waggoner, Lewis - Sally Underwood	5- 5-1813
Walker, Alfred - Malinda Philips	12-27-1819
Walker, Lewallen F. - Martha Ann Suttle	12- 4-1823
Walker, Luallen F. - Lucy Comstock	7-27-1818
Walker, William - Nancy McCaslin	11-22-1823
Wallace, William B. - Rebecca Miller	4-13-1829
Wallis, Samuel - Elizabeth Hay	4- 8-1824
Walton, Abraham - Nancy Hays	12-23-1828
Walton, Comfort - Nancy E. Sprague	2-17-1821
Walton, Euphratus - Mary Ann Hoagland	1- 1-1824
Walton, John - Susannah Roseberry	2-13-1820
Warrell, Joshua - Mary Dunbar	3-22-1827
Washburn, William A. - Mary S. Deming	3-20-1830
Washer, Alexander - Clarissa Barber	9-11-1821
Washer, Stephen - Polly Buckhanan	7- 9-1818
Waters, George - Hester Rush	12- 4-1827
Watson, Ebenezer - Ann McCrory	12-20-1821
Watson, Robert - Nancy McKinley	6-22-1828
Watson, Robert - Eleanor Portor	4-27-1829
Watson, Samuel - Mary Cunningham	12-10-1825
Watson, William M. - Sally Talbott	6-14-1831
Watts, John - Rutha Cox	9-22-1824
Way, Ira - Elizabeth Sutton	8-31-1819
Wear, Samuel - Polly Roberson	9-27-1828
Weatherford, Hardin - Rebecca Smith	8- ?-1831
Weaver, Michael - Polly Scott	11-24-1823
Webb, Henry - Julia Ann Branham	3-21-1830
Webb, John - Susan Buchanan	5-10-1831
Webb, Mordicai - Jane Humphries	9-25-1827
Weir, William - Hanah Cully	7- 6-1823
Wellington(?), John P. - Isabel Lott	8-30-1821
Wells, Samuel - Elizabeth Baker	4-26-1822
Wells, Samuel - Polly Wilton	9-16-1824
Wells, Squire - Joanna Mikesell	8-18-1829
West, Isaac - Sarah Rodger	5-28-1819
West, Isaac - Hannah Miles	6-24-1819
West, James - Elizabeth West	4-15-1829

West, John - Martha Benefield	1-12-1816
West, John - Patsy Howard	8-24-1819
West, John T. - Ursula Degonet	1-25-1831
West, John - Mary Lewis	2-16-1823
West, Reuben - Frances Davis	2-13-1823
West, Thomas - Ann Glover	11-31-1831
West, William - Narcissa Jackson	5- 6-1824
West, William N. - Eliza Wichita(?)	10-18-1828
Whare, Samuel H. - Abigail Ambrose	8-15-1819
Wharton, William G. - Elizabeth Blackmore	2-19-1829
Wheadon(?), William - Frances B. Ennington	8-11-1831
Wheatly, George - Mary Mills	3-13-1821
Whitaker, Nathaniel - Matilda Whitaker	10- 1-1829
White, Alexander - Margaret McCaslin	10-25-1829
White, John - Nancy Stamper	8- 1-1825
Whiteside, Newton - Priscilla Denica	10-13-1827
Whitesides, John - Polly Blankenship	5-30-1816
Whitham, James - Martha Bolin	1-17-1827
Whitham, John - Elizabeth McIntosh	1- 9-1817
Whitlow, Matthew H. - Cynthia Nicholson	5- 6-1830
Whitsitt, William - Lucinda Whitsitt	5-25-1828
Wier, William M. - Cassandra Robertson	5-19-1831
Wiere, John - Polly Crim	2-21-1828
Wildman, James - Nancy Edwards	1-24-1825
Wildman, James - Almyra Barber	12-11-1828
Wildman, John - Elizabeth Underwood	12-28-1815
Wiles, David - Catherine Bear	9-20-1827
Wiley, Cyrus - Rosannah Baker	2- 9-1812
Wiley, Washington - Jane Tull	1-18-1827
Wilhite, George H. - Louisa Coffman	4-21-1825
Wilhite, President - Sarah Plunket	2-22-1831
Wilkins, Stovall - Anna Vernon	12-31-1829
Wilkinson, John W. (or D.) - Mary Barns	3- 2-1831
Wilkinson, Joshua - Elizabeth Culbertson	4-29-1829
Willey, Dennis - Margaret Gasaway	7-13-1826
Williams, Allen - Margaret Stiver	4-26-1827
Williams, Bluford - Mary Mitchell	9-13-1831
Williams, Fielding - Eleanor Jones	5- 6-1830
Williams, John - Ann Pritchard	12-27-1826
Williams, John - Elizabeth Giltner	2- 7-1823
Williams, John - Nancy Scaggs	9-29-1830
Williams, Matthew - Sally Starlen(?)	6-16-1814
Williams, Richard - Nancy Underwood	8-20-1816
Williams, Robert - Sarah McDonald	8-20-1818
Willis, Abiah M. - Eliza Thomas	10-18-1823
Wilson, Abraham - Catherine Bell	3-23-1830
Wilson, Alexander - Frances Stewart	10-20-1814
Wilson, Alexander - Nancy Wilson	3- 4-1823
Wilson, Andrew - Jane Sage	10-19-1820
Wilson, Isaiah - Susannah Hollinsworth	9- 6-1827
Wilson, James - Patsy Dunn	1- 7-1830
Wilson, Jesse M. - Polly Cortney	4-24-1828
Wilson, John - Betsey Herod	1- 1-1812
Wilson, John - Jane Bramwell	1- 6-1812
Wilson, John - Mary Park	5- 2-1822
Wilson, John - Catherine Cane	5- 5-1825
Wilson, John - Elizabeth S. Spann	11-10-1830
Wilson, Joseph - Nancy Wilson	3- 5-1822
Wilson, Levi - Matilda Windson	8- 4-1825
Wilson, Nathaniel - Susannah G. Woodfill	3-30-1826
Wilson, Robert - Rebecca Rich	1-14-1819
Wilson, Samuel - Ruhamma Chinowith	11-22-1821
Wilson, William - Sarah Hamilton	5-25-1820
Wilson, William - Polly Showders	3- 7-1822
Wilson, William F. - Polly Boyd	9-10-1829
Winkler, Godfrey - Lear Huddleston	5-19-1823

Wise, James - Rachel Watts	12-25-1814	Woody, James - Mary L. Houston	6-18-1819
Wise, Thomas - Jane McDaniel	6- 1-1817	Wright, Thomas - Ann Rector	4-26-1825
Wood, Andrew - Nancy Monroe	3- 5-1829	Wyatt, George - Elizabeth Utt	11-18-1830
Woodard, Charles - Deborah Wood	1- 9-1821	Wyatt, Richard H. - Martha A. Dorsey	8-31-1826
Woodard, William - Priscilla Monroe	12-14-1820	Wyne, Bennett - Nancy Sullivan	10- 7-1831
Woodburn, Culver - Rhoda Hubbard	11-16-1831		
Woodfill, Andrew - Mary C. Ryker	3-17-1827	Yates, Isaac - Rebecca Glasgow	7- 4-1819
Woodfill, Daniel - Betsy Davis	5-13-1819	York, Amos - Catherine Vandever	12-29-1830
Woodfill, Daniel - Julian French	12- 4-1823	Yost, Charles - Sarah Ann Staton'	8-12-1830
Woodfill, Ephraim - Mahulda W——	5-20-1830	Yost, Jesse - Maria Holcomb	12-10-1829
Woodfill, Gabriel - Polly Wilson	8-10-1819	Yost, Thomas - Matilda Sheets	2- 1-1837
Woodfill, Gabriel - Elenor Pullem	1-20-1824	Young, Hezekiah - Sarah Coplen	6-13-1816
Woodfill, James M. - Mary Ryker	8- 2-1827	Young, Mitchell D. - Elizabeth Radikin (?)	6-23-1831
Woodfill, John S. - Jane Wilson	4-22-1830		
Woodfill, William - Hannah Stevens	1- 1-1824	Zenor, Edward - Sallie Miller	10-15-1829
Woods, Joseph - Mary Snodgrass	8-21-1828		
Woodward, Henry - Sabina Strickland	1-11-1829	(blank in MS), James - Ailsa Chitwood	6- 1-1817

CORRECTION IN JEFFERSON COUNTY MARRIAGES. In the marriages, 1811-1831, printed in the October-December, 1973, *Hoosier Genealogist*, the name Gerardus RYKER should be Gerardus RYKER R. MEDDISC; he married Jane Eatin 29 March 1825. Thank you Mrs. Marion Ryker Chiarello for the correction.

NICHOLSON FAMILY BIBLE AND OTHER RECORDS

Contributed by Mrs. William B. Adams, Muncie. The births and deaths were copied from a Bible before the book was destroyed about 1900.

Births

John Nicholson, Sr. b. 12-12-1790; ... Oct. 1870
Sharlotte (Connell) Nicholson b. 10-5-1788; d. March 1863
Greenup Nicholson b. 1-25-1810; d. Oct. 1870
Sarah Nicholson b. 10-22-1811; d. Aug. 1881
Nancy Nicholson b. 10-15-1814; d. 1873
James D. Nicholson b. 8-8-1816
Elijah Nicholson b. 3-14-1818
Benjamin Nicholson b. 10-28-1819; d. 11-17-1864
March Q. (?) Nicholson b. 9-20-1822; d. July 1880
Mary E. Nicholson b. 4-4-1824; d. 4-14-1880
Emly C. Nicholson b. 1-17-1829; d. 1886.
John E. Nicholson b. 5-13-1831

Land Records

"Know ye, that John Nicholson of Jessamin County, Kentucky, having deposited in the General Land Office, a certificate of the Register of the Land Office at Jeffersonville, whereby it appears that full payment has been made for the southeast quarter of section eleven of township three north of the baseline in range three east of the meridian line [in Jefferson Twp., Washington Co.] of the lands directed to be sold at Jeffersonville by act of Congress. Given under my hand at the City of Washington, 27 Day of June, 1816." Signed by James Madison & Josiah Meigs, Comr. G.L.O.

————————

Elijah Nicholson to Wm. McCully (McCoully), Mortgage, dated March 1, 1849. "Wm. McCully of the City of Pittsburg, State of Pennsylvania, land in Jefferson Co., Indiana, east half of southeast quarter of section 12, town 4, north of range 9 east, in Jeffersonville land district, except 20 acres off east side—for $100 with interest at 6 per cent per annum" [the location of land would have been near Wirt].

————————

Will of Priscilla Nicholson received for probate by clerk of Jefferson County, March 5, 1886.
Marriage license for Elijah Nicholson and Lucy A. Hill, Nov. 16, 1886, returned by W.Y. Monroe, Minister, Jefferson Co.

Contributed by Mrs. Everett Huntzinger, Pendleton, Indiana.

Mikael Mitschelen b. Jan. 11 1826 in Germany, d. at his home northeast of Wakarusa, Ind. Aug. 3, 1896.

Rebecca Hively b. Feb. 19, 1837 in Ohio, d. July 14, 1861.

Mikael Mitschelen & Rebecca Hively m. Sep. 30, 1855.

Children:

    1. Mary Elizabeth b. Dec. 16, 1856 Elkhart Co., Ind.; d. Mar. 8, 1936

    2. John b. Dec. 12, 1859 Elkhart Co.; d. Mar. 31, 1863

Maria Culbertson b. Oct. 3, 1837 in Ohio; d. Aug. 19, 1894

Mikael Mitschelen & Maria Culbertson m. Mar. 30, 1863

Children:

    3. Levi b. Jan. 21, 1864 Elkhart Co.; d. May 17, 1916

    4. Katie Ann b. Oct. 25, 1866; d. Jan. 19, 1888

    5. Martha b. Jan. 30, 1868; d. May 19, 1932

    6. Margaret b. Jan. 11, 1870; d. Nov. 13, 1947

    7. Anna b. Dec. 23, 1873; d. Sep. 13, 1937

    8. Jacob b. Sep. 6, 1876; d. May 16, 1960 at Plymouth, Ind.

HENDRICKS COUNTY WILLS, 1822-1846

Compiled from microfilm of Hendricks County Will Records, Vol. I, in Genealogy Division, Indiana State Library.

ALDERSON, MOSES. Will dated July 29, 1825; date of probate not given. Heirs: wife, Phebe; children: Mary M. & Aaron (oldest), Harriet & Amos (youngest); brother, John. Mary M. to have linens & other items that belonged to her mother, my former wife. Executors: wife, John Alderson, John Carter. Witnesses: John R. Porter, Ephraim Doane, James Clark. Will Record, pp. 4-5.

BARNETT, JUDITH. Will dated May 21, 1842; proved May 8, 1843. Heir: sister, Winaford Bargo, wife of Jacob, to have my personal belongings. Samuel, a black man in Ky., willed to me by my father Daniel Barnett, to have & enjoy the proceeds of his labors for the years 1841 & 1842. No executor. Witnesses: Simon T. Hadley & Daniel Bargo. Will Record, pp. 126-127.

BLANTON, JOHN. Will dated Oct. 10, 1844; proved Nov. 11, 1844. Heirs: sons, Thomas & William; daughters, Belinda Sumner, Catharine Murphy, Margaret Thomas, Mary Alison, Jane Moss. Executor: Charles Reynolds. Witnesses: James Ritter, John J. Jessop. Will Record, pp. 140-41.

BLANTON, WILLIAM. Will dated Feb. 20, 1840; proved Apr. 13, 1840. Heirs: wife & children, names not given except for son John. Executor: Edward Strange. Witnesses: James W. Shannon & James B. Williams. Will Record, pp. 81-82.

BRIGGS, THOMAS P. Will dated June 8, 1839; proved Aug. 5, 1839. Heirs: wife, Margaret; children, Elizabeth Ann, Stephen, William, Alfred, & perhaps others whose names are not given. Executors: sons Stephen & William. Witnesses: William Gladden, Joseph Richards. Will Record, pp. 65-66.

BURT, BENJAMIN. Will dated Sep. 16, 1832; proved Oct. 2, 1835 in Scott Co., Ky. Heirs: wife, Margaret; children, Joseph, Hannah Ballard, Elizabeth Stout, Sally Ballard; grandsons, James, Joses, Benjamin, & John, sons of John, decd.; granddaughter, Sally Peck; stepson, Andrew McClure. Executors: John Duvall, Beverly Ballard. Witnesses: James Scruggs, Lemuel Triplett. Will Record, pp. 22-24.

CARTER, JOHN. Will dated Jan. 27, 1841; proved Aug. 14, 1844. Heirs: wife, Sarah; children, Elizabeth, Benajah, Enoch, Jesse, William, Margaret, Susannah, Sarah (the last six $1.00 each). Executor: son William; witnesses: S. T. & N. T. Hadley, Samuel Melogue. Will Record, pp. 137-39.

COOK, JOHN. Will dated Nov. 13, 1841; proved Jan. 5, 1843. Heirs: wife, Lydia; children, Jesse, Levi, Stephen, Henry, Nathan, Mary Marshall. Executor: son Jesse. Witnesses: William Pope, George Carson, Jediah Hussey. Will Record, pp. 108-110.

COX, EZRA. Will dated May 23, 1835; proved June 1, 1835. Heirs: wife, Susanna, & sons & daughters, names not given. Executor: Charles Reynolds. Witnesses: Caleb Sumner, William Peasce, Thomas Cary. Will Record, pp. 20-21.

COX, WILLIAM. Will dated Sep. 11, 1838; proved Oct. 1, 1838. Heirs: brothers & sisters, Herman of Hendricks Co., Thomas & Abel of Randolph Co., N. C., Benjamin of Indiana, Mary Moffitt, wife of William

Moffitt of Randolph Co., N. C., Martha, widow of Nathan Allen of same place, Amy, wife of Levi Stout of Randolph Co., Ind., Ruth, wife of William Newby of Hendricks Co. Deceased wife's apparel & bed to be given to her sister Hannah, wife of Jonathan (?) Johnson. Executors: brother Herman & John Airy. Witnesses: Elijah Coffin, Nathan Moffitt, Thomas & Mary Rolinds. Will Record, pp. 59-61.

DARNALL, AMOS. Will dated Nov. 29, 1836; proved Dec. 20, 1836. Heirs: wife & children, names not given except William & Franklin, two oldest sons, & James Harrison, youngest son. Executors: Amos S. Wills, Lewis Pannels (?). Witnesses: Thomas Potts, Reuben Darnall. Will Record, pp. 32-35.

DARNALL, HENRY. Will dated Feb. 29, 1844; proved May 22, 1846. Heirs: wife (name not given); children, Turpin, William Harrison, Matilda Swain, Polly Flathers, Elizabeth Hyton; granddaughter, Maria Darnall, heir of Zachariah deceased. Executors: sons Turpin & William Harrison. Witnesses: Thomas Gatson, Martin L. Green, Nathan Swain. Will Record, pp. 162-68.

DAVENPORT, WILLIAM. Will dated Sep. 30, 1839; proved Oct. 25, 1839. Heirs: wife & seven children (names not given), & nephew, Greenville Keith. No executor. Witnesses: Gordon Walker, Samuel W. Walthall, Stephen Floor. Will Record, pp. 69-70.

DeHAPPART, JOSEPH WILLIAM, of Brown Twp. Will dated May 28, 1836; proved July 19, 1836. Heirs: wife, Helen Maria; daughters, Maria Theresa & Venerolia (?) de Happart. No executor. Witnesses: John & James Ward, Ann Marry. Will Record, p. 25.

DOLLARHIDE, LARKIN. Will dated Sep. 23, 1837; proved Nov. 7, 1837. Heirs: wife & children (names not given). Executors: David Sparks, James Wm. Hooper. Witnesses: Griffith Dickerson, John W. Ray. Will Records, pp. 46-48.

DOWNEY, ALEXANDER, of Bellville. Will not dated; proved Dec. 5, 1836. Heir: wife, Ann P. Executor: wife. Witnesses: Homer Johnson, Caroline Ballard. Will Record, pp. 28-29.

DUNCAN, SAMUEL A. Will dated Jan. 28, 1846; proved Mar. 3, 1846. Heirs: wife, Elizabeth, & son Robert, a minor. Executors: George Kreigh, Erastus B. Duncan. Witnesses: David Boswell, Joseph P. Bishop. Will Record, pp. 154-56.

FARMER, WILLIAM. Will dated July 20, 1840; proved Nov. 14, 1840. Heirs: wife, Ruth, & children, Rebecca & Daniel. Executors: Jesse Blair, Eli Newlin. Witnesses: Samuel Carter, Jr., Mordecai Carter, Eli Newlin. Will Record, pp. 91-93.

FITZSIMMONS, THOMAS. Will dated Feb. 10, 1840; proved March 28, 1840. Heirs: wife, Mary, & children (names not given). Executor: son-in-law William Pearson. Witnesses: H. Brittain, George Crow. Will Record, pp. 79-80.

FLETCHER, WILLIAM, SR. Will dated Sep. 20, 1843; proved Dec. 2, 1843. Heirs: wife, Sarah, & children, names not given except for son Eli. Executors: wife & William B. Smith. Witnesses: John M. Garrison, Nathan Philips. Will Record, pp. 124-26.

FLORENCE, WILLIAM, of Woodford Co., Ky. Will dated Oct. 13, 1839; no date of probate. Heirs: wife, Elizabeth; children, Elizabeth Ross, Lilly Anderson, William, Obadiah, Katherine Reardon, Willis, James, Nelly, Lane (?), Eliza, Cynthia. All but last two to receive $1.00. Executor: wife. Witnesses: Alexander Duningford (?), Isaac Howard, Jacob Kenneday, George Hickman (?). Will Record, p. 74.

FOWLER, SKELTON, of Bellville. Will dated Dec. 18, 1842; proved July 12, 1845. Heirs: wife, Juliana D.; nephews, George R. & Benjamin F. Fowler; niece, Ann Fowler, Caroline Marquiss, now Caroline Schively, who lives with me. No executor. Witnesses: Noah Day, Charles Wallace. Will Record, pp. 148-49.

FOX, DAVID. Will dated Aug. 14, 1838; proved Oct. 8, 1838. Heirs: wife, Martha; sons, Oliver, Henry B., Manassah. Executor: wife. Witnesses: Joseph & Hiram Tomlinson. Will Record, pp. 58-59.

FOX, JACOB. Will dated July 15, 1837; proved March 5, 1838. Heirs: wife, Mary; sons, Jacob, David, Nemuth (?), Manasseh; daughters, Mary, Hannah, Elizabeth, Margaret. Executor: Asher Hunt. Witnesses: Zimri Hunt, Beulah Hunt, S. T. Hadley. Will Record, pp. 56-57.

GARDNER, ABSALOM B. Will dated Jan. 24, 1838; proved Feb. 27, 1838. Heirs: wife, Jane; children, Eliza (wife of Wesley Bowen), Madison, John C., Martha, Evaline, Darius; brother, James; grandchildren, William Benjamin & Evalina Ganno, children of John F. Ganno. Executors: Joel Wilson, Hudson Mary. Witnesses: James M. Gregg, Robert N. Richardson. Will Record, pp. 49-53.

GRAHAM, YOUNG W. Will dated Apr. 4, 1846; proved May 12, 1846. Heir: wife (name not given). Executor: Taliafero B. Miller. Witnesses: Lemmon Christie, John Houston, Nichodemus Harris. Will Record, pp. 159-161.

HADLEY, SIMON T. Will dated Nov. 15, 1832; proved Apr. 26, 1843. Heirs: wife, Elizabeth; children, William, Martha, James, Ruth, Jonathan, Joshua, Sarah, Elizabeth, Simon, John, Mary, Thomas. To heirs of Benjamin Pickett & Jesse Dixon "my part of the $500 which my brother Joseph is to pay to legatees of my father's estate at the death of my stepmother." Executors: sons James & Joshua. Witnesses: James & Nancy Tolbert. Will Record, pp. 111-13.

HAMBLETON, DANIEL. Will dated July 27, 1840; proved Apr. 18, 1845. Heirs: wife, Martha; children, James Y., Matilda Foster, William, Susan McCracken, Mary Burks, Daniel D., Abraham H., Amanda Gorrel, John, No executor. Witnesses: J. M. Gregg, Simon T. Hadley. Will Record, pp. 142-44.

HANNAH, JOHN. Will dated Feb. 12, 1840; proved Mar. 5, 1840. Heirs: wife, Elizabeth; children, Patterson, Thomas, John, William, Mariah, Jane, Elizabeth, Nancy, Lucinda, Mary. Executor: wife. Witnesses: Robert Cooper, Benjamin Hiatt. Will Record, pp. 75-77.

HARBISON, THOMAS, of Brown Twp. Will dated Jan. 31, 1846; proved Feb. 25, 1846. Heirs: wife, Permelia; children, Mary & Elizabeth. No executor. Witnesses: Joseph Willson, Robert Harbison. Will Record, pp. 150-51.

HAWORTH, JAMES, of Randolph Co., Ind. Will dated May 20, 1826; date of probate not given. Heirs: wife, Mary; children, Levi, Rees, Eli, Sarah, Charity, Margaret, Ann, Elizabeth. Sons William, James, George, David, & Jonathan (?) have already received their share. Executors: wife & son James. Witnesses: David & George Haworth. Will Record, pp. 10-11.

HOLSCLAW, JACOB. Will dated Mar. 13, 1846; proved Mar. 30, 1846. Heirs: wife, Elizabeth, & children (names not given). Executors: John Collins, Blain (?) Mills. Witnesses: Stephen Hale, William McLeod. Will Record, pp. 157-159.

HOOSER, WILLIAM. Will dated Feb. 22, 1836; proved June 27, 1837. Heirs: wife, Sarah, & children (names not given). Executor: wife. Witnesses: Samuel Shannon, Elijah Tinder. Will Record, pp. 36-37.

HULTS, URIAH. Will dated Aug. 28, 1822; date of probate not given. Heirs: wife, Abigail; children, Daniel C., Nathaniel W., Uriah S., Charity, Abigail, Susan, Jerusha; grandson, Silas, son of Nathaniel; Sally Mariah, relationship not given, probably daughter. Executors: wife, son Nathaniel, Jeremiah Cox. Witnesses: Moses Cook, Jeremiah Collis (?), J. B. Crumbaugh. Will Record, pp. 1-3.

JACKSON, WILLIAM. Will dated July 28, 1842; proved Aug. 20, 1842. Heir: wife (name not given). Executor: Jesse McMahan. Witnesses: T. C. Williams, William Leake. Will Record, pp. 102-103.

JESSOP, TIMOTHY. Will dated Jan. 31, 1844; proved Feb. 23, 1844. Heirs: wife, Susannah; children, Rachel Ritter, Ammy Rich, Rhoda Snow, Susannah Jessop, Lewis, John J., Samuel, Timothy, Jesse; sister, Avis Jessop. Owned land in Hamilton & Hendricks cos. & a tanyard. Executors: Joseph Jessop, son Samuel. Witnesses: Matthew Stanley, Adin Ballard. Will Record, pp. 128-31.

JESSUP, JACOB. Will dated ——19, 1827; date of probate not given. Heirs: mother; sisters, Polly Lockhart, Anna Chandler, Sarah ——, Edith Cook of Surrey Co., N. C., "money which her husband John owes me"; brothers, John, Levi. Executors: brother John, Thomas Lockhart. Names of witnesses not readable. Will Record, pp. 9-10.

JESSUP, JONATHAN. Will dated Jan 1, 1826; date of probate not given. Heirs: wife, Sarah; children, Ruth, Lucy, Rachel, unborn child. To receive land in Stokes Co., N. C., given him in his father's will, after death of mother. Executors: Elihu Jackson, Samuel Jessup. Witnesses: Abijah Pinson, Joseph Cloud. Will Record, pp. 5-8.

JONES, MATTHEW. Will dated July 11, 1836; proved Aug. 8, 1836. Heirs: sons, Thomas, Wiley, Matthew, John, Bessant; daughter, Sally Sturgeon. Executor: son John. Witnesses: James Campbell, Samuel C. Mitchell, Samuel Barber. Will Record, pp. 30-31.

JONES, SAMUEL. Will dated Mar. 3, 1838; proved Mar. 20, 1838. Heirs: following children to receive $1.00 each: Polly, Margaret, Orpha, Sarah, Elizabeth, Matilda, Mourning, Wynn, William, Josiah, Samuel; remainder of estate to wife & sons John & James Harvey. Executor: Samuel, Jr. Witnesses: John Spears, Emanuel Lockhart. Will Record, pp. 54-55.

KELLY, WILLIAM. Will dated Sep. 19, 1840; proved Oct. 13, 1840. Heirs: wife, Malinda, & children (names not given). Executors: John Houston, Daniel Liming. Witnesses: Wesley Morgan, Isaac R. West, Archibald West. Will Record, pp. 85-86.

LEMON, ROBERT. Will dated Feb. 15, 1837; proved Apr. 6, 1837. Heirs: wife, Mary; children, John, Lavina Merritt, Sarah Merritt, George, Martha Merritt, Elizabeth Lemon, Cornelius, William, Jane Lemon. Executors: sons John & Cornelius. Witnesses: David Ballard, John Pinson, Samuel Starbuck. Will Record, pp. 38-40.

McCRACKEN, ROBERT. Will not dated, probably 1826 or 1827 (?). Heirs: wife, Mary, and children, Susannah, William, Samuel, Nelson, Robert. Executors: Pollard Baldwin, William McCracken. Witnesses: William Townsend, Mary McCracken. Will Record, pp. 8-9.

McKINLEY, WESLEY. Will dated Aug. 24, 1839; proved Sep. 14, 1839. Heirs: wife, Nancy, & children (names not given). Executor: Andrew B. Shallody. Witnesses: Charles F. Sitzman, S. T. Hadley, George McCoy. Will Record, pp. 67-68.

MAHAN, JOHN. Will dated Apr. 24, 1837; proved May 10, 1837. Heirs: wife, Nancy; daughters, Elizabeth Ann West, Mary, Elizabeth, Sally, Emily, Indiana; sons, James, John B., Woodson, William. Executors: wife & Simon T. Hadley. Witnesses: Moses Cavett, Thomas Higgins. Will Record, pp. 41-43.

MILES, JOHN. Will dated Aug. 15, 1843; proved Oct. 5, 1843. Heirs: sons, John, Samuel, Elisha, Isaac; grandson, Alfred Cook, son of daughter Hannah & William Cook; heirs of sons William & David, $1.00 each; William M. & Naomi Rogers (relationship not given). Executors: William M. Rogers, David Downs, Sr. Witnesses: Richard Christy, Elias Rodgers. Will Record pp. 123-24.

MILLIKEN, ANN. Will dated July 27, 1830; date of probate not given. Heirs: sons, William, Benjamin, Jesse, heirs of John; daughters, Elizabeth Mary, Jane Hoggatt, Mary Tomlinson, Sarah Hoggatt, Ann Bales. Executors: Abner & Solomon Blair. Witnesses: S. Galisbury Moore, Enoch Jessup. Will Record, pp. 14-15.

MILLHOUSE, ROBERT. Will dated Apr. 11, 1839; proved Dec. 13, 1841. Heirs: wife, Sally, & children, Robert, Rebecca, Elizabeth, Arin. Sons Henry, Samuel, & John have received their share. Executors: wife & son Samuel. Witnesses: Samuel Starbuck, William Newby, Joseph Ballard. Will Record, pp. 101-102.

MOBERLY, JOHN. Will dated June 2, 1843; proved July 17, 1843. Heirs: wife, Elizabeth; sons, Benjamin N., William, Joseph F., John C., Simeon E.; daughters, Martha Ann Tout, Lavina M. Tout, Elizabeth A. West, Susan A. Barlow, Amanda, Paulina T., & Samantha A. Moberly. Executors: wife & son Benjamin. Witnesses: S. T. Hadley, W. A. Baugh. Will Record, pp. 117-21.

MONTAGUE, THOMAS. Will dated Aug. 6, 1837; proved Aug. 25, 1837. Heirs: wife (name not given); children, William, Clairmont, Nancy, Hannah. Executors: Benjamin M. Logan, Clairmont Montague. Witnesses: Valentine B. Cress, Robert Davison, Jr. Will Record, pp. 44-45.

NICHOLS, JAMES. Will dated Sep. 8, 1834; proved Feb. 7, 1835. Heirs: wife (name not given); children, Andrew, James, Harriet, Eleanor, Erasmus, Thomas, Sally, Betsy, Jane (last five to receive $1.00 over & above what they have already received). Executors: sons Erasmus & Thomas. Witnesses: S. T. Hadley, Edward Strange. Will Record, pp. 18-19.

OWEN, BENJAMIN. Will dated Mar. 8, 1845; proved Dec. 9, 1845. Heirs: wife, Hannah, & other heirs (names not given). Executors: Samuel Owen, Jr., Caleb Easterling. Witnesses: Samuel, David, & Sarah Mendenhall. Will Record, pp. 150-51.

PATTISON (or Patterson), WILLIAM. Will dated Mar. 11, 1841; proved June 28, 1841. Heirs: John Moses Mathias (relationship not given); sisters, Jane & Elizabeth Pattison. Executors: John M. Mathias, Elias Hadley. Witnesses: Joel Hodgin, David Carter. Will Record, pp. 93-95.

PINSON, ABIJAH. Will dated June 24, 1830; proved Aug. 13, 1832. Heirs: wife, Ann, & children, Eliza Ballard, John. Executor: son John. Witnesses: James M. Gregg, John Ballard, William Newby. Will Record, pp. 13-14.

RAMSEY, BARTHOLOMEW. Will dated June 15, 1833; proved Aug. 12, 1833. Heirs: wife, Catharine; sons, James, Samuel, John, Daniel; daughters, Elizabeth Jones, Nancy Jones, Sarah Jane Ramsey. Executors: wife & David Jones. Witnesses: Edward Bray, John B. Hadley, Mary White. Will Record, pp. 16-17.

RICHARDS, NAOMI. Will dated June 27, 1841; proved Nov. 10, 1842. Heirs: children, Samuel, Joseph, Ruth, Lydia; grandchildren, Elizabeth Ann, Naomi Ann, & John W. Campbell, Large P. Noble (?), Joseph R. & William H. Cain. Executors: 2 sons. Witnesses: Aaron Homan, Samuel Spray. Will Record, pp. 106-108.

RICHARDS, REUBEN. Will dated Sep. 27, 1839; proved Nov. 16, 1839. Heirs: wife, Susan; son, George; daughters, Christiana, Nancy, Lucinda, Sarah Jane, & Cintha Richards. Executors: wife & brother-in-law John Baker. Witnesses: William Hinton, William Faught. Will Record, pp. 71-73.

SACREY, CHARLES. Will dated Apr. 1, 1843; proved Apr. 22, 1843. Heirs: wife, Elender; children, Benjamin, Charles, Polly, Elizabeth Jane; stepson, Stephen Green. Executor: Stephen Stephenson. Witnesses: George Darnall, Allen Powers, William Faught. Will Record, pp. 113-115.

SCAMAHORN, NATHANIEL. Will dated July 18, 1828 (?); no date of probate. Heirs: wife (name not given); younger sons, Nathaniel & Joseph; names of other sons not given; daughters, Mehally & Sally, an equal portion to what I have given my older daughters (their names not given). No executor. Witnesses: William Buckhart (?), Thomas Tadlock, Henry Byers. Will Record, p. 12.

SHANNON, SAMUEL. Will dated Oct. 1, 1841; proved Oct. 20, 1841. Heirs: sons, William, Thomas, John, Samuel, Russell, James, $1.00 in addition to what I have already given them; other son, Harvey G.; daughters, Polly A. Bowen, Nancy, Margaret, & Sarah Jane Shannon. Executor: Edward Strange. Witnesses: John R. Lamb, William Bowman. Will Record, pp. 95-98.

SIMMONS, EZEKIEL. Will dated June 7, 1838; proved Nov. 11, 1840. Heirs: wife, Martha; sons, George, Josephus; daughters, Nancy, Margaret, Elizabeth, Eleanor, Lucy Mattox, wife of Jesse; Delphi, once a slave, "whom I raised." Executor: Charles Ventrees. Witnesses: Joel Nelson, Nicholas Lawler. Will Record, pp. 87-90.

SIMPSON, JOSEPH. Will dated March 26, 1845; proved Apr. 25, 1845; Heirs: wife, Sarah Jane, & son, Alexander L., a minor. Executor: Alexander Little. Witnesses: Samuel Jessup, Francis F. Sheldon. Will Record, pp. 145-147.

SMITH, JOHN M. Will dated Sep. 7, 1843; proved Sep. 30, 1834. Heirs: wife, Martha; niece, Margaret Green, daughter of Nelly Sacrey; nephew, Christopher Hilton, son of John. Witnesses: L. Christie, John Bush. Will Record, pp. 121-22.

TAYLOR, ISAAC. Will dated Dec. 15, 1839; proved Jan. 4, 1840. Heirs: wife, Mary; son, Fountain B.; daughter, Mary Duncan (?); grandson, Carter Taylor. Executor: wife. Witnesses: William Townsend, Josiah Hodson. Will Record, pp. 78-79.

THORNBROUGH, ELIZABETH. Will dated Jan. 20, 1842; proved Feb. 25, 1843. Heirs: children, William, Clark, Hannah, Diadamia. Executor: Preston Brown. Witnesses: Jeremiah Johnson, Jane Mills, Esther A. Kellum. Will Record, pp. 110-11.

TOUT, BENJAMIN G., of Danville. Will dated Jan. 13, 1838; proved Mar. 5, 1839. Heirs: wife, Sally, & children (names not given). Executors: wife & Simon T. Hadley. Witnesses: Edmund Clark, James M. Gregg. Will Record, pp. 62-64.

TOUT, JOHN. Will dated Jan. 5, 1844; proved Mar. 15, 1844. Heirs: wife & children (names not given). Executors: John Henry, John Triggs. Witnesses: Henry Muller, James N. Tout, Hugh G. Larimore. Will Record, pp. 134-37.

TRYER, DANIEL B. Will dated July 23, 1839; proved May 29, 1840. Heirs: wife, Cynthia; children, John & Aleary(?) Ann. Executor: wife. Witnesses: William Gladden, David Faucett. Will Record, 83-84.

WALL, JAMES. Will dated Nov. 13, 1841; proved Dec. 13, 1841. Heirs: wife (name not given); son, Reuben Parks. Executors: David Boswell, Abraham Bland. Witnesses: Berry Burks, John W. Brown, Aaron Wilcookson. Will Record, pp. 98-100.

WILLSON, THOMAS. Will dated Aug. 20, 1842; proved Oct. 10, 1842. Heirs: wife, Nancy; children, John, William, Emily Willson, Esther, wife of John T. Trotter; Shannon Willson, Anna, wife of Thomas H. Howell; Jane, wife of Nelson T. Trotter, Squire H. Willson. Executor: Jeremiah Tinder. Witnesses: Simon T. Hadley, William Brown. Will Record, pp. 103-105.

WILSON, BETSY. Will dated Oct. 25, 1836; proved Nov. 23, 1836. Heirs: John Wilson, son of Hannah, deceased; brothers, John & Robert; sisters, Polly Smith, Hannah Lawrence. Executor: David Vestal (?). Witnesses: Ezekiel Williams, Sally Carpenter. Will Record, pp. 26-27.

The following wills were found in the Hendricks County Deed Records:

ALDRIDGE, ELIZABETH. Will dated May 30, 1829; proved July 4, 1829. Heirs: father & mother, Daniel & Polly Higgins; brothers (names not given). Executor: father; witnesses: J. F. Beckett, John Scoot (Scott). Deed Records, I, 331-32.

BALLARD, WILLIAM. of Morgan Co. Will & codicil dated Oct. 21, 1823; proved Jan. 26, 1824 in Morgan Co. Heirs: wife, Mary; son, Thomas; daughters (names not given). Executors: wife & son. Witnesses to will: Levi Jessup, Nathan Kirk. In the codicil he specified that his interest in south half of north fraction of section 6, T14N, R1E, held by Thomas Hinton & himself, together with lots remaining in town of Hillsborough, be offered as a donation to the county provided the county seat be established at Hillsborough; also he gave to Nathan Kirk half of the above lands "agreeably to note he holds against me." Witnesses to codicil: Levi Jessup, George W. Pope. Deed Records, I, 39-40.

MATLOCK, GEORGE. Will dated Sep. 20, 1825; proved Feb. 23, 1827. Heirs: wife, Sally; sons, Thomas, George (to receive $1.00); daughters, Susan, Nancy, Matilda. Executors: David & Thomas J. Matlock. Witnesses: Amilia & Nathan Kirk. Deed Records, I, 231.

WALKER, THOMAS. Will dated June 30, 1830; proved Jan. 3, 1831. Heirs: wife, Elizabeth; daughters, Sarah, Elizabeth, Matilda, Martha; son, William. Other children: John, Thomas J., William P., Nancy Dunn, Margaret Fowler, to receive $1.00 each. Executor: William P. Walker. Witnesses: Thomas J. Matlock, Jacob Kennedy. Deed Records, I, 390-91.

HARRISON COUNTY MARRIAGES, 1809-1817

Compiled from microfilm copy of Volume I of the Harrison County Marriage Records in the Genealogy Division, Indiana State Library. The names have been checked with the compilations made by the Harrison County Chapter of the D.A.R. and by the compilation made by Mrs. Ruth M. Selvin for the Fort Wayne Public Library. The latter covers Volume II (1817-1832) as well as Volume I.

Albin, Philip C. - Hanah Williams   5-17-1817
Allin, Marshel - Polly Dailey   4-10-1817
Allison, Richard - Amy Tracy   8-14-1817
Anderson, John - Louisa Cuzee   8-14-1817
Armstrong, Robert - Priscilla Steele   8-21-1817
Armstrong, Thomas - Elizabeth Guine (?)   lic. 11- 7-1813
Arnold, George - Betsey Stephens   7- 6-1815
Askren, David - Nancy Davis   lic. 8-18-1817
Aynthay (?), Thomas - Elizabeth Guine (?)   lic. 1-11-1814

[Page damaged] - Magdaline Baker, daughter of Henry   9- 5-1817
Balinger, Joseph - Elizabeth Webb   11-13-1812
Barker, Henry - Elizabeth Willard   1-19-1813
Barker, Moses - Crissy Willard   lic. 4- 8-1813
Barkshire, John - Nelly Stevenson, daughter of James   lic. 2-20-1814
Barkshire, Joseph - Margaret Stephenson   6-16-1814
Barkshire, Richard - Sarah Jackson, widow   lic. 3-13-1811
Barnett, David - Polly Hone   11-23-1814
Barton, James - Mary Conway   lic. 9- 3-1814
Bates, Samuel - Polly Rice   3- 3-1816
Batman, John - Rutha Harrison (?)   4-28-1815
Beanblossom, Martin - Lucinda Huffman   9-30-1813
Beard, John M. - Lucy Spoone, widow   1- 4-1816
Beeman, Stephen T. - Jane Smith   lic. 5- 3-1810
Bell, Daniel - Nancy Spencer   12-24-1811
Bell, Philip - Polly Polke   7-25-1811
Bennet, Johnston - Mary Yatsler   lic. 3- 2-1816
Bentley, George - Metilda Ludlow   12-24-1815
Berington, Samuel J. - Elizabeth Armstrong   1-2-1817
Berry, Ezekiel - Nancy Byrn   lic. 1- 7-1817
Berryman, Francis - Barbara Boodin   6-13-1817
Beshang, John - Jenny Buckhannon   5- 7-1811
Bierly, John - Katy Frank   3- 5-1812
Blackburn, Hugh - Polly Totten   lic. 8-22-1817
Bluery (?), Isom - Anny Oldman   lic. 11-18-1814
Blunk, Moses - Anne McCullock   lic. 8-24-1816
Bogard, Jacob P. - Patsey Ewing   6-19-1817
Boone, Hiram C. - Fanny Boone, daughter of Jonathan   lic. 3-17-1813
Boone, Squire - Nancy Cotner   5-16-1817
Boone, William - Elizabeth Spencer, widow of Spier Spencer   3-17-1816
Boston, Beverly B. - Elizabeth Boston   6-15-1812
Bounty, Jacob - Sarah Young, daughter of James   lic. 11- 4-1810
Bowman, Christopher - Lucinda Long   4-24-1817
Bowman, James - Lydia Springer   lic. 2- 3-1817
Brandenburgg, Absolom - Esther Frakes   8-15-1815
Brandenburgh, Solomon - Alazina Williams   9-25-1814
Branham, Alpheus - Polly Shaw   1- 1-1815
Branham, Paydon - Jane Richardson   5- 3-1812
Breeze, John - Sarah Hallowell   9-13-1810

Brooks, William - Susannah Marian, daughter of Henry   lic. 11- 9-1809
Brown, David - Abigail Spivey   lic. 9-30-1811
Brown, Dickson - Jane Bruce   10-31-1811
Brown, Henry - Elizabeth Cole   2- 7-1813
Brown, James - Patsy Sands, daughter of William   lic. 1-17-1810
Brown, John - Syntha Butler   lic. 10-30-1812
Brown, Samuel - Polly Bell   12-25-1811
Bruice, James - Sarah Davis   12-14-1815
Bryles, Ephraim - Susanah Fleshman, daughter of Susanah Coopriter   lic. 5-10-1817
Buchannan, James - Jane Smith   1-24-1811
Buckanan, Alexander - Elizabeth Smith   12-25-1814
Buckhart, David - Molly Smith   lic. 2-17-1817
Bugher, David - Marian Sapenfield   7-20-1816
Bugher, Henry - Lauretta Branham   2-14-1811
Bush, William - Caty Bacon   lic. 10- 4-1811
Butler, William - Mary Carr   lic. 10-11-1813

Calloway, Samuel - Cath Evans   lic. 12-29-1809
Car, John - Nancy Carter   12-16-1810
Care, Jacob - Susannah Coonrod   lic. 8-21-1816
Carpenter, William - Ruth Wheeler   9-25-1814
Carr, Thomas - Polly Allen   lic. 12- 7-1814
Carter, John - Nancy Fleener, daughter of W. J. Fleener   lic. 7-26-1813
Carter, Robert - Eday Wilcox   7-24-1811
Carter, Thomas - Sarah Richardson   lic. 7-29-1816
Charles, William - Polly Dougherty   10-20-1811
Charley, Peter - Caty Bell   lic. 3- 7-1814
Chuam, John - Margaret Tibbs   lic. 3-29-1816
Clarke, William - Jean Blair   7-30-1817
Clendennan, John G. - Deborah Lindley   lic. 1-19-1814
Clerk, George - Jean Galy, widow   9-17-1812
Cloud, William - Polly Willson, people of color   lic. 2- 6-1813
Collins, Andrew - Ellender Faith   8- 3-1817
Colvin, John - Elizabeth Noble   lic. 8-19-1815
Combs, William - Elizabeth Barbary   7-23-1813
Conley, Robert - Liddy Hopper   1-22-1811
Cooly, Thomas - Mary Evans   lic. 8-16-1813
Coonts, George - Elizabeth Boggett   3- 9-1817
Cooper, John - Milly Ruth   lic. 12-14-1813
Coopriter, John - Elizabeth Fleshman   5-27-1810
Coopriter, Peter - Susan Fleshman, widow   5-30-1810
Cotner, David - Rachel Denboe   lic. 10-22-1814
Cotton, John C. - Elizabeth Noble   lic. 8-19-1816
Craig, John - Nelly Waller, daughter of Thomas   lic. 4-10-1816
Crandall, Nathaniel - Gracy Stevens   2-14-1817
Crawford, William - Nancy Lahue   10-30-1817
Crecelius, Philip - Rebecca Enlow   2- 6-1817
Crofton, William - Mary W. McIntire   lic. 2-28-1816
Curry, Thomas - Sally Emmons   3-28-1812

Danley, William L. - Martha Davis   lic. 8- 5-1811
Daugherty, John - Mary Hallowell,
    daughter of John Hallowell   2-11-1810
Davidson, Daniel - Aribella Dawson (?)   7-14-1811
Davidson, Daniel - Caty Beryman   1-15-1817
Davidson, James - Polly Hardin,
    daughter of Cathrine Hardin   10-29-1815
Davidson, Peter - Sally Daggs   1-29-1813
Davidson, Samuel - Elizabeth Bareley   12-29-1814
Davis, Evan - Elizabeth Ballard   7-31-1817
Davis, John - Nancy Willson,
    daughter of Samuel   lic. 3- 3-1813
Davis, Milo R. - Jane Spencer   lic. 12-22-1816
Dawson, James - Sally Vaughan   lic. 2- 1-1815
Dawson (or Davison), John - Hepsey Onion 3-12-1809
Deal, D. - Barbary Keller(?)   lic. 8-12-1816
Deal, Daniel - Barbery Keller   lic. 8-12-1815
Deal, George - Frances Wright   lic. 12- 7-1815
Decker, Joseph - Elizabeth Wheat   3- 5-1812
Denton, Burkett Handford - Rebecca Cooper
                                            11- 5-1812
Diken, Archibald - Rachel Fotzer   lic. 5-18-1813
Dirbin, Melvin - Isabella Latta   lic. 11- 4-1812
Doan, Archibald - Rebekah Spiver(?)   5-31-1812
Dodd, William - Sarah McKee   10-14-1813
Downs, Ezekiel - Charlotte Rollings   3- 8-1814
Downs, William - Hannah Berry,
    widow of Thomas   lic. 12-14-1813
Downs, Zachariah - Rachel Huston,
    daughter of Isaac   lic. 9- 9-1817
Duvalt(?), John - Jane Johnson   lic. 12-31-1813
Dyer, Charles, Jr. - Margaret Kepley lic. 9-19-1816

Eads, Thomas - Juda McFarland   7- 6-1814
Eastridge, James - Mary Wells   lic. 8-21-1810
Echert, Moses - Sarah Kellion   lic. 7-20-1816
Echord, Joseph - Polly Cotner   10- 5-1815
Edwards, Cassius - Lydia Thompson lic. 11-10-1814
Edwards, Griffith - Rachel Hinton   9-10-1812
Edwards, John - Margaret Brinley   3- ?-1817
Edwards, William - Agnes Tipton   10-10-1811
Elliott, James - Polly Cooprider   lic. 11-23-1815
Elliott, Thomas - Elizabeth Sheets   5-28-1812
Ellison, Isaac - Patsey Hoff   lic. 12-25-1815
Engram, William - Polly Fouts   lic. 1-10-1817
Enlow, Henry - Rebecca Mattocks,
    daughter of Edward Mattocks   lic. 6-28-1810
Enlow, John - Jenny Paisley   12-24-1812
Enos, Peter - Polly Jones   7-11-1812
Evans, Evan - Mariah Bugher   3-27-1817
Evans, George - Susannah Armstrong   8- 4-1814
Evans, James - Ann Carr   lic. 3-12-1816
Evans, John - Polly Willson   lic. 12-28-1810
Evans, Joseph - Edith Hoggatt(?)   lic. 3-14-1810
Evins, John - Nancy Oxendine   11- 8-1811

Farmer, John - Catherine Zenor   lic. 5-19-1809
Flanagan, Patrick - Catharine French,
    daughter of Daniel   lic. 11-21-1814
Fleshman, Jacob - Polly Charley   10-21-1813
Fleshman, Jonas - Sally Pittman   11- 1-1810
Fleshman, William - Sarah Charley   lic. 12-25-1815
Forsythe, William - Jane Ludlow   10-14-1811
Fowler, Benjamin - Mary Davis   8-28-1817
Fowler, William - Anny Tuell   6-13-1812
Fox, John - Elizabeth Cunningham   2- 8-1810

Frake, Peter - Nancy Vanwinkle   lic. 5-26-1815
French, Daniel, Jr., son of Daniel
    - Sarah Smith   11-10-1814
Funk, Harry - Elizabeth Smith   4-23-1814
Funk, John - Rebecca Pagget   6-22-1809
Funk, Peter - Nancy Enlow   lic. 8-29-1816
Funk, William - Sarah Martin   lic. 1-24-1817

Gaither, James W. - Mary Hunter   lic. 3-21-1814
Gamer, Henry - Nelly Dunlap   1-25-1810
Garrison, Reuben - Ann Sturgeon   lic. 4-30-1811
Gentle, Fielder - Sarah Onstot   lic. 4- 7-1814
Gibbs, James - Nancy Niel   lic. 1- 7-1817
Gibbs, Thomas - Rebekah Beard   1-26-1814
Gibson, John - Nancy Ash   3-31-1816
Glover, Joseph - Polly McManas   lic. 5-11-1813
Goodman, William - Farebee Jones   lic. 8-28-1814
Gortney, Thomas - Sarah Crawford   lic. 12-23-1815
Gregory, J. - E. Edwards   lic. 5- 6-1814
Gregory, John - Mary Vaughn   lic. 9- 2-1817
Gregory, William - Lucy Moffett, widow   9- 1-1814
Grigsbey, John - Heather Sharp   lic. 4-15-1817
Grisham, Phillip - Elizabeth King Crutchfield
                                            12-10-1812
Grose, Conrad - Susan Miller   3-26-1812
Gullett, Joshua - Barbary Haush   12- ?-1812
Gwin, Edmond - Rachall Harberson,
    daughter of John Harberson   lic. 1- 2-1811

Hadrick, Jacob - Polly Brisben   lic. 1-10-1809
Hamilton, Jamison - Nancy Boldon   12- 9-1813
Hancock, John - Mary French   1- 7-1813
Harberson, John - Patsy Randall   lic. 2- 1-1810
Harberson, John - Nancy Morgan   lic. 7-28-1814
Harbison, James - Anna Rice,
    daughter of Henry Rice   7-18-1809
Hargrave, James - Rebecca Gibs   lic. 8-26-1816
Harminson, Peter - Anny McGee   8- 4-1815
Hattabaugh, Jacob - Mrs. Jane Spear,
    daughter of William Logan   lic. 2- 7-1812
Hawkins, David - Nelly Sturgeon   lic. 10-25-1813
Heady, James - Polly Bugher   lic. 10- 8-1816
Heckman, James - Mary Moser   2-10-1811
Heckman, John - Elizabeth Duncan   12-31-1815
Henery, Hiram - Sally Person   lic. 10-28-1815
Henry, William Jr. - Hannah Williams lic. 9-12-1816
Hensley, Edmond - Elizabeth [blank]   5-10-1812
Henson, Isaac - Charity Hill   9- 2-1813
Henson, James - Servilla Roden   lic. 1-13-1817
Henson, Joseph - Dolly Heslapp   lic. 9-20-1814
Hessey, John - Sally Kennedy   5-25-1811
Hickman, James - Elizabeth Siselove lic. 6-22-1813
Hinton, Thomas - Rutha Reede   lic. 10-17-1812
Hoback, Mark - Nancy Lynch   lic. 1-19-1816
Holdcroft, Nathaniel - Elizabeth Applegate 3-24-1814
Holly, Ephraim - Peggy Guffey,
    daughter of James Guffey   lic. 10-22-1810
House, George - Mary Flaner   lic. 6-14-1811
How, James - Jane Dotson   lic. 12- 3-1813
Howell, Abatha - Hannah Swinford   lic. 9-21-1816
Howell, Joseph - Mary Buckhannan   10- 6-1812
Hubbard, James - Bersheba Hurst   3-10-1816
Hughes, John - Mary Daggs   1-28-1812
Hughs, Nathan - Elizabeth Daggs   lic. 12-21-1816
Humprey, Lewis - Celey Carpenter   9-22-1817
Humphreys, Charles - Mary Stewart   5-29-1810

Hupp, James - Myra Bird   3-13-1817
Hurst, William - Nancy Dyer   lic. 8- 7-1816
Hyrall, Hodgeman - Elizabeth Allin   4- 4-1816

[Page damaged] - Mary Ingram   9-11-1817

Jenkins, Jeremiah - Patsey Spencer   lic. 5-29-1815
Jinkins, Josiah - Polly Hicky   3-25-1813
Johnson, James - Hessy Light   lic. 3- 3-1814
Johnson, James - Elizabeth Reede,
    daughter of David Reede   lic. 3-15-1814
Johnston, William - Dorinda French   1-20-1817
Jones, David - Susan Potter   lic. 2-24-1812
Jones, George - Lydia McMirtry   2-13-1817
Jones, Pierce - Lettie Melton   12-26-1816
Jones, Richard - Cath. Branes   3-23-1810
Jones, Rob - Elizabeth Chappell   1- 2-1817
Jones, Westley - Allis Luther   lic. 1-27-1817
Jyles, John - Hannah Harriman   12-23-1811

Keeth, Jack - Malinda Mattingley   7-14-1812
Kellem, William - Arabella Davidson   3- 4-1816
Keller, Jonathan - Polly Fleshman   8-16-1810
Kelley, Joshua - Rebekah Brown   lic. 4-28-1816
Kelly, James - Alsey Leston   10- 6-1812
Kelsey, Daniel - Sarah Wattson   lic. 9-28-1816
Kennedy, Samuel - Alsey Turner   lic. 8-18-1812
Kenser, Micheal - Polly Morgan   lic. 8- 9-1816
Kepley, Andrew - Sarah Mozer   lic. 4-10-1816
Kepley, George - Molly Young   1- 4-1813
Kesner, Christopher - Barbery Bayles   7-18-1816
Kesner, Jacob - Polly Ewen   lic. 1-16-1817
Killion, David Adam - Solomy Ahard   9- 4-1817
Kilton, Robert - Ara L. Malry   lic. 12-17-1815
Kirkham, Henry - Stacy Stephens   1-10-1813
Kishline(?), Peter - Nancy Frakes   lic. 9-11-1813

Lane, Edward - Caty Standage   1-15-1815
Lane, John - Charity Standage   3-16-1817
Lang (or Long), James - Sarah Armstrong   8-19-1813
Lashbrook, John - Hetty Hopkins   lic. 6-22-1814
Lauery, David - Sally Poston   lic. 2-20-1814
Lawrence, Landon - Caty O'Banion   lic. 4- 4-1816
Lee, John - Rebekah Berkens   lic. 7-22-1814
Lee, John - Delfa Scott   lic. 2-10-1815
Legesaw, Lewis - Charity Lee   lic. 5-14-1813
Lemey, Nathan - Jenny Jones   lic. 8-20-1814
Lesley, Levi - Sarah Windle   lic. 8-16-1817
Lewis, Thomas - Betsey Tibbs   1-18-1815
Light, Abner - Elizabeth Burkett   lic. 5- 8-1814
Littell, Samuel - Rachel Lang   10- 5-1816
Long, Anderson - Elizabeth Richardson
                               lic. 4- 5-1813
Long, Thomas - Anna Allison   7- 4-1816
Long, Thomas - Sarah Peters   lic. 8-17-1816
Long, see also Lang
Lopp, Jacob - Mary Conrad   lic. 9- 4-1817
Lovell, Rubun - Elizabeth Bradberry   lic. 4-23-1814
Luther, George - Sarah Downs   9- 4-1817

McBee, John - Hannah Evilsizer   6- 5-1817
McAdams, Samuel - Eliza Nottingim   5-25-1810
McCarty, William - Elizabeth Willson   5- 1-1817
McClelan, Marstin - Roda Buckhanan,   8-19-1813
    by consent of Alex Bohanan

McCown, Rezin - Elizabeth Pifer   6-20-1811
McCoy, George - Lydia Wolf   10-26-1813
McCullum, James - Abigail Sharp   lic. 3- 3-1817
McCune, Andrew Jr. - Sarah Perkins,
    widow   9- 9-1815
McFall, Barnebas - Rebekah Royes   7-29-1813
McFarling, Robert - Betsey Bullington
                               lic. 2-24-1813
McGaughey, Arthur - Sally Bell   lic. 12-25-1811
McGee, James C. - Margarate Thompson
                               lic. 8-31-1816
McGee, John - Edna Fields   lic. 4- 2-1815
McGee, Samuel - Catharine Hardin   lic. 8- 9-1816
McGee, Washington - Sally Harrison   7-12-1815
McIntire, John - Margaret Brown, widow
                               lic. 7- 1-1812
McIntosh, George - Elizabeth Boone   lic. 7-27-1811
McKabe, John - Nancy Branham   lic. 3-26-1814
McKee, James - Patsey Logston   11-23-1815
McKelroy, James - Barbery Friedley   11-11-1813
McKintosh, William - Jane Boone   lic. 12-29-1810
McMahan, John - Patsy McMahan,
    widow of Richard   6- 7-1813
McMannas, Thomas - Sally Peters   8-12-1813
McVey, James - Sarah Linley   10- 1-1811

Macune, William - Susan Pipher   9-18-1814
Manwaring(?), James H. - Elizabeth Branham
                               7-18-1817
Mars, John - Mary Reams   lic. 12-20-1813
Martin, John - Polly Evans,
    widow of David   lic. 4-12-1810
Maxedon, Robert - Mary Pearson   lic. 1-22-1816
May, William - Pheba Vanwinkle   1-11-1816
Mefford, John - Susan Byrn   5- 9-1815
Melton, David - Catherine Pfrimer   11- 4-1810
Melton, James - Mary Kendall   lic. 6- 7-1812
Melton, Jesse - Sally Keller   lic. 2- 2-1812
Mickleberry, George - Elizabeth Sellers   2-19-1815
Miller, Andrew - Nancy Garrison, widow   7-17-1817
Miller, Jacob - Elizabeth Liston   9-12-1811
Miller, Jacob - Anna Willcoxon   12-20-1812
Miller, John J. - Elizabeth Hurst,
    daughter of Henry   lic. 10- 6-1815
Miller, Martin - Elizabeth Hoebach   lic. 11-22-1816
Miller, Samuel - Nancy Miller   lic. 11- 7-1813
Miller, Valentine - Elizabeth Coprass   3-12-1816
Mills, Joseph - Nancy Owens   lic. 10-15-1814
Mitchel, James - Nancy Burton   lic. 10-12-1816
Mitchel, Robert - Juda Goldsmith   8- 9-1816
Moore, Edward - Abigal Reede   7-16-1812
Moore, James B. - Luran Smith   12-31-1815
Morgan, Ebenezer E. - Lucretia Stroud   1-27-1814
Morgan, John - Mary Lehue   3-10-1816
Morrice, Maurice - Rebecca Wilcox   lic. 12-20-1811
Moser, Frederick - Elizabeth Smith   11-30-1815
Moser, John - Elizabeth Kepley   8-11-1814
Mulky, James - Elizabeth Wyman   8-25-1814
Mundle, Andrew - Rachel McKauen   lic. 6-18-1816
Murphy, Daniel - Polly Henton,
    daughter of George   9-10-1812

Nance, Clement - Patsy Chamberlain   6- 7-1810
Nance, James R. - Polly McNary   lic. 6- 5-1815
Nash, William - Sary Cromell   7-17-1813

Neal, Samuel - Keziah Hup   lic. 8-24-1815
Newman, Caleb - Patsy Handcock,
    daughter of Vachel Handcock   2- 8-1809

Oatman, George - Rachel Baird   lic. 5-14-1811
O'Banion, James - Mary Waller   lic. 4-13-1816
Osborn, Philip - Jane Bodine   lic. 1-23-1816
Osbourn, Samuel - Liddy Maxwell   lic. 12-17-1816

Paddacks, John - Sarah Ewing   lic. 3-20-1816
Pagget, William - Mary Smith   lic. 6- 7-1811
Parker, Mathew - Teny Holmington   9- 9-1814
Patin, Lewis - Nancy Batman   1- 6-1815
Pavy, Samuel - Barbery Bolan   8-13-1812
Payne, James - Judith Hurst,
    daughter of William   lic. 12-29-1814
Payne, John - Jane Lerton   3-30-1817
Pennington, Zack - Lettice Morgan   lic. 8-20-1817
Pfrimmer, Samuel - Rebeckah Wright   4-16-1815
Phillips, Aron - Mary Ann Clark   2- 3-1816
Pierce, John - Lorana Smith   7-26-1812
Pile, James - Nancy Reede,
    daughter of James Reede   lic. 8-12-1813
Pitman, John - Susannah Oatman   3- 9-1817
Pittman, John - Christiana Oatman   lic. 8-27-1814
Pittman, Lawrence - Caty Lopp   8- 8-1813
Pollard, Jesse - Polly Linch   lic. 1- 4-1815
Poole, John - Eleanor Perkins Thornton
                                        lic. 7- 6-1816
Pope, George F. - Susan Fates   5- 5-1811
Popham, James - Mary Davidson   1-26-1816
Porter, Joseph - Leddy Swinny   lic. 9-23-1812
Potter, William - Elizabeth Funk   7-15-1812
Potts, David - Elizabeth Rogers   2- 4-1816
Purcell, Henry - Caty McCune   4-30-1812
Purcell, M. - Peggy Nighton   lic. 1-22-1814
Purdue, Uriah - Sarah Byrn   10- 8-1815

Ram, David - Phebe Mansee(?)   8- 6-1812
Ransdall, Edward - Susannah Sampson   4-18-1813
Rawlins, James - Jane Sharp   lic. 3-19-1816
Redis, John - Polly Pifer(?)   8-17-1815
Reede, Caleb - Prudence Kirkham(?)   3-19-1812
Renard, John - Sarah Wilkins   11-24-1816
Rice, Abraham - Sarah Gwartney   3- 6-1817
Rice, Martin - Catherine Evans   lic. 1-22-1811
Rickham(?), Mikeal - Nancy Pearson   2-18-1816
Riney, Joseph - Margaret Willard   10-20-1816
Roades, Michael - Sarah Crable   12-10-1815
Roads, William - Elizabeth Riley   lic. 12-27-1814
Robertson, George - Frances Westfall   lic. 1-18-1814
Robinson, Benjamin - Sarah Bell   9-30-1816
Robinson, Bolden - Sally Phillips   lic. 6- 4-1811
Roden, James - Nancy Long,
    daughter of John   8-26-1813
Roden, James - Elizabeth Lashbrooks   lic. 5-30-1814
Roe, Stephen - Susanah Wood   12-29-1816
Ross, James - Delilah Ashcraft   lic. 12-19-1814

Saffer, James - Mary Rogers   lic. 11- 5-1813
Sampson, John - Betsy Brightman   lic. 2- 6-1811
Sampson, Wyatt - Sarah Tabler   12-30-1813
Samuels, Robert - Jane Gilmore   11-28-1813
Samuels, William - Jane Martin   11-29-1816
Sands, James - Nancy King   10- 8-1817

Sapinfield, Mathew - Elizabeth Foutz   12-24-1816
Savage, Chapnes - Catherine Stroud   lic. 10-10-1810
Schepple, Henry S. - Mary Smith   6-12-1810
Scot, Martin - Elizabeth Samuels   lic. 12-23-1813
Scott, William - Sophia Fields   lic. 12-15-1813
Scott, Willson - Dorinda Sharp   lic. 11-23-1815
Seselove, John - Christina Kepley   lic. 10- 7-1817
Shackleford, John - Elizabeth Brisco   lic. 10-13-1813
Shacklet, Jesse - Sally Dotson   6-15-1811
Shaver, Peter - Hanah Grey   3-28-1812
Shaw, William - Mary Webb   lic. 1-18-1810
Shepherd, John - Mary Roden   lic. 6-30-1814
Shepherd, John - Caroline Nichleson   1-16-1817
Shields, William - Betsy Logan   2-23-1813
Shuck, Christopher - Susanna Zenor   12- 5-1813
Shurley, Henry - Catharine Wiman   lic. 12-19-1812
Simmons, John - Elizabeth Coonrod   lic. 6-25-1812
Skeene, John - Rebecca Walker   4-20-1812
Slaughter, James B. - Delilah Spencer   1-16-1814
Smith, Abraham - Sally Berry   lic. 11- 8-1815
Smith, James - Sally Long,
    daughter of James   7- 2-1812
Smith, John - Jane Long,
    daughter of James   12-10-1810
Smith, John - Nancy Spencer   10- 8-1815
Smith, John - Nancy Flemon(?)   6-10-1817
Smith, Moses - Fanny Lardiss   lic. 5-25-1814
Smith, Nathan - Polly Weathers   9-11-1814
Smith, Samuel - Margaret Buckhanan   lic. 8-20-1811
Smith, Thomas - Catharine Wiggins   lic. 1- 6-1816
Smith, William - Sarah Hupp   lic. 2-27-1811
Smith, William - Elizabeth Friedley   lic. 10-28-1815
Smoot, Alexander - Kitty Erickson   lic. 4-12-1813
Snell, John - Barbery Ruth   2-21-1813
Snelling, John Berryman - Hannah Bohall
                                        lic. 12-14-1814
Snider, George - Cathy Bierly   3- 2-1812
Sparks, Westley - Anne Mitchel   lic. 9-14-1816
Speaks, Aquilla - Jane Boston   lic. 5-29-1816
Spencer, Elisha - Nancy Hupp   lic. 8-18-1811
Spencer, James(?) - Polly Hupp   lic. 3-22-1812
Spencer, Major - Polly Robins   lic. 7-26-1815
Spurgin, Joseph - Elizabeth Brenneman
                                        lic. 7- 7-1812
Stalkup, Henry - Juda French   lic. 3- 2-1813
Stalkupp, Isaac - Polly Craig   lic. 9-18-1816
Standage, William - Neoma Stilwell   lic. 8- 2-1815
Stanley, Robert - Delfa Boston   7- 7-1812
Starr, John - Nelly Padget   lic. 2-16-1817
Steale, Stephen P. - Susan McCarty   8-17-1814
Stephens, Benjamin - Nancy Arnold   2-16-1811
Stephens, James - Sally Bruice   lic. 10-27-1812
Stephens, William - Louisa Bell   lic. 2-18-1813
Stevens, Benjamin - Susanah (or Sarah) Hughs
                                             10-11-1816
Stevenson, James - Elizabeth Uts   lic. 9-23-1816
Stevins, John - Abigal Stevins   10-17-1816
Stewart, John - Sarah Guffey   lic. 12-24-1810
Stewart, Robert R. - Matty Beard   lic. 10-26-1813
Stilwell, Henry - Sarah Simons   9-15-1816
Stonesipher, John - Betsey Young, widow   11-18-1813
Stovall, Bartholomew - Mary Mcak,
    daughter of Sylvester Mcak   10- 4-1810
Stroud, Abourn - Susannah Goldman   7-18-1817
Stroud, Isom - Sarah McCrany   lic. 8-24-1811

Stroud, Joseph - Polly Kelly		5-15-1810
Sturgeon, Nathan - Mary Combs	lic.	3-21-1817
Tadlock, Alexander - Polly Bullington		6-16-1816
Tadlock, Jeremiah - Sarah Suddath	lic.	2-20-1817
Tatman, Nathan - Sarah Reams	lic.	1- 8-1814
Tibbs, John - Elizabeth Harrington	lic.	7-22-1816
Todd, William - Nancy Stucker,		
daughter of Phillip		6- 3-1813
Toops, Henry - Elizabeth Tabler		12-12-1814
Townsend, Silas - Hanna Voiles	lic.	4- 1-1813
Tuell, Elijah - Bridget Zenor, widow	lic.	1- 2-1815
Tuell, Elijah L. - Ann Stephens	lic.	1- 6-1816
Tuell, John - Elizabeth Mchu (?)	lic.	7-24-1810
Vanasdall, Jacob - Elizabeth Infield		5- 9-1816
Vanasdall, Simeon - Nancy Walker	lic.	9-21-1814
Veatch (Veach), Elijah - Sarah Danner		12-24-1816
Veatch, Nathan Jr. - Betsey Fane Evans		12-21-1815
Veneret, William - Aggy Mitcham	lic.	2-25-1815
Vert, Samuel - Jane Boston	lic.	7- 5-1813
Voiles, Moses - Ruth Townsend		5-26-1812
Waller, Thomas C. - Jane McNary	lic.	6- 5-1815
Waltz, Henry - Elizabeth Russel		5- 7-1812
Warnell, Nolley - Margaret Dills		9-29-1817
Watson, James - Margaret Kennedy,		
daughter of William Kennedy		3-22-1810
Watson, James B. - Polly Long		12-19-1816
Watson, John - Pheribe Pope		11-21-1816
Watson, Nathan - Caty Bugher, widow	lic.	3-25-1815
Watson, Perigo - Nancy Brown	lic.	4- 4-1815
Watson, William - Rachel Jones		7-10-1817

Weaks, Joseph - Lydia Herrell	lic.	8-26-1812
Weedman, (?) Nicholas - Elizabeth Charley		
	lic.	9-21-1815
Westfall, Daniel - Nelly Popham	lic.	5-26-1814
Westfall, Samuel - Elizabeth Robinson		9-22-1814
Wheeler, John - Cath. Zenor, widow of George		
Zenor, daughter of David Tanner (?)		2- 6-1810
White, George - Margaret Davidson		3- 5-1812
White, Richard - Barbery Barnum		12-11-1814
Williams, John - Molly Combs	lic.	8- 4-1810
Williams, Thomas - Hannah Byrn		3-13-1817
Willson, Jesse - Katy Vandier	lic.	2-29-1812
Willson, Joseph - Margarete Armstrong		7-25-1815
Wilton, John - Sarah Davis	lic.	4- 1-1813
Winager, Samuel - Nancy Young	lic.	1-24-1817
Wingate, Henry - Sarah Brown		4-15-1817
Wise, Coonrod - Elizabeth Mitchell		7-12-1812
Wise, John - Rebecca Morgan	lic.	1-15-1817
Wolf, Samuel - Elizabeth Bufford	lic.	5-12-1815
Worlan, Peter - Pheba Coprass		9-25-1815
Wright, Eli - Christina Pfrimmer	lic.	9- 5-1816
Wright, Jonathan - Elizabeth Kirkham		6- 7-1812
Wright, Joseph - Sally Allen		10-20-1814
Wright, Peter - Rachel Wood		3-26-1812
Wright, Ruben - Elizabeth Randall	lic.	3-22-1811
Wright, Thomas - Anne Light		1- 9-1814
Yanawine, Jacob - Charity Sizelove		5-18-1817
Yandle, Jesse - Sarah Purcell		4-16-1816
Zenor, John - Mary McIntosh,		
daughter of Peter		1- 1-1815

WILSON BIBLE RECORD

Copied by Mrs. Alfred L. Moudy, Indianapolis, from a Bible purchased in 1872 at Richmond, Indiana. The Bible was found in an antique shop on East Washington Street in Indianapolis; the names Mr. & Mrs. Perry H. Wilson appear on the cover.

MARRIAGES

Perry H. Wilson to Miriam Martha Ream — 11-9-1869.
Guy S. Wilson to Ella Mary Bagley — 10-14-1903.
Perry H. Wilson to Margaret S. Baird — 2-1-1905.
Norton H. Wilson to Ina Autumn Travis — 8-23-1911.

BIRTHS

Perry H. Wilson, b. near Milton, Wayne Co., Ind. —
   9-21-1846.
Miriam M. Ream, b. Dublin, Wayne Co. — 5-8-1850.
Guy S. Wilson, son of Perry and Miriam Wilson, b.
   Dublin — 8-21-1879.
Norton H. Wilson, son of Perry and Miriam, b. Dublin,
   4-27-1890.

Margaret S. Baird, b. Dublin, 9-1-1852.
Ella M. Bagley, b. Fayette Co., Ind. — 6-16-1880.
Ina Autumn Travis, b. Indianapolis — 8-23-1895.
Ruth M. Wilson, dt. of Guy and Ella Wilson, b. Dublin
   — 7-4-1906.

DEATHS

Miriam Martha Wilson, wife of Perry H., d. at her home
   in Dublin — 9-28-1903.
Perry H. Wilson d. at his home in Dublin — 7-31-1926.
Ella M. Wilson, wife of Guy S. Wilson d. at her home in
   Phoenix, Ariz. — 6-4-1915.
Guy S. Wilson d. at South Bend, Ind. — 5-31-1924.

INDIANANS AND DIRECT INDIANA DESCENDANTS IN THE PANHANDLE OF TEXAS, 1880

This compilation is drawn from Ernest R. Archambeau, "The First Federal Census in the Panhandle, 1880," *Panhandle-Plains Historical Review*, XXIII, 1950, 23-132.

Out of a total population of 1613 recorded for the Panhandle of Texas in 1880, 60 persons were either born in Indiana or were of parents one or both of whom had been born in Indiana. The map of the Panhandle shows the counties in which they were living in 1880. The large number of persons in Wheeler County is partially attributable to the existence of Fort Elliott, the first military post to secure the Panhandle from further Indian troubles. Seventeen of the twenty-five persons credited to Wheeler County were associated with Fort Elliott. Settlements in the Panhandle were very young as the problems with the Indians had been solved less than five years before.

Texas Panhandle residents in 1880 who were born in Indiana:

Name	County	Color	Sex	Age	Marital Status	Occupation	Self	Father	Mother
							Place of Birth		
Brewer, William A.	Donley	W	M	26	S	Printer	Ind.	Ind.	Ind.
Caldwell, James	Wheeler	W	M	22	S	Soldier	Ind.	—	—
Clampett, B. F.	Wheeler	W	M	30	M	Livery Stable keeper	Ind.	—	—
Clampett, J. J.	Wheeler	W	F	29	M	Keeping house	Ind.	N.C.	Tenn.
Dill, Daniel	Hutchinson	W	M	23	S	—	Ind.	—	—
Fisher, Margaret	Wheeler	W	F	25	M	Keeping house	Ind.	Ire.	Ire.
George, David	Wheeler	W	M	34	S	Soldier	Ind.	—	—
Gibson, F. H.	Wheeler	W	M	22	S	Soldier	Ind.	Ind.	Ind.
Green, C. T.	Ochiltree	W	M	19	S	Herder	Ind.	N.Y.	N.Y.
Green, Otis	Hemphill	W	M	21	—	Herder	Ind.	—	—
Grimes, Gillead S.	Gray	W	M	28	S	Carpenter	Ind.	Md.	Ohio
Hama, S. C.	Lipscomb	W	M	29	S	Herder	Ind.	Ind.	Ind.
Hill, H. M.	Childress	W	M	28	S	Herding cattle	Ind.	Pa.	Canada
McFadden, S. C.	Wheeler	W	M	24	S	Soldier	Ind.	Ohio	Ohio
Mitchell, Frank	Armstrong	W	M	21	S	Herding cattle	Ind.	Ohio	Vt.
Murphy, Charles	Wheeler	W	M	19	S	Laborer	Ind.	Ind.	Ind.
Rainey, H.	Ochiltree	W	M	24	S	Herder	Ind.	Ind.	Ind.
Reinhardt, G. W.	Wheeler	W	M	26	S	Teamster	Ind.	Scot.	N.C.
Shoup, James S.	Donley	W	M	22	S	Farmer	Ind.	Pa.	Ind.
Smith, G. M.	Wheeler	W	M	31	S	Clerk in store	Ind.	—	Ohio
Stewart, Francis	Roberts	W	M	48	S	Raising cattle	Ind.	Ky.	Ky.
Weind, Charles E.	Wheeler	W	M	19	S	Cook	Ind.	Pa.	Ind.
Williamson, Martial P.	Donley	W	M	27	M	Teamster	Ind.	W. Va.	W. Va.
Woods, Ellen	Wheeler	W	F	53	M	Keeping house	Ind.	—	—
Woods, Samuel	Wheeler	W	M	52	M	Farmer	Ind.	Tenn.	Tenn.
Wright, Mattie M.	Donley	W	F	17	S	At home	Ind.	Ohio	Ind.
Wright, Susah H.	Donley	W	F	40	M	Keeping house	Ind.	Ky.	Mo.
Young, L.	Lipscomb	W	F	34	M	Keeping house	Ind.	Ky.	Ind.
Young, W. A.	Lipscomb	W	M	37	M	Stone mason	Ind.	Ohio	Ky.

Texas Panhandle Residents in 1880 who were born outside Indiana of Indiana-born parentage:

Name	County	Color	Sex	Age	Marital Status	Occupation	Self	Father	Mother
Anderson, M. M.	Hemphill	W	F	39	M	Keeping house	Mo.	Ind.	Ind.
Campbell, James M.	Armstrong	W	M	23	S	Herding cattle	N.C.	Ind.	Ind.
Clampett, H. C.	Wheeler	W	M	4	S	—	Tex.	Ind.	Ind.
Clampett, Loula	Wheeler	W	F	2	S	—	Tex.	Ind.	Ind.
Day, D. F.	Lipscomb	W	F	28	M	Keeping house	Tex.	Ind.	Ind.
Day, J. T.	Lipscomb	W	M	1	S	—	Tex.	Tex.	Ind.
Esterbrooks, Capitola	Wheeler	W	F	3	S	—	Tex.	Ind.	Minn.
Fisher, Emily M.	Wheeler	W	F	5	S	—	Kan.	N.Y.	Ind.
Fisher, Henry M.	Wheeler	W	M	6 mo.	S	—	Tex.	N.Y.	Ind.
Fisher, Lenora	Wheeler	W	F	3	S	—	Tex.	N.Y.	Ind.
Leforce, Isaac	Armstrong	W	M	22	S	Laborer	Ark.	Ind.	Tenn.
Lewis, H. A.	Wheeler	W	M	31	S	Attorney	Ky.	Ind.	Va.
McKenzie, A. F.	Hemphill	W	M	21	S	Teaching school	Ill.	Ind.	Ind.

62

Name	County	Color	Sex	Age	Marital Status	Occupation	Place of Birth Self	Father	Mother
Miller, J. W.	Hemphill	W	M	22	S	Herder	Tex.	Ind.	Ind.
Morgan, John B.	Lipscomb	W	M	6 mo.	S	–	Ill.	Ind.	Ky.
Palmer, S. P.	Wheeler	W	F	37	M	Keeping house	Ill.	Mo.	Ind.
Parks, Vasha W.	Donley	W	F	31	M	Keeping house	Ill.	Ind.	Ohio
Patton, F. M.	Wheeler	W	M	39	M	Freighter	Ill.	Mo.	Ind.
Reed, Samuel P.	Donley	W	M	26	M	Farmer	Ill.	Ky.	Ind.
Woods, Abe	Wheeler	W	M	14	S	–	Col.	Ind.	Ind.
Woods, John	Wheeler	W	M	25	M	Farmer	Ark.	Ind.	Ind.
Woods, Lucy	Wheeler	W	F	13	S	–	Mo.	Ind.	Ind.
Woods, Samuel, Jr.	Wheeler	W	M	9	S	–	Col.	Ind.	Ind.
Wright, Julia E.	Donley	W	F	14	S	At home	Ill.	Ohio	Ind.
Wright, Martial L.	Donley	W	M	6	S	In school	Ill.	Ohio	Ind.
Wright, Mary L.	Donley	W	F	10	S	In school	Ill.	Ohio	Ind.
Wright, Maud H.	Donley	W	F	3	S	–	Ill.	Ohio	Ind.
Wright, Pearl R.	Donley	W	F	8 mo.	S	–	Tex.	Ohio	Ind.
Young, C.	Lipscomb	W	M	12	S	At home	Kan.	Ind.	Iowa
Young, G.	Lipscomb	W	M	11	S	At home	Kan.	Ind.	Iowa
Young, R.	Lipscomb	W	M	6	S	At home	Col.	Ind.	Iowa

INSCRIPTIONS FROM PROTESTANT GERMAN CEMETERY, VANDERBURGH COUNTY

Contributed by David Becker, Evansville. The cemetery is located at the intersection of Highway 65 and the turnoff to the town of St. Joseph in German Township.

Elisabeth C. Bank
21 Mai 1868 - 14 Juni 1909

Mutter Philippina Hahn
9 Juni 1849 - 28 Nov 1935
Vater Friedrich Hahn
3 Marz 1836 - 14 Marz 1910

Johann Konrad Cramer - Vater
17 Juli 1845 - 29 Marz 1910
Margaretha Cramer geb. Gobel-Mutter
16 Okt 1847 - 19 June 1923

Bena G. wife of H. Wehmer
1. 24, 1886 - 5. 27, 1916

Fred Cramer
Sept. 11, 1847 - June 1, 1922
Katherine his wife
March 27, 1854 - 8 Dec 1926

Christina Gattin von Ludwig Happe
18 Nov 1836 - 21 Marz 1909

Friederike L. Umbach
15 Dec 1834 - 26 Sept 1905
Georg F. Umbach
24 Mai 1824 - 8 Feb 1907

Magdalene Gattin von Jacob Pfettscher
geb. Muller
July 21, 1821 / July 19, 1903

Friedrich Cramer
Geb 24 Feb 1815 in Schnabelweid, Baiern - gest. 12 Jan 1892

? wife of F. Kramer
9 Aug 1811 - 3 June 1871

Johann Koffher
1 Sept 1846 in Linsenhofen, Wurtenberg - 28 Oct 1880

Henriette Gattin von Carl Strube
15 Nov 1805 - 17 Dec 1886
(the place of birth was on the stone but unreadable)

Karl Strube
10 Oct 1805 (the date of death is not readable)

Georg Bernhard sohn von Fr. und ? Umbach
2 Aug 1856 - 20 Dec 1881

Fredinant Sohn von Fr u Frke Umbach
21 Feb 1861 - 18 Jan 1882

Johan Adam Schlessler
15 Juni 1856 - 7 Sept 1857

Hier Ruht Carolina Gattin von Franz Hahn
geboren 1811 - gestorben 25 Nov 1864

Johannes Hoffherr
30 July 1812 - 24 Dec 1892
Friedarika Beh Gattin von J.H.
16 Juni 1827 - 6 Jan 1913

Franz Hahn
Gestorben 16 Jan 1859
58 Jahren 10 Monaten und 24 Tagen

Johne H. son of h & B Wehmer
23 Oct 1915 - 15 May 1916
Edward C. Sohn von Johann u Augusta Hoffherr Jr.
1 Sept 1877 - 30 Aug 1878

Sadie Fetscher
21 Oct 1893 - 1 Jan 1894

Johanna K. Hahn
18 Juli 1872 - 28 Oct 1877

Christine K. Hahn
27 Aug 1876 - 7 Dec 1877

Johann Hahn
11 Oct 1880 - 6 Jan 1881

Edward Hahn (no dates)

Christian Bredenkamp
18 June 1809 - 28 Oct 1859

Katharine C. Cramer
8 Nov 1876 - 16 March 1878

Veda Mae Reynolds - Daughter
27 May 1934 - 10 Aug 1940

Maria Toch. von Heinrich u H. Bank
17 Oct 1867 - 16 Oct 1874

Ludwig Sauer
geb zu Beittenfeldt, Wurttemberg 9 Aug 1815
    gest 8 Dez 1887

Karolina Sauer
6 October 1852 - 16 February 1859

Johann Jacob Bauer
18 Sept 1802 - 1 Dez 1858

Carolina Gattin von Gottleb Duerst
13 June 1799 - 1 Sept 1858

SCHOOL ENUMERATION, HARRISON TOWNSHIP, HENRY COUNTY, 1919

This is a later record than any that has heretofore been published in the *Hoosier Genealogist*, and is included because it shows the type of information available in school enumeration records, and because it supplements birth records that are often incomplete. The present document was created under the act of 1865 which required that such an enumeration be taken by township trustees each year between April 10 and 30. All unmarried persons between the ages of six and twenty-one were to be included, giving date and place of birth, even though some of the older ones were no longer in school. The names of parents, guardians, or persons having charge of the children were to be recorded, and, in addition, the person giving the information was required to certify under oath to the correctness of the same (this last requirement being an amendment of the original law). Usually the person signing was the one listed as parent, guardian, or person having charge of the children, but sometimes it was another member of the family. Proof of birth as furnished in school records is accepted by the Social Security Offices. The original record reproduced here is in the Indiana Historical Society Library.

CORRECTIONS: The Henry County School Enumeration, Harrison Township, for the year 1919, published in the March 1974 issue of the *Hoosier Genealogist*, is an enumeration for Greensboro Township instead of Harrison according to Mr. Richard P. Ratcliff of the Henry County Historical Society. He states that all the people listed were residents of Greensboro Township. The original record from which the enumeration was taken stated it was for Harrison Township and we failed to check further.

Name of parent, guard-ian, head of family, or person in charge of children	Names of children	Year and place of birth		Correctness of informa-tion sworn to
Adams, J. Q.	Thelma	7-16-1904	Howard Co.	John Q. Adams
	Mildred	4-11-1907	" "	
Addison, Geo.	Mary	6-18-1902	Henry Co.	Dora L. Addison
	Edward M.	12-22-1903	" "	
Addison, Geo. W.	Myrtle L.	4-22-1906	" "	
Anderson, Lewis	Veva	2- 8-1901	" "	Muriel Anderson
Archey, Charley	Helen	10- 2-1902	" "	Ella Archey
	Oakley	6- 6-1904	Rush Co.	
	Louis[e]	9-19-1908	Henry Co.	
	Wilber	11-30-1906	" "	
Bailey, Aulbert (?)	Hubert	7-15-1909	" "	Hattie Bailey
Bales, Clara	Chloea	1- 8-1912	" "	Clara Bales
	Inez	3-17-1904	" "	
Ballenger, Ora	Chas Hilton	7- 3-1910	" "	Ora Ballenger
Barrett, Glen	Edith	7-20-1910	" "	
Bassett, James	Syras Colter	1- 8-1910	Hamilton Co.	Mary Bassett
Bean, Nora	Mable	9- 3-1903	Henry Co.	Nora Bean
	Carrie	8-15-1905	" "	
	Ralph	11-13-1906	" "	
Beeson, Gus	Ruth	10- 7-[1905]	" "	Addie Beeson
Bickel, Merl, see Judge, Len				
Bicknell, Orlie	Martha	4-10-[1904]	" "	Jessie Bicknell
	Morris	6-30-[1906]	" "	
Bolen, Obe	Homer	7-30-1901	" "	Obe Bolen
	Parvin	4-12-1904	Hancock Co.	
	Gunivere	6- 2-1909	" "	
	Jenivere	6- 2-1909	" "	
Boman, H. W.	Walter	2-11-1910	Henry Co.	H. W. Bowman
Bowman, Ray	George	1- 5-1902	" "	Florence Bowman
	Horace	9-28-1903	" "	
	Russel	3-31-1909	" "	
Burris, Mina, see Hoosier, Bryant				
Bussell, Stella	Delmar Hodshire	11-14-[1910]	Allen Co.	Stella Bussell
Byers, Samuel	Boyd Cullum	5-30-[1907]	Ohio	Samuel Byers
Byers, Walter M.	Lois	2-21-1910	Hancock Co.	Viola O. Byers
Carmichael, E. A.	Donald	8-17-1900	Henry Co.	Lottie Carmichael
	Dorothy	2-19-1906	" "	
Carmichael, Rollie	Carl	12-30-1900	" "	
	Ruby	5-17-1903	" "	
Casey, Charley	Gilbert	6-25-1902	" "	
	Rowena	2-13-1909	" "	
Casey, David	Howard	8-29-1905	" "	David Casey
	Horace	7- 2-1900	" "	
Casey, Emery	Wayman	4- 9-1901	" "	
	Ralph	12-22-1908	" "	
	Max	10-14-1912	" "	
Chew, Martha	Gerald	6-30-1901	" "	in Army
	Garnet	3- 7-[1904]	" "	Martha Chew

Chew, Mary J.	Ethel M.	8- 9-1905	Minnesota	Mary J. Chew
Cleek, Alice	Warner	5- 9-1902	Delaware Co.	Alice Cleek
	Howard	7-24-1903	Blackford Co.	
	Arlen	11-24-1906	" "	
	Blanche	6- 8-1910	Henry Co.	
	Paul	10-18-1912	" "	
Collins, Chas.	Mary Ada	8- 3-1904	" "	
Collins, Elmer	Franklin	12-23-1911	Rush Co.	
Collins, Frank	Donald	7-13-[1905]	Henry Co.	Bertha Collins
Collins, Milton	Howard Haden	7-28-1907	Madison Co.	Sadie Collins
Collins, Ollie	Grace	12- 2-1902	Henry Co.	Ethel Collins
	Horace	11-11-1908	" "	
Colter, Syras, <u>see</u> Bassett, James				
Comer, Chas.	Wm. Shipley	9- 8-1909	Hancock Co.	Eliza Comer
Cook, Chas. L.	Russell	4-17-1900	Henry Co.	Chas. L. Cook
	Joseph	11-26-1907	" "	
	Cameron Edward	11- 7-[1903]	" "	
Cook, Jackson	Wade	8-11-1900	" "	A. J. Cook
	Hortence	1-31-1902	" "	
	Reva	10-19-1905	" "	
	Dewey	5-13-1898	" "	
Coon, Lafe	Ruth	2-22-[1906]	" "	Minta Coon
	Robert	5- 8-[1908]	" "	
	Ines	9-18-[1910]	" "	
Coon, Lawrence	Dale	2- 4-1911 ·	" "	
Copeland, Glen	Elizabeth J.	4-22-1903	" "	Effa Copeland
Copeland, Herman	Carrol	4-18-1911	" "	Crystal Copeland
	Forest	7-21-1912	" "	
Copeland, Mearl	Vaughn Miller	10-10-[1911]	" "	Hattie Ford
Cox, John	Geo. McGrady	5-20-1899	" "	working on farm
Craig, Arlie	Gerald	8-27-1900	" "	
	Mildred	1-12-1904	" "	
	Gladys	2-16-1907	" "	
Craig, Charles	Clyde	5-15-1903	" "	Emma Craig
	Grace F.	3-10-1905	" "	
	Clifton	11- 4-1906	" "	
Craig, Jake	Ralph	4- 5-1900	" "	Jacob Craig
Craig, Mary	Velva Ratcliff	7- 2-1899	" "	employed
Cronk, Walter	Paul	1-10-1903	" "	
	Daisy	11-23-1904	" "	
Currey, Florence	Lucy	10-20-1910	Madison Co.	Florence Currey
	Fred	2- - 1903	Tipton Co.	
	Frank	6- 1-1900	" "	
Daniels, May	Wells	12- 3-1906	[blank]	
Darling, Claude	Wilber	1-13-1911	Henry Co.	Claude Darling
Darling, Frank	Paul	1-26-1912	" "	Frank Darling
Darling, Onedia	Ruth	3- 1-1899	" "	Onedia Darling
	Mary	3-24-1901	" "	
	Fay	3- 7-[1905]	" "	
	Floyd	8- 1-1908	" "	
Darling, Quincy	Murray	3-18-1905	" "	Quincy Darling
Davis, Arthur	Mildred	12- 5-1908	" "	Arthur Davis
Dean, William	Doris	9-17-1902	" "	
	Walter	5-14-1907	[blank]	

Dean, William	Evalin	9-14-1910	Hancock Co.	William Dean
Delon, Geo. W.	James W.	9-23-1912	Henry Co.	Nellie Delon
De Rome, Malene	Dale	8-16-[1909]	" "	Malene De Rome
	Alice	5-25-[1910]	" "	
	James	3-25-[1912]	" "	
Dishman, W. H.	Lloyd	6-29-1908	" "	Wm. H. Dishman
	Evelyn	12- 9-1912	" "	
Drysdale, John	Glen	4- 7-1900	Rush Co.	John Drysdale
Dudley, Jackson	Myrtle	7-26-1898	Henry Co.	Jackson Dudley
	Ethel	1- 4-1900	" "	
Dudley, Ross	Olen	9-27-1908	" "	Grace Dudley
	Donald	3-26-1911	" "	
Dudley, William	Ralph	1- 9-1902	" "	Bill Dudley
Duncan, Edna, see Garner, Walter				
Elliott, Clint	Basel Vance	11-28-1899	" "	Bertha Elliott
	Ethel May	5- 8-1910	" "	
	Paulene	2- 8-1912	" "	
Elliott, Coit	Elva Lucile	4-11-1913	Hancock Co.	Laura Elliott
Flemming, Evelyn, see Madison, Perry				
Frazier, Joseph C.	Jesse	7-29-1899	Madison Co.	Lula E. Frazier
	Ruby	3-12-1901	" "	
	Victor	3- 1-1903	" "	
	Opal	1-31-1905	" "	
	Fred	2-22-1908	" "	
	Grace	1- 1-1911	Canada	
Garner, Walter	Wilma	7- 5-1904	Henry Co.	Gertrude Garner
	Lowel	7-25-1903	Wabash Co.	Bert Boune
	Edna Duncan	1- 5-[1905]	Henry Co.	Maggie Hosier
Garret, James	Dan	7- 5-[1908]	Madison Co.	Julia Garret
	Ralph	10- 8-[1910]	Hancock Co.	
	Paul	1-31-[1913]	" "	
Garriott, Homer	Naomi	2-15-1902	Henry Co.	Homer C. Garriott
	Kenneth	3- 9-1905	" "	
George, Irb	Pauline	9-11-1905	" "	Irb George
	Eugene	2- 8-1908	" "	
George, Oscar	Ruth	2- 3-1900	" "	Minnie George
	Paul	10-25-1901	" "	
	Harriott	2-28-1904	" "	
	Mildred	11- 1-1907	" "	
	Kathern	7-29-1912	" "	
Graham, O. E.	Earl	10- 5-1899	Hendricks Co.	Balta Graham
	Ruth	8- 9-1903	" "	
	Ollie	4-11-1907	" "	
Groves, Maxine, see Kern, Herbert				
Hardin, John	Charles	3- 4-1909	Henry Co.	John Hardin
Harrison, Laurence	John A.	8-24-[1912]	" "	L.E. Harrison
Harter, Norman	Harriet	5-11-1900	" "	Norman M. Harter
	Horace M.	10- 5-1903	" "	
	Clara Belle	10- 4-1912	" "	
Harvey, Mike	Nellie	3- 3-1902	" "	Myrtle Harvey
	Jesse	2-11-1906	" "	

Hiatt, Ethel	Blane	2-21-[1908]	Hancock Co.	Ethel Hiatt
Hiatt, Frank	Thelma	6-11-1911	Michigan	Maude Hiatt
Hill, Adolphus	Olive	4- 4-[1906]	Henry Co.	
Hinshaw, Bert	Howard	8-12-1903	" "	R. L. Hinshaw
Hinshaw, Jesse	Robert	12-25-[1898]	" "	
Hinshaw, Russel	Vivian	12- 1-1912	" "	Russel Hinshaw
Hodshire, Delmar, see Bussell, Stella				
Hooker, Lon M.	Reba	3-20-1906	" "	Lon M. Hooker
	James R.	6-20-1908	" "	
	Martha E.	1-28-1912	" "	
Hoosier, Bryant	Mina Burris	3-26-1911	" "	Elizabeth Hosier
Hosier, Wilber	Carl Wright	6-26-1906	Grant Co.	W. J. Hosier
Hutson, Charley	Elbert	4-20-1902	Henry Co.	
Jackson, Chas.	Mable	10- 9-1904	" "	Chas. E. Jackson
Jacobs	Clarence	2-28-[1904]	" "	Louie Jacobs
	Gladis	4- 6-[1902]	" "	
	Markus	8-14-[1907]	" "	
	Nellie	6-21-[1909]	" "	
Jacoby, Murray	Loys	3-28-1915	Grant Co.	Anna Jacoby
	Lillian	1- 4-1913	" "	
	Wilfred	8-14-1910	Delaware Co.	
James, A. L.	Earl E.	4-10-1906	Henry Co.	A. L. James
James, Robert	Mary L.	8-26-[1909]	" "	Mrs. R. James
	Pauline	10-24-[1912]	" "	
Jarvis, Wile	Elva	6- 5-1907	" "	Emma Jarvis
	Kenneth	8- 3-1904	" "	
Jarvis, Will	Vernis	7-13-1904	" "	Vercie Jarvis
	Ralph	3- 6-1906	" "	
	Wilburn	3-23-1908	" "	
	Raymond	8-26-1910	" "	
Jay, Joe	Dorothy	6-22-1908	" "	Mary B. Jay
Jessup, Warren	Margaret	4-19-[1906]	" "	Warren Jessup
	Walter	9-22-[1909]	Clark Co.	
	Omer	4- 4-[1911]	" "	
Johnson, Claude	Ruth	6-26-1911	Rush Co.	Claude Johnson
	Russel	3-20-1913	Wayne Co.	
Johnson, Roe	Howard	1-17-1903	Hancock Co.	J. M. Johnson
	Jula	3-13-1911	Henry Co.	
Johnston, George	Mary	9- 6-1912	Rush Co.	George Johnston
	George	2- 8-1909	" "	
Judd, Chilton	Alfred	3-29-1912	Henry Co.	Chilton Judd
Judge, Bert	Gladys	7-23-1902	Hancock Co.	Bert Judge
	Lavon	5-20-1905	Henry Co.	
	Gerald	11- 1-1908	" "	
Judge, Len (or Lew)	Merl Bickel	age 15	Hancock Co.	employed
Judge, William	Robert	12- 1-1916	Henry Co.	Willie Judge
Keesling, Chas.	Kenneth	9- 4-1906	" "	Clara Keesling
	Elizabeth	9-14-1910	Hancock Co.	
	Gerald	3-26-1913	Madison Co.	
Kern, George	Obed	11- 1-1899	[blank]	
Kern, Herbert	Maxine Groves	8- 4-1910	Henry Co.	

Keslar, M. W.	Murray	10-14-1899	Henry Co.	M. W. Keslar
	Miriam	3- 9-1901	" "	
	Hilda	7-22-1903	" "	
Kirk, Milt	Edna Trice	4-17-1913	" "	Milt Kirk
Kirkpatrick, Walter	Thelma	4- 6-1910	" "	Walter Kirkpatrick
Koons, Clifford	George	6- 2-1912	Delaware Co.	Linnie Koons
Laremore, Frank	Ruth B.	1-29-1904	Henry Co.	Frank Larmore
Laremore, Ike	Orville	age 19	" "	
	Mearl	9-22-1901	" "	
	Claude	3- 8-[1904]	" "	
	Leonard	6- 2-1905	" "	
	Donald	age 12	" "	
	Elmer	1- 6-1908	" "	
	Eva	age 6	" "	
Laremore, Stella	Fred	3-23-1900	Madison Co.	Stella Larmore
Laremore	Elijah	4-13-[1903]	" "	Mary Larmore
	Retha	4-24-[1907]	Hancock Co.	
Leakey, Frank	Orice (?)	9-10-1901	Henry Co.	Mrs. F. M. Leakey
Leavitt, Elmer	Ralph	5-23-1903	Tipton Co.	Mrs. E. D. Leavitt
	Paul	1-15-1907	" "	
	Lester	4- 4-1909	Miami Co.	
Lee, Harrison	Marion	9-11-1908	Kansas	Mrs. Harrison Lee
Lee, Marion T.	Harrold	12-23-1898	Henry Co.	Marion T. Lee
Lockridge, Evert	Elbert	4- 3-1913	" "	Della Lockridge
Lockridge, George	Carrol	5-21-1903	" "	George Lockridge
	Herald	2-19-1909	" "	
Lockridge, Jesse	Claude	10- 3-[1899]	White Co.	Etta Lockridge
	Rollie	10- 2-[1901]	" "	
	George	5-21-[1903]	" "	
	Mary	9- 9-[1908]	" "	
Lockridge, Will	Harold	1-20-1903	Henry Co.	Wm. Lockridge
	Ines M.	6- 2-1904	" "	
	Bernetha	1-19-1911	" "	
Long, A. P.	Charles Edwn	10-31-1904	Grant Co.	A. P. Long
	Edith	10-26-1905	" "	
	Harry	9-21-1907	" "	
	Mildred	10- 1-1909	" "	
	Freda	1-31-1913	" "	
Lowe, Eva	Edith	6-13-1903	Henry Co.	Eva Lowe
	Mildred	9-10-1905	" "	
	Milford	9-10-1905	" "	
McArren, Stanley, see McGrady, Roland				
McCaslin, Claud	Agnes May	11- 5-1908	" "	Claud McCaslin
McClamner, Charles	Evert	age 11	[blank]	
	Verlin	age 10	"	
	Susie	age 8	"	
McCormac, Warner	Hallard	3- 8-1908	"	W. McCormack
	Ermall	11- 8-1911	"	
McDaniels, Joe	Roy	9-21-1899	Hancock Co.	Ida B. McDaniel
McDonald, Martin	Lillie	11- 3-[1903]	Cincinnati	Martin McDonald
	Pancy	1-17-[1907]	"	
	Raymond	5- 7-[1909]	"	
	Violet	2-14-[1912]	"	
McGrady, George, see Cox, John				

McGrady, Roland	Stanley McArren	8-17-1908	South Bend	R. V. McGrady
McGrath, John	Anna	4-10-1910	Cook Co., Ill.	Bessie McGrath
	John	10-20-[1912]	" " "	
McIlvain, Rosco	Charles	10- 6-1910	Henry Co.	Flossie McIlvain
	Harold	1- 2-1912	" "	
McKnight, Oscar	Roy	9-20-1907	Rush Co.	Oscar McKnight
	Blanche	1- 3-1909	" "	
	Hazel	4- 2-1911	" "	
McShirley, Loring	Agness	10-20-1902	Henry Co.	
	Opal	11- 5-1905	" "	
McVicker, Marie, see				
Walker, John				
Madison, Lew	Allen	1- 2-1902	" "	
Madison, Perry	Evelyn Flemming	8-28-1908	" "	Perry Madison
Maines, Paul	Lester	1-16-1908	Ohio	
	Gearold	8-26-1911	"	
Marrell, Albert	Raymond	7-29-[1907]	Rush Co.	Pearl Marrell
	Beatrice Raines	4-19-[1910]	Henry Co.	
Melson, Kale	William	6-24-1900	Madison Co.	Jennie Melson
	Ezra	6-28-1902	" "	
	Bertha	4-16-1904	Henry Co.	
	Jonas	10-18-1905	" "	
	Francis	5-21-1909	" "	
Miller, Vaughn, see				
Copeland, Mearl				
Millis, Arthur	Irven	12-24-[1900]	" "	Maud Millis
	Walter	9-14-[1902]	" "	
	Marguerite	12- 4-[1906]	" "	
	Cathern	3-21-[1913]	" "	
Modlen, Jason	Edith	8-24-1899	" "	Mary Modlen
Moulton, E. M.	Ruth	7-26-1901	Decatur Co.	E. M. Moulton
Murphy, George	Mossie	12-30-1898	Henry Co.	Myrtle Murphy
	E. Lucille	11-30-1903	" "	
	Horace A.	3- 9-1913	" "	
Muterspaugh, J. C.	Helen	3- 6-[1910]	Hancock Co.	Nancy Muterspaugh
Newby, Mort	Ward	10- 2-1901	Henry Co.	M. E. Newby
	Dale	8-26-1903	" "	
	Paul	8-30-1904	" "	
Newson, Fowel	Irene	3-22-1902	Rush Co.	
Nicely, Earnest	Doris A.	9-29-1911	Hancock Co.	Mrs. Earnest Nicel
Oalden, Ray	Robert	11-24-1910	Henry Co.	Lulu Oalden
Oaldon, Grant	Ruth	8-20-1904	" "	Laura B. Oaldon
	Glen	4- 2-1907	" "	
	Lynn	6-11-1911	" "	
Peacock, William	Emma	11-12-1904	Hancock Co.	
Peters, Clarence	Roy	6-11-1911	Henry Co.	Clarence Peters
Pierson, Chas.	Imogene	1-27-1908	" "	Chas. H. Pierson
Poe, John	Jessie	5-25-1901	" "	
	Lester	8-10-1906	" "	
Raines, Beatrice, see				
Marrell, Albert				
Ratcliff, Velva, see				
Craig, Mary				
Ratliff, Lawrence	Alleane	11-29-1910	Hancock Co.	Lawrence Ratliff

Ratliff, William	Morris	12- 1-1903	Henry Co.	Wm. Ratliff
	Edna Mae	7-29-1906	" "	
	Viola	2- 5-1912	" "	
Redick, Frank	Lois	9-24-1912	" "	Frank Redick
Reece, Ed	Gladis	10-26-1902	" "	Ed M. Reece
	Dorothy	4-28-1910	" "	
Rhoades, Belle	Reff	9-17-1898	Hamilton Co.	Belle Rhoades
	Vernon	2-20-1900	Indianapolis	
Ricks, Charley	Levi	1-11-1903	Henry Co.	C. E. Ricks
Ricks, Joe	Laura	5-13-[1902]	" "	
Riggs	Ruth	2- 3-[1905]	" "	Mrs. Peter Riggs
Riley, Marshall	Wilber	3- 9-1908	" "	Marshall A. Riley
	Mildred	11-27-1909	" "	
Roahrig, Webber	Mary	1-13-1911	Marshall Co.	Webber Roahrig
	Erdine	5-15-1909	" "	
Rood, John	Girald	12-17-1903	Henry Co.	J. H. Rood
Shipley, William, **see** Comer, Chas.				
Short, Albert	Francis	6- 4-1910	" "	Albert Short
Smith, Carl	Lloyd	2- 1-1912	" "	Carl Smith
Smith, John A.	Hallie	4-26-1900	Rush Co.	John A. Smith
	Howard	7-16-1904	Hancock Co.	
	Kenneth	12-13-1907	Henry Co.	
	Merrell	10-10-1909	" "	
	Sarah	2-14-1912	" "	
Smoot, Georgia	Mattie	3-21-1908	Kentucky	Mrs. Georgia Smoot
	Addie May	3- 2-1910	"	
	Sherman	1- 3-1913	Henry Co.	
Stafford, Chas.	Harrold	6- 6-1902	" "	Chas. A. Stafford
Stafford, Milton	Lowell	1- 3-1901	" "	Minnie Stafford
	Edith	12- 6-1903	" "	
	Ethel	12- 6-1903	" "	
Starbuck, Earl	Harry W.	12-31-1902	" "	Bertha Starbuck
Steel, Charley	Howard	6-29-1899	Madison Co.	Mrs. Chas. Steele
	Ralph	2-19-1901	" "	
	Henry	5-30-1905	" "	
	Raymond	8-18-1907	" "	
	Fred	7-26-1910	" "	
Stone	Fanny	5- 6-[1902]	Henry Co.	Pink Saul
	Hazel	6- 1-[1904]	" "	
Storch, Leona	Mary Helen	11- 4-1910	Indianapolis	
Templeton	Marguerite	9-17-1905	Hancock Co.	Sarah Templeton
	Lawrence	10-24-1911	Henry Co.	
Thomas	Norris	12-10-1907	" "	Lola Thomas
Thomas, Mary	Nonie	11-29-1902	" "	Mary A. Thomas
	Ester	1-25-1906	" "	
Tracy, S. H.	Olive	10- 9-1900	Hancock Co.	S. H. Tracy
Trail, A. W.	Chlotile	4-21-1904	Henry Co.	
	Arthenia	7- 6-1908	" "	
Trice, Edna, **see** Kirk, Milt				
Turner, Lane	Walter	6-20-1905	" "	Flora Turner
Ulmer, Chas.	Walter Ratcliff	9-15-1907	" "	
Ulmer, L.	Alice	6-11-1900	Hancock Co.	S. Lou Ulmer

Vandament	Geneva	6-12-1911	Indianapolis	Gretta Vandament
Vanduyn, Mart	Ople	9-24-[1901]	Madison Co.	
	Mary	1-10-[1906]	Hancock Co.	blind
Van Meter, Benton	Robert	8-22-1899	Henry Co.	Benton Van Meter
	Ethel	12-10-1904	" "	
	Riley	2- 3-1907	" "	
	George	5- 4-1909	" "	
Walker, John	Marie McVicker	5-17-1902	" "	John Walker
Walker, Len	Mary	10- 8-1906	" "	Ruth Walker
Ward, Willard	Bernice	5-20-1911	Wayne Co.	
Weaver, Henry	John	2-16-1903	Rush Co.	Maud Weaver
Wells, Ray	Imogene Ruth	1-30-[1912]	Henry Co.	Valletta Wells
Wilcox [illegible]	Clifford	8- 6-1902	Shelby Co.	
Wilkinson, Bert	Hilda	6-26-1904	Henry Co.	Bert Wilkinson
	Inez	10- 2-1906	" "	
	Blanche	2-13-1909	" "	
	Lucile	9-26-1911	" "	
Williams, Orval	Clark	6- 8-[1911]	" "	Orval Williams
	Herbert	2- 4-[1912]	" "	
Williamson, Jesse	Ralph	12-25-1907	" "	Mrs. Jesse E.
Willis, Jim	Donald	4- 5-[1902]	[blank]	Williamson
	Lester	age 14	"	
	Millard	age 11	"	
	Ruby	age 6	"	
Wills, Arthur	Monroe	11-20-1908	Henry Co.	
	Howard	9-23-1912	" "	
Wilson, Ralph	Ralph D.	10-31-1903	Hancock Co.	Mrs. Ralph Wilson
	Max M.	11-13-1911	" "	
Wilt, Charles	Clemence	3-29-1900	Randolph Co.	Carrie Wilt
	Vere	1- 7-1902	" "	
	Violet	9-27-1903	" "	
	Andrea	10-11-1905	Hancock Co.	
	Keith	12- 2-1911	" "	
Winslow, Frank	Frank	9-17-1909	Philippine Is.	Frank Winslow
	Joseph	3-17-1910	" "	
Winters, Alvin	Robert	7-11-1900	Henry Co.	Ella H. Winters
Wisehart	Homer	4-20-1899	" "	Luther Wisehart
	Alta	2- 3-1902	" "	
	Ralph	11-12-1907	" "	
Wolfe, Ben	Nola Cathern	11-23-1907	Randolph Co.	Hazel Wolfe
	Pauline	3- 6-1910	Henry Co.	
Wolfe, Charles	Margerite	8-26-1906	Kansas	Mrs. Charles Wolf
	Mildred	4-26-1908	"	
Wood, F. A.	Wilber	4-10-1909	Hendricks Co.	F. A. Wood
	Cloyce	1- 6-1911	" "	
	Eilen	12-17-1911	" "	
Wood, O. B.	Goldie B.	11- 1-1900	Henry Co.	O'Sean B. Wood
	Wilber	10- 1-1910	" "	
Wright, Carl, see Hosier, Wilber				
Wright, Cora	Rex	4-23-1903	" "	
Wright, Ray	Malcomb	4-10-1912	" "	Ray Wright

SHARON BAPTIST CHURCH, BARTHOLOMEW COUNTY

Written by Dr. J. C. Beck of Cincinnati, Ohio, and published in the Columbus *Daily Evening Democrat,* December 26, 1881. Dr. Beck was a former resident of Bartholomew County and was personally acquainted with some of the members of the Sharon Church. Mrs. Herschell Murphy of Columbus copied the article from the newspaper exactly as it was written.

Having given the readers of the DEMOCRAT the history of Flatrock Baptist church and Friends society in Sandcreek township and Azalia, I will give a sketch of Sharon church. It is very difficult to give it as complete as desirable, as the record of twelve years between April, 1844, and 1857 is lost, and also the first few months after its organization.

The last male member born on thr first church roll, which is still in existence, died some time ago. I allude to John Miller. He was the ninth male member in a total of fourteen. Miss Rachel Robertson was the ninth female member in a total of twenty-five lady members on this first roll. This young lady was the daughter of Joseph Robertson. Rachel Robertson sr., her mother, was numbered the eighth.

Several of the lady members of this roll are living. Mrs. Yealy, the wife of John Yealy, is one, and her sister Rachel, now living at Springville, Utah Ter., is another. Peggy Yealy is numbered twenty-one, and her sister, Elizabeth Robertson, who joined Nov. 25, 1826, closes the first roll of members.

Jesse Spurgin, who joined Dec. 23, 1826, is not enrolled in any of the lists of members. April 18, 1829, he "positively" withdrew from the Sharon church. During his brief membership he had antagonized Samuel Nelson, the clerk and principal member, but subsequently failing to have his views of church government sustained withdrew as stated. However I am anticipating and this is given as an apology for the loss of the early records of the church.

It is believed that Sharon was organized at the residence of Samuel Nelson, January 1, 1823. Many of the early settlers believed in taking especial care to do on New Year's day what they ought to do every day in the year, and it is well known after the split in Sharon church that the Reformers, Disciples, or as called by some, Campbellites, organized at Esquire Nelson's, January 1, 1833. The former members from Sharon instituted the Clifty church, of which Elder George D. Roland is now the representative or ruling Bishop.

The meetings were at first held at the houses of members Wm. McFall, Sanders, Kent, Henry, and others, oftenest at Samuel Nelson's, where Thomp. New now resides, southeast of Petersville, on the Newbern and Columbus pike.

The first list or roll of members and many facts here related are substantiated by the record of living witnesses. I have recently received a long letter from Mrs. Spofford, who was Rachel Robertson jr. on this first roll. She afterwards married Jonathan Ford, joined the Clifty church, and afterwards the Latterday Saints and moved to the West, and finally to Utah and married Spofford after Ford died.

It is interesting to look over the old roll of members, and I give them as they stand on the record.

Male Members [Read across]

Samuel Nelson,	Thomas Dudley,
William Robertson,	Joseph Keller,
Wm. Dudley,	Samuel Phillips,
John Keller,	Wm. McFall,
John C. Miller,	Joseph Robertson,
Thos. Henry,	Joseph Phillips,
Thomas Dudley,	Martin Keller.

Female Members [Read across]

Charity Dudley,	Sally Dudley,
Nancy Nelson,	Lydia Spurgin,
Mary Turner,	Polly Roland,
Jemima Nelson,	Rachel Robertson, sr.
Rachel Robertson, Jr.	Rachel Keller,
Jemima Miller,	Polly Miller,
Abigail Nelson,	Jane McFall,
Elizabeth Keller,	Ruth Kellar,
Elizabeth Wharton,	Hetty Hart,
Nancy Phillips,	Caty Arthur,
——Dudley,	Peggy Yealy,
Esther Robertson,	Lucinda Kent,
Elizabeth Robertson.	

Who were these people? Samuel Nelson was born July 26, 1769 in Bucks county, Penn., and was one of the first, if not the first, justice of the peace for Clifty township, in this county. He was the honored clerk of Sharon church for nearly ten years. He died March 2, 1844, and is buried in Flatrock church graveyard.

Nancy Nelson, his wife, was born in Culpepper county, Virginia, March 24, 1771, died April 12, 1849, and was buried near her husband.

Their daughter Jennie became the second wife of Joseph H. VanMerer, but died soon after in 1835, aged 33 years. She is also buried in Flatrock cemetery.

Lydia Spurgin was the highly respected wife of Judge Jesse Spurgin. Polly Roland was Esquire Nelson's eldest daughter and the wife of Geo. Roland. Rachel Robertson, sr., was the wife of Joseph Robertson, sr. Mrs. R. died Dec. 18, 1847, aged 78 years, and is buried in the Clifty "meeting house" graveyard. She was the mother of seventeen children, and lived to see them all raised and all married except Henry. Her daughter Rachel married first Jonathan Ford, and after his death married Mr. Spofford, and now lives at Springville, Utah county, Utah Ter. A few days since I received a long letter from her, written by her excellent grand-daughter, Miss Annie Johnson.

Peggy Yealy is the venerable wife of John Yealy, both old pioneers of our county, and when I last visited them they were in excellent health. Mrs. Yealy is also a daughter of grandmother Rachel Robertson, sr.

ROBERTSONS

Joseph Robertson sr. was born in New Jersey, but with his parents removed to Maryland, where his wife was born and where they were married, and removed to Warren county, O., and from there to this (Bartholomew) county. They landed at their future home at the ford of Clifty, east of Petersville, April 10, 1820. Joseph Robertson was a son of David Robertson and Elizabeth Marsh. David R. Trotter and Andrew B. Trotter are sons of William Trotter and Martha Marsh. These two Marsh girls were the legal heirs to ninety acres of land in the city of Philadelphia and six hundred acres about six miles from Philadelphia. David Robertson, a brother of Joseph, had all the papers showing the title to the land and gave them to a lawyer named Pack, who went to Philadelphia at the expense of the estate, and Joseph's children have had no report from the lawyer and this is over forty years ago. Archie Thompson's wife is a daughter of Martin Keller, and grand-daughter of John Keller.

WILLIAM MC FALL

Married Jane Fenton, and her sister, Isabel Fenton, became the wife of John McFall. These two are brothers to Col. Joseph McFall, who married Jane Greaves, and Jonathan McFall, who married Ruth McEwen.

But I must limit my statements as much as I can to the members of Sharon church. Wm. McFall moved from Switzerland county, near the Ohio river, and settled near Columbus in 1820, on the south bank of Clifty, nearly opposite John Keller's east of Columbus, after his marriage with Miss Fenton. He remained in this county until 1846, when he removed to Iowa, and six years later to Missouri, settling in Harrison county, where he died in 1870. He left six children, three boys and three girls. His son Joseph married Polly Williams, and his daughter Polly Ann married Wm. McEwen. Susan, another daughter, married G. Wash. May. His son Gideon, married Polly Newsom. Samuel, Polly Gaston, and his daughter Sarah married John Lindsey. The pioneer Wm. McFall left thirty-nine grand-children, and fifteen great-grand-children. This was the number six years ago, and I have no doubt there are by this time several times fifteen of the great-grand-children. It is said that Wm. McFall was of the opinion that he encamped on Tipton Knoll in an expedition against the Indians during the last war with England.

CENSUS OF TOWN OF SPEEDWAY AT THE TIME OF ITS INCORPORATION IN 1926

The town of Speedway, located west of downtown Indianapolis and north of Tenth Street, received its name from the famous Indianapolis Motor Speedway which was completed in 1909. The first automobile race was held there that year and the first 500 Mile Race in 1911. The town was platted in 1912 by the same men who built the race track. The original plat contained 1,255 acres but the boundaries have been greatly extended since that time. At the time of its incorporation in 1926 the population was approximately five hundred. The census printed below and other documents concerning the incorporation of Speedway are in the Marion County Commissioners Record, Book 57, pp. 181-90.

Names of Heads of Families in Speedway in 1926	No. of Voters	No. of persons belonging to each family			
			Malcolm, Earl	2	2
			Mann, O. R.	2	3
			Martin, Frank R.	2	2
			Marvel, Ida	1	1
			Milburn, C. D.	2	5
Babb, Oretta	2	3	Miller, John	2	5
Ballard, Eliza	8	9	Moldthan, Mary S.	1	1
Baxter, Wayne	2	3	Moore, John W.	2	2
Beeler, A. V.	2	2	Ness, Charles	2	3
Bilbee, Dwight B.	2	5	Newman, David	2	2
Broom, John C.	2	2	Otto, Merle	1	1
Christian, Joseph E.	2	2	Pearcy, John	1	1
Daupert, Harry C.	2	6	Perkins, Herman	2	2
Denton, John W.	2	3	Peterson, H. W.	2	3
Deqweg, J. M.	2	2	Phillips, Downing	4	6
Dietz, Henry	2	3	Phillips, Robert	2	5
Doughty, L. H.	2	2	Phillips, Wm.	2	6
Edwards, S. E.	2	3	Pieper, Herman	2	3
Ferguson, Harold	2	3	Piner, Harold	2	2
Ferguson, Hattie	3	4	Piric, Jasper C.	2	3
Ferguson, Paul	1	1	Powell, H. Dilly	2	2
Ferree, Edgar L.	2	2	Prince, Donald		
Frazier, E. W.	2	2	Quick, Jean	2	4
Fyster Theo R.	2	5	Raider, Mary	1	4
Grande, J. A.	3	3	Rauck, Oscar	2	2
Halfman, John	2	2	Reid, W. M.	2	2
Hall, J. H.	2	4	Renard, Eugene	2	3
Harrison, Jack	1	1	Rice, Luey	1	1
Hatfield, Ed	1	4	Rice, T. E.	2	3
Hayes, R. Alfred	2	4	Roberts, Oliver	2	4
Henry, Lewis	4	5	Rosner, August	2	6
Hentzel, Chas.	1	1	Rosner, Frank	1	1
Hibner, Carol	2	2	Rosner, Wm.	2	6
Hockensmith, Byron	2	2	Ryan, John	2	4
Hodgson, Wm.	2	3	Sehi, Anna	3	5
Hogue, Frank C.	2	4	Sharp, J. D.	2	2
Hold, Sheldon	1	1	Skinner, O. H.	2	5
Hollinger, James	2	3	Smith, Butler	1	1
Hooker, Robert J.	2	3	Smith, Roy	2	2
Hopkins, A. L.	3	5	Spencer, Chas.	2	3
Hostetter, Lewis	3	6	Spencer, Marshall G.	2	4
Hunt, Virgil	2	5	Srader, Oscar	2	5
Irwin, Ida	1	1	Staum, Francis E.	2	4
Isreal, Kenneth	2	5	Stallwood, Geo.	2	5
Jennings, Benjamin V.	2	3	Stewart, Maxwell D.	2	4
Jennings, Newell	2	3	Strebe, George	3	9
Johnson, Nora	1	1	Thompson, H. A.	2	3
Keogh, Thomas	2	2	Trosky, Charles L.	3	6
Lantry, John	1	5	Urban, Charles C.	2	5
Larsen, James	2	3	Wagner, L. W.	2	2
Leonard, John	2	7	Wall, H. L.	2	2
Love, Joseph	1	1	Wenz, Kenneth	2	2
Love, Thomas	2	3	Winner, Dwight	2	2
McCrea, John A.	—	2	TOTALS 148	307	507
McKenna, R. F.	2	4			

THE FIGHTING QUAKERS
IN THE AMERICAN REVOLUTION

There is a general opinion that those having Quaker ancestry are not eligible for membership in patriotic organizations. There are exceptions, however, in the Fighting Quakers of the American Revolution, who were known as Free Quakers and came into organized existence during the latter years of the American Revolution. The groups throughout the Colonies were mostly made up of those who had been disowned by the Quakers for participating in some manner in the War.

The principles for which they were disowned were not new to Quakerism. Friends had been disowned for the same reasons almost from the beginning of the Quaker movement, but the large number of disownments of the Revolutionary period was caused by circumstances which put many a young Quaker in an almost untenable position.

Quakers of Revolutionary times have been considered by some historians to have been Tories, and many of them were. It is also true that the great majority of the Quakers did support the Crown during those years, but in doing so they were upholding one of the Quaker principles which we have to go back to their earliest years to understand. In England one of their doctrines was that they had no responsibility for the creation of any government, and their only duty was to be obedient, to the extent their conscience would allow, to the government which then existed. They were never revolutionaries and tranquilly transferred their support from Cromwell to Charles II, and so on, as soon as each successful political movement was accomplished.

Of course, some of the responsibility placed upon them when they first came to America, especially in Penn's Colony, somewhat altered their attitude toward government. But when the American Revolution arrived the old testimony against plotting and revolutions was brought out again and was the basis for the neutrality which all the Quaker Meetings adopted. They officially supported the Crown and it was for this reason they refused to pay taxes required by the Continental Congress, or state governments, or to take office under the new government, or to support it in any way.

Another principle of long standing which always caused Quakers trouble was the matter of taking an oath. Under no circumstance might a Friend take an oath; he was under a sacred obligation to make his ordinary word as true as a bond. Therefore, a Quaker could hold no office, the obligation of which was administering oaths, nor would he take an oath required to hold an office. The various Colonial legislatures side-stepped this issue by allowing Friends to make an affirmation—a formal declaration that he would perform his duties to the best of his ability.

The Quaker principle we know best, of course, is that they would take no part in warfare. They said, "We can not fight, for we believe that fighting itself is immoral, and we will not do wrong even for a righteous cause." Prior to the Revolution there were a few Quakers in Pennsylvania who attempted to alter this doctrine. Around 1775 James Logan advanced the idea that offensive war was never to be considered, but that a war of defense was Christian and therefore justifiable. His proposal to the Philadelphia Yearly Meeting was not even read.

Dr. John Fothergill was an English Friend who visited the Colonies and was one of few who maintained a correspondence with Friends here. When the movement for independence began he wrote urging them to maintain their opposition to war, but otherwise to yield to the "voice of America." He felt the cause of liberty in England, as well as in America, was bound up with the success of the movement. Had they taken his advice, it would have saved them a great deal of trouble. However, at the Yearly Meeting held in Philadelphia in 1774, a letter was ordered sent to all meetings of Friends in America, warning members not to take part in any of the political upheaval, and strongly suggesting the propriety of disowning all who disobeyed the orders issued by the Yearly Meeting.

Perhaps you can understand somewhat the predicament in which a young Quaker found himself when required to join the militia, or at least pay a fine for not so doing, or when he was required by law to take an oath of allegiance, and if he felt he should pay taxes to the state or Continental Congress. If they did any of those things, then they were virtually cut off from their own society, for they were disowned by the Quakers. If they did not—well, then they faced a jail sentence. It was not a comfortable position in which to be. Disownment of many Quakers was the primary reason for the formation of the organization of Free Quakers. [Miss Luke here spoke of the disownment of Thomas Bryant as an example.]

Most of what has been written about Free

Quakers has been about those in Philadelphia. However, there were organizations elsewhere in the Colonies. In Virginia and the Carolinas some of the young Quakers entered the American Army, were disowned, and formed organizations of Free Quakers. There were groups in New York, also, and in Maryland there were Free Quakers at Deer Creek and West River Meetings. In New England the question upon which division came was payment of taxes to the new government. Throughout the controversy the disowned New Englanders exchanged correspondence with leaders of the movement in Philadelphia and in 1781 a Free Quaker organization was formed at Dartmouth, Massachusetts. They received a copy of the discipline outlined by the Philadelphia group, and although they did not entirely agree with it, they kept in touch with them. The New England organization continued until at least 1802.

[Miss Luke here told of her research on the family of Mordecai Yarnall, a Quaker of Chester County, Pennsylvania, and Philadelphia; several of his family became Free Quakers.]

While they agreed with their elders that war was wrong, many of the young Quakers in Philadelphia believed it was not consistent to accept the protection of Congress and the Army and refuse to help them. Especially after the Declaration of Independence was adopted in 1776, some accepted active military duties, others served in non-combat capacities, while those who felt no inclination to serve at all willingly paid the militia taxes and fines. When it became the law in 1777 that all residents of Pennsylvania must take the oath of allegiance, some did take it secretly, but many publicly obeyed the law. Consequently disownments were rampant. But, since they were reared in the Quaker discipline, those who were disowned were not inclined to join other denominations, and they missed their meetings and the fellowship of the meetings. In the autumn of 1780 a small group of disowned Quakers began meeting together for worship in the homes of Samuel Wetherill and Timothy Matlack, and after a short time decided to form a meeting of their own.

In forming the new religious society they felt they should publicly make known their cause for doing so. Samuel Wetherill, Timothy Matlack, and his brother, White Matlack, were appointed to write this message, which was approved by the Free Quakers on April 24, 1781. It was printed as a broadside, or handbill, and was addressed to those who had been disowned. It stated that

their separation had been forced upon them and they had no design to promote schisms in religion; but that they would endeavor to support and maintain public meetings for worship, and invited those who wished to join them. By this time their meetings had grown and Timothy Matlack, who was a trustee of the University of Pennsylvania, obtained permission for them to meet in the University's building.

One of their first concerns was forming a discipline or plan of organization, which they worked on for many months. In August of 1781 they adopted a discipline similar to the original discipline, but differing in two respects. They believed that "no man who believed in God, in the supreme, wise and benevolent Ruler of the Universe," should be disowned for any cause whatsoever. It was this principle with which the New England Free Quakers disagreed. The other difference was their belief that they were obligated to serve their country in the time of war.

Within a short time the membership of the Free Quakers had grown to over one hundred members, and the accommodations of the University of Pennsylvania were not adequate. A formal, printed letter was prepared in September 1781, addressed to "Those of Our Brethren Who Have Disowned Us," requesting the use of one of the meeting houses held by the parent group, which was not then in use. They also requested permission to use the Quaker burial ground for interment of members of the Free Quakers. The appeal was presented to the three Monthly Meetings of Philadelphia by the Matlack brothers and Moses Bartram, who were later advised by the clerks of the various Meetings that their "paper" had been considered by committees and had been found improper to be read to the Meetings. One sentence of their appeal certainly was worth consideration: In their request for use of the burial ground they pointed out: "For, however the living may contend, surely the dead may lie peaceably together."

As was permissable by Quaker custom, the Free Quakers next presented their request to the Yearly Meeting. This time they were advised their request "was not fit to be read." While later on the Friends tried to refute it, there is evidence in the Meeting records that the rulings against them were made by only a few of the leading Quakers.

Next they petitioned the General Assembly to recognize the rights of the Free Quakers in the property held by the parent group, and that the Friends be forced by law to grant the privileges requested. Some of the Free Quakers were subscribers to the common stock of the Friends and also subscribers for particular purchases of property, so they really did have a right in the property. The Friends replied to the petition with a lengthy memorial setting forth their position, and the whole matter was referred to a committee. When you stop to think of it, this action by the Society of Friends was almost impertinent; they refused to take any part in the new government, or support it in any way, yet there they were asking its help and requesting the assembly not to grant the request of the Free Quakers. Altogether the situation was a very hot potato for the Assembly. The committee did meet with both groups, but in the end the General Assembly failed to act. After almost two years in attempting to get the matter settled, the Free Quakers finally realized they must build their own meeting house. They solicited subscriptions among their members and others in sympathy with them and by July, 1783, had purchased a lot at the corner of 5th and Arch Streets in Philadelphia. The Free Quakers were immensely popular in Philadelphia so that within the same year they had sufficient funds to begin construction. It is said both General Washington and Benjamin Franklin contributed to these funds.

Over two hundred people attended the first Meeting for worship in the new meeting house on June 13, 1784, but thereafter the usual number was from thirty to fifty. After the war some returned to the parent organization. Gradually over the years the original members of the Free Quakers died and their descendants drifted into other religious organizations. The attendance became less and less until in 1836, the last Meeting for religious worship was held with only the clerk and one other person present. That one other person was Elizabeth Claypoole better known as Betsy Ross.

Before the building was even completed Clement Biddle rented the basement and storage vaults two levels below the street. The balcony originally planned was boarded up and an upper floor for many years housed a school for young ladies. When the Meetings for worship were discontinued, the Apprentices' Library occupied the premises for over fifty-five years; then for another sixty years the building was rented to various business tenants. When Independence Mall was planned the building was moved about thirty-three feet west, and it was restored to appear as it was in Samuel Wetherill's original plans of 1783. The Junior League of Philadelphia now has offices in the basement and provides guides for visitors.

After Meetings for worship were discontinued, the business meetings of the Free Quakers continued through descendants of original members. A Committee for Charity distributed the income from rent of the building and other invested funds received over the years. Both the Yearly Meeting and the Charity committee still function. The roll of members and other records of the Free Quakers are at the American Philosophical Society in Philadelphia.

The Free Quaker Meeting House still standing on the northeast corner of Independence Mall in Philadelphia, bears "silent testimony to men and women whose conscientious bravery wrote a vital chapter in the religious history of Philadelphia," and of the United States.

GRANT COUNTY MARRIAGES, 1831-1853

Compiled from microfilm of the original record of Marriages, Book C, in the Grant County Courthouse. The county was formed in 1831 and this is the first book of Marriages. The compilation was made by Mrs. Ruth Slevin for the Fort Wayne Public Library.

Adamson, David & Bever, Didema	12- 1-1844
Adamson, James & Roberds, Nancy	10- 3-1843
Adamson, Joseph & Hines, Sarah	12- 5-1839
Adamson, Joseph & Jacks, Martha	11-19-1846
Adamson, Moses & Johnson, Mary Ann	6-10-1852
Addington, Thomas & Mason, Mary	2-27-1840
Addington, William S. & Moorman, Senah	1-15-1853
Allen, Amer & Daily, Malinda	3-10-1842
Allen, Jonathan & Beachem, Malinda	7-24-1839
Allen, Jonathan & Cook, Rebecca	4-24-1846
Allen, Robert W. & Duke, Matilda	10- 9-1851
Allen, Samuel & Thomas, Mary	11- 7-1849
Allison, James J. & Case, Sarah	1- 6-1842
Anderson, Isaac & Camblin, Eliza	8-17-1841
Anderson, Isaac & Roberds, Lydia	11-15-1849
Anderson, James & Druck, Susanna F.	3-14-1847
Anderson, John & Jacks, Phebe	1-25-1844
Anderson, Mordica & Moorhead, Susannah	3-15-1846
Anderson, Moses & Roberts, Rachel	3- 1-1834
Anthony, William & Stackhouse, Clarinda S.	9-14-1843
Antrim, Mahlon & Stair, Margaret	1-13-1848
Antrim, Thomas & Massey, Lucinda	12-27-1838
Arnet, Lindley & Jones, Eleanor	4- 7-1853
Arnett, Phillip & Bruner, Catharine	11-12-1846
Arthurhultz, David & Cravens, Ruhey	11-12-1846
Atchison (or Atkison), James & Roberds, Mary J.	12-13-1840
Atchison, Silas & Adamson, Anna	7- 1-1841
Ayres, Stephen D. & Brandon, Matilda	9- 9-1838
Badger, Ebenezer & Wiant, Margaret	1-10-1836
Badger, Reason & Curtis, Mary	5-28-1840
Baird, Morgan & Fear, Mahala Frances	6-19-1848
Baldwin, Ahira & Newby, Jane	7- 9-1840
Baldwin, David & Coalman, Elizabeth	1-29-1846
Baldwin, Elias & Tharp, Harriet C.	10-15-1840
Baldwin, Jonathan & Dillon, Sarah Ann	4-19-1849
Baldwin, Joseph & Stanfield, Lydia Jane	4-16-1840
Baldwin, Moses & Stephens, Dorothy R.	3-25-1847
Ballenger, James & Marine, Julia A.	12-20-1849
Ballenger, Josiah & Cook, Tamer W.	4-14-1842
Ballinger, Jesse & Walker, Mariann	2-1-1846
Ballinger, John & Mitchell, Melinda	11-13-1851
Bardue, Benjamin & Beaty, Lucy Ann	1- 6-1848
Barkdall, Joseph & Perry, Mary Ann	8-16-1849
Barkley, Henry & Todd, Rhoda	4-28-1840
Barley, David & Lenfesty, Ann	10-17-1849
Barley, George W. & Line, Mehettable	2-25-1852
Barley, Jacob & Rix, Elizabeth	3- 3-1853
Barnes, Joshua & Moorhead, Rosannah	11-18-1847
Barnet, William J. & Vohras, Jane lic.	3-27-1836
Barnett, John W. & See, Elizabeth	1-16-1838
Barns, Cyrus & Campbell, Matilda A.	5- 6-1852
Barr, Reuben H. & Owings, Elizabeth	6-14-1838
Bates, Daniel & Smith, Rixey	10-19-1834
Bates, William & Qualls, Malinda	8- 6-1840

Bates, William & Jones, Elizabeth	11-16-1843
Baxter, Louis & Belveal, Wiminda	3-18-1852
Bayles, Enoch & Crist, Sarah	2-20-1851
Beauchamp, Charles & Thomas, Tamer	6-15-1843
Beauchamp, Curtis & Schooly, Rachel	1- 4-1841
Beauchamp, David & Smith, Sarah	2-22-1844
Beauchamp, John & Dille, Lovina	9-21-1843
Beauchamp, Miles & Small, Lydia	10-26-1843
Beauchamp, Wilson & Small, Rachel	12-17-1840
Beauchamp, William & Small, Mariam	5-11-1843
Beckford, William & Stout, Ann	3-23-1846
Beeman, John & Wall, Mary Ann	6-22-1848
Bell, Lancaster & Baldwin, Mary	7-19-1838
Belveal, Landen & Frantz, Susannah	3-25-1851
Benbow, David & Osbom, Lydia	4-16-1846
Benbow, Jesse & Jessup, Nancy	9-27-1849
Benbow, John Jr. & Modlin, Leah	4-19-1838
Benbow, Moses & Lytle, Jane	5-18-1843
Benefield, John H. & Mullins, Mary M.	7- 8-1841
Bennett, Silas & Spond, Casander	6-18-1837
Benoy, Edward & Millhollen, Sarah Ann	3- 6-1851
Benoy, George & Walker, Catharine	12- 2-1847
Benoy, Thomas & Heele, Elizabeth	3-13-1848
Beony (Benoy?), Thomas & Furnish, Essignor	8-27-1840
Berry, Jonathan & Welsh, Sally	1- 2-1839
Berry, William & Malott, Submit	9- 3-1837
Berry, William J. & Martin, Polly Ann	11-20-1851
Bett, John & Druley, Martha Jane	5-20-1847
Bevard, David & Garret, Nancy	1-20-1853
Bevard, John & Marsh, Matilda A.	11- 5-1851
Bevard, William & Wortman, Louisa	10- 1-1848
Bird, Benjamin & Monroe, Eliza lic.	9- 8-1852
Bird, Garret & Hardesty, Rebecca	8-12-1841
Bird, James W. & Williams, Caroline	1-20-1850
Bish, Abraham & Hendrix, Lucinda	2- 2-1842
Bish, David & Dunn, Elizabeth	3-26-1835
Bitezell, Jonathan & Cain, Sarah	8-22-1846
Bocock, Achilles & Newland, Eliza	1- 5-1840
Bocock, George & Line, Sarah	4-29-1849
Bocock, James & Shannon, Hester Ann	1-30-1852
Bocock, William & Daily, Matilda	10-31-1839
Bodkin, Hamilton & Conner, Julian	10- 5-1845
Bodkin, Thomas Allen & Conner, Phebe	8-16-1840
Bogue, Jesse & Webb, Ann	6- 4-1840
Bole, Lorenzo & Evans, Hannah	3-17-1850
Bond, Joseph & Rich, Susannah	8-14-1851
Boozer, Peter & Arthershults, Marie	2- 8-1853
Boots, Caleb S. & Johnson, Amanda	3-25-1849
Boots, Caleb S. & Hodge, Eliza Jane	1- 5-1853
Boots, John O. & Conner, Katharine	10-23-1836
Boots, Martin & Norman, Nancy	6-20-1833
Boots, William & Hurley, Juliann	7- 4-1833
Boots, William & Bocock, Eliza	5- 3-1849
Bowers, G.H. & Jones, Evalina	4-12-1838
Bowman, George & Walker, Mary	10- 4-1851
Bowman, John C. & Dills, Rosanna	2-17-1850
Boxell, Joseph & Welsh, Anna	9- 9-1852

Boxell, Robert B. & Rea, Elizabeth   12-25-1851
Bradberry, John L. & Wilson, Casander 7-27-1847
Bradfield, Birkley T. & Wright, Margaret 4-26-1849
Bradfield, Eli & Simson, Fanny   1-31-1843
Bradfield, James & Martin, Elizabeth   10-31-1844
Bradford, Casper & Watkins, Nancy V.   2-15-1853
Bradford, John M. & Pully, Sarah Rebecca
    1-16-1848
Bradford, Joseph & Woolman, Sarah   10-29-1848
Bradford, William R. & Gaines, Elizabeth
    7-27-1848
Braffet, John & Wood, Elizabeth   7-12-1849
Branson, Crumes & Stout, Phebe   3-28-1849
Branson, David & Stout, Neoma   5-8-1845
Branson, John & Burget, Malinda   7-25-1844
Braselton, Robert & Hill, Ruth   lic. 6-14-1845
Braton, James & Wall, Hannah   7-12-1835
Brewer, Aaron & Thomas, Anna   2-1-1849
Brewer, Aaron & Lanson, Louisa Jane   9-23-1851
Brewer, John & Davis, Permelia   2-16-1837
Brewer, Stephen & Leach, Jane   3-31-1842
Bright, Michael & Bevard, Nancy   11-15-1845
Brodrick, George & Thomas, Orp'ah   2-18-1847
Brodrick, George & Davis, Piety   2-23-1850
Brodrick, Robert & Coppock, Mary   1-26-1850
Broils, Handley & Seely, Elizabeth   9-29-1842
Brooks, Jesse & Havens, Rebecca   9-4-1842
Brooks, John & Russell, Elizabeth   2-10-1842
Brown, Henry & Lytle, Anna   11-11-1847
Brown, John & Garret, Hester   12-5-1837
Brown, John R. & Dailey, Rebecca   10-31-1848
Brown, Mason & Carter, Mary   11-10-1844
Brown, Thomas & Magee, Eliza   8-17-1852
Brown, William R. & Ridwell, Rebecca   4-23-1851
Brownlee, James & Goldthait, Lucey   11-30-1840
Brownlee, John & Goldthait, Mary   7-21-1839
Brownlee, John & Weeks, Mary Louisa   10-13-1845
Bruner, Samuel & Griggs, Catharine   1-7-1841
Bruner, Lemuel & Mercer, Mary Ann   8-2-1846
Brunson, Milton & McNeal, Elizabeth   4-7-1853
Bubick, Senah & Hummel, Mary   8-17-1837
Buchanan, Alexander & Eltzroth, Julia   9-9-1841
Bukdull, Albert & Swan, Nancy Ann   1-1-1851
Buller, Andrew & Lamb, Rebecca   1-6-1849
Buller, John & Thomas, Jane   2-16-1843
Buller, Linsey & Lytle, Mary   4-17-1837

Burden, Elberd & Smith, Martha J.   4-10-1853
Burk, Robert H. & Camblain, Elenor   2-20-1840
Burket, Daniel & Owings, Henrietta   3-17-1853
Burnett, Franklin & Chavois, Rachel   5-15-1851
Burns, Anthony & Tyler, Vazippe   1-1-1852
Burns, James & Horine, Ellanor B.   6-7-1853
Burson, Eden & Ballinger, Anna   8-13-1848
Burson, Henry & Hozier, Elizabeth   7-6-1843
Burson, John & Vandeventer, Jane   1-22-1849
Burson, Joseph & Hiatt, Lydia   2-19-1852
Burson, Joshua L. & Pearson, Matilda   7-2-1840
Burson, Samuel & Brodrick, Rebecca   12-15-1848
Burson, William R. & Johnson, Jane   3-3-1853
Bussey, Thornton & Lamb, Rachel   7-30-1846
Byerly, Noah & Stackhouse, Mary   8-2-1844
Byres, Isaac & Pendry, Elizabeth
    (of Delaware Co.)   2-20-1834

Cable (or Cabel), Emanuel & Brownfield, Margaret
    10-21-1852

Camblin, David J. & Duckwall, Mary Ellen
    12-13-1842
Camblin, Enoch E. & Lugar, Sarah Ann 12-5-1852
Camblin, George W. & Bradford, Rebecca5-20-1849
Camblin, Thaddeus & Lugar, Mary Jane 7-4-1852
Campbell, Alexander & Lamey, Evaline 2-8-1849
Campbell, Charles & Dawson, Sarah   11-23-1848
Campbell, Joseph & Campbell, Judith   11-11-1841
Campbell, Samuel A. & Lugar, Sarah   12-7-1845
Campbell, Shesbadger B. & Jackson, Emily
    10-31-1841
Campbell, Thomas P. & Spears, Rebecca
    9-18-1852
Campbell, William J. & Braffet, Salina   2-6-1853
Capper, Archibald & Smith, Jane   7-8-1847
Carson, Joseph & Troth, Mary   10-5-1851
Carson, Thomas & Troth, Catharine   12-7-1851
Carter, Asa & Thomas, Agnes   4-27-1852
Carter, George & Buller, Mary   11-25-1836
Carter, Henry & Morris, Celia   6-18-1835
Carter, Howard & Layon, Eleanor   2-18-1851
Carter, Ira J. & Conn, Eliza Ann   7-25-1844
Carter, Isaac & Reynolds, Mary Ann   6-2-1853
Carter, Jonas & McClure, Sarah   5-1-1834
Case, Elijah & Starkey, Margaret   10-22-1840
Case, John & Dalrymple, Elizabeth Jane 2-11-1846
Case, Samuel & Hurley, Matilda   2-6-1834
Case, Simeon & Owings, Eliza J.   2-20-1848
Cary, Ebenezer & Eltzroth, Mary   1-30-1836
Cary, Oliver H.P. & Hall, Lois S.   11-10-1840
Cavanet, Jacob & Huffman, Nancy Hulda 3-11-1852
Chambers, Elijah & Clark, Sally   4-29-1833
Chambers, Pleasant & Norman, Rixyan 10-18-1835
Chance, Stephen & Hodgens, Elizabeth 6-11-1848
Chance, William & Badger, Judah Ann   5-24-1846
Chandler, John & Riffe, Rebecca   4-1-1851
Chany, Charles E. & Stair, Drusilla   8-23-1845
Chapman, Norman & Jackson, Sarah   4-22-1841
Chavis, John & Wallis, Ann   3-4-1852
Clanin, Samuel & Duffield, Susan   2-17-1848
Clanin, Thompson & Buroaker, Elizabeth 7-8-1852
Clawson, Shadrach & Pricket, Phebe   12-18-1834
Clevenger, Job & St. Clair, Mahala E.   8-19-1852
Cloud, Joseph & Matheny, Jane   10-6-1850
Cluster, Daniel & Flumer, Barbary Ellen
    11-24-1850
Cluster, Thomas & Miller, Elizabeth   3-10-1848
Coate, Allen & Shugart, Abigail   6-28-1850
Cochran, William & Anderson, Levina Jane
    12-18-1851
Coffield, Alexander & Reeves, Mary Ann 4-16-1846
Coffield, Samuel & Clark, Rebecca   12-29-1840
Coffman, Aaron & Knight, Buela   12-25-1851
Cole, Charles & Creviston, Melissa   9-12-1842
Cole, Samuel L. & Connett, Elizabeth   2-29-1843
Coleman, Daniel & Johnson, Mary Ann   7-23-1843
Collins, Andrew & Moore, Nancy   5-9-1844
Collins, John K. & Fields, Sarah A.   8-30-1848
Collins, John W. & Paris, Mary L.   2-14-1850
Collins, Moses & Shuman, Malinda   9-9-1846
Cone, Christopher C. & Lewis, Mary   7-28-1849
Conger, Calvin & Stevens, Rebecca H.   9-30-1852
Conn, Ephraim & Harlan, Perlina   4-21-1842
Conn, Ezra & Gaines, Susannah   11-5-1843
Conn, Stephen & Love, Minerva   4-8-1849

Conner, Jeptha & Housden, Margaret   10-23-1847
Conner, John & Low, Eleanor   10- 9-1834
Conner, John Moses & Sutton, Ann   4- 3-1832
Conner, Lewis & Reeves, Orpha   7- 5-1840
Conner, Trustum & Gamer, Rhoda   8-25-1850
Conner, William & Fagan, Elizabeth   9-17-1838
Conner, William & Allen, Mary   6-11-1840
Cook, George R. & Speelman, Susan   3-23-1851
Cook, Isaac & Miller, Elizabeth   6- 9-1842
Cook, Seth & Pearson, Huldah   9-10-1844
Cook, Silas & Benbow, Sarah   8-15-1845
Copp, Chrisman & Thomas, Sarah   5-14-1846
Copp, Christman & Rush, Elizabeth   9-23-1847
Coppock, Aaron & Edgerton, Ruthanna   12-24-1840
Coppock, Philomon & Bowman, Elizabeth
    6-29-1851
Corey, William D. & Duckwall, Amanda M.
    10- 2-1851
Cosand, Edwin D. & Hiatt, Abana   11-23-1851
Cottrell, Albert & Stout, Elizabeth   10-10-1850
Couch, David & Eltzroth, Anna   7-15-1838
Coulter, James & Howe, Jane   4-26-1838
Covey, John & Walton, Margaret   4-18-1852
Cowgill, Joseph & Johnston, Francis Ann
    8-26-1841
Cox, Abijah & Long, Nancy   7- 8-1841
Cox, David & Fear, Armilda C.   4-24-1853
Cox, Jacob & Conner, Lydia   8-23-1851
Cox, Nathan & Thomas, Malinda   2-19-1852
Cox, Vinnadge, & Reitch, Christena   3- 9-1851
Cox, William & Wilson, Elizabeth   10-23-1845
Crane, Richard & Fisher, Martha   1-15-1852
Cravens, James H. & Lugar, Louisa   2-27-1848
Cravens, Joseph & Janes, Sarah J.   11-26-1846
Creamer, Harrison & Swan, Louisa   10- 6-1851
Crawford, Cyrus & Kessinger, Katharine B.
    2-15-1840
Crawford, Joseph & How, Margaret   8-23-1838
Creason, Willis & Bailey, Rachel Ann   1-29-1848
Creek, Isaac & Thomas, Martha   6-30-1842
Creek, Isaac & Moore, Martha   12-27-1849
Creviston, Henry & Slagle, Polly   4-13-1837
Creviston, James & Garver, Mary   8-13-1850
Creviston, Thomas & Slagel, Margaret   1-21-1837
Creviston, William & Latridge, Minerva   6-15-1850
Crist, George W. & Petty, Mary Jane   4- 7-1853
Cubberly, David P. & Frazier, Charlotte J.
    7-19-1849
Cuberly, William & Line, Dulierma   7- 3-1842
Culp, George W. & Mittank, Hannah   2- 7-1846
Cunningham, George & Wallace, Nancy   12-23-1841
Cunningham, Joseph & James, Ellen   11-27-1851
Cunningham, William & Knox, Rachel   1- 1-1852
Curtis, Alfred & Minick, Ann   4-19-1846
Cutsinger, John & Havens, Martha Ann   2-16-1851

Dailey, John F. & Slagal, Susannah   7-20-1837
Darbey, Thomas & Morris, Margaret   8- 1-1850
Darby, William & Beaty, Rachel   3- 6-1851
Davis, Job & Buller, Polly   4- 1-1838
Davis, Jonathan B. & Hiatt, Nancy   3-11-1835
Davis, Richard & Thomas, Sidney   4- 7-1836
Davis, Thomas & Gauntt, Bathsheba   3- 7-1850
Davis, Thomas & Fees, Anna   4-25-1850
Davis, Thomas & Booher, Julia Ann   2-17-1852

Davis, Wilson & Tharp, Elizabeth   3- 7-1847
Dawson, Garrison & Owings, Elizabeth   9-24-1848
Dawson, Thomas S. & Pricket, Elizabeth
    10-11-1842
Dawson, William & Collins, Sarah   10-29-1848
Day, Joseph & Roberds, Lydia   10- 5-1843
Dean, Thomas & Anderson, Hannah   10-20-1847
Dehavens, John & Elliott, Mary   9- 6-1845
Demoss, Joshua & Heaverlo, Rachel   11-30-1851
Denison, Andrew J. & Mason, Lamira   12-30-1847
Dille, Jacob & Smith, Rachel   7-25-1840
    (Ichabod Dille on return)
Dille, James & Morris, Anna   6-27-1844
Dillen, John & Foster, Sarah   4- 9-1840
Dillen, Albert & Johnston, Julianna   8- 9-1849
Dodd, John W. & Seward, Eliza J.   2-27-1844
Dollar, James & Leonard, Sarah F.   7-26-1849
Doty, Peter & Cary, Mary (Mrs.)   1- 8-1849
Downs, Alen B. & Pence, Phebe A.   2- 1-1849
Draper, Elias J. & Hobaugh, Elizabeth   1- 1-1851
Draper, John & Douglass, Margaret   4-26-1850
Draper, Josiah & Forney, Mary   1-13-1848
Draper, Josiah & Price, Nancy   1-15-1853
Draper, Noah & Douglass, Sarah E.   6-11-1853
Druck, Jacob & Taylor, Nancy   5-28-1846
Duckwall, William L. & Cloud, Sarah   9- 8-1844
Duffield, Johnson & Hamden, Jane   3-11-1852
Duglas, Henry & Malcom, Elizabeth   12- 1-1842
Dunlap, James W. & McKeever, Minerva   9-25-1849
Dunn, Alexander & Baldwin, Sarah   8- 7-1845
Dunn, James & Moore, Precilla   7-10-1836
Dunn, John & Murray, Mary   7- 3-1834
Dunn, John & Bryan, Miranda   12-30-1847
Dunn, John & Line, Lucinda   10-28-1852

Edge, John Brownlee & Goldthait, Mary   7-21-1839
Edgerton, Owen & Rich, Mary   2- 3-1843
Edgerton, Samuel & Lytle, Winney   1-25-1844
Edmonds, Robert & Badger, Anna   11-23-1849
Eliston, Amos & Norman, Elizabeth   10-14-1834
Elliot, Shadarick & Murray, Rosannah   9-25-1848
Ellis, Jonathan M. & Jones, Jemima Ann   6-22-1851
Eltzroth, Nicholas & Prickett, Lucinda   10- 7-1843
Embree, John & Swift, Hannah H.   11- 9-1845
Embree, John & Yount, Sophia   11-25-1849
Endsley, Elihu & Logan, Margaret   5-23-1852
Endsly Elihu & Parsons, Sidney   12- 2-1838
Entsminger, David & Johnson, Mary Ann
    10- 3-1850
Entsminger, David E. & Adamson, Melvina
    12-26-1844
Entsminger, William & Wallace, Jennet W.
    6-27-1840
Evans, Calvin J. & Knox, Comfort   4-19-1853
Evans, Elijah & Johnson, Frances   5- 1-1849
Evans, Henry & Rood, Hannah   8-10-1848
Evans, John & Horton, Martha Ann   1-15-1853
Evans, Perry & Evans, Rachel   1- 1-1849

Fankboner, John & McCormick, Anna   8-24-1837
Fankboner, Levi L. & Moreland, Rachel J.
    8- 3-1852
Fanning, Jacob & Rood, Marinda   4-29-1838
Farbanks, William & Dunlap, Sarah   10- 3-1839
Farnash, William H. & Wine, Susannah   4- 7-1842

Farr, Samuel & Morgan, Rachel   11-23-1851
Farr, Smiley & Camblin, Mary J.   9-21-1851
Farver, Reuben & Pearson (or Peirson)' Anna
     5-18-1848
Fees, John & Collins, Mary Ann   1-10-1849
Felton, Robert & Daily, Eliza   2-22-1842
Fentrell, Jacob & Nelson, Mary Ann   1-18-1851
Fields, John H. & Foster, Martha   4-22-1852
Finkle, David & Dalrymple, Rebecca Ann 3-2-1844
Finkle, David & Shanehulser, Mary J.   1-15-1847
Fleming, Elmers W. & Badger, Juliann   3- 3-1836
Flin, John & Boots, Rebecca   10-21-1841
Flinn, John W. & Ceily, Sarah   3-20-1849
Flinn, Peter & Grandy, Emily E.   5-19-1852
Flock, Isaac & Galer, Sarah   4- 7-1847
Flummer, Jacob & Badger, Susan   6- 2-1853(3)
Forehand, James & Roberts, Anna   11- 7-1833
Fornash, William H. & Wineburner, Aley A.
     7-30-1849
Forney, Christian S. & Iams, Mary   9-26-1847
Fornshell, Robert D. & Pilcher, Mary Ann
     8-19-1847
Foster, Elijah C. & Prickett, Mary   10- 7-1852
Foster, Jacob & Fields, Wilmath M.   8- 8-1848
Foster, John & Foster, Mary Ann   3- 1-1853
Foster, Lewis & Coppock, Mary   6-16-1839
Foster, Stephen & Littler, Mary Catharine
     11- 7-1844
Foster, William & Fields, Massilva   12- 6-1849
Fox, Edward & Hummel, Julet Ann   1- 7-1836
Fox, John & Hummell, Hester   7-16-1843
Frazier, Nathan W. & Boots, Martha   8-18-1841
Freeman, Joshua & Lytle, Elizabeth   5-20-1845
Freeman, Winfield S. & Vanborn, Casander
     8-16-1846
Futrell, Abraham & Burson, Jane   7-20-1848

Gage, Henry & Atkinson, Phebe   6- 8-1850
Gains, Oliver & Bradford, Mary Jane   1- 1-1852
Gerrard, Lloyd & Creviston, Amanda   1-11-1838
Gettes, John & Moore, Elizabeth   1- 7-1849
Gifford, Bedford W. & Phebe B. Pearson 1- 8-1852
Gilbreth, Joseph & Prickett, Catharine   9-22-1843
Gillet, John & Arthurhelts, Rebecca   3- 7-1850
Gillett, William & Clark, Welthy Ann   6-22-1848
Glass, John & Hamden, Harriet   2- 5-1850
Goldthait, Cimon & Stevens, Martha E.   11-12-1848
Goldthait, Oliver & Eward, Marilla Ellen 4-11-1847
Gonnerknight, Sebborn & Parsons, Elizabeth
     7-15-1847
Goodykoontz, Abram B. & Phillips, Margaret
     4- 8-1848
Gowdy, Robert S. & Hurley, Elizabeth   3- 2-1839
Grant, John A. & Hurley, Sarah   7-20-1844
Grant, Washington S. & Hurley, Lavina   8-22-1847
Green, Mahlon & Lundy, Lydia W.   4-24-1852
Green, Robert & Wallace, Elizabeth   10- 7-1849
Gregg, Solomon & Bails, Sarah   7-30-1849
Gregg, William & Starkey, Lydia   9- 5-1841
Griffin, James & Murdock, Rachel   9-27-1833(?)
Griffin, Martin & Nelson, Penninah   4-13-1836
Griffin, Robert & Hines, Eleanor   4-24-1834
Grow, John & McCracken, Anna   10-22-1848
Guilinger, Thomas & Coppack, Martha   10- 8-1846
Guillinger, James & Coppock, Sarah   4- 2-1846
Guinin, Edward & Strieb, Sophiah   2-16-1843

Hale, James L. & Utter, Anna   10-26-1843
Hall, James & Moorman, Rachel   4-29-1833
Hall, John F. & Hurley, Lovica   12-12-1841
Hamaker, Benjamin M. & Curtis, Phebe   4-27-1848
Hamaker, Jefferson & Woolman, Martha 10-13-1850
Hamaker, John B. & Williams, Mary Ann 6-27-1850
Hamilton, William & Branson, Drucila   7-22-1838
Hammer, William & Moon, Clarinda   10- 3-1843
Hampton, John & Dehaven, Lydia   10- 3-1844
Hardy, Noah & Case, Jestina   8-15-1849
Hardy, Otha & Dowden, Jane   3-26-1843
Harenden, Jeduthan & Clanin, Susan   3- 8-1849
Harlan, Andrew J. & Hendrix, Delila   9-19-1839
Harlan, Isaiah M. & Oppy, Melissa   8-17-1843
Harlan, Isaiah M. & Counett, Mary Allena
     11-29-1849
Harper, Joseph & Creviston, Catharine 12-13-1846
Harper, Mordacai & Ross, Charlotte   2-10-1853
Harrison, John & Barnett, Jane   4- 1-1846
Harrison, Lewis & Searl, Elizabeth   11-25-1841
Harrison, Stephen S. & Cloud, Mary Ann 7- 4-1852
Harrold, Andrew & Wellington, Hannah 10-29-1851
Harvey, James & Hiatt, Leuzena S.   2-25-1847
Harvey, Michael & Hodge, Sarah C.   2- 1-1852
Haskel, Jabez & McDaniel, Elizabeth   8-18-1833
Havens, Jonathan & Clark, Gabrilla   4- 7-1842
Hawket, Joseph & Tharp, Emaline   11-23-1843
Hayworth, Richard & Meek, Ruey   12-27-1840
Heaverlan, William & Baty, Emily   4-20-1846
Heavilin, Abram J. & Heal, Harriet   11-18-1852
Heavilin, Ephraim & Cowgill, Susana   1-17-1847
Heel, William & Anderson, Elizabeth   3-26-1845
Hendricks (Hendrix), William F. & Young, Elizabeth
     12-22-1851
Hendrix, William E. & Hurly, Margery   10- 8-1840
Hendrix, William E. & Lawson, Mary   3-25-1844
Hendrix, William E. Jr. & Sutton, Ellen   3-25-1848
Henly, John R. & Newby, Sarah   3- 6-1851
Hess, Abner & Ward, Sarah J.   12-13-1849
Hess, R.S. & Massey, Sarah   6-12-1839
Hess, Roley & Branson, Phebe   5-17-1836
Hess, Roley S. & McKray, Mary Jane   12- 3-1837
Hiatt, Alfred & Thomas, Lucinda   11- 4-1847
Hiatt, Aram & Roberds, Lucinda   9- 1-1836
Hiatt, Bartly & Johnson, Priscila   4-29-1838
Hiatt, David & Lee, Barbara   4-19-1846
Hiatt, Elam & Patterson, Loiza   10-25-1838
Hiatt, Eli & Patterson, Corinda   11-28-1838
Hiatt, Eli & Nelson, Martha   6-22-1850
Hiatt, Elias & Walker, Rachel A.   5-21-1852
Hiatt, Elihu & Macy, Lydia   11-16-1851
Hiatt, Jesse & Pearson, Rebecca J.   11-30-1848
Hiatt, William & Huffman, Sarah Ann   8-27-1846
Highley, James & Myer, Sarah   5- 9-1847
Highley, John & Pence, Mary   11-24-1849
Hill, Charles W. & Willcuts, Lucy Ann   6-29-1848
Hill, Charles W. & Gardner, Martha J.   8- 5-1852
Hill, Ezra C. & Stewart, Nancy E.   9-10-1852
Hill, Jackson & Wallis, Lucy   1-29-1852
Hillman, Abijah & Smith, Amanda   11-18-1852
Hillman, Daniel & How, Sarah E.   1-21-1847
Hillman, Loami O. & Coate, Elizabeth 10-15-1846
Hillman, Phineas R. & Benbow, Ann   1- 4-1852
Hindman, John & Troxell, Polly   9-18-1832
Hines, Mahlon & Adamson, Mary   7-15-1841

Hinshaw, Levi & Hodgson, Martha	3-10-1850
Hite, David C. & Foster, Mary	1- 1-1839
Hite, Isaac & Lamey, Mary Ann	7-14-1843
Hobaugh, George W. & Malott, Lydia	1- 8-1852
Hobaugh, John R. & Woolman, Lucy	1-16-1842
Hobaugh, Van D. & Conn, Sena	6- 6-1843
Hobaugh, William H. & Parks, Eliza Ann	1- 4-1846
Hockett, Elijah & Tharp, Julia	7-13-1842
Hockett, Elijah & Hinkley, Mary	11- 3-1850
Hockett, Elijah & Waldren, Mary Ann	7-31-1852
Hodge, William B. & Stephenson, Sarah C.	
	1-25-1842
Hogin, David S. & Vantilburg, Elizabeth J.	
	6-22-1852
Hollcroft, Seely & Payne, Joanna	4- 6-1842
Holliday, Joseph W. & Campbell, Elizabeth J.	
	12- 5-1848
Holliday, William L. & Fleenor, Susan	4-24-1853
Hollingsworth, Enos & Hiatt, Elenor	6-27-1844
Hollingsworth, Ira & Russell, Phebe	9-21-1848
Hollingsworth, Isaiah & Morris, Mary	11-28-1850
Hollingsworth, Joseph & Benbow, Lydia	6-28-1843
Hollingsworth, Moses & Russel, Sarah Ann	
	6-23-1844
Holman, Nicholas D. & Massey, Manerva	9- 2-1847
Holt, Emanuel & Bevard, Maria	12-31-1851
Homes, William & Love, Elizabeth	12- 8-1842
Horine, James H. & Davis, Rachel	2-24-1848
Horton, Levi & Stebben, Rosey	4-22-1849
Hosier, Pearson & Rigdon, Elizabeth	4- 5-1838
Hosier, Wilson & Creviston, Harriet	1- 1-1843
How, Edward & Pierce, Elizabeth	10-25-1847
How, William & Duhadway, Emerilas	2-21-1850
Howard, William & Woolman, Ruth	2-12-1845
Howell, Robert & Leuell, Elizabeth	10-14-1846
Hozier, Pearson & Overman, Sarah	8-17-1843
Hubert, John & Clark, Caroline E.	7-24-1849
Huff, Hiram & Wine, Adaline E.	11- 4-1846
Huff, John & Briggs, Mary	10-15-1840
Huff, John & Zuck, Mary Ann	8-19-1847
Huffman, Thomas J. & Knight, Lucinda M.	
	9-23-1850
Hull, Cyrus & Hall, Sarah J.	2-13-1853
Hullinger, Reuben & King, Lydia	2-15-1852
Hullinger, William & Heavilo, Jane	3- 8-1849
Huls, Richard & Olinger, Julia Ann	7-18-1847
Hults, Joseph H. & Kenneday, Amanda M.	
	11- 7-1833
Humbee, Charles & Clarke, Hannah	5-20-1847
Humes, Thomas & Brown, Jemima	2-16-1848
Humes, William & Massey, Mary Ann	10- 3-1844
Hunnel, John & Wise, Eliza A.	1- 2-1847
Hunt, Zeri & Moorman, Elizabeth	12-22-1836
Hurley, Elijah & Rent, Anna	9- 8-1838
Hurley, Joshua & Half, Catharine	12-30-1847
Hurley, William & Wall, Rebecca	11-27-1834
Hurley, William & Boots, Mary	12- 1-1836
Hurray (or Harry), John & Klean, Mary	3- 2-1839
Hutton, Basil W. & Tyler, Lucinda	8-10-1848
Iams, George W. & Overman, Matilda	9- 3-1846
Jacks, Greenberry & Cole, Cyndarilla	9- 6-1839
Jacks, Jeremiah & Ballenger (or Bullenger), Hester	
	3-30-1843

Jackson, Griffith & Nelson, Mahala	2-25-1847
Jackson, Jesse & Lash, Catharine	6-13-1853
Jackson, Mathias & Egbert, Rebecca	8-28-1851
Jackson, Robert & Prickett, Mahala	10- 5-1848
Jackson, William & Levell, Laura J.	4-18-1850
Jacobs, Charles T. & Hummel, Veleria	12- 6-1848
Jay, Denny & Cogshell, Anna	7-31-1851
Jay, Isaac & Davis, Ruth	9-24-1852
Jay, Richard & Cogshell, Mary	4- 2-1852
Jay, Thomas & Russell, Nancy	2- 2-1845
Jessep, John & Small, Kezia	2- 3-1848
Jessop, Jonathan & Lloyd, Mary J.	5- 4-1848
Jessop, Mahlen & Jessop, Isabel	7-13-1845
Jessop, Zenis & Edgerton, Martha Ann	4-11-1846
Jessup, William & Lee, Abigail	8- 1-1852
Johnson, Dixon & Neal, Caroline S.	11-11-1852
Johnson, Isaac K. & Russel, Mary Jane	5-12-1850
Johnson, James & Anderson, Nancy A.	1- 6-1849
Johnson, John & Nelson, Lourana	10-19-1851
Johnson, John & Duffield, Margaret	9-13-1852
Johnston, Benjamin & Moore, Mary Ann	7-15-1849
Johnston, William E. & Dunn, Melissa	
	lic. 8-25-1842
Jones, Abijah F. & Hollingsworth, Sarah	4-19-1848
Jones, David Winston & Atkinson, Jane	9- 3-1840
Jones, Ellis & Morehead, Elizabeth J.	12-25-1851
Jones, Henry & Staley, Eliza	3-18-1847
Jones, Hiram H. & Dolman, Mary M.	3-25-1844
Jones, Joseph & McCormac, Catharine	11-26-1839
Jones, Joshua (of Blackford Co.)	
& Owens, Malinda	2-23-1843
Jones, Lewis & Lytle, Nancy	11- 5-1846
Jones, Nathan & Bailey, Laura A.	2-28-1849
Jones, Richard Jr. & Webb, Martha Ann	11-25-1841
Jones, Robert B. & Wall, Amanda	11-22-1849
Jordan, William & McClain, Rachel	10-29-1848
Jourdan, Alexander & McClain, Sarah	8- 5-1847
Juks, Joel & Martin, Susan	4-23-1846
Jumper, George & Laughrage, Elizabeth	8-15-1848
Jumper, John & Pixler, Sarah J.	1- 8-1849
Keeler, George & Wilkins, Nancy	7- 1-1838
Keever, William & Wimmer, Phebe	3-31-1853
Kelley, David & Thomas, Charlotte	9-10-1848
Kelley, James & McClain, Susanna	12-22-1850
Kelsay, William & Edgerton, Mary Ann	4- 3-1842
Kenedy, Aaron & McKee, Sarah J.	11-24-1844
Kenneday, John W. & Parker, Sarah Ann	8- 8-1844
Kennedy, Charles P. & Johnson, Sarah J.	8-15-1852
Kerlin, Joseph B. & Small, Mary	4-11-1850
Kesler, John C. & Miller, Elizabeth	3-17-1843
Kessinger, David & Nelson, Harriet Ann	5-12-1852
Kessinger, John A. & Jackson, Neoma	1- 6-1841
Kessler, Ulrich & Whiteneck, Margaret	11-30-1848
King, Anthony & Martin, Rebecca J.	11- 8-1849
King, Charles A. & Dodd, Mary	8- 1-1847
King, Jonathan & Love, Elenor	8-24-1849
Kinsey, Samuel & Saxon, Lucretia (or Luticia)	
	5-12-1853
Kirkpatrick, Edmund & Needler, Eliza Jane	
	4-10-1851
Kirkwood, John R. & Brown, Hannah	6- 1-1849
Knight, Manoah & Wilcuts, Martha	3-24-1836
Kretzinger, Henry & Renberger, Matilda	9-16-1849

Ladd, Samuel & Cook, Charity 5-12-1850
Lamb, Eli & Bowman, Mary Ann 12-14-1851
Lamb, Hezekiah & Small, Hannah 5-20-1836
Lamb, Jacob & Yates, Sarah 3-26-1850
Lamb, John & Dille, Mary Ann 3-25-1844
Lamb, Josiah & Lamb, Ruth 9-21-1836
Lamb, Nathan & Jones, Anna 4- 6-1848
Lancaster, Joshua & Hale, Darcus 1-27-1848
Landes, Lewis & Whinnery, Phebe 3-17-1848
Lawson, Aaron & Madden, Mahala 12- 2-1849
Lawson, Joseph & Marks, Margaret 4-29-1847
Lay, John W. & Owings, Rachel 2-12-1851
Leach, Edmund & Brewer, Emly 6- 6-1841
Leach, Esom & Corn, Lucinda 8-28-1838
Leach, John & Feare, Martha Ann 3- 9-1843
Leas, Francis J. & Brandon, Mary J. 8-19-1851
Ledman, Eugenius & Whinery, Selina W. 11-18-1849
Lee, Marma Duke & Barkley, Sarah 9-19-1844
Lemons, George & Bryant, Martha 4-15-1848
Lenfesty, William F. & Barley, Catharine R.
12- 2-1852
Lenox, Hamilton J. & Hall, Mary Eliza 2-27-1844
Levall, Henry & Smithson, Mahala 12-14-1843
Levall, Henry & Morgan, Melvina 6-15-1851
Levingston, Aaron & Edgarton, Nelly 10- 8-1840
Lewallen, Benjamin F. & McClain, Harriet
4-27-1852
Lewis, George & Montgomery, Rachel 7-15-1852
Lewis, Henry & Cline, Elizabeth 3-22-1841
Lewis, Jacob & Cline, Lydia 1-18-1841
Lewis, James & McClure, Rosannah 3- 2-1834
Lewis, John & Jobes, Martha 11-25-1847
Lewis, Nathan & Richards, Catharine 7-19-1834
Lewis, William G. & Orsborn, Emiline 6-23-1853
Life, Christian & Sutton, Mary Ann 8-19-1841
Lindsey, James H. & Swayzee, Malinda A.
8-15-1839
Lindsey, Robert H. & Hall, Ellen 9-14-1851
Line, Eastin & Stair, Elenor 12- 7-1847
Little, Daniel & Cloud, Nancy 12-28-1852
Little, John & Endsley, Sarah 12-30-1852
Lloyd, Samuel & Glessner, Cerena 10-31-1852
Loney, William & Creviston, Lydia Ann 5- 4-1837
Long, Ellis & Huff, Malinda 6- 8-1843
Long, Philip & Roush, Dianna 1-27-1853
Lorain (or Loring), Hudson & Beeson, Sarah
1- 9-1853
Lotherage, Levi & Burns, Harriet 7-16-1851
Loundsbury, Truman & Fry, Sarah 4-23-1851
Lovall, Edward & Adkins, Eliza Jane 5- 1-1851
Love, Frame & Brown, Hannah 1-30-1844
Lowe, John & Marshall, Mary 10-20-1847
Ludwick, Joseph M. & Malcom, Rachel 4-11-1844
Lugar, John & Roberds, Darcus 9-16-1838
Lugar, John & Long, Elizabeth 11- 4-1847
Lugar, Jonathan & Gard, Margaret 11-30-1848
Lung, Henry H. & Said, Malinda 9-14-1845
Lynch, Edward W. & Lucas, Mary 12-16-1852
Lyon, William & Barrett, Hannah 2-20-1840
Lytle, Andrew J. & Hardricks, Catharine 4-2-1853
Lytle, George & Huff, Leah 9-23-1851
Lytle, Harman & Wilson, Nancy 8-26-1843
Lytle, James & Buller, Easter 5-15-1837

McCuin, Henry & Miller, Elsy 3-31-1853
McCarty, Joseph & Kidwell, Mary 1-25-1851
McClure, David R. & Fisher, Phebe Ann 6-10-1852
McClure, John & Carter, Recy 8-24-1836
McClure, Joseph & Keller, Elizabeth 8-18-1833
McClure, Joseph & Conner, Electa Ann 8-10-1848
McClure, Nathaniel & Smith, Caroline 12-25-1845
McCormick, John L. & Lee, Diana 1-31-1847
McCormick, Lewis N. & Turner, Rebecca 4-18-1851
McCracken, Alexander & Hannah, Ann 1-11-1844
McCracken, David & Allen, Esther 8-17-1851
McCracken, John & Fairbruther, Anna 2- 6-1853
McCreery, James & Leach, Mary 5- 7-1846
McCullah, Achilles & Copley, Mary Adaline
10-12-1848
McFadden, George & Boxell, Margaret 12-23-1849
McFadden, George & Boxell, Sarah 6-15-1853
McFarland, Uriah K. & Tharp, Ursly W. 6-17-1852
McGuire, Oliver & Stackhouse, Pricilla 8-24-1851
McKinney, David R. & Hogin, Emily E. 6-20-1848
McKinney, Elias W. & Barley, Ottillia 11-26-1848
McKinney, Fielding S. & Oppy, Sarah 3-23-1841
McKinney, Leander M. & Toba, Alcina 10-28-1845
McKinstray, Joseph & Patterson, Margaret
3-21-1844
McMillen, Alexander & Farr, Narcissa M.
12-28-1843
McNary, Samuel & Hite, Susannah 12-20-1848
McNeal, Alfred & Berry, Martha Ann 1-16-1853
McVicker, Archibald & Perfect, Sarah Jane
1-29-1846
McVicker, David & Deane, Anne 5-28-1846
McVicker, William & Foster, Phebe 2-14-1843
Macey, Oliver H.P. & Addington, Mary Ann
2-15-1843
Machatton, Alexander & Lomax, Elizabeth S.
4-29-1852
Mackey, Joshua M. & Malott, Mary 5- 6-1851
Macy, Oliver H.P. & Hocket, Elizabeth 3-24-1846
Maggert, David & Heavilon (?), Ann Mariah
10-13-1850
Malcom, Forgason & Roush, Nancy lic. 11- 8-1852
Malcom, Samuel & Gifford, Mary 8- 5-1847
Malcom, William & Hays, Crissa 2-16-1843
Malcomb, John & Roberds, Martha Ann 6- 4-1853
Malott, Abner & Dailey, Mary 2-26-1837
Malott, Hiram & Pearson, Mary 2-27-1845
Malott, Reason, Jr. & Marks, Rachel 3- 1-1838
Malott, Robert & Draper, Melisan 1-24-1850
Malott, Squire & Lugar, Susannah 10-31-1833
Malott, Wilton & Piatt, Elizabeth 5- 3-1843
Mann, Richard & Jones, Mary Ann 8-25-1852
Mansfield, James & Fees, Susannah 10-12-1843
Mansfield, James & Payton, Ann Jane 12-26-1851
Mansfield, John & Madden, Delilah 3-21-1846
Maple, Mentilla H. & Hendrix, Margaret 9-16-1845
Marine, Jonathan & Forehand, Mary 3-18-1853
Marks, Elisha & Julan, Minerva J. 4- 4-1849
Marsh, Elisha & Tidrick, Charity lic. 5-24-1849
Marsh, Enoch & Martin, Sidney 2-22-1838
Marsh, Isaac & Thompson, Martha 11- 9-1843
Marsh, Lorenzo D. & Moore, Hannah 10-28-1841
Marshall, James & Newcomb, Mary 6-11-1837
Marshall, James & Dennis, Elizabeth 9-27-1849

Marshall, John D. & Roberts, Mary Ann 12-13-1842
Marshall, John M. & Small, Malinda   1-29-1852
Marshall, Joseph & Bird, Elanor   8- 9-1838
Marshall, Joseph & Scott, Phebe Jane   10-11-1843
Marshall, Robert & Cue, Rachel   11- 9-1837
Marshall, Robert & Fanning, Jane   5-17-1840
Marshall, Samuel & Nelson, Sarah Jane   1- 6-1853
Martin, David H. & Bocock, Sarah   2- 8-1852
Martin, William & Hummel, Eliza   9-25-1834
Mason, Elihu & Collins, Elizabeth   5- 3-1846
Mason, John C. & Coleman, Mahala   8-25-1844
Mason, Michael S. & Colman, Anna   10-11-1849
Massey, Enos & Lane, Elanor   2- 8-1838
Massey, Even E. & Stephens, Rosaline   3- 3-1842
Masters, Daniel & Fullis, Sarah   7-10-1833
Masterson, Vack & Rhoads, Naomy   2- 4-1849
Matchett, William J. & Chipet(?), Catharine
                                            3-17-1839
Meek, Isaac & Jones, Ruth   7-13-1836
Meek, Jacob & Murray, Sarah   10- 8-1844
Meek, Jacob & Cooper, Tirzey Ann H.   6-11-1848
Meeke, George W. & Keyes, Ann   3-30-1843
Mercer, Aaron & Life, Mary Ann   12-20-1845
Metank, David & McKeever, Margaret   10- 3-1850
Metcalf, Jacob & Watson, Mary   1-16-1851
Michael, Peter & Simpson, Phebe   5- 8-1845
Middleton, Bethuel & Weaver, Nancy J.   1- 1-1852
Miles, Alfred & Gillespie, Lucinda   7-13-1845
Miles, William C. & Moore, Mary Jane   9- 9-1838
Miles, William C. & Pierce, Rebecca K.   8-19-1849
Miller, Daniel B. & Boots, Mary   5-24-1832
Miller, Henry & White, Mahala   12-31-1850
Miller, Isaac Newton & Corn, Martha Jane
                                            6- 8-1848
Miller, John J. & Cane, Virginia   5- 4-1848
Miller, John S. & Myers, Mary A.   3-28-1850
Miller, Paul & Parker, Mary   10-10-1850
Miller, Sylvester C. & Janes, Susannah   1-18-1849
Mills, Job S. & Willcuts, Elizabeth   10- 6-1851
Mills, Joseph & Lugar, Margaret   5-27-1841
Mills, William & Holloway, Margaret   5-12-1849
Mire, Thomas & Hodgins, Lucinda   3-13-1843
Modlin, Elias & Ratcliff, Mary (or Martha)
                                            6-18-1840
Modlin, Jacob & Kenneday, Eliza J.   8- 8-1844
Monahan, Larkin & Martin, Sarah   6- 2-1842
Montgomery, James & Thomas, Mrs. Hannah
                                            11-26-1833
Moody, George & Hurley, Syntha   11-25-1839
Mooraw, Mark F. & Burson, Jane   6-17-1852
Moore, Benjamin & Williams, Effa A.   1-16-1850
Moore, Francis A. & Weaver, Rosanna   8- 1-1850
Moore, George & Case, Rebecca   3-10-1842
Moore, James W. & Wright, Marada   3- 6-1845
Moore, Jesse & Massey, Jane T.   1-31-1850
Moore, John & Montgomery, Hannah   11-12-1846
Moore, John W. & Egbert, Maria   11- 7-1848
Moore, Samuel & Douglass, Jane   7- 4-1852
Moore, Samuel & Nixon, Serrelda   12- 5-1852
Moore, Samuel G. & Blinn, Julia Ann   7- 1-1852
Moore, Thomas C. & Eyestone, Rose   5-19-1853
Moorman, Cuzee & Hobbs, Amanda   10- 2-1847
Moorman, Philip D. & Gilbert, Sarah Jane 6-9-1853
Morehead, William & Sutton, Sarah Jane 12-17-1850
Morgan, Benjamin & Hobaugh, Rachel   9- 7-1841

Morgan, Robert H. & Davis, Rebecca   4- 3-1852
Moris, Jesse & Lamb, Sarah   5- 2-1847
Morris, Jesse B. & Jones, Catharine   6-15-1845
Morris, William & Jones, Margaret   12-14-1843
Morrow, Robert S. & Elliott, Elizabeth   11-30-1848
Mote, James & Coppock, Margaret   9-15-1841
Mote, Jesse & Coppock, Darcus   6-25-1838
Mullens, Jesse & Rader, Catharine C.   1- 1-1843
Murphy, James & Harrington, Sarah   1- 5-1853
Murray, Abram & Barns, Sarah   3-16-1848
Murray, David & Hummel, Katharine   2-29-1844
Murry, Abraham & Beard, Nancy   1-13-1852
Murry, Abraham & Creasun, Rachel Ann
                                     lic. 1-25-1853
Murry, James & Hobaugh, Lydia   1- 8-1843
Myer, Noah & Powell, Malvina   10- 3-1852
Myers, Jacob & Martin, Sarah Ann   8-17-1845
Myres, Jacob & Lefler, Hannah   6-30-1840
Myres, Soloman & Martin, Nancy J.   4-22-1850

Neadler, David & Walters, Maranda   1- 6-1839
Neadler, John & Adset, Mary Jane   4-10-1841
Neal, Charles W. & Roberts, Nancy   8-18-1850
Neal, James & Adamson, Anna   11-16-1837
Neal, Thomas J. & Brownlee, Elizabeth   7- 4-1841
Neal, William & Presnal, Julia   8-19-1847
Needham, Jesse & Winslow, Sarah   2-18-1841
Needham, John & Winslow, Mary   11- 2-1843
Nelson, Hezekiah & Busson, Rebecca   1- 2-1840
Nelson, James R. & Patent, Alvira   1-29-1846
Nelson, James W. & Jay, Susannah   3- 9-1851
Nelson, Lawrence & Wilson, Clarissa   12-24-1846
Nelson, Mathew & Hays, Martha   1-24-1839
Nelson, Stephen & Nelson, Elizabeth   6-19-1852
Newcom, John & Barnard, Mary C.   9-29-1849
Newel, Daniel & Smith, Elizabeth   10-25-1849
Newport, Daniel & Coal, Perlina T.   2-14-1847
Niccum, Robert R. & Coal, Elizabeth Jane
                                            12-17-1846
Nickles, Ousborn & Weaver, Sarah J.   5-30-1852
Noble, James & Cochran, Jemima   9-17-1846
Norton, Eugene & Morgan, Elizabeth   3-23-1847
Nottingham, Owen P. & Couch, Mary Ann 2-24-1853
Nun, John & Rood, Lucinda   5-15-1853
Nun, Riley & St. Clair, Nancy Ann   3-20-1851
Nusbaum, Henry S. & Stair, Elizabeth   5-4-1848

O'Harra, John & Stripe, Catharine   7- 3-1842
Okeley, Abraham & Bash, Elizabeth   9-26-1844
Okley, Abraham & Bash, Lidia   11-14-1848
Olinger, Henry & St. Clair, Rebecca   9-12-1847
Olinger, John & Wood, Susan   9- 4-1848
Oliver, Edmund & Hill, Seneah R.   8- 5-1852
Oliver, John & Pearson, Elizabeth   4- 7-1853
Oppey, Jacob & Neal, Amanda   2- 2-1840
Oppy, Jacob & Briggs, Elizabeth T.   1- 8-1843
Oren, Alexander & Philips, Ann   7-10-1853
Orr, Robert & Marks, Eliza   10-18-1842
Osbum, David & Harris, Mary   6- 6-1844
Overman, Benjamin & Burson, Rebecca 12-13-1846
Overman, Benjamin & Marshall, Clarissa 1-12-1851
Overman, Ephraim & Jones, Martha Ann 7-29-1841
Overman, Ephraim C. & Jones, Elizabeth 6- 4-1851
Overman, Jesse & Griffin, Jane   5-10-1838
Overman, Jesse & Clark, Sarah   2-21-1839
Owings, Thomas & Roberds, Elizabeth   2-14-1850

Palmer, John & Dunlap, Athalinda 3-22-1850
Palsley, Robert W. & Fergus, Mary 2-22-1849
Parker, Charles & Toler, Elizabeth 4- 8-1841
Parker, Daniel & Parker, Cintha A. 10-14-1847
Parker, James G. & Parris, Milly 11-27-1851
Parks, John & Smith, Frances 1-24-1850
Parks, John W. & Creviston, Lydia Ann 11- 6-1851
Parris, Berry & Dwiggins, Sarah Jane 12-31-1851
Parsons, William & Newby, Rebecca 6-13-1839
Parsons, William & Hobbs, Ann 9-12-1843
Patterson, Andrew & Turner, Lucina 10-14-1846
Patterson, Amos & Roberts, Esther 8-11-1852
Patterson, Henry K. & Adamson, Sarah Ann
9-17-1840
Patterson, John & Zook, Jerusha 9-19-1852
Patterson, John C. & Babb, Anna 12-19-1850
Patterson, Philip & Baldwin, Mary 10-30-1851
Patterson, Samuel & Iams, Sarah 1- 2-1840
Patterson, Samuel & Draper, Lucinda 11-23-1848
Patterson, Samuel & Messersmith, Emily E.
10- 4-1849
Patton, Wesley L. & Moomaw, Catharine 5-20-1852
Pearson, Bailey & Jones, Elizabeth 9-26-1849
Pearson, Thomas & Draper, Sarah 10-20-1836
Pearson, William & Patton, Mary A. 1-18-1849
Pegg, Wiley J. & Nelson, Julia Ann 1- 9-1848
Peirce, Henry & Austin, Telitha Ann 3- 7-1841
Peirce, Levi & Entzminger, Matilda 8-10-1840
Pence, Lewis & Fisher, Elizabeth 1-26-1851
Pennington, Aaron & Barnes, Margaret 12-16-1851
Peril, James C. & Walker, Elizabeth 12-27-1849
Perry, Andrew J. & Lloyd, Elizabeth 9-16-1852
Perry, Richard & Stanley, Rebecca 9-28-1839
Peterson, George D. & Fees, Sarah 5- 3-1849
Peterson, William & Wright, Julia Ann 4-15-1847
Pilcher, Charles D. & Smith, Sarah 10-18-1849
Pixler, Robert & Wood, Mary 10-15-1846
Plaster, John & Buller, Rebecca 2-10-1853
Poe, John & Philips, Sarah 3-18-1852
Pope, Robert M. & Martin, Mary Ann 3-20-1851
Porter, Reuben W. & Woolard, Rachel Jane
7-27-1852
Potter, Earl & Powell, Sally 3- 2-1850
Powell, Harrison & Hale, Nancy 3-23-1843
Powell, Joel F. & Hooper, Henrietta C. 10-17-1848
Presnall, Absalom & Beauchamp, Tamer 8-19-1847
Presnall, Elihu & Davis, Mary Ann 8-16-1849
Price, Joab & Massy, Lovina 2-11-1838
Price, Levi & McCoy, Eliza 8-24-1851
Price, Samuel & Poe, Nancy 6-13-1844
Price, William & Starkey, Mary 12-31-1846
Price, William & Badger, Lovina 3- 8-1851
Price, William L. & Dalrymple, Catharine 9-28-1851
Pricket, Benjamin & Moor, Rebecca 11-14-1845
Pricket, Perry & Watkins, Sarah A. 5-27-1850
Pricket, Thomas & Alexander, Susannah 5-23-1848
Prickett, Adolphus & Prickett, Lydia 9-18-1851
Prickett, Fleming & Bruss, Ann Catharine
10-24-1852
Prickett, John & Hall, Betsey 10- 5-1848
Prickett, John F. & Hendrix, Rhoda E. 3-20-1852
Prickett, Levi & Fees, Catharine 4- 2-1846
Prickett, Nathan & Malott, Winney 1-31-1839

Pritcett, Jonathan R. & Collins, Julia Ann
10-30-1851
Pugh, Josiah & Walker, Margaret 8-15-1848
Pulley, James & Marsh, Elizabeth 9-23-1846
Pulley, Jonathan & Marsh, Martha Jane 3- 3-1853
Pulley, Samuel & Boxell, Olive Emily 8- 1-1844
Pully, Adam & Wiant, Keturah 4- 9-1840
Pully, James & Hendrixson, Eliza 2-14-1847
Pyle, Jesse K. & Nelson, Elizabeth S. 12-18-1851
Py' Nathan & Milligan, Maria 6- 6-1853

Rader, James S. & Riffle, Nancy 1-15-1848
Reasner, Noah & Slater, Matilda 7-11-1839
Reasoner, Richard & Capper, Lydia 4-13-1852
Reasoner, Samuel & Perrell, Mary Jane 10-28-1844
Reavis, Asberry & Saine, Aberiah 6-16-1850
Reed, Levi & Lugar, Martha Ann 11-16-1848
Reeder, William H. & Said, Mary Elizabeth
10-27-1850
Reel, Henry S. & Said, Nancy 8- 9-1843
Reeve, Benjamin C. & Simons, Alma 12-21-1848
Reeve, Joseph T. & Simons, Cynthia A. 12-20-1848
Renaker, James & Marks, Lucy 1-31-1850
Renbarger, Edward & Prickett, Mary 1-21-1838
Renbarger, George & Pricket, Jemima 11-23-1834
Renbarger, Henry & Diller, Susannah 6-13-1843
Renbarger, Henry & Martin, Louisa Jane 9- 7-1851
Renbarger, Isaac & Lugar, Nancy 3- 3-1842
Renbarger, Charles & Egbert, Eliza 11-16-1848
Reynolds, James & Shearman, Minerva Ann
10-13-1844
Rhodes, Adam Evan & Trask, Abigail 5-20-1845
Rich, George & Buller, Elizabeth 6-14-1844
Rich, John & Hix, Susannah 2-10-1853
Richards, Henry & Reader, Mary J. 5- 7-1849
Richards, Jacob & Gillispie, Susan 3-23-1848
Richardson, Jonathan & Winslow, Lydia 8-20-1846
Richardson, Zimri S. & Newby, Rebecca 1-10-1850
Richardson, Zimri S. & Harvey, Martha 8-18-1852
Riggs, Andrew R. & Brandon, Mary C. 3- 4-1852
Riggs, John W. & Harrison, Martha Ann 2-27-1851
Ritter, Jacob & Rood, Selestina 8-23-1849
Rix, John & Nelson, Milla 8-31-1848
Rix, Jordan & Feutrel, Martha Ann 3-11-1852
Roberds, Benjamin & Rood, Lydia 11-16-1841
Roberds, Elijah & Mitchell, Evaline 10-13-1850
Roberds, Joseph & Simons, Ann 9- 9-1847
Roberds, Phineas & Brooks, Elizabeth 8-29-1846
Roberds, Timothy & Whitson, Phebe 3-29-1838
Roberts, Ashford & Simons, Matilda 1- 1-1849
Roberts, Benjamin & Hiatt, Lydia 2- 7-1836
Roberts, Edward & Hodgson, Darcus 3- 1-1843
Roberts, Edward & Malcom, Mary Ann 12-15-1850
Roberts, Isaiah & Burson, Rebecca 3- 2-1834
Roberts, Michael & Bird, Sarah 1- 8-1845
Roberts, William M. & Marzley, Elvira 3- 1-1849
Rogers, Branson & Monroe, Julian 4-16-1843
Rood, Christopher C. & Druley, Elizabeth
3-11-1849
Rood, George H.D. & Malcom, Margaret 6-11-1840
Rooks, (?) Thomas & St. Clair, Rachel 2-14-1833
Rooks, Thomas & Miller, Clarrissa 4-12-1849
Rouch, William & McCormack, Jane 3-25-1841
Ruley, Alexander J. & Spence, Rebecca A.
9-12-1848

Rupe, George & Sertan, Sarah 12-23-1849
Russel, Samuel & Smith, Lutitia 8-27-1835
Russel, Samuel A. & Hogin, Catharine A. 3-8-1842
Russell, Ithamer & Dolman, Harriet 5- 7-1848
Russell, John & Collins, Nancy 3-15-1849
Russer (Rouser), Peter & Miller, Catharine
2-12-1847

St. Clair, James & Branson, Lydia 2- 4-1835
St. Clair, James & Braffet, Evaline 2- 2-1853
St. Clair, William & Rood, Sarah 5-14-1837
Sarfo, John & Hurley, Samantha 2-18-1837
Saunders, Joseph & Nixon, Sarah 3-30-1849
Scott, Allen C. & Johnson, Matilda 1-13-1839
Searl, Elijah M. & Lanson, Rachel 6-19-1845
Selby, Otho & Allen, Jane Caroline 9- 2-1845
Shaffer, David & Pemberton, Jane 5-16-1852
Shanhan, Amos B. & Niccum, Marilla 4-16-1849
Shanon, Reuben R. & Crown, Jane 3-16-1850
Shaw, William S. & Tharp, Ceila 3- 7-1850
Shear, Nicholas & McFarren, Elizabeth 10- 7-1852
Shetler, Hezekiah & Sutton, Nancy A. 6-10-1849
Shetler, William & Harrison, Jane 7- 8-1848
Shipley, James & Lyon, Rachel Ann 11-16-1851
Shipley, Samuel & Curtis, Sarah 7-22-1852
Shively, James S. & Marshall, Harriett 4-16-1837
Shockey, John & King, Catharine 3-30-1852
Shoemaker, William H. & Wellington, Valleriah
5-15-1851
Shuff, David H. & Bradford, Catharine 1- 6-1850
Shuman, Joseph & Wilson, Eliza 4- 6-1843
Shupe, Tunis A. & Pugh, Margaret 3-28-1852
Simons, Benjamin & Davis, Rebecca 1-16-1840
Simons, James & Hinkley, Elizabeth 10-29-1851
Simons, Nathan & Burson, Mahala 6-11-1840
Six, James & Miller, Eliza M. 2-12-1852
Sizmore, William & Fields, Judiah 11-28-1850
Skinner, John & Wallace, Perscilla 5-28-1846
Slagel, Frederick & Parker, Mary Elizabeth
8- 1-1851
Slagle, Conrad & Clanan, Sarah 11-11-1852
Slagle, John & Creviston, Christina 3- 6-1837
Slagle, Joseph & St. Clair, Sarah 1-21-1842
Slater, Jacob & Shields, Harriett 4-19-1838
Slater, John N. & McFarren, Sarah J. 3- 7-1850
Small, Benjamin & Addington, Hannah 4-25-1840
Small, Isaac H. & Campbell, Hester Ann 5- 7-1846
Small, Jabez & Dailey, Eliza J. 9- 8-1850
Small, James B. & Beauchamp, Matilda 3- 3-1842
Small, Josiah & Boxell, Nancy Jane 1-28-1850
Small, Josiah & Simons, Sarah 11-3-1850
Small, Nathan M. & Perry, Ruhama 9- 9-1852
Small, Reuben & Davis, Melissa Jane 1-20-1853
Smith, Amos & Slagle, Avirvilla 8- 3-1851
Smith, Caleb & Dilla, Nancy 9-20-1832
Smith, Caleb & Hiatt, Elizabeth 2-13-1837
Smith, Edward B. & Newell, Manerva 3-20-1851
Smith, George & Berry, Sarah M. 3-30-1851
Smith, George W. & Murray, Elizabeth 8-10-1848
Smith, George W. & Brodrick, Catharine 7-29-1849
Smith, Henry W. & Smith, Emily 7-20-1848
Smith, John & Thomas, Mary Ann 9- 8-1831
Smith, John & Vanhom, Jemima J. 5- 6-1849
Smith, John A. & Dawson, Elizabeth J. 11-14-1849
Smith, John Barkam & Dilla, Rachel 9-20-1832

Smith, John V. & Levall, Evaline 1-20-1853
Smith, Lewis & Webb, Elizabeth 8-31-1848
Smith, Mathew & Jourdan, Mary lic. 12-13-1848
Smith, Matthew & Taylor, Keziah 1-10-1849
Smith, Oliver A. & Thompson, Mary E. 3-20-1853
Smith, Parker & Thomas, Sophrona 3-22-1838
Smith, Thomas E. & Leach, Martha A. 5-26-1852
Smith, William & Bradfield, Thurzy 11-20-1842
Smithson, Judiah & Neal, Lydia 7- 8-1852
Snyder, John & Smith, Nancy J. 3- 8-1849
Spell, Spencer & Knox, Margaret 7-16-1851
Springer, Jesse M. & Doty, Jane A. 12-31-1848
Spurgeon, Ebenezer S. & Lammey, Terrissa
8-26-1852
Stackhouse, George W. & Adamson, Polly
10-26-1834
Stair, Joseph & Pearson, Mary Ann 2-15-1846
Stallard, Jacob M. & Thornton, Louisa 8-12-1851
Standley, John & Nun, Nancy 1-16-1851
Standley, John & McCreery, Mary 5-26-1851
Stanfield, William W. & Wright, Jemima 11-19-1843
Starbuck, Elisha & Pearson, Susan 12-12-1850
Starbuck, Gayer & Shaw, Cynthia A. 2-24-1848
States, Albert W. & Cougal, Rebecca J. 1-24-1850
Stephens, Alfred M. & Porter, Catharine 5-29-1849
Stephens, Isaac & Cain, Nancy 11-18-1849
Stephenson, William & Bash, Mary 10-22-1848
Stevens, William & Cain, Mary 12-21-1851
Stevenson, John N. & Goldthait, Margaret
10- 7-1838
Steward, Thomas & Green, Elsy 3-11-1846
Statler, John & Fleming, Elizabeth 4- 1-1852
Stout, John & Yont, Catharine 10- 9-1850
Summers, Elijah & Reeves, Susannah 9-13-1840
Sutton, Jeptha & Eltzroth, Sarah 11-28-1835
Sutton, Jeptha & Brandom, Mary 6-14-1840
Swafford, Marion F. & Williams, Elizabeth
3-28-1852
Swan, Cyrus A. & Lewellen, Rebecca 11-25-1852
Swayze, Aaron C. & Hodge, Minerva A. 2-16-1841
Swayze, John B. & Simons, Fidelia 7-11-1841
Swift, Stephen & Scott, Sally Ann 5-20-1841
Swisher, Anthony & Shideler, Sarah Jane 4-18-1848
Symons, Bethuel & Hunt, Amy 1-29-1835

Taylor, Daniel W. & Alexander, Cintha 10-14-1852
Taylor, Isaac & Speelman, Adaline 11-25-1852
Taylor, James & Myers, Martha 12-17-1844
Taylor, John & Burson, Nancy 1-11-1851
Taylor, Joseph A. & Tippey, Margaret 6- 1-1849
Taylor, Mathew & Hullinger, Catharine 2- 8-1852
Taylor, Robert & Druck, Myrrillus F. 1-16-1845
Taylor, William & Ritch, Rebecca 3-12-1851
Taylor, William J. & Hindman, Rebecca J.
1-26-1851
Tharp, Thomas & Howell, Rachel 10-19-1837
Thomas, Amos & Presnall, Emily 5-31-1851
Thomas, Henley & Holler, Catharine 7-15-1849
Thomas, Isaac M. & Moore, Jane 2- 9-1841
Thomas, John & Jones, Nancy 8-22-1844
Thomas, John & Brown, Anna 7-29-1847
Thomas, John & Clark, Eleanor 10- 3-1852
Thomas, Milton & Way, Martha 6-15-1837
Thomas, Milton & Stackhouse, Mary Jane
12-14-1850

Thomas, Solomon & Moorman, Ruth   3-18-1850
Thomas, Timothy & Carrothers, Eliza   12- 2-1845
Thomas, William & Addington, Martha Ann
                                         6- 6-1839
Thomas, William B. & Brown, Polly   9- 3-1847
Thomason, James & Stebbens, Catharine 6-19-1853
Thompson, Howel D. & Butler, Eliza Jane
                                        12- 5-1852
Thompson, Jesse W. & Mullins, Catharine
                                        12-12-1852
Tippy, Henderson, & Marsh, Vashti   4- 8-1841
Todd, Adreal & Raynalds, Elizabeth   3-19-1840
Todd, Jonathan & Reeve, Sarah   10-13-1850
Tomlinson, Wilie & Hammer, Margaret   3-27-1851
Toohee, David & Littler, Adaline   1- 9-1851
Toomire, Bryant & Cole, Rebecca   5- 9-1846
Townsend, James & O'Haver, Jemima   3- 2-1851
Townsend, Uriah & Taylor, Rachel   6- 7-1849
Trent, Alexander & Smith, Sophrona   12- 5-1850
Tribbey, Thomas M. & Ward, Priscilla A. 9-20-1852
Tribet, William & Conway, Nancy   4-18-1835
Trimble, Peter & Marquis, Mahala Ann   1- 1-1840
Truax, Isaac & Hillman, Anna   8-13-1848
Turner, Henry & Adkin, Margaret   7-23-1849
Turner, John & Crawford, Margaret   9-10-1843
Turner, Joseph P. (or B.) & Covey, Mary Ann
                                         4-10-1853
Turner, William H. & Jordan, Mary   1-14-1851
Tyson, Thomas & Poe, Louisa   7-10-1845

Vannard, Samuel & May, Jane   12-24-1846
Vanscoyoc, Aaron & Benbow, Charity   3- 2-1844
Varner, Hiram & Rodgers, Lucinda   1-20-1845
Vernon, Ira & Miles, Emily   1-30-1848
Vinson, Nathan & Hobbs, Lucinda   3-17-1849
Voris, William R. & Newell, Rhoda L.   12- 4-1851

Walker, Arthur & Rogers, Rebecca lic. 11-27-1847
Walker, James & Smith, Eliza   12-17-1840
Wall, Alson R. & O'Haver, Elizabeth   3- 6-1851
Wall, Dugan & Wall, Susan   2- 2-1853
Wall, William & Malott, Mariah   12-24-1835
Wallace, Alexander S. & Loman, Prucilla 2-6-1840
Wallace, Benjamin F. & Steer, Celinda G.
                                         5-16-1848
Wallace, Robert & Weaver, Julia Ann   10- 9-1851
Wallace, William & Brownlee, Catharine 12- 2-1841
Wallace, William L. & Wallace, Elizabeth
                                         7-29-1839
Wallis, Aaron & White, Eliza   4-25-1852
Wallis, Elisha & Birden, Phebe   3- 4-1852
Wallis, Isaac & Wood, Eliza   1- 4-1852
Walters, Warren N. & Pully, Elizabeth Ann
                                         1-29-1846
Ward, Obediah & Burk, Caroline   7-21-1833
Ward, William & Cravens, Martha   3- 3-1853
Ware, John A.J. & Vanhorn, Rachel   4-28-1850
Warrenburg, David & Work, Ruey Ellen   6-30-1851
Watson, John & Adset, Harriet Elonina   2- 2-1840
Watson, Robert & Hendrix, Mary   10-30-1850
Watson, William & Curtis, Louisa   1-17-1850
Weasoner, Joseph & Walker, Mary Jane   6-19-1843
Weaver, Byrd L. & Chavois, Sarah Ann   11- 7-1850
Weaver, Henry & Burden, Sarah M.   12-14-1852
Weaver, John F. & Stokes, Leanna   7-24-1851
Webb, Floyd H. & Jenkins, Mary   9-28-1851

Webster, Harrison B. & Scott, Mary E.   11-23-1841
Weesoner, David & Dille, Susannah   7-13-1837
Welch, Andrew & Hite, Mary   3-11-1841
Welsh, Jonah & Horton, Juliet   9- 2-1845
Weston, John & Montgomery, Jane   6- 8-1837
Wharton, William & Grayham, Rachel   7- 2-1835
Wheat, Thomas & McKeever, Sarah   9- 3-1851
Wheeler, George B. & Coon, Suzellen   10-30-1851
Whinerry, Mills & Light, Jane   3- 3-1846
Whisler, Samuel & Harlan, Eliza Maria   1- 2-1851
Whistler, Andrew & Creviston, Delila   7- 4-1841
Whistler, Henry & Jackson, Rachel   11- 9-1845
Whistler, Jacob & Horton, Wealthy Ann   1- 9-1844
White, Alexander & Phillips, Eliza Ann   7-18-1839
White, George & Green, Hannah J.   12-27-1849
Whitson, John & Draper, Mariam   1-30-1837
Wiant, Isaac & Woolman, Eliza   11- 9-1845
Wiant, Jacob & Gains, Melinda   1-27-1842
Wickersham, Noah L. & Ward, Mary J.   9-18-1851
Wilcuts, John & Moore, Jerusha   12- 2-1847
Wilcuts, John & Morris, Sally   12-16-1847
Wilcuts, John W. & Baldwin, Pelinia   12-23-1851
Wilcutts, John & Crutchlow, Milly E.   3-31-1853
Willcuts, Jehu & Scott, Martha Ann   2-11-1852
Williams, David W. & Bradford, Mary C.   2- 4-1849
Williams, Isaac & Jones, Rebecca   11-11-1847
Williams, Joseph & Chambers, Nancy   4-29-1833
Williams, Levi & Carter, Mary A.   12- 5-1844
Williams, Lewis & Howard, Mary   3-28-1848
Williams, Lewis & Burns, Elizabeth M.   4-10-1852
Williams, William & Foy, Julia Ann   9-12-1852
Willson, Thomas & Wills, Mary   2-27-1840
Wilson, Henry & Parsons, Kesiah   8-22-1844
Wilson, James M. & Renbarger, Martha   1-11-1846
Wilson, James S. & Morgan, Eveline   10-12-1844
Wilson, John & Rigdon, Hannah   lic. 9- 1-1834
Wilson, John M. & Lucas, Mary Ann   6- 3-1841
Wilson, Micajah & Neal, Margaret   4- 9-1846
Wilson, Samuel & Knox, Dorothy   12-11-1851
Wilson, William & Ruley, Sarah Elizabeth 9-12-1850
Wine, Benjamin & Long, Mary Ann   3-25-1841
Wine, George W. & Bevard, Elizabeth   3-21-1844
Winebruner, William & Bevard, Nancy   4-30-1846
Winslow, Jesse H. & Johnson, Susanna   8-25-1849
Winslow, William & Neal, Sarah   10-21-1841
Wise, John & Marine, Mary Ann   8- 6-1851
Wonderly, Isaac & Moore, Mary Ann   5- 1-1851
Wood, Hiram & Olinger, Mahala   11-20-1847
Wood, William & Braffet, Lavina   4-12-1849
Wood, William & Braffit, Marinda   11- 7-1852
Woodring, Benjamin & Payne, Celia   2- 1-1846
Woodring, Valentine & Bates, Mary   10-18-1849
Woollman, Benjamin & Murray, Lydia   1- 4-1849
Woolman, Burr & Conger, Elizabeth A.   9-10-1851
Wooton, Henry & McCracken, Rachel   8-17-1851
Work, Henry & Holman, Sarah J.   11-20-1851
Worthen, James P. & Snider, Elizabeth   11- 2-1848
Wright, Charles & Reynolds, Betsheba   10-27-1850
Wright, David & Lytle, Mary Jane   12-10-1848
Wright, Joel & Said, Susannah   2-17-1842
Wright, John E. & McKee, Syntha Ann   2- 5-1849
Wright, Robert & Wright, Margaret   12-29-1842
Wright, Robert & Bradfield, Amanda   12-16-1847
Wrightsman, Abraham & Davis, Judah   3-10-1848

Yont, Andrew & Bevard, America   11-20-1850   Zeek, John & Smith, Rixia A.   12-30-1849
Young, John A. & Johnson, Melissa   11-11-1852
Young, William & Bash, Hannah   2- 7-1850

CORRECTIONS IN GRANT COUNTY MARRIAGES

The following corrections should be made in the marriages as printed in the April-June, 1974, issue of the *Hoosier Genealogist:*

    Bruner, Samuel - Catherine Briggs (not Griggs)

    The surnames Benoy and Beony should be Beuoy or Beouy, according to Mr. Gordon P. Tierney of Inverness, Illinois.

THE HOOVER FAMILY

The following account appeared in the Paris (Ky.) *Western Citizen,* January 12, 1855, taken from the Dayton (Ohio) *Gazette* of January 1. It was reprinted in *Kentucky Ancestors, Vol. X, No. 3 (January, 1975).*

A PIONEER FAMILY PARTY — A party of nine — David, Frederick, Henry and Andrew Hoover, with their sisters Elizabeth Bulla, Susannah Wright, Rebecca Julian, Catharine McLean and Sarah Sanders — met last week at the residence of the latter, in the vicinity of Richmond, Ia., and by way of reviving past recollections for comparison with the present, visited Dayton on Friday, by railroad, taking dinner at the Phillips House.

Fifty-two years ago, before Ohio was a State this same party emigrating from North Carolina, passed through Dayton then a small log-house village and stopped 10 miles north on Stillwater. Owing, however, to the prevalence of the ague, they settled in the Spring of 1803 at the head of Clear Creek. Having remained there four years they removed to White Water, Indiana Territory — now Wayne County — in the neighborhood of Richmond; where most of them have resided to the present time. But one of the family is dead — the mother of John Newman, esq., President of the Indiana Central Railroad and a distinguished member of the Indiana Bar. The oldest of those living, is now seventy-six, and the youngest fifty-six — all, except the oldest sister, being in robust health. In connection with their residence in this region, they relate many incidents and trials peculiar to pioneer life. It is among the agreeable reflections in which they are permitted to indulge in the evening of life, that they have contributed their share in subduing nature and reducing the forests to fields, while the records of both Church and State testify in their service in each.

DEARBORN COUNTY MARRIAGES, 1826-1833

Compiled by Mrs. Ruth Slevin from microfilm of Books 1 and 2 in Genealogy Division, Indiana State Library. The marriage records prior to 1826 were lost in the fire that destroyed the courthouse on March 5, 1826. A few were rerecorded in Book 2 and additional ones were taken from the Lawrenceburg newspapers available in the Archives Division. A few of the earliest marriages in the county were preserved in the papers of William Major, a justice of the peace, and are in the Tippecanoe County Historical Museum. The marriages from the above three sources appear at the end of the 1826-33 listings.

Abbott, Isaac - Elizabeth Faulkner		10-14-1827
Abbott, Richard - Sarah Amanda Cornelius		
		12-29-1831
Abbott, William - Frances Bruce	lic.	7- 7-1829
Abercrombie, Samuel - Mary Purcell		2-14-1828
Adams, Jacob - Harriet Tanner	lic.	9-30-1827
Adams, Moses - Sarah Cain		4-26-1829
Adkins, John H. - Mary Ann Dudley		8-22-1830
Akers, Benjamin L. - Elizabeth Bogard		10-25-1829
Allemong, Henry - Rebecca Masten		3-21-1830
Allen, Joseph - Dorcas Williams		6-28-1831
Allen, Wiatt - Anne Carleton		2- 1-1829
Allington, Thomas - Rebeccah Disberry		
	lic.	2- 9-1830
Anderson, Howell - Sarah Stockton		9- 2-1833
Andrews, Bazil - Mary Jackson		9- 3-1829
Andrews (or Anderson ?), Peter - Jane McClary		2-23-1832
Andrews, Robert R. - Maria Freeland		11- 8-1827
Antrim, Joel - Mary Morgan		3- 6-1828
Archibald, Edmund - Belinda Calhoun		12- 6-1827
Archibald, William - Polly Carmichael		12-28-1826
Armstrong, John - Margaret Sutton		1-17-1832
Armstrong, Thomas - Catharine Ivins		7- 9-1832
Armstrong, William - Clarissa Clark		8-19-1832
Arnold, Benjamin F. - Amanda Richardson		9-11-1832
Arnold, Charles, of Hamilton Co., Ohio - Eliza Hartpence		5-11-1828
Arnold, Richard - Nancy Bromwell		10-22-1829
Arnold, William B- Elizabeth D. Hennegin		
		12-16-1828
Atkeson, Robert - Syntha Switzer		8- 5-1833
Aylesberry, Frederick - Nancy Whitley		3-15-1832
Bacon, Alexander - Eunice W. Beach		6-20-1833
Bailey, Henry - Elizabeth Curtis		10-12-1826
Bailey, John L. - Eleanor Birdsell		9- 6-1829
Bailey, Richard - Sarah Hamilton	lic.	1-24-1829
Bainum, Conanery (?) - Sarah Dashiell		4-11-1832
Baker, John - Louisa Howard		11- 4-1832
Baldwin, Philemon P. - Lorena Love		11-25-1832
Ball, Aaron I. - Mary Cannon		6-17-1831
Barber, Eliphalet - Ann Chappelow	lic.	12-17-1832
Barber, William - Maria Hinkston		1-12-1832
Barkdall, David - Abigail Hamblin		5-25-1833
Barkdall, John - Mary Hall		3-27-1831
Barkhurst, George - Rachel Richardson		6-25-1829
Barkhurst, Isaac - Jane Davidson		6-19-1828
Barkhurst, Samuel - Sarah Hodge		7-24-1831
Barklow, Harman - Rebecca Thom		10-23-1828
Barnhart, David B. - Sabra Sill		3-23-1828
Barrickloo, John - Ruth Mayall	lic.	11-13-1829
Barricklow, Farrington - Elizabeth Perkins		
		4-10-1832

Barricklow, Farrington - Martha Buchanan		4- 4-1833
Barricklow, Henry - Mary Lutton (or Sutton)		
		1-14-1827
Barricklow, Henry - Sarah Ellis		7-25-1833
Barricklow, John - Frances Thompson		1-25-1830
Barricklow, John Jr. - Mary Emmerson		9-21-1826
Barricklow, Joseph - Catharine Buchanon		2-21-1833
Barricklow, William - Nancy Miles		4- 7-1831
Bartholomew, Gilead - Sarah Roseberry		
	lic.	1-28-1831
Bartholomew, Samuel - Susan Hibbetts		6- 6-1833
Bartlett, John William - Catharine Carmichael		
		3- 2-1830
Barton, John - Delina Ferris	lic.	6-16-1829
Bayley, Obadiah - Martha Hall		7- 2-1829
Baylor, Jacob - Agnes Hume		3- 8-1831
Bean, Robert - Parmilea Beach	lic.	5- 1-1828
Bear, Ezra - Priscilla French		3-31-1833
Beatty, John - Hewitt, Ruth		5-25-1826
Beeson, Amos - Helen Maria Test		5-25-1829
Belles, Daniel - Nancy Hume		8- 2-1827
Bennet, Thomas - Chloe Ann Mason		9-13-1829
Best, Samuel - Sarah H. Green		12-11-1828
Bettis, Philip - Lettecia Pate		6- 6-1830
Bevan (or Bevins), Thomas - Elizabeth Dean		
		5- 4-1826
Biddle, George - Hetty Cameron	lic.	9-20-1826
Bigley, Charles - Peggy McBride		5-18-1826
Billingsley, James - Sarah Hayes		10- 4-1832
Birdsel, William C. - Louise Emerson		5-17-1832
Birdsell, Isaac - Elizabeth Burnes		3-19-1829
Blake, Stephen - Elizabeth Seward		1- 5-1832
Blasdel, Ambrose - Sophia Dean		4-15-1832
Blasdel, Enoch - Eleanor Cooper		2- 1-1827
Blauvelt, James - Maria Wright		4-18-1827
Bledsoe, Joseph - Rachel Hathaway		4-10-1828
Blue, Uriah - Elizabeth Smith		3-11-1830
Blue, William - Mary Roseberry		12-25-1828
Bobbs (or Babbs), George - Fanny Sefton		
	lic.	12- 6-1832
Bolander, Jacob - Margaret Davis		12-26-1830
Bostwick, Jacob - Maria Daniels		4-17-1831
Bostwick, James - Elizabeth Heavrin	lic.	11-10-1832
Bottz, Peter - Hannah Michael		9-27-1832
Bowan, Samuel - Elizabeth Leonard		3- 8-1827
Bowen, John D. - Mary Ann Smith		2-16-1832
Boyce, Alexander - Virginia Bradley	lic.	9-18-1826
Boyd, John H. - Isabella Jane Furgason		
	lic.	7- 9-1827
Boys, William - Mary Durbin	lic.	10-21-1826
Bradford, Eli - Mary Ann Wright		3- 9-1829
Brady, John - Mary Levitt		8- 9-1827
Bramble, Ayers - Nancy Abraham		6- 7-1832
Brasher, Charles - Eliza Danford		9- 4-1828

Brasher, Charles L. - Mary Cook	6-12-1828
Brewington, Benjamin - Martha Benham	3-10-1832
Briggs, Charles - Anne Hambleton lic	3-25-1833
Brookes, John - Anne Jones	1-19-1832
Brown, James - Elvey Trulock	8- 9-1832
Brown, James - Harriet Conaway	12-13-1832
Brown, John P. - Ammaranda Holford	7-21-1831
Brown, William - Maria Kincaid	4- 3-1828
Brown, William - Amanda Kincaid	4- 8-1832
Brown, Zebedee - Pamelia Hardin	8-12-1827
Bruce, Isaac - Julia Ann Farrand	8-27-1829
Bruce, Torrence C. - Pertama Pate	8- 9-1832
Buble(?), George - Anne Leavitt lic.	7- 9-1832
Buchanon, Samuel - Sarah Johnson	8-31-1832
Buchanon, William - Lucinda Douglass	4- 1-1827
Buckanon, George - Maria Gerrard	5- 5-1829
Buffington, Stephen - Nancy Flake	9-13-1827
Bunce, Alonzo - Sarah Teny	6-22-1828
Burk, Daniel Cᵣ - Sarah Cranzee	8- 8-1826
Burk, Jesse - Elizabeth Harris	10-28-1830
Burke, Baylous C. - Jane Shelby	1- 1-1829
Burroughs, Elhanan - Angelina Peck	1-19-1832
Cable, George W. - Mary Baker	2- 6-1833
Cage, Israel - Sarah Green	5-26-1833
Cairnes, William - Mary Ingles	4- 8-1828
Cameron, Henry - Nancy Foster	12- 5-1832
Campbell, Caleb - Matilda Jones	6-11-1829
Canfield, William - Matilda Riggs	2- 6-1832
Cannon, Charles B - Belinda Cochran	
	lic. 10-19-1830
Cannon, Holman B. - Maria S. Ball	1-22-1833
Carman, Amos - Mary Huffman, by consent	
of guardian John Boyer	lic. 9-11-1827
Carmichael, Hugh - Elizabeth Chappelloo	5-29-1831
Carpenter, Joseph - Isabel Purdy	12- 9-1832
Casady, William - Sarah Henderson	12-27-1827
Casidey, Robert - Margaret Morgan lic.	11-23-1830
Casseldine, Henry - Eleanor Walton	1-27-1831
Cassidy, John - Sarah Morgan lic.	5- 7-1832
Chalmers, Andrew - Rachel K. Heuston	8-29-1833
Chamberlin, Robert - Elizabeth Reed	9-25-1828
Chance, Robert - Ann Maria Champeon	1- 3-1833
Chapman, Thomas C. - Mehaley Abbott	7-15-1832
Chappelow, John - Mary Routh lic.	12-17-1832
Cheesman, Edmond - Abigail Cozene lic.	12-24-1827
Cherry, Thomas - Zipporah, Ripley	4-24-1826
Chinn, Ellis - Anne Williamson	7-12-1827
Chisman, Elias - Elizabeth Baker	9-20-1832
Clark, Eli - Sarah Miller	11-13-1828
Clark, Hardin - Rachel Williams lic.	4-11-1827
Clark, James M. - Mary Mason	1-26-1832
Clark, William Alfred - Angelina Roberts	2-26-1829
Clarke, James - Sarah Stoneking	3-24-1827
Clarke, John B. - Sophia Abright	5-24-1827
Clarke, Linus A. - Agnes Nelson	10-27-1831
Cloud, Daniel - Neoma Hathaway	3-21-1833
Cloud, Vivian - Sarah Gibson	2- 7-1833
Cochran, Isaac - Eleanor Large	7-19-1832
Cochran, Joseph - Polly Large	10- 8-1829
Coldwell, Bartholomew - Eleanor Stage	12-25-1828
Cole, Benjamin D. - Elizabeth Hume	5-11-1830
Colshear, Jesse - Melinda Green lic.	8-29-1833
Coman, Russel - Ann McMath	3-12-1829
Conaway, John - Nancy Wilson	4-15-1832
Cone, Thomas - Mary Maria Stuart	10- 3-1827

Conner, Daniel - Julia Ann Bigley lic.	10-20-1830
Conner, John - Sarah Goodner	12-23-1828
Cook, Elisha - Charlotte Briddle	9- 5-1833
Cook, Sylvester - Lydia Stevenson	2-19-1827
Coon, Josiah - Mary Nelson	3-24-1829
Cooper, Henry - Nancy Ellis	12-24-1828
Cornwell, Elijah - Mary Bromwell	4-24-1831
Cory, Parks - Margaret Sill	4- 9-1826
Cottingham, George - Hester (Hetty) Wooley	
	11-19-1829
Cottingham, William - Elizabeth Maple	12- 6-1829
Cox, William - Eliza Borvin	7- 2-1828
Cox, William - Anny Peters	7- 3-1832
Coyle, Amos T. - Sabrina McCardel	10-17-1830
Cozine, Cornelius S. - Mary Ann Miller	11-22-1831
Craft, John B. - Mary Hastings	11-26-1826
Craig, Daniel - Hannah Philbrick	1- 4-1831
Crandall, Crockett - Hannah Kelsey	1- 6-1831
Crandall, Nathaniel - Mary Pate	10-20-1827
Criswell, David - Elizabeth Lynn	2-25-1830
Croel, Hiram - Mary Conger	12-22-1830
Cross, Aaron S. - Elizabeth Barns	5- 1-1828
Crouch, Nehemiah - Mary Clarke	11- 5-1826
Crouch, William - Elizabeth Malott lic.	1-21-1828
Crozier, George - Hetty Souders	9-30-1830
Cry, Ephraim - Sally Hall	4-28-1831
Crysonburry, Benjamin A. - Rebeccah	
Sunderland	11- 1-1827
Cure, Justus M. - Mary Norris	11-16-1826
Cure, Justus M. - Nancy Briddle	11-24-1829
Curtis, John - Purthena Davis lic.	9-27-1827
Curtis, Samuel - Agnes Curry, Negroes	6-16-1829
Cusack, Michael - Jemima Lacey	2-16-1829
Danford, Hollis - Bolinda Brown	10- 9-1828
Daniel, John - Harriet Demoss	4- 5-1827
Daniels, James - Paulina Morris lic.	2- 4-1828
Daniels, William - Rebeccah Crowl	
(or Cowl)	11-23-1828
Daniels, William Jr. - Mary Griffith	2-19-1829
Darling, Alfred - Charlotte Tibbets	6- 7-1832
Darling, George H. - Maria Snell	5-16-1833
Darling, John - Abigail Gibson	1-18-1827
Darling, Peter H. - Harriett Freeland	11-18-1830
Darling, Thomas - Juliann Martin lic.	3-31-1827
Darragh, Charles - Sarah Bruce	7-29-1830
Darragh, James M. - Margaret Griswold	7-16-1826
Darragh, Jesse - Mary Winings lic.	1-13-1830
Dart, Nimrod - Mary Foster	8-24-1828
Daubenheyer, Peter - Nancy March	10-25-1826
Daugherty, John - Christiana Carabaugh	6-13-1830
Daugherty, John - Martha M. Hogshier	1-19-1832
Davidson, William - Mary Hogshear	10-15-1832
Davis, David D. - Hannah Donohoe	2-22-1831
Davis, Zimri Nelson - Jane Arthurs	5-21-1829
Dawson, Harrison - Charlotte Jane Dowden	
	7-22-1833
Dawson, Noble - Sarah McGarvey	1-29-1832
Dawson, Thomas - Sarah Ann James	10-26-1826
Day, Stephen M. - Emily Wilson	6-16-1831
Dazey, Jacob - Nancy Beach	8-11-1830
Dazey, James H. - Mary Ann Goble	7-24-1828
Dement, Benjamin - Elizabeth Coy	6- 9-1832
Dennis, Benjamin - Anna Downey	9-29-1831
Dennis, George B. - Margaret Ann Cloud	10-31-1830
Dewitt, David - Hannah Ann Scofield	3-21-1832

Dill, Abner - Mary Roberts   lic. 7-16-1833
Dill, Alexander Hamilton - Gertrude Pearson
                                                      3-11-1827
Dill, Benjamin - Elizabeth Roberts   10-18-1832
Dils, Albert D. - Parmelia Jaquith   12- 6-1828
Dils, Henry - Clarissa Hasty   lic. 6-18-1831
Dils, Jacob - Teny Dawson   7- 1-1827
Dils, Stokely - Aurora Plummer   5-12-1829
Dils, William - Ann Morgan   10-26-1826
Disborough (or Disbury), John -
     Mary C. Gibbs   9- 2-1830
Dixon, William - Juliann Round   1- 1-1833
Dolph, Jacob - Charity Spoor   3-31-1831
Donahoe, James - Sarah Beach   8-22-1833
Dorman, John - Mary Jane Truitt   1-17-1833
Downey, James M. - Eliza Phelps   3- 3-1831
Downey, John - Sarah Gibson   2- 4-1830
Drake, Enoch - Sarah Hueston   11- 7-1829
Drake, Benjamin - Nancy Lathrop   4-28-1832
Driver, Harvey - Sarah Williams   6- 2-1832
Drake, James P. - Priscilla Buell   1-23-1831
Dudley, Francis Danna - Mary Ann Palmer 10-8-1828
Duncan, William - Charlotte McCurdy   6-28-1829
Dunkin, John - Nancy McCaslin   2-25-1830
Dunlap, Archibald - Elmira Chandler lic. 10-30-1829
Dunn, Gersham G. - Jane Freeland   6-20-1833
Dunn, John P. - Almira J. Buell   6-11-1826
Durbin, William S. - Eliza A. Sparks   11- 2-1828
Duskey, Enoch - Sarah Fryer   2-15-1827
Dyer, David - Priscilla Henry   2-26-1829

Eastman, Joseph - Lorena Richmond   1-13-1830
Eastman, Nelson - Mary E. Pugsley   7- 4-1833
Elder, Charles - Jemima Carmichael   2-12-1829
Elder, John - Jane Williams   6- 7-1832
Elder, Lemuel G. - Jane Record   12- 5-1826
Elkins, William - Susan Smith   10-20-1830
Elliott, John Jr. - Rhoda Dexter   7-30-1829
Elliott, Samuel - Lavenia Chandler   7-10-1833
Ellis, Blake, - Elizabeth Griffin   3-29-1832
Ellis, David - Mary Bartor   2-24-1831
Ellis, Hezekiah - Amanda Tower   10- 2-1832
Ellis, William - Joanna Whitten   lic. 9- 8-1829
Elsbury, Isaac - Martha Ann Bennett   8- 5-1830
Espy, David - Maria Showers   3-16-1826
Evans, Samuel - Hanna Michael   lic. 2- 8-1831
Evill, Luke - Susannah Lindsay   lic. 10-16-1829
Ewbank, Martin C. - Rebeccah Clark   4-15-1828
Ewbank, Robert - Jane Milburn   6-19-1832
Ewbank, Thomas - Lois Frances Fitch   5- 7-1827

Faduree, John - Elizabeth Hill   12- 6-1830
Fairbanks, Alexander - Catharine Perdun 2- 2-1832
Fairbanks, Solmon - Paulina Jaquith   11- 1-1827
Farran, Isaac - Lydia Switzer   1-17-1828
Farrar, Taylor - Jane Todd   7-28-1831
Ferris, Marmaduke E. - Sarah Jane Hunter 9-18-1828
Finley, Mahlon - Margaret Fall   7-24-1827
Finley, Squire B. - Sarah Ann Williams   1- 1-1833
Fisher, Cyrenus - Nancy Finch   lic. 9-30-1826
Fisher, Emmerson - Sarah Fisher   1-20-1831
Fisher, Witt - Sally Robinson   12-25-1826
Fitzgerald, Aaron - Mary Reed   9- 5-1832
Flake, Adam Jr. - Elizabeth Brewington   9- 6-1827
Flake, Amer - Nancy Golding   11-22-1827
Flake, Michael - Elizabeth Moore   5-13-1827

Fleming, John - Catharine Bowers   lic. 11-11-1829
Foster, John - Abigail B. Parris   3-14-1833
Foster, Lowry - Susannah Showalter   8- 5-1830
Foster, William - Susannah Flenegin   6-14-1829
Foulk, Aaron - Eliza Holman   11- 6-1832
Fowler, James - Eliza Evans   7- 1-1830
Fowler, Robert H. - Mary Ann Butterfield 10-12-1826
Fox, James - Sarah Tinker   lic. 6- 1-1828
Frazier, Rollin T. - Mary Ronalds   12-22-1831
Freeland, Lyman S. - Christiana Perdun   1-10-1828
Freeman, Adam H. - Sarah Marsh   11- 4-1829
Freeman, Benjamin - Elizabeth Moore   9-10-1829
Freeman, Isaac - Hannah Jane Snell   12-14-1828
Freeman, William - Nancy Tucker   5-16-1833
French, James - Mary Ann Parker   lic. 8-23-1833
French, John - Eliza Swift   1-15-1826
Froman, Isaac - Frances Rand   lic. 5-20-1826
Fryor, John Jr. - Lucy Whitley   9-19-1830
Fulton, John - Mary Welch   1-15-1832

Galbreath, James - Mary Ann Farrand   3- 8-1832
Garret, John - Margaret Vansickle   3- 8-1827
Garrison, Alfred - Louisa Melcom   lic. 3- 6-1831
Garrison, James - Eleanor Leming   10-29-1826
Garrison, William - Hannah Morgan   1-21-1830
Gaylor, Jacob M. - Cynthia Crouch   11-18-1830
Gerrard, Richard L. - Rebecca Scott   4-13-1829
Gibb, Samuel - Mary Alpha   7-27-1828
Gibson, David - Mercy Allee   5-29-1833
Gibson, Robert - Ann Henry   lic. 1- 1-1829
Gibson, Whalan - Polly McGahan   10- 5-1826
Gibson, Whalen - Mrs. Elizabeth Graham 7-28-1831
Gibson, William - Mary Ann Clarke   1- 7-1827
Gidney, Charles - Phoebe Upjohn   1-12-1831
Gilbert, Oramel - Mary Ann Hutcheons   3- 4-1830
Gladwell, George Washington -
     Lucinda Jarred   lic. 5-29-1827
Glardon, Peter - Mary Forton   2-18-1828
Glore, Henry - Emeline E. Calkine   4- 1-1831
Gloyd, Noah - Elizabeth Johnson   6-21-1827
Gobel, Ebenezer - Mary Renno   lic. 12-22-1829
Golden, James - Sarah Wilson   8-11-1829
Goodner, John - Jane Latta   11- 9-1826
Goodner, Michael - Catharine Conner   12-24-1828
Gottenby, John - Celia Baxter   5-10-1827
Grace, John - Eliza Ann B. Hall   8-22-1833
Graham, William - Betsy French   11-21-1826
Granger, William - Elizabeth Jackson   9-16-1831
Grant, Daniel - Caroline Bonker   3-28-1832
Grave, Lavantus - Cynthia Oliver   11- 3-1831
Gray, Thomas - Elizabeth Farren   12-25-1827
Gray, Thomas - Susannah Lindsey   9-13-1832
Green, Alexander - Eleanor Lamb   8-12-1827
Green, Hiram Hamilton - Tabitha Carabaugh
                                                 12- 2-1830
Green, Page - Mary Cochran   lic. 3-26-1828
Green, Robert - Nancy Green   11-22-1832
Green, William - Laura Toler   3- 6-1828
Gregg, Milton   [Lucy B. Dennis]   [12-25-1828]
Gregory, Joseph - Clarissa Shaw (or Shane?)
                                                 1-13-1828
Griffin, Samuel - Rachel Conaway   9-10-1829
Groff, James - Elizabeth Holden   10-24-1830
Grove, Daniel - Catharine Wing   6- 6-1830
Grubbs, John - Jane Casady   12-28-1826
Guess, Levi P. - _____   [4- 1830]

Guigurs, Joseph - Sarah Sharabough lic. 11-17-1829

Hail, James - Polly Killum   11-29-1826
Haines, Henry - Caroline Holliday   4-15-1828
Haines (Haynes), Joseph - Lavina Johnson
                                                       11- 4-1830
Haldren, Moore A. - Elizabeth Fowler
                                                  lic. 1-29-1831
Halford, Hiram - Martha Ann Dougal   4-16-1826
Hall, David - Eunice Sanders   lic. 8-20-1830
Hall, George - Nancy Mead   5-17-1829
Hall, Lyman B. - [Sarah Laten]   [4-15-1830]
Hall, Peter - Mary Cluxton   4- 3-1828
Hall, Thomas - Elizabeth Bennett   11- 4-1830
Hamblen (or Hamlin), Linus - Theodosia
   Jaquith   1-26-1832
Hamilton, Allen - Emmerine J. Holman
                                                  lic. 10-23-1828
Hamilton, Charles - Nancy Barricklow   7-28-1830
Hamilton, James Harvey - Amanda Pease
                                                  lic. 10-30-1829
Hamilton, Jarred - Arah Shook   9-12-1830
Hamilton, John - Electra Fisher   8- 6-1829
Hanes, John - Rebecca Wheeler   5-10-1827
Hannah, John - Margaret Jenkins   7-16-1831
Hannah, William - Marybe Barricklow   2-25-1827
Hansell, Francis H. - Anna F. Plummer   1-13-1831
Hansell, John - Jane Cornforth   10-18-1827
Hansell, Thomas - Elizabeth Smith   12- 8-1829
Hanson, Bartlett - Nancy Pressley   5-20-1832
Harbert, Caleb - Sarah Downey   10-19-1826
Harbert, Samuel - Mary McCabe   lic. 10-29-1829
Harbert, —— - —— Moore   4-   1833
Harker, Daniel - Hannah Craw   6-16-1833
Harrawood, John - Gwenay James   10-19-1826
Harrawood, Joseph - Nancy Cheesman   9- 4-1828
Harris, Francis - Catalina Harris   8-10-1830
Harwood, Daniel - Elizabeth Burns   lic. 8-10-1829
Harwood, Frederick - Harriett Powell   6-16-1833
Hathaway, Reuben - Mary Hill   8-14-1828
Hathaway, Reubin - Elizabeth Callahan   7- 1-1832
Hayes, Elijah - Eunice Willey   lic. 6- 6-1826
Hayes, Jacob - Leah Hayes   6-10-1829
Hayes, James B. - Jane Bennet   lic. 12- 2-1832
Hayes, Mahlon - Sarah Miller   6-27-1832
Hayes, Silas - Rachel Hayes   5-31-1832
Henderson, Samuel - Susannah Longdecker
                                                      10-18-1832
Henrill (?), Robert - Elizabeth Morgan   6-11-1829
Henry, Aaron B. - Lydia Small   1- 8-1829
Henry, Samuel - Rebecca Conaway   8-13-1829
Heustis, Elias - Margaret Clarke   11- 8-1826
Heustis, Elias - Sarah Ellis   5-19-1831
Heustis, Henry - Elmira Plummer   12-25-1828
Heustis, Major - Sally Runolds   11- 9-1826
Hewitt, Jesse - Margaret Beaty   8-14-1827
Hill, Ira - Violet Gaw   lic. 4- 4-1833
Hill, John - Elizabeth Daniels   7-15-1830
Hill, Jonathan - Sarah Walden   11- 6-1831
Hinds, James - Mary Brumley   1-20-1830
Hinesley, Joshua - Nancy White   2- 1-1827
Holland, William - Rachel Bowman   3-31-1831
Holliday, Dorman - Julian Little   2-19-1833
Holliday, Sterling - Urania Ball   2- 5-1829
Holliday, Sterling - Juliann Purdy   3-21-1833
Holmes, William - Celia Ricketts   2-20-1832

Hood, John - Mary Ann Bedford   1-24-1833
Hopkins, Henry - Maria Stone   lic. 6-14-1831
House, Eli - Nancy Thompson   11- 6-1831
Howard, John W. - Elethea Marsh   8-11-1833
Howe, Jonathan - Clarissa Cruger   9-13-1832
Howe, Sylvanus - Sarah Ann Scranton   10- 5-1828
Howell, Chatfield - Ann French   1-25-1829
Howlet, Benjamin - Jemima Howlet   3-17-1831
Hubbard, Nehemiah - Elizabeth Inman   11-22-1832
Hubbell, Enoch J. - Polly Bowen   3- 6-1833
Hueston, Thomas W. - Isaphena Couch   12- 4-1826
Hueston, Wilson B. - Jane Boyle   8-15-1833
Hulse, Edmund - Lydia Ann Loder   2- 2-1832
Hume, George - Lucinda Powell   3- 5-1829
Hume, Madison - Eliza Bowers   3-23-1828
Hunter, Abner - Lancy Vargison   lic. 1-27-1833
Hunter, Alanson - Prescilla Havern   9-10-1829
Hunter, Joseph - Rhoda Ann Conger   7- 9-1833
Huston, Christopher - Susannah Lemon   12-27-1827
Huston, Thomas W. - Iyphena Couch   lic. 12- 1-1826
Hutchings, Jonathan - Hettey Whetsei   1-28-1830

Ingle, Ralph - Betsy Mason   lic. 9- 4-1826
IsGrigg, Washington - Laura Jane Castle   1-17-1833

Jackson, Asa - Rachel Powell   lic. 1- 8-1827
Jackson, Enoch - Elizabeth Hardisty   3- 8-1827
Jackson, Enoch - Elizabeth White   3-19-1829
Jackson, Enoch Jr. - Catharine Garrison   7-22-1830
Jackson, Ezekiel - Elizabeth Andrews   12-25-1828
Jackson, George G. - Thomasion Bean   9- 9-1832
Jackson, John Randolph - Charlotte Guthridge
                                                       5- 2-1833
Jackson, Martin - Delia Dils   lic. 6-12-1827
Jackson, Washington C. - Nancy Moore   2- 3-1829
Jackson, William - Polly Wilkinson   1-19-1826
James, Pinkney - Mary Ann Craft   11- 9-1828
Jane, John - Lucretia Newton   11- 5-1829
Jaqueth, Nathaniel T. - Harriet L. Neal   10-16-1827
Jarvis, Squire - Julian McIntosh   10-   1832
Jenkins, Ira - Sarah Matthews   10-19-1830
Jenkins, John - Malinda Cooper   7-18-1833
Jennings, Thomas - Emmeline Jones   8-14-1833
Johnson, David - Elizabeth Guile   lic. 9- 5-1829
Johnson, James F. - Elvira Gibbs   3-19-1831
Johnson, John D. - Sarah Brownley   10-23-1828
Johnson, William - Elizabeth Mendal   11-23-1828
Johnson, William P. - Maria L. Olmstead   3- 8-1832
Johnson, William - Sarah Spangler   8-16-1832
Johnson, Young - Mary Spangler   7- 5-1832
Johnston, David - Charlotte Cheeseman   4-16-1829
Johnston, Jacob - Mary Thornton   lic. 6-12-1829
Johnston, John - Eliza Standifird   8-25-1831
Jolly, Charles - Martha Southard   5- 2-1833
Jones, Elisha - Lucinda Chance   11- 4-1832
Jones, James - Sarah Hudson   7-11-1830
Jones, Lewis - Winifred Curtis   11-20-1832
Jones, Richard - Mary Coen   9- 9-1830
Jones, Theophilus - Margaret Williams   9-10-1829
Jones, Thomas - Emily Wilkins   lic. 10-26-1832
Judd, Roswell - Elizabeth Liddle   3- 8-1827
Jurdon, Rufus - Parmelia Mapes   11- 9-1826

Keighan, Daniel B.W. - Mary Williamson   4-30-1827
Kell, Benjamin - Rheuma Beckner   9-13-1832
Kelso, Joseph - Margaret Stone   8- 4-1831

Kenneday, Thomas - Mary Ann Madden   8-10-1829
Kenton, James - Emily Bromwell   4-24-1831
Kersey, Daniel T. - Louisa Parris   8- 9-1832
Kilcheel (Kitchell?), Joseph -
    Catharine Carmichael   lic. 8- 7-1827
Kincaid, Warren - Lucinda Peck   8- 7-1828
Kinney, Cornelius - Nancy Fuller   lic. 7-13-1826
Kins, John A. - Matilda Morford   3- 4-1827
Kirtly, Larkin - Nancy Wilson   9- 3-1829
Kitchell, Joseph - Harriet Dils   8-12-1830
Kittle, Daniel - Mary Anne Downey   8-21-1831
Kittle, Jacob - Mary Boyce   12-27-1827
Knapp, Ezekiel - Charlotte Myrick   7-30-1829
Knapp, Nehemiah - Clarissa Frazier   10-19-1828
Kneeland, George - Celikey Edwards   1-11-1827

Lamb, Alexander - Martha Varguson   12- 9-1830
Lamb, George - Elizabeth Shepherd   6- 7-1827
Lamb, George - Rachel Larrison   3-15-1831
Lambertson, James - Hetty Dickinson   1-21-1830
Lamkin, Hiram - Catharine Graves   11- 4-1829
Lanes, James - Maria Claspill   7-12-1829
Laniess, William - Jane Ann Atheam   2-23-1828
Larabee, Charles - Lucinda Faulkner   4- 1-1830
Larew, Jacob - Rebecca Read   5-27-1830
Larrison, George - Leah Glenn   12- 2-1830
Lathrop, Erastus - Juliet Fenton   8- 5-1833
Lawrence, Daniel - Magdalene Bargin   2-14-1830
Lawrence, David - Elizabeth Kyle   8-23-1826
Lawrence, John - Magdalena Showalter   4-17-1828
Lawrence, Jonathan - Catharine Yeager   9-14-1826
Lawson, John - Margaret Sells   lic. 5-20-1833
Leavitt, Asaph - Caroline Whitten   3-15-1832
Leming, Harvy - Eliza Golden   lic. 9-12-1827
Lemmons, James, of Boone Co., Ky. -
    Catharine Love   3-15-1832
Lemons, John - Frances Plummer   9-21-1828
Lemons, Samuel - Esther Farr   lic. 6-19-1828
Lenover, James - Sarah Helms   9-15-1833
Lenover, John - Elizabeth Boyce   5-26-1833
Leonard, James - Mrs. Abigail Hilderback 5-18-1826
Lewis, John K. - Lucinda Isabel Best   9-24-1829
Lewis, —— - ——Mason   4- 1833
Liddle, John - Martha O'Conner   10-12-1826
Liming, Lorenzo D. - Elizabeth Knowland
                              lic. 6- 6-1829
Lind, Joseph - Sarah Smith   2-13-1831
Lindsay, Solomon - Mary Vincent   4-14-1831
Lindsey, Cyrus - Mary Jackson   lic. 10-24-1826
Lindsey, Elijah - Araminta Frazier   4-11-1833
Linn, Leroy W. - Delilah Craft   9-24-1831
Lippard, Jacob E. - Elizabeth Thornton   6- 1-1828
Little, Elias - Nancy Wallace   10-13-1828
Little, Ephraim - Lucinda Shed   2-28-1833
Littlefield, Harvey - Mary Ann Bovard
                              lic. 5-21-1832
Longley, Thomas - Lydia Shafer   6-18-1828
Longwood, Milo - Rebeccah Scott   5- 6-1829
Loring, Bradley - Emmeline French   6-19-1831
Lose, John - Lucinda Burns   11-16-1826
Lounsbury, Joseph - Palmira Herrick lic. 1- 2-1830
Low, John - Eleanor Duncan   1- 1-1830
Lowe, Harrison - Frances Coldwell   4-26-1832
Lowe, William - Abigail Roberts   12-20-1832
Ludwick, Jacob - Hester Myers   9-25-1828
Luke, George - Betsey Rudisel   1- 7-1830

Luther, Abraham C. - Rebecca Downey   11-27-1827
Lynas, Joseph - Sarah White   8- 9-1826
Lynes, George - Lucinda White   4-12-1832
Lynn, George W. - Phila Vanworner   9- 7-1830
Lyons, James - Rhoda Conaway   10-27-1831
Lytle, Thomas C. - Mildred M. Bootts   8- 4-1831

McBride, Robert - Sarah Fuller   10- 2-1832
McCabe, John - Margaret Stewart   lic. 12-20-1830
McCardell, Philander - Polly Scranton   2-21-1832
McClaine, Samuel - Jane Harbert   2-19-1829
McClean, Conrad - Elizabeth Walden (or Weldon)
                                    11- 3-1829
McClure, William - Eliza Trumbull   6- 8-1826
McCullum, John - Rebecca Dixon   2-17-1828
McGahan, James - Mary Ruth Williams   10-18-1832
McGloughlin, Hiram - Elizabeth Cox   9-25-1828
McGrew, Thomas - ————   [12- 1828]
McGuire, Michael - Nancy Blue   1-13-1831
McGuire, William - Maria Blue   7-24-1831
McIntire, James - Polly Miller   lic. 1- 5-1833
McKinney, James - Abigail Miller   6-25-1826
McKittrick, James - Penelope Linn   5-29-1828
McKittrick, William - Zerelda Allen   4- 7-1833
McManaman, James - Margaret Runyon   3- 6-1828
McMullen, Daniel - Nancy Fox   5-16-1826
McMullen, Samuel - Nancy Dunn   3- 6-1826
McNeely, Elisha - Catharine Thornsburgh 8- 5-1827

Mahan, Daniel - Sarah McKenzie   2-17-1833
Manley, Martin - Huldah Halford   10-16-1830
Mapes, James Jr. - Ema (Ana) Roberts   8-26-1827
Mapes, William - Mary Jurdon   10-26-1826
Marshall, Thomas - Lucretia Protzman   7-16-1826
Martin, James Montgomery - Sarah Hodge
                              lic. 3-15-1832
Mason, Isaac - Mary Ann Lynch   9-16-1830
Mason, Jacob - Rebecca Showalter   5-14-1831
Mason, Jacob - Charlotte Dart   8-28-1833
Mason, John - Elizabeth Sanks   2-27-1831
Masters, Joseph - Elizabeth Cairnes lic. 12- 7-1832
Matthews, James - Elizabeth B. Anderson 5-27-1830
Mead, Allen - Rhoda Crouch   1- 5-1832
Meeker, William - Sarah Jane Shane   8-28-1831
Merryman, Aaron Y. - Margaret Elliott
                              lic. 5- 5-1826
Mettler, Isaac - Hannah Banister   3-18-1827
Michael, Casper - Hetty Battz   10-18-1832
Middleton, Isaac - Frances Bennett   12-11-1828
Milburn, David - Harriet Coldwell   6-19-1828
Miles, John - Harriet Hayes   4-19-1827
Miles, Levi - Catharine Durbin   lic. 4-24-1833
Miller, Aaron - Eleanor O'Conner   lic. 5-14-1832
Miller, Daniel - Sarah Roberts   5- 2-1828
Miller, Daniel - Eleanore Clore   2-11-1830
Miller, George - Margaret Douglass   9- 7-1826
Miller, Job - Sarah Morison   12-24-1829
Miller, John - Eliza McCardell   9-17-1827
Miller, Mahlan - Eliza Hayes   10- 6-1831
Miller, Michael H. - Matilda Colwell   4- 5-1832
Miller, Thomas - Eliza Moore   5-26-1833
Milliken, James - Priscilla Noyes   4-12-1827
Mills, John - Anne B. Marshall   11-15-1832
Mineman (?), Henry - Margaret Ringer   8- 4-1833
Mitchell, Samuel H. - Margaret Wining,
    (daughter of John Wining)   3-16-1826

Moers, Herman - Mary Sullivan	8-13-1829
Montgomery, James - Electa O. Wilson	2-26-1828
Moodey, George E. - Rachel Harbert	2-14-1833
Moore, Henry B. - Huldah Stroud	7-25-1830
Moore, David - Mirah ——, Negroes lic.	9-22-1831
Moore, Robert - Helen Maria Gidney lic.	1- 1-1828
Morford, Caleb - Charlotty Harris	11- 8-1827
Morgan, John - Mary Osburn	9-24-1829
Morgan, Lewis D. - Mary Ann B. Farrell	4-17-1828
Morris, Bethuel F. - Mrs. Margaret E. Noble	
	7- 1-1832
Morris, John - Sarah Miller	7-23-1830
Morrison, William - Mary Ann Stewart	3-19-1833
Morton, William - Mary Manlief	11-16-1826
Moss, Harvey - Elizabeth Stevens	7-25-1833
Moss, John - Elizabeth Jordan	8-29-1833
Moss, Thomas L. - Rachel Donahoe	8-15-1833
Mouk, Jacob - Delia Jackson lic.	8- 3-1831
Moulton, Levi - Rebeccah Lacey	7-16-1832
Mounts, Charles - Catharine Wicks	8-11-1829
Moys (or Mays ?), Simon - Jane Manliff	
	lic. 2-22-1830
Muir, Thomas - Eliza Frazee	3-25-1832
Murphy, Peter - Drusilla D. Wolf	3-10-1833
Musgrave, Eli - Elizabeth Flake	1-14-1830
Myers, Henry - Margaret Hogshire	5- 4-1828
Myers, John - Rebecca Ann Weaver	2-10-1831
Myers, Manuel - Ann Carman	5- 8-1828
Nelson, Benjamin - Charlotte Sharp	8- 3-1826
Nelson, John - Elizabeth Pearce	11-11-1826
Nelson, Jonathan Ross - Huldah Hunter	1- 4-1829
Nelson, Samuel - Sarah Wells	10-11-1828
Nelson, Thomas - Elizabeth Blackburn	
	lic. 9-17-1830
Nelson, Thomas - Harriet Watson	7-10-1833
Nelson, Zachariah - Emmeline Wooley	11-19-1829
Nevins, Charles S. - Margaret Bennet lic.	11-24-1828
Nichols, Elikam - Hannah Dolson	11-11-1832
Nichols, Lewis - Elizabeth Wheeler	12- 5-1829
Nichols, Ninnan - Jane Hogshead lic.	9-25-1826
Noble, Benjamin S. - Mary Jane Armstrong	6- 6-1831
Noble, Jonathan - Elizabeth Dashield	5-30-1833
Norrick, Peter - Mary Ann Freeman	4- 9-1829
Norris, Joseph - Sarah Ward	12-28-1826
Norris, Joseph - Lydia Wilcox	10- 5-1828
Norris, Richard - Margaret Wilcox	1-24-1828
Norris, Richard - Clarina Porter	12- 1-1829
Norris, Stephen - Esther Davis	8-26-1830
Nowland, Jeremiah - Parmelia Blasdel	9- 2-1827
Noyes, Amos - Sarah Crocker	12-22-1831
Noyes, Amos - Lavinia Crocker	4- 6-1833
Noyes, Talmae - Nancy Brimhall	2-23-1832
Nye, Zadok Allen - Kitty Ann Hinkston	
	lic. 9- 2-1828
O'Brian, Moses - Matilda Holland	8-30-1832
Ocley (or Odey), Nathaniel - Martha Suits	10-20-1830
Oliphant, James M. - Caroline Tousey	4-12-1832
Oliver, John - Polly Craw	5-17-1827
Oliver, Simeon - Mahitable Hobert	9-11-1828
O'Neal, Benedict B. - Jemima Santee	4-20-1826
Osborn, Abraham - Mary Shepherd lic.	1-24-1829
Osburn, Bennajah - Tonnsen(?) Garrison	
	lic. 9-10-1831
Osgood, Samuel - Huldah Cheek	3-18-1830

Owen, Allen - Margaret Vansickle	10- 9-1831
Owens, James - Ruth Freeman	9- 6-1829
Owens, Robert - Margaret Barttell lic.	6-24-1833
Owens, William - Mary Lance	9-19-1832
Pain, Decalvas - Deborah Cartwright	8- 8-1829
Palmer, Prentice T. - Eleaner B. Dazey	4-27-1828
Pardun, Jesse - Tacy Maria Ketchun	7-30-1831
Parker, Daniel - Mary Songer	4- 8-1830
Parker, Peter - Rachel Kittle lic.	10-16-1832
Parker, Samuel - Minerva Melvina Clarke	11-10-1831
Parvis, Guessport - Mary Abell	2-19-1829
Pate, Amster - Christiana Fox	7-31-1828
Pate, Hamilton- Parthenia Conaway	5-23-1833
Pate, Henry Jr. - Electra Peas lic.	2-17-1827
Pate, William Simpson - Catharine Goodner	
	1-18-1827
Patterson, James - Sarah Swift	1-14-1827
Patterson, Robert - Sarah Nelson	3-15-1832
Payne, Lewis - Catharine Robinson	6-20-1830
Payne, Morgan Lewis - Rebeccah Adams	7-20-1826
Payne, William Milton - Eliza Hamilton	7-29-1830
Pearce, Joseph - Lucy Brace	4-18-1833
Pearce, William - Joannah Brace	11-27-1828
Pearson, Abel - Esther Ann Miller	7-14-1833
Pearson, Joseph T. - Nancy Givan	1- 1-1830
Peaslee, Abraham Jr. - Charlotte Fulton	7-24-1828
Peasley, Isaac - Eleanor Hannah	7- 1-1830
Peasley, Jacob - Nancy Winters	8-14-1831
Peck, William - Susan Stevenson lic.	11-11-1826
Percival, Jared - Millicent Bedford	3-10-1831
Perdun, Abraham - Anne Coledin	7-30-1826
Perdun, Abraham - Elizabeth Thompson	12- 9-1826
Perrine, David W. - Caroline Maynard lic.	10-12-1826
Peters, Henry - Rachel Myers	11-24-1829
Peters, Joseph - Ailsey (alias Alice) Miller	
	lic. 10-14-1826
Peters, Robert - Elizabeth McGlaughlin	
	lic. 9-24-1832
Peters, Robert - Catharine Cox	8-18-1833
Peters, Stephen - Susannah Moore	7-30-1832
Pettigrew, Ezekiel - Emmeline Beach	11-18-1827
Phelps, William B. - Amelia Gibson	3- 1-1827
Phillips, John - Rebecca Smith	3-16-1827
Phillips, Thomas (of Ohio) -	
Nancy Herrington	5-21-1826
Phillips, Woodford W. - Dorcas Russell	12- 5-1829
Phillis, Thomas A. - Margaret R. Hall	7-12-1832
Piatt, John B. - Emily Scott	9- 4-1829
Piatt, Samuel - Barbara Law	5-20-1831
Pinckard, Thomas B. - Catharine L. Vance	
	11-28-1826
Pippin, Zebulon - Rebeccah Lambden	3-29-1832
Plummer, Sewell - Mary Lozier	2-25-1828
Plumer, Benjamin - Hannah Huestis	6-20-1833
Porter, Alvin - Sarah Lore	1-17-1828
Porter, Andrew - Lucy Ann Botts	3-10-1831
Powell, Elihu - Jane Clark (dt. of	
George Clark)	3-15-1826
Powell, George - Sarah Griffon	8- 2-1827
Powell, John B. - Caroline H. Brewington	9-20-1832
Powell, Mahlon - Elizabeth Coldon	9- 6-1826
Powell, Van Vactor - Temperance Smith	12-14-1832
Pratt, Edwin G. - Frances E. Wright	5-30-1828
Price, Samuel - Joanna Peek	3-10-1830
Priest, William - Nancy Patterson	1-29-1829

Purcel, Thomas - Mary Boyce	1- 1-1833
Purcel, Thomas Jr. - Charlotte Robinson	
	lic. 11- 9-1827
Purcell, Aaron - Jane B. Allen	11-25-1832
Purdey, Alexander - Jane Buffington	4-15-1830
Quinlan, John - Melysa Scranton	lic. 6-25-1827
Rabb, James - Frances S. Weaver	3-12-1829
Radley, Jacob - Amanda Thompson	7- 1-1830
Ramer, Henry - Mary McCune	3- 8-1827
Rand, Carder - Mary Anne Keffer	11-15-1827
Rand, Thomas - Lydia Lyons	3-30-1830
Record, Thomas - Hanna M. Sanders	
(Hannah M. Sanford in return)	7-10-1832
Record, Sampson (alias Thomas) -	
Maria Smith, Negroes	5-30-1830
Redding, James - Hannah Buffington	lic. 10-13-1832
Redlen, John - Margaret Robinson	9-28-1828
Reed, Addison - Rachel Yerkas	1- 3-1832
Reed, John V. - Tarissa Irwin	lic. 1- 9-1830
Reede, Gershum - Margaret Gould	lic. 9-22-1832
Reeder, Stephen W. (of Hamilton Co., Ohio)	
- Matilda Larew	lic. 7-11-1827
Regan, Joseph - Harriett Cairnes	lic. 6- 8-1826
Rees, John Frederick - Nancy Kersey	3- 1-1833
Reynolds, John - Phoebe Grant	8-16-1829
Richards, Isaac - Experience O'Brian	
(or Brian)	10-17-1831
Richards, John - Mary Ann Jordon	6-21-1829
Richards, Philip - Sarah Grant	3-29-1832
Richardson, Orison - Harriet Kimbal	5-14-1829
Richardson, Peter - Malinda Musick	3-25-1830
Ricketts, Andrew - Eliza Payne	1-16-1831
Ricketts, William - Harriet Dean	2- 5-1832
Riggs, George A. - Jane McCullough	7-26-1832
Riggs, Henry - Azuba Richardson	9-28-1826
Ripley, Joseph S. - Joanna Kneeland	1-10-1827
Rittenhouse, Jefferson - Mary Moore	5- 2-1832
Roberts, Arthur P. - Meralice Freeman	10-18-1832
Roberts, Daniel - Louisa Littlefield	lic. 12-11-1832
Roberts, David M. - Hannah Tibbetts	10-14-1830
Roberts, James Jr. - Martha Freeman	12-22-1831
Roberts, Moses M. - Almira Clarke	3- 1-1827
Roberts, Thomas - Sarah Medd	lic. 2-21-1833
Roberts, Vinson - Dorcas Roberts	4-16-1832
Roberts, Zebulon H. - Catharine Clarke	10-13-1830
Robinson, James B. - Martha T. Foster	
	lic. 4-20-1828
Robinson, Morgan H. - Sarah Holmes	11-18-1832
Robinson, Nathan - Elizabeth Devar	2- 7-1828
Robinson, William - Maria Nevins	5-29-1828
Rodgers, Parker - Hannah Blue	4-25-1830
Rogers, Nelson - Harriett Wright	2-25-1831
Rogers, Peter - Janet Boyle	4-30-1829
Rollins, George S. - Isabella Fuller	8-12-1831
Rood, William - Sarah Stewart	3-26-1827
Ross, James - Elizabeth Pate	5-27-1830
Ross, Philander - Anne Kelso	1-13-1828
Ross, William - Maria Beachum	5- 1-1833
Rozell, Abednego - Sarah Lamb	lic. 5-28-1826
Rozell, Abednego - Mary Diggs	lic. 5-25-1827
Rude, Richard - Jane Gold	12-11-1828
Runnells, David - Elizabeth Tozier	12- 3-1832
Runnells, George - Catharine Johnston	5- 1-1833
Runnion, William - Drusilla Darragh	12-16-1832

Runyon, Absalom - Polly Asken	4-15-1832
Russel, Ephraim - Harchulanium Fuller	8-23-1832
Ryal (or Ryle), Larkin - Eliza Watson	9-16-1827
Saine, Jacob - Mary Vanzile	5-10-1827
Saltmarsh, George - Mary Percival	10-13-1831
Sanks, George - Barbara Stevens	7- 4-1830
Sanks, Joshua - Susannah Rees	11-23-1826
Sawdon, William - Mary Liddle	lic. 3-27-1831
Scantling, John - Eleanor D. Wolf	6-28-1832
Schooley, Elias - Rebecca Plummer	3-18-1830
Scott, Alexander - Margaret Linch	2-15-1833
Scott, Jesse - Margaret McCamron	1-27-1833
Scott, Samuel - Mrs. Sophia Cole	7-22-1833
Scranton, Almon - Rachel Pierce	12-30-1832
Scranton, Levi - Mary Peirce (or Pierce)	4-24-1828
Scranton, Munson - Julia Howe	11-29-1827
Scroggins, Merrit - Maria Crozier	11- 3-1831
Seeley (?), Samuel - Sarah Brisbane	1-29-1832
Seward, Mason - Sarah Cage	3-10-1833
Shane, George Washington - Sylvia Hubbell	
	lic. 3- 4-1833
Shearin, Thomas - Jamima Hues	1-18-1827
Shed, Daniel - Elizabeth Adams	8-21-1828
Sheets, William - Mary S. Randolph	5-29-1833
Shephard, Joel - Charlotta Gibson	7-31-1828
Shepherd, Alonzo - Sarah Hume	5- 9-1830
Shepherd, Dacid - Mary Bowers	2- 1-1832
Shepherd, Russel - Martha Hume	lic. 4-16-1827
Shepherd, William - Isabella Chidester	6-24-1831
Sherrin, Abner R. - Nancy Morris	12-11-1829
Shields, Edward (or Edmund) T. -	
Electra Lindsay, by consent of	
her uncle, Stephen Wood	6-14-1826
Shoemake, Blackley Jr. - Elena Dawson	1-10-1830
Shoemake, Enoch - Dedemiah Michael	4-11-1833
Shoemake, John - Cynthia Dawson	1-29-1832
Shook, Lloyd - Sarah Ann Carson	5-27-1830
Shook, Wilson L. - Catharine Jane Bigley	11-21-1830
Shoppel, David - Lavina Sanderson	10-23-1828
Short, Adam - Nancy Bennett	lic. 1-16-1827
Showalter, Abraham - Frederica Christina Kyle	
	9- 7-1826
Showalter, Jacob - Eliza Coen	6-17-1832
Sidle, John - Mary Todd	10-25-1832
Sill, Thomas - Jane Fulton	1-10-1828
Simmonds, Silas - Elizabeth Morrow	lic. 7-17-1833
Simons (or Simmons), John - Mary Lewis	11- 8-1827
Simpson, Isaac H. - Phebe Garrison	12- 7-1826
Simpson, Mathias - Sina Garrison	8- 5-1827
Simpson, Nathaniel - Ruth Symmes	7-11-1829
Slater, James - Thankful Juliann Whitten	12- 1-1827
Small, John - Nancy Kilgore	6-27-1830
Smiley, James - Delilah Walden	11-13-1832
Smith, Aaron - Lavinia Jane Huffman	2-10-1831
Smith, Cyrus - Delilah Dunkin	11- 8-1832
Smith, Daniel - Rachel Dawson	lic. 2- 4-1828
Smith, Daniel - Olive Eastman	9- 5-1833
Smith, Eli - Elvey Henry	8- 4-1833
Smith, George - Anna Bella McDonough	11-27-1826
Smith, George - Elizabeth Wilson	11-26-1827
Smith, George - Ann Michael	4- 3-1829
Smith, George - Amanda Hull	2- 9-1830
Smith, George - Sylvia Layton	10-31-1831
Smith, Hamilton - Nancy Cheek	lic. 11-19-1831
Smith, Honley - Eliza Molson	3-25-1829

Smith, James P. - Eliza Ann Beachum	8-27-1826
Smith, John - Catharine Tucker	2-23-1832
Smith, John - Phoebe Glass	4- 4-1833
Smith, John C. - Mary E. Dunn	5-28-1833
Smith, John M.T. - Alcinda Lahue	10-17-1827
Smith, Joseph H. - Asenath Rowling	9-21-1831
Smith, Lyman T. - Sarah Hinds	lic. 12-22-1827
Smith, Oliver H. - Elizabeth Speer	lic. 3-16-1832
Smith, Samuel M. - Lucy Andrews	1-28-1830
Smith, Thomas - Jane Collier	8-28-1828
Smith, Willis R. - Mary Gould	2- 5-1833
Snell, Abraham B. - Jane Susannah Perrine	
	12-17-1828
Snell, Henry - Emerline F. Clarke	1- 4-1830
Songer, Samuel - Sarah Parker	8-13-1829
Southard, David - Sarah Colwell	12-27-1827
Spangler, Peter - Mary Ann Shepherd	7-15-1832
Sparks, Jesse - Jemima Thorn	9- 2-1827
Speer, John - Pamelia Conoway	5- 8-1831
Spencer, John W. - Fidelia Falls	4-29-1832
Spencer, Matthew - Leah Briddle	3- 8-1827
Spencer, William C. - Rispey Allee	11- 7-1830
Spialman, Jacob - Juliann McAdams	4-19-1829
Spicknall, Leonard - Emely Horham	12-14-1828
Spicknall, Thomas - Elizabeth Williams	5-18-1826
Springer, David - Sarah Brewington	lic. 11-20-1832
Squibb, Nathaniel L. - Rhoda M. Henegin	
	lic. 1-30-1832
Stage, Hugh - Elizabeth Daugherty	12- 8-1831
Standford, Thomas - Isabella Blue	7-30-1829
Stark, Washington - Nancy Cochran	12-14-1826
Starkey, Jesse - Barbary Elliott	12-25-1828
Stevens, Andrew N. - Sarah Dashiell	11-25-1830
Stevens, Justice - Rebecah Rude	11-20-1828
Stevenson, Andrew - Rachael Early	10-29-1826
Stevenson, Armer - Caroline Riggs	6-22-1826
Stevenson, Sylvanus - Lavinia Louderbough	
	4- 4-1832
Stewart, John - Priscilla Stewart	
(of Hamilton Co., Ohio)	3-20-1828
Stewart, John - Catharine Boyd	lic. 9- 1-1829
Stinson, Spencer - Nancy Lose(?)	2-15-1827
Stockdale, Benjamin - Mary Wilson	10- 1-1829
Stockton, William L. - Susan C. Mills	6-20-1833
Stoddard, John W. - Mary Ann Cox	10-28-1829
Stone, Elijah - Elizabeth Taylor	12- 8-1831
Stone, Francis W. - Lydia P. Loring	12- 6-1829
Stone, John - Margaret Hodge	12- 4-1828
Stoneking, Samuel - Susannah Boyd	11-13-1828
Stradder, John - America Lassety	lic. 10- 3-1831
Stroud, Allen - Jane Smith	7- 4-1833
Stubbs, John - Nancy Heavrin	12-28-1826
Sullivan, James - Nancy Reeves	2-12-1829
Summers, Thomas - Nancy Tate	6-14-1832
Sumner, Leonard - Elizabeth Mills	2- 4-1827
Surbar (Surber), Henry - Mary Conner	2-19-1829
Suttles, Uriah - Elizabeth Johnson	5-28-1833
Sutton, Ephraim - Sarah O'Harrah	7-18-1830
Sutton, John - Juliann Fowler	6-19-1831
Sutton, William - Sarah Masten	11-16-1826
Swanger (Swangor), Abraham - Rachel Bruce	
	10-21-1830
Swatfager, Lewis - Eustena Busen	6- 6-1833
Swift, Mason - Mary Hammond	10-27-1830
Swift, Samuel - Rachel Backhurst	3-26-1829
Sykes, John - Elizabeth Langdon	10-15-1830

Tague, George W. - Sophia Ricketts	7-25-1833
Tanner, Pierce Lacy - Mary Ann Carpenter	3-11-1832
Tate, John - Harriet Stewart	9- 6-1827
Taylor, Isaac - Lavenia Sacket	8-11-1831
Taylor, Lucius - Isabella Roseberry	8- 6-1829
Taylor, Thomas S. - Elizabeth Bainum	4-25-1833
Teney, Henry - Ann Hagerman	1-10-1828
Teney, John - Esther Hubbard	2-21-1833
Terrill, Benjamin - Frances M. Bishop	
	lic. 1-26-1833
Thatcher, Harvey - Milly Bear	lic. 3-13-1828
Thompson, Albert - Sarah Wilber	8-29-1830
Thompson, George - Alice Ann Murray	10- 9-1828
Thompson, James - Eliza Porter	8- 9-1829
Thompson, Joseph - Harriet M. Baxter	5- 6-1832
Thompson, Matthew - Mary Lindsay	8-18-1831
Thompson, Robert - Elvirah Dexter	7-11-1833
Thompson, Smith - Frances Fulton	6- 2-1831
Thorn, Daniel - Zedah Calkins	4-12-1832
Thorn, Stephen - Jane Lewis	2- 5-1829
Thornton, John S. - Amelia Nelson	lic. 9-10-1832
Thorrington, Alexander - Martha Webb	4-15-1827
Tinker, Ira - Abby McMullen	4-24-1829
Tinker, Stephen - Submittance Hall	5-14-1829
Torbet, Nelson H. - Eliza Brooks	6- 6-1826
Torbet, Nelson H. - Eliza W. Lewis	11-22-1832
Todd, Henry - Nancy Williams	6-23-1831
Todd, James - Jane Alexander	6-18-1833
Toussey, George - Hannah Ann Dunn	3-13-1828
Tower, John Z. - Lucinda Guice	6- 2-1833
Trader, John - Elizabeth Johnson	1-26-1831
Trester, Samuel - Sophia Briddle	lic. 3-31-1828
Trester, William - Catharine Cheesman	8-29-1833
Tryon, Lucas - Sarah Huffman	5-17-1832
Tryon, Thomas - Catharine Norrick	5-21-1830
Tucker, Nathaniel - Phoebe Blauvelt	10-13-1831
Tull, Isaac - Maria S. Roach	3-28-1833
Tumey, William - Rachel Whitford	8-12-1829
Turner, Robert Jr., of Switzerland Co. -	
Mary F. Dean	11-30-1828
Vanarsdale, John - Nancy Gibson	9-21-1826
Vance, George - Susan Hunt	11-13-1828
Vancicle, John Jr. - Mrs. Mary Kneeland	6-14-1829
Vancleves, John - Pamela Cole	9-13-1826
Vanclief, Garret - Polly Wright	4-29-1833
Vanhorn, Abraham - Nancy Henry	9-11-1828
Vanhouten, Cornelius W. - Maria Isabella Ray	
	2- 8-1827
Vansickle, James - Elizabeth James	8-22-1832
Vaughn, David - Cornelia Hamblin	lic. 7-20-1829
Voshell, Obadiah - Ann Williams	lic. 8- 3-1829
Wade, James - Hannah M. Sampson	11- 1-1832
Wade, William - Rosannah Batey (Beatty)	5- 9-1831
Walden, James - Priscilla Philbrick	9- 2-1827
Walden, Jedediah - Mary Danford	1-15-1829
Walden, Josiah - Sarah Bean	12-29-1831
Walker, Benjamin - Eliza Ann Wilber	lic. 3- 6-1833
Wallingsford, William T. - Mary Cloud	6- 3-1833
Walliser, Francis A. - Elizabeth Shively	
	lic. 4-11-1833
Walser, James - Mary Bailey	1- 5-1832
Walton, Andrew - Melinda Lacy	3-21-1833
Walls (or Watts), John - Sophia Anabal	12-25-1828
Walser, Burrel - Polly Peters	lic. 5-20-1826

Walser, David - Elizabeth Van Middlesworth
1-23-1827
Ward, George Washington - Susan McLister 1-10-1833
Ward, John - Hannah Ward 11-12-1829
Wardell, Zebulon Pike - Mary Bowers 11- 3-1831
Warner, Hiram - Alenia Arthurs   lic. 4-20-1830
Warner, Israel - Clarissa Helmes   lic. 11-14-1829
Warnock, John Elgin - Sarah Bruner 6-10-1829
Watts, Harrison W. - Lavinia Guard 9-30-1830
Watts, Hiram - Charlotte Finley 8-17-1828
Watts, Squire - Isabella Hayes 9-11-1828
Weathers, Jesse - Eleanor Taylor 7-22-1832
Weckerby, William - Mary H. Druse 10-17-1831
Welch, Daniel - Nancy Davis 11-29-1827
Welch, John - Sarah Fulton 1- 3-1828
Welch, Matthew - Demila Peasley 9- 9-1832
Welch, Noah M. - Mary Peasley 5-18-1828
Wesley, Alexander - Margaret Harrawood 9- 1-1826
West, Norman - Diedamia Sartwell 6-10-1830
West, Samuel - Lucinda Gadley (?) 10-11-1829
Westbrook, John - Deborah Halford 5-13-1827
Wharton, Johnston - Matilda Wilson lic. 5-22-1828
Wheeler, Jabez - Mary Erving 6-28-1827
Wheeler, John - Martha Miller 1-28-1830
Wheeler, Piercy - Jerusha Holliday 10- 4-1832
Whetstone, John - Mary Whetstone 2- 3-1833
Whipple, David - Selvia Swift   lic. 1-31-1828
Whipple, Elias - Sally Babbit 12-14-1826
Whipple, Luman C. - Martha Gaw   lic. 3- 4-1833
Whipple, William - Margaret Hubbard 8-20-1829
Whitaker, James W. - Eleanor Hubbard 11- 8-1832
Whitcum, Orin - Elizabeth Heeton 4-10-1828
White, Alexander - Deborah Lake 12- 9-1831
White, Henry - Elizabeth Hunter McGahan 12-13-1832
White, John - Rebecca Drake 1-29-1829
White, John Jr. - Rhoda Lindley 12-10-1826
White, Joseph - Jane Lynes 4-19-1832
Wiant, Isaac - Margaret Lawrence   lic. 3-31-1830
Wilber, Shadrach - Agnes F. Watts 10-30-1828
Wilcox, Hiram M. - Mary Anne Cure 3-11-1830
Wildredge, Ralph - Eliza Bowman 11-20-1831
Wiley, Elhanon - Margaret Fowler 1-18-1829
Wiley, Hiram - Mary Cozine 11- 3-1829
Willey, Renslaer - Athey Lyon Weathers 7-12-1829

Williams, Archibald - Catharine Shull 3-20-1828
Williams, Edward - Sarah Stewart 9-30-1832
Williams, James - Elizabeth Denison 11-16-1828
Williams, Joseph - Catharine Clements
lic. 5-18-1833
Williams, Lewis - America Moore 2- 3-1828
Williams, Thomas - Paulina Pate 3-23-1826
Williams, Thomas N. - Mary Jane Blasdel 8-23-1832
Williams, William, of Ohio - Nancy
Thorrington 3-16-1826
Williams, William - Mary Cheek   lic. 2-10-1827
Williamson, David - Silence Spencer 3-27-1828
Williamson, Isaac W. - Mary Eggleston 3-18-1832
Williamson, Joachim - Elizabeth Vandolah
11-27-1828
Willing, Nelson - Mary Myers 11- 6-1826
Willman, Christian - Rozetta Buffington 6- 4-1829
Wilson, David - Susannah Poe 3-22-1829
Wilson, Jesse - Catharine Jones 8-14-1828
Wilson, John - Sarah Smith 12-25-1827
Wilson, Levi - Sarah March 12-30-1830
Wilson, Thomas - Matilda Weathers 11- 1-1829
Wilson, Thomas - Mehalah Neel 2- 7-1833
Wilson, Valentine - Mary Ann Rowland 12- 6-1832
Winscott, John - Eliza Buffington 2-28-1828
Wolcot, Daniel (of Switzerland Co.) -
Mary Daugherty 5-17-1826
Wood, Isaac - Lucinda Beach 11- 8-1829
Wood, Valentine - Mary Neely   lic. 8-20-1830
Woolley, George - Rebeccah McClure 6-18-1829
Works, John - Elizabeth Greathouse 7-23-1831
Worley, Andrew - Margaretta Harwood lic. 9- 6-1826
Worley, Francis - Jane Dils 5-10-1832
Wright, Charles W. - Louisa Palmer lic. 11-24-1827
Wright, John C. - Joanna Norris 10-11-1831
Wright, Thomas F. - Electa Shed 5-28-1826
Wymond, Gilbert Hodge - Mary Buell 4- 8-1830
Wymond, John - Margaret Johnson 1-29-1833
Wymond, William - Sarah G. Elder 10- 1-1830

Yeager, Nicholas - Susannah Lawrence 5-26-1833
Yerkes, Nathaniel - Elizabeth Medd 4- 4-1833

Zinn, Jacob - - Luvisa Pate   lic. 2-12-1827

EARLY DEARBORN COUNTY MARRIAGES

Marriages performed by William Major, Dearborn County justice of peace, 1806-15. Some of these people became residents of Franklin County when it was organized out of Dearborn County.

Allen, William - Elizabeth Eades 9- 5-1815
Alverstatz, John - Charlotte Shank 10- 3-1807
Battiest, Moses - Fanny Stout 12- 7-1807
Bullock, Jacob - Betsy Edwards 12- 1-1809
Cornelius, James Terrel - Jane Cloud 10-30-1813
Eads, William H. - Jane Adair 1-10-1807
Farrand, Michael - Sarah Fowler 2-13-1815
Fred, William - Abigail Rockafeller 10-30-1810
Garey, David - Prudence White 12-17-1814
Gayness, Richard T. - Catharine Vincent 9- 1-1806
Gould (?), James, Jr. - Charlotte Marchant 5-30-1814
Hardin, James - Catharine Cloud 9-15-1813
Johnson, Samuel - Betsy Farrar (or Farran)
11- 6-1810

Logan, James - Liddy McCarty 11-28-1807
McCarty, Enoch - Elizabeth Logan 10-10-1807
Myers, Henry - Lucinda Mundy 10-29-1813
Norris, John - Rebecca Skinner 4-11-1808
Parks, Joseph - Sarah Johnston 3-22-1815
Razor, Simeon - Polly Allensworth 10-29-1814
Remy, James - Rebeckah Adair 2-10-1807
Richardson, Benoni - Ruth Adair 4-14-1810
Rollf, Asa - Celany Eads 5-28-1810
Scotton, Eli - Isabella McElvy 12-26-1807
Simmons, William - Nancy Kyger 1-10-1810
Tibbs, Warren - Elizabeth Ashby 1-26-1815
Wiley, James - Elizabeth Williams 4- 6-1811

Marriages prior to March 5, 1826, taken from Lawrenceburg newspapers in Indiana State Library.

Baker, William - Mrs. Elizabeth Carlough	9- 8-1825	Reynolds, Benjamin J. - Elizabeth Guest,	
Brasher, Charles L. - Elizabeth Cole	12- 8-1825	dt of Moses	3-10-1826
Brasher, Jacob - Jemima Spurior, of Ohio	7-28-1825	St. Clair, Arthur - Mary Lane, dt of Amos	9-29-1825
Brasher, James M. - Amelia Worrell	7- 7-1825	Saltmarsh, Elijah - Rachel Carman	12- 8-1825
Burke, James - Nancy Grubbs	3- 9-1826	Saltmarsh, Joseph - Isabella Bedford	6- 2-1825
Burrows, James - Nancy Leggett	3-31-1825	Sanks, Zachariah - Julian Gaw	6- 9-1825
Cole, Samuel - Sophia Watson	2- 9-1826	Shepherd, George - Phebe Hudgson	2-14-1826
Culley, David V. - Mary Ann Brown	12- 8-1825	Sparks, Norval - Jane Johnson	7- 7-1825
Fanar, Henry - Ann Brown	8-20-1825	Towsey, Omer - Lucinda Johnson, of Boone	
Hanna, I. N. - Martha Knight, both of		Co., KY	10-16-1823
Brookville	9-18-1825	Tyner, Richard, Brookville - Martha Noble,	
Hays, Isaac - Presilla Miller	7-31-1825	Boone Co., KY	10-15-1823
Morgan, William - Jane O'Farrell	5-19-1825	Utz, Frederick - Mrs. Catharine Lord	10-20-1825
Morrell, Jacob - Mary Bowman	10- 6-1825	Vance, Arthur St. Clair - Lavenia Noble of	
Nevitt, David - Eliza Thar	6-19-1825	Boone Co, KY	2- 8-1826
Porter, David - Mary Leason	10-14-1823	Wright, James - Lucy Brasher	10-16-1823
Park, Harris - Huldah Curtis	8-14-1825		
Ray, James B. - Mrs. Booker of Centerville	9-15-1825		

Marriages prior to March 5, 1826, that were rerecorded in Book 2 of Dearborn County Marriages.

Abbercrumbie, John - Rebecckah Pierce	1-12-1826	Hinesly, John - Almira Gold	2-23-1826
Barricklow, Conrad - Jane Stewart	11-21-1822	Hollowell, William - Celestia Allington	7-31-1825
Brown, Robert E. - Mary Ann Stockdon	7-18-1824	Hunter, Hiram - Huldah Fisk	2- 1-1823
Clements, James - Sally Dixon	3- 3-1825	Kelso, James - Ruth Carman	2-20-1826
Connell, William L. - Clarissa Chase	1-30-1825	Lotton, Samuel - Cosiah Douglass	7-30-1823
Doughterman, Charles - Rebeccah Sanderson	2- 5-1826	Lotton, William - Juliann Jinkins	8-12-1824
Easdale, Robert - Jane Vaners(?)	9- 8-1822	Porter, William - Mary Oglevee	11-25-1824
Ewbank, Benjamin - Ann Smith	8-27-1825	Powell, John - Grace Williams	12-14-1825
Fulton, William - Mary Ann Meeker	5-29-1823	Shepherd, George - Pheba Hudgson	2-14-1826
Hamlin, Alfred - Sarah Duncan	12-16-1825	Tinker, Samuel - Jane Jinkins	3- 3-1823
Hannah, Samuel - Jane Mosby(?)	9-30-1824	Warnock, Samuel - Mary Cory	10-14-1823

DEATHS REPORTED IN INDIANAPOLIS *LOCOMOTIVE*, 1845-1860

One method of collecting death records in Indiana prior to 1882 (the year the counties began keeping official records) is by checking local newspapers. The following list, taken from an Indianapolis paper, is an example. Probably only about one tenth of the deaths were recorded. Information given has been shortened in most instances to save space. The *Locomotive* also recorded births and marriages. The Index of births, deaths, and marriages from 1845 to 1860 was compiled by Mrs. Elizabeth Best Coffin of Indianapolis and is in the Archives Division, Indiana State Library.

Abbett, James Eddy, infant of Dr. L.	8- 6-1853	Anderson, Charles, inf. of J.H.P.	7- 5-1851
Ackley, Dr. A. A., in California	2-23-1850	Apple, Solomon	6-24-1848
Adams, Mary E. (Mrs. George H.)	9-18-1858	Appleton, George, age 10	6-10-1848
Alford, Lilian, inf. of John T.	6-19-1852	Armintrout, David	11-11-1848
Alldredge, Aaron	11-26-1853	Armitage, Benjamin, age 41	5-21-1853
Alldredge, Nancy (Mrs. Aaron)	4-13-1850	Armstrong, Charlie, inf. of L J.	7- 9-1853
Allen, Calista (Mrs. Nathan), formerly		Armstrong, Thomas, age 85, b. Berks Co.,	
of Norfolk, Conn.	10- 4-1851	Pa., d. Franklin, Ind.	2-16-1856
Allen, Mary (Mrs. Thomas L.)	4-20-1850	Asky, Mary Ann, age 37	8- 5-1848
Allen, Nathan, formerly of Conn.	12-23-1854	Astley, George, in California	12-21-1850
Alley, Bentley	10-11-1845	Athon, —— (Mrs. James S.)	6-13-1857
Ames, ——, dt Rev. Edward R.	4-22-1848	Atkinson, Arabell (Mrs. Alonzo)	5-17-1856
Ames, Aquilla	8-10-1850	Atkinson, Lucy C., age 4	3- 3-1855
Anderson, Christinia (Mrs. Joseph)	5-25-1850	Atkinson, Mary, dt of Eli & Marg.	9-20-1851
Anderson, George, bank director	5-17-1856	Avery, Lillie, age 7, dt of L.S.	12-24-1859

Axtell, Mary E. (Mrs. Charles),
  dt of Douglass Maguire   10-20-1849
Aylesworth, Mrs. Anna E., age 21,
  dt of J.W. Borden, Fort Wayne   3-26-1853
Axtell, Miss Mary Jane, in Fla.   1-19-1850

Babb, Mary Ella, inf. of Rev. C.E.   5-11-1850
Bacon, Horace   1- 1-1853
Baker, Mary C. (Mrs. James)   3-14-1857
Baldwin, E.J., age 29, jeweler   1- 1-1859
Baldwin, Edwin J., son of E.J.   3-12-1859
Baldwin, Mrs. J.C., widow of Dr. Baldwin
    12-15-1849
Ballenger, ——, inf. son of E.M.   1-28-1854
Bane, Mattie (Mrs. L.G.), age 19   6-14-1856
Banta, Kitty (Mrs. Daniel)   12- 4-1852
Banta, Peter A., Johnson Co.   10- 4-1851
Barbour, Wm. W., son of Lucian   8- 2-1851
Barr, Dallie D., son of Jacob   5-10-1856
Barr, Jemima, inf. of Jacob   9- 8-1855
Barth, Elizabeth (Mrs. J.H.),
  dt of Jacob Birkenmayer   3- 6-1858
Barth, Jacob, inf. of John   6- 3-1854
Barth, John Newton, inf. of John
  & Elizabeth (dec'd)   3-20-1858
Beach, Hannah (Mrs. Walter E.)
  of Elkhart Co.   1-11-1851
Beach, Naomi Juliette, dt of Wm.   1-27-1855
Beaty, Mrs. Elizabeth, mo of David   6- 5-1852
Beeler, Joseph, Decatur Twp.   7-19-1851
Belles, Eddie, son of Dr. Joshua   12-31-1859
Belles, Emma E., dt of Dr. Joshua   1-28-1854
Berry, Sarah, inf. of Benjamin   7-26-1856
Biddle, Benjamin, son of Wm.   10- 4-1851
Biehler, S.S., age 25   1-17-1852
Bilby, Edward, son of Elisha (dec'd)   9- 9-1848
Bingham, Mary (Mrs. J.J.), of Lafayette 9-20-1851
Birkenmayer, Jacob, formerly of
  Jefferson Co., Ky.   3-17-1860
Birkenmayer, Nancy (Mrs. Jacob)   9-22-1855
Bisghmann, Peter, of Evansville, at
  School for Deaf   7- 8-1848
Black, Nancy Wingate (Mrs. Joshua)   2- 8-1851
Blackledge, Mrs. Alvin   9-30-1848
Blake, Glovina, dt of Thomas H.   2- 5-1853
Bland, James, of Stilesville   2- 8-1851
Blythe, Samuel, age 53   12-14-1850
Bodkin, Lucinda (Mrs. Alexander)   8- 6-1853
Boetticher, Oscar, son of Julius   11-17-1855
Bonnet, Thomas "Fancy Tom" negro   6- 9-1849
Booth, Alfred   10-13-1855
Bosworth, J. Theodore, in Alexandria,
  Va., formerly of Indianapolis   10-29-1853
Bowers, Daniel, Washington Twp.   10-30-1852
Bowers, Kate, Williamsport, Md.   4-26-1856
Boyd, Martha (Mrs. Ezekial)   3-22-1851
Brackenridge, Mrs. Caroline, dt of
  Isaac N. Phipps   11- 3-1855
Braden, Eliza (Mrs. William)   12-20-1856
Bradley, Debbie H., dt of John H.   7-26-1851
Bradley, James of Perry Twp.   2-22-1851
Bradley, James, son of Caleb H.   5-21-1853
Bradshaw, ——, in R.R. accident   6- 4-1853
Bradshaw, Albert, inf. of Wm. A.   9-20-1856
Bradshaw, Jennie (Mrs. James)   9-15-1860
Bradshaw, Martha (Mrs. William)   11- 6-1858
Breg, William, teacher Deaf Sch.   5-19-1849
Brenneman, Fanny (Mrs. Henry)   11- 7-1857
Bricket, Dr. William A.   3-29-1851

Brickett, Dr. T.M.   4- 5-1851
Bridgeford, Mary (Mrs. Charles)   6- 7-1851
Bridges, Mrs. Jesse   2-22-1851
Bright, Ella, dt of Major   12-17-1859
Broadway, John A., son-in-law of
  Phillip Landis   9-23-1854
Brown, Hiram, age 61, b. Pa.,
  came to Indianapolis 1823   6-18-1853
Brown, Kate, dt of Austin H.   6-10-1854
Brown, Lucina, age 73   3- 1-1856
Brown, Mary Warrick, widow of Bazel   8-11-1849
Brown, Nehemiah age 67   6-22-1850
Brown, Susan, inf of Wm. J.   7-28-1849
Browning, Eliza (Mrs. Edmund)   7-19-1851
Browning, Marquet, son of Robert   1-20-1849
Browning, Mary D. (Mrs. Robert)   3-22-1856
Browning, Lt. R.L., in Calif.   6- 8-1850
Browning, Woodville, age 34   6-30-1860
Browser, ——, son of Daniel   8- 5-1848
Bruce, Eliza, age 46   6- 4-1859
Bruner, Chas. F., son of Chas.   8- 5-1854
Bryan, Elizabeth (Mrs. Thomas)   9-11-1852
Bryan, Luke, of Perry Twp.   3-28-1857
Bryan, Thomas, of Perry Twp.   12- 5-1857
Bryant, Lucinda Patton (Mrs. A.C.)   8-25-1860
Buchanan, ——, inf of Washington   5-13-1848
Buchanan, Elizabeth (Mrs. C.F.)   10- 8-1859
Buchanan, Electa (Mrs. Joseph)   8-29-1857
Buchanan, Martha, dt of Joseph   7-21-1855
Bullard, Alice Kate, dt of Dr. T.   1-23-1858
Bullard, Charles, inf of Dr. T.   6-19-1858
Bullard, Sed. Alice, dt of Dr. T.   8-19-1854
Bullen, Frank, inf of J.A.   9-27-1856
Burgess, Cornelia, inf of C.N.   7-17-1852
Burk, Lusullus,P., son of John   8-26-1854
Burns, A.F.   4- 5-1851
Burns, Sarah J., age 26   5-19-1855
Bush, Daniel, of Rockville   8-12-1848
Bustle, William, of Hancock Co.   5-27-1848
Butch, John   11-11-1848
Butterfield, ——, dt of T.P.   6-30-1855
Butterfield, Mary A.F. (Mrs. T.P.)   4- 7-1855
Butterfield, Sarah, dt of M.   1-26-1856
Byrkit, Valentine, age 31   3-26-1853

Cady, Albemarle C., inf of Charles   1-13-1849
Cady, Charles W.   11-24-1859
Caldwell, Joseph, son of Timothy   2-12-1859
Campbell, Charles S., son of Wm.   11- 4-1854
Campbell, Jane (Mrs. William)   6-13-1857
Canady, Joshua, of Boone Co.   12-21-1850
Canoll, Henry (coroner's inquest)   12-22-1855
Cantwell, ——, age 2, dt of Marg.   7- 7-1855
Carle, Mrs. Mary, pioneer resident   9-22-1855
Carlisle, Mrs. Elizabeth, age 62   8- 6-1859
Carnahan, Andrew M., in Covington   3- 2-1850
Case, Mrs. Josephine G.   1-13-1849
Case, Thomas Granby, inf of T.R.   9-30-1848
Cathcart, Ellen (Mrs. Andrew)   8- 7-1858
Catterson, Mary E., inf of Cyrus W.   9-20-1851
Caylor, Jacob, age 44   12-18-1852
Chapman, George A.   3-22-1851
Charles, Esther (Mrs. John), age 52   7-22-1854
Charles, Susan, inf of Abraham   7-21-1860
Chase, Mrs. Abigail, age 82   6-21-1856
Cherry, Thomas P.   7- 6-1850
Clarige, Amelia (Mrs. Daniel)   6- 9-1860
Clark, Joseph   10-25-1851
Clark, Rebecca (Mrs. Silas)   6-28-1851

Cline, James, age 27   5-20-1854
Cline, James Wesley, inf of James   7-30-1853
Cline, Nicholas, age 22   6-16-1855
Cline, Phoebe Bethia, inf of Peter   9- 3-1853
Coates, Deborah, age 71   3-24-1855
Coen, Mary Frances, dt of John   9-17-1859
Coffman, Charles S., inf of Jacob   7-28-1855
Coffman, Emily, inf of Jacob   7-17-1852
Coffman, Emily Allen (Mrs Jacob),
   formerly of Norfolk, Conn.   8- 6-1853
Coffman, Henrie E., inf of Jacob   7-30-1853
Colestock, James, age 31   3-31-1855
Collett, Enoch, from Calif.   12-21-1850
Collins, Jeremiah, age 75   7-22-1854
Comegys, Nancy (Mrs. Levi)   9-20-1851
Conarroe, Nancy (Mrs. Samuel)   7-31-1858
Conduitt, Mary (Mrs. W.L.), of
   Mooresville, dt of Samuel Moore   10-22-1853
Connard, Charles, 5 mi s.w. Indpls.   10-27-1849
Conner, Mrs. R.J., formerly of
   Noblesville   5-23-1857
Cook, Anna Dowling, inf of Lewis M.   7-12-1851
Cook, Carrie W., inf dt of James   3-31-1860
Cook, Louis E., inf of Isaac L. Cook
   of Dover, N.J.   7-19-1851
Coonfield, Geo. W., inf of Wm. C.   9-16-1854
Coonfield, Leannah, age 25   6- 3-1854
Coonfield, Nancy Jane (Mrs. Wm. C.)   6-17-1854
Coonfield, William, age 28   2- 9-1856
Cooper, Rev. Samuel E., in Greencastle   7-26-1856
Corbaley, Eliza J. (Mrs. John B.)   1-23-1858
Corbaley, Fannie B., dt of Samuel   9-24-1859
Corbaley, Mary, dt of John B.   6-20-1857
Cornelias, Benson   8-27-1853
Cottman, Preston S., inf of John   10-11-1851
Cox, Henry, age 45, Noblesville Rd.   5-17-1851
Cox, James, age 7, son of Jacob   9-23-1848
Cox, Sarah L. (Mrs. Asher), age 49   5- 8-1852
Cramer, ——   9-27-1851
Craner, George, of Terre Haute   8-14-1852
Crawford, Frank S., son of Rev. C.   2-25-1854
Crow, James   8-16-1851
Culley, John, son D.V., in Calif.   11-30-1850
Cunningham, Mary F. (Mrs. T.M.)   3-20-1858

Dailey, ——, inf dt of Hugh   8-12-1848
Danaldson, Fleming, son of D.S.   2-15-1851
Daniel, L.P.H., son of John J.   7-19-1851
Daniels, Barbara (Mrs. Samuel P.)   10-25-1851
Danforth, James, son of J.K.   10- 8-1853
Darrach, William H., son of G.M.   10- 3-1857
Davenport, Henry, age 30   8- 2-1851
Davenport, Jacob, in Oregon Terr.   2-26-1853
Davenport, Martin, Jr., age 12   8- 7-1852
David, William M., age 50   10- 8-1859
Davidson, Catharine M. (Mrs. Alex.),
   dt of Gov. Noah Noble   5-31-1851
Davis, Oleatha, inf of J.W. & Eliza   9- 6-1851
Dawson, Elijah, pioneer res., age 78   7-24-1858
Day, Margaret Young (Mrs. Lot), of Calif.   5- 9-1857
Day, —, inf dt of Mrs. Lot Day   12-21-1850
Deford, Purlina (Mrs. M.R.)   6-12-1852
Defrees, Amanda M., dt of John D.   7-30-1853
Defrees, James S., of Kosciusko Co.   5-18-1850
Defrees, Mary D. (Mrs. Anthony)   5-31-1851
Delano, Albert M., inf of J.A.   7-29-1854
Delano, Sarah A.M. (Mrs. J.A.)   7-29-1854
Delzell, John, age 27   3- 8-1851
Delzell, John H., inf of Samuel   6-17-1854

Denny, Theodore V., age 54   1-28-1854
Dewels, J.W., in Sacramento, Calif.   12-21-1850
Dickey, J.R., son of James of
   Mercersburgh, Franklin Co., Pa.   6-17-1854
Dinwiddie, W.N.G., formerly of Cambridge
   City, in Paris, Ky.   9-11-1852
Dixon, James P., formerly of Frederick Co., Md.,
   recently of Weston, Mo.   9- 6-1856
Dogget, Louisa J. (Mrs. Richard)   7-29-1854
Doil, Jane (Mrs. Michael), dt of
   Samuel & Mary Long   8-15-1857
Doll, William H., in Harrisburg, Pa.   9- 4-1852
Donalin (Donellan?), Thomas   5- 3-1851
Donellan, A. (widow of Thomas)   1-27-1855
Donellan, Alice, dt of Thomas   5-25-1850
Donavan, Elizabeth (Mrs. James)   9-20-1856
Donavan, Fidelis, dt of Harvey   9-17-1859
Donavan, Obid S., inf of Harvey   3-31-1855
Dougherty, Roland O., inf of Dr. Z.   7-23-1853
Douglass, Arthur S., son of Wm. H.B.   8- 9-1851
Douglass, Jesse, in Logansport   10-25-1845
Douglass, John   7- 5-1851
Douglass, Maria Jane, age 22   1- 1-1848
Douglass, Martha (Mrs. Wm.)   10-12-1850
Douglass, William H.B., in Calif.   11-20-1858
Downey, S.P.   6- 2-1855
Downie, Prof. George B., in Calif.   11-18-1854
Drum, Eliza (Mrs. James J.)   6- 5-1852
Drum, Hattie, dt of James S.   9-15-1860
Drum, Martha (Mrs. Simon, Sr.)   3- 3-1860
Dudley, Alvin, inf of Alvin & Sarah   7-10-1852
Duffield, ——, inf son of Geo. D.   9- 1-1849
Duncan, Mary, dt of Robert B., age 7   1- 7-1860
Dunlap, ——, in R.R. accident   7- 9-1853
Dunlap, Henry L., in Calif.   6-23-1849
Dunn, Fanny J. (Mrs. George H.)   2- 3-1856
Duzan, F.A.   11-20-1858
Duzan, John W., near Maysville, Ky.   6-17-1854

Eaglesfield, George   6-23-1849
Easterday, John Calvin, Wash. Twp.   9-11-1852
Easterday, Rebecca J., dt of Wm. L.   10- 4-1851
Easterday, Samuel W., son of Solomon   4-24-1852
Easterday, Solomon, age 53,
   formerly of Frederick Co., Md.   2- 4-1854
Eastman, ——, inf son of Levi   1-27-1849
Easton, Miss E. M., nr Shelbyville   11-29-1851
Eckert, William, saddler   10-11-1851
Eckert, William, son of Eliza   10-30-1852
Eden, Ann (Mrs. Charleston), age 29   9-29-1860
Edwards, Elizabeth M. (Mrs. A.W.),
   formerly of Madison, Ind.   9-13-1851
Elder, Henry D., son of John R.   3-12-1853
Elder, John, age 61, in Calif.   12-19-1857
Elder, Julia Ann (Mrs. John R.)   4-16-1853
Elder, Julia Ohr, dt of John R.   10-28-1854
Elder, Mrs. Margaret, in Harrisburg, Pa.   9-27-1851
Elder, Samuel P., in Bradford, Iowa   10-17-1857
Elliott, Christopher C., age 34   8-19-1854
Elliott, Mary H., inf. of Byron K.   12- 5-1857
Elliott, Mary M., inf of Calvin   1- 2-1858
Ellis, Hannah Brown, age 2   8-23-1851
Ellis, Jennette M., wife of Dr. E.W.H.   6-21-1856
Ellsworth, Mary G., dt of Henry W.   9-24-1853
Espy, George, age 63   11-14-1857
Espy, ——, inf of Samuel   7-24-1858
Espy, Mary, age 7, dt of Samuel   7-17-1852
Evans, Charles P., inf. of Thomas   8-17-1850
Evans, Peter, inf. of William D.   12-23-1848

Fairchild, Mrs. Eunice Adams, age 76   7-31-1858
Fairchild, Joseph   9- 8-1849
Fatout, Mrs. Irene, age 54   3-15-1851
Ferguson, Henry Clay, age 20   9-13-1851
Ferguson, Isabell, dt of James C.   6-30-1860
Ferguson, see also Furgason
Ferris, Amanda, age 7, dt of Alfred   11- 5-1853
Fike, Vashti (Mrs. J.W.), age 25   3-17-1855
Finch, H.G., at Centerville   10-20-1855
Finch, Mary Theresa, dt of Hampden   12- 2-1854
Fitler, Mary (Mrs. Jacob B.)   4-22-1848
Flack, Moses   5-31-1849
Fleetwood, Mary,
    dt of William C. of Lexington, Mo.   6-10-1848
Fletcher, Fanny, inf. of Calvin, Jr.   8-17-1850
Fletcher, Eunice Allen (Mrs. Elijah)   5- 5-1855
Fletcher, Julia (Mrs. Stoughton A.)   4- 5-1856
Fletcher, Richard   8-18-1849
Fletcher, Richard F., of Boston   7-22-1854
Fletcher, Sarah H. (Mrs. Calvin)   9-30-1854
Foltz, Henry W., son of Frederick   8-11-1855
Foos, Caroline, inf. of T.J.   6-14-1851
Foos, Rebecca, inf of T.J.   no date
Ford, Rebecca (Mrs. John)   6-30-1860
Forsythe, Charles, inf.of William   3-17-1860
Foudray, John W.   8-31-1850
Foudray, inf. son of John E.   1-15-1859
Freeze, Perry A., at Tiffin, Ohio   4-17-1858
Fridley, George   3- 4-1854
Fry, Mrs. Mary E., age 83   10-29-1859
Fuqua, Josephine (Mrs. Andrew)   4-10-1852
Fultz, Hiram, inf. of Frederick   9- 6-1851
Furgason (Ferguson), Charles C.   8-10-1850
Furgason, Druzilla, widow of John   8-28-1852

Gall, Lewis W., inf. of Dr. A.D.   7-19-1851
Galway, Anne M., dt of Moore & Mary   11-18-1848
Gamer, Mary, age 20   9-24-1853
Gates, Martha (Mrs. Uriah)   10- 4-1851
Gause, Isaac, age 68, in Richmond   5-31-1856
Geddes, Agrippa, formerly of Pa.   12-29-1849
Gennaty, Thomas, age 24   7-23-1853
George, David   9-30-1851
Gilbert, Martha (Mrs. Richard)   6- 2-1849
Gillespie, James   11- 3-1849
Glazier, Jacob   11-17-1849
Glazier, Mary, age 8, dt of Chas.   12- 6-1851
Glenn, Archibald, of Johnson Co.   7- 4-1857
Goble, Philip (R.R. accident)   5-14-1853
Good, Margaret A. (Mrs. Charles)   8-18-1855
Goode, D.B. (wife of Rev. W.H.)   3- 5-1859
Goode, Eliza (Mrs. W.V.)   6- 2-1855
Goodwin, Ella, age 6, dt of Rev. T.A.   2-26-1859
Goree, Emma M. (Mrs. J.A.)   6-24-1854
Gorham, Willie M., inf. of Wm. H.   9-19-1854
Goss, David, age 63, of Portage, O.   10-28-1848
Graham, Alexander, printer, in N.O.   9-16-1848
Graham, Laura U., inf. of Dr. Thomas   9- 4-1852
Graves, Donavan, age 53, in Rush Co.   6- 7-1851
Gray, Jemimah, dt of Robert P.   7-19-1851
Graydon, Edward, son of Alexander   8- 4-1849
Graydon, Jane, dt of Alexander   10-22-1853
Graydon, Theodore, son of Alexander   9-14-1850
Graydon, Vincent, son of Alexander   7- 6-1850
Green, John A., of Brownsburg   3-27-1852
Green, R.B. (R.R. accident)   4- 9-1853
Greene, Mary, inf. of James & Mary   6-26-1858
Greenfield, Elizabeth (Mrs. Robert)   4- 5-1850
Greer, Elizabeth (Mrs. John), age 38   1-19-1856

Greer, John, pioneer resident   11-26-1853
Gregg, Lucy A., dt of Milton   4-14-1855
Gregg, Mrs. Myrilla, age 34   7-15-1854
Gregg, Oscar, age 23, at New Albany   10-29-1859
Griffing, Michael   9-14-1850
Griffith, Edwin, in Illinois   1-17-1857
Griffith, John, nr. Merom   9- 6-1845
Griffith, Mary I., dt of Humphrey   7- 7-1860
Griffith, Thomas, age 7, bro. of John   9- 6-1845
Groff, Jacob, native of Md.   5-15-1847
Grooms, Moses, Sr., age 77   9-17-1859
Grubbs, Theodore, son of Richard   3-12-1853
Guilford, Catharine E. (Mrs. Simeon)   11- 6-1858
Guiney, Rev. Edmund R., Lutheran   11-14-1857

Hall, Edward S., age 36   9-20-1851
Hall, Fred, son of E.A. & S.A.   12-22-1855
Hall, Mrs. Martha   12-28-1850
Hamilton, Diantha (Mrs. Charles C.),
    dt of James Perham   10-15-1853
Hamilton, Sarah (Mrs. John W.)   7-26-1851
Hammond, Rebecca (Mrs. U.J.B.),
    dt. of Mrs. Mary Cannon   1-24-1852
Hanch, William D., formerly Indpls.   8-14-1858
Hanna, Adolphus, son of V.C.   2- 3-1849
Hanna, Eliza, widow of Jas. F.   7- 2-1853
Hanna, James F., age 32   5-28-1853
Hanna, Milburn, inf. of Wm. H.   4-22-1848
Hannah, Israel, son of Samuel   8-14-1852
Hannaman, Mason J., son of Wm.   7-19-1851
Harding, Robert   10-13-1849
Harkness, Isaac M., son of Thos.   3-27-1852
Harley, Miss Mary Jane, Delphi   6- 7-1851
Harn, Lawson, in Iowa, accident   9- 9-1854
Harrison, Alice T., dt of A.W.   8-18-1855
Harrison, Cornelia, dt of James   8-18-1849
Harrison, Emma, dt of Mary   9-15-1860
Harrison, Mary, dt of James S.   12- 1-1855
Harrison, Joanna M. (Mrs. Abram)   5-24-1851
Harrison, Louisa, inf. of John C.   5- 7-1853
Hart, Col. James B.   9-20-1851
Hart, William Alex (son of Wm.)   4-10-1852
Hascall, Chauncey, son of E.W.H.   3-11-1853
Haverstick, George, age 69   2-25-1860
Haverstick, Michael, age 19   9-23-1848
Haugh, Adam, Jr.   7-20-1850
Haugh, Margaret (Mrs. Emanuel)   4-19-1856
Hausman, Henry, merchant, age 29   9-22-1860
Havens, Daniel, age 35, in Iowa   9- 9-1854
Hawkins, Maria, of consumption   2- 5-1848
Hawkins, Mrs. Ruth, mo of Mrs. Nicholas McCarty
    1- 1-1853
Hay, Mrs. Harriet, in Vincennes   9-15-1849
Haynes, Ada, dt of Philip & Sarah   2-19-1859
Haywood, ——, child of John   9-25-1858
Headley, Samuel, in Franklin   4-26-1851
Heath, ——, inf dt of Charles   8- 5-1848
Hedges, Eliza (Mrs. Elijah), dt of
    James & Maria Hill, age 19   10-14-1854
Henderson, Martha A. (Mrs. Wm.)   5-27-1854
Henley, E., in Sacramento, Calif.   12-21-1850
Herring, Mrs. ——, in Pittsburgh,
    former principal of Female College   8- 3-1850
Herringlacke, ——, inf dt of Henry   8- 5-1848
Herritage, Elvira   6-24-1848
Hetiselgesser, Mary, dt of Samuel   5-30-1857
Hildebrand, Martha, dt of Uriah   2-12-1853
Hill, ——, inf dt of James   4-15-1848
Hill, Calvin F., age 17   7- 8-1848
Hill, S.C., bro of G.W., age 48   11-21-1857

102

Hills, Clarinda, dt of Rev. A.F.	8-28-1852
Hines, Julia, inf. of J.C. & Mary	8-27-1859
Hines, Maria (Mrs. Cyrus), dt of Calvin Fletcher	5- 5-1860
Hinton, Ida, inf. of James & Mary	4-30-1859
Hockman, Sarah F., dt of J.M.	8-25-1849
Holbrook, William, son of A.S.	12-18-1852
Holcombe, W., of La Porte	4-14-1855
Holland, M—— (Mrs. John W.)	6- 3-1848
Holliday, Lucia, dt of Rev. Wm.	4- 9-1853
Hollingshead, Mrs. Josephine B.	9-16-1854
Holloway, Sarah (Mrs. Elisha)	12-28-1850
Holman, Solomon, son of Joseph	8-21-1852
Holman, B.B.	10-12-1850
Holmes, William, age 69, pioneer	2-26-1859
Holt, Mrs. Isabella R., age 64	4-12-1851
Holt, Miss Margaret R., age 31	8-18-1849
Hooker, James, age 28	10-30-1858
Hooker, Katy, inf. of James	4-10-1858
Houghteling, Ernest, son of Cyrus	9-17-1859
Housum, Philip, son of George	7-17-1858
Howe, M.W., of Cincinnati	9-24-1853
Huffman, Christina (Mrs. Jacob)	6- 9-1849
Huffman, Julia, inf. of Jacob	4-14-1849
Hughes, Francis M.	4-20-1850
Hughes, James T., son of Nixon	1- 8-1859
Huggins, Edward, age 65	7- 1-1848
Hunt, Dr. D.P.	9-16-1848
Hunt, Isaac P., son of P.G.C.	8-27-1853
Hunter, Martha, inf. of William	9-18-1858
Hunter, Nancy J. (Mrs. A.B.)	1-21-1854
Hunter, William H., nr Greenwood	12- 4-1852
Hurd, Mary A., dt of Daniel	8-11-1855
Hurley, Orintha, dt of G.W. & Ivy	8-30-1851
Idler, Laura, dt of Clinton	3- 3-1855
Irwin, James B., age 49, in Pa.	5-10-1851
Irwin, Mrs. Jemima, sister of Benjamin L. Blythe	2-16-1856
Irwin, Joseph D., of consumption	3-26-1859
Jackson, Joseph L., at Puebla, Mexico, last August	1- 8-1848
Janeway, John, b. Cambridge, England	8- 8-1857
Jefferson, Cornelia J.	11- 4-1848
Jenkins, Miranda H. (Mrs. W.A.)	9- 6-1845
Jenks, James P., in Lafayette	10-12-1850
Johnson, Hannah (Mrs. James)	9- 8-1860
Johnson, Mrs. John	4-15-1848
Johnson, Margaret (Mrs. Henry S.)	2-21-1857
Johnson, Rev. Samuel Lee	12-30-1848
Johnston, Charles E., age 19	2-16-1856
Johnston, McKinna L., age 4	6-11-1859
Jones, Albert E., in Chicago	3-28-1857
Jones, Edwin, b. Litchfield, Conn.	9-22-1860
Jones, Joseph C., in Noblesville	4-25-1857
Jones, Martha A., dt Albert E.	7-29-1854
Jordan, Elizabeth	9-20-1845
Jordan, James G.	4- 5-1851
Jordan, Miss Margaret	8-18-1849
Kartheus, Gabriel E., from France, late of Pittsburgh	12-13-1851

Keeley, Samuel, age 58	8-25-1849
Kemper, Daniel, inf. of Henry	8-28-1852
Kentzell, Anna Maria (Mrs. John)	5-29-1858
Kern, J.S.K., of N.W.C. Univ.	2-18-1860
Ketcham, Samuel M., son of John	7-15-1848
Kavanaugh, ——, inf. dt of B.T.	4- 1-1848
Kimberly, Tilghman H.	9-15-1849
Kinder, Isaac	12- 8-1849
King, Elizabeth (Mrs. Francis)	2-11-1860
King, Harriet, widow of David	12-22-1855
King, John H., age 17, in Ky.	6-10-1854
Kingsbury, Frances (Mrs. John E.)	9- 3-1853
Kinsley, Clara, drowned	7-10-1852
Kline, Nicholas, age 60	4-15-1848
Knepfler, Flora (Mrs. Joseph), dt of Royal Mayhew	10-18-1856
Kneppler, Dr. Nathan, age 56	1-15-1859
Knodle, Esther C., dt of Adam	11-20-1858
Knotts, Nathaniel, age 33	2-12-1859
Koontz, Maria	7-12-1851
Kyle, Phoebe, dt of John & Eliz	6- 5-1852
Lamasters, Mary Ellen, age 21	8- 9-1851
Lamb, Isaac, of St. Joseph Co.	7-28-1849
Landers, F., in California	12-21-1850
Landis, Emma C., dt of J.M.	5- 5-1849
Landis, Joseph	10-11-1851
Landis, Joseph H., inf. of Milton	3-13-1858
Landis, Juliet, dt of Dr. Landis	9-23-1854
Landis, Dr. Phillip L., in Ill.	9-23-1854
Laux, Joseph, native of France	11- 5-1859
Lawrence, Mrs. Lucinda King, dt of James Vanblaricum	6-14-1851
Lay, Cyllan (Mrs. George)	7- 9-1853
Leatherman, Sampson, negro	3- 3-1849
Lee, J. Vinton, son of Royal	1-15-1859
Lee, Margaret (Mrs. George)	7-19-1851
Lefever, Mrs. Joseph, age 50	3-18-1848
Leonard, Luther, inf. of John D.	11-26-1859
Lewis, Ann, dt of G.M. Beswick	12-16-1848
Lewis, John J., Washington Twp.	6-17-1854
Lindley, Catharine (Mrs. Jacob)	4-12-1856
Lindley, Mary E., dt of Jacob	4-16-1853
Lindley, Sarah, inf. dt of Jacob	12-18-1852
Lingenfelter, Mrs. Archibald	3-15-1851
Lingenfelter, Edward, inf. of D.	9-27-1856
Lingenfelter, George, shoemaker	8- 6-1853
Lingenfelter, Mrs. John W.	11-16-1850
Lingle, Simon	4-30-1853
List, Conrad, late of Pittsburgh	6-25-1853
List, Henry, age 32	11- 9-1850
Lister, Maria (Mrs. John)	6-18-1853
Lister, Nathan	4-28-1849
Little, Joseph	12-20-1856
Little, Margaret (Mrs. John)	11-11-1854
Lockerbie, George, age 86	6-21-1856
Looker, Altha, dt of Robert	8-25-1860
Lowe, Mary C., dt of George	7- 9-1853
Luce, Eleazer, murdered	2-26-1848
Lutz, Conrad, cabinet maker	5-19-1855
Lynn, Josiah, age 46	4- 7-1855

McArthur, Rev. John, formerly
of Oxford, Ohio   8-11-1849

McCarty, ——, inf. of Wm. & Aurelia   6- 3-1854

McCaslin, Elizabeth, dt of Hervey,
in Johnson Co.   10- 5-1850

McCaslin, Rebecca (Mrs. John)
died in Franklin   9-18-1852

McChesney, Mrs. Hannah, age 65   3- 4-1854

McChestney, Charles Colfax, inf.
of J.B.   7-17-1852

McClellan, Margaret Ann (Mrs. Joseph
S.), in Franklin   7-24-1858

McClellan, Ophelia (Mrs. H.L.),
in Franklin   8-13-1859

McClellan, Robert H., age 29, from
Johnson Co.   8-23-1851

McClintock, M. Thomas   8- 9-1851

M'Clong, Quill, accident on Cumber-
land Road, 1 mi. E. of Philadelphia   8-18-1849

McCluer, Mrs. Margaret D., age 25   2-25-1854

M'Clung, Mrs. Susan, widow of
Judge Wm., d. in Maysville   11-20-1858

McCollum, John, of Kosciusko Co.   4-28-1849

McConnell, Mary, age 78   12- 2-1848

McCormick, Samuel, of Tippecanoe Co.   3-12-1853

McCoy, John, an accident   4-27-1850

McCready, James E., son of James &
Eliza, age 16   12- 3-1859

McCutcheon, John, age 49, b. Ireland   2-14-1852

McDonald, Alice, dt of David & Mary   8- 5-1854

McDowell, James A., age 89   2-25-1860

McDowell, Mary Ursule (Mrs. John)
of Franklin   5- 7-1853

McFarland, —, wife of D.L.   1-13-1855

McFarland, Sarah   3-25-1848

McFarland, Sarah R., dt of J.S.   2- 9-1850

McFarlin, Mrs. Sarah   6-16-1849

M'Gaffey, O.H., age 21, drowned,
Putnam Co.   5-26-1849

McGill, John, age abt. 35   10-22-1853

McGuire, Elizabeth (Mrs. John D.)   5- 6-1848

McGuire, Jackson N.,   8- 5-1848

McGuire, Lucy (Mrs. James E.)   4-28-1849

McHattan, Mary E. (Mrs. Jesse),
age 25   4-10-1858

McIlvain, James   4- 8-1848

McIlvain, ——, inf. son of James   4-15-1848

McKay, George, in Philadelphia, Pa.   6-17-1854

McKay, Mrs. Hugh, in El Dorado,
Calif., dt of Rev. C.W. Ruter   9- 8-1855

McKissick, Dr. David, age 45   4-16-1853

McLain, Robert M., age 39   8-23-1851

McLaughlin, Aley (Mrs. F.P.), age 43   8- 6-1859

McLean, Florence, sister of Rev. C.G.   4-23-1853

McLene, Sarah, widow of Gen. Jeremiah
of Revolutionary War, age 86   1- 8-1859

McMahan, Newton, age 20   5-24-1856

McMahon, Darlington   9-15-1855

McMullen, Mr. ——, of Montgomery Co.   4-22-1848

McNabb, James M., age 4, son of
Stephen & Jane   7-26-1851

McNabb, William S., age 1, son of
Stephen & Jane   7-26-1851

McNeely, Florence, inf. of James H.
& Margaret P.   4-18-1857

McNeely, Parke, son of James H. &
Margaret   1- 5-1856

McRae, Sanders, son of John H.
& Agnes   6-14-1856

McRae, Sarah Agnes (Mrs. John H.)   10-17-1857

Magill, Samuel   6-28-1851

Maguire, Rebecca (Mrs. Douglas)   1-13-1855

Major, ——, inf. son of Stephen   8- 5-1848

Manley, William, a barber   9-13-1856

Mansur, James F., son of Wm. & Hannah   6-5-1858

Manwaring, Francis C., dt of Wm H.
& Margaret, age 14   4-17-1852

Marcus, ——, wife of Joseph, age 26   4-22-1848

Marrs, Clarence W., son of W.A. & C.M.
     12-29-1855

Marrs, M. David, age 65   5-14-1859

Marrs, Martha (Mrs. John), age 59   8-18-1849

Marrs, Rachel (Mrs. David), age 61,
of Franklin   9- 8-1855

Marshall, Joseph G., of Madison   4-14-1855

Marshall, Thomas L., Franklin Co.,
Ohio   9- 3-1859

Martindale, Joseph, in Marion Iowa   12- 2-1854

Matlock, Wm. L., Danville, age 43   1-10-1852

Maugham(?), Wm., age 70, a printer   5-12-1855

Mavity, Robert, age 18   3- 8-1856

Maxwell, Sarah T. (Mrs. Samuel D.),
of Clinton Co.   1-19-1856

May, ——, inf. son of Edwin   9-23-1848

Meeker, Thomas N., in Louisville   12-30-1848

Meikel, John, age 35   11-27-1858

Melville, Mary, inf. of Calvin A. &
Martha Elliott   12-26-1857

Melville, Sarah E., dt. of R.B. &
M.A., age 10   3-28-1857

Millard, Alfred Henry, son of Wm. J.
    & Paulina, near Millersville   2-12-1853
Miller, Davis T.   3-25-1848
Milless, Mary Ann (Mrs. Laertes O.),
    of Baltimore, Md.   4-12-1856
Mills, Elizabeth C. (Mrs. C.L.)   7-12-1851
Mills, William Jackson, son of H.W. &
    A.F., at Morristown, N.J.   10- 6-1860
Montague, Sarah Catharine, dt. of
    John & Phebe Ann   3-17-1855
Moore, Charles Ray, son of J.M.   11-17-1849
Moore, Mrs. Mary H., of Genesee, Ill.   9- 8-1860
Morely, William   9- 9-1848
Morgan, Courtney L., son of Samuel C.
    & Susan   8- 8-1857
Morley, C., late of Madison, age 17   7-19-1851
Morley, Mrs. Lavina, age 63   9-25-1858
Morris, Alexander M., son of Ann E.   7-29-1854
Morris, Austin W.   7- 5-1851
Morris, Catharine P., dt. of B.F.   7-22-1848
Morris, Elizabeth (Mrs. Sanford), age 23
                            8-17-1850
Morris, Margaret (Mrs. Bethuel F.)   2-26-1853
Morris, William L.   2-26-1853
Morrison, Alexander F., age 53   1- 2-1858
Morrison, Elizabeth, dt. of W.H. &
    Mary, age 3   3-24-1860
Morrison, Elizabeth, dt. of Michael   10-22-1853
Morrison, Mary L. (Mrs. Wm. A.),
    dt. of N.B. Palmer   9-24-1859
Morrow, ——, wife of Rev. Wm.   9-22-1849
Mothershead, Amanda M. (Mrs. J.L.)   2-15-1851
Mothershead, J.L.   11-11-1854
Mounts, Mrs. Almira M., widow of Wm.   11- 4-1854
Munsell, Dr. Luke, in Jeffersonville   7-15-1854
Murphy, Mary Ann, wife of D.W.
    Umberhime, of Wexford, Ireland   1-28-1860
Murphy, Peter, accident   9-14-1850
Murray, Mary E. (Mrs. Maj. E.)   1-17-1852
Mussulman, George W., in Calif.   5-31-1851
Myars, Elizabeth Cornelia, age 1   7-15-1848
Myers, George, age 59   10-22-1859
Myers, Minerva (Mrs. James),
    Harrison Co., Ky.   3- 3-1860

Nave, Lurena (Mrs. C.C.), in Danville   6-26-1852
Neal, John, formerly of Pa.   9-28-1850
Negley, Albert, inf. of George M.
    & Jane   7- 5-1856
Neighbors, John M., son of Chas.
    & Jane   8-24-1850
Nelson, Albert, son of Henry   10-11-1851
Nettleton, Sister Ann Eliza, age 19,
    left a husband   9-30-1854
Newberry, Nathaniel, at Pendleton,
    from Michigan, age 37   1-22-1853
Newhouse, Lewis Albert, son of Lewis
    Y. & Drusilla, near Lanesville   7-19-1856
Newkirk, Charles, age 50   12-14-1850
Noel, Nellie Campbell, dt. of S.V.B.
    & Elizabeth G., age 3   9- 8-1855
Nofsinger, Mrs. Evaline Howard, age
    25, dt. of Tilghman A. Howard   4-24-1852
Nofsinger, William B., son of Dr.
    Wm. R. & Emeline B.   8-15-1857

Norman, Joseph, formerly of N.Y.   11-26-1859
Norman, Mrs. Juanna P., age 71   11- 7-1857
Norman, Lucy A., (Mrs. J.B.),
    in New Albany   1-20-1855
Norman, Mary S., inf of John B.
    & Lucy A., in New Albany   2-12-1853
Norris, Wm. L., son of S.W.,
    on way home from Calif.   12-28-1850
Norwood, Newton N.   7-13-1850
Nowland, Mrs. Elizabeth   12-13-1856
Nowland, James R.   4-26-1851

Ogilsby, Charles Henry, son of J.H.
    & Mary, age 9   8- 5-1848
Ogle, Mrs. Amanda M., at Carrolton, Ky. 4-18-1857
Ohr, Frank W., son of John H. &
    Sarah   9- 4-1858
Ohr, Geo. D., son of John H. & Sarah   12-10-1859
Ohr, Jacob I., age 69, from Maryland   9- 9-1854
O'Kane, Sister Julia A., dt. of Elder
    O'Kane, age 20   6-28-1851
Oliver, Martha Ann (Mrs. D.H.),
    dt. of Judge Harding   9-17-1859
Orr, Benjamin, age 29   9- 6-1845
Osgood, Wm. O., son of J.R. & O.L.   11-12-1853
Outley, David   5-13-1848

Palmer, Lucy Louisa, dt. of Wm. H.H.
    & Amanda, age 1   7-23-1853
Palmer, Nathan B., age 20   4- 4-1857
Palmer, Rebecca Ann (Mrs. E.)   3- 6-1858
Parker, Daniel, age 78   11-13-1858
Parker, ——, dt. of James, age 7   8-12-1848
Patt, Susanna, dt. of Charles &
    Margaret, age 17   4- 7-1855
Patterson, Christian Newton, son of
    Samuel & Adaline, age 3   8-16-1851
Patterson, Elliott M., accident   8- 9-1851
Patterson, Henry C.   8-30-1856
Patterson, Robert, age 76   5-29-1852
Peck, Anna P., dt. of Wm. H.
    & Julia E.   8-11-1849
Peck, Julia (Mrs. Wm. H.)   1-26-1850
Peirce, Louise Smith (Mrs. Joseph C.),
    dt. of Dr. Edwin Smith, Dayton   10-31-1857
Pellet, Elizabeth Jane (Mrs. Wm. A.),
    dt. of Jacob Huntington   10-31-1857
Pendergeist, John   5-28-1859
Penington, Otho, age 65   12-18-1852
Peoples, Josiah, age 20   5-21-1851
Perkins, Amanda J., dt. of Judge
    Perkins, age 2   12-19-1857
Perkins, Amanda J. (Mrs. Samuel E.)   4-19-1856
Petro, Charles W., son of Louisa
    Shirley, at Orphan Asylum   1-12-1856
Phelps, Wm. Terry, son of Wm. &
    Susan, age 2   12-10-1859
Phillips, Mrs. Hannah   3-29-1851
Phillips, Israel, murdered   11-10-1849
Phipps, Eunice Ellen, dt. of John M.
    & Mary A.   7-15-1854
Phipps, John B., age 64   2-11-1860
Pierce, Mrs. Georgiana A., age 28   12-30-1854
Pitts, Stephen, age 61   10- 6-1860
Pleas, Wm., age 54, in Hamilton Co.   3- 8-1856

Pleasants, Arthur Reeves, son of
   Dr. John & Ann M. 10-17-1857
Poak, James, suicide 5- 4-1850
Pogue, Malinda (Mrs. John), age 44 3- 2-1850
Ponteney, James, in Calif., age 45 5-31-1851
Pope, Daniel, inf. of Abner J. 12-17-1853
Pope, George F., son of Abner J.,
   age 3 12-17-1853
Porter, George 2-21-1852
Pottage, Mary Ann, inf. of Benjamin 8-24-1850
Potter, John, of Washington Co. 11-24-1849
Potts, John D., son of Chas. & Martha 2-13-1858
Pratt, Miss C.C., sister-in-law of
   Rev. S.L. Johnson 5- 6-1848
Price, Mrs. Sarah, widow of Clarkson
   Price, formerly of Ohio 2-11-1860
Pugh, Lucina (Mrs. Jacob), in
   Marion, Iowa 12- 2-1854
Pugh, Malinda (Mrs. Isaac), age 43 10- 2-1852
Pugh, Margaret, dt. of Isaac & Mary 7-23-1853
Pugh, Mary (Mrs. Isaac), age 55 3-15-1851
Purcell, Edgar 5- 3-1856
Purnell, Milby Francis, son of Thomas
   Purnell of Maryland, age 21 8- 2-1851
Pyle, Phebe W. (Mrs. E.C.), age 31 11- 3-1855

Quarles, John W., accident 4-17-1852
Quarles, Luke, age 19 11- 6-1858
Quarles, William 12-22-1849
Quinn, ——, inf. son of Philip 7-15-1848
Quinn, Patrick, drowned 5-15-1852

Rains, Harvy, in Calif., age 23 12- 2-1854
Rains, Martha A., age 23 3-26-1853
Ransom, Ada, age 15, dt. of J.L. &
   Rebecca A., at Burdett, N.Y. 7- 2-1853
Ransom, Hiram 12-25-1852
Ransome, Jane (Mrs. John), dt. of
   Samuel & Sarah Cones 4-26-1851
Rariden, James, of Cambridge City 11- 1-1856
Ray, Emma Montfort, dt. of James M. 8-31-1850
Ray, Esther, (Mrs. James B.) 8-17-1850
Ray, James Mills, son of Chas. B. 11- 5-1859
Ray, James Brown, late governor
   of Ind., in Cincinnati 8-12-1848
Ray, Julia Potter, dt. of James M. 1-15-1853
Ray, Laura Kate, dt. of Charles A. &
   Laura A., age 2 2-11-1860
Ray, Margaret (Mrs. James M.), dt. of
   Rev. Elias & Margaret Riggs 8- 5-1854
Ray, Wm. J., son of John & Isabella 9- 9-1854
Rea, George West, son of Sampson &
   Martha West, age 2 6- 3-1854
Ream, B.O., age 31 10-22-1853
Ream, Nancy A. (Mrs. Benjamin) 9-18-1851
Redpath, James, in Barry Co., Mich. 9-21-1850
Reed, James, age 17 8-12-1848
Reveal, Margaret, dt. of Thomas &
   Elizabeth, in Wappelo Co., Iowa 7- 3-1858
Reynolds, Elizabeth M. (Mrs. John L.),
   dt. of Wm. Bradshaw 10-20-1855
Rhoads, Hannah (Mrs. James) 7-28-1849
Rickets, Mary Ann (Mrs. George),
   dt. of G.L. Strang 7-30-1859
Rider, Caroline (Mrs. Lawrence), Iowa 5-21-1853

Rider, Lawrence, Iowa 5-27-1854
Ritchey, Margaret (Mrs. John),
   b. Pa. 6-30-1849
Rives, Mary E. (Mrs. John F.), dt. of
   Rev. R.W. Bailey, in Hind Co., Miss.
   10-15-1859
Roberson, Julia, dt. of Charles
   & Mary Ann 3-18-1848
Roberson, Mary E., dt. of Wm.
   & Nancy 3-18-1848
Roberts, Mrs. Margaret, age 76,
   mother of Joseph T. 4- 9-1859
Robson, ——, (Mrs. Wm.) 4-22-1848
Rockey, Betsey (Mrs. Henry) 4-30-1853
Roe, James 3-30-1850
Rooker, Letita Jane (Mrs. C.F.),
   St. Joseph, Missouri, age 32 3-22-1856
Rooker, Mary Anna, dt. of A.J. &
   Henrietta 11-18-1854
Rooker, Nina Beatrice, dt. of Calvin
   & Lydia 5-12-1860
Rooker, Capt. John, of Howard Co.,
   Missouri 2-22-1851
Roop, William M., age 18 10-14-1854
Rose, ——, dt. of Wm. R., age 2 4-22-1848
Rosengarten, Ernst, son of Henry &
   Mary 3- 3-1855
Rosengarten, Mary Ann (Mrs. Samuel) 4-24-1858
Rousseau, Mrs. Elizabeth Jane, age 20 12-14-1850
Russell, Alexander W. 10- 2-1852
Russell, Catharine (Mrs. A.W.) 9-20-1845
Ryan, Elizabeth (Mrs. James B.),
   b. in Johnson Co., age 34 2- 5-1859

Sanders, Dr. John N. 5-25-1850
Seaman, Hiram B., age 50, in Morgantown
   3- 2-1850
Selly, Mrs. Jane B., age 109 9-17-1859
Serbin, Samuel B. 5-10-1851
Seward, Rachel, widow of Wm. 4-21-1860
Seymour, Lizzie D. (Mrs. E.P.), dt. of
   late Capt. Isaac Vanhouten, in
   San Francisco 9-25-1858
Shark, Mary Ann (Mrs. John), formerly
   of Wayne Co., age 40 1-11-1851
Sharp, Vincent, inf. of J.K. & M.E. 2-25-1854
Sharpe, Mrs. Eliza, widow of Ebenezer,
   age 69 6-11-1853
Sharpe, Ellen, dt. of Thomas H. &
   Elizabeth 1-28-1854
Sharpe, Sophia W., dt. of Thomas H.
   & Elizabeth, age 13 12-25-1858
Sharpe, Thomas H., inf. son of
   Thomas H. & Elizabeth 12-29-1849
Sharpe, Wm. Graydon, inf. son of
   Joseph K. & Mary E. 8- 4-1849
Shaw, Mrs. Elizabeth 10-14-1848
Shaw, Mary (Mrs. Victor) 1-20-1855
Shearer, Mary (Mrs. W.F.) 12-16-1848
Sheets, David Eldridge, son of late
   Jas. A. Sheets of Madison 9-25-1858
Sheets, Eliza (Mrs. David), age 31 12-14-1850
Sheets, Jacob, Boone Co., age 60 4-19-1851
Sheets, James Dill, son of Wm. &
   Mary S. 4-28-1849

Sheets, Willeana, dt. of Wm. & Mary, age 7   3- 6-1858

Shelby, Elizabeth (Mrs. Benjamin), Henry Co.   12-11-1858

Shoemaker, Silas   6- 8-1850

Shortridge, Albert C., son of A.F. & Nancy   7- 3-1852

Shortridge, Caroline Lister, dt. of A.F. & N.T., age 12   4- 8-1854

Shute, Wm., age 59, from N.J.   1-19-1850

Siler, Wm., son of Daniel   9-29-1849

Silvey, John T., near Millersville   6- 5-1858

Silvey, Nancy, dt. of Hillary & Patience, age 20   8-11-1855

Sinker, ——, inf. son of Edward & Sarah   8-31-1850

Sloan, Stephen, son of John & Louisa M.   7-19-1851

Sluker, Sarah Jane, dt. of E.T. & Sarah, age 6   11-13-1858

Smallwood, Matilda L., dt. of Rev. Wm. A., of Zanesville, Ohio   12-30-1848

Smart, Frances Ann (Mrs. Humphrey)   10-27-1849

Smith, Augustus   8-20-1853

Smith, C., age 85, father of T.M.   1-28-1854

Smith, Charlotte Davis, dt. of Hugh H.   3-27-1852

Smith, Colone Taylor, son of Hugh H., age 9   9-10-1853

Smith, Elenora, dt. of Isaac & Eliza Jane, age 5   5-13-1848

Smith, Elizabeth Jane (Mrs. Elisha)   5-21-1859

Smith, Elizabeth (Mrs. Peyton H.)   3-14-1857

Smith, Hannah Maria, dt. of Hugh H.   9-13-1851

Smith, Hattie W., dt. of Rev. John C. & Margaret, age 7   12-10-1859

Smith, James, accident   9- 2-1848

Smith, Jane (Mrs. Wm.), age 31   4-15-1848

Smith, Margaret Nesbit (Mrs. D.R.)   8-26-1854

Smith, Martha (Mrs. Thomas M.)   1-25-1851

Smith, Wm. J., age 59   7-17-1858

Smock, ——, inf. son of John & Rebecca   7-20-1850

Smock, Rebecca Jane (Mrs. John)   7-20-1850

Socks, John, son of Philip, age 18   8-28-1852

Southard, Emma, dt. of J.P. & Ann   9-15-1855

Southard, Louis P., son of J.P. & Ann   8- 5-1854

Spann, Eliza Lake, dt. of John S. & Hester A.   8-25-1855

Spann, George, son of John & Hester   11-10-1860

Spann, Wm. E., inf. son of John & Hester   ———

Sparlan, John, murdered   7- 6-1850

Spencer, Amanda M. (Mrs. E.S.)   12-25-1858

Sponable, Mary Ann, niece of Philip   3-31-1860

Springer, John, age 56, early settler of Warren Twp.   7- 8-1854

Stapp, George Dallas, son of James H.   7-24-1852

Staten, Elizabeth, age 15   9- 7-1850

Stephens, Alfred   10-18-1856

Stephenson, Isabella, b. 1756   2- 9-1850

Stevens, Alanson J., age 30, at Salem   2-24-1849

Stevens, Charles, age 52   2-23-1856

Stevens, Margaret (Mrs. Joshua)   7- 1-1848

Stevens, Thomas, son of Charles & Ann, at Madison   5- 6-1848

Stewart, Harriet Ellen, dt. of Robert & Nancy, age 1   9-11-1852

Stewart, Wm., age 55, b. Pa.   11-12-1859

Stone, Charley M., son of Geo. & Lucy, in Minneapolis   9- 4-1858

Stowell, James Telford, inf. son of Myron A. & Elizabeth   4- 9-1859

Stretcher, Joseph I.   9-15-1849

Swift, Mrs. Anna, age 66   2-26-1859

Swords, Mary (Mrs. John)   6-12-1852

Talbott, John Coran, inf. son of W.H. & Elizabeth   3-13-1852

Talbot, John Saunders, of St. Louis, brother of Rev. Talbot of city   11-15-1856

Talbot, Mrs. Sarah, mother of Rev. J.C., of Christ Church   8-11-1855

Talbott, Mrs. Mary, age 62   3-15-1851

Tanner, Andrew J., Jackson Co.   7-31-1858

Tanner, Mary J., age 16   9-11-1858

Tarlton, Helen M. (Mrs. John)   2-27-1858

Taylor, Eliza J. (Mrs. Napoleon B.)   7-12-1851

Taylor, Jerome B., of Franklin   4- 2-1853

Taylor, Mary M., dt. of Robert A. & Mary, in Ky.   6-20-1857

Taylor, Robert S., age 42   8-28-1858

Teal, D.C., age 29, Noblesville   7- 2-1853

Test, Hon. John, nr. Cambridge City   10-20-1849

Thalman, A.M. (Mrs. J.J.), nr. Seymour   1- 1-1859

Thayer, Ira, age 47, at Evansville   10- 9-1858

Thompson, Ruth (Mrs. John), formerly widow of Rev. John Strange   2-16-1850

Thompson, Thomas   8- 4-1855

Thorp, Sarah (Mrs. John D.)   6-19-1852

Thorpe, Ella, inf. dt. of John D. & Sarah   11-24-1849

Thorpe, Sarah Cornelia, inf. dt. of John D. & Sarah   8-16-1851

Tilley, Amelia L.M., inf. dt. of Herman & F.   9-29-1860

Tinsley, Lucinda (Mrs. Wm.), age 47   11- 7-1857

Tomlinson, John, son of Stephen D. & Mary T.   7-26-1851

Toon, Josiah B., in Iowa   5-20-1854

Tousey, Mary E. (Mrs. Oliver)   1-25-1851

Travis, E. Ellen, at Knightstown   9-30-1854

Trester, Sarah (Mrs. Wm. D.), age 26   12-17-1853

Trester, Sarah (Mrs. Silas G.)   6-25-1853

Tucker, Elizabeth C. (Mrs. Robert)   8-19-1848

Tully, Wm. H.C., son of Wm. & Eliza A., age 4   10- 3-1857

Turner, Louisa, dt. of Deacon James & Malinda, age 19   3- 6-1858

Tutewiler, Mary Jane, inf. dt. of Henry & Nancy   2-10-1849

Tutewiler, Nancy (Mrs. Henry)   2-16-1850

Tutewiler, Nancy Ellen, inf. dt. of Henry & Nancy   7-22-1848

Tutewiler, Samuel, son of Henry & Mary I.   3- 4-1854

Tuttle, Amasa M., son of B.W. & Polly   10-6-1848

Tuttle, Nelly F., dt. of P.E. & Julia, age 13, in Peru   9-29-1855

Updegraff, Phoebe W. (Mrs. J.I.), at Mt. Pleasant, Ohio;; dt. of Robert R. & Sarah W. Underhill   2- 9-1850

Vale, Nicholas, age 14   5-11-1850
Vanblaricum, James, age 53   8-21-1858
Vanblaricum, ——, inf. son of Wm. G.
&. Caroline   9- 7-1850
Vance, Arthur S., nr. Allisonville   9-29-1849
Vance, Ella, inf. of L.M. &. Mary J.   9-11-1852
Vanhorn, Sarah (Mrs. Wm. H.)   5- 7-1853
Vanhorn, Wm., son of Wm. &. Sarah   6- 7-1851
Vanhouten, Cornelius B., son of C.W.
&. Rachel M., age 1   2- 4-1854
VanHouten, Maria J. (Mrs. Cornelius W.) 1-4-1851
Varner, Elias, in Calif.   10- 4-1851
Vaughn, Julia, inf. of Jacob &. Jane   3- 6-1858
Vice, Mrs. Hannah, age 70   2-19-1859
Vinton, Eddie, son of A.E. &. Therese   8- 6-1853
Voorhees, A.M. Bellamy Storer, son
of Capt. A.L., age 12   3- 8-1851
Voorhees, Abraham L., age 63   1-15-1859
Voorheese, Abraham D., age 75, formerly
from N.J.   10-25-1851

Wainscott, —— (Mrs. T.)   8-12-1848
Wainwright, —— (Mrs. Samuel)   2- 3-1849
Walker, Harry A., son of Harry &.
Sarah   2-25-1860
Walker, Jane, inf. of W.F. &. Mary   3-20-1858
Walker, ——, dt. of W.F. &. Mary   5- 5-1860
Wallace, Cordelia, dt. of Wm.   6-25-1853
Wallace, David, former governor   9-10-1859
Wallace, Sanders, inf. son of Gov.   10- 9-1858
Walls, Sarah Ann, Greencastle   8-30-1851
Walpole, John G., age 29, from
Fort Wayne   9-27-1851
Ward, John P., age 20   9- 5-1857
Ward, Robert in Calif.   1- 4-1851
Warenfelc [sic], Peter, nr. Allisonville   5- 6-1848
Warfel, Esther (Mrs. Martin B.), dt
of John Charles   9-30-1854
Warfell, Mary Jane, inf. dt of Martin B.
&. Esther   7-22-1854
Warner, ——, dt. of Charles   1-19-1850
Warner, Caroline G., dt. of Charles G.
&. Mary, age 13   12-22-1855
Warner, Mary (Mrs. —— G.)' age 40   5-10-1856
Waterman, George F., age 62, nr.
Pendleton   1-29-1853
Waters, Florence, dt. of W.W. &. C.A.   10-13-1860
Waters, Harrie G., son of John G. &.
Anne Lee   7-22-1854
Watson, Indiana, inf. of Joseph &.
Sarah Jane   3-20-1852
Watson, Joseph, age 51, at Miamisburgh
                                           9-28-1850
Weaver, Kate, dt. of Wm. W. &. Elmira   8-21-1858
Weaver, Caroline C.P., dt. of Wm. W.
&. Elmira, age 2   7-15-1854
Webb, Mary L. (Mrs. John W.O.),
in Franklin   8-14-1852
Webb, Mary Virginia, age 12   4-19-1851
Weeks, Mary Francis, dt. of John G.
&. Rachel, age 7   8-16-1851
Weiand(?), Levi, son of Isaac &.
Elizabeth, age 5   1-15-1853
Weiand(?), George H., son of Isaac
&. Elizabeth   1-15-1853

Wells, Clara Bell, inf. of W.F. &.
Rebecca   8- 7-1858
Wendworth, Ellen (Mrs. Julius), age 29 10-22-1859
Wesley, James, son of James &. Mary
A. Clines, age 1   7-30-1853
West, Abner F., age 35   5-30-1857
West, Charlie H., in Chicago, age 22   10-31-1857
West, Harry, in Cincinnati   6- 9-1849
West, Louisa, dt. of Harry &. Mary   6-12-1852
West, Margaret J. (Mrs. Nathaniel)   8-14-1858
West, Mary Bowles, widow of Nathaniel
                                           11- 4-1854
Wheatley, John, age 54   3-18-1854
Wheatley, Milton, age 17   3- 6-1858
Wheeler, Anna W., dt. of Prof. John,
late of Asbury Univ.   10-14-1854
Wheeler, Mary Y. (Mrs. John), dt. of
Daniel Yandes   9- 9-1854
Whitcomb, James, former governor   10- 9-1852
White, ——, dt. of Pres. White of
Wabash College   11- 9-1850
White, Mary, widow of George, age 71,
formerly of Philadelphia   5-15-1858
White, Samuel E., age 61   3- 9-1850
White, William, son of James   2-21-1852
White, William, age 76   12- 9-1854
Whitefield, George, Chippeway Indian,
age 50   1-17-1852
Whitford, Mr. E., age 65, from N.Y.   7-16-1853
Wickoff, James H., age 38   8-27-1853
Wicoff, Mrs. Sarah, age 75   7- 5-1851
Wiggens, Margarette Jane (Mrs. Lytle) 10- 6-1855
Wiley, ——, inf. dt. of Wm. Y. &. M.C.   4-12-1851
Wiley, Horatio O., age 25   5- 5-1860
Wiley, James R., son of Wm. Y. &.
Margaret C.   10-28-1848
Wiley, Willie, son of Wm. Y. &. M.C.   3- 6-1858
Wilkins, Mary Ellen, dt. of John &.
Eleanor, age 9   3-11-1848
Willard, Thomas Henry, son of Albert
G. &. Marcia D.   9- 8-1849
Williams, Samuel, son of J.T. &. Ann M. 7-12-1851
Williams, John Merrill, son of Freeman
&. Sarah, age 2   9- 5-1857
Williams, Matthew, age 60   5-20-1848
Williams, Welter G., age 25, b. Conn.   2-23-1856
Williams, Wm. Wyley, son of Jacob &.
Ann Maria   2- 3-1849
Williamson, Asa   1-20-1852
Williamson, Howard, inf. son of L.D. &.
Minerva, age 3   1-28-1860
Wilson, Adaline, dt. of Andrew   5-13-1848
Wilson, James H., son of Andrew   9-29-1855
Wilson, Sallie, dt. of Andrew, age 19   11-24-1855
Wilson, Wm., son of Rev. Wm. &. Mary   3-26-1853
Wilson, Wm. Garrison, son of James G.
&. Sarah   1- 1-1859
Winchell, ——, dt. of Jackson   8- 5-1848
Winchell, B.F., in Lafayette   8-11-1849
Windle, Frederick, nr. Pendleton   12-28-1850
Wingate, Ann Ellen (Mrs. Wm. L.),
daughter of E. Colestock   5- 5-1855
Wingate, Joseph, inf. son of Wm.
&. Ellen   10-13-1849
Wiseman, Jacob J.   8-23-1851

Wood, —, inf. son of John M. &
    Margaret, d. Frankfort, Ky.   6-21-1856
Wood, Mary, dt. of Ely A. & Sarah   9-13-1851
Wood, Mary Anna, dt. of John M. &
    Margaret A., age 10   2-25-1854
Wood, Sarah Stevenson, dt. of J.F. &
    E.M., age 1   1- 9-1858
Wooley, Henry, son of John & Mary   1-28-1854
Woollen, Thomas, age 87   5-31-1856
Worn, Mrs. Mary J., in San Francisco   2-18-1860
Wright, Adam, age 52   11-22-1851
Wright, Charles A., son of Wm. A.
    & Sarah L.   2- 3-1849
Wright, Emsley, of Washington Twp.   8- 9-1851
Wright, Fannie Eliza, dt. of Dr.
    Augustus S. & Ellen R.   8- 4-1855
Wright, Lavinia G. (Mrs. Willis W.)   1-26-1850
Wright, Marion, Washington, Ind.   1-22-1853
Wright, Mary A. (Mrs. Williamson), in
    Logansport, age 26   6-22-1850

Yandes, Mrs. Anna, age 56, b. Pa.   3- 1-1851
Yandes, Lafayette, at Havana, Cuba   2- 9-1850
Yerrell, Samuel S., inf. son of
    Solomon & Elizabeth   8-25-1849
York, Jane (Mrs. Jennings)   5-25-1850
Young, Julia (Mrs. John H.), in St. Louis
    9-18-1851
Young, Martha (Mrs. John)   9-25-1858
Youngerman, Addie Emeline, dt. of
    George, age 10   8-18-1860
Youngerman, Margaret Ann, inf. dt.
    of Charles & Susan   5-28-1853
Youngerman, Mary Eveline (Mrs. John)   8-17-1850
Youngerman, Susan (Mrs. Charles)   11-12-1853
Yount, Jesse   3- 7-1857

Zimmerman, Margaret (Mrs. J.S.)   4-24-1858

JUSTICE FAMILY BIBLE RECORDS

Copied by Larry V. Richardson, Paradise, California, through courtesy of Mr. & Mrs. Roger Norlie; the Bible was found in a used-book store in Chico, California.

Marriages

Benjamin F. Justice to Sarah Ann Webb 4-25-1847
Sarah A. Justice to George Brown 5-24-1855
John Q. Justice to Eudore Emmons 6-1-1880 at Bedford
John Q. Justice to Flora B. Lewis 7-25-1897 at Terre Haute

Births

Benjamin F. Justice b. 8-28-1821 Fayette Co.. Ind. near Connersville
Sarah M. Justice b. 5-14-1827 Fayette Co.
John Quincy Justice b. 1-18-1848 near Connersville
Junius Justice b. 5-23-1851 near Connersville
Forest W. Brown, son of Geo. & Sarah A. Brown, b. 9-6-1856 at Noblesville, Ind.
George Brown, husband of Sarah, b. 5-13-1811
May Emmons Justice b. 5-1-1881 in Bedford, Ind.
Daniel Rainey Brown b. 9-20-1883 in Bedford
Telford Forest Brown b. 1-5-1885 in Bedford
Georgia Brown b. 10-21-1887 in Bedford
May Emmons Justice, b. 5-1-1881 at Bedford
John Quincy Justice, Jr. b. 4-8-1900 at Malott Park, Marion Co.
Eudora Emmons b. 10-16-1851 Darlington, Ind.
Flora B. Lewis b. 8-12-1862 Marion Co.

Deaths

Junius Justice d. 2-23-1852, aged 9 months in Rush Co.
B.F. Justice d. 5-31-1853
George Brown d. 4-14-1857 of chronic bronchitis
Eudora Justice d. 1-17-1894 at Indianapolis
Flora Belle Justice d. 8-2-1908 at Indianapolis.
J.Q. Justice d. 4-9-1914 Indianapolis; buried Crown Hill
Mother S.A.W. Brown d. Gulfport, Miss. 8-2-1910; buried Crown Hill

KNOX COUNTY MARRIAGES, 1807-1832

Compiled from photostats of Knox County Marriage Certificates, 1807-32, and Knox County Marriage Licenses, Volume I (1807-20) and II (1820-39), in the Genealogy Division, Indiana State Library. The original volumes of marriage licenses for the above years are no longer in existence; the photostats were made from volumes apparently prepared at a later time. The earliest licenses, dating from the time Knox County was created in 1790 down to 1807, have not been found.

There are some marriage returns for which there are no licenses, and likewise, some licenses for which there are no returns. In some instances where there are both returns and licenses the names are spelled differently; the fact that many of the applicants were French complicated the recording. We give the date of marriage when it was available; otherwise, the license date is given. We have not tried to indicate all variant spellings.

Although the civil marriage records were not found prior to 1807 (except for one in 1806), the records of St. Francis Xavier Catholic Church in Vincennes have been preserved back to 1749. Photostats of these are in the Genealogy Division; they are printed in American Catholic Historical Society *Records*, XII (1901), 46-60. 193-211, 322-36 for the period 1749-1778.

Prior to 1817 the area of Knox County exceeded its present boundaries. The formation of Gibson and Warrick counties in 1813, and Daviess and Sullivan counties in 1817 changed respectively the southern, eastern and northern boundaries of the county and reduced it approximately to its present size.

Adams, Amos - Rachel Wood   lic. 1-31-1815
Adams, Amos - Annea Decker, Widow
      lic. 2-29-1820
Adams, Amos - Betsy Ann Read   9-18-1831
Adams, John - Catharine Gilmore   lic. 2- 9-1814
Adams, Joseph - Betsy Key   9-26-1810
Adams, Robert - Easter Ellen Graham
      lic. 11-10-1810
Adams, Samuel - Sally Wood   4- 6-1813
Adams, William - Grance Robins, Widow
      lic. 4-28-1819
Ails, Robert - Mary Ann Mallet   2-24-1831
Alcutt, Horace - Nancy Holly   3-25-1825
Alexander, Asbury - Betsy Lindsey   lic. 5-22-1812
Alexander, Samuel R. - Nancy Ann Scott
      lic. 1-19-1829
Allen, John - Dotie Cartright   lic. 8-17-1808
Allen, John W. - Mary C. Brewer   9-30-1831
Allen, Prince - Susan, Negroes   lic. 10-23-1830
Allen, Prince - Elizabeth Nyus, Negroes
      lic. 10-25-1830
Allen, Prince - Ann Redman, Negroes   1-22-1831
Allis, James - Margaret Maltman   2-11-1829
Allison, Daniel - Polly Mills   5-11-1815
Allison, John - Lydia Mills   lic. 12-16-1812
Allison, Robert - Mary Amn Buntin   lic. 12-18-1814
Allman, Thomas - Ruth Martin   12-12-1812
Allman, William - Sarah Murphy   2-25-1813
Allsop, Thomas - Zilpah Anthony   8-12-1812
Allsop, Willis - Jannett Ash   2- 4-1813
Almon, John - Hollan Murphy   lic. 6-29-1812
Almy, Harvey - Mary McCullough   9- 8-1824
Almy, Seneca - Elizabeth Tice   7-19-1812
Alton, Benjamin - Bellammer Johnson   9-21-1820
Alton, John - Margaret Barkman   11- 4-1829
Alton, Samuel - Sally Neel   lic. 4-24-1815
Amlin, Lawrance - Nancy Johnson   1- 3-1826
Amos, Jesse - Barbary Cardinal   9-14-1830
Anderson, Isaac - Rachel Rittenhouse,
   Widow   lic. 5-11-1816
Anderson, John - Welthy Knight   8-19-1810

Anderson, Joshua - Mary Ann Anderson,
   Negroes   6-27-1816
Anderson, Pinkney of Ohio Twp. -
   Elizabeth Boom   7- 2-1812
Anderson, Walter - Cloe Stapleton   8- 3-1809
Anderson, William D. - Sarah Clark   1-23-1827
Andre, Amable - Elizabeth Daniel   lic. 5- 2-1831
Andre, Jacques - Rosanna St. Mary   9- 3-1815
Andre, Joseph - Catharine Valle   8-18-1823
Andre, Pierre - Barbara Bonhom   2-20-1815
Andre, Pierre - Olive Reeves   5-11-1828
Andrews, David - Mary Ann McFadden
      lic. 3-25-1824
Andrews, Ebenezer F. - Mary Ann Fisher
      lic. 12- 6-1811
Anston, Joseph - Rachel Jones   4-20-1810
Anthis, Francis - Polly Ripenbark   2-11-1810
Anthis, Jacob - Clarissa Browning   lic. 4- 5-1819
Anthis, John - Sarah Johnson Filpot   lic. 9-20-1817
Anthis, Martin - Sally Jacobus   1-28-1830
Archer, Charles K. - Mary McClure   lic. 11-30-1814
Archer, Jesse K. - Jane McDonald   11-30-1825
Archer, William - Anna Chambers   6-16-1812
Armstrong, Elsberry - Betsy Landers
      lic. 11-17-1810
Armstrong, Thomas - Martha Balch (?)
      lic. 8-29-1827
Arnet, William - Polly Starman   4-18-1813
Arnold, Jeremiah - Barbary Coonrod   4-27-1809
Ashby, Joseph - Matilda Timmons   1-27-1830
Ashby, Noah - Mary Beard Emison   lic. 12- 4-1821
Ashby, Noah - Mary Widner   lic. 1- 1-1827
Ashley, Benjamin - Peggy Bardett   2-22-1816
Atkinson, Jesse - Frances Andre   7-12-1811
Austin, Joseph - Sarah Dickson   6-28-1827

Babcock, Jonathan - Nancy Long   8-24-1818
Badger, William - Nancy Bedell   10- 7-1815
Badollet, Albert - Jane M. Agun   lic. 2-13-1817
Badollet, Albert - Relief Burtch   lic. 12-16-1823
Badollet, Algemon Sidney - Julia Armstrong
      lic. 1- 2-1822

Badollet, James P. - Malinda McClure
                             lic. 1-18-1820
Bailey, John - Annie Butler   lic. 10-28-1807
Bailey, John L. - Mary Voshan, called
   St. Antoine   3-17-1817
Bailey, John T. - Phillis Villnave lic. 3- 8-1820
Bailey, Nathaniel B. - Frances B. Olds 12-30-1816
Bailey, Thomas C. - Eveline Purcell   12- 8-1824
Baird, Thomas, of Daviess Co. -
   Polly Stork   9-18-1823
Baker, Harris - Susan Chandler   9-24-1818
Baker, John - Nancy Danford   4- 2-1811
Baker, Nathan - Rebecca McBean lic. 8-22-1816
Baldwin, Daniel - Hannah Butler lic. 12-16-1811
Baldwin, James C. - Acey Ann Applegate 1-2-1825
Ball, Joseph - Sarah Palmer   lic. 5- 5-1810
Baldwin, William A. - Sally Bartlow   10-20-1825
Ballard, Stephen - Rachel Waldrond   2- 9-1812
Ballou, Nathan - Jane Martin   5- 1-1828
Ballow, George D. - Nancy Ann Sherkliff 9- 1-1830
Balthis, John C. - Sally Benedict lic. 12-23-1818
Bamford, Moses - Elizabeth Moppin   5-23-1822
Bamford, Robert - Matilda Ludington   6-17-1817
Banks, Alexander-- Nancy Rawlings lic. 10-29-1816
Banks, James - Rebecca Jonston   5-13-1812
Barbeaux, Francois - Angelique Degan
                            lic. 12-23-1807
Barikman, John - Jane Hanna, both of
   Palmyra Twp.   7-24-1810
Barker, Jesse - Betsy Key   3-23-1812
Barkman, John - Lydia Johnston   lic. 4- 7-1823
Barnaby, Antoine - Mary Lovellett   8- 8-1825
Barr, William - Eliza Sloan   9-24-1812
Barrois, Francois - Maryanne Andre   8- 7-1826
Barrois, Jean Marie - Adelaide Gamelin 2-24-1824
Barrois, Lombard, Jr. - Mary LaPlante 1-20-1817
Barron, Joseph - Maria Joseph Gamelin
                           lic. 8- 4-1807
Bartlow, Jacob - Kitty Harman   lic. 3-14-1811
Bartlow, William - Elizabeth Odley lic. 6-25-1810
Bass, Small - Sally Wease   11-20-1829
Bass, William T. - Dorothy Pancake lic. 12- 8-1810
Batson, Jonathan - Rachel Marney   10- 4-1819
Bayard, Jean Francois - Mariane Boneau 7- 7-1823
Bean, Jacob S. - Betsey Glen   4- 4-1827
Bease, John - Cassey Robins, both
   of Palmyra Twp.   7-23-1812
Beazley, Robert - Casa Bedell (or Beedle)
                           1-28-1831
Beckes, Benjamin V. - Sarah Harbin   2-13-1807
Beckes, Benjamin V. - Elizabeth Pea   5-27-1812
Beckes, Benjamin V. - Sarah Browning,
   Widow   lic. 9-16-1815
Beckes, William - Margaret Jordan lic. 4-26-1814
Becknell, Alfred - Betsy Hullen   4- 7-1817
Becknell, John - Patsey Goodman   4-14-1822
Becknell, Micajah - Permelia Willis 11- 3-1828
Becknell, Mumphard - Nancy Ashby   5-25-1820
Becraft, Benjamin - Polly Foulger   11-18-1808
Bedell, William - Rachel Toure (or Touer)6-21-1824
Bedwell, Enoch - Eleanor Milam   6-19-1816
Beedel, William - Nancy Curry   lic. 5-21-1821
Beedle, Charles W. - Eliza Boyer lic. 7-28-1829
Beedle, John - Rachel Beedle   7-12-1827
Beedle, Samuel - Harriet (or Hannah) Johnson
                           3-28-1830

Bell, Francis - Nancy McComb   4-20-1827
Bemis,(Beamis), Levi - Rebeckah Secret 1-21-1827
Benedict, Benjamin - Christina Fox   9-10-1831
Benham, John - Maria Alton   9-16-1830
Bennett, Lewis - Susan Wisner   2- 8-1827
Bennock, Jean B. - Marie Toulon lic. 6- 7-1813
Benson, Henry - Rohena Bishop   6-17-1830
Berry, Andrew, of Daviess Co. -
   Mary McDonald   lic. 10-11-1819
Bilderback, James - Darky Woods   7-29-1819
Bilderback, John - Katherine Catte lic. 2-11-1822
Billings, Noyez - Mary Ann Duffee lic. 1-16-1812
Bishop, Benjamin - Betsy Palmer   7-14-1814
Black, Asa - Lavina Burress   6- 3-1830
Black, James - Milly Becknell   4-20-1831
Black, John - Elizabeth Mathoney lic. 5-30-1820
Black, Thomas - Sarah Heathman lic. 1-27-1810
Black, Thomas - Peggy Row   lic. 4- 8-1812
Black, William - Judy Rowe   lic. 3-21-1812
Blackburn, ––– - Francis Ann Emison
                          lic. 8-19-1826
Blackburn, Alexander - Delilah Polke 1-15-1828
Blackburn, James M., of Sullivan Co. -
   Cassandra Widner   lic. 12-17-1819
Blackburn, Thomas H. - Polly Marney 7-19-1818
Blackford, Isaac - Caroline McDonald
                          lic. 12-23-1819
Blackman, Trueman - Patience Cunningham
                           4-14-1816
Blankinship, John - Diana Drennon   2-21-1829
Blessing, Daniel - Polly Francis   6- 1-1819
Blessing, Daniel - Rebecca Wyant   1-26-1830
Blevens, James - Elizabeth L. Robbins 10- 6-1831
Bloxsome, James - Ann Robinson   3-30-1830
Boatright, Alexander - Hannah Councilman
                          lic. 10-12-1831
Bogard, George - Barbary Warner   3-17-1812
Bolds, Zachariah - Deby Hazelton   6-18-1808
Boneau, Lambert - Mary Ann Boyer lic. 8- 9-1824
Boner, James - Kitty Scott   6-10-1819
Boner, James - Hannah Fisher   11-28-1824
Booth, Charles - Susana Butler   lic. 8- 1-1816
Booyer, Pleasant - Margaret Huffman 10- 1-1829
Boswell, Ladock - Patsy McKee   4-10-1822
Bouche, Vital - Barbary Gregory lic. 1-20-1827
Bouche, Vital - Lapeal Bernard lic. 5-28-1827
Bouche, Vital - Ursula Chabot, of
   Lawrence Co., Ill.   5-28-1827
Boucher, Amable - Angelique Mallet 5- 3-1824
Boucher, Francois - Lalite Voudre   2-27-1816
Boucher, Francis - Mary Dequinte   9- 9-1820
Boucher, Jean Baptiste - Mary Kirby 2-24-1811
Boucher, Joseph - Mariette Tromblis 5-29-1811
Boucher, Vital - Mary Vallee   1- 3-1816
Boudinot, Elisha - Elizabeth Cannavar
                        lic. 11- 3-1820
Bougher, George - Nancy Redinghous
                       lic. 4-25-1812
Bourdelow, Antoine - Amelia Cross   3-18-1826
Bourdelow, see also Burdelow
Bourgard, Antoine - St. Genevieve Querrie
                         10- 1-1818
Bowers, George - Sally Wilmore   3- 2-1826
Bowman, John - Mary Goforth   2-15-1813
Boyer, Francois H. - Motette Grimard 1-10-1826
Boyer, Gabriel - Archange Metlaye(?) lic. 2-26-1824

Boyd, James, Jr. of Sullivan Co. -
  Mariah Young   5-30-1822
Bradley, Valentine L - Eliza Ann Clark
                              lic.   7-12-1817
Brady, John - Deborah Mallery   7-27-1828
Brazelton, John - Margaret Evans lic. 5-23-1811
Bready, Samuel - Annie Curry   lic. 9- 3-1810
Brenton, Robert - Betsy Pryde   3-26-1809
Brewner, Frederick - Mary Wright   4- 5-1812
Brinton, Henry - Esther Baird   lic. 6-14-1814
Brodie, James - Sally Curry   12-21-1815
Brodie, William - Susannah Ashmore   7- 8-1815
Brokaw, Henry - Sarah Ruble   lic. 10- 3-1822
Brooks, James - Mary Landsdown   2- 5-1808
Brooks, Samuel - Elizabeth Hall   12-17-1818
Brotherton, Trueman - Nancy Thorn   5-30-1824
Brown, Bazel - Polly Hamilton   6-16-1811
Brown, Elisha U., of Vigo Co. -
  Fanny Hains, Widow   11-19-1823
Brown, James - Nancy Southwick   9- 4-1831
Brown, John - Elizabeth Youngman,
  both of White River Twp.   3-28-1813
Brown, John - Temperance Medley   11-26-1815
Brown, John B. - Louisa Freeland   4-15-1813
Brown, Mannasah - Peggy Wyatt   lic. 2-23-1813
Browning, Marshall - Rebecah I. Patterson
                              lic. 11- 9-1826
Bruce, John - Willemena Lassa   5- 6-1813
Bruce, Spear - Rachel Chambers   lic. 2-26-1827
Bruce, Squire - Polly Lucas Bruce   1-15-1822
Bruce, William - Nelly R. Holmes lic. 1-27-1818
Brumbaugh, Joseph - Nancy Hempsteal(?)
                              lic. 12-21-1818
Brumfield, David - Polly Patton   1-23-1812
Bruner, James - Patience Blackman, widow
                              lic.   1-22-1823
Bruner, Samuel - Sarah Cunningham   2-23-1816
Buchanon, Joseph - Rebecca McBride
                              lic.   4- 2-1808
Buckels, Robert - Sarah Becknel   4-14-1817
Buckhanon, John, Wabash Co., Ill. -
  Elizabeth Ginn (or Guinn)   11-27-1827
Bullar, John, Jr. - Peggy Harbison,
  both of White River Twp.   11- 7-1809
Burdelow, Emez(?) - Frances Compo lic. 2-14-1825
Burdelow, John - Banan (or Belan) Johnson
                                     5-24-1826
Burdelow, Michel - Theresa Derosier 10-26-1825
Burgin, Isaac - Sarah Horrell   3- 8-1815
Burnside, James - Eliza Wilson   lic. 4- 1-1817
Burtch, William - Margarette Hannah lic. 10-14-1819
Bushey, Francis - Mary Decant   lic. 9-18-1820
Butler, William - Betsy Macceda   10-17-1808
Butterfield, Supply - Jensey Storman
  (or Slurman)   7-25-1815
Buzan, John - Leah Rodarmel   lic. 7- 9-1817
Byergon, Nicholas - Pelage Vallie lic. 1- 5-1808

Cabassier, Pierre - Elisabeth Ravalette 7-26-1820
Caderett, Louis - Constance Cardinal
                              lic. 11- 2-1830
Cain (Cane), Felix - Nancy VanMeter   8-20-1829
Caldwell, Asahel C. - Ann Maria Johnson
                              lic. 11- 1-1828
Caldwell, John - Sarah Badolett   lic. 2-10-1814

Caldwell, John - Rebekah Barkman   12-23-1807
Caldwell, William - Rachel E. Harper
                              lic.   1- 4-1827
Campbell, Joseph - Lucinda Williams   10- 3-1816
Campeau, Antoine - Susan Bordeleau   1-10-1820
Cannon, John - Elizabeth Kimmons   2-17-1829
Cantwell, James - Mary Smith   lic. 12-19-1821
Car, Thomas G. - Catherine Willson lic. 10-21-1807
Cardinal, Joseph - Catherine Delorier
                              lic.   7-12-1823
Cardinal, Joseph - Betsy Cary   lic. 10-19-1829
Cardinal, Medard - Mary Bouche,
  widow of Joseph   1- 2-1826
Cardinal, Nicholas - Ursulla Davis lic. 9-28-1807
Carel, Anthony - Frances Lavellett lic. 6-28-1828
Caris, Peter - Mary Ann Junkins   lic. 4-21-1807
Carlin, Daniel - Ruth Purcell   6- 3-1808
Carr, see Car, Karr
Carrico, Rezin - Elizabeth Engle lic. 12-11-1814
Carson, John - Hannah Castleberry lic. 2-25-1812
Carter, Dick - Becky Springs   1- 3-1831
Carter, Elizar B. - Dorcas Armstrong
                              lic.   2-17-1817
Carter, Jacob - Rachel Hammond   2- 3-1812
Carter, Richard - Susan Gibson, Negroes
                              lic.   1-28-1832
Cartier, Isadore - Victoire Baillar   4-25-1820
Cartier, Joseph - Mary Amlin   lic. 10-22-1827
Cartier, Louis - Mary Cabacier   12-30-1825
Cary, John - Susan Tougas   lic. 5-31-1830
Case, Abraham - Sally Hogue   12-19-1811
Castleberry, Thomas - Rachel Jane Carson
                              lic.   9- 1-1812
Catt, George - Rebecca Pea   lic. 8-12-1817
Catt, Louis - Jane Moore   11-11-1824
Catt, Michael - Christian Maltman   1-27-1831
Catt, Phillip - Sally Kimmons   lic. 11-14-1820
Catt (or Catte), Pierre - Ebby Decker 8- 1-1827
Catt, William - Margaret Philips   2- 4-1830
Catte, Daniel - Charity Lindy   lic. 3-17-1818
Catte, John - Susan Catte   lic. 8- 7-1811
Catte, Moses - Rebecca Catte   lic. 3-11-1812
Catte, Sebastian - Sebra Conger   lic. 1-30-1814
Catte, Sebastian - Mary Fredrick lic. 7-11-1807
Catte, Solomon - Kitty Rederick   lic. 4- 8-1815
Cauthorn, Gabriel T. - Susan S. Stout
                              lic.   4- 5-1827
Chambers, James - Lydia Hollingsworth 10-17-1816
Chambers, Levi - Jane Hollingsworth   6- 9-1823
Chambers, John - Nancy Hollingsworth 6-29-1815
Chambers, Levi - Mary Hopkins   11-15-1829
Chambers, Philip - Sally Miner   10-15-1829
Chambers, Samuel F. - Anna Piety lic. 12-24-1831
Chambers, Willis - Anny Barton   lic. 1-15-1812
Chancellor, Jesse - Jane Chesney lic. 5-17-1823
Chapard, August, son of Nicholas & Cecile
  (Languedock) Chapard - Balbe Denot, dt
  of Reney & Cecile (Seyen) Denot   10-12-1818
Chapman, Elijah - Mariah Johnson   12-24-1817
Chapman, George - Sally Jones   6-23-1808
Chapman, Jesse - Elizabeth Wallace
                              lic.   2-21-1817
Cheeck, Joel - Leander Brown   1-16-1812
Cheek (or Check), Nathan - Peggy Price 11-10-1814
Chenett, Anthony Zepherin called St. Mary-
  Marie Louisa Racine   4-18-1809

Chevalier, see Shevalier

Chinn, Jesse - Petsey Pitmana, Negroes
    lic. 10- 4-1819
Chrisman, William - Melinda Irvan   9-23-1818
Clark, Charles A., of Louisville -
  Virginia LeRoy   lic. 9- 4-1824
Clark, Samuel - Mary Bateman, Negroes
    lic. 7-12-1817
Clark, Westley - Sarah Osman lic. 12-15-1816
Clark, William A. - Sophia Terman 1-11-1814
Claycomb, Adam - Mary Welton   1-14-1812
Claycomb, Andrew - Sally Reel lic. 8-30-1825
Claycomb, Elias - Elizabeth McKinley 6-19-1828
Claycomb, Frederick - Katherine Barrackman
    7-29-1823
Claycomb, Frederick - Agnes McKinley 3- 4-1826
Claypool, George - Hannah Putnam lic. 5-27-1813
Claypoole, John - Bridget Donlin lic. 1-31-1827
Clement, John A. - Elizabeth Devin lic. 10- 7-1809
Cochran, John - Betsey Seaton   11-21-1819
Cochrane, Jeremiah - Francoise Cardinal 8-14-1815
Colbert, Daniel - Mary Flint   3-25-1815
Colbert, John - Sidney Lashley   3-24-1814
Colbert, Toliver - Sarah Miller lic. 2-10-1817
Colegrove, George W. - Sally Buchanan 12- 6-1823
Coleman, Christopher - Peggy Baird
    lic. 7- 8-1816
Coleman, John - Maria Thixton   10-14-1828
Collins, Absolom - Polly Like   6-27-1830
Collins, Charles - Sarah McLane   7- 9-1812
Collins, David - Lucinda Hunnicut 4-29-1821
Collins, Hiram - Elizabeth Francis lic. 11-11-1831
Collins, John - Rachael Armstrong lic. 2- 4-1815
Collins, Madison - Jane Pinkerton 1-30-1812
Collins, William - Viney Kuykendall lic. 9- 6-1810
Colman, William L. - Eunice Burtch lic. 5-10-1816
Colvin, Peyton - Malinda Smith lic. 1-21-1832
Comer, Samuel - Sarah Coleman lic. 3-18-1811
Commack, Michael - Sarah Milburn 9-17-1807
Compagniott, Peter - Ellen Rachambale
    lic. 6-29-1830
Compagniott, Ustache - Marianne Mallet
    lic. 1-17-1829
Conaway, Samuel - Ruby Austin   5-14-1822
Condren, James - Polly Miner lic. 9-15-1821
Conner, David - Cynthia Huff   2-23-1808
Conoyer, Pierre - Mary Page lic. 7-10-1829
Conway, Isaac S. - Peliga Kabaskia 12- 4-1821
Cook, Andrew - Elizabeth Morris 8-11-1829
Cook, James H. - Margaret Reel   3-23-1824
Cooke, William - Peggy Pea lic. 7-23-1812
Coon, Isaac - Susannah Drenning, widow 5-11-1823
Coonrod, George - Betsey Miley   2-16-1809
Coonrod, Mark - Peggy Kuykendall lic. 1- 2-1814
Coply, Gustavus - Elizabeth Chadwick 2-14-1831
Correll, Andrew - Sally McGowan 8-30-1829
Cotrell, Wilson - Esther Cluster 3- 5-1825
Couch, David - Mariah Roler lic. 4- 8-1829
Coughman, Isaac - Elizabeth Blevins 9-16-1824
Courtright, John - Rheuhemah Devore
    lic. 11-29-1816
Courtright, Luke - Katherine Devore
    lic. 7-31-1823
Courtright, Peter - Betsey Devore lic. 5-22-1815
Coutchman, Benjamin - Polly Claycomb
    lic. 2- 9-1819

Cowden, John - Rebecca Richey   11-12-1815
Cox, Jesse - Rebecca Langon, Negroes 10-12-1826
Cox, Richard - Amey Hollingsworth 2- 8-1816
Cox, William - Hannah Hollingsworth 1-23-1819
Creely(?), Charles, son of Gerome & Therese
  (Leforce?) Creely - Marguerite Richard, dt
  of Peter Richard   7- 6-1818
Crisman, William - Mary Minnis   4- 8-1808
Critchell, Caleb - Hannah Nate lic. 4-15-1812
Crooks, Michael - Nancy Timmons 1- 7-1826
Crosby, Leonard - Sarah Purcell lic. 3-16-1814
Crow, James, Jr. - Annie Kirk   2-20-1812
Crow, John - Esther Catt   4-25-1830
Crow, Joseph, of Gibson Co. -
  Sally Wheeler   8- 3-1828
Crow, Robert - Polly Kirk lic. 7-25-1808
Cruft, John F., of Vigo Co. -
  Elizabeth Armstrong lic. 12-17-1823
Crumb, Conrad - Anna Williams 11-28-1827
Crunk, John - Patsy Price lic. 11-19-1812
Cubra, Elikam - Betsey Jackson lic. 3-29-1812
Cumstock, William - Martha Hollingsworth
    7-20-1823
Cunningham, Alexander - Nancy Archibald
    5- 4-1820
Cunningham, John - Cynthia Purcell 11- 4-1825
Cunningham, Payton - Betsey Beedle
    lic. 10-13-1814
Cunningham, Payton - Polly Anderson
    lic. 10-24-1816
Curry, James - Isabella Hogg   4- 8-1813
Curry, John - Sarah Ingle, widow lic. 12-24-1816
Curry, Samuel - Polly Watson   3-18-1813
Curry, William - Anny Butler   3-19-1808
Curry, William - Polly Hogg   12-27-1808
Curtain, Daniel - Suzan Davis lic. 11-11-1814

D'Alby, Joseph - Mary Cabacier lic. 4-28-1831
Dale, Jarvis - Mary Holems lic. 3-24-1814
Daniel, Richard - Ann Chew (or Nancy)
  Johnston   4-24-1818
Danion, Touisaint - Mary Benack lic. 4-26-1813
Dardenne, John A. - Jane Godere 9-13-1824
Dardenne, John A. - Josephine Boyer
    lic. 1-18-1830
Dauphin, Jean Bapte. - Marriann Laforest 2-7-1820
Davis, Francis - Catherine Bailey lic. 2-15-1821
Davis, John - Christina Bayley 10-16-1812
Davis, Owen - Nancy Dunkin lic. 7- 5-1816
Davis, Phenias - Esther Fuller   4- 7-1817
Davis, William - Betsey Young   1-27-1831
Decker, Abraham - Nancy Catte lic. 2-28-1814
Decker, Asa - Catherine Decker 7-10-1825
Decker, Daniel (son of Abraham) -
  Cinthiana Soden lic. 9-17-1821
Decker, Daniel - Polly White   6-12-1825
Decker, Hiram - Eliza Kuykendall lic. 9-14-1819
Decker, Isaac - Barbary Kuykendall lic. 10-25-1810
Decker, Isaac T. - Hannah Dunham 7-31-1810
Decker, John - Barbary Sillard   7-28-1807
Decker, John - Diana H. Reiley, widow
    lic. 10-11-1821
Decker, John - Ellen Johnson lic. 11-18-1815
Decker, Luke - Trenney Claypoole lic. 12-18-1807
Decker, Nicholas - Polly Thomas lic. 7-27-1812
Deen, William - Carey Shirley   6- 1-1807

Defendall, Simon - Nancy Johnson   4-26-1819
Dejean, Antoine - Francois Amlan(?)   12- 4-1826
Deleau, John - Isabella Hunter   6-11-1826
Deligne, Joseph, son of Louis & Mary (Thomas)
    Deligne - Cecille Delisle, dt of Charles &
    Jeanette (Bercelott) Delisle   2-22-1819
Delisle, Charles - Angelique Danneau
    lic. 1-28-1814
Delisle, John Baptiste, son of Charles &
    Jeanette (Bercelott) Delisle - Victoria
    Valley, dt of Alexander & Catherine
    (Langton) Valley   10-19-1818
Dellinger, Christian - Polly Myers   9- 2-1819
Delorier, Francois Xavier - Cisselle Racine
    lic. 8-23-1820
Delorier, Joseph - Elizabeth Lafon lic. 2-19-1830
Denny, John - Rachael James   9- 6-1808
Denny, William - Betsey Bates   lic. 9-26-1811
Denny, William - Catherine Cook   2-24-1825
Deshane (or Deshaw), Alexis -
    Leona Bonhomme   lic. 2-23-1829
Depriest, Green - Polly Crosby   3-21-1813
Dequier, Francis, son of Francis & Felicity
    (Cardinal) Dequier - Pelagie Huno, dt of
    Gabriel & Mary Ann (Compagniot) Huno
    7-19-1819
Devore, John - Nancy Selvy   lic. 6- 5-1815
Devore, Philip - Susannah Minnis   lic. 5- 9-1812
Dickson, Joseph - Emily Lambert   4- 8-1812
Dillworth, Samuel - Marcia Brooks lic. 3-26-1818
Dinwiddie, William - Martha E. Burnsides
    12-14-1828
Dolby, Antoine - Mary Villeneuve   11-22-1825
Dollahan, John - Elizabeth Glover, widow
    lic. 12-11-1819
Donnovan, Jeremiah - Susan Wyant lic. 10-19-1823
Dono, Charles - Mary Ann Cornoyer lic. 11-10-1828
Dono, Pierre - Mary Shunette   12- 4-1830
Dooley, James - Polly Milam   lic. 3- 8-1816
Dougherty, John B., of Sullivan Co. -
    Hetty Hogg   lic. 1-25-1820
Douglas, Jonathan - Betsey W. McComb 11-27-1827
Douthit, Solomon - Nancy Simpson   12- 7-1820
Dowden, John H. - Emily McNamee   2-16-1830
Downey, John - Nancy Benson   lic. 6- 6-1812
Drake, Samuel - Nancy Purcell   2- 6-1812
Driskel, Elias - Christinah Heaton lic. 5-16-1812
Drouet, Henry, called Richardville -
    Marie Bouchez   8- 7-1822
Drouette, Michel, called Roucherville -
    Catherine Boucher   lic. 2- 3-1818
Dubois, Charles - Susan Moyense   lic. 6-14-1828
Dubois, Henry - Maria O. Clarke   lic. 8-27-1814
Duchere (or Duchene), Alexis (or
    Alexander) - Patsey Lindsey   1-24-1811
Duckworth, James - Rebecca Gibbons
    lic. 2- 7-1810
Duncan, James - Sarah Foulger   lic. 3- 5-1807
Dunn, Andrew - Eliza Jane Denny   2-14-1831
Dunn, James - Polly Steen   10-20-1825
Dunn, Joseph - Mary Hawkins   5- 2-1830
Duprese, Louis, Jr. - Francis Seemore
    (or Seamon ?)   3-16-1827
Duquinder, Francois - Eureuel Lefevre
    lic. 11-28-1814
Dushane, Tousaint - Mary Laplante   2- 8-1832

Duty, Matthew - Matilda Shaner   lic. 10-23-1829

Edmonson, Charles - Rebecca Edmonson
    lic. 7- 4-1817
Edmundson, William - Nancy Sharp   12-29-1815
Edwards, James - Rebecca Chambers
    lic. 3-20-1815
Edwards, James - Abigail Lockwood   6-27-1816
Edwards, Joseph - Hannah Morgan   12-30-1815
Elliott, James - Patsy Engle   10-30-1809
Elliott, James - Elizabeth McClure   12-11-1824
Elliott, John - Polly Engle   8- 6-1815
Elliott, John - Rachel Hanley   8- 4-1808
Elliott, John - Frances Marta   3-25-1829
Elliott, Levi - Elizabeth Watson   2- 2-1812
Elliott, Robert, Jr. - Silby Hollingsworth 4- 7-1825
Elliott, William - Lydia Ruble   6-22-1820
Elsey (or Elsea), John - Eliza Ferguson 8-19-1830
Elzy, Robert - Elizabeth Taylor   12- 5-1816
Embry, John - Mary Thompson   12- 2-1824
Emison, Wm. W. C. - Betsey Posey 11-10(?)-1825
Emmerson, Allen - Nancy Mounce   9-17-1810
Emmerson, Jonathan - Elisabeth Alsop   9- 2-1810
Emmison, Samuel - Polly McClure   lic. 4- 8-1812
Engle, Richard - Sally McElroy   2-13-1816
Ensminger, Emanuel - Catharine Davenport
    7- 5-1808

Fairhurst, Alfred - Elizabeth Hollingsworth
    10- 3-1830
Fairhurst, George - Matilda Garrett   10-26-1823
Fairhurst, George - Ann Hollingsworth   8-21-1828
Fairhurst, John - Sarah Westfall   6-26-1817
Fairhurst, John - Susan Roller   lic. 7-27-1830
Fairhurst, Samuel - Isabella Vanmeter   3-28-1829
Fairhurst, Wilson - Polly Jarrell   5-10-1827
Farnhan, Joshua - Betsey Harrington
    lic. 12-16-1819
Farrington, James - Harriet Ewing lic. 11-29-1826
Feezel, John - Jane VanKirk   lic. 1-17-1817
Fellows, Louis - Mary Zomber   12-12-1827
Fellows, Silas - Sofiah Brooks   10- 5-1817
Fellows, Willis, Sr. - Sarah Parker, widow
    lic. 1-31-1821
Fenimore, John B. - Rebecca Handy   12-25-1814
Ferguson, Thomas - Fanny Flinn   5-25-1829
Findley, John - Martha Welton   4-25-1814
Finley, John - Susan Spencer   2- 5-1808
Fisher, John - Sally Stapleford   8- 8-1812
Fisher, William - Sarah Goodall   6-13-1811
Fitch, Wm. Geo. Washington - Jane Jordan
    12- 1-1823
Fitzgerald, Johnson - Margaret Eyers   1-30-1812
Fitzhugh, Thomas - Polly Kennerly lic. 3- 3-1817
Fitzpatrick, John - Nancy McGowan lic. 11- 9-1816
Fitzpatrick, John - Polly Becknell (dt of
    Thomas Clark)   3-25-1819
Fitzpatrick, John - Catherine Warner   12-29-1825
Fitzpatrick, John - Sally Pender   8-20-1829
Fleanor, John - Eleanor McMullin   3-19-1812
Flint, John - Nancy Edwards   2-15-1817
Flower, George - Eliza Julia Andrews
    lic. 7-15-1817
Flowers, John - Elizabeth Huffman lic. 1-24-1832
Flowers, William - Sarah Harbin   4-17-1814
Foreman, Gabriel - Rhoda Hathaway   4-27-1820

Foreman, James - Rachel Trimble   2-14-1831
Foucher, Tanerelle - Mary George Sequin 7-19-1827
Francis, George - Elizabeth Whetstone   7-16-1812
Francis, James - Sarah Duty   12-31-1818
Frederick, Andrew - Elizabeth Miner   9-19-1830
Frederick, Boston - Margaret Stark lic. 11-17-1810
Frederick, Henry - Caty Willmore   2-28-1828
Frederick, Isaac - Eliza Miner   2-15-1826
Frederick, Michael - Mary Claycomb   4-24-1828
Frederick, Phillip - Lucy Philips   lic. 9-29-1810
French, David - Rebecca Hudson, widow 2- 4-1816
French, Joseph - Mary Thomas   12-29-1816
Fry, Solomon - Susan Snapp   4- 6-1826
Fugate, Samuel - Catharine McCoy, widow
                                          7- 7-1815
Fuller, Charles - Pheby Stewart   lic. 4- 7-1812
Fuller, Jacob - Ruth Davis   3-15-1821
Fuller, William - Betsey White, widow
                                     lic. 11-20-1815
Fullerton, John - Nancy Mathiney, widow,
   of Sullivan Co.   lic. 4- 4-1823
Fullerton, William - Francois Theldkill
                                     lic. 2-28-1821

Galligar, William - Mary M. Clark   lic. 4-16-1832
Gamble, Lorenzo - Lucinda Willmore   1- 6-1828
Gamelin, Pierre - Francoise Vilenhauve
                                     lic. 6- 7-1813
Gano, James - Martha Medley   lic. 3- 3-1832
Gardiner, John - Ruth Doherty   3-24-1809
Gardner, Andrew - Hannah Swift   6- 3-1819
Garner, Walter - Mary Thompson   12-17-1807
Garrett, William - Calista Durell   12-23-1828
Garrett, William - Elizabeth Steward   1-11-1820
Garwood, John - Peggy Applegate   2- 9-1825
Garwood, John - Rachel Davis   2- 3-1831
Genery, Francis - Barbary Lognion   5-25-1829
Gibson, James - Mary Lamot   7-29-1812
Gibson, Robert - Jane Hughs   10-15-1811
Gilham, Henry - Fanny Badollet   lic. 4- 1-1815
Gill, Robert - Rebecca Gill   lic. 11- 6-1816
Gillmore, John - Sally Vankirk   10-14-1830
Gilmore, Ephraim - Sally Sitzer,
   both of Palmyra Twp.   10-27-1807
Gilmore, John - Nancy Dillon   12-29-1831
Gilmore, Robert - Mahalah Johnson   7-21-1825
Glass, Hiram - Kitty Pea   lic. 2- 8-1822
Glass, John - Polly Dobbins   lic. 8-17-1810
Glass, Thomas - Sofiah Fredrick   lic. 12-15-1821
Goble, George - Nancy Arnold   12-10-1812
Godare, Alexis - Felice Villneuve   lic. 9-19-1829
Godare, Pierre - Frances Dilean   lic. 1-25-1832
Godfrey, Eleazer - Polly Ashby   6-21-1818
Gold, Calvin - Hannah Leech   8-22-1825
Goldman, Simon - Nancy VanKirk   10-16-1828
Goldman (or Goolman), Solomon - Peggy Thorn
                                          3-25-1830
Goldsmith, Henry - Elizabeth Ferguson   3-11-1832
Good, Jesse - Anna Farris   11-28-1824
Goodman, John - Nancy Becknell   1-26-1826
Goodman, Milchage (or Micage) -
   Malinda Black   11-14-1813
Gordon, Joseph - Hannah Frazier   4-27-1825
Goyean (?), Burway - Elizabeth Doneau   8-24-1826
Goyer, Antoine - Louisa St. Mary   lic. 11-29-1830

Graeter, Christian - Margrette McClure
                                     lic. 1- 8-1812
Graeter, Christian - Rosean Coulter lic. 1- 2-1827
Graham, Ebenezer - Annie Weas   5-18-1819
Graham, Jonathan - Anny Hill   2-13-1811
Grant, Charles - Liddy Stoddard   lic. 2- 3-1820
Grant, John - Hannah Kirby   4-27-1817
Gray, James - Elizabeth Brown   8- 5-1810
Gray, John - Susan Catte   4-12-1812
Gray, Solomon - Melinda Bratton   11-30-1829
Gray, William - Julia Soden   3-26-1829
Greentree, Richard - Polly McGowan   6-17-1814
Greer, Richard - Mary Smith   lic. 6- 7-1812
Gregory, Charles - Catherine Kuykendall 9-16-1826
Gremore, John - Barbary Boyer   5-23-1827
Gremore, Joseph - Sopha LaPlante   lic. 11- 2-1824
Griffin, Arthur - Sarah Creek   5-28-1812
Griffin, Ira - Elizabeth Dolohan   3-18-1828
Grigsby, Tolliver - Winy Johnson   11-28-1811
Groves, Elisha - Sarah Case   12-13-1824
Groves (or Graves), Nero - Sally Thomas
                                     lic. 4-18-1826
Gun, Jacob - Hannah S. Jones   11-24-1831

Hadden, Jared P. - Olive Spratt   2-15-1824
Hadden, Jesse - Betsey Piety   4-16-1815
Hagan, Theodore - Eliza Davis   11- 3-1831
Hale, David M. - Esther Scribner   lic. 10-22-1816
Hall, William - Mary Elliott   2-10-1808
Hampstead, Thomas - Cornelia Vanderburgh
                                     lic. 11-16-1814
Hancock, William - Nancy McReynolds   7- 4-1815
Hand, Enoch B. - Mrs. Sarah Francis
                                     lic. 2-11-1832
Hand (?), Peter - Elizabeth Light   8- 8-1820
Handcock, John - Nancy Siles (or Liles) 1-25-1827
Handy, Stephen D. - Margaret Dickson   7-18-1815
Hanks, Peter - Elizabeth Ramsey   11- 4-1814
Hanlen, Mathew - Nancy Palmer   3- 4-1814
Hannegan, Edward - Margaret C. Duncan
                                     lic. 4- 4-1829
Hansborough, John - Delila Polke   5-25-1815
Harbin, Jesse - Sally Curry   6-30-1830
Harbin, Joshua - Eliza Beedel (Bedle)   3-28-1830
Hardison, Hardy - Betsey McGowan lic. 3-10-1819
Hardy, William Allen - Nancy McJunkin
                                     lic. 1- 2-1812
Hargrave, Richard - Nancy Ann Posey   3-10-1829
Harned, William, of Kentucky -
   Margarette Piety   9-28-1820
Harnis, Adam, Jr. - Polly Kuykendall
                                     lic. 8- 2-1815
Harniss, Job - Betsey Purcell   6- 7-1818
Harniss, Michael - Peggy Reel   3-14-1816
Harniss (or Harness), Michael -
   Penny Kelly   lic. 4-25-1823
Harper, Henry - Eliza Hadden   12- 6-1825
Harper, Jacob - Jemima Rose   11-20-1817
Harper, James - Margrette Curry   lic. 12- 4-1812
Harper, John T. - Caty Glass   2- 2-1830
Harper, Joseph - Martha Palmer   11- 9-1830
Harper, Thomas - Polly Sullinger   lic. 4- 2-1821
Harper, William - Elizabeth Dunn   1-29-1813
Harrington, Thomas - Sally Philips   11-11-1829
Harris, John - Elizabeth Church   2-25-1817
Harrison, Benjamin - Louisa S. Bonner   4-24-1828

Harrison, Benjamin L. - Susan Racine   7-21-1814
Harrison, Robert - Jerusha Chatsey   6-12-1816
Hart, Gideon W. - Nancy Langton   lic. 11-24-1818
Hart, William - Hannah Davis   lic. 8-23-1817
Harvey, John - Pheby Warner   12- 8-1822
Hathaway, Joseph - Sally Vankirk   3-11-1819
Hawkins, Charner - Jane Steen   lic. 2-27-1827
Hawkins, Jacob - Nelly Ember, Negroes 11- 1-1821
Hawkins, Jesse - Elizabeth Mastison   6-12-1812
Haynes (or Hayne), Jacob -
    Catharine Vanarsdall   11- 2-1830
Haynie, Stephen - Sally Patterson, widow 7-14-1815
Hazleton, Stephen - Parmelia Chisum   7- 2-1829
Hearn, Edmund - Susanna Heaton   lic. 8-13-1812
Heberd, William J. - Charlotte Burtch   10-14-1824
Hicklin, James - Permelia Black   1-24-1819
Hiers, William - Elizabeth Murphy   9-16-1813
Hill, Frank - Milly Thomas, Negroes   4-24-1823
Himrod, Andrew - Sally Crawford   4-16-1817
Hobbs, Joseph - Anna Jones   7-12-1811
Hodge, John - Mary Devore   lic. 4- 1-1812
Hogue, David - Sarah Welton   lic. 7- 1-1808
Hogue, Joseph - Nancy Parker   4-21-1816
Holbrook, William - Nancy Potter   4-29-1812
Holland, John C. - Elizabeth McClure
                                     lic. 2- 7-1820
Holland, John C. - Indiana Posey   4-20-1830
Hollems, William - Polly Rose   lic. 12-29-1813
Hollingsworth, Abraham - Sally Dunn
                                     lic. 2-15-1819
Hollingsworth, Abraham - Mary Clark   1- 6-1830
Hollingsworth, Bernard - Nancy Ann McKee
                                            3-28-1816
Hollingsworth, Jackson - Margaret Dunn 4- 3-1831
Hollingsworth, Jesse (or Moses) -
    Mary Lindsey   7-28-1816
Hollingsworth, John - Nelly Polke   lic. 2-16-1807
Hollingsworth, Joseph - Polly Harper   3-16-1828
Hollingsworth, Peter - Sarah Young   9- 8-1808
Hollingsworth, Thomas - Amy (or Anny)
    Keith   5-28-1829
Hollingsworth, Washington - Hannah Hill
                                     lic. 2-23-1831
Holloway, James - Violet Smith, Negroes 9-22-1814
Holmes, John A. - Delilah T. Bruce lic. 8-31-1819
Holmes, Josiah L. - Margarett McClure
                                     lic. 6-16-1818
Holtsclaw, William - Rebecca Watson   11-28-1816
Honeycutt, William - Elizabeth Melton   9-23-1830
Hoover, Peter - Frances Siminson   3- 5-1826
Hopewell, Henry - Rachel Edmondson   9-14-1815
Hopewell, John - Catharine Lisman lic. 9-14-1816
Horrell, James - Sarah Horrell   3-10-1814
Horrell, William - Peggy Stone   5-11-1815
Horton, Ebenezer - Elizabeth Allison,
    dt of Frederick   7-29-1818(1819?)
How, John - Ann Wheeler   1-28-1830
Howard, David - Rosa Chinn   11-30-1827
Howard, John - Betsey Chandler   3-21-1815
Howard, John S. - Jane Ann Caruthers
                                     lic. 7- 5-1827
Howard, William - Nancy Young   9-19-1820
Howard, William - Latitia Thorn   5-20-1824
Hubbs, Pompey - Mariah Parker, Negroes 7-28-1829
Huffman, James - Juliet White   6-30-1829
Huffman, Joseph - Milly Bodlin, Negroes 5-15-1821

Huffman, Solomon - Fanny Ann Purcell
                                     lic. 2-20-1827
Huling (or Hulling), Edmond -
    Nancy Cunningham   4- 7-1817
Huling, Wiat - Hannah Johnson   12-11-1816
Hull, Abijah - Phila Burtch   4-24-1817
Hummer, Harvey - Cynthia Cook,
    dt of David   lic. 9- 3-1822
Hummer, James - Polly Burns   lic. 6-21-1820
Hummer, John - Ann Dunn   lic. 6- 5-1823
Humphreys, Joseph - Peggy Lynn   lic. 6- 1-1808
Hunt, James - Mary Jordan   lic. 12-19-1816
Hunter, James - Parmelia Westfall   7-10-1831
Huse, Absolem - Rosey Gray   5-13-1823
Hutch, David - Maria Rober   4- 9-1829
Hutchinson, James - Julia Ann Malbeauf
                                     lic. 5- 3-1814
Hutson, Isaac - Rebecca Sturman   5-11-1813
Hutson, John - Sarah Westfall   lic. 8-28-1817
Hyneman, John - Elizabeth Melbourn,
    widow   5-12-1807

Ingle, Aaron - Margaret Shimp   lic. 3-31-1817
Illicot, Joseph - Elizabeth Galvin   lic. 7- 4-1807

Jackson, Abram - Eliza Anne Gifford lic. 2-9-1832
Jackson, Francis - Hannah Caty   9-10-1814
Jackson, Jeremiah - Betsey Jones   12-18-1807
Jackson, Joseph - Nancy Ann Hanes   5- 2-1822
Jackson, William - Eliza G. Olds   9- 8-1816
Jacobus, Daily - Eliza Anthis   12-24-1830
Jacobus, Peter - Margaret Warth   5-20-1829
Jacobus, Thomas - Barbary Crock   8- 5-1825
James, James - Margaret Bowen   4-12-1812
James, James - Rachel Price   lic. 10-20-1821
James, Jonah - Elizabeth Murry   11-26-1823
Janes, Fletcher B. - Ann Miller   9-16-1827
Jaradaw, John Baptiste - Francis Barbo
                                     lic. 5-31-1831
Jarrel, Charles - Sally Becknel   lic. 4- 3-1816
Jarrel, Eli - Nancy Cox   2-15-1827
Jarrel, Elijah - Catherine Ralph Snyder
                                     lic. 12- 1-1828
Jarrel, John - Nancy Chamberlain   6- 2-1831
Jefferson, Thomas - Susanna Tevebaugh
                                     lic. 1- 2-1818
Jemison, Samuel - Rachael Handy   12-25-1814
Jenckes, Daniel - Rachel Ewing   lic. 5- 7-1820
Jenkins, John - Polly McClure   11-15-1831
Jerue, Andrew - Therase Longdo   lic. 6-16-1829
Jerue, Louis - Frances Burdelou   lic. 4-26-1827
Jerue, Louis - Susan Compo   lic. 5-31-1830
Johnson, D.C. - Mary Beckes   11-14-1830
Johnson, David - Ruth Potter   4- 4-1813
Johnson, Jacob - Matilda Hopewell   11- 9-1829
Johnson, James - Anny Banks   lic. 7-23-1811
Johnson, James - ―――, Negroes   6- 3-1815
Johnson, James - Jenny Needy, Negroes
                                     lic. 4-19-1825
Johnson, James J. - Betsey Moore   1-19-1819
Johnson, James L., of Sullivan Co. -
    Hannah Watson   lic. 5-24-1822
Johnson, John - Nancy Wilson   lic. 7-29-1809
Johnson, John - Mary Moutney   4-16-1812
Johnson, John - Peggy Anderson   2- 1-1816
Johnson, Jonathan - Elizabeth Rogers   3-10-1812

Johnson, Joseph - Nancy Cunningham
           lic. 4-16-1814
Johnson, Reuben - Polly Whitlock   4- 5-1818
Johnson, Robert - Jane Ruby   lic. 2-22-1819
Johnson, Thomas - Martha Brees   8-31-1820
Johnson, William - Sarah Goodman   3- 2-1816
Johnson, William - Lettitia Porter   2- 7-1822
Johnston, General Washington -
    Eliza Beckes   lic. 1- 4-1817
Johnston, Robert - Nancy Minor   lic. 1-10-1812
Johnston, Thomas - Sarah Richey, widow
           lic. 8- 6-1808
Johnston, William - Christian Anthis   8- 9-1808
Jolly, Benjamin - Margrette McDaniel
           lic. 9- 1-1812
Jones, Edward - Patsey Jones   2-11-1813
Jones, James - Lucretia Smith   lic. 8- 1-1821
Jones, James W. - Louisa McClure   6- 7-1829
Jones, Josiah - Elizabeth Counselman   9- 8-1829
Jones, Levin - Julia Ann Mallett   6- 8-1814
Jones, Lewis - Betsey Barr   1-12-1815
Jones, Lewis - Anny Brown   4-21-1818
Jones, Morgan - Parsassa(?) Patterson
           8-13-1825
Jones, Morgan - Eliza Snapp   lic. 6-19-1830
Jones, Thomas, Jr. - Elizabeth McClure 12-30-1809
Jones, William - Susan Dubois   4-26-1807
Jordan, James - Melinda Scott   8- 5-1825
Jordan, James - Nancy Simpson   8-11-1824
Jordan, John - Jane Gamble   10-15-1826
Jordan, John - Louisa Gordon   5-14-1819
Jordan, Robert - Polly Snider   11-27-1817
Jordan, Thomas, Jr. - Malinda McCoy   8-21-1828
Jordan, William - Jane Hunter   11- 6-1828
Joyeuse, Joseph - Susanna Bonhomme   1- 2-1828
Joyeuse, William - Francoise Derome
    (or Doram)   2-14-1820
Joyeuse, William - Jessett Deline   5-10-1830
Junkins, David - Elizabeth Patterson   11- 9-1928
Junkins, James - Nancy McCoy   2- 1-1818
Junkins, William - Isabel Cynthia Gamble 4- 4-1824
Justice, Daniel - Mary Lite   lic. 2-28-1811

Karr, Robert - Hannah Crealey   5- 7-1818
Keith, John - Delilah Ruby   lic. 8- 2-1822
Kelly, David - Ruth Armstrong   lic. 6-23-1817
Kelly, Thomas - Betsy Wooddes   lic. 6-21-1830
Kelly, William - Mary Washbum   lic. 9-11-1824
Kelso, Joseph - Mary Foster   lic. 12-18-1816
Kelso, William - Julian Hogue   lic. 8- 7-1827
Kenall, Robert - Elizabeth Morrison lic. 3- 8-1809
Kennedy, Samuel - Margery Black   lic. 10- 9-1810
Key, John - Mary W. Hardy   lic. 7-17-1821
Kigan, Amable - Francis Racicot   lic. 2-16-1829
Kimball, Jesse - Sally Kimball   11-21-1811
Kimmons, Henry - Eliza Pea   6- 4-1825
Kimmons, Joseph - Betsy Catte   lic. 1- 2-1823
Kinder, George - Elizabeth Clark   5- 2-1811
King, Seth - Mary Ann Patterson   6- 8-1829
King, Thomas A. - Mary Douthard   lic. 6-30-1817
Kinney, Amory - Hannah Bishop   lic. 1- 6-1821
Kirk, Henry - Margarm McGary, widow   1-29-1807
Kirk, John - Susanna Hyneman   lic. 2-22-1810
Kirkey, Antoine - Julia LaForce   lic. 9-25-1826
Knight, William - Fanny Harris, Negroes 12-12-1822

Knolin, Samuel - Phyllis —, Negroes   6-14-1816
Knox, George - Mary McClure   2- 5-1824
Knox, John - Mercy Tevebaugh   lic. 3-18-1822
Knox, John - Phebe Thomas   lic. 1-16-1832
Kurtz, John H. - Isabel Hannah   6-10-1830
Kuykendall, George - Patience Gregory
           lic. 12-10-1822
Kuykendall, George - Barbary Gregory   11- 4-1830
Kuykendall, Henry - Elizabeth McFall,
    widow   4- 4-1811
Kuykendall, Henry - Sally Smith   lic. 4-15-1816
Kuykendall, Jacob - Delilah Collins   8-23-1826
Kuykendall, John - Elizabeth Vankirk   6-30-1809
Kuykendall, Nathaniel - Vicry Langsdown
           11-30-1812
Kuykendall, Peter (or Henry) -
    Julia Spencer   3- 4-1810

Lacroix, Dommique - Henriette Petit   9- 3-1821
Lafond, Jean Antoine - Cecille Boyer   4-14-1814
Lafond, John Antoine - Babie Racine   9-27-1819
Laforce, Xavier - Hanna Lamphier   5-11-1820
Lagow, Alfred G. - Sarah Kuykendall
           lic. 1-17-1827
Lagow, John - Anna Maria Elizabeth Wise
           lic. 3-14-1827
Lamotte, Joseph - Eliza Richardson
           2-25-1818 (1819?)
Lander, Levi - Matilda Lindsey   1-29-1811
Landman, John - Martha Thresher   3- 3-1808
Landon, Thomas - Hester Willks   lic. 4-16-1813
Lane, Daniel - Susannah Lane, widow
           lic. 9-28-1816
Lane, Daniel - Sarah Purcell   2-18-1829
Lane, Samuel - Elizabeth Danford   lic. 1-26-1809
Lane, William Carr - Mary Ewing   lic. 2-25-1818
Langton, Samuel - Emelia Baird,
    dt of Thomas   lic. 9-30-1818
Lansdown, James - Sarah Philpot   8-11-1812
Laplante, Hyacinthe - Mary Ann Compagniott
           lic. 5-31-1830
Laplante, Jean B. - Elizabeth Martin
           lic. 12-27-1826
Laplante, Pierre - Elizabeth Gamelin   1-16-1820
Lashly, George - Polly Bradford   lic. 11- 5-1816
Lathorn, Jonathan - Delilah Potter lic. 10-29-1808
Latour, Amable - Felicite Cadarette   11-15-1825
Latour, August, son of Joseph & Angellique
    (Leveille) Latour - Margarethe Lavillette,
    dt of Louis & Jeanne (Christome) Lavillette
           1-20-1819
Latour, Henry - Josette Delisle   6-19-1820
Latoure, Pierre - Marie Barsalon   lic. 7-16-1822
Lavillette(?), Anthony, son of Louis &
    Agnes (Godder) Lavillette - Adelaide
    Cabassier, dt of Charles & Mary (Mallet)
    Cabassier   7- 6-1818
Law, Charles - Locha Steffee   lic. 8-18-1830
Law, John - Sarah Ewing   lic. 11-28-1822
Lawson, John - Elizabeth Miller   11-20-1823
Laycie(?), Tedar - Sales Joyie   lic. 1-12-1824
Leach, Jonathan - Sally Groves   9-30-1815
Ledgerwood, Joseph - Nancy Gill   5- ?-1810
Ledgerwood, Samuel - Nancy Leman   9-27-1810
Ledgerwood, William - Catharine Jenkins 9-26-1810
Lee, John - Phebe McCarter   3- 2-1817

Leech, George, Jr. - Jane Junkin   12-23-1819
Lefollet, John - Betsey Bruce   lic.   9-19-1827
Lemmon, William - Rebeccah Boswell   1- 1-1818
Lemon, David - Sarah Harper   lic.   10- 3-1821
Lemon, Friend - Polly Hansbrough   10- 8-1812
Lemon, Friend - Achsah Polke, widow   3-15-1816
Lemon, John, Jr. - Easther Kaufman   5-15-1817
Lemontaine, George - Jane Howard   5-30-1824
Leonard, Clement - Lucinda Woodrow   2-19-1824
LeRoy, Alexis - Elizabeth Vanderburgh
                                     lic.   2-17-1819
Lett, James - Nancy Veale   1-24-1813
Lettson (or Setson ?), George -
    Rachel Mannin   1- 6-1825
Lewis, Benjamin - Lucy Ritchey   8-27-1829
Light, John - Polly Groves   10-28-1821
Light, Russel - Mary Hollingsworth   12-19-1826
Lilley, Andrew - Barbary Claycomb,
    both of Palmyra Twp.   12-23-1810
Lillie, Solomon - Sarah Huffman   lic.   10-15-1814
Lindsey, George W. - Susanah Polk   lic.   11-19-1822
Lisman, Adam - Jane Ledgerwood   lic.   4-27-1809
Lisman, James - Margrette Ledgerwood   10-10-1810
Lisman, Peter - Catharine Fredrick   6-23-1814
Litsey, Henry - Nancy Carrico   12-14-1815
Loes, Thomas - Sally Robbins   6- 8-1817
Logue, Thomas - Selberry Sanders   lic.   6-10-1807
Longuedoc, Louis - Francoise Delorier 12-27-1815
Louis, Abner - Caty Springs   6-25-1825
Love, William - Jane Denny   lic.   7-13-1811
Lownes, Caleb - Francoise Vanderburgh 2-14-1817
Lucas, Zachariah - Elizabeth Gambel
                                     lic.   10-19-1809
Lukins, Jesse - Sarah Wright   8-21-1810
Lumsden, Cosby D. - Harriet Luke (or Luker)
                                            11-13-1815
Luzader, Isaac - Sally Engle   9-10-1809
Luzader, Isaac - Sally Vail   5- 4-1813

McCall, James B. - Julia Vanderburgh
                                     lic.   5-29-1813
McCall, William R. - Betsey Wyant   lic.   12-30-1815
McCarter, Jesse - Mary Dale   lic.   4- 2-1831
McCarty, Lemuel (or Samuel) -
    Polly Canan   9-15-1827
McClanahan, Thomas - Sally Engle   3-12-1812
McCliefe, William - Nancy Benefield   3-16-1821
McClure, Andrew - Anny Hogg   1- 4-1810
McClure, Charles - Margaret McDonald   5- 2-1813
McClure, Daniel - Esther Thompson   2-14-1831
McClure, James - Polly Campbell   1-12-1815
McClure, James - Elizabeth Ross (?) lic.   7-12-1810
McClure, James - Anne Warrick   6-12-1808
McClure, John - Eliza Armstrong   2- 5-1824
McClure, John, of Clark Co., Ill. -
    Priscilla Morrison   10-31-1826
McClure, John - Rebecca Seaton   lic.   2- 7-1818
McClure, John A. - Jane McClure   3-16-1826
McClure, Joseph - Mary Going   lic.   5-28-1817
McClure, Robert - Jane Thompson   lic.   2-12-1820
McClure, Samuel - Elizabeth Purcell
                                     lic.   11-14-1810
McClure, Thomas - Betsey Handly   1-18-1810
McClure, William G. - Elizabeth Purcell 2- 2-1830
McCord, Asa - Rachael Duty   4-19-1817
McCord, George - Maria Smith   8-17-1820

McCord, William, Jr. - Sarah Hollingsworth
                                            12-11-1814
McCormick, Andrew - Hannah Gollaber
                                     lic.   8- 6-1817
McCoy, Alexander - Sarah Claycomb   3-24-1831
McCoy, James - Sopha Myers   4- 8-1830
McCoy, Robert - Ellen Ray   9-20-1830
McCoy, Robert - Louisa Steen   10-26-1830
McCoy, William - Melinda Jordan   6- 1-1825
McCrea, Alexander - Drusilla Sullivan
                                     lic.   7- 8-1824
McCullough, John L. - Jane Matilda Richardson
                                            2- 6-1817
McCutchen, James - Nancy Ledgerwood
                                     lic.   2- 6-1808
McDonald, D. P. - Lucretia Johnson lic.   6-19-1822
McElroy, Henry - Rebecca Ingle   4- 5-1817
McFall, Esau - Indiana Hannah   lic.   6-16-1831
McGlochlon, Henry - Ann Noriton   4-12-1813
McGowan, James - Sarah Bilderback   2-24-1820
McGowan, William - Elizabeth Shannon   7-31-1828
McHenry, Samuel - Dorcas Carter   10-19-1826
McKee, Archibald B. - Julia Smith   10- 3-1831
McKee, John H. - Patsy Hollingsworth   9- 2-1830
McKinney, Daniel - Mary Westner   lic.   2- 3-1817
McKowen, Morgan - Hetsey Decker   lic.   5-27-1820
McMahan, Andrew - Nancy King   lic.   6-26-1816
McMillan, Jesse - Catherine Pea   1- 1-1826
McNally, Peter - Judy Newton   2-16-1830
McNeeley, James - Sally Haynie, widow 5-24-1818
McNeeley, Jeremiah - Mary Jacobus   9-16-1826
McNeeley, Jeremiah - Teeney Kuykendall
                                            12-14-1819

Macy, Obed - Lucinda Polke   10-17-1824
Maddox, John W. - Jane Warrick   2- 7-1813
Mahan, Alexander - Ann Crocker   6- 4-1812
Mahel, Frederick - Polly Foster, widow 1-18-1820
Mahel, Isaac - Julian Springer   1- 2-1827
Mail, Charles - Elizabeth Shepherd   lic.   3-31-1817
Mail, Solomon - Susanna Spain   lic.   7-26-1816
Malcom, William - Polly Thickston   12-26-1819
Mallate, Louis - Jenevi Querrie   lic.   2-25-1808
Mallery, Hiram - Eleanor Smith   11-15-1825
Mallet, Ambroise - Angelique Comoyer
                                     lic.   11-15-1810
Mallet, Francis - Marie Delorier   8-14-1817
Mallet, Peter - Hannah Ramsay   lic.   10-17-1811
Mallett, Francois - Cecilia Louval   4-15-1826
Mallett, Francois - Sarah Ramsey   lic.   2-21-1807
Mangam, William - Polly C. Douglas   3-29-1812
Manning, Samuel - Catherine Smith   6- 4-1828
Manville, Charles - Sally Allen   4- 8-1819
Marney, John - Mary Marrow   7-22-1825
Marrs, John - Margaret Marrs   5-17-1812
Marsh, George, Jr. - Elizabeth West   7- 9-1815
Marsh, William - Lodicia Knight   lic.   1- 5-1814
Marshall, Samuel - Sarah Hannah   2-13-1820
Marshall, Samuel - Sally White   lic.   4- 5-1815
Martin, Charles - Franky Rook   7-16-1812
Martin, John - Nancy Anderson   1-22-1813
Martin, John B. - Eunice Colman   1- 6-1825
Massey, Alexander - Mary Ann Alison,
    widow of Dr. Robert Alison   4-12-1823
Masters, Richard Lee - Catherine Gray,
    dt of Betsy Ann Gray   12-30-1819

Matler, Frederick - Lila Owens		8-27-1817
Matson, Luke - Delila Stewart	lic.	10-12-1810
Mattingly, Thomas - Nancy Gollerber		2-10-1815
Maumanee, August - Bridget Boneau		6- 7-1830
Maxwell, Alexander - Susan Decker		2- 4-1813
Mayes, Henry - Rebecca Baker		3-18-1829
Mayho, Simon - Fanny Johnson, Negroes		11-3-1826
Mays, Elijah - Polly Mahel	lic.	8- 2-1816

Mayse, Charles, son of Charles & Francois
   (Bayerjean) Mayse - Genevieve Grimard,
   dt of Peter & Josette (Delisle) Grimard 1-7-1819

Mead, Israel - Jane Jordan		3-11-1819
Medley, James - Polly Carrico		6-10-1815
Medley, Joseph - Rachel Stewart		6-30-1825
Melson, Mias - Silvy Williams		4- 3-1812
Melton, Abner - Jane Elliott		10-14-1830
Melton, Alexander - Hannah Ruble	lic.	7-30-1825
Merry, Calvin - Isabel Hanks		9- 6-1812
Merry, Cornelius - Henry(?) Sulivan	lic.	5-13-1813
Metcalfe, John E. - Rachel Cox	lic.	7- 9-1821
Mette, Pierre - Mary Lafayanne		3-22-1827
Mettie, Pierre - Marie Ravillette		10- 2-1820
Michel, John - Mary Fredrick	lic.	10- 6-1809
Middleton, Samuel - Chloe Black		2-22-1813
Milburn, David - Milly Key		4-24-1811
Miles, George - Phelina Danford (or Miles?)		
		2-11-1830
Miley, Henry - Nancy Pride		3-23-1811
Millburn, Robert - Nancy Archer	lic.	2-29-1812
Miller, Abraham - Maria Lemon		8-26-1830
Miller, Jacob - Nancy Shook		11-23-1815
Miller, John - Elizabeth Melvin		10-20-1809
Miller, Joseph M. - Peggy L. West	lic.	10-13-1816
Miller, Philip - Elisabeth Westfall	lic.	2- 8-1817
Miller, Richard - Polly Johnson	lic.	7-21-1824
Miller, Samuel - Polly Lemond	lic.	8- 4-1819
Mills, Henry I. - —— Decker, widow	lic.	6- 6-1807
Mills, John - Lucinda Highsmith		8-23-1812
Miner, George - Catharine Plough	lic.	7- 6-1811
Miner, Stinson - Betsy Craft		3-26-1829
Miner, Thomas - Fanny Chambers		3-11-1828
Miner, William - Nancy Frederick		11-11-1827
Mitchel, Robert - Margaret Adams		2- 2-1815
Mitchel, Stephen - Hariot Delorier		12-14-1815
Moes, Joseph - Jane Dubois	lic.	1-17-1829
Moffatt, James - Julia Bouidinot	lic.	12-17-1822
Mondo, John M. - Madelaine Mitte		5- 7-1821
Montgomery, Robert - Patience Marvel		4-30-1812
Montgomery, Walter Crocket -		
Nancy Roberts	lic.	8-17-1808
Montmany(?), John - Josette Dielle		9-12-1818
Moore, Hiram - Nancy Catt		8-12-1824
Moore, John - Anna Scott	lic.	4- 6-1820
Moore, Samuel - Nancy Booth		9-20-1807
Morgan, Randle E. - Susannah Johnston		6- 6-1820
Morgan, Sympson - Elizabeth Fredrick		7- 7-1811
Morris, Michael - Roady Stewart	lic.	8-18-1821
Morris, William - Lovina Roberts		4-16-1829
Morton, Francis - Ruth Powell		4-13-1808
Moutney, William - Nancy Allmon		1-14-1813
Mulloy, David - Sarah Freeman, widow		5- 2-1819
Musick, Asa - Sarah Lucas		1-14-1809
Myers, Frederick - Micah Gouthury		
(or Macha Gaultney)		6- 3-1830
Myers, Jacob - Peggy McCrackin	lic.	10-20-1818
Myers, John - Julia Crealy		12- 9-1812

Myers, John - Mary Williams		3-23-1825
Myswanger, Joseph - Elizabeth Huffman		
	lic.	3- 8-1820
Nabb, James - Barbary Dagnion		11-11-1814
Nash, Allen R. - Matilda Flowers	lic.	9-13-1831
Neal, Wilson - Louisa Honeycutt	lic.	2-20-1826
Needy, Ned - Rachel Baldwin		6- 2-1824
Nesler, John - Susannah Garner	lic.	4-21-1807
Newport, William - Mary Rankin		4-17-1829
Newton, Isaac - Judy ——, Negroes		5-29-1823
Newton, Jesse - Pricilla Brock		4-22-1829
Newton, Nathaniel - Pricilla Embry,		
Negroes		6- 1-1826
Newton, Nathaniel - Jane McNeely		8-31-1820
Ney, William - Polly Mamey	lic.	8- 6-1811
Nicholas, Martin - Elizabeth Cobb	lic.	9-16-1815
Nolin, Henry - Harriet McKown		5-10-1821
Nolin, Henry - Cassandra Miner		11-19-1824
Nott, Sylvester - Rachel Jane Gardner		
	lic.	1-31-1820
O'Neile, Joseph - Victoria Delisle	lic.	8- 3-1808
O'Neille, Hugh - Polly Wells,		
both of White River Twp.		5-10-1810
Onyotte, Joseph - Margaret Cardinal,		
widow		11-20-1818
Osburn, James - Isabel Sherman		
(Isabel Hill on return)	lic.	6-30-1815
Otter, Charles - Sarah Applegate		4-15-1820
Owens, Moses - Catharine Anthis		12- 8-1824
Owens, Thomas - Sally Tevebaugh	lic.	8- 9-1824
Owens, Thomas - Dorothy Bass		7- 1-1827
Page, Dominique - Marie Villeneauve		4-27-1809
Page, Dominique - Pleage Valle	lic.	11-28-1828
Palmer, Elijah - Berthshebe Sharp		12-30-1817
Palmer, Martin - Hetty Morgan		12-25-1814
Pancake, Jacob - Barbary Gaultney,		
widow		12- 5-1819
Pancake, Jacob - Catharine Schrader		4-10-1817
Parker, Bazil - Naomi Risley		4-11-1820
Parker, Daniel - Mariah Kilecare,		
Negroes	lic.	5-31-1825
Parker, James - Delilah Cartwright	lic.	10-25-1830
Parker, John, of Illinois -		
Sally Duty	lic.	3-21-1825
Parr, Samuel - Sally Scott	lic.	11-26-1808
Partelow, Jacob - Ketty Harman		3-17-1811
Patlow, William - Sally Thixton		10- 6-1817
Patterson, Baptist - Nancy Collins	lic.	8-13-1815
Patterson, Samuel - Fanny A. Blackburn		
	lic.	8-15-1831
Pea, Abraham - Susanna Selvy	lic.	1-16-1808
Pea, Jacob - Susan Barkman		5-31-1820
Pearson, Enoch - Sarah Leach		3-17-1816
Peckham, Louis, son of Thomas & Anna		
(Weaver) Peckham - Mary Dague - dt of		
Ambrose & Mary (of the Many Nations)		
Dague		9-27-1819
Pelletier, Louis - Peggy Bolden, Negroes		
		9-17-1821
Pennington, Charles - Mary Trotter		10-29-1812
Perdue, Edward - Lydia Goodman		5- 1-1814
Perry, William N. - Catharine McClure		
	lic.	11-29-1820

Person, William - Patsy Stricklin 2-15-1810
Petit, Anthony, son of Anthony & Josette
   (Villeray) Petit - Susanna Cartier, dt
   of Peter & Versnique (Mallet) Cartier 10-19-1818
Pew (or Pugh), David - Elizabeth Morrell 9-19-1831
Philips, John - Almeda Herrington 2- 2-1832
Phillips, David - Polly Duckworth 1-10-1822
Philpot, John - Sarah Johnson,
   both of White River Twp. 5- 4-1810
Picard, Alexander - Mary Petit 10-23-1820
Picard, Alexis - Francis Pezion lic. 5- 3-1827
Pickle, Henry - Elizabeth Lawson 9- 4-1828
Pickle, John - Jane Johnson 7-21-1825
Piety, Samuel D. - Eliza Ann Hodgins 12- 3-1828
Piety, William - Sally Ann Threlkeld 1- 5-1830
Pin, German - Jane Levellie 7-26-1831
Pitcher, John - Matilda Coulter 12-26-1819
Plough, Isaac - Polly Holladay 11-13-1807
Podvink, Pierre - Victoire Cardinal lic. 10- 6-1823
Pogue, James - Emet Thomas 8-10-1815
Poidvin, Francois, son of Francois &
   Teresa (Benacky) Poidvin - Victoire
   Lanson(?), dt of Alexander & Archange
   (Bordeleau) Lanson 7- 6-1818
Polk, Adam G. - Caroline Burnsides 6- 2-1831
Polke, James - Harriet (or Elizabeth)
   Shepherd 10-30-1829
Polke, Robert - Betsey Widner 5- 1-1815
Poore, Zachariah, of Sullivan Co. -
   Mary Kaufman 11-15-1821
Poorman, John - Mary Ann Scomp 1-16-1825
Porier, Francois - Teena Baker, Negroes 3-26-1815
Porier, Francois - Nancy LaMontain 4-24-1818
Porier, Toussaint - Silvey Hopkins lic. 3-28-1820
Portee, John - Charlotte Anderson,
   Negroes 6-27-1816
Porter, David - Nancy Berry, widow 3-28-1816
Potter, George W. - Mary Ann Carruthers 10-11-1830
Potter, Robert - Nancy (or Mrs. Ann)
   Thing lic. 1-24-1831
Pressey, Charles - Catharine Stork 4- 3-1825
Price, David - Nancy Dougherty 4-28-1818
Price, Isaac - Margaret Shook 5-30-1811
Price, James - Mary Collins lic. 3-17-1809
Price, Peter - Nancy Rector lic. 8-24-1816
Price, Samuel - Nancy Mays 2- 1-1820
Price, William - Cinthia Durham 6-24-1819
Price, William, of Sullivan Co. -
   Eliza Ann Patterson 2- 2-1824
Pride (Pryde), Thomas - Caty Miley 7-12-1809
Probst, William - Sally Ann Bailey lic. 2-27-1827
Pryor, Benjamin - Julia LaPlante 9-30-1829
Puckett, Thomas - Nancy Early, widow
   lic. 1-20-1817
Pugh, see also Pew
Pugh, David - Eliza Long lic. 6-13-1816
Pulham, Zachariah - Lavina Lindsey 7-22-1816
Purcell, Adam - Frances Kuykendall 10-20-1825
Purcell, Edward - Abigal Williams 7- 5-1814
Purcell, Elijah, of Daviess Co. -
   Susannah Wiles 9-15-1825
Purcell, Isaac - Sarah Catt 2-18-1830
Purcell, Isaac - Jane Hogue 11-24-1831
Purcell, Isaac - Elizabeth Wheeler 8- 9-1825
Purcell, James - Catherine Reedy 9- 5-1811
Purcell, Jesse - Delila Freeland lic. 4-24-1812

Purcell, John - Hannah Hollingsworth
   lic. 3- 1-1807
Purcell, John - Betsey Ready 6-22-1815
Purley, George W. - Lucretia Landers 8- 1-1827
Putman, Reding - Stacy Combs lic. 6- 6-1812
Putnam, Howard - Rosy Washburn 7-24-1824

Quarque, Elezidore - Victoire Bayerjon
   lic. 4-26-1820
Querrie, Antoine - Catherine Frederick 7- 2-1823
Querrie, Pierre - Jane Mallett, widow
   lic. 4-17-1817

Racico, Antoine - Mary Lognion lic. 1-23-1832
Racine, Francis - Angeline Jalbar lic. 7-27-1829
Racine, Francois - Lagette Delorier 7-26-1824
Racine, Jean Baptiste - Mary Ann Urneau 7- 3-1820
Ramsey, Allen - Elizabeth Reedy 5-20-1820
Ramsey, John - Mary Cardinal 1- 7-1829
Ramsey, John - Sharlotte Hazleton lic. 1- 8-1831
Ramsey, William - Susannah Hall lic. 9- 9-1809
Randolph, Robert - Martha Gamble 11-22-1812
Raper, William - Mary McClure lic. 9-27-1815
Ravellate, Antoin - Deleyite Cabasier
   lic. 6-30-1818
Rawlings, Moses - Nancy Badger lic. 7- 5-1824
Rawlings, Moses - Joice (or Jane?)
   Colvin lic. 3-29-1825
Rawlings, Moses - Charlotte Reed lic. 10-11-1813
Ray, Martin - Margaret McCoy 11-14-1825
Ray, Nimrod - Delphia Smith 8- 4-1831
Ray, William - Polly Lamon 1- 2-1812
Reaugh, David - Mary Tevebaugh lic. 6-10-1809
Reeds, William - Charlotte Thixton 9- 4-1831
Reel, Aaron - Sena Gaultney 12-24-1829
Reel, Abraham - Emily Welton lic. 11-14-1831
Reel, Absolom - Malinda Jordan 2-23-1824
Reel, David - Sarah McCoy 2-17-1825
Reel, George - Catherine Decker 6- 7-1829
Reel, John Jr. - Sally McCoy lic. 2- 2-1816
Reeves, Allen - Margaret Carrico 2-28-1815
Reeves, John - Osse Cochran 9- 3-1822
Regenbold, Antoine - Helen Desbrens
   lic. 7-16-1828
Reiley, David B. - Diana Decker 11-19-1819
Reiley, John C. - Susan Bailey 2- 8-1829
Reiley, John C. - Maria McCall lic. 12- 4-1818
Reneau, Joseph - Julie Bisayon 7-29-1815
Rhoadarmel, John - Mary Adams 12- 8-1807
Rice, Isaac - Margaret Shook 5-30-1811
Rice, James - Nancy Armstrong lic. 11-20-1810
Rice, Samuel - Amy Landers 4-15-1811
Richard, John Baptiste, son of John
   Baptiste and Elizabeth (Mallette)
   Richard - Julie DesJean, dt of Philip
   & Victoire (Cornoyer) DesJean 11- 1-1819
Richards, William M. - Sally Long lic. 7- 1-1816
Richardson, James - Mary Hathaway,
   widow lic. 1-20-1816
Richardson, Louis - Sarah N. Bonner 3-20-1829
Richardville, Antoine - Clamas Cornoyer
   lic. 5-31-1830
Richardville, John Bpte. - Mary Bonhomme
   11- 4-1825
Richardville, see also Drouet, Henry
Richey, David - Cinthia Alton 10-26-1815

Richey, David - Scinthe McClure lic. 9-30-1819
Richey, Samuel - Matilda Sill, Negroes 9-22-1825
Riley, Jonathan - Louisiana Black 12- 1-1814
Risley, David - Nancy Harsha 12-17-1829
Risley, James - Sarah Piety 2- 7-1828
Risley, Samuel - Polly Thompson lic. 1-27-1816
Risley, Silas - Catharine Adams 12-26-1807
Risley, William - Eliza Welton 2-10-1830
Ritchey, John - Elizabeth Steen lic. 1-11-1820
Ritchey, William - Jane F. Jones,
 Negroes 1- 9-1832
Rittenhouse, Elias - Sarah Ackley 11- 4-1825
Roach, Griffin T. - Mary Wingate 9-18-1818
Roads, Henry - Mary Fisher 5-14-1810
Robb, James - Elenor Warrick lic. 6-15-1811
Roberts, Alanson G. - Mary Fairhurst 12-25-1821
Robertson, Thomas - Kitty Thorn lic. 11-15-1815
Robins (Robbins), Elbert W. - Cynthia Biggs
  6-12-1828
Robins, Nathaniel - Lydia Graham 9-20-1810
Robins, Thomas - Anne Pogue 5-15-1816
Robinson, Alfred - Mary Johnson 10- 2-1828
Robinson, Harmon B. - Eleanor Steen
  lic. 10- 7-1822
Rodarmel, Abraham - Nancy Hanna 6-16-1811
Rodarmel, Joseph - Nelly Trigger lic. 1-11-1809
Roderick, Francis - Elinor Johnson lic. 5-25-1816
Roderick, Semien - Nancy Clarke 3-17-1819
Rodgers, John - Sally Martin 5-24-1811
Root, Simean - Hariot Langton lic. 3-12-1822
Rose, Peter F. - Barbary Snyder 6-15-1829
Roseman, Joseph - Minerva Hanah lic. 11- 7-1822
Ross, John - Mary Beamon 12-16-1824
Ross, Russell - Elizabeth Almy lic. 1-27-1823
Ruble, David - Nancy Piety 2-17-1825
Ruble, George - Indiana Westfall 6- 8-1827
Ruby, Franklin - Lucy Lemon lic. 12- 6-1830
Rue (or Roux), Emanuel - Elen
 (or Helen) Coulter 8-11-1825
Russell, Charles - Nancy Palmer 4-17-1817
Russell, Robert W. - Susana Kirky lic. 9-13-1828
Russell, William - Rachel Davis 4-20-1814

Sacrest(?), Joseph - Mary Ann Roquest
  lic. 1-30-1832
St. Clair, Damiel - Sarah Sanders 2-18-1819
St. Mary, Henry - Barbary Dubois lic. 2-12-1827
St. Mary, see also Anthony Chenett
Salter, Washington - Jane Scott lic. 8-30-1809
Sampson, Jesse - Rebecca Snider 8-26-1827
Sarters, John - Sally Hollingsworth 1-16-1831
Scales, Benjamin - Patsy Roberts 4-19-1812
Scales, William - Nancy Ann Haynes 4-24-1831
Scott, A. D. - Frances Purcell lic. 6-16-1830
Scott, Archibald - Kitty Purcell lic. 2- 8-1819
Scott, Charles - Sally Widner lic. 3-27-1816
Scott, George - Elizabeth Rose lic. 8- 9-1820
Scott, Thomas - Rebecca Hadden lic. 10-24-1810
Scott, Thomas - Polly Holmes lic. 5-30-1821
Scott, Thomas - Martha Norwood 11-20-1831
Seeds, James - Prudence Powers
 (dt of John) 2-13-1822
Seily, Edward R. - Peggy Crosby 2-24-1811
Selby, Joseph - Mary Johnson lic. 12-20-1809
Selvy, Joshua - Polly Pea 4- 4-1813
Selvy, William - Rachel Johnson lic. 10-28-1809

Sernino(?), Ambrose - Angelique Trembly
  9-16-1830
Setzer, John - Margaret Barkman 10-11-1827
Severens, John - Elizabeth Murphy 5-25-1811
Seyen(?), Louis, son of Louis & Mary Ann
 (Denoyon) Seyen - Clariss DesJean, dt
 of Phillippe & Victoire (Cornoyer)
 DesJean 11-23-1818
Shaw, Henry M. - Elisa M. L. Smith lic. 12-17-1823
Shaw, Hoseah - Nancy Leonard,
 of Illinois lic. 1- 1-1823
Shaw, Hugh - Kitty Applegate lic. 6- 1-1813
Shaw, Joseph - Mary F. White lic. 1-27-1817
Shearer, Adam - Susanna Jenny, widow
  lic. 8-21-1821
Shearman, Benjamin - Rebecca Jessup
  lic. 6-26-1816
Sheilds, Booker - Patsy Cunningham 11-30-1809
Sheilds, Thomas C. - Mary Dagenet lic. 7- 3-1817
Sheilds, William - Jane Grant 3-23-1817
Shepherd, Horace B. - Patsy Harper lic. 11-12-1827
Shepherd, William D. - Cynthia Polke 10- 8-1820
Shevalier, Jean Baptiste - Kitty Burges
  lic. 4-26-1817
Shields, James - Margaret Lane lic. 5-20-1817
Shields, John - Polly McBain 3- 6-1819
Shippy, Seth - Polly (or Hannah) Dixon 3-24-1830
Shook, William - Rachel Wease lic. 1-18-1812
Shoults, Mathias - Nancy Marricle lic. 7- 2-1816
Shuler, Lawrence S. - Sarah Cunningham
  lic. 11-28-1820
Signer, George - Sarah Burnham 6-22-1828
Silence, David - Polly Carter 10-21-1829
Silence, Jacob - Sharlotte Louis 10-14-1830
Simms, Cornelius - Betsy Embree 10-28-1831
Simpson, Charles - Elizabeth Stucky
  lic. 7-10-1810
Simpson, John - Polly Wilkinson 8- 6-1810
Skelton, Ralph - Fanny Lathom 1-16-1810
Slawson, Jesse - Rachel Reeves 3-24-1809
Sleavin, Samuel - Catharine Conner 12-22-1812
Slinkard, Frederick, of Greene Co. -
 Catherine Skomp 9-22-1825
Slinkard, Moses, of Greene Co. -
 Mary Skomp 11-29-1827
Sloo, Albert G. - Harriett G. White 2- 6-1826
Small, Jacob - Elizabeth Mayes 2- 5-1829
Small, John - Anne Frederick, dt of Lewis
  lic. 4- 5-1821
Small, William M. - Elizabeth Reiley
  lic. 11- 5-1827
Smith, Abraham - Philey Mallary lic. 12-23-1823
Smith, Bastion - Hannah Nicholson 7-16-1829
Smith, Charles - Mary Carpenter 12-15-1822
Smith, Garris - Mary Jenks lic. 8- 8-1827
Smith, George - Sally Armstrong lic. 5-14-1810
Smith, James - Eliza Jones lic. 10-24-1822
Smith, John A. - Anna Durell lic. 10-28-1820
Smith, Merit - Janny Smith lic. 8- 8-1827
Smith, Minard P. - Matilda McClure lic. 10-29-1923
Smith, Moses - Mary Goldman 9- 3-1820
Smith, Thomas - Betsy Frederick 7-22-1828
Smith, William - Eliza Hogue 10-14-1824
Smith, William - Elizabeth Jourdan lic. 6-28-1814
Snapp, Abraham F. - Martha Baird 12-27-1827
Snapp, John F. - Jane McCord 12-18-1829

Snider, John Ralph - Nancy Wily Sampson 4-28-1825
Snyder, David - Eliza Miller, widow   2- 1-1824
Snyder, David, Jr. - Sally Lillie   1-22-1822
Snyder, Henry - Amanda Whitcomb   9-22-1824
Soden, William - Hannah Westfall   lic. 9-17-1823
Sommes, Joseph - Frances S. Vanderburgh
                      lic. 12- 6-1831
Sowden, Hiram - Sally Beedle   lic. 10- 9-1828
Spade, Daniel - Youthey Catte   4-22-1819
Spain, Archibald - Sally Woods   5- 6-1819
Springs, Henry - Judy ——, Negroes lic. 11-26-1815
Sprinkle, Michael - Mary Ann Bayers
                      lic. 8-22-1808
Sprowl, James - Nancy Ledgerwood   4-26-1814
Srader, Jacob - Kitty Reel, widow   8- 7-1817
Stafford, Benjamin - Clarra Maxfiel   4- 1-1832
Stafford, Thomas - Priscilla Horrall lic. 3-15-1817
Stafford, William - Rachel Horrel   6-23-1815
Staggs, Abraham - Caty Garner   lic. 12-11-1824
Staggs, Edward - Elizabeth Mail   6-23-1823
Stainer, Michael - Hannah McCarter lic. 2-10-1813
Stallings, John - Celia McAdoo   lic. 1-31-1812
Stanley, Needham - Polly Barton   lic. 7-24-1811
Stapleton, Frederick - Jane Musick lic. 5- 6-1811
Starnater, Andrew - Elizabeth Hunt lic. 12- 4-1816
Starner, Michael - Margaret McCord   10-27-1816
Steen, James - Polly Dunn   lic. 8-11-1817
Steen, John - Ruth Robinson   lic. 4-14-1820
Steen, Samuel B. - Mary Alsop, widow
                      lic. 6-14-1822
Steen, William - Naomi Robinson   4- 4-1832
Stephens, Ezra - Betsey Ludington   6-12-1820
Stevenson, Samuel H. - Eunice McArthur 4- 8-1829
Steward, William - Sarah Ann Duty lic. 11- 2-1825
Stewart, Arnstead - Ede Embry   2-26-1830
Stewart, Ichabod - Lily Jarrel   2-15-1827
Stewart, James - Elizabeth Laplante
                      lic. 4-16-1814
Stewart, William, Jr. - Angelique Tromblis
                      1-20-1815
Stoker, Benjamin - Betsy Dudley   1-21-1813
Stoker, Joseph - Peggy Hill   5-14-1812
Stoner, John - Margaret Robinson   lic. 4- 6-1812
Stork, John - Betsy Risley   12-12-1824
Stork, John, Jr. - Mary VanKirk   6-15-1820
Story, Smith - Elizabeth Ferguson lic. 6- 9-1811
Stropes, Adam - Penelope Lockwood   6- 5-1816
Stropes, John - Serinda Chatsey   5- 5-1816
Stroud, William - Nancy Jarrold   2-13-1824
Struple, John - Polly Dixon   2-27-1816
Stuckey, Jacob - Polly Tevebaugh,
  dt of William   lic. 1-16-1822
Stuckey, Samuel - Rebecca Gregory,
  widow   11-20-1815
Sturgis, Robert W. - Jane Braden   lic. 2- 1-1827
Suhebriette, John Baptiste -
  Elizabeth Grant   3-28-1827
Sullivan, Daniel - Susan Sullivan lic. 2-27-1808
Sullivan, George R. C. - Helen Vanderburgh
                      lic. 11- 2-1813
Sullivan, James - Nancy Helderman   3-15-1828
Sullivan, William - Durscilla Tevebaugh 7- 8-1821
Summers, Dempsey - Elizabeth Forsithe 4-25-1811
Symms, Edward - Julia Catee   lic. 3- 3-1815

Taylor, Edmund - Mary Anne Perkins,
  Negroes   4- 6-1826
Taylor, Francois - Nancy Embry,
  Negroes   9-20-1825
Taylor, Frank - Susan Jefferson,
  Negroes   7-13-1816
Taylor, Isaac - Sarah Kirkpatrick   11-14-1830
Taylor, Jacob - Elizabeth Price   11-26-1812
Taylor, John - Nancy Kelly   7-16-1828
Taylor, John - Nancy Mattingly, widow
                      lic. 9-13-1817
Taylor, Jonathan - Rhody ——, Negroes 4-16-1816
Taylor, Thomas - Rebecca Taylor   7- 6-1814
Teague, Elijah - Caty Rudycill   2-20-1831
Teriack, James - Margaret Mallet   lic. 11- 2-1829
Teriack, Joseph - Ellen Vilnave   lic. 5- 1-1827
Tessier, Francois - Victoire Cabassier 1-10-1820
Tevebaugh, George - Patience Severns
                      lic. 9- 5-1811
Teverbaugh, George - Maria Miller   8- 3-1828
                      (1829?)
Teverbaugh, Nimrod - Sally Sampson   10- 6-1824
Thing, Samuel - Mrs. Nancy Norton   12- 4-1826
Thixton, Bluford - Elizabeth Welton   8-13-1823
Thomas, Abijah - Nancy Hansbrough   8- 5-1813
Thomas, James Evans - Nancy Wiley Sampson
                      6-13-1824
Thomas, Jesse - Phebe Snyder
  (dt of Ralph)   6-13-1819
Thomas, Joseph - Mary Chambers   7-12-1810
Thomas, Joseph (or Joshua) -
  Rebecca Owens   5- 3-1818
Thompson, Cyrus - Mary Hodgen   lic. 7-24-1823
Thompson, Isaac - Mary Wiley   lic. 8-27-1812
Thompson, James - Lavinia Boals   lic. 5-10-1813
Thompson, Samuel - Laura Roberts   lic. 2- 4-1822
Thorn, Absalom - Eliza Billings   4-13-1815
Thorn, Afsiah - Senia Cutright   6- 5-1817
Thorn, Elijah - Sally McFall   8- 2-1825
Thorn, George - Mary Wilson   11- 2-1826
Thorn, James - Anna Douthard   lic. 8-19-1817
Thorn, James - Polly Garrett   2-22-1825
Thorn, Joshua - Margrette Baker   lic. 4-18-1811
Thorn, Michael - Elizabeth McBeene   8-24-1830
Thorn, Samuel - Polly Huffman   lic. 7-13-1808
Thorn, Solomon - Nancy Flinn   10-25-1818
Thorn, William - Barbary Thorn   lic. 9-22-1827
Tigert, William - Nancy Keith   9-22-1831
Timms, James - Polly Reeves   11-15-1812
Timms, Littleton - Louisa McCollough 12- 6-1827
Tindal, William - Otha McDonald   10-18-1806
Tollagier, Abraham - Polly Stewart   5-13-1819
Tougas, Alexis - Elizabeth Boye   lic. 8-21-1826
Tougas, Augustus - Widow Mallet   12- 5-1825
Tougas, Guillaime - Angeline Borrois   8- 7-1826
Tracy, Alvin - Lucinda Thorn   9- 9-1829
Trombly, Mitchel - Elizabeth Racicot
                      lic. 2-12-1827
Truckie, Nicholas - Lassuel Longdo   2-18-1828
Trusler, George - Sally Loomis   12-20-1824
Turbet, Henry - Nelly Mays   7- 7-1827
Turman, Benjamin - Prudence Nash   11-10-1824
Turner, —— - Sarah Thompson   lic. 11-17-1825
Turpin, Louis - Sally Joyeuse   lic. 5-24-1830
Tyler, Samuel - Amelia Lindsay   3- 2-1819

Tyler, William - Loucretia Tusser,
    Negroes   6-19-1823

Underwood, John - Liddy Hollingsworth 12-11-1821
Urneau, Antoine - Mary Bordeleau,
    of Illinois   9-12-1822

Valle, James - Eleanor Aikman   lic. 8-22-1813
Vanderhoaf, Harvey - Catharine Crock 1- 6-1831
Vangordon, William - Mary Wyatt   6- 3-1825
Vankirk, John - Ann Risley   2- 9-1813
Vankirk, Joseph - Anne Beamon   3-18-1830
Vanzantt, John - Ann Vining   10- 1-1821
Veale, Daniel - Mary Coleman   6-23-1813
Villmere, Nicholas - Margaret Malbeauf 4-18-1808
Visinon (or Fisinon), Francois -
    Scynthy Fasset (or Foset) lic. 10- 4-1808

Wade, Hiram - Lucy Neal   2-18-1819
Waldrop, John - Sally Eaton   9-15-1814
Walker, Abraham - Diana String, widow,
    Negroes   5-20-1820
Walker, Isaac - Susanna Risley lic. 10-24-1810
Walker, Jonathan - Polly Brinton   5- 9-1811
Walker, Oliver - Mariah ——, Negroes 1-30-1828
Wallace, Morgan - Betsey Lucas   2- 3-1815
Wallace, Nicholas - Polly Bellew   5-28-1815
Waller, Jack - Heziah Westfall   3-17-1816
Walters (or Waller), Isaac - Sarah Jeffres,
    of Illinois   4-18-1825
Walters, Mathias - Betsey Neill   6-25-1818
Wardon, Elisha - Agnes Dubois lic. 7-19-1813
Warner, Alanson - Jane McGiffen lic. 8-16-1821
Warner, John - Sarah McGowen   10- 1-1812
Warner, Joseph - Elizabeth Jones   6- 3-1824
Warrick, John - Anny Johnston lic. 8-17-1808
Watson, Frederick - Sarah Dyer lic. 4-21-1808
Watson, Isaac - Mary Ann Souligne 7-26-1825
Watson, Luke - Delila Stewart   10-14-1810
Watson, William T. - Margaret Thompson
                      lic. 6-13-1814
Wease, David - Elizabeth Harbison lic. 4- 7-1812
Wease, John - Polly Jerrold   lic. 7-17-1810
Wease, Preston - Elizabeth Collins 7- 1-1827
Weathers, John G. - Mittean Beacher 7-25-1831
Weaver, John - Elizabeth Harper   11-15-1812
Webb, David - Sally Bass   7-12-1818
Weddes (or Wooders), William -
    Ana Rebecca Boyd   7-27-1830
Welham (Welman), Barnabas - Jane Brown 8-30-1819
Wellman, Barnabas - Sally Stewart lic. 4-16-1821
Wells, William - Susanna Fredrick   7-13-1820
Welton, David - Rachel Philips lic. 11-10-1810
Welton, James - Mary Ann Hershey lic. 2-11-1823
Welton, William - Rebecca Setzar   12-23-1819
West, Alexander - Polly Fuller   4-13-1816
Westfall, Abel - Polly Rumsour lic. 8- 3-1811
Westfall, Abel - Indiana Thorn lic. 3-29-1830
Westfall, Abraham, Jr. - Sally Rumsour
                      lic. 10- 7-1817
Westfall, Isaac, Jr. - Sally Westfall lic. 1-28-1818
Westfall, James - Rebecca Furguson
                      lic. 1-24-1815
Westfall, John - Eliza Foster   11- 4-1829
Westfall, Thomas - Elizabeth Myers lic. 4-18-1820
Westfall, Thomas - Polly Springer lic. 2-20-1812

Westrope, Richard - Margaret Lansdown 4-22-1813
Wheeler, Henry D. - Esther Polk   1-23-1817
Wheeler, John - Polly Catt   2- 8-1824
Wheeler, Peyton - Catherine Key   5-15-1812
Wheeler, Samuel - Nancy Key   5-31-1812
Whipple, John - Mary Ann Haynes   1-12-1829
Whitaker, Edward - Elizabeth Neal lic. 8-14-1815
White, George - Jane Herrington   2-28-1824
White, John, Sr. - Ann E. Crowel   3-19-1830
White, John - Letitia White lic. 8- 5-1816
White, John Couret - Nancy Willison Johnson
                        5-12-1814
Whitmore, Daniel - Virginia Westfall 3-26-1829
Whitneck, Andrew - Catharine Rodarmel 9-19-1825
Whitney, James - Elizabeth Dixon   1-10-1819
Whittelsey, Isaac N. - Elizabeth Buntin
                    lic. 4-12-1831
Whitten, Elisha H. - Ann Mi(MS torn) 11- ?-1827
Whitten, James - Mary Frakes   1- 1-1828
Widner, John W. - America Shepherd 12- 1-1831
Wile, Andrew - Almey Van Kirk,
    dt of Joseph   11-10-1823
Wiles, Andrew - Zelpha Herrington lic. 12-10-1831
Wiles, Andrew - Susannah Kaufman 7-13-1826
Wiles, Andrew - Sophia Liles lic. 2-18-1832
Wiles, George (?), Philena Wiles lic. 2-10-1830
Wiles, Michael - Betsey Stipes   3-16-1828
Wiley, William - Rachel Jessop   1- 1-1816
Wilkes, Edward - Mary Watson   1- 1-1811
Wilkes, Willis - Nancy Jacobus lic. 3-31-1832
Wilkie (or Wilkin), Andrew -
    Sarah Manville   8-18-1830
Wilkins, Andrew - Elizabeth Thomas 12-24-1812
Wilkins, William - Hetty Carruthers lic. 5-18-1818
Willard, Titus B. - Hannah Elsworth 5-20-1821
Williams, Holloday - Nancy Cabbage
                  lic. 6- 6-1810
Williams, James D. - Nancy Huffman 2-17-1831
Williams, John - Nancy Johnston   5-29-1820
Williams, Welton - Susanne Myers   1-12-1826
Williams, William B. - Cinthia Larkins
                lic. 10-23-1813
Williamson, Isaac - Betsey Fisher 1- 3-1830
Willson, Jerry - Ann Taylor   lic. 4-22-1815
Willy, Jonathan - Frances Palmer   5-15-1812
Wilmore, Jacob - Mary Fortenburgh 1- 9-1820
Wilson, David - Phebe P. Morrell 10- 9-1830
Wilson, Edward - Mary Sampson lic. 9-13-1816
Wilson, Edward - Mary R. Snider   5-10-1825
Wilson, James - Sarah Powel   11-13-1812
Wilson, John - Ruthy Wease   12- 7-1826
Wilson, Samuel N. - Sarah Baker lic. 8-24-1811
Winkler, Adam - Nancy Brooner lic. 3- 9-1812
Winters, William - Sylvia Akin,
    widow   lic. 6-21-1817
Wise, John - Hannah McCall   2-12-1824
Withers, William L. - Christina Snapp 6- 4-1815
Wolf, George - Christena Frederick 10-22-1829
Wolverton, John D. - Adeline McNamee
                  lic. 6-20-1822
Wood, Jeremiah - Elizabeth Scribner lic. 3-30-1818
Wood, Joseph - Leah Greathouse   7-14-1808
Wood, Joseph - Peggy McDowell   10-24-1816
Wood, Spencer - Matilda Flowers lic. 5- 2-1810
Wright, David - Elizabeth Brewner,
    both of White River Twp.   7- 4-1811

Wright, William, of Pike Co. -
     Catharine Bass, widow   lic.   3- 4-1825
Wyant, George - Eliza Douthart   9-21-1825
Wyant, Henry - Julia Douthet   4- 4-1821

Yeats, Isaac - Nancy Rollins, widow   3-23-1816
Yenvin, Mathew - Anna Ellis   12- 3-1816

Young, Garret - Susannah Crook   2- 1-1823
Young, Mathew - Sarah Berry   5-25-1812
Young, Robert - Polly Snider   3-24-1822
Young, Sparling - Peggy Cochran   2-21-1813
Young, William - Betsey Jones   4- 9-1812
Youngman, James - Rebecah Stout   4-15-1827

Zevely, Alexander M. - Rebecca West   12- 3-1816

"GONE WEST," HOOSIERS IN CALIFORNIA, 1856

Compiled by Effingham P. Humphrey, Jr., editor of the *Pennsylvania Genealogical Magazine*.

A phrase that occurs often in genealogies, in the pre-Civil War period, is "Left home when a young man and was never heard from again." These men often went to sea, to the "big city," and, especially in the 1849-60 period, to California as part of the Gold Rush.

Some of the latter group can be identified in the *Index to the 1850 Census of the State of California*, compiled by Alan P. Bowman (Genealogical Publishing Co., Baltimore, 1972). This census (the count was taken in 1850 and into the spring of 1851) gave not only the name of the individual, but also his age and state of origin.

Equally helpful, though for a limited area, is the somewhat later *Miners & Business Men's Directory. For the Year Commencing January 1st, 1856. Embracing a General Directory of the Citizens of Tuolumne, and portions of Calaveras, Stanislaus and San Joaquin Counties. Together with the Mining Laws of Each District, A Description of the Different Camps, and Other Interesting Statistical Matter.*, by Heckendorn & Wilson (Columbia: Printed at the Clipper Office, Fulton St., Near Main. 1856).

This small pamphlet, in the Rare Book Room of the New York Public Library, consists of 104 pages, plus paper covers, four pages of advertising, a title page, and a view of Columbia, one of the richest and most important settlements of the Mother Lode. The brief preface disclaims completeness and accuracy, because of the lack of cooperation in certain mining camps, and states, "we have not given over one-eight [sic] part of the population."

Nonetheless, several thousand names, with occupations and states of origin, are included, listed by town, mining camp, or district. The names of the men from Indiana (either born there or previous residents) are presented here as in the original, with occasional omission of initial(s).

Tuolumne County, one of the original 27 counties of California, was organized on 18 February 1850, and the county seat in 1856 was Sonora. It lies at the southern end of the gold mining area, and the three other counties mentioned are neighboring areas to the west and north.

Grateful acknowledgment for valuable assistance is made to Carlo M. De Ferrari, Tuolumne County Historian, Sonora.

Columbia District
Daubney, Geo., Printer
Foster, G.D., Miner
Kincaid, S., Miner
Nale, N., Miner
Robinson, G.N., Carpenter
Toman, M.S., Miner

Sonora
Anderson, B.A., Brewer
Cooper, W.H., Livery Stable
Griffin, Wm., Clerk
Martenstein, J., Butcher
Martenstein, P., Butcher
McClary, Robt., Miner
Taylor, John, Butcher
Woodruff, M.W.H., Miner

Jamestown
Russell, C., Miner

Montezuma
Cartright, J., Miner
Clark, L.P., Ditchman [1]
Fail, G.W., Miner
Farrens, N.J., Miner
Maxson, E.R., Miner
Mott, A., Miner

Chinese Camp
Graham, M.R., Post-master
Meeher, J., Blacksmith

Shaw's Flat
Clark, W.A., Miner
Cubberly, Miner
Ellison, M., Miner
Hannah, A.G., Miner
Helt, H., Miner
Lucas, M., Miner
Milner, N., Justice of the Peace
Mitchell, G., Teamster
Robinson, J., Blacksmith
Vanarsdall, W.H., Miner
Warner, J., Miner

Springfield
Barrow, J., Blacksmith
Brasher, T.R., Miner
Chapman, J., Miner
Elliott, G.S., Miner
Hildebrand, A., Miner
Jewett, G.E., Miner

Melcher, Jno., Blacksmith
Sines, J., Miner

La Grange
Hanie, W.C., Deputy Sheriff
McGarvey, R., County Clerk
Turner, David, Miner

Murphy's Camp
Hunsdorff, J., Baker
Parsons, E., Miner

Loveland, W.R., Miner
Shaff, W., Miner
Stevenson, V., Miner
Stewart, T.B., Miner
Swank, P., Miner
Whitfield, J., Boot Maker

Gold Springs
Oliphant, —, Miner

Yankee Hill
Fleehart, W., Miner
Hunter, I.K., Miner
Jones, H.L., Miner
Mondary, J., Miner

Brown's Flat
Bales, W.M., Miner
Berringer, Jacob, Miner
Chase, J.W., Miner

Similair, Z.B., Grocer
Stuart, W.W., Miner
Vaughan, J.D., Soda Manufacturer

Douglass' Flat
Been, G.A., Miner

Empire Diggings
Griswell, R.M., Miner

NOTE: [1] A ditchman was employed to walk the lines of the hydraulic ditches serving the mines, check them for breakage and water stealing, and collect the fees for the water, which was sold at so much a ''miner's inch'' - the price usually being whatever the market would bear.

THE BLESSINGER FAMILY OF DUBOIS COUNTY

Excerpts from a longer family sketch written by Joan A. Fischer of Jasper, Indiana

John Blessinger was born in the town of Bensheim in Baden, Germany. In 1832 at the age of eighteen he came to America with his widowed mother and several brothers and sisters. The family had sold their possessions in Germany to acquire enough money for the trip across the Atlantic; after they had paid their passage money to the ship's owner they had only $1.25 left from their savings. The Blessinger family landed at Baltimore and then moved on to Pennsylvania. Since John was the oldest child, it was his responsibility to help support the family and he found employment in an iron mine. There was practically no safety equipment in mines at that time. Narrowly escaping death in an explosion that occured in the mine where he was working, he quit and traveled down the Ohio River in a flatboat to Troy, Indiana. From Troy he traveled to Evansville with the intention of purchasing land for farming in that vicinity but was advised by the Catholic priest that the Evansville area was wet and swampy and that Dubois County would be a better area to establish a farm and home because there the land was higher and better drained. Also, there had been an outbreak of fever in the Evansville area which had caused many deaths. John Blessinger accepted this advice and bought forty acres of land in Dubois County from the government at $1.25 per acre. This was in 1838; he had saved the purchase price from his earnings in the iron mine. Later on he purchased more acreage and cleared the land to raise a corn and navy bean crop. At this time farmers generally traded their farm produce for supplies at a general store. John traded the corn and beans he raised for clothing, flour, sugar, salt and other needed supplies.

During the fall and winter, John walked to and from Louisville to work in a meat-packing house. Hogs were butchered and the meat was cut and salted. This was the method of preserving meat, since there was no type of refrigeration available at that time. He earned $50 for approximately six weeks of labor. This money was used to pay taxes and to buy supplies.

In late October, 1845, John Blessinger and Katherine Schmitt were married in the log church in St. Joseph's parish at Jasper. Katherine had come from Germany at the age of fifteen with her parents. She worked as a maid for a wealthy family in Kentucky before her marriage. After their marriage they lived on a farm in Dubois County, close to Huntingburg, and were the parents of eleven children that lived to adulthood; one son, Frankie, died in infancy. After the death of this child another son was given the name of Frank.

John Blessinger died in 1891 and Katherine in 1898. They are both buried in the old cemetery of St. Joseph's parish in Jasper. John donated labor to the building of the present St. Joseph's Church and also donated one of the long logs for the 12 large pillars in the church.

Frank Blessinger, the second youngest son of John and Katherine Blessinger, was born in 1868. He attended the Rose Bank School in Bainbridge Township, Dubois County, and then became a rail splitter, making railroad ties for railroads in Kentucky. He always received his salary in gold coins. During the summer months, in partnership with his brothers, he operated a threshing machine for his Dubois County neighbors.

Frank married (1) Elizabeth Hopf, daughter of John and Margaret (Dick) Hopf; they were the parents of a son, Paul and one set of twins, Anna and Mary, and two other children, Benno and Margaret. Elizabeth died in August 1905 of typhoid fever, attributed to impure drinking water. Frank married (2) Josephine Schmidt on January 22, 1907, the daughter of John and Sophia (Wenzel) Schmidt. The Schmidt and Schmitt families were not related; John Schmidt had emigrated from Bavaria and lived in Louisville before settling on a farm in Dubois County. Frank and Josephine had four children: Tillie, Louise, Alfred and Lorene. Frank Blessinger was engaged in farming all his life.

Joan A. Fischer (author of article) is a daughter of Lorene, and granddaughter of Frank Blessinger.

BENTON COUNTY MARRIAGES, 1840-1858

Compiled by Mrs. Ruth M. Slevin from microfilm of Book 1 in Genealogy Division, Indiana State Library. Benton County was organized in 1840 out of Jasper County. The population in 1850 was only 1, 144.

Adsit, John P. — Gray, Hannah	12-19-1850
Adsit, Silas — Waldrup, Mahala, P.	2-10-1853
Abernethe, Samuel — Hickman, Mary Ann	3-29-1857
Ale, John — Liptrap, Rebecca Jane	10-29-1857
Allman, Isaac — Denton, Mary Ann	8-16-1854
Anderson, John C. — Campbell, Eliza A.	11-28-1856
Atkinson, Cephas — Burch (or Birch), Rachel	7-29-1852
Atkinson, Zimri — Buckley, Mary Jane	8-30-1857
Baker, Charles — Watters, Elizabeth C.	12-18-1856
Baker, Stephen Edward — McQueen, Margaret	3- 9-1852
Barnes, James W. — Scott, Opha Ann	5-21-1858
Baugh, Jonathan — Nolen, Ruth Ann	10- 1-1840
Besser, Frederick — St. John, Jane	7-16-1854
Binney, Samuel — Cole, Sarah Ann	9-30-1858
Blades, Franklin — Holton, Sarah Jane	9-29-1850
Blanchfill, George S. — McClure, Susan E.	8-13-1854
Blessing, Marcus — Ladd, Mary Ellen	3-25-1858
Blessing, Reuben — Burch, Mary Ann	12-30-1855
Bone, Joseph — Monroe, Nancy	6-22-1854
Bottsford, William W. — Robertson, Martha Ann	2- 9-1854
Bowen, Peyton — McClure, Serrilda	9- 7-1852
Brier, George D. — Hawkins, Elizabeth	7- 7-1855
Brier, Mark J. — Lain, Martha A.	7-22-1858
Brittinham, Samuel — Hallam, Martha	10-20-1853
Bromley, Edward M. — Pearce, Lucinda	2-28-1856
Brown, Isaac — Shafer, Caroline	11-13-1851
Brown, John — Wilson, Mrs. Sarah	3-16-1848
Buck, George W. — Erick, Jane	4-27-1858
Bunnell, Elijah — Robertson, Martha	8-27-1846
Burns, John — Conklin, Harriett	10-17-1854
Carnahan, Abraham P. — Benedict, Juliett	1-24-1858
Carney, Edmund — Miller, Julia Ann	7-24-1853
Carter, Andrew L. — Ladd, Lucinda	9-20-1855
Carter, Thomas — Jolly, Martha Jane	6-27-1846
Charlesworth, John — Hopkins, Hannah J.	8-30-1855
Cheadle, Martin Luther — Bannon, Jocasty	8-19-1852
Claig, Benjamin H. — Wood, Mrs. Elizabeth	6-15-1851
Clarke, William Henry — Knouse, Sarah	6-16-1852
Cochran, John H. — Johnston, Mary Magdalene	9-24-1848
Coffenberry, Benjamin Franklin — Oilar, Bethsheba	1-31-1842
Cole, Thomas — Gillespie, Minerva	9-18-1856
Cook, James W. — Lank, Susannah	4-11-1854
Courtney, Oron — Griffin, Elizabeth	8-26-1858
Courtney, William — Robertson, Nancy Ann	10- 3-1849
Cozad, James — Beales, Minerva	8-29-1855
Crab, Vinson — Sargent, Catharine	10-26-1856
Curl, Frank — Swift, Lucy	6-27-1858
Davis, Isaac M. — Franklin, Judah Ann	1-10-1858
Dawson, Noah J. — Denton, Esther	3-18-1858
Dehart, Strawder — Ford, Mercy	9-23-1858
Denton, Elijah — Miller, Mary Ann	11-11-1849
Downey, John — Harkrider, Polly	3-21-1857
Edmonson, Robert F. — Timmons, Mary D.	10- 2-1851
Evans, Joseph — Moore, Sarah	12- 3-1854
Everhart, Adam — Cozad, Catharine	12-18-1853
Fenton, Enoch — Crawford, Julia Ann	10-10-1849
Ferguson, Joseph M. — McConnell, Mary Jane	6- 2-1850
Finey, John A. — Lane, Amanda D.	7- 1-1847
Ford, Charles — Myers, Belinda	9- 9-1858
Ford, Mortimore — Cozad, Elizabeth	6-11-1853
Freeman, George W. — McIlvain, Abigail L.	2-22-1849
Freeman, William — Marvin, Elizabeth	11-24-1853
Funk, Henry B. — Myers, Mary Jane	2-26-1852
Gefney, Thomas — McCurtain, Lucinda	4- 2-1846
Gillespie, Stephen — Minnicks, Mrs. Elizabeth	7- 3-1858
Glass, John — Thomas, Letitia	3- 5-1857
Gray, Chancy M. — Charlesworth, Elizabeth	6-25-1857
Gray, John — Lewis, Hannah	4-20-1848
Gross, Morris — Lindsey, Lydia Jane	7-10-1856
Gwinn, Daniel S. — Lank, Phebe	2- 8-1853
Harmon, John — Staton, Mary Jane	3-31-1853
Hawkins, James — Sumner, Jane	8- 3-1858
Hawkins, John — Sheetz, Margaret Rebecca	11- 1-1849
Hawkins, William — Sheetz, Nancy	9-25-1850
Hawley, Luther D. — Sheetz, Hannah	5- 6-1858
Hazlett, Hugh — Graham, Margaret	12-15-1857
Hickman, Albert — Ale, Elizabeth	12-17-1854
Hilton, John — Garland, Margaret	6-20-1841
Hix, William — Liptrap, Lavina	7-30-1856
Hixson, Franklin — Hopper, Martha F.	11- 6-1853
Hoover, James — Logan, Elizabeth	10-23-1856
Hoover, Milton — Craft, Mary	11-13-1856
Hurd, Ansun — Cell, Amanda	6-16-1853
Jackson, Alexus M. — Williams, Margaret E.	4- 3-1855
Jaspers, Henry — Luken, Mary	2-18-1855
Jennings, Elnathan C. — Baugh, Nancy Jane	1-28-1858
Jennings, Marmaduke — Robertson, Elizabeth	10- 1-1840
Johnson, William R. — Finch, Margaret	6- 2-1842
Johnston, Peter — Vanhorn, Adaline	4- 4-1854
Jones, Tarpeley — Hopper, Mary C.	1- 7-1858
Kelly, John — Wood, Sarah Ann	9-29-1845
Keys, Isaac — Solomon, Lucinda	2-15-1854
Kincade, Francis M. — Markel, Isabella	10-29-1857
Kincade, James — Foster, Mrs. Finetta Jane	12-13-1853
Lacount, George W. — Pennywell, Narcissus	2-13-1852
Ladd, Thomas, Jr. — Hawkins, Jane	4-11-1858
Lane, William W. — Vanhorn, Caroline	5- 3-1852
Lewis, Isaac W. — McConnell, Lavicy	5-30-1850
Lewis, Thomas — McConnell, Elizabeth	2-15-1842
Liggett, Alexander — Sunderland, Mary Jane	2- 5-1852
Lister, John Calvin — Ross, Martha	6- 2-1853
Littler, Elijah — Adams, Louisa	9-15-1858
Littler, Elisha — Crosson, Margaret Jane	1- 7-1851
Loring, Thomas — Roberts, Elizabeth	4- 8-1858
McComb, Samuel — Curtis, Mary Ann	9-10-1857
McConnell, David — Blanchfill, Mrs. Sarah	10- 7-1852
McConnell, David J. — Howard, Mary Lavina	3-27-1851
McConnell, Hugh — Johnston, Margaret M.	4-20-1848
McConnell, Hugh — Jolly, Melissa M.	4-27-1854
McConnell, James A. — McIlvaine, Sarah	3- 2-1848
McConnell, Jasper N. — Wilson, Sally M.	11-17-1853
McConnell, John L. — Johnston, Elizabeth B.	8- 3-1848
McConnell, William B. — Howard, Frances Jane	4- 7-1846
McDade, John — Martin, Esther	4-16-1846
McDade, John — McConnell, Mrs. Margaret	11-16-1854
McDaniel, Jackson — Sargent, Nancy Ann	3-28-1852
McElheny, Andrew — Ford, Lydia	2-28-1856
McElheny, James — Hoddy, Mary E.	6-19-1856
McIlvain, Samuel — McConnell, Margaret Jane	11- 5-1846
McMillen, Sampson — Chancellor, Ann Fox	4-26-1857

Marvin, William — Johnston, Lovia N.	10- 9-1853	Smith, Emri A. — Cell, Judith	9-22-1851
Melvin, Noble A. — Ladd, Angeletta	2-22-1855	Smith, Thomas — Martin, Margaret	3- 8-1849
Mendenhall, Eli — Williams, Sarah	10- 8-1842	Stanley, Sims — Beard, Amanda	2- 5-1846
Merritt, Nathaniel P. — Chenowith, Eliza	6- 1-1851	Stedham, William — Ryan, Joanna	2-25-1858
Metsker, Abraham — O'Dell, Elizabeth	8-27-1845	Stow, Eben — Howard, Catharine E.	2-25-1851
Miller, James — Williams, Mary	12-30-1852	Sullivan, Timothy S. — Kerins, Mrs. Mary	4-15-1857
Miller, John — Rommell, Barbara	4-28-1855	Sumner, Nelson — Boswell, Elizabeth B.	11-17-1850
Miller, John Henry — Harper, Nancy Jane	12-26-1853	Sutton, Rinaldo — Denton, Virena Crayton	2-10-1848
Mills, James F. — Young, Martha L.	11-23-1852	Swank, John H. — Crawford, Miranda Jane	6- 7-1857
Mitchem, Westley — Frazier, Maria Elizabeth	9-16-1852	Swift, Alphonso — Curl, Susan Emiline	10-12-1856
Monroe, Milton L. — Odell, Margaret Jane	4-12-1855	Templeton, Isaac — Jennings, Mrs. Maria	1- 2-1849
Morgan, Henry C. — Liptrap, Mary Elizabeth	4- 5-1849	Templeton, William J. — Jennings, Melissa Ann	9-14-1851
Morrison, Archibald — Groom, Tamson	3-21-1843	Terwilliger, James Henry — Griffin, Mary	9-17-1845
Myres, John — Noles, Sarah	9- 5-1844	Thompson, Evan E. — Stow, Mary Ann	5-11-1854
Nolen, Richard N. T. — Coffelt, Elizabeth	3-23-1854	Thompson, Joseph — McConnell, Elizabeth	2-26-1845
Nolen, William James — Lank, Sinderilla	5- 4-1854	Timmons, Thomas — Coffett, Leannah	9-22-1850
Norman, John — Charlesworth, Elizabeth	9- 1-1858	Umpstead, Starks — Edmondson, Sarah Jane	7-29-1852
Norris, Bradford Q. — Griffee, Elizabeth	3-18-1857	Vance, Robert A. — Hopper, Elizabeth Ann	11-30-1854
Odell, James R. — Monroe, Mary Ann	11-16-1854	Vanhorn, Henry — Rose, Luiza	12-14-1843
Odell, James S. — Monroe, Sarah Ellen	1-12-1854	Wattles, Charles — Littler, Leah	2- 6-1848
Odle, Andrew C. — Ross, Mary Jane	11- 8-1856	Westover, Hiram — Gibson, Elizabeth	5- 8-1856
Oliver, John S. — Crawford, Martha Jane	4-14-1852	Whinnery, Allen — Atkinson, Mary	1-31-1858
Oungst, William G. — Mills, Mary	10-23-1850	Whitakker, John — Smith, Sarah	9-15-1844
Parker, Henry C. — Boswell, Harriett Maria	1- 9-1855	White, Amos — Earhart, Mary	8- 2-1840
Parker, James F. — Justus, Rachel N.	8-25-1842	Whitesel, James — Cheney, Synthia Ann	9-23-1857
Prechel, Christopher — Wolfer, Dola	8-21-1856	Whitmore, Martin — Dehart, Elizabeth	2-16-1854
Retner, James — McClure, Elizabeth	3-25-1858	Wilkinson, William — Johnston, Nancy P.	8-10-1848
Robertson, Charles — Mitchell, Eliza Ann	2-25-1841	Williams, Adison — Martin, Catharine	9-10-1846
Robertson, James E. — Alexander, Jane	2- 1-1842	Williams, D. McArthur — Boswell, Elisabeth	3-27-1853
Robertson, Samuel — Alexander, Sabria	2-25-1841	Wilson, Moses A. — Martin, Mrs. Armintha	lic. 8-17-1848
Ross, Daniel — Cozad, Minerva L.	8-22-1858	Wilson, Nathan — Howell, Aseneth M.	8- 4-1853
Runner, Isaac — Brake, Charlotte	1-25-1855	Wilson, Sanford H. — Cell, Martha Jane	lic. 2-22-1854
Ryon, John — Philips, Emiline	9-21-1856	Woglan, Frederick E. O. — Laforce, Mary	8- 5-1857
Sargent, Simeon — Calahan, Dorinda	3-26-1857	Wood, Bartlet Y. — Howard, Martha Jane	8-18-1850
Scovill, Elbert A. — Thomas, Mary Ann	5-12-1850	Wray, William — Carson, Sarah Jane	lic. 11- 3-1845
Shambaugh, George — Shoemaker, Louisa	1- 6-1848	Wray, Zebulon M. — Arehart, Mary Ann	3-26-1848
Sheetz, John R. — Templeton, Lucy	11-28-1852	Wright, Elias M. — Ford, Martha	6- 8-1851
Slagal, Alcana — Griffin, Mary	8-26-1858	Wright, Ezdail — Hopkins, Mary	8-26-1855
Smiley, James — Littler, Tabitha	12- 6-1849	Wylie, James — Davis, Mary	5-27-1847

CLARK COUNTY ESTRAY BOOK, 1801-1817

Estray books were kept in each county to record the finding of stray animals. The early settlers had no fences in which to confine their hogs, sheep, cattle, and horses so it was necessary for each family to have particular markings for their animals and these marks were made a matter of record. Persons taking up stray animals were required to advertise the same in their neighborhood and if not claimed they were to make oath before a justice of the peace that an animal with certain markings had been taken up; the justice then issued a warrant for three disinterested householders to appraise the same. The returns made by the appraisers were entered in an estray book kept by each justice and a copy of the report was transmitted to the clerk of the county court who also entered it in a county estray book. Similar provisions were made regarding stray boats that were found.

Since Clark County was the second oldest county to be organized in Indiana Territory, its estray book is especially valuable. The boundaries of the county at the time of its formation in 1801 included all the area east of the Blue River and the East Fork of White River to the boundary line between the Indiana and Northwest territories. From this area Harrison County was formed in 1808, Jefferson in 1811, Washington in 1814, and Jackson in 1816. In the beginning Clark County had three townships: Clarksville, Springville, and Spring Hill; Bethlehem, Harrison, Madison and Silver Creek townships were organized as settlements increased.

A microfilm copy of the Clark County Estray Book is in the Genealogy Division, Indiana State Library. The names of the following individuals were noted in the book as finders of live stock or boats, appraisers of the same, as recording their marks, as justices of the peace, or in some miscellaneous record, including one marriage. The dates are those of the first appearance of the name. The residence of the individuals is included whenever it was given, even though it may not have been noted on the first appearance of the name.

Abbet, James, Spring Hill Twp.	5-30-1810
Abbet, James, Jr., on 14 Mile Cr.	10-20-1816
Abbott, Jonson	11- 5-1814
Adams, John	1- 7-1815
Adams, Samuel, Living on Big R., Spring Hill Twp.	11-15-1813
Adkins (Akin), Disamus (?)	12-10-1816
Akin, Joseph	1-30-1816
Akin (Eakin), William	1-11-1809
Aldridge, Christopher	2- 8-1812
Allen, Moses, on Bull Cr.	11-10-1814
Allen, Thomas	11-29-1813
Allgood, Prestly, Silver Cr. Twp.	12-30-1814
Allhands, Jacob, on Owens Cr.	2-19-1814
Allhands, John	11-28-1815
Alpha, Peryagrin (?)	11-18-1816
Anderson, Graham	1-17-1809
Anderson, James	1- 3-1811
Anderson, John & Noah	5- 7-1810
Anderson, Thomas	2- 5-1815
Apple, John	6- 6-1808
Applegate, Aaron	11-24-1810
Applegate, Hezekiah	12-18-1810
Applegate, John	6- 4-1803
Applegate, Samuel & Thomas	2- 2-1813
Arbuckle, James	12-16-1809
Armstrong, Thomas, on 14 Mile Cr.	2-13-1813
Arnold, Ephraim, Justice of the Peace	1808
Ashebrannah, Henry	12- 7-1815
Aston, John	1- -1813
Aston (Asten), Richard	9-11-1809
Bailey, James	3-30-1812
Ballard, John	12-11-1816
Barickman, Frederick	3-13-1812
Barnaby, John	1-13-1810
Barnes, David, Living 14 Mile Cr., near Capt. Gulick's carding machine	11-16-1814
Barnes, John	3- 6-1815
Beabout, Jacob	12-26-1814
Beargard (or Boangard), Philip	1-21-1815
Beckett, William A.	1- 3-1811
Beedle, Luther	8-17-1813
Beeler, George, Indentured to Daniel Graham by his father, Thomas Beeler	3- 9-1812
Beeman, Andrew	4- 5-1809
Beeman, Stephen	5- 1-1809
Beggs, George	7- 3-1813
Beggs, James, In Spring Hill Twp., nr Armstrong's Sta.	6-10-1811
Beggs, John, justice of peace	1809
Belding, Oliver	11- 9-1815
Belpha, Jeremiah	2-12-1808
Berkshire (Barkshire), Henry	7- 5-1808
Bigger, David	12-12-1810
Bigger, James	2- 8-1810
Biggs, John	1-20-1809
Biggs, Robert	1- 8-1811
Bishop, Philip	2-25-1812

Blackburn, John	5-15-1813
Blair (Blare), John	12- 6-1811
Blan, James and William	5- 3-1810
Bland, Abel, Living nr Bethlehem in 1815	2-27-1810
Bland, John	12- 8-1812
Bland, Thomas, Living T. 1, R. 9	10-13-1810
Blankenship, Lewis	1-25-1808
Blizzard, John	10-21-1809
B[l]ume, Elexander	1-24-1812
Blunt, Samuel, in Cain settlement	4-21-1809
Boiles, Charles, on Indian Cr.	12-12-1814
Bollbe (Bolesby ?), Enos (?)	2-29-1816
Booker, Odon, on Bull Cr.	11- 8-1814
Borden, Stephen	1-25-1817
Boston, Benjamin	6- 4-1807
Bottorff, Andrew	10- 6-1815
Bottorff, John, Receives deed for lot in Charlestown	5- 9-1812
Bower, Adam	2-11-1813
Bower, Joseph	2-25-1812
Bower, Levy	1-24-1817
Bowl, John	1-27-1817
Bowland, John	12-13-1815
Bowman, Aaron	5- 1-1809
Bowman, John	3-29-1810
Bowman, Leonard	12- 8-1812
Bowman, Samuel	1-14-1815
Bowyer, Levi	2-12-1810
Boyer, Christopher	12-29-1810
Boyer, Henry	1-25-1814
Boyer, John, Living T. 1, R, 10	5- 5-1810
Boyer, Philip	1-25-1814
Bradford, William, On Sinking Fork of Silver Cr.	11-16-1803
Bratton, George W.	11- 9-1814
Brenton, William	4-13-1812
Brewer, Henry	1-12-1812
Bridgewater, Chrisley (?) May be same as Christian	2-25-1812
Bridgewater, Christian	5-17-1815
Bridgwater, Elias	12-29-1814
Brightman, Walter, On Ohio R., 2 mi below mouth of Middle Cr.	2-12-1808
Brookart, Jacob	11-23-1816
Brown, Elisha	1- -1817
Brown, James, justice of peace	3-30-1810
Browne, William	5- 7-1810
Bullock, Charles	1-22-1811
Burge, Isaac	10-25-1814
Burge, James	12-15-1809
Burge, John	1- 8-1817
Burk, Lewis (same as Lucas?)	11- 5-1812
Burk, Lucas, Springville Twp.	11-21-1814
Burnett, Moses	11-20-1812
Burnett, Thomas	12- 8-1812
Butler, Jesse	4-16-1808
Cameron, Robert	1- 6-1814
Campbell, John	9-12-1817

Car, Greer, in Madison Twp. On Saluda Cr., nr Ohio River — 1-20-1810

Carlisle, Thomas, on Camp Cr. — 3-21-1811

Cairns (Carns), John, on Indian Cr. — 12-12-1814

Cairns (Carns), Robert — 12-26-1814

Carns, Joseph — 3- 7-1816

Carr, Elisha — 1- 3-1810

Carr, Jonathan — 4-24-1813

Carr, Thomas — 2- 4-1812

Carr, Thomas G. — 5-14-1810

Carr, William — 4- 6-1812

Carril, Edward — 11-10-1814

Carson, Greze (?) — 9-11-1809

Carson, Jonathan — 12-12-1814

Carson, William — 2- 9-1813

Cassady, George — 12-25-1815

Cater (Ater?), Peter — 2-25-1812

Chambers, James — 5- 7-1810

Chambers, John — 1-27-1809

Chanery, Edward — 12- 6-1811

Chappel (Chapple), Thomas — 1- 8-1814

Chew, John, on Elk Run — 1-26-1816

Chunn, John Thomas, Justice of peace — 1810

Clark, Esliten (?) — 5-17-1815

Clark, James — 1-11-1814

Clark, John — 9-23-1816

Clark, Joshua — 7-16-1817

Clendennon, Elizabeth — 12-14-1814

Cleveland, Ab _____ — 11-22-1816

Clifton, Elias — 11- 6-1817

Coble, John, in Springville Twp. — 1-17-1811

Coble, John — 9-28-1811

Collings, Richard — 1-14-1811

Collings, Spencer — 11-24-1807

Collings, Spencer, Jr. — 9-30-1817

Collings, William E. — 2-27-1812

Collings, Zebulon — 1-15-1812

Collins, Harris — 1- 7-1815

Collins, Kaney — 10-27-1815

Collins, William — 1- 7-1815

Combs, Benjamin, On Ohio R. at upper end of Clark Co. — 11-18-1808

Combs, William — 9-28-1811

Comer, Thomas — 12-23-1811

Common, John — 11- 9-1815

Conner, John — 3-30-1813

Conner, Lewis, on Indian-Kentuck — 3- 9-1810

Cooke, Moses — 1-15-1812

Coombs, Jacob — 12- 4-1814

Coombs, Joel — 2- 3-1813

Coombs, John — 1-27-1813

Coombs, Joseph — 12-20-1814

Coons, Charles, in Springville Twp. — 12-17-1814

Cooper, Isaiah — 8-10-1812

Cooper, James, Living on Camp Cr. 1 mi from Ogle's Mill — 11- 8-1816

Copple, Jacob and Thomas living on Camp Cr. — 1-27-1812

Copple, John — 1-27-1812

Cornett, William, nr Woods' ferry — 1-27-1813

Corson, Henry — 11-29-1811

Covert, Daniel and Bargon — 3-19-1817

Covert, John — 11-30-1809

Cowan, John, in Charlestown — 11- 9-1814

Cox, Daniel — 12-10-1814

Cox. Phineas and Samuel — 12-15-1816

Crafford, James — 3-21-1815

Crenmon (Crenmore ?), John, Living in Clarksville Twp. — 3-14-1812

Crist (Christ), Nicholas — 11- 7-1815

Crocket, John — 1-24-1812

Crown, Jacob (same as Crum?) — 1- -1815

Crum, Jacob — 11- 5-1811

Crum, John, on Owens Cr. — 2-13-1809

Crum, John, Jr., in Spring Hill Twp. — 2-28-1813

Crum, Mathias — 1-20-1812

Cunningham, Aaron — 4-18-1812

Cunningham, James — 12- 2-1815

Cunningham, Joseph, in Silver Cr. Twp. — 12- 4-1816

Cunningham, William — 12-18-1816

Cunningham, Robert — 11-24-1815

Curry, James — 1-20-1814

Dailey, Charles — 1-17-1811

Dailey (Dayley), Philip — 2-22-1811

Damron, Robert — 1-18-1815

Davis, James — 3- 6-1807

Davis, Joseph — 12-19-1812

Davis, Levy — 3- 3-1815

Davis, Samuel R. — 12- 7-1815

Davis, Sila H. — 12-20-1815

Davis, Thomas, nr mouth of Silver Cr. — 3-30-1810

Deatz (Deets), John, Sr. — 1-17-1811

Deatz, John, Jr. — 1-27-1815

Dean, David, on Camp Cr. R. 9, T. 1 — 1-30-1809

Deen, Daniel — 1-27-1810

Den (Deen ?), Robert — 11-25-1816

Denning, Anthony — 12-26-1814

Denslow, Chapman — 1-30-1813

Devour (Devore), Samuel — 1-27-1812

Detzler, Peter — 12- 7-1815

Douthitt, John — 7- 3-1809

Dowden, Thomas and Zephaniah — 10-21-1809

Downs, Thomas, Judge — 1801

Drummond, James — 12-30-1809

Drummond, John — 6- 1-1811

Dumont (or Dement), George — 1-13-1810

Dun, Alexander — 2-27-1812

Dunn, Williamson, in Madison Twp. — 1- 6-1810

Earl (?), Jacob — 7- 3-1809

Easton, John — 3- 2-1815

Edwards, David — 1-23-1818

Egirald (?), Jacob — 1-29-1810

Elliott, Absalom and John — 1-16-1817

Ellis, William — 1-12-1816

Elwood, James — 11-29-1814

Emmons, Jonathan — 9-23-1816

English, see Inglish

Eppler, Abraham, animal taken up 2 miles from Woods' ferry on Ohio R. — 8-23-1808

Etter (or Etten), Peter — 7- 3-1809

Estill, Isaac — 12- 2-1816

Esom, Barrack — 12-26-1812

Esom (Esum), Elisha — 12-25-1813

Evans, Moses — 11-30-1812

Evans, Robert, on Bull Cr., Spring Hill Twp., in in Clark's Grant — 2-23-1809

Evans, William, nr mouth 14 Mile Cr. — 9-30-1810

Fait, Andrew received deed for lot in Jeffersonville — 6-16-1812

Fannin, David, Justice of Peace — 1813

Farris, David	1-16-1813
Ferguson, James	3-19-1812
Ferguson, John	11-24-1807
Ferguson, William	7- 4-1807
Fifer, Christopher	3-29-1815
Findley, Abel	1- 3-1810
Findley, Alexander	12-20-1813
Findley, John	12-26-1814
Fipes (or Tipps?), Aaron Living on	12-26-1813 [1812]
Elk Run, Silver Cr. Twp.	1817
Fisher, Frederick	9-11-1809
Fislar, Jesse	12-26-1815
Fislar, John, Sr., on Owens Cr.	1- 6-1810
Fislar, John, Jr. of Bethlehem	1- -1817
Flanagan, Elijah On Silver Cr., 1 mile from Hogland's mill	1- 8-1814
Flanagan, Richard Living near Hogland's mill	3-16-1812
Flouven (Flower?), Thomas	3-31-1815
Floyd, Davis	12-31-1801
Foland, James	1-11-1815
Forbes, Ebenezer	1- -1816
Ford, Lemuel and Thomas	11-20-1816
Foredyce, James	2-26-1813
Fouts, David	6- 6-1808
Fouts, Jacob	10-26-1809
Fouts, Jacob, Jr.	9- -1808
Fouts, Lewis	12-20-1808
Froman, John, Henry (or John Henry), and Paul	11-14-1810
Fry, George	6-17-1817
Fuller, Salmon, justice of peace	1811
Gallen (?), Charles	12-26-1812
Garner, Wyalt	10-28-1815
Gassaway, Nicholas on 14 Mile Cr., Spring Hill Twp.	1-11-1811
Geabriel (Gabriel?), Nathaniel	1-11-1815
Gelwick, Andrew	3-29-1810
Gibbense, James, in Springville Twp.	12-20-1811
Gibbons, Thomas	2-27-1810
Gibson, Burwell on Muddy Fork of Silver Cr.	3-11-1812
Gibson, John, Judge	1802
Gilbreath, Samuel	2- 7-1812
Giltner, Jacob	12-25-1809
Giltner, John	2-11-1817
Giltner, Michael on Camp Cr., Bethlehem Twp.	12- 2-1816
Glass, David	11- 8-1814
Glynn, Joseph H.	1- 1-1812
Goben, John, Sr. and Jr.	2- 9-1815
Goben, William, Sr. and Jr. Living on 14 Mile Cr.	11-26-1814
Goodman, George Living near mouth of Bull Cr.	1-14-1815
Goodman, Thomas	1-14-1813
Goodwin, Thomas, on Owens Cr.	12- 4-1814
Goodwin, William, on Pleasant Run	8- 3-1813
Goodwin, Willis W.	5- 1-1809
Gore, Frederick	1-14-1811
Graham, Daniel, George Beeler indentured to	3- 9-1812
Gray, Daniel	1-31-1815
Gray, David	12-31-1814
Gray, John	1-22-1814
Green, Elisha	12-16-1814
Green, Elijah	11-12-1814
Green, Joseph	12-17-1814
Greer, Robert	1-25-1808
Griffin, David	3-17-1809
Griffin, Ralph	11-18-1808
Griffith, William N.	4-24-1813
Grismore, Jacob	11- 8-1814

Grost, (Gross?) David Living on Elk Run, Silver Creek Twp.	1-29-1817
Groves, George	5- 1-1809
Guleck, William	11-25-1816
Guyer (Guier), Aaron	1813
Guyer (Guier), Jesse	12-17-1812
Hall, Isaac	2-17-1809
Hamilton, William	1-24-1814
Hanchier (?), John	12-25-1809
Handlin, James on 14 Mile Cr. near Capt. Gulick's carding machine	1- 4-1815
Handlon, Darby	12- 1-1815
Harmon, John	11- 9-1811
Harrison, Christopher	2-17-1809
Harrison, Nicholas, justice of peace	1807
Harrod, John	2-20-1813
Harrod, William	1-15-1814
Hart, Philip	5- 1-1809
Hartley, Daniel	10- 5-1814
Haun, Henry	3- 5-1814
Hawkings, Thomas, Bethlehem Twp.	11- 7-1814
Hay, John, justice of peace	11- 6-1809
Hay, Samuel	12-25-1809
Heath, William, on 14 Mile Cr.	1-22-1814
Heath, William	1815
Henderson, James	6- 1-1810
Henderson, John, Madison Twp.	12- 1-1814
Henley (Hendley), Jesse	4- 5-1809
Hensley, George living on Ohio R., 2 mi from Urbandus (?) ferry	11-21-1808
Hensley, Samuel	3- 7-1808
Hester, Matthias	1-29-1810
Henthorn, Abraham	9-21-1816
Henthorn, Robert	11- 6-1816
Hickman, Jacob	11-24-1815
Hickman, John	6- 4-1807
Hickman, Nicodemus	5-19-1812
Hikes, Jacob	4-22-1809
Hiler (Hyler), William	12-21-1812
Hilton, John, justice of peace	1814
Hobson, Milburn	2-13-1816
Hoke, George	1- 9-1813
Hoke, Henry	2- 7-1812
Holeman, Isaac	1- 2-1810
Holmes, Fergus	4- 6-1812
Holmes, William P.	1-12-1816
Holt, Jacob S.	2- 6-1813
Hood, John, on Ohio R. nearly opposite Westpoint	12-18-1816
Hooker, Odon	11-10-1814
Hopkins, Robert 11-13-1815	
Hoten, Joel	2- 6-1813
Hougland, James	11-13-1815
Hougland, Moses, on Silver Cr.	2-13-1812
Hougland, Spencer	6-13-1816
House, Andrew	2-23-1809
Houston, Leonard	5-30-1810
Howard, Jonas	9-14-1809
Howard, Joseph	12- 8-1812
Huckleberry, David	3- 5-1810
Huckleberry, Henry	1-27-1815
Huckleberry, John	2-22-1811
Huckleberry, Martin	9-10-1810
Huckleberry, Peter	4-13-1810
Hudson, Dan[ie]l	4-26-1810

Huff, Jesse	2-23-1809
Huff, John	11- -1814
Huffman, Catharine	12-10-1814
Huston, Samuel	1-22-1813
Hutchinson, Thomas	4-13-1812
Hutson, Daniel Living in Cane settlement	12- 7-1811
Inglish, Leon (or Levin)	1-14-1815
Irwin, David	2-22-1811
Izzard, William	3- 1-1813
Jackson, Daniel	1-21-1815
Jacison, John, on Silver Cr.	3-16-1812
Jackson, Robert	9-26-1812
Jackson, William Living on Silver Cr. near Hoglan's mill	11- 9-1811
Jacobs, Edward G.	10-28-1809
Jacobs, Ely	12-17-1814
Jacobs, Jeremiah, Sr.	1-20-1809
Jacobs, John D.	11-23-1809
Jacobs, Joseph, justice of peace	1817
Jacobs, Thomas	5-22-1809
James, William	7- 3-1809
Jamison, Neeh (Nehemiah ?)	11-24-1810
Jenkins, Bartholomew, on Elk Run	1-26-1816
Jenkins, Ezekiel	1- 5-1811
Jennings, Elnathan	11- 5-1814
Johnson, Baley May be same as Balas Johnston	12-17-1814
Johnson, Charles	4- 4-1808
Johnson, Daniel	3- 2-1815
Johnson, Elias	3-25-1815
Johnson, George	3- 2-1812
Johnson, John	11-29-1811
Johnson, Jonathan	3- 2-1815
Johnson, Joseph	5-17-1815
Johnston, Balas	12-15-1808
Johnston (Johnson), Charles On headwaters of 14 Mile Cr. near falling timber	11-20-1810
Johnston (Johnson), Daniel	11- 6-1813
Johnston (Johnson), George	11-30-1809
Jones, James	10-14-1812
Keene, Henry	5- 7-1810
Keller, Adam	3-31-1815
Kelley, David	12-26-1812 [1813]
Kelly, Hugh and Joseph	2-26-1816
Kelly, John	1- 1-1810
Kelly, Nathan	6- 3-1817
Kelly, William, in R10, T1	12-15-1808
Kemp, Reuben	8- 5-1817
Kerns, John	12-16-1816
Keynon, William	12-18-1816
Killian, Jacob	11-25-1816
Kimberland, Abraham	2-22-1812
Kimberland, Daniel	1-19-1809
Kimberland, Isaac On Muscatatuck R., Springville Twp., 1 mile from Abraham Kimberland	12- 6-1814
Kimble, Isaac	3-21-1815
Lamaster, James	1-19-1809
Lamb, Isaac	12-12-1814
Lamb, Thomas On Indian Cr. in Lamb settlement	12- 6-1813
Landon, see London	
Lappolet (Lafollet ?), Robert	2-12-1808

Leeds (?), Charles Gives deed to lot in Jeffersonville	6-16-1812
Lemon, William	2-25-1812
Levor, John	9-16-1811
Lewis, Jacob	3-27-1811
Lewis, Jonathan	1-29-1813
Lewis, Richard	2- 5-1813
Lewis, Samuel	1- 2-1810
Lewis, William	6- 1-1810
Lewisdon (?), Richard	2-12-1815
Lindsey, Joshua	5-18-1812
Lingan, Joseph A.	1-27-1812
Little (Littell), Abraham, Jr.	1-31-1809
Little (Littell), Absalom	4- 7-1807
Little, Amos	1-20-1809
Little (Littell), John T.	2-17-1812
Lockhart, Enoch	1-23-1813
Lockhart (Lockhard), William, in R.9, T.1	5- 5-1810
London (Landon), Charles living in Silver Cr. Twp.	5-19-1812
London (Landon), Thomas On Saluda Cr. near Ohio R., Madison Twp.	3- 1-1810
Long, Abraham living Swartz settlement on White R.	11-30-1809
Long, Anderson	12-12-1814
Long, Anthony and Andrew	11-12-1814
Long, Elisha	1- 9-1816
Long, George	3-11-1815
Lowden, Thomas	2-12-1810
Lutz, David	5- 2-1812
Lynn, Joseph	7-29-1814
McBride, John	3-14-1812
McCafferty, living on Muddy Fork of Silver Creek	1-27-1810
McCalla, Hugh	1- 2-1808
McCallen, Hays	9-15-1808
McCampbell, James, justice of peace	12-18-1810
McCarty, Enoch	11-14-1810
McCarty, Johathan, living on Indian-Kentuck Cr.	3- 9-1810
McCauley, William, Jr.	2-20-1813
McClain, Barnard, living on Crooked Cr. near Ohio River	4-10-1809
McClelland, William	11-30-1809
McClintick, Samuel	6-10-1809
McClure, Zechariah	3- 7-1816
McConnel, John	1- -1813
McConnell, Walter	11-10-1815
McCombs, William	12-26-1815
McCormack, Joshua	6-10-1811
McCoy, James, living on muddy Fork of Silver Cr.	1-10-1810
McCoy, John	1-10-1810
McCullough, James B.	2- 8-1810
McDonald, James	1-19-1811
McDonald, Peter	3- 5-1810
McGuire, Elizabeth, on Elk Run	1-20-1816
McGuire, Francis, deeds land	8-15-1812
McKinley, Samuel	2-12-1810
MacKinley, Thomas, living on Muddy Fork of Silver Cr.	10-25-1816
McKinney, John	11- 1-1815
McNaught, John, near Springville	2-15-1813
McNaught, Thomas	2-15-1813
McNew, Jeremiah, in Springhill Twp.	1- 8-1813

McNew, Richard, in Spring Hill Twp.	2- 7-1812
McQuillin, John	1- 4-1817
McTagert, James	3-30-1812
McWilliams, William, justice of peace	1813
Mainon (?), John	12-30-1816
Malott, Joseph	2-22-1811
Marrs, James	1-19-1815
Mart (?), Philip, on Pleasant Run	1-18-1802
Mathes, Robert	12-18-1816
Mathews, Robert, living near mouth of Camp Cr.	1-18-1815
Matthews, Charles	11-20-1802
Maxwell, John	1- 6-1810
May, George	1-12-1812
Mearmart (?), Joshua	2-13-1809
Meredith, W. P.	3-30-1812
Metts, Peter	11-25-1814
Michel, William	10- -1815
Miller, Christley	10-27-1815
Miller, David in Lamb settlement on Indian Cr.	11-26-1813
Miller, John	4-19-1810
Mires, Isaac	1-12-1815
Mitchell, Andrew	1-22-1811
Mitchell, William, living near Armstrong's Sta.	12-17-1812
Monrow (Monroe), Michael	1- 6-1810
Montgomery, Alexander, living R. 9, T. 1, New Purchase	12-28-1808
Montgomery, John	12-15-1813
Montgomery, William, on 14 Mile Cr.	6-17-1809
Mooney, Nathaniel	12-23-1815
Mooney, William	11-26-1812
Moony, James	1-24-1812
Moore, James B.	1-23-1818
Moore, Levy, living in Pigeon Roost	2-11-1814
Morgan, William	3-25-1814
Morris, Alexander, near Hogland's mill	1-20-1809
Morris, Jefferson D.	3-11-1815
Morris, John	3- 6-1815
Morrison, Absolom B.	1-20-1816
Mosley, Richard	2- 2-1809
Myner (?), George	5- 5-1807
Nay, Jacob	9- 2-1809
Naylor, John	3-30-1812
Needham, Joseph	11-28-1815
Neeld, William	2- 1-1809
Neil, Archibald	1-13-1813
Neker, Dorrell	12- 8-1812
Newland, George	5- 5-1807
Newland, Joel	6-15-1816
Newland, John, Sr.	8-15-1811
Newland, John H.	10-28-1815
Newman, Caleb	7- 3-1809
Nicelas (?), John, nr Charlestown	11- 6-1809
Nugent, Bennet	12-28-1814
Nugent, David	1-29-1816
Nugent (Newgent), John	3- 9-1814
Nugent, Levi A.	4-18-1816
Ogle, John, in Spring Hill Twp.	9-24-1812
O'Kaupman (?), James	12-20-1811
Owens, David, Jr., married to Rebeckah Goben	1-22-1812
Owens, David, Jr.	1-22-1812
Owens, David, married to Rebeckah Goben	5-13-1813
Owens, James, leases lot in Clarksville	5-25-1812
Owens, John	1-17-1809

Packwood, Samuel	1-20-1817
Pantrick, William	3-20-1803
Parker, Absalom	2-11-1812
Parker, Alexander	12-23-1815
Parkey, Christian	12-29-1811
Parkey, Samuel	11- 5-1811
Parks, John	1-24-1815
Parks, Matthew	1-17-1812
Finds animal on road between Charlestown & Royse's Lick	
Paron, Aaron, living 1 mile from Henley's mill nr. line of Clark's Grant	12-30-1816
Parvin, John, justic of peace	1811
Parvin, Mary	11-18-1811
Parvin, Thomas L. (or S.)	10-18-1811
Parvin, William	3-21-1812
Passwaters, Zael	10-20-1815
Paton, Richard	2-5-1811 [1812]
Patrick, William	6- 8-1809
Patterson, Robert, on Camp Cr.	12-28-1811
Patterson, Samuel	1-20-1813
Pattor (Pattose ?), Andrew	10- -1815
Payne (Paine), Jeremiah	1-12-1812
Pearceall, John	5-27-1809
Peck, Adam	1-26-1816
Pennington, Dennis, justice of peace	1808
Perdue, Jesse, Spring Hill Twp.	6-19-1813
Perry, William	3- 7-1812
Person, Joseph	2-26-1816
Pettit, John, Living on Ohio R. at mouth of Bull Cr.	3-21-1812
Pettyjohn, William	12-15-1813
Peyton, Daniel	1-19-1815
Peyton, Micajah	1-16-1815
Piersal, Jacob	1- -1815
Pile, Richard	2- 2-1809
Pile, William	12-22-1812
Pinison, Benjamin	11-22-1816
Pinny, John	3- 6-1815
Pittman, John	1-22-1814
Pittman, William L.	5-27-1816
Plasket, Robert L., on Owens Cr., Spring Hill Twp.	2-13-1809
Plasket, Samuel, on Owens Cr. near Armstrong's Sta.	12-29-1811
Poindexter, Gabriel	11-12-1814
Pool, Ephraim, in Spring Hill Twp.	8-17-1815
Pool, Joseph, on 14 Mile Cr., in Clark's Grant	2- 2-1811
Pope, Gaser	11-22-1816
Porter, Forest (?)	8-27-1814
Pound, Joseph	1-16-1813
Prather, Basel	1-29-1810
Prather, Basel R.	6-10-1809
Prather, John	5-27-1809
Prather, Walter	6- 8-1809
Prather, Loyd	5- 9-1815
Prather, William	6- 4-1803
Prewet (Prewitt), Archibald, on Camp Cr.	12-28-1811
Provine, William	3- 4-1815
Pursil, William	8-27-1814
Ramsey, James, Springville, Twp.	11- 2-1811
Raney, Robert	12-18-1816
Rannels, Bowman, Springville Twp.	1- 9-1816
Ranney, Stephen	3- 2-1816
Rayment, Timothy	10-14-1812
Recoesin (?), Jabez	11-20-1816

Redman, Reason	1-20-1809	Simmons, John	1- 1-1812
Redus (?), George	12-25-1812	Sivers, Nathan	2-12-1815
Reed, George	11-16-1813	Skelton, John	2- 4-1812
Reed, John, Sr.	1-15-1817	Sleed, Charles	4-12-1815
Reed, William	12-30-1809	Slider, Richard	7- 5-1808
Reese (Reace), Joseph	11-20-1810	Smallwood, David	12-28-1810
Reilly, John	1-14-1813	Smith, John	9- -1808
Restine, Henry	3-13-1809	Smith, John W.	1-21-1815
Reynolds, Samuel	5-15-1817	Smith, Thomas	1-10-1810
Richards, Alexander	3-11-1815	Smith, William	4-16-1808
Richardson, Dan	11- 4-1815	Smock, Jacob	1-27-1809
Richy, John	1-18-1815	Smock, Peter	12-16-1809
Ricketts, Rezin	1- 3-1811	Smock, Samuel	4- 4-1808
Rider, George	3- 5-1814	Sotherlin, James	1- 4-1815
Ridge, Samuel, on 14 Mile Cr.	3- 2-1812	Spangler, David	1-20-1812
Ritchey, James	4-13-1812	Sparks, Baxter	2-25-1808
Roads, Jacob	12-28-1808	Sparks, Orson, on Muscatatuck R.	11-10-1816
Robb, James, on Ohio R., 16 mi. below mouth of Kentucky R.	3- 7-1808	Sparks, William	11-18-1808
		Sparling, George	1-11-1814
Robbins (Robeans), Jacob	2- 2-1811	Spear, Andrew & Samuel	3- 6-1813
Robbins, Phillimon	8-17-1815	Spear, Richard	11-23-1813
Roberson, Joseph, on 14 Mile Cr. near Capt. Gulick's carding machine	4- 9-1815	Speer (?), Daniel	5-14-1810
		Sperry, Jose	12-27-1815
Roberts, Sevestel	9-24-1812	Springer, Charles	3-30-1816
Robertson, Eli & Hezekiah	3-27-1811	Sproat, Benjamin & John	12-18-1812
Robertson, Jeremiah & Nathan	12- 7-1811	Sprowl, John	12- 5-1812
Robertson, Middleton & Zephaniah	11-25-1809	Stacey, Catherine	1-22-1814
Robertson, Robert	4- 5-1809	Stacy, Peter, on Pleasant Run Cr.	3-20-1803
Robnett, Enoch	12- 2-1816	Stacy (Stasy), William	5- 7-1810
Robson, William L.	12-18-1816	Stagherwalt, Peter	11-10-1815
Roby, Absalom	3-30-1816	Stark, Abraham	3- 1-1813
Rodgers, Samuel	1- 6-1814	Stark, Daniel & James, on Camp Cr.	2-17-1812
Rodman, Benjamin, on Pleasant Run Cr.	11- 6-1801	Stark, Enoch	1- 1-1817
Rodman, William	2-11-1813	Stark, John	1- 4-1810
Rogers, John, on Camp Cr.	3-30-1816	Steed, Reuben	7-28-1813
Romain, Abraham	3-20-1815	Stephenson, Lanson (or Lawson ?)	1- 4-1817
Rood, George	1- 1-1813	Stewart, Isaac	11-27-1815
Rose, Francis	10-26-1815	Stewart, John	1-30-1816
Ross, Charles	1- 1-1813	Stewart, Samuel	1-20-1817
Ross, Charles F.	3- 2-1816	Stilwell, Jacob	8-11-1815
Rowland, David	11-15-1813	Stoner, Valentine	11-26-1814
Ruddell, William	2-13-1816	Stonesipher, Adam	1-20-1815
Rush, George, at Armstrong's Station	10-18-1811	Stonesifer, Henry, Sr., & Jr.	1- 1-1813
Russell, William & Robert	1-24-1812	Stroud, Joseph	2-24-1810
Ryker, Gerardus	3- 9-1810	Stuart, David	3-20-1803
Ryker, John, justice of peace	1809	Stuart, James	2- 2-1809
Ryon, Thomas	12-21-1812	Stutsman, Daniel	12-29-1811
Sage, Jeremiah	3- 5-1810	Stutsman, Jacob	2- 8-1810
Sargent, Melson	5- 5-1810	Stutsman, Samuel, on Owens Cr.	2- 9-1813
Saunders, Benjamin, on 14 Mile Cr.	11-24-1814	Sullivan, Joseph	3- 4-1815
Saunders, Thomas	12-16-1816	Sullivan, Willis, on Ohio R. 16 mi. below mouth of Kentucky R.	11-21-1808
Schwarz, John	2-13-1809		
Scifres, Joseph	1-30-1815	Summers, George	2-11-1812
Scott, James	5-25-1812	Swartz, Christian	3- 8-1816
Scott, John, Silver Creek Twp.	1- 8-1815	Swartz, John	1-10-1816
Searls (Serrels), Ebenezer	12-19-1814	Swarz, Michael	3-25-1809
Shake, Widow	1-16-1813	Sweney, James	6- 4-1803
Shannon, James	11-12-1814	Sylvester, Emory, see Silvester	
Sheets, Andrew	1-14-1813		
Shelby, Isaac, county clerk	1816	Taffe, James	11- 9-1811
Shew, Joseph	3-23-1807	Taylor, James	2- 7-1812
Shields, Patrick	6- 4-1807	Taylor, William	3- 2-1813
Shute, Andrew	2- 9-1813	Teple, Jacob	2-22-1816
Sigman, Barnet	11- 9-1810	Thomas, Evan, on branch of White R.	1-25-1808
Silvester (Sylvester), Emery	3-30-1809	Thomas, Jonathan, Jr.	1-20-1817
Simonton, Robert, in R. 10, T. 1	12-26-1811	Thomas, Josiah	12-25-1813

Thomas, Plano	2-15-1810	Welch, John	1- 1-1812
Thompson, John	3-30-1810	Welch, Patrick	5- 7-1810
Thompson, John H., Justice of Peace	1813	Wells, Francis	2- 1-1809
Thompson, Joshua	1-30-1813	Wells, Thomas	12-30-1814
Thompson, William, on Camp Cr. R. 9, T. 1	3-21-1811	Whirl (?), James	2- 3-1813
Tingle, Thomas	3- 3-1817	White, John	12-19-1812
Tipps, Conrad	2- 4-1812	Whiteman, John	12-19-1814
Tipps, see also Fipes		Whitson, Thomas	2-11-1812
Tolkin, James	11-19-1816	Wickhens, Josiah	5- 3-1810
Travers, Robert	3-21-1816	Wiggins, Aaron, near mouth of Salt R.	4-16-1808
Trinnel, Alexander, near Springville	1-31-1816	Wilkey, William	2-27-1810
Troutman, Leonard	1-13-1817	Wilkil (?), John, on Bull Run	11-26-1816
Trueblood, Josiah	5- 1-1809	Willey, Barzilla	12-11-1813
Trueblood, Mark	2- 5-1813	Willey, Minard	1- 6-1815
Tucker, Leonard, in Charlestown	3- 9-1815	Williams, Daniel	9- 6-1817
Tuell, Jesse	2-22-1811	Williams, Isaac & Jacob	11-25-1814
Tuley, Charles P., judge, died prior to 9-29-1802	1801	Williams, James	1- 1-1812
Turner, Richard	1- 8-1814	Williams, John, on Muddy Fork of Silver Cr.	3-14-1811
		Williams, Josiah & Reece	3-30-1811
Vance, David	11- 9-1814	Williams, William	1-11-1814
Vancleve, Thomas	6-14-1813	Wincio (?), Jeremiah	1-28-1817
Vandeventer, John	1-30-1814 [1815]	Wiseman, Andrew & Isaac	1-27-1816
Vanskiver, Oliver	12- 5-1814	Withers, John	12-15-1809
Vawter, James	3-13-1809	Wood, George & Moses G.	2-19-1816
Vawter, Jesse	2-12-1810	Wood, Henry	9-14-1809
Vawter, John	5- 1-1809	Wood, James N., Clarksville Twp.	3- 3-1802
Vest, William, on Post Road	6- 4-1807	Wood, William	11- 2-1810
		Woods, Nancy, Silver Creek Twp.	1-21-1815
Wainman (Waynman), Emanuel	1- 5-1811	Woods, William	12-18-1812
Walker, Alexander	8-18-1815	Worden, Samuel	3- 2-1816
Walker (Waker), Samuel	12-23-1811	Work, John, Springhill Twp.	1-17-1809
Wardell, John	12-10-1814	Work, John, Jr.	9-12-1810
Wardle, Leonard & Robert	5-30-1810	Work, Joseph (or James)	6-19-1815
Warman, James	3-11-1812	Work, Samuel, on Ohio R. 2 mi. above mouth of 14 Mile Cr.	3-11-1811
Warman, Wilson	2-13-1815		
Warren, Aaron	8- 2-1817	Worrall, James	7- 4-1807
Watts, Mason	3- 7-1808	Wright (Right), James	11-25-1809
Weathers, John	2-15-1813	Wright, Philbert	3- 7-1815
Weathers, Samuel	1- 6-1815	Wright, Philip	11- 5-1811
Web, John	8-18-1815		
Weer, Andrew	11-27-1815	Yates, William	11-21-1814
Weir, James	2- 9-1813	Yunt, Benjamin	6-13-1816
Weir (Wier), Robert	1-17-1812		
Welborn, John	2- 5-1817	Zilling, George	1-16-1817

PIKE COUNTY MARRIAGES, 1817-1844

Compiled by Mrs. Ruth M Slevin from microfilm of Book 1 in Genealogy Division, Indiana State Library. Pike County was organized in 1817 out of Gibson and Perry counties.

Abbott, Edwin - Susan Adams   1-29-1833
Abbott, James M - Betsey Keith   3- 8-1835
Abbott, Leonard - Hannah Arnold   11-26-1839
Ainley, Joseph - ElizabethChappell
                                  7-27-1840
Ainley, Matthew - Nancy Fowler   5- 4-1834
Alexander, James H - Mary Case   11-27-1839
Alexander, Jesse H - Emily Buddington
                                  9-27-1840
Alford, Thomas - Priscilla Williams
                              12-27-1817
Allen, Francis D - Ann Jane Debruler
                                 2- 6-1842
Allen, William - Rebeckah Swearingen
                                 3- 3-1841
Alton, James - Kizziah Hisic   10- 4-1840
Anderson, Andrew - Mary Bontey   9-11-1823
Armstrong, James - Mary Scales   12-11-1821
Armstrong, Madison - Jane Chew   12-22-1839
Arnold, Calvin - Emeliza Arnold   7-23-1843
Arnold, Jackson - Nancy Keith   9-12-1840
Arnold, James - Martha Hays   5-29-1839
Arnold, John - Emiley Cross   1- 4-1835
Arnold, Josiah - Elizabeth Kuglscott
                         lic. 7-17-1841
Arnold, William H - Priscilla Arnold
                                 7-23-1843
Ashby, James - Elizabeth A Coonrod
                              10- 9-1836
Ashby, Joshua - Susan Tisdale   10- 2-1831
Ashby, Peyton - Louiza Crow   10- 4-1837
Ashby, Robert - Elizabeth Caldwell
                                 1-16-1828
Ashby, William - Peggy Johnson   2-15-1822
Atkinson, Andrew - Hester Wyatt   5-22-1843
Aulton, William H - Martha VanCamp
                         lic. 1-28-1838
Avery, Elisha - Martha Ann Stucky
                               12-20-1840
Baker, John - Milley Malinda Barnet
                               7- 1-1838
Ballard, Amos - Sally Hawkins   4-24-1827
Ballard, James - Tamar Morgan   2-13-1841
Barbour, Allen - Lucinda Horrell   12-24-1837
Barnes, Alexander - Elizabeth Woodrey
                               11- 4-1830
Barnes, Joseph - Mary Ann Cline   3- 1-1838
Barnet, James H - Sarah Hargraves
                               8-18-1836
Barns, Thomas - Rebeckah Evans   10- 5-1839
Barrett, Richard - Mary Black
                      lic. 10-12-1829
Barrett, Richmond - Matilda Quiggins
                               3-14-1834
Barrett, Richmond - Catharine Kinman
                               5-31-1843
Barrett, Spencer - Catharine Lee   9- 6-1839
Barrett, Wilson - Nancy West   6- 7-1838
Battles, Newit - Susan S Harrison
                               3-10-1842
Beans, Henry - Emeline Ferguson   11- 7-1833
Beard, Thomas - Zipporah Griffith
                               2- 6-1839

Beck, Ambrose - Elizabeth Wright   12- 2-1841
Beck, Fredrick - Sophia Hill   4-13-1829
Beck, Henry Jr - Elizabeth Helsley
                               11- 9-1837
Beck, Jacob - Dolley Robling   6-28-1837
Beck, John - Catharine Winkler   9-26-1827
Beck, John - Jinney Barret   2-24-1830
Beck, Lewis - Delilah Lovelass   1-10-1822
Beck, Lewis Jr - Mary Hensley   12-29-1836
Beck, William - Betsey Brenton   7-21-1825
Benedict, Nathaniel - Zerilda Mead
                               3- 5-1839
Bilderback, David - Phoebe Lemasters
                               6-19-1824
Bilderback, Thomas - Sally Colman
                               2-16-1826
Black, Daniel C - Lucinda Coonrod
                              10- 3-1841
Black, David - Martha Colman
                         lic. 1-14-1819
Black, David A - Jane Souvercool   12-29-1841
Black, Henry - Elizabeth Colman   1-12-1824
Black, Robert - Polly Hedges
                         lic. 3-16-1833
Black, Robert A - Martha Melton   12-18-1838
Black, William - Elizabeth Hardin
                               5- 8-1819
Blagrave, James - Peggy Curry   6- 6-1817
Blaze, George W - Susan Rumble   1-15-1840
Blaze, Tevalt - Susan Simpson   11- 3-1829
Boger, Fredrick - Peggy Risley   5- 9-1825
Boger, Reuben - Mary Arnold lic.   8-16-1838
Boon, Elisha B - Mary Ann Parham   3-10-1839
Borders, Henry Jr - Susanna Snyder
                               2- 5-1835
Borders, John - Patsey J Brenton   8-24-1820
                         or 8-24-1821
Bowman, Jonathan J - Elizabeth Miley
                               1- 5-1839
Brenton, George - Mary Hawkins   4- 9-1829
Brenton, Henry - Susan Borders   7-28-1820
Brenton, Henry - Matilda Parker   9- 6-1829
Brenton, James - Mary Ainsley   9-21-1830
Brenton, James M - Lucy C Black   6-20-1833
Brenton, John - Anna Ferrell   3- 2-1837
Brenton, Newton - Juliann Masters   2-17-1841
Brenton, Peter - Elizabeth Robbins
                               4-23-1826
Brenton, Peter - Rachel Chappell   5-15-1828
Brenton, Peter Jr - Nancy Tislow   12-23-1841
Brenton, Robert - Catharine Borders
                               10- 7-1819
Brenton, Wesley - Polly Ann Kirk   12- 5-1836
Brewster, James - Catharine Corn   9-14-1834
Bright, Jacob - Priscella Miley   9-12-1841
Brittingham, William - Savara Johnson
                               12-26-1839
Bruister, Elijah - Susan Corn   2-28-1839
Bruister, Solomon - Mary Bryant   1-18-1835
Bryant, James - Margarett Scott   7-21-1842
Bullard, Allen - Nancy Miller   12-19-1841
Burditt, Thomas - Sally Ashby   2- 9-1830
Burkhart, Emsley - Mary Snyder   10-25-1842

Burkhart, Silas - Louisa Selby   9- 2-1841
Butler, John - Elizabeth Masters
                                        12-26-1826
Campbell, Henry K - Mary Ogden   4-14-1833
Capehart, George - Caroline DeBruler
                                        2-11-1841
Capehart, George - Mary Gray   2- 5-1843
Case, Abraham - Elizabeth Russell 8- 3-1831
Case, Abraham - Mary Stubblefield 9-10-1840
Case, Ebenezer - Elizabeth McBride
                                        1- 5-1818
Case, Thomas - Minerva Russell   9-22-1842
Case, Washington - Sally Russell 1-26-1831
Case, William G - Nancy Caldwell 10-29-1840
Catt, Amos - Elizabeth Decker   4- 7-1840
Catt, Bartley - Elizabeth Borders
                                        4-29-1841
Catt, Henry - Alleigh Selby   2- 1-1835
Catt, Thomas H - Susan Catt   11- 1-1842
Chambers, Andrew B - Catharine Grubb
                                        12-13-1835
Chambers, Edmond - Anna Meddis   1-19-1830
Chambers, James - Mary Romine
                                   lic. 7-24-1822
Chambers, John - Ruth Curtis   4- 2-1826
Chambers, John - Polly Ivy   8-27-1843
Chapman, Justus - Nancy Pain   11-20-1834
Chapman, Samuel - Elizabeth Briant (?)
                                        11-26-1839
Chappel, Job - Appama Brenton
                                   lic. 10- 5-1828
Chappell, Joab - Hannah M Chapman
                                        12-21-1838
Chappell, Stephen - Hannah Miller
                                        12-19-1832
Chew, Joseph - Mary Barnett   11- 3 1828
Chew, Marcellus - Mary Coonrod   1- 1-1837
Clark, Henry - Phoebe Benedict   9- 7-1843
Clark, Miles - Lydia Hayden   1-29-1840
Clarke, Jacob - Betsey Scamahorn   4-16-1821
Clifford, Allen W - Susan Moor   6-25-1835
Cline, Henry - Phoebe Johnston   7- 5-1835
Cline, Lewis - Sally Lovelass   6- 4-1835
Clutz, Henry - Elizabeth Goodbry 1-25-1843
Coan, Isaac - Thirza Kinman   1-19-1820
Coan, Isaac - Elizabeth Stone   3- 2-1834
Coker, Aaron - Temperance Tisdale
                                        8-29-1839
Coleman, Hasting - Sarah Lucas   10- 5-1837
Coleman, John - Frances Trayler   1-26-1832
Coleman, Page M - Mary T Bass   8-11-1835
Coleman, Thomas J - Elizabeth Bord
                                        8- 8-1839
Colman, Conrad - Elenor Coleman   3-17-1831
Colman, Samuel D - Charlotte Bass 5-11-1837
Colvin, Alfred - Betsey McCray   1- 4-1835
Colvin, Elisha - Maria Barnes   3-29-1838
Colvin, George - Abigail Lindy
                                   lic. 10-11-1829
Colvin, Moses - Mary Smith   11- 7-1832
Colvin, Richard - Dorcas Hillman 1-16-1831
Colvin, William - Elizabeth Hillman
                                        4-26-1827
Combs, Benjamin - Priscilla Scott 7- 5-1838
Conger, Jonathan - Hannah Crow   2-23-1840
Conger, Levi - Jeniah Small   6-15-1827
Conn, Andrew C - Mary Cooper   4- 3-1827
Conn, Hiram S - Elizabeth Pride   1-24-1827
Cook, Thomas - Mary Ainley   11-22-1834
Coonrod, Christopher I - Louisa Evans
                                        7-13-1843

Coonrod, Daniel - Elizabeth Pruett
                                   lic. 9-26-1840
Coonrod, David - Tillitha Millburn
                                        7- 7-1837
Coonrod, Henry - Elizabeth Soverigns
                                        2- 4-1819
Coonrod, Henry - Elizabeth Sovreigns
                                        8-23-1832
Coonrod, Henry H - Malinda Moor 10-24-1836
Coonrod, James J - Sarah Devabah 10-25-1840
Coonrod, James N - Catharine Stuckey
                                        5- 4-1831
Coonrod, John D - Sally Harden   7-24-1828
Coonrod, John D - Bethsaida Harrell
                                   lic. 5-31-1838
Coonrod, John D - Catherine Cowgill
                                        5- 5-1839
Coonrod, John F - Ellender Moore 10- 5-1833
Coonrod, John M - Lydia Kinman   7-15-1830
Coonrod, William H - Parthina Harding
                                        9-30-1829
Coonrod, William L - Margaret Keith
                                        12-17-1843
Coons, Alexander - Elizabeth White
                                        12-20-1835
Coonts, Alexander - Mary Kisiah Skinner
                                        2-28-1841
Cooper, Joseph - Mary Kinman   5-15-1831
Corby, Jacob - Lurena Lett   12- 1-1831
Corn, Aaron - Polly Coleman   6- 8-1830
Corn, James - Rebecca Scott   10-20-1833
Corn, William - Mary More   12-19-1839
Cox, Hezekiah - Elizabeth Lovelass
                                        9-28-1837
Cox, Isaac - Lucinda Harding   5- 3-1835
Crayton, Calvin - Anna Whaley   9- 1-1836
Crayton, Josiah - Louisa Thomas   9-20-1834
Crayton, Thomas - Patsey Wyatt
                                   lic. 6- 9-1827
Crosier, James M - Elizabeth Barnet
                                        3- 3-1842
Cross, Joseph - Epsey D Kinman   1-20-1838
Crow, James - Harriet Townsend
                                   lic. 10-18-1832
Crow, James D - Rebeckah Knight 10-27-1825
Crow, John Jr - Joanna Alexander
                                   lic. 11-17-1836
Crow, Robert Sq - Abigail Hayden 7- 2-1843
Crow, William - Mary Shaw   11- 5-1823
Cummins, Charles - Delilah Rhodes 7- 4-1837
Curtis, William H - Lucinda Anderson
                                        4-20-1843
Custin, Henry B - Elizabeth Alexander
                                        2-12-1843
Davenport, William C - Sarah Miley
                                        8-16-1835
Davidson, Alfred G - Eliza Williams
                                        11-12-1843
Davidson, John - Elizabeth Hulen 8-27-1833
Davis, Isaac I - Ann Posey   11-24-1842
Davis, Jesse G - Martha M Clanahan
                                        10-19-1842
Davis, John - Prudence Overton   5-26-1842
Davis, John I - Elizabeth Black   9- 6-1838
Davis, Philip - Nancy Corn lic.   1- 9-1836
Davisson, James - Nancy H Cooper
                                   lic. 3- 6-1838
Davisson, Josiah - Emeline
  Sawyer   1- 5-1838
Deadrick, John - Anna Taylor   8-23-1825
Deafindoll, Joseph - Patsey Johnson
                                        2- 6-1825

Deavendoll, Joseph - Eliza Smith 10- 7-1820
DeBruler, George W - Abarilla DeBruler
                                  8- 8-1839
DeBruler, Harberd - Polly Trayler
                                12- 3-1818
DeBruler, Thomas F - Ann R Bailey 4-26-1843
DeBruler, William G - Rebeckah
  Stublefield   6- 3-1841
DeBruler, William H - Nancy Alexander
                                8-10-1843
Decker, Abraham - Harriet Catt   4-18-1833
Decker, Abraham S - Sarah Jane Wyatt
                                5-11-1842
Decker, Johnson - Rebeckah Crow   6- 9-1832
Decker, Presley - Nancy Colvin   8-24-1826
Dedman, Elijah H - Elizabeth Wright
                                8-17-1820
Dedman, Franklin T - Elizabeth Hedges
                              10-14-1838
Dedman, John E - Cynthia Trayler 11-14-1833
Dedman, Samuel C - Minervia Davisson
                              11-13-1828
Dedrick, Samuel P - Elizabeth Coonrod
                              1-18-1831
Defendoll, James - Polly Hillman 3-15-1831
Defindoll, James - Lucinda Dorsit
                              10- 4-1841
DeJarnett, Christopher - Christine
  Beck   10-18-1838
Denson, Joshua - Anna Cummins   4-29-1830
Depree, Henry - Sally Defendoll 11- 6-1831
Devin, Alexander - Caroline Augusta
  Glezen   8-18-1842
Dial, Reuben - Rebeckah Draper 8-30-1825
Dickerman, Cyrus B - Winnie Blaze
                            12-14-1843
Dillon, Hezekiah - Cynthia Willis 8-19-1842
Dillon, Jonathan - Patsey Garner 10-28-1841
Dobbins, William - Sally Dedman
                   lic. 12- 5-1828
Dockins, Travense - Mahuldah Kinman
                              5- 5-1828
Douchan (?), Edward - Ellen Cronen (?)
                   lic. 4-11-1839
Douds, William - Eliza Luff   4- 7-1842
Doughten, William T - Susan Rysinger
                              9- 7-1840
Drennon, Abraham S - Caroline R
  Sawyer   lic. 4- 5-1838
Drennon, Benjamin V - Juliann Kinman
                              4- 7-1842
Duffner, George - Susan Tislow 4- 2-1838
Duncan, David - Catharine Foster 11- 9-1822
Dunning, Henderson - Marthy Pea 11- 4-1828
Dyer, Isaac - Orpha Ainsley lic. 6-19-1827
Edmondson, James - Eliza Ann Hargraves
                              3-25-1840
Edwards, James - Eliza Barr   3-23-1837
Edwards, Levi - Emerina Blanton
                   lic. 12- 2-1827
English, David D - Crosha Coleman 2- 6-1825
English, Thomas J S - Nancy Johnson
                   lic. 9-15-1826
Ent, Charles - Winnie B Kinman 2-17-1831
Evans, Dennis - Juliann Grissom 12-25-1836
Evans, Hinton - Rachel Griffith 9-28-1839
Evans, Nathan V - Lucyann Adyer 5- 7-1843
Evans, Wesley - Nancy Tourtelott 2-21-1840
Evans, William L - Margaret Barnet
                              3- 1-1824

Falls, Felix S - Angeline Johnson
                              3- 6-1842
Farmer, Fleming - Louisa Clifford 5- 1-1842
Farr, Archibald - Phoebe Risleye 11-24-1825
Farrell, William - Polly Ann Bryant
                              10-14-1840
Ferrell, Hugh S - Minerva Dedman 1-22-1832
Fettinger, George - Hannie Ann Hillman
                            10-10-1839
Fettinger, Henry - Mahala Robling 3- 2-1843
Ficklin, Joseph - Elizabeth Stewart
                            6-24-1828
Fickling, John H - Elizabeth Feltner
                            6-26-1842
Fields, Benjamin - Nancy J Mount 9- 8-1825
Fields, Keen - Malinda Johnson 6-30-1836
Finn, John - Elizabeth Osborn
                     lic. 9- 7-1824
Flinn, James - Ellen Clark lic. 8-12-1839
Ford, Samuel A - Harriet E Campbell
                            11-25-1830
Foster, Isom - Elizabeth Miley 9-26-1836
Foster, James - Polly Teague   12-11-1839
Foster, Joel - Elizabeth Gray   7-22-1830
Foster, Matthew W - Ellen Johnson 6-18-1829
Foster, Robert - Drusilla Teague
                     lic. 3-30-1840
Foster, William - Elizabeth Chappell
                            12-10-1840
Foster, William - Mary Ward   9- 3-1835
Fouts, Daniel - Nancy Simpson 12-27-1827
Fouts, David - Christian Trayler 4-20-1840
Fouts, John - Peggy Lindsey   8-16-1821
Fouts, John - Nancy McCrary   2-19-1831
Fowler, Edmond W - Drusilla Selby 9- 1-1827
Fowler, Elijah - Elizabeth Beck 2-17-1824
Fowler, James - Polly Brenton 9-26-1824
Fowler, James Jr - Nancy Willis 12-30-1841
Fowler, Jonathan - Martha Ann Thomas
                            9-14-1843
Fowler, Warren - Nancy Pride   3-17-1833
Fredrick, Andrew - Elizabeth Colvin
                            11-16-1843
Fredrick, Jacob - Polly Reedy   3-22-1832
Fredrick, John - Sally Kennedy 2-17-1831
Fredrick, Joseph - Elizabeth Ann
  Smith   4-16-1843
Fredrick, Lindy - Ellenor Decker 7-23-1835
Fredrick, Michael - Mary M Gray 8-21-1836
Gamble, Oliver - Dulcenia Jerrold 9-29-1831
Gibbins, Julius - Catharine Barns 4-24-1836
Gillmore, Samuel - Sarah Evans 3- 3-1840
Gladish, Henry - Eliza Jane Crow 1- 6-1842
Gladish, James - Anna Weas lic. 10-29-1831
Gladish, Richard - Eliza Ann Foster
                            12-17-1839
Gray, James - Eliva Trayler   11- 8-1832
Gray, James - Lavina Trayler 12-22-1842
Gray, William - Mary Trayler   4-12-1838
Gray, William - Priscilla
  Fredrick   1-26-1841
Green, Napoleon - Elizabeth Shawhan
                            2-27-1844
Greene, William - Susanna Fergerson
                            3-29-1830
Gregory, Jeremiah - Martha Caldwell
                            4- 7-1843
Griffith, John - Nancy Maxwell 8-26-1840
Griffith, Thomas - Nancy Colfax 10-18-1832
Grubb, George Sr - Polly Robling 4- 3-1842
Grubb, Henry - Elizabeth F Garwood
                            8-27-1840

Grubb, Lewis - Minerva Hartley   11- 2-1843
Grubb, Valentine - Margaret Shoults
                                   4-12-1837
Gwinnup, Samuel - Melissa Jane Smith
                                  10-17-1839
Hager, Simon - Elizabeth Defindoll
                                   9- 7-1843
Hale, Richard - Elizabeth Chambers
                                   8-10-1830
Hammond, Lester - Nancy Case   8-24-1838
Hammond, Perry C - Nancy Edmondson
                              lic. 9-13-1837
Hammonds, Albert - Elizabeth Case 7-29-1831
Harbison, James - Elizabeth Coonrod
                                   6-15-1834
Harden, Henry - Mary Crow   11-10-1822
Harden, John - Elizabeth Thompson 8-26-1824
Harden, Nicholas - Milley Rutherford
                                   1-23-1843
Hardin, John - Mary Kinman   1-28-1838
Hardin, Squire - Polly Curtis   7- 6-1843
Hardin, William - Tillithianna
   Tisdale   12- 8-1830
Hargraves, Miles B - Martha B Dedman
                                   5- 9-1839
Hargrove, Lemuel P - Susanna W
   DeBruler   12-25-1832
Hargrove, Thomas - Patsey Trayler
                                  10-25-1821
Harper, Robert - Patsey Colman   9- 4-1828
Harrell, Hosea - Susan Gainey   3-19-1840
Harrell, Whitson - Mary Teverbough
                                   5-18-1834
Harris, James - Charity Brenton   8-21-1818
Harris, James - Patsey Finn lic. 1-29-1821
Harris, Richard - Elizabeth Trayler
                                   9-17-1833
Harris, Richard - Sarah Kirkland 2- 6-1840
Harris, St Clair - Mary Johnson 10- 7-1841
Hart, Thomas - Sarah West   6-20-1843
Hartley, Benjamin- Martha Ann Hill 6-23-1841
Hartley, Reuben - Nancy Hill   6-17-1841
Hartley, Thomas - Nancy Real   1-19-1825
Hartley, William - Malinda Coonrod
                                   7-29-1842
Harvey, John - Mary Pride   lic. 12-22-1830
Hathaway, John - Michee Harrell   9- 1-1833
Hathiway, John - Elizabeth Trayler
                                   3- 3-1836
Hawkins, Allen - Rosanna Collins
                              lic. 1-18-1838
Hawkins, William - Elizabeth Kinman
                                   1- 6-1838
Hays, Elias - Malinda Lett   5-28-1820
Hays, Ezekiel - Lydian Pride   10- 3-1841
Hays, Ezekiel G - Betsey Teague   7-11-1833
Hays, James - Polly Trayler   8- 2-1827
Hays, John - Anna Rogerson   3- 9-1823
Hays, Philo - Nancy Tislow   8- 2-1821
Heacock, Edwin - Mary Corn   11- 5-1843
Heartley, Reuben - Polly Trayler   4- 6-1828
Hedges, James - Sally Trayler   4-25-1839
Hedges, Jefferson - Rhoda Kinman   8- 7-1828
Hedges, John - Indiana Mead   8-20-1839
Hedges, Peter - Polly Bright   5-26-1836
Hedges, William - Patsey Bright   3-31-1831
Helsley, William - Mary Dejarnett 11-23-1843
Henderson, William - Elizabeth
   Herald   lic. 2- 1-1840
Hendricks, John - Nancy Jane Taylor
                                   3-21-1839
Hendrix, James - Malinda Roundtree
                                   6- 8-1837

Hewens, Darwin - Emeline Merchant
                                  11- 5-1840
Hewens, Erwin - Maria Merchant   1- 1-1840
Hicks, Allen - Catharine Duncan   1-12-1835
Hightower, Pleasant - Elizabeth
   McAtee   10-27-1833
Hill, Alexander - Peggy Lovelass 8-13-1839
Hill, Richard - Catharine Hill   3-11-1839
Hillman, Daniel - Mary Ann Lane   7-17-1834
Hillman, Henry - Rebeckah Deal   7-22-1830
Hillman Joseph D - Mary Flenor   1- 2-1840
Hiser, Jacob - Hannah Dunn lic. 8-17-1826
Hobble, Francis - Margaret Atkinson
                                   4-16-1840
Hoggatt, Josiah - Martha Johnson 7-14-1842
Hollingsworth, Samuel - Louisa Lett
                              lic. 12- 5-1829
Hope, Adam - Sally Crozier   8- 6-1817
Hopkins, Stephen N - Nancy Pride 3-25-1840
Hopkins, Wesley D - Mary Ann Cutright
                                  12-24-1840
Horniday, Josiah - Maria Smith   7-25-1841
Horrell, Cleaver - Mary Kinman   12-15-1831
Horrell, Coleman - Lucinda Lett   1-18-1824
Horrell, James - Elizabeth Capehart
                                   4- 4-1824
Houchins, Clifford - Sarah M Taylor
                                   1-14-1841
Howard, Merideth - Elizabeth Kinman
                                   3- 2-1826
Huff, Ovid - Dilley Beck   9-28-1841
Hulen, Hiram - Eunic S Osborn   8-28-1836
Hulin, Wyatt - Elizabeth Deadrick
                                  12-18-1825
Hulings, Jacob - Belinda Cutwright
                                   8-23-1839
Hummer, Harvey - Elizabeth Bishop 2-24-1836
Humphreys, Abijah - Sebra Garwood 8-13-1829
Hurst, Charles - Susanna Lindsey 12-24-1818
Hurst, Ira - Phebe Ann Brenton   12-20-1837
Hutchens, Thomas - Chloe Thomas   5-19-1834
Ive, Wilson - Lydia Woods   5-14-1823
Jaco, Cornelius - Betsey Tisdale 6-12-1833
Jaco, John - Mary Coburn   2-15-1829
Jacobs, Samuel H - Mary McCarty 12-10-1840
Jerauld, Elijah - Harriet Leslie 2-28-1839
Jerel, Jefferson - Polly Colvin   6-10-1822
Johnson, Abner R - Mirian Miller 8-29-1841
Johnson, John - Sarah Jane Colman
                                  10-23-1841
Johnson, Josiah - Elizabeth Walron
                                  10-10-1839
Jones, John M - Elizabeth Jerrell
                                  12- 5-1843
Keith, Jeremiah - Mary Keith   7-24-1839
Keith, William - Elizabeth Arnold
                               7-24-[1829?]
Kelso, Andrew F - Susanna Hargrave
                                   9-17-1829
Kent, John W - Susan Hill   9-28-1842
King, Marcus - Roxanna Morrison   2-12-1840
Kinman, Archibald - Ascenath Kinman
                                   4-30-1829
Kinman, Elijah - Phoebe Henry   5-28-1823
Kinman, Henry - Sally Coonrod   11- 6-1831
Kinman, Hiram - Hannah Goodin
                              lic. 3-29-1817
Kinman, Hiram W - Matilda Coonrod
                                  11- 6-1828
Kinman, Jackson - Emeline Cougill
                                  10-13-1839
Kinman, James - Nancy Kinman   8-20-1828
Kinman, James - Catharine Vaughn 9-28-1828

Kinman, James - Polly Johnson
lic. 3- 2-1837
Kinman, Jeremiah - Mary Crayton
lic. 4-25-1820
Kinman, Jeremiah - Sarah Dockens 6- 8-1832
Kinman, Jesse R - Mary West 10-13-1836
Kinman, Joel - Jaralia McCane 12-31-1818
Kinman, John - Delilah Miley 4-25-1839
Kinman, John Jr - Nancy Kinman 9-15-1824
Kinman, Joseph - Charity Boleyn 2- 2-1836
Kinman, Josiah - Rebeckah Stuckey 3-13-1840
Kinman, Leonard - Sally Whitehead
lic. 3-15-1837
Kinman, Samuel - Caroline Traylor
lic. 10-11-1817
Kinman, Samuel W - Manda M Wyatt
lic. 7- 8-1837
Kinman, Seburn - Bersheba Noflet 4-16-1826
Kinman, Seburn - Patsey Risley 1- 8-1829
Kinman, Syrus - Sally Adams 2-11-1819
Kinman, Thomas M - Rachel Shaw 6- 4-1843
Kinman, William - Jane McCain 3- 6-1826
Kinman, William - Mary Ann Coonrod
7-14-1831
Kinman, William - Delilah Arnold 2-24-1833
Kinman, William H - Rebecka Tislow
10-22-1843
Kirk, Edward - Sarah Kime 6-12-1834
Knight, Andrew - Betsey Crow 10- 6-1825
Knight, John - Lucy Decker 5-11-1837
Lamb, Nixon - Elizabeth Eaton 10-22-1829
Lamb, Stanton - Elizabeth Bright 5-25-1826
Lambert, Thomas - Catharine Hardison
2-11-1837
Lance, Benjamin - Joanna Beatty 10-16-1839
Lane, Elijah - Susan Hawkins 6-24-1834
Lee, Henry - Rebeckah I Barnes 4-24-1838
Lee, John - Susan Cline 2-19-1829
Leet, Aaron - Rebeckah Coleman 7-30-1825
Leet, Charles - Catharine Corn 8-23-1823
Leet, John - Rebeckah Stewart 8-29-1830
Lemasters, Simeon - Nancy Almon 10-20-1831
Leslie, Alexander - Rowene Hewins 4- 4-1841
Leslie, Alexander - Harriet Crow 5- 7-1835
Lett, Jessee - Priscilla Alford 4-23-1820
Lett, John A - Mary Thomas 10-20-1831
Lett, Randle - Jane Conn lic. 11-12-1831
Lett, Whitfield - Elizabeth Halbert
3-17-1833
Lewis, John W - Ellen T Cooper 9- 6-1833
Lindey (?), Fredrick - Matilda Catt
8-20-1828
Linn, Isum - Lydia Garwood 12-22-1825
Linn, see also Lynn
Loan, Joseph W - Susan Potts 7-28-1818
Lovelace, Henry - Susanna Beck 3-12-1830
Lovelace, Isaac - Phoebe Young 1-10-1828
Lovelace, John - Peggy Beck lic. 10-26-1825
Lovelace, William - Susanna Lee 11- 6-1828
Lovelass, Henry - Elizabeth A Barnes
10-31-1839
Lovelass, Joseph - Elizabeth Beck
3-18-1824
Lovelass, Luke - Christian Winkler
8-11-1836
Lovelass, William - Lucinda Cox 9-14-1843
Lownsdale, John J - Nancy Thomas 6-24-1840
Lownsdale, Thomas - Maria Wright 3-17-1831
Lynn, Sylas - Susanna Bilderback 10-26-1823
Lynn, see also Linn
McAtee, Benjamin - Ellen Decker 10-25-1832
McAtee, Josiah - Biddy Miller 6- 4-1835
McAtee, William - Susan Shoults 1-30-1838

McBay, Robert - Mary Pancake 2-11-1843
McBride, James - Rachel Russell 7-12-1832
McCain, Hamilton - Mary Brinton 6-30-1825
McCain, Hamilton Jr - Mary Wood 7-31-1834
McCain, Hugh - Hannah Crayton 9- 9-1827
McCain, Hugh - Eby Kinman 9-17-1829
McCain, James - Delilah I Kinman 2-21-1833
McCain, Thomas - Asceneth Kinman 11-15-1836
McCain, William - Sally Duncan 9-24-1826
McCalister, Elijah - Elizabeth Cox
6-16-1838
McCormick, James P - Ann Maria Whight
2-24-1842
McCoy, James - Mary Moor 1-14-1831
McCrarey, Joel G - Rebeckah Coats
12-15-1843
McDonald, Alexander - Rachel Harbison
2- 1-1818
McDonald, William - Lucy Frederick
9- 6-1824
McGowen, William - Elizabeth Wyatt
1- 2-1826
McGrigrd, Daniel - Martha Campbell
9-29-1831
McIntire, John - Frances D Elder 6-21-1825
McKinney, John - Louisa McCray 5-15-1840
McLean, Ephraim - Jenny Blagrave 3-29-1817
Malott, Elijah - Lelah Kinman 1-11-1818
Manning, Joseph - Naomi Almon 2-12-1838
Marker, Benjamin - Elizabeth Brenton
3- 1-1824
Martin, Thomas - Mary Ann Trayler 1-23-1840
Mason, James - Tasa Wilhes 12-21-1841
Masters, Gabriel H - Winnie B Miley
4-20-1843
Maxian, Enoch K - Lavinia T Sawyer
5-19-1824
Maxwell, John W - Nancy Miley 1-16-1836
Mead, Graves - Aceneth Adams 12-19-1825
Mead, Thomas Jr - Sarah Moor 5- 3-1824
Melton, Austin - Olivie Greenaway
lic. 9-13-1823
Merrick Malachi - Lydia Ogden 8-15-1824
Merritt, David - Elizabeth Kinman
lic. 5- 4-1840
Miley, Alexander - Sarah Teague
lic. 11-27-1841
Miley, David - Nancy McMannus 7-24-1817
Miley, David - Elizabeth Lane 1-14-1830
Miley, David - Elizabeth Finn 10-16-1831
Miley, George O - Elizabeth Hays 7-18-1820
Miley, Harrison - Elizabeth Pride 4- 1-1841
Miley, Henry - Sally Kinman 8-28-1836
Miley, Henry Jr - Polly Foster 1- 1-1837
Miley, Henry C - Eveline Davisson 6-25-1840
Miley, Jacob - Mercy VanCamp 4- 6-1828
Miley, Lewis - Winnie Miley 4-15-1843
Miley, Martin - Nancy Soverigns 8-26-1824
Miley, Peter - Sally Pride 4-11-1830
Miley, Samuel - Catharine Brenton
12-30-1838
Miley, William - Frances Smith 2-28-1836
Miley, Woolsey - Matilda Abbott 4-16-1837
Millburn, James - Catharine Brenton
9- 9-1836
Miller, Jack - Rebeckah Miller
lic. 1- 5-1839
Miller, Robert Q - Cynthia Lamb 9-15-1842
Miller, Thomas - Rody Lindy 8-12-1817
Miller, William - Mary Martin 1- 5-1832
Mitchell, Thomas - Elizabeth Hartley
2-26-1839
Miner, St Clair - Matilda Conger 9-22-1825

Money, James - Phoebe Harris   7-30-1840
Montgomery, Archilles - Rachel Pancake
                                     10- 4-1836
Morehead, Thomas B - Jane Clayton
                                      3-27-1842
Mount, James - Mary Miley   9-27-1840
Mount, Mathias - Sarah Osbourn
                                 lic. 9-13-1829
Niblack, John - Patsey Hartgrove   8- 9-1821
Nichols, John L - Elizabeth Miley 8-14-1823
Noland, John W - Nancy Robling   4- 4-1843
Ogden, Nehemiah - Elizabeth Pride
                                 lic. 1-17-1827
Oliphant, George E & Mary Ann Lownsdale
                                     11- 8-1835
Oliphant, Nathaniel B - Leathey
     Lownsdale   6- 6-1833
O'Rear (?), William - Maria T Sawyer
                                      3-17-1825
Osborn, Elias - Maria Mount   3-22-1829
Osborne, Eber - Elizabeth Campbell
                                      7- 2-1829
Owens, Thomas - Sarah Stafford   6-27-1836
Palmer, Allen - Eveline Campbell   12-24-1840
Palmer, Hiram W - Celia Rix   11- 9-1829
Palmer, John - Fruzam Campbell   8-13-1833
Palmer, John S - Sally Sullivan   7-22-1834
Palmer, Jonathan - Polly Chembley   5- 1-1818
Palmer, Parmenas - Sarah Campbell 1-10-1835
Pancake, William - Mary Thompson
                                 lic. 11-29-1833
Parker, Charles L - Lucintha Trayler
                                     10-15-1829
Parker, George - Harriet Trayler   11-27-1832
Parker, Lorenzo D - Betsey Forguson
                                      4-10-1828
Parker, William - Sally Dunning   7-28-1828
Patton, David - Elizabeth Adams   12- 9-1841
Payne, William - Rebekah Hays   3- 4-1841
Pea, Daniel - Elizabeth Lett   10-26-1820
Pea, Jacob Jr - Polly Buckhannon   3- 3-1824
Perdue, Henry - Rachel Garwood   9-16-1838
Peters, William S - Maria Lockhart
                                      2-26-1822
Polk, Samuel - Mary Young   1- 4-1823
Poor, James - Juliet Williams   8-29-1817
Posey, Harrison - Eliza Campbell   5-29-1839
Postlewait, Jonathan - Mary Foster
                                      5-29-1833
Postlewaite, Richard W - Mary McCain
                                      9-28-1839
Powers, Major T - Mary Crayton   2- 2-1826
Price, Hiram - Elizabeth Ferrell   6-25-1840
Pride, Benjamin - Catharine Trayler
                                      5-26-1822
Pride, Henry - Rhoda Fowler   9-24-1837
Pride, William - Alley Adams   3-15-1838
Pride, William G - Emma Conn   9-27-1827
Pride, Wilsey - Elizabeth Whitehead
                                      4-14-1842
Pride, Woolsey - Mary Ogden   11-13-1820
Pride, Woolsey - Mary Trayler   9-24-1837
Pride, Woolsey B - Mahala Dockins   6-22-1831
Proffit, George H - Mahala Wyatt   9- 1-1830
Quinn, Patrick - Ann Agin   lic.   2- 7-1839
Rainey, Matthew - Polly Johnson   9-15-1836
Reedy, George B - Susan Crow   4-26-1838
Reedy, John - Sarah Cunningham   7-24-1823
Reed, Green - Virginia Withers
                                 lic. 1-29-1832

Reel, Lewis - Margaret Lindy   9-12-1830
Reel, Moses - Sally Catt   11-25-1830
Reeves, Isaac - Sarah Huff   1-16-1839
Rhoades, John - Sarah Millburn   12- 9-1841
Rhoads, Henry - Hannah Clayton   6-16-1840
Rhoads, Lewis - Nancy Keith lic.   12-30-1829
Rice, William - Jane Moor   7-26-1838
Rich, Hiram H - Susanne Johnson   1-14-1837
Richardson, William J - Nancy Tislow
                                      7- 4-1839
Risley, Charles - Sally Ann Arnold
                                     12- 1-1836
Risley, Daniel - Nancy Bryant   3-16-1831
Risley, John - Mary Rodgerson   8- 7-1821
Risley, Matthew - Matilda Wallace 9-21-1832
Roberts, Norman - Temperance Lockhart
                                      1-25-1821
Robling, James - Rachel Lee   2- 9-1834
Robling, John - Anna Simpson   1- 1-1839
Robling, John L - Elizabeth Fettinger
                                      1- 5-1843
Robling, Peter - Sally Beck lic.   8-27-1828
Robling, William - Drusilla Hartley
                                      7- 4-1838
Rogerson, Solomon - Betsey Risley 8-26-1824
Rumble, Alexander - Cynthia Lovelass
                                      1- 4-1838
Rumble, Charles - Polly Blaze   2-12-1833
Rumble, Eli - Susan Hawkins   3-19-1837
Rumble, Samuel - Sally Blase   3-21-1833
Rumble, William - Susan Lovelass   5- 3-1835
Rush, John C - Mary W Stewart   5-10-1838
Russell, Charles - Sarah Woods   2-16-1837
Russell, John - Frances Pride   6-10-1830
Russell, William - Sally Pride   1-27-1831
Rutherford, Hiram - Anna Stewart   7-26-1838
Rutherford, Robert - Pamela Clayton
                                      4-17-1839
Sampson, Aaron - Mary Sullivan   9-14-1834
Sawyer, Franklin F - Mary Means   11-15-1820
Scott, Samuel - Phoebe Woolsey   12-28-1838
Scraper, John - Huldah Hays   1-11-1827
Scraper, John - Peggy Trayler   2-16-1832
See, James - Irene Stuckey   1- 2-1836
Selby, John - Jane Cooper   5-17-1829
Selby, John O - Nancy Brenton   11-19-1824
Selby, Richard - Betsey Ann Gladish
                                      8-21-1823
Selby, Samuel - Nancy Reidy   6-23-1831
Selby, Zepheniah - Ellenor Reidy   2- 6-1823
Servis, Stephen - Nancy Pinkleton
                                      5-11-1840
Shafer, Levi - Catharine Brown   2- 5-1837
Shaver, Henry - Elizabeth Hill
                                 lic. 4-30-1839
Shaver, William - Sophia Brown   3-14-1837
Shaw, Alfred - Susan Bruister   11-27-1841
Shaw, Elvis - Elizabeth Davisson   6-30-1825
Shaw, Hugh - Sally Brewster lic.   2-25-1830
Shiddy, John - Emeline Pruett   6-20-1839
Short, William - Malinda Knight   2-27-1826
Short, William - Jane Fredrick   5- 6-1839
Simpson, Bazzle - Elizabeth Knight
                                      4-16-1829
Simpson, Humphrey - Polly Young   1-23-1827
Simpson, Robert - EllenorLemasters 4- 7-1831
Skidmore, Arthur - Mary Abbott
                                 lic. 10-15-1822
Smith, Albert - Elizabeth Stuckey
                                     12-10-1839

Smith, Henry - Polly Campbell   11- 1-1821
Smith, Hosea H - Nancy Williams   10-16-1842
Smith, John - Penninah Chappell   8-12-1827
Smith, Joseph - Susanna Crayton   10-27-1839
Smith, Moses - Sally Wingate   11-29-1837
Smith, Onias - Mary Adams Wyatt
                           lic. 11-12-1829
Smith, Thomas - Lucy Wyatt   9- 6-1833
Smith, Warren - Narcissa Trayler   10-22-1830
Snider, John - Mary Grubb   10-11-1838
Snyder, Daniel - Sally Brenton   2- 3-1842
Snyder, Joseph - Tryphena Selby   5-24-1842
Soverigns, Archibald - Elizabeth
   Hardin   8-26-1828
Spade, John - Margaret Dobbing   7-29-1821
Spade, John - Polly Curtis   1-15-1830
Spade, John - Nancy Edwards   8-19-1842
Spurgen, James - Christine Blaze   6- 7-1838
Spurgeon, Jacob - Nancy DeJarnell   4- 5-1838
Steel, William - Mary Jane Dean   3-19-1840
Stewart, Henry H - Ruth Lownsdale
                                     12-16-1830
Stewart, James - Jane Hammond   8-24-1837
Stewart, James - Phoebe Richardson
                                      7-22-1839
Stewart, Martin W - Harriet Collins
                                      9-28-1837
Stewart, Thomas C - Elizabeth
   Simington   8-29-1817
Stone, Henry - Priscilla Trayler   8-31-1826
Stone, John - Elizabeth Trayler   7-25-1822
Stone, William - Maria Lamb   1-15-1837
Stoner, John W - Nancy Maria Hillman
                                      4- 9-1843
Strong, Joel - Mary Pride   8-22-1839
Stuckey, John S - Huldah Alexander
                                     12-27-1835
Summers, James - Jane Laster   1-15-1824
Swan, John - Eliza Carlisle   10- 4-1840
Taylor, Benjamin - Polly Hendricks
                                      2-18-1836
Taylor, Benjamin S - Eliza Wright   5-18-1841
Taylor, Francis - Sarah Brannen   9-22-1838
Taylor, Joseph - Lucinda Houchin   5-16-1839
Teague, Henry - Martha Teague   3- 8-1838
Teague, John - Matilda Evans   10-30-1831
Teverbaugh, Jacob - Betsey Sullivan
                                      8-23-1821
Thomas, Fleming - Nancy McCain   5-29-1832
Thomas, Isaac F - Susan Chew   5-18-1843
Thomas, John - Mary Griffith   3-29-1829
Thomas, John M - Ann Eliza Johnson
                                      6-20-1837
Thomas, Joshua - Milley Hassell   11-11-1832
Thomas, Malachi - Ruth Hillman   5-17-1842
Thomas, Michael - Patsey Hedges   5-26-1836
Thomas, Samuel H - Sally Marrick   9-12-1824
Thompson, Arthur - Adah Almon   9-24-1837
Thompson, James - Birella Emily
   Clifford   4-17-1842
Thompson, William - Elizabeth Borden
                                      2-29-1824
Thornton, James - Monice Lownsdale
                                      8-20-1829
Tisdale, Runison - Nancy Pry   2- 3-1824
Tisdale, William - Fanny Thomas   4-28-1836
Tisdale, William - Elender Davis   4-10-1839
Tislow, Christopher - Polly Hesse   3- 3-1825
Tislow, Paul - Ellenor Ashby   4-12-1821
Tislow, Paul - Sarah Osbourn   12-25-1831

Tislow, Paul - Nancy Griffith   1-30-1834
Tislow, Peter - Willery Hardin   8- 9-1821
Tislow, Peter - Degeneray Shoemacher
                                      5- 9-1839
Tourtelott, Abraham - Nancy VanCamp
                                      6-19-1825
Tourtelott, Abraham - Nancy
   Chappell   9-15-1833
Townsend, Osmer O - Harriet Campbell
                                     11-25-1828
Trayler, Barton - Mary Ann Chew   10-21-1839
Trayler, David - Hannah Willis   3-15-1843
Trayler, Elias D - Elizabeth Fowler
                                      9- 1-1836
Trayler, George - Zipporah Catt   1-15-1829
Trayler, Jesse - Mary Campbell   8-29-1839
Trayler, Jessee - Mary Hardin   2-27-1842
Trayler, Lewis - Margaret Campbell
                                      1-21-1830
Trayler, Madison - Mary Timberlake
   Case   7-29-1841
Trayler, Matthew - Lucinda Case   12-19-1831
Trayler, Richard - Sarah Ann Mead   2-14-1830
Trayler, Thomas - Catharine Shoultts
                                      2-24-1836
Trayler, Willis - Patsey Finn   2- 6-1821
Twitty, Allen - Betsey Gears   10-28-1841
Twitty, Barford - Rebeckah Brittain
                                      9-23-1817
Upton, David - Almira Defindoll   8- 4-1841
Upton, Joseph - Eliza Elizabeth Fowler
                                     11-23-1843
Vaughn, John - Catharine Selby   7-23-1823
Vinanner (?), George - Ruth West   7- 6-1823
Walh, David - Susanna Higgens   5- 5-1839
Wallace, Harrison - Ellen Cummins
                                     12-19-1841
Ward, John - Elizabeth Ann Hardin
                                     12- 1-1842
Ward, Levin - Sina Lett   11- 1-1832
Weaver, John - Rachel Harbison   9-16-1817
Wells, Daniel - Joanna Roberts   11-10-1825
West, Alexander - Arpy Marvil   5-22-1842
West, Tilmon - Nancy O Kinman   5-15-1842
Whaley, Elijah - Catharine Adams   11- 4-1833
Whaley, John - Margaret Watson   9-17-1843
Whaley, Stephen - Hannah Miller   12-19-1833
Whaley, Thomas - Betsey Kinman   9- 5-1830
Whaley, William - Bersheba Crayton
                                      7-26-1824
White, Alvin T - Elizabeth Thomas   3- 1-1838
White, Charles F - Betsey Colvin   1- 5-1826
White, Charles F - Henrietta Ward   8-15-1840
White, Henry - Susanna Johnson   7- 2-1837
White, John - Catharine Johnson   1-26-1837
White, Lewis - Lucretia Burkhart   5-24-1835
Whitehead, Silas - Emily Young   1-13-1823
Whitehead, Solomon - Sophia Lamb   8- 7-1825
Wilkins, Thomas F - Mary Elizabeth
   Miller   3-29-1843
Williams, James - Mary Alexander   1- 3-1841
Williams, John W - Angeline Oliver
                                     12-18-1838
Williams, Joseph - Elizabeth Yates
                                      4-28-1825
Williams, Joseph - Rueyann Parker   3-24-1833
Williams, Thomas - Mary Foster   6-17-1841
Williams, William H - Manilla Lane
                           lic. 3-25-1838
Willis, George - Elizabeth Johnson
                                     12-10-1833

Willis, Hazel - Sarah Ann Fowler
lic. 9-29-1841
Willis, Jessee - Mary Elizabeth
Fowler 6-17-1842
Willis, Maxwell - Nancy Fowler 10-22-1839
Wilson, Andrew - Mary Selby 9-28-1830
Wilson, Peter - Mary Pride 11- 7-1824
Withers, James R - Jane Campbell 7-10-1836
Withers, William L - Christiana
Withers 4-27-1819
Wixon, John - Mahala Coonrod
lic. 12-29-1830
Woodrey, Isaac - Nancy Knight 1- 5-1837
Woods, William - Elizabeth Corn 12-29-1839
Woolf, Peter - Mary Fredrick 10-10-1817
Wright, George - Edith Whips 2-14-1820
Wright, George - Jane A Bee 11-18-1841
Wright, Hiram - Sally Wyatt lic. 9-11-1827
Wright, Jackson - Lucinda Baltch (?)
lic. 9-10-1839

Wright, John - Mary Deadman lic. 12-31-1829
Wright, William Jr - Nancy Hardin 4- 1-1819
Wyatt, Benjamin F - Patience Scott
4-17-1839
Wyatt, Emanuel - Harriet Cummings 4-22-1843
Wyatt, William - Caroline Battles 4-18-1841
Wyatt, William H - Mary Dedman
lic. 6- 7-1837
Wyley, Theodore - Mary Kinman 5-21-1840
Young, David - Elizabeth Hawkins (?)
3- 3-1828
Young, David - Polly White 3-14-1837
Young, David Sr - Polly Beck 5- 3-1832
Young, Jacob - Margaret Blase 9-15-1833
Young, Jonathan - Harriet Withers 3- 3-1822
Youngman, Jacob - Anna Dilley 6- 3-1827
Youngman, John - Amelia Curtis 1-31-1830
---, James - Rachel A ---Negroes 10-29-1820

GENEALOGICAL RESEARCH IN FEDERAL DOCUMENTS

Mr Volkel in his recent talk at the Genealogy Symposium mentioned the printed Federal Documents as a source for genealogical material. To test this we checked at random some of the Congressional Documents, and while we found more for other states than for Indiana in a very limited search, it is surprising what can be found. The Documents are indexed by subject in Ben Perley Poore, A Descriptive Catalogue of the Government Publication of the United States, 1774-1881 (Washington, D. C., 1885). Among the Documents relating to Indiana were the following:

From Senate Documents, 15 Congress, 1 session, Vol. II, Doc. 170 [1818]

List of Invalid Pensioners, belonging to the State of Indiana,
and payable at Vernon, Indiana, with the annual allowance to each . . .

[Only the names are reproduced here]

George Antis
Thomas Almon
Robert Baird
Joseph Bartholomew
John V Buskirk
Guydon Branham
Henry Bateman
Robert Briggs
Mathew Byrns

Godfrey Hall Balding
Hugh Barns
William Crist
William Collins
Samuel Little
Zachariah Lindley
Peter M'Mickle
Daniel Minor

John Norris
Samuel Potter
Adam Stropes
Silas Stansbury
William Samuels
Joseph Wasson
Humphrey Webster
William B Welsh

Statement showing the Widows and Orphans who are inscribed on the books of this office as half-pay pensioners for five years, conformable to the laws of the U. S. especially the first section of the act of April 16, 1816 . . . [The Indiana list appears on pp. 353-54; the amount each received is omitted. Many of those listed were widows of men killed in the Battle of Tippecanoe, November 7, 1811]

Name of Pensioner	Commencement of pension	Remarks
Asbury, James, widow	7 Nov. 1811	See act of Apr. 10, 1812
Butner, Edward, widow & children	same	Widow remarried Sept. 26, 1813
Berry, Thomas, widow	same	See act of Apr. 10, 1812
Clendenin, Thos., widow	same	same
Drummons, John, widow	same	same
Fisher, Daniel, widow	11 Nov. 1811	same
Hanks, Porter, widow	7 Nov. 1811	same
Hickey, Henry, widow	same	same
Howell, Adin, widow	16 July 1814	same
Kelly, William, widow	7 Nov. 1811	same
Lang, John, widow	22 Nov. 1812	See act of Mar. 3, 1812
Milholland, widow	23 Jan. 1814	

Music, Jesse, widow	7 Nov. 1811	See act of Apr. 10, 1812
McCoy, John, widow	same	same
McMahon, Richard, widow	same	Widow remarried June 7, 1813
Spencer, Spier, widow	same	See act of Apr. 10, 1812
Warrick, Jacob, widow and children	same	Widow remarried Feb. 7, 1813

From House Reports, 16 Congress, 2 session, No. 37 [1820]

Report of the Committee of Claims in the case of Benjamin Freeland, accompanied with a bill for his relief.

The petitioner states that, with his family, in the year 1818, he emigrated from the state of Maryland to the state of Indiana, with a view of settlement for life, and with the hope of obtaining a small tract of land for each of his children, some of whom are married. That with this view he attended the late sales of public lands at Terre Haute, having made several selections, which he describes: that he attended during the first week of the sales, waiting an opportunity to purchase the quarter sections he wished; that he was a few minutes absent at the time a new township was offered for sale, and, being informed by a friend that the lands he wished were then "crying," he instantly bid for them, and purchased them; when, in fact, there was a mistake of a whole range, the lands which he wanted being in range two, and not in range one, which he purchased; that, as soon as he discovered his mistake, he applied to the Register and Receiver for redress, but, having paid for the lands, they declared it out of their power to afford relief: that his object was not speculation, but cultivation, and that if the lands he purchased were fit for that purpose, he would not trouble Congress with his misfortunes; but that they are utterly unfit for farming purposes: he prays for permission to locates within the same district, to the amount of those purchased through mistake. . . .

From Senate Documents, 23 Congress, 2 session, Doc. No. 141

Memorial and Resolution for the benefit of Madison Collins, Feb. 25, 1835.

Whereas it is represented to this General Assembly, that Madison Collins, late of the county of Knox, and now of the county of Warren, has served his country as a common soldier at different periods: that said Collins was in the battle of Tippecanoe, and in that of the spur defeat, and was in the service of his country from the commencement to the close of the late war with Great Britain; through all which service he escaped unhurt, and was honorably discharged in January, 1815. That in the February following the said Collins, in company with a neighbor, was attacked by four Indians on Busseron creek, in Sullivan county, when riding from his father's to Gill's Fort, in which attack his neighbor Dudly Mack was killed, and Collins shot through the shoulder, from which wound he was compelled to undergo surgical treatment for a period of twelve years, which has not only reduced him to poverty, but disabled him from making exertions for his support; therefore, your memorialists would respectfully, but earnestly recommend that the name of said Madison Collins be placed on the pension roll with full pay as a private inasmuch as the said Collins, at the time of receiving said injury was on the western frontier when depredations were continued by the Indians, after the conclusion of peace with Great Britain until June 1815;

From House Reports, 24 Congress, 1 session, Vol. III, No. 759 [1836]

The Committee of Claims, to which was referred the petition of Dr. David H Maxwell, report:

That the petitioner states he entered the service of the United States on or about the 13th day of April, 1813, as a private in Captain Williamson Dunn's company of mounted rangers, and continued in the service of the United States until the 16th day of March, 1814; that said company, with other companies of rangers, were employed in traversing the frontiers, in occupying the different stations and block houses, so as to protect the inhabitants from the hostilities of the Indians. That as no provision had been made by Government for affording medicines and medical attendance for the sick and wounded of said companies; and as from the nature of the service and the wilderness country, through which they had to act, both medicines and medical attendance were indispensably necessary, and without which, individuals and the service would suffer, said petitioner, at the instance and request of the officers and privates, furnished medicines and surgical instruments, and performed the duties of surgeon and physician to said company; that he continued to perform those duties from within a few days after he entered the service until discharged therefrom, in March, 1814; That for a long time he rendered like services for two companies of rangers under the commands of Captains Biggers and Peyton, as also for the volunteer militia under the command of Col. William Russell an officer of the United States army, while on an expedition against the principal Indian towns on the Wabash river, and other frontier places; and that he afterwards performed like services for a company of United States infantry, stationed at Fort Harrison, most of whom were in a deplorable state of sickness, without medical aid, as the physician at said fort had been for many weeks confined to his bed with sickness. The petitioner further states, that he furnished medicines at his own expense for said companies of rangers, volunteer militia, and infantry, to the amount in cost or value, of two hundred and fifty dollars; and the surgical instruments used in said service, and destroyed, or rendered valueless by it cost him seventy dollars; of these sums one hundred and fifty dollars was repaid by the officers and men of his company. Petitioner also alleges, that while in the service at Fort Harrison, he was attacked with fever, which afflicted him for about fourteen months, and broke and impaired his constitution, in consequence of which, he has suffered from ill health ever since and is thereby compelled almost wholly to quit the practice of his profession, on which a large family depends for support. His present situation induces him to present his claim to Congress for such compensation as his services, and said expentitures of money, may justly and equitably entitle him to.

In support of his claim, petitioner produces the certificate of the honorable John Tipton, who states that he was an officer of volunteer militia in the service of the United States against the hostile Indians, in the Indiana Territory, during the summer of 1813, and that a corps of United States rangers were on the same tour, in which, Dr. D. H. Maxwell served; that he attended to the sick and wounded, furnishing his own medicines and surgical instruments, for all which he received no compensation from the volunteers.

The certificate of Captain Williamson Dunn, and other officers of the company of rangers of which petitioner was member, certifies that practitioner furnished medicines and surgical instruments, and attended to the sick and wounded of said company, from the 13th of April 1813, until the March following, when the company was disbanded; that when other companies were associated he extended like services to them, particularly to the United States infantry at Fort Harrison, at which place petitioner was sick himself.

Captain Bigger, who commanded a company of rangers, and Joseph Bartholomew, colonel of a regiment of militia, both certify to the value of the medical services rendered by petitioner.

The petitioner also produces the certificate of the honorable William Hendricks, proving his entering said service, and the great value of his professional services, not only to said Dunn's company, but to the other companies united with it. Mr. Hendricks speaks of the petitioner as a man of much medical reputation and respectability of character, who was for many years president of the State Medical Society of Indiana; was a member of the convention which formed the State constitution, and often a member of the legislative body of that State.

The committee are satisfied that the medical services rendered by the petitioner were very valuable to the service, and that he is entitled to compensation for the same; and for the medicines and damage to surgical instruments, furnished by him, for the benefit and use of the troops, deducting from the amount to be estimated, the sum repaid him by his company for medicines, and his regular pay as a private ranger, heretofore received by him from Government.

As the committee have not sufficient data before them to ascertain the just amount that should be paid, a bill is reported referring the settlement of the claim to the proper accounting officers of the Treasury.

Vols. VII and VIII of the Territorial Papers of the United States compiled and edited by Clarence E. Carter and published by the U. S. Government Printing Office, relate to Indiana Territory and contain a great many petitions directed to the Congress or the President. The following is a sample from Vol. VIII pp. 102-104.

Petition to Congress by Inhabitants of Dearborn, Franklin, and Wayne Counties, from House files 11 Congress, 3 session.

To The Honourable the senate and House of Representatives of the United States of America in Congress assembled, the Humble petition of the subscribers, inhabitants of Dearborn, Franklin and Wayne Counties in the Indiana Territory most respectfully sheweth.

That at a late session of our Territorial Legislature the two latter above named counties have been formed out of the North end of Dearborn and organized as seperate counties; from which circumstance Your Honourable body will perceive the propriety of extending the line of Post offices and Post roads throughout those counties, as the communication of those with the old county of Dearborn is in a great measure cut off, and in order too that political and private information may be more generally diffused through out those counties, than can possibly be under existing circumstances, they being (as before observed) now detached and organized--seperate from all others. We therefore pray that Your Honourable body will be pleased to extend the line of Post roads, from Lawrenceburgh in Dearborn County so as to pass through Brookville in Franklin county, thence through the seat of Justice in Wayne County--and from thence it might with propriety be extended so as to intersect the Ohio Mail at the Town of Eaton in Preble county, Your petitioners therefore Humbly pray that if, (as Your petitioners believe) the above extention of Post roads shall seem reasonable You will be pleased to establish a Post office at Brookville in Franklin county--and authorize the Post Master General, so soon as the seat of Justice shall be fixed in Wayne, to establish a Post office, at the seat of Justice in the said county of Wayne, and Your petitioners as in duty bound will pray &c &c

James Dill	Jabez Winship	Robert Russel
Wm Wilson	John Perkins	Richard Lions
John R. Beaty	John Tomptson	Marton Higgins

Thos. Wardel	Uel Stephens	Nathaniel Winchel
Cyrus Moore	Samuel Brown	John Winchill
Thomas Miller	W. Hamilton	Stephen Law
S. Evans	John James	Wm. Davis
Ulysses Cook	Henry Barnhart	Elias Davis
Chambers Forster	Jonathan Orr	Geor. Steward
Stephen Ludlow	John Huston	Robert Steel
John Lindsay	Stephen Stites	Henry Doubigin
Nh. Davis, Jr	John W. Dorsey	Saml. C. Vance
James Adair	Asahel Churchil	Jacob Horner
Saml. Rockafellar	Samuel Arnett	Isaac Dunn
James Knight	Jacob Hackleman	Wm. Daubigin
John Allen, Jr	Thomas Henderson	Enoch Russel
Joseph Gifferd	Joel Davis	George Guiltner
John Allen	John Vincent	John H Rockafellar
Fieldin Teter	Alekander Higgins	George Wilson
William Henderson	Jacob Hetrick	Robert Hastey
Jeremiah Cary	James Hall	William Logen
Greenbery Lyons	Stephen Winchil	Stephen Lacey
Chilon Foster	Thomas Williams	Davis Milton
Elliott Herndon	James McCoy	Wm. Wilson
John Richerson	David Bradford	Isaac Wilson
George Martin	James Tyner	James Remy
Jesse Winship	Benjn Smith	John Clinton
John Lefforge	Giles Martin	John Login
Saml. Thompson	William Wilson	William Dottar
John Philips	Jno. Lovell	Josiah Allan
John Brown	John Hylum	Harland Brown

PETITIONS TO INDIANA TERRITORIAL GOVERNORS WILLIAM HENRY HARRISON AND THOMAS POSEY

The original petitions are in the Archives Division, Indiana State Library; we appreciate the opportunity to reproduce them in the Hoosier Genealogist. This type of material is very fragile as well as valuable and obviously the use of it has to be restricted. The original wording and spelling of the petitions has been preserved; some of the names have been very difficult to decipher; some were illegible.

The first and earliest petition presented here is one from the newly organized county of Dearborn in 1803. Though Governor Harrison had the power to make all civil and military appointments, license ferries, etc. he usually accepted the recommendations of the petitioners. The counties of Knox, Clark, and Dearborn from which many of the petitions originated covered a much larger area than that included in their present boundaries.

[August 12, 1803]

To William Henry Harrison Esquire Governor of the Indiana Territory

Your petitioners sheweth that a Ferry kept at the upper end of the Commons of the Town of Lawrenceburgh across the Ohio River, and one other across Tanners creek at or near the mouth will be of great publick utility by facilitating the progress of passengers to and from said Town and that Samuel C. Vance Esquire wou'd be a proper person to entrust with the same.

That your Excellency may grant licence agreeable to the above petition, your petitioners will ever pray &c

Thomas O'Brien	Samuel Elliott	Francis Haines (?)
Stephen Stites	Jacob Horner	John Gordon
Joseph Hayes	Hugh Carson	Justus Gibbs
Caleb Hayes	W. Wilson	C. TrusMoore (?)
Jabez Percival	Orin Floury	William Caldwell
Nicholas Lindsey	Jesse B Thomas	James Hamilton

[February the 14 1807]

To his Excelency [William Henry] Harrison esquire Governer and commander in chief of the Indianna Territories

We your humble Petitioners living in the Bounds of your Dominions on the Waters of the Ohio between the red-Bank and the Wabash; are destitute of a Majistrate amongst us. We therefore desire you to authorize Jabez Jones whom we whose names are here written recommend to you for that place

Andrew Mcfadin	Warner Clark	Reuben Fox
Hugh Todd	Jesse Cavins	George Chapman
Gipson Moore	Squire McFadin	Joshua Cavens
Charles Vandaver	Michael Jones	Samuel Jones
John Enyart	Thomas Givens	John Burlison
Absalom Chapman	Samuel Aldredge	Andrew Mcfadin

Indiana Territory Clark County

To his excellency William Henry Harrison Governor of the aforesaid Territory

The memorial of sundry inhabitants and citizens living in the aforesaid Territory & county Your petitioners humbly sheweth you that we are destitute of a justice of the peace amonguest us and are at the distance of twenty miles from any to administer the necessary duties of that office We therefore pray that your wisdom may deem it prudent to send forward a commition for John Vawter as he is the choice of his fellow citizens in these parts as will bee seen by the list of names hereto annexed done in presents of Abraham Huff Esq. a resident in the Illinois grant this 24th October 1807

Gideon Underwood	Jas. Vawter	Jas. Underwood
Wm. Offall	Jas. Edwards	John Lively
Elzaphan Jackson	Joshua Jackson	Ralph Griffin
William Hall	Jesse Vawter	Esquire Hall
John Griffin	John Davis	James Robb
Mason Watts	John Ryker	Stephen Green
James Grissom	John Hall	Samuel Smock
Wm Vawter	Joseph Laine	Peter Laine
Isaiah Blankinshipp	Joel Jackson	Colby Underwood
Bernard McKlain	Robert Greer	Isaac Green

To his Excelancy William H. Harrison Governor of the Indiana Territory

The Petition of a number of the Inhabitance Knox County on the Ohio River in the 12th Range humbly sheweth that by means of Rong or Pertial information Given to your Excelancy a Certain Jacob Windmiller [Winemiller] was appointed a justice of the peace for Sd county. Your Petitioners Humbly Represent that the said Windmiller Cannot or at least does not speak or write any language so as to be understood--Your petitioners therefore Recommend Paul Castelbery as a Gentleman of good charrector Education and Information and has made himself a pirmement setler in our Sd County. your Petitioners therefore pray that your Excelancy will take this matter into consideration and make such appointments as you shall think wright and your Petitioners as in duty Bound will Ever Pray

James Denny	Robert Denny	John Simpson
Amos Kuykendell	James McGuire	Joseph Griffin
John Landers	James McGuire senour	John McGuire
Thomas McGuire	Henry McGuire	Thomas Choat
John Crump	Adam Kuykendall	Jonathan Hampton
Jacob Landers	Abner Kuykendall	Robert Kuykendall
James Strain	Moses Benson	Nickles Long
William Sritle (?)	John Slover	John Slover Sr.
Daniel Miller	Isaac Slover	Saremia (?) Rust
Charles Carson		

Knox County Indiana territory

To all to whom these presence shall come Greeting

That whereas we the pertitioners of our sd county and in the inhabittance of the Afforesaid territory in the united states of America that it appears greatly to us that we stand in need of some person authorised in our sd settlement as a justice of the peace for our sd county of Knox and in our inhabittance for we the above pertitioners and it appears to us that Mr Robert Warfth a citizen of our sd county and territory being the most fitting for the office for we hath suppose him to be a punctual honest man and a good citizen to the sd territory and we the sd pertitioners doth hereby recommend him the sd Robert Warfth unto you William Henry Harrison our Governor of the sd territory and it is our wish desire and request that you will appoint him the sd Robert Warfth as a justice of the peace for us the sd people of your township on white river . . Given and certifyed by us the above subscribers this 3th day of May 1808 and in the independence of the united states of America to William Henry Harrison Captain General and Cheif Commander At the town of Vincennes

William H Harrell	William A Hardy	Nichilass Johnson
Jacob Anthis	Peter Daryon	Jacob Satterly
Elias Satterly	Joseph Johnson	Francis Anthis
John Anthis	Daniel Decker	Levi Selers
Philip Almy	Lot Baldwin	John Daryen
Phinehas Clark	George Fidlen	J B Drennin
Thomas Banks	David Crock	Armstead Bennet
William Haney (?)	Joseph Bowman	Joseph [illeg.]
Thomas Hardy	John Bowman	James Deal
Nat Claypool	Squi[?] Ramy	Jacob Plough
John Decker	Nat Harness	James Percell
John Satterly	John Banks	Seneca Almy

Indiana Territory Knox County hawkins township

To his excellency the governor and commander in cheaf of the indianna

We the under subscribers do recomend to his excellency a very worthy citizen John Wallas a preacher of the gospel to be a justice of the peace in the fork of white river in hawkins township to which we hope his excellency will grant and appoint

Frind Spears	Samuel Conner	Thomas Aikman
John Aikman Junr	Wm Ragsdal	Hezekiah Ragsdal
M[illeg.] Ragsdal	Wm Ballow	Robert Ragsdal
Vance Jones	Robert Bar[?]	Hery Johnson
John Aikman	John Horrall	John Dassy
Thomas Horrall	Martin Redman	Daniel Gregory
Robert Elsey	Jona W Gowen	William Wallis
Josiah Wallis	James C. Veale	John Coleman
Thomas Horrde	James Horrell	John W. Horrell
Wm Horrall	Danl Conner	John Smith
Wm Smith	Wm Brown	Joseph Hobbs
Robert Hays	Alexr. Hays	Henry [illeg.]
Richard Steen	Clariton Steen	Lager Peek
[illeg]	Christopher Coleman	

To his Excellencey William Henery Harrison Governor of the Indianna territory,

The Citizens of the town of Madison humbly sheweth unto your Excellencey that theay haive grate neede of another Majustrate in this plaice for to discharge the ordanary buisness of this town and agreeable to [your] own request we the undersigners do recommend our worthey friend Abraham T. Fisk to your Excellencey to serve us as a majustrate if your Excellencey will gratify your patitioners request in this purticular theay will feall them selves in duty bound to pray
patitioners names this 28th Day of January 1812

Charles Eastin	David Vancleave	Phil Eastin
William Downey	Abraham Smock	Jacob Smock Senr
Jacob Smock junr	Jacob Yunt	Jno. Ryker
Gerardus R. Robbins	Jacob Kelly	John Storm
Lewis Waggener	Leonard Barnes	Samuel Hensley
Benjamin Devawon (?)	Robert Manchus	

The document is endorsed: Commission Issued 5th March 1812

To his Excellency Governor Harrison of the Indiana Territory

We the inhabitants of Ohio Township County of Knox have great reason to complain for want of a Justice of the peace. . . and we the subscribers do recommend Adam Young of the Township above mentioned as a suitable person for that office and we the subscribers do humbly pray you will grant us this request

Danl Grass	Payton Thrailkill	John Meeks
Charles Meeks	Peter Tucker	William Meeks
Athe Meeks	Wiatt Anderson	William Mcfadin
Gulmas Wiggins	A. B. Saburn Dover	Hiram Tarrant
Harrison Hendrick	Joseph McDonald	Amos Critchfield
Thomas Scott	Baily Anderson	Pinkney Anderson
Ratliff Boon	Thos. Hudspeth	William Hammond
John Boon	John Lout	Joshua Anderson
John Luce (?)		

To the Honourable the Governor of the Indiana Territory, Greeting

We your petitioners of Franklin County & territory aforesaid, beg leave to represent that as John Hall Esqr. feels it inconvenient to serve any longer (he being a magistrate of the peace) we therefore Humbly request that you would commission Dr John Bradbourn of this place to that office; we believing, from his deportment in life &c that he will fill the place with benefit to the community &c. And your petitioners as in duty bound will ever pray &c

John Hall	Landon Robinson	John Tyner
Jacob Youngblood	Lewis Deweese	

To the Right honourable [illeg.] the commander in Chief of the Indianian Territory

We your humble petitioners being under command of your excellencies [illeg.] beg leave to state that whereas we your petitioners having been Calld on to serve the country in which we live, & to defend our Rights & privileges have come far hence even to this place as tho our own places had been in safety But Alass horrid news awakes our sensibility by an undoubted assersion that An awful savage outrage has taken place in the bounds of our own company (when at home) the awful consequences of which are that some of our (fellows when at home) such as parents wives children brethren, & friends have become a victim to the savage [illeg.]; & houses burned & beasts destroyed & much robberies in house & other propperty taking place much of which has undoubtedly taken place for want of men to guard the frontier from which we were taken.

We your petitioners inhabitants of Clark County Indianian Ty Imploring mercy from your excelences honour & humanity have hope & therefore pray that our company may be ordered immediately to march in haste to that frontier so that we may assist in the preserverence of our helpless families & to prevent the horrid [illeg.] from extending with savage yells to spred desolation over the face of our part of the Territory as it has now began at pigeon Roost a place in which some of the greatest danger lies

John B. Pittman Capt.	Benjamin Pool	Levi Johnston
Henry Giles Lieut.	Levi Bridgwaters	Phillip Beerguard
Richard Aston	James Robertson	Richard Collins
Thomas Montgomery	Aaron Cunningham	Moses Allen
Alex Montgomery	Wm. Wilky	Isaac Clark
Thomas Pool	Wm. N. Griffith	Joseph Johnston
Jonathan Carson	Benj. Sanders	Danl. W. Williams
Jonathan Carr	Edward G. Jacobs	Elijah Randels
Aaron Holdman	Wm. Pittman	James Sumers
Saml. Plasket	Frederick Bayer	Wm. B. Guthrie
William Ferguson	Wm. G. Gulick	Jno. Jackson
David Huckleberry	Andrew Fait	Barwell Prather
Reuben Steed	Charles Steed	Thomas Sweny
Eli Jacobs	Jeremiah Jacobs	Absalom Parker
John Huffman	John Reed	Wm. Montgomery
John Jeffries	Thomas Mathews	George Huklebery
Thomas Mathews	Jeremiah Robertson	John Anderson
Josiah Williams	Daniel Field	Jonathan Hartley

Walnut Ridge 2nd June 1813

To his Excellency Thomas Posey

We of the citizens of Harrison County being an entire frontier and intirely destitute of any guard and have been very much harrassed by the enemy this season and are probably as much exposed as almost any part of our Territory We pray you if in your power to give us what aid you can from Capt. Biggers company of Rangers that have just been organized as they are not yet disposed of The citizens adjacent Valonia wish to be remembered as there is a probability of their being left destitute also And we your humble petitioners are ever bound in duty &c &c

Demsey Rice	John Ramsey	William Logan
Jacob Hattabough	Thomas Denney	Elijah Driskell
Mical Ring	Richard Newkirk	Elijah Rinker (?)
George Hattabough	Robt. Ellison	James Ellison

A VERMONT EMIGRANT LIVING IN CRAWFORD COUNTY WRITES HOME

In sending in a correction on Dubois County Wills published in the December 1975 issue of *THG*, Mrs. Lora Arms Peters of San Antonio, Texas, a descendant of America Ann Arms (not Annis as in *THG*), heir of James Newton, also sends us two interesting letters. One is from Charles R. (Charleroy) Arms, America's husband, to his brother Richard in Brandon, Vermont. It was written August 6, 1844, and postmarked Fredonia, August 19, 1844. The second letter from Finch ? Barlow, a brother-in-law of Arms, was enclosed. The original letters are in the Vermont Historical Society State Library, Montpelier.

August the 6th 1844

To Mr Richard Arms Brandon Vermont

Deer Brothers and sisters and friends I will inform you all that I am in good health and hope these lines may find you all in health and prosperity I went to kentucky last spring to see the Widow Arms, Mary, and hir people Benoni,s children are all dead this news may cause you to think that this is a sickly countery Whare I live is very healthy wee have had no sicknice in our family whatever

I have recievd 4 leters from Samuel Arms since he left this countery in his last he informs me that you have sold youre farm and intend to come to the west next spring Samuel requested me to wright to you if I knew of any good farms for sale, I will now inform you that thare is good chances here of farms with apple and peach orchards good buildings for sale and very cheap 4 or 5 hundred Dollers

149

is it not passing strange that Samuel in passing thru the States of New York Ohio Indiana and as far as the City of Neworlenes and back thru the state of Indiana east and West north and south and then to the state of michigan is it not strange I say that in pasing so many thousand good farm,s he cannot lik eny but reccomendes one that he never saw I have traveld the most of this (Samuels travels) and I like this countery very well for mildnice of Climate productive soil and good water divercifide with hills and dales brooks and rivers the beautiful Ohio river with hir 500 steemboats and as meny flat boats freight with all kinds of produce, and passingers the busyness that is a going on in the west will surprise a Vermont it surprised Barlow and Naoma perhaps you would [like] to here more about Barlow and Naomi they live in the town of fredoni on the ohio river 40 miles below New Albany 20 miles from me if you come down the river thare is youre best place to land

Finch Barlow come here 18 months ago they landed at fredona he likes this countery very well they hav ben to ce me Naoma wanted to live by me but Barlow pre fired living nere the river to sell wood to the steemboats they get two Dolers a cord for wood I got word yesterday that he was sick of a feaver I must go and see him soon they have 5 girls and wee have 4 make 9 no boys somutch for Barlow and Charli

I will now give you some of the outlines of my affares in 2 weeks i will raise my mill 40by 46 feet it is a very heavy frame for sawmill and gristmill I have one span of mares two yoke of oxens 4 cows 15 head of sheep and hogs without numb number i killed and sold 26 head last fall and 2 beeves 150 bushels of corn worth 37½ cents per bushel this sold and for sale I have a good crop this year the rise of 20 acres of corn 6 of flax 2 of oats my oats fell down the land is to rich for oats to bad to ceep my oats that is not prophitable N.B. I do all this work my self if i have ^{eny} thing to sell it Does not go ti hirelings wheat took the rust this year is not good

now Richard the time is come that you ^{can} come here with a good piece of mony which goes a good ways in this cou ntery and Noah I would like to see you in this wide extended countery school teaching is good bussyness here taylering is good busyness the young men have to go 15 or 20 miles to get a coat cut and made they are still dressing beter some broad cloth is worn and the making costs very high you have now good learning and a good trade come a head this from youre broher in the west

CHARLEROY ARMS

Mr. Richard Arms Sir As I was out Charleys the time or soon after he had wrote this letter and he told me what he had herd from you and wished me to fill out this letter and I took it but did not reede it till sense I have been home and I find some of it not agreeble to mi mind As for land there is farms for sale here A Most Every one wonst to Sewl and there Is A farm for sale nere here with a good orchard Peach Aples one hundred and twenty Acers but now I will give you A Discripshion of the Country it is hiveley and broken and this Soil b (a or e) ing but light broke And A plenty of Milk Sick fever nere Charleys this seson but Charleys four have not had it yet And there is a Nother little plage the tick which is a litle criter about the sise of a fleas Said if you go in the wode this time of the year they will be thousens on you at once and the storet biten Chicker that you Ever saw to Conclude the hole it is the minest Part of the world I Ever was in Charley wrote that I wis well Satisfie in this country But am Satis fide to guit out of it and that will be soon for I huv sold and Start movin soon you will do well to wait til you here from me again our family Ar all well at the Presant Except me and I am A getin better fast Considrin if you dont believe com and see this from your friend

FINCH ? BARLOW

(Polke) Family

Copied from an old Bible found in an antique shop in Menlo Park, California, and sent to the Indiana Historical Society by the Santa Clara County (California) Historical & Genealogical Society.

Family Register

Adam G. Polk b. 2-11-1807, Shelby Co., Ky.

Coraline [or Caroline] Burnside b. 11-25-1815, Franklin Co., Ind.

Adam G.Polke (1) Caroline Burnside 6-21-1831; (2) Otelia Winchill Cullen, dt of Nathaniel & Maria Barbara Winchill, 5-12-1842

Otelia Winchill b. 1-23-1814, Franklin Co., Ind.

Francis DeWitt b. 2-14-1817, Emden [   ]

Otelia Polk b. 1-23-1814, Franklin Co., Ind.

Francis DeWitt & Otelia Polk m. 7-17-1848

Maria Barbara DeWitt b. 7-26-1849

Francis M. DeWitt b. 5-19-1852, Portland, Oregon Territory

Otelia Viola DeWitt b. 12-23-1854, Washington Co., Oregon Territory

VANDERBURGH COUNTY MARRIAGES, 1818-1840

Compiled from a microfilm copy of loose manuscript material. such as applications for marriage licenses, marriage returns, consent papers, affirmations of age, etc. in the Genealogy Division, Indiana State Library. For the period 1835 through 1839 the marriages were checked with a compilation made in 1949 by the Vanderburgh Chapter of the Daughters of the American Revolution from the first bound volume of marriages. It is quite likely that the marriages are incomplete for the early period since no record of them has been found in a bound volume.

Acheson, William - Amelia F. McJohnston
    9-11-1840
Aeikley, Jacob - Anne Shafner   2-24-1835
Alcorn, Thomas, Jr. - Jane Haynes   7- 8-1833
Alexander, George - Jane Swaney   3-12-1829
    John Wilson attests to their ages
Allen, Edward - Rebecca Palmer   2-10-1819
Alverson, Davis - Jane H. Hopkins   7- 2-1840
Amory, George W. - Mary Phillips
    Eliza Phillips, mother of bride
    consents on   8- 9-1834
Anderson, Thomas - Mary Johnson   5-20-1819
Angel, Anderson - Matilda Chriswell 6-11-1835
    Elizabeth Chriswell, mother of bride,
    consents
Angel, John W. - Lorana Darby   10-18-1832
    Timothy Judd, guardian of bride, consents
Anson, Abraham W. - Ruthy Stout   8- 4-1819
Anthony, John - Hope Wilson   2-12-1829
Archer, Thomas M. - Kezia Taylor   11- 1-1836
Armstrong, Neely - Katharine Armstrong
    Abraham Dudley attests to   12-15-1833
    their ages
Austin, David - Nancy Dickerson   12- 4-1825
Austin, George - Alesana Shelton   6-17-1831
Austin, William - Sally Tickner   11-29-1833
    Thomas Dunk attests to their ages
Bacharach, Joseph - Mary Bittrolff 9- 2-1838
Baker, George - Catherine Henry   6-12-1839
Baker, William - Sarah Shults   6-12-1832
Baker, William M. - Sarah Pennington
    3-17-1839
Balding (or Baldwin), John - Almira Paul
    8-26-1819
Ball, William - Sirkle   4-15-1834
    consent of parents (names not given)
Ballard, John - Anna Lankton lic. 4- 8-1830
Barber, Avery - Nancy Dean   8-12-1823
Barker, Thomas - Mary Cutright   12-26-1818
Barker, William - Elizabeth Onyett 10-29-1839
Barker, William H. - Jane McCorcle 1-21-1836
    Patsey Hawkins, mother of groom, consents
Barlow, Anderson - Melissa Lane   1- 1-1840
Barnard, George - Grace Balsden   11-15-1828
Barnet, James A - Sarah A. McCrilles
    Jesse & Elizabeth Gay,   6- 1-1837
    parents of groom, consent
Barnett, Joseph A. - Esther Anne Jones
    8-31-1826
Barnett, Joseph Clemment - Abigail Gillett
    10-12-1837
Barnett, William - Calesta Kinyon   7-13-1826
Barnett, William - Maryetta Knapp   7-26-1832
Bass, William - Sarah Maxey
    Ages attested to 8-14-1832
Basselton, James - Elizabeth Rappelyea
    5- 6-1840
Bates, George - Mary E. Martin   4-22-1840

Bates, Isaac - Judy Green   10- 4-1823

Bates, William - Elizabeth Martin   1-16-1838
Bauer, John August - Margaret B. Hein
    9-20-1840
Beach, Alvin - Sally James   9-18-1825
Beal, George - Cynthia Shultz   10-30-1827
    Abraham Franceway attests to her age
Beatty, Henry - Sally Hirons   12-24-1829
Behagg, John - Amanda Leftridge   5- 9-1836
Bell, Charles - Margarett Whitstone 2-25-1830
Benjamin, Elijah - Sarah Waters   3- 6-1838
Biers, Henry - Margaret Hubener   6-30-1839
Bigham, John - Mahala Childers   6-27-1837
Bippus, Gottlieb - Catherine Loften 12-10-1837
Blackburn, Bryson - Sarah Stanchfield
    4- 9-1840
Blackburn, Hervey - Ann Balsdon   9-13-1832
    Grooms father, consents; name not given
Blackburn, Hugh - Polly Tyler   7- 2-1826
Blackburn, Hugh - Mahatable Paul 11- 3-1835
Blackburn, James - Anna Robe   1-14-1830
Blackburn, James - Mahala Sutton   8- 3-1837
Blackburn, Plasant - Nancy Bates   3-21-1839
Blanchard, Samuel - Sarah Young   6-13-1840
Blevins, William - Lavina Fairchild 2- 6-1825
Boardman, Charles G. - Mary Scott 12- 2-1838
    Sylvester & Susan Boardman, parents of
    groom, consent
Boardman, Edward T. - Elizabeth Scott
    Jane Kennedy, mother of bride, 4-25-1839
    consents
Bohall, David Ross - Susanna Smith 2-16-1832
Bohall, John - Hannah Crow   1- 1-1840
Boiquet, Conrad - Sabine Geyer   4- 7-1840
Boner, Charles - Peggy Asa   4-22-1827
Boswell, George W. - Martha Hutchinson
    9-30-1838
Boyrne (or Boren), Jesse J. - Catharine
    Fairchield   11-27-1837
Bowyer, William - Elizabeth Crisp 11- 8-1834
Brainbridge, John - Mary Rocket   9-11-1830
Brown, George - Eliza Peck   6-14-1833
Brown, James S. - Francis Bugg   5-28-1829
Brown, William - Rebecca McIntosh 12- 4-1836
Brown, William - Polly Ann Thomas   7-26-1838
Bryant, George W. - Anna Hays   8- 4-1831
Bugg, John - Martha Johnson   3-27-1835
    Jacob D. Bugg attests for their ages
Burch, Walter - Lavicia Diana Davis 5-29-1831
    Levi Davis consents for bride
Burcklow, James - Elizabeth Burcklow 8-16-1836
    John V. Burcklow attests their ages
Burris, John - Louisa Dissinger   8- 8-1838
Burtis, Edward - Delia Ann Hale   4- 1-1831
Burtis, Jesse - Hannah Hayhurst   10-25-1832
Butcher, Thomas J. - Mary Mallard 10-20-1836
Butler, Richard L. - Frances King   8- 8-1836
    Agnes Butler, mother of groom, consents
Butler, Thomas - Polly Ann Chapman
    Joseph & Ibby Chapmen, parents of bride,
    consent on   8- 8-1836

Caldwell, Joseph M. - Julia C. Dupuy
 7-22-1840
Caldwell, William - Clementine A. Hopkins
 5- 9-1833
Calloway, Harvey T. - Armilda Stinson
 12-24-1840
Calvert, James - Martha Jane Ewin   7-20-1836
 Henry Ewin, Sr., father of bride, consents
Cannon, Curtis - Eliza Shaw   7-19-1833
Cannon, Russell - Harriett Palmer   10-30-1837
Carlile, Richard - Prescilla McNew   3-25-1825
Carlile, Richard Jr. - Elizabeth Whetstone
 Richard Carlile, Sr., father of 6- 8-1834
 groom, consents; George Francis attests
 to age of bride
Carosen, Thomas - Sarah Jane Wright   1- 7-1839
Carson, Robert G. - Martha Wright   3-25-1834
Carter, John - Eliza Arburn   3-12-1838
Cashman, Elisha P. - Esther Knapp   7-24-1821
Caslur, James, see Kausler
Catlin, William - Catharine Blevins   3-20-1828
Cavens, Joshua - Rachel Stinchfield   3-19-1840
Cavins, Ira - Lavinia Hooker   12- 1-1833
 Ruth Cavins, mother of groom, consents
Cavins, Shelby - Sarah David   8- 2-1838
Chamber, John - Malinda Hogue   2-16-1837
Chapman, James - Fanny Mills   10-28-1824
 William Chapman attests to age of groom;
 Nancy Mills for bride
Chapman, Jeremiah - Sarah Henson   4-19-1832
 Dorcas Chapman & Jesse Henson, parents,
 consent
Chapman, John - Eliza Sprinkle   2-11-1836
 Joseph & Ibby Chapman, parents of groom,
 consent
Chase, Joseph P. - Rosetta Hutson   1-28-1821
Childers, Joseph C. - Mahala Casy
 Nicholas Long, guardian   lic. 8- 8-1831
 of bride, consents
Childs, Thomas - Mary Pleck (or Peck)
 8- 4-1831
Chrisp, William - Eves Arb   9-14-1837
Clark, John - Rachel Williams   1-16-1839
Clark, Solomon S. - Lamira Woodworth
 John Clark, father of   lic. 11-14-1838
 groom, & Horace & Phebe Woodworth, parents
 of bride, consent
Clay, Benjamin M. - Arbiah F. McDowell
 11- 6-1838
Clighman, George - Mary Ann Henson   10-21-1839
Cobble, Adam- Eliza Webb   7-30-1830
 Eliza Webb has neither parents nor
 guardian in Indiana
Cockrum, James, Sr. - Hopy Eaton   10- 2-1834
Cockrum, Jonathan W. - Katharine Garrett
 John Garrett, father of   6-30-1831
 bride, consents
Coda, Barna - Susan Burtes   8-30-1825
Coim, Jacob -   Rufbolton
         (or Rushbotton?)   9-20-1819
Coker, Thomas I. - Nancy Lyel   12-24-1840
Cole, James - Ruth Scott   11-29-1819
 Hugh Coal (Cole) & Belitha Scott, parents,
 consent
Collins, Thomas C. - Martha Jane Miller
 Willey Miller, mother of bride,   8-13-1835
 consents
Collins, Wilson - Sibble Kenyon   2- 2-1837
Colquit, Vincent F. - Catharine Miller
 6-11-1832
Colvin, Charles G. - Margaret A. McCorcle
 3-25-1838

Combat, Peter - Parby Hauft (?)   12-16-1838
Compton, Joseph - Rebecca Peck   8- 4-1825
Cook, Henry - Margaret Davis   6-14-1838
Cook, John - Elizabeth Dausman   1- 9-1840
Copy, Hudson - Martha Jane Hightower
 12-12-1836
Cory, Samuel - Sarah Faree   8-10-1838
Cothan (or Gotham), George - Susan Watts
 11-21-1837
Cotton,(?) James - Lucinda Burk   12- 9-1840
Cowl, William - Julia Ann Ewing   5- 7-1835
Cox, Isaac - Sarantha Benjamin   3-23-1840
Cox, James - Franky Miller   4-22-1822
Cox, Joseph - Sally Miller   3-21-1822
Craddock, Daniel B. - Mary Jane Gilmore
 2-22-1838
Craig, Jesse R. - Eliza Richardson   1- 7-1828
Craig, Joseph - Hannah Hutchinson   6-26-1836
Criderfield, Jesse - Nancy Robertson
 9-27-1840
Crist, James - Nancy Levingworth   10-23-1839
Crow, Benjamin - Clarissa Murphy   12-18-1840
Crow, Phillip - Margaret Eliza Lane   5-29-1836
Cruse, see Kruse
Cummings, Ambrose - Polly Turpin   9-10-1829
Cutler, Jarvis - Eliza Chandler   9-29-1821
Daniel, William - Betsy McGiffin   6- 5-1823
Darby, Ezra - Achsash Emily Judd
 Timothy & Judy Judd,
 parents of bride, consent   lic. 11-26-1829
Darby, Reubin - Peggy Noble   6-30-1822
Darby, Reubin - Sarah Wood   8- 1-1825
Darby, Reuben - Mary Wood   3-27-1832
Darnel, James - Thankful Gillaspey   1- 3-1839
 J. P. Gillaspy, father of bride, consents;
 William Darnel attests to age of groom
Darnel, William - Melissa Sillman   12-31-1829
 Ephraim Darnel, father of groom, consents
Darnell, John - Eliza McCallister   4-18-1830
Davis, George - Martha Powell   2-22-1835
Davis, Robert - Ann Maria Fairchield
 Seth Fairchild, father of   12-25-1832
 bride, consents
Davis, Thomas - Nancy Martin   6-20-1824
Davis, Thomas - Frances Price   lic.10- 5-1830
Day, Phillip - Elizabeth Hayman   9-13-1838
Dean, William - Nancy Bass   10-21-1830
Dean, William - Eliza Wallers   6-20-1838
Decker, Christian - Ann Mary Griesz   8-18-1837
Decker, Phillip - Caroline Cook   9- 6-1839
Degel, George - Mary Deidrich   6- 8-1840
Delger, John - Dorothy Hipner   11-12-1840
Depoyster, John - Elizabeth Robeson
 11- 4-1818
Dhemer, Heinrich - Margaret Hakjler   6- 9-1838
Dixon, Roger - Eliza Brown   1-22-1828
Dobyns, Thomas I. - Clarisa McGary   9-29-1825
Dodge, Richard - Rebecca Warren   10-23-1833
Donaldson, Charles - Ellen Dupray   5-16-1838
Dougherty, William - Nancy Johnson   8-13-1828
Douglas, Albert W. - Nancy Rose   12-21-1826
Duffy, Aaron - Deborah Ann Prince   7- 3-1839
Dukes, Britain - Melissa Ann Wiley   11-17-1833
Dukes, Hezekiah - Priscilla Jane O'Neal
 John O'Neal, father of bride,   7- 1-1830
 consents
Dukes, Hezekiah - Nancy Whetstone   1-26-1837
 Mary Whetstone, mother of bride, consents
Dukes, William - Louiza France   3- 3-1836
 William & Catharine France, parents of
 bride, consent
Duncan, John - Harriett Stroud   10-13-1836

Caldwell, Joseph M. - Julia C. Dupuy
                  7-22-1840
Caldwell, William - Clementine A. Hopkins
                  5- 9-1833
Calloway, Harvey T. - Armilda Stinson
                12-24-1840
Calvert, James - Martha Jane Ewin   7-20-1836
   Henry Ewin, Sr., father of bride, consents
Cannon, Curtis - Eliza Shaw   7-19-1833
Cannon, Russell - Harriett Palmer 10-30-1837
Carlile, Richard - Prescilla McNew 3- 3-1825
Carlile, Richard Jr. - Elizabeth Whetstone
   Richard Carlile, Sr., father of 6- 8-1834
   groom, consents; George Francis attests
   to age of bride
Carosen, Thomas - Sarah Jane Wright 1- 7-1839
Carson, Robert G. - Martha Wright 3-25-1834
Carter, John - Eliza Arburn   3-12-1838
Cashman, Elisha P. - Esther Knapp 7-24-1821
Caslur, James, see Kausler
Catlin, William - Catharine Blevins 3-20-1828
Cavens, Joshua - Rachel Stinchfield 3-19-1840
Cavins, Ira - Lavinia Hooker   12- 1-1833
   Ruth Cavins, mother of groom, consents
Cavins, Shelby - Sarah David   8- 2-1838
Chamber, John - Malinda Hogue   2-16-1837
Chapman, James - Fanny Mills   10-28-1824
   William Chapman attests to age of groom;
   Nancy Mills for bride
Chapman, Jeremiah - Sarah Henson   4-19-1832
   Dorcas Chapman & Jesse Henson, parents,
   consent
Chapman, John - Eliza Sprinkle   2-11-1836
   Joseph & Ibby Chapman, parents of groom,
   consent
Chase, Joseph P. - Rosetta Hutson 1-28-1821
Childers, Joseph C. - Mahala Casy
   Nicholas Long, guardian   lic. 8- 8-1831
   of bride, consents
Childs, Thomas - Mary Pleck (or Peck)
                  8- 4-1831
Chrisp, William - Eves Arb   9-14-1837
Clark, John - Rachel Williams   1-16-1839
Clark, Solomon S. - Lamira Woodworth
   John Clark, father of   lic. 11-14-1838
   groom, & Horace & Phebe Woodworth, parents
   of bride, consent
Clay, Benjamin M. - Arbiah F. McDowell
                11- 6-1838
Clighman, George - Mary Ann Henson 10-21-1839
Cobble, Adam- Eliza Webb   7-30-1830
   Eliza Webb has neither parents nor
   guardian in Indiana
Cockrum, James, Sr. - Hopy Eaton 10- 2-1834
Cockrum, Jonathan W. - Katharine Garrett
   John Garrett, father of   6-30-1831
   bride, consents
Coda, Barna - Susan Burtes   8-30-1825
Coim, Jacob -   Rufbolton
      (or Rushbotton?) 9-20-1819
Coker, Thomas I. - Nancy Ann Lyel 12-24-1840
Cole, James - Ruth Scott   11-29-1819
   Hugh Coal (Cole) & Belitha Scott, parents,
   consent
Collins, Thomas C. - Martha Jane Miller
   Willey Miller, mother of bride, 8-13-1835
   consents
Collins, Wilson - Sibble Kenyon   2- 2-1837
Colquit, Vincent F. - Catharine Miller
                6-11-1832
Colvin, Charles G. - Margaret A. McCorcle
                3-25-1838

Combat, Peter - Parby Hauft (?)   12-16-1838
Compton, Joseph - Rebecca Peck   8- 4-1825
Cook, Henry - Margaret Davis   6-14-1838
Cook, John - Elizabeth Dausman   1- 9-1840
Copy, Hudson - Martha Jane Hightower
               12-12-1836
Cory, Samuel - Sarah Faree   8-10-1838
Cothan (or Gotham), George - Susan Watts
               11-21-1837
Cotton,(?) James - Lucinda Burk   12- 9-1840
Cowl, William - Julia Ann Ewing   5- 7-1835
Cox, Isaac - Sarantha Benjamin   3-23-1840
Cox, James - Franky Miller   4-22-1822
Cox, Joseph - Sally Miller   3-21-1822
Craddock, Daniel B. - Mary Jane Gilmore
               2-22-1838
Craig, Jesse R. - Eliza Richardson 1- 7-1828
Craig, Joseph - Hannah Hutchinson 6-26-1836
Criderfield, Jesse - Nancy Robertson
               9-27-1840
Crist, James - Nancy Levingworth 10-23-1839
Crow, Benjamin - Clarissa Murphy 12-18-1840
Crow, Phillip - Margaret Eliza Lane 5-29-1836
Cruse, see Kruse
Cummings, Ambrose - Polly Turpin   9-10-1829
Cutler, Jarvis - Eliza Chandler   9-29-1821
Daniel, William - Betsy McGiffin   6- 5-1823
Darby, Ezra - Achsash Emily Judd
   Timothy & Judy Judd,
   parents of bride, consent lic. 11-26-1829
Darby, Reubin - Peggy Noble   6-30-1822
Darby, Reubin - Sarah Wood   8- 1-1825
Darby, Reuben - Mary Wood   3-27-1832
Darnel, James - Thankful Gillaspey 1- 3-1839
   J. P. Gillaspy, father of bride, consents;
   William Darnel attests to age of groom
Darnel, William - Melissa Sillman 12-31-1829
   Ephraim Darnel, father of groom, consents
Darnell, John - Eliza McCallister 4-18-1830
Davis, George - Martha Powell   2-22-1835
Davis, Robert - Ann Maria Fairchield
   Seth Fairchild, father of 12-25-1832
   bride, consents
Davis, Thomas - Nancy Martin   6-20-1824
Davis, Thomas - Frances Price lic.10- 5-1830
Day, Phillip - Elizabeth Hayman   9-13-1838
Dean, William - Nancy Bass   10-21-1830
Dean, William - Eliza Wallers   6-20-1838
Decker, Christian - Ann Mary Griesz 8-18-1837
Decker, Phillip - Caroline Cook   9- 6-1839
Degel, George - Mary Deidrich   6- 8-1840
Delger, John - Dorothy Hipner   11-12-1840
Depoyster, John - Elizabeth Robeson
               11- 4-1818
Dhemer, Heinrich - Margaret Hakjler 6- 9-1838
Dixon, Roger - Eliza Brown   1-22-1828
Dobyns, Thomas I. - Clarisa McGary 9-29-1825
Dodge, Richard - Rebecca Warren   10-23-1833
Donaldson, Charles - Ellen Dupray 5-16-1838
Dougherty, William - Nancy Johnson 8-13-1828
Douglas, Albert W. - Nancy Rose   12-21-1826
Duffy, Aaron - Deborah Ann Prince 7- 3-1839
Dukes, Britain - Melissa Ann Wiley 11-17-1833
Dukes, Hezekiah - Priscilla Jane O'Neal
   John O'Neal, father of bride, 7- 1-1830
   consents
Dukes, Hezekiah - Nancy Whetstone 1-26-1837
   Mary Whetstone, mother of bride, consents
Dukes, William - Louiza France   3- 3-1836
   William & Catharine France, parents of
   bride, consent
Duncan, John - Harriett Stroud   10-13-1836

Dunk, John - Rebecca Watts   12-31-1838
Durbrow, James - Ann M. Foal   1-28-1820
Earl, Robert - Ann Boyd   11-29-1838
Earskin (or Erskin), Andrew - Abigal Ewing
    (or Ewin)   12-25-1825
    Henry Ewin, father of bride, consents
Earskin, William - Elizabeth Hemingway
                                     2-14-1825

Earskin, see also Erskin
Eaton, Allen H. - Zilpah Barker   10-11-1835
Eaton, George W. - Malinda Walker   6- 3-1829
    Thomas Walker, father of bride, consents
Eaton, William - Lucy Barker   11- 3-1833
Edmond, George, Sr. - Polly McDonald
                                lic. 9-26-1835
Edmond, Thomas - Mary Tupman
    James & Elizabeth Tupman, parents of bride,
    consent   2-24-1829
Edmonds, George - Charlotte Gothard
                                    11- 4-1831
Edmunds, John - Litha Sirkles   3-15-1823
Edwards, Hardy - Eliza Wagnon   1-29-1829
    William Wagnon, father of bride, consents
Edwards, James - Lucinda Miller   7- 5-1827
Edwards, Samuel - Susan Englett   8-19-1839
Eisle, Andrew W. - Rosina Losa   2-23-1839
Elderfield, Thomas - Jane Tupman   6-27-1838
    James & Ann Tupman consent (relationship
    not given)
Elderfield, Thomas - Bathsheba Hooker
                                     6-14-1840
Eliot, Lewis - Rhoda Thomas   1-19-1839
Elliott, George - Susan Blackler (or Blackla)
                                     4-27-1833
Elliott, Joseph P. - Mary Ann Harrison
                                    10-19-1837
Elliott, Joseph P. - Mary L. Wheeler
                                    12- 7-1839
Elliott, Josiah - Elizabeth Powell
    David Powell, father   lic. 2-26-1831
    of bride, consents
Elsworth, Aaron - Elizabeth Parker   2-14-1819
    George Parker, father of bride, consents
Ely, Jesse - Sally Cummings   8-16-1829
Endicott, Joseph - Nancy Calvert   11- 6-1834
    William (or Patrick?) Calvert, father of
    bride, consents
Endicott, Moses - Elizabeth Calvert
                                    12- 4-1825
    Patrick Calvert, father of bride, consents
Endicutt, Henry - Jane Calvert lic. 9-28-1829
English, David D. - Sarah McClanahan
                                     6-11-1837
Ennest (?), Jacob P. - Ruth Oily
                                lic. 7-14-1821
Enyart, Carlon - Sophia Ragan   8- 2-1838
Erskin, Alfred - Rose Phearon   4-10-1840
Erskin, see also Earskin
Evans, Camillus C. - Saleta Stinson
                                    10-28-1830
Everets, Alfred L. - Rachel Gentry 11-23-1840
Fairchild, Charles - Rachel McCorkle
                                     3-25-1838
    James McCorkle, father of bride, consents
Fairchild, Gasham H. - Sarah McCann
                                    11-29-1837
Fairchild, Orman - Hannah Wagnon   1-11-1820
Fairchild, Shearman - Diantha Cody 10-28-1824
Fairchild, Sherman - Louisa Knight   4-15-1834
Fairchild, Timothy - Nancy Blevins   2- 3-1825
Fairchild, Walter - Maryann Pritchett
                                     1-26-1826

Faith, Josiah (or Tobias?) - Nancy Mills
                                    11-25-1827
Fearling, George Peter - Lucy Ann Olur (or
                            Obur) 12-17-1837
Ferguson, Joseph - Tabitha Lyle   3-22-1839
Fetta (Fetty) Philo - Margaret Boger
                                     1-21-1822
Fewquah, Henry - Nancy France   10-24-1839
Fields, Edmond - Cinthia Sullivan   5- 3-1821
Fisher, John T. - Emaline Cloud
    H. W. Cloud, father of bride, gives
    consent   10-11-1837
Fisher, Joseph - Adeline Evans   8-23-1835
Fitzgarrel, Morrison - Rachel Hooker
                                     4- 1-1818
Fitzgarrold, James - Ruthy Hooker   1-25-1821
Fitzgerald, Asa - Julia Warren   2-17-1830
Folmer, Charles - Catharine Humbold
                                    12-22-1836
Forrest, John - Mary Ann Bullett   12- 3-1832
Forrester, Benjamin - Rebecca Shaw
    (negro)   9-11-1838
Forth, Robert - Mary Warren   12- 6-1829
Foster, Weeden - Rebecca Harvey (or Hewey)
                                     7-29-1832
Fowler, Frederic F. - Susanna McQuin
                                     8-29-1837
Fowler, Martin - Nancy Wakelin   8-21-1838
France, Alfred - Mary Ann Hopkins   12- 1-1833
France, James - Elizabeth Beach   6-21-1832
Freeman, William - Elizabeth Arburn
                                     7-25-1839
Fritch, Joseph - Barbara Vinson
    George P. & Sarah Vinson, parents of bride,
    give consent   6-11-1838
Fuller, Lewis - Harriett K. Pettis
                                    10-17-1833
Fuqua, Stephen - Elizabeth Peck   6-28-1825
Furgason, Peter - Peggy Twiford   7-27-1826
Furgeson, Thomas - Catharine Decker
                                     5-18-1829
    Nancy Decker, mother of bride, consents
Garrett, Corydon - Sally James   2-23-1837
    Henry James, father of bride, consents
Gasser, John - Fanny Sweetzer
    Benjamin Gasser attests to her age
                                    12-28-1840
Gates, Joshua - Mary Blackburn   2-25-1834
Geisler, Jacob - Catharine C. Bettroeff
                                     2- 5-1837
Gentry, Enos - Rachel McNeely   9- 6-1827
Gibson, Robert - Frances Knapp   4- 7-1825
Gillett, Aremah - Euranah Knight   8- 6-1829
Gillman, William - Anna Robinson   3-12-1829
Gipson, Elijah - Rebecca Hayhurst   9- 5-1831
Gipson, Robert - Anna Knight   3-21-1821
Glazebrook, William A. - Mary Ann Stapp
                                     6- 2-1830
Gobin, Joseph D. - Frances Stroud   4- 2-1833
    Joshua & Mary Stroud, parents of bride,
    consent
Goldsmith, Daniel F. - Melissa Hopkins
                                     3-27-1823
Good, Andrew - Mary Bruner   6-16-1839
Goodrich, Dempsey - Jane Robinson   4- 4-1834
Goodwin, Ephraim C. - Susan Bohall
                                    10- 7-1834
Goodwin, Ephraim C. - Martha Ann Ross
                                     3-25-1837
Goodwin, Jarre - Sarah Wilkerson   12- 5-1833
Goslee, Ferdinand D. - Ann Amelia Wheeler
                                     6-29-1837

Goss, William - Permelia Rouse   11-22-1835
Gotham, see also Cothan (or Gotham)
Graff, George - Katharine Kollenburgh
                                  10-30-1840
Graften, William - Hannah Russell 4-15-1819
Granger, Ira P. - Phebe Jane Brunfield
                                  5-13-1832
Grant, Thomas - Mary Ann Crisp   5- 8-1837
Greathouse, John - Rachel Isabella Fenton
                                  4-19-1837
Green, Robert - Mary Ann White   4- 9-1840
Green, Thompson - Nancy Ruby   6-10-1828
Green, Thompson T. - Elizabeth McCann
                                  10-26-1837
Gresham, John - Henrietta Yerkes   3- 9-1839
Grim, Calvin - Matilda Fields
    Joseph & Barbary Grim & Cynthia Fields,
    parents of bride & groom, give consent
                                  3-24-1840
Grimwood, James - Hannah Grant   12-15-1838
Gumbert, Abraham - Catharine Hackman
                                  10- 1-1838
Gyon, Peter - Elizabeth Weiden Kopt 5-21-1839
Haas (?), Christopher - Amanda Gates
    Susanna Cline, mother of bride, gives
    consent   12-31-1840
Hale, Abijah - Arena Cavens   2-23-1840
Hale, Nathan - Delia Ann Hopkins   7- 4-1827
Ham, William K. - Jerusha Elmira Monroe
                                  3-11-1836
Hancock, Charles - Mary Ann Mandell
                                  8-22-1833
Hardy, Jubelee - Sarah Gibson   1- 8-1829
    Elijah Gibson attests to age of bride
Haribold (?), Andreas - Eva Hauck 5-22-1838
Harmon, John - Sally Casey   3-30-1828
Harrington, James L. - Isabella Whistler
                                  5-31-1839
Harris, John - Lydia Saunders   10-29-1836
    John R. Hord attests to their ages
Harrison, Elisha - Juliana Fairchild
                                  2-16-1819
Harrison, Zepheniah - Elizabeth Saunders
                                  3-13-1823
Hauser, Philip - Margaret Smidt   4-11-1838
Hayhurst, John - Ellen Carson   8- 4-1838
Hays, Ephraim - Nancy Williams   4-19-1838
Heddenburg, Christian - Elizabeth Schmoll
                                  2-18-1838
Heem, David - Susanna Fink   8-21-1840
Held, Jacob - Louisa Lohmiear   5- -1839
Hemmingway, Israel - Hannah Hall 12- 8-1831
Henning, Arnold - Katharine Olds   9- 9-1832
Henson, John - Mary Chapman   7- 4-1820
Henson, John - Rebecca Wooton   12-25-1820
Herschelman (?), Henry - Elizabeth C. Candee
                                  1- 2-1840
Hess, Henry - Catharine Myer   5-19-1838
Hibbard, Charles - Mary Durphy   7-11-1822
    Elisha Durpee attests that bride is of age
Higgins, Dennis - Eliza Welsh   9- 7-1839
Hill, Samuel - Katey (or Catharine) Sherwood
                                  11- 1-1818
Hillyard, Alexander - Edith Ewin   3- 2-1826
    Henry Ewin, father of bride, consents
Hillyer, William - Mary Conlee   2- 4-1821
Hilyard, James - Mary Erskine   10- 5-1826
Hindman, Alexander - Sarah Ramsey 8- 1-1839
Hisoner, John - Maria Taylor   8- 9-1840
Hoffman, Jacob - Eliza Davis   5- 9-1839
    John Davis, father of bride, consents

Holcom (Holcomb), Benjamin - Lydia Patten
                                  10-19-1821
Holder, James - Hester Ann Noble   3-30-1828
Holloway, Jesse - Mary Fitzgarrel 6-10-1819
    John Fitzgarrel, father of bride, consents
Holzel (or Halsel), Alford - Peggy Fairlee
                                  2- 3-1831
Hooker, Levi - Amelia Perry   6- 7-1840
Hooker, Samuel - Elizabeth Hughs   8-25-1830
Hooker, Thomas - Marietta Eaton   7- 4-1833
Hooker, William - Mahala McCauley 3- 7-1820
Hooker, William - Mary Ann Foster 6- 5-1830
Hoover, George - Elizabeth Hennezin (or
              Hunezin)   2- 7-1840
Hopkins, Hiram - Matilda Fauquer   9-23-1832
Hopkins, John S. - Mary Ann Parrott
                                  12- 9-1834
Hopkins, Lorenzo - Orilla Richey (or Ritchey)
                                  11- 8-1832
Hopkins, Rubin - Juliet Ewin (or Ewing)
                                  4-27-1823
    Henry Ewin, father of bride, consents
Hopkins, William Henry Harrison - Eliza Scott
                                  3-28-1833
Hord, Harrison - Eliza Dunk   10-29-1835
    Charles & Sophia Dunk, parents of bride,
    consent
Hornbrook, John - Margaret B. Knowles
                                  5- 4-1823
Hornby, Henry - Caroline Hornby (alias
              Caroline Mansell)   10- 4-1832
Horner, Thomas - Elizabeth Harrington
                                  4-24-1835
Horsley, John - Anna Wilkins   11- 4-1824
Hotman, Lawrence - Barbara Lisz   1-30-1840
    Richard Horsley, father, consents
House, Andrew - Polly Connelly   12- 3-1836
Hudson, William - Susannah Brown   2-20-1840
Huey, Enoch - Harriet L. Knap   4- 5-1838
    Rebecca Foster, mother of groom, consents
Hughey, Joseph - Betsy Bryant   1-24-1822
    John Bryant, father of bride, consents
Hugo, John - Jane McCallister   8-25-1835
Hunnel, William - Mary McCorcle   12-24-1835
Hurley, Lewis - Catharine Rasune
                     lic.   7-19-1832
Hutchcraft, William - Jane Smith   6- 4-1839
    Thomas Smith, father of bride, consents
Hutchinson, Daniel - Eliza Hooker 12-27-1838
Hutchinson, Isaac - Miriam G. Gavit
                                  10- 8-1837
Hutchinson, Josiah - Eliza Cane   11-20-1831
Hutchinson, Josiah - Mary Palmer   5-28-1837
Hutchinson, Jothum C. - Cynthia Martin
                                  1-20-1831
Ikely, Mathew - Christiana Combs   5-10-1822
Ingle, James - Eliza Wheeler   8-14-1834
Ingle, William - Eliza Neel   11-20-1837
                     Filed   6- 3-1839
Inwood, John - Harriet M. McJohnston
                                  8-17-1836
    William Inwood, father of groom, consents
Ireland, William - Jane Henson   9-18-1838
Isbell, George - Nancy France   4-13-1832
    Daniel Isbell, father of groom, & bride's
    mother, (name not given) consent
Jackson, Isaac - Ann Carlin   9-26-1839
Jacobs, Joseph K. - Sarah Webster 8-15-1819
Jaky, George - Sarah Caton   5-30-1839
James, Henry - Matilda Shultz   6-24-1824
    Daniel James, father of groom, and Sally
    Shultz (no relationship given) consent
James, Henry - Lucy Henberman   4-20-1839

James, Henry Sr. - Cynthia Beal   4-12-1832
James, Lewis - Gemima Whetstone   4- 5-1835
James, William - Savilla Hay   3-19-1828
James, William - Winna A. Lane   1-15-1835
Jared, Ervin - Sarah McShain   3-31-1836
    Samuel & Harriet, parents of groom,
    consent
Jarret, John - Lydia Stanchfield   8-24-1837
Jimerson, William - Hannah Hardisty   6- 9-1838
Jimerson (or Jamerson), William P. -
    Margarett James   2-16-1826
    Daniel James, father of bride, consents
Johnson, James - Martha Washum   12-31-1835
Johnson, James M. - Delila Phillops
                                       11- 8-1837
Johnson, Pleasant - Sarah Jones   1-10-1835
Johnson, William - Catharine Haun   7-29-1819
Jones, Alexander - Minerva Delaney   9- 4-1839
Jones, Charles - Missouri Amazan Miller
                                       3- 8-1837
    Daniel & Sarah Miller, parents of
    bride, consent
Jones, Eli C. - Frances Carson   5-19-1834
    Robert Carson attests to their ages
Jones, James G. - Rose Ann Rappelyea
                                       2-15-1838
Jones, John - Pamela McDaniel (negro)
    (negro)   8-28-1840
Jordan, William - Susannah Armstrong
                                       8- 4-1835
    James Hill, vouches for ages
Judkins (or Judgkins), Lewis - Rachel
    Blackburn   6- 7-1840
Judkins, Hiram - Serena Martin   6-20-1829
Kaffer, John - Catharine Earg   10- 6-1837
Kausler (or Caslur), James - Betsy Harmon
    (or Hannon)   12-23-1830
Keagin, Patrick - Eliza Matilda Johnston
                                       10-12-1829
Kelly, John - Ledoiska Waters
    Daniel Waters, father of bride, gives
    consent   4-27-1832
Kelsey, Lorin A. - Mary M. Williams   2- 4-1838
Kennedy, Jacob - Elizabeth (?) Harris
                                       5- 9-1836
    Ann Richey vouches for brides age
Kennerly, Everton - Jane Scott   9-16-1830
Kesselring, Jacob - Nancy Aydelott   10-25-1832
Kidd, William - Nehoma Edwards   2-21-1838
Kimball, Alvey - Polly Fleeharty   7-22-1818
King, Felix G. - Mary E. Jones   4- 2-1833
King, John - Judith B. Neale   10-20-1836
King, Oliver - Sarah Jane Gobin   12-24-1835
    James & Jane Gobin, parents of bride,
    consent
Kingsbury, Hiram - Rhoda Barker   12-26-1828
Kitchen, John - Claressa Neal   12-25-1833
    John Neal, father of bride   [1834?]
    gives consent   12-23-1834
Knapp, Davis - Delila G. Anderson   8- 4-1836
Knight, Abram - Polly Kimball   3-17-1821
Knight, James - Hannah Hooker   3-24-1833
Knight, William - Elizabeth Darnell
                                       10- 6-1836
Knowles, Daniel - Mary Kingsberry   5-23-1826
Kramer, Philip - Doratha Kollenberg   1-28-1839
Kruse, Frederick - Catherine Schmidt
                                       1-15-1838
Kruse, Henry - Charlotte Bockhouse   12- 9-1838
Lacy (or Lay), William A. - Mary Ann Miller
                                       12-23-1834
Laforge, Joseph - Martha Ludwick   10-18-1835
    Craven Carlin attests to their ages

Lair, William - Martha Logan (or Loger, or
                Lozer)   5-16-1839
Lamb, Bowen - Mary Laffery   9- 2-1830
Lamb, Eli - Lydia Thomas   4-18-1833
Land, James - Sarah Goodman   5-18-1836
Lane, Anthony Floyd - Cynthia Barnet
    John Lane & Nancy Barnet, parents of groom
    & bride, consent on   3-29-1822
Lane, Daniel S. - Sarah Wheeler   1-18-1833
Lane, Jesse - Ulila Parker   lic.   9- 6-1828
Lane, Joseph - Polly Hart   6-23-1820
    John Lane, father of groom, consents
Langford, William - Anna Alarish   7-17-1835
Larance (or Lorance?), John - Indiana
    Whetstone   6-24-1830
Latimore (or Ledermere), John - Betsy
    Stanley   3-11-1823
Lean, John - Louisa Tackett   1- 3-1819
Leffler, Joseph - Martha Gratz   11-20-1838
Leforgee, William - Lucinda Beach   6-13-1832
Leister, William - Mary Rogers   7-25-1839
Leneve (?), Thomas L. - Mary Ann Neale
                                       1-20-1833
    Richard Neale attests to age of bride
Lenn, Josiah - Olive Van Bever   5-26-1831
Lennon, George W. - Hetty Black   3- 7-1830
    William Black, father of bride, consents
Lennon, Joseph - Sarah Davis
    Stephen Woodrow attests they are of age
                                       4- 6-1833
Leonhardt, Christian F. - Christian Genisch
                                       3-25-1838
Lewellen, Wiley - Jane Fleming   7-11-1822
Lewellen (Luallen), Wiley - Ann Barnett
                                       8-17-1828
Lewis, Hiram - Anna Mathews   2-25-1838
Lewis, James - Octavia E. Newman   4-27-1826
Lewis, William - Jane Conner   2-17-1820
Lile, John - Minerva McDaniel   7-28-1836
    (negro)   (negro)
Lindsay, George W. - Sarrah Conner   1-30-1820
Lingist (?), Jacob - Elizabeth Hetther
                                       1-15-1837
Linkswiler, Christopher - Maryan Rose
                                       10-16-1823
Linxswiler, Isaac - Sally Rose   3-31-1825
Linxwiler, Jacob (or Peter) - Mariah Curtis
                                       4-22-1819
Linxwyler, William - Jane Clinton   2-10-1833
Litchfield, Joseph - Lucy K. Browning
                                       6-18-1840
Livingston, John - Abigael Cross   2-11-1839
Livingston, Thomas - Kizia McNew   6-16-1825
Lockhart, James L. - Sarah C. Negley
                                       9- 1-1835
Lockwood, John M. - Caroline Newman   4-24-1834
Long, John Franklin - Sarah Alexander Patton
                                       2-23-1826
    Robert Long, father of groom, states he
    is age 21
Long, Levi - Rachel Ferrel   8-18-1831
Long, Reuben - Eliza Barnet   4-18-1824
Long, Simeon - Aseneth Lock   10-19-1819
Loomis, Albert - Sarah Onyet   4- 7-1835
Loomis, Solon - Sarah Hutchinson   5-30-1837
Love, William M. - Nancy Cavins   12-13-1838
Lyon, George F. - Harriet T. Clark   10-20-1836
McAlpin, Thomas - Margaret McCutchan
                                       4- 5-1838
McBride, Robert - Julia Ann Conner   7-24-1836
McCallister, Clark - Catharine Saunders
                                       12-10-1835

McCallister, Joseph - Polina Hoskins
    12- 4-1820
McCallister, Thomas - Fidelia Boardman
    2-13-1833
McCann, John - Elizabeth Knight   2- 3-1821
McCarty, Silas - Olivia Edwards   12-31-1829
McCasland, James - Jane Wright   10-31-1839
McClain, Mathew - Mary E. Stone   9- 5-1837
McClanahan, John - Sarah Ring   3-23-1821
    James Ring consents
McClure, Edwin - Mary Ann Newman   12-17-1835
McCollum, John - Elizabeth Rhodes   8-26-1833
    David Rhodes attests to their ages
McCorcle, James - Mary Ann Weger   5- 7-1835
McCorrie, William - Ann Knight   11-15-1832
McCullough, Robert - Mary Jane Reynolds
    2-14-1840
McDonald, Doran J. - Lucinda Catlin   7-27-1837
McDowell, George - Ann Rockett   6-14-1840
McDowell, William G. - Susan Neale
    Richard Neale attests to ages of both
    parties   8-23-1834
McGary, Hugh - Polly McClain lic.   9- 7-1826
McGlothlin, Hughey - Rebecca Miller   5-28-1832
McIntire, James - Cynthia Ann Livingston
    9- 9-1837
McJohnston, Kinlock - Mary Ann McCutchan
    10-14-1839
McKnitt, William - Sally Stinson   12-30-1819
McLaughlin, Hugh - Rebecca Miller
    Mother, only surviving parent of bride,
    consents   5-18-1832
McNew, Eli - Jane Kelly   3- 6-1832
    Matilda Wooten, mother of bride, consents;
    groom has no parents or guardian in Ind.
McNew, John - Rachel Bowling (age 18)
    3-16-1821
McReynolds, John - Lydia Ann Clinton
    8-28-1836
    Jonathan Clinton father of bride, consents
McReynolds, Peter A. - Clarissa Prince
    10- 1-1840
Mackey, James - Eliza Aydelott   7- 4-1821
Maidlow, Edmond - Ann Hornbrook   4-10-1822
    J. Hornbrook, father of bride, consents
Maidlow, James - Mary P. Hornbrook   4- 3-1820
Maidlow, John Spencer - Barbara Hornbrock
    5-11-1824
    Saunders Hornbrook, father of bride,
    consents
Manley, James - Cynthia Ann Darby   7- 6-1837
Mansell, John B. - Ann Watts   3- 9-1836
    William & Susan Watts, parents of bride,
    consents
Mansell, Samuel - Lucy Powell   10- 1-1836
Marcus, John - Mary W. Neely (or McNeely)
    2-19-1823
Marquis, James - Sarah Rogers   3- 4-1820
Marrs, Samuel R. - Rachael Stinson   5- 5-1836
    Mary Marrs, mother of groom, consents
Marsh, Franklin - Clarinda Ferril   2-25-1822
Marshall, James - Manesa Armstrong   8- 1-1838
Marshall, William - Jemima Ross   2- 9-1837
Martin, John S. - Lydia Taylor   5-11-1834
Martin, John - Asenath Tyler
    Dinah Tyler, mother of bride consents on
    9-30-1840
Martin, Nathan - Elizabeth Stinson   4-29-1837
Martin, Reuben - Caroline Knight   10-13-1839
Martin, Thomas - Mary Tyler   12- 9-1829
Masel, Phillip - Mary Folz   3-10-1838

Match, French B. - Anna Mary Kurtz   2- 2-1839
Maxbury, Arasha - Margaret Divine   8-12-1823
May, George W. - Eliza Long   8- 9-1840
Meek, Samuel - Delila Hubbard   6-13-1829
Melvin, James - Sarah L. Roberts   5-27-1819
    Hazeal Putnam, guardian of bride, consents
Melvin, John - Lucy Vanderventer   8-29-1819
Metzger, Theobald - Margaret Steiner
    12-21-1837
Milburn, Hiram - Mary Ann McCoy   6-11-1836
    Robert & Nancy Milburn, parents of groom,
    & A. L. Evans, guardian of bride, consent
Miller, Charles J. - Martha Wilson   5-27-1839
Miller, George - Malinda Wagnon   7-10-1825
Miller, Jacob - Mary Cline   3-26-1838
Miller, Martin - Isabella Barnet   8-21-1824
Miller, Peter - Martha Hooker   6-17-1832
Mitchell, John - Elvira Seely   12-10-1829
Moffett, James - Wilhelmina McJohnston
    8-17-1836
Moffett, Samuel - Margaret Sleeth   7-11-1839
Moll, John Henry - Christina Gottschalk
    8-29-1837
    Catharine E. Gottschalk, mother of bride,
    consents
Monroe, John - Rebecca Courmes   7-23-1826
Montgomery, John - Rachel B. Brumfield
    10-15-1840
    Mary Brumfield, mother of bride, consents
Montgomery, Preteman - Martha Prewett
    both of Gibson Co.   12- 1-1837
    [1838?]
Montgomery, Smith - Minerva Hawkins   9- 4-1833
Moore, John - Mary Brown   7-28-1839
Morefield, John - Ann Davis   10- 5-1833
Morgan, George W. - Mary Ann Branham
    12- 1-1840
Morgan, John - Eliza Eaton   12- 8-1835
    Groom has no parents or guardian in Ind.
Morris, Benjamin - Rosella Sullivan   9-12-1835
    Elizabeth Sullivan, mother of bride,
    consents
Morris, John - Mary Marshall   3-20-1837
Moss, Benajah - Maryann Simmons
    Eliza Simmons, mother of bride,
    consents on   11-12-1838
Moylen, Edward - Hannah Record   9- 4-1837
Muir, Washington - Sarah Way   4-14-1839
Murphey, John - Polly Lane
    consent of John Murphey & John Lane,
    parents, on   11-19-1822
Murphy, Ethan - Claricy Parker
    George Parker, father of bride, consents
    return filed   2-19-1819
Murphy, Peter - Peggy Wilkins   7- 8-1825
    John Murphy & Nancy Wilkins, parents,
    consent
Murray, John S. - Isabella McClain   10- 7-1837
Myre, John - Margaret E. Ohlingen   4-11-1837
Neal, Alexander H. - Elizabeth Negley
    D. Negley, father of bride, consents
    lic. 12- 8-1832
Neal, Thornton - Elizabeth Cloud
    H. W. Cloud, father of bride, consents on
    5- 6-1840
Neale, Richard - Polly McDowell   11- 3-1835
    Joseph M & Amelia McDowell parents of
    bride, consent
Nesler, Wade H. - Nancy Wesley   8-10-1837
Newman, Esau - Elizabeth Rocket   11-10-1833
Newhouse, John - Dinah Elam   8-17-1839

157

Newman, John M. - Elizabeth Harrison
9- 7-1837
Newman, Mason O. - Elizabeth Price 3- 5-1835
Newman, Peter - Elizabeth Bess (or Bates)
11-25-1833
Thomas Rockett attests to their ages
Nightingale, Elias - Bathona Coleman
11- 6-1838
Noas, Jacob - Margaret Schmahl 4-15-1838
Noble, Moses - Abigail Corbin 8-12-1828
John Garret attests that bride is age 17,
has no parents or guardian in Ind.
Noble, Moses - Polly Crow lic. 8-23-1835
Corydon Garret attests to their ages
Noble, Noah - Mary O'Neal 4-14-1836
Noble, Washington P.? - Nancy Dukes
3- 2-1826
Parmelia Noble & John & Hager Dukes,
parents, consent
Noble, Washington P. - Ann Dukes 3- 3-1836
Norse, Frederick - Malinda Wise 12-29-1839
Nunn, David - Jane Shelby 12- 2-1831
Ober, Jack - Mary Davis 6- 4-1839
Oglesby, John - Nice Taylor 8-15-1833
O'Hara, John - Elizabeth Sullivan 3- 3-1836
Olds, Jackson - Betsey Peters 5- 1-1834
Catharine Hening, mother of groom,
consents
Olds, William H. H. - M. J. McCrary 2- 5-1835
Catharine Henning & Marion McCrary,
parents, consent
Onyet, Thomas - Silvey Cody 4-24-1829
John Cody, father of bride, consents
Oynet (Onyet?), John - Elizabeth Hall
6-22-1826
Parker, Alva - Rebecca Stines
Prudance Parker consents on 9-23-1826
Parker, John - Ruthy Zarnes 4- 1-1819
George Parker, father of groom, consents
Parker, Lorenzo D. - Lorena Lane 9-25-1828
Elizabeth Lane, mother of bride, consents,
groom has no parents or guardian in Ind.
Parker, William - Yalila Garret 3-20-1825
George Parker & Polly Garret, parents,
consent
Patterson, Andrew - Elizabeth McCausland
(or McCaslin) 3-25-1838
Patterson, John - Martha Reynolds 8-11-1840
Paul, Cyrus - Mahatable Rosenburgh 4-19-1821
Paul, Cyrus - Ann Hayhurst 2-16-1832
Pauley, William - Margaret Fitzgerald
age of both vouched for 8- 5-1833
Payne, Fielding - Letitia Russell 8-13-1837
Moses Payne vouches for both parties
Payton, Edward - Angeline Baty 4- 4-1840
(Negro) (Negro)
Peck, Charles - Polly Beach 6- 6-1819
John Beach, father of bride, consents
Peck, John - Esther Marshall 4- 6-1834
Peck, Richard - Mary Ann Earl 12-12-1839
Pecke, Landon - Charity Smith
Harriet Smith consents on 12-19-1838
Pelham, John - Anna Pelham 1-23-1827
Pennell, Rev. Lewis - Esther Slocumb
7- 3-1838
Perry, James - Ann Morris 1- 4-1836
Perry, John - Margaret Wood 10- 7-1839
Pew, William - Lucy Reeder 11-30-1832
Thomas Biggs certifies they are of age
Phar, Ephraim - Mahala McCallister 6-21-1829
Phar, Ephraim - Asaneth Marrs 6- 1-1837

Phar, John - Harriet Caroline Kelsey
Maria Kelsey, mother of bride consents
2- 1-1840
Phar, Josiah - Upha(?) H. Lane 6-21-1829
Phar, Vicissimus K. - Polly Rice 12- 4-1820
Phelps, Abraham - Francis Johnson 7-17-1827
Phelps, Joseph H. - Elizabeth Ann Barker
5- 6-1840
Philips, David - Anna Kenerly 2-24-1825
Philips, William P. - Mary E. Coker 8-10-1837
Phillips, James - Elizabeth Lanus (?)
11- 4-1830
Pine, James - Sarah B. Town 5- 8-1837
Potts, George - Mary Ann Maidlow 4- 6-1820
Powell, Alexander - Mary Burns 3-22-1838
Powell, John H. - Margaret Price 2-11-1836
Prewit, Willis - Jane Mordock 11-19-1831
Prewitt, John - Mahala Green 10- 5-1826
Moses Prewitt, father of groom, consents
Prewitt, John - Elizabeth Holcom 8-10-1837
Pritchett, John H. - Emily Saturley 4-27-1826
Prichett, John H. - Margaret Tanater
9-13-1836
Ragan, John - Elizabeth Williams 1-13-1837
Ragan, Samuel K. - Maria Reynolds 4-21-1840
Redman, Absolom - Juliet Prewett 10-16-1839
Reed, John N. - Jane McAlpin 7-27-1839
Reeves, John C. - Elizabeth Witherow
6- 9-1832
Reilly, William - Mary F. Willson 12-31-1840
Reitz, John - Catherin Freiser 8- 4-1839
Renslar, Peter - Catharine Snyder 4- 8-1839
Rensler, John - Margaret Boneckel 6-30-1839
Rhodes, Joseph R. - Jane Price 4-28-1836
Rich, John William - Sarah Stratton 1-14-1836
John Nightingail attests to both of their
ages
Rich, John W. - Eliza Hord 12-10-1840
Ring, James - Elizabeth Hall 4- 9-1828
Ritchey, Westley - Harriet Burtis 8-27-1836
Ritchey, William - Nancy Rogers 4-18-1839
Ritchie, Samuel - Jane Bradley 1- 4-1840
Thomas McReynolds attests to both of their
ages
Ritner, Isaac - Lavina Edwards 5- 5-1837
Robb, Peyton W. - Susan Finch 5-15-1836
Robb, William S. - Lavinia Finch 4- 1-1830
Robbins, William - Sarah Ann Powell 5-23-1825
Robert, George - Catharine Monrowe 5-26-1839
Robertson, Anthony - Polly Saunders 8-19-1822
Jeffrey Saunders, father of bride, consents
Robertson, George - Mary Johnson 11- 5-1818
Robertson, Jonathan - Mary Renard 10-18-1829
Robeson (or Robinson), Abner - Anna Gibson
10- 7-1824
Robinson, Burrel T. - Margaret Martin
12- 8-1833
Robinson (or Robertson), James - Nancy
Stinson 3-13-1823
Robinson, John J. - Ruth Burns 12-27-1838
Thomas & Nancy Burns, parents of bride,
consent
Robinson, William Ford - Julian McCann
10- 8-1822
John McCann, father of bride, consents
Robison, Achillis E. - Amanda France
1-27-1833
Rockett, George - Sally Salsbery 11-12-1834
Rogers, Edwin - Phebe Harrison 9- 3-1826
Rogers, Preston C. - Emelia Calvert 4-20-1840
Patrick Calvert, father of bride, consents

Rogers, Rhodes - Anne Littlepage   11- 2-1826
Rogers, Samuel K. - Maria Reynolds 4-21-1840
Rohmann, Charles - Catherine Wilhelmie
                                    10- 1-1838
Roland, Morgan - Matilda Kelly   12-30-1830
Rollins, Reuben - Priscilla Scott   2- 6-1839
Rose, Benjamin - Phebe Linkeswiler 2-14-1821
Rose, Joseph - Alcy Oglesby   9-14-1837
Rose, Willis - Mary Lynxwyler   4-28-1825
Ross, David A - Priscilla Dukes
   Amos Clark, guardian of bride, consents
                          on   1-20-1833
Ross, James - Sarah Ann Wicheight (or
   Wilheight)   4-25-1837
Ross, Levi - Elizabeth McCarty   2-16-1832
Rupp, Nicholas - Elizabeth Fredinck
                                    9- 9-1837
Rusden, William - Martha Peck   9-18-1834
Russell, James - Elizabeth Rinerbiger
                                    5-20-1819
Ruston, Robert - Isabella Whitehead
                                    12- 8-1838
Ryan, James - Margaret Miles   12-19-1838
Sanders, John S. - Nancy Roberson   8- 1-1819
Saterlee, Abel - Elizabeth Griffith 2- 6-1822
Saterlee, Varner - Betsy Long   5-10-1827
Saunders, James - Ziba Sirkl   10-21-1818
Saunders, Peter - Sarah Slover (or Stover?)
                                    12-15-1825
Saunders, William C. - Lydia E. Fauquher
                                    9-10-1835
Schenck, William B. - Elizabeth Willhight
                                    12- 6-1838
Schmitter, Stephen - Ann Mary Folz 8-18-1838
Schmoll, Martin - Sarah Ann Schoffner
                                    4- 6-1839
Schnur, George - Elizabeth Kalpfleisch
                                    12-22-1840
Schroads, David H. - Mary Householder
                                    7- 9-1835
Schustuis, Lear - Lizabeta Harman   4- 8-1839
Schwyver, Michael - Elizabeth Hann 9-23-1839
Scott, Grandville - Ann Farr   5-29-1836
Senatt, John - Elizabeth Hallaman   8-31-1840
Senson, Benjamin - Mary Burgess   10- -1837
Shabner, George M. - Barbara Fuchs 12- 7-1839
Sharland, Edward H. - Emily Dunham 2- 7-1821
Shaver, George L. - Mary Skidmore   5-12-1819
Shaver, Harman - Sally Marks   5-26-1833
Shaver, John - Mary Hall   5-23-1821
Shaw, William - Martha McCallister 1-19-1836
Shearwood, Eli - Polly Wilson   5-26-1824
Sherwood, Marcus - Prudence Johnson
                                    11-27-1834
Sherwood (?), Reuben C. - Jane F. Johnson
                                    5-10-1840
Shirman, Samuel - Mary D. Shaffer   11-28-1837
Shook, Wilson - Malinda Hamsley   7-11-1839
Sirkel, Lewis - Sarah Saunders   8-11-1818
Skeels, William - Ann Young   11-21-1839
Skelton, James - Louisa Jane Combs 7-19-1838
Smith, Conrad - Maria Schwab   9- 5-1839
Smith, Henry D. - Sarah Tupman   7-14-1822
Smith, Hiram - Mary Ann Robinson   3-24-1839
Smith, John - Poly Ross   9-27-1820
Smith, Joseph - Eliza Baldwin   3- 3-1820
   Joseph Baldwin, father of bride, consents
Smith, Michael - Ann Marony   4- 9-1839
Smith, Thomas - Elizabeth Newman   2-25-1840
Smith, Thomas - Ann Horsley   3- 8-1840
Smith, Wilson - Laura Eoff   9- 4-1825

Sprinkle, William - Susan Cody   2- 2-1832
Spyker, John - Octavia Steel   1- 9-1840
Stahlhofer, Mathus - Gertrude Henrich
                                    1- -1839
Stanchfield, David - Mary Elliott   9-27-1838
Stanfield, Ashley - Mary Franceway 11-18-1818
Stansbury, Silas - Sarah Wilkins   1-16-1837
Staser, John C. - Margaret Clinton 4-13-1837
Steel, Ninian - Eliza Williamson   1-29-1827
Steele, James - Mary A. McKnitt   12-19-1839
Stephens, Charles - Sophia M. Dunk 2-18-1833
Stephens, David - Frances Cox   8-11-1836
Stephens, Griffin - Sarah Hayhurst 3-13-1839
Stephens, Joshua W. - Nancy Gipson 12-28-1820
   Julius Gipson, father of bride, consents
Stephens, Silas - Juliene Evans
                          lic.   2-12-1829
Steward, John - Catharine Whetstone 6-12-1828
Stewart, Charles - Catharine Phillips
                          lic.   6-18-1833
Stewart, William T. - Eliza Huey   4-13-1837
   Rebecca Foster, mother of bride, consents
Stinchfield, Daniel - Mary McClary 10-28-1838
Stinettler, David - Caroline Sinzich
                                    1-16-1840
Stinson, John - Rebecca Wilkins   8- 8-1824
Stinson, John W. G. - Missouri Stinson
                                    7-27-1837
   Consent of J. B. & Matilda Stinson
Stinson, Lewis W. - Sarah Ann Gillett
                                    6-17-1832
Stinson, W. H. - Elizabeth C. McCorkle
                                    5-23-1839
Stockwell, John M. - Ann Eliza Duncan
                                    3- 1-1838
   John M. & Rebecca Duncan, parents of
   bride, consent
Stockwell, Robert - Martha L. Negley
                                    4- 5-1831
Stoner, John - Sarah France   7- 6-1837
Stover, Preston - Catharine Henson 6- 7-1821
Stratmatter, Frederick - Sibila Miller
                                    11- 4-1839
Stratton, William - Charlotte Watts 6-26-1840
Strong, Simon - Mary Catlett   5-29-1839
Stroud, Hiram - Amand C. Catlett   3- 9-1837
Stroud, Nelson - Sarah Stroud   8- 3-1838
Stull, George - Catharine France   8- 9-1829
Suiten, George W. - Alcinda Deal   4-11-1838
Sullivent (or Sillivent), Adam - Nelly
   Blevins   2-13-1823
Sullivent, Samuel - Violet Chapman 9-10-1822
   William Chapman, father of bride, consents
Surkel, George - Milancan Mitten   7- 3-1819
Sutchell, Joseph - Mary Cain   11-19-1840
Sutton, Ebenezer - Polly Myers   4-20-1831
Swain, Anthony - Rachel Stout   5-23-1820
Sweasor, Peter - Nelly Webster   1-17-1819
Talbott, James - Mary Scantlin   11- 9-1837
Taylor, Alfred - Sarah Linn   2-13-1836
   both of Henderson Co., Kentucky
Taylor, John - Mary Magdaline McGee 5-24-1825
   Samuel & Nanse Taylor vouch for age of
   both parties
Taylor, Tarpley E. - Polly S. Baker
                                    10- 9-1823
   George S. Baker, father of bride, consents
Taylor, William - Rachel Stinson   4- 1-1821
Taylor, William - Jane Wyat   2-25-1825
Taylor, William - Malinda Loyd   10-11-1835
   James & Rachel Taylor & James & Catharine
   Loyd, parents, consent

Taylor, William L. - Lucinda Barnett
                                8-31-1838

Teal, William - Sephia Gauch
   Affidavit as to age & residence filed
         no other date   9-20-1830

Templeton, James - Elizabeth Brown
                 lic. 9-12-1821

Terry, John S. - Thirza Rice   3-20-1836

Terry, John S. - Juliet E. McCallister
   Paulina McCallister, mother of bride,
   consents   6-18-1838

Thompson, James - Anna McClanahan 1-19(?)
                                     1821

Thompson, John, of Daviess County -
   Elizabeth Wheeler   9- 9-1828

Todd, John - Malinda Parker   8-21-1838

Tompkin, Peter - Peggy Wyatt
   Affidavit of age by William Taylor
        no other date   1-17-1832

Tompkins, William - Sarah Wyatt 9-16-1832

Tool, Daniel - Ann Thompson   7-18-1821

Tool, Daniel - Lucy (?) Samuels   1- 3-1826

Townsend, Leander W. - Ann Eliza Wood
                          12-24-1838

Trafton, William - Hannah Russell 4-15-1819

Trewitt (or Truitt), Samuel - Rebecca
   Chapman   4-21-1836

Tubbs, Nathan H. - Sarah Stinson 12-10-1837

Tully, Lewis - Amila Brumett   4- 9-1840

Tupman, Edward - Elizabeth Pritchett
                          12-23-1824

Tupman, Edward - Polly Carter (?) 11-14-1828

Tuttle, Olney F. - Eleanor Herod (or Herd?)
                          10-29-1839

Van, Absalom - Delighe Williams 8-21-1820

Van, John - Frances Carlin   11-17-1835
   both ages sworn to by Craven Carlin

Van Bibber, Peter - Lavinia Phillips
                        10- 4-1836
   Jonathan Van Bibber vouches for age of
   both parties

Van Bibber, William - Obedience Watson
                          7- 1-1834

Van Duson, Jacob - Martha Jane Kirkpatrick
                        10-27-1835

Vany, Jarret - Elizabeth Woodside 7- 2-1840
                (negro)

Varner, Jacob - Polly Webster lic. 11-29-1823

Vaughan, Henry P. - Hannah T. Knight
                          9-10-1840

Vaughn, Lewis - Mary Williams   7-18-1839

Vincent, Isaac - Rebecca Housman 9-26-1834
   Henson Housman vouches for ages

Voris, William - Terresa E. Head   2-26-1837
   Andrew C. White vouches for ages of both

Waggoner, Henry J. - Matilda Hemingway
                          8-27-1832

     Henry G. Waggoner in return filed
                          7-15-1832

Wagnon, John P. - Mary Tupman   3-25-1824
   Edward Tupman consents

Wagnon, William - Polly Kennidy   3- 7-1833

Wagonen (?), George B. - Anna Tylor
                        12-18-1819

Walden, George - Mary Coffitt   7-10-1836

Walker, James T. - Henrietta McCallister
                         7- 6-1837

Walker, Thomas - Maria Ingle   6-17-1839

Ward, George - Hetty Polley   10-14-1829

Ward, James - Jane Carlisle   3-20-1828

Ward, Thomas - Elizabeth Hornbrook 10-27-1819

Ward, Thomas - Nancy Carlile   11-12-1824

Warren, Alexander - Nancy Mace   8-16-1829

Warren, Levi - Polly Farler   5- 1-1828

Warren, Stephen - Mary Sutton   3-14-1830

Warren, William - Sarah Peck   9-24-1829

Washington, George - Amy Bluford 4- 3-1825

Washum, Daniel - Elizabeth Stinson 1-29-1826

Wasson, William C. - Emelina Prewett
                          10-16-1839

Waters, Elijah   Sophia Heminway 4-10-1823

Watson, Daniel - Sarah Kisinger (or Risinger)
                          4-19-1840

Watson, Isaac - Judith Wann   8-11-1831

Watts, James - Elizabeth Decamps 2-18-1838
   married at home of A. Decamps

Weatherow (Withrow?), Robert F. - Malinda
   Gipson   1-28-1830
   Nancy Withrow, mother of groom, consents

Webster, Levi - Sarah Jane Barnard 5-18-1836

Wells, William - Mary Gallagher 5-12-1831

West, William - Elizabeth Kimmel 9-24-1835

Westfall, James - Keziah Barker 2- 4-1836
   D. Grimes swears that Keziah Barker who
   lives with him has no parents living &
   no guardian, and is 17 yrs. old

Wheeler, Joseph, Jr. - Eliza J. Hopkins
                         12- 4-1834

Wheeler, Mark - Sarah Cowl   10- 3-1823

Whetstone, David - Mary Bigham 2-28-1833

Whipple, Willard - Mary Bigley 10-29-1837
                           [1839?]

White, James - Sarah Hornbrook 7- 6-1838

White, Timothy W. - Caty Dimsey 2-14-1819

Wigginton, William G. - Eliza King 5-23-1822

Wilkins, Jonathan - Nancy Wilkins 6-18-1832
   James Wilkins certifies they are of age

Wilkinson, Isaiah - Polly Prewitt 6-20-1837
   both are from Gibson Co.

Willhight, William - Catharine Brilles
                        10-16-1837
                         [1836]

Williams, Harry - Sarah Beach   1-27-1831

Williams, Jesse C. - Elizabeth Sprinkle
                        11- 8-1836

Williams, Shareman - Harriet Kinyon
                        12- 2-1830

Williams, William H. - Elizabeth W. Scates
                        11- 9-1837

Willkins, George - Nancy Pendleton 10-21-1834

Wills, William - Hariett Judkins 6-22-1826

Willson, Adam - Alsy Austin   7-27-1837

Willson, Lemuel - Lucinda Coker 12- 6-1837

Wilson, Elijah - Ann Grady
   John Wilson consents on   7-28-1829

Wilson, Enoch - Maria Scott   5-29-1828

Wilson, James - Hopy Thatcher   1-23-1825

Wilson, John - Catherine Sevire 4- 6-1825

Wilson, William V. - Elizabeth Stallings
                        6-15-1836

Wingleman, Jacob - Catharine Bruner 9-26-1839

Witherspoon, James - Maria Wilson 12-25-1836

Withins, Jesse - Eliza Tyner   8-16-1840

Withrow (or Witrow), William J. - Hannah
   Gibson   4- 6-1831
   Elijah Gibson certifies bride is of age

Wood, James - Catharine E. S. Perry 1-24-1822
   Katharine Olds, mother of bride, consents

Wood, James - Sophia Holder   2-29-1828

Wood, John E. - Nancy Fauquher 10-24-1839

Wood, William - Eliza Kirkpatrick 11-17-1836
   James R. & Sarah Kirkpatrick, parents of
   bride, consent

Wood, Young - Esther France   5-22-1833
Woodrow, Stephen - Judith McGehee
     Elijah Waters vouches for ages of both on
     no marriage date   3-25-1834
Woodruff, Matthew - Ruby L. Bell   10-23-1839
Woods, John - Polly Bingham   10- 9-1828
     John is of Gibson Co.
Woods, Silas - Lucinda Darby
     parents of groom consent on   1- 3-1829

Woolf, Daniel - Drusilla McVine   8-31-1840
Worth, - Richard K. - Nancy Simpson 3- 8-1838
Wright, Joseph T. - Elizabeth Wright
     7-19-1835
Young, John James - Priscilla Ross   9-20-1835
Young, John - Elizabeth Stafford   6-17-1839
Young, Morgan - Caty Bleavens   3-30-1819
Zeigenhagen, Francis - Leisa Leseria
     1- 7-1839

DEATHS IN RUSH COUNTY, 1823-1856

Abstracted from Rush County Complete Probate Books I-XII [1830-1857] by Maurice Holmes of Shelbyville. The abbreviation c. for circa is used when the date given is the approximate date of death. The deceased may not have lived in Rush County but had property or heirs there.

Name of Deceased	Date of Death	Probate Record
Aldridge, John	c. 2-22-1842	7:526
Aldridge, Mary	c. 11-27-1843	4:535
Alexander, James M.	11- 9-1845	6:625
Allen, John	c. 6-18-1850	10:32
Allen, Theophilus	11- 3-1847	7:640
Allen, William	5-20-1844	12:8
Anderson, Cornelius	c. 5-28-1841	7:390
Anderson, George	8- -1846	6:1
Anderson, George	c. 8-24-1846	:116
Anderson, Mary wife of Nathaniel	1846	6:1
Anderson, Nathaniel	12-29-1845	6:1
Arnold, Isaac	9-26-1851	11:500
Arnold, William	c. 7-24-1832	1:93
Aspy, George	12- 5-1842	4:101
Baker, James	4-23-1843	4:249
Balser, Jacob	8-28-1844	5:38
Barbour, John W.	3-23-1850	12:140
Barger, Phillip	5-30-1843	6:218
Beason, Junius	2-16-1853	11:259
Beaver, Abraham	7- 7-1849	10:317
Bebout, Benjamin	9-16-1851	9:357
Bentley, Reuben	9- 3-1839	5:75
Berry, Thomas	1847	12:46
Binford, Joshua	1- 5-1844	4:531
Bingaman, Allen	c. 12- 1-1841	8:217
Blanks, John	c. 4- 1-1841	4:327
Bowden, John	3- 8-1843	8:259
Bowlby, Joseph	10-12-1846	7:104
Bowen, John W.	4-26-1844	5:1
Bowen, Solomon	4- 6-1840	5:98
Bowen, Thomas son of Sol.	1838	5:98
Bowen, William T.	2-14-1843	5:338
Bowne [or Bowen], Cornelius	2- 5-1852	10:535
Bravard, Rachel	10-16-1854	12:120
Brown, Evander	5 or 6- -1855	12:545
Brown, John	9-14-1846	5:378
Brown, John	2-15-1852	10:578
Brown, John Jr.	c. 11-20-1839	3:322
Brown, Mathias	9-26-1846	6:374
Buell, Israel Sr.	11-24-1845	8:298
Bundy, Josiah	4-17-1846	10:357
Burton, Thomas	3-18-1855	12:235
Bussell, Levi	12-21-1844	5:170
Bussell, Samuel	2-23-1843	4:24
Butler, William	2- -1851	10:373
Caldwell, William Jr.	10-17-1845	5:424
Calpher, Albertson	9-29-1849	7:257
Campbell, Francis Sr.	2- 8-1852	11:20
Carr, Sarah of Henry Co.	c. 1826	2:346
Carter, Joseph	1-26-1849	8:90
Cartmel, John	1843	11:145
Carothers, Harvey	c. 7-27-1844	4:545
Carothers, Hugh	9- -1836	2:192
Coffin, Barzilla	9- 8-1849	10:112
Collins, James	1844	6:453
Collins, Thomas	12- 3-1842	5:152
Commons, John	c. 6-11-1854	12:105
Conaway, Henry	c. 9- 1-1837	3:37
Cooper, Asa	c. 8-14-1838	4:279
Cooper, Experience	10-18-1847	8:533
Cooper, Merill	8-27-1845	7:379
Conde, Norman	6- -1839	12:14
Conde, William A.	6-12-1842	8:204
Cowan, Hugh	6- 1-1838	5:451
Cowger, David	7- 9-1842	4:341
Cowger, Gustavus	10- 2-1843	4:373
Cowger, James	8-16-1847	6:464
Cox, Benjamin	10-17-1840	4:308
Cox, Isaac S.	c. 4- 5-1841	6:191
Creed, Colby	c. 2-10-1855	12:555
Crim, David	1- 6-1856	12:561
Cross, Ebenezer	11- 2-1843	5:534
Cross, James	9-25-1842	5:93
Culbertson, Marg. S.	1- 2-1855	12:352
Culbertson, William	11-16-1854	12:355
Cunningham, James	c. 7-11-1852	10:71
Curry, Robert	Fall of 1844 in Iowa	4:410
Danner, Samuel	9-29-1855	12:596
Daugherty, Eleanor	4-11-1852	10:498
Day, Elizabeth	6- 5-1850	9:443
Day, John	4- 6-1845	9:404
Decker, Johigley	8-14-1847	10:97
Deem, Adam	9- -1848	8:224
Doty, John and wife Rosannah	1842	5:552
Dougherty, Joseph	12- 7-1848	7:95
Doughty, Thomas	1846	7:184
Douglass, John	6-28-1850	8:287
Durham, George	c. 4- 1-1847	7:217
Dyer, Edward	1- 4-1850	7:632

Eck, Jacob		9-16-1846	6:474
Elder, James		1840	5:552
Elder, William J. D.		10-26-1850	9:436
Endicott, John		1840	4:94
English, Hugh B.		1-10-1850	12:258
English, Hugh L.		1- 1-1849	8:293
English, James H.		1849	8:359
English, John		8- 2-1853	12:66
English, Robert		7-14-1854	12:567
Ewing, William		3-24-1840	3:45
Fairley, James		8-27-1838	4:6
Fancher, Benjamin	c.	8-18-1853	11:397
Fancher, David		3- -1850	8:517
Farran, Mathew	c.	7- 9-1825	2:56
Farran, Valentine		2- 1-1842	5:518
Farrow, William S.	c.	11-17-1849	12:342
Ferree, William		4-19-1855	12:647
Fleenor, Adam		[1833?] 1823	2:195
Fox, Ellis		8-22-1852	10:399
Frame, William		10-11-1849	11:515
Gifford, Annaniah		1- 9-1854	12:618
Gilbert, Charles	c.	1-15-1854	11:483
Gilliam, Andrew		7-24-1852	11:96
Gilson, Mary widow of Andrew		8-11-1845	5:48
Gilson, Samuel	c.	5-12-1838	3:129
Giltner, George		8- 7-1845	5:574
Glore, Alexander		11- 7-1841	4:118
Gordon, John	c.	11- 7-1841	5:197
Gordon, Josiah		7-12-1849	9:316
Gray, John		11- 3-1854	12:581
Gray, Thomas		8-30-1838	4:109
Green, Lot		7-12-1845	6:108
Gregg, James		1828	1:309
Grimes, John L.		1835	2:235
Guffin, George		8-30-1845	5:507
Hale, Conrad		5- 5-1851	10:335
Harcourt, Richard		11-21-1847	10:254
Hargitt, George W.		4-29-1855	12:315
Heflin, Reuben		11-22-1848	11:61
Heflin, William	c.	11-21-1846	6:204
Helms, David		8-22-1852	11:52
Henley, Elias Sr.		9-15-1848	10:349
Henley, Elias Jr.	c.	10-27-1850	10:342
Henry, Alexander C.		1836	2:182
Hewitt, Israel		8-20-1843	10:220
Hewitt, Moses		3-22-1840	4:105
Hewitt, Olive		11-18-1854	11:142
Higgins, Jesse		10- 8-1845	8:156
Hill, Jonathan		11-12-1844	6:182
Hill, Samuel		12-23-1851	10:631
Hill, Thomas		9- 1-1840	4:506
Hill, Zilphah		9- 6-1846	6:174
Hilligoss, Conrad		9- 7-1844	5:20
Hinkson, Thomas		6- 4-1849	8:12
Hite, Catharine	c.	7-15-1854	11:481
Hollingshead, Thomas		1-25-1848	7:119
Holloway, Dayton		5-18-1847	11:5
Honaker, William		5- -1841	6:726
Houston, Jane		11-18-1845	5:417
Huddleson, Alexander		10-22-1846	6:640
Huddleson, Samuel		5-11-1853	11:284
Hume, Aquilla		12-11-1849	9:428
Hunter, Eleanor		1843	10:233
Huntley, Parker		4-23-1843	4:428
Hurley, James	c.	6- -1837	2:371
Inlow, Edward		5- -1850	10:472
Innis, James		12- -1842	4:618
Innis, John		7-24-1841	4:30
Innis, Joseph		7- 5-1841	4:68
Irvin, Elam		10- 1-1841	10:438
Isham, George		1842	7:308
Isham, George J.	c.	8-26-1843	5:531

Jackson, Joseph		7-20-1851	9:472
Jackson, Jos. M. son of Jos.		6- -1856	12:483
James, Elisha		10-14-1841	4:162
James, Madison		1- 3-1848	10:27
Johnson, Jacob		5- 2-1855	12:435
Johnson, John		2-23-1855	12:373
Johnson, Nancy G.		1846	8:222
Johnson, Reuben H.		3- 5-1846	11:159
Jones, James		1-13-1842	4:286
Jones, John Sr.		Fall of 1828	2:222
Jones, John A.		11-28-1852	10:656
Junken, Joseph B.		1- 7-1850	8:335
Keeler, Caleb	c.	11-28-1842	5:394
Keeler, Ira		2-2 or 3-1843	11:106
Keighler, John		7- 1-1851	11:451
Kellogg, Burgess		3-30-1842	4:258
Kelsey, Adin		12- 3-1846	7:28
Kelso, Levi in Illinois		1- -1843	6:697
Kennedy, James		3-28-1846	8:521
Kennedy, Samuel		4-30-1840	4:115
Kennedy, Walter O.		6-26-1843	4:160
Kennedy, William C.		1846	8:330
King, Joseph		8-22-1852	10:396
King, Peter C.		6-10-1838	3:102
Kiplinger, John		9- 3-1844	12:426
Kiplinger, John Sr.		1844	4:448
Kiplinger, Katharine minor heir of John		1847	6:785
Kirkpatrick, John		9- 8-1848	12:572
Kizer, George		6- -1842	6:667
Kizer, Joseph		8-30-1837	5:488
Kizer, Rebecca Jane		8- -1848	12:205
Kizer, Willis		8- -1842	7:442
Knox, George		1828 or 1829	2:346
Knox, John		3- 4-1841	4:145
Lacy, Pearson		5-28-1844	4:541
Lacy, Samuel		5-18-1852	10:663
Laden, Perry M.		4-12-1845	8:33
Laughlin, Ruth		5- 4-1851	10:415
Lee, Elzy C.	c.	11- 7-1846	6:435
Legg, Thomas		9-28-1847	10:424
Leisure, John H.	c.	12-27-1851	10:287
Leisure, Thomas J.		5- 3-1848	10:127
Lewis, William C. at Hamilton Co., Ohio		8- 5-1850	8:445
Lines, Greenberry		4-14-1838	11:89
Lines, Henry	c.	8 or 9-1835	2:491
Lines, John J.		1845	11:89
Lines, John L.		5-22-1845	12:123
Linville, Edward		7-13-1840	10:74
Long, John		9-26-1845	7:274
Looney, David W.		5-11-1855	12:612
Love, Henry		1847	7:46
Lower, James		1-13-1844	7:155
Lower, John Jr.		9-11-1838	3:117
Lowery, John of Missouri		8-18-1845	11:401
McBride, Robert Y.		7-18-1848	11:311
McCabe, John of Fayette Co., Kentucky		5-27-1833	3:286
McClintock, Elizabeth		11-13-1849	7:628
McComas, Nathaniel	c.	5- 1-1835	1:436
McCord, John		1-14-1850	12:56
McCorkle, John		1849	7:479
McCormack, John [in Illinois?]		1838	3:34
McCullough, Simeon		4- 8-1839	5:43
McCullough, William		1839	2:599
McDaniel, James		2-21-1851	9:117
McDaniel, Robert		l1-15-1845	6:303
McDaniel, William A.		4- 6-1842	6:501
McFarland, Thomas		1836	2:176
McKinney, Robert	c.	11- 6-1842	8:119
Macklin, John Sr.		11-17-1839	5:69
Macklin, Sarah Sr.		1-16-1849	7:651

McKown, John	7- -1841	3:403
McKown, Pleasant	c. 8-27-1840	3:294
McManus, Martha	1836	2:249
McMillen, John	5-29-1850	9:123
McRoberts, Jane	6- 2-1852	10:676
McRoberts, Samuel	10- 9-1838	2:538
Malaby, Richard	10-15-1839	6:209
Mappin, James	7-16-1844	6:309
Martin, James	8-11-1843	4:206
Maxwell, William	4- 8-1841	4:32
Mayne, Hugh	c. 10-12-1852	11:406

Union Co., Ill.

Mayse, Samuel	11-22-1854	12:385
Maze, John Jr.	4- 2-1842	3:437
Maze, William Riley	c. 12-20-1855	12:211
Meek, Samuel	c. 6-21-1850	12:81
Messersmith, Samuel	9-25-1844	5:333
Miller, George	10- 6-1853	11:437
Miller, Jacob R.	7-12-1851	9:460
Minks, Jacob	6-29-1851	10:278
Mitchell, David C.	3- 2-1854	12:361
Mock, John	9-18-1842	4:379
Moffett, John	12-25-1845	6:557
Moffett, Robert D.	3- 3-1844	6:746
Moffett, Thomas	1836	2:142
Moore, Benjamin D.	4-17-1855	12:266
Moore, Elijah	c. 7-20-1843	8:234
Moore, George W.	10- -1849	10:1
Moore, Margaret	1843	8:213
Moren, David	1846	6:455
Morgan, Amaziah	10-10-1839	7:164
Morgan, Evan	c. 7- 7-1851	10:304
Morgan, John T.	c. 11- 1-1842	4:13
Morris, Thornton	c. 6-29-1851	10:109
Morriss, Caroline widow of William	8-31-1849	7:428
Morrison, Matthew	1-26-1846	6:60
Mowry, Valentine	bet.1 & 2-20-1838	4:54
Mullen, John	3- 6-1850	8:274
Murphy, James	c. 8-11-1854	12:320
Newbold, Francis	9- -1839	7:569
Newby, Henry	c. 12-25-1833	2:103
Newhouse, John	1835	4:410
Newhouse, John	4-22-1852	10:187
Newton, John	7- -1835	2:289
Nixon, Joseph	8-29-1840	4:240
Nixon, Thomas	2-15 or 13-1849	12:19
Ocheltree, Cath	6- 1-1855	12:643
Ochiltree, James	10- 1-1841	6:702
Oldham, Jesse	4-17-1848	7:504
Oldham, Mary Ann	5-19-1845	6:103
Oliver, John	1-15-1849	9:446
Oliver, William	10- 9-1840	4:383
Overman, Nathan	6- 5-1851	10:83
Oxley, Joseph	1839	3:136
Parker, Asa	1- -1839	4:318
Parker, John	11- 3-1843	10:45
Parker, North	8-10-1849	8:366
Parker, Samuel	6-13-1847	11:151
Parker, Thomas	7-12-1839	2:581
Parkhurst, William	12- 1-1840	4:128
Parrish, David	11-11-1843	5:420
Parson, Milton	2-16?-1852	12:112
Parsons, John	10- 1-1846	6:587
Patterson, Elihu	10-14-1843	4:420
Patterson, Ledgerwood	1842	10:159

in Henry Co., Iowa

Patton, Nathaniel	7- 3-1844	5:50
Patton, Polly	1- 5-1847	6:170
Peake, Samuel	9-17-1838	6:38
Perkins, Jehu	5-31-1836	2:354
Phillips, Valentine	3-27-1841	5:88
Pike, William	9- 1-1844	6:607

Plummer, Benjamin	7-27-1844	6:266
Pogue, William	7-26-1851	10:20
Powers, James	c. of 10-1837	3:204
Prehm, John B.	c. 10- 5-1843	4:112
Price, James	3-15-1854	12:304
Priest, Benjamin F.	2-21-1849	8:114
Priest, John W.	9- -1842	4:22
Priest, William P.	c. 4-14-1833	1:323
Pugh, Job	8- 9-1847	10:260
Pugh, Leri [or Levi]	11-19-1841	4:73
Pugh, Leroy	5-19-1854	12:41
Pugh, Reu	8- 3-1837	10:260
Query, George	7-10-1843	5:310
Query, Josiah in Texas	10-11-1852	11:376
Rariden, James	8-21-1838	2:448
Rariden, William	c. 4- 9-1845	5:429
Rawlings, Aaron	8-20-1849	8:319
Rawlings, John	8-17-1843	8:410
Rawlings, Preston	1847 or 8	10:488
Redden, Nathaniel	10-16-1844	7:489

in Iowa Territory

Reeder, George	c. 5-13-1845	4:514
Reel, Solomon	1836	3:76
Reid, Alexander	4-16-1847	6:23
Reynolds, Edward H.	12-25-1847	11:335
Rhodes, Smith M.	12- 6-1843	5:4
Rich, Tilghman	2-12-1852	10:170
Ricketts, Edward	c. 10 or 15- 9-1838	3:264
Roberts, Benjamin	4-28-1846	5:504
Roberts, James D.	5-29-1849	7:623
Roberts, Willis	3- 3-1846	6:11
Robinson, Fanny	3-27-1843	4:91
Robinson, Osmyn	6-10-1842	7:363
Rowland, Richard	8-19-1847	6:18
Rumbley, James	11- 5-1843	4:237
Runley, James	5- -1853	11:404
Sailors, Hezekiah	c. 1835	7:474
Sampson, Benjamin	9- 1-1845	6:150
Scott, Jesse	c. 5- 1-1850	9:303
Scott, Joshua	9-30-1842	7:349
Scott, Matthew	1-12-1838	5:369
Scott, Robert	c. 10-21-1850	8:511
Scott, Robert H.	12-23-1841	5:166
Scott, William H.	4-13-1845	8:414
Selby, William	4- 7-1844	8:257
Sharp, John	11- 1-1836	4:64
Sharp, Julius	c. 7-23,1846	10:542
Shaw, Albin III	9- 4-1847	7:222
Shaw, Thomas C.	c. 8-21-1846	6:386
Shawhan, Daniel	c. 1- 2-1840	8:232
Shawhan, Mary widow of Daniel	c.-1848	8:232
Shields, Samuel	10-18-1849	10:124
Shelton, David	12-17-1847	10:464
Shelton, Joel	10-31-1847	7:331
Shoppell, Elizabeth	10-16-1845	5:85
Shultz, Sarah	6-28-1853	11:389
Sidwell, Elizabeth widow of Thomas	10-24-1851	9:233
Sidwell, Thomas	6- 4-1849	9:144
Siler, Ulery	4-24-1849	7:606
Six, John	8-11-1850	9:466
Slane, William T. ?	5-28-1839	9:365
Smelser, George Andrew	7-24-1842	4:414
Smelser, Mary Gilson	8-11-1845	5:48
Smiley, John	1-24-1846	8:73
Smith, Nancy widow of Michael	12-25-1850	9:223
Smith, Robert H.	c. 3-15-1833	2:97
Smith, Seneca E.	3- 2-1846	12:450
Sparks, Joshua	4-20-1850	10:307
Springer, Barnabas	9- 9-1840	6:28
Springer, Nathan	c. 5- 2-1845	6:367

Staggs, David	1842	5:62
Staggs, Sarah widow of David	6- -1843	5:62
Stapleton, Frances	9- 8-1843	5:341
Steckman, Frederick c.	12- 9-1851	12:101
Stephens, Ezekiel	6-27-1843	4:451
Stevens, Elijah of Fayette Co.	3- -1843	5:359
Stewart, Fidelius c.	11-26-1841	5:34
Stewart, Franklin G.	4- 8-1848	6:352
Stewart, James R.	1-24-1845	5:514
Stewart, James Wilson	12- 4-1854	12:33
Stewart, Moses M.	8- -1836	3:28
Stewart, Robert	5-25-1850	10:312
Stewart, Samuel	4-14-1845	4:455
Stiers, Samuel	11-25-1853	12:240
Stockwell, William d.	c. -1835	2:94
Street, James M.	8-23-1840	3:400
Street, John	7- -1842	6:49
Summers, Elijah	11-26-1847	8:502
Sutton, William c.	7-14-1844	4:339
Swain [or Sweam], Thomas	1- 7-1846	6:284
Talbott, John	3- 4-1843	11:69
Tevis, John D.	8- -1849	8:267
Tharp, Andrew J.	1830	2:406
Thomas, Daniel	8- 9-1846	6:141
Thomas, Mary	1-15-1843	4:432
Thompson, James	9-28-1838	3:168
Thompson, James c.	11-18-1838	3:64
Thompson, Samuel	1830	4:244
Thrasher, Stephen	3- 1-1841	4:49
Tolle, Benham	10-20-1853	11:292
Trees, Peter	6- -1841	5:114
Tribby, Thomas	12-10-1848	8:352
Trimble, Alexander	11-14-1837	2:466
Tryon, William	4- 2-1853	11:40
Tullis, Isaac	9-19-1842	4:218
Tullis, Jonathan c. 10 years ago[1825]		1:368
Turner, Willis	1844	5:367
Tweedy, Aaron	7-28-1849	10:364
Tyler, John .c.	9- 1-1844	7:24
Tyler, Joseph	1845	9:56

Virt, Adam	9-26-1845	5:439
Wadkins, David	1841	3:209
Waggoner, Catharine	10-23-1841	8:262
Waits, William	8-29-1844	4:539
Waldron, Bryant c.	9- -1844	5:106
Watkins, Daniel	6- 7-1852	12:272
Weasner, Jesse	8-28-1848	8:449
Webster, Henry	10-28-1851	10:243
Weed, Reuben	6-30-1842	4:122
Weir, Sarah wife of John	8- -1844	6:323
Westerfield, John M.	9-16-1840	9:451
White, Henry	5- 9-1839	2:576
White, Joseph M.	3-13-1852	10:380
White, Robert	10-24-1847	10:454
Wiggins, Joseph c.	7-16-1842	5:537
Wilhoit, William	1-11-1832	4:227
Wilson, Anna	2-13-1842	4:303
Wilson, Mary	11-30-1840	4:269
Wilson, Matthew of Wayne Co	2- 4-1851	10:190
Wilson, Wesley	3-16-1847	12:442
Wilson, William	9- -1844	8:340
Wiltse, Martin	8-20-1840	3:377
Wiltse, Simeon Sr.	5-25-1837	5:156
Winship, Jesse Sr.	11-18-1854	12:332
Winslow, John	10- 9-1841	5:582
Wood, John	12-29-1851	11:378
Worth, Levi	4-29-1837	2:469
Worth, William	2- -1855	11:256
Wrightsman, Abigail	1850	9:486
Wyatt, John	1-10-1844	6:483
Wyatt, Lewis	8-28-1847	6:488
Wyatt, Rebecca	9-11-1854	12:94
Wyatt, William S.	8-23-1843	5:57
Yeager, George of Porter Co.	1844	6:789
Young, Alexander c.	9- -1847	10:610
Young, James	11-15-1839	6:513
Younker, Peter c.	11- 6-1843	4:470
Zornes, William	4-28-1848	8:1

Lawrence Family

Contributed by Clyde H. McClure, Artesia, California. Information in ( ) was added by Mr. McClure.

Joseph Lawrence b. 11-24-1834 (Cabell Co., Va.) m. Eliza Catharine (Black) b. 2-1-1844 (Cabell Co., Va.). Their children:

Miles Monroe b. 5-15-1861 (Va.)
Alais Amanda b. 2-10-1863 (Kansas)
Florence Ann b. 3-3-1865 (Kansas)
Rebecca Virginia b. 3-5-1867 (Kansas)

Rosa Bell b. 5-18-1869 (Kansas)
Permelia Catharine b. 8-30-1871 (Kansas)
Joseph Dickson b. 5-24-1873 (Kansas)

FRANKLIN COUNTY, INDIANA NATURALIZATION RECORDS
Book 1, 23 Sept. 1826 - 11 March 1839

Franklin County, formed 1811 from Clark, Dearborn & Jefferson Counties, was an important early gateway to the Indiana Territory. The immigrants reflected in these records came first to the eastern seaboard, then usually moved westward. A spot check of the 1840 Indiana census shows many still in Franklin County, some of the same names in other Indiana Counties, others gone, the migration was still on.

Not all of the aliens appearing before the Circuit Court of Franklin Co. were residents of that county, some were from Pipley and Dearborn, others just residents of Indiana. The Intentions, often termed "first papers," contain different information than the "second papers" when citizenship was finally granted Frequently the "second papers" were filed in another state or a different county.

These Declaration of Intentions in Franklin County beginning in 1826 are unique because they are extant and are so early. Except for Dearborn Co., whose records start the same year, we know of no others, though we may find some hidden away. Dearborn's records will be published in subsequent issues. The WPA Inventory of Naturalization Returns (see **THG** Dec. 1976) with few exceptions list any before the early 1850s, and of course these may no longer be available in the county court houses.

The testimony was oral, the Clerk of the Court recorded it as he heard it. Enoch McCarty & Robert John, the clerks, probably struggled to understand those who spoke little or no English, resulting in many strange spellings of names and places. No attempt has been made to change these; hopefully they are presented accurately.

Date and place of birth, arrival in the United States, residences thereafter, and in some instances names of other members of the family are important clues for family historians. The path is opened for bridging the Atlantic for those who did not have colonial ancestors.

23 Sept. 1826	SAMUEL BARBER, b. Co. Sligo, Ire. 24 Mar. 1781, from Donogold July 1819, to N.Y. 1819, to Franklin Co., Dec. 1819.
25 Sept. 1826	JAMES McCLURE, b. Co. Letevia (?), Ire., age 47, from Donegald 1819, to Franklin Co. Dec. 1819.
13 Mar. 1828	JAMES BARBER, b. Co. Sligo, Ire, 26 May 1777, from Belfast 11 Apr. 1811, to Norfolk, Va. 20 June 1811, to Franklin Co. 1 Feb. 1815.
17 Mar. 1828	CHRISTOPHER WHITEHEAD, b. Yorkshire, Eng. 25 Apr. 1770, from Liverpool 18 June 1822, to Philadelphia Aug. 1822, to Franklin Co. Mar. 1822 [sic] (1823?).
19 July 1830	JOHN BLACKBURN, b. Leeds, Yorkshire, Eng., 10 Mar. 1794, from Londonderry 17 May 1817, to New York, 6 Aug. 1817, to Franklin Co. 1820.
30 July 1830	WILLIAM STERRIT, b. Co. Donegal, Ire. 1784, from Londonderry, to Blackrock, New York [now part of Buffalo] 1821 to Franklin Co., Jan. 1827.
30 July 1830	JOHN MITCHELL, b. Co. Faranagh, Ire., 1776, from Londonderry 1 June 1824, to Blackrock, N.Y. ca 17 Aug. 1824, to Franklin Co. ca 16 Sept. 1824.
30 July 1830	WALTER MITCHELL, b. Co. Faranah, Ire. 30 May 1807, from Londonderry 5 May 1821, to Blackrock, N.Y. ca 17 Aug. 1824, to Franklin Co. ca 16 Sept. 1824.

30 July 1830   GEORGE DICKSON, b. Fermagh, Ire. Oct. 1787, from Londonderry 5 May 1821, to State of N.Y. July 1827, to Franklin Co., 5 July 1829.

9 Mar. 1832   WILLIAM HEAP, b. Lancashore, Eng. 1777, from Liverpool 7 July 1819, to Alexandria, D.C. 5 Sept. 1819, to Franklin Co. 20 Aug. 1820.

25 Apr. 1832   ALEXANDER CRAWFORD, b. Co. Landrick, Scot., 1800 or 1801, from Glasgow 20 Apr. 1817, to N.Y. ca June 1817, Franklin Co. summer 1822.

5 Sept. 1832   WILLIAM HUTCHINSON, b. Co. Yorkshire, Eng. 1808, from Liverpool 16 May 1831, to Norfolk, Va. ca 20 June 1831, to Franklin Co., fall 1831.

5 Sept. 1832   CHARLES HUTCHENSON, Junior, b. Co. Yorkshire, Eng., 1810, from Liverpool 16 May 1831, to Norfolk, Va. ca 20 June 1831, to Franklin Co., fall 1831.

5 Sept. 1832   CHARLES HUTCHENSON, b. Co. Yorkshire, Eng. 1769, from Liverpool 16 May 1831, to Norfolk, Va. ca 20 June 1831, to Franklin Co., fall 1831.

5 Nov. 1832   WILLIAM BANES, b. Co. Derham, Eng. 1786, from New Castle 23 Mar. 1820, to Baltimore 23 May 1820, to Indiana 1820.

5 Nov. 1832   WILLIAM WHITEHEAD, b. Co. York, Eng. 1802, from Liverpool ca 18 June 1822, to Philadelphia ca 31 Aug. 1822, to Indiana 1823.

17 Nov. 1832   ROBERT BLACKER, b. Co. Armagh, Ire 1799, from Belfast, spring 1816, to Amboy, N.J. Sept. 1810, then to Ohio, to Indiana spring 1828.

12 Dec. 1832   THOMAS ELDEN, b. Co. York, Eng. 1790, from Sunderland Apr. 1820, to Canada, to Sodus, New York (Wayne Co.) ca 1 July 1820, to Franklin Co. Sept. 1820.

12 Dec. 1832   JOHN ELDON, b. Co. York, Eng. 1797, from Sunderland 27 May 1821, to Black Rock, N.Y. June 1822, to Franklin Co. June 1822.

12 Dec. 1832   JOSEPH ELDON, b. York Co. Eng. 1794, from Sunderland 27 May 1821, to Black Rock, N.Y. June 1832, [sic] (see above), then directly to Franklin Co.

17 Feb. 1834   GEORGE O'BYRNE, b. Ire. 15 Feb. 1770, from Sligo 10 May 1831, to New York City ca 22 June 1831, to Franklin Co. ca 22 Aug. 1831.

14 Apr. 1834   GEORGE H. FITTIG, France.

14 Apr. 1834   BENDICK WINKLEMAN, Switzerland.

14 Apr. 1834   ADAM SCHLIGHT, MICHAEL RIPPERGER, HENRY HOOVER, IGNAS RIPPERGER, JOHANNES FUSNER, WILLIAM GEIS, ALOIS BAUER, late of Kingdom of Beiern.

14 Apr. 1834   JACOB FRUGER & JOHN FRUGER, Weddingbrough.

14 Apr. 1834   WILLIAM FISHER, Kingdom of Prussia.

25 May 1834   PHILIP HYDE, b. Lancaster Co. Eng. 8 Apr. 1797, from Liverpool 9 Apr. 1830, to New York 2 June 1830, immediately to 12 miles of Dayton, O., 29 June 1830, to Franklin Co., ca 1 Apr. 1831.

19 Apr. 1834	FRANCIS DOWNING b. Co. Londonderry, Ire. Oct. 1797, from Belfast 13 May 1820, to Quebec, Canada 24 June 1820, to Moose Island, Maine June 1821, to Baltimore 1821 one month, thence to Pa., to Franklin Co. by way of Cincinnati spring 1825.
2 Oct. 1834	WILLIAM KERR, b. Co. Mid Lothian, Scotland 1803, from Liverpool Apr. 1834, to Philadelphia May 1834, to Franklin Co. June 1834.
3 Oct. 1834	PATRICK BLACKER, b. Co. Armagh, Ire. 1803, from Belfast, spring 1810, to Amboy, N.J. fall 1810, to Ohio until spring 1828, to Franklin Co.
13 Oct. 1834	ROBERT SPEERS, b. Co. Lenack, Scotland 1793, from Belfast May 1819, to New York 19 July 1819, to New Jersey, Pennsylvania, Ohio & Franklin Co. spring 1830.
13 Oct. 1834	GABRIEL GILMORE, b. Airshire, Seat. 1800, from Grenock May 1832, to New York, City July 1832, to Conneticut, to Franklin Co. May 1834.
28 Jan 1835	JOHN H. MILLER, b. Lancashers, Eng. 1784, from Liverpool 23 May 1818, to Philadelphia July 1818, to Ohio 2 years, to Indiana 1821.
28 Jan. 1835	JOHN HEAP b. Co. Lancashire, Eng. 1789, from Liverpool 4 July 1819, to Alexandria, Va Sept. 1814, to Franklin Co.
17 Feb. 1835	JOHN SOUTER b. Co. Yorkshire, Eng. 1807 or 1808, from Hull 9 May 1832, to New York 10 June 1832, to Franklin Co. July 1832.
14 Apr. 1835	WILLIAM WOOD, b. Gr. Britain 28 Mar. 1808, to New York 1831.
17 Apr. 1835	HUGH SLEVENS b. Co. Terone, Parish Cogher, Ire. 1807 or 1808, from Belfast 19 Apr. 1828, to Quebec, Canada 2 June 1828, to Philadelphia Aug. 1828, to Cincinnati, O. 1829 and after going to New Orleans, to Franklin Co. spring 1832.
— — 1835	JOHN CARTER, b. Co. Yorkshire, Eng. 1803, from Hull 9 May 1832, to New York, 15 June 1832, to Cincinnati 12 July 1832, to Franklin Co. Apr. 1833.
11 Aug. 1835	WILLIAM CRAIG b. Airshire, Scotland 1800, from Greenock Mar. 1820, to Rhode Island 1820, to Franklin Co. Sept. 1830.
12 Oct. 1835	CONRAD WILER, JOHN SLEIGHT, GODFRED HOOBER, BLESSE JACK-AL, ADAM BROSEY & JOHN WEST. Conrad Wiler, John Sleight, Godfred Hoober, John West natives of Kingdom Bayern, Ger. Conrad, age 29, left Bayern 1830 & lived in New York same year. John Sleight, age 27, left Bayern 1831, landed in New York 1831. John West, age 60, left Bayern 1834, arr. Baltimore (no date). Said Godfred Hoober, age 27, left Bayern 1828, landed New York last of the year. Said Blesse, age 30, left Baden 1834, landed in New York. Adam, age 53, native of Kingdom of Wertenberg, left 1835, landed in Baltimore. Subscribed and sworn to in open court the 12 Oct. 1835, the contents being made known to and explained by an interpreter to the signers of the above declaration. Robert John, Clk. F.C.C.
16 Oct. 1835	LEWIS SCHNEIDER, b. Kirchemboland, Bavaria 1804. Sailed from Havre de Grace, France, 10 Oct. 1833, to New York 29 Nov. 1833, to Northampton Co. Pa. Dec. 1833, to Butler Co. Oh. June 1834, to Franklin Co. June 1835.

16 Oct. 1835   JOSEPH BEICH, b. Cloverburgh (?), Baden 1802, to Havre de Grace, France 3 Oct. 1830, to New York 3 Nov. 1830, to Cincinnati, Oh. 6 Dec. 1830, to Franklin Co. Nov. 1834.

17 Oct. 1835   THOMAS MITCHELL, b. Co. Tyron, Ire. 1798, from Belfast 1819, to New York 1819, to Cincinnati 1820, to Natchez, Miss. 1825, back to Cincinnati 1826 to Huntsville, Ala. 1830, to Franklin Co. spring 1835.

17 Oct. 1835   ISAAC BEASLEY, b. Lancashire, Eng. 1800, from Liverpool July 1830, to New York Aug. 1830, to Franklin Co. Sept. 1830.

17 Oct. 1835   WILLIAM ASHTON, b. Yorkshire, Eng. 1803, from Liverpool 8 Apr. 1834, to Philadelphia May 1834, to Franklin Co. June 1834.

30 Jan. 1836   JONATHAN HART, b. York Co. Eng. from Liverpool May 1819, to Philadelphia June 1819, to Franklin, Butler Co. Oh. fall 1819, to Franklin Co. Ind., spring 1823.

3 Mar. 1836   CHARLES MITCHELL, b. Ireland 13 Nov. 1774, from Sligo 21 June 1830, to St. Johns, New Brunswick, Aug. 1830, to Eastport, Maine, Oct. 1831 to Cincinnati, Oh. Nov. 1831, to Louisville, Ky. 1833, to Franklin Co. Sept. 1834.

15 Aug. 1836   HENRY STOCKMEYER, JOHN STOCKMEYER, PHILIP GESELL, PHILIP RUPP and HENRY ACKLES (?). Henry and John, natives of Beyern, Ger. Henry, age 29, left Beyern 8 May 1831, landed New York 24 July 1831. John Stockmeyer, age 21, left Beyern Mar. 1834 landed New Orleans 11 June 1834. Philip Gesell and Philip Rupp natives of Darmstadt, Ger., both left 20 Apr. 1836, landed New York 12 June 1836. Gessell, age 46, Rupp, age 39. Henry Ackles, native Hessecastle, Ger., left Aug 1833, landed Baltimore fall 1833. All now residents of Indiana. (Oath and declarations through interpreter.)

7 Oct. 1836   JOSEPH BEESLEY, b. Lancashire, Eng. 1802, from Liverpool Aug. 1831, landed Baltimore Sept. 1831, to Franklin Co. Nov. 1831.

13 Oct. 1836   JOSEPH WYNN, b. Yorkshire, Eng. 1803, from Sunderland 8 Apr. 1820, landed Suckers Harbour, N.Y. ca July 1820, to Franklin Co. ca Sept. 1820, being then underage 18 yrs.

18 Oct. 1836   ISAAC HART, b. Co Armagh, Ire. ca 1780, best information he has, age about 56 years. From Belfast June 1817, to Baltimore, to Franklin Co. Oct. 1819.

24 Oct. 1836   GOTTLIEB EKERT, b. Wertenburgh, Ger., age 27, left June 1833, to New York Aug. 1833, to Franklin Co. May 1836.

24 Oct. 1836   AUGUST VOGEL, b. Saxony, Ger. age 35, left June 1834, to Baltimore Sept. 1834, Franklin Co. since May 1836.

21 Oct. 1836   JOHN ILIF, from Kingdom of Bavaria Mar. 1833, age 40, to Baltimore June 1833, to Franklin Co. 22 Oct. 1836. Family came with him, wife and 3 children, Anna Magdalena; b. Bavaria, age 42; son, George, age 16; John age 12; Nicholas, age 8, all b. Bavaria.

21 Oct. 1836   JACOB WALTERS, b. Hesse Darmstad, Ger. age 36, left Mar. 1832, arr. New York May 1832. In Franklin Co. since May 1836.

31 Jan. 1837   JOHANNES SIMON, b. Kingdom of B..., Ger. 1808, left May 1834, arr. New York July 1834, to Franklin Co. Jan. 1837. (Prb. from Bavaria as he renounced King Ludwick I.)

21 Feb. 1837   JOHN BARBER, b. Co. Sligo, Ire. June 1785. Is about 5'6" tall, sandy complexion. From Londonderry 11 May 1833, arr. New York ca 16 June 1833 with family; wife and Jane Barber, age now ca 19, Joseph age ca 18, Francis age ca 14, John age ca 12, Eliza, age ca 5, all b. Sligo, direct to Franklin Co. 1 Aug. 1833.

22 Feb. 1837   THOMAS SHERA, b. Co. R..., Ire. 1811, left 1831, to Quebec, Can. 1831, to Butler Co. Oh., then Franklin Co. 1836.

23 Feb. 1837   JOHN HUTCHINSON and MATHEW HUTCHINSON. John b. 12 Sept. 1812, Yorkshire Co., G. B., is son of Charles Hutchinson, who reported himself to Clk. of Court 5 Sept. 1832; is 5'6" high, light complexion. Sailed with father from Liverpool 16 May 1831, arr. Norfolk, Va. ca 1st June 1831, then age 18, came immediately with father to Franklin Co. 1831. Said Mathew, son of Charles, age 17 when arr. in U.S. Became 21 fall of 1834.

11 Mar. 1837   JOHN MITCHELL, b. Ire. Apr. 1804. From Sligo 21 June 1830, to Stephens, New Brunswick Aug. 1830, to New York Sept. 1830, to Cincinnati, then to Louisville, Ky, Nov. 1833, to Franklin Co. Sept. 1834.

21 Mar. 1837   JOHN SHEANLOAB reports for self and minor son; b. Bavaria, Ger. 1785, left Apr. 1837, arr. New York July 1832, to Cincinnati Aug. 1832, then to Dearborn Co. Ind. 12 Apr. 1833 where now lives with son, Michal, age 18 last Dec.

9 June 1837   SAMUEL McCURDY, b. Co. Antrim Ire., 1799. From Belfast spring 1831, to New York May 1831, following April to Ohio, to Franklin Co. Mar. 1836.

7 Aug. 1837   CONRAD SHUMBAD, b. Co. [sic] Wazen Umstead, Ger. 1799. From Bremen May 1831, to Baltimore Sept. 1831, to Cincinnati 7 Mar. 1832, to Franklin Co. Feb. 1835.

7 Aug. 1837   ADAM CLURE, b. Baden, Ger. 1812, from Bremen 14 Aug. 1832, arr. Baltimore 13 Dec. 1832, to Cincinnati 1 Sept. 1833, to Franklin Co. fall 1836.

14 Aug. 1837   HENRY WOLBER, b. county of Brechhaven, Kingdom of Hanover 1810. From Bremen June 1832, landed Baltimore Aug. 1832, to Cincinnati Sept. 1834, to Franklin Co. Jan. 1836.

14 Aug. 1837   HENRY MINS, b. Co. Dupaltz, Kingdom of Hanover, 1798. From Bremen Sept. 1832, arr. Baltimore January 1832, to Cincinnati Mar. 1832, to Franklin Co. Aug. 1836.

14 Aug. 1837   JOHN ELLERMAN, b. Co. Osnabruck, Kingdom of Hanover 1802. From Bremen, arr. New York Oct. 1834, arr. Cincinnati Nov. 1834, Franklin Co. Feb. 1834 (1835?)

17 Aug. 1837	FREDERICK DOBBELING, b. Co. Dupholtz, Kingdom of Hanover 1791. From Bremen Oct. 1831, arr. Baltimore Jan. 1832, to Cincinnati, Oh. where since and now resides.
14 Aug. 1837	HENRY WILLIAMS, b. Co. Dupholtz, Kingdom of Hanover. From Bremen Oct. 1831, arr. Baltimore Jan 1832, to Cincinnati 1832, to Franklin Co. Aug. 1836.
14 Aug. 1837	HENRY BAKEMAN, b. Co. Dupholtz, Kingdom of Hanover. From Bremen Oct. 1831, arr. Baltimore Jan. 1832, to Cincinnati fall 1832, to Franklin Co. fall 1837.
14 Aug. 1837	HENRY ELLERMAN, b. Co. Onabruck, Kingdom of Hanover 1800. From Bremen May 1835, arr. New York June 1835, arr. Cincinnati July 1835, Franklin Co. Feb. 1835 (1836?)
14 Aug. 1837	PETER RITINGER, b. Co. of Winham (?), Dukedom of Baden, 1805. From Bremen Aug. 1832, arr. Baltimore Nov. 1832. To Cincinnati Nov. 1835, to Franklin Co. Mar. 1836.
14 Aug. 1837	HEROD ELLERMAN, b. Co. Omabruck, Kingdom of Hanover, 1783. From Bremen 1834, arr. New York Oct. 1834, to Cincinnati Nov. 1834, to Franklin Co. Aug. 1836.
14 Aug. 1837	LEWIS SCHOCKEY, b. Co. Islinger, Kingdom of Hanover, 1805. From Bremen Apr. 1832, arr. New York June 1832, arr. Franklin Co. Apr. 1832 (1833?)
19 Aug. 1837	PHILIP SEVENDOLLAR, b. Permaans, Kingdom of Bavaria 1805, left Jan. 1831, arr. Philadelphia Aug. 1831, arr. Cincinnati Feb. 1832, to Franklin Co. Feb. 1834.
19 Aug. 1837	ADAM DIM, b. Co. Aschfenburgh, Bavaria 1802, left Aug. 1836, arr. Baltimore Oct. 1836, to Franklin Co. Feb. 1837.
19 Aug. 1837	GEORGE SCHINDELDECKER, b. Co. of Permaans, Kingdom of Bavaria 1794, left Mar. 1837, arr. Baltimore May 1837, to Franklin Co. Aug. 1837.
19 Aug. 1837	GEORGE SEVENDOLLAR, b. Co. Permaun, Kingdom of Bavaria 1810, left Jan. 1831, arr. New Orleans May 1831, arr. Cincinnati May 1831 to Franklin Co. Feb. 1834.
——Aug, 1837	JOHN HENRY WEACHER, subject of Great Britain, b. in Hanover, one of dependencies of the Kingdom aforesaid, 1809 or 1810. Embarked for U. S. 1829, arr. Baltimore, ship Minerva 1830, since resided U. S. and now of Franklin Co.
19 Aug. 1837	The Declaration of Wm. Wright for Naturalization filed 22 Aug. 1828 which was omitted, to be entered 19th day Aug. 1837, done nunc pro (blotted out) which follows in these words and figures to wit: b. Co. of Lancaster Eng. 18 Feb. 1734, from Liverpool 14 June 1819, arr. Philadelphia 30 June 1819, thence to Ohio & Franklin Co. ca 26 April 1824.
21 Sept. 1837	GEORGE ADAM RIPP, b. town of Klongenburgh, Kingdom of Byern, 1812, from Bremen Aug. 1834, to Baltimore arr. 26 Aug. 1834, thence to Wheeling, Va, then to Cincinnati, to Franklin Co. fall 1835.

11 Oct. 1837	STEPHEN BOLINGER, b. Co. of Aergau, Switzerland, 1804, left 1834, arr. New York July 1834, to Pittsburgh Sept. 1834, thence Collumbia Co. Oh, Oct. 1834, to Franklin Co. 1837.
21 Oct. 1837	CHRISTIAN BOHRER, b. Kingdom of Beyrne, Ger., 1810, left Nov. 1832, arr. New York Jan. 1833, to Cincinnati ca Feb. 1833, to Franklin Co. July 1837.
21 Oct. 1837	PHILIP BAYER, b. Co. Hesse Darmsted, Ger., 1788, left July 1837, arr. New York Sept. 1837, arr. Cincinnati 5 Oct. 1837, to Franklin Co. 10 Oct. 1837.
3 Nov. 1837	JACOB CLASS, b. Kingdom Wittenburg 1795 about 25 Dec., from Havre de Grace, France, winter 1829 or spring 1830, arr. Philadelphia spring 1830 about 15 weeks after he sailed. After 14 days, to Cincinnati until 1 July 1837, arr. Franklin Co. 4 July 1837. No wife or children, is about 5'7" high, sandy complexion.
4 Nov. 1837	JOHN MICHAEL KREGER, b. Wittenburgh 22 Oct. 1797, from Amsterdam June 1816, arr. Philadelphia 14 Aug. 1816 where resided. 29 Aug. 1835 left Philadelphia sailed to West Indies, resided Cuba ca 9 mos, to New Orleans 14 Aug. 1836, Vicksburg Oct. 1836, then to Cincinnati and Franklin Co. 4 July 1837. No wife or children.
3 Jan. 1838	GEORGE ADAM KUHN, b. Kingdom Beyrn 1798, left June 1837, arr. Boston Sept. 1837, to Franklin Co. Nov. 1837.
22 Jan. 1838	JOHN PETER, b. Co. of Gelhausen, Dukedom Hesse 1773, left May 1836, arr. Baltimore Aug. 1836, arr. Pittsburg Sept. 1836, Franklin Co. Sept. 1837.
22 Jan. 1838	ADAM KLANFELTER, b. Co. Gelhausen, Dukedom of Hesse 1790, left May 1837, arr. Baltimore 12 Sept. 1837, arr. Cincinnati 29 Sept. 1837, to Franklin Co. Oct. 1837.
5 Feb. 1838	HENRY BRINKMEYER, b. Prussia 1813, left Oct. 1834. [no port of arr.], to Wheeling, Va. Apr. 1835, to Cincinnati July 1836, to Franklin Co. Dec. 1837.
6 Feb. 1838	JOHN BART, b. Kingdom Beyrn, Ger. 1788, left May 1837, arr. New York July 1837, to Cincinnati Aug. 1837, to Franklin Co. Oct. 1837.
7 Feb. 1838	JACOB BARKER (signature is Berger) b. Kingdom France 1813, left July 1837 [sic] arr. New York Aug. 1837, to Wilmington, Del. Feb. 1836 [sic], Pittsburgh June 1837, Franklin Co. Nov. 1837.
8 Feb. 1838	CHRISTIAN FRITSCH, b. France 1783, left 7 Aug. 1834, arr. New York 11 Nov. 1834, to Buffalo, N.Y. until July 1837, to Pittsburgh, arr. Franklin Co. Nov. 1837.
20 Feb. 1838	JOHN HEAP, Jr., b. Eng. 1808, left July 1819, arr. Baltimore Aug. 1819, arr. Cincinnati Sept. 1819, to Franklin Co. Jan. 1828.
20 Feb. 1838	JOHN BERTINSHAW, b. Eng. 1802, left July 1819 arr. Alexandria, Va. Sept. 1819, to Cincinnati and Franklin Co. Mar. 1820.
21 Feb. 1838	FREDERICK JACKSON, b. Ire. 1814, left Feb. 1832, arr. N.Y. Mar. 1832, arr. Cincinnati Apr. 1832, to Franklin Co. July 1837.

21 Feb. 1838	THOMAS WHITEHEAD, b. Eng. 1805, left Apr. 1830, arr. N.Y. June 1830, thence Cincinnati June 1830, to Franklin Co. Mar. 1836.
21 Feb. 1838	WILLIAM BEASLY, b. Eng. 1797, left July 1830, arr. N.Y. Aug. 1830, Cincinnati Aug. 1830, to Franklin Co. Sept. 1830.
22 Jan. 1838	[sic] FRANCIS MATTHIAS MILLER, b. Co. of Ammerbach, Bavaria 1797, left May 1837, arr. Baltimore 12 Sept. 1837, to Cincinnati 29 Sept. 1837, to Franklin Co. Oct. 1837.
1 Mar. 1838	TIMOTHY CRONIN b. Ire. 1798, left May 1828, arr. N.Y. July 1828, to Philadelphia Aug. 1828, thence to Miflin Co. Pa. Aug. 1828, to Montgomery, Md, then Washington City, D.C. 1830, to Richmond, Va. Apr. 1835, to Franklin Co. Dec. 1837.
7 Apr. 1838	ANTHONY WOLFORD, b. Bavaria, Ger., left 10 Aug. 1836, arr. Baltimore 18 Oct. 1836, to Cincinnati Nov. 1836, Franklin Co. ca 2 June 1837.
15 Apr. 1838	FREDERICK KLEMM, b. Bavaria 1792, left May 1837, arr. Baltimore Aug. 1837, thence to Franklin Co. same month.
26 Apr. 1838	FREDERICK BEZNER, b. Kingdom of Wirtenburg, Ger., 1794, left Apr. 1837, no place of arrival, to Franklin Co. Aug. 1837.
27 Apr. 1838	MICHAEL HUBER, b. Switzerland 1787, left Apr. 1836, arr. N.Y. 5 May 1836, thence to Franklin Co. July 1836.
20 June 1838	JOHN MAURER, b. Kingdom of Wirtenburg, Ger. 26 Sept. 1807, left 27 May 1832, arr. Baltimore 1 Sept. 1832, removed to Pa., then Ohio and Franklin Co. Dec. 1835.
22 June 1838	MATTHIAS GEIS, b. Bavaria, Ger. 10 May 1800, left June 1837, arr. Boston, Oct. 1837, thence to Franklin Co. 26 May 1838.
13 July 1838	JOHN R. DARKERSON, b. Kingdom of Aldenburg, Ger. 1792, left May 1833, arr. Baltimore July 1833, to Cincinnati Aug. 1833, to Franklin Co. Mar. 1838.
13 Feb. 1838	[sic] JOHN J. DARKERSON, b. Kingdom of Aldenburg, Ger. 1800, left June 1834, arr. Baltimore Aug. 1834, to Cincinnati Sept. 1834 and Franklin Co. Feb. 1837.
16 July 1838	ADAM SMITH, b. Bavaria, Ger. 25 Jan. 1797, left 18 Mar. 1834, arr. Baltimore 8 June 1834, to Franklin Co. ca 1 Oct. 1834.
23 July 1838	JOHN BOLINGER, b. Co. Argau, Switzerland 1803, left July 1833, arr. N.Y. Sept. 1833, to Columbiana Co., Oh. Nov. 1833, Franklin Co. Aug. 1837.
23 July 1838	JOSEPH SMID, b. Co. Argau, Switzerland 1788, left May 1838, arr. N.Y. July 1834, to Collumbiana Co., Oh. Nov. 1834, Franklin Co. Aug. 1837.
24 July 1838	MICHAEL FRIES, b. Bavaria, Ger. 11 Feb. 1788, left 26 June 1837, to Boston 16 Sept. 1837, arr. Franklin Co. Oct. 1837.
21 Aug. 1838	WILLIAM GEIS, b. Big (?) Mall... (?) Kindgom of Beirn, 1783, 5'6" high;

sailed from Bramist (?) Ger. 3 May 1833, arr. Baltimore 15 Aug. 1833, went directly to Cincinnati, then Franklin Co. Oct. 1838.

21 Aug. 1838 ALOIS BAUER, b. Mansborough, a town about 2 miles from Big Malltown, Kingdom of Beirn, 1780, name Alois Bauer in German, but English is Alphonse Bauer. About 6 feet high. Sailed from Braman (Bremen?) 30 May 1833, arr. Baltimore 15 Aug. 1833, direct to Cincinnati, then Franklin Co. Oct. 1833.

25 Aug. 1838 JOHN BARBOUR, b. Co. Sligo, Ire. Nov. 1811. Sailed from Donegal June 1819, landed City of Washington Sept. 1819, to Franklin Co. Dec. 1819 where he has since and now resides. Age ca 8 yrs. when arrived. Also came Rebecca O'Bryan b. Co. Sligo, Ire. 1813, now aged 25; from Donegal June 1819, arr. Washington City Sept. 1819, to Franklin Co. Dec. 1819. Age about 6 years when arrived. Francis Barbour, b. Co. Sligo, Ire. 1819, arr. Washington City 1819, to Franklin Co. Dec. 1819.

15 Sept. 1838 JOHN ADAM KUHN, b. Bavaria 1790, arr. Baltimore Oct. 1836, to Franklin Co. Feb. 1837.

no date PETER GERBER, b. Bavaria 1799, arr. Baltimore Nov. 1836, Franklin Co. Mar. 1837.

21 Sept. 1838 GODFREY GRAMMEL, b. Bavaria 1796, left Apr. 1837 arr. Baltimore June 1837, Franklin Co. Aug. 1837.

21 Nov. 1838 [sic] MICHAEL HOFF, native of Heinwerler in Rhine, Bavaria, age about 24 yrs. From Havre de Grace 15 May 1838, arr. N.Y. 6 July 1838, thence to Dearborn Co. Ind. (Ia) where he now resides and intends to reside.

22 Sept. 1838 GEORGE NORT, b. Bayern, Ger. 1810, arr. Baltimore Sept. 1837, to Franklin Co. Dec. 1837.

21 Nov. 1838 ANDREW LOGEE, b. Heinweiter in Rhine, Bavaria, from Havre de Grace 1 Apr. 1836, arr. New Orleans 25 June 1836, thence to Dearborn Co. Ind. (Ia) where now resides and intends to reside.

24 Mar. 1838 PETER CONRAD, b. Kingdom Hesse Darmstadt 1810, arr. Baltimore Aug. 1833, thence to Dearborn Co. Oct. 1838, where since and now lives.

24 Nov. 1838 GEORGE AHL, b. Hesse Darmstadt 1788, arr. Baltimore Aug. 1833, thence to Ripley Co. Ind. Sept. 1839, where since and now lives.

28 Nov. 1838 JOHN LOGEE, native of Rhine Bavaria, age ca 60, from Havre de Grace 1 Apr. 1835, arr. New Orleans same year, thence to Dearborn Co. where now resides and intends to reside. Petitioner has sons Zuba Philipp, b. 6 Mar. 1821, Barnard, b. 23 Sept. 1823.

28 Nov. 1838 MICHAEL SCHRUNK, b. 1813, Bavaria, left May 1832, arr. Baltimore Aug. 1832, thence to Wheeling, Va. Aug. 1832, to Cincinnati 1835 and Franklin Co. Sept. 1838.

3 Dec. 1838 PHILIP HITTLE, b. Dukedom Hesse Castle, Ger. 1804, left 15 May 1835, arr. N.Y. Oct. 1835, thence to Cincinnati Oct. 1835, to Franklin Co. Nov. 1836.

10 Dec. 1838	GEORGE SHILLING, b. Kingdom of Baden 1804, left June 1830, arr. Baltimore Dec. 1830, thence to Huntingdon Co. N.J. Jan. 1831, to Philadelphia Apr. 1836, to Franklin Co. Sept. 1837.
10 Dec. 1838	HENRY SNIDER, b. Kingdom of Berne, Ger. 1811. Left May 1836, arr. New Orleans Aug. 1836, thence Cincinnati Apr. 1837, to Franklin Co. Sept. 1837.
22 Dec. 1838	JACOB KNER, b. Kingdom of Berne, Ger. 1820, left Apr. 1835, to Baltimore, arr. Aug. 1835. To Cincinnati Oct. 1835, to Franklin Co. June 1838.
22 Dec. 1838	CHRISTIAN DENNY, b. Kingdom of Berne, Ger. 1818, left 1835, arr. New Orleans Dec. 1835. Thence to Cincinnati Mar. 1836, to Franklin Co. Sept. 1838.
22 Dec. 1838	JOHN GEORGE BETZNER, b. Wittenburg, age ca 30, from Bremen 5 July 1837, arr. Philadelphia 30 July 1837, to Franklin Co., to date.
31 Dec. 1838	JOHN KLEIN, b. Bavaria 1772, left Oct. 1830, arr. N.Y. Nov. 1830, lived state of N.Y. until 1833, thence to Franklin Co. 1833.
1 Jan. 1839	PATRICK CORCORAN, b. city of Waterford, Ire. 1812, left July 1832, arr. Burlington, Vt. Oct. 1833, thence to Albany, N.Y. Nov. 1833, to Franklin Co. Dec. 1838.
1 Jan. 1838	[sic] PATRICK LYNCH, b. town of Tipperary, Ire. 1811, left Aug. 1831, arr. Boston Mar. 1832, to Albany, N.Y. Nov. 1835, thence to Franklin Co. Dec. 1838.
1 Jan. 1839	JEREMIAH O'SULLIVAN, b. Co. Tipperary, Ire. May 1814, left 23 Apr. 1831, arr. N.Y. 4 July 1831, thence to Harrisburgh, Pa. July 1831, to Columbus, Oh. Jan. 1836, to Franklin Co. Nov. 1838.
2 Jan. 1839	PHILIP ARIAN, b. Bavaria, Ger. 1781, Left May 1833, arr. Baltimore Aug. 1833 thence to Franklin Co. Nov. 1834.
4 Jan. 1839	MORRIS SCHANDLIN, b. Co. Kerry, Ire. 1806, left May 1830, arr. Mass. Apr. 1832, thence to Clear Spring, Md. July 1837, to Franklin Co. Apr. 1838.
8 Jan. 1839	PETER FISHER, b. Bavaria, Ger. 1791, left Aug. 1836, arr. Baltimore Oct. 1836, to Franklin Co. Feb. 1837.
14 Jan. 1839	JOHN EPPECK, b. Bavaria, Ger. 1800, left June 1837, arr. Boston Sept. 1837, to Franklin Co. May 1838.
17 Jan. 1839	JOHN KERN, b. Kingdom of Berne, Ger. 1 Nov. 1814 arr. Baltimore 12 Aug. 1837, thence Franklin Co. Nov. 1838.
21 Jan. 1839	TETRICK RINEHART, b. Hesse Castle, Ger. 1807, left 1834, arr. Baltimore July 1834, to Wheeling, Va. May 1831, to Franklin Co. Oct. 1837.
21 Jan. 1839	JOHN SCHRUICHT, b. Kingdom of Bayern, Ger. 1801, left 2 Apr. 1836, arr. N.Y. 5 June 1836, to Franklin Co. Oct. 1836.
21 Jan. 1839	HENRY PAUSCH, b. Hesse Castle, Ger. 1785, left May 1834, arr. N. Y. 1834, to Wheeling, Va. Oct. 1835, to Cincinnati June 1837 and Franklin Co. Nov. 1837.

21 Jan. 1839   MATTHEW FISHER, b. Kingdom of Bayern, Ger. 1799, left July 1838, arr. Baltimore 8 Oct. 1838, Franklin Co. Nov. 1838.

22 Jan. 1839   BELTHASSAR BERG, b. Hesse Darmstadt 1791, left May 1831, arr. Baltimore Aug. 1831, thence to Fredericktown, Md. Aug. 1831, to Wheeling, Va. May 1838, Franklin Co. Sept. 1838.

11 Jan. 1839   JOHN A. BRINKMAN, b. Kingdom of Oldenburg, Ger. 1815, left July 1838 [sic], landed Baltimore Sept. 1834, to Cincinnati Oct. 1834, to Franklin Co. Sept. 1837.

28 Jan. 1839   LEWIS DOLT? (Dott?) b. Baden 1790, left Sept. 1832, arr. Baltimore Jan. 1833, to Fredericktown, Md. Apr. 1833, to Cincinnati Dec. 1834, to Ripley Co. Apr. 1835 where has ever since resided.

15 Feb. 1839   JOHN KARLENBACH, b. Kingdom of Wertenburgh 1811, left 1 July 1837, arr. Philadelphia 30 July 1837, to Franklin Co. Aug. 1837.

18 Feb. 1839   JOHN KING, b. Dorsetshire, Eng. 1807, left 1830, arr. Norfolk, Va. June 1830, to Cincinnati Nov. 1830, to Franklin Co. Mar. 1834.

18 Feb. 1839   JOSEPH T. HOOVER, b. France 1811, left 1835, arr. N.Y. July 1835, to Franklin Co. Aug. 1835.

19 Feb. 1839   JOSEPH BOWER, b. Bavaria, Ger. 16 Apr. 1813, left May 1833, arr. Baltimore 17 Aug. 1833, to Wheeling, Va. Sept. 1833, thence to Franklin Co. 3 May 1834.

27 Feb. 1839   JACOB TRAGER, b. Wirtenburgh, Ger. 1781, left Aug. 1832, arr. Baltimore Dec. 1832, Franklin Co. Apr. 1838.

27 Feb. 1839   HENRY HOOVER, b. Kingdom of Baiern, Ger. 1784, left June 1828, arr. N.Y. Oct. 1828, thence to Cincinnati Feb. 1832, to Franklin Co. Aug. 1834. Also reports sons, Lewis, age ca. 20 yrs. John age ca. 18 yrs, George age ca. 12 yrs.

27 Feb. 1839   CONRAD WILDER, b. Rosbeck, town in Kingdom of Baiern, 1806, left 1830, sailed from Havre de Grace, France 2 May 1830, arr. N.Y. 6 Aug. 1830, directly to Philadelphia where resided until 14 Sept. 1832 when came to Cincinnati; 15 Aug. 1834 to Dearborn Co. Ind. where has since and now resides.

27 Feb. 1839   GODFREY HOOVER, b. Kingdom of Bayern, Ger. 1808, left June 1828, arr. N.Y. Oct. 1828, to Cincinnati Feb. 1832, to Franklin Co. Aug. 1834.

27 Feb. 1839   MICHAEL RIPPERGER, b. Kingdom of Baiern 1792, left May 1833, arr. Baltimore 15 Aug. 1833, thence to Franklin Co. Oct. 1833. Reports his children, John Adam, age 18; Michael, age 16; George age 14; Ysidor, age 10, Anthony, age 6.

27 Feb. 1839   BLAIS YAKLE, b. Kingdom of Baden 1797, left May 1834, arr. N.Y. Aug. 1834, thence to Franklin Co. Sept. 1834. Reports sons, Valentine, age 19; Mathias, age 16.

1 Mar. 1838	JOHN SLEICHT, b. 1808, Kingdom of Bairne, Ger., left Apr. 1832, arr. N.Y. July 1832, thence to Cincinnati Aug. 1832, to Franklin Co. Oct. 1838.
6 Mar. 1839	JOHN F. HELIS [Allis?], b. Hanover, Ger. 1804, left 1832, arr. Baltimore Jan. 1833, thence to Cincinnati Feb. 1833, to Franklin Co. Oct. 1833.
6 Mar. 1839	PETER HOFMANN, b. Kingdom New Bearne, Ger., 1797, left June 1838, arr. Baltimore Sept. 1838, thence to Cincinnati Oct. 1838, Franklin Co. Nov. 1838.
8 Mar. 1839	JOHN A. RIPPERGER, b. Kingdom of Beiern, 1815, left May 1833, arr. Baltimore Aug. 1833, to Cincinnati Sept. 1833, to Franklin Co. Oct. 1833.
11 Mar. 1839	ADAM BROSA, b. Wertenburg, Ger. 1782, left May 1835, arr. Baltimore July 1835, to Franklin Co. Aug. 1835. Reported children, Adam, age 13; Matthew, age 19 in June 1839.

PIONEER PHYSICIANS OF BARTHOLOMEW COUNTY, INDIANA

The following notes were made by Mrs. Jane Murphy of Columbus from articles published in the Columbus *Evening Republican*, July 25-26, 1911. The articles were prepared by Dr. George T. MacCoy (more often spelled McCoy), giving credit to notes of the late Dr. John C. Beck, George Pence, and W. H. Terrell.

Dr. Hiram Smith. Dr. Smith was the first physician to locate in Columbus, arriving April, 1821 from Mercer Co., Ky. He was the unanimous choice for Master of St. John's Lodge No. 20, F. & A. M. of Columbus when Grand Lodge met at Corydon, Oct., 1822 and granted its charter. After his wife's death, he relocated in Mooresville, but shortly afterwards, moved to Edinburg and died there Oct. 1, 1869, from gastric ulcer, aged 79.

Dr. Joseph L. Washburn. The next physician to locate in Columbus was Dr. Joseph L. Washburn, in the autumn of 1821. He was born and educated in Vermont. He taught school earlier at Middlebury, Vt. In March, 1822, he served as senior deacon of our St. John's Lodge. He died Oct. 9, 1828, and is buried in Thompson Graveyard, one mile south of Columbus.

Dr. Wm. V. Snyder. Dr. Snyder came here from Virginia in 1822, but returned there, where he died many years ago.

Dr. Joseph Rose. Dr. Rose and his junior brother, Dr. E. Rose, located here about 1822.

Dr. John Ritchie. Dr. Ritchie located here about 1827. His wife was an educated woman and was first of her sex to teach higher branches in the public schools of Columbus. Dr. Ritchie was born in Adams Co., Pa., Jan. 5, 1782. He studied medicine twenty miles west of Pittsburgh and practiced a few years in Ohio. In 1832 he moved to Franklin, Ind. and died there Oct. 10, 1857.

Dr. James Ritchie. Dr. James Ritchie, son of John, was born in Erie Co., Pa., June 6, 1804, and studied medicine with his father. Afterwards moved to Edinburg, and later, to Rensselaer, Ind., where he died some years ago.

Dr. Wm. P. Kiser. Dr. Kiser came to Columbus about 1828. He studied medicine in the office of Dr. Cravens of Shenandoah Co., Va., having as fellow office student, Dr. Joseph A. Baxter, who also located here in 1829. The two men formed a partnership, which lasted several years. Dr. Kiser died many years ago in Rockport, Ind.

Dr. Joseph A. Baxter. Dr. Baxter established the first drug store in Columbus. He was a strict Presbyterian and served as elder. He was one of the leading physicians in the state and died in 1839.

Dr. Tiffin Davis. Dr. Davis came from Ohio in 1830. He was a classmate of Dr. James Ritchie, 1828-29, in Ohio. His mother was a sister of Edward Tiffin, the first Governor of Ohio. Dr. Davis died in Edinburg, Ind. about 1871.

Dr. Henry B. Roland. Dr. Roland came at about the same time as Dr. Tiffin Davis, coming from Virginia and locating between Columbus and Newbern. He moved to Bloomfield, Iowa, in 1848.

PHYSICIANS LOCATING IN COLUMBUS BETWEEN 1839 and 1850

Dr. Samuel M. Linton, first located in Azalia, 1839, and to Columbus in 1842, died there Dec. 28, 1889.

Dr. Samuel Barbour came in 1843 from Rush Co., Ind., returned there, and later moved to Indianapolis, where he gave up practice and became the proprietor of the Palmer House.

Dr. George C. Comstock graduated from Louisville Medical College, came to Columbus in 1841. He was an artist—moved to Illinois, where he died Jan. 28, 1845.

Dr. Robert M. McClure came from Madison, Ind. where he was born, graduated from medical college of Philadelphia—came here in 1843, returned to Madison in 1853.

Dr. Isaac Fenley came here from Jackson Co., Ind. about 1844; volunteered for Mexican War in 1847, raised a company in 4th Ind. Regt. and was commissioned lieutenant. Returned in 1848. In 1849 cholera was brought to Columbus by German immigrants from New Orleans, via the Mississippi and Ohio rivers. Dr. Fenley was among the many who died of it.

Dr. Homer T. Hinman first located in Hope, coming to Columbus in 1848. He traveled one year as Grand Masonic lecturer, visiting all lodges in the state, then resumed practice until his death in 1859.

Drs. Isaac Fenley and Homer T. Hinman were present at the formation of the Indiana State Medical Society, June, 1849.

EXTRACTS FROM THE INDIANA GAZETTE

The *INDIANA GAZETTE* was the first newspaper printed in the new Indiana Territory, capital Vincennes, by Elihu Stout. The first issue appeared in August 1804 and continued until 1805 when his print shop and all equipment burned. By 1807 he had again transported down the Ohio River and up the Wabash, new type, hand press, supplies and started a new paper, the *WESTERN SUN*.

A few copies of the *GAZETTE* have been preserved and microfilmed by the Indiana State Archives. From them we have attempted to cull those items of local interest which reflect the life and times of these early Hoosiers, their disputes, concerns, activities, even the kind of crops they raised, making them vibrant personalities rather than statistics in official records. Family historians, besides recognizing the well known public figures, may see the name of a lost ancestor who paused here then moved on.

Indiana Territory, fct. "Whereas a writ of foreign attachment has issued out of the court of Common Pleas of the said county of Knox against the lands in tenements, goods, chattels and effects, rights and credits of JEAN MARIE ROUILLE, at the suit of THOMAS JONES, in a plea of trespass on the case, by virtue of which writ the sheriff of the said county has attached sundry goods, chattels & effects, as the property of the said defendant—now notice is hereby given, that unless the said defendant shall appear by himself or attorney to give special bail to answer the said suit, judgement will be entered against him by default, and the property so attached will be sold for satisfaction of all the creditors who shall appear to be justly entitled to a demand theron and shall apply for that purpose, dated 3d August, 1804. R. Buntin, Prothy, John Rice Jones, Attor for the plaintiff." Vol. 1, No. 2.

Owner of Dark Bay Horse...delivered by Wea Indians to Governor, is requested to call for him on [sic] JOSEPH BARRON, Interpreter. Vincennes, 21 July 1804. Vol. 1, No. 2.

Writ of Foreign Attachment, issued General Court, directed to Sheriff of Clarke Co. against JOHN HOLKER & NICHOLAS VICTOR MUHLBERGER at suit of JOHN EDGAR...broken covenant. Dtd 16 July 1804. H. HURST, c.c.c., JOHN RICE JONES, Attor. Vol. 1, no. 2.

Writ of Foreign Attachment, issued General Court, directed to Sheriff of Knox, aginst FRANCIS MITCHELL at suit of JACQUES & FRANCOIS LASSELL, plea trespass. H. Hurst C.G.C. John Rice Jones, Attor. Vol. 1, No. 2.

JOHN GIBSON reappointed secretary for Indiana Territory, July 31st. Vol. 1, No. 3.

"Died on Tuesday last after a long and painful illness MR. ISAAC DECKER, an industrious & respectable farmer; he has left a wife and family of small children to deplore his untimely end." Vol. 1, No. 5, 28 Aug. 1804.

JOHN HULING announces purchase possessions of MR. SMALL at Amboy & will furnish traveler grain there. 28 Aug. 1804.

WILLIAM PRINCE, shff Knox Co. Proclaimation... honorable HENRY VANDER BURGH & JOHN GRIFFIN, Esquires, Judges...to hold Court in Vincennes, Tues. Sept 4th...

(Advertisement) "Circumstances have recently occurred, which authorise me in pronouncing and publishing WILLIAM M'INTOSH, an arrant knave a profligate villain a dastardly cheat, a perfidious rascal, an impertinent puppy, an absolute liar: and a mean, cowardly poltroon. B. PARKE, Vincennes, Aug. 27, 1804."

"The lotts No. 68, 81, 88, 89, 101, 146 containing Four Hundred Acres each granted by the United States to heads of family at Vincennes on or before 1783 & laid out for them according to law... will be sold together or separately at a low price by the subscriber, agent for the proprietors. WILL M'INTOSH, Vincennes 9 Aug. 1804 (Adv. appeared several issues.)

(Adv.) $20.00 Reward. Runaway from Carkasaw (?) Bluff on the Mississippi, a likely young negro fellow named J O E, about 20 yrs of age, 5'9" or 10", very dark, smooth face, smiling countenance, especially when spoken to, lump on shoulder...if enters Tennessee, Indiana Territory or lower part of Kentucky... reward $20.00. JOHN INSTONE, Frankfort, Ky. Aug. 28, 1804.

For the Indiana Gazette—Word to the Public at parting with M'INTOSH. Follows an exchange of letters between PARKE & M'INTOSH.

(Adv.) Ten Cents Reward. Ran away from subscriber, living in town of Vincennes, an apprentice boy by the name of JAMES CARRICO, bound to learn the trade of Hatting—all persons are hereby cautioned against harboring or unlawfully detaining said apprentice as they will be dealt with according to law. JAMES HALL, Vincennes, 10th Sept. 1804.

(Adv.) G. WALLACE, Jun & Co. Have just received a Good Assortment of Fall & Winter Goods. Will dispose of on reasonable terms for Cash, Pork, Wheat, Flour, Beef, Corn etc etc. Vincennes, Aug. 1804.

The subscriber has lost or mislaid a warrant drawn on the government, or the Treasurer of the Territory for fifty-two dollars for my services...HENRY HURST.

(Adv.) $5.00 Reward. Runaway from Subscriber living in town of Vincennes, an apprentice JOHN MATSON, bound to learn the House Carpenter business...JOSHUA BOND.

(Adv.) $50.00 Reward. Ran away from Subscriber living in Upper Louisana and district of New Bourbon on the night of the 10th instant, negro man named S A M, about 28, 29 yrs of age, about 5'10" high, stout made, both feet and legs have been severly scalded. ALSO, a negro woman named R E B E C C A, about 19 or 20 years of age, she is very remarkable, was born black but has turned white except a few black spots, her hair is curly, the same as another negro...but quite gray, generally keeps her head tied up... may attempt to pass for a free woman & mistress of the other. They took away with them a rifle gun & a number of cloathes... EZEKIEL ABEL, Little Saline, 14 Sept. 1824.

...Now pending in general court of Indiana Territory an action of trespass on the case, in the name of JAMES N. WOOD, esq. of Clarke Co. against me, PETER SMITH of said county for scandalous words by me against said JAMES N. WOOD...when I uttered said words...was at a time I was intoxicated... PETER SMITH, 23 Aug. 1804, signed and sealed in the presence of DAVIS FLOYD & SAMUEL GWATHMEY.

Notice. Co-partnership of WILLIAM BULLITT, CUTHBERT & THOMAS BULLITT, under name of WILLIAM BULLITT & CO. is this day dissolved by mutual consent. Vincennes, 11 Sept. 1804. The business in future will be carried on in name of WILLIAM BULLITT & C. SMITH who have on hand large quality of Fall & Winter Goods, Whiskey & Salt...sell low for cash, Wheat, Flour, Beef, Pork, Corn, Peltry & Fur...

The business in future will be done and carried on at Kaskaskia & St Genevieve in name of WM. BULLITT & C. SMITH...goods imported from Baltimore, 11 Sept. 1804.

Post Office, Vincennes, Oct. 18, 1804. A List of Letters Remaining in this office the last quarter, which have not been taken out before the expiration of three months, will be forwarded to the

General Post Office as dead letters, viz.

B. BROOKS, James; BENN, Jonnithan; BENN, Henry; BAIRD, Joseph; BRAZELTON, William; BOUSIER, George; BAKER, Mathias; BIDEL, Jean Bpe.

C. CHASE, Tome, alias THOMAS JONES; COULTER, Joseph; CAHEEN, Jo'n; [sic] CRUM, Conrad.

D. DUBOIS, Toussaint.

G. GIBSON, Sarah mrs; GREATER, Frederick.

H. HODGE, William

J. JOHNSON, John

K. KUYKENDALL, Jacob; KELLY, Hugh.

L. LONGHEAD, William; LEMARDE, Francois.

M. M'DANNEL, John

N. NEELY, Thomas

P. PRICE, Benj.; PARKE, Benjamin

S. SMALL, John; STEWART, William; SPENCER, William

V. VANNORDSDELL, Simon

W. WARSON, David; WHITSON, John; WESTFIELD, Abraham.

Genl. W. Johnson, p.m.

"Vincennes (I.T.) Oct. 16, 1804. Died On Friday morning the 12th inst PIERRE GAMLIN, esq. long a respectable citizen of this place. "Mr. G." has ever been distinguished as a good citizen, an affectionate husband & father, and a faithful public officer. He has exercised the duties of the First Judge of the Court of Common Pleas almost ever since this country belonged to the United States... ."

"Indiana Territory—St Vincennes, Sept. 15, 1804. This day ROBERT SLAUGHTER (who had been demanded by the governor of thie territory from the governor of Tennessee...) was brought to trial before Judges GRIFFIN & DAVIS, (Judge VANDER BURGH withdrew because of prisoner's having objected to him...)" Was indited for murder of JOSHUA HARBIN. Defense objected, says was committed on Indian lands... at Gross Pointe, Randolph Co. Testimony by JOSEPH BAIRD, ROSINA DOLOHAN, interpreter BADOLLET. (The testimony of the entire trial is reported in full.)

Vincennes, (I.T.) Oct. 23, 1804, Married Saturday eve last Mr. JOHN M'GOWAN to the amiable miss [sic] SALLY BALTIS, both of this county.

Writ of foreign attachment has issued from the count of Common Please for said county of Knox, returnable Nov. 1804 term, against ROBERT DUNBAR at suit of JOHN HARBIN in an action of debt...sheriff has attached certain monies in hands of GEORGE LEECH & LUKE DECKER...E. BUNTIN, Prothy, Gen. W. JOHNSON, Attny. for plntf. Vincennes, July 15, 1805.

Beef, pork, bacon, corn, cotton, whiskey, wheat, sugar, potatoes, butter, eggs, chickens, tobacco, tallow, flour & oats will be received in payment of the Subscription to this Paper, delivered at the Office in Vincennes. Wednesday, Aug. 14, 1805.

From the Ky. Gazette, Lexington, July 23. Suicide. On Saturday last...Mrs. Eve, a widow woman in the prime of her life put a period to her existance by hanging herself... Been in a melancholly state... over death of her husband & subsecquent loss of property...

Five Dollars Reward. Run away from subscriber on the fourth inst out of Mr. JOSEPH BARRON'S yard, a large bay horse...about 14 hands high, the brand of a turtle on his right shoulder...JOSEPH BARRON, Vincennes, 15 Aug. 1805.

ADAMS COUNTY MARRIAGES, 1836-1844

Adams County was organized in 1836 from Allen & Randolph Counties, county seat Decatur. These marriages are from Book A, copied from microfilm in the Genealogy Division, Indiana State Library. The dates are those of the marriage returns unless otherwise indicated.

A few of the very earliest records show the father's name as consenting; others have witnesses of "willingness of parents" or lawful age. W.P.A. complied an index to later marriages, (1845-1920) which is available in the Genealogy Division, Indiana State Library and at the Fort Wayne-Allen Co. Library, Fort Wayne, Indiana, for later search.

The handwriting is crabbed, the writing dim. Other sources were searched, attempting to verify names. In a few instances supplementing the marriage record we have cross references to Wills, Books A & B (1837-1888) compiled by the Antione Rivarre Chapter D.A.R., Decatur, Indiana.

Ames, George - Mary Ann Hooper   9-28-1843
   [Mary Ann named in will of Ezekiel Hopper,
   proved 2 June 1871]
Andrews, Jonathan - Jane T. Niblock 3-18-1841
   [Both mentioned in will of Robert Niblick,
   proved 13 November, 1848]
Andrews, Jonathan - Susannah Gwin (Grim?)
                                    1- 6-1842
Andrews, Thomas - Deborah Gwin (Grim?)
                                    2- 4-1840
Ball, William - Hetty Pillars   11-12-1839
Barnhart, Daniel D. - Mary Russel (lic.)
        Margaret Russell (ret.)   4-20-1843
Beineke, Ernest Wilhelm - Soppia Peck
                                    5-25-1843
Bell, James - Clemency Mann   8-20-1840
Belt, Charles N. - Margaret Cofelt 8- 5-1841
Belt, John N. - Margaret P. Shepard 9-16-1840
Blossom, Benjamin F. - Nancy Ann Browning
                                    1-30-1842
Blossom, Horatio - Mrs. Nancy Forsythe
                                    3-17-1842
Bowen, David - Elizabeth Shafer   12-15-1842
Brittain, Benjamin - Rachel Major 6-25-1838
   [A daughter Rachel named in will of
   William Major, proved 24 Jan. 1855]
Brown, Nicholas - Elisabeth Scott 5- 4-1843
Brown, William - Margaret Barnhart 2- 1-1843
   [A William Brown left will, proved
   19 Mar. 1878, wife unnamed]
Browning, Alexander H. - Nancy Ball
   consent, father William Ball   6- 4-1837
Bultimer, Conrad - Louisa Miland   10-15-1841
   [Conrad Bultemeier, exec. will of William
   Panne, prob. 19 Nov. 1852 witnessed will
   Elenore Kenemann 11 Mar. 1867]
Bushnell, Homer - Pheby Jane Stacey
                lic.   10-12-1841
   [Homer wit. will Mahulda Douglas,
   proved 11 Nov. 1844]
Campbell, Conrad - Mary Sample   1-10-1843
Carpenter, Ira - Martha Ann Teeple 6-24-1844
Carpenter, William - Anna Teeple   4-21-1844
Carrington, Freeman P. - Elizabeth Belt
                                    7- 7-1842

Casky, Samuel - Sarah Ann Fredrick 6- 8-1843
Chambers, Samuel - Martha Selby   3-16-1839
Christannen, Frederick Wilhelm -
   Anamarie Enger Knapp   12- 4-1840
   [Wm. Knapp will proved 6 Nov. 1851
   mentions daughter, Ann Mary Engel]
   [A Frederick Christianer wit. will
   Leonard Schatzer, proved 1 Sept. 1854
   & Harmon Garke's, proved 19 Oct. 1864]
Cline, George - Margaret Crozier   7- 7-1844
   [Leonard F. McConnehay's will names uncle
   George Cline, proved 19 Mar. 1879]
Coffee, Timothy - Margaret Miller   1- 9-1841
   [Timothy's will proved 20th April 1871,
   wife, Margaret, gdn. minor children]
Coffee, Timothy - Gardina Brake   2- 2-1844
Cowan, Israel - Eliza Allen   5-12-1842
Crabs, Joseph - Betsy Evans   10-25-1841
   [A Joseph Crabs exec. will Daniel Gaunt,
   proved 11 Apr. 1859]
Crabtree, Ephriam - Ester Hill   5-26-1844
Crawford, John - Caroline Bunker   10-19-1841
Crawford, John - Mary Ann Abnet   9-16-1843
   [Will Jacob Abnet names daughter, Mary
   Ann Crawford, dated 15 July 1848]
Crawford, Josiah - Rosannah Abnet   3-10-1841
   [Will Jacob Abnet names daughter Rosa
   Ann Crawford, dated 15 July 1848]
Deen, Samuel, Jr. - Catharine Roe   8- 1-1841
Deerman, Conrad - Willhelmina Durick (lic.)
   Willhelmina Zwick (ret.)   4-15-1842
   [Will Henry Zwick mentions daughter
   Sophia Wilhelmina married to Doehrman
   proved 10 Feb. 1846]
Dickson, Charles - Mary Heart   1- 7-1841
Doherty, Jacob - Nancy E. Cole   1- 5-1843
Downs, Samuel - Ester Jane Scales   2- 8-1844
Dunbar, Lucien - Philenia French   10-24-1840
   [Lucien wit. will Holman Reynolds,
   proved 27 Oct. 1855]
   [Philena named in will of Joseph French
   proved 11 Apr. 1845]
Elifrits, William - Polly Longnecker 2- 3-1844
Elliott, Richard - Sarah Hankins (Hawkins?)
                                    9-23-1839

Elzey, Elisha V. - Mary Roe   5-14-1840
Elzey, Elisha V. - Comfort Ann Whitehurst
                                        3-22-1842
Elzey, William, Sen. - Barbary Fisher
                                        3- 4-1840
Elzey, William, Jr. - Sarah Anne Andrews
                                        3- 5-1840
Etienne, Francis - Margaret Mangeot 3-26-1842
Evans, John K. - Barbary Kinsey   7- 8-1840
Evans, Robert 2nd - Elizabeth Sparks
                                        9- 3-1843
Everman, Philip - Lydia Lister   8- 4-1836
    Wit. Enos W. Butler
    [Will John Reynolds, prvd 12 Aug. 1844
      mentions a daughter, Lydia Everman]
Fields, Andrew - Philindia Boles   2-17-1842
Filling, John Henry - Anna Maria Reinerts
                                        7-27-1842
    [John H. wit. will Nicholas Holbrook
      prvd. 6 Jan. 1870]
Fitzgerald, David - Hannah O'Connel 2-21-1842
Flagg, Alwin - Mily Hill   10-22-1839
Fleming, Jonathan - Susannah Lemasters
                                       11-10-1842
    [Will John LeMaster names son-in-law
      Jonathan Fleming married to dtr.
      Susannah. Prvd. 31 Aug. 1846]
Foster, Samuel - Mrs. Mary Ann McCue
                                        7-25-1839
Frank, George - Nancy Sacket   9-29-1839
    [Will Peter Frank, Sr. names son, George
      Frank, exec. prvd. 17 Oct. 1872]
Frecht, John Eberhardt - Catherine
    Elizabeth Fothermark   5-28-1843
    [One John Fruchte wit. will William
      Hilgeman, Sr. prvd. 28 Apr. 1888]
Frederick, Alfred - Sophia Tehtmeier
                                        5-28-1843
Fuller, James - Martha Madison   8-20-1840
Gable, Christian - Mary Ann Hall   10-14-1842
Gable, Peter - Sophia France   6- 4-1844
    [Will, Garret Henry France names dtr.
      Sophia France, dtd. 15 Aug 1866, prvd.
      20 June 1874]
Gasse(?), Joseph - Mary Acremet   1-12-1841
    [A Joseph C. Gass exec will Henry Gass,
      prvd. 7 Nov. 1882]
Gesinger, John - Caroline Matilda Warner
                                        4-16-1840
Gessinger, John - Phebe Wilban(lic.)
        Phebe Brieban (ret.)   9- 4-1838
Grim, Jacob - Sophia Stoops   5-12-1844
    [Will Edwin S. Metzger, Jacob W. Grim
      & wife Sophia, among heirs, no
      relationship noted. prvd. 19 Dec. 1865]
    [Sophia Grim will mentions her father
      Joseph Stoops. Prvd. 22 Jan. 1878]
Halk, John - Susannah Make (?) Wake(?)
                                       12- 2-1841
Halmire, Conrad Deitrick - Christine Craft
                                        7-11-1841
Harper, John - Marie Eliza Stoops   6-21-1838
Harper, Joseph - Elizabeth Bloom   7- 9-1843
Harris, Loyd - Susan Coffalt   9-19-1843
Haughton, Roswell - Sabine Sheldon   12-30-1840
    [A Roswell Houghton was exec. will
      Geo. French, dtd. 25 June 1852]
Hawkins, Albert O. - Margaret Ann Hill
                                        2-16-1839

Heath, Daniel - Harriet Gable   6- 4-1844
Henderson, William - Rachel Baker   1-27-1842
Hilgerman, William - Sophia Goreneker
                                       10-10-1842
    [Will William Hilgeman, wife Sophia
      prvd. 28 Apr. 1888]
Hill, John Adam - Elizabeth Mewhorter
                                       11-14-1841
Hill, Martin - Mary Burwell   8-11-1842
Hobbs, John - Catharine Sheline   10-24-1840
Hooper, Ezekiel - Amy Ames   8-17-1843
    [Will, Ezekiel Hooper, wife, Almira,
      proved 2 June 1871]
Houdyshell, Andrew - Elzey Mace   2-23-1841
Huffman, Peter - Maria Foreman   12-15-1841
Johnson, Levi - Mrs. Emily Skinner   1- 1-1842
Jones, William - Martha Loofbourrow   2- 3-1841
Kieffer, Jacob - Susannah Spangler   7- 9-1844
King, John - Sarah Lenhard   1-31-1841
    [Will, John Lenhart names dtr.
      Sarah. Prvd. 11 May 1877]
Kinneman, Frederick - Lena Hatfield   4-21-1842
    [Will, Conrad Konermann, names son
      Frederick. Prvd. 3 Dec. 1860]
Kinsay, George - Mary Ann Hooper   9-28-1843
Kinsey, William L. - Nancy Dill   3-15-1841
    [Wm. & Nancy Kimsey wit. will Wm.
      Cyphers, prvd. 1 Dec. 1853]
    [Will, William Kimsey, wife Nancy,
      proved 14 Mar. 1871]
Kohne, Antoin - Elizabeth Menton   10- 7-1842
    [Will, Anton Kohne, no wife named,
      prob. 1 Nov. 1882]
Lehrman, John - Mary Yeager   2-21-1839
Lewis, Frank (?) - Ruth Pillars   2-18-1844
Lewis, Sherborn - Sophrona O'Harra   12-22-1843
Loofbourrow, John - Mariah Shepherd   3- 8-1842
Luckey, Andrew - Elizabeth Baune   12-26-1841
Lung, David - Elizabeth Hawk (Halk)   7-12-1838
Lung, Jacob - Clarinda Counterman   8-13-1840
Lung, Noah - Sarah Hawk (Halk)   11- 4-1838
McDonald, William - Irene Drake (lic.)
        Jane Drake (ret.)   3-18-1840
Major, Daniel - Margaret Brittian   6-24-1838
Major, David - Evaline Julick(?) Gulick (?)
                                        4- 4-1844
Major, James - Mary Sacket   11-30-1843
    [Will, William Major, names son, James
      dtd. 24 Jan. 1855]
    [Will, Mary Major, proved 16 Oct. 1878]
Major, James, Jr. - Nancy Brittian   3- 5-1844
Major, Joshua - Harriet Dulick   3-25-1841
    [Will, William Major, names son, Joshua.
      Dtd. 24 Jan. 1855]
Mann, Joseph - Sarah Jane Mewhorter 5-11-1841
    [Will Justen Mann, names son Joseph K.
      Dtd. 1 Mar. 1876]
    [Joseph E. Mann, wit. will Charles O. Bly,
      prvd. 17 May 1886]
Mead, Nathan C. - Emma Webster   10-13-1842
Mewhorter, John - Huldah Mann   9- 9-1841
Meyer, John Frederick Christian -
    Milbelaine(?) Alfeld   lic.   8- 4-1840
Middleton, Humphrey - Mary Smith   9-30-1838
Milans, John - Catherine Heiderman   2-25-1843
Miller, Samuel P. - Ann Mary Hill   8-10-1839
Miriam, Giles V. - Maria Ames   3-26-1843
Mix, Michael - Elizabeth Jones   12-13-1842
Montgomery, William H. - Elizabeth Springer
                                        5- 3-1842

More, Aaron - Sarah Ann Syfers   5-23-1844
Morningstar, George - Mrs. Elanor Breaghled(?)
    James W. Ryan - wit.   12-24-1837
Morningstar, Jacob - Catherine Abnet(t)
                                        4-23-1840
    [Will, Jacob Abnet names Catherine
       Morningstar, dtd. 15 July 1848]
Morningstar, Samuel - Sarah Johnson 6-10-1841
Moyer, William - Willhelmina Moyer
                        lic.   8- 2-1844
Neimond, Rinhard - Rosavilla Flagg 10-12-1844
    [Names & date appear at top of page but
       lic. application not filled out. Last
       listing in Book A]
Nelson, Edward - Catharine Rader   5- 6-1841
Niblock, James - Sarah Ann Ball   2- 3-1839
    [Will, James Niblick, wife Sarah Ann,
       prvd. 15 Dec. 1869]
    [Will, Robert Niblick, names son James
       prvd. 13 Nov. 1848]
Norville, Abraham - Arminda Hawley
    Wit. William Norville   10-23-1837
Odle, Zaphaniah B. - Mary Adams   2-11-1838
O'Harrah, Hugh - Sarah Hoppel   1- 3-1839
Peterson, John - Hannah Smith   6- 4-1840
Pirdy, Edward - Lucinda Blauvelt   3- 7-1844
Pomeroy, Henry - Esther Carpenter   5- 2-1843
Pring, William - Rebecca Lyster   8-26-1841
Randall, Alvin - Hannah Dehaven   12- 5-1843
Randall, Joshua A. - Sarah Goodspeed
                                        2-20-1842
Reynolds, John - Melinda Andrews   8-14-1838
    [Will, John Reynolds, names son, John
       prvd. 12 Aug. 1844]
Rice, Benjamin - Mary Kimsey   8- 8-1839
Rice, Benjamin James - Elizabeth Pillars
                                        9- 6-1838
Rigby, Jonathan - Philena French   7-18-1838
Roberts, Abraham - Elizabeth Everman
    consent, father, Philip Everman   8-22-1836
Robinson, Abraham - Nancy Zimmerman 9-17-1843
    [Will, Eli Zimmerman, names Nancy
       Robinson, dtr. prvd. 7 Nov. 1878]
Roe, Jeremiah - Ursula Selby   3-28-1839
Roe, Joel - Malinda Andrews   1-13-1839
Roe, Joel - Mary Odle   8-31-1841
Roe, Michael - Anne Hopple
    Wit. Zepaniah Odle   12-29-1836
Roebuck, Garrison - Sarah Caroline Everitt
                                        3-24-1839
Rogers, Benjamin H. - Mary Davis   1-26-1841
Rogers, Joseph S. - Elizabeth Turner
                                        1-18-1838
Rose, Charles M. - Christina Mearing (?)
                                        5- 2-1844
Rugg, Stephen S. - Elizabeth Wise   2-25-1841
    [Will, Elizabeth Leatherman, grandchildren
       Elizabeth M. Wise]
Sacket, Samuel - Julia Ann Heath
    Wit. George T. Heath   3-28-1837
Selby, George - Peggy Roe   7-11-1840
Severns, Jonathan - Harriet McReynolds
                                        4-28-1839
Sheets, Christopher - Margaret Perkins
                                        3-30-1843
Sheline, John - Huldah Mewhorter   1-22-1843
Shepherd, William P. - Emily Loofborrow
                                        11-14-1838

Skeels, Sylvester - Eliza Loofburrow
                                        9-12-1839
Smith, James C. - Lavina Vandevent   3-30-1843
Smith, Samuel - Nancy Rhea   8-23-1838
Spangler, Peter - Hannah Mewhorter   6-27-1843
Spelman, Robert - Abigail Stoops   10-20-1839
Stauffer, John - Anne Stiver lic.   8- -1844
    [Will, John Stauffer, wife Anna,
       prvd. 18 Apr. 1887]
Stewart, Wellington - Sarah Barnhart 6-26-1842
Stoppenhagen, Ernest - Charlotte Book
                                        9-12-1841
Strong, Ephriam - Angeline Hill   7- 2-1840
Summers, William - Emaline Rock   6- 2-1842
Swartzendrouber, Christian -
    Susannah Baker   11- 8-1840
Tinkham, Dennison - Margaret Ann Scales
                                        1-25-1844
Tisdale, Robert - Florilla Lewis   3-11-1844
    [Will, Florilla Tisdale, dtd 1858,
       proved 7 May 1883]
Todd, Reasin - Mary Bitler   1- 1-1840
Trout, William - Mary Welch   3-22-1842
    [Will, William Trout, wife Mary
       prvd. 7 July 1884]
Troutman, Joseph - Sarah Wimer
    consent father, George Wimer   7- 3-1836
Wade (?), George - Hannah Halk lic. 8-17-1844
    [Will, William Wade names son, George
       prvd. 3 June 1841]
Wagers, Samuel - Mary Hawk (Halk)   7-26-1838
Walters, David - Charlotte Loofborough
                                        11-10-1842

    [A David Walters is exec. will of
       Robert Tisdale, prvd. 10 Nov. 1856]
Watkins, Caleb of Ohio - Mary Jane Neptune
                                        10-29-1837
Watkins, Joshua - Mary Peterson   10-16-1839
Watson, John - Margaret Brant   7-19-1838
Watterman, David - Nancy E. Cole
                        lic.   3-30-1842
White, James T. - Sarah Heath   8- 3-1843
Whitehurst, Jacob W. - Rachel Ball   4-14-1842
Whitemore, George W. - Hannah Peterson
                                        4- 4-1843
Winans, Benjamin B. - Jane Miller   9-17-1843
Winans, Joseph R. - Nancy Heath lic.10-20-1838
Winans, Samuel - Lydia Neptune   12-24-1840
Wisner, David - Lydia Allen   11-26-1840
Wyneker, Frederick - Sophia Book   8-31-1841
Yaeger, Samuel - Mary Soest (?)   3-10-1840

FOREIGN IMMIGRATION INTO INDIANA BEFORE 1860

Foreign immigration into Indiana has played an important part in the cultural, economic, political, religious, and social life of the state. From the time of the coming of the French to Post Vincennes in the middle of the eighteenth century down to the latest arrivals, the Vietnamese in the 1970s, Indiana has witnessed a continuous stream of foreign immigrants. In the middle 1800s the Germans and Irish led the way; later it was those from eastern Europe, and in more recent years Asia has contributed to the state's foreign population. No one has undertaken a comprehensive study of foreign immigration into the state, but some work has been done which we would like to call to the attention of our readers; also, the resources that are available for further studies. Individuals familiar with research in foreign countries all point to the need of family historians doing their home work in the United States before venturing abroad, i.e. learn all you can about your family after their arrival in this country before trying to trace their roots in their native country.

The 1850 census was the first to record the birthplaces of residents but the totals were tabulated only by states and not by counties. For Indiana the following pattern was shown:

Native Born		Foreign Born	
Indiana	541,079	Germany	28,584
Ohio	120,193	Ireland	12,787
Kentucky	68,651	England	5,550
Pennsylvania	44,245	France	2,279
Virginia	41,819	British America	1,878
North Carolina	33,175	Scotland	1,341
New York	24,310	Prussia	740
Tennessee	12,734	Switzerland	724
Maryland	10,177	Wales	169
New Jersey	7,837	Belgium	86
Illinois	4,173	Holland	43
South Carolina	4,069	Mexico	31
Vermont	3,183	Norway	18
Delaware	2,737	Austria	17
Massachusetts	2,678	Sweden	16
Connecticut	2,485	West Indies	12
Michigan	1,817	Denmark	10
Missouri	1,006	Italy	6
Maine	976	Portugal	6
New Hampshire	886	Russia	6
Georgia	761	Africa	4
Rhode Island	438	Asia	4
Iowa	407	South America	4
Alabama	395	Spain	3
Louisiana	321	Other Countries	108
Mississippi	287		
District of Columbia	227		54,426
Arkansas	151		
Wisconsin	99	Place of birth not known	2,598
Texas	44		
Florida	21		
Territories	11		

Elfrieda Lang, who has done more research than any other person on Indiana's foreign immigrants, has recorded the numbers in 1850 for the northern counties by going back to the original returns. No one has made a similar study for the middle or southern counties. Her tabulation (from *Indiana Magazine of History*, XLIX, 27) shows the following:

Inhabitants in Northern Indiana by Counties from the Foreign Countries in 1850

County	Canada	England	France	Germany	Ireland	Scotland	Switzer-land	Other Foreign Countries*	Total
Allen	124	197	554	2,439	424	56	96	12	3,902
Cass	21	96	19	178	243	11	3	3	574
De Kalb	30	33	10	112	22	9	12	0	228
Elkhart	178	35	10	196	57	20	6	16	518
Fulton	44	15	7	85	32	12	2	2	199
Jasper	33	19	0	8	6	0	0	5	71
Kosciusko	22	53	4	119	53	5	15	5	276
Lagrange	66	181	2	38	15	19	1	6	328
Lake	171	60	5	560	60	3	0	3	862
La Porte	155	173	17	122	249	46	0	21	783
Marshall	45	25	3	187	17	4	0	3	284
Miami	3	34	4	254	46	9	9	1	360
Noble	15	35	4	158	14	2	11	0	239
Porter	226	46	2	23	100	9	0	10	416
Pulaski	11	9	9	69	8	1	5	1	113
St. Joseph	91	78	43	415	149	31	7	19	833
Starke	2	2	0	0	4	0	0	1	9
Steuben	45	92	2	51	22	8	15	0	235
Wabash	18	34	10	138	190	4	15	4	413
White	8	22	1	13	19	4	2	1	70
Whitley	15	11	9	168	36	1	0	2	242
Total	1,323	1,250	715	5,333	1,766	254	199	115	10,955

In 1860 the National Bureau of the Census tabulated those of foreign birth by counties. In Indiana the ten counties with the largest number of foreign born were:

Vanderburgh	8,374	Tippecanoe	4,126
Allen	6,842	Floyd	3,836
Marion	6,395	Jefferson	3,571
Dearborn	5,871	Ripley	3,299
La Porte	5,008	Franklin	3,124

The twelve counties with the largest number of foreign born in relation to their total population were:

Vanderburgh	40 per cent	La Porte	22 per cent
Lake	28 " "	Tippecanoe	22 " "
Dubois	26 " "	Floyd	19 " "
Dearborn	24 " "	Porter	17 " "
Perry	24 " "	Ripley	16 " "
Allen	23 " "	Franklin	16 " "

After finding the name of your foreign immigrant in a census record, the records that will be most helpful in learning more about him or her will be church and cemetery records, naturalization records, letters, personal memoirs, and biographical sketches in county and family histories. To cite an example we might take the little known Scotch settlement on the boundary between Jefferson and Switzerland counties, where the first settlers arrived between 1815 and 1820, after coming overland from the East coast to Pittsburgh and then down the Ohio River to Vevay and Madison. It is said they chose this locality because it reminded them of their home land. Their description of the area in letters to their relatives in Scotland led others to join them. They were Presbyterians and worship services were first held in various homes until a log church or "kirk" was built in 1819 or 1820 called Caledonia; this original building has been replaced several times and the present one is in Switzerland County and the cemetery is across the road in Jefferson County. The first names on the church roll were those of Anderson, Crawford, Culbertson, Dow, Glen, Graham, Gray, Gunnion, Daglish, Irvine, Jamison, Kirkwood, McKeand, Morton, Ralston, Shaw, Spier, Sterritt, Storie, Thompson, Tait, Weir, Welch, Wilkie, and Witherspoon.

The inscriptions on the markers in the cemetery often give the birthplaces as well as birth and death dates of the founders of the church:

Mary Culbertson, native of Argileshire, Scotland, d. 1821, age 74.

William Culbertson, native of Argileshire, Scotland, d. 1836, age 74.

James Glen, native of Ayr, Scotland, d. 1838, age 29.

Agnes Graham, wife of Alex Graham, native of Edinburghshire, Scotland, d. Sep. 22, 1836, age 58.

Alexander Graham, native of Scotland, b. Mar. 17, 1776; d. June 9, 1860.

Marrion Robertson, native of County Renfrew in Scotland, and wife of Robert Spiers, d. 1839, age 39.

Jane, wife of Hugh Stevenson, native of Ayrshire, Scotland, d. May 24, 1829, age 42.

Agnes, wife of Thomas Thompson, native of West Galter, Scotland, d. 1848, age 43.

William Wilkie, native of Queen's Ferry, Scotland, d. Nov. 28, 1831, age 42.

Hellen Morris, wife of William Wilkie, native of Leith, Scotland, died Dec. 21, 1832, age 46.

On the sides of a rather imposing monument are these inscriptions: S.F. Morton, d. July 27, 1856, age 25; Ann Morton, wife of Andrew, d. Dec. 1843, age 54.

A record of all the inscriptions in the Caledonia Cemetery are in the Genealogy Division, Indiana State Library. The naturalization records for Jefferson and Switzerland counties are in the respective county courthouses. Records of the Jeffersonville Land Office, where the Scotch emigrants entered land, are in the Archives Division, Indiana State Library.

From Family Records collected by Miss Mary Hill of Madison and given to the Genealogy Division, we can learn more of some of the families. These show a great deal of intermarrying between the Scotch families. The four Culbertsons listed in the 1850 census were sons of James Culbertson, born Argyle, Scotland, married Janet White; came to America with four sons in 1818, landed in Philadelphia, traveled overland with team and wagon until they reached the Ohio River, which they descended in a skiff; purchased land in Jefferson and Switzerland counties in 1820-21; James died 1821; Janet in 1834.

John Tait (1776-1861) grew up in Ayrshire, Scotland; came to America on the advice of Mr. Dow who preceded him; married Jean McKay; waiked from Cincinnati to the Scotch settlement.

Dr. William Ralston was born in Paisley, Scotland; graduated from the University of Edinburgh; married the daughter of Decision and Jeannie Buchanan Laing of Balfron; sailed from Glasgow with two children and a number of relatives in April, 1825. After a journey of six weeks they landed in Newfoundland whence they followed the St. Lawrence and Hudson rivers and the Erie Canal to Buffalo, then smaller streams to Pittsburgh and down the Ohio to Madison where they landed fourteen weeks after leaving Scotland. An article about him in the Society of Indiana Pioneers *Year Book*, 1943, was prepared by Anna C. Malloch, a descendant.

Also in Switzerland County, around Vevay, was the Swiss settlement which is unique in that these people came for the express purpose of introducing the culture of the grape. The United States government gave them an extended length of time in which to pay for their extensive land purchases of some 3,500 acres. The site had been chosen by John James Dufour in 1802 after an earlier site in Kentucky had proved to be unprofitable. The first group of seventeen men, women, and children from Canton de Vaud in Switzerland had landed at Norfolk, Virginia, in May, 1801, after a difficult voyage of one hundred days; they crossed the Alleghany Mountains in wagons to Pittsburgh, then by boat to Maysville, Kentucky, and overland to Lexington in that state. After a brief time at the Kentucky site they moved over into Indiana where they were joined by other relatives and friends from Switzerland. They built substantial brick homes instead of the usual log cabins of the first settlers, and produced their first wine in 1806 or 1807. The story of this Swiss colony was written by Perret Dufour, son of the leader, and was published in book form in 1925; numerous articles have also been written about it, many appearing in the *Indiana Magazine of History*. Another colony of Swiss immigrants came to Tell City in Perry County in the 1860s.

The English settlement in Vanderburgh County, known as McCutchanville, is another example of a well-documented immigrant group. Ken McCutchan has told their story in *From Then 'Til Now*, published by the Indiana Historical Society in 1969.

The account of the German immigration to Dubois County is told by Elfrieda Lang in articles in the *Indiana Magazine of History*, Vol. XLI, taken from her M.A. thesis. She begins with their residence in the German states, their preparation for the voyage, the voyage itself, their arrival in America, travel to Indiana, and their life in Dubois County, including the founding of a number of Catholic churches. The naturalization records for Dubois County were published in the *Hoosier Genealogist*, December issue, 1976.

The German immigration into Dearborn, Franklin, and Wayne counties is touched on in a series of articles on the Whitewater Valley by Chelsea Lawlis in Vols. XLIII-XLIV, of the *Indiana Magazine of History*. These Germans were both Catholic and Lutheran and the records of their churches are an important source. The Oldenburg community was settled almost exclusively by Catholics. The naturalization records for Franklin County will be published in the December issue of the *Hoosier Genealogist*.

In Allen County, where there was another concentration of Germans, they were specifically invited to come and help clear the land. Henry Rudisill, writing in 1837, said he would prefer the Wurtembergers as they "are the most industrious and temperate;" he was also interested in attracting this group because they were Lutherans. Other factors which influenced German immigration into Allen County was the fertile soil and the comparatively easy route from New York by way of the Erie Canal, Lake Erie, and the Wabash and Erie Canal. In the end, all parts of Germany came to be represented in Allen County as well as the various professions in addition to farmers.

The steel industry in Lake County drew a large influx of immigrants from eastern Europe in the early 1900s, but they were not the first to settle there. Germans began coming to the county in the 1840s, both Catholics and Lutherans. Some had first settled in Chicago and from there backtracked into the Calumet Region on learning of the opportunities offered there. Among the towns largely settled by Germans were Whiting, Tolleston, Miller, Hessville, and Schererville. After the meat-packing industry was started at Hammond in 1869, many Germans were drawn to that town where they were recognized as experts in that industry. A group of Dutch immigrants directly from Holland established the village of Munster. Dingernon Jabaay, Antonie Bonevman, and Widert Munster were leaders of this group.

Miss Lang's study of the population of Center Township, Lake County, compiled from the 1850 Census is published in the *Indiana Magazine of History*, Vol. XLIV, 281-304.

No study of the Germans in Vanderburgh County has been found even though it leads the list of counties in the number of foreign born, most of whom were Germans.

Likewise, no statewide study has been made of Indiana's second largest group of immigrants, the Irish. Many left their home land because of famine; they often stopped in the East and worked on the canals and railroads there before coming to Indiana to engage in the same type of work. Nearly all were Catholics, and a study of church records should reveal information about them in addition to the naturalization records.

What about Indiana's first immigrants, the French, who came to what is now Fort Wayne and Vincennes in the early eighteenth century. While the former place was largely a trading post, and a very strategic one because of its location, the French at Vincennes acquired land, built a church, and acquired a degree of permanence. The first census taken in 1746 showed only numbers, listing 46 "Habitans" and 5 Negroes. The records of St. Francis Xavier Catholic Church go back to 1749. When the last French commandant left the post in 1765, only two names were mentioned in his instructions, those of Le Caindre and Richardville. Two years later the population was given as 232 inhabitants (men, women, and children) and 168 "strangers," the latter probably being English traders, travelers, and adventurers. In 1769 we have the first list of names of the heads of families. When the English were considering deporting the inhabitants of Post Vincennes in 1772, they prepared a lengthy remonstrance signed by 88 citizens telling how they obtained their lands. Their appeal proved successful and they were allowed to remain.

It was not until 1777 that the English sent any one to assume control of the French village. When Lieutenant General Edward Abbott arrived from Detorit in May of that year, the inhabitants presumably took an oath of allegiance to the government of Great Britain, but we have no record of those who might have taken the oath. Abbott's stay was short; he left early in February, 1778, and after a painful journey of thirty-three days reached Detroit. We next come to the stirring days of the American Revolution in the West with which everyone is familiar. Following George Rogers Clark's capture of Kaskaskia on July 4, 1778, Father Pierre Gibault and a small group went from that place to Vincennes where they were welcomed by the citizens who then took an oath of allegiance to Virginia, a record of which is preserved.

The records for the period when Vincennes was a part of Virginia are very scarce; we know that two of the nine judges were J.M.P. LeGras and Francis Bosseron. The French were not happy with the treatment accorded them by the military establishment which Clark set up and sent a memorial to the Governor of Virginia on June 30, 1781, telling how they had been forced to take depreciated currency in payment for provisions, how their property had been seized, etc., but the memorial was signed only by the principal citizens.

With the establishment of the Northwest Territory in 1787, the records for Vincennes become more plentiful including those of the French citizens. In their effort to perfect their titles to their lands numerous petitions were forwarded to the new American government; these and the subsequent settlement of these claims provide a basis for research. References for a study of the French in Indiana may be found in the bibliography in Barnhart and Riker, *Indiana to 1816*, published by the Indiana Historical Bureau and Indiana Historical Society in 1971.

The articles on the Richardville family of Vincennes and Fort Wayne in the June, 1978, issue of the *Indiana Magazine of History*, is an excellent example of research on a French family. We hope other similar studies will be undertaken.

LA PORTE COUNTY MARRIAGES, 1832-1844

Compiled from microfilm of Book A of La Porte County Marriage Records in Genealogy Division, Indiana State Library.

Alderman, Isaac W. - Harriet Young   2- 8-1844
Aldrich, Jesse W. - Sarah A. Bates   7- 7-1842
Alldrich, Joshua - Harriet Goodrich   12-30-1841
   Harriet Goodwin in return
Allen, Burrel - Ann Adamson   3-30-1837
Allen, John - Julidia Bonesteel   5-31-1838
Allen, John W. - Martha E. Lemon   10- 5-1837
Allen, William - Sarah E. Shotwell   5- 4-1837
Alyea, John L. - Mary Ann Warren   3-14-1839
Ames, Charles - Cynthia Truell   7-27-1837
Ames, Fisher - Marietta White   3-19-1839
Anderson, Andrew - Isabel Valentine   7- 2-1840
Anderson, George C. - Marietta Willett
                               11-18-1841
Anderson, George W. - Martha Jane Norcot
                               7- 8-1840
Anderson, John - Betsy Burlingame   3-10-1841
Andrews, Jacob P. - Eliza Eager   9-27-1843
Ashton, Gallatia - Susan Ritter   5- 6-1840
Austin, William G. - Polly Plank   12-19-1843
Averill, Caleb N. - Sarah H. Sprague   12-31-1838
Averill, Charles K. - Jane M. Sumner   4- 9-1838
Bailey, David A. - Olive H. Lyon   4- 2-1838
   consent of adopted parents of bride
Bailey, John - Matilda Bryant   5-19-1833
Bailey, Volney W. - Phebe Ann Hendricks
                               5- 5-1841
Bailey, William - Nancy Ann Farmer   1-16-1842
Baily, Lewis - Eve Henry   10-15-1837
Baker, George - Rhoda Ann Thompson   10-25-1840
   Ezra Thompson, her father, consents
Baker, George - Hannah Peer   10-13-1841
Baker, Lewis V. - Elizabeth Rose   3-31-1842
Baker, Stephen T. - Margaret McLane   12-13-1838
Ball, John - Nancy Glover   5-18-1836
Ball, William D. - Drusilla Mix   12-11-1839
Ballow, Hosea - Juliana Clark   7-25-1841
Balser, Abraham A. - Lucy Johnson   1-25-1835
Banks, John - Malinda Banks   3- 1-1836
Barclay, John N. - Sarah A. Welch   1-17-1839
Barker, John - Cordelia E. Collumer   6-28-1841
Barnard, James - Angelina Winchell   9- 7-1837
Barns, Ezra H. - Catharine S. Blaney   9- 6-1838
Barr, Joseph - Caroline Nickell   11-16-1843
Bassett, Thomas H. - Julia Ann Woodbury
                               1-16-1844
Bathrick, Otis - Mary Miller   12-17-1836
Batterson, John - Nancy Luther   4-20-1837
Batterson, William - Arbelia Clyburn   9-10-1839
Baumgarten, Morris - Mary McLane   8- 8-1839
Bay, Joseph - Elizabeth Cissne   10-13-1833
Bear, Benjamin F. - Rachel Summers   2-12-1840
Bear, James D. - Charlotte L. Smith   6-25-1839
Bebee, Daniel N. - Alzina Spafford   5-13-1838
Beckner, John - Susan Beckner   7- 2-1840
Beckner, Jonathan - Lydia A. Stanton   1- 5-1842
Behan, Luke - Sarah Alexander   2- 7-1839
Belden, John - Mary M. Lane   2-12-1836
   Mary McClane in return
Belden, Philo of Michigan - Mary F. Belden
                               6- 6-1839

Benedict, Levi - Holly Ann Tabor   2-27-1840
Bennet, Nelson - Mary Titus   1- 1-1840
Bennett, Ezra H. - Frances Winchell
                               2-26-1837
Benson, Roland - Elizabeth Richardson
                               2- 5-1837
Bently, Irwin N. - Louisa Ballou   3-17-1838
Bentley, Joseph - Eunice Evans   1-23-1842
Bently, Wheeler - Mariah Decker   3-25-1841
Beny(?), Jacob - Keziah Houston   2-19-1843
Billington, Elam - Mary White   9-23-1841
Billington, Lorenzo - Catharine Dunham
                               9-28-1843
Bilmore, Michael - Mary Judah   2-18-1839
Black, James - Jane Elliott   11-11-1835
Blain, William A. - Patty Hull   12- 3-1842
Blair, Chauncy B. - Caroline De Graff
                               6-11-1844
Blake, Jesse - Amanda Griffin   10-13-1841
Bliss, Nathan P. - Arbrilla Hains   4-16-1843
Bliven, Robert C. - Mary A. Norris   9-25-1842
Blue, John - Nancy Griffin   1-25-1838
Bolster, Thomas E. - Catharine Eaton
                               6- 5-1835
Bond, David Y. - Ann Janette Pierce
                               11-23-1834
Bond, William - Mary Hitchcock   12-31-1835
Bonesteel, Noah - Anna D. Norris   4-10-1840
Bosserman, George - Francis Tony
   no return   lic.   2-26-1838
Bosserman, George - Minerva Walker   3-16-1843
Boucher, Stephen - Zoe Lemas   11-20-1838
Boutwell, Enoch - Elizabeth Fravel
                               11-19-1840
Bowers, James - Ruth Fletcher   7-11-1839
Bradley, James - Anna Maria Reid   3-24-1842
Brand, Michael - Susanna Webster   12- 4-1834
Brayton, Gideon F. - Amelia Crane   10-14-1840
   parents, Gideon Brayton & Shadrach
   Crane, consent
Brayton, Joseph - Pamela Spencer   1-30-1835
Brewer, Enoch - Caroline Gwinn lic.
   no return   10- 3-1837
Briant, Benjamin S. - Affa Maria Benedict
                               12- 6-1834
Brinkerhoff, Derrick - Adelia Griffin
                               11- 3-1840
Brooks, Benjamin - Rebecca Brown   5-30-1841
Brown, Amos, Jr. - Melissa Hyde   5-26-1839
   John L. Hyde, her father, consents
Brown, David - Lydia Parsons   4-14-1836
Brown, David - Henrietta Howell   9- 2-1842
Brown, Dexter - Sarah Wright   8-20-1843
Brown, Elisha K. - Sarah E. Summers
                               12-17-1840
Brown, James - Susan Evans   7-28-1836
Brown, Jerry F. - Lois Nichols   12-17-1840
   Nathan B. Nichols, her father, consents
Brown, Manuel - Pricilla Burdyle   2- 9-1843
Brown, William - Philema Collins   1-19-1840
Brush, Samuel R. - Sarah Ann Corey   9-24-1836

Burch, Henry - Sylvia Hill   10-11-1835
Burlingame, Wanton - Abigail Watkins 3-15-1838
Burner, Abram - Mary Long   1-28-1841
Burnie, William - Abigail Morris   3-18-1844
   Abigail Moore on return
Burns, James - Maria L. Gilbreath   5- 4-1837
Burns, Lewis, of Vermillion Co. - Maria Brown
                                     5-21-1834
Burr, Horace - Martha Atkins   7- 4-1843
Burson, Samuel - Elizabeth Everhart 4-13-1842
Bush, David - Elizabeth Miller   1-10-1844
Bussey, George - Emily Gaba   8-25-1836
Bussey, John R. - Catharine Decker   9-22-1836
Butler, Drury - Matilda Coon   10-11-1835
Butler, Hiram - Nancy Crumpacker   11-22-1838
Butler, Nathan - Milley Skipwell   3-24-1842
Butt, George W. - Mary Thorp   9-18-1844
Cadwallader, Moses - Rachel Greir   3-28-1844
Cain, James P. - Rebecca Sparks   11-22-1842
Calkins, Cornelius - Maria Chambers 11-21-1840
Callison, James - Polyna Philips   8-20-1838
Campbell, David - Ginsey C. Fouts   4-19-1838
Campbell, Horace - Mary Jane Francisco
   Aaron Kidder, uncle & adopted   6-13-1839
   father of bride, consents
Campbell, Isom - Rebecca Richardson 12-25-1833
Campbell, John - Amanda Shaw   7- 4-1839
   Charles Campbell & Benjamin Shaw,
   parents, consent
Campbell, William - Margaret Griffith 6- 3-1835
Cannon, George N. - Mary Robinson   1- 1-1835
Carmichael, Charles - Saratta Mix   12-31-1842
Carpenter, Daniel - Mary S. Waggoner 5- 4-1840
Carruth, James K. - Mary A. Johnson 7- 4-1843
Carter, John E. - Elizabeth Jacobus 8-18-1836
Case, Aurora, Jr. - Abigail M. Tryon 9-11-1843
Casewell, Luther R. - Mary Ann Blaney
                                     12-13-1838
Cathcart, Charles W. - Josephine Lemon
                                     2-16-1837
Cathcart, Henry N. - Nancy B. Eaton 1- 4-1844
Catlin, Nicholas M. - Helen A. Mears 9-18-1844
Catlin, Theodore - Matilda C. Wyllys 1-17-1838
Cator, William H. - Dianah Borst   12-26-1836
Cattron, John G. - Elizabeth Eahart 10-29-1840
   William Eahart, her father, consents
Cattron, William - Judy Eahart   4- 9-1843
Chamberlain, Joseph W. - Carolyn Tryon
   no return   lic.   11-20-1837
Chapman, John - Lucinda Atkins   10- 1-1839
Chapman, Reubin - Matilda Bailey   7- 7-1840
Chase, Enoch - Nancy Bromly   9-24-1837
Church, John - Lydia Ann Coggswell   6- 6-1844
Cissne, John - Ruth Austin   3-22-1838
Clark, Amos - Sarah Weed   8-22-1844
Clark, Elam - Rebecca V. Harmon   9-29-1842
Clark, George - Polly Ann Nickerson 8- 9-1843
Clawson, Clark - Hester Hale   7- 7-1835
Closser, Andrew F. - Rebecca J. Sweat 9-22-1844
Closser, David M. - Mary Ann Osborn 11-10-1836
Closser, John - Esther Ann Moulton   2-15-1838
Closser, John - Bridget Forrister   10-10-1842
Clough, Rufus - Phebe Ashton   10-17-1839
Clyburn, William - Amanda Clyburn   7- 4-1841
Cogghill, Paschall - Rebecca Ship   1-21-1836
Colby, Solomon - Mary Webb   10- 1-1842

Cole, John - Elizabeth Morden   9-18-1839
Cole, John W. - Eliza Payne   4- 6-1834
Cole, Pembrooke S. - Effe Orick
   no return   lic.   9-20-1837
Coleman, Jesse - Dorcas Dawson   10-29-1836
Coleman, John - Sarah Hesser   11-30-1834
Colgrove, Caleb - Rachel Vandermark
                                     9- 7-1840
Conant, Daniel - Mary Ann Renn   12-25-1834
Conaway, John - Elizabeth Thornburg
                                     1- 9-1836
Condon, Richard - Mary Griffin   10-13-1844
Conner, Cader - Rebecca Hulbert   5-23-1844
   Rebecca Herbert on return
Cook, David - Sarah M. Goodrich   11-11-1835
Cooper, Charles - Betsy Philips   2-12-1840
Cooper, Henry - Cynthia Bolster   8-28-1834
Cooper, John - Mary Waldriff   10-20-1836
Coplin, Isaac - Levina Evans   9- 1-1836
Coplin, Joseph - Harriet S. Wait   12-24-1839
Corliss, Jesse E. - Elsey Jessup   8-28-1836
Cory, Oliver H. - Rachel Jones   6-24-1841
Cottam, John - Susah Kellog   11-30-1841
Couchman, David - Mary E. Harman   12-27-1838
Cowan, James - Cynthia Casteel   2- 5-1837
Cowan, James S. - Sarah Redding   2- 1-1842
Cowden, Reynolds - Margaret S. Marshall
                                     1- 9-1839
Coy, Nathan - Wealthy E. Smith   6-24-1840
Crane, Alexander - Huldah Jane Closser
                                     2- 1-1844
Crane, Edwin J. - Mary E. Johnson   7-11-1844
Crane, Henry - Mary Closser   12-24-1840
   Daniel Closser, her father, consents
Crane, Richard - Mary Ragan   8- 3-1844
Crane, Shadrack - Sally Plank   8- 6-1837
Crane, William T. - Phebe Keith
   no return   lic.   7-26-1836
Cranney, Russel - Emily Wallace   1-21-1840
Crawford, William - Margaret Ann Whitmore
                                     12- 9-1837
Crawl, Benjamin - Martha Finley   9- 5-1839
Critchet, Peter - Margaret Rittenhouse
                                     1- 1-1835
Crook, A. B. - Margaret Ann Teeter   3- 4-1840
Crook, William H. - Emily Rooks   11-12-1841
Cross, Hiram - Mary Ann Wilson   9-26-1840
Crouse, George - Mary Gossett   7-15-1839
Crumpacker, John - Elizabeth Emmons
                                     1-21-1844
Cullen, John - Otilia Winchel   3-20-1836
Culveyhouse, Elias - Lydia Highly   8- 9-1838
Cummings, Allen - Eliza Stephenson   1- 1-1843
Cutler, Alonzo R. - Sarah Church   12-30-1842
Danforth, Cyrus - Mary Jones   7- 1-1838
Davis, Arod - Mary Tyler   3-17-1844
Davis, Christopher L. - Mary Conner
                                     2-28-1841
Davis, John - Nancy Leggitt   5-18-1837
Dawson, Joseph - Mary Ann Burden   1- 8-1843
Dawson, Lucas - June Hollingshead   7-12-1836
Dawson, Obediah - Sophia E. Warren   7- 8-1841
Dawson, Saul - Nancy Miller   11- 9-1836
Decker, John F. - Sarah Dewitt   9-19-1836
Decker, Michael - Eliza Jane Harrison
                                     10-21-1836

Denham, Ferdinand - Angeline Lewis 9-14-1840
Denham, John - Rachel Ballard Johnson
                                    12- 3-1836
Denslow, Henry, of St. Joseph Co. -
                Sarah Cisnee   5- 5-1839
Dewitt, Archibald - Olive Below   1-24-1835
Dewitt, Benjamin - Sarah M. Burcham 9-29-1841
Diggins, Joseph - Clarissa Mears
    no return   lic.   4-20-1836
Dingman, William - Corinthia Hibbard 7-18-1838
Diserd, John - Hester Hunter   7- 4-1838
    Hester Turner in return
Doran, Patrick - Mary McCulloch
    No return   lic.   7-11-1839
Downing, Benjamin F. - Melinda Baldwin
                                    4-14-1839
Downing, Joshua F. D. - Eliza Jane Meeker
                                    9-28-1844
Downing, Samuel - Eliza Wagner   11-12-1840
Downs, Edmond M. - Caroline Lathrop 5- 1-1841
Draper, John - Elizabeth Bolster   10- 8-1833
Droolinger, Gabriel, of St. Joseph Co. -
                Mary Elizabeth Chapman 4-27-1834
Drummond, John B. - Orvilda Bowell 4- 4-1844
Dudley, William - Abigail Bickel   2-14-1839
Dumond, Archer G. - Elizabeth Martin 5-12-1834
Eahart, William - Emily Cassaday   11-19-1843
Earl, George M. - Sarah Booker   12-24-1833
Edrall, William S., of Allen Co. -
                Louisa McCarty   6-11-1839
Egbert, Charles - Mary Thomas   4-11-1833
Elliott, Benjamin - Mary Griffin   3-23-1843
Elliott, Benjamin - Almyra Hill   9-17-1844
Ellithorp, Samuel - Matilda Snodgrass
                                    1-13-1840
Elston, James K. - Lucinda Ann Salisbury
                                    1-18-1837
Emmerson, Moses - Elmira Wheeler   12- 7-1834
Emory, Alvin - Susan Haines   12-21-1842
Evans, David - Elizabeth Thomas   4-12-1837
Evans, Edward - Mary Snavely   3-24-1842
Evans, Robert F. - Permelia Long   1-22-1843
Evins, John H. - Melissa Mix   6-27-1839
Farmer, Henry E. - Mary Walbridge   2- 5-1840
Faulkner, George W. - Lydia A. Payne
                       lic.   12-28-1835
Fear, John P. - Electa Sprague   2- 3-1839
Fees, Samuel - Adaline M. J. Bias   4-10-1842
Ferguson, Jonathan - Mary Smiley   12- 7-1834
Finch, William - Nancy Young   8-22-1835
Finley, John - Jane Fleming   9- 6-1837
Finn, Enos - Almyra P. Lower   2- 1-1835
Fisher, Thomas - Amanda Dudley   7-29-1841
Fisk, Samuel - Martha S. Maxon   5-26-1836
Fletcher, John A. - Eliza H. Newkirk 8- 5-1835
Fletcher, Peter E. - Sarah Messenger 4-14-1842
Fletcher, Peter - Isabelle Kimberly 4-18-1844
Flint, Miner - Serena Walker   10-15-1843
Flood, Benjamin - Matilda Reed   8-27-1837
Fogle, Levi - Sarah Anderson   3- 3-1841
Follett, Ureal C. - Matilda Travis 10-11-1842
Forrester, James - Margaret Frazier 8-24-1835
Forrester, James - Lavina White   8-15-1844
Fosdick, John S. - Mary M. Collins 11-21-1842
Foster, Aaron - Phebe Hunt   8-11-1839
Foster, Andrew - Cynthia Reynolds   2- 2-1837
Foster, George P. - Mary Dalrymple 1-22-1836
Foster, Scipha - Isabella Warwick   2-13-1843
Fox, William - Diane Corey   3- 8-1836

Francis, Thompson - Esther Francis
    no return   lic.   9-21-1837
Fravel, Charles - Sarah Baker   11- 5-1839
Fravel, John B. - Sophia E. Fravel 1-18-1838
Frye, Azariah - Naomi Speakman   7- 6-1844
Frye, William - Zamira Clarkson   12-11-1838
Fullington, Bradbury - Electa A. D.
                Wallbridge   9-26-1839
Fulton, Robert - Catharine Carpenter
                                    11- 1-1842
Gains, James - Mary J. Gibson   11-16-1842
Gardner, Edmund S. - Polly Haskill 5-12-1839
Garg (?), Caleb - Cynthia Norton   9-12-1844
Garner, William G. - Elizabeth Richards
                                    6-17-1834
Garwood, Levi - Charity Reed   9- 2-1834
Garwood, William - Catharine Forrester
                                    4-29-1841
Gibson, Jabez W. - Emily Crawford   11-14-1842
Gibson, William - Juliana Rose   11-18-1840
Gilchrist, William H. - Nancy Webster
                                    2-10-1842
Giles, Dearborn - Esther Franklin   10- 8-1837
Gillam, Hiram - Juliza Speaks   5-21-1838
Godfrey, Miles J. - Elizabeth Oliver
                                    6-22-1837
Goodall, William - Sarah Mann   5- 1-1842
Goodrich, Joseph M. - Catharina M. Weed
                                    2-13-1843
Gordon, James - Sally Ann Quick   11-27-1834
Gould, Ingrahan - Mary Leaming   6- 7-1835
Gould, Zebina - Jemima Green   3-14-1842
Greenwood, James - Matilda Reynolds
                                    11-12-1843
Gregory, Elnathon - Amelia C. Fletcher
                                    4-12-1842
Gregory, Niles - Matilda Swope   5-14-1836
Gregory, Samuel - Sarah Ann Evins   12-12-1840
Griesell, John - Elizabeth Kitchell
    no return   lic.   3-12-1835
Griffin, Aristarchus - Anna Rose   3- 5-1844
* Griffin, Sylvester, Jr. -   1-16-1844
Griffith, Isaac - Susan Sweet   5- 9-1836
Griffith, John - Sarah Herbert   9-22-1839
Griffith, Warren - Catherine Prentice
                                    4-11-1844
Gunn, Isaac S. - Melinda Galyean   2- 2-1840
Gustin, William B. - Ann Eliza Booth
                                    1-12-1840
Haas, Samuel G. - Sarah Everts   5-20-1844
Hackley, Joseph H. - Selina Fuller 1-12-1836
Hale, Silas F. - Milicent F. Johnson
                                    7-22-1844
Hale, Timothy W. - Mary D. Cornwall
                                    10- 9-1834
Hale, William B. - Clarenda Walker 3-21-1844
Hall, Banks - Parthenia H. Boggs   4-13-1837
Hall, George - Nancy Fouts   10- 3-1843
Hall, Samuel D. - Sarepta Heald   9-28-1834
Hamilton, David S. - Hannah Linn   2-18-1841
Hamilton, Robert - Ann Stewart   9- 4-1838
Hampton, John B. - Mary Ann Monahan
                                    8-17-1837
Hannah, William C. - Sarah Clement 5-12-1836
Hannum, James - Louisa Bartlett   11-19-1842
Harding, Charles W. - Esther T. (?) Jones
                                    10- 1-1844
Harding, Henry - Hulda Pinnes(?)   8- 2-1844
Harmison, Isaac - Eunice Barrett   9-14-1837
    * Catharine E. Hunt

Harness, Andrew - Amanda Powers   9-11-1842
Harness, James - Alsy Dawson   1-19-1843
Harness, John - Phebe Dawson   9- 1-1842
Harper, Archibald - Balinda Foster   2-20-1838
Harper, Asa - Margaret Dunn   7- 3-1843
Harris, David - Julia Rust   10-22-1837
Harris, John - Hester Cannon   11- 1-1835
Harris, Nathaniel - Nancy Clark   1-20-1833
Hartford, James M. - Polly Austin   11- 3-1842
Hartwell, William C. - Ruth Ambler   9-13-1840
Harvey, Anson - Lucy Ann Stephenson   7- 4-1843
Hatfield, Richard - Catharine Rose   7-16-1840
Hathaway, Abram - Ann Cannon lic.   12-30-1835
Hayes, William W. - Amanda M. Warner 6- 2-1844
Haywood, Wesley - Amanda Elliott   9- 4-1837
Heald, Chester - Sarah Cadwallader 12- 1-1840
Heath, Richard - Elizabeth Scarce   10- 8-1843
Hemenway, Ansel A. - Abigail Whitmore
                                         1-22-1834
Henry, George - Phebe Titus   9- 9-1840
Henry, Miles S. - Philena Mann   7- 3-1843
Herbert, Richard - Jane Jones   9-29-1836
Herrold, Henry - Belinda Dorr   4-18-1835
Higgins, William W. - Cornelia A. Howes
                                         5- 8-1838
Hill, David S. - Lawson(?) E. Harvey 9- 8-1844
Hill, Joseph A. - Susan Bothwell   4- 1-1839
Hitchcock, James M. - Hellen M. Chittenden
                                         3-23-1843
Hitt, Washington W. - Ellen T. Shotwell
                                         3-10-1840
Hixon, Lucas - Elizabeth Wright   10-13-1842
Hixon, Thomas I. S. - Elizabeth Haskell
                                         6-24-1841
Hobbs, Charles - Susan Vandermark   9- 7-1840
Hoffman, Syrenus C. - Lydia Haper   2-16-1839
Holder, Absolom - Mary Blivin   5- 8-1834
Holland, David S. - Hannah Cooper   8- 2-1837
Holland, Samuel Johnson - Maria Clement
                                         3-24-1836
Holliday, John - Mary Raymond lic. 11-13-1837
   no return
Holliday, John - Caroline A. Low   2-24-1840
Holliday, Stephen J. - Lydia Wilson   1-11-1838
Holliday, Sterling - Sarah Welch   8-26-1841
Holliday, William J. - Mila Lucas   4-23-1839
Hollingsworth, Frederick - Elizabeth Brown
   no return   lic.   4-14-1836
Holloway, Jason - Harriet M. Dodd   1-28-1841
Holloway, Nathan - Susannah Pagin   2-23-1843
Holmes, John D. - Hannah Richards   5- 7-1834
Hooten, John - Lucy Sprague   12-10-1840
   Eleazer Sprague, her father, consents
Horner, Emanuel - Lucintha Jane Stillwell
                                         8-25-1833
Housmer, Austin - Nancy Concannon   1- 3-1844
   Hosmer in return
How, Amos Judson - Mary Jane Smith   7- 1-1837
Howell, James C. - Helen M. Newell   1-23-1836
Hubbard, John K. - Elizabeth E. Watkins
   Isaac Watkins, her father,   6-29-1840
   of Cook Co., Ill., consents
Hudson, David - Louisa Marston   10- 1-1844
Hunt, David M. - Hannah J. Holbrook 10-14-1841
Hunt, Isaac E. - Eliza A. Patterson 2-20-1844
Hunt, Jonathan S. - Elizabeth Hudson 1-27-1842
Hunt, Seth W. - Sarah Rose   3-11-1841
Hunt, Stephen G. - Louisa Salisbury 8- 8-1838

Hunt, William H. - Sophia Galyean 4-21-1841
Hupp, Abram - Louisa Gardner   7- 9-1837
Hurlbut, Jacob - Susan P. Sheffield
   Jacob Holbert in return   3-24-1836
Hutchins, Isaac - Catherine Norton 2- 6-1840
Hutson, Solomon - Eliza Runey   3-27-1840
Ingalls, Benjamin - Mary Smith   10-26-1842
Ingram, William - Betsy Smith   8-12-1841
Inman, Hiram - Mary Young   7-25-1838
Inman, Richard C. - Margaret Martin
                                         6-10-1836
Inman, Richard C. - Mary Jane Petro
                                         4-15-1842
Ireland, William - Mary Houseman   6-19-1834
Isham, Abel - Amanda Heaton   1- 1-1839
Ives, Frederick - Mary Sutherland   5- 5-1842
Jacobs, James - Jerusia Johnson   6-27-1839
Jacobus, Isaac - Rachel Carter   11-17-1836
James, Eli - Sarah Ann Robinson   12-11-1837
James, William - Elizabeth Johnson
                                         11-23-1834
Jessup, George - Susan Howard   6-21-1842
Jessup, James - Nancy Callison   4-15-1838
Jessup, John - Mary Young   10-18-1840
Jewett, Orin P. - Phidelia Cross   lic.
   no return   5- 8-1836
Johnson, Eli S. - Sally Ann Alysa 12-31-1842
Johnson, George - Polly Courier   5-11-1843
Johnson, Isaac - Elmyra Hale   6- 5-1838
Jones, Alfred D. - Rebecca DiPatrie
                                         1-10-1839
Jones, Christopher W. - Susan Talbott
                                         6-21-1843
Jones, Eli - Amanda F. Armitage   7-20-1837
Jones, James - Cynthia Ferguson   6-28-1835
Jones, Theodore - Phebe Johnson   12-21-1834
Jones, Thomas D. - Eunice G. Swain
   no return   lic.   3-16-1836
Jones, Wilie - Sabra Richardson   9-28-1837
Jordan, Edwin - Mary C. Norton   12-16-1841
Jordan, Joshua - Delia Gregory   6- 9-1836
Keely, Levi W. - Charlotte H. Crandal
                                         3- 6-1844
Keely, William - Hannah Moore   2- 3-1838
Kennedy, David - Clarissa Hunt   4-30-1835
Kennedy, Robert W. - Mary Ann Bentley
                                         11- 2-1837
Kewley, Thomas - Frances M. Fritts
   Nancy Forkes, mother of bride, 12- 3-1840
   consents
Kimball, Daniel - Jane C. Heald   4-24-1842
Kimberly, George M. - Harriet Harrison
                                         2- 2-1837
King, William H. - Melissa Drum   2-27-1840
   Jacob Drum, her father, consents
Kingsbury, Daniel B. - Malinda Morris
                                         2-11-1840
Kingsbury, Stephen - Clarissa Jackson
                                         4-26-1840
Kitchen, Charles - Catharine Mowrey
                                         1- 7-1836
Knaggs, James - Clarrisa Low   1- 6-1835
Knapp, James E. - Mary Chrisman   12-13-1840
Knot, John M. - Lucinda Bery   3-28-1844
Lampkin, John - Lydia Thayer   3- 9-1840
Lane, Robert R. - Leah Modlin, of
   Berrien Co., Mich.   8-11-1836
Lang, Stansbury - Patience Carter   5-25-1835

Large, Cary - Mary Wilson   9- 6-1840
Layman, Abraham - Phila D. Barns   9-27-1840
    Solomon Barns, her father, consents
Layman, Joshua - Cynthia Ann Mead   7- 6-1842
Leaming, Harvey - Sophronia Shippee   3-14-1837
Leaming, Jeremiah - Jane Reynolds   3-25-1838
Leaming, Judah - Rosanna Reynolds   10-15-1835
Leclear, George - Ursula Hosmer   3-26-1840
Lemon, John M. - Mary R. Hannegan   6-13-1839
Lemon, Orange V. - Charlotte Warnock   6- 1-1837
Lewis, Jabez - Angeline McCollum   6-19-1836
Lewis, John - Mary McKinstry   7- 3-1834
Lewis, Moses - Lucy M. Randall   1-17-1837
Livings, James - Eliza Stilson   10-17-1836
Livingston, John - Anna Boret   1-18-1839
Livingston, John - Rachael Nickerson   4-14-1839
Looker, James - Isabella Patten   6-13-1839
Love, Hiram - Jane Brown   8-24-1843
    Jane Brewer on return
Low, Harvey - Emily Classon   7- 4-1833
Low, Peter - Elizabeth Anscomb   1- 1-1835
Lucas, Albert - Catharine Robertson   3-13-1836
    Catharine Robinson in return
Ludlow, Oliver P. - Eliza Walker   9-29-1842
Macadoo, James - Nancy C. Goodhue   6- 1-1840
McBride, William - Mary Ann Proud   3-21-1844
McCafferty, Edward - Elizabeth Ballard
                                             3- 5-1836
McCall, Ervin - Harriet Griffin   5-19-1839
    Irwin McCall in return
McCall, John, of Niles, Mich. -
    Margaret Somerville   11-12-1835
McCartney, Nathaniel - Abigail Parker
                                             7- 1-1841
McClain, Bird - Abby W. Wills   9-20-1844
McClellan, Joseph - Phidelia Reed   3-18-1835
McClintock, John A. - Sarah Broaded   3- 5-1840
McClintock, William - Phebe McClain   4-16-1843
McClure, Christopher - Sarah Ann Robertson
    McCluer in return   1-15-1841
McCollum, George - Ellendy Dukes   10- 7-1837
McEnterfer, John - Lydia Winchell   1-29-1840
McIntyre, Spaulding - Emily Wheeler   2- 4-1841
McKlewrath, James - Thankful O. Griffin
                                             3-26-1839
McLain, John - Clarkey Warrel   11- 2-1836
McLane, Samuel - Margaret Wilcox   4-14-1839
McLane, William - Hannah Wills   5- 5-1839
McLaughlin, William W. - Emelina Hazelton
                                             5-30-1838
McVoy, Richard - Elizabeth Evans   10-19-1844
Main, William - Lydia Parker   9- 9-1837
Mallet, Christmas - Eliza Ann Hobough
                                             3-24-1838
Mallet, Nicholas - Mariah Wilcox   4- 8-1841
Mallory, Burdette - Penelope Pratt   5-26-1842
Mandevill, Simeon D. - Helena Kalder
                                             5-20-1840
Mane, Daniel - Mary Cattron   7-14-1839
    William Cattron, her father, consents
Mann, Jacob J. - Maria McCall   11-19-1843
Mansfield, Robert - Mary Fees   8- 5-1841
Mares, Samuel - Elizabeth Pagin   11-27-1834
Maricle, George - Sally Mariah Brown   3-26-1842
Markham, Hiram - Jane Ann Bill   1-24-1844
Markham, Israel - Thankful Sperry   2-19-1837
    Horace Markham in return
Marks, Ives - Emily Leaming   12-20-1835

Marshall, William K. - Sarah Morrison
                                             4-22-1839
Martin, Asa T. - Harriet A. Branch
                                            10- 8-1840
Martin, Charles R. - Mareia Parsons
            (or Maria)   1-13-1842
Martin, Gale - Marilla Woolsey   12-22-1836
Martin, John - Sarah Bunton   8- 8-1844
Martin, Stephen - Mary Parsons   12-15-1842
Mason, Aaron - Sarah Mix   8-22-1839
Mason, Arthur - Bridget Flynn   7- 2-1840
Mathews, Abner T. - Lucretia Chuney
    no return   lic.   11- 6-1837
Matthews, Asahel H. - Sally M. Millspaugh
                                             3-14-1840
Matthews, Edwin G. - Martha A. Bigelow
                                            8- 6-1843
Matthews, Lyman - Ann Lightner   6-26-1839
Maulsby, Benjamin - Rhoda Williams   1-13-1838
Mayes, Matthew - Mary W. Herbert   1-16-1839
Mayhew, Elisha - Mary Ann Shirley   10-16-1836
Mayse, Alexander - Sarah Hayes   10-12-1843
Mears, Losias - Harriet McLane   5- 1-1836
Melville, John - Catharine Forrester
                                            12-31-1837
Milford, Abram - Ann Brooks   7-14-1839
Miller, Denton - Almira Miller   10-30-1839
Miller, Henry - Polly Miller   3-14-1839
Miller, John - Sendarilla Bowell   12-27-1843
Miller, Samuel - Emily Kimberly   8-17-1834
Mills, Amos F. - Mary Ann Knapp   4-14-1839
Mills, John P. - Ruth June Thomas   6-22-1843
Mitchell, Amos - Mary Behan   6-27-1839
Mix, Ira - Trissey Ann Brown   6-26-1842
Mix, John - Charlotte Longshore   8-19-1841
Mix, Orange R. - Sarah Ann Livingston
                                             6-12-1842
Mix, Samuel R. - Eliza Thompson   2-18-1841
    Ezra Thompson, her father, consents
Mix, Stephen - Louisa Sawin (or Lawin)
                                             8-15-1839
Monroe, Henry - Angeline Griffin   4- 9-1840
Moore, Charles - Elizabeth Niel   11-28-1843
Moore, John S. - Margaret McClain   9- 6-1835
Morden, Ralph - Martha Broaded   12-29-1836
Morehead, William - Minerva Pottinger
                                             5-29-1839
Morgan, Wesley - Hannah Johnston   12- 5-1839
Morgan, William - Mary Dusenbury   12-22-1836
Morse, Alonzo - Esther Sprague   1-29-1844
Mowlan, Charles - Charlotte Rambo   10-23-1832
Mulks, John - Philo Mela Norton   11-23-1837
Munday, Reubin - Eleanor Wair   8-13-1840
Murray, Luke - Mary McNamara   10-13-1844
Nelson, William - Ann Pierce   5-19-1836
Nelson, William C. - Margaret J. Dinwiddie
                                             8-27-1844
Newkirk, Benoni M. - June Moore   5- 6-1841
Nichols, Stephen D. - Mary Van Matre
                                             9-10-1834
Nicholson, James - Catharine Utley   1-30-1840
Nickerson, Chauncey B. - Mary Broaded
                                             3- 5-1840
Niles, John B. - Mary Polke   12-16-1834
Noble, John P. - Mary Ann Smith   7- 9-1836
Norris, Harvey - Sarah Miller   2- 2-1840
Norris, William - Jane Mix   6-12-1842
Norton, David H. - Betsy M. Evans   12-18-1839

Noyes, Luke W. - Nancy Herbert	2-28-1841
Oakman, Joseph - Dinah Bayles	2- 1-1837
Oaks, Orrin - Phebe M. Johnston	8-16-1838
Olinger, George - Rachel Marshall	4-23-1840
Oliver, John C. - Lydia M. Fellows	12-15-1835
Oliver, Thomas - Deborah Martin	5-29-1834
Omstead, Jacob, of La Grange Co. - Margaret Woodward	9-23-1839
Organ, Edmund S. - Catharine N. Early	9-26-1844
Orton, Myron H. - Mary Ann Brown	7- 2-1840
Osborn, Andrew L. - Lucy Northam	3-14-1840
Osborn, Joseph Pitman - Urzilla Eahart	2-14-1833
Osborn, Joseph P. - Naomi Leigh	4-26-1838
Osborn, Reuben - Clarissa F. Sims	4- 3-1844
Owen, Asa F. - Ellen Taylor	7-11-1844
Owen, Milton - Desdemonia Fail	3-11-1844
Owen, Owins A. - Sarah McGivin	11- 5-1835
Pagin, David - Rebecca Gifford	5-19-1842
Pagin, Joel - Harriet A. Chisbee	6-16-1841
Pagin, Lewis - Elizabeth Justice	12-22-1842
Paine, Erastus H. - Mary Ann Rhodes	10-28-1843
Palmer, Charles, Jr. - Susan Miller	12-24-1839
Palmer, Harvey - Thankful Tuttle	5- 2-1839
Palmer, Milton - Sophrona Smith	11- 4-1843
Pangman, Philo B. - Polly Palmer	1-30-1841
Parker, Joel - Leah Smith	12-10-1836
Parkinson, Samuel R. - Harriet Norris	6-28-1840
Parmer, Charles - Maria B. Walbridge	9- 8-1840
Charles Palmer in return	
Parrott, John - Mary Wills	11-29-1834
Parvey, James - Hetty H. Burch	5-26-1838
Patrie, Jeremiah - Harriet Pomeroy	2-25-1844
Patten, John - Lodiska Reynolds	2-16-1840
Patten, Mathew W. - Eliza Griffin	7- 1-1840
Patterson, Darwin H. - Mary Smith	3-29-1844
Payne, Alonzo D. - Mary Jane McClintock	9-24-1839
Pearse, Amos B. - Elizabeth Cornell	10-24-1843
Peas (Pease), Enos - Matilda Russell	
no return	lic. 11-23-1835
Peas, Enos - Isabelle Myers	1-25-1836
Peas, Enos A. - Lucy Ann Finley	3-26-1836
Pease, Asa C. - Martha Smith	12-21-1837
Peck, Doomes - Deborah Behan	10-25-1837
Penwell, John N. - Rachel Penwell	11-22-1835
Pepper, William - Mary T. Hatfield	2-18-1836
Perkins, Jeremiah - Eliza Kennedy	2- 4-1841
Perkins, Norris - Cynthia Ann Wright	9-17-1843
Perkins, William - Mary Reynolds	11-24-1839
Perry, Willard - Lucinda Duerden	12-10-1837
Petrie, Conrod - Ruth Everts	6-25-1837
Phelps, Myron - Elizabeth Kennedy	4-16-1843
Pichert, Peter - Rebecca Rohrer	5-29-1836
Peter Prichet in return	
Pinney, Horace - Angelina Haskill	5- 4-1843
Pinney, William - Cynthia Long	12-23-1841
Piper, Orlando F. - Mary A. Hawkins	7- 1-1844
Place, Nelson T. - Elizabeth Spalding	3-31-1839
Plumteaux, John - Hannah Miller	12-28-1835
Plymale, John B. - Elizabeth Blake	3-20-1834
Polke, Adam G. - Otelia Cullen	5-12-1842
Porter, Abel D. - Electa Wells	11-28-1843
Pound, Elijah - Prudence Jones	12-28-1843
Powers, David - Julian Tuley	1- 1-1839
Powers, James - Elizabeth Mullen	2- 7-1837

Pratt, John - Margaret Kellison	12- 2-1838
Pratt, John - Laura Ewing	1-21-1840
Preston, Vickers - Charlotte E. Fouts	3-14-1841
Price, John - Margaret Burton	8- 5-1835
Purse, Charles - Hannah Leyman	10- 3-1837
Pursell, Abram - Juliana Rose	3-22-1838
Randle, Roswell - Nancy Carlisle	6-30-1839
Daniel Carlisle, her father, consents	
Ranson, Levi - Amanda Root	3-10-1842
Redding, Josiah - Caroline Griffin	2-22-1842
Redding, Lewis - Malissa Rood	3- 7-1843
Reed, George - Margaret Ann Marguson	7- 3-1841
Reeve, Amos - Lydia Harding	8- 5-1843
Restorick, Samuel - Louisa Baker	4-24-1844
Reyley, Alonzo - Martha G. Jackson	8-23-1837
Reynolds, Asahel - Hethey Hogan	7-19-1837
Reynolds, George W. - Cynthia Winchell	6-23-1836
Reynolds, Ranson H. - Matilda Russell	4-20-1837
Rhinehart, John - Deborah Campbell	6- 2-1836
Rhoades, John S. - Susannah Culver	8-25-1836
Rhodes, Adam E. - Jane E. Bear	1- 1-1819
Rhodes, Benjamin - Latisha Miller	4-14-1837
Rice, James E. - Nancy Bear	5-20-1835
Rice, William S. - Mary St. Clair	10- 2-1834
Richardson, Ira - Hannah Teaney	8- 4-1835
Hannah Teator in return	
Richardson, Likens - Josephine Tuley	12-31-1835
Ridgely, Asa D. - Martha Willets	11- 9-1839
Riley, Matthew - Margaret Griffin	10-26-1839
Ring, Joshua - Sarah A. Mix	8-25-1843
Ritter, Simon - Martha Jessop	4-11-1844
Robb, John W. - Sarah Hitchcock	3-13-1834
Roberts, Charles S. - Elizabeth Cain	3-17-1842
Roberts, Coral G. - Ann Marcia Evans	10- 5-1841
Robins, Benjamin C. - Isabella Fulton	11-29-1838
Rodefer, Harrison - Eliza Ann Ruggles	10- 8-1840
Rodgers, Lewis - Nancy Eaton	1- 7-1836
Rood, Leonard - Catharine Foley	11-29-1840
Root, Sylvanus - Frances J. Gwinn	9- 6-1838
Rose, Elisha - Elizabeth Haseltine	5-11-1837
Rose, Gilbert - Louisa Haseltine	7-18-1841
Ross, Abner - Hester A. Ross	9- 1-1835
Ross, David C. - Lydia Richardson	10-13-1842
Rowen, Daniel - Mary Jane Oathet	7-17-1839
Russell, Francis M. - Nancy Newhouse	6-11-1837
Rust, John Van - Amanda M. Andres	10-22-1839
Sale, Francis A. - Mary Ann Warnock	10-22-1844
Sargent, Albert - Mary Jane Moore	9-10-1840
Satterlee, Milton - Rebecca Pease	5-23-1837
Satterlie, Ossian - Susan Pease	11- 7-1835
Scott, Samuel - Louisa Jackson	1- 1-1838
Seffens, George - Mary Belshaw	11- 1-1835
Self, Joseph B. - Nancy Hall	3-30-1837
Selkregg, George R. - Emily Hackley	lic. 12-30-1835
Selkregg, Mark H. - Amelia Minor	12-22-1841
Serwell, William - Sarah Stanton	6- 1-1843
Shannon, James - Mary Garwood	2-25-1841

Sharp, Julius - Mary Lawman 4- 1-1840
Sharp, William - Mary Louisa Finly 6-18-1840
    James Finley, her father, consents
Shedd, Erasmus N. - Malissa Totten 10-26-1842
Shaw, Daniel - Julia Ann Reynolds 11- 6-1839
    Abram A. Reynolds, her father, consents
Shepherd, John E. - Martha Jane Winchell
           10-16-1839
Sheridan, William - Minerva Reynolds 9- 6-1837
Sherley, Lewis - Mary Ohara 9-10-1843
Sherman, James - Hannah L. Bentley of
    Mich. Territory 4-24-1836
Sherman, Thomas H. - Mary Bias 11-18-1843
Shigley, Samuel - Sally C. Weed 5-21-1837
Shinebarger, Simeon - Esther R. M. Tabor
           10-20-1844
Shippee, George W. - Eliza Ann Bently
           2-24-1839
Shipworth, Benjamin - Milly Brown 6-17-1837
Shrimp, Jacob - Ann Drolliner 2-22-1838
Shults, Jacob M. - Catharine Ann Burger
           2-16-1843
Simms, Presley - Nancy Coghill 12-10-1835
Simons, Asa - Anna Smith 12-12-1839
Sims, John B. - Anna Graham 7- 4-1844
Singer, Michael - Ruth Farewell 11- 8-1838
Singleton, Thomas - Equella Hanon 10-13-1833
Skinner, Henry C. - Susan D. Moody
        lic. 8- 2-1837
Slater, David A. - Adaline Shippee 12-13-1838
Slipher, David - Mary Scott 3- 1-1838
Small, Phineas - Mary Pinney 6-25-1840
Smith, Alanson - Julian Drumm 10- 8-1840
Smith, Alexander - Elizabeth Bickel
           7- 6-1844
Smith, Eldridge G. - Mary Fowler 8- 3-1841
Smith, George - Rebecca Goodrich 1-16-1836
Smith, Hiram - Nancy Dawson 6-12-1834
Smith, James Y. - Oliva Brown 6-13-1840
Smith, Joseph W. B. - Henrietta Washburn
           10-15-1844
Smith, Merit - Anna Austin 5- 5-1839
Smith, Purdy - Surenna Beatty 3-23-1834
Smith, Truman - Roxy Ann Herrington 12-19-1843
Smith, William - Mary Ann Roney 3-21-1839
Smith, William V. - Elizabeth Gibson
           10- 8-1840
Snavely, Willis K. - Selestine Clark 9- 5-1844
Snell, William - Margaret Earls lic. 5-31-1841
Snow, Alva L. - Sylvina Cole 5-14-1844
Snyder, Henry - Margaret A. Brown 2-17-1842
Spear, William - Mercy Ann Austin 11-24-1840
Spencer, Henry G. of Wis. Territory -
    Margaret P. Campbell 6-22-1839
Sperry, Aurea - Lucinda M. Duerden
    no return lic. 12-29-1835
Sperry, Aurea - Mary Ann Caldwell 10-18-1840
Spurlock, Burwell - Margaret Blake 2-27-1836
Stanfield, Eli - Laura Ann Phelps 1-28-1836
Stanfield, Eli - Harriet Tompkins 10-10-1839
    Harriet Thompson in return
Stanfield, Robert - Angeline Conner 11-20-1836
Stanton, Aaron - Martha A. Fosdick 5-16-1843
Stanton, Amos - Jane Fail 6- 9-1833
Stanton, Benajah - Cynthia Clark 10-20-1837
Stanton, Elijah - Charlotte Bond 4-10-1834
Stanton, Joseph - Elmira Leaming 12- 8-1835
Starratt, Alexander - Tharissa McLain
           10-25-1836

Stebbins, Joseph S. of Mass. -
    Ann M. Kent 5-30-1839
Stephens, Darwin A. - Delia C. Porter
           4-15-1840
Sterling, Francis - Mary Fisher 11-24-1843
Sterling, Isaac - Ruth Bolster 8-17-1836
Sterling, Samuel - Mary Denton 3-13-1840
Stevens, Gilbert - Deborah Ann Russell
           2-25-1836
Steves, Daniel C. - Almira Dutton 12-25-1843
Stewart, Austin - Susannah Metts 10- 6-1842
Stewart, Ivey - Sarah R. Osborn 4- 9-1835
Stewart, Samuel - Phebe Norton 3- 7-1839
Stewart, Thomas A. - Mary S. Cobbs 3- 6-1844
Stewart, William O. of Warren Co., Ill. -
    Salome Bentley 10- 3-1839
Stilman, Jarod A. - Fanny Shumway 9- 8-1840
Stocking, William H. - Mary Ann Walbridge
           11- 3-1842
Stockton, Henry P. - Mary E. Conklin
           3-22-1843
Stockton, William - Mary Martin 1-15-1835
Stockwell, Loriston - Clarissa Gardner
           10-19-1841
Stover, Alexander - Catharine Whitenbeck
           11-30-1843
Strong, Dewit - Susan M. Low 12- 2-1835
Sturin, John I. - Mary Ann Jaquett 7-27-1843
Surdam, Bishop - Mary Letcham 12-14-1840
Taylor, Abram - Samantha P. Wood 3-31-1844
Taylor, James A. - Mary E. Evans 1-29-1844
Taylor, Richard - Caroline Thompson
           6-23-1842
Taylor, William B. - Rebecca A. Niece
           9-18-1837
Teegarden, Abraham - Lara Treat 9-22-1840
Teeple, Charles - Rue Ann Bryant 12-24-1839
Teeple, James W. - Clarissa Bunce 10-11-1835
Teeter, Henry - Catherine Fail 10-30-1836
Teeter, Jacob - Lucy Clark 2-18-1841
Teeter, Zachariah - Frances Russell
           3-23-1836
Teeter, Zachariah - Martha Vanorden
           4-13-1840
Templeton, John A. - Cornelia Sherman
           4- 8-1835
Thompson, Andrew - Malvina Clark 3-10-1841
Thompson, Henry - Mary Randall 2- 8-1835
Thompson, John - Mary Ann French 8-10-1843
Thorp, Horace L. - Mary Fosdick 2- 8-1840
Tinkey, George - Cynthia Little 9- 1-1844
Titus, Horace W. - Mary Ann Swett 6-11-1840
Titus, James - Mary Barns 12-23-1842
Tolbert, Jeptha - Elizabeth Leslie
           12- 5-1839
Tomlinson, John - Catharine Drom 9-17-1844
Toney, Sebert - Jane E. Ryon 12-24-1840
Toney, Sebert - Adaline Douthett 1-13-1842
Towle, Samuel S. - Maria Stevens 12- 9-1841
Tozier, Reuben - Elizabeth Farlow 6- 4-1840
Tratebas, Edmund - Hannah Thomas 6-24-1834
Travis, Curtis - Mary Ann Miller 2- 8-1838
Travis, John R. - Catharine M. Drew
           5- 1-1838
Travis, Joshua - Angeline Williams
           10-15-1840
Troxel, David - Dorothy Fravel 1-12-1843
Truesdell, Harvey - Catharine Tryon
           10-28-1838

Tuley, Simon P. - Mary Bone   12-21-1836
Turner, Samuel - Abigail Jackson   1- 1-1840
Turner, Thomas J. - Adeline R. Burnside
                                      2-19-1840
Tuttle, Guy W. - Lucy Hamishaw   3-11-1839
Tyrrell, Andrew J. - Sarah Blake   11-28-1837
Underwood, Barclay - Amelia Jackson   9- 8-1842
Utley, Sanford - Catharine Burnet   10-20-1835
Vail, Charles, of St. Joseph Co. -
   Olive M. Stanton   7- 1-1832
Vail, Thomas D. of St. Joseph Co. -
   Elizabeth Droliner   1-31-1837
VanArsdoll, William - Mercy Miller   6-12-1834
Vanpelt, Sutton - Hannah S. Bridge   10-31-1842
Vantassel, Henry B. - Maryiana Mulks 1-11-1837
Van Winkle, Lewis C. - Mary Hittle   6-21-1838
Vaughan, John M. - Hannah Clark   10-19-1844
Veneman, John - Matilda Harper   3-29-1836
Voice, John - Jane Muzzell   5-15-1840
Wagner, Alpheus I. - Eleanor Fail   3- 4-1841
Wagner, Benjamin F. - Mary C. Hunt   12-15-1836
Wagner, David F. - Angelina Cadwallader
                                      9- 1-1840
Waldo, Jesse H. - Clarissa M. Ward   3-19-1840
Waldrip, Clark C. - Sarah Martin   8-27-1834
Walker, Mathew L., of Trumbull Co., Ohio -
   Eleanor H. Dinwiddie   6- 6-1837
Walker, William - Permelia Harris   10-17-1840
Walker, William J. - Caroline M. Rose
                                      5-31-1838
Walton, William - Sarah Webster   2-26-1840
Warner, David - Almyra Weed   7-14-1839
   Lewis Weed, her father, consents
Warnock, John - Ellen Steele   6-22-1841
Warren, Charles - Martha Little   7-18-1841
Wart, Warren S. - Melinda Peek   12-30-1840
   Francis Peek, her father, consents
Wasson, Jesse - Mary Cadwallader   1- 1-1840
Watkins, J. Thamer - Ann Sharp   6-22-1844
   Thomas Wadkins in return
Way, Isaac - Rosana Wellman   8-29-1841
Weast, Joshua - Prudence Sweat   6-25-1837
Webb, Andrew - Margaret Smith   12-26-1842
Webster, Harlow S. - Mary J. Block   11-10-1842
Webster, John M. - Martha McLucus   8-22-1844
Webster, Reuben H. - Elizabeth C. Patterson
   Elizabeth C. Elliott in return   4-20-1843
Webster, William A. - Nancy McCall   2-28-1841
Weed, Lewis O. - Emily Warner   10-27-1839
Welch, William A. - Sarah Ann Lemon   4-21-1835
Weller, Joseph - Susan Ann Sergeant
                              lic.   5-22-1837
Wells, Amos - Janet Willis   3- 6-1839
West, Daniel - Elizabeth Crumpacker   4- 1-1838
West, Joseph - Susan Dinwiddie   2- 3-1835
Westerwelt, Joseph - Sarah Cooper   3-16-1843
Whallon, Alfred - Ann L. Monahan   4-22-1841
Wharton, Robert - Nancy Starbuck   1- 4-1844
Wheeler, Levi - Elizabeth Stone   5-31-1840
Wheeler, Philander - Elizabeth McIntyre
                                      7- 2-1840
Wheeler, William - Mary McIntyre   12- 3-1840
Whetzel, Joseph - Mary Ann Nations   6- 7-1843
Whitcraft, John - Alluna Shaw   6-12-1839
   Marquis D. Shaw, her father, consents
White, Frederick A. - Louisa Buck   2-18-1840
White, Henry F. - Susan Jacobs   1-27-1839
White, Jacob H. - Abigail Closser   3- 1-1840
White, John - Ann Horner   12-23-1840

White, Robert - Mary Ann Travers   8-23-1836
Whitehead, Hampton B. - Margaret Hastings
                                     11-15-1838
Whitehead, William H. H. - Mary Ann Hastings
                                      9-12-1837
Whitman, Russell - Lustina P. Wheaton
                                      2-17-1841
Whitmore, Daniel W. - Rebecca Ives   3-23-1838
Whitner, Robert C. - Susannah Hobaugh
                                      1-15-1843
Whittlesay, Eliphalet W. - Catharine E.
   Shinmin   10-24-1841
Wilcox, Hiram - Sabrina J. Webster   9- 8-1844
Wilder, Hiram - Martha Ann Wood   2- 4-1837
Willfong, Elijah - Elizabeth Argabright
                                      7- 2-1840
Williams, James H. - Louisa Flint
   no return   lic.   6- 2-1836
Williams, John C. - Mary Wilson
   no return   lic.   1- 6-1838
Williams, Samuel E. - Evilina Bridge
                                      4- 6-1843
Willis, Stephen R. - Maria Carter   7- 3-1842
Willis, Thomas H. - Elizabeth Snodgrass
                                      3-29-1837
Willits, James - Margaret Ann Fenner
                                      2-29-1840
Wills, James - Mary Cissney   12-20-1835
Willson, William - H. Monell   2-17-1841
Wilson, Charles - Sarah Brough   10-26-1838
Wilson, David - Rebecca Owen   10- 9-1833
Wilson, Jeremiah - Abigail Wills   3-29-1835
Wilson, Joshua M. - Emeline Winchell
                                      6-16-1833
Wilson, Samuel, of St. Joseph Co. -
   Alzina Burch   7-29-1839
Wilson, William M. - Eliza Aspinwall
                                      2-16-1843
Wiltfond, Samuel - Barbary Hostetler
   Barbary Hollister in return   1-29-1843
Winchell, Jesse H. - Lucy Ann Francis Smith
                                      7-29-1835
Winchell, John B. - Harriet Holmes   9-24-1837
Winchell, William H. - Louisa Osborne
                                      4- 5-1840
Windham, Joseph - Eliza Ann Contee   1-19-1841
Winslow, Jason - Rhoda Skinner   9-17-1838
Winter, Alfred R. - Cornilia I. Payne
                                     12-21-1835
Wittenbury, Wellington W. - Sarah Swain
                                     12-18-1837
Wolfe, John - Mercia Wells lic.   11-10-1834
Wood, Horace - Elizabeth McClane   12-23-1834
Wood, James D. - Harriet Reynolds   9-31-1842
Wood, Leonard - Catharine T. Faulkner
                                      8- 2-1835
Wood, Silas - Sarah Hale   12-22-1836
Woodbury, Jesse, Jr. - Julia Ann Porter
                                     12-16-1834
Woodman, Edwin - Almyra Warner   10- 8-1839
Woodruff, Henry E. - Achsah Ann Everts
                                     11- 6-1842
Woods, Bartlett - Sally Ann Griffin
                                      4-17-1841
Woodworth, Ansel - Sarah Baldwin
   no return   lic.   10- 3-1837
Woodworth, Louis - Louisa Parenton(?)
                                     10-18-1842
Woolley, Daniel - Rachel McHoney   5-23-1843
Young, Florius B., of Cook Co., Ill. -
   Huldah E. Joyner   4-18-1839
Young, Robert - Sarah Walker
   no return   lic.   1- 1-1839

Woolley, Finley Y. - Jane Hogan   8-11-1842
Wright, Edward - Angeline F. Paine   12-25-1834
Wright, Harry H. - Elizabeth Myers   2-13-1836
Wright, Newton - Cynthia Foutz   6- 2-1836

CRAWFORDSVILLE DEATHS

I had hoped that the Crawfordsville _Locomotive_ would be like its counterpart the Indianapolis _Locomotive_ in reporting local news, including births and deaths, but was disappointed in checking the microfilm copy of the paper from June, 1853, through April, 1855, in the Indiana State Library. The Crawfordsville _Review_ from January, 1855 through December, 1858, which was also available on microfilm, was likewise disappointing in death notices but did carry the notices of appointment of administrators of estates, and advertisements of sales of personal property and real estate. Apparently, only paid death notices were inserted in these papers.

ALEXANDER, JAMES
W. C. Layton, admr.
4-12-1856

ALLEN, JUDGE WILLIAM
d. 3-11-1857, age 76
formerly of Tipp. Co.
3-21-1857

BAKER, NICHOLAS
John S. Gray, admr.
11- 7-1857

BALDWIN, ELIAS
Geo. Bratton, admr.
12- 6-1856

BARGELT, ABRAHAM, of Middletown
John M. Fisher, Admr.
6-12-1858

BARTON, JOSEPH
A. Gaddes, excr.
5- 2-1857

BECK, DURHAM, of Walnut Twp.
Jeptha Beck, admr.
3- 3-1855

BIRT, THOMAS
Henry Parrish, admr.
10-18-1856

BOWEN, FRANCIS ALBERT
Inf. son of Chas. H. & Martha E.
d. 8- 9-1853, age 2 mos.
8-13-1853

BOWEN, MARTHA E.
wife of Charles H.
d. 6-30-1856   7- 5-1856

BRENTON, THOMAS
Samuel Brenton, admr.
4- 7-1855

BRITTS, JOHN
James H., Jane, Vincent P.
Britts, minor heirs
Zachariah Mahorney & Thomas
Roberts, guardians of above
4- 7-1855

BRITTS, SAMUEL
Matthias Frantz, excr.
9-19-1857

BROWN, WILLIAM M.
G. M. Brown, admr.
10-18-1856

BRUSH, MARY
D. C. Stover, excr.
2-16-1856

BYRD, JAMES R. of Clark Twp.
Oliver B. Wilson, admr.
11-28-1857

CAMPBELL, MRS. SARAH G.
d. 12-31-1855
1- 5-1856

COSHOW, THOMAS
John Coshow, admr.
3-21-1857

CRAIG, HUGH N.
Robert C. Craig guardian
of Elizabeth, minor heir
1-26-1856

CROY, ALEXANDER
David Long, admr.
12- 6-1856

DECK, ELIZABETH
Samuel Deck, admr.
2-23-1856

DEWEY, JAMES
Margaret Dewey guardian
of Anthony, minor heir
1-26-1856

DOCTERMAN, CHARLES
of Middletown
Samuel Poth, admr.
1-24-1857

DOYEL, FARMER
Joseph Allen, excr.
2- 9-1856

DUNN, STRANGE S.
Cornelius O'Brien, admr.
6-30-1855

DUNWIDDIE, WILLIAM
Levi Curtis, admr.
9- 8-1855

ELLIOT, JOHN
Samuel Gilliland, admr.
1- 9-1858

EVANS, CHARLES
Inf. son of I. C. & S. U.
Adams   d. 6-14-1854
6-17-1854

FARLEY, JOHN
Robert W. McMakin, excr.
3- 6-1858

FIELDS, ELIZABETH
Wife of Stephen
d. 2-14-1855, age 49
2-24-1855

FINNELL, DAVID, of Whitesville
killed on railroad
12-20-1856

FLANIGAN, JOHN
Archibald Flanigan, admr.
1-26-1856

FOUST, SEBASTIAN, of Wea Plains
d. 5-3-1857, age 25
b. Pickaway Co., Ohio; to Ind.
in 1854; wife, father, child
survive   5- 9-1857

GALEY, LUCY
wife of W. W.
d. 9-1-1853, age 44
b. Oldham Co., Ky. to Ind. 1823
5 Children survive   9-17-1853

GALEY, SAMUEL
d. 2-15-1857, age 81
2-28-1857

GILKEY, SAMUEL, of Coal Cr. Twp.
Aaron Gilkey, admr.   11-17-1855

GOTT, DAN B.
William Hanna, admr.
5-19-1855

GROENENDYKE, PETER
final settlement of estate
2- 9-1856

HALL, BENJAMIN
Samuel Gilliland, admr.
9- 4-1858

HARLOW, GARRET W.
Garret Harlow, excr.   9-13-1856

HARN, EDWARD
Clement Johnson, admr.   11- 1-1856

HARSHBARGER, ISAAC
John W. Blankenship, admr.
11-17-1855

HARTER, WILLIAM B.
inf. son of Mr. & Mrs. D. Harter
d. 8-15-1856 at Toledo, Ohio
8-23-1856

HARTMAN, JOHN, SR.
d. 5-17-1858, age 80
b. Botetourt Co., Va. 3-24-1778
5-22-1858

HELM, WILLIAM
Naomi, guardian of minor
heirs, Elizabeth & John D.
5- 5-1855

HIPES, SAMUEL
Robert Finch, admr.
10- 2-1858

HORNER, MRS. A.
d. 10-1-1855, age 63
at residence of late husband
10- 6-1855

HUFFMAN, ISAAC
well digger, d. 6-28-1855
6-30-1855

HUDSON, HENRY O.
inf. son of Montgomery E. & Mary J.
d. 6-7-1854   6-10-1854

HUFFMAN, CATHERINE
wife of Henry
d. 1-14-1854, age 26
1-21-1854

INGERSOLL, MARTHA
wife of I. D. Ingersoll
d. 10-23-1854 at parents' home
dt of O. P. & Margret Jennison
of Oskaloosa, Iowa
11- 4-1854

JACKSON, ELIZABETH
Stephen Allen guardian of Joseph
& Nancy, minor heirs
1-26-1856

JARRET, MERCHANT
Jonathan Vancleave, admr.
5- 9-1857

KEARAN, SUSAN C.
wife of John V.
d. 1-19-1854   1-21-1854

KENDALL, SAMUEL
John Graves, guardian of
Samuel A. & David, minor heirs
1-26-1856

KERR, JOSEPH
David Long, admr.
10- 9-1858

KIRKPATRICK, ABSALOM
John Kirkpatrick, admr.
9- 1-1855

KNOX, CASSANDER
wife of James, Ladoga merchant
d. 10-10-1854   10-28-1854

LAYMON, JOSEPH
d. 4-21-1856, age 56
David A. Laymon, excr.
11-11-1856   5- 3-1856

LAYTON, FANNY PIATTE
inf. dt. of Sarah & W. C.
Layton   d. 12-27-1854
12-30-1854

LONG, NEWTON
Thomas Long, admr.
4-28-1855

LYNN, ANDREW P.
James W. Lynn, excr.
4-11-1857

McBROOM, PHEBE ELLEN
inf. dt. of Wm. & Emily
d. 8-10-1853   8-20-1853

McDONALD, SARAH E.
dt of John & Elizabeth
d. 11-29-1857   age 11
12- 5-1857

MARLOW, WILLIAM, of Walnut Twp.
Robert M. Higgins, admr.
4-25-1857

MASTERSON, JOSEPH D.
printer; d. 5-3-1858
5- 8-1858

MICK, LAVINA
wife of James F.;
dt of Mrs. Laura Mitchell
d. 8-8-1854, age 24
8-19-1854

MICK, MAGGIE W.
wife of James F.
d. 6-14-1858, age 19
6-19-1858

MIKELS, WILLIAM H., of Franklin
Twp.; Daniel Shaver, admr.
11- 1-1856

MILLER, JOSIAH
William Bowman, admr.
12- 6-1856

MILLER, NOAH,
of Coal Cr. Twp.
Levi Curtis, admr.
9-13-1856

MITCHELL, ANDREW
Alexander Mitchell, admr.
3-29-1856

MORGAN, ENOCH
Edward S. Morgan, admr.
12- 1-1855

MORRISON, THOMAS
Thomas T. Morrison, excr.
9-20-1856

MOUNT, ALFRED G.,
of Clark Twp.
Elijah Mount, admr.
12-18-1858

MURPHICS, JAMES
George Vandevander, admr.
4- 7-1855

NAUMAN, JOHN
Valentine Miller, admr.
8-11-1855

NORMAN, JOHN
Valentine Miller, excr.
12-25-1858

OLIVER, ELIAS
Dice Oliver, admr.
1- 2-1858

OLIVER, MINERVA
Elias Oliver, guardian
of Mary J. & Joseph E.,
minor heirs
2- 9-1856

PIERCE, JOSEPH
Elisha G. Pierce, admr.
10-20-1855

POWERS, DAVID, SR.
Thos. W. Florer, admr.
9- 4-1858

PREWIT, JOSEPH W.
Alfred Rose, admr.
4-18-1857

PRYOR, LUCINDA
Wiley G. Bell, admr.
11-21-1857

REITZEL, JOHN
David Rusk, admr.
9-15-1855

RICE, ELIZABETH J.
wife of Isaac A.,
edtr. Attica Ledger
d. 6-28-1857 7-11-1857

RIDGE, CYNTHIA ANNE
wife of Benjamin F. Ridge
d. 6-1-1854 at home of
father in Tipp. Co.
6-10-1854

RISTINE, MAJ. HENRY
d. 10-8-1854, age 74
of cholera   10-13-1854

ROBERTSON, E. M.
wife of W. Robertson
d. 4-5-1858, age 32
Piqua, O. papers please copy
4-10-1858

ROYALTY, JOHN M.
Wm. D. Royalty, admr.
3-29-1856

SCHENK, WILLIAM M.
inf. son of R. & Mary A.
d. 2-23-1857   2-28-1857

SCOTT, JENNIE
wife of Uriah M. Scott
d. 7-31-1858, age 22
8- 7-1858

SMITH, CHARLES
Benjamin Smith, admr.
12- 8-1855

SMITH, HENRY
George Smith, admr.
1-27-1855

SMITH, JACOB
John Britton, admr.
9-12-1857

SNOOK, DR. H. T.
d. 11-12-1856, age 59
11-22-1858

SPARKS, THOMAS
Joseph Swearingen, admr.
6-14-1856

STIPE, JOSEPH, of Franklin Twp.
John & William Stipe, admrs.
2- 6-1858

STONER, BARBARY, of Clark Twp.
David Stoner, admr.
4-17-1858

SUTTON, DAVID
Jonas Sutton, admr.
3- 3-1855

TAYLOR, THOMAS
William H. Taylor, admr. 11-17-1855
Sarah Taylor, guardian of Sarah,
minor heir   1-26-1856

THOMAS, ABRAHAM
John M. Thomas admr., sale of
personal property at home of
William Thomas, Coal Cr. Twp.
1-10-1857

THOMASON, LEWIS
William F. & Lewis M., admrs.
6- 2-1855

THORN, GEORGE
Thomas Davis, admr.
3-24-1855

VANCE, DAVID
Samuel W. Austin, admr.
2- 9-1856

VANCLEAVE, RALPH
John Canine, admr.
3- 3-1855

VANHOOK, MILTON HERNDON
Son of Archelus & Martha
d. 7-8-1858, age 20
7-17-1858

WASSON, WILLIAM, JR., of
Brown Twp., d. 12-1-1856, age 32
12-6-1856   12-27-1856
*
WATTS, JOHN, of Coal Creek Twp.
Jane Watts, admr.
3-13-1858

WEATHERS, WILLIAM, of
Madison Twp.
John I. Weathers, admr.
4-12-1856

WILHITE, JULIA ANN
Paschal F. Wilhite, admr.
1- 9-1858

WILSON, WILLIAM
Ludlow K. Thomas, admr.
1-30-1858

WOOD (OR WOODS), BARTHOLOMEW
d. 12-19-1856   12-20-1856
John Lee, admr. 1-24-1857

WORL, THOMAS
James Gilkey, admr.
7-21-1855

WORTZ, WILLIAM S.
William F. Thomason,
guardian of minor heirs,
Mary E. & Amanda, adv. lot in
Ladoga   5- 2-1857

WYSE, JOHN, of Madison Twp.
Coroner's inquest 11-24-1855
Jacob Stingley, admr.
1- 5-1856

YERIAN, JANE
wife of William
d. 8-6-1857, age 19
8- 8-1857

ZOOK, JACOB
John S. Gray, admr.
12- 8-1855

ZUCK, GEORGE, of Wayne Twp.
John S. Gray, admr.
1-16-1858

*Jeremiah Stillwell, admr.

SOUTH BEND DEATHS

OBITUARIES, ADMINISTRATION NOTICES, AND OTHER NEWS ITEMS ABSTRACTED FROM
EARLY SOUTH BEND NEWSPAPERS, NOVEMBER, 1831, THROUGH DECEMBER, 1854

Reprinted from a 1977 issue of the Quarterly of the South Bend Area Genealogical Society.
The dates are taken from obituaries, administration notices, and general news items from four
newspapers on file at the Northern Indiana History Society Museum. The numbers preceding the
dates indicate the name of the newspaper in which the article appeared: (1) St. Joseph Valley
Register; (2) South Bend Free Press; (3) Northwestern Pioneer; (4) St. Joseph Beacon. The dates
are those of the newspaper, not of the death. The South Bend Area Genealogical Society has also
published later deaths, 1855-63, and 1863-69 in the issues of their Quarterly.

The Genealogical Society was organized in January, 1976; meetings are held on the fourth
Monday of each month (except in July, August, and December) in the auditorium of the South Bend
Public Library. Dues are $5.00 (individual), $7.00 (family), and $3.00 (junior). Mrs. Mary
Thornsen is the 1978 president; Mrs. F. A. Lies is editor of the Quarterly magazine. Publica-
tion of queries is free to members.

The Indiana Historical Society wishes to express their appreciation for permission to
reprint from their Quarterly, this first segment of Deaths and Other Notices from South Bend
newspapers.

ABBITT, Mrs. Roxanne E.	1	8 Jul 52	BIRD, John	1	24 Oct 50
ABSHIRE, Lucy M.	1	8 Jun 54	BLAIR, Amos	2	16 Dec 37
ALEXANDER, B. F.	1	4 Sep 5?	BOLES, John	1	23 Nov 54
ALEXANDER, Charles Edwin	1	13 Sep 49	BONEBRAKE, Henry	1	5 Jun 51
ALEXANDER, Mrs. Eliza	1	11 Oct 49	BOOKEY, Frank	1	6 Jan 53
ALEXANDER, Mrs. Sarah	1	18 Aug 53	BOWEN, John	1	20 Nov 46
AMMEN, William	1	13 Feb 51	BOWERS, Theresa	1	9 Oct 46
ANDERSON, (Male)	1	24 Oct 45	BOWLSBY, Levi	2	Sep 38
ANDERSON, J. G.	1	21 Dec 48	BOYD, Elizabeth	1	22 Jan 47
ANDREW, Daniel	1	9 Apr 47	BOYD, William S.	1	22 Jan 47
ANDREWS, Isaac	1	13 Mar 51	BRACKBILL, James	1	10 Oct 45
ANDREWS, Mrs. Nancy	1	13 Mar 51	BRADLEY, Herman A.	1	3 Aug 54
ANDRUS, Harvey	1	11 Apr 50	BRATT, Jacob	1	30 Oct 46
ANTRIM, William	1	23 Feb 54	BRAY, Tyra W.	2	12 Sep 44
ARMSTRONG, Simon	1	22 Jul 52	BRIGGS, Mary	1	4 Oct 49
ARMSTRONG, Thomas P. Esq.	1	14 Nov 50	BRISET, L.	1	9 May 50
ASHBY, John	2	6 Oct 38	BRISET, Mrs. Mary	1	10 Feb 53
ATWELL, Norman E.	1	10 Sep 47	BRONSON, Tyra	1	10 Jun 52
AUTEN, Schuyler	1	18 Sep 46	BROOK, Samuel	1	8 Nov 49
AUTEN, William	1	3 Feb 53	BROOKFIELD, Noah	1	15 May 51
AVERY, Nathan	1	12 Feb 52	BROOKS, Samuel	1	20 Sep 49
AVERY, Seth	2	6 Jan 38	BROWER, John P.	1	30 Nov 48
AYER, Darious	2	15 Sep 38	BROWER, John P.	1	10 Jan 50
BADIN, Father Stephen A.	1	5 May 53	BROWN, W. B.	1	17 Oct 45
BAKER, Charles	1	19 Sep 50	BRUNSON, Warren	1	26 Jul 49
BAKER, George	2	20 Oct 38	BUCK, Jonathan	1	22 Nov 49
BALDWIN, William	1	18 May 54	BUCK, Ruth	1	3 Apr 51
BALL, William E.	1	6 Feb 46	BURNETT, Abraham	3	14 Mar 32
BARBER, Mrs. Prudence M.	1	11 May 54	BURROUGHS, Mary Frances	1	12 Mar 47
BARTLETT, Mary S.	1	10 Mar 48	BUSHA, George	1	13 Mar 51
BASHFORD, Eleanor	1	30 Jul 46	BUTLER, Mrs. Mary	1	9 Jun 53
BASHFORD, Eleanor	1	20 Feb 51	CALDWELL, Joseph Defreese	1	5 Dec 50
BAUKER, Mrs. (Judge John)	4	15 Aug 32	CAMERSON, M. S. Representative	1	12 Nov 47
BAURGELT, Mrs. Elizabeth	1	23 Aug 49	CAMPBELL, Mrs.	2	26 May 38
BEACH, Mrs. Hannah	1	23 Jan 51	CAMPBELL, Harriet	1	30 Jun 53
BEAUTILLEIR, Francis	4	15 Aug 32	CAMPER, Mrs. Elizabeth	1	5 Apr 49
BECKWITH, of Kalamazoo, Mich.	1	10 Oct 50	CAMPER, William	1	12 Dec 50
BEEKMAN, Miss Catharine	1	31 Oct 50	CARLISLE, Achsah	1	5 May 48
BEESON, Job John	2	30 Dec 37	CARPENTER, Edward	1	27 Mar 51
BELL, (Male)	1	5 Sep 50	CASE, Theophilus	1	30 Jul 46
BEMENT, Mrs. H.	1	13 Sep 49	CASEY, Mr.	2	12 May 38
BENNETT, Arthur G.	1	14 Sep 48	CHALFANT, Mrs. Anna	1	12 Apr 49
BENNETT, Friar	1	28 Aug 51	CHAMBERLAIN, Freegift	2	20 Jan 38
BENNETT, H. G.	1	19 Feb 47	CHANDONIA, John B.	1	12 Sep 45
BERTRAND, (Notre Dame Std.)	1	21 Oct 52	CHANDONIA, John B. Estate notice		
BIGGER, Samuel (Gov.)	1	18 Sep 46		2	9 Nov 37

CHAPIN, Martha Emaline	1	27 Feb 46
CHAPMAN, George A., Esq.	1	27 Mar 51
CHAPMAN, Henry Eugene	1	29 Apr 52
CHAPMAN, Pardon S.	2	12 May 38
CHESS, Anna May	1	11 Dec 51
CHILDS, James M.	1	26 Aug 52
CHILSON, John	1	16 Jun 53
CHIPMAN, Halton (Bristol)	1	16 Jul 46
CHORD, Isaac	1	13 Feb 46
CHORD, Mrs. Isaac	2	4 Sep 40
CHORD, Jacob	2	9 Sep 37
CHORD, Jonathan (first name not clear tear in paper)	2	23 Sep 37
CHORD, Jonathan	1	12 Sep 45
CLAPP, Otis of Egypt, NY	1	3 Dec 47
CLARK, Annie	1	4 Nov 52
CLARK, Charles Titus	1	6 Jun 50
CLARK, Ebenezer B.	1	10 Dec 47
CLAY, Winfield	1	22 Mar 49
COBB, Dudley	1	10 Jun 52
COBB, Lewis	1	27 Sep 49
COLE, Anzel	1	14 Jun 49
COLFAX, Mrs. Catharine	1	26 Apr 49
COLFAX, Richard of NY	1	24 Jan 50
COLFAX, Mrs. William W.	1	19 Jul 49
COLLINS, Benjamin	1	12 Feb 52
COLLINS, Eli V.	2	22 Sep 38
COLLINS, LaFayette	1	6 Mar 46
COLLINS, Tabitha Dorcas	1	15 Aug 50
COMPARET, Frances	1	24 Jul 51
COMPTON, Mrs. Sarah	1	6 Mar 51
CONNER, Clarence	1	27 May 52
COOK, Arthur	1	5 Sep 50
COONLEY, Benjamin	1	7 Oct 52
COPELAND, (Male)	2	12 May 38
COPELAND, Joshua	2	19 May 38
COPELEN, (Male)	2	10 Feb 38
COROTHERS, Thomas	1	15 Nov 49
COSGROVE, Mrs. Elizabeth	1	15 Aug 50
COSGROVE, John	2	15 Sep 38
COSGROVE, Josephine	1	17 Oct 45
COTTON, John Francis	1	14 Apr 53
COTTRELL, Lemuel	2	22 Sep 38
COVERT, Alfred	1	6 Apr 54
CRAHEN, (Student Notre Dame)	1	21 Oct 52
CRIPE, Benjamine	1	13 Mar 51
CRIPE, Mrs. Fanny	1	23 Feb 54
CRIPE, Jacob	1	12 Mar 47
CRIPE, John	1	24 Mar 48
CRIPE, John Jr.	1	1 Mar 49
CRITCHFIELD, Dr. A. M.	1	22 May 51
CROCKER, Mrs. Mary Norton	1	16 Apr 47
CROCKETT, Garland	1	10 May 49
CROCKETT, Mrs. Martha	1	4 Oct 53
CROCKETT, Mrs. Mary	1	19 Feb 47
CRONE, William	1	18 Jan 49
CRONE, William	1	17 Nov 53
CULVERSON, Samuel	1	27 Nov 51?
CUMMING, H. H.	1	25 Apr 50
CURTIS, Ida B.	1	2 Sep 52
CURTIS, Lewis Andrew	1	13 Nov 51
CURTIS, Marquis R.	1	11 Apr 50
CURTIS, Susan	1	17 Nov 53
CUTLER, Mrs. Mary Jane	1	16 Dec 52
DAVIS, Mrs. Altha C.	1	3 Nov 53
DAVIS, Mrs. Elizabeth	1	26 May 53
DAVIS, James A.	1	15 Jun 54

DAVIS, Joshua	1	27 Aug 47
DAVIS, Joshua	1	17 Dec 54
DAVIS, Clark	1	20 Sep 49
DAY, Emma	1	20 Jun 50
DAYTON, Catherine S.	2	31 Jul 40
DEARDOFF, Mrs. Hannah	1	26 Jun 51
DEARDOFF, Mary Hannah	1	31 Jul 51
DEFREES, Mrs. Anthony	1	5 Jan 51
DEFREES, Elizabeth	1	27 Feb 54
DEFREES, Mrs. Jane	1	3 Aug 54
DEFREESE, James S.	1	23 May 50
DELAMATER, Cornelia Miss	1	23 May 50
DENNOR, Michael	1	10 Oct 45
DIBBLE, Edward	1	21 Oct 52
DIEHL, Henry	1	3 Dec 47
DIVELY, Abraham	1	7 Nov 50
DIVELY, Abraham	1	8 Jul 52
DOBLAR, Rosannah	1	19 Jul 54
DOTS, Elijah	4	8 Aug 37
DOTY, Mr. and dau.	1	10 Oct 50
DOUGHMAN, Jacob	1	12 Sep 45
DOUGHMAN, Jacob	1	20 Dec 49
DOWLING, Andrew	1	14 Nov 45
DOXTATER, Mr.	1	19 May 53
DRAPIER, Ebenezer	1	10 Mar 53
DRYER, Thomas	1	25 Nov 52
DUFF, Capt. on Ship, Berald	2	19 May 38
DUNN, Frank	1	2 Jun 53
DYER, Edgar Walton	1	21 Sep 54
EAKER, Erastus	1	23 Oct 46
EARL, Edgar B.	1	28 Feb 50
EARL, William L.	1	3 Jul 46
EDGE, Charles Elliott	1	10 Sep 47
EDWARDS, Lewis Cass (infant)	4	11 Jul 32
EGBERT, John	1	1 Feb 49
EGBERT, John	1	8 Jul 52
ELDER, Alexander	1	11 May 54
ELLIS, Mrs. Mary Maria	1	1 May 46
ELLSWORTH, J. P.	1	18 Aug 53
EMMONS, Wales	1	13 Apr 54
EUTSLER, Enos	1	12 Aug 52
FARNSWORTH, Ebenizer	1	14 May 47
FARNSWORTH, Silvia Caroline	1	3 Sep 47
FARRAND, Mrs. Martha J.	1	17 Apr 51
FERGUSON, William	1	11 Dec 45
FERRIS, Isaiah	1	3 Feb 53
FERRIS, John	1	11 Jun 47
FERRIS, John	1	6 Dec 49
FERRIS, Morton E.	1	9 Mar 54
FINLEY, Dr.	1	22 May 51
FINLEY, Mrs. M. T.	2	9 Jun 38
FISHER, Elias	1	17 Oct 50
FISHER, John	1	1 Jan 50
FISHER, John	1	5 Dec 50
FISHER, Joseph	1	24 Jan 50
FISHER, Joseph	1	4 Sep 51
FITCH, Dr. Frederick	1	28 Mar 50
FLANEGAN, Hugh C.	1	3 Oct 45
FLANEGIN, Hugh C.	1	23 Aug 49
FORD, John	2	20 Oct 38
FOWLER, Thomas	1	9 Apr 47
FOX, Peter	1	2 Sep 52
FRAME, Daniel	2	20 Oct 38
FRAME, Jesse	1	1 Apr 52
FRAZIER, Louisa	1	15 Nov 49
FRETIZ, Mary	1	17 Sep 47
GARST, Abraham	2	15 Sep 38

GARST, Mrs. Anna	1	23 Nov 54
GARVEY, Matthew (murder)	2	14 Oct 37
GARWOOD, Jonathan	3	11 Jan 32
GARWOOD, Joshua	2	Oct 38
GIBBONS, William	1	7 Dec 54
GIBBS, Francis Edwin	1	22 Jun 54
GILMORE,	1	3 Apr 51
GISH, Mrs. Sarah	1	9 Feb 54
GOOD, Mr. (died 21 Oct 1836)		
GOOD, Samuel	2	17 Mar 38
GOODENOW, Hon. John M.	2	18 Aug 38
GOODING, Ephriam	1	26 May 48
GOODMAN, Mr. (Soldier of Niles)	1	1 Oct 47
GORDON, Ann	1	1 Feb 49
GORDON, Mrs. Hannah	1	21 Sep 54
GOUCHER, Romi	1	28 Dec 48
GRANNIS, Solon A.	1	4 Dec 46
GRANT, John	1	7 Jan 48
GRANT, Mary	1	15 Jan 46
GRAVES, W. J.	1	5 Oct 48
GREELEY, Son of Horace	1	9 Aug 49
GREEN, Delphi	1	12 Jun 46
GREEN, John	2	19 May 38
GREEN, Nathan	1	17 Oct 45
GREEN, R. C. (wife & 3 ch)	1	12 Jun 46
GRIFFITHS, Ann	1	2 Jan 51
GRIFFITH, J. B.	1	29 Aug 50
GRIFFITTS, Samuel	1	25 Sep 46
GRIMES, Lucien	1	16 Oct 51
GROSENICKLE, David	2	6 Jan 38
HACKNEY, Obadiah	1	4 Dec 46
HAGER, Thomas	1	27 May 52
HAIN, Maria Louisa	1	21 Sep 50
HALL, Inf. Son	4	8 Sep 32
HALLOCK, ?	1	24 Jan 50
HALSEY, A. B.	1	26 May 53
HALSEY, Daniel	1	20 Mar 51
HARDMAN, William Henricks	2	25 Aug 38
HARPER, John Abraham	1	23 Apr 47
HARPER, Louisa Ellen	1	23 Oct 51
HARRIS, Ellen Marie	1	22 Apr 52
HARRIS, George Washington	1	21 Aug 46
HARRIS, John W.	1	3 Sep 47
HARRIS, Leonard G.	1	17 Nov 53
HARRIS, Margaret	1	13 May 52
HARRISON, ?	2	16 Jun 38
HARTPENCE, John	1	16 Nov 54
HARVEY, Ithamer	1	3 Mar 48
HATCH, Tresa	1	16 Jun 53
HATFIELD, Thomas Sr.	1	Feb 47
HAUPTMAN, Family of St. Louis	1	26 Sep 45
HAWLEY, Carlos A.	1	19 Feb 47
HAZLETTE, Miss Lydia D.	1	15 May 51
HEATON, James	2	9 Apr 41
HENRICKS, Emma Louise	1	7 Apr 48
HENRICKS, Mrs. Harriet A.	1	24 Jun 52
HENRICKS, Julia Ann	2	5 May 38
HENRICKS, Mary Catherine	1	1 Mar 49
HENRY, David	1	17 May 49
HENRY, Peter	1	29 Aug 50
HESTEN, Malen	1	7 Sep 54
HILDEBRAND, Jonathan	1	14 Jan 48
HOLLOWAY, Mrs. Mary	2	25 Aug 38
HOOD, William N. of Peru Esq.	2	24 Jul 38
HOOPER, Alice E.	1	7 Jul 48
HOOPER, John C.	1	30 Jul 46
HOOPER, Phebe	1	7 Jul 48

HOOTEN, Thomas	1	22 Apr 52
HOPKINS, Jay	1	17 Mar 53
HOPKINS, Mrs. Margaret	1	26 May 53
HORRELL, Mrs. Matilda	1	19 Feb 47
HOUGHTON, Mrs. Elizabeth	1	11 May 54
HUGGINS, Charles E.	1	3 Aug 52
HUGGINS, Clara L.	1	3 Aug 54
HULETT, John M. (4 year old)	4	15 Aug 32
HUMPHREY, Dr. Harvey	1	27 Nov 51
HUMPHREYS, Edward	1	9 Apr 47
HUMPHREYS, Dr. Harvey	2	1 Sep 38
HUMPHREYS, Harvey	1	21 May 47
HUNTSINGER, Henry	1	18 Apr 50
HURD, Elliott	1	29 Oct 47
HYLER, Mrs. Margaret	1	22 Dec 53
IRELAND, James	2	9 Sep 37
IRWIN, Amos	1	17 Jun 52
JENKS, James P.	1	10 Oct 50
JODAN, Edgar Roberts	1	18 Mar 52
JOHNSON, Chancy	1	13 Nov 51
JOHNSON, John	2	29 Sep 38
JONES, Mrs. Elizabeth	1	15 Mar 51
JONES, Samuel	1	15 Aug 50
JUDSON, Mary Elizabeth	1	6 Mar 51
KANE, Maria Louisa	1	30 Apr 47
KEELER, Alice	1	7 Aug 46
KELTNER, Miss Elizabeth	1	27 Apr 51
KENNEDY, Cong.	1	7 Jan 48
KENNEDY, Henry D.	1	18 Aug 53
KILKENNY, James	1	23 Aug 49
KILMORE, John	2	28 Jul 38
KIMBALL, James	2	13 Oct 38
KING, Miss	2	4 Nov 37
KING, Thomas	1	22 Dec 53
KINGERY, Eliza C.	1	23 Jun 48
KINSING, John	1	15 Dec 45
KNIGHT, Mary Hattle	1	3 Aug 54
LANSING, Susan Platt	1	28 Jun 49
LAPIERRE, Joseph M.	1	21 Sep 48
LAWRENCE, James Grove	1	19 Sep 45
LAWRENCE, Morris	1	28 Apr 48
LEER, Stephen	1	4 Feb 48
LELAND, Dr. Dexter F.	1	15 Jun 52
LEMON, John	1	21 Feb 50
LENTZ, Christopher	2	15 Sep 38
LINEBACK, Elijah	1	27 Feb 46
LISTON, Henry	1	24 Mar 53
LISTON, Mrs. Margaret	1	22 Jan 46
LISTON, Mrs. Margaretta L.	1	19 May 53
LISTON, William Morris	1	15 Jan 47
LOWRY, Leola	1	9 Oct 51
LOWRY, Lorenzo	1	1 Oct 47
LUCE, Mary Caroline	1	10 Aug 48
MCBRATNEY, Samuel	1	3 Oct 45
MCCARTNEY, (?) Sanuel	1	3 Oct 45
MCCARTNEY, William	1	26 Aug 52
MCCARTY, Nicholas Esq.	1	25 May 54
MCCHESNEY, Charles Colfax	1	15 Jul 52
MCCLELLAND, John T.	1	12 Sep 45
M'CORMICK, Julia (3 yr old)	3	14 Mar 32
MCCULLOUGH, Helen	1	7 Aug 51
MCGOGY, James F.	1	22 Aug 50
MCINDOFFER, J.	1	21 May 50
MCKINLEY, James	1	24 Sep 47
MCMICHAEL, Mary Ann	1	20 Apr 54
MCMILLAN, Milton	1	2 May 50
MCNABB, John	1	25 Nov 52

MCNEISH, Rev. D.	1	7 Sep 54
MCNEISH, Mary	1	27 Mar 51
MABEE, John P.	1	9 Oct 46
MACK, Andrew	1	18 Sep 46
MALBUFF, Alex	1	3 Feb 53
MARSTON, Nelson E.	1	2 Oct 51
MARTIN, Corbly	1	19 Oct 54
MARTINDALE, William	1	23 Feb 54
* MASSEY, Robert	1	23 Feb 54
MATHEWS, Mary	1	5 Mar 47
MATTHEWS, Mary	1	26 May 48
MAUDLIN, Barnabas	1	9 Nov 54
MEAD, Charles L.	1	24 Aug 54
MEAD, John	1	2 Jan 46
MEIXELL, John	1	13 Jun 50
MELLING, Andrew	1	19 Jun 51
MEREDITH, Jehu	1	14 May 47
MERRITT, William P.	1	31 Mar 53
MESSNER, Evelyn Colfax	1	25 Nov 52
METZGAR, Enock	1	27 Jul 54
METZGER, Jacob	1	26 Feb 47
MILLER, Amos	1	23 Apr 47
MILLER, Andrew	1	7 Jan 48
MILLER, Mrs. Barbia	2	9 Jun 38
MILLER, Elizabeth	1	23 Apr 47
MILLER, Frank	1	18 Aug 53
MILLER, Henry	1	8 Jan 52
MILLER, James Henry	1	19 Jun 51
MILLER, Jonas	2	29 Sep 38
MILLER, Mary Ellen	1	20 Nov 47
MILLER, Samuel M.	2	20 Oct 38
MILLIKAN, Dr. Jesse	1	28 Mar 50
MILLIKAN, Mrs. Sarah	1	22 Jan 46
MILLIS, Amanda	2	24 Jul 38
MILLIS, Mrs. Emeline	1	19 Sep 50
MILLS (?), Amanda	2	24 Jul 38
MITCHELL, William B.	1	31 Mar 48
MONSON, Albert	1	19 Dec 50
MONSON, Albert	1	25 Mar 52
MOORE, William H.	1	11 Sep 51
MONTGOMERY, William	1	9 Nov 54
MOREY, Charles	1	10 Oct 50
MORGAN, Mary Agnes	1	31 Aug 54
MORRELL, Charles H. Esq.	2	3 Feb 38
MORRELL, Thomas	1	19 May 53
MORRIS, Aaron P.	2	9 Sep 37
MORTON, George W.	1	23 Jun 53
MULLIGAN, Patrick	1	27 Nov 51
NANAUQUAY, (Murdered)	4	13 Jun 32
NELSON, Albert D.	1	10 May 49
NEWELL, John C.	1	24 Apr 51
NEWTON, Henry	1	9 Feb 54
NEWTON, Joseph	1	26 Nov 47
NEWTON, Willard Martin	1	20 Oct 53
NORRIS, Lusaby	1	7 Apr 48
* NUNNELLY, Samuel P.	1	24 Jun 52
PALMER, John Thomas	1	31 Mar 53
PALMER, Mary Elizabeth	1	1 Mar 49
PALMER, Rev. Truman Fayette	1	23 Jan 51
PARKINSON, Mrs. Sophia W.	1	8 Jan 52
PATTESON, Mary A.	1	27 Feb 46
PATTESON, Mary A.	1	6 Mar 46
PATTINGALE, Daniel	2	25 Nov 37
PATTINGALE, Daniel	2	9 Dec 37
PAYNE, John W.	1	20 Feb 46
PAYNE, William E. (Salem, MA)	2	1 Sep 38
PEMBROKE, James	2	6 Oct 38
PERKINS, Mrs. Lucy	1	1 Apr 52
PETTIT, Amos	2	1 Sep 38
PHILLIPS, Anthony	1	4 Sep 46
PICKETT, Mary	1	27 Feb 46
PICKETT, Mary Evelyn	1	24 Mar 53
PICKETT, Mrs. Sarah	1	3 Apr 51
PIERT, J. S.	2	19 May 38
PILSON, Hugh	1	19 Sep 45
PIPER, John S.	1	1 Feb 49
POLK, William	1	27 Jun 50
POMEROY, Grove Judge	1	9 Nov 54
POMEROY, Mary	1	27 Oct 53
PRESTNA, John	1	23 Feb 54
PRESTON, Mrs. Keziah Brown	1	18 Mar 52
PROFFIT, George H.	1	17 Sep 47
PRUNIER, Bosile	4	6 Jun 32
REAMER, Mrs. Rebecca	1	16 Aug 49
REASONER, Garret S.	1	11 Apr 50
RECTOR, Mark	1	4 May 54
REED, Robert	1	9 Nov 54
REEVES, Obadiah	1	5 Oct 54
REPLOGLE, Jacob	1	3 Jul 46
RESTORICK, Samuel	1	29 Mar 49
RHODES, Flora	1	10 Mar 53
RHONE, Benjamin	1	21 Jun 49
RICHARDSON, Charles A.	1	31 Dec 47
RICHARDSON, David	1	13 Jun 50
RIGGIN, William Roderick	1	9 Nov 54
RING, Jefferson	1	20 Mar 46
RITTER, Samuel	2	26 May 38
RITTINGER, Female	1	10 Nov 53
ROCHE, Dr. Matthew	1	13 Mar 51
ROCKHILL, (child)	2	4 Nov 37
ROCKHILL, William	2	26 Apr 41
ROCKHILL, William	1	18 Oct 49
RODEBAUGH, Susannah	1	31 Aug 48
ROE, Charles	2	1 Sep 38
ROE, Elijah	1	25 Dec 51
ROE, Ella Sophia	1	7 Apr 53
ROGERS, Jonathan	1	1 May 46
ROHRER, David	1	1 May 46
ROHRER, John	1	12 Sep 45
ROHRER, Mrs. Joseph	2	5 Mar 41
ROHRER, Joseph Sr.	1	28 Nov 45
ROLLER, John	1	19 Jan 54
ROOF, David	3	14 Nov 31
ROOT, Syverius	1	23 Apr 47
ROSE, Nathan	1	1 Dec 53
ROSE, Rhoda	1	1 Dec 53
ROSE, Oliver	2	28 Jul 38
RUNYAN, Henry	1	2 Nov 53
RUPLE, John	1	23 Jun 54
RUSH, Isaiah	1	23 Feb 54
RUSH, Israel H.	2	4 Nov 37
RUSH, Leonard R.	1	14 Nov 45
RUSH, Dr. Mahlon	1	6 Jun 50
RUSSEL, Elisha	1	10 Oct 50
RUSSELL, Mrs. Caroline C.	2	15 Sep 38
RUSSELL, Mrs. Jacob (?)	1	23 Feb 54
RUSSELL, Mrs. Isaac R.	2	15 Sep 38
SADD, Catherine M.	1	12 Jun 51
SALVAGE, Orion	1	19 Jul 49
SAMPLE, Frederick	1	18 Mar 52
SAMPLE, John	1	16 Oct 46
SANCOMB, Edwin	1	19 Jun 54
SCHAEFER, Mary Ann	1	19 Sep 45
SCHELL, Anna Marie	1	16 Apr 47
SCHNIERLE, Fred	2	19 May 38
SCOTT, David (sentenced)	2	19 May 38

Name		Date
SCOTT, William	1	20 Oct 53
SEARLE, Robert	1	21 Nov 45
SEEBER, Rev. Safrenus	1	27 Mar 51
SEIGFREID, Mrs. Mary S.	1	17 Oct 50
SHANK, Infant son	1	19 Feb 52
SHANK, Mrs. Mary Ann	1	2 Jan 51
SHEFFIELD, Dr. E. S.	1	2 Apr 47
SHEFFIELD, Dr. Eliphalet S.	1	27 Jun 50
SHEFFIELD, Eliphalet S.	1	12 Oct 48
SHERMAN, Alvin B.	2	9 Dec 31
SHERMAN, John M.	1	16 Jul 46
SHORT, Theophilas	1	20 Mar 40
SHURTER, Mrs. Sarah	1	10 Aug 54
SIMONTON, Samuel	1	21 Nov 50
SINGER, Henry	1	23 Jun 48
SISSON, William	1	22 Feb 49
SLOCUM, John	1	17 Apr 51
SMITH, Alfred	2	19 May 38
SMITH, Miss Christena	3	14 Mar 32
SMITH, George	1	11 Sep 51
SMITH, Jane	1	12 Sep 45
SMITH, Jacob	1	5 Jun 51
SMITH, Loly Ann	1	1 Sep 53
SMITH, Wilfred	1	6 Jan 53
SNIDER, Henry	1	16 Jan 51
SNODGRASS, James	1	19 Aug 52
SNURE, Henry	1	19 Aug 52
SPAULDING, T. Elder	2	11 Aug 38
SPONSLER, Abraham	2	9 Dec 37
SOPER, Reuben	1	21 Oct 52
STAILEY, Sarah	1	19 Nov 47
STANFIELD, George W. (infant)	4	15 Sep 32
STANFIELD, John V.	2	18 Nov 37
STAPLES, Austin	1	3 Aug 54
STAPLES, Mrs. Harriet	1	26 Jul 54
STAVES, Francis	2	24 Jul 38
STEEDMAN, Col. C. J.	2	19 May 38
STILES, Dr. John	1	27 Nov 50
STILES, Mrs. Mary Ann	1	25 Jul 50
STONE, Elizabeth Noble	1	25 Nov 52
STOVER, Catharine	1	12 Feb 47
STOVER, Emmeline Virginia	1	24 Sep 47
STOVER, Mrs. Nancy	1	31 Dec 47
STOVER, William R.	1	7 Aug 46
STUART, Mrs. Elizabeth	1	17 Aug 54
STUDYBAKER, Samuel	1	30 Jan 46
SUDDARTH, Abraham	1	28 Sep 48
SULLIVAN, John	1	21 Jun 49
SUMPTION, Charles	2	12 Apr 49
SUMPTION, George	1	20 Aug 47
SUTHERLAND, Ellen Amelia	1	4 Nov 52
TATMAN, Mrs. Harriet	1	10 Jun 52
TAYLOR, Asa	2	19 May 38
TAYLOR, Mrs. Jane	1	26 May 53
TAYLOR, Willias H.	1	13 May 52
TERRILL, J. Morris	1	13 Apr 54
TERRILL, Nathaniel B.	1	27 Feb 51
THOMAS, Mrs. Emma B.	1	28 Dec 54
THOMPKINS, William Sanford	2	9 Dec 37
THOMPSON, Davis	2	16 Oct 40
THOMPSON, John R.	1	28 Sep 48
THOMPSON, John R.	1	10 Nov 53
THOMPSON, Mrs. John R.	2	6 Jan 38
THOMPSON, Lewis G.	1	25 Jun 47
THOMPSON, William B.	2	4 Aug 38
THORP, Mrs. Phebe	1	30 Mar 54
THURBER, John D.	1	17 Apr 46
TOMPKINS, Henry (3 year old)	2	7 Oct 37
TOWLE, Maria	1	30 Jul 47
TRUE, Henry Martyn	1	17 Sep 47
TUTT, Mary Howard		
USHER, Perry	1	17 Jun 52
VALENTINE, Theodore	1	31 Dec 47
VANDEN BOSCH, John W.	1	25 Jul 50
VANSTEIN, Albert	1	10 Oct 50
VESEY, Mrs. Mahala	1	18 Oct 49
WADE, Robert	1	19 Jun 51
WAGGONER, Charles Traver	1	21 Nov 50
WAGNER, Andrew	1	16 Oct 54
WALKER, Charles	1	28 Apr 48
WALL, John	1	13 Mar 51
WALL, William	1	16 Jan 51
WALLACE, Gibson	1	12 Oct 48
WALLACE, James H.	2	9 Jun 38
WARD, James Edwin	1	12 Jun 46
WARD, Mrs. Mary Ann	1	26 Sep 50
WARD, Parsons Pratt	1	17 Sep 47
WARREN, Daniel	2	30 Dec 37
WARREN, David	2	30 Dec 37
WARREN, Miss Sarah	1	8 Oct 47
WATKINS, William	1	2 May 53
WEAVER, William	1	7 Aug 46
WEBSTER, Mrs. Elizabeth	1	23 Jan 51
WENGER, Mrs. Christian	1	20 Feb 51
WESSKLS (?), Rebecca	1	19 Jul 49
WESTERVELT, James	1	1 Oct 47
WHARTON, Jonathan	2	6 Oct 38
WHARTON, Joshua	1	31 Aug 54
WHARTON, Samuel B.	1	
WHEELER, Mr. (mate on Ship)	1	28 Apr 48
WILDER, Asa	1	15 Jul 52
WILLIAMS, Florence Helen	1	12 Jul 49
WILLIAMS, John	1	17 Oct 45
WILLIAMS, Morton	1	23 Oct 51
WILLIAMS, Smith estate notice	2	4 Nov 37
WILLOUGHBY, Sarah H.	1	16 Apr 47
WILLS, Asahel	1	24 Sep 47
WILLS, Levi	1	7 Nov 50
WILSON, Florence	1	24 Jul 51
WILSON, Matthew	2	19 May 38
WITTER, Emeline	1	23 Nov 54
WITTER, Jacob	1	6 Mar 51
WITTER, Lucinda	1	14 Oct 52
WITTER, Phillip	1	16 Nov 54
WITTER, Phoebe Jane	1	24 Jun 52
WOODHULL, Catalina Delamater	1	24 Mar 53
WOODWARD, William L.	1	27 Dec 49
WOOLMAN, Eber	1	17 Mar 48
WRIGHT, (Murdered)	1	5 May 53
WRIGHT, Mary (Mrs. William)	1	20 Jun 50
WRIGHT, Silas	1	3 Sep 47
WYLLYS, Chas.	1	26 Jul 49
ZIGLER, James L.	1	10 Mar 48
ZIGLER, Michael	1	7 Apr 48
ZIMER, Sebastian	1	4 Jan 49
* MATTHEWS, Leonora	1	27 Feb 51
* NYE, Ludlow	1	20 Feb 46

HUNTINGTON COUNTY MARRIAGES, 1837-1852

Compiled from microfilm copy of Book I, Huntington County Marriage Records, 1837-44, and pages 1-152 of Book II, 1844-1859. The latter volume is not an original record, but was compiled from the original by order of the court in 1968.

Ackerman, Jacob - Elizabeth Saul   11-22-1849
Adams, Daniel - Juliann Hart   10- 7-1847
Allen, William C. - Mary Wilson   2-17-1843
Allman, Tipton - Jane Klingel   8-26-1849
Alsop, John - Elizabeth Ann Baumhart
                                   6-10-1847
Ambur, William - Martha Barnett   12-15-1842
Anderson, J. L. - Sarah J. Goddin   7- 3-1851
Angel, Artamus W. - Mary A. Leach   5-23-1852
Anthony, Charles - Mary Chernut   6-13-1839
Arick (or Erick), James C. - Ruth I. Vohres
                                   9-26-1850
Armstrong, Abraham - Mahala Johnson 1-28-1846
Aumock, Josiah - Margaret Wolf   4- 5-1849
Ayres, Porter - Catherine Kenower 10- 1-1844
Back, John A. - Mary Ann Swaim   4-22-1841
Bagley, Chester P. - Elizabeth M. Thompson
                                   5-14-1846
Bagley, Leonard C. - Mary Ann Thompson
                                   1-19-1849
Bair, Peter - Eliza Kimble   12- 5-1848
Baker, Frederick - Rosannah Earhart
                                   10- 5-1852
Baker, Jacob R. - Sarah Ann Simonton
                                   8-24-1848
Ball, David - Sophia V. Farry   2-17-1838
Balts, Marmaduke - Selinda Twining 2- 9-1845
Bane, William J. - Elizabeth C. Hedrick
                                   12- 4-1849
Barker, Isaac - Hannah Fisher lic. 10-26-1850
Barnes, Amos - Nancy Housman lic.   1-13-1848
Barnet, Jacob - Martha A. Powell   6-27-1839
Barnett, William - Sarah Louiza Purviance
                                   12-29-1838
Barnhart, George - Ann Mary Shively
                                   10- 5-1851
Barrick, Eli - Elizabeth Williamson
                                   8-13-1851
Beal, William - Catharine Sprinkle 7-21-1852
Beam, Daniel - Sarah Jain Coffield 4-14-1844
Beard, Andrew - Susana Matilda Platter
                                   1-25-1844
Beard, George - Mary Ann Dalrymple 1-24-1847
Beard, John - Melissa Ann Buse lic. 8-19-1848
Beard, Joshua - Susanah Dalrimple
                   lic.   10-18-1848
Beasly, William - Amy Ann Young   3- 7-1850
Beaver, Samuel - Mary Wilhelm   8- 1-1850
Belt, Jesse W. - Lucinda Crandal   1-19-1845
Belt, John W. - Hannah Beauchamp   2-12-1852
Benjamin, John - Rachel Hight   9- 7-1846
Bennett, Isaac - Mary Fullhart   9-14-1843
Bennett, William - Eliza Phillips
                   lic.   11-15-1840
Binkley, Abraham - Leahann Emily
                   lic.   2- 8-1845
Blair, James A. - Mary I. or J. Helton
                   lic.   10- 2-1851
Blair, Joseph - Mary Stanton   9- 4-1845
Blair, Lot - Caroline Fleming   10- 3-1839
Blair, Thomas - Cynthia Irwin   2- 5-1843
Blount, Albert S. - Elizabeth Campbell
                                   4-10-1845
Blunt, Joseph A. - Electa Friend   4-23-1841
Bodine, Thomas S. - Elizabeth Parke
                                   10-25-1849
Bond, Joshua - Mary Walton   9- 2-1850

Boon, Joseph - Elizabeth Hudson   6- 6-1850
Bower, Benjamin - Elizabeth Hayward 3-12-1846
Bower, Joseph - Mary Knop   10-18-1849
Bowin, Charles F. - Marshia H. Murray
                                   3- 7-1852
Boxell, James - Jane Shuman   11-18-1848
Boylan, Daniel - Elizabeth Monch   11- 9-1843
Boyle, Lawrence - Jain Dennaly (or Temalye)
                   lic.   7-25-1845
Boyle, Patrick - Elizabeth Ellingham
                                   8- 3-1851
Branstrater, James - Sarah Slone   9-17-1848
Brown, Henry - Sarah Ann Pomray   11- 7-1846
Brown, John - Julia Harden lic.   7- 1-1848
Brown, Robert B. - Ruth B. Brown   7- 7-1842
Brownlee, James - Lydia Ann Parker
                   lic.   12- 2-1850
Brubaker, Noah - Mary Ann Awmock   8-15-1852
Bruce, George W. - Cendrilla Biniger
                                   4-14-1847
Bruss, Simon - Susanah Wintrade   5-17-1846
Buck, William - Rebecca Albertson   11- 1-1852
Burgess, William - Mary McElen (?)   2-20-1839
Burket, Absalom - Susanna Detrow   5- 3-1850
Buzzard, George - Mary Amanda Cline 7-25-1844
Buzzard, Henry - Elison Purviance   1-14-1845
Buzzard, John - Sabina Denton lic. 2-18-1850
Cain, Alonzo D. - Catharine C. McClelland
                                   7-15-1849
Cain, Joseph - Mary Frederick   8-17-1852
Campbell, John D. - Mary Fisher   7-18-1839
Carmony, William - Rosannah Myres   1-29-1852
Carpenter, George W. - Elizabeth Stroup
                                   5-21-1846
Cass, James - Jain Maddock   2- 4-1846
Cass, John - Christina Hartman   11- 3-1848
Caylor, Michael -   lic.   4-24-1849
Cecil, John - Lydia Waggoner   12- 1-1849
Cecil, Joseph - Eliza Denton lic.   3- 3-1849
Cecil, William - Dillard Denton   2-12-1852
Chadwick, Michael Richard - Caroline Gadden
                   lic.   12-14-1848
Chambers, Isaac - Ruth Jane Wells   11- 3-1850
Chany (or Chary), David - Martha Ann Wood
                                   8- 8-1847
Chapson, William - Ruth C. Swaim   1-29-1852
Charles, David - Sidney Ann Coon
                   lic.   10-21-1851
Chenoweth, Joel - Elizabeth Leviston
                                   10-14-1847
Chenoweth, Hezekiah - Sarah E. Parker
                                   5- 9-1847
Chrisman, James C. - Sarah Jane Priddy
                                   1-30-1851
Churchill, Nelson - Maria Epply   3-21-1852
Clark, William - Artamasy Fox   12- 1-1841
Clements, Samuel I. - Martha Bennett
                   Pinkerton   8-23-1850
Clinginpeel, John - Martha Jane Purviance
                                   1- 2-1851
Clone (?), Henry S. - Amanda Vandike
                                   12-30-1849
Cloud, Noah - Elizabeth Little (or Litler)
                                   2-20-1851
Coffee, David - Sarah Little lic.12-31-1850
Coffield, Charles W. - Emily Parker
                                   12-11-1852
Coffroth, John Randolph - Mary E. Slack
                                   4-13-1852

Cole, Eri - Mary Slagal   5- 2-1841
Cole (or Cale?), Eri - Jane McCarty 11-22-1850
Coll, William - Cornelia Harris   8- 7-1843
Collins, Moses - Eliza Ann Bowman   12-30-1852
Collins, William R. - Ann McClure   11- 3-1846
Collins, William S. - Lucinda McQuery (?)
                                           2- 7-1849
Colter, Lawrence - Elizabeth Boyle   9-23-1849
Columbia, David (or Dana) - Elia Ward
                                           5- 7-1840
Cook, John - Ann Dunman   5-27-1847
Cook, William - Elizabeth Cox   2- 2-1845
Coon, George W. - Elizabeth Herrald 6-11-1848
Cooper, Jonathan - Mahala J. Dial   9-29-1850
Copenhafer, Martin - Elizabeth Crull
                                          11-18-1849
Corbett, William - Elizabeth Cox   10-22-1850
Cox, Jacob - Sarah McFaren   10- 6-1850
Crago, John S. - Sarah Stephens   11-18-1841
Craig, Joseph - Emily Johnson   4- 4-1852
Crakes, Richard - Margaretta Holt   10-26-1848
Crakes, Robert - Catherine Hunt   9- 3-1846
Crakes, Watson M. - Eliza W. Hambleton
                                           6- 9-1849
Crandal, Samuel F. - Dorris Hayward 10-15-1850
Crane, Thomas B. - Amanda Actordyke
           lic.   8-11-1852
Crapo, Joseph - Margaret Valacut lic.5- 2-1845
Crawford, Andrew I. - Mary Anne Hale 1-31-1850
Croningon, Marchin - Lydia A. Parker 4-29-1851
Crum, Richard - Manerva Ford   10-30-1845
Custance, James B. - Huldah Ann Barnes
                                           3-21-1850
Cutter, Josiah C. - Elizabeth H. Purviance
                                           5-15-1851
Danome (?), Derias C. - Eliza Ann Morrison
                                           1-28-1847
Davis, Jesse - Jane Orton   8-12-1849
Davis, Lewis - Sarah Ann Sornus (?) 10-13-1846
Deckard, Jacob - Margaret Westover   4-30-1843
Decker, Henry E. - Martha Shookman   10-28-1849
Deems, Darius - Nancy Jane King   3-21-1852
DeLong, Alexander W. - Elizabeth Morgan
                                           5-23-1850
Delvin, William - Susan Sellars   8- 3-1837
Delvin, William - Rachel S. Newcomb 6-20-1850
Denand, James - Catharine Cook lic. 8- 4-1848
Dening (Denand), Humphrey - Elizabeth Winten
                                           9-24-1840
Dening (Denand), Umphre - Ruth Wright
                                           2-28-1846
Dening (Denand), William - Mary Ann Ketner
                                           2-17-1850
Denton, Daniel S. - Nancy Herrald   5-27-1847
Denton, William - Elizabeth Stevens 12-30-1848
Detrow, John - Catharine Miller   12-23-1849
Dillon, Thomas E. - Mahala Whitestine
                                           4-18-1847
Dimius, Levi - Sophia Alerton   12-20-1849
Dolon, Lewis - Barbary Nair (or Nain)
                                          10-21-1849
Donaldson, James - Lucinda Groves   11- 4-1847
Dougherty, Henry - Mariah Jane Miller
                                           9-13-1846
Dougherty, Salamon - Harriet Bazel
                                      3[12]-26-1844
Dungan (?), Josiah - Henrietta Belt 12-27-1849
Dunigan, Mathim - Hannah Barker   12-19-1852
Duper, Francis - Sarah Chaddin   12- 8-1841
Dwiggins, John - Ellen McGinnis   3- 3-1850
Dyel, Jehu - Matilda Slusser   6-23-1849
Eddy, William M. - Ellenor Rouch   8-24-1837
Edgar, Atkinson - Jain Mounsey   1-15-1846

Edwards, Jesse - Rebecca Jeffrey   12-21-1848
Elkins, John H. - Martha Ann Chaney
                                           9-21-1852
Ellingham, Charles - Hannah Scotten 8- 1-1847
Emely (Emley?), Anthony - Evaline Herendon
                                           6-18-1843
Emery, John - Sarah Ann Crandal   8-31-1852
Endsley, Abraham - Mary Ann Hedrick10-16-1845
Enyard, Levi - Elsa A. Powel   6- 9-1842
Enyart, Silas - Sarah Retner (?)   6-24-1847
Ervin, John - Mahala Payton   8- 9-1849
Evins, George W. H. - Elizabeth M. Mooler
              lic.   9-10-1844
Ewart, Joseph E. B. - Sarah Eliz. Mitchel
                                          11-14-1852
Ewart, Lemuel - Sarah Flemming   11-22-1848
Fernandez, Joachum - Hannah Rathman
                                          11-14-1846
Fidler, Curtis - Mary Maddock   10-13-1840
Filson, Jeremiah E. - Nancy D. Long 2-21-1850
Fisher, John - Susannah Gurly   1- 1-1845
Fisher, John - Phebe Irwin lic.   9- 9-1849
Fisher, John D. - Lucinda Rinerson 12-28-1845
Fisher, Samuel - Elizabeth Beauchamp
                                          12-25-1845
Fisher, Samuel - Mary Ann Rauch   2-19-1850
Fisher, Simon - Emeletta Cummons   2-27-1842
Fisher, Simon - Mary Miller   2- 3-1850
Fisher, Thomas - Susannah Dwiggins 12-12-1844
Ford, William - Precilla Casey   10-21-1841
Foreman, Andrew - Lucinda Mitchel   7-23-1846
Foust, Jacob - Ruth Wilson   9- 8-1851
Fout Peter - Jarusha Durend (Denand?)
                                           3-31-1839
Fraim, Abner D. - Nancy Mitchell   2-18-1847
              lic.   [1848]
France (Fraim?), Simon W. - Barbara Newman
                                           3-27-1849
Free, Daniel - Mary McCarty   5-25-1845
Freel, James - Mary Morton   8-22-1852
Freel, Stephen - Sarah Ann Bellows   7-11-1852
Friend, Harvey - Jain Hollowell   9-28-1843
Fulhart, Jacob - Nancy Hilderbrand   3-26-1840
Fullhart, Nicholas - Arminta Ann Moore
                                           7- 4-1852
Fulton, John - Sarah Clayton   2-29-1852
Galier (?), James - Martha Bales   11-14-1839
Gamble, John G. - Prithena O. Robbins
                                           8-14-1852
Gamble, Samuel - Wethra Ann Robbins
                                          12-25-1852
Gamble, Shedrick - Lydia Stoniker
              lic.   12- 4-1852
Gay, Zebulon - Maryan Miller   6-16-1840
Gebo, Charles - Adaline Reame   7-28-1847
Gebo (?), Lewis Guzua (?) - Harriet Peters
                                           6- 6-1839
Gephart, Lewis - Sarah Miller   7-12-1849
Gettys, William - Sarah Eliz.Bevington
                                          10-20-1850
Gilman, John B. - Mary Eliz. Clem   12-27-1851
Good, Joseph F. - Frithena Carel   10- 3-1851
Goodson, Bennett - Margaret Sinnitt 7-19-1850
Griffith, Chilion B. - Sarah Ann Eddinfield
                                           4- 3-1851
Griffith, David - Orpha Cole   9-12-1841
Groves, Emanuel G. - Margaret Ann Griffith
                                           5- 6-1849
Guire, David - Harriet Ann Senate (Sinnit?)
                                           8-17-1851
Guthery, John - Castary Wallace
              lic.   10-23-1847
Hacker, Silas C. - Rebecca Slagle   11-29-1851

Haffer, Abraham - Margaret Thomas   8-29-1852
Hale, George - Mary Ann Brooks lic.   4- 6-1849
Hall, Whitson - Mary Jane Morrison   4-26-1848
Hallcom, Benjamin - Caroline Kitner   8-29-1851
Halsted, Lewis I. - Mary Ann Harter   6- 1-1848
Hannar, John - Martha Fugy   1- 2-1851
Harker, Nathaniel W. - Sarah Ann Smith
                                      2-13-1851
Harrell, Jesse D. - Mary D. Webb   10-19-1848
Harrison, William - Sarah Jane Webb   7- 9-1846
Hartman, John - Catherine Creigh   8-15-1851
Haugh, Franklin - Lydia Martin   8- 7-1842
Haughtelling, Stephen - Clarissa Cummings
                                      8-10-1848
Hawkins, Uriah P. - Martha Ellen Price
                                      9-28-1851
Hayward, George - Mary Hall   1-14-1847
Heckkle, David - Elizabeth Boyer   1- 1-1851
Hefner, Frederick - Nancy Cook   6-23-1839
Hefner, Isaac - Martha A. Clanahan   1-24-1847
Hefner, Peter - Sarah Hawkins lic.   10-10-1851
Heiny, David - Julia Ann Slagle   4- 8-1847
Heiny, John H. - Mary Boyd   4-15-1852
Helser, David - Elizabeth Delvin   10-20-1850
Henderson, James C. - Elizabeth Barnes
                                      6-31-1849
Henderson, Thomas - Sofiah Harris
                       lic.   11-29-1851
Hinckle, Samuel - Delila Hull   9-28-1848
Holler, Augustus - Nancy Luper   7-26-1846
Hoover, Benjamin - Margaret Newman   5- 4-1845
Hoover, Henry - Elizabeth McRinny   10-17-1843
Hoover, Jacob - Mary Dinius   10- 4-1849
Hoover, Jonas - Nancy Ann Jones   12-25-1842
Housel (Houser?), Jacob - Christina Sellers
                       lic.   7- 5-1851
Houser, Francis - Elizabeth Zahn   11- 2-1846
Houser, Thomas - Elizabeth Beal   4-19-1852
Howel, Nathan P. - Elinor Fry lic.   4-10-1850
Howenstein, John - Amanda Briant (?) 12-18-1849
Hubbell, Alfred A. - Rosamond E. Dunton
                                      9-24-1850
Hughs, James O. - Frances Barnes   12-13-1851
Humes, Thomas - Sarah Bane   5- 3-1844
Hunt, Horace - Mary E. Jones   2-12-1838
Huston, William - Elizabeth McGinnis 2-13-1851
Irwin, Cornelius N. - Elizabeth Swain
                                      8-31-1848
Irwin, George S. - Ruth Stanton   10- 6-1845
Irwin, John L. - May Edgar   4- 7-1850
Irwin, Lewis - Anabel Black   9- 7-1848
Irwin, Moses - Susannah Herald lic.   9-15-1852
Irwin, Robert Y. - Angeline A. Alexander
                                      5-14-1846
Irwin, Samuel - Mary Carpenter   6- 6-1844
Jackson, Amos - Clarissa Baker lic.   1-22-1849
Jessup, Jehial - Nancy Sutton   7- 8-1852
Jester, John - Adaline Harry   7-18-1847
Johnson, Henry - Mary Freel   8-18-1845
Johnson, Henry - Margaretta Prince
                       lic.   1- 6-1848
Johnson, Henry - Margaretta Harris
                       lic.   10-20-1851
Jones, John - Elizabeth Linn   9-16-1852
Jones, Silas - Eliza Jane Dillon   11-13-1840
Jones, Smith - Emphema Gibson   3-28-1850
Jones, William - Margaret S. Provines
                                      8-20-1850
Kanff, Christian - Caroline Saal   11-23-1850
Kauss (?), Jacob - Mary Ann Yanger   8-19-1847
Kennedy, A. E. - Elizabeth Barnhart   5-31-1849
Kenower, Adam Q. - Ann Mariah Taylor 9-28-1851

Kenower, John - Lucy H. Montgomery 3-17-1842
Kenower, John - Flarancis M. Bineger
                                    4-13-1847
Kenower, John - Sarah Purviance   4-15-1851
Ketring, Adam - Elizabeth Weber   6-29-1848
Klingle, Jonathan - Elizabeth Jett 10-18-1850
Knose (?), Harmon - Catharine Ritter
                                    4-12-1850
Koffman (?), Godfrey - Susannah Windermuth
                                    2-12-1852
Lafontaine, Lewis - Mary Birdan (or Burden)
                                    5-22-1847
Lafountain, Francois - Catharine Richardville
                       lic.   5- 3-1843
Lamson, Noah S. - Margaret Lewis   4-12-1846
Larabee, Stephen M. - Catharine E. Yahne
                                    11- 4-1852
Large, John R. - Margaret Park   5-20-1852
Larh, Philip - Mary Knoblock   6-17-1851
Lassell, Francis - Catherine Lafontain
                                    9-26-1848
Lauduback, Daniel - Maria Alexander 2-10-1850
Laughlar, John - Lydia M. Johnson   4-29-1841
Laughridge, Wilson B. - Eliza Ann McCleland
                                    6-10-1845
Lavery, A. M. - Ann Dewit   10-22-1849
Lawler, Patrick - Mary Ann Johnson 9- 8-1850
Laymon, John - Nancy Irwin   10- 7-1847
Lee, Adam U. - Sarah Long   10-12-1848
Leech, Jacob - Eliza A. Johnson lic. 7- 1-1849
Lefler, Henry - Sarah Ann Zent lic. 11-10-1849
Lefler, John - Barbara Zent   12-28-1848
Lent, Conrad - Mary Ackerman   10-11-1852
Leonard, Abner - Ruth Irvin   6-15-1841
Leonard, Richard - Catharine Grass 10-21-1848
Leonard, Thomas - Eliza Price (or Prine)
                                    9-17-1843
Leverton, George - Letticia Barker
                       lic.   11-12-1850
Leverton, James - Lucinda Mahoney   2- 4-1844
Lewis, Abel M. - Lavina Smith   1- 7-1849
Lewis, John - Catharine Dillon   5- 4-1845
Lewis, William H. D. - Celinda Swail
                                    12- 7-1851
Lickinteller, Jonathan - Hannah Wade
                                    1-25-1850
Lininger, William - Elizabeth Dishong
                                    2- 1-1852
Loegler (?), George - Louiza Shaffer
                                    4-30-1850
Luse, William P. - Jain Boles   1- 2-1844
McCallister, George - Rebecca Jain
                       Rittenhouse lic. 12-28-1848
McCindy (?), Henry - Elvira Brooks 12-23-1851
McClure, Alfred H. - Mary Wintrode 5- 2-1841
McDaniel, Alexander - Mariah Johnson
                                    3- 1-1846
McEawan, Samuel - Lucinda Jones   7- 5-1838
McGreve, Noah - Lydia Pribble   11-18-1840
McKachin, Daniel - May Barnhart   5-31-1849
McKinstry, Neil - Julia A. Davis
                       lic.   3-25-1851
McNamara, James - Abigail Gay   2-18-1841
McPherson, Jacob - Harriet Ann Dillon
                                    2-25-1841
McTaggart, John H. - Catharine E. Lewis
                                    12-13-1843
Maddux, Simon - Jane L. Wright   9- 6-1852
Madock, Jonathan - Hannah Tilberry 1- 4-1851
Mahony, Hugh - Ruth E. Johnson   4-16-1848
Mahony, Philip - Sarah Gurley   9- 1-1852
Manford, David - Sarah Jane Thomas 3-21-1852

Manning, Gabrial - Susan Delvin   6-15-1843
Maren, Elisha - Katharine Miller   8-19-1850
Marker, David - Catharine Yahne   7- 1-1852
Marks, William - Sarah Miller   7-17-1842
Marshall, James - Catharine Broombaugh
                              lic.   9- 8-1849
Marshall, Samuel G. - Levina Rittenhouse
                                         1- 1-1843
Masters, G. W. - Sarah Ann Gay   2-10-1838
May, Nehemiah - Catherine Davis lic. 9-27-1848
May, William - Louisa Jane Dodd   7-22-1852
Mendenhall, Joshua - Elizabeth Yougger
                                         5-24-1849
Miles, John - Mary Billetter   1-28-1851
Miller, Harrison - Elizabeth Jane Layman
                                         6-29-1841
Mills, James R. - Mariah Louise Alexander
                                         9-17-1846
Minor, Harvey - Mary Crakes   9-26-1850
Mitchel, Elijah - Elizabeth Ireland
                              lic.   3-26-1849
Mohn, John - Rebecca Truly (?)   6- 2-1850
Moore, Aaron - Mary Zent   12-15-1842
Moore, Daniel A. - Alsey Mariah Irwin
                                         8-10-1852
Moore, Samuel - Mary Ann Fox   5-24-1837
Moore, Samuel - Belinda Anderson   8-16-1846
Moreland, John J. - Phebe Ann Poynter
                                         9-19-1850
Morgan, Samuel T. - Waty Comstock   9-11-1851
Morris, Christopher C. - Nancy Alexander
                                         12-27-1845
Morrow, Elihu - Catharine Sutton
                              lic.   8- 2-1852
Morrow, Levi - Martha Barnes   9-16-1852
Moslander, Abraham - Deborah Youghgar (?)
                                         6- 2-1850
Mowrey, Nicholas - Julia Ann Ebersole
                              lic.   7-18-1851
Moyer (?), Jacob - Mary Ann Fogstater
                                         6-15-1851
Moyer, Jesse - Margaret M. Ritner   2-17-1850
Murray, Byron - Maria O. Thompson   2-27-1850
Myres, David S. - Sarah McCleland   9-19-1848
Newman, Jacob - Pauline Dimius   1-27-1850
Newman, John - Lydia Stanton   11- 9-1848
Newman, Samuel - Caroline Agar   6-17-1852
Nick, William S. - Abigail Herald
                              lic.   5- 5-1851
Ogdin, David O. L. - Mary Jain Ridgley
                              lic.   9-16-1848
Ossen, Henry - Susan Richardville   12- 8-1842
Owing, William D. - Elizabeth Large   8-30-1849
Pain, James - Mary Masters   3-21-1838
Palmer, Samuel - Elizabeth Snider   8- 3-1848
Palmer, Samuel - Ruth Ann Riggs   4-18-1852
Parker, Albert G. - Cynthia A. Swaim 9- 9-1851
Parker, John J. - Celia Jane Penland
                                         10- 5-1848
Parker, Silas H. - Mary C. Taylor
                              lic.   9-22-1851
Patty (Patly?), Lot P. - Sarah Jane Dortch
                                         8- 6-1846
Pelky, James - Josephine Shirly lic.11-15-1845
Pence, William H. - Susannah Whaley 7- 3-1849
Penn, James - Catherine Ware   2- 8-1849
Pershing, Samuel S. - Sarah Sellers 10-19-1839
Peyser (Paizer, Pizer), Isaac - Sarah Ann
                              Downs   5-14-1843
Peyser, William - Susanna Bolinger   8-15-1850
Piles, John - Sarah Ann Price   1- 7-1847
Poarman, John - Henrietta Brinaman   5- 9-1852

Poulson, William - Martha Jane Griffith
                                         3-16-1851
Powell, John - Catharine Hefner   4- 1-1852
Powell, Joshua - Mary Ann Fisher   2-19-1850
Powers, Jacob - Christina Smith   1- 3-1850
Presler, Jacob - Christine Waggoner 3-14-1841
Price, George - Elizabeth Croll   12-15-1844
Price, Veazey - Mahala Skinner   3- 1-1848
Priddy, James W. - Lydia E. Irwin   1-23-1845
Purviance, George I. - Elizabeth R. Clark
                                         12-19-1852
Purviance, Samuel H. - Elizabeth J. Montgomery
                                         6- 8-1843
Raney, Aaron C. - Hannah Jones   11-18-1847
Ream, Joseph - Mary Eliz. Brown   3- 6-1851
Ream, Samuel - Louisa Dial   10-25-1840
Reame, Jacob - Henrietta Crumrine 10-23-1845
Reame, Noah - Sarah Angeline Crumrine
                                         10-30-1845
Rebadue, Joseph - Matilda Reame   11-30-1845
Reed, William G. - Mary Ann Holmes 2- 2-1840
Rees, Thomas - Mary Ann Shupplehathan
                                         2- 6-1841
Reid, Isaak - Rosanah Sprowl   8-18-1842
Reneanon (Rinearson?), Hiram - Mary Snider
                                         7-18-1839
Reome (Reous), Francis - Jain McClure
                              lic.   11-21-1843
Richard, John Peter - Mary Mohn   9-10-1848
Richardville, Mitchel D. - Margaret Lafabyer
                              lic.   4-11-1842
Richardville, Thomas - Celestine Ocher
                                         7- 7-1851
Riddle, William - Anna Mary Provines
                                         8-21-1850
Ridgway, Job - Elmira McCampbell   3-20-1850
Riggs, Kinsey - Louisa Ann Taylor 5-25-1852
Rinearson, Allen - Sarah Ann Parrott
                                         12- 7-1850
Rinearson, Jedin - Elizabeth Barratt
                              lic.   7-26-1848
Rittenhouse, Aaron - Christeanne Zent
                              lic.   7-22-1848
Rittenhouse, Daniel - Mary A. Johnson
                                         10-10-1851
Rittenhouse, James B. - Mary Fox   10-22-1842
Rittenhouse, Nathan A. - Eliza Scott
                              lic.   9- 2-1848
Rittenhouse, Peter - Barbara A. Zent
                                         6- -1851
Rittenhouse, William - Martha Jane Gill
                                         8-10-1842
Roberts, Henry - Amelia Ann Coffield
                              lic.   6- 7-1849
Roberts, Samuel S. - Mary Eliz. Coon
                                         11-28-1847
Rosengrant, Charles - Phebe A. Joice
                                         8-19-1850
Rowe, John O. (?) - Priscilla Dewitt
                                         3- 7-1850
Ruggles, William - Mary Kesiah Purviance
                                         9-23-1847
Rugles, George - Christina Crull   1-21-1850
Runnels, Perry - Mary Blount   9- 9-1845
Ruth, Evan - Margaret Frankfather or
      Frankfadder in lic.   3-10-1850
Sawtell, Joseph C. - Sarah W. Darrow
                                         5- 2-1839
Saylar, Thomas - Elizabeth Zent   2-13-1847
Schlosser, Isaac K. - Caroline Klingel
                                         8-26-1849
Schoolcraft, John - Maria Adams   4-24-1839

207

Scott, Andrew - Catharine Binkley   9-26-1850
Scott, George W. - Elizabeth Harm   3- 7-1849
Scott, John S. - Jemima Chesnut   12-25-1851
Scott, Joseph - Susannah Griffith   1-23-1851
Seely, Joel P. - Malisa Twining   9- 6-1843
Sellers, John - Rebecca Marker   10-24-1850
Shaffer, Charles - Caroline Rugles   1-21-1850
Shearer, Homan S. - Sarah Russell   11- 6-1849
Shearer, Jacob - Jane Leverton   11-12-1847
Shearer, William - Nancy P. Betts   2-17-1846
Shelly, Lewis - Sarah Hefner   12-16-1841
Shideler, Amos - Elizabeth Heaston   1-29-1852
Shirley, Andrew - Josephine Carna   10-31-1839
Shirley (Shurly?), Lorenzo - Lauean Reaume
                                         4-21-1844
Shively, Jacob - Rebecca Herrin   4-27-1845
Shively, Jacob - Julia Ann Bruss   2-13-1851
Shively, Owen - Mary McClure   6-29-1848
Shookman, Eleazer S. - Martha Sulivan
                                         10-20-1844
Shuman, Washington - Angeline Harden 4-23-1849
Sibolt, John - Christina Weber   7- 3-1850
Sickapoos, Jacob - Elizabeth Dimmis (Dimius)
                        lic.   4- 6-1852
Siely (?), John L. - Tirzah M. Shearer
                                         11-26-1840
Siling, John A. - Hannah Cloud   6-15-1851
Sires, Thomas - Mary Jane Staley   8-29-1852
Slack, James R. - Ann P. Thompson   10- 5-1843
Slagle, William - Mary Jain Fisher   9-22-1844
Slusser, Daniel - Lydia Deal   9-23-1849
Slyter, Seth - Catharine Poff lic.   8- 1-1848
Smith, Amos - Rebecca Parke   6-24-1852
Smith, Ebenezer - Jane Wiley   3- 6-1851
Smith, James M. - Mary Howe   2-13-1851
Smith, George W. - Mary Fagstater   1- 1-1846
Smith, John - Catharine Roach   1-22-1842
Smith, Nathan - Susan McConner   4-16-1851
Smith, William - Julia Ann Koontz   2-16-1851
Snider, Henry - Margaret Morrow   1-30-1851
Snider, Lini - Sarah Ann Buzzard   4-19-1850
Sowers, Simon P. - Mariah Rittinhouse
                                         11-30-1841
Spacy, William H. - Margaret Stephen (Stepton)
                                         7-26-1846
Sparks, Jacob J. - Ellen Jane McCarty 1-25-1852
Sprinkle, Solomon H. - Maria H. Sinnitt
                        lic.   7-28-1851
Sprowl, Davidson - Mary Eliz. Beal   6-30-1852
Sprowl, James - Elizabeth Waggoner   12- 3-1840
Sprowl, Robert - Hanah Shaffer   8-21-1849
Sprowl, William M. - Mary Waggoner   12-22-1844
Stackhouse, Nathan - Iryliann Snider   2-23-1843
Stallsmith, John - Ann Boles   10-16-1848
Stentz, James F. - Mary I. Krebbs   9-21-1852
Stephens, James - Elizabeth Stephens 10- 3-1841
Stetcel, Philip - Susanah Dexhimer   4- 7-1846
Stewart, John - Sophia Wiley   11-14-1844
Stovich, Daniel - Margaret Drushal   6-15-1852
Stricker, John - Caroline Smith   5- 5-1849
Strickler, Henry - Regina D. Dericut   5-25-1850
Stroup, Reverend A. - Elizabeth Cupp   8-19-1852
Stults, Jacob - Margaret E. Best   3-25-1852
Sutton, Nathan - Katharine Hefner lic.
                                         11- 1-1851
Swaim, Samuel W. - Elizabeth P. Back 11-15-1841
Swartz, Henry - Wilhelmine Long   6-30-1850
Swazey, Samuel C. - Catharine Anderson
                                         3-30-1851
Swisher, Isaac - Mary Blair   1-16-1842
Tait, Hugh - Welthy Hayward   12- 3-1846
Taylor, James - Malissa Marshall   10-26-1845
Taylor, James - Mary Thrailkill   8- 3-1848

Taylor, Samuel - Mary Ann Irwin   9-30-1847
Thompson, Ebenazer - Permelia Blair 3-12-1845
Thompson, Ezra - Jain Blair   9- 2-1845
Thompson, Franklin - Mary Skinner   5-12-1850
Thompson, George S. - Lydia Helton   8-10-1851
Thompson, James H. - Mary Ann Hollowell
                                         2-22-1844
Thompson, John H., Jr. - Lucretia Prible
                        lic. 12-31-1852
Thompson, Robert - Mary I. Campbell 4- 3-1851
Thompson, William - Elizabeth Klemm 3- 3-1850
Trickler, John - Elizabeth Lahr   8-20-1842
Trotter (?), Jonathan B. - Nancy Shooman
                                         9-29-1850
Trout, Andrew L (or J.), - Elizabeth Shult
                                         4-25-1852
Trovinger, Amos - Hannah Freel   6-18-1848
Trovinger, David - Mary Jane Freel 6-22-1851
Trovinger, Hiram - Sarah A. Freel 11-18-1852
Turny, David - Abigail Mann lic.   2-20-1848
Twining, Dewit C. - Susanah Hamilton
                                         9-23-1848
Valecat, Peter - Margaret Collins
                        lic.   10-16-1844
Vanantwerp, Lewis W. - Rebecca Anderson
                                         11- 2-1852
Vanbuker, Lorenzo - Eliza Jane Pense
                                         11-19-1848
Waggoner, John - Armind Vandyke   9-21-1848
Waggoner, Joseph - Margaret Hildebrand
                                         1-27-1842
Walker, James - Jane Olvin   3-22-1852
Walker, John B. - Margaret D. Smith 4-29-1847
Warner, Luzon - Cintha Crandal   12-15-1850
Warner, William - Sarah Klingle   5-18-1851
Washburn, Levi - Ellin Terry   6-27-1846
Waters, Jonathan - Margaret Williams
                        lic.   3-22-1851
Watson, Joseph - Sophida Masters   4-10-1842
Weaver, Joseph - Margaret Snider
                        lic. 10-31-1851
Webb, James - Cynthia Ann Freeman 9- 7-1852
Weber, Michael - Barbary Smith   6-30-1850
Wenrick, Benjamin - Martha Jane Stewart
                        lic.   4-21-1848
Whitestine, David - Julia Ann Delvin
                                         3- 4-1848
Whitestine, James - Lucinda Campbell
                        lic.   10-28-1848
Whitestine, William - Martha Herrin 4-27-1845
Whitman (Whitmore?), Edwin - Harriet Ream
                                         4-23-1848
Whitmer, Ferdinand - Magdaline Stedsal
                                         7-28-1850
Wickum, Thomas - Isabella Mackie   12-31-1846
Wiley, Caleb - Elizabeth L. Sprowl
he of Preble Co., Ohio   8-16-1838
Wiley, Joseph, Jr. - Mary Jain Riggs
                                         1- 1-1852
Wiley, William - Nancy Laymon   2-10-1852
Wilkerson, William M. - Frances Thompson
                                         2-24-1852
Williams, Thomas R. - Mary A. Best 4-27-1848
Wilson, Isaac A. - Mary E. Sewell   6-31-1851
Wintrode, Daniel - Hannah Beauchamp 1-11-1849
Wire, Jonah - Eliza Ann Fisher   12-29-1844
Wolf, Jacob - Lydia Ann Aumoch lic. 6-14-1848
Wolf, William - Julia Louisa Anemock
                        (Aumock)   10-23-1851
Wolfgang, Henry - Mary Foust   9-17-1844
Worden, Sylvester - Mary D. Glanton 2- 8-1846
Wright, Elwood - Ruth Cook   5-16-1841
Wright, Lindsey E. - Sarah E. Pinkerton
                                         8-30-1851

Wright, Ralph - Anna Fulhart	12-12-1849	Zahn, Jacob - Mary Nook	6-16-1845
Yahne, Emanuel - Emily Gettis	12- 7-1843	Zahn, John - Esther Lafontain	4-12-1850
Yahne, John - Lucinda Viberg	11- 1-1849	Zeigler, Andrew - Martha Campbell	9-11-1852
Yantiss, Jacob - Nancy Truly (or Freely?)		Zellars, George - Rebecca Staly	5- 2-1843
	4-13-1851	Zent, Jacob - Sarah Huffman	12- 6-1848
Young, David - Mary Ann Tharp	4-22-1849	Zent, John - Mary Ann Foster	10-14-1852
Young, William - Phebe Rebecca Webb	12- 6-1849		

KIMBALL SERENDIPITY

As so often happens in historical research, in looking for one thing you come across some unrelated item that you can not resist stopping to read. Such was the case in finding the autobiographical sketch of Nathan Kimball in the William H. English Collection in the Indiana Historical Society Library. Kimball's life touched many different phases of Indiana history and leaves one with a desire to know more of this little known Indianan.

Nathan Kimball's father Nathaniel and grandfather emigrated from Massachusetts in 1815, settling near Jeffersonville in Clark County where they engaged in making brick. After the death of the grandfather in 1817, Nathaniel and his brother Eleazer moved to Salem and there engaged in merchandising. Nathaniel married on May 13, 1821, Nancy Ferguson, daughter of James Ferguson, who had been one of Clark County's earliest settlers, settling near Clarksville on the Ohio River before 1800; Nancy was born there on December 9, 1801.

The mercantile firm of Coffin, Kimball, and Parker was among the most enterprising in that section of the country, buying products of all kinds from the farmers and shipping them to New Orleans. On one of these trips Nathaniel Kimball died on January 12, 1829. Nancy had died earlier on January 25, 1825, leaving Nathan Kimball, born November 22, 1822, an orphan at the age of seven. He lived with his grandfather Ferguson who had moved to Fredericksburg, working on his farm and attending what schools were available. For a few terms he attended the Washington County Seminary under the direction of John I. Morrison and for a short time in 1838-39 attended Asbury (now DePauw) University but for want of funds had to go to work, finding employment as a clerk in the store of Lee and Ash in Greencastle; he then taught school in western Missouri from 1840 to 1843. On returning to Indiana he studied medicine under Dr. Alexander McPheeters of Fredericksburg and in 1844 attended Louisville Medical College. The following year he began the practice of medicine in partnership with Dr. McPheeters and on September 23 of that year married Martha McPheeters, daughter of James McPheeters of Livonia; they became the parents of one son James. Following Martha's death, Nathan married Emily McPheeters in 1850, daughter of John C. McPheeters of Livonia.

Kimball served in the Mexican War in Company G, Second Regiment, under Col. W. A. Bowles, taking part in Zachary Taylor's campaign and was in the battle of Buena Vista "where I knew every officer and man did his duty excepting the Colonel, who coward as he was, attempted to disgrace his command and brought reproach on Taylor."

After being discharged from service he resumed his profession, practicing medicine at Livonia and then at Loogootee. He was a presidential elector on the Whig ticket in 1852. At the outbreak of the Civil War he was commissioned colonel of the Fourteenth Regiment and was promoted to brigadier general on April 15, 1862, and served throughout the war. He devotes several pages of his autobiography to his service in the war, following which he served as treasurer of Indiana for two terms, 1867-1871, and as a member of the House of Representatives from Marion County in 1873. In 1874 he was appointed by President Grant surveyor general of the Territory of Utah, serving four years, and then was appointed postmaster for Ogden City, Utah, following which he retired to private life.

At the time he wrote the sketch in 1886, Kimball was living in Ogden City "broken in health and physically about used up." He considered his life "of not much importance to the public" but "an eventful one" to me. The Historical Society also has a photograph of Kimball in his army uniform. The Lilly Library, Indiana University, has some five hundred of his letters, but they relate mostly to his military life.

RECORDS OF JACKSON TOWNSHIP, GREENE COUNTY, 1860-1876

Compiled from a xerox copy of the Trustee's Account Book, Jackson Township, Greene County, 1859-1876, in the possession of Willard Heiss.

The office of township trustee is one with which most of us are familiar. The duties of the office have changed from time to time but in the 1860s they consisted chiefly of receiving and disbursing school funds, appointing and paying teachers, enumerating school pupils, establishing roads, appointing supervisors to keep up the roads, and recording the names of persons working under these supervisors. Very few of the records kept by township trustees have survived except as they are contained in the records of county officials to whom they made reports; for example, he was required to make reports concerning shcools to the county superintendent of schools or to the school examiner.

Although the covering dates of the Jackson Township Trustee's Book are 1859-76, the school enumeration and lists of road workers were only for the years 1864-66. Other payments were made which may have been for teachers but only those specifically stated as being for teachers are included in the list below. The records from this one Indiana township are presented here as a sample of the information one might expect to find in the trustee records.

Teachers In The Public Schools And Years In Which They Taught

Alexander, John, 1861, 1862
Armstrong, Elizabeth, 1860, 1862
Ashcraft, Joseph, 1865
Ashcraft, Lewis, 1865
Baker, S. W., 1861
Batts (or Battin), Anna, 1864, 1866
Bennet, George, 1860
Dobbis, William, 1865
Dugger, Francis, 1860
Dye, William S., 1860
Edington, Elijah, 1860
Edington, Thomas, 1860, 1862, 1865, 1866
Emery, John, 1866
Fields, Thomas, 1865
Finell, N. R., 1860
George, Jasper, 1866
George, Joseph F., 1864, 1866
George, Josiah, 1860, 1861, 1862
Graham, Avariler, 1866
Hardesty, Martha Jane, 1860
Harris, Robert, 1862

Jackson, Theophilis, 1861, 1865
Kale, John, 1861
Leonard, Nancy, 1862, 1866
Lam (Lamb), John T., 1865, 1866
Lam (Lamb), Thomas 1864, 1865
Murray, Lydia, 1862
Parke, L., 1861
Pate, John, 1865, 1866
Records, Absalom, 1862
Records, Samuel, 1860
Riley, John H., 1862
Roberts, Thomas C., 1861, 1866
Short, Lucinda, 1861
Stone, John, 1865
Todd, John, 1860
Waker (Walker?), Mary, 1860
Whitworth, Joseph, 1864
Winders, L. D., 1860
Woodward, Elzey, 1862
Wort (or Worts), Rebecca, 1865, 1866
Woolam, John F., 1865

School Enrollment, 1864-1866

The names of the parents are given, the school district in which they were located, and the number of children in school in a particular year. Sometimes it is the mother's name that is given, sometimes the father's; we have made no attempt to try to pair the two together. In some instances the father may have been away from home serving in the army.

	District	1864	1865	1866		District	1864	1865	1866
Alcorn, James A.	4	4	--	--	Ashcraft, Jacob	6	6	3	6
Allcorn, Jerry	7	4	--	--	Ashcraft, Joseph	12	4	5	5
Allcorn, Jesse	7	4	--	--	Ashcraft, Lewis	11	2	3	3
Alexander, J. J.	5	--	--	2	Ashcraft, Robert	9	5	5	4
Armstrong, Robert	1	5	--	--	Barker, O. T.	5	2	1	2
(Transferred from					Barto, James	11	--	--	2
Lawrence Co.)					Beaty, Elenor	4	1	--	--
Ashcraft, Daniel	6	4	4	5	Beaty, John, Jr.	5	4	3	3
Ashcraft, Elijah	9	2	2	2	Beaty, John, Sr.	5	1	1	1

Name	District	1864	1865	1866
Beaty, William	4	5	5	5
Bectal, James	11	4	4	4
Beswick, Elisabeth	5 & 7	3	3	3
Beyers, Isaac	10	--	--	1
Beyers, Joel	2	5	5	5
Beyers, Phillip	1	--	1	1
Boruff, Ann	11	--	2	--
Boruff, Daniel	11 & 2	3	2	2
Boruff, Rebecca	11	--	--	3
Boruff, Wesley	11	2	2	--
Boruff, William	2	--	1	1
Brandon, Ellis	2	1	--	--
Brandon, James	13	4	--	5
Brandon, Lawrence	13	5	5	--
Brandon, Levi	5 & 10	1	1	1
Bridges, Mathis	4	--	--	1
Brock, Emory	10	1	--	--
Brock, Newel	10	--	1	1
Brown, Harmon	11	1	1	1
Brown, Noah	5	3	1	2
Bruce, Henry	7	2	--	--
Bruce, Hugh	7 & 10	4	4	4
Bruce, Jacob	3	4	5	5
Bryles, Mrs. Mary	3	4	3	3
Busenburg, Hugh	2	3	3	3
Calkins, Catharine	2	--	1	--
Calkins, Nelson	2	--	--	1
Carr, James	8	--	--	1
Carr, Jeremiah	10 & 11	6	5	5
Carter (or Courter), Thomas	1	--	1	1
Carter (or Courter), William	2	--	1	1
Chesnut, Thompson	5	3	--	--
Chesnut, W. P.	5	--	3	--
Clemons, Mrs. Roseann	9	5	6	5
Cobb, Mary Ann	6	--	--	2
Cobb, Samuel, Jr.	7	2	2	2
Cobb, Samuel, Sr.	5	--	3	--
Cobb, Semor (?)	7	--	1	--
Cole, Ezra	4	2	3	1
Cole, Thomas	4	--	--	1
Connell, Stivert (or Stuart)	9	--	--	4
Cook, Aguston	2	1	--	2
Cooper, John	12	4	4	4
Cooper, Joseph T.	12 & 13	5	4	--
Cooper, Rebecca	9	--	--	1
Cooper, Spencer	9	--	1	--
Corban, Albert	8	3	3	4
Corban, Benjamin F.	8	--	--	3
Corban, Franklin	8	2	--	--
Corban, Mrs. George	8	--	2	--
Corban, James	8	2	2	--
Crow, Constantine	6	--	1	--
Crow, Mansfield	12	--	--	4
Davis, Levi	8	5	3	4
Davis, Milford	2	--	1	--
Dawson, Mary	7	4	4	3
Dishman, Jeremiah	2	5	6	6
Dobbins, Daniel	11	4	4	3
Dobbins, William	5 & 6	4	4	5
Donahey, William	9	1	--	--
Doney, Elizabeth	3	--	--	2
Doney, Elizabeth	5	2	2	--
Dugger, Harden	2	--	--	5
Dugger, Thomas	2	5	4	4
Duke, John	11	5	5	4
Dye, George	3	4	--	--
Dyer, Ann	11	--	--	4
Dyer, James	11	--	--	1
Eason, Haydon	4	--	5	--
Edington, Aquilla	6 & 7	--	1	3
Edington, Edward	9	3	3	--
Edington, Elijah	5 & 6	3	--	3
Edington, Elisa Ann	7	2	--	--
Edington, Mary	12	3	--	--
Edington, Thomas	9	4	5	5
Emory, John	9 & 13	6	5	5
Ferguson, Andrew	8	3	4	3
Ferguson, Drusilla	2 & 11	3	--	3
Ferguson, Richard	6 & 11	2	2	--
Fields, John	5	--	1	1
Fields, Thomas H.	5	3	3	3
Fields, William	5	4	3	4
Fish, H.	4	--	1	--
Fish, John H.	4	--	--	2
Fitzpatrick (or Patrick), James	2	4	3	3
Fitzpatrick (or Patrick), Henry	2	--	--	1
Fitzpatrick (or Patrick), Joseph	2	6	6	5
Flinn, Franky	9	2	3	2
Flinn, William	9	5	5	--
Floyd, Enoch H.	2	8	6	6
Fordice, Abraham	10	5	5	5
Frazier, William	5	--	--	4
Frazier, William	10	2	--	--
Freeman, William	1	2	3	3
Fulks (or Fults?), Daniel	7	6	6	--
Fuller, Elijah	10	2	--	--
Gabbert, Peter	8	2	2	3
Gardner, David	7	--	3	--
Gardner, F. S.	6	3	3	--
Gastineau, Charles	4	5	5	3
George, David	7 & 12	2	3	3
George, John	5	3	1	2
George, John E.	8	--	3	3
George, Joseph	10	4	4	--
George, Josiah F.	10	--	--	3
George, T. H.	5	--	2	--
George, Thomas D.	7	5	5	5
George, William	5	--	2	--
Gilleland, Harvey	3	2	3	--
Gilleland, James H.	3	--	--	3
Goodin, William	2	6	--	--
Graham, Abigail	4 & 5	3	3	3
Graham, Basil	5	1	2	2
Graham, F. M.	10	--	--	1
Graham, Jane	5	--	1	--
Graham, Lafayette	10	1	1	2
Graham, Samuel	5	2	1	1
Hall, George	13	--	1	1
Hall, James C.	7 & 8	1	1	--
Hamilton, John	8	1	--	--
Hardesty, Harriet	9	3	3	3
Hardesty, Jane	12	6	6	6
Hardesty, Joseph	9	5	5	5
Hardesty, William	9	4	5	5
Hardin, William	2 & 10	1	2	--
Harper, Bayless	2 & 10	5	4	4
Harper, Lewis	8	4	4	4
Harshfield, David D.	6	4	3	--
Harshfield, James	11	--	1	--
Hatfield, Ale	5 & 6	3	2	2
Hatfield, Ale, Jr.	8	2	2	2
Hatfield, Armsted	5	4	3	3
Hatfield, Daniel B.	8	--	--	1
Hatfield, Emanuel	5	2	2	1
Hatfield, George W.	3	--	--	3
Hatfield, Jeremiah	5	3	3	3
Hatfield, Mordica	8	7	7	--
Hatfield, Washington	3	5	5	--
Hatfield, William	5	3	4	--
Haydon, Frances	5	--	--	4
Haydon, Martin	3 & 5	3	3	--
Haydon, Thomas G.	5	2	3	--

Name	District	1864	1865	1866
Herron, Richard	3	3	--	--
Herron, Richard	4	--	3	--
Herron, Richard	10	--	--	4
Hert, William	5	2	2	2
Hill, B. F.	5	1	1	--
Hill, David	13	3	4	3
Hitchcock, Samuel	4	5	4	4
Holder, Benjamin	1	4	4	3
Holder, George	6 & 9	--	5	5
Holder, John	6	--	1	--
Holder, Zachariah	1	--	--	1
Horn, Abraham	11	1	1	2
Howel, Alfred	12	3	3	4
Hudson, Hale	6 & 10	6	4	--
Hudson, James	6	3	3	3
Hudson, John	2	4	4	4
Hudson, William	2	3	3	3
Hudson, Lankston	10	2	2	2
Hudson, Lankston, Jr.	11	--	4	--
Humrickhouse, George	8	--	--	5
Imhuff, Isaac	9	2	3	--
Inman, Jackson	7	1	1	2
Isenhour, George	11	8	7	5
Jackson, Alfred	7 & 10	4	4	4
Jackson, Elbridge	7 & 10	4	5	5
Jackson, James	7	4	--	--
Jackson, Jefferson	7	2	3	2
Jackson, John	7	1	1	--
Jackson, Moses	10	--	2	4
Jackson, Nicholas	3 & 12	--	1	2
Jackson, William	3	4	3	--
Jackson, William P.	7	--	--	4
Jamison, J.	8	5	4	--
Jamison, Rid	8	--	1	1
Jones, Henry	5	1	2	--
Jones, Thomas F.	5	3	3	3
Kirkpatric, David	11	3	3	3
Lamb, Calvin	3	2	--	2
Lamb, Hiram	3	1	1	1
Lamb, John	3	3	1	1
Lamb, Mrs. Manerva	11	1	2	1
Lamb, Rebecca	3	4	4	3
Lancaster, Henry	8	2	1	--
Lanter, Archibald	11	2	2	2
Lanter, Bluford	6	--	2	--
Lanter, William B.	6	--	--	3
Laughlin, Lindsy	10	--	--	3
Lee, Enoch	5 & 7	6	--	5
Leonard, Joseph	3	4	4	4
Litton, Mrs.	7	2	--	--
Loflin, Linsey	4	4	--	--
Long, Israel	2	6	6	6
Love, A. H.	5	3	4	--
Love, Howard	5	--	--	4
Love, J. P.	5	5	5	5
Loveall, Abraham	11	--	3	--
Lynch, Nathaniel	13	4	4	4
McCan, James	1	5	4	--
McCan, James	10	--	--	5
McColip (?), John W.	1	--	1	2
McDaniel, Rebecca	1	4	3	3
McGill, William	11	2	--	1
McGlaughlin (or McLaughlin), Mrs. John	13	4	3	--
McHurter (or McWhirter), Robert	9	2	2	2
McKee, James	3	--	1	--
McKinzie, Augustus	11	1	--	--
McQuillin, David	11	1	--	--
Mansfield, Jacob	12	2	2	2
Mansfield, Riley	12	2	2	3
Martindale, John J.	2	1	1	2
May, Amandy	13	2	--	--
May, Mary	13	3	--	--
Merideth, Franklin	13	--	--	4
Merrit, Richard P.	6	2	3	2
Miller, Alfred	9	5	--	--
Miller, Mrs. Alfred	9	--	4	--
Miller, Henry H.	6	6	5	6
Miller, Hiram	7	--	4	4
Miller, Jacob	5	1	--	1
Miller, Job	3 & 4	7	6	6
Miller, Nancy	9	--	--	4
Minix, Cyntha	4	5	--	--
Minix, Isaac	4	--	5	5
Mosier, John	5	--	--	2
Mullis, Albert	9	--	--	1
Niel (or Neal), James	11	4	6	3
Niel (or Neal), Jacob	11	--	--	1
Niel (or Neal), Washington	12	2	2	--
Neldon, George	6 & 12	3	3	4
Neldon, John	13	4	--	4
Nowel, Mitchel B.	10	2	1	1
Odell, A. G.	5	--	--	2
Odell, Stanhope S.	5	5	7	4
Organ, Thompson	8	2	--	--
Overmen, Margret	13	--	--	5
Owens, Lilburn	5	5	5	6
Owens, Mary	5	3	2	2
Page, E. F.	6	--	1	--
Page, Edward	6	--	--	2
Page, Jesse	5	2	2	--
Page, Jesse	6	--	--	2
Paget, James	8	1	--	3
Paget, Martha	13	--	1	2
Parker, Jacob	2 & 11	6	5	4
Pate, Minor	6	6	6	6
Patrick, see Fitzpatrick				
Peen (?), Francis	4	--	--	3
Peran, Thomas	5	--	--	2
Phillips, M. H.	5	2	2	2
Pigman, Joseph	9	4	--	--
Poole, Lethy Ann	1	--	4	5
Potter, John P.	5	3	3	4
Price, Moses	10	6	6	7
Price, Landon	10	4	4	4
Priest, William	6 & 10	3	3	3
Pugh (Pew), John	8	--	4	4
Pugh (Pew), Lewis	8	--	2	3
Rainbolt, Solomon	1	2	3	3
Records, Absalom	6	--	--	1
Records, Henry	6	--	--	1
Records, James M.	10	2	2	4
Records, Jane	8	1	1	1
Records, Samuel	7 & 8	3	4	4
Records, W. W.	8	5	4	4
Reid, Nathaniel	7	5	5	5
Richeson (or Richardson), William L.	1	3	3	3
Riley, Elzy	8	5	6	6
Riley, Frances	11	--	--	1
Rooch, Thomas	6	--	--	1
Roberson, Thomas	11 & 12	2	2	--
Roberts, Henry C.	6	--	--	1
Roberts, Richard	7	2	2	--
Roberts, Thomas	7	2	3	3
Roberts, Richman	5	--	--	2
Roberts, Shelby	11	1	--	--
Rollins, Allen	3	6	--	4
Rollins, Daniel	7	4	4	3
Rose, T. J.	7	3	3	3

District	1864	1865	1866
Ross, William	6	2	2	--
Rush, G. G.	5	2	--	--
Rush, John C.	3	5	6	7
Rush, Louis	3	6	--	6
Rush, Louise	3	--	5	--
Sanders, Jane	8	4	--	--
Sanders, John	8	--	4	--
Sebern, (or Sebring), Henry	8	3	2	3
Sentney, John	5	2	--	--
Sexson, L.	B 1	3	3	4
Shanklin, Abraham	10	4	4	4
Shanklin, Nero	11	4	4	4
Shoptan, A. H.	6	4	--	--
Shrout, Jesse	12	2	--	--
Shrout, Catharine	13	--	3	4
Simson, Levi	8	--	--	2
Smiley, Nathan	7	3	3	3
Smyth, Henry	4	--	--	4
Sparks, Jerome	11	2	3	--
Spears, Wash, Jr.	5	2	2	2
Spears, Wash, Sr.	5	--	2	1
Spinks, Marium	9	--	--	1
Stanley, J.	1	1	1	--
Stone, Jeremiah	4	2	1	--
Stone, John	6	--	1	--
Stone, William W.	3	3	3	3
Strosnider, Charles	4	1	1	2
Strosser, Joel	11	4	3	5
Terrill, Mrs. Elizabeth	1 & 7	3	--	--

District	1864	1865	1866
Tetrick, John	11	3	4	3
Todd, Loyd	8	2	2	--
Toomey, Nancy	9	--	--	3
Veach, Jane	5	--	--	1
Vest, James G.	1	--	3	3
Vest, Fielding	7	--	8	3
Vest, Washington	13	4	--	--
Wade, Henry	10	2	2	2
Wade, Noah	10	--	--	1
Waggoner, Henry	9	2	3	3
Walker, Rebecca	1	--	--	5
Wall (or Wals), David	5	--	2	2
Walters, Aaron B.	7	--	--	6
Wharton, Larance	5	4	4	2
Wharton, John	6 & 7	--	2	2
White, Luther F.	10	6	4	5
Whitworth, Henry	7	4	4	--
Whitworth, Thomas H.	7 & 10	4	--	3
Williams, V. W.	5	4	3	3
Willson, Lawson	2 & 10	3	--	2
Wilson, James	2 & 11	1	1	1
Wilson, William	2 & 3	1	4	4
Winders, Henderson	12	5	5	--
Winders, Charity	12	--	--	4
Winders George	9	3	4	--
Woolhams, Sarah	8	4	4	3
Wright, Edward F.	13	1	1	1
Wright, John	12 & 13	2	2	4
Wright, Joseph	12 & 13	--	2	1
Wright, Loyd	12	9	8	8
Wright, Luvena	13	--	1	--

Enumeration of Persons Working on Roads, 1864-66

Some of the men were listed as working in only one of the above years, some in two of the years, and some in all three. In order to save space the names have been combined into a single list. There appeared to be enough additional names that were not on the school enumeration to justify the duplication that appears. All able-bodied men between the ages of eighteen and fifty were required to work on the roads or pay a road tax.

Alexander, Columbus
Allcorn, J.
Ashcraft, Daniel
Ashcraft, Jacob
Ashcraft, Joseph
Ashcraft, Lewis
Ashcraft, Martin
Ashcraft, Robert
Ault, Esarl
Baker, David
Barker, O. T.
Barnes, W.
Barto, James
Beaty, John
Bectil (or Beghtal), James
Bennet, J. W.
Beswick, Jerry
Beyers, George
Beyers, Isaac
Beyers, Joel
Beyers, Philip
Bobbit, Columbus
Boriff, William
Brandon, Ellis
Brandon, James
Brandon, Lee
Brandon, Levi
Brannon, John
Brannon, William
Bridges, John
Briles, A. S.
Brock, David
Brock, N.
Brown, Noah

Bruce, Henry
Bruce, Hugh
Bruce, Jacob
Burchem, Adam
Burges, Joseph
Busenburg, Hugh
Calkins, Nelson
Carr, James
Cobb, Samuel, Sr.
Cobb, Samuel, Jr.
Cobb, Semer
Cole, Thomas
Connel, Inerd
Cook, Augustine
Cooper, John
Cooper, Joseph
Cooper, Paris
Corbin (or Corban), Albert
Corbin, B. F.
Corbin, George
Cot, Daniel
Courter, Thomas
Courter, William
Crow, Constantine
Crow, Mansfield
Darbro, William, Sr.
Darbro, William
Davis, Allison
Davis, Harrison
Davis, Milford
Dawson, Joseph
Dishman, J. B.
Dobbins, Samuel
Donaha, Henry

Donahey, William
Dowden, W.
Dugger, F. M.
Dugger, Thomas
Duke, Henry
Duke, John
Duke, Richard
Dye, George
Dye, William S.
Dyer, James B.
Edington, Aquilla
Edington, Elijah
Edington, Thomas
Ferguson, Andrew
Ferguson, James
Ferguson, Richard
Fields, E. H.
Fields, John
Fields, M. G.
Fields, Thomas H.
Fine, Abraham
Fish, Andrew
Fish, Harrison
Fisher, Nathaniel
Fitzpatrick, Henry
Fitzpatrick, James
Fitzpatrick, Joseph
Flin, William
Floyd, E. H.
Floyd, Henry
Floyd, F. M.
Foredice, Sanford
Frazier, William
Freeman, Lewis
Freeman, William

Fults, Daniel
Gardner, David
Gardner, F. S.
Garrey, A. J.
Gastineau, Charles
George, B. F.
George, J.
George, J. F.
George, John E.
George, Josiah
George, T. F.
George, T. H.
George, Thomas D.
(Some of George names may be duplicates)
Gillian, H.
Gilliner, James H.
Goodin, William
Graham, Basel
Graham, Charles
Graham, F. M.
Graham, Lafayett
Hall, James
Hamilton, John
Hardin, Alexander
Hardin, William
Hardisty, Edmond
Hardisty, Jasper
Harper, Balas
Harper, William
Harshfield, James
Harshfield, William
Hatfield, Ale, Sr.
Hatfield, Ale
Hatfield, Andrew

Hatfield, Daniel B.
Hatfield, F. M.
Hatfield, Jasper
Hatfield, Jeremiah
Hatfield, Joel
Hatfield, Mordecai
Hatfield, W. H.
Hardon, M. C.
Henderson, Robert
Herron, Richard
Hert, William
Hill, B. F.
Hitchcock, Samuel
Holder, John
Holder, Robert
Holder, Zachariah
Homerickhouse, George
Horn, Abraham
Horn, Sampson
Hudson, J. M.
Hudson, James
Hudson, Jeremiah
Hudson, John R.
Hudson, Joshua
Hudson, Stephen P.
Hummer, K.
Ikard, Erastus
Inman, Jackson
Inman, John
Isenhour, George
Isenhour, Martin
Jackson, Alfred
Jackson, Alpheus
Jackson, E.
Jackson, Granville
Jackson, Jacob
Jackson, Jefferson
Jacobs, Johanes
Jamison (or Jimerson)
Jamison, Jackson F.
Jamison, Jacob
Jamison, John
Jamison, Reese
Jamison, Urice
Kid, Peter
King, G.
  (Kirkpatrick?)
Kirk, Henry
Kirkpatrick, Henry
Lamb, Calvin
Lamb, Hiram
Lancaster, D. P.
Lancaster, M.

Lancaster, Pendleton
  (may be same as D. P.)
Lancaster, Samuel
Lanter, Bluford
Laughlin, Linsey
Lee, Enoch
Leonard, Joseph
Long, Edward
Long, John W.
Long, Reuben
Love, Howard
Love, J. P.
Loveal, Isaah
Lynch, Nathaniel
McBride, Isaac
McCan, James
McCothlin, -----
McKinney, Augustine
McKinzie, B. G.
McWilliams, Elijah
Mansfield, A. R.
Mansfield, Riley
Martin, Joseph
Martindale, Jacob
Martindale, John
Martindale, Thomas S.
May, Augustin
Meredith, Ambrose
Mereth (Meredith?),
  Franklin
Merrit, William
Miller, Andrew
Miller, Hiram
Miller, Jacob
Miller, Job
Miller, John
Miller, Solomon
Miller, William
Miller, Zachariah
Minicks, Isaac
Mosier, Bent
Mullis, Robert
Neal, Jacob H.
Neal, Thomas Y.
Neal, Washington
Neldon, George
Neldon, John
Nicholson, Abraham
Noel, Jonathan
Noel, Mich (or M.B.)
Noel, William
Odell, A. G.
Odell, S. S.

Ogden, Joshua
Organ, Thompson
Owen, R. D.
Owens, Lilburn (or
  Silburn)
Padgett (or Paget),
  Edward
Padgett, James
Page, Jesse
Parham, Lewis
Parker, Francis M.
Parker, Jacob
Pate (or Pait), Minor
Patric, Henry
Perin, T. W.
Pigman, Joseph
Porter, Malicier
Potter, John
Potter, John P.
Potts, John
Price, Hamilton
Price, James
Price, L. C.
Price, Moses, Jr.
Pugh, William
Quilling, David
Rainbolt, John, Jr.
Rainbolt, Solomon
Raney, Melchert
Reaves, Jefferson
Records, Absalom
Records, H. C.
Records, James M.
Records, L. M.
Records, P. A.
Records, Samuel
Records, Will W.
Reed, Nathaniel
Richardson, Leflet
Richeson, O. B.
Richeson, William L.
Rigney, Joab
Roach, Thomas
Roberts, Henry C.
Roberts, Richard
Roberts, Richmond
Roberts, Shelby
Roberts, Stephen
Roberts, Thomas
Rollins, A.
Rose, T. J.
Sanders, John
Sentney, John

Sexson, Alen
Sexson, L. B.
Shacklet, Homer
Shanklin, Abraham
Shanklin, Nero
Shelton, Anderson
Shoptan, A. H.
Shrout, Jesse
Simpson, Levi
Singer, John
Smiley, Nathan
Smith, Henry
Sparks, Jerome
Spears, W.
Stark, Mordecai
Stone, Wesley
Stone, William W.
Strosnider, Charles
Strosser, Joel
Swango, J.
Tetric, John
Todd, Loyd
Vest, Washington
Wade, Dr._____
Wade, Andrew
Wade, Noah
Wagner (or Waggoner),
  Henry
Wall, David
Wharton, John
White, L. F.
Whitworth, James
Whitworth, Joseph
Williams, N. W.
Williams, William
Wilson, G. W.
Wilson, James
Wilson, Samuel
Wilson, William
Winders, George
Winders, William
Woody, William
Woolam, John F.
Wright, Alexander
Wright, Edward
Wright, Elli
Wright, John
Wright, Joseph
Wright, Samuel
Wright, William

1810 CENSUS OF HARRISON COUNTY

(Harrison and Exeter Townships)

Head of Household	Township	Males (Under 10 - 10 to 16 - 16 to 26 - 26 to 45 - Over 45)	Females (Under 10 - 10 to 16 - 16 to 26 - 26 to 45 - Over 45)
Able, Ignatius	E	3-0-0-1-0	1-3-1-1-0
Albin, George	E	3-0-0-2-0	2-0-1-0-0
Albin, John	E	2-0-0-1-0	2-0-0-1-0
Armstrong, James	H	0-0-0-0-1	1-1-1-0-0
Armstrong, James	H	2-0-1-0-0	1-0-1-0-0
Arnold, Richard	H	3-2-0-0-1	2-0-1-1-0
Austin, David	E	2-0-0-1-0	0-0-0-1-0
Ballard, William	E	2-1-0-1-0	1-2-0-1-0
Bannister, Henry	H	1-0-0-1-0	3-0-0-1-0
Barkshear, Charles	H	1-0-1-0-0	1-0-2-0-0
Barkshear, Henry	H	0-0-2-0-1	0-1-0-0-1
Barnaby, Robert	H	3-0-0-1-0	2-0-1-0-0
Barnett, George	E	0-0-0-1-0	2-0-1-0-0
Barnett, James	E	3-1-0-1-0	4-0-0-1-0
Barnett, William	E	2-0-0-1-0	0-0-1-0-0
Bartmess, George	E	3-2-1-1-0	0-1-0-1-0
Bass, John	E	1-0-1-0-0	1-0-1-0-0
Bateman, William	H	2-2-1-0-1	2-0-0-1-0
Bates, Dolly	H	1-0-0-0-0	1-0-0-1-0
Bates, Rachel	E	0-0-0-0-0	0-0-0-0-1
Batman, Henry	E	1-0-1-1-0	2-1-0-1-0
Beanblossom, Jacob	E	0-2-2-0-1	0-1-0-0-0
Beard, James	H	0-0-1-0-0	1-0-1-0-0
Beard, Samuel	H	1-0-0-1-0	2-0-0-1-0
Beard, Thomas	E	1-0-0-1-0	1-0-1-0-0
Beard, William	H	1-0-0-1-0	0-1-1-0-1
Bell, Samuel	H	1-1-2-0-1	3-2-0-1-0
Berry, Thomas	H	3-0-0-1-0	1-1-0-1-0
Bertley, Robert	E	3-0-0-1-0	1-0-1-0-0
Best, Enos	H	1-0-1-0-0	0-1-1-0-0
Biggs, Robert	E	1-0-0-1-0	0-0-1-0-0
Black, Moses	H	2-0-0-1-0	4-0-0-1-0
Blunk, Aaron	E	3-0-0-1-0	1-0-1-0-0
Blunk, Amos	E	2-0-0-1-0	1-0-1-0-0
Bogard, Benjamin	H	2-1-0-1-0	1-0-0-1-0
Boone, George	E	2-0-1-1-0	2-0-0-1-0
Boone, John	E	1-0-0-1-0	4-0-1-0-0
Boone, Jonathan	E	0-1-1-1-0	1-1-0-1-0
Boone, Moses	E	3-1-0-1-0	2-3-2-1-0
Boone, William	E	1-0-0-1-0	0-1-1-0-1
Boothe, James	E	1-0-1-0-0	2-0-1-0-0
Boston, Benjamin	H	3-2-0-0-1	3-1-2-0-1
Bowman, John	H	2-0-0-1-0	2-1-0-1-0
Branham, William	H	1-0-1-0-1	0-2-0-1-1
Bright, David	E	1-0-0-1-0	3-0-0-1-0
Brindley, Henry	E	2-0-0-1-0	0-1-0-1-0
Brindley, John	E	3-0-0-0-1	1-0-0-1-0
Brown, James	H	3-0-0-1-0	0-0-0-1-0
Brown, Margaret	E	1-0-0-0-0	2-0-0-1-0
Brown, William	H	2-0-0-1-0	2-0-0-1-0
Bruce, James	H	2-2-1-0-1	0-1-2-0-1
Buchanan, Agnes	E	0-0-1-0-1	0-0-1-1-1
Buchannan, James	E	0-0-2-0-1	0-0-3-0-1
Bufford, Melton	H	1-0-0-1-0	3-0-0-1-0
Burckhartt, Frederick	H	1-0-1-0-0	0-0-1-0-0
Burkett, John	H	0-1-1-1-0	2-2-0-1-0
Burkhartt, Jacob	H	2-0-0-1-0	1-0-0-1-0
Burton, Joseph	H	1-3-0-1-0	3-1-0-1-0
Burton, Levi	H	1-0-0-1-0	2-0-1-0-0
Buskirk, Absalom	H	0-1-2-0-0	2-1-1-0-0
Buskirk, Isaac	H	2-1-1-0-1	0-2-0-0-1
Butler, Jesse	H	1-2-0-1-0	3-0-0-1-0
Butt, Israel	E	0-0-1-0-0	0-0-1-0-0
Byerly, Philip	H	1-0-0-1-0	3-0-0-1-0
Byrn, Charles L.	H	3-0-0-1-0	0-1-0-1-0
Byrn, Temple	H	3-0-0-1-0	0-0-1-0-0
Byrn, William	H	2-1-2-0-1	1-1-0-0-1
Carr, James	H	0-0-1-0-0	0-0-0-0-0
Carr, Thomas	E	1-0-0-1-0	3-0-0-1-0
Carter, Shadrack	E	0-0-0-0-1	0-0-0-0-1
Case, Ichabud	E	0-0-1-0-0	1-0-1-0-0
Case, James	E	1-0-0-0-1	0-0-0-0-1
Castile, Zach	E	2-0-0-1-0	1-1-0-1-0
Chamberlain, Pierce	H	1-1-0-1-0	3-1-0-1-0
Chamberlain, Robert	H	1-1-0-1-1	0-0-0-0-1
Clark, George	E	1-1-1-0-1	2-1-0-0-0
Cline, Daniel	H	0-0-1-0-0	2-0-1-0-0
Cline, Daniel	H	0-0-1-0-0	0-0-1-0-0
Cline, John	H	2-1-1-0-1	1-0-1-0-1
Coffinower, John	E	2-0-0-1-0	1-0-1-0-0
Cohoon, Robert	H	1-0-0-1-0	2-0-1-0-0
Coonrad, George	E	0-0-0-1-0	3-2-2-1-0
Coonrad, Henry	E	2-0-0-1-0	0-0-1-0-0
Coonrad, Jacob	E	1-0-0-0-1	0-0-0-0-1
Coonrad, Jacob	H	2-2-0-1-0	1-0-0-1-0
Coonrad, Jacob	E	0-0-1-0-0	2-0-1-0-0
Coonrad, John	E	1-0-1-0-0	1-0-1-0-0
Coonrad, Philip	E	4-1-0-1-0	0-2-0-1-0
Coopriter, John	E	1-0-1-0-0	0-0-0-1-0
Coopriter, Peter	E	0-3-0-1-0	3-1-0-1-0
Copperas, Peter	H	2-1-0-0-1	3-2-2-1-0
Crabill, Benjamin	H	2-1-0-0-1	1-1-2-1-0
Criswell, Elijah	H	0-0-1-0-0	3-0-1-0-0
Crooks, Jeremiah	H	4-1-0-1-0	2-1-0-1-0
Crutchfield, George	H	1-1-0-0-1	3-2-0-1-0
Cunningham, Elizabeth	E	0-2-0-0-0	0-0-0-0-1
Cunningham, Thomas	E	2-0-0-1-0	1-0-1-0-0
Cunningham, William	E	3-2-0-1-0	1-0-0-1-0
Daggs, William	H	0-1-1-1-0	1-1-2-1-0
Davis, Thomas	E	1-2-0-1-0	0-0-0-1-0
Davis, William	H	0-0-1-0-1	0-0-1-0-1
Davison, Hezekiah	E	0-0-2-0-0	0-0-0-0-0
Davison, Thomas	E	2-0-1-1-0	3-2-1-0-0
Dawson, John	E	1-1-0-1-0	0-1-0-1-0
Dean, Nathan	H	3-0-0-1-0	2-1-0-1-0
Dean, Richard	E	0-0-1-0-1	0-0-0-0-1
Dean, William	E	1-0-1-0-0	0-0-1-0-0
Decker, Joseph	H	0-0-1-0-1	0-0-1-0-1
Denbo, Joseph	E	2-0-0-1-0	3-0-0-1-0
Denbo, Robert	E	3-0-0-2-0	2-2-0-1-0
Duggins, Reuben	E	0-0-1-0-0	0-0-1-0-0
Duncan, David	E	1-1-2-0-1	3-1-0-1-0
Dunn, Levi	H	0-0-1-0-0	3-0-1-0-0
Edwards, Cassins	H	1-0-1-0-0	0-0-1-0-0
Elliott, Samuel	H	1-0-0-1-0	1-0-1-0-0
Enfield, Thomas	H	2-2-0-0-1	1-1-0-1-0

Head of Household	Township	Males Under 10	10 to 16	16 to 26	26 to 45	Over 45	Females Under 10	10 to 16	16 to 26	26 to 45	Over 45
English, see Inglish											
Enlow, see Inlow											
Erick, John	H	0	0	1	0	0	0	0	0	0	0
Erwin, John	H	0	3	1	1	0	2	0	0	1	0
Erwin, William	H	2	0	0	1	0	3	0	1	0	0
Evans, John	H	0	1	0	1	0	2	0	0	1	0
Fenton, Joseph	H	2	0	1	1	0	2	0	1	0	0
Flannagan, Samuel	H	4	0	0	1	0	0	0	0	1	0
Fleshman, Jonas	E	0	0	0	1	0	0	0	1	0	0
Fort, Christopher	E	0	0	0	0	1	0	1	1	1	0
Fossett, Thomas	E	2	0	0	1	0	2	1	0	1	0
Fowler, Jacob	E	1	2	0	1	0	3	0	0	1	0
Fox, John	E	0	0	1	0	0	0	0	1	0	0
French, Paul	E	2	1	0	1	0	3	0	0	1	0
Friedley, Jacob	E	0	2	0	0	1	3	2	1	0	1
Funk, Daniel	E	2	0	0	1	0	0	0	0	1	0
Funk, Henry	E	2	1	1	0	1	0	0	1	0	1
Funk, Isaac	E	1	0	1	0	0	1	0	1	0	0
Funk, Jacob	E	0	1	1	0	1	0	0	0	0	1
Funk, John	E	0	0	1	0	0	0	0	1	0	0
Goodwin, Abraham	E	3	0	0	1	0	1	1	1	1	0
Goosenberry, Henry	E	1	0	0	1	0	2	0	0	1	0
Gresham, George	H	4	0	0	1	0	2	0	0	1	0
Gresham, Lawrence	H	0	2	1	0	1	0	0	0	0	1
Gunn, Elisha	H	0	0	0	1	0	0	0	0	1	0
Gwinn, John	H	0	1	2	1	1	0	2	1	0	1
Gwinn, John Jr.	H	3	0	0	1	0	1	0	0	1	0
Hallowell, Henry W.	H	2	0	1	0	0	0	0	1	0	0
Hallowell, John	H	1	1	1	0	1	0	0	0	0	1
Harbison, James	H	0	0	1	0	0	0	0	1	0	0
Harbison, John	H	0	1	0	0	1	0	1	2	0	0
Harris, William B.	E	1	0	0	1	0	3	0	1	0	0
Harrison, Caleb	H	2	0	0	1	0	3	0	1	0	0
Harrison, Joshua	H	1	1	1	0	1	0	0	0	0	1
Haston, Joseph	H	1	0	0	1	0	1	0	1	0	0
Henson, Jeremiah	H	1	0	1	0	0	0	0	1	0	0
Henson, John	H	3	1	0	1	0	1	0	0	1	0
Henson, John Jr.	H	1	0	1	0	0	1	0	1	0	0
Henson, William	H	3	1	1	0	1	1	1	1	0	0
Heth, Henry	E	2	2	0	1	0	0	0	1	0	0
Heth, Richard M.	E	3	1	0	1	0	1	0	0	1	0
Hickman, John	H	1	1	0	1	0	3	1	1	0	0
Hickman, Sarah	H	0	0	2	0	0	0	0	0	0	1
Highfill, Henry	H	0	0	1	0	0	0	0	1	0	0
Highfill, William W.	E	1	1	0	1	0	2	1	2	1	0
Highslip, James	H	2	1	0	1	0	0	1	0	1	0
Hoback, Andrew	E	0	0	1	1	0	3	3	0	1	0
Hooten, George	E	1	0	0	1	0	2	0	1	0	0
Hopson, John	H	2	0	0	1	0	1	0	1	0	0
Hornbeck, William	E	3	0	0	1	0	2	0	1	0	0
Housley, John	H	3	0	1	0	0	1	0	0	1	0
Huff, Abraham	H	1	1	1	1	0	1	0	0	1	0
Hughes, Benjamin	H	1	0	0	0	1	2	1	0	0	0
Hurst, Abraham	H	2	0	0	1	0	3	0	0	1	0
Hurst, Elijah	H	3	2	0	1	0	1	0	1	0	0
Hurst, Henry	H	1	0	0	1	0	0	1	0	1	0
Hurst, John	H	0	0	0	0	1	0	0	0	0	1
Hurst, John Jr.	H	3	0	1	0	1	3	0	0	1	0
Hurst, William	H	4	1	0	1	0	1	1	1	1	0
Inglish, Stephen	E	0	0	1	0	0	1	0	1	0	0
Inlow, David	E	2	1	0	1	0	2	0	0	1	0
Inlow, Henry	E	0	0	0	0	1	2	0	0	1	1
Inlow, Henry Jr.	E	0	0	1	0	0	0	0	1	0	0
Inlow, Jesse	E	3	0	0	1	0	3	2	0	0	0
Johnston, Andrew	E	3	0	0	1	0	2	0	0	1	0
Johnston, Daniel	H	4	1	0	1	0	1	0	0	1	0
Jones, Polly	E	1	0	0	0	0	0	0	0	1	0
Jones, Richard	E	0	0	1	0	0	0	0	1	0	0
Jones, Williamson	E	0	1	0	1	0	0	1	1	0	1
Keller, John	E	2	2	1	0	1	1	1	2	0	1
Keller, Jonathan	E	0	0	1	0	0	0	0	1	0	0
Kelly, Andrew	E	1	0	0	1	0	4	0	0	1	0
Kendall, Allen	H	1	1	0	1	0	1	0	0	1	0
Kendall, James	E	0	0	1	0	0	3	0	1	0	0
Kendall, William	E	1	1	0	1	0	1	2	0	1	0
Kennedy, William	E	2	3	0	0	1	2	0	1	1	0
Kepley, John	H	4	1	0	1	0	2	1	0	1	0
Kimberlin, Henry	H	5	2	0	1	0	0	0	0	1	0
Kingery, Tobias	E	4	0	0	1	0	1	0	0	1	0
Kirkham, Robert	E	1	1	1	0	1	0	1	1	0	0
Lamb, Joshua	H	0	0	0	0	1	0	0	0	0	1
Lane, Stephen	E	0	0	1	0	0	0	0	0	1	0
Lang, John	E	2	0	0	0	1	2	3	0	1	0
Langford, Mason	E	0	2	0	0	1	4	0	0	0	1
Lee, John	E	0	1	2	0	1	1	0	1	0	1
Lefollett, Robert	E	0	0	0	1	0	2	0	1	0	0
Light, Mary	H	4	2	0	0	0	1	1	0	1	0
Lindsay, Jesse	H	1	0	0	1	0	4	0	0	1	0
Lindsay, Nathan	H	2	0	0	1	0	1	0	1	0	0
Liston, Ebenezer	H	4	0	0	0	1	1	2	2	1	0
Littell, William D.	E	1	0	0	1	0	0	0	1	0	0
Long, James	E	2	1	0	1	0	1	1	2	1	0
Lopp, Jacob	E	0	2	2	1	0	0	3	0	0	1
Lopp, John	E	1	3	0	0	1	1	1	1	0	1
Lopp, John	H	3	0	0	1	0	2	0	0	1	0
Ludlow, Sarah	E	0	1	0	0	0	1	1	0	0	1
Marley, John	H	1	1	1	0	1	0	1	2	0	1
Martin, John	H	4	0	1	0	0	0	1	0	1	0
Mathena, James	E	0	0	1	0	1	0	0	0	0	1
Mathena, Samuel	E	1	0	1	0	0	1	0	1	0	0
Mathena, William	E	0	0	0	1	0	2	0	1	0	0
Mattocks, Edmond	E	1	0	1	0	0	0	0	1	0	0
Mattocks, Edward	E	0	0	0	0	1	1	2	0	0	1
Mayall, Joseph	H	1	0	0	1	0	2	0	0	1	0
McAdams, John	E	2	0	0	1	0	2	1	0	1	0
McCallen, Hayes	H	4	0	0	1	0	0	2	0	1	0
McIntire, Jacob	E	1	1	0	1	0	1	0	1	0	0
McIntire, William	E	0	1	4	0	1	0	1	2	0	1
McIntosh, Peter	E	0	0	2	0	1	0	0	1	0	0
McKee, Thomas	E	3	1	0	1	0	2	0	0	1	0
McKee, William	E	1	0	0	1	0	2	0	0	1	0
McKune, Andrew	E	1	1	2	1	0	2	1	1	1	0
McMahon, Richard	H	0	0	0	1	0	3	1	1	0	0
McMickle, John	H	2	1	0	1	0	1	0	0	1	0
McRae, Alexander	E	2	2	0	1	0	0	0	1	0	0
McRae, Daniel	E	0	0	1	0	0	0	0	0	0	0
Meek, Isaac	E	0	0	1	0	0	0	0	1	0	0

Head of Household	Township	Males (Under 10–10 to 16–16 to 26–26 to 45–Over 45)	Females (Under 10–10 to 16–16 to 26–26 to 45–Over 45)
Meek, Sylvester	E	1-1-0-1-0	3-2-1-1-0
Melton, David	H	0-0-1-0-0	0-0-1-0-0
Melton, Eli	E	2-3-0-0-1	2-0-0-1-0
Miller, William	E	2-0-0-0-1	2-0-0-1-0
Mock, Jonathan	H	3-2-0-1-0	1-1-1-1-0
Moffett, John	E	1-0-0-0-1	0-0-1-0-0
Moore, John	E	2-1-0-1-0	1-0-0-1-1
Moore, William	H	1-1-1-0-1	0-1-0-0-0
Morris, Gare	E	0-0-1-0-0	0-1-0-0-0
Moser, Philip	H	2-0-1-0-1	0-2-2-0-1
Mowrer, George	H	3-1-0-1-0	1-0-0-1-0
Mowrer, Jacob	H	2-0-0-1-0	0-0-1-0-0
Mundle, James	H	4-1-0-1-0	0-0-0-1-0
Nance, Clement	H	3-2-1-0-1	0-0-2-0-1
Nance, Clement Jr.	H	0-0-1-0-0	0-0-1-0-0
Nance, William	H	2-0-1-0-0	1-0-1-0-0
Oatman, John	H	3-0-1-0-0	3-0-1-1-0
Onion, Charles	E	0-0-0-0-1	0-0-0-1-1
Onion, William	E	1-1-0-1-0	3-1-0-1-0
Owens, Thomas	H	2-1-1-1-0	3-2-0-1-0
Paddocks, Joseph	E	3-0-0-1-0	2-0-0-1-0
Parmelle, Joseph	H	1-2-0-1-0	0-0-1-0-1
Patrick, Brice	E	1-0-0-1-0	0-0-1-0-0
Pennington, Dennis	H	2-0-0-1-0	3-0-0-1-0
Pennington, Sack	H	0-0-0-1-0	0-0-1-0-0
Pennington, William	H	1-0-0-1-0	1-0-1-0-0
Perkins, John	E	1-0-0-1-0	4-0-1-0-0
Pfrimmer, J. George	H	1-0-1-2-1	0-2-0-0-1
Philips, Sarah	E	0-0-1-0-0	0-0-1-0-0
Phipps, Stephen	H	0-0-2-0-0	0-0-1-0-0
Pipher, Henry	E	0-1-1-0-1	0-0-3-0-1
Pittman, John	H	3-1-1-0-1	0-2-0-0-1
Potter, Elisha	E	0-1-0-1-0	0-2-0-1-0
Potts, Joseph	E	4-0-1-1-0	3-0-1-1-0
Prather, Archibald	H	3-1-1-1-0	2-0-1-0-1
Purcell, Jesse	E	0-0-1-0-0	0-0-1-0-0
Purcell, Lawrence	E	0-1-4-0-1	4-1-2-0-1
Quinley, Richard	H	3-0-0-1-1	1-0-0-1-0
Ransdall, Edward	H	0-0-0-1-0	0-0-1-0-0
Ransdall, Sandford	H	0-0-0-1-0	1-0-1-0-0
Ray, John	E	1-0-1-0-0	1-0-1-0-0
Ray, Samuel	E	4-1-0-1-0	0-1-0-1-0
Reagan, Amos	E	3-0-2-0-1	1-1-0-1-0
Rice, Henry	H	3-2-0-0-1	0-2-0-1-0
Riley, James	E	3-0-0-1-0	3-0-1-0-0
Rinkle, Frederick	H	0-0-1-0-0	0-0-1-0-0
Ripperdan, John	E	1-0-0-1-0	1-0-1-0-0
Rogers, Thomas	E	2-0-0-1-0	3-2-1-1-0
Royse, John	H	1-0-0-1-0	1-1-0-1-0
Rusk, Robert	E	3-1-0-2-0	2-0-0-1-0
Russell, John	H	1-0-1-0-0	1-0-1-0-0
Saffer, John	E	2-0-2-0-1	2-2-0-0-1
Sampson, John	E	0-0-0-1-0	0-0-0-0-0
Samuels, John	H	1-1-2-1-0	1-2-1-1-0
Sands, William	E	4-3-0-1-1	0-1-1-1-0
Scarmahorn, Joseph	E	0-1-0-1-0	2-0-0-0-0
Scraper, George	E	3-0-0-1-0	1-0-0-1-0
Scott, Martin	E	2-2-1-0-0	0-0-1-0-0
Sevedge, Champness	H	0-0-2-0-0	0-0-1-0-0
Shaw, William	H	1-0-0-1-0	2-2-0-1-0
Shields, Benjamin	E	4-0-0-1-0	1-0-0-1-0
Shields, James	H	2-1-0-1-0	2-1-0-1-0
Shields, James	E	2-1-0-1-0	0-2-1-1-0
Shields, Jesse	E	1-0-0-1-0	4-0-1-0-0
Shields, Joseph	E	3-0-0-1-0	1-0-0-1-0
Shields, Josuha	E	2-0-0-1-0	0-0-1-0-0
Shields, Patrick	H	4-1-0-1-0	1-0-0-1-0
Shirley, Christian	H	3-1-0-1-0	1-0-1-1-0
Shirley, John	H	0-0-1-0-0	2-0-1-0-0
Shook, Christopher	H	2-0-2-0-1	2-1-0-1-0
Simbler (?), John	H	2-0-1-0-0	0-0-1-0-0
Simmons, Moses	E	2-2-1-1-0	1-1-1-1-0
Smith, Edward	H	0-1-1-1-1	1-2-1-0-1
Smith, Frederick	H	3-0-0-1-0	0-2-0-1-0
Smith, James	H	0-1-1-0-0	2-0-1-0-0
Smith, John	H	1-1-0-0-1	3-1-0-1-0
Smith, John	H	0-2-1-1-0	3-2-3-1-0
Smith, John	E	1-0-0-1-0	2-0-1-0-0
Smith, John	E	2-0-0-1-0	1-1-0-1-0
Smith, John	H	0-0-1-0-0	0-0-1-0-0
Smith, William	E	1-0-0-1-0	1-0-1-0-0
Smith, William	H	1-0-1-0-0	1-0-1-0-0
Snider, John	H	1-2-1-0-1	0-1-1-1-0
Southard, Jacob	E	0-0-0-0-1	0-0-0-0-0
Southerland, Philip	H	6-1-0-1-0	1-1-0-1-0
Sparks, Baxter	H	1-0-0-0-0	1-0-1-0-0
Speak, Aquilla	H	0-0-0-1-0	3-0-2-0-0
Spencer, Spier	H	0-2-2-4-0	2-2-2-1-0
Standiford, Ephraim	E	0-0-0-1-0	5-0-1-0-0
Stephens, Abraham	H	1-0-1-0-0	2-0-1-0-0
Stephens, Jacob	H	1-0-0-1-0	2-0-1-0-0
Stephens, James	E	1-1-1-1-0	0-0-0-1-0
Stephens, Stecy	E	2-0-0-0-0	4-0-0-1-0
Steward, Matthew	H	2-0-2-0-0	1-0-0-1-0
Stewart, James	H	0-2-0-1-0	0-0-0-1-0
Stewart, William	H	0-0-1-0-1	0-0-0-0-1
Stillwell, Richard	E	1-0-0-1-0	3-2-0-1-0
Stonesypher, John	E	0-0-0-1-0	0-0-1-0-0
Stout, Daniel	H	0-0-1-1-0	2-0-0-1-0
Stroud, Jesse	H	3-3-0-0-1	1-0-0-1-0
Stroud, John	H	2-1-0-1-0	0-3-0-1-0
Stroud, Thomas	H	2-1-0-1-0	2-0-0-0-0
Sturgeon, Jeremiah	E	2-0-0-0-1	1-0-0-1-0
Sturgeon, John	E	2-2-0-0-1	3-1-0-1-0
Styne, Philip	H	4-1-0-1-0	1-0-0-1-0
Suttles(?), Jesse	E	2-0-0-1-0	1-0-0-1-0
Swank, John	H	2-1-0-1-0	4-1-0-1-0
Swassack, Richard	E	1-0-0-1-0	2-0-0-1-0
Tanner, David	E	2-0-0-0-1	0-2-1-0-1
Tanner, John	E	1-0-1-0-0	0-0-1-0-0
Taylor, John	H	4-0-0-1-0	2-0-1-0-0
Thompson, Lawrence	E	1-0-0-0-1	1-0-0-0-1
Tipton, Janet	E	0-1-0-0-0	0-2-0-0-1

Head of Household	Township	Under 10	10 to 16	16 to 26	26 to 45	Over 45	Under 10	10 to 16	16 to 26	26 to 45	Over 45
		Males					**Females**				
Tipton, John	E	1-0-1-0-0					0-0-1-0-0				
Toops, Henry	E	1-0-2-0-1					1-0-2-0-1				
Torr, James	E	1-0-0-1-0					0-0-1-0-0				
Totton, Jonas	H	2-0-0-0-1					3-2-0-0-1				
Tuell, John	E	0-0-1-0-0					0-0-1-0-0				
Vanarsdall, John	H	2-2-1-0-1					1-0-0-1-0				
Vanwinkle, Abraham	E	2-0-0-1-0					1-0-1-0-0				
Vanwinkle, James	E	2-0-0-1-0					1-3-0-1-0				
Vest, William	H	0-1-3-0-1					0-2-0-0-1				
Walk, Abraham	H	0-0-0-1-0					0-0-1-0-0				
Walker, Robert	E	1-1-1-1-0					0-3-2-1-0				
Waltz, George	H	2-2-1-0-1					0-0-0-1-0				
Watkins, John	H	0-0-0-1-0					1-0-1-1-0				
Watson, James	E	0-0-1-0-0					0-0-1-0-0				
Watts, James	H	1-0-1-0-0					0-0-1-0-0				
Weedman, Jacob	H	0-0-0-1-0					3-0-1-0-0				
West, John	E	0-0-0-1-0					1-0-1-0-0				
Westfall, Hiram	H	0-0-0-1-0					1-0-1-0-0				
Wheeler, Benjamin	E	2-1-0-0-1					2-1-1-0-1				
Wheeler, John	E	0-0-1-0-0					0-0-0-1-0				
Wheeler, Thomas	E	1-0-0-1-0					0-0-1-0-0				
Wilkins, Alexander	E	0-4-0-1-0					3-1-0-1-0				
Wilkins, George	E	0-1-0-0-1					1-1-0-0-1				
Williams, Griffith	E	0-0-0-0-1					1-2-0-0-1				
Williams, John	H	1-1-1-0-0					1-1-0-0-0				
Williams, Peter	E	0-0-0-1-0					0-0-0-1-0				
Williams, Richard	H	2-0-0-1-0					1-3-0-1-0				
Winegamer (?), John	E	1-0-0-1-0					2-0-1-0-0				
Winters, John	H	1-0-0-1-0					1-0-1-0-0				
Withers, John	E	1-0-0-1-0					3-0-1-0-0				
Wright, Eli	H	1-2-2-0-1					1-1-1-0-1				
Wright, Greenberry	H	1-1-0-1-0					4-1-0-1-0				
Wright, Peter	H	0-1-0-0-1					0-0-0-0-0				
Wright, William	H	4-0-0-1-0					0-0-1-0-0				
Young, David	E	0-1-1-0-1					1-0-1-0-1				
Zenor, George	E	3-1-0-1-0					1-0-0-1-0				
Zenor, Jacob	E	1-0-1-0-1					0-1-1-0-1				
Zenor, Jacob Jr.	E	3-1-0-1-0					2-0-0-1-0				

The last two columns of the census showing "Slaves" and "Other free persons, except Indians, not taxed," are not reproduced here.

The following persons were listed as holding slaves: Jonathan Boone, 1; John Hurst, 1; Joseph Parmelle, 2; John Pittman, 5; Thomas Rogers, 1; Patrick Shields, 1; John Smith, Exeter Twp., 1; Peter Williams, 3. Total number of slaves, 15.

Other free persons, except Indians, not taxed, were listed in the following households: Benjamin Bogard, 1; Moses Boone, 2; John Hurst, 1; J. George Pfrimmer, 8. These may have been former slaves who had been freed.

HARRISON TOWNSHIP

Males		Females	
Under 10 yrs. of age	280	Under 10	214
10 to 16	106	10 to 16	94
16 to 26	95	16 to 26	102
26 to 45	102	26 to 45	90
Over 45	50	Over 45	30
Free persons not taxed	10	Slaves	10

EXETER TOWNSHIP

Males		Females	
Under 10	241	Under 10	237
10 to 16	80	10 to 16	95
16 to 26	82	16 to 26	115
26 to 45	116	26 to 45	88
Over 45	47	Over 45	38
Free persons not taxed	2	Slaves	5

Total for the two townships   2338

The number of persons within my Division consisting of Two thousand three hundred thirty eight appears on a schedule hereto annexed. Suscribed by me Twenty Sixth day of December 1810.

Geo. F. Pope
Assistant to the Secretary
of the Indiana Territory

BROWN COUNTY MARRIAGES, 1836-1855

Compiled from microfilm of Marriage Records in Genealogy Division, Indiana State Library.

Adams, Charles G. - Sarah Fosselman   2-22-1849
Adams, J. L. - Jane Pricket   4-18-1853
Adkins, Michael - Nancy Kemp   8-15-1847
Admier, Jacob - Mary J. Callahan   12-15-1849
Admier, James - Elizabeth Dean   1-29-1854
Admire, George - Rosanne Sparks
                          lic. 4-24-1841
Allen, David - Lydia Whitehorn   10-12-1843
Anderson, Elijah - Elizabeth Cordery
                          6-15-1854
Anderson, James - Martha Walker   4-15-1852
Anderson, William - Martha S. Weddel   6-15-1854
Anspach, Peter - Amilda Barnet   9-16-1855
Applegate, Richard - Nancy Ann Park   11- 2-1853
Arter, Samuel - Margaret Fleetwood   1-24-1847
Arthur, Alexander - Elizabeth White   7-10-1843
Arvine, John - Musnervey Quick   12- 4-1836
Arwine, John S. - Harriet A. Manville   5-30-1854
Axson, Joseph - Martha A. Hall   2-12-1855
Axson, Samuel - Malvina Fleetwood   10-15-1851
Aynes, John - Sarah A. Honeycutt   3- 1-1855
Aynes, Peter - Rebecca Helms   8-26-1855
Aynes, Reuben - Bathsheba Hall   10- 5-1847
Aynes, William - Susannah Chafin   3- 7-1855
Ayres, Edmond - Dorcas Dotson   8-29-1840
Ayres, Henry - Katharine Duckworth   12-19-1847
Ayres, James - Martha Gosvenor   4-28-1845
Bails, James - Martha Elkins   8- 7-1847
Baker, John B. - Winny Myers   9-20-1845
Barger, Joseph - Hannah Jackson   6-24-1852
Barker, John - Matilda Hicks   4- 8-1852
Barker, William R. - Harriet F.
                   Everling   7-12-1846
Barnes, David - Mary Jane Hillman   8-18-1852
Barrow, Daniel - Rachael Long   1-24-1853
Barton, Basel - Mahala Jane Hicks   6- 8-1852
Baughman, Jacob - Eliza Snider   3-23-1846
Beacham, William R. - Sarah Ann Trail   3-16-1854
Beal, William - Mary J. Johnson   12-21-1851
Beck, David L. - Margaret L. Wagoner   5-14-1853
Beck, William P. - Mary Brown   3-29-1855
Bell, David - Elizabeth Orchards   8- 2-1837
Bender, William, Jr. - Ellen Jane
                   Morris   5-18-1850
Benner, Peter - Elizabeth Stillower   6-13-1851
Bergen, George - Margaret Eoff   4-24-1846
Bergen, Peter - Emily S. Guinn   3-30-1848
Berry, James T. - Sally Mattey   10- 6-1842
Bird, Henry - Matilda Cobb
                          lic. 1- 1-1839
Blackburn, John N. - Elizabeth Wooten
                          10-25-1855
Blackburn, Robert J. - Mary Ann
                   Bracken   7-26-1853
Boles, Benjamin - Susan Morgan   11-23-1843
Boner, Mathew - Sarah Miller   11- 7-1853
Bonta, Jacob - Sarafine Waltman   1-22-1852
Boruff, Greenbury - Elizabeth Marshall
                          4-10-1855
Bott, Isaac - Martha A. Hughes   10-22-1843
Bracken, William D. - Margaret Coatney
                          4-30-1846
Bradley, Daniel D. - Sinia Williams   6-20-1841
Bradley, Granson G. - Frances Cleaveland
                          2- 5-1854

Bradley, Milton S. - Arah Dawson   6-20-1844
Branyan, Joseph - Mary Ann Neidigh   8-12-1849
Breedlove, John - Orinda Followell   12-28-1837
Breedlove, Theodore S. - Lucinda Followell
                          6-22-1844
Breedlove, Thomas J. - Mary Ann Sturgeon
                          3-31-1842
Bright, Zachariah - Ann Arnold   8-14-1855
Briles, William - Martha Porter   3-20-1851
Brooks, Lewis - Ann Sullivan   4-10-1852
Brown, Alexander - Mary Ann Lawless
                          10-24-1850
Brown, George W. - Lydia A. Nickerson
                          3- 1-1855
Brown, Henry - Elizabeth David   7-26-1855
Brown, John - Adaline Mathis   4- 3-1852
Brown, John - Mary Lefevre   11- 1-1852
Brown, John - Nancy Rippee (or Rippel)
                          9-15-1853
Brown, Thomas - Sarah Floyd   1-26-1839
Brown, William - Louisa David   12-14-1845
Brown, William - Lilley Fleetwood   3-12-1854
Broyles, James - Sarah Ann Dickinson
                          lic.3-11-1853
Brummet, Banner - Sarah Ann Parker   6-26-1844
Brummet, George - Emily Marshall   2-10-1838
Brummet, Granville - Miriam Conner   2-24-1848
Brummet, Henry - Alcinda Stephens   10-25-1830
Brummet, Joseph - Elinor Rains   1-21-1846
Brummet, Joshua - Mary W. Prosser   2-24-1850
Brummet, Lewis - Viney Robertson   4- 8-1855
Brummet, Loyd - Jane Hickman   9-19-1846
Brummet, Rees - Orry Long   1-15-1846
Brummet, Robert - Amanda Harris   12-18-1845
Brummet, Ron S. - Margaret Prosser   11-29-1842
Brummet, Solomon - Esther Marshall   8- 1-1847
Brummett, Lewis - Elizabeth Prosser   1-17-1839
Brummett, Lloyd - Margery Williams   4- 8-1853
Burns, James - Sarah Redwine   5- 9-1847
Bush, David - Sinthy Wagoner   10- 2-1853
Byers, Philip - Sarah Followell   8-24-1838
Byrd, Vardaman - Nancy Merit   1-13-1853
Callahan, John T. - Ellen Admier   11- 8-1849
Callon, Leonidas - Elizabeth Burget   9-26-1855
Calvin (or Colvin?), James - Rachael
                   Prosser   4-11-1839
Calvin, Squier W. - Martha Gillaspy   3-23-1854
Campbell, David - Mary Jenkins   3- 5-1840
Campbell, Robert W. - Harriet Waltman
                          1-23-1852
Cannull, Jacob - Amanda Wilkerson   7- 2-1854
Cardwell, Thomas - Julia Ann Gilespie
                          12-19-1844
Cardwell, Thomas J. - Luticia J. Hemphill
                          1-14-1851
Cardwell, William - Sarah Ann Sparks
                          1-14-1838
Carmichael, Benjamin F. - Elender
                   King   3- 5-1854
Carmichael, Robert - Hannah Powell   4-10-1851
Carmichael, William - Nancy S. Calvert
                          11- 1-1852
Carter, Elam - Mary Henry   3- 7-1844
Carter, James - Jane Henry   3-25-1847
Carter, Robert - Cynthia Sturgeon   12-30-1847

Chandler, James B. - Hannah Woods   6- 7-1840
Chandler, Matthew - Mary Jane
                    Anderson   9-21-1845
Chandler, Shadrach - Usley Robertson   3-31-1844
Chandler, Silas - Elizabeth Scott   12-29-1853
Chandler, William K. - Malinda Pawley
                                         3-17-1853
Chappell, Abraham - Eleanor Huff   11-16-1854
Chittenden, Daniel B. - Ann Mason   8-22-1847
Christy, John - Rachel Matheny   3-17-1855
Clapton, Jesse - Maria J. Followell   8-25-1840
Clark, Asa - Maria Headrick   2- 6-1845
Clark, Robert - Ruth Crouch   12- 3-1854
Coffland, Thomas - Lorena Dolsberry   4- 7-1855
Coffman, Samuel - Hester J. Calvert   11- 1-1852
Collins, Sy - Cyntha Clark   3- 4-1855
Colvin, John - Catharine Millis   1-16-1848
Colvin, John - Sarah Conner   12-14-1848
Colvin, John H. - Eliza Newkirk   2-17-1848
Coonfield, John - Ann Winkler   4-13-1840
Coons, Philip J. - Mary Cain   7-16-1854
Cooper, Abraham - Euphama Decker   10-19-1854
Cordrey, Bennett - Mary Wineman   3-31-1853
Cordrey, Hiram W. - Nancy J. McCain   8- 2-1851
Cordrey, William - Margaret Waltz   3- 2-1844
Cornet, John - Sarah Ann Brown   4-28-1853
Costlow, Edward - Nancy Furgerson   8- 8-1854
Cottel, James - Mary Ann McIlvaine   8-26-1841
Coulson, Thomas - Nancy Taggart   8- 6-1840
Coulson, Thomas - Hannah Lover   6- 6-1855
Coy, Samuel - Martha Anderson   8-29-1850
Crane, Caleb, Jr. - Anne Kelley   3-31-1847
Critchfield, John - Emily Philips   4-18-1854
Cross, Henry - Mary Clark   10-12-1845
Crouch, Daniel - Nancy Ping   9-12-1850
Crouch, Moses - Christena Ping   1- 9-1842
Crouch, Washington - Elizabeth Floyd   2- 5-1846
Crouch, Zacharia - Elizabeth Lawless   8-26-1847
Cummings, Malichier - Elizabeth A.
                    Robertson   11-30-1854
Cummons, John - Amanda Headrick   8-19-1847
Curry, Elijah - Mary Richards   9-15-1836
Daggy, Andrew L. - Mary Parsley   11-29-1855
Daggy, Jacob - Mary McFarlin   9-25-1849
Daggy, Samuel - Sarah Myers   10-31-1844
Darling, Rolly J. - Mary Jane Young   1-17-1850
Davenport, Edward F. - Margaret Cully
                    lic. 3-10-1840
David, Edward, Jr. - Irena Mathis   1- 1-1845
David, George W. - Mary Hampton   9- 2-1847
David, Louis H. - Mary J. Tomy   3-23-1848
David, Thomas W. - Sarah E. Tomy   2- 3-1848
Davidson, John - Rachel A. Applegate   1-15-1852
Davidson, Josiah - Katharine Lawson   2-10-1839
Davis, James - Elizabeth Crouch   6-30-1853
Davis, James T. - Catherine Prosser   2- 9-1852
Davis, Jarome B. - Hannah Townsend   11- 4-1855
Davis, Jesse - Inda Phillips   10-12-1843
Davis, Michael - Hannah Womach   9-30-1855
Davis, Stephen C. - Delilah Floyd   1-14-1848
Davison, William - Rachael L. Gray   3- 5-1853
Deboard, Dawson - Mahala Woods   4- 8-1837
Denton, David - Eliza Emeline Bolt   4-21-1841
Deringer, Mathias - Orea Brummett   1-24-1853
Devore, James H. - Sarah Logue   5-20-1849
Devore, John - Nicy Ping   3-31-1851
Dewit, James - Sarah K. Kinzy   10- 1-1848
Dickerson, James - Indiana Sturgeon
                    lic. 1-21-1851
Dickinson, Spencer B. - Clarinda
                    Sturgeon   lic. 4- 1-1853

Dine, Peter - Mary Jane Fricker   2- 1-1853
Dodson, Henry - Polly Conley   7-11-1840
Dodson, Henry - Elenor Nelson
                    lic. 8-20-1853
Dodson, Henry - Nancy Fleetwood
    (Henry Dotson on return)   2-18-1855
Doherty, John - Nancy Rawlings   11- 4-1851
Donelson, John - Eliza Jane Daggy   11-14-1850
Dorts, Philip H. - Melinda Ann Hamblin
                                         2-26-1850
Dotson, George W. - Rachel Nelson
    (George W. Dobson on return)   2- 8-1851
Dotson, Henry - Martha Bailes   5-23-1850
Douglas, C. G. - Harriet Parmerle   1- 8-1851
Douglass, James - Sarah Ann Daggy   3-15-1849
Dover, John - Sarah Stump   4-13-1848
Dunaway, Benjamin - Margaret Mowry   5- 5-1843
Dunean, Jesse - Katharine Cardwell   3- 1-1838
Dunn, Felix - Margaret Gould   10-26-1841
Dutten, Samuel L. - Sarah Weddel   8-14-1850
Eaton, Harvey - Eliza J. Speaks   2- 8-1851
Eddell, McCallen W. - Sarah Fleener
                                         12-23-1852
Edwards, William - Tincy Ann Guy   10-10-1839
Elkins, Drury - Nancy Uley   10-31-1839
Elkins, James - Morning Weddel
                    lic. 1-15-1852
Elkins, Joseph - Tabitha Fergason   3-10-1840
Elkins, Richard - Margaret Uley   2-21-1841
Elkins, Richard - Eliza Wilson   8-29-1847
Elkins, Robert - Mary Sullivan   6-28-1855
Elkins, Thomas - Ruany Medlock   9-13-1855
Elkins, William - Margaret Polly   7-20-1837
Everling, Samuel - Revina Munden   7-19-1851
Eytcheson, Jefferson S. - Elizabeth Stiver
                                         1-12-1847
Ferguson, Samuel - Lucinda Polly   3-24-1842
Finley, William - Sarah Fleetwood   10-29-1848
Fitzgibbon, Edward - Salina Mathis   9-19-1853
Fleener, Jacob H. - Sarah Rude   9-10-1854
Fleener, Samuel W. - Nancy Rude   1- 1-1852
Fleetwood, General - Sharlotta Pawley
    (Sharlotta Polly on return)   7- 5-1854
Fleetwood, Isaac - Emerine Wilkison   1-23-1839
Fleetwood, Isaac - Luvina Hall   4- 5-1845
Fleetwood, James - Louisa Tabor   1- 8-1854
Fleetwood, John - Ann Johnson   4- 1-1852
Florer, Robert - Lovisa Porter   1-16-1844
Flowers, Solomon - Elizabeth Griffen
                                         11-22-1855
Floyd, Mathew - Zillah J. Bidwell   1-20-1845
Followell, Alexander - Debby Ann Wise
                                         11-23-1839
Followell, Cornelias - Mary Jane Quinn
                                         10- 1-1848
Followell, James H. - Letitia Breedlove
                                         6-22-1844
Followell, James H. - Lydia Ann Mavity
                                         12-18-1850
Followell, Joseph D. - Esther Percifield
                                         9-21-1850
Followell, Lewis B. - Sarah Marshall
                                         5-24-1845
Followell, Samuel R. - Elizabeth Taggart
                                         3-12-1846
Foot, Edward A. - Hannah Mathis   2-10-1845
Foreman, William - Margaret J. Hanvey
                                         7-13-1854
Fortenburg, Benjamin - Sintheann Bradly
                                         6- 2-1844
Fowler, Samuel - Mary Murphy   6-26-1851

Fowler, Washington T. - Elizabeth I. Ross
                                    3-15-1846
Fox, Isaac - Delila Newkirk   3-30-1841
Fox, John - Louisa Pike   1-28-1844
Fox, Joseph - Harriet Porter   1- 1-1854
Frad, Joseph - America Burget   2-12-1854
Fraker, Joseph - Mary Ann Gillaspy 9- 9-1852
Fread, John - Lydia Guthery   12-19-1840
Freed, John, Jr. - Mary Chase   3-11-1841
Fricker, Ambrose - Margaret A. Dine 2- 6-1855
Fricker, Joseph - Manerva Duncan   2-21-1855
Fricker, William - Sarah Jane Walker
                                   12-31-1853
Fry, Andrew - Elizabeth Bales   12-15-1853
Fuller, David - Hellena Andrews   11- 4-1855
Furgerson, John - Elizabeth Elkins 7-29-1849
Fussleman, William - Elizabeth Anders
                                    5- 7-1848
Gale, Jarvis - Margaret Quinn   7- 1-1849
Gallion, Thomas - Rebecca Eddy
                              lic. 6- ?-1852
Gardenner, Leroy - Sarah E. Frad   5-17-1855
Gillaspy, John W. - Rachael A. Wells
                                   12-15-1854
Gilpin, Joshua - Martha Day   3-24-1851
Givens, Thales - Julia Carter   7-27-1842
Goforth, Richard - Mary F. Hamblen 1-23-1849
Goins, John - Belinda Baker   10- 5-1853
Good, Samuel M. - Nancy M. Henry   5- 4-1851
Gooding, James M. - Mary Deans   2-24-1852
Goss, Daniel - Elizabeth Goss   1-16-1842
Goss, William - Anna Matney   6-19-1842
Gosvenor, George - Lydia Whitehorn
                              lic. 12- 7-1840
Gosvenor, George - Jemina Hampton   4-11-1842
Gosvenor, John - Fanny Kinworthy   4-11-1839
Gosvenor, Richard - Elizabeth Hill 12-28-1848
Gould, John C. - Margaret Prosser   9- 6-1842
Gourly, Robert - Lucinda Melton
  (Robert Gowerly on return)   1- 1-1854
Graham, Harrison - Sarah Ann Lawless 6-25-1840
Gray, Josephus - Elizabeth Stump   1-20-1853
Greenlee, Alfred - Almeda Womack   11- 4-1855
Greenlee, Amos - Mary Ann Mathis   10-14-1855
Gregg, Mark T. - Sarah Hicks   12-21-1853
Grey, Hamilton - Elizabeth Fry   11- 5-1842
Griffin, James - Sarah Pace   2- 8-1848
Griffin, William - Margaret Woods 10- 8-1851
Griffith, Valentine - Susan Adams 11-22-1855
Griffith, William - Katharine Jackson
                                   12-24-1838
Grigsby, Jesse - Sintha Ann Frad   4-13-1854
Grimes, John - Eliza Brummet   9-26-1850
Grove, Garrison - Sally Ann Stivers 11-11-1843
Guffy, Henry - Ruth Blocker   3-23-1848
Guffy, Joshua P. - Sarah A. King   9-27-1853
Guffy, Thomas M. - Susanna King   9- 8-1850
Guffy, Thomas M. - Nancy Millsaps 11- 3-1853
Guy, Lillman - Dulcena Richardson   2-19-1843
Guy, Wiley - Anna Davis   1-19-1854
Hacker, Charles - Anna Followell   6-27-1850
Hackney, John R. - Mary Jane Rogers 12- 1-1854
Hagar, John - Lucinda Henry   12-14-1853
Hamblen, David S. - Nancy Coulson   4- 8-1849
Hamblen, Pleasant - Angeline Murphy 10-14-1847
Hamblen, William - Nancy Goforth   1-10-1839
Hamblen, William - Elizabeth Burkhart
                                    5-22-1839
Hamblin, David L. - Nancy Watson   10- 1-1843
Hamblin, Elikim - Elizabeth Minard 5-30-1855
Hamblin, Jesse - Milly Rice   1-13-1850

Hamblin, Uriah - Mary Ann Chappel 10- 1-1854
Hamblin, William - Elizabeth Huff   2-13-1855
Hampton, James - Martha Followell   9-23-1852
Hampton, Levi - Elizabeth Hill   7-13-1848
Hampton, William - Lucinda Rogers
                              lic. 6- 2-1851
Handy, William - Rachel Dine   6- 9-1845
Hanway, Amos - Catharine Neidigh   2-10-1845
Hardin, Ferrel - Elizabeth Jones   4-19-1843
Harris, John - Sally Berry   3-22-1842
Hartman, Peter - Phebe Jane Lamb   8- 5-1855
Hatchet, Bartlet - Elizabeth Percifield
                                    3-12-1854
Hatchet, John - Nancy Jeffers   7-10-1845
Hatchet, William G. - Catharine Jeffers
                                    3- 5-1848
Hatchet, William G. - Elviry Elkins 9-25-1853
Hatten, Jonathan - Sarah Ayres   8- 1-1850
Havens, Alexander - Anna Maxwell
                              lic. 4-13-1843
Havens, Joel - Dolly Scroghan   11-27-1851
Havron, Elijah - Margaret Henry   7-21-1850
Hays, William W. - Martha Huntington
                                    2-22-1846
Hays, William W. - Elizabeth M. Dutz
                                   12-29-1846
Head, Loranza D. - Indiana M. Hotchkiss
                                    5-18-1846
Headrick, Joseph - Sally Ann Mullis
                                   12-26-1839
Hedrick, Benjamin F. - July Ann Brown
                                    7- 3-1853
Helton, John S. - Martha Jane Woods
                                   12-11-1842
Hemphill, James - Elizabeth Hicks   3-25-1851
Hemphill, Joseph - Sarah Ann Friker
                                   10-25-1849
Hemphill, Thomas - Katharine Sleighter
                                   12-15-1849
Henderson, James M. - Jane Bright   8-19-1855
Henderson, Robert - Mary Ann Davis 12-13-1849
Henderson, William - Emeline King   1-18-1852
Henly, Davidson - Melinda Noblet   8-21-1842
Henry, John - Nancy Scarbrough   8-22-1850
Henry, Murray - Caroline Branaman 11-21-1852
Henry, Philip - Lucinda Young   9-26-1852
Hensley, Richardson - Matilda Ann Tharp
                                    1-27-1842
Hicks, Amos - Mary Cardwell   12-22-1842
Hicks, Henry - Arrena Kemp   11-12-1848
Hicks, Robert - Druzilla Mitchell   1-10-1847
Hicks, William - Armity Bell   2-29-1840
Hill, John - Nancy Fleetwood   4-11-1854
Holmes, John Q. - Barbary Bozzell   7-27-1853
Holms, Hugh Allen - Mary Phillips   7-29-1849
Honeycutt, Michael - Eliza Costtow 6-29-1855
Honeycutt, Sterling - Lucy Helms   2- 8-1855
Hooper, Isaac - Lydia Gould   12-25-1844
Hoover, Sandford - Naome Keeney   11-19-1846
Hoover, William - Nancy Watts   2-23-1855
Hopkins, James - Juliana King   7-21-1844
Hubbard, Allen - Ary Fleener   11- 3-1839
Hubbard, Jesse L. - Lucinda King   11-19-1839
Hubbard, Simeon G. - Martha Ann Weddel
                                   12-18-1847
Hubbard, William C. - Margaret Kennedy
                                   12- 5-1839
Huff, Theodrac - Mary Keefe   2-13-1852
Huntington, Ozi C. - Nancy J. Jackson
                                    5-20-1849
Huntington, William O. - Sarah I. Adams
                                    2-19-1846

Hurkey, Elisha - Catharine Ping   8-30-1841
Hurley, Ephraim - Mary E. Mabe   6-24-1840
Hurley, Dr. James - Mary Wyse   12- 7-1845
Hurley, Joseph M. - Elizabeth Hedrick
                                  lic. 4-16-1839
Hurley, Moses F. - Susannah Trua   4-13-1854
Isreal, John W. - Maria E. Colvin   9- 9-1855
Jackson, George - Margaret Yates   8- 9-1850
Jackson, Granville - Rebecca Jackson
                                       12-21-1848
Jackson, James - Sarah Dawson   7-28-1847
Jackson, John - Rachel Taggart   2-19-1852
Jackson, Joshua - Nancy Jane White   1- 6-1848
Jackson, Martin B. - Mary Jane Taggart
                                        6-28-1855
Jackson, Thomas - Christina Chester   2- 7-1850
Jackson, Wilson - Violinda Edwards   8-17-1850
Jeffers, John - Margaret Wise   4-27-1848
Jeffers, Paul - Sarah Scott   10-31-1852
Jenkins, Alexander H. - Eliza Jane Devore
                                        1-14-1849
Jenkins, Joshua - Cerrena Elder
  (Caroline Elder on license)   1- 1-1849
Jimison, Charles - Ann Keefe   3-21-1852
Johnson, Israel - Nancy Duggans   8- 1-1839
Johnson, Temple - Ruth Scarbrough   4-12-1855
Johnson, William - Aly Wilson   7- 4-1852
Johnston, Harvy - Rody Elkins   9-10-1854
Jones, James - Elizabeth Tidd   9- 9-1852
Jones, Thomas W. - Juliana Hopkins   11-13-1845
Jones, W. G. - Margaret Honeycutt   7-13-1855
Jorad, Stephen - Eliza Ann Chase   11-16-1848
Keeling, Ambrose - Nancy Hurley   1-30-1846
Keeney, George - Ruanna Hoover   12-19-1846
Kelley, Edwin B. - Orpha Rains   9-30-1847
Kelly, John C. - Hannah E. Cox   7-10-1855
Kelly, Richard E. - Nancy J. Butcher
                                       11- 4-1855
Kelly, Zachariah - Jane Taggart   3-22-1852
Kemp, Thomas D. - Eliza Jane Franklin
                                        7-23-1846
Kemp, Thomas D. - Sarah Ann Franklin   9-15-1847
Kennedy, John - Martha McQuinn   2-25-1855
Kennedy, Moses - Lucy Kennedy   2-23-1852
Kennedy, Stephen - Susannah Taggart   7-29-1847
King, Coonrod - Eliza Shafer   5-28-1854
King, Daniel - Abigail M. Carmichael   6-11-1848
King, Henry - Rosanna Joslin   7-31-1845
King, Isaac - Violet Porter   12-31-1840
King, Isaac - Elizabeth Henderson   3-19-1852
King, John - Nancy Baker   4-21-1837
King, William - Mary Ann Park   8-29-1845
Kinsey, Thadeous - Margaret Hancher   12-24-1854
Kirts, Daniel - Catharine Petro   8- 3-1854
Kirts, John - Nancy Joslin   10-21-1851
Kirtze, Coonrads - Jane Rariden   4-19-1837
Knight, Joshua - Mary Ann Johnson   8-15-1852
Kridelbough, Andrew J. - Mahala Colvin
                                        2- 8-1849
Lamb, George - Phebe Jane Bright   12-17-1840
Lamb, Yancy - Margaretty Flowers   2-16-1853
Lambert, Matthias - Sarah Lair   12-11-1845
Lane, Gilman - Emily Henry   1-11-1851
Lane, Ralph - Susan Cobb
                                  lic. 8-13-1844
Lawless, Abraham - Elizabeth Ping   1-16-1839
Lawless, Jacob - Elizabeth Matney   5-31-1844
Lawrence, Manuel P. - Mary Waltz   9- 7-1848
Lee, Joseph - Phebe Goss   3- 5-1840
Lee, William G. - Mary Gosvenor   3- 4-1847
Lefonce, Samuel - Rebecca Sherrill   10-19-1848

Legans, James - Mary Handy   2-23-1843
Lemmon, Isaac - Elizabeth Morgan   7-31-1855
Lemon, William P. - Lucinda Walden   6-29-1843
Lingo, John S. - Asherine Richardson
                                        1-28-1852
Lockridge, William - Hannah Mordock   9-14-1851
Long, Andrew - Nancy Myers   9-20-1848
Long, Christopher - Elizabeth Harris
                                        2-29-1844
Long, Hamilton - Sarah Ann Prosser   2- 9-1852
Long, Willie - Mrs. Eliza O'Haver   12- 6-1845
Long, Willis - Hannah Cox   5-17-1843
Long, Willis - Hannah Foot   9-17-1848
Loy, David - Elizabeth Crouch   3- 6-1850
Lucas, Jonathan - Elizabeth A. Petro
                                  lic. 4- 5-1844
Lucus, Solomon - Aly Johnson
                                  lic. 1-27-1855
Luts, George - Mary Noblet   11-10-1853
Luts, Philip - Mary Ann Brown   12- 1-1853
McCarty, Samuel - Angeline Douglass   3- 2-1854
McCarty, William H. - Martha Ann Rude
                                        9-30-1849
McColip, Huston - Margaret M. Pendleton
                                        8-28-1855
McCord, Steward B. - Rachel Huntsinger
                                       11-21-1852
McCoy, Cornelius - Mary Ann Weddell   6- 3-1855
McFarlin, Henry - Margaret J. Tuttle
                                       11- 7-1850
McFarlin, William - Harriet Kemp   4-10-1849
McIntosh, Peter - Anna Elkins   9-10-1844
McKinney, Daniel - Jane Henderson   9-20-1840
McKee, Ephraim - Phebe Ann Stillabower
                                        2-17-1853
McKinney, John - Sarilda Weddel   9-10-1850
McLaughlin, David - Ann Fancher
                 (or Hancher?)   7-19-1852
McLaughlin, Thomas - Catharine Parks
                                        6-20-1847
McQuality, George - Jane Graham   10-30-1844
McQuinn, Birkert I. - Elizabeth Wooten
                                       10-24-1855
McQueen, Uriah - Malvina Henry   12-16-1852
McWilliams, James - Elenor Hampton   7-15-1855
Mabe, James W. - Anna Noblet   11- 3-1842
Male, William F. - Elizabeth Clark   8-10-1848
Marcum, Elisha - Sarah Redwine   2- 5-1855
Marlett, Jared - Jemima S. Rush   10-27-1855
Marsh, Daniel - Sarah Cox   11-22-1853
Marshall, George - Adaline Hodge   9- 4-1850
Marshall, James - Artimacy Followell
                                        8-18-1839
Marshall, Robert - Martha E. Knight   3-22-1849
Marshall, Robert - Elizabeth Brown   1- 8-1850
Martin, Benjamin - Levisa Ann Sherrill
                                        9-26-1849
Mathis, Jacob - Nancy W. Edgington   7-19-1852
Mathis, Jeremiah - Nancy Wilkinson   1- 5-1854
Mathis, Martin - Nancy Brooks   8-15-1843
Mathis, Mathew - Eliza Ann Williams
                                       12- 1-1839
Mathis, Reuben - Hannah McIntire   6-30-1839
Mathis, Riley - Elizabeth Edgington
                                       12-29-1853
Matlock, David - Nancy Mabe   10-11-1849
Matney, Daniel - Rebecca Goforth
                                  lic. 9- 4-1844
Matney, John - Catharine Goss   4-18-1841
Matney, Joshua - Susannah Rogers   4-15-1838
Matney, William A. - Catharine Summy
                                       12-29-1842

Matthews, Joseph - Mariah Mahonney   10-30-1848
Mayfield, David F. - Nancy Fry   2-22-1854
Mead, Hannibal I. - Nancy Jane Hamblen
                                      10- 4-1848
Mead, Joseph - Rebecca Kennedy   3-19-1851
Mellatt, Aaron - Mary Truax   8-11-1853
Micham, Christopher - Keziah Spriggs
                                      11-13-1851
Millens, John G. - Elizabeth Ann Porter
                                       9- 6-1854
Miller, Isaac - Elizabeth Jeffers   1-14-1850
Miller, William - Sally J. Debord   6-10-1849
Millsap, Robert M. - Nancy Weddel   2-24-1848
Mitchel, James A. - Mary Jane Skidmore
                                      10-27-1850
Mitchell, Richard - Phebe Dire   8-17-1851
More, Samuel L. B. - Lucinda Cordell 9- 3-1853
Morgan, George - Elizabeth Everling   9- 7-1847
Morgan, Zedekiah - Miriam Robertson   3-30-1845
Morris, Nathaniel - Mary Richardson   11-14-1854
Morris, William - Dosha Bently   6-28-1855
Morrison, James - Sally Wooten   12-22-1853
Moser, Washington - Delila Followell 3-24-1851
Mullis, Franklin - Margaret Rogers   6- 5-1848
Mullis, John - Indiana McKinney   3- 6-1846
Mullis, Richard - Jeriah McKinny   5-22-1844
Murphy, James - Nancy Kenkins   2- 3-1848
Murphy, William - Mary Jane Gray   5-20-1852
Myers, John - Sarah Ann David   3-21-1850
Neal, Linsey M. - Catharine Bockman
  (Catharine Baughman on return)   9-29-1853
Neff, Oliver A. - Sarah E. Campbell   5- 9-1853
Neidigh, Abraham - Mary A. Fleener   2-15-1846
Nelson, Samuel - Catharine Crider   9-24-1850
Newkirk, Henry - Hannah Waggoner   5-24-1840
Nickerson, Isaac - Alecy Matley   9-21-1842
Noblet, John - Henrietta Lawless   8-26-1847
Noblet, Levi - Maude Ripple   6- 9-1853
Noblet, William - Lucinda Womack   3-16-1848
Orchard, James - Mary Hicks   10-21-1847
Page, Timothy - Sarah Crim   9- 9-1847
Painter, Benjamin - Jane Mundane   12-22-1850
Paris, William - Lorinda Hawkins
                (or Hankins?)   6-16-1846
Parks, Samuel - Dorcas Henry   8-20-1841
Parmerlee, James C. - Nancy Neely   6- 9-1846
Parr, Robert - Jane Hicks   5-26-1851
Parris, Isom - Mary Ann Lane   11- 6-1853
Parsley, Columbus - Elizabeth Chapell
                                       1- 5-1853
Parsley, Daniel - Ann Thomas   2-21-1838
Parsley, John - Martha Chapple   11-21-1852
Paskins, John W. - Anna Fricker   1-28-1848
Paskins, Thomas - Sarah Ann Mathis   10-10-1850
Pawley, David J. - Eliza Jane Brenton
                                       5-31-1846
Payne, Jesse R. - Margaret Shoock   1-23-1845
Payne, Joseph W. - Amanda Abby   11-19-1854
Payten, Craven - Mary Watson   9-25-1851
Percifield, Blevins - Nancy Hampton   10-10-1849
Percifield, Gilbert - Jane Neampton   12-21-1850
Percifield, Marlin - Orinda Hoover   9-12-1850
Percifield, Marlin - Sylvania Huff   10- 4-1855
Percifield, Missener - Sally Turk   8-17-1845
Percifield, William - Emily Percifield
                                       9- 1-1844
Percifield, William - Josey Percifield
                                       9-13-1853
Perry, John - Scharlotte Rambo   6-10-1855
Persifield, George - Elizabeth Clapton
                                       3- 4-1847

Peters, Phillip S. - Sarah Brown   12-23-1847
Petro, Benjamin - Catharine David   1-28-1854
Petro, George - Saphira Calvin
                (or Colvin)   11- 5-1846
Petro, Nicholas - Elizabeth Brown   3- 2-1854
Philips, Silas - Leanah Coonfield   11-24-1851
Picher, Franklin - Alsey Stufflebean
                                      12- 6-1838
Pike, Phillip - Nancy Crouch   8-24-1848
Ping, John, Jr. - Elizabeth Lawless   9-15-1842
Ping, Richard - Sarah Rogers   7-15-1838
Ping, William - Elizabeth Bender   1-30-1844
Ping, William - Martha Chambers   5-17-1849
Pitcher, Benjamin F. - Eliza Dean   9-25-1852
Po, John - Rebecca Cumaford   4- 3-1855
Polly, James - Lucinda Furguson   4-22-1843
Porter, Henry - Harriet L. Newkirk   6-21-1840
Powell, John W. - Rhoda B. Gray   9-23-1847
Powell, Moses - Sophronah Weddell   10-12-1854
Prewitt, Laomi - Eliza Jane Davidson
                                       4-10-1845
Price, Wilson - Mary Kelly   7-19-1855
Pricher, Jonathan - Anne Stiver   6-28-1846
Pricket, Jacob W. - Margaret Corn   1-10-1848
Prosser, Abraham - Martha Wilkins   10-12-1841
Prosser, Daniel - Minerva Brummet   12- 5-1843
Prosser, Daniel, Jr. - Hannah Swift   5- 2-1842
Prosser, Daniel D. - Matilda Jenkins
                                       6-18-1840
Prosser, Daniel W. - Bethany Hubbard
                                      11- 7-1852
Prosser, Isaac - Elizabeth Kelly   6- 2-1840
Prosser, James - Margaret Jane Kelly
                                       4-15-1841
Prosser, Joseph - Melissa Brummet   3-12-1846
Pruitt, James - Roseann Wadworth   3-17-1853
Pruitt, Thomas L. - Rachael Hankins
                                      11-28-1852
Pryer, James A. - Elenore F. Davis   6-23-1853
Pryor, John B. - Lucinda Davis   6-11-1854
Quick, Littleton - Mary Ann Wells   1-21-1855
Quinn, Hugh - Eliza Kennedy
                               lic.   4-27-1844
Quinn, John - Maria Bright   12- 9-1847
Ragsdale, George - Rebecca Ann Woods
                                       2-16-1851
Rains, Wiley - Orphea Brummet   4- 1-1845
Rairden, Jefferson - Minerva Chapell
                                      12-13-1854
Raper, John - Mary Campbell   7-31-1851
Raper, Lewis F. - Hester Ann Loudermilk
                                       4- 9-1846
Rariden, Henry - Margaret J. Rariden
                                       4-29-1848
Rawlings, George W. - Vesleny Dehart
                                       7- 5-1849
Rawlings, Page - Rachel Daggy   11-23-1847
Ready, William - Maria Gable   10- 7-1847
Reynolds, Hiram - Sarah Jane Raper   2-24-1848
Reynolds, John - Milinda Reynolds   8-15-1846
Reynolds, Jorden - Sarah Orsben   6- 4-1850
Reynolds, Miriam - Priscilla Tull   10-18-1853
Rice, Joseph - Rachel Henderson   2- 9-1840
Rice, Joseph H. - Ursula Satterthwait
                                       8-18-1853
Richards, David - Rebecca Grove   7-18-1844
Richards, Jesse - Anna Grove   11-23-1836
Richards, Stephen - Elizabeth Weddle
                                       5- 4-1837
Richardson, James - Rebecca Robertson
                                      11- 1-1849

Richardson, Jeremiah - Mary E. Fleenor
                                8-25-1848
Richardson, Joel - Miriam Robertson 12-27-1849
Richardson, John N. - Lydia Mathis 11- 8-1853
Richardson, William N. - Harriet A. Beaty
                                12-19-1850
Richison, John S. - Sarah E. Straw   9-22-1854
Rider, George W. - Jane Johnson   2-17-1848
Ritter, Jesse - Frances P. Owen   9-16-1852
Robbins, William - Matilda K. Umphrey
                                9-18-1842
Roberts, Benoni S. - Susannah Elson 10-30-1853
Roberts, Richard - Rachel A. Henry 10-30-1851
Roberts, Silvester - Lethea Ann Holeman
                                2- 7-1850
Robertson, Daniel - Margaret Keith 11-19-1847
Robertson, John - Malinda McCoy   12-21-1848
Robertson, John - Lucy Ann Botts   3-18-1849
Robertson, John - Phebe Tabor   4-24-1851
Robertson, Joseph - Eliza Ann Whitney
                                4-23-1848
Robertson, William - Charlotte Vites 4- 7-1840
Robertson, William - Rebecca Sutfin 6- 6-1844
Rodgers, Jesse - Margaret Robertson 7- 3-1842
Rogers, William - Mary Ann Cobb   3-30-1837
Roy, William J. - Nancy C. Cobb   11- 6-1842
Runde, Worden - Vina Ann Reynolds
   (Worden Rude on return)   4- 7-1854
Ryker, John - Margaret Cooper   4-19-1855
Scaggs, John - Prudy Kemp   5- 6-1852
Scott, Lewis - Martha Patterson   11-14-1837
Scotten, William - Kiziah Percifield 9-14-1848
Scugs, Marcus - Dicy Kemp   2- 1-1851
Sexton, David - Ann Rogers   12-20-1853
Shannon, Robert - Sarah Susan Gray   7-18-1846
Shannon, William - Mary Prosser   5-13-1841
Shelton, James - Olla Brummet   1- 2-1848
Shepard, Josiah - Rachael Eddy   4-25-1854
Shipley, Jesse - Mary Ann Hall   3-23-1845
Shipley, Jesse - Emarine Lash   11-24-1854
Shipley, John - Nancy Kinworthy   11-18-1849
Shipley, Nelson - Canzady Harper   9- 7-1850
Shipley, Samuel - Sarah Shipley   1- 6-1854
Sipe, Thomas J. - Hannah Tharp   3- 2-1853
Sixtine, Joseph - Esther Scripture   1-26-1845
Skidmore, William - Lucinda Mitchell
                                12-17-1846
Slack, Jacob - Eliza A. Bott   3-26-1843
Smith, Charles - Irenah King   9-10-1836
Smith, Jesse - Elizabeth Quinn   2-16-1842
Smith, John - Catharine Preston   8- 9-1846
Smith, Jonathan - Mary M. Howard   3- 6-1843
Smith, Samuel - Ally Johnson   1-29-1855
Smith, William - Sarah Ellis   3- 1-1843
Smith, William - Susanna M. Smith   1- 6-1853
Smith, William J. - Angeline Barnett 4-15-1852
Snider, George W. - Louiza Parker   5-15-1844
Snider, Harmon - Sally Long   9- 8-1842
Snider, James - Elizabeth Brummet   9-27-1853
Snider, John - Elizabeth Murphy   5-19-1852
Snider, John - Elizabeth Brummet   12- 1-1853
Sparks, George M. - Elizabeth Harris
                                10-30-1836
Spitzner, Frederick - Susannah Stillabower
                                12- 6-1855
Spurgeon, Eli - Parmelia Guy   4- 2-1848
Staal, Peter - Mary Schroghan   2-23-1855
Staples, Joseph - Elizabeth Brooks   5-23-1852
Step, John - Jane Chapell   3-16-1851
Stephens, James - Sarah Fleetwood   4-13-1848
Stevens, Jourdan - Zilpha Huff   9-22-1853

Steward, Benjamin - Lucretia Jenkins
                                3-16-1845
Stewart, Benjamin - Mahala Spears   1-19-1837
Stillabower, John - Catherine Stillabower
                                12-11-1853
Stivers, George - Nancy Petro   12-12-1852
Stivers, Henry - Sary Harris   7-28-1836
Stufflebean, John - Mary Stivers   5-26-1849
Stults, William - Olive A. Frad   2-10-1855
Stump, George - Minerva Huff   4-11-1846
Sturgeon, Alexander - Jane Mavity   10- 3-1847
Sturgeon, James - Nancy Reynolds   7- 3-1851
Stuts, George - Eliza Conner   10-23-1855
Sullivan, Isaac - Lucinda Harper   3-24-1854
Sullivan, Isaac - Margaret Percefield
                                8-14-1855
Sullivan, James E. - Elizabeth Hall
                          lic. 6- --1854
Sullivan, James T. - Anna Weddel   8- 4-1844
Sullivan, James T. - Emily Jane Elkins
                                7-21-1850
Sullivan, William, Jr. - Nancy Elkins
                          lic. 8-10-1855
Summa, George - Mrs. Margaret Mavity
                                1-25-1846
Swift, Thomas - Elizabeth Dickerson 8- 6-1840
Syra, Thomas - Mary Ann Weatherman   8-20-1846
Tabor, James - Polly Shipley   2-14-1852
Tabor, Joshua - Elizabeth G. Noblet 4-11-1851
Tabor, Joshua - Martha Elkins   5- 6-1853
Tabor, Martin - Susan Noblet   9-30-1847
Taggart, James, Jr. - Nancy H. Daver
                                2-29-1844
Taggart, James W. - Hannah Newkirk   3- 4-1847
Taggart, John - Nancy Hubbard   5- 6-1848
Taggart, William - Leah F. Gillaspy
                                12- 5-1852
Taggert, William P. - Sarilda Hamblin
                                8- 6-1851
Taylor, Archibald - Elizabeth King   1-26-1837
Taylor, Hery - Katharine Davidson
                          lic. 4- 5-1838
Thomas, John H. - Nancy R. Tomey   6-29-1854
Thomas, William - Spicy Schrougham   7-17-1844
Thompson, James - Phebe Ann Hicks   12-29-1850
Tinkey, David - Margaret E. Cordry   1- 3-1846
Todd, Wellington - Mariah Johnson   1- 5-1854
Tomlinson, John - Polly Joslin   8-11-1842
Tomy, Samuel - Eleander Myers   8-24-1847
Toney, William - Eliza Wiatt   2-18-1844
Tony, Reubin - Mary Bell   2-20-1838
Tremly, Levi - Mary Harmon   9- 5-1850
Truax, John W. - Sarah E. Haislup   4-17-1853
Tucker, Cornelius - Mary Hamblin   1-19-1837
Tucker, John - Emily Hatchet   5- 8-1845
Tucker, John - Mary Jackson   3-13-1851
Tull, Levin - Luvina Reynolds   9-16-1846
Tull, Lewis J. - Indiana Williams   2-13-1850
Tull, William - Elizabeth Mathis   4- 9-1851
Turk, Samuel - Maria Percifield   6-20-1842
Vance, Silas - Catharine Bozzel   5-21-1848
Vawn, Stockley D. - Amanda J. Sullivan
                                7-26-1850
Waggoner, Elisha - Margaret J. Vance
                                7-16-1848
Waggoner, George W. - Mary Ann Vance
                                8-11-1850
Walker, James - Louisa Rawlings   2-10-1848
Walker, Landy B. - Rachel Young   10-24-1839
Walker, William T. - Mary Davidson 12- 3-1851
Wallace, Joseph L. - Julia Ann Waltman
                                3-30-1848

Waltman, Hiram - Sarah Jane McIlhenney
                                1-11-1852
Waltz, Absalom - Nancy King   12-20-1846
Waltz, John - Eliza Rude   9-16-1851
Waltz, Simon P. - Semantha Weddel 9-25-1853
Watson, Darius M. - Lucinda Richards 1- 6-1842
Watson, James - Frances Cleavelin 11-25-1851
Watson, James C. - Sarah Cox   2- 9-1854
Weatherman, Harrison - Harriet Robertson
                                11- 5-1850
Weddel, Francis M. - Martha Sullivan
                                10- 7-1853
Weddel, James A. - Mary Robertson 7-19-1855
Weddel, John - Geriah Hatten   6-21-1849
Weddel, John - Malinda C. Kelley 1- 6-1853
Weddel, John - Malinda Hatten   1- 6-1855
Weddel, Mordecai - Martha S. Smith 9-12-1850
Weddel, Richard B. - Catharine Hurley
                                6- 4-1848
Weddel, William E. - Polly Turk   3-10-1846
Weddel, William G. - Sabine Jeffers 3-12-1844
White, Ellis - Martha Johnson   10- 3-1849
White, Henry - Elizabeth Broyles 4-22-1852
White, William H. - Margaret Rogers 2- 8-1847
Whitehorn, Elijah - Lucy J. Weddel 2-25-1853
Whitney, James - Mary Helms   5- 3-1855
Whitney, Theodore - Isabelle Quinn 1-20-1850

Wilkerson, Hammond - Margaret White 6-25-1848
Wilkerson, James - Polly Rogers   3- 7-1844
Wilkerson, William H. - Mary Ann Ritter
                                9- 2-1852
Wilkins, James W. - Sarah Callahan 10-28-1847
Williams, Alfred - Nancy Ann Mathis
                             10-27-1844
Williams, John B. - Susanah Robertson
                              1- 4-1844
Willison, James - Dorcus Cordial 2- 1-1838
Wilson, George W. - Susan Mathis 10-11-1844
Wink, Isaac D. - Nancy Ann Foreman 4-12-1855
Wise, Bennet - Tilitha Lane   5-22-1853
Wise, James, Jr. - Lucinda Lemons 6-30-1854
Wise, Matthew - Katharine Brown 11-16-1848
Wolf, Otho - Elizabeth Smith   9-22-1842
Woods, Andrew - Margaret McChase 11-11-1839
Woods, Felix - Rebecca Dawson   6- 2-1850
Woods, Jackson - Eliza Ann Roberts 2-12-1846
Woods, Jackson - Sarah M. Roberts 4-10-1849
Wright, David F. - Margaret Ann Knight
                                1-11-1849
Yoder, John - Mary Ann Tull   3-19-1853
Yost, James A. C. - Catharine Truax 7-12-1855
Young, Bazel - Julia Fancher (?) 12- 4-1851
Young, Evin - Elizabeth Hovis   4- 2-1854
Young, John - Sarah McNeel
      (McNeely on return)   1-23-1839

MARRIAGES PERFORMED BY REV. PETER H. GOLLADAY, 1839-1867

The marriages were performed while Reverend Golladay was serving as pastor of the Presbyterian Church in Harrison, Ohio. They were contributed for publication by Mrs. Marjorie B. Burress, Cincinnati, Ohio.

The Reverend Peter H. Golladay was born in Augusta County, Virginia, April 10, 1802, the son of David and Rebecca Golladay. He graduated from Washington College (Md.) in 1828 and Union Seminary in 1831. After being ordained at Oxford, Ohio, in 1832 he pastored Presbyterian churches at Camden and Venice, Ohio, before becoming pastor of the Harrison church in 1839 where he remained until 1856. The following eight years were spent in Decatur and Franklin counties, Indiana, after which he returned to Harrison for two more years. On April 27, 1833, he married Eliza M. Doughty of Butler County, Ohio, a native of Prince William County, Virginia.

The town of Harrison lies partly in Ohio and partly in Dearborn County, Indiana. The congregation of the Presbyterian church was drawn from Dearborn and Franklin counties, Indiana, and from Hamilton County, Ohio. Reverend Golladay was called on to perform marriages in all this area. He died December 17, 1883, and his wife in 1895. The marriages performed while pastor at Harrison were kept in a ledger and were published in the Harrison News, December 11 and 16, 1890 from the ledger. The present whereabouts of the ledger is not known. Mrs. Burress copied the marriages from the newspaper.

Armstrong, James - Letitia McClure 12- 6-1849
Arnold, Richard - Julia Ann Shroyer 2-19-1840
Arnold, George - Hannah Herron   12-21-1842
Arnold, Samuel B. - Elizabeth Hann 8-19-1839
Arnold, George W. - Harriet B. Herider
                                3- 1-1854
Atherton, Elijah - Mary Arnold   8- --1843
Baldridge, John - Agnes Henderson 9-25-1855
  (Nancy A. Henerson in return)
Ball, Samuel - Mrs. Ruth Horney   8- 8-1865
Barret, John - Rachel Palmer   11- 8-1846
Barrow, John - Mary Pruden   1- 2-1851
Barrow, Joseph - Hannah Keen   2-11-1848
Baton, William - Rebecca Kirkpatrick
                                1----1846
Benton, A. - Margaret White   2- 3-1852
Bonham, Eugene W. - Sarah Penny 7-23-1865
Bonnel, Seneca - Martha Rifner 12- 8-1842

Bowler, Harry - Jane Simonson   5- 2-1866
Branson, Dr. -- - Eveline Arnold 5- 3-1853
Brown, John - Sarah Ellis   1-19-1851
Bruner, Thomas - Nancy Wildridge 1-15-1867
Burk, Elisha M. - M. E. Crets   5-24-1865
Burk, Ulick - Mary Calloway   2- 9-1848
Calvin, Robert - Angeline Rifner 9-13-1853
Campbell, John - Abigail Sowders 9-12-1841
Cavender, W. P. - Emma Baldridge 12-25-1866
Charlton, James - Jane Brown   11-13-1847
Cheek, Davis - Mary Andrews   7- 9-1866
Clark, William - Sarah Cloud   3----1849
Clark, William - Rachel A. Watkins
                              10- 9-1849
Cloud, Lawson - M. J. Gibson   11- 5-1846
Craig, William - Eliza Ann Otto 12-28-1848
Curry, Asa - Amanda Dair   3- 6-1851
Dair, James - Charlotte Briggs 11- 7-1847

Dayton, Sherman - Eliza Ditmars   3- 2-1854
Denny, Jacob - Margaret Wakefield   10- 2-1850
Dobel, Joseph - Margaret Sowder   12-13-1848
Doughtry, Augustus - Mary P.Tutman
(James A. Doughty in Franklin Co.
                marriages)   9-20-1847
Dowdell, Isaac - Rebecca Hall   8- 1-1841
Elliott, James - Susan Purcell   2- --1845
Fleming, Thomas - Sarah Pelton   6-19-1849
Follinsbee, William - Salome Brown   8- 3-1845
Ford, A. M. - Mary E. Reeves   9- 7-1846
Forsythe, William - Fidelia Young   10-15-1849
Foster, James - Hannah Pruden   1-20-1848
Friend, John - Isabella Hardin   2-21-1850
Frost, Abraham - Naomi Hutchinson   2-13-1840
Fuller, E. E. - Cecelia Gerard   6- 1-1849
Fuller, James D. - S. Bolander   3- 1-1848
Garriott, James - Matilda Scudder   11-19-1842
Gibson, John - Elizabeth McShane   12-21-1842
Gibson, William - Lottie McConnell   9-20-1866
Gould, William - Abaline Kirker   2- 7-1843
Graham, Robert - Mary Walsh   1-20-1851
Green, Stephen - Anna Kiser   3-15-1866
Griszly, George - M. L. Starkey   2--- 1867
Gwaltney, R. - Mary Wakefield   10- 9-1866
Hamilton, W. - Mrs. -- Sampson   11-19-1842
Hensley, Samuel -   -- Rowe   12----1851
Herider, William - Sarah Snider   2-22-1848
Hobson, Richard - Rosanna Yeager   3-15-1866
Holland, James - -- Wildridge   9-25-1865
Homan, Jeremiah - Mary A. Murbarger   1-13-1840
Homer, Francis - Susan Pierce   -----1846
Horner, William - Mary J. Kelso   4- 8-1849
Huffman, N. M. - Marne Oyler   1-19-1851
Hull, William - L. A. Row   1-16-1851
Hunt, Benjamin - M. E. Godley   7----1843
Hutchinson, Charles - Frances Sampson
                                         9-10-1841
Hutchinson, William - Emma Hopkins   6-16-1865
James, William M. - L. Marsh   7- 4-1865
Johnson, William - Virginia Smith   6-14-1866
Jones, Daniel - Juliet Wiley   12-13-1848
Jones, Dewitt C. - Ellen A. Wallace   12- 9-1848
Keen, Bruce - Drusilla Campbell   9-11-1866
Kelso, Harvey - Mary Jane McClure
                          lic. 11-23-1843
Kincaid, William - Mary Kirkpatrick   11- 4-1841
Kirkpatrick, John B. - Honer Grubbs   11----1853
Knox, John - Susan Ditchler   2- 3-1848
Larimore, James - Catherine Cann   3-21-1850
Laughlin, James - Phebe Rourk   1-28-1847
Lazur, Rev. H. S. - Emma John   5-23-1850
Leonard, N. - Helen Brackenridge   2-29-1848
Little, Asa - Elizabeth McCullough   5- 1-1851
Little, Charles - Catharine Wilson   2-17-1846
Lowes, William - E. Frazee   6-15-1855
McCasky, John - Jenetta H. Pruie (?)
                                         10----1851
McReedy, Jacob - Harriet Updike   9-25-1866
Macy, Simeon - A. H. Doughty   8-19-1846
Marshall, William - Cynthia A. Dondree
                                         12-21-1846
Mayall, James - Mary Ann Craig   9-23-1840
Maynard, -- - E. Butterfield   4-29-1852

Mettler, Asa R. - Euphemia Rittenhouse
                                         ---- 1854
Mettler, George W. - Amanda Mettler
                                         11- 2-1853
Miller, Thomas - Elizabeth Garrison
                                         10- 7-1841
Norris, John P. - Isabel Roudebush   9- 5-1850
Ogden, Isaac - Elizabeth A. Ford   6-21-1854
Osage, Jacob - Dorcas Clark   12-17-1848
Oyler, William - Eliza Vantrees   7-26-1850
Paull, T. T. - Mary S. Oyler   2-24-1848
Pearson, John - Martha Fondree   12-18-1848
Phares, John H. - Hannah Butler   10----1842
Phares, John P. - Maria J. Pelton   4----1845
Phares, S. S. - Frances C. Rust   8-27-1851
Phares, William - Sarepta Frost   10- 9-1866
Pierson, Adam - Rebecca Helmick   8- 2-1865
Porter, Morgan - Christina Elder   12- 1-1848
Porter, William H. - Sarah Oyler   9-10-1854
Ramsdell, John - Elizabeth Dodge   11- 8-1849
Reed, Henry - Mary E. Odenbaugh   8----1853
Rice, Solomon G. - Louisa L. Fuller
                                         12-31-1846
Richmond, -- - Kate Carpenter   5----1867
Rifner, J. M. - Martha Hollowell   2----1852
Rifner, Peter P. - Elizabeth Riley   3- 7-1845
Rittenhouse, E. T. - M. L. Schroyer   2-15-1855
Robertson, W. - Mary Swales   8-31-1848
Robinson, Asa - Martha Butler   12-25-1839
Ross, John P. - Adeline Guise   6----1845
Ross, William F. - Electa West   8----1847
Rowe, Ed - Sarah Johnson   1----1852
Sater, Nathan - Eliza Hutchinson   3-11-1840
Schroyer, William - Elizabeth McFeely
                                         5-29-1850
Scoggins, Aaron - Sarah Kirkpatrick   6- 3-1849
Slete (?), Henry - Caroline Phares   11- 5-1846
Smith, Nathan - Naomi Wheeler   3----1847
Snyder, John - Elizabeth Hassed
(Elizabeth Wasson in Franklin Co.
                marriages)   5----1843
Stansbury, -- - -- Craig   1----1851
Stillwell, Joshua - Margaret Kilgore
                                         11- 3-1849
Swales, George - Mary Burk   3----1849
Swales, James - Harriet Watkins   11- 3-1849
Swales, Wilson H. - Sarah Ann Pruden
                                         2-10-1842
Tebbs, James - Sarah Craig   3----1849
Tebbs, John - Ellen Dalton   11- 7-1849
Thompson, Jackson A. - Hannah Sheckles
                                         11-26-1848
Thompson, William - Priscilla Bramble
                                         7-31-1845
Thornberry, Rev. James L. - Martha C. Baldridge
                                         11-22-1854
Turrell, Lyman - Jane Adair   6-27-1850
Turrell, Milton - E. Penny   10----1855
Vanansdol, John L. - Hannah Brown   3- 7-1866
Van Cleve, Joseph - Susan Corgell   2-28-1850
Van Doler, James - Ruth A. Cloud   1- 7-1849
Vansickle, Baxter - Rachel Vancleve   7-15-1845
Wakefield, William - Jane Hughes   1----1852
Wellman, Lewis - Sarah Linn (or Dunn?)
                                         9----1852

Whipple, A. - S. Gibson   3- 2-1848
White, Alex - Mary J. White   11-25-1846
Williams, Jonas - Mary Burton   11----1850
Williams, Owen - Elizabeth Dair   12-16-1847
Wood, Thomas - Matilda Cross   9- 5-1850
Zeamer, Ferdinand - Jane Bledsoe   12- 8-1846

BIBLE RECORDS

Allbright—Gerhart Families

Copied from Bible of Carrie Marie Allbright (Albright) by her grandson Stephen M. Warren, 4725 S. Castle Rock Court, Las Vegas, Nevada 89117, and sent to the *Hoosier Genealogist* by Mr. Warren   The Bible is in the possession of his aunt, Mrs. Mary Beverage, Plattsmouth, Nebraska. The birth, marriage, and death entries in the Bible have been combined here.

Gerhart Family Births, Marriages, Deaths

Elias Gerhart b. 7-26-1818, N. Heidleburg, Berks Co., Pa.; d. 2-4-1868

Maria C. Keohler b. 9-26-1819, Lebanon, Pa.; d. 10-2-1852

Sarah J. McCorkle b. 4-23-1829, Preble Co., Ohio; d. 6-28-1906

Stephen Augustus b. 11-13-1841, Lebanon, Pa.; d. 1-13-1842

Regina Amelia b. 11-30-1842, Lebanon, Pa.; d. 8-23-1860

John Ranatus b. 3-7-1845, Lebanon, Pa.; d. 1-1-1884

Louisa Catharine b. 12-8-1847, Lebanon, Pa.; m. William R. Allbright 4-16-1872
   at Thorntown, Ind.; d. 2-18-1904, Plattsmouth, Neb.

Calvin Elias b. 7-18-1852, Lebanon, Pa.; d. 10-5-1852

James Edward b. 8-12-1854, Thorntown, Ind.; d. 8-31-1854

Theophilus Jay b. 5-8-1856, Thorntown, Ind.; d. 3-20-1889

Eddie Millard b. 11-28-1858, Thorntown, Ind.; d. 3-1-1924

Ormsby Mitchell b. 2-18-1863, Thorntown, Ind.; d. 4-2-1891

Albert Hall b. 3-11-1866, Thorntown, Ind.; d. Feb. 1914

Allbright Family Births, Marriages, Deaths

William Reese Allbright b. 4-30-1844 in Alabama; m. Louisa Catharine Gerhart 4-16-1872, Thorntown, Ind.

Carrie M. Allbright b. 12-5-1872, Thorntown, Ind.; m. Frank Enos Warren (b. Bedford, Iowa, 3-21-1872) 9-15-1897 at Golden, Colo.; he d. 3-5-1939, Plattsmouth, Neb.; she d. same place 5-4-1951. [The marriage date in the Bible is wrong; the correct date is 3-21-1898]

Edna May Warren b. 7-4-1898, Denver, Colo.; m. (1) Earl C. Marler 12-19-1917; (2) Leo Boynton 9-6-1947; she is living in Plattsmouth, Neb.

Frederick Valley Warren b. 4-21-1902, Plattsmouth, Neb.; m. Bernice C. Frombola 6-17-1929, Reno, Nev. [he changed his middle initial to J.]

James Archie Warren b. 8-4-1904, Plattsmouth; m. Helen O. Forsythe 1-27-1934 San Francisco

Mary Louisa Warren b. 6-29-1908, Plattsmouth; m. Richard E. Beverage 12-28-1928, Plattsmouth

Francis Earle Warren b. 3-28-1911, Plattsmouth; m. Elaine Robertson 12-5-1946, Glendale, Calif.

Minnie Eleanor Warren b. 6-9-1912, Plattsmouth; d. 7-18-1912

Margaret Ellen Warren b. 6-9-1912, Plattsmouth; d. 7-15-1912

Robert Allen Warren b. 8-10-1913, Plattsmouth; d. 2-28-1932

Frederick DeWitt Harris b. 1-18-1851, South Bend, Ind.; m. Louisa C. Allbright 4-1-1884, Denver, Colo.

John Calvin Harris b. 5-2-1887, Denver, Colo.; d. 6-10-1887

Albert Edwin Harris b. 4-7-1892, Davenport, Iowa; d. 9-29-1892

Guy Mannering b. 8-26-1891, Denver, Colo. (adopted); d. 7-13-1903

Mary Marshall Hanna Warren Blount d. 3-8-1920, age 64, Lincoln, Neb. [her maiden name was Mary Marshall Hanna, dt of Francis Marshall Hanna & granddt of John Hanna, of Jackson Co., Ind.]

Fred J. Warren d. June 1916, Denver, Colo.; [b. 1874 in Iowa]

Charles E. Warren d. 10-31-1926, age 86

Sybil Warren Head d. June 1928, Plattsmouth; [b. 1876 same place]

Leo M. Boynton d. 11-11-1950, Lincoln, Neb.

Edna M. Warren Taylor d. 12-14-1950, Plattsmouth; [b. 1879 same place]

Helen Forsythe Warren d. 8-14-1960

Adam Black Family

Contributed by Clyde H. McClure, Artesia, California. The Bible is in possession of a family member in West Virginia. Amanda Ann Black who married Samuel Carroll moved to Indiana where most of their children were born. In 1848 they moved to Kansas with her sister Elizabeth Black Lawrence.

Register of Adam Black b. 1-14-1779 & wife Elizabeth b. 1-14-1783. Their children:
*James Cockburn b. 4-14-1806
John b. 2-13-1808
Robert & Abraham (twins) b. 7-2-1810
Sally b. 5-12-1813
Tyre Brown b. 10-1-1815

Daughter b. 8-4-1817; d. 2-2-1818
William b. 3-26-1819
Eliza b. 1-27-1821
William Cambell b. 7-6-1827

---

*James Cockburn Black b. 4-14-1806; m. 9-16-1828 to Lucy E. M. J. Brown b. 4-7-1811. Their children:
Mary Harris b. 9-17-1829
Lucinda Adaline b. 2-20-1831; m. Joseph L. Sexton 3-19-1847
Amanda Ann b. 10-23-1832; m. Samuel Carroll 7-29-1848
George Anderson b. 3-4-1834
Permelia Agnes b. 2-20-1836
Adam Clark b. 1-21-1838
Betsy b. 1-14-1840

Sarah Jane b. 10-22-1841
Eliza Catharine b. 2-1-1844
John Wesley b. 10-20-1846
*William Fletcher b. 11-8-1848
Caroline Melitta b. 3-28-1851

---

*William Fletcher Black b. 11-8-1848; m. (1) 11-7-1869 to Adaline Alice Ashworth b. 3-5-1849. Their children:
William Tyre b. 9-25-1870
Faralee b. 12-12-1872
George Adam b. 3-15-1875

Rosa Ellen b. 1-14-1878
Albert Franklin b. 6-18-1880

---

*William Fletcher Black m. (2) 1-18-1888 to Emma Jane (Eden) Davis. Their children:
Hattie Lucy b. 11-3-1888
Mattie b. 1-29-1891
James Leslie b. 6-8-1896

Eddie b. 7-26-1901
Eugene Davis b. 12-29-1879

(her child by previous marriage?)

Other Births

George A. Brown b. 7-15-1809

Adam Clark Welch b. 3-10-1867

Deaths

Abraham d. 8-24-1834
Robert d. 9-4-1834
Betsy d. 10-15-1840
George Anderson d. 3-31-1860
Sarah Jane d. 3-10-1867
Lucinda Adaline Sexton d. 11-19-1884
Adaline Alice d. 5-25-1885
James C. d. 5-17-1893
Emma Jane d. 6-12-1929

William Fletcher d. 3-4-1932 in Hamlin, W. Va.
John Wesley d. 3-1-1932
George Adam d. 11-7-1939
William Tyre d. 6-18-1896
Eddie d. 7-26-1901
Eugene Davis d. 2-13-1904
Faralee Black Eden, n. d.
Hattie Black Scites, n. d.

PORTER COUNTY MARRIAGES, 1836-1850

Compiled from Marriage Book A in Porter County Courthouse, Valparaiso. The County was organized January 28, 1836, effective February 1, 1836.

Adams, David - Margaret Jane Buck	5-30-1845	
Adams, John Q. - Mary G. Seymour	2-13-1847	
Adsit, Elijah N. - Charlotte Hicks	1-12-1848	
Alder, Thomas - Currence Bradley	8-25-1850	
Alexander, James - Elizabeth McAfee	9- 3-1849	
Allen, Charles - Hetty Ann Witham	10-19-1836	
Allen, Josiah - Katharine Rinker	10- 2-1842	
Allen, Thomas - Rachel B. Chandler	10-30-1842	
Alyea, David, Jr. - Tamer Parker	10-12-1841	
Alyea, Elias J. - Hannah Lumly	3- 5-1848	
Alyea, Humphrey - Sarah Williams	8-26-1847	
Alyea, John - Hannah Alyea	4-12-1848	
Alyea, Samuel - Deborah Alyea	3-15-1845	
Alyea, William - Deborah Jane Beeson	9- 8-1849	
Anderson, Mathias - Rachel Cheney	6- 6-1850	
Andrews, Amos H. - Susannah Hughes	12-28-1842	
Anthony, Samuel I. - Nancy B. Emery	5-19-1846	
Atkins, Lyman - Catharine Vandalsen	2-27-1845	
Ault, Andrew - Mary Jane Bradshaw	11-29-1846	
Ault, Franklin - Margaret Eaton	10-30-1842	
Ault, Washington - Elizabeth Brewer	2-11-1841	
Austin, Joseph C. - Katharine Adams	2-22-1842	
Axe, Elias - Elizabeth Pennock	7- 6-1847	
Bagley, Daniel - Ann Eliza James	11-28-1847	
Baker, Hiram - Mrs. Lucenia Thomas	9-18-1848	
Baker, William - Anna Morgan	1- 6-1848	
Barrens, Joseph D. - Emily M. Price	10- 3-1848	

Bartholomew, Artillus V. - Elizabeth Stephens
              4- 4-1844

Bartholomew, George W. - Caroline Stevens
              3-22-1849

Bates, Christopher - Hannah Adams	4-18-1850	
Baughman, John - Sarah Goodwin	1- 1-1850	
Beach, Lyman - Mary Billings	12-25-1841	
Beauchamp, Martin - Sarah Allen	9- 9-1850	
Beebe, Isaiah S. - Deborah Dustin	6-15-1839	
Beedle, Abraham - Emiline Ross	2-17-1839	
Bell, Henry - Margaret Graybell	1-16-1848	

Bell, Ludlow - Rosina Caswell (or Cadwell?)
              10-18-1845

Bell, Simeon - Nancy Graybell	1-13-1848	
Berrier, John - Elmyra Salsberry	5-30-1850	

Berrier, William - Margaret E. Keeler
              11-16-1843

Biggs, Asa - Susan Watson	11- 9-1848	

Billings, William H. - Mary E. Miller
              11- 1-1846

Binnyon, Richard - Mary Hale (or Hall?)
              10-24-1847

Blachley, Oram - Belinda J. Bartholomew
              12-10-1848

Blachly, Boyd - Katharine Laughlin	4- 4-1841	
Blachly, Ebinezer - Susan Butler	2-16-1837	
Blake, Perry - Clorinda Cleveland	4- 5-1848	

Boger (or Bayer?), Thomas - Mary Smith
              12-26-1847

Boothe, Alfred - Rachel Houston lic.
              12-21-1839

Bowman, Calvin W. - Rebecca J. McCurdy
              12- 6-1850

Bowman, Isaac W. - Elizabeth Herr	12-25-1845	
Bowman, William - Mary McCurday	1- 9-1848	

Brandded, John of La Porte Co. - Mary Adams
              lic.   5-21-1842

Brady, John J. - Abigal E. Lightfoot
              10- 6-1850

Branen, James - Minerva Lahew   3- 9-1843

Brewer, Abraham - Hannah M. Bunnell
              6- 8-1843

Brewer, Isaac - Susan Barton	1-28-1841	
Brewer, Isaac - Mary Ann Blake	11-16-1845	
Brewer, Jacob - Lucinda Patterson	12-25-1839	

Brewer, Mathew W. - Ann Barbary Minnick
              11- 7-1839

Brewer, William - Jane Schultz	5- 7-1843	

Bristol, Newton - Calista Ann Bolster
              6- 6-1843

Brittain, Joseph - Hannah Myres	4- 2-1837	

Bronson, John A. - Betsey Ann Miller
              4- 1-1847

Brough, John - Elizabeth Castleman
              9-19-1847

Brown, Miner - Hannah E. Billings	12-10-1840	
Brown, William - Cornelia Finney	4-14-1842	

Bryant, David - Margaret Steinbrook
              11-20-1836

Bryant, Zephaniah S. - Hannah Walker
              2-15-1838

Buel, Andrew Jackson - Aurelia Stoddard
              1- 1-1845

Buel, Henry M. - Mary Herr	1- 5-1843	
Burd, Thaddeus - Orinda Parker	2-28-1841	
Burge, Richard - Alvina Underwood	5- 7-1848	
Burns, Samuel - Charlotte Stoddard	8-19-1838	
Bush, Reuben H. - Lecticia Taylor	5- 1-1841	
Cabler, Charles S. - Mary E. Cobb	7- 2-1850	
Cadwell, Hiram - Nancy Jane Gates	11-22-1849	
Cadwell, James - Nancy O. Gates	9-19-1844	
Cain, Theophilus - Ruamy Cook	5- 9-1850	
Calhoon, William - Sarah Sefford	4- 6-1837	

Cameron, Robert A. - Jane E. Porter
              3-27-1849

Campbell, Samuel - Harriet Cornell	3-18-1847	

Campbell, Thomas A. E. - Margaret Parkison
              3-25-1841

Campbell, William H. - Clarissa A. Keelen
              12- 7-1848

Cannon, Richard - Rachel M. Wright	8-28-1842	
Carl, Alexander - Jane Blalock	8- 5-1838	

Carmack, Abram of La Porte Co. -
  Ruth Massey, dt Samuel   5-16-1836

Carman, Anson G. - Hannah Young	12-24-1846	

Carman, Anson G. - Cornelia Hoffman
              3-28-1850

Carr, Hiram - Mary Emily Robbins	11-15-1849	
Carr, Silas S. - Zadah Ann Oaks	12-31-1846	
Carryl, Orrin - Nancy M. Parker	10- 9-1847	

Carter, Philo - Abagail M. Johnson
              11-22-1849

Cason, Joseph - Annette Hays	2-10-1848	
Cass, Levi A. - Levisa S. Porter	12-28-1848	

Casteel, Lewis - Caroline Todhunter
              7- 3-1836

Caswell, John J. - Frances Stoddard
          lic.   5- 4-1842

Cathcart, John P. of La Porte Co. -
  Jane Jones   12-15-1840

Chester, Daniel - Mary A. Pennock	5-30-1844	
Chester, William - Mary E. Case	11- 1-1843	

Churchill, James - Eliza Ann Jones
              12-12-1844

Clark, Joseph of Lake Co. - Eliza Ann
  Hodgman   10-31-1839

Clark, Lafayette - Sarah B. Stannard
lic. 10-23-1846
Clark, Thomas S. - Delila Saddoras 2- 6-1837
Clement, Cyrus N. - Lucinda Eglin 8-27-1850
Clement, James M. - Harriet Dilley 1- 4-1849
Clifford, John C. - Lucinda Simpson 8-27-1843
Cline, George - Jane Bushnell 12-17-1840
Cline, John M. - Nancy Trim 1- 4-1844
Coghill, George W. - Julian Ault 12-24-1836
Colerick, William - Mavis M. Spray 12-18-1848
Collins, Alexander - Nancy Jane Kinne
10- 4-1848
Collins, Andrew J. - Maranda Wheeler
9- 5-1850
Colrick, William - Charlotte Stearns
10- 1-1846
Concannon, Thomas - Rhoda Williams 5- 7-1846
Congdon, James - Orra Burge lic. 11-28-1848
Connett, James P. - Cynthia Morris 3-30-1837
Cornell, Alvin - Lydia Lightfoot 1-29-1843
Cornell, Morgan - Louisa Stackers 10-26-1843
Craig, Robert H. - Amela Enoch 5- 4-1850
Crane, David - Charity Eaton 2-14-1848
Crawford, Calvin - Anna Lyons 1-24-1839
Cripe, John - Eliza Petrie 5-19-1847
Currier, John M. - Laura M. Oliver 10-24-1847
Curtis, Alonzo A. - Sarah McAfee 1-16-1848
Curtis, James - Emaransa Cadwell 11-24-1842
Cuthbert, Royal - Esther Burge 6- 3-1840
Daniels, Charles W. - Maranda Curtis 4- 6-1845
Darling, William M. - Almira Young 12-24-1846
Davidson, David - Martha Lee 4-14-1850
Davis, Richard H. D. - Dorothy Grout 8-27-1843
Davis, Thomas - Nancy Alyea 5-15-1845
Davis, William L. - Helen Gordon 8-13-1848
Deerland, Samuel - Minerva Jane Billings
9-30-1850
Delap, William - Melinda Crofert 3-24-1842
Dewolfe, Charles E. - Mary Baum 4-16-1840
Dille, Hiram - Mary Jones 6-25-1848
Dilley, James - Sarah Richards 8-23-1838
Dilley, Solomon - Julia Denton 3- 7-1844
Dillingham, Olcott - Hannah A. Hale 6- 5-1848
Dillingham, John, Jr. - Emaline Carter
6- 7-1840
Dillingham, John, Jr. - Electa M. Ketchum
1-14-1849
Dinwiddie, David T. - Elsey Hildreth 4-25-1844
Dolson, George H. - Naomi Stevens 1-29-1841
Dorr, Edward - Eliza Bull 6- 4-1846
Dorr, Russell - Emeline James 12-27-1837
Dothman, Stephen - Hannah Sprague 9- 5-1847
Doty, Wesley - Ortha Ann Bagley 7-11-1847
Doty, Westley - Mary Ann Cline 7-13-1844
Drellinger, Daniel - Mary Ann Brown 2-26-1847
Drew, Noah - Lucinda Patterson 11-14-1844
Duck, William - Susannah Snodgrass 8-13-1837
Dunham, Rodney D. - Rosea Ann Frame 4-11-1839
Dutton, John - Zuba Winslow 2-27-1846
Dye, Daniel - Debby Ann Church 4- 2-1847
Dye, Ira J. - Mary Ann Lightfoot 2-14-1846
Dye, Otis - Eliza Jane Folts 9-23-1849
East, Jesse - Anna Osborn 3-25-1850
Eaton, William - Susannah Ault 6- 4-1836
Eaton, William - Julia Hulbert 12- 4-1837
Eaton, William J. - Lucinda Coleman 5- 2-1850
Edwards, Enoch - Hannah Robinson
(or Robison?) 5-16-1839
Edwards, Isaac, Jr. - Isabel Lambert 6-28-1846
Edwin, Randall - Eliza A. Hulings 7-25-1847
Egbert, Jacob - Mary Service 7- 6-1844

Eglin, John - Mahaleth C. Edwards 2-26-1846
Eglin, Thomas - Phebe Blachley 10-29-1848
Ensign, Edwin - Eveline Curtis 8- 4-1844
Ensign, Lucius - Avis Ellen Morrison
3-13-1845
Fancher, William H. - Eliza Ann Campbell
5-28-1846
Farnum, David - Rachel H. Jessup 11-17-1842
Farr, Ralph - Hannah Jane Servis 1-11-1850
Faulkner, George W. of La Porte Co. -
Harriet P. Smith 7- 3-1841
Finney, Charles G. - Elizabeth Bartholomew
4- 3-1844
Fishburn, John - Abagail Weeks 10-23-1845
Fleming, James - Maria Morgan 6-23-1844
Fleming, Robert - Margaret Ann Sayler
11-30-1836
Forbes, Sylvester - Levina Service 8-25-1839
Frame, Jeremiah - Lourena Forbes 2-26-1837
Frame, William - Jane McCarrihan 9-12-1839
Frasier, Andrew - Catharine B. Tremen
(or Turnen?) 4-23-1846
Fravel, Harrison - Nancy Jones 8-21-1844
Freed, Paul - Nancy Lee 10- 3-1847
Freeman, Lorenzo - Harriet Cheney 9-12-1843
Freeman, Truman - Mary Cheney 1-28-1845
French, Luther - Mary Sephia Hatch 8-25-1839
French, Silas - Martha Tyler 11- 3-1849
Fry, Ira - Lydia Dole 2-14-1849
Garlin, George - Susan Rittenhouse 5-12-1839
Garrison, William - Nancy Fulton 8-17-1847
Garvey, William - Comfort Dillingham
9-23-1847
Gibbs, David - Betsey Safford lic.10- 5-1846
Gilson, Joel G. - Elanor H. Sweney 7- 7-1840
Goold, George W. - Mary M. Hammond 8-20-1837
Graves, James B. - Elizabeth Ault 3- 9-1845
Graybill, Duncan - Phebe Charlton 10-15-1848
Griffith, Samuel - Elizabeth Williamson
5-22-1849
Grout, Chester - Rachel Young 2-28-1849
Hall, Ephraim - Louisa Plympton 9-29-1839
Hall, Horatio - Orvilla Webster 12- 3-1849
Hansford, John - Hannah Dillingham
4- 4-1844
Harding, Ebenezer S. - Naomi Wilson
6- 1-1845
Harding, Eldridge T. - Martha Willey
4- 8-1849
Harker, Daniel - Julianna Coghill 10-22-1843
Harlan, Joseph - Rebecca Ann Fleming
3-18-1840
Harlan, Joshua - Cordelia Blachley
10-27-1844
Harper, Archibald R. - Emily Atwater
7- 7-1845
Harrison, Lawson N. - Mary Jane Gilman
7-12-1840
Hartford, Amos S. C. - Eunice N. Laurence
8-12-1845
Hartford, John N. - Charity Salyer 7-31-1840
Hartman, George W. - Frances Jane Nephis
2-23-1846
Hatch, Jeremiah S. - Sarah Addams
lic. 7-12-1842
Hathaway, Joseph C. - Gemima Frakes
12-21-1839
Hathaway, Oliver H. P. - Mary E. Drake
4- 1-1850
Hathaway, Simeon B. - Mary Frakes
lic. 3-30-1842

Haviland, Samuel - Phebe Ashton
    lic.   9- 2-1839
Hawkins, Elkanah - Mary Hawkins   9-16-1838
Hays, Almon J. - Eliza Wheelen   12-29-1844
Hayward, Henry - Mary Fifield   5- 6-1846
Hazleton, Lemuel - Jane Gould lic. 5-30-1838
Hendricks, Eli - Mrs. Nancy Beeson 8-20-1848
Hendricks, Henry - Susannah Bundy 4- 9-1844
Henthorn, Richard - Jane Spurlock 5- 5-1836
Hesser, Alexander - Elizabeth Hammond
                   7- 6-1846
Hesser, George - Mary Ann Hall lic. 4- 2-1842
Hicks, Lewis - Eliza Bell   1-20-1848
Higgins, John - Diantha Tumper (or Fumper?)
                 3-18-1847
Highland, Henry - Sarah Jane Jones 7-12-1846
Hill, Elijah P. - Jane A. Rose   4- 4-1850
Hilton, William - Mary Ann Barr 12- 7-1843
Hodgeman, Lawrence - Mary Taylor 5-17-1840
Holden, Lewis A. - Mary Ann Reiden 6-12-1847
Holmes, William - Jane Ann Rugar 7- 5-1836
Horner, Amos - Mary White   7- 4-1844
Hoskins, Barney - Caroline Walton 2-26-1843
Hoskins, Nicholis - Jane Childers 11-11-1850
Hough, Ellis P. - Mary Robinson (or Robison?)
                 5-24-1840
House, Augustus R. - Sophia Dye 10- 7-1849
Houseland, William - Peggy Steel 9-19-1850
Howe, Francis - Rose Bailly lic. 11- 8-1841
Hubbard, James H. - Julia S. Barr 5-12-1844
Hugheart, William - Elizabeth Zane 6-14-1836
Hughes, Gabriel B. - Electa Augusta Kenney
               11-28-1850
Hughes, William C. - Melissa Gossett 1- 1-1847
Hulburt, David - Elizabeth Spafford 4- 7-1850
Hume, George W. - Rebecca Crawford 4- 6-1837
Ingram, James W. - Sarah Jane Beck 8-19-1847
James (or Jones?), Allen B. - Roxina Griffin
                 9-17-1842
James, Benjamin - Iley Vina Robison 5- 4-1839
James, Stephen - Charlotte Reynolds 11-28-1849
Johnson, Nathan - Esther Dillingham 1- 5-1845
Johnson, Philander - Phebe Banker 12-19-1847
Johnson, Stephen R. - Juliann Bundy 9-27-1846
Johnson, Thomas R. - Hannah Alyea 11- 8-1846
Johnson (or Johnston?), William -
    Prudence Currier   3-29-1838
Johnson, William - Sybil Curtis 12-31-1839
Jones, Alvy - Sarah Jane Lee   3-26-1840
Jones, Daniel - Martha Ann Lee lic. 4-11-1842
Jones, David - Eliza Ann Olinger 6-18-1846
Jones, Erasmus J. - Maria McNutt 3-25-1849
Jones, Jackson - Huldah C. Eaton 9- 5-1847
Jones, John - Martha Weeks   5-25-1843
Jones, Robert - Clarissa Dillingham 5-17-1845
Keeler, Ira B. - Mary Ann Hughart 10- 1-1848
Kelsey, Charles P. - Sophiah Adams 2-24-1839
Kimball, George W. - Adelia A. Dillingham
                9- 8-1844
Kimble, Harry - Harriet Dillingham 1-28-1838
Kingsbury, Charles - Louisa Cornell 1- 1-1846
Kinsey, Aaron - Elizabeth Bhymer 9-28-1847
Kinsey, David - Rebecca Duey 12-18-1844
Kinsey, Jacob, Jr. - Harriet Tenice 11-26-1848
Kinsey, William - Margaret C. Worley 3-24-1844
Kinzie, Joel - Delila Witham 10-19-1836
Kirk, Edward J. - Minerva J. Kessey (?)
                 3-27-1849
Knight, Jonathon - Beeda A. Merine 7- 5-1849
Lambert, Lacount - Amanda M. Campbell
                 3-29-1849

Lansing, Aratus - Maria Johnson 1-28-1849
Laurence, Henry - Delilah Harris 2- 2-1846
Lee, David - Rebecca Oliver 12-15-1842
Lee, Solomon - Elizabeth Draper 5-21-1843
Lee, William D. - Phebe Carpenter 11-12-1840
Leland, Charles - Jane L. Smith 4-15-1846
Lewis, Benajah - Caroline Williams 4- 1-1847
Lewis, Orrin - Eliza A. Bartholomew
                 7-26-1836
Lightfoot, John - Atha Ann Walters 3-14-1847
Line, Silas C. - Catharine Hearing 3-18-1847
Lith, Thomas G. - Idilla Allen 4-13-1847
Long, Samuel of La Porte Co. -
    Parmelia Rogers   3- 1-1843
Longyear, Solomon - Katharine Sadorrous
               4-28-1838
Lowe, James M. - Mary Ann Hesser 1- 8-1848
Ludy, Henry G. - Sarah Stoner 9-19-1839
Luther, Caleb C. - Rebecca Comer 7- 3-1849
Lyons, Daniel W. - Anna Dillingham 2- 9-1837
McAlpin, John L. (?) - Eliza Ann Dinwiddie
               3-28-1843
McAlpin, Joseph L. - Sarah A. Dinwiddie
              10-12-1848
McClung, Eastman - Hannah Spooner
        lic.   3- 3-1848
McCord, George of La Porte Co. - Eleanor
    Blair   1- 3-1842
McCoy, Andrew J. - Elizabeth Metts 4-28-1846
McCurday, John - Orinda Burd 7-17-1845
McNee, William - Eliza Cline 6-25-1847
McPherson, John - Rebecca Morgan 8- 9-1849
McPherson, John H. - Mercey E. Curtis
               1- 9-1850
Mahaney, Edward - Mildred J. Hughes
             12- 9-1844
Mahoney, Daniel - Mary Ann Walton 12-31-1839
Malone, Francis W. M. - Rebecca Jane Wilcey
               7- 2-1846
Malone, Franklin W. W. - Lydia S. Billings
               6-18-1848
Malone, Leslie - Emily Billings 9- 2-1849
Malsby (or Maulsby), John H. - Sarah
    J. Reynolds   9- 3-1848
Martin, Jasper - Eleanor J. Miller 5-28-1848
Martin, Lyman - Jane Banker 3-17-1850
Martin, William - Elizabeth Blair 10- 5-1837
Mason, Alfred J. - Ann Maria Keeler
               3-28-1850
Mason, Stephen D. - Rebecca Dillingham
              4- 8-1838
Massey, David - Elizabeth Reed 7- 1-1838
Massey, Joseph - Adaline Sanford 7-14-1839
Massey, Joseph F. - Esther Johnson 10-10-1847
Massey, Levi - Jane Crawford lic. 11- 2-1837
Masum, Philip - Elizabeth Finney 4- 3-1850
Matthews, David - Jane F. Crooks 3-30-1843
Matthews, David - Jane Slover 8-22-1846
Maxwell, William - Biddy Sweeney 9-16-1838
Miles, Harvey - Phebe Massey 4- 6-1848
Millard, John - Silva Ann Wells
          lic.   8-26-1839
Miller, Isaac - Susannah West 3- 2-1843
Miller, Isaac - Catharine Cuson 3-11-1846
Miller, Milo - Cynthia Sprague 7- 2-1849
Morgan, Joseph C. - Nancy Ann Knapp
               7- 4-1848
Morris, Absalom - Mary Jane White 4- 2-1849
Morrison, John M. C. - Susan Blair 11- 2-1848
Morrison, Thomas M. of Illinois -
    Katharine Blair   7- 4-1837

Moser, George - Christena Firman   10-28-1850
Mulinex, Charles W. - Sarah Ann Banker
                                    12-19-1847
Murray, Michael - Martha McAffee   1- 1-1843
Muselman, David - Harriet Chenay   9- 8-1848
Nelson, John C. - Eliza Collins   9-14-1847
Nephis, John C. - Rosannah Chandler 5-20-1846
Nickerson, Clark - Sarah Frakes   7-18-1847
Nickerson, Thomas - Sally Edwards   5- 7-1845
Nowland, Francis of La Porte Co. -
    Alecy Coghill   8-24-1837
Ohara, Edward - Ruth Dixon   4-25-1850
Oliver, George W. - Susannah L. Peters
                                    7-12-1846
Olmstead, Jabez - Didamia Ensign   1-13-1848
Orton, Harlon (or Harlow?) S. -
    Elizabeth Cheney   7- 2-1839
Orum, Joshua - Martha McNutt   6- 4-1840
Palmer, Edmund W. - Eliza Jane Sweeney
                                    4-21-1840
Parkinson, William - Nancy C. Morris 1- 8-1845
Parriott, Adam H. - Sarah Hall   7-25-1850
Parshall, George L. - Elizabeth Bundy
                                    10-27-1844
Patterson, Alfred - Sarah Jane Hough 9- 3(?)
                                    1840
Patton, George - Nancy Ann Adams   12-13-1846
Pearce, Michael of Lake Co. -
    Margaret Jane Dinwiddie   11-19-1840
Peek, Hubbard - Ann Harrison   10- 1-1848
Peer, Samuel M. - Jane Cook   2-26-1846
Pennock, William - Mary Ann Hopkins 4-27-1840
Peters, Aldrich - Susannah L. Shepard
                                    1-29-1841
Petree, William - Harriet Riley   10- 6-1846
Philips, Wear - Sarah Kinsey   12-12-1844
Philo, Edward S. - Emeline Hopkins 8- 4-1848
Pickrell, Daniel - Mary Bell   7- 3-1849
Pierce, Alanson W. - Mary Winslow   3- 2-1843
Pierce, Rufus of Lake Co. - Mary Hodgman
                                    10-31-1839
Piper, Caleb - Jane A. Hale   11-12-1839
Price, Andrew B. - Louisa Dye   10-15-1848
Pumer (?), John - Sophia Riley   8- 7-1843
Purdy, James - Elizabeth Adams   8- 2-1846
Purdy, William - Margaret Breyfogle 11-12-1847
Randall, Edwin - Paulina Hewlings   1-19-1850
Randel, Mason - Rosine Bailly lic. 1-27-1840
Reeder, Thomas - Abigail Marine   8-29-1848
Renney, Peter - Delila Walton   3-15-1838
Reynolds, Azariah W. - Catharine Grist
                                    6-16-1850
Riley, Hugh W. - Martha Price   3-23-1848
Robison, Henry - Parmelee Randall   10-14-1847
Robison, Jacob - Jane Hathaway   1- 9-1843
Robison, Thomas - Rebecca Dye   6-15-1841
Root, William - Samantha Alyea   3-26-1849
Ross, Calvary - Mary Ellen Beedle   9-24-1848
Ross, Jesse - Fanny Jane White   1-21-1849
Ross, Thomas L. - Lydia Hatch   12-24-1845
Russell, Newell - Pauline Blachley 6-11-1850
Russell, Solomon - Rosina Barnard   lic.
    both of the territory attached to Porter Co.
                                    3- 7-1837
Russell, Solomon of Lake Co. -
    Elizabeth Sweeney   10- 7-1840
Russell, William of La Porte Co. -
    Margaret McCarrihan   4- 2-1839
Salisbury, John - Polly Ann Berrier 7- 3-1844
Sandford, Isaac - Ann Eastman   2-10-1839
Sanford, David - Polly Ann Morford 10- 9-1847

Sawyer, Daniel F. - Susan Maria Taylor
                                    11-27-1842
Sawyer, Isaac - Almira M. Harris   12-16-1849
Sawyer, Nathaniel - Eliza Randel   1-14-1849
Sawyer, Nathaniel - Sarah Ann Hodgman
                                    2- 9-1840
Sawyer, Samuel M. - Nancy Spafford
                                    10-26-1845
Saylor, Benjamin - Elizabeth Jane Jacobs
                                    6-21-1838
Service, Albinus P. - Mary J. A. Gilson
                                    1-24-1843
Servis, Aaron - Lydia Gilson   6-30-1840
Sheffield, Jesse - Ellen Hughes   8-22-1844
Shepard, Philo - Elizabeth Ronzer   3-20-1848
Sherman, Amasso J. - Delilah M. Curtis
                                    3-23-1848
Shinebarger, James - Alecta Blachley   lic.
                                    7-31-1846
Shinebarger, William - Levisa Eastwood
                                    5-18-1845
Shintaffer, George S. - Amanda Blachly
                                    7-30-1848
Shoemake, Edwin - Martha M. Jones 10-20-1850
Shoults, John - Deborah Hesser   7-12-1840
Shreve, Richard - Susannah Hulin   12- 8-1850
Shuey, George - Winneford Jones   1- 2-1845
Sigler, William - Catharine Parrott
                                    12-31-1844
Skidmore, Henry - Amelia Ault   8-12-1848
Skinner, David - Susannah Beck   4- 7-1841
Skinner, Truman - Sarah Johnson   10-16-1849
Slawson, Manassar B. - Amelia Tibbetts
                                    5-14-1848
Slover, Isaac - Peggy Thatcher   12-31-1849
Smith, Abraham - Eunice Tree   9-17-1848
Smith, Andrew J. - Elizabeth Sade
                        lic.   5-16-1845
Smith, Henry - Samantha Spafford   3-23-1845
Smith, Horace F. - Mary Olinger   12-18-1839
Smith, Stephen - Adeline Wright   9- 5-1844
Smith, Sylvester W. - Louisa A. Pennock
                                    11-29-1846
Spencer, Francis - Anna Blalock   9-21-1837
Spencer, Stuart R. - Elizabeth Jones
                                    10-24-1847
Sprague, Samuel - Emeline Frye   6-24-1847
Sprague, William F. - Jane Austin 11-16-1843
Spray, George L. - Phebe Hunt lic.10-27-1848
Stanley, John - Susan E. Heath   3-13-1845
Stanley, Solomon - Martha Witham 10-29-1842
Starkie, David - Martha Jones lic.10- 6-1848
Starr, Orson of Lake Co. - Julia M. Hatch
                                    9-14-1843
Steele, Reuben - Eliza Ann Horner   3-10-1850
Stephens, Furnando C. - Hester Edwards
                                    10-30-1850
Stevens, Oren, see Stephens
Stephens (or Stevens), Oren - Elizabeth
    Moore   3-29-1837
Stock, William B. - Elizabeth Morford
                                    8-18-1847
Stoddard, William - Ann Rinker   6- 7-1840
Stoner, Jacob - Mary Stanley   8-27-1842
Stoner, Samuel - Sally Harlan   2-16-1840
Stoner, Samuel - Rachel Williams   3-17-1850
Strong, Orson W. - Emaline Cadwell 6-11-1840
Stump, William - Lucy Page   11- 9-1849
Swank, Michael - Catharine Servis
                        lic.   3- 1-1849
Sweet, Elhannan W. - Tamar Alyea   6-29-1846

Swin, Isaac - Caroline Martin   8-22-1837
Tabor, George W. - Cloe F. Holister   1-30-1839
Tabor, Jonathan - Hannah Shinebarger
                            lic.   7-17-1847
Tabor, William - Sarah Lawrence   11-27-1844
Talbott, William K. - Sinai Ann McConnell
                                       7-13-1836
Talcott, William C. - Maria Luther   5- 1-1838
Taylor, David N. - Margaret A. Blain 3-23-1847
Taylor, Israel S. - Hannah McCarty   6-20-1840
Thomas, Herbert - Polly Starr   11-22-1848
Thomas, Samuel H. - Luzinia Hale   4- 7-1840
Thomas, William - Ann Morgan   7-12-1845
Thompson, John C. - Catharine M. Cameron
                                       1-29-1849
Thompson, Leonard W. - Prudence Muzzall
                                       8-12-1839
Thompson, Reuben - Jemima Knight   5-18-1845
Tree, John W. - Jane Smith   2-17-1848
Tuplo (?), Henry T. - Paulina Morgan
                                       4- 2-1846
Turner, David - Caroline Bissell   10-17-1844
Tyler, Erastus - Isabella Blain (or Blair?)
                                       3-11-1847
Tyler, Hiram - Elizabeth Blachley   1-14-1849
Van Horn, Cornelius C. of Will Co. Illinois -
       Mary M. Richards   1-23-1842
Walton, Lewis - Sarah Blake   9-18-1836
Warnock, Aresly - Dorotha Davis   4- 9-1846
Warnock, John - Helena Dorr   3-24-1840
Waters, William B. - Margaret Davidson
                            lic.   7-31-1849
Watts, Thomas, Jr. - Julia Ann Allen 2-14-1847
Wauhob, William - Betsy Electa Dillingham
                                       3-28-1837
Webster, John E. - Rebecca Witham   2-24-1850
Weeks, William - Lovina Baum   5-12-1850
Welch, Stephen - Elizabeth Magee   6- 4-1846
Welch, William C. - Phebe Lee   9-15-1842
Wells, Harlow M. - Chloe D. Robinson 1- 2-1842
Wells, Hiram - Julia Ann Jones   2-25-1847
Wells, Jesse F. - Fanny Campbell   5-17-1849
Wells, John - Ruby Johnson   11-22-1849
Wells, Rufus P. - Maria Ann Smith   9-30-1849
West, Erasmus - Susannah Hughart   5-14-1845
Wheeler, Chauncey - Jerusha A. Curtis
                                       2- 2-1846
Wheeler, James - Elizabeth Peer   5-10-1846
White, David W. - Lydia Taylor   10-31-1849
White, James G. - Mary Ann Clement
                            lic.   7-31-1847

White, James G. - Mary Jackson   8-12-1849
Whittemore, Edson - Mary Wells   5-22-1845
Wicker, Joel H. - Josephine Hortense Bailly
                                       7-24-1849
Wilie, George - Katharine Snyder   5-18-1837
Williams, Alexander - Elizabeth Jones
                                       2- 2-1837
Williams, Alfred - Nancy E. Beeson (?)
                                       7-10-1845
Williams, Elam - Elizabeth McChristy
                                       4-19-1846
Williams, Elisha - Samantha Arvin   11- 6-1844
Williams, George R. of Elkhart Co. -
       Rhoda Hathaway   7-23-1836
Williams, James H. - Frances A. Dewey
                                       2-23-1848
Williams, Milliken - Nancy Lansing   7- 9-1848
Williamson, Azariah - Margaret Couts
                                      11-23-1848
Wills, Charles of La Porte Co. -
       Susan Cross   7- 3-1841

Wilsey, John - Caroline Curtis   4-12-1840
Wilsey, Josiah - Rebecca Jane Billings
                                       8-25-1841
Wilson, Amos - Melinda Blachley   10-29-1848
Wilson, James H. - Mary Dinwiddie   9- 8-1842
Winchell, George W. - Eunice A. Vandalsem
                                      11- 2-1845
Winslow, Seth - Amy B. Andres   4-25-1850
Witham, Alfred - Drucilla Allen   9-15-1842
Witham, James - Drusilla Patton   4- 2-1837
Witham, Joseph - Barbary Harlan   12-15-1839
Witham, Simon - Belinda Jane Bartholomew
                            lic.   1-25-1847
Witham, Simon - Dinah R. Spencer   10-22-1848
Wood, Martin - Susannah G. Taylor   8-26-1849
Woodbridge, George A. - Jane M. McConnell
                                       5- 8-1844
Wolf, Edmund D. - Louisa Beebe   12-30-1838
Worly, John L. - Neomi Hathaway   12-21-1842
Wortman, Milton L. - Lucinda Doud
                            lic.   2- 9-1839
Wright, Alexander L. - Sidney Jones
                                       5- 7-1840
Wright, Andrew J. - Laura Ann Atkins
                                      12-25-1845
Wright, Edward - Lavina Jones   8-25-1839
Wright, Lattin - Susan McKinney   9-20-1847
Young, James - Sally McCarty   10- 1-1837
Young, William - Ann Hough   3- 7-1839
Zimmerman, John - Sarah Jane Arthur
                                       9-26-1850

ENUMERATION OF CHILDREN BETWEEN THE AGES OF FIVE AND TWENTY-ONE IN
WABASH TOWNSHIP, ADAMS COUNTY, TAKEN FEBRUARY 16, 1846

Compiled from xerox copy of original record in Archives Division, Indiana State Library; the original is in the Auditor's Office, Adams County Courthouse, Decatur. Sex designated when there might be uncertainty.

Name of Parent	Child	Age	Name of Parent	Child	Age

District 1

Name of Parent	Child	Age	Name of Parent	Child	Age
Abnet, William	Mary	9	Moore, Oliver	Henery	7

233

Baker, George F.	Marguit (f)	20	Morningstar, Jacob	Leesis (f)	5
	Corneilous	18			
	Eave	13	Roads, Elizabeth	Frederic	6
Baker, Henery	none		Shrull, Jacob	Jane	16
Crawford, John	none			Barbara	14
Crawford, Josiha	none				
			Wilson, Joseph	Thomas	17
Gallaway, Covey	Amos	20		Nancy	15
	Mary	17		Abraham	13
	Nancy	12		Hariet	10
	Elizabeth	9		Covey	7
twins	(Elisha	6			
	(Marguit	6			

District 2

Ash, Christian	Joseph	13	Rich, John	Mary (?)	18
	Jacob	11		Christan	13
	Daniel	9		Anna	10
	Noah	7		John	7
	Barbara	5		Jacob	5
Baker, Hars (?)	none		Salt, Michel	Marguit (f)	14
				Sarah Jane	10
Iker, John	Barbara	17		Susan	8
	Jacob	10		Jacob	5
	Christan	8			
	Mary	5	Swatinstrove, Christain	none	
McDonald, David	Rebecca	16			
	Absolum	14			
	Sharlota	9			
	Levi	7			

District 3

Barber, John	James	17	Vance, William	James M.	19
	David	13		David	17
	Halet	12		William C.	15
	Enos	10			
	Richard	6	Vance, William	(Mark T.	12
	Pruda (f)	15	twins	(Marchal P.	12
				Joseph Noblen	7
McHugh, William	Arther	18		Catharine	6
	Elizabeth	12			
	Susanah	9	Wheeler, Amos	Isral	19
	Thomas	7		Charles	17
				Manerva	15
Sprunger, Abner	Sarah Jane	17		Jane	13
	Shedrick	15		Isaac	11
	Martha Ann	13		Mary	9
	James	12		Elza (f)	7
	Hiram	9			
	Henery	6	Wheeler, Isaac	David	14
				Mariah	9

Studabaker, Mary	David	18
	Elizabeth	16
	John	14
	Catharine	12
	Abram	9

District 4

Conkle, Jacob	Louisa	10	Linton, Samuel	Haner (f)	13
	Elizabeth	8		Jane	12
	Jamima	5		James	9
				Wilia (m)	7
Hill, Sarah	Obed	18			
	Eunice	16	Mitchel, William	John	8
	David	14		David	5
	Edward	11			
	Martha	9	Scot, John	George	17
				Marion (m)	14
Imble, Michael	John	14		Angeline	12
	2 girls	—		Eliza	10
				Elizabeth	8
Judy, Henery S.	Elizabeth	12		Marguit (f)	6
	Daniel	10			
	John	6			

District 5

Burdy, William	Henery P.	15	Nelson, Charles	Isaac	18
	Catharine	14		John	16
	Nathaniel	11		James	11
	Isaac	6		Mariam (f)	9
				Charles	7
Buskirk, Daniel	John	7			
	Adam	5	Nelson, Elias	John	20
				Mary	11
Cook, Jacob	Otha	18		Levi	9
	Elizabeth	13		Barbara E.	7
				Sarah	5
Cook, John	Jacob	5			
			Shane, Cyrus	William	5
Hiltton, Mathias	Samuel	12			
	Susanna	6	Shepherd, William	Alen T.	12
Macklin, Jacob	Noah	12	Shepherd, William Jr.	Edward	19
				Mahala	14
				Alford	9
			Williams, James	David	11

Total amount in the above list is 133 schollars   Covey Gallaway T Clk

NEGRO REGISTERS

Article XIII of the Indiana Constitution of 1851 provided that "No negro or mulatto shall come into, or settle in the State, after the adoption of this Constitution. At the first session of the General Assembly after the adoption of the new constitution, legislation was passed to implement Art. XIII. Negroes were prohibited from coming into the state in the future and those who were residents prior to November, 1851, were required to register with the county clerks, producing witnesses to prove their right to reside in the state. This latter provision appears not to have been strictly enforced. Although registers were begun in most counties, the names of only a small fraction of Negro residents were recorded. We are reproducing below the names recorded in three of the registers with ages and birthplaces of the registrants. In addition, the registers give the physical characteristics of registrants. For example, John Blanks of Bartholomew County was "six feet high; has no hair on top of his head; left wrist is crooked; his right leg has been wounded with an axe." Relationship is given where it appeared. Persons of the same name are grouped together but may not have been related.

Bartholomew County Register

Copied by Maurice Holmes from the original volume in the clerk's office, Bartholomew County Courthouse, Columbus. All registrants were residents of Bartholomew County unless otherwise indicated.

Name of registrant	Age	Place of birth	Name of witness	Date of registration
Blanks, John	54	Rockingham Co. Va.	Edward A. Herod	9-21-1853
Blanks, Christy	__	Robeson Co. N.C.	Edward A. Herod	9-21-1853
Blanks, Willis	21	Robeson Co. N.C.	Edward A. Herod	9-21-1853
Blanks, Elizabeth	15	Robeson Co. N.C.	Edward A. Herod	9-21-1853
Blanks, Eli, son of John	13	Robeson Co. N.C.	Edward A. Herod	9-21-1853
Bolden, Daniel	28	Ohio	Henry Bryant	9-30-1853
Curzy, Edward	43	Bladen Co. N.C.	William Atkinson	11- 5-1853
Curzy, Dolly, wife has 3 children	26	not given	William Atkinson	11- 5-1853
Curzy, Eliza	3	Bartholomew Co.	William Atkinson	11- 5-1853
Curzy, John	4½	Jennings Co. Ind.	William Atkinson	11- 5-1853
Hatcher, John	40	Darlington Dist. S.C.	James Hobbs	10- 4-1855
Hatcher, Sophia	38	Nashville, Tenn.	James Hobbs	10- 4-1855
Hatcher, Geo. W., son	3	Columbus, Ind.	James Hobbs	10- 4-1855
Galbraith, Edmund	70	South Carolina	James Hobbs	9- 1-1853
Galbraith, Dianah, wife	50	Perquimans Co. N.C.	James Hobbs	9- 1-1853
Hill, Abraham	53	Washington Co. Va.	James Hobbs	9-16-1853
Hill, Catharine	32	Perquimans Co. N.C.	Joshua V. Horn	3-20-1854
last 5 residents of Johnson Co.				
Hill, Mary Eveline	18	Jackson Co. Ind.	Wm. H.H. Terrell	3-20-1854
Hill, Andrew Jackson	8	Bartholomew Co.	Joshua V. Horn	3-20-1854
Hill, Susan Henrietta	4	Bartholomew Co.	Joshua V. Horn	3-20-1854
Hill, Abraham Augustus	2	Bartholomew Co.	Joshua V. Horn	3-20-1854
Jones, William Riley	40	Robeson Co. N.C.	George B. Gaines	8-22-1853
Jones, Lucy Ann	40	Halifax Co. Va.	George B. Gaines	8-22-1853

Jones, Irvin, son	14	Robeson Co. N.C.	George B. Gaines	8-22-1853
Jones, Enoch, son	13	Robeson Co. N.C.	George B. Gaines	8-22-1853
Jones, Willis, son	11	Robeson Co. N.C.	George B. Gaines	8-22-1853
Jones, Thomas, son	9	Richmond Co. N.C.	George B. Gaines	8-22-1853
Jones, Oliver, son	7	Richmond Co. N.C.	George B. Gaines	8-22-1853
Jones, Lucinda, dt	5	Scott Co. Va.	George B. Gaines	8-22-1853
Jones, Mary H., dt	3	Bartholomew Co. Ind.	George B. Gaines	8-22-1853
Jones, William R., Jr.	1	Bartholomew Co. Ind.	George B. Gaines	8-22-1853
Leevy, Alexander	6	Robeson Co. N.C.	Edward A. Herod	9-21-1853
son of Louis Leevy				
Mitchell, Priscilla	45	Halifax Co. N.C.	Wm. H.H. Terrell	11-10-1853
Newby, Penina	50/60	Perquimans Co. N.C.	Joshua V. Horn	3-20-1854
Newby, John	20	Jackson Co. Ind.	William Ruckle	12-28-1853
Newby, Jemima	15	Jackson Co. Ind.	Joshua V. Horn	3-20-1854
Osborn, Thomas	15 mo.	Bartholomew Co.	Joshua V. Horn	3-20-1854
Oxendine, Daniel	37	Robeson Co. N.C.	John B. Abbett	8-19-1853
Oxendine, Priscilla	10	not given	James Hobbs	4-10-1854
Oxendine, Sarah L.	9	Robeson Co. N.C.	Thomas Hays	10-5-1855
Oxendine, Seneth E.	7	Franklin Co. Ind.	Thomas Hays	10-5-1855
Oxendine, Lucy M.	4	Franklin Co. Ind.	Thomas Hays	10-5-1855
all children of Daniel				
Simmons, Meredith	37	Fayette Co. Ky.	James Hobbs	4-10-1854
Simmons, Susan, wife	36	Henry Co. Va.	James Hobbs	4-10-1854
Simmons, Margaret	22	Brown Co. Ind.	James Hobbs	4-10-1854
Simmons, Sarah Jane	14	Greene Co. Ill.	James Hobbs	4-10-1854
Simmons, Lawson	47	Caroline Co. Va.	James Hobbs	4-10-1854
Simmons, Caroline, wife	27	Warren Co. Miss.	James Hobbs	4-10-1854
Simmons, Betsy, dt	13	Bartholomew Co. Ind.	James Hobbs	4-10-1854
Simmons, Mary Ann, dt	9	Bartholomew Co. Ind.	James Hobbs	4-10-1854
Simmons, James, son	4	Bartholomew Co. Ind.	James Hobbs	4-10-1854
Simmons, Williams, son	4 mo.	Bartholomew Co. Ind.	James Hobbs	4-10-1854
Turman, Harry	53	Rockingham Co. Va.	James Hobbs	9-17-1853
Turman, Clarissa, wife	53	Clark Co. Ind.	Wm. A.T. Greene	9-17-1853
Turman, Samuel, son	12	Jennings Co. Ind.	Nathan Graves	9-29-1853
Turman, James	21	Jennings Co. Ind.	Nathan Graves	9-29-1853
Turman, Henry	20	Jennings Co. Ind.	Nathan Graves	9-29-1853
Wheeler, Ephraim	18	Johnson Co. Ind.	James Hobbs	9-27-1853

Franklin County Register

Copied from xerox of the original record in the Indiana Division, Indiana State Library. All of the registrants gave Franklin County as their residence. There was no date of registration for the first names in the book, but it apparently was prior to July 5, 1853, the first date given.

Name of registrant	Age	Place of birth	Name of witness	Date of reg- istration
Banks, Britton	72	North Carolina	Benjamin D. Goodwin Henry George	n.d.
Bass, Alexander	32	North Carolina	Robert Pugh William Maxwell	n.d.
Brayboy, Stephen	34	North Carolina	William Maxwell Israel Goble	n.d.
Day, Donaldson	53	South Carolina	Israel Goble Andrew J. Ross	n.d.
Edrington, Gustavus	41	Virginia	George M. Byram Nathaniel M. Crookshank Samuel Murphy	n.d.
Fant, Willis	41	Kentucky	John C. Burton Andrew Grob	n.d.
Freeman, Archibald	42	North Carolina	Robert Pugh William Maxwell	n.d.
Hays, James	39	North Carolina	William Maxwell Israel Goble	n.d.
Hood, Josiah	30	On the ocean	Jacob Guard Hiram Brison (?)	7- 5-1853
Holley, Rode	60	Virginia	Michael Batzner Isaac Jones	7- 7-1853
Holley, Sarah	60	Virginia	Aaron Ailes	4- 8-1856
Holley, Sanford	20	Franklin Co.	Aaron Ailes	4- 8-1856
Holley, Nancy	17	Franklin Co.	Aaron Ailes	4- 8-1856
Morgan, Matthew	52	North Carolina	Robert Pugh William Maxwell	n.d.
Morgan, Nancy	42	North Carolina	Robert Pugh John S. Simonson	9-16-1853
Morgan, James Wesley	14	North Carolina	John S. Simonson	9-16-1853
Morgan, Sophronia	12	North Carolina	Robert Pugh John S. Simonson	9-16-1853
Morgan, Joseph	11	North Carolina	Robert Pugh John S. Simonson	9-16-1853
Scott, Philip	73	Virginia	Andrew R. McCleery Thomas Gard	n.d.
Short, Henry	49	Maryland	Richard & William T. Tyner	7- 7-1853
Short, Jane	18	Dearborn Co.	Aaron Ailes James Evans	4- 8-1856
Shorts, Henry	12	Dearborn Co.	James Johnson	10-31-1856
Sibley, Henry	53	Virginia	William Robeson James Fordice	n.d.
Smith, Benjamin	46	New Jersey	Branson Lawson Oliver M. Bartlow	7-27-1853

Name	Age	Place	Witness	Date
White, James B.	26	North Carolina	John S. Simpson Robert Pugh	9-16-1853
White, William B.	21	North Carolina	John S. Simpson Robert Pugh	9-16-1853
Williams, Jesse	24	New Jersey	William Maxwell Israel Goble	n.d.
York, Joshua	34	Franklin Co.	William Roberson Richard S. Lines	9-16-1853

Jennings County Register

Compiled from a copy of the original record in the Genealogy Division, Indiana State Library. The copy was made by Maurice Holmes from the original in the Jennings County Courthouse, Vernon.

Name of registrant	Age	Place of birth	Name of witness	Date of registration
Anthony, David	53	Elbert Co. Ga.	Thomas Grissom William B. Hagins	7-22-1853
Anthony, Charlotte	38	Elbert Co. Ga.	Thomas Grissom William B. Hagins	7-22-1853
Anthony, William	22	Elbert Co. Ga.	Thomas Grissom William B. Hagins	7-22-1853
Anthony, Nancy	22	Jennings Co.	Joseph Fellinger Harvey M. Cowell	8- 6-1853
Brandon, Lemuel	17	Jackson Co.	Levi W. Todd Henry House	8-24-1853
Carsey, Alexander	19	Jennings Co.	_____	4-30-1853
Carsey, Dennis	64	Georgia	Robert D. McCammon James H. Biggs	4-25-1853
Carsey, Ephraim	60	Georgia	Achilles & David Vawter	4-30-1853
Carsey, Ephraim	32	Jennings Co.	Solon Cowell Achilles Vawter	8-30-1853
Carsey, Eliza Jane	18	Jennings Co.	Solon Cowell Achilles Vawter	8-15-1853
Carsey, George	54	Wilkes Co. Ga	Levi W. Todd Henry House	8-24-1853
Carsey, Hulbert	21	Jennings Co.	Harvey Boner Charles Rust	8-20-1853
Carsey, Mariah Jane wife of Hulbert	19	Elbert Co. Ga.	Harvey Boner Charles Rust	8-20-1853
Carsey, Sally	60	Georgia	Joseph Cowell Thomas J. Story	5- 3-1853
Carsey, Stephen	70	North Carolina	Robert D. McCammon Asa Haney	5- 2-1853
Carsey, Willis	17	Jennings Co.	Achilles Vawter James M. Baldwin	8-18-1853
Dennis, Peter	41	South Carolina	Achilles Vawter Robert D. McCammon	5- 5-1853
Dennis, Margaret	37	South Carolina	_____	9-16-1853
Dennis, John William	15	South Carolina	Achilles Vawter Robert D. McCammon	5- 5-1853

Dennis, Sarah Elizabeth	13	South Carolina	Achilles Vawter Robert D. McCammon	5- 5-1853
Dennis, Mary Eliza	11	South Carolina	Achilles Vawter Robert D. McCammon	5- 5-1853
Dennis, James Walter	9	South Carolina	Achilles Vawter Robert D. McCammon	5- 5-1853
Dennis, Enoch Wagner	7	Kentucky	Achilles Vawter Robert D. McCammon	5- 5-1853
Dennis, Margaret Ann	4	Jennings Co.	Achilles Vawter Robert D. McCammon	5- 5-1853
Dennis, Robert Mazwell	2	Jennings Co.	Achilles Vawter Robert D. McCammon	5- 5-1853
Dunlap, Peter	63	Abbeville Dist. South Carolina	Smith Vawter Harvey Boner	8-20-1853
Dunlap, Jane	51	Abbeville Dist. South Carolina	Smith Vawter Harvey Boner	8-20-1853
Dunlap, Martha	30	Abbeville Dist. South Carolina	Smith Vawter Harvey Boner	8-20-1853
Dunlap, Nancy	20	Abbeville Dist South Carolina	Smith Vawter Harvey Boner	8-20-1853
Dunlap, William	5	Jennings Co.	Smith Vawter Harvey Boner	8-20-1853
Dye, Daniel	44	Warren Co. Ga.	Achilles Vawter Robert D. McCammon	6-11-1853
Dye, Nancy Jane	13	Jennings Co.	Achilles Vawter Robert D. McCammon	6-11-1853
Dye, Acquilla Ann	9	Jennings Co.	Achilles Vawter Robert D. McCammon	6-11-1853
Dye, James William	8	Jennings Co.	Achilles Vawter Robert D. McCammon	6-11-1853
Edwards, Grace	18	Elbert Co. Ga.	Joshua & Margaret Palmer	8-18-1854
Evans, Zebidee	19	Halifax Co. N.C.	Achilles Vawter James M. Baldwin	8-16-1853
Harper, Grigg	82	Prince Edward Co. Va.	Asa & John Skinner	7-22-1853
Harper, Jane	56	Elbert Co. Ga.	Milton & Harvey Boner	8-12-1853
Harper, Riley	28	Elbert Co. Ga.	Arad Parks John Skinner	7-11-1853
Harper, Thomas	29	Elbert Co. Ga.	Arad Parks John Skinner	7-11-1853
Henderson, Harrison	42	Garrett Co. Ky.	Achilles Vawter Harvey M. Cowell	8-20-1853
Henry, Thomas J.	33	Bourbon Co. Ky.	Achilles Vawter George M. Payne	8-29-1853
Hill, Ananis	51	Maryland	George M. Payne Avery W. Bullock	8- 5-1853
Hill, Bluford A.	28	Elbert Co. Ga.	Ebenezer Baldwin Smith Vawter	8-15-1853
Hill, Jefferson	20	Jennings Co.	James M. Baldwin Elisha Boner	9- 1-1853
Hill, Lewis	69	Culpeper Co. Va.	_____	8-26-1853

Hill, Agrippa, son of Lewis	15	Jennings Co.	Achilles Vawter Levi W. Todd	8-26-1853
Hill, Mary Ann	23	Elbert Co. Ga.	Achilles Vawter Thomas McGannon	9-20-1853
Hood, Ephraim	59	Rockingham Co. N.C.	Achilles Vawter Elisha Boner	12-26-1853
Hood, Fanny	46	Virginia	Harvey M. Cowell Elisha Boner	1-28-1856
Hood, Hannibal	41	Jefferson Co.	Achilles Vawter Robert D. McCammon	6-19-1855
Hood, James H.	11	Jennings Co.	Achilles Vawter Thomas McGannon	9-20-1853
Hood, John	20	Jennings Co.	Achilles Vawter Morrow McMindes	8-12-1853
Hood, Mary	16	Jennings Co.	Achilles & Henry J. Vawter	12-27-1853
Hood, William	55	Rockingham Co. N.C.	Achilles Vawter Elisha Boner	12-26-1853
Hullam, Jasper	10	Elbert Co. Ga.	Thomas Grissom William B. Hagins	7-22-1853

[registered with Anthony family]

Johnson, Judah	72	Tennessee	Achilles Vawter Joseph Cowell	9-16-1853
Johnson, Thomas L.	29	Jennings Co.	Achilles Vawter Robert D. McCammon	9-14-1853
Johnson, Mary	30	Fauquier Co. Va.	Achilles Vawter Robert D. McCammon	9-17-1853
Johnson, Sarah Esther dt of Thomas & Mary	4	Jennings Co.	Achilles Vawter Robert D. McCammon	9-17-1853
King, Emeline	24	Jefferson Co.	Harvey M. Cowell Achilles Vawter	9- 5-1853
King, Jane	26	Jefferson Co.	Thomas McGannon Achilles Vawter	9-20-1853
King, Spencer	68	Culpeper Co. Va.	Levi Todd Thomas Walker	8-30-1853
King, Spencer Beverly	19	Jennings Co.	Achilles Vawter Levi W. Todd	8-26-1853
Lee, Ellen	__	Jennings Co.	William B. Hagins David Merrick	7-18-1853

[registered with Norman family]

Lee, William	54	Rockingham Co. Va.	Robert D. McCammon Avery W. Bullock	2- 1-1854
McCoppin, Marshall	38	South Carolina	William B. Hagins David Merrick	7-18-1853
McCoppin, Sarah wife of Marshall	35	Elbert Co. Ga.	William B. Hagins David Merrick	7-18-1853
Newby, James	16	Jackson Co.	William B. Hagins Henry L. Arnold	2-13-1854
Newsom, Emily	19	Jennings Co.	Achilles Vawter Harvey M. Cowell	8-15-1853
Norman, Nancy	47	Elbert Co. Ga.	William B. Hagins David Merrick	7-18-1853
Norman, Augustus	15	Elbert Co. Ga.	William B. Hagins David Merrick	7-18-1853
Norman, Willis	13	Elbert Co. Ga.	William B. Hagins David Merrick	7-18-1853
Pettiford, Drury	41	Stokes Co. N.C.	Levi W. Todd David Merrick	7-28-1853

Phillips, Henry	31	Warren Co. Ga.	Ebenezer Baldwin Joseph Fellinger	8- 1-1853
Phillips, Rosa, wife	23	Jennings Co.	_____	8- 6-1853
Phillips, Elzora, dt	5	Jennings Co.	Joseph Fellinger Harvey M. Cowell	8- 6-1853
Phillips, Cynthia, dt	3	Jennings Co.	Joseph Fellinger Harvey M. Cowell	8- 6-1853
Phillips, Emily, dt	1	Jennings Co.	Joseph Fellinger Harvey M. Cowell	8- 6-1853
Phillips, Wesley	25	Warren Co. Ga.	Ebenezer Baldwin Solon Cowell	8-26-1853
Phillips, Joseph, son	2½	Jennings Co.	Ebenezer Baldwin Solon Cowell	8-26-1853
Phillips, Jesse	21	Warren Co. Ga.	Ebenezer Baldwin Solon Cowell	8-26-1853
Phillips, Silvester	18	Warren Co. Ga.	Ebenezer Baldwin Solon Cowell	8-26-1853
Phillips, Stephen	15	Jennings Co.	Ebenezer Baldwin Solon Cowell	8-26-1853
Stafford, Martha E.	20	Abbeville Dist South Carolina	Achilles Vawter Thomas McGannon	9-20-1853
Stafford, Richard	30	Fauquier Co. Va.	Manlove Butler Robert D. McCammon	9-19-1853
Valentine, Andrew	23	South Carolina	Commodore C. Root William B. Hagins	7- 9-1853
Valentine, Samuel	28	Abbeville Dist. South Carolina	Harvey Boner Smith Vawter	8-20-1853
Valentine, Caroline	34	Abbeville Dist. South Carolina	Harvey Boner Smith Vawter	8-20-1853
Valentine, Martha	5	Jennings Co.	Harvey Boner Smith Vawter	8-20-1853
Valentine, James	3	Jennings Co.	Harvey Boner Smith Vawter	8-20-1853
Valentine, Jesse	4 mo.	Jennings Co.	Harvey Boner Smith Vawter	8-20-1853
Vickery, Allen	39	Abbeville Dist. South Carolina	Achilles Vawter Thomas McGannon	9-20-1853
Vickery, Addis	18	Abbeville Dist. South Carolina	Achilles Vawter Thomas McGannon	9-20-1853
Vickery, Oliver	17	Abbeville Dist. South Carolina	Achilles Vawter Thomas McGannon	9-20-1853
Vickery, James	49	Abbeville Dist. South Carolina	Thompson Grissom William B. Hagins	7-22-1853
Vickery, Rhoda, wife	49	Elbert Co. Ga.	Thompson Grissom William B. Hagins	7-22-1853
Wallace, Elias	19	Jennings Co.	Joseph Cowell Era Rosa	8-19-1853
Wallace, Isaiah	19	Jennings Co.	John S. Basnett Levi W. Todd	9-19-1853
White, William	50	Virginia	Thomas Grissom William B. Hagins	7-30-1853

ORANGE COUNTY MARRIAGES, 1816-1835

Compiled from microfilm copy of Book 1 and pages 1-67 of Book 2 of Orange County Marriage Records in Genealogy Division, Indiana State Library. Many of the names may be found in the Lick Creek and Paoli Monthly Meeting records published in Volume V of the Indiana Quaker Records.

Able, Andrew, Jr. - Rebecca Link	10-15-1835	
Able, Hiram - Elizabeth Ware	8-28-1828	
Able, William - Millie Link (?)	3- 1-1833	
Adams, David - Abigail S. Chapman	10-13-1829	
Agen, John - Nancy Lockhart	2- 2-1832	
Alderson, Moses - Ruth Dicks lic.	2-10-1817	
Alexander, Walter - Catherine Jolliff		
	4-11-1822	
Allegir, Robert - Nancy Philips	10-30-1833	
Allen, Charles - Mary Carroll	10-23-1834	
Allen, Jesse - Matildy Fort	1-12-1821	
Allen, John Rice - Jane Morris	11-22-1832	
Allen, William - Eleanor Seybold	3- 2-1824	
Allen, William - Elenor Ann Harris	2- 8-1829	
Allen, William - Deborah Hobson	8-24-1831	
Allgood, Robert - Hannah Buckhannon	12-18-1834	
Alten (?), Samuel - Polly Benson	1-29-1829	
Anderson, Abel - Jane Roberts	1-12-1832	
Archer, James M. - Jane Glover	1- 7-1835	
Archer, William - Mary Saunders	1-31-1818	
Archy, Moses - Polly Roberts	11-15-1829	
Armstrong, Felix - Isabell Bland	3- 9-1820	
Arten, Daniel - Milly Ann Moyer	7-24-1831	
Athon, Alfred - Betsy Hazlewood	2-25-1823	
Atkinson, Arthur - Abigail Doan	1- 1-1835	
Atkinson, Elijah - Rachel Reed lic.	7- 1-1830	
Atkinson, Robert - Rebecca Crow	1-29-1829	
Atkinson, Rochester - Sarah P. McDonald		
	11-28-1823	
Atkinson, Thomas - Margery Lindley	3- 6-1823	
Atkinson, Thomas - Rachel Evans	7- 7-1825	
Baker, James - Sally Burgess	7- 3-1834	
Baker, James H. - Elizabeth Moyer	4-24-1832	
Baker, John - Anna Erwin	10-12-1823	
Baker, William - Harriet Cowherd	11-24-1825	
Baldwin, Eli - Betsey Pinoll	3- 6-1823	
Baldwin, Elisha - Rachel Bland	2-13-1821	
Ballard, Andrew J. - Elizabeth Shephard		
	9- 3-1833	
Barnet, Jesse - Polly Stroud	1-16-1821	
Barns, Dean - Mahala Athon	11-26-1823	
Barnum, Ebenezer - Tempy Smith	9-29-1831	
Bateman, William - Catherine Robbins	7- 4-1822	
Baxter, Dennis - Margaret Wilson lic.		
	10-22-1828	
Beach, John - Rebecah Steward	3-31-1825	
Beasley, Charles - Polly Lock	4- 5-1825	
Beasley, Daniel - Rachel Tearra	3- 9-1835	
Belcher, Berry - Jane Trimble	3-11-1824	
Belcher, John - Eunice Pitman	12-14-1826	
Belcher, Joseph - Ruth Wall	3-20-1820	
Belcher, Moses - Eliza Belcher	7- 9-1835	
Belcher, William - Susannah Ingram lic.		
	7-21-1830	
Bell, James - Margaret Stines (?) lic.		
	10-19-1835	
Bell, William - Susan Dougherty	10-18-1834	
Benjamin, John B. - Jane Moser	6- 9-1825	
Bennett, John - Sally Berry	12-11-1827	
Bennett, John - Sarah Keysee	2- 8-1835	
Benson, Thomas - Polly Allen	7-12-1829	

Berry, William W. - Christiana Holler		
	6- 9-1831	
Bilyeu, William - Polly McCart	5-27-1831	
Bingamon, Peter - Gilly Lynch	3-18-1824	
Blackburn, Robert L. - Lucinda Rigny lic.		
	11- 8-1830	
Blackwell, Benjamin - Mary McCune	4- 9-1833	
Blackwell, Lewis - Olive Pedigo	8-14-1834	
Blake, James - Mary Padget	2- 2-1826	
Blake, William - Mary Piles	12-22-1825	
* Bland, Francis - Elizabeth Lane	1- 7-1819	
Bland, John - Polly Jervis	3-12-1819	
Bledsoe, Lewis A. - Mary Hobson lic.		
	10- 9-1835	
Bobbitt, Harrison - Lydia Boswell	11-15-1832	
Bobbitt, John - Catharine Gobble	5-21-1835	
Bolton, Abnatha - Fanny Stone	12- 6-1832	
Bolton, James - Elizabeth Leathers lic.		
	8-25-1830	
Bonds, Fradarack - Sarah Means		
People of color	11-12-1835	
Bonds, Reuben - Penellepe Hill	6- 7-1832	
Boon, Hezekiah - Jenny Duncan	6- 7-1821	
Boon, John - Catharine Edwards lic.		
	12-22-1831	
Boon, Solomon - Sarah McNaminee	8-12-1829	
Bosley, Gideon - Martha Flint lic.		
	8-15-1829	
Boswell, Thomas - Elizabeth Ann White		
	3-26-1835	
Bowles, Andrew - Huldy French lic.		
	3- 2-1835	
Branen, Kane - Mariah Lee	5-14-1829	
Brantram, John F.(or T.) - Nancy Martin		
	3-29-1821	
Braxton, William - Sally Moulder	12-21-1826	
Bredwell, James - Mariam Osbourn	3- 1-1835	
Breeze, James - Charity Handley	10-23-1825	
Britton, John - Elizabeth Mackelmas		
	10-13-1825	
Breeze, Richard - Berdina Self	11- 9-1832	
Bridgewater, William - Priscilla Boon		
	2-13-1834	
Briner, George - Sally Denny	5-31-1827	
Briner, George - Mary Clements lic.		
	8-30-1830	
Briner, Isaac - Polly Denny	8- 3-1832	
Britton, John - Eliza Spragal	11- 3-1831	
Broadwell, John - Rebecca Allen	3-14-1823	
Brooks, Daniel - Mary Vanator	11-26-1833	
Brooks, Jacob - Susannah Grimes	1-24-1829	
Brooks, Thomas J. - Susannah Poor	8- 5-1830	
Brothers, William - Rebecca Keller	1-10-1828	
Brothers, Wilson - Sally Lewis	11-28-1827	
Brown, James M. - Charity Hopkins	9- 6-1828	
Brown, John - Matildy Boone	3-13-1817	
Brown, William - Rebecca Crumb	6- 6-1824	
Brown, Zachariah - Betsy Blevins	10-24-1835	
Brumet, John - Polly Gadd (?) lic.		
	2-22-1817	

Bruner, John - Deborah Hodges lic.
                                1-10-1828
Bryner(?), John - Lucinda Roberts lic.
                                2- 1-1834
Buckner, Henry - Elizabeth Scott   8-16-1817
Bugg, Sampson - Delilah Roberts   12- 2-1824
Bullington, Alfred - Delila Manly(?)
                                7-27-1826
Bullington, Benjamin - Rosannah Hutchison
                          lic. 12- 9-1829
Bullington, Isaac - Mahala Aston lic
                                9-11-1833

Bullinton, John - Rachael Evans   6-24-1821
Bullington, Robert - Nancy Wells   9-18-1828
Bullington, William - Polly Hopkins 11-23-1826
Bunch, Israel - Lydia Taylor   3- 7-1828
Bundy, Gideon - Elizabeth Fort   9- 9-1819
Bundy, Gideon - Peggy Reynolds   1-11-1834
Bundy, Jesse - Sarah Lee lic.   5- 4-1816
Bundy, Reuben - Anna Smith   4-24-1834
Burgar, John - Martha Rogers   7-24-1825
Burgess, Dobson - Roda Robbins   11-20-1829
Burnet, David - Elizabeth Cole   3-13-1826
Burton, George - Lucinda Burch   12-18-1831
Bush, Isaac - Elizabeth Melton lic. 7-29-1834
Busick, Joseph - Nancy Jones   10- 5-1821
Busick, Kindred - Hester Ann Millis 10- 7-1826
Busick, Thomas W. - Eliza Hackney 8- 6-1835
Busick, William - Sidney Hackney   2- 7-1833
Butler, Thomas - Anna Martin   8-30-1835
Caddell, William - Diana Pitman   9- 4-1828
Cadell, John - Ginny Seybold   12-18-1830
Calter (or Colter?), Samuel - Sally Vest
                                4-20-1817
Campbell, Adlai - Lavisa Galbreath 8-16-1835
Campbell, Maxwell - Sarah Field   12- 6-1827
Canaday, Henry M. - Mary E. Evans 5- 9-1828
Cantril, Abraham - Rebecah Williams 7-27-1820
Canttor(?), Charles - Betsy Fisher 4- 9-1818
Carl, William - Elizabeth Simmons 7-10-1831
Carlisle, John - Louisa Strange   1-18-1825
Carlisle, William - Nancy Jackson lic.
                                2-22-1830
Carr, Elisha - Elizabeth Lucas (or Lewis)
                               12-31-1818
Carr, George - Eliza B. Busick lic.
    consent of her guardian   5-11-1835
Carr, Linsey - Nelly Chambers lic. 8- 2-1830
Carr, Thomas G. - Margaret Ribble 5- 7-1833
Carroll, Benjamin - Sally Sinclear 9- 9-1832
Carroll, James - Fernally McCoy   2-27-1834
Carter, John - Hannah Holloday lic. 6- 9-1827
Case, Josiah - Polly Neal lic.   6- 3-1831
Case, Washington - Rachel Porter 10- 6-1831
Cates, Prier - Nancy Robbins   3-28-1833
Chace, Michael - Polly Gattin (?) 12- 5-1822
Chambers, Jonathan - Deborah Stalcup
                               12- 9-1832
Chancey (or Chaney), William - Jane Blackwell
                                9-22-1831
Charles, Azor - Rachel Cobb   1-17-1820
Charles, William - Margaret Brown 2-13-1834
Chasteen, Daniel - Betsy Lewis   10-18-1821
* Chatham, John - Nancy Maxwell   2-20-1817
Chenoworth, Elias - Elizabeth McIntosh lic.
                                8- 9-1829

Chenoworth, James - Elizabeth Stallcup
                                1-11-1835
Chenoworth, Levi - Susanna McIntosh lic.
                                7-28-1835
Chess, Thomas - Delila Gasaway   2- 3-1831
Child, Royal B. - Mahala Reed lic. 2-13-1832
Childers, John - Usley Demoss   7-20-1826
Childers, Richard - Margaret McCauley lic.
                                2-13-1828
Childress, William - Sally Bosley lic.
                                9- 9-1829
Chisham, Uriah - Catherine Busick 4-15-1830
Chisher, James - Susannah Brooks   7- 4-1826
Christopher, John - Margaret A. Walls
                                5-12-1831
Clampit(?), Thomas - Nancy Woods   2- 6-1823
Clark, James - Lydia Dicks   7- 2-1818
Clark, James - Catherine Harmin   2- 4-1819
Clark, Thomas - Reese Trueblood lic.
                                9-16-1826

Claxton, Jeremiah - Delilah Pearce
                               12- 1-1835
Cleaveland, Joshua - Sarah Jenkins 8- 3-1834
Clegg, Thomas - Sidney Biggs   12-18-1822
Clemens, Thomas - Winford Richardson
                                5-25-1825
Clements, Francis - Annis Martin   9-28-1831
Clements, John - Nancy Copeland   4-15-1827
Clendenin, John G. - Mary Fustad   2-25-1819
Clendenin, John G. - Dovey Cook   11-16-1830
Clendenin, Joseph - Polly Hollowell
                               10- 6-1829
Clendenin, Peter - Polly Gorden   2-11-1826
Cleveland, Marvin - Patsy Noblett 1- 5-1830
Cleveland, Mathew - Elizabeth Jenkins
                                2- 3-1833
Clifton, Calya - Letitia Halfacre 4-11-1833
Clifton, Henry - Elizabeth Cauble 3-31-1835
Clinton, Henry - Delpha Sherrod(?) lic.
                                4-23-1829
Cloud, James - Sarah Pitts   12-27-1832
Cloud, John - Hannah Newlin   12-29-1825
Cloud, William - Jane Pruett   1-26-1832
Cobb, Ara(?) - Elizabeth McCr____ 6- -1835
Cobb, Henry - Permelia Tanner   12- 7-1820
Cobb, William - Lucinda Pinnick   1-29-1824
Cochran, Thomas - Polly Dickens   8-17-1824
Coffin, William - Eunice Alfred   6-23-1819
Colclasure, Jacob - Ruth Stalcup (?)
                               11- 5-1823
Collins, Findly - Rebeckah Black   6-21-1829
Collins, James - Susannah Carter lic.
                                4- 9-1816
Collins, Quash - Lavinah Harris   9- 4-1822
Collun, Cyrus - Eliza Jane Maxwell 7-24-1834
Colvin, Lewis - Susan Ray   9-27-1821
Conder, John - Elizabeth K. Carter
                               11-13-1828
Conder, William - Margarett Cunningham
                               11- 2-1834
Conklin, Charles - Mary Ann Halfacre
                                5-31-1827
Conrod, George - Levina Harris   1-18-1827
Cook, Absalom - Polly Bobbitt   12-11-1834
Cook, David J.(or L.) - Nancy Lingle
                                9-15-1831
Cook, George - Jane McCauley   9- 5-1824

Cook, Isaac - Catharine Wininger   11- 3-1831
Cook, Jacob - Catherine Wise lic. 8-24-1829
Cook, Philip - America Tillery   6-15-1831
Cook, Valentine - Polly Bobbett   lic.
                                   8- 9-1830
Cook, William - Lavina Charles   2-13-1821
Coonrod, Philip - Lucinda Connel 10-13-1825
Cooper, Hiram - Kesiah Wills (or Wells)
                                    5-26-1825
Cooper, Jacob - Sally Bryant   2-15-1821
Cooper, Jacob - Betsey Wilkey   12-21-1823
Cooper, James - Janthe Malena   3-23-1828
Cooper, William R. - Anna Cay   10-30-1834
Copeland, Elias - Sarah McCune   9-10-1833
Copple, William - Abbe Handley   1-23-1831
Cornwell, Edward - Nancy Johnson   10- 6-1831
Cornwell, Harrison - Nancy Cornwell
                                   12-23-1827
Cornwell, Harrison - Rebecca Fulfer
                                    3-25-1834
Cornwell, Payton - Elizabeth Moyers(?)
                                    9- 6-1827
Cornwell, Simon - Polly Wolf   2- 5-1824
Cornwell, William - Matilda Johnson
                                    1- 8-1830
Cox, Lewis - Sally Danner   6-24-1824
Cox, Solomon - Nancy Cloud   10-30-1834
Craig, William - Sophia Davis   10-25-1832
Craig, William - Nancy Busick   10-16-1834
Crawford, Jesse - Elizabeth Wright lic.
                                    1-22-1827
Crumbi, Robert - Sarah Boon   8-30-1821
Cully, John - Elizabeth Ingram   10- 7-1819
Cunningham, John T. - Polly Overby 8-17-1828
Cunningham, Lindsey P. - Hester Ann Britton
                                    2- 7-1832
Cunningham, Woodson - Margaret M. Coward
                                    8-18-1831
Cutshaw, Samuel - Angeline Turner   7-29-1831
Cutsinger, Michael - Susannah Willaby
                                    4-12-1827
Dales(?), William - Elizabeth Ingram 2-24-1831
Damewood, Henry - Elizabeth Rader   8-16-1828
Danner, Solomon - Sarah Cates   5- 8-1834
Daugherty, Milton T. - Mary Dougherty
                                    8- 2-1832
Daugherty, Warden - Elizabeth Dunbar
                                    3- 1-1832
Davis, Asahel - Emeriah Rigney lic. 1- 9-1832
Davis, Barnett - Catharine Davis   10-14-1824
Davis, Blueford - Polly Bush   12-20-1832
Davis, Edmund - Nancy Wadomans(?)   1-29-1822
Davis, John - Rebecca Mayfield   2-27-1833
Davis, Joseph - Mary Smith   3- 9-1832
Davis, Thomas J. - Margaret Abel   9-30-1835
Dawson, Benjamin - Prissilar Fincher(?) lic.
                                    4-19-1816
Dawson, Daniel - Elizabeth Holloday 9-30-1819
Dawson, John - Nancy Lindly   6- 9-1825
Dayhuff, Daniel - Rachael Smith   8-15-1822
Dellender, James - Nancy Vandever   3-19-1833
Denton, Andrew - Rebeckah Oborn (or Osborn)
                                   10- 7-1819
Denton, George - Arretta Weathers lic.
                                    7-19-1830
Depew, Isaac - Sarah Vantrese   3-28-1822
Depew, James - Judy(or Indy?) Hill 10-23-1831

Deweez, Dubelius - Ellander French 9-24-1816
Dewey, Charles - Sarah Liggett   2-11-1824
Dickens, Ephraim - Rachal Mayhoe lic.
                                    7- 7-1827
Dicks, Zachariah - Peggy Trueblood 2-11-1819
Dillard, William - Hetty Samuelson 2-11-1831
Dishon, William - Deannah Lowell   12-12-1829
Ditto, Shadrick - Mary Atkinson   4-19-1821
Dixon, Carrentan - Rachel Williams 8-25-1822
Dixon, Jacob - Rebecca Patton   3-23-1831
Dixon, Jacob - Elizabeth Wood   1-12-1832
Dixon, Joseph - Phebe Stallings   6-16-1833
Dixon, Solomon - Elizabeth Hill   4-28-1825
Doan, Jacob - Anna Culberson   1-14-1820
Doan, Jonathan - Polly Leonard   1- 2-1825
Doan, Joseph - Sally Pascall   8-25-1822
Doan, Joseph - Rachael Hobson   12-10-1829
Doan, William - Ruth Dixon   5-20-1819
Dodds(?), R. C. - Elizabeth Tate   8-28-1834
Doggatt, Isaac - Nancy Head   11-14-1833
Done, Malen - Jane Freeman lic.   11- 8-1826
Dougherty, Gabriel - Sally Lafferty lic.
                                    7-26-1831
Dougherty, John - Mahala Havens   3- 6-1827
Dougherty, Samuel - Mary Bland   11- 5-1819
Downs, John - Belura Bishop   4-11-1818
Drake, Jefferson - Elizabeth Flick 12-27-1829
Drake, Ransom - Eliza Flick   4- 5-1829
Dunkan, David - Hannah Inman   1-13-1825
Dunkin, James - Mary Cleavland   12-22-1824
Edwards, Edward - Margaret Worrell 12- 4-1832
Edwards, Griffith, Jr. - Rebecca Johnson
                                    3- 6-1821
Edwards, Thomas - Lucy Nugent   4-11-1834
Edwards, William - Elvira Jenkins   1- 8-1835
Eldridge, Levi A.- Mary Holbert   12- 3-1835
Elgan, John - Sarah Pound   4- 1-1819
Elkins, _____ - Grasillah Ratliff
                             lic.   4- 4-1829
Elkins, Archibald - Mariah Oston   8-16-1829
Elkins, Stephen - Dorothy Fulfer   5-15-1833
Elkins, Wesley - Anna Pickens   11- 9-1826
Ellexson, Ezekiel - Polly Nidiffer
                             lic.   12-12-1831
Ellis, Daniel - Sarah Brown   7-30-1835
Ellis, Isaac M. - Jane Ratcliff   4-22-1827
Ellison, James - Rachel Ward lic. 4-19-1816
Ellison, Thomas - Nancy D. Huddleson
                                    2-26-1835
Elrod, James M. - Delila Noblett   5-14-1835
Elrod, John - Sally Stultz   8- 4-1824
Elrod, Noah - Polly Hoots   12-14-1828
Erly, James - Caty Washburn   8-16-1817
Evans, Joshua - Nancy Dunkin   5-18-1826
Evans, Strond - Rebecca Knight   9-22-1822
Faris, Nathan - Susannah Pinnick   12-11-1823
Farlow, Jonathan - Ruth Maris   11-15-1832
Farlow, Nathan - Mary Ann Moulder 11-13-1834
Farris, Young - Polly Dunbar   7-26-1831
Farus, John - Lavina Mullins   10- 5-1820
Faulkner, William - Anna Harned   11-18-1818
Feather, Jacob O. - Matila Copeland
                                   12- 5-1829
Ferris, Hardy H. - Nancy Ferris   1-23-1834
Fetherkile, George - Margaret Robberts
                                   12-27-1826
Field, Jesse - Mary Bailey lic.   2-23-1831

Fields, Benjamin H. - Rachel Wilson
1-15-1819
Fields, George - Elizabeth Rankin 2-18-1834
Fields, Jeremiah - Margaret Wilson 7- 3-1817
Fields, John - Catharine Crutsinger
6-30-1820
Findley, Cyrus - Rachel Dasoney 12-17-1818
Fisher, William - Susan Campbell 5-10-1825
Fisher, Zelotek - Elizabeth Glenn 8- 5-1819
Fitsgerald, Allen - Nancy Baker 5- 3-1832
Fleming, David - Fanny Bell 7- 9-1826
Flick, Jonathan - Fanny Elkins lic.
1-15-1835
Flick, Washington - Martha Drake 10- 8-1835
Foust (or Faust), John - Luisa Haudishelt
lic. 8-22-1827
Frazure, Elijah - Dorinda S. Piggott
7-19-1835
Frazure, John - Elizabeth Freeman 3- 5-1835
Freed, Daniel- Elizabeth Kutsinger 8- 7-1828
Freeman, Abner - Polly Spiceley 6-25-1835
Freeman, Alfred - Elizabeth Stanfield
7-22-1831
Freeman, Benjamin - Martha Frost 7-30-1829
French, Haden - Mary Boswell 11-22-1827
French, Robert - Nancy Kirk 1-17-1833
French, Tanely(?) - Lydia Stroud 1- 4-1821
Frost(?), Isaac - Franky Henderson 8- 7-1817
Fulfer, John - Elizabeth Osborne 1-14-1817
Fulfer, John - Tobitha Kidd 12-27-1825
Fulfer, Joseph - Massa Chaney 9- 2-1824
Fuller, John - Elizabeth Killiam 7-28-1828
Fulton, Alexander - Margaret Depew 1-20-1829
Furgeson, Thomas - Betsey Self 8-18-1819
Gadd, Robert - Nancy Demoss 3- 8-1817
Galbreth, Andrew - Laricy Porter 8-27-1829
Gammon, Harris - Margaret Cutsinger
1-28-1830
Gammon, Silas - Margaret McElyea (or McAlya)
5-21-1833
Gasaway, Nicholas - Margaret Matthew
lic. 2-10-1831
Geans(?), Jefferson - Elizabeth Speakes
lic. 7- 6-1827
Gee, John - Rebecca Ann Tate lic. 9-18-1829
Gerken, Jonathan - Nancy Moyer lic.
11- 3-1834
Gerking, Samuel - Anna Williams 5-13-1835
Gifford, Levi - Sarah Baker 4- 1-1824
Gillum, James - Elizabeth Warren 1-18-1835
Gilpin, Curtis - Polly Shaiger(?) 2- 8-1823
Girkin, Samuel - Rachel Myers 12-17-1830
Givins, Elisha - Hannah Holoday 5-13-1828
Glenn, David - Susannah Reaves 4-20-1823
Glenn, Samuel - Lydia Shields 5-31-1827
Glover, Jonah - Evlen Vandover(?) 9-10-1818
Glover, Jonah - Lydia Ann Wallace 11- 1-1821
Goliman, Jacob - Susannah Weathers 2-27-1828
Golman, Moses - Catharine Savage 2-14-1825
Gobble, Adam - Julia David lic. 8-19-1830
Gooly, William - Harriet Athon 6-19-1821
Graham, Nelson - Zelphe Boswell lic.
8-17-1831
Gray, William - Caty Osborn lic. 10-22-1816
Green, Elias D. - Lewana(?) Vickery
lic. 9-18-1834
Greenstreet, John - Clarissa Pipher 5-17-1824

Gresham, Esau - Lydia Dark 11-19-1835
Griffey(?), Luke - Elizabeth Holt 12-24-1828
Grigsby, Moses - Delilah Strange 2-16-1828
Grimes, George - Nancy Patton 3-20-1831
Gross, Absalom - Polly Tegarden 5-29-1828
Gross, Hiram - Peggy Leatherman 3- 1-1821
Gross, Jacob - Ally Marlow 10-23-1832
Grubb, Virgil - Delilah Saunders 2-16-1832
Guthrie, William - Elizabeth Rigney 1- 9-1823
Gwin, Isom - Betsy Snowden 3- 1-1824
Habban(?), Michael - Mary Wells 3- 7-1819
Hackney, John - Sarah Lambden 7-23-1818
Hadley, John - Mary Hadley 6-27-1818
Hains, John - Mary Speaks 7- 3-1826
Halfacre, David - Polly Moore 9-25-1834
Hall, John - Elizabeth Kellems 2-19-1818
Hall, Joseph - Polly Wilson 3-12-1821
Hamblin, Uriah - Clarrey Calyon(?) 9-28-1820
Hamilton, Stephen - Polly Duncan
lic. 2-15-1832
Hamersley(?), Andrew - Lucy Roberts 12- 8-1824
[1825?]
Hammond, Aaron - Mary McKern 10-22-1829
Hammond, John - Sarah Gobble 1-24-1833
Hampton, Jesse - Catharine Brooks 6- 9-1831
Hancock, Benjamin - Polly Bingaman 4- 8-1828
Handcock, Martin - Margaret May 3-13-1823
Harden, Stephen - Mary Vandeveer 9-14-1825
Hardin, John - Clon(?) Colelashure 10-12-1817
Hardman, Daniel - Elizabeth Hosteller
9- 1-1831
Hardman, William - Susannah Keedy 3-31-1831
Harmon, William - Phebe Steck 7-22-1827
Harned, Charles F. - Lucinda Stallcup
lic. 8-26-1834
Harned, Samuel - Ann Lindley 3-18-1824
Harrell, David - Maria Fuller 3-24-1833
Harris, George W. - Cynthia Richerson
10-17-1833
Hart, Joseph - Sally Riley 12-25-1817
Harvey, Michael - Polly Knight 3- 7-1824
Hatfield, John - Malinda Davis lic. 3-31-1830
Hazlewood, Josiah - Levisa Johnson
lic. 8-27-1830
Head, William - Sally Phillips 5-21-1827
Heath, James - Naomi Grogan 11- 5-1826
Helphinstine, John - Mary Singleton 10- 7-1830
Henderson, David - Grace Crow 10- 7-1816
Henderson, James F. - Deborah Jane Fisher
9- 5-1835
Henderson, John - Margaret Busick 1-26-1832
Henderson, Oren - Rebecca Hart lic.10-22-1829
Henderson, Robert - Elizabeth Ford 5-24-1824
Hendley, Joseph - Sarah Lindley 1-12-1826
Hendricks, Isaac - Nancy Hawood(?)
11-15-1820
Henry, William - Betsy Berry 9- 2-1833
Henson, Jesse - Jemima Cobb 12-11-1834
Hill, Jesse - Lydia Millis lic. 8-29-1830
Hill, Joseph - Nancy Davis 1-30-1823
Hill, Leonard - Susannah Bundy 1-14-1823
Hill, William - Prudance Brooks
lic. 3-18-1817
Hinton, George - Polly White 4-23-1818
Hinton, Guy - Mary Dillard 1-19-1830
Hix (Dix?), Willis - Rebecca Breeze
8-23-1820

Hobson, Baly - Clercey Stroud   3- 9-1821
Hobson, George - Polly Holt   9-20-1829
Hobson, John - Margaret Boswell
                        lic.   8-20-1829
Hobson, John - Nancy Haga   2-18-1832
Hobson, Joseph - Rachael Reynolds   7-13-1824
Hobson, Nathan - Elizabeth Sims   2- 8-1827
Hoggatt, Robert - Rachael Johnson   9- 7-1834
Hoggatt, Wilford - Betsy Wells   10- 7-1830
Holdsclau, James - Anny Inlowe   2-20-1823
Holland, John - Patsy Rooke   4-29-1833
Hollen, Arthur - Polly Belcher   8- 3-1835
Hollen, Markham - Rachael Pilgrim   1- 9-1834
Holler, Absolam - Nancy Lipins   6-28-1828
Holler, Israel - Susan Miller   8-22-1833
Holley, John - Mary Parks   7-17-1834
Holloday, John B. - Maria Crittenden
                                       12-12-1830
Holloday, Samuel - Absilla Boswell
                                       11- 7-1827
Holloday, William - Miriam Hollowell
                        lic.   6-24-1830
Hollowell, James - Agnus Lambdin   1-26-1832
Hollowell, Jesse P. - Sarah Maxidon
                                       10-14-1824
Hollowell, John - Hannah Self   11-16-1820
Hollowell, John - Urchel(or Michal?) Stout
                                       11-20-1828
Hollowell, John - Elizabeth Lindley
                        lic.   8- 9-1831
Hollowell, Jonathan - Jane Cantrel   8-14-1817
Hollowell, Jonathan - Hannah Sanders
                                       12-16-1835
Hollowell, Malachi - Elizabeth Tarr
                                       10- 8-1835
Holmes, Henry - Hannah Lindly lic.
                                       12-27-1828
Holmes, Jacob - Aseneth Wood   1- 4-1821
Holmes, William S. T. - Polly Duncan
                                       4-10-1827
Holsclaw(?), John B. - Elizabeth Owens(?)
                                       2-28-1819
Holt, James - Sarah Shields   5-24-1829
Holt, Joseph - Elizabeth Wilson   2- 9-1826
Hooten, Noah - Mary Adaline Mayfield
                                       11-20-1832
Hopper, John - Susan Lankford   10- 8-1835
Hopper, Raleigh - Rebecca Malone   11-18-1824
Hoskins, William - Mary Russell lic.
                                       12-23-1830
Hostetter, Jonathan - Elizabeth Leatherman
                                       9- 4-1823
* Huddleson, Thomas - Lydia Elrod lic.
                                       3- 4-1834
Hudelson, William H. - Elizabeth H. Springer
                                       6- 7-1831
Huffman, William - Lavisa Davis   9-30-1827
Hufford, Jacob - Elizabeth Burtner   7- 8-1824
Hughes, James H. - Nancy F. Boon   3-16-1820
Hughston, James B. - Nancy Hill   12-29-1831
Humphry, Alfred B. - Sally M. Luckey
                                       11- 6-1828
Hunnel, Frederick - Ruth Marshall   10-21-1824
Hunt, John - Anna Maxadon(or Maxident)
                                       11- 5-1826
Hunt, William - Betty Williams   2-28-1819
Hunter, Thomas - Caroline Bowles   4-30-1835

Husband, John - Judy Hall   10-28-1828
Huston, Squire - Nancy Gwin   10-27-1822
Hutchison, Joseph - Sarah Sutton   10-21-1824
Hutslar, James - Susanna Mayo   5-17-1835
Idings, David - Mary Voris   9- 2-1820
Ingram, Hurd - Malinda Lagle lic.   12-27-1828
Ingram, William - Caty Booffer   8-22-1822
Inlow, George - Mahala Atkins   2- 9-1834
Irvin, Samuel - Mary Smiley   12-26-1834
Irvin, Samuel F. - Iris G. Hoggatt   9-23-1827
Jackson, Nathan - Martha Johnson   7- 8-1832
Jenkins, Jeremiah - Elizabeth Smith   10-15-1835
* Jenkins, Thomas - Elenor Smart lic. 10-20-1828
Jervis, Edward - Susannah Tindle   4-22-1819
John(?), John - Mary Cullums   9-10-1824
Johnson, Benjamin - Elizabeth Meacham
                                       11-16-1828
Johnson, James - Lucy Lock   2- 7-1833
Johnson, Lancelott - Nancy Vest   5-17-1821
Johnson, Levi - Anna Roberts   7- 2-1829
Johnson, Martin - Dycey Smith   6-20-1822
Johnson, Richard - Catherine Fox   6-25-1827
Johnson, William - Polly Harden   10- 5-1828
Johnson, William - Parmelia Dougherty
                                       8- 1-1833
Johnson, William - Sarah Hardesty   10- 1-1835
Jones, Allen - Altha Luther   6-19-1824
Jones, Eli - Hannah Snyder   1-17-1833
Jones, John - Mary Hadley   7- 9-1820
Jones, Jonathan - Elizabeth Stalcup   1-22-1833
Jones, Moses - Polly Vance   7-25-1833
Jones, Philip - Rebeckah Taylor   11- 3-1825
Jones, William - Polly (Mary) Fisher
  John Jones in license   4-28-1829
Justice, James - Malinda Pitman   7- 7-1825
Kearby (Kerby?), Elias - Sally Nichols
                                       9-10-1830
Kearby, William - Rachel Moore   6- 5-1834
Kee, William - Sarah Stroud   6-16-1834
Keith, Alexander - Susannah Wilson   3- 3-1822
Keith, James - Polly Parsons   8-19-1824
Kellams, James - Delilah Copelin   10- 7-1823
Kelms, Gilbert - Mary Pippin   6-29-1817
Kellums, Martin - Sarah W. Bolan(?)
                        lic.   4-19-1830
Kellums, Pleasant - Mary Ann Connell   8-26-1834
Kendall, Hiram - Nancy Gregory   11-19-1829
Kerby, Giles H. - Mary Depew   12-22-1825
Kerby(?), Lewis - Polly Boon   12-28-1826
Kerby, William - Harriet Bigle   11- 6-1828
Kimbley, Isaac - Elizabeth Spicely   10- 6-1828
King, Cornelius - Mary Vandever   4- 8-1819
King, Russell - Susannah Briggs   10-25-1835
* King, William - Ann King   5-27-1817
Kinkade, Andrew - Barbary Landis   8-20-1817
Kinley, James - Mary Jane Gill   3-19-1835
Kinley, Lewis - Agnes Riley lic.   3- 9-1832
Kirby, Joel - Sally Duncan   7-30-1818
Kirk, William - Elizabeth Shackles   10-21-1835
Knight, Jonathan - Lydia Knight   10- 7-1823
Knight, Jonathan H. - Betsey Sumner   9-29-1825
Knight see also Night
Knoblet, John - Jane Furgeson   6-22-1823
Kreitzinger, Jacob - Sally Lee   11-25-1819
Lambdin, Daniel - Rodoh Stone lic.   1- 5-1828
Lambdin, Lewis - Mary Johnson lic.   8- 8-1831
Lamdin, David - Rosana Pinnick   12-23-1827
Landreth, Allen - Oma Burton   3-22-1831

Lane, Daniel - Mary Collins	6-11-1835
Lane, Jonathan - Rebecca Giles	2- 2-1832
Lankford, John - Mary Brooks	9-12-1833
Lankford, William - Lemander(?) Brooks	
lic.	2- 1-1833
Laughlin (or O'Laughlin), Hiram -	
Rhody Patton	12- 9-1830
Lay, Joel - Sarah Gooden	4-25-1829
Lay, Thomas - Patsy Sinclair	10-21-1832
Leatherman, David E. - Elizabeth Smith	
	3-30-1831
Leatherman, Henry - Fanny Bland	3-29-1820
Leatherman, John H. - Polly Lee	5-14-1829
Lee, Andrew - Silvey Scags	12-17-1818
Lee, Benjamin - Queen Anna Lindley	9-18-1828
Lee, Clement - Maria Welleby	1-12-1824
Lee, Dickerson - Sally Lindley	10-26-1826
Lee, Isaac - Dolly Leatherman	7- 7-1825
Lee, Jesse F. - Martha Lee lic.	2- 1-1834
Lee, John - Nancy Wilson	6-25-1835
Lee, Joseph - Nancy Roberts	10-25-1829
Lee, Josiah - Elizabeth Wilson	
lic.	11- 3-1831
Lee, Moses - Polly Griffin	11- 2-1820
Lee, Samuel - Elizabeth Lindley	12-28-1834
Lee, Spencer - Elizabeth Tegarden	6-10-1819
Lee, William - Mary Lindley	2-29-1820
Leffler, Jonathan - Peggy Jackson	7-25-1832
Lefler, Daniel - Anna Morgan	11- 9-1834
Lefler, David - Sarah Hazlewood	7-17-1821
Lefler, George - Hannah Harden	3-25-1829
Lemmond, Clark - Eliza Campbell	12- 4-1832
Lemon, James - Amy Rollins	4- 2-1818
Leonard, Bayley - Lucinda Trimble	
lic.	10-16-1827
Leonard, Jabez - Barbara Moore	12-20-1833
Leonard, James - Oly Moon(?)	11-28-1822
Leonard, Jeruel - Nancy Litteral	12-31-1828
Leonard, William - Sally Giles	8-12-1829
Lewis(?), Adam - Eliza Oston	10-15-1825
Lewis, James - Bethilda Rayborn	8-10-1824
Lewis, James T. - Perlina Hokstetler	
	2-12-1831
Lewis, Moses P. - Polly Hardman	5-28-1831
Lewis, William - Susannah Colclasure	
lic.	4-17-1816
Lewis, William D. - Helen S. Miriam	
	11-27-1834
Lindley, David - Jane Wilkins	11-27-1827
Lindley, David, Jr. - Ruth Lee	12-22-1831
Lindley, James - Sally Britten	10-29-1828
Lindley, Jefferson - Miriam Brooks	
	12-27-1825
Lindley, Jonathan - Lydia Moulder	1- 8-1830
Lindsey, James - Charlotte Anthony	
	4- 6-1835
Line, Joab - Nancy Morris	11-11-1819
Lingle, Joseph F. - Ruth Cook	8- 9-1831
Liston, Henry - Anna Kelly	9-11-1828
Liston, John - Constance Bowles	12- 8-1835
Litterel, John - Betsey Harmon	7-27-1826
Livengood, David - Elizabeth Tillery	
	7-19-1831
Livings(?), John - Morning Brown	
Livace on return	1-25-1832
Lock, James - Mariah Fisher	7- 1-1832
Lock, Samuel - Delila Edwards	1-14-1819

Lockhart, Eleazer - Susannah Agan	2- 8-1827
Lockhart, Mitchel - Delia Cline	4-13-1834
Logan, David - Fanny Jenkins	4-21-1825
Lomax, Essex - Abigail Davis	8-23-1827
Lomax, Quinten - Nancy Davis	6- 2-1825
Loveless, Zadock - Elizabeth Lasswell	
	10-26-1835
Lowe, Jonathan - Elizabeth Vance	4-24-1823
Luttrell, Willis - Nancy Silvers	8-23-1829
Lynch, Claton - Anna Crim	3- 2-1820
Lynch, George - Jenetta Dickerson	2- 5-1829
Lynch, James - Nancy Noblitt	12-15-1833
Lynch, John - Elizabeth Tate	10-15-1826
Lynch, William D. - Mary Lindley	10- 3-1822
Lynd, Samuel of Washington Co. -	
Uphamie White	3- 6-1832
Lynd, Samuel - Jane Doak	12-19-1833
McBride, Francis - Ruth McGee	12-11-1828
McBroom, Jesse - Susannah Sowers	12-28-1824
McCabe, Absalom - Anna Cook lic.	9-15-1830
McCart, John - Lucretia Shearon	3- 8-1832
McCart, Pleasant - Lucy Lee	7-21-1833
McCarty, John L. - Margaret Gammons	
lic.	1-18-1834
McChoe(?), John - Ann Green lic.	2-28-1827
McClain, Cornelius - Rachel Vails	12- 3-1829
McClain, William - _____Fisk(?)	
lic.	4- 5-1816
McClintock, Robert - Lorain Ribble	9- 1-1832
McClintock, William A. - Barbara Ribble	
	3- 9-1833
McCoy, George - Polly McKinney	11-21-1822
McCracken, James - Betsey Pinnick	1- 8-1829
McCracken, William - Mary Abel	10-10-1835
McCune, James - Nancy Nichols lic.	11-17-1830
McCune, William - Sarah Walker	6-16-1831
McDaniel, Alexander - Priscilla Smith	
	11-28-1821
McDonald, Abner - Betsy Newkirk	3-15-1825
McDonald, Daniel - Catharine A. Haller	
	3-13-1828
McDonald, David - Susannah Williams	10-21-1832
McDonald, Eli - Harriet Lane	2- 8-1827
McDonald, Elihu - Mary Veach	7-21-1831
McDonald, Isaac - Eliza Edwards	
lic.	11- 3-1828
McDonald, James - Margaret Newkirk	7-13-1822
McDonald, James - Elenor Quackenbush	
lic.	3-17-1827
McDonald, James - Rodah Quakenbush	7-28-1829
McDaniel in return	
McDonald, John - Nancy Mode	8- 9-1821
McGahan, Valentine - Cynthia Pipher	
lic.	11-14-1831
McGahan, William - Rachel McCracken	6- 1-1823
McGauhey, John - Nancy Fulton	4-14-1831
McGee, Elijah - Elizabeth Shields	11- 8-1821
McGee, Elisha - Lucy Vandeveer	3-12-1829
McGee, Henry - Elizabeth Walden lic.	
	6- 3-1831
McGee, Jesse - Elizabeth Kellums	8- 5-1827
McGee, Samuel - Elizabeth Bullington	4- 6-1820
McGee, William - Serena Tungate	5- 6-1832
McGill, William - Hannah Boon	12-18-1823
McGrew, Elisha - Sarah King	4-28-1825
McGrew, Felix - Julyan Pound	12-23-1827
McGrew, Fielden - Sarah Glover	10-24-1826

McGrew, Findley - Elizabeth Glover   9-10-1824
McGrew, Jefferson - Delila Dickerson
                                      12- 3-1829
McIntire, David - Barbary Leatherman
                     lic.   1-15-1832
McIntire, William - Emley Jones   4-19-1821
McIntosh, William - Melinda Rigney   10- 4-1832
McKever, Kenneth - Elizabeth Coy   12-12-1832
McKillip, William - Sally Johnson   11-18-1827
McKinney, James Wallace - Jane White
                                      8-27-1833
McKinney, Thomas - Jane McGrew   8- 2-1827
McKinney, William W. - Martha Quinn   4-26-1827
McKnight, Christopher - Rebecca Vontress
                                      3-22-1821
McKnight, James - Martha Webster   12- 4-1828
McKnight, Joseph L. - Elizabeth McCollough
                                      11- 2-1828
McKown, Thomas H. - Casey Davis   2-26-1835
McLane, Cornelius - Polly Ard   9- 3-1835
McNelly, Daniel - Sally Cleveland   10-27-1835
McNary, John - Betsey Griffin   5-26-1820
McPheeters, Alexander R. - Elizabeth
     Hutchison   9- 1-1831
                  _____
McVey, Edward - Catherine Lindly   6-13-1822
McVey, John - Ruth Michum   4- 2-1822
Macumber, Levi - Betsy Gentry   11- 6-1821
Magner, John A. - Sarah Campbell   12- 4-1834
Mahan, John - Clarisa Moore (or Moon?)
                                      6-14-1832
Mann, John - Katsey Halfacre   12-12-1821
Manship, Charles - Polly Foster   6-23-1827
Manship, Charles - Elizabeth Hooten
                                      4- 7-1833
Maris, Aaron - Kesiah Millus   12-13-1826
Marley, Michael - Susannah White   3-19-1830
Marshal, Hiram - Susannah Snider   2-14-1828
Martin, Hiram - Peggy Cloud   8- 2-1818
Martin, Reuben - Jane Beasley   12-31-1818
Martin, Samuel - Mary Hutchison   12- 6-1832
Martin, Samuel A. - Julian Edwards
                     lic.   11- 6-1832
Marts, Chamberlin - Emily Pounds   5-26-1831
Mason, Andrew - _____ Casey lic.
                                      3-12-1816
Mason, John - Caroline Spears   9-17-1833
Massey, John - Kissa Spicly   2-22-1829
Massie, Samuel - Elizabeth Shirrer(?)
                                      2-27-1831
Massy, Charles - Catherine Piles   9-30-1827
Mattox, Nathaniel - Elizabeth Danner
                                      3-13-1834
Maxadant, John - Lourranna Stephens
                                      3-16-1821
Maxadon, Thomas - Nancy Alan   3-11-1819
Maxident, James - Jane Forte   12-30-1820
Maxwell, Nimrod - Jane Riley   8- 7-1828
Maxwell, William - Leodicea Sanders
                                      3-24-1819
May, Andrew - Elizabeth B. Bingamon
                                      12-23-1823
May, George - Polly Wood   10-21-1833
May, Silvester - Lucinda Blackburn
                                      4-14-1831
Mayo, James - Margaret Clarke   2-23-1831
Mecham, Anderson - Lucinda Wasson   11-26-1822

Meece, John - Mary Tipton lic.   3-23-1835
Melton, Edmund - Nancy Kendall   12-30-1832
Melton, John - Polly Gregory   12-30-1832
Merritt, Jeremiah - Catherine Pitts
                                      9- 5-1833
Millis, Enoch - Susannah Moulder   10-31-1822
Miller, Jesse - Sarah Crawford   10-10-1833
Miller, Michael - Patsey Daugherty
                     lic.   9-30-1826
Millis, Nickison - Elenor Maris   11-18-1819
Mills, Samuel - Mary Ann Cox   1-26-1834
Millsap, William - Elizabeth Smith   4-10-1828
Mitchel, James S. - Margaret Carr(?)
                                      6-10-1817
Moad, Henry - Polly Young   2-20-1827
Moad, Samuel - Peggy Breedlove
          Breadwater on return   2-28-1833
Moad, William - Sarah Riley   1-31-1829
Mobly, Edward - Matildy Jones   3- 7-1820
Mock, George - Lucy Pipins   3- 4-1819
Mock, John - Betsy Pippin   lic.   2-17-1829
Moffit, Samuel - Elizabeth Wiseman   3-27-1829
Monarch, George - Sally Bishop   12-24-1816
Mongomery, Robert - Nancy Roberts   7- 5-1825
Montgomery, Joshua R. - Ebeline Shoars
                     lic.   8- 3-1835
Moon, Jahue - Charlotte Walker lic.
                                      12-17-1834
Moon, John - Sarah Pirtle   9-13-1832
Moon, Silas - Mary McClelland   3-20-1821
Moore, Benjamin - Charity Marshall   8- 7-1823
Moore, Charles - Ruth Doan   7-19-1831
Moore, Edward - Susanna Brient(?)   9-24-1823
Moore, Francis - Elizabeth Reed   4-14-1831
Moore (More), George W. - Jane Campbell
                     lic.   10-23-1829
Moore, Henry - Elizabeth Snider   12-31-1833
Moore (More), James - Peggy Cummins   6-15-1826
Moore, Jefferson - Mary Dixon   2-23-1832
Moore, John - Rebecah Aulspaw lic.   2-10-1817
Moore, John - Pheby Boner   3-15-1828
Moore, John Delila Dark   3-24-1831
Moore, John - Polly Breedon   4-29-1832
Moore, Reuben - Jane Cattin   4-12-1829
Moore, Robert - Sarah Cameron   3-25-1825
Moore, William - Hester Gifford   8-27-1824
Moore, William - Jane Throop   7- 2-1828
Moorman, Zachariah - Hannah Osburn   10-22-1835
Morgan, Samuel - Polly Taylor   3-25-1830
Morris, Alexander - Mary M. Davis   12-18-1828
Morris, Eli - Sarah Thomas   3- 6-1822
Morris, James - Ruth Bundy   11-21-1822
Morris, Thomas - Jemimah Bobbitt   12-22-1831
Morris, Washington - Sally Thomas   3- 5-1818
Morris, William - Mary Jones   2-19-1822
Morris, William - Catharine Davis   5-11-1825
Morris, William - Nancy Lane   1-23-1834
Morrison, Zachariah - Marian Skaggs
                                      11-22-1835
Moser, John - Charity Walker   4- 3-1823
Moser, Robert W. - Elizabeth Brown   1- 8-1829
Moulder, John - Elender Maris   2- 1-1827
Moyer, Daniel - Polly Keisey   2-12-1834
Moyer, David - Sussanah Pinkley
                     lic.   11- 4-1830
Moyer, George A. - Nancy Malloney   2-16-1830
Moyer, Paul N. - Sarah Pippin lic. 9- 8-1830

Moyers, Joseph - Ellenor Thomas   1- 4-1827
Moyres, Moses - Patsey Brothers   1- 6-1820
Mudal(?), John - Mathlin Redick
        (or Redish?)   7- 5-1821
Mullins, Isaac - Eliza Hollis lic. 1-22-1831
Murphy, John - Christenah Vantrese   7-17-1828
Murray, John - Elizabeth Trueblood   4- 8-1824
Nale, George - Priscilla F. McElyea   3- 4-1831
Neidever, Jacob - Polly Willoughby
        lic.   5-16-1832
Newkirk, John - Nancy Snowden   3-15-1825
Newkirk, Thomas - Rachel Snowden   4-12-1835
Newton, Bing - Permelia Chittenden(?)
        11-28-1830
Nichols, Martin - Rachel Fields(?) 1-27-1825
Nichols, Nathan - Sarah G. Kerby   10-23-1828
Nichols, Thomas - Matilda Wasson   7-31-1823
Nicholson, Harvey - Maria Connell   6-26-1834
Nicholson, Samuel - Peggy Ann Collins
        5- 8-1834
Night, Absolem - Polly Patten   3-20-1828
Noblett, Joseph - Elizabeth Reynolds
        10- 6-1831
Noblett, Ransom - Malvena Elrod   9- 4-1831
Norman, William - Nancy Blair   1- 8-1824
Nunnally, Nelson W. - Letty S. Hicklin
        4-14-1825
Oaks, John - Mary Shaver(?)   2-26-1818
Orton, Joshua - Susannah Farris   2- 7-1830
Osborn, David - Mary Miller   12-10-1829
Osborn, William - Elender Smith   9- 3-1817
Overby, William - Milly Boswell
        lic.   8-10-1830
Palmer, Jonathan - Elizabeth Hunt 1-10-1830
Parker, James - Jane Butler   10-10-1824
Parks, Andrew F. - Eliza Overling 9-19-1824
Parks, Samuel - Polly Overton   1-23-1823
Parks (or Sparks?), Thomas - Eveline
   Bledsoe   9-29-1831
Parks, William - Polly Freeman   6-18-1829
Pascal, Robert - Mary Robbins   [11]-2-1826
Paskil, John - Patsey M. White   11-17-1825
Patten, James - Polly Summers   8- 3-1824
Patton, James - Ceola Cooper lic.
        11-25-1834
Patton, William - Lueasy Laswell   2- 1-1835
Payne, Barzilla - Sarah Johnson   4- 4-1834
Payne, William - Sarah Wells   6- 9-1834
Payton, James - Kisiah Cooper   7-26-1829
Payton, Luis W. - Elizabeth Baker 1- 3-1822
Payton, Nathan - Rebeckah Danner
        lic.   7-29-1829
Payton, William - Rahab Marshall
        lic.   3- 2-1831
Pearce, George R. - Mahala M. Shively
        11-22-1829
Pearson, Benjamin - Peggy Lakey   7- 3-1824
Pearson, Elias - Priscilla Hazlewood
        4-17-1833
Pearson, Elihu - Mary Ann Cloud   8-15-1822
Pearson, Elijah - Elizabeth Kindle
        6-26-1823
Pearson, Isaac - Keziah Livingston
        11-26-1835
Pearson, Jacob - Terena Vandeveer 4- 2-1833
Pearson, James - Mary Jane Agin 12-10-1835
Pearson, Peter - Jane Prewit   1-30-1824
Peck, Joseph H. - Peggy Depew   1-22-1819
Pence, William - Ellis Winter   10-21-1832
Pertell, Bazell - Lydia Moon   3-14-1833
Peters, Abraham - Joanna Burt   4- 5-1827

Peters(?), Abraham - Maryan Bosley
        lic.   1- 6-1830
Peters, Abraham - Elizabeth Bosley
        12- 1-1835
Philips, Leonard - Lucinda Leonard
        8-22-1833
Phillips, George - Jane Hodges
        lic.   10-26-1826
Phillips, John - Sarah Cobb   12-20-1824
Phillips, John - Melissa R. Lewis 6- 5-1834
Phillips, Joshua - Sally Boon   2-11-1831
Phillips, William - Susan Head   1- 3-1822
Phiper, Jacob - Sarah Holms   3-29-1821
Pickens, James - Fanny Cowherd   6-15-1820
Pickens, Lemael - Mahaly Speer   7-29-1830
Pierson, Allen - Sarah Case   1-11-1827
Piggott, Jacob J. - Mahala McCulla
        8- 4-1831
Piles, Peter - Margaret Skaggs   10-15-1826
Pinick, Elijah - Lucinda King   4- 3-1823
Pinkley, George - Ritty Myres   2- 6-1826
Pinnick, Isaac - Polly Charles   9-10-1824
Pinnick, James - Mary Cobb   9- 4-1817
Pinnick, John - Jane Faris   12- 9-1830
Pinnick, William - Susanna Harmon 1- 9-1820
Pitman, George - Fanney Kindell 12- 6-1821
Pitts, Thomas - Abigail Bridwell
        lic.   7-23-1827
Potter, Isaac H. - Mary Jane Smith
        lic.   5-13-1834
Pound, James F. - Eleanor Case   3-21-1833
Pounds, Thomas - Nancy Johnson   2- 8-1821
Powers, Daniel B. - Jane Sutherland
        3-31-1822
Prewett, Andrew - Rebeccah Prewett
        9-10-1829
Prewett, Elijah - Jane Moore   1-18-1829
Prey, Hezekiah - Elizabeth Biggs   2-13-1823
Pruett, William - Nancy Cloud   2-27-1834
Purkins, William - Elizabeth Daugherty
        8-11-1825
Quinette, Charles - Sally Hodges   2-28-1821
Radcliff, William V. - Sinthey Dillard
        1-23-1834
Ragan, Hiram - Polly Pendleton   6-16-1834
Ragle, John - Eliza Webster   6-18-1829
Ragle, Nicholas - Delila Samuels   10-29-1829
Ragle, Peter - Peggy Wadsworth   3-20-1828
Ragle, William - Polly Ann Edgington
        7-15-1830
Rainbolt, John - Freelove Boon   6-28-1827
Ratliff, Richard - Louisa Mills   5- 2-1830
Rawlins, Joseph - Sally McManise   1- 5-1817
Rawlins, see also Rollins
Ray, Daniel - _____ Stephens lic.
        8-20-1829
Ray, Daniel - Camma Eliza Gillian 12-30-1830
Readick, Jonathan - Nancy Allen   2- 7-1822
Reddick, Jonathon - Betsy Seybold 11-11-1826
Redman, Thomas - Belinda Sorrels   7- 5-1827
Reed, Elias - Polly Newgin   12-31-1820
Reed, Jana(?) - Ann Johnston lic. 4-25-1827
Reed, Jesse - Elizabeth Wilson   9-12-1822
Reed, Johnson - Elmira Moyer   4- 1-1831
Reed, Joshua - Susannah Lucus
        (or Lewis)   2-12-1818
Reed, Joshua - Hannah Grayham   4- 6-1826
Reed, William B. - Sophiah Moyer   3- 5-1829
Reynolds, Parker - Mary Lockhart
        lic.   3- 9-1830

Reynolds, William - Polly Huchinson 2- 6-1817
Rhodes, William - Jane Mitchum   5- 9-1820
Richardson, John - Mary Perrigo   8-20-1824
Riddle, Caswell B. - Nancy Spicly   10-13-1829
Rife, William - Fanny Potter   8- 4-1825
Rigney, Isaac - Phebe Cornwall(?)   10- 8-1823
Riley, Charles M. - Emily B. Duncan 3- 5-1833
Riley, Daniel - Elizabeth Duncan   9- 2-1824
Riley, David - Sally Lowe   4- 3-1823
Riley, Ezekiel S. - Peggy Gray   1- 8-1818
Riley, James - Sally Pitman   1- 4-1821
Riley, Thomas - Esther Moad   2-22-1827
Riley, William - Thirsey Brooks   11-30-1823
Ring, James - Lurany Blackwell   1-26-1818
Robbins, David - Arriana Gillum   1-22-1835
Robbins, Ezekiel - Polly Burgess   1-29-1835
Robbins (Robins), George - Martha Giles
                                     11-26-1835
Robbins, Isaac - Nancy Kerby   8-13-1829
Robbins, William - Margaret Marshall
                                      3- 1-1825
Roberts, Cornelius - Polly Martin   12-13-1818
Roberts, Elias - Priscilla Frost   5-13-1824
Roberts, Jacob - Polly Marshall   2-21-1830
  James Roberts in return
Roberts, James - Elizabeth Allagay 4-15-1824
Roberts, James - Emelia(or Emily) Clements
                                      3- 6-1828
Roberts, Jesse - Nancy Brinigar   12-13-1826
Roberts, Lewis - Margaret Marshall 10- -1830
Roberts, Shadrack - Mahala Lee   4- 1-1819
Roberts, Thomas C. - Charlotte Temple
               Brininger   11-11-1830
Roberts, William - Ann Featherkile   3-30-1826
Roberts, William - Lydia Buckner   12-23-1830
Roberts, Wily - Mary Thomas   lic.   8-21-1830
Roden, Allen - Patsy Weathers   8-16-1821
Rollins, Aaron - Franky Rollins   11- 6-1823
Rollins, see also Rawlins
Ruberson, Jonah - Mary Stout   3-14-1833
Russell, William - Judith Weathers   2-24-1822
Sanders, Henry - Sally Laswell   1-29-1829
Sanders, Isaac - Avarillar Boling
                                      6-16-1821
Sanders, John - Sarah Copple   10- 8-1829
Sanders, Samuel - Polly Laswell   4-17-1825
Sanderson, Robert - Priscilla Ann Kirby
                                      1-13-1825
Sands, John - Polly Sands   2-14-1817
Saunders, Aaron - Nancy Hollowell   9-12-1833
Saunders, Miles - Mary Copple   2-24-1831
Saunders, Wright - Polly Fritz   6-27-1816
Savage, Ogleby - Catharine Stroud
                      lic.   10-14-1835
Scarlet, Samuel - Jemima Dunbar   9-30-1824
Scarlett, Samuel - Rachael Atkins 3- 3-1832
Scarlott, William - Delilah McGrew
                      lic.   9- 8-1830
Scott, William - Hannah Henry   8- 8-1816
Scott, William - Nancy Scott   8- 8-1816
Self, George - Barbara Mull   11-21-1832
Self, Philip - Amy Underwood
                      lic.   11-11-1834
Self, Thomas - Delitha Underwood 11- 7-1828
Self, William - Rebecca Sanders   8-21-1829
Self, William A. - Peggy Allen   12-24-1820
Self, William A. - Nancy Davidson
                      lic.   11-25-1834
Sewell, John - Delight Pipher   12- 2-1819
Seybold, Jasper - Nancy Leonard   11- 9-1828

Seybold, John - Jane Leonard   10- 6-1817
Seybold, Joseph - Jane Leonard   8- 7-1828
Scribnor, William A. - Caroline M. Chapman
                                     10-25-1827
Shade, William - Lucy McCracken   8- 7-1834
Shaw, John - Louisa Pearce   11- 2-1819
Shearer, John - Sarah McCart lic. 1-23-1833
Shearer, Lorenzo D. - Polly Hammersly
                                      8- 5-1833
Sheeks, George C. - Artmesha Crawford
                                      6- 8-1833
Shelton, John - Precious Stephen 8-22-1820
Shelton, John A. - Elizabeth Franklin
               lic.   5-16-1832
Shelton, Joseph - Elsie Sutton Philips
               lic.   7- 1-1826
Shepard, Hiram - Susannah Ragle   12-15-1831
Shepherd, James - Polly Sears
               Betsy in return   10- 8-1829
Shepherd, Thomas - Nancy Walls   9- 5-1826
Sheppard, William - Edith Wolf   12-20-1821
Sherwood, Daniel - Delila Copelain
                                     12-16-1819
Shieks, Denton - Emily Right   4-13-1826
Shields, Daniel - Polly Welch   5- 5-1825
Shields, James - Seila Fisher   4-22-1819
Ship, Ambrose - Margaret Baker   6-13-1832
Shively, Philip - Penelope Busick 9-12-1827
Shoafe, Henry - Elizabeth B_____   3-15-1834
Sholts, Jacob - Polly Demos   12- 1-1818
Shroyer, Cyrus - Jane Bingamon(?)
               lic.   5- 3-1834
Shryer, John D. - Sarah McGrew   2-22-1832
Simmons, Benjamin - Frances Shurwood
                                      3-28-1823
Simpson, Arthur J. - Mary Ann Campbell
                                     12-17-1833
Sinex (Knox?), John - Irena Shroyer
                                      4-19-1834
Siske, Willis - Anna Wilson lic. 6-28-1830
Skaggs, Wesley - Hannah Shields   12-11-1817
Smith, James - Elizabeth Allgood
               lic.   6-12-1834
Smith, Jesse - Susannah Williams 1-11-1821
Smith, John Ahart - Sena Miller
               lic.   4-16-1828
Smith, John H. - Malinda Redman   12-23-1831
Smith, John W. - Paloner(?) Hamilton
               lic.   4-17-1833
Smith, William - Jane Fortner   7-12-1821
Smith, William - Maria Hoggatt   11-29-1830
Smithey, Reuben - Hannah Tarr (or Torr?)
                                     10-20-1825
Snipes, John - Nancy Crow   8-22-1816
Snowden, David - Polly Vannest   11-27-1823
Snowden, Joseph - Sarah Overby   5-28-1835
Sorrels, Charles - Jane Patton   11-11-1824
Sorrels, Hiram - Mahaly Redman   2-13-1827
Sorrels, John - Sally Redman   7-19-1827
Sorrels, Joseph - Nancy Redman   2-15-1833
Sorrels, Peter - Sarah Head   8- 5-1830
Sorrels, Richard G. - Mary Head   11-10-1831
Southerlin, Thomas S. - Polly Crawford
                                     10-14-1824
Southern, James - Ann Kirk   7-23-1835
Spaldon, Nelson - Elizabeth Litterel
                                      6-20-1826
Sparlin, Archibald - Lovisa Mullins 4-14-1827
Sparling, Edward - Mary Kretsinger 5-13-1821
Speaks (or Specks), Thomas - Rhody Adams
                                      4- 3-1825

Speaks, Thomas - Sally Haynes   7-20-1834
Spear, Jesse - Jemima Gregory   9-30-1834
Spears, Andrew - Winny Manley(?)   7-27-1826
Spears, Lovell - Eliza Ellen Irvine
                        lic.   12-18-1831
Speer, Ashberry - Margaret Booth   3- 2-1828
Spencer, Joseph - Elizabeth Kenly   12-10-1826
Spooner, Benjamin - Martha Ware   1- 9-1823
Spooner, William W. - Caroline Burts
                                  8-18-1831
Spooner, William W. - Elizabeth Millis
                                  1-24-1822
Spriggs, David - Mary Montgomery   4- 5-1823
Springer, John S. - Susan L. Nichols
                                  2-10-1831
Springer, Nicholas - Elizabeth Nichols
                                 10-30-1820
Spurling, Moses - Levisa Duncan   11-23-1826
Srawyers, Levi - Rebeccah Ann Tate   2-14-1830
Stalcup, John - Jane Stalcup lic.   3-24-1830
Stallcup, Eli - Rhoda Hunt   lic.   12-19-1835
Stallcup, Samuel - Jane Harned   8- 6-1830
Stallians, Stephen - Polly Martin   7-13-1820
Standiford, Vincent - Johannah White
                                 10-26-1826
Starks, Absalom - Sarah Lee lic.   11-24-1831
Starks, Thomas - Nancy Foster   4-18-1824
Starks, William - Kiseah Kindal   3-28-1825
Stephens, Jacob - Eliza Baker   8-21-1821
Stewart, Elijah - Minerva Atkins   2-17-1831
Stoner, Peter - Polly Wells   8- 3-1827
Stotts, Robert C. - Ellender Laughlin
                                 12-30-1816
Stout, David - Moranda Reed   1-18-1828
Stout, Hiram - Nancy Thomas   10-13-1831
Stout, Sylvanus - Rebecca Stanfield
                                  8- 6-1835
Strain, James - Rebecca Dix   8- 2-1825
Strain, Robert - Clarissa Burt   2-10-1825
Strange, Edward - Fanny Wolfe   9- 2-1824
Strange, Joel - Glathey Weathers   2-14-1825
Strange, Joseph - Polly Cornwell   2-20-1828
Strange, William - Sarian Woolf   1-14-1819
Street, James - Elizabeth McCracken
                        lic.   4-16-1834
Stringer, George - Sally Smith   9- 6-1835
Stroud, Abraham - Tessa Seasking(?)   2-10-1825
Stroud, Allen - Arsa Askin   2-10-1825
Stroud, Westley - Nancy Brown   2- 9-1832
Strouse, Jacob - Rachael Noland
                        lic.   5-27-1833
Stutesman, Elaxander - Rebecca Seybold
                                  1-26-1826
Sullivan, Evan - Susan Wininger   4-25-1833
Sullivan, Henry - Polly Ann Rutherford
                                  4-15-1832
Sutherland, Sampson F. - Elizabeth Crawford
                                  3-20-1820
Sutherlin, Irvin - Susannah Keith
                                 11-27-1821
Sutherlin, Owen - America Crawford
                                  8-17-1834
Swayne, Jonathan H. - Elizabeth Bean
                                  8-26-1835
Talbot, Thomas - Margaret Trobridge
                        lic.   6-15-1830
Tate, John D. - Lucinda Sayers   12-10-1829
Taylor, Benjamin - Elizabeth Peare(?)
                                  1-29-1824
Taylor, Eleazer H. - Elizabeth Lingle
                                  1-27-1831

Taylor, Henry - Lydia Elkins   6-23-1828
Taylor, Samuel - Elizabeth Young   7- 3-1823
Taylor, Thomas B. T. - Jane Moore 1- 1-1835
Taylor, Uriah - Rachel Leonard   12- 1-1825
Taylor, William - Delilah Rigny   12-30-1832
Tegarden, Abraham - Elizabeth Lee 3-31-1831
Tegarden, Andrew - Sarah Lee   12-25-1823
Tegarden, Andrew - Mirian(?) Finley
                        lic.   9-13-1832
Tegarden, John - Lucinda Erwin   12-14-1820
Thomas, Mathew - Polly Roberts
                        lic.   12-10-1834
Thomas, Tildon F. - Ruth Lynch   12-16-1829
Thomlinson, James C. - Nancy Doan 1-14-1819
Thompson, James - Sarah Towel   6- 1-1826
Thompson, Michael - Betsy Thely(?)
                                  8-27-1817
Thornton, Thomas V. - Clarinda Coffin
                                  2-19-1835
Throop, John T. - Sarah Johnson   1-14-1835
Tindal, Thomas - Betsy Faris   8-10-1817
Tolbert, Hinson - Polly Alliger
                        lic.   12-28-1831
Toliver, James - Elizabeth Maxwell
                                  6-19-1821
Tomlinson, John - Martha Pearson   4-18-1822
Tomlinson, Moses - Sebia Demoss   1-23-1823
Toton, John - Nancy Smith   lic.   7-14-1826
Towell, Isaac - Elizabeth Cox   9-25-1834
Treadway, Thomas - Louranna Connell
                                  2-16-1832
Truaxe, Zebulon - Margaret Davis 12-24-1822
True, William D. - Sarah Weir   2-26-1835
Trueblood, William - Deborough Chambers
                                  4-28-1825
Trueblood, William - Margaret Morris
                                 11-17-1825
Trusty, Temple - Jemima Walls
                        lic.   3-11-1830
Tucker, John W. - Almira Maxwell 9-26-1833
Tungate, Dennis - Polly Skidmore 7- 3-1831
Tungate, Lewis - Levisa Millis
                        lic.   4-21-1827
Tungate, Robert - Elizabeth Clayton
                        lic.   10-21-1830
Tungatt, William - Colley Beasly 9-26-1822
Turley, Benjamin - Pamelia Right 2-23-1826
Underwood, Alfred - Sara Ann Walker
                                  9-23-1832
Vails, Lewis - Rhody Coggs   3- 8-1835
Vancleave, Aaron - Nancy Galoway 6- 5-1827
Vancleave, David - Jane Vancleave 8-16-1831
Vancleave, James - Mary Lynn
        Martha Lynd on return   3-14-1833
Vancleave, John - Nancy Nicholas 12-15-1831
Vandeveer, Lovil - Mary Handly   10-30-1828
Vandever, Thomas - Hannah Glover 12-13-1818
Vanfranklin, Richard - Elizabeth Nidoffer
                                  9-10-1824
Vantrece, William - Eliza Lindley   2-10-1826
Veatch, James - Patsy Allen   12- 3-1835
Verden, Hugh - Patsy Early(or Easly?)
                                  3-20-1831
Vest, Nathaniel - Livina Duncan   5-25-1818
Vest, Samuel - Sarah Smith   10-18-1827
Vickers, James - Lettitia Pruett   8-21-1831
Vickery, Jesse - Mary Johnson   12-25-1828
Vickery, Nelson - Elizabeth Brooks 3-16-1834
Vontress, William - Elizabeth K. Kinder
                                  3-16-1834
Voris, Abraham - Delilah Pipher   9-21-1820

Voris, Garrett - Fariby Inman   11-10-1831
Voris, Isaac - Sally Warren   11-20-1820
Voris, Jacob - Delilah Ashcraft   11-15-1818
Wade, Jonathan F. - Elsina Vantress 2-20-1825
Wadsworth, Robert - Nancy Riggs
                                lic.   11-20-1832
Walker, Alexander - Elizabeth Standiford
                                        6- 4-1829
Walker, John - Sarah Ann Blackwell 3-18-1824
Wallace, James - Reyna Beman   9- 4-1824
Walling, James - Catharine Ribble 12- 1-1833
Walls, Samuel B. - Eleanor Averil   2- 7-1830
Walls, William - Mahala Gillum   5-13-1832
Ware, James - Polly Busick lic.   2-25-1833
Ware, William - Perlina True   3-20-1835
Wasson, Miles - Cintha Ann Daugherty
                                        2-28-1828
Weathers, Benjamin - Jane Tipton
                                lic.   12-22-1827
Weathers, Daniel - Polly Russell   8- 5-1823
Webb, Benjamin - Mrs. Polly Spencer
                                       11-27-1829
Webb, John - Sally Noblett   7- 8-1828
Webb, Samuel - Merrah Smith lic.   8- 1-1835
Webster, Wilson - Susannah Skaggs   4-12-1828
Wellman, Joseph - Sarah Pittman   5- 2-1833
Wellman, Samuel W., Jr. - Amanda A. Pittman
                                       11- 5-1835
Wells, _____ - Sarah Allen   4-14-1823
Wells, Jesse - Polly Moore   1-29-1818
Wells, Jesse - Martha D. Overlin   9-27-1832
Wells, Jonathan - Eulicia Way   1- 8-1824
Wells, Joseph - Mary Cates   1-21-1827
Wells, Joseph - Sarah Smart   12-19-1835
Wells, Levi - Mary Lambden   9- 6-1821
Wells, Nathan - Sally Overlin   11-15-1832
Wells, William - Mary McCoy   7-27-1829
Welsh, S. B. - Elizabeth Taylor   10-20-1835
White, Drury - Elizabeth Bird   4-14-1833
White, Henry Harrison Green -
       Patience Overbe   8-20-1831
Whitten, John - Polly Beaver   10-16-1834
Wilkey, Horace - Elizabeth Yount
                                lic.   3-19-1831
Wilkey, Joshua - Jane Marshall   6-24-1828
Wilkey, Willis - Mary Lindley   3-16-1834
Wilkins, Benjamin - Louisa McDonald
                                lic.   7- 8-1830
Wilkins, George - Polly Wilkins
                                lic.   7- 8-1830
Wilkins, William - Grace Lindley   1-31-1832
Williams, David - Susannah Hunt   6- 8-1817
Williams, David - Betsey Young   3-15-1825
Williams, Denton - Jane Williams   5- 9-1828
Williams, Dwir(?) - Vina Collins   7-15-1832
Williams, Eli - Sary White   3-22-1817
Williams, Jesse - Celia Overton   1-14-1826
Williams, Joel - Nancy Allen   10-11-1832
Williams, John - Mary Ann Allen   3- 2-1828
Williams, Joseph - Elizabeth Johnston
                                       11-28-1822
Williams, Jonathan W. - Elizabeth Williams
                                        9-22-1832
Williams, Matthias - Elizabeth They(?)
                                       10-12-1818
Williams, Robert - Mary Harned   9- 3-1829
Williams, Thomas - Tabitha Williams
                                        3-13-1831
Williams, Washington - Susannah Berry
                                       12-25-1828
Williams, William - Rachel Berry   4- 1-1830

Williamson, Tucker W. - Caroline Depew
                                        8- 5-1834
Wilson, Alexander - Leurancy Cornwell
                                       12-12-1833
Wilson, David - Elizabeth Cornwell
                                lic.   1-25-1835
Wilson, Edward - Betsy Hall   4-24-1829
Wilson, George - Amereca Black   11- 2-1832
Wilson, James - Mary Edwards lic.
                                        2- 5-1833
Wilson, James, Jr. - Sarah Wilson   8-30-1834
Wilson, Jesper - Mary Underwood   11-10-1825
Wilson, Nathaniel - Jane Kenley   6-11-1835
Wilson, Samuel - Permendia Charles
                                        1-15-1820
Wilson, Samuel - _____ Brooks
                                lic.   6-22-1827
Wininer, John - Sally Rutherford   8-17-1825
Wininger, Jacob - Julian Sullivan   2-11-1830
Witsman, Jacob - Rebecah Williams   7-15-1819
Wolf, Anderson - Polly Ford   3- 8-1829
Wolfington, Amesby - Nancy Lane   6- 3-1824
Wolfington, David - Isabella Trimble
                                        5-20-1824
Wolfington, Eleazor - Margaret Burns
                                        9-20-1829
Wolfington, George - Prudance Taylor
                                        3- 2-1820
Wolfington, James - Nancy Payne   1-20-1831
Wolfington, William - Glase Giles   4-18-1833
Wood, Elijah - Polly Sutherland   4-12-1827
Wood, James C. - Sally Pipher   2-15-1827
Wood(?), John L. - Ann R. Troop
                                lic.   9- 6-1831
Wood, Jonas B. - Polly Inman   1-20-1828
* Wood, Thomas - Sarah Pearson lic.
                                       11-20-1816
Wood, Thomas - Sarah Pearson   3- 8-1817
Woodard, Littleton - Elizabeth Jones
                                        4- 8-1824
Wooton(?), John - Polly Starbuck
                                lic.   10- 8-1830
Wright, Elijah - Lucinda Crawford
                                        8- 5-1823
Wright, Elijah - Minira Grew(?)
                                lic.   7-31-1827
Wright, Elijah - Melinda Tegarden   2-12-1834
Wright, Freman - Mary Sprogles
                                lic.   7-23-1829
Wright, Jonathan - Drusilla Roberts
                                        7-17-1828
Wright, Robert J. - Elizabeth Walker
                                lic.   8-31-1830
Wright, Warden H. - Eliza Ann Glover
                                        9- 3-1835
Wright, William - Nancy Reedy   10-30-1823
Young, Hugh H. - Mahala Wolf   11-26-1835
Young, Mathew - Betsey Moore   3-16-1820
Young, Sampson - Polly Williams   12-15-1819
Zabriskey, Henry - Nancy Nugent   11-20-1822

* Bland, Henry - Keziah Tomlinson 12-23-1819
* Chatham, Reuben - Elizabeth Busick
                                       12-15-1825
* Hubbs, Joshua - Sally Harmon   2-13-1823
* Jenkins, Wesley - Margaret Underwood
                                       12-27-1821
* King, William - Malinda Shields   5-19-1825
* Wood, Lewis B. - Mirah Hall   3-31-1825

253

By an 1805 act of the Indiana territorial legislature, persons owning or purchasing slaves were allowed to hold or bring them into the Indiana Territory and bind them to service. If the slaves were over fifteen years of age, the owner could make a contract for service with them for any term of years. This indenture was to be recorded with the clerk of the county in which they resided within thirty days after the arrival of the slave into the territory, and if the slave refused the terms offered him, the master could have him taken out of the territory within sixty days without losing his title. Slaves under the age of fifteen were to be registered and required to serve until the age of thirty-five if they were males, thirty-two if females. Children born to the slaves after they were brought into the territory were to serve the master of the parent until they reached the age of thirty for males, or twenty-eight for females.

The act was amended in 1806 to permit the time of service of anyone bound under the 1805 act to be sold as part of a personal estate. An unsuccessful attempt was made in 1808 to repeal the 1805 act, but a second attempt in 1810 was successful thus prohibiting any future contracts with slaves; nothing was said about pre-existing contracts.

During the period in which the law was in effect, there were four counties in Indiana Territory: Clark, Dearborn, Harrison, and Knox. Registers have been found for Clark and Knox Counties; Dearborn County did not have any slaves in 1810; the formation of Harrison County was not effective until 1809 and some of the slaves registered in Clark County were living in that portion of Clark that became Harrison County. The 1810 census showed 81 slaves in Clark County, 21 in Harrison, and 135 in Knox. The number registered between 1805 and 1810 (33 in Clark and 44 in Knox) apparently was only a fraction of those held. However, the Knox County register only covers the period 1805-1807; if there was a later record it has not been found.

When Indiana became a state in 1816, Art. XI, Sec. 7 of its constitution reaffirmed the action of the 1810 territorial legislature by decreeing that "there shall be neither slavery nor involuntary servitude in this state, otherwise than for the punishment of crimes, whereof the party shall have been duly convicted. Nor shall any indenture of any Negro or mulatto hereafter made, and executed out of the bounds of this state be of any validity within the state." Though definitely settling the question of future importations, the effect of this provision on pre-existent slavery and servitude was left open to various interpretations. In the eastern counties it was generally considered that slaves and servants were emancipated and their masters acted on that theory. In the western counties a few masters removed their slaves from the state, and some of these were afterwards released by the courts of southern states. The great majority, however, simply continued to hold their slaves, believing that property in slaves was a vested right secured by the Ordinance of 1787 and could not be impaired.

The census of 1820 still showed 190 slaves in the state, only 47 less than in 1810. Desiring to make a test case of the provision in the constitution, a group of attorneys in 1820 arranged for Polly, a slave of Hyacinth Lasselle of Vincennes, to sue her master for her freedom. The case was decided in favor of Lasselle in the Knox County Circuit Court, but when an appeal was taken to the Indiana Supreme Court, the decision was reversed and Polly was set free. This decision brought to an end the slavery question in Indiana so far as any legal right was concerned; however, Negroes continued to be held as slaves for many years. A local census of Vincennes in 1830 showed 32 slaves, but the federal census of the same year made no mention of these. By 1840 the federal census listed only two slaves in the state (Barnhart and Riker, *Indiana to 1816*, pp. 347-48, 350, 354, 360, 457-59).

CLARK COUNTY REGISTER, 1805-1810

Compiled from the original manuscript in the Archives Division, Indiana State Library. The first contract in the Register has been copied verbatim; contents of the other contracts are summarized.

> This day Evan Shelby, and York, a Negro Boy, the property of said Shelby, of about seventeen years old, came before me Samuel Gwathmey Prothonotary of the Court of Common Pleas of Clark County, and it is agreed between the said Shelby and the said Negro York that the said York will serve the said Shelby His Heirs &c from this time until the 21st day of October in the year one thousand Eight hundred and thirty five, as pointed out in a Law of this Territory entitled 'an act concerning the introduction of Negroes and Mullattoes into the Territory.'

Name of Master	Name of slave	Age of slave	State from which brought	Years of service	Date registered
Evan Shelby	York	17	[not given]	30	10-21-1805
James Arbuckle	Isaac	16		44	5-6-1806
William Bullitt	Jemime	36		20	7-24-1806
Mary Provine	Aaron	6		—	10-6-1806
" "	Sam	5		—	10-6-1806
William Berry	Sarah	13		—	11-13-1806
John Evans	Willis	14	N. Carolina	—	11-16-1807
John Jackson	Betty	55	Kentucky	10	3-16-1808
Aaron Willcoxen	Judy	29	"	30	3-16-1808
Waller Taylor	Gabriel	19	Virginia	42	6-15-1808
James Bruce	Moses	15		40	10-29-1808
Frederick Fisher	David	17	Kentucky	23	5-8-1809
(late of Nelson Co., Ky. David a mulatto)					
John Harrison	James	23	"	32	5-25-1809
Willis W. Goodwin	Anthony	45	"	16	5-30-1809
(Purchased from Baley Marshall of Shelby Co., Ky.)					
Joseph Oatman	Sam (mulatto)	23	Kentucky	26	6-7-1809
James Clark	Sam	9	"	—	7-3-1809
Samuel Ledgerwood	Adam	42	Knox Co., Ind.	—	7-20-1809
" "	Poll[y]	27	" " "	—	7-20-1809
John Harrison	Dick	55	Kentucky	10	7-31-1809
Edmund H. Taylor	Anne	48		21	10-18-1809
John Chunn	John	7		—	12-27-1809
John Maxwell	Rachel	10		—	1-1-1810
Daniel Speer	James	20		60	5-14-1810
(Purchased from Reuben Samuel)					
Samuel Gwathmey	Fanny	17	Kentucky	33	7-5-1810
(Purchased from William A. Booth of Jefferson Co., Ky.)					
Joseph A. Lingan	Ama	31		30	9-5-1810
" "	Fanny	7		—	9-5-1810
Williamson Dunn	Isaac	8		—	9-17-1810
Bezaleel Maxwell	Dick	14		—	9-28-1810
" "	girl	13		—	9-28-1810
David H. Maxwell	Maria	10		—	9-28-1810
" "	Sarah	19		12	9-28-1810
Isaac Shelby	Harry	16		21	10-30-1810
" "	Alley(f)	17		25	10-30-1810
Fvan Shelby	Julia	15		40	11-12-1810
Edmund H. Taylor	Ben	15		40	11-13-1810

KNOX COUNTY REGISTER, 1805-1807

Compiled from microfilm of the Register in Archives Division, Indiana State Library. The first contract in the Register has been copied verbatim; contents of the other contracts are summarized.

Be it remembered that on the twenty-eighth day of November, one thousand eight hundred and five, before me Robert Buntin clerk of the Court of Common Pleas of the County of Knox in the Indiana Territory personally came Elli Hawkins of the said county and a Negro lad of the age of sixteen years being a slave named Jacob belonging to the said Elli Hawkins and by him brought into this Territory from the State of South Carolina, which said Hawkins and the said Jacob in pursuance of a law of the Territory in that case made and provided determined and agreed among themselves in my presence in manner following, that is to say, that the said Jacob shall and will serve the said Elli Hawkins and his assigns for the term of ninety years from the day of the date hereof, he the said Elli Hawkins and his assigns providing the said Jacob with necessary and sufficient provisions and clothing washing and lodging, according to his degree and station, & from and after the expiration of which said term the said Jacob shall be free to all intents and purposes —and the said Elli Hawkins enters into a Bond with sufficient surety conditional that the said Jacob shall not after the expiration of his time of service become a county charge.

Name of Master	Name of slave	Age of slave	State from which brought	Years of service	Date registered
Elli Hawkins	Ann	17	S. C.	90	11-28-1805
Mathias Rose	Milly	15	Ky.	70	11-28-1805
Thomas Jones, Sr.	Salia	18	Md.	10	12-6-1805
Salia brought to Indiana Territory by William McCandless & sold to Jones					
Elihu Stout	Pheby	16	Ky.	60	12-11-1805
Joseph Hollingsworth	Jeffrey	30	S. C.	20	2-1-1806
Joseph Hollingsworth	Sena	30	S. C.	20	2-21-1806
William Hawkins	Marget	28	S. C.	20	2-21-1806
Hawkins also registered Marget's children, Jane, a mulatto, b. S. C. 1800, Judy, Negro, b. 1802, & David, Negro, b. 1804					
Daniel Smith	Annes (f)	16	Ky.	99	5-2-1806
John Hadden	Franky (f)	30	Va.	30	5-2-1806
John Hadden	Isaac	15	Ky.	40	5-2-1806
John Hadden	James	16	Ky.	36	5-2-1806
Samuel Ledgerwood	Adam	40	Ky.	12	7-26-1806
John Murphy	Watt	38	Ky.	18	9-10-1806
James Ford	Dinah	17	Ky.	30	9-23-1806
James Ford	Fanny	20	Ky.	30	9-23-1806
Brought to Indiana Territory by George Vann & sold to Ford					
Francis Jordan	Ned	16	—	30	9-23-1806
James Ford	Bob	22	Ky.	30	9-23-1806
Brought to Indiana Territory by Hugh White & sold to Ford					
Thompson Harris	Nan	25	Tenn.	38	10-6-1806
Thomas Montgomery	Eve	30	Ky.	99	10-17-1806
James Johnston	Judy	30	Ky.	18	10-23-1806
Her four-year-old son Nero also registered					
John Johnston	Fame	33	Ky.	21	11-8-1806
John Grant	Will	36	Ky.	20	11-18-1806
John Grant	Vine	32	Ky.	20	11-18-1806
Richard Boyd of Davison Co. Tenn.	Henson	22	Tenn.	—	12-26-1806
Philip Trowell (?)	Janie	17	Tenn.	40	12-28-1806
Brought to Indiana Territory by Lazarus Powel & sold to Trowell					
Philip Trowell	Adam	29	S. C.	35	12-28-1806
Brought to Indiana Territory by [Champ?] Langford & sold to Trowell					
Philip Trowell	Patience	16	Tenn.	40	12-28-1806
Philip Trowell	Cloe	17	Tenn.	40	2-5-1807
Joshua Sexton	Mournen	48	Ga.	14	1-24-1807
Brought to Indiana Territory by John Depriest & sold to Sexton					
Benjamin D. Price	Milly Gorden	60	Ky.	20	2-10-1807
Benjamin D. Price	Milly	20	Ky.	40	2-10-1807
Milly's son, a mulatto age 8, also registered					
Robert Elliott	Jack	25	S. C.	20	2-14-1807
Robert Elliott	Betty	20	S. C.	20	2-14-1807
Samuel Ledgerwood	Polly	24	Ky.	11	2-26-1807
James Robb	Ally	24	Ky.	40	3-5-1807
Martin Rose	Pomp	21	Ky.	40	3-6-1807
Martin Rose	Ned	27	Ky.	40	3-6-1807
Martin Rose	Bob	20	Ky.	40	3-6-1807
James Scott	Ruben	16	Ky.	50	3-23-1807
Joel Collins	Patrick Smith, mulatto	—	—	20	3-28-1807
Walter Montgomery	Mime	17	Ky.	40	4-7-1807
John Warrick	Flora, mulatto	30	Ky.	20	4-7-1807
John Warrick	Lemon	32	Ky.	20	4-7-1807
Adam Goodlet	Dick	18	Ky.	14	4-10-1807

ST. JOSEPH COUNTY MARRIAGES, 1830-1838

The original Marriage Book I covering the years 1832 through 1838 was lost sometime before the WPA inventory of St. Joseph County records was published in 1939 and the individual marriage licenses disappeared many years earlier. The present volume labeled Book I has been made up from the general index of marriages, from newspaper notices, wills, deeds, cemetery records, the 1850 census, county histories, etc. The local chapter of the D.A.R. helped in the work, which required twelve years; additional information obtained about the parties was included in the new volume. The record printed below was compiled from a microfilm of the new Book I in the Genealogy Division, Indiana State Library. Most of the additional information about the parties has been included.

Adkins (or Adkinson, Nathaniel - Amanda Evarts
           2-20-1834
Akins, Robert - Sarah Ann Hardin 1-25-1838
Andre, Joseph - Mary Ann Wallace 1-17-1836
 Joseph b. 1806; d. 1-1-1866; bur. City
 Cemetery, S.B.; Mary b. 1820 Pa.; d. before
 1850
Antrim, William - Sarah Whorton 2-18-1835
 William b. 1804 Ohio; Sarah b. 1814 Ohio
Arnold, Levi F. - Mariah Skinner 8- 6-1833
Austin, James - Lucy Lord   9- 5-1836
 James b. 1803 Md., lived Penn Twp.; Lucy
 b. 1813 N.Y.
Backus, Abijah - Melinda Norris 11-15-1838
Backus, Joseph - Araminta McCombs 10-19-1837
Bainter, Frederick - Delilah Roof 6- 5-1837
 Frederick (1786-1838) bur. City Cemetery,
 S. B.
Baker, Joshua - Rebecca Sumption 8-30-1835
 Joshua b. 1812 Va., lived Green Twp.;
 Rebecca b. 1816 Ohio
Ball, Harmon - Rachel Hatfield 12-25-1834
Baltimore, James - Rachel Jones 9- 8-1833
Baltimore, Philip - Polly Hardman 1-20-1833
 Philip b. 1806 Ohio; Polly b. 1816 Ohio
Baugher, David - Mary Mote   12-30-1834
Beck, James - Sarah West   9- 7-1834
Becraft, John - Elizabeth Roof   1-21-1833
 John b. 1804 Ky., d. 12-21-1871;
 Elizabeth b. 1814 Ohio
Belding, Zenas - Hannah J. West 9-25-1838
Bell, John - Nancy Ring   4- 6-1837
Bell, Samuel - Sally Harris   12-9-1830
 Samuel b. 1807 Va., d. 1-30-1851, bur.
 Salem Cem.; Sally b. 1810 dt of Jacob Harris
Black, John, Jr. - Araminta Hague 9-19-1833
Blades, David - Sarah Ward   12- 8-1835
Bloomer, Daniel I. - Betsy Ferris 3- 5-1838
 Daniel b. 1817 N.Y.; d. 5-13-1882; bur. City
 Cem., Mishawaka; Betsy b. 1820 Ind.
Bourrisau, Lazarus - Mary Ann Haremson
 Lived Olive Twp.   6-29-1836
Bowen, Thomas (1814-1876) - Mytilene Rambo
 (1818-1868)   8-11-1836
 Both bur. Sumption Cem., Green Twp.
Bowers, Isaac - Elizabeth Edwards 8-21-1838
Brayton, Stephen, of La Porte Co. - Catherine
 Coleman   11-27-1831
Brown, Asa - Lucy Baker   2-14-1838
Brown, Henry (1812-1884) - Elizabeth Ritter
 (1816-1877)   5-15-1834
Bulla, Thomas P. (1814-1886) - Hannah Draper
 dt of Gideon, b. N.Y. 1810; d. 12-18-1891
           1-15-1835
Burden, William - Catherine Salladay
 William b. 1815 N.J., lived Olive
 Twp., Catherine b. 1818 Ohio 11-18-1837
Burroughs, George H. of Zanesville, Ohio -
 Rebecca J. Bell   12-28-1837

Campbell, Peter - Elizabeth Winn 1-24-1836
Carrick, Elijah - Nancy Ireland 7-24-1834
 Elijah b. 1810 Ohio, lived Penn Twp.;
 Nancy b. 1816 Ohio
Cartwright, William - Sally Swift 8- 5-1837
Castle, Lisander - Amanda Harvey 9- 2-1837
 Living Elkhart Co. 1838
Chandler, Uriah - Mary Hughs 5- 5-1836
 Uriah b. 1814 Ohio, lived Penn Twp.; Mary
 b. 1817 N.Y.
Chapin, Horatio - Martha E. Story 12- -1835
 Horatio b. 1803 Mass., d. 1871, bur. City Cem.,
 S.B.; Martha sister of Wilber Story, founder of
 Detroit *Free Press*, b. 1809; d. 2-15-1846
Chord, Jonathan - Mary Ann Cox 8-20-1837
 Jonathan b. 1812, d. 9-17-1837; Mary b. 1820
Christman, David - Elizabeth Smith 3-26-1837
Cissne, Robert G. - Anna Miller 11- 6-1836
 Robert son of John & Jane (Glass) Cissne of
 Hudson Lake
Clark, James - Emmeline Millis 12-10-1837
 Both of Mishawaka
Cleavland, B.J. - Rebecca Frazier 1- 9-1837
Cobb, Dudley - Elizabeth Martin 8-31-1837
 Dudley d. before 1850; Elizabeth b. 1811 Pa.
Cope, Daniel T. - Julia Ann Cottrell 9-11-1836
Cosgrove, William - Lydia Ann Carter 5-31-1838
Coveny, Joseph - Mary Louisa Roe 10-29-1837
Cramer, Thomas C. - Matilda Cottrell 11-26-1836
Cratee, Madore (1802-1894) - Elizabeth Reynolds
 He bur. City Cem., S.B.
Cripe, Jacob - Polly Rench   10-15-1835
Crocket, Shellin - Louisa Ireland 5-25-1836
 Shellin b. 1812 Ky., d. 1893; bur. City Cem.,
 S.B.; Louisa d. 1848 Penn Twp.
Crow, Isaac - Nancy Grant   6-30-1836
 Isaac b. 1810 Ohio; Nancy b. 1811 Ohio
Crum, William - Anna Radabaugh 6- 3-1838
 William b. 1809 Ohio, lived Warren Twp.;
 Ann b. 1812 Ohio
Curry, James (1814-1897) - Elizabeth Nickerson
 (1818-1885)   4-19-38
 Both bur. New Carlisle
Custer, John R. - Catherine Grossnickle 1- 1-1837
Day, Abram - Betsy Runion   6-28-1837
 Abram b. 1814 Ohio; Betsy b. 1817 Ohio
Dayton, Hiram - Lucinda Alwood 4-11-1837
Dean, Thomas - Julia A. Lincoln 4-3-1834
Dinely, Abraham - Malvina Snell 4-26-1838
 Abraham b. 1819 Ohio; Malvina b. 1821 Ohio
Donney, Richard - Mary Puterbaugh 3- 4-1835
Dorsey, John - Mary Reese   12-31-1836
Dukes, John - Nancy McCoy   11-22-1836
Dunham, John - Eliza Cobbler 11- 2-1838

Eaton, Samuel - Jane Russell 12-24-1835
 Lived Lake Co.
Eberly, Godfrey - Mary Sayers 12-31-1837
 Godfrey b. 1809 Canada; Mary b. 1809 Va.

Edson, Henry - Delitha Powell   lic.12-5-1835
Edwards, Daniel W. - Susan Sherer   9-25-1837
Egbert, Elisha - Eliza McCartney   11-16-1831
    Elisha b. 3-25-1806 N.J., d. Nov. 1870; Eliza b.
    1814, d. 1846
Edgington, Daniel - Delilah Johnson   4- -1834
Elder, John - Emily A. Sweet   4- 2-1838
    John b. 11-11-1808 Scotland, d. 10-7-1896;
    Emily b. 3-20-1816 Conn., d. 12-20-1894;
    both bur. City Cem., S.B.
Englewright, Jacob - Anna Weaver   5-17-1836
    Jacob d. 11-11-1846 Berrien Co., Mich.
Englewright, *see also* Inglewright
Falta, Peter - Rachel Mote   5-30-1834
    Lived Elkhart Co.
Farnum, Matthias - Dimee Finch   10-25-1837
Finch, Walter, of Penn Twp. - Marvilla Adkins
                         4-20-1834
Finley, Andrew - Mary Harris   7-11-1837
Fisk, Daniel - Lucinda Plats   1- 7-1838
Fox, Jonas - Nancy Mitchell   12-22-1836
Fullerton, Daniel A. - Zilpha M. Stillson   4-18-1832
Furguson, George - Sarah Wittfong   4-18-1837
Garroute, James S. - Charlotte Richards   1-11-1832
Garwood, Joshua (1810-1854) - Mary Peacock
    He bur. Sumption Prairie   lic. 5-7-1835
Gaugh (or Goff), David - Malinda Hatfield 2-20-1834
Gephart, William - Margaret Wilson   11-12-1837
Gillrich, John, of Marshall Co. - Mary Case 3- 1-1835
Good, James - Catherine Miller   2-12-1835
    James b. 5-11-1802 Va., d. 4-11-1867;
    Catherine b. 9-8-1815 Ohio, d. 3-24-1879;
    both bur. Mt. Pleasant Cem.
Gordon, John - Barsheba Roe   3-1-1835
Green, Ezekiel - Sarah Garwood   7-9-1835
    Ezekiel b. 1810 Del., d. 6-21-1891, bur. City
    Cem., S.B.; Sarah b. 1812 Ohio, d. 1854
Guinn, Peter - Jane Brown   5-29-1834
Hagle, George B. - Lucinda Griswold   lic. 8-15-1835
Hague, William - Sarah Miller   4- 1-1832
    William b. 1813 Ohio; Sarah b. 7-26-1807
    Ohio, d. 8-10-1872, bur. Mt. Pleasant Cem.
Hall, Charles - Sarah Ann Chandler   8-16-1838
Hardman, Philip (1810-1852) - Sarah Witter
    He bur. Mt. Pleasant Cem.   11-23-1834
Harris, John - Lovina Miller   1- 4-1831
Harris, Jonathan - Sible Hamilton   5-16-1835
    Lived Marshall Co.
Harris, Thomas - Janie Finley   10-13-1836
Harvey, Andrew (1814-1839) - Martha Stull
    He bur. Sumption Prairie   12- 7-1837
    Martha m. (2) David Ruple   12-3-1840
Hathaway, Isaac of Berrien Co., Mich. - Catherine
    Huff   12-11-1832
Haynes, Samuel - Rebecca Woolman   1-23-1836
Helmick, Nathan - Susannah Ross   9-20-1835
Henderson, John - Olive Smith   5-2-1837
    Olive dt of George Smith
Henrick, John A. - Julia Comparet   12-2-1833
    John b. 8-10-1811 Pendleton Co., Ky.
High, James - Betsy H. Jenkins   1-1-1838
Hildreth, Levi - Mary Replogle   4-20-1837
Holler, Christian (1794-1867) - Elizabeth
    McMullen (1813-1852)   4- 1-1838
Hollingshead, George (1812-1857) - Martha Rays-
    den (1814-1898)   1-21-1836
    Both bur. Eustler Cem.
Hopkins, Jacob - Serena Scott   3-19-1835

Hopkins, John W. (1788-1892) - Mary Solladay
                         11-10-1836
Howe, Lumin - Anna C. Goodrich   2- 9-1836
Huntsinger, John - Kiziah Pettis   6-23-1836
    John b. 1814 Ohio; Kiziah b. 1818 Ohio
Huntsinger, Levi - Rachel Ireland   8- 2-1835
Huntsman, Howell - Barbara Rupel   10- 6-1833
    Howell b. 1801 N.J.; Barbara b. 1807 Pa.
Huston, James (1812-1891) - Margaret McMullen
    (1816-1890)   8- 3-1834
    Both bur. Dunkard Cem., German Twp.
Huston, John (1814-1896) - Rhoda Johnson
    (1818-1865)   12-26-1835
    Both bur. Dunkard Cem., German Twp.
Hutchens, James - Mary Drapier   5-15-1838
Inglewright, Andrew, of Buchanan, Mich. - Betsy
    Weaver   4-17-1833
Inglewright, *see also* Englewright.
Inman, Aaron of Elkhart Co. - Lorahana Mote
                         6-27-1833
Ireland, Lewis - Rebecca Pettit   12-31-1837
Ireland, William (1807-1851) - Polly Ireland
                         7-23-1833
Irvine, Hood H. - Wliza Ann Terrill   8-25-1838
Jay, Anderson-Margaret Gilliam   8-25-1838
Johnson, James - Esther Pemberton   5- 7-1835
Keefer, Peter - Susanna Mufflin   2-24-1835
Keith, Adam - Hannah Harris   11-18-1830
    Keith b. 11-15-1795 Huntington Co., Pa.,
    d. 1883 Nebraska; Hannah, dt of Richard of
    La Porte Co., from Union Co., d. Kansas before
    1904
Kern, Abram - Martha Lucas   2-13-1838
    Abram b. 1810 N.Y.; Martha b. 1821 Pa.
Kilgore, John (1806-1848) - Rosanna Vinnedge
    (1816-1879)   8-20-1835
    Rosanna m. (2) John Plake; both bur. Polk Twp.,
    Marshall Co.
Lamb, Emsley H. - Lydia Davis   1-20-1836
    Emsley b. 1818 Ind.; Lydia b. 1818 Ky.
Lamb, Josiah G. - Maryanna Van Winkle   8-17-1837
    Josiah b. 1817 Ind.; Maryanna b. 1820 Ind.
Layton, George F. - Mrs. Laura M. Stewart 1- 3-1838
Leach, Joshua - Matilda Smith   6-18-1837
Lesh, Isaac N. - Mahala Hanes   6-26-1836
Lewis, Enoch - Laura L. Magness   6- 5-1837
Liggett, Eli - Nancy Tong   4-27-1837
    Eli b. 10-8-1815 Warren Co., Ohio; d.
    11-24-1903, bur. Riverview Cem., S.B.
Lobdell, Daniel - Lucy True   9-19-1838
    Both b. N.Y.
Lottrara, George - Lois Benton   4- 3-1834
Luther, Edmund (1812-1892) - Elizabeth Trowbridge
                         2-23-1837
    Edmund bur. Hamilton Cem., Olive Twp.;
    Elizabeth b. 1820 Pa.
Lykins, Joseph, of La Porte Co. - Margaret Nixon
                      6- 5-1831
McCartney, William - Nancy Egbert   3- 8-1833
McConnell, Richard - Elizabeth Cripe   9- 9-1834
    Richard b. 1811 Ohio; lived Elkhart Co.
McCoy, Russell - Fanny Kingery   1- 7-1836
McCracken, Charles - Julia Adkins   6-28-1835
McIntire, Joseph - Fatima C. Stover   2-28-1837
McLaughlin, Robert - Lucinda Shaw   7- 1-1835
    Robert b. 1796 Vt.; Lucinda b. 1819
    Ohio

McMichael, John - Mary Level　　　　8-23-1838
　　John b. 1813 Pa., d. 1905;; Mary b. 1820 Ky.,
　　d. 1868; both bur. Harris Prairie Cem.
McMullen, Samuel (1808-1848) - Caty Holler
　　　　　　　　　　　　　　　　　　12-15-1833
　　Samuel bur. Dunkard Cem., German Twp.
McMullen, William - Elizabeth Ritter (1816-1849)
　　Wm. b. 1812 Va.　　　　　　　　8-21-1836
　　She bur. Mt. Pleasant Cem.
Main, John - Sally Ann Halstead　　　5-13-1838
　　John b. 1816 Ohio; Sally d. before 1850
Mannering, John - Julia Ann Garwood　9- 4-1834
Mason, Simeon - Joanna Carlton　　　2-15-1837
Massey, James W. (1816-1892) - Elizabeth
　　Smith (1812-1897)　　　　　　　8- 5-1835
　　Both bur. New Carlisle
Massey, William C. - Elizabeth Hamilton (1821-
　　1885)　　　　　　　　　　　　　11-26-1837
Merenis, Harvey - Mariah Hardy　　　12- 2-1836
　　Mariah dt of Jonathan Hardy
Metzger, Ferdinand - Barbara Zehuby　2-19-1835
Metzger, Joseph E. - Eliza Harris　　　3-17-1836
　　Joseph b. 1815 Germany; Eliza b. 1818 Ohio
Michael, Andrew - Biddy Curtis　　　11-25-1836
Michael, Lee - Eliza McDonald　　　　9-15-1836
　　Lee b. 1811 N.Y.; Elizabeth b. 1822 Nova
　　Scotia
Middleton, William - Rebecca Gillam　1-17-1833
Miller, Aaron - Elizabeth Smith　　　11-28-1833
　　Aaron b. 1811 Ohio, d. 1890, bur. Mt. Pleasant
　　Cem.; Elizabeth b. 1814 Ohio, lived German
　　Twp.
Miller, Benjamin - Margaret Wagoner　1 -1-1832
Miller, Charles W. - Ovanda Lamb　　11- 2-1837
Miller, David D. (1788-1842) - Martha McMichael
　　　　　　　　　　　　　　　　　　10-24-1833
　　David bur. Mt. Pleasant Cem.
Miller, Henry, Jr. - Margaret Roof　　12-15-1836
Miller, Isaac - Susanna Hardman　　　4-28-1833
Miller, Solomon - Elizabeth Hardman　7-26-1834
　　Solomon b. 1814 Ohio, d. 10-1-1862; Elizabeth
　　b. 2-3-1813 Ohio, d. 4-1-1879; both bur. City
　　Cem., S.B.
Miller, William W. - Phoebe Ann Hathaway 9- 8-1837
Moore, Joseph - Permelia Ferris　　　12- 7-1837
Monson, Alonson W. - Mrs. Eliza J. (Brown)
　　Perry　　　　　　　　　　　　　2-14-1837
Morgan, Charles - Sarah Shumard　　3-15-1837
　　Charles b. 11-1-1801 N.C., d. 6-3-1885;
　　Sarah b. 11-9-1814 N.J., d. 12-24-1873;
　　both bur. City Cem., S.B.
Morgan, William - Angeline Bannick　2- 2-1832
Morris, Charles - Elizabeth Hollingshead 6-12-1836
Morse, Daniel - Marina Sanders　　　5-13-1838
Muffley, Isaac - Mary Yocky　　　　　2-13-1838
　　Isaac b. 1811 Pa., to Cass Co., Mich. 1838;
　　to Marshall Co., Ind. abt 1851; Mary b.
　　1815 Pa.
Needham, John - Nancy Wilson　　　　9-22-1832
Nichol, Solomon - Sarah Wilson　　　9- 3-1837
Nichols, Thomas S. (1804-1852) - Rachel Crammer
　　Thomas bur. Hamilton Cem.　　　10- 2-1837
Nickerson, George - Sophia Wilson　　4-18-1838
Nixon, Robert - Elizabeth Haslett　　7-22-1838
Orr, John Louisa Battle Taylor　　　　12- 7-1835
Overacker, Barton - Sarah Martindale　11-10-1831
Owen, Francis W. - Eliza Willmington　9-14-1835
　　Eliza d. before 1850
Owen, Thomas P. - Sally Ann Trowbridge 2-21-1836

Palmer, Asher H. - Nancy Odell　　　5- 5-1836
Palmer, David - Elizabeth Ruple　　　12-13-1834
Pease, Jesse T. - Lemry Ann Mallett　　10-14-1833
Peek, James - Cynthia Jay　　　　　　9-30-1837
Pershing, James - Susan Halstead　　　7- 6-1834
Phillips, Isaac - Sally Wilson　　　　　11- 7-1833
　　Isaac b. 1810 N.C.; Sally b. 1817 Ohio
Phillips, James H. - Ann Forgison　　　3-11-1836
Phillips, John - C. Harris　　　　　　1-11-1838
Phthoxton, William - Nancy A. Smith　8-13-1837
Pierce, Daniel N. - Harriet Sherwood　10-31-1837
Pilibeam, Benjamin - Pamelia Doolittle　6- 7-1838
Pren (or Prue), Gabriel - Margaret Page 6-28-1834
Price, Jacob - Sarah Bennett　　　　　8- 3-1836
Purdy, Isaac - Eliza Ann Jay　　　　　6- 7-1838
Puterbaugh, Jacob - Sarah Roof　　　3-30-1837
　　Sarah b. 11-6-1822 Ohio, d. 11-30-1893
　　Berrien Co., Mich.
Radabaugh, William - Eliza Randall　　8-20-1835
Randall, Isaac - Susan Replogle　　　　4- 2-1837
Raysden, Shelrich - Rose Hollenshead　lic. 3-30-1837
　　Shelrich b. 1808 N.C.;　　　　　lic. 3-30-1837
　　living La Porte Co. in 1850
Redding, Matthias, of Marshall Co. - Elizabeth
　　Higans　　　　　　　　　　　　6-27-1833
Redding, Samuel - Mary Egbert　　　3- 8-1838
　　Samuel b. 9-17-1815 Ohio, d. 9-27-1838,

　　bur. Dayton, Mich.; Mary b. 1817, d. 1884,
　　m. (2) Peleg Slocum, bur. Hamilton Cem.
Replogle, George - Sarah Grossnickle　9-27-1835
　　George b. 1810 Ohio; Sarah b. 1817 Pa.
Replogle, Michael - Christine Smith　　8-27-1835
Ring, James - Mary Pearson　　　　　3- 2-1837
Rockhill, Thomas - Elizabeth Martin　11-25-1834
　　Thomas b. 1800 N.J., d. 1889; Elizabeth b.
　　1812 N.J., d. 4-11-1883, bur. City Cem., S.B.
Roe, James - Susan Hardman　　　　lic. 10- 7-1837
Roherer, Robert (1815-1845) - Elizabeth Bowman
　　(1817-1843)　　　　　　　　　　3-24-1836
　　Both bur. Roherer Cem.
Roof, Daniel - Margaret Yager (or Mary Yaga)
　　Daniel b. 1812 Zanesville,　　　　10-27-1835
　　Ohio; d. 1-31-1899; Margaret b. 1814 Zanes-
　　ville, d. 7-9-1895; both bur. City Cem., S.B.
Roof, Henry, Jr. - Anna Mabbit　　　10-22-1835
Roof, James - Betsy Puterbaugh　　　3 or 4 1837
Roof, John - Rachel Price　　　　　　9- 4-1836
　　John b. 1815 Ohio
Roof, William - Sarah Hatfield　　　　9-17-1835
　　Wm. b. 1811 Ohio; Sarah b. 1817 Ohio
Root, Hiram - Jane McMichael　　　　10- 7-1835
Ross, Robert S. - Maria Mitchell　　　1-17-1838
Royal, John - Jane Smith　　　　　　9- 7-1837
Ruddock, John (1809-1882) - Elizabeth Rupe,
　　dt of Jacob & Susanna (1810-1874)
　　Both bur. Sumption Prairie　　　8- 1-1833
Rupel, Samuel - Eleanor Chord　　　11-27-1833
　　Samuel b. 1805 Pa.; Eleanor b. 1809 Va.
Ruple, David - Sarah Milling　　　　　1-10-1836
　　David b. 1811 Somerset Co., Pa., d. 1-24-1894;
　　Sarah b. 1817, dt of Andrew & Margaret,
　　d. 2-21-1875; both bur. Liberty Twp.
Ruple, Matthew - Rachel Tong　　　　5-31-1838
Rush, Hiram - Ann Inwood　　　　　2-13-1835
　　Israel b. 1805, d. 1837, bur. Hamilton Cem.;
　　Mary, dt of Thomas & Rachel Clark; m. (2)
　　Wilmot C. Monson 1842

Russell, Moses C. - Catherine Weand   3-22-1838
Sandilands, Alexander - Dorothy Irwin Oliver
          Alex. b. 1807 Scotland;   10-24-1837
          d. 1-10-1871; Dorothy b. 1815 England, d.
          9-17-1899; both bur. City Cem., Mishawaka
Salee, Stephen - Susan Shook   1- 7-1838
Sanger, Horatio P. - Julia Ann Sherwood 11- 9-1835
Searell, John W. - Sarah Smith   1-25-1837
Shepley, Jacob - Susan Swift   7-23-1837
          Jacob b. 1810 Ohio; Susan b. 1822 Ohio
Sherman, Monroe C. - Cornelia Hurd   6- 3-1838
Shirley, John A. - Lydia Blakely   lic. 10- 8-1835
          Lived Marshall Co.
Shoe, Daniel - Ruth Crissman   lic.10-31-1837
Shoemaker, Elias - Rebecca Radabaugh   3-15-1838
Sisson, William - Charlotte Bennett   1-25-1838
Skinner, Zina - Lois Henniman   5- 5-1836
Smith, George W. - Elizabeth Case   lic. 10-31-1836
Smith, John T. - Harriet D. Willard   9- 6-1838
Smith, Jonathan - Sarah Yockey   11-24-1836
          Lived Marshall Co.
Smith, Jonathan - Susannah Runion   fall 1838
Smith, Martin - Eliza Jane Michell   1-22-1835
          Martin b. 1816 Ohio, lived Union Twp.
Spillman, Jacob - Ruth Althur   5-14-1835
Sprague, William - Mary West   4-13-1837
Staley, Joseph W. - Sidona Fleehart   lic. 10- 2-1835
Stanton, Alfred - Pheby Fail   1- 9-1831
          Alfred of La Porte Co., formerly of Union Co.

Stutsman, John C. (1815-1888) - Elizabeth Ulrich
          (1814-1887)
          Both bur., Ullery Cem.   4-13-1837
Suddarth, Thomas - Nancy Eaton, dt of Isaac
                                                   11-27-1836
Sumption, Abijah (1818-1890) - Rachel Rupe (1820-
          1886)   9- 3-1834
          Both bur. City Cem., S.B
Swan, Charles - Mary Wilson   7- 9-1838
Sweet, Elhannan - Margaret Harvey (1816-1843)
          His 1st wife was Malinda Hill who d. 1831
Taylor, Edmund Pitts - Phoebe Stanfield
          (1818-1891)   2-29-1833
          Taylor b. 1810 N.Y.; d. 1887
Taylor, Israel (1769-1841) - Abigail B. Phillips
                                                   6-11-1835
Taylor, Lathrop M. & Mary Johnson (1818-1879)
          Lathrop b. 1805 N.Y., d. 1892;   5-15-1833
          Both bur. City Cem., S.B.
Teel, David W. - Mariah Louise Mallett   9-16-1835
          David b. 1817 Pa.; Mariah b. 1820 Ohio
Teel (or Tell), William - Rebecca Burkit   5- 8-1834
          Wm. d. before 1850; Rebecca b. 1814 Ohio,
          dt of Jacob (b. 1777 N.C.) & Elizabeth
          (b. 1780)
Terrill, Nathaniel B. (1808-1851) - Sarah Garrett
          (1810-1860)   7-16-1836
          Both bur. New Carlisle
Thompson, George (1814-1884) - Martha Cottrell
          (1818-1880)   8-10-1837
          Both bur. Mt. Pleasant Cem.
Thompson, John R. - Betsy Antrim   1-9-1833
Thompson, John R. - Mrs. Susannah Love 9- 2-1838
Tong, Joseph - Sarah Collins   1- 9-1837

Tutt, Thomas R. - Mary J. Hardy   3-16-1837
          Thomas b. 1814 Va.; Mary b. 1820 Va., dt
          of Capt. Jonathan Hardy
Ullery, Jacob - Lovina Stutsman   6-22-1837
          Jacob b. 1811 Ohio, d. 4-26-1865; Lovina
          b. 1817 Ohio, d. 3-19-1886; both bur. South
          Lawn Cem., S.B.
Varney, Harlow - Polly Swangin   4- 6-1836
          Harlow b. 1808 N.Y.; Polly b. 1812 N.C.
Vinnedge, David (1792-1853) - Lurina Baker
          David bur. Marshall Co.   3-15-1835
Wall, John - Mary Smith   3-15-1838
          John b. 1811 Ohio; Mary b. 1822 Pa.
Ward, James H. - Mary Ann Millis   11-8-1837
Ward, William & Margaret Huston   12-11-1836
Washburn, David - Elizabeth Austin   6-30-1836
          David b. 1801 Ohio; Elizabeth b. 1810 Md.
Watkins, William - Hannah Parks   12-17-1837
Weaver, David - Mary Wilfong   1-25-1835
          David b. 1811 Ohio; Mary b. 1816 Ohio
Weaver, Jacob (1813-1882) - Susanna Englewright
          (1820-1846)   5-17-1836
          Both bur. Oak Ridge Cem., Berrien Co., Mich.
Weiler (or Witter, Miller), John - Sarah Miller
                                                   9-4-1834
Welsh, Samuel - Clarissa Vann   5-10-1835
Wenger, Christian - Esther Studybaker
          Christian b. 1814 Lebanon   9-20-1838
          Co., Pa., d. 11-2-1876; Esther b. 1817 Ohio,
          d. 1851; both bur. Bowman Cem., S.B.
Whinery, John - Sarah Norton   9-19-1835
White, Jacob - Rachel Egbert   6-14-1832
White, Jacob (1777-1861) - Alenia Trowbridge
          b. 1791 Warren Co., Ohio d. 2-2-1865
          Both bur. Hamilton Cem., Olive Twp. 3- -1836
White, Willian - Charlotte Garrett   8- -1835
          Wm. b. 1815 N.J., Charlotte b. 1816 N.J.
Wickerham, Robert - Jane McClary   4-28-1836
Wiggins, Thomas - Lucinda Singleton   lic. 8-29-1836
Williams, John - Deborah Austin   lic. 4-16-1836
Wilson Abraham - Lydia Chord   1-12-1837
          Abraham b. 1805 Pa., Lydia dt of Isaac
Wilson, Daniel T. - Sarah Ann Benton   6- 4-1837
          Adm. papers 1895 Marshall Co.
Wilson, James H. - Nancy Kingery   4-19-1838
Winans, James - Martha Ashley   9-28-1837
          James b. 1810 Ohio; Martha b. 1820 Ohio
Wing, Andrew M. - Mariah E. Tuttle   8-14-1837
Witter, Jacob - Rebecca Miller   8-24-1837
          Jacob b. 1791 Pa., d. 2-10-1851
Witter, John (1782-1864) - Hannah Shepley (1778-
          1854   7- 5-1836
          Both bur. Mt. Pleasant Cem.
Wright, Alfred - Jane Wilson   5-10-1838
          Alfred b. 1813 Ky.; Jane b. 1823 Ky.

_____ - Prudence Dawson   5- -1838
_____ - Sarah A. Thomas   12- -1837
_____ - Mary Zigler   7- -1837

Compiled from microfilm of Book II, St. Joseph County Marriage Records, in Genealogy Division, Indiana State Library.

Adams, George W. & Lydia Ann Harris	2-23-1839
Adams, Isaac & Margaret Rossell	7-29-1841
Akins, Samuel & Sarah Byrket	8-15-1839
Alfont, John & Nancy Mikesel	11- 2-1843
Allen, Charles & Eve Roof	11-22-1840
Alward, Samuel & Melinda A. Vanwinkle	5-14-1840
Anderson, Samuel M. & Florella Chandler	12-9-1843
Andrews, Hiram & Rebecca Ann Haynes	10-31-1839
Andrews, James E. & Harriet Webster	10- 8-1843
Annis, Jacob E. & Margaret J. Watson	1-24-1844
Anthony, John & Rachel Price	lic. 10-23-1839
Atwell, Hiram & Julia Ann Jane Lamb	7- 6-1843
Austin, Cain & Mary T. Bowker	12-7-1843
at home of Michael Bowker	
Austin, Daniel & Margaret M. Cooper	6-13-1841
Avery, Daniel & Lucinda Ferris	[11- -1839?]
Backus, Gideon & Mary Ann Hardman	9-24-1840
Bainter, Jacob & Mary Hoover	7-28-1839
Baker, Joseph & Almira Whitman	4-29-1841
Ball, Herman & Hannah Nelson	6-2-1842
Ball, William E. & Eunice Hildreth	2-19-1842
Barns, John E. & Ann West	2- 1-1842
Barton, John D. & Betsy Stevens	4-23-1843
Beas, Garret & Mary Gosset	10- 4-1841
Beck, Albert & Lovina Pettit	2-18-1841
Beck, Noah & Joannah Jenkins	2-16-1841
Beck, William & Huldah Swabb	1-19-1843
Beer, William & Isabel Agins	3- 1-1842
Berger, Henry & Sophia Cimmer	5- 1-1843
Bingham, Alfred & Anne Miller	8- 6-1846
Bly, William T. & Elizabeth Miller	5- 5-1839
Bolden, John & Harriet Smith	8-11-1840
Bowen, John & Elizabeth Russell	1- 6-1842
Bowen, Lot & Phebe Cottrell	9-15-1841
Bowman, John & Margaret H. Sutphin	12-15-1842
Bramsmaid, Alfred L. & Martha Belden	2-18-1840
Brockhill, James & Electa Pinnell	10- 5-1842
Brower, Washington J. & Louisana Vaughn	10- 4-1840
Brown, George & Phebe Clark	11-22-1838
Brunson, Perry & Catharine Calkins	5- 1-1842
Buck, Edward A. & Julia Ann Mead	12-25-1843
Bugbee, Almand & Adelia Crocker	4-28-1844
Bunker, Macy & Margaret Jackson	8-22-1844
Burns, James & Phebe Ann Clark	5-30-1844
Busha, George & Tallee Durkee	3- 1-1840
Butler, William S. & Sophronia Harris	7- 3-1842
Calvert, Isaac D. & Mary Ann Defrees	1- 6-1842
Calvert, Thomas & Sarah Cuny	11-26-1842
Carty, Joseph & Eliza Cond	5-26-1840
Casper, Winfield & Rosanna McNalley	2- 9-1840
Cass, Albert & Jane Pettinger	2- 4-1841
Castle, George & Lourehanz Dawson	7-13-1843
Chambers, Charles & Sidney Jane Stringer	3-10-1844
Chandler, Peter & Sophia Sherryman(?)	12- 1-1840
Chapin, Reuben & Sarah Pratt	12-31-1843
Chess, John W. & Olivia A. Winans	3- 4-1841
Childs, James M. & Julia A. Brown	5-15-1839
Chord, Samuel M. & Lydia Throckmorton	5-29-1841
Christian, Robert & Mariah Miller	8-22-1844
Cissne, Joseph & Phebe Miller	10-28-1839
Clark, Alonzo & Mariah Holdridge	11-11-1840
Claypool, Hiram & Sarah Hall	8- 5-1839
Coe, Benjamin W. & Hylanda Ireland	4- 9-1839

Coil, Francis & Rachel Bates	3-21-1844
Cole, Alvah & Betty Mariah Jones	7-16-1840
Coleman, Peter & Mariah White	6-16-1839
Collins, Jesse H. & Margaret A. Gish	8-11-1842
Connor, Benton & Maria Usher	8-13-1840
Cook, William & Melissa Caldwell	4-23-1844
Cooke, Elias & Sophia Eberhart	2-24-1842
Cooper, William & Sarah Ward	lic. 1-23-1839
Copper, William & Elizabeth Male	6- 9-1839
Cory, Silas & Louisa Bratt	9-28-1843
Cosgrove, Bradford G. & Mary Phelps	9- 8-1841
Crawford, Samuel R. & Bellila Cotton	4-22-1841
Crews, Jonathan & Polly Mira Ireland	12- 2-1842
Cripe, Benjamin & Mary Jane Fulmer	11-17-1842
Cripe, Daniel & Mary Skiles	6-25-1840
Cripe, Rinehart J. & Sarah Jane Hopkins	1- 1-1844
Curtis Chancey & Malina Ferris	8- 7-1844
Curtis, Reuben B. & Eliza Hackney	3-10-1841
Curtis, Seth B. & Mary Doolittle	8-28-1842
Cutting, Jonas & Aurilla Mattoon	1-25-1843
Dalrymple, Oliver & Ann Mariah Malcum	1- 4-1843
Dashnie, Peter & Elizabeth Lucie	lic. 7-12-1844
Dawley, William & Malfina Fuller	6- 6-1841
Day, John & Elmira Phelps	12-21-1842
Day, Russell & Hannah Sherman	9-15-1842
Dayton, Daniel & Nancy Maria Wade	1-11-1844
Dayton, Frederick A. & Mary Ann Porter	6-28-1839
Dealman, Adam & Elizabeth Kiefer	4- 8-1842
Deno, Peter & Lucy Jaquith	9-18-1843
Dolly, Horace & Abigail Cunningham	3-13-1844
Doolittle, Uri & Eliza Jane Fields	12-21-1843
Drake, John M. & Barbra Huntsinger	2-20-1840
Dunbar, Archibald & Eliza Ann Myler	6-22-1843
Dunn, Reuben & Mary Jane Dunn	11-12-1840
Dunning, Barton B. & Laura Stiles	12-29-1840
Eaton, John & Mahala Barns	10-10-1842
Eberhart, Jacob W. & Louisa Ferris	6-28-1843
Eckman, William & Catharine Ullery	10-13-1842
Edwards, Andrew & Huldah Ferry	8-26-1839
Egbert, Asher & Elizabeth Dunn	5-21-1844
Eller, Philip & Elsa Michael	8-29-1843
Elliott, Frances N. & Adelia M. Cutting	1- 1-1843
Ellis, Artemus C. & Elizabeth Ann Pembroke	6-11-1842
Ellis, James & Sarah Wharton	12- 5-1839
English, George & Susannah Hetrick	8- 1-1844
Enos, Orville A. & Mary Ann Ivens	12- 7-1841
Eslinger, Christopher & Mary Yost	11-14-1842
Farneman, Joseph & Barbara Ullery	2-29-1844
Farnsworth, Reuben L. & Sylva Parker	4-18-1840
Ferris, David & Lucy Vaughn	4-12-1840
Fields, Stephen, of Kalamazoo Co., Mich. & Nancy Bronson	2-11-1839
Fields, Stephen & Charlotte H. Rush	2- 1-1844
Finley, Henry A. & Jane Fox	6-22-1843
Finley, Samuel & Jane C Marchant	8-19-1841
Fisher, Henry & Rosanna Gitchell	4-21-1844
Foot, Alexis & Christiana Millis	9- 4-1843
Forgason, George & Mary Ann Wilson	3-18-1841
Fouts, William D. & Charity Wharton	5-19-1844
Frame, Jesse & Susannah Ranstead	5-29-1839
Frame, Nathaniel & Caroline Main	5- 8-1842
French, Alpheus & Sylvia Chandler	3-27-1844
French, Dennis & Mary Johnson	5-21-1843

Garard, Henry & Elizabeth Pettit	10-12-1840
Garrigus, James & Katharine Barns	11- 5-1840
Garrison, Lewis & Catharine Mead	3-28-1842
Garwood, Jonathan & Martha Rupe	1-21-1841
Garwood, Stacy & Clarissa Throckmorton	4-14-1842
Garwood, William & Patsey Montgomery	10-14-1841
Gibson, John & Katharine Witter	7-16-1839
Gish, George & Elizabeth Chalfant	4-18-1839
Gish, Joel & Sarah Jane McCartney	9-23-1841
Gitchell, David D. & Rebecca Curtis	5- 7-1844
Griffin, William & Amy Clark	12-30-1841
Griffith, Caleb B. & Matilda P. Smith	lic. 12-21-1840
Grimes, Joshua S. & Louisa D. Camp	3-21-1844
Guberick, David & Fanny Miller	7- 1-1840
Hackney, Thomas & Laura Caldwell	10- 1-1840
Hagle, George B. & Martha Gillam	1-17-1841
Hahn, Jacob & Catharine Stutsman	lic. 4-27-1844
Hanson, William H. & Ann Burk	2-18-1841
Hardman, Aaron & Eunice Backus	12- 9-1838
Hardman, David W. & Malinda Roe	3-29-1840
Hardman Joshua & Martha McCombs	12-11-1838
Hardman, Samuel & Mary Backus	9- 8-1842
Hardy, Hiram & Harriet Jones	9- 7-1839
Hardy, Joseph & Margaret Ann Jones	2-17-1844
Harris, George & Priscilla Tritt	12-24-1840
Harris, Jacob & Elizabeth Ann Harmon	lic. 8-24-1839
Harris, Jacob & Barbary Ketring	2- 6-1842
Harris, James & Mary Ann Funston	2- 6-1840
Harris, Timothy & Harriet Baird	6-27-1844
Hartwell, James & Mary Keating	7-28-1843
Hathaway, Henry & Nancy Moon	5-27-1841
Hays, Thomas & Mary Adney Chandler	9- 5-1843
Herrington, Anthony & Amanda Skinner	4-16-1840
Hetrick, Philip & Susannah McMullen	7-19-1840
Hicks, Martin & Sarah Edwards	lic. 7-14-1842
High, Jesse & Hester Ann Jenkins	3-28-1844
Hill, Herbert H. & Charity White	3-20-1844
Hollar, Jonas & Sarah Price	5-20-1841
Hollingshead, Matthias & Mary Moon	12-16-1841
Hollingshead, William & Barbara Moon	3-25-1841
Hollister, Justus E. & Alma H. Bancroft	11-17-1840
Holloway, George & Eliza C. McCullough	7- 9-1839
Holloway, Thomas L. & Drusilla McCollough	10-4-1842
Hooper, John & Phebe Smith	4-14-1840
Hooper, Thadius M. & Mary S. Earl	9- 2-1841
Hoover, David & Rebecca Overfield	7-25-1841
Hoyt, John J. & Eliza Wood	12-24-1842
Hubbard, Ransom & Marriett Whitlock	12- 5-1842
Hughs, Thomas & Ann Gillen	11- 7-1841
Hummer, Washington & Mercy Garwood	3-19-1840
Hunt, Charles W. & Rhoda Weakley	12-11-1843
Huntley, Benjamin & Rhoda Baldwin	1-27-1842
Huntsinger, Samuel & Sally Ann Pettit	4-21-1844
Huntsinger, William & Elizabeth Jones	11-25-1841
Huston, Abraham & Sarah Robbins	
Sarah Roberts in return	8-18-1842
Huyck, William F. & Abby Alger	5-18-1843
Hyler, Harrison & Elizabeth Frame	11- 7-1839
Inman, John & Jane Garwood	2-24-1842
Inwood, Richard & Catharine Ann Rush	5- 2-1844
Ireland, David M. & Elizabeth Swabb	9-19-1839
Ireland, Maxwell & Sally Ann Pettit	9-19-1839
Jackson, Amos & Emily Jane Harvey	3-14-1844
Jackson, William & Mary B. Platts	12- 8-1840
Jacobs, Daniel & Sarah Edwards	8-23-1843
Jennings, Samuel R. & Matilda Bargdoll	6- 8-1841
Johnson, Lea P. & Luna L. Perry	9- 8-1841
Jones, Elias D. & Annis Cole	7-23-1840
Jones, Harrison & Lucinda Ritter	4-21-1844

Jones, Samuel Z. & Mary Mechlin	12-14-1838
Jones, William & Susannah Hathaway	12-12-1839
Judson, Adoniram B. & Eliza Ann Smith	3- 2-1841
Kendrick, Francis & Anna Wilson	1-23-1844
Kingery, John & Eliza C. Jenkins	3-24-1840
Kinney, Franklin & Eliza Nickerson	1-19-1843
Kinney, John & Elizabeth Emberling	11-28-1839
Kinyon, James & Nancy Case	12-21-1843
Kirkwood, Robert & Catharine Crull	12- 5-1841
Klinger, Philip & Elizabeth Miller	1-15-1839
Knapp, Asa P. & Rebecca Chrisman	6- 7-1840
Lambert, Oliver C. & Eleanor McMullen	7- 2-1840
Landon, Robert & Salina Wilmington	1-20-1839
Lane, William & Sally Scott	4-15-1840
Laning, Robert C. & Mary Ann Cooper	1- 5-1840
Lamport, Ansel M. & Roxy Ferris	4-11-1844
Leach, George & Lurana Ann Shelton	5-27-1843
Lehr, Samuel & Malinda Geisleman	1- 6-1842
Lichtenberger, Adam & Sophia Russell	11-22-1842
Lichtenberger, John & Lodema Fowler	5-28-1840
Ligget, Isaac & Anna Cole	10- 2-1839
Lindsey, John T. & Sarah Cond	10-17-1843
Longley, Levi & Julia Jewell	11-21-1841
Loomer, George P. & Almira Mellin	2-25-1843
Lowery, John & Mary A. Coverdal	lic. 8-17-1841
Lowning, George & Lydia Cole	3- 6-1843
McCartney, James & Louisa Clark	12-19-1843
McCombs, William & Eve Cripe	9-12-1839
McGlaughlin, Wm. & Bloony Jane Wakman	1-26-1840
McMullen, David & Elizabeth Bainter	8-21-1842
Main, Christopher Sr. & Elizabeth Backus	8-19-1841
Malbof, Lewis & Lemah Burtro	2-14-1844
Malcum, James E. & Elizabeth Dalrymple	11-13-1842
Malcum, John W. & Emeline Everts	1- 2-1839
Mallery, Simmons & Thankful Willis	3-25-1842
Martin, Charles W. & Jane Buck	9- 8-1842
Martin, Henry & Julia Ann Lashbough	5- 4-1840
Mason, Josiah B. & Sarah Vaughn	3-19-1840
Meek, Richard C. & Eliza Tatman	6-22-1841
Mikeal, Edward & Eliza Noffsinger	2-29-1840
Edmund Michael in return	
Mikesell, Garret & Deborah Bunker	5-18-1843
Mikesell, Hiram H. & Sarah Byers	1-18-1844
Miksel, Hiram & Elizabeth M. Vicory	8-27-1840
Millburn, William & Sarah Chandler	7-14-1844
Miller, Adam & Mercy Ann Mead	4- 2-1839
	lic. 12- 1-1838
Miller, Asher & Elizabeth Ann Watson	1- 1-1840
Miller, Daniel & Margaret Hollingshead	11- 7-1843
M. at home of Daniel Hollingshead	
Miller, David & Elizabeth Hoover	3-31-1844
Miller, Henry B. & Esther Bowman	1-21-1841
Miller, Isaac & Hannah Smith	12-14-1843
Miller, Jacob & Charlotte Berry	2-25-1839
Miller, Jacob E. & Sarah Blackford	lic. 4-16-1841
Miller, James & Sarah Young	10-27-1839
Miller, James H. & Mary Huston	3-11-1841
Miller, John & Sarah Rohrer	10-28-1841
Miller, John H. & Elizabeth Studybaker	11-26-1840
Miller, Noah & Clarissa Drullinger	7-24-1844
Millikan, John & Joannah R. Lewis	11-27-1839
Millis, William J. & Margaret Lace	12-30-1842
Minor, John D. & Catharine Utsler	1- 8-1841
Monson, Albert & Sarah M. Sample	8-24-1843
Monson, Wilmot C. & Mary O. Rush	4-17-1842
Montgomery, Joseph & Ann Garwood	3-24-1842
Moon, Eli & Louisa Hathaway	5-25-1842
Moon, Patrick & Mary Ann Sherdon	4-15-1843
Moon, Wanton & Alvina Pikard	11-30-1843

Moon, William & Lenny Utsler 6-7(?)-1843
Moore, William H. & Lucinda Kemp 1-21-1840
Morehouse, Joseph B. & Martha Swabb 6-27-1844
Morris, Garret & Sarah Ann Copper 4- 3-1842
Morss, Thomas E. & Rosanna Buck 1-17-1843
Mufley, Joseph & Rebecca Christian 1-27-1842
Mundy, David & Elizabeth Crone 2-28-1842
Murphy, Hiram & Martha Jane Sherman 7-12-1843
Murphy, William & Margaret Craper 8-23-1840
Murtin, William & Permelia Harris 10-24-1839
Myers, Cornelius & Isabella Cooper 10- 8-1843
Myler, Calvin & Mary Jane Scott 3-24-1842
Myler, Matthew & Polly Wilson 10-19-1843
Neal, Henry & Mercy Armstrong 7-23-1843
Neal, James & Mrs. Lucy Hawkins 3-10-1843
Newton, Joseph & Susannah Pershing 10- 6-1839
Nickerson, Henry & Nancy Mole [1- -1839]
Nicol, William & Harriet Cody 8-14-1842
Norton, William & Mary Ann Day 9-10-1841
O'Connor, John & Lucy Benner 8-12-1842
Odell, William P. & Maria Wallace 5-15-1844
Oliver, Andrew & Amanda Ford 10-20-1839
Oliver, James & Susan Doty 5-13-1844
Oliver, William I. (or J.) & Lucinda Ford 10- 6-1842
Ovitt, S.A. & Celestia Durrell lic. 2- 8-1840
Page, Richmond F. & Almira Griffin 4-30-1844
Parker, Valney & Sophia Konklin 1- 1-1844
Parker, William M. & Ann Leonard lic. 1- 4-1843
Parkinson, John & Mary C. Anderson 12-25-1842
Parks, George W. & Malinda E. Sherman 8- 4-1839
Parnell, Thomas & Susannah Wilfong 4- 1-1841
Parrett, William & Catharine Rogers 8-12-1843
Parsels, Isaac & Rosanna Knapp 8-12-1841
Peck, Morgan & Sarah W. Crane 1- 2-1842
Penwell, David W. & Susannah Rupe 12-19-1839
Penwell, Enos & Martha Holloway 6- 7-1842
Picket, Joseph & Sarah Hildreth 12-30-1841
Pickett, Edwin & Mary Rohrer 10-29-1840
Postley, William A. & Elmira Wheeler 1- 8-1844
Price, James & Mary Smith 2- 1-1843
Price, John B. & Susan Ullery 7- 3-1842
Price, Thomas & Tabitha Emberling 9-26-1839
Ranstead, James & Cyntha Bixley 7-12-1840
Rarrick, Henry & Phebe Ann Miller 8-24-1843
Reamer, Henry & Abigail Ligget 9- 1-1844
Rearick, Jacob & Mrs. Elizabeth Sherman 9- 8-1842
Rector, Jacob & Fanny Little 5-28-1839
Rector, Mark & Elizabeth Lineback 9-16-1841
Redding, George W. & Mary Eller 4-18-1844
Redding, Lewis H. & Mary Jane Trowbridge 1- 3- 1839
Redding, Wesley & Nancy Egbert 7-15-1839
Reynolds, Charles & Elizabeth Linch 1-26-1843
Reynolds, John & Clarissa Egbert 4-16-1844
Reynolds, Waterman & Elizabeth Eutsler lic. 3-23-1839
Ribble, Tobias & Rebecca Watson 6-15-1841
Richardson, Augustine P. & Harriet Egbert 2-24-1839
Riddle, Wiley & Marinda Price 9-30-1841
Rinard, Benjamin & Catharine Stutsman 10-20-1842
Ringle, Samuel & Elenor Bennett 12-22-1841
Ringle, Simeon & Nancy Yockey 2-14-1839
Ritter, David & Eunice Graves 10-10-1844
Ritter, John H. & Rachel Hardman 8- 1-1839
Ritter, Samuel & Sally Jones 4-10-1844
Ritter, Solomon & Elizabeth Hardman 7- 4-1839
Robison, Abraham G. & Angeline Pierson 11-23-1843
Rodebaugh, Samuel & Anna Bowman 10-27-1839
Roe, Ethan A. & Jane Rebecca Lambert 8-27-1840
Roe, Jeremiah B. & Elizabeth H. Clark 11-22-1842
Rogers, John & Jane Oliver 7-23-1842

Rohrer, Joseph & Sarah Miller 7- 9-1839
Roof, Jacob & Elizabeth Chamberlain 9-22-1842
Roof, John & Rebecca Roof 2- 4-1842
Ruggles, Philo E. & Ann Leach 4-20-1843
Runyan, Henry & Melissa Price 3-28-1839
Runyan, Isaac & Mary Jane Chamberlain 10-17-1841
Rupe, Daniel & Martha Harvey 12- 3-1840
Rupe, Samuel & Sally Ann Owen 9-10-1840
Ruple, Benjamin & Nancy McLaughlin 10-20-1843
Ruple, John & Susannah Chord 10-21-1841
Rush, Squire & Lovina Williams 4- 1-1840
Russell, James S. & Deborah M. Cates 1- 1-1839
Russell, John H. & Elizabeth Bowen 10-24-1839
Sale, Thomas W. & Anna Stewart 7-17-1843
    Anna Stuart in return
Sample, Andrew R. & Mary H. Defrees 6- 6-1843
Scott, George & Elizabeth Leer 11-21-1839
Shanahan Peter & Sarah Nichol 4- 2-1840
Shaw, Silas & Eliza Jane Ireland 8- 6-1844
Sherman, Cornelius V. & Mary M. Long 11-22-1840
Simms, John & Harriet Cates 3-10-1840
Skinner, James F. & Elizabeth Bowker 4-14-1842
Slocum, Peleg & Esther P. McLaughlin 12-16-1838
Slocum, Peleg & Mary Redding 8-29-1840
Smith, Alexander H. & Dolly Ann Lilly 6-23-1844
Smith, George & Ann Heston 7-22-1840
Smith, Jacob D. & Sarah Stuart 1-19-1840
Smith, Job & Eliza Jane Lancaster 6-27-1844
Smith, Jonathan & Susan Jane Runyan 1-24-1841
Smith, Michael & Margaret Roads 4-10-1843
Smith, Samuel J. & Susan Davis 1- 6-1842
Snell, Jacob & Elizabeth Ligget 11- 4-1841
Snyder, Adam & Jane Wilcox 5-25-1844
Stanfield, Eli & Sarah Mikesell 7-14-1842
Stanfield, William & Mary Garwood 11-11-1842
Steel, Nicholas & Mary A. Harvey lic. 4- 6-1840
Stevens, James & Mary Ann Cobbler 9-19-1839
Stevenson, Amos L. & Priscilla King 7-11-1839
Stewart, Daniel & Mary Henry 2- 9-1840
Stiles, John A. & Mary Ann Keyes 1-23-1841
Stover, David & Lucinda Whitman 3-12-1840
Stutsman, Joseph & Lavina Smith 9-29-1842
Sumption, Charles & Mrs. Mary Bainter 10-30-1842
Swabb, William & Nancy Ann Beck 12-21-1843
Swartwout, Henry B. & Lois M. Palmer 11-23-1843
    (alias Lois M. Oliver)
Sweeney, Robert & Margaret Rogers 1-25-1839
Sweet, Elhanan W. & Margaret Tritt 1-23-1844
Tatman, John & Harriet A. Cosgrove 6-11-1843
Taylor, Andrew & Jenett Armstrong 5-28-1842
Taylor, James & Jane Leach lic. 5- 8-1841
Tipton, John & Laura Sherman 2-22-1844
Todd, Henry & Clarissa Weaver 11- 2-1843
Tutt, Francis R. & Martha Jane Hackney 4- 9-1839
Unruh, John & Hannah Sophis 3- 2-1839
Usher, Andrew J. & Louisa Falmer 7- 4-1840
Vail, William S. & Sarah W. McClelland 10-31-1840
Vanderhoof, Gilbert & Emiline Rose 2-29-1844
Vaughn, Edward & Priscilla Ann Wycoff 10- 5-1843
Vincent, Benjamin H. & Betsy Ellis 12-15-1842
Voughsburgh, Nelson & Eliza Ann Turner 1-24-1839
Wagner, Andrew & Mary Ritter 3-28-1840
Wagner, David H. & Mary Witter 12-12-1839
Wagnor, William & Eve Ritter 12-16-1838
Ward, Franklin & Susannah McMullen 10-22-1843
Wharton, William & Charity C. Throckmorton 2- 6-1844
White, David & Lamenta Copper 5-16-1839
Wilder, Reuben B. & Nancy Ann Parks lic. 1- 8-1840
Wiley, Augustin & Susan Gish 6-18-1840

Wilkeson, George & Margaret Keefer	11-26-1843	Wilson, Robert & Adaline Fox	11- 5-1840
George Wilkerson in return		Witherley, William P. & Elizabeth Smith	lic. 5- 5-1841
Willfong, Noah & Elizabeth Hostettler	6-27-1844	Witter, Abraham & Elizabeth Radabaugh	2- 3-1842
Williams, Christopher & Mary Keefer	4-8-1842	Witter, George & Sarah Miller	2-16-1840
Williams, James & Sarah Jane Martin	5-23-1839	Witter, Jacob & Margaret Bainter	10-24-1839
Williams, James A. & Elizabeth Hatfield	9-10-1843	Wright, Stephen L. & Almira Bancroft	6-25-1840
Williams, William C. & Elizabeth Simpler	10- 7-1839	Wycoff, Peter & Louisa Wilson	10-22-1840
Willoughby, Dewit C. & Sarah H. Meredith	2-15-1842	Zimmer, Michael & Sophia Helmberger	10-12-1843

LEGISLATION OF LOCAL AND GENEALOGICAL INTEREST, 1800-1825

Believing that the printed volumes of Indiana *Laws* contain information of interest to family researchers, we are beginning in this issue a digest of items that seemed most likely to be of help to local historians and genealogists. The printed volumes are very rare and largely inaccessible, but the Indiana Historical Society now has a microfilm of the *Laws* through 1851. The *Laws of Indiana Territory* have been printed in two volumes: the first covering the years 1801-1809, by Francis Philbrick, and the second, 1809-1816, by Louis W. Ewbank. For legislation of the territorial period we have used these reprints.

Subjects chosen for inclusion were those relating to specific counties and their residents; divorces (in some instances the county of residence was not indicated); relief laws (these are under the counties if the residence was given), and legislation regarding roads. The latter took up much of the time of the General Assembly and has been included since it gives the routes by which settlers traveled, and it gives the names of those appointed to lay out the roads. In the case of the system of state roads mapped in 1821-22, we have also given the names of the contractors as listed in the *Senate Journal* in connection with the payments they received. We will be happy to have the reactions of our readers to the listings, as this will be a guide to the continuation of the digest in following issues of *THG*.

LEGISLATION REGARDING SPECIFIC COUNTIES OR THEIR RESIDENTS

Clark County

Formation by proclamation of Governor William Henry Harrison, Feb. 3, 1801. Executive Journal.

Act for regulation of town of Charlestown. Trustees: James M'Campbell, James M'Faggert , William Bowen, Andrew P. Hay, James Bigger. *Laws* 1813-14 (Ewbank), pp. 463-66.

Incorporation of borough of Charlestown. Trustees: Lemuel Ford, Benjamin Ferguson, John Carr, Jr., Joseph A. Lingan, Alexander S. Henderson, William Duerson, Charles B. Naylor. *Laws*, 1819-20, pp. 41-47.

Incorporation of town of Charlestown. Trustees: James Sharp, Littleton Howard, John Carr, John M. Lemon, Alevitus T. Green, James C. Caldwell, William McMillen. *Laws*, 1825, pp. 30-32.

Board of trustees appointed for town of Jeffersonville. Thomas T. Davis, James Lemon, Davis Floyd, Marston G. Clark, Samuel Gwathmey. *Laws*, 1807 (Philbrick), pp. 564-66.

County comrs. to make allowance to Westill S. Caulkins, a pauper. *Laws*, 1822-23, p. 140.

Admrs. of estate of Simpson Charlton—Samuel Patterson & John Rodgers—authorized to convey certain land to Levi & Thomas Ogle. *Laws* 1822-23, pp. 137-38.

Execr. of will of John H. Crane deceased authorized to sell lot in Clark's Grant. *Laws*, 1823-24, pp. 74-75.

John Fishlie authorized to keep ferry below & adjoining town of Jeffersonville. *Laws*, 1821-22, pp. 146-48.

Marriage of Catharine Moore with John Prince dissolved & her marriage with Robert K. Moore legalized. *Laws*, 1808 (Philbrick), pp. 648-49.

Relief of securities of William H. Moore, late tax collector (James C. Caldwell, John Carr, Benjamin Ferguson, Francis Ratliff, John H. Thompson, Isaac Howk). *Laws*, 1825, p. 59.

George White authorized to keep ferry at Jeffersonville. *Laws*, 1820-21, pp. 120-22.

William Wright authorized to build toll bridge over Silver Creek. *Laws*, 1817-18 (special), pp. 43-46.

Marriage of William Smith and Elizabeth Wood performed by Leroy Smith, legalized. *Laws*, 1810 (Ewbank), p. 706.

Clay County

Formation of, effective April 1, 1825. *Laws*, 1825, pp. 17-18.

Crawford County

Formation of, effective March 1, 1818. *Laws*, 1817-18 (special), p. 27.

John Sturgeon, father of Edmund, authorized to sell land. *Laws*, 1818-19, p. 131.

David Stewart & Lucinda Wyman, admrs. of estate of George Wyman, authorized to convey land to James Flynn. *Laws*, 1822-23, pp. 126-27.

Daviess County

Formation of, effective Feb. 15, 1817. *Laws*, 1816-17, p. 192.

Dearborn County

Formation by Governor's Proclamation, March 7, 1803. Executive Journal.

Incorporation of Aurora Seminary. Trustees: Jesse L. Holman, James Walker, Robert M'Kettrick, James W. Weaver, Richard Norris, Edward Fairchild, Timothy Brown, Daniel Bartholomew, John C. Lewis, David Fisher, Elias Conwell, Martin Cosine. *Laws*, 1822-23, pp. 119-21.

Incorporation of New Hope Baptist Church on Deer Creek. Trustees: John Brown, George Harlin, John Ewing. *Laws*, 1810 (Ewbank), pp. 706-11.

Abel C. Pepper, _____ Decoursey, & Lot North authorized to build toll bridge over Arnold Creek. *Laws*, 1818-19, pp. 132-33.

Robert Wright, Thomas P. Metcalf, Caleb Hayes, Joseph E. Milburn, & Jesse L. Holman authorized to erect bridge over Hogan Creek. *Laws*, 1815 (Ewbank), pp. 660-66.

John Barricklow & Gideon Cummins authorized to build toll bridge over Laughery Creek. *Laws*, 1818-19, pp. 135-38.

Board of comrs. (Stephen Ludlow, Isaac Dunn, James Dill, George Weaver, Jacob Weaver, Jacob Blasdall, Sr., David Reese, & Elijah Sparks) authorized to build bridge over Tanner's Creek. *Laws*, 1814 (Ewbank), pp. 737-47.

Incorporation of Tanner's Creek Bridge Co. Comrs.: Stephen Ludlow, Daniel Brown, Jesse Hunt, George H. Dunn, Daniel Plummer, Davis Weaver. *Laws*, 1825, pp. 40-43.

Dubois County

Formation of, effective Feb. 1, 1818. *Laws*, 1817-18 (special), pp. 16-17.

Fayette County

Formation of, effective Jan. 1, 1819. *Laws*, 1818-19, pp.103-107.

Floyd County

Formation of, effective Feb. 1, 1819. *Laws*, 1818-19, pp. 99-103.

Incorporation of Indiana Cotton Mfg. Co. in New Albany. Trustees: John Badger, Charles Paxton, Joseph Whitcomb, James Besse, Ebenezer Baldwin. *Laws*, 1820-21, pp. 74-79.

Incorporation of New Albany school. President & managers: Seth & Charles Woodruff, John Eastborn, Samuel C. Miller, & Samuel Marsh. *Laws*, 1820-21. pp. 72-74

Relief of James, Joel, & Elizabeth Scribner, admrs. of estate of Nathaniel Scribner. *Laws*, 1819-20, pp. 9-10.

Franklin County

Formation of, effective, Jan. 1, 1811. *Laws*, 1810 (Ewbank), pp. 108-111, 190.

Regulation of town of Brookville. Trustees: Benjamin Smith, Arthur Dixon, Joshua Harlan, William H. Eads, & James Knight. *Laws*, 1813-14 (Ewbank), pp. 437-42.

Incorporation of East Fork of Whitewater Toll Bridge Co. Incorporators: Robert John, Samuel Goodwin, Robert Breckenridge, James S. Coalscott, John Jacobs. *Laws*, 1822-23, pp. 97-100.

Admrs. of estate of Thomas Osborn to complete conveyance of land known as Osborn's Mills to David & Joseph Alyea & Joseph Love. *Laws*, 1825, pp. 7-9.

Relief of William & Larkin Simms who undertook to build courthouse in 1814. *Laws*, 1819-20, pp. 119-20.

Gibson County

Formation of, effective April 1, 1813. *Laws*, 1813 (Ewbank), pp. 348-50.

Jesse Emmerson, supt. of seminary twp., authorized to settle with Henry Ayres. *Laws*, 1820-21, p. 111.

Edmund Hogan & Thomas Neely authorized to build toll bridge over Patoka River. *Laws*, 1813-14 (Ewbank), pp. 434-35.

Fence to be erected around grave of Edmund Hogan, late representative. *Laws*, 1818-19, p. 144.

Polly Mosely, admr. of estate of Enos Mosely, authorized to sell part interest in Patoka or Columbia mills. *Laws*, 1822-23, pp. 124-25.

Greene County

Formation of, effective Feb. 5, 1821. *Laws*, 1820-21, p.114.

Hamilton County

Formation of, effective April 7, 1823. *Laws*, 1822-23, pp. 100-103.

Harrison County

Formation of, effective Dec. 1, 1808. *Laws*, 1808 (Ewbank), pp. 645-46.

Incorporation of Corydon Seminary. Trustees: Davis Floyd, George F. Pope, & Richard M. Heth. *Laws*, 1814 (Ewbank), pp. 729-31.

Payment to Harbin H. Moore for use of his house by the governor. *Laws*, 1820-21, p. 138; 1821-22, pp. 176-77.

Relief of Benjamin Adams, minister of the gospel. *Laws*, 1821-22, pp. 170-71.

Rebecca Heth & Fielding M. Bradford, admrs. of estate of Hervey Heth, authorized to convey lots, etc. *Laws* 1816-17, pp. 233-34; supplementary act, 1821-22, pp. 24-25.

Elizabeth Heth, Nathaniel Holcroft, & Henry W. Heth, admrs. of estate of Richard M. Heth, authorized to sell bank stock. *Laws*, 1819-20, pp. 123-24.

For benefit of Henry Kimberlin. *Laws*, 1823-24, pp. 73-74.

Relief for Samuel Little & Thomas Highfill for damage to their land caused by construction of road. *Laws*, 1823-24, p. 71.

Richard M. Heth & Jonathan Wright, guardians of Maria, Rosanna & Nancy McMahan, infant heirs of Richard McMahan, authorized to buy land. *Laws*, 1816-17, pp. 236-37.

Hendricks County

Formation of, effective April 1, 1824. *Laws*, 1823-24, p. 111.

Henry County

Formation of, effective June 1, 1822. *Laws*, 1821-22, p. 115.

Jackson County

Formation of, effective Jan. 1, 1816. *Laws*, 1815 (Ewbank), pp. 601-603.

Thomas Ewing & John McAfee authorized to lay off town in section 29, T5N, R4E [Vallonia] for heirs of Samuel Ewing, some of whom are minors. *Laws*, 1810 (Ewbank), pp. 711-13.

Relief of William H. Ewing. *Laws*, 1821-22, pp. 101-22.

Relief for securities of Samuel Powell, tax collector (William Marshall, William Williams, John Elliott, Robert Burge & Francis Elliott). *Laws*, 1823-24, pp. 67-69.

Jefferson County

Formation of, effective Jan. 1, 1811. *Laws*, 1810 (Ewbank), pp. 104-105, 190.

Incorporation of Farmers and Mechanics Bank. Subscriptions to be received by John Paul, John McIntire, John Ritchie, Christopher Harrison, Alexander A. Meek, Henry Ristine, Nathaniel Hunt, John Sering, Dawson Blackmore. *Laws*, 1814 (Ewbank), pp. 747-54.

Incorporation of town of Madison. Trustees: Israel T. Canby, Dawson Blackmore, John Sering, David M'Clure, Andrew Collins, Brook Bennett, & Martin Rowser. *Laws*, 1823-24, pp. 84-88.

Incorporation of Madison Academy. Trustees: John McIntire, John Paul, Israel T. Canby, Thomas Douglass, Thomas Crawford, Jeremiah Sullivan, Robert Cravens. *Laws*, 1819-20, pp. 15-17.

Leases of Jacob Lewis & Willis Law of school section, obtained in 1811, extended. *Laws*, 1818-19, pp. 116-17.

Marriage of William Field to Elizabeth Arbuckle, performed by Michael Monroe, legalized. *Laws*, 1823-24 (special), pp. 13-14.

John Burns, execr. of will of John Smith, permitted to sell land for heir. *Laws*, 1820-21, p. 113.

Paxton W. Todd authorized to erect toll bridge over Indian Creek. *Laws*, 1817-18 (special), pp. 46-49.

Jennings County

Formation of, effective Feb. 1, 1817. *Laws*, 1816-17, p. 197.

Johnson County

Formation of, effective May 5, 1823. *Laws*, 1822-23, pp. 22-24.

Knox County

Formation by proclamation of Governor of Northwest Territory, June 20, 1790. *St. Clair Papers*, II, 166n.

Incorporation of borough of Vincennes. Trustees: Robert Buntin, Joshua Bond, William Bullitt, Henry Hurst, Charles Smith, Jacob Kuykendall, Hyacinth Lasselle, Toussaint Dubois, Peter Jones. *Laws*, 1807 (Philbrick), pp. 513-16.

Incorporation of Bank of Vincennes. Comrs.: William Jones, Charles Smith, Wilson Lagoe, John D. Hay, Nathaniel Ewing. *Laws*, 1814 (Ewbank), pp. 754-63.

Incorporation of Roman Catholic Church at Vincennes. Trustees: Jean Baptist Delorier, Toussaint Dubois, Francis Racicot, Louis Delorier, Alexander Valle. *Laws*, 1810 (Ewbank), pp. 716-21. Act reviving 1810 act of incorporation names trustees Anthony Blane, Francis Vigo, Hyacinth Lasselle, Peter Brouillet, Peter Andre, Ambrose Mallet, John Baptist Laplante. *Laws*, 1818-19, pp. 121-23.

Incorporation of Vincennes University. Trustees: William Henry Harrison, John Gibson, Thomas T. Davis, Henry Vanderburgh, Waller Taylor, Benjamin Parke, Peter Jones, James Johnson, John Badollet, John Rice Jones, George Wallace,

William Bullitt, Elias McNamee, Henry Hurst, General Washington Johnston, Francis Vigo, Jacob Kuykendall, Samuel McKee, Nathaniel Ewing, George Leach, Luke Decker, Samuel Gwathmey, John Johnson. *Laws*, 1806 (Ewbank), pp. 178-84.

Incorporation of the Indiana Church (Presbyterian). Trustees: John Gibson, William McClure, Samuel Thompson, John Ockiltree, & Joseph Williams. *Laws*, 1810 (Ewbank), pp. 192-94. Act to amend 1810 act names trustees Thomas Posey, Samuel Thompson, John McClure, Daniel Smith, Samuel Adams. 1817-18 (special), pp. 39-41.

Incorporation of Wabash Baptist Church in Palmyra Twp. Trustees: Robert Elliott, John Alton, William Bruce. *Laws*, 1807 (Philbrick), pp. 572-74.

Relief of Claudius G. Brown, trustees of Vincennes University required to pay. *Laws*, 1823-24, p. 66.

Admrs. of estate of Toussaint Dubois authorized to convey property to George R. C. Sullivan & John Aikman. *Laws*, 1817-18 (special), pp. 54-56.

Admrs. of estate of John Francis Hamtramck authorized to sell certain lands. *Laws*, 1807 (Philbrick), pp. 576-78.

Admrs. of estate of William Jones authorized to sell certain land. *Laws*, 1819-20, pp. 128-30.

Guardians of Francis V. & Archibald McKee, minor children of Dr. Samuel McKee, authorized to sell land. *Laws*, 1819-20, pp. 77-78.

For relief of Benjamin Olney & Patrick & Rachel Simpson who paid duplicate taxes on same land. *Laws*, 1822-23, pp. 12-13.

Several acts for benefit of widow & children of Henry Vanderburgh. *Laws*, 1817-18 (special), pp. 38-39; 1818-19, pp. 129-30; 1823-24, pp. 62-63.

For relief of securities of David Whitinghill who absconded (Samuel McClure, William Brandy, John Curry & John Hogue). *Laws*, 1810 (Ewbank), pp. 721-22.

Daniel M'Clure, Thomas Emison, James Watson, Samuel Chambers, Henry Ruble, William Gamble, Thomas Jordan & Abraham Kirkendall appted to select a site for erection of bldgs. for employment of poor. *Laws*, 1820-21, pp. 102-10.

Lawrence County

Formation of, effective March 16, 1818. *Laws*, 1817-18 (special), p.12.

For relief of Thomas Beezley. *Laws*, 1821-22, pp. 25-26.

For benefit of Polly Brown & infant heirs (Lewis, Morris, Benjamin, John, Berry, Polly & Margaret Brown) of Henry Brown, deceased. *Laws*, 1823-24, pp. 14-16.

Madison County

Formation of, effective July 1, 1823. *Laws*, 1822-23, pp. 94-97.

John McDonald & William McCartney authorized to erect mill at Falls of Fall Creek. *Laws*, 1821-22, pp. 99-101. See also, 1825, p. 107.

Martin County

Formation of, effective Feb. 1, 1820. *Laws*, 1819-20, pp. 54-58.

Monroe County

Formation of, effective April 10, 1818. *Laws*, 1817-18 (special), pp. 14-15.

For relief of James Thompson, Jesse W. Knighten, & David Downs, trustees of state seminary authorized to pay. *Laws*, 1820-21, pp. 118-19.

For relief of William Jackson who leased old Indian salt lick. *Laws*, 1823-24, p. 61.

Montgomery County

Formation of, effective March 1, 1823. *Laws*, 1822-23, pp. 7-10.

Morgan County

Formation of, effective Feb. 15, 1822. *Laws*, 1821-22, pp. 35-36.

Orange County

Formation of, effective Feb. 1, 1816. *Laws*, 1815 (Ewbank), pp. 643-45.

Joel Charles authorized to enter & enjoy pt. of section 3, T1N (?), R2W for 3 years in consideration of exertions made & confiscations suffered in late war. *Laws*, 1822-23, pp. 134-35.

For benefit of Benjamin Vancleave & heirs of Hugh Holmes, deceased—authorized to build mill dam on Stampers Creek. *Laws*, 1823-24, pp. 99-101.

Owen County

Formation of, effective Jan. 1, 1819. *Laws*, 1818-19, pp. 96-99.

Parke County

Formation of, effective April 2, 1821, *Laws*, 1820-21, p. 63.

Mary & James Brooks, execrs. of will of Andrew Brooks, authorized to sell lands held in company with Moses Robbins & Chauncey Rose. *Laws*, 1822-23, p. 130.

Perry County

Formation of, effective Nov.1, 1814. *Laws*, 1814 (Philbrick), pp. 529-32.

Jesse Upton authorized to erect mill dam across Anderson's River at place known as Upton's Mill. *Laws*, 1822-23, pp. 135-36.

Pike County

Formation of, effective Feb. 1, 1817. *Laws*, 1816-17, p. 208.

Posey County

Formation of, effective Nov. 1, 1814. *Laws*, 1814 (Philbrick), pp. 529-32.

Putnam County

Formation of, effective April 1, 1822. *Laws*, 1821-22, p. 65.

Randolph County

Formation of, effective August 10, 1818. *Laws*, 1817-18 (special), p. 18.

For benefit of infant heirs of Jesse Roberts, deceased; Lucy Roberts, guardian. *Laws*, 1823-24, pp. 101-102.

Ripley County

Formation of (effective date not given). *Laws*, 1816-17, pp. 197, 199. The county was organized a year later, effective April 10, 1818. 1817-18 (special), pp. 32-33.

Rush County

Formation of, effective April 1, 1822. *Laws*, 1821-22, pp. 61-62.

Scott County

Formation of, effective Feb. 1, 1820. *Laws*, 1819-20, pp. 51-54.

Regulation of town of Lexington. Trustees: James Ward, Samuel Patterson, Daniel Searles, Jacob Rhoads, & William Pringle. *Laws*, 1815 (Ewbank), pp. 621-25.

Shelby County

Formation of, effective April 1, 1822. *Laws*, 1821-22, p. 52.

Spencer County

Formation of, effective Feb. 1, 1818. *Laws*, 1817-18 (special), pp. 20-21.

For benefit of Samuel Goldsmith, builder of courthouse. *Laws*, 1819-20, pp. 122-23.

Sullivan County

Formation of, effective Jan. 15, 1817. *Laws*, 1816-17, p. 205.

Morgan Eaton & William Ledgerwood authorized to build bridge over Busseron Creek. *Laws*, 1817-18 (special), pp. 50-53.

Election of following trustees for county library legalized: David Harbour, James Wason, Abraham M'Clelland, David Wilkins, Josiah Mann, James Drake, Charles Fullerton, & Samuel Judah. *Laws*, 1821-22, pp. 132-33.

For relief of securities of Robert Gill, late agent (William Caruthers, Thomas Turman, Isaac Brocaw). *Laws*, 1822-23, pp. 122-23.

Switzerland County

Formation of, effective Oct. 1, 1814. *Laws*, 1814 (Ewbank), pp. 538-42.

Regulation of town of Vevay. Trustees: John Francis Dufour, Thomas Gilleland, Benjamin Norton, Walter Clark, & Thomas Armstrong. *Laws*, 1815 (Ewbank), pp. 674-79.

Incorporation of Literary Society of Vevay. Directors: John Dumont, Daniel Dufour, Robert M. Trotter, Elisha Golay, Philo Averil, John F. Seibenthal, & George Coggshell. *Laws*, 1814 (Ewbank), pp. 735-37.

Incorporation of Seminary of Vevay. Trustees: James Rouse, John Dumont, Philo Averil, Elisha Golay, Daniel Dufour. *Laws*, 1815 (Ewbank), pp. 679-82.

Union County

Formation of, effective Feb. 1, 1821. *Laws*, 1820-21. pp. 126-27.

Joseph Hanna of Franklin Co., Beal Butler of Wayne Co., & Allen Crisler of Fayette Co. appted. to locate & establish seminary in Union Co. *Laws*, 1825, pp. 94-95.

Vanderburgh County

Formation of, effective Feb. 1, 1818. *Laws*, 1817-18 (special), p. 22.

John G. Chandler, admr. of estate of Asaph Chandler, authorized to sell land. *Laws*, 1818-19, pp. 119-21.

William Marrs of Washington Co. authorized to sell lots in Evansville conveyed to heirs of James Marrs. *Laws*, 1819-20, pp. 14-15.

Vigo County

Formation of, effective Feb.15, 1818. *Laws*, 1817-18 (special), p. 34.

Warrick County

Formation of, effective April 1, 1813. *Laws*, 1813 (Ewbank), pp. 348-50.

For relief of securities of John Upham, deceased, late tax collector. *Laws*, 1819-20, p. 8.

For benefit of heirs of Daniel Rhodes, deceased. *Laws*, pp. 65-66.

Jesse Gay, admr. of estate of John Sprinkle, authorized to make deeds for lots to John Upp & Ezekies (alias Ezekiel) Smith. *Laws*, 1823-24, p.60.

Relief of John Hunter, who purchased land with Jacob Warrick, deceased, *Laws*, 1813 (Ewbank), pp. 354-55.

Washington County

Formation of, effective Jan. 17, 1814. *Laws*, 1813-14 (Ewbank), pp. 446-48.

Regulation of town of Salem. Trustees: Thomas Beesley, Simeon Lamb, John DePauw, James Ferguson, & Thomas Weathers. *Laws*, 1814 (Ewbank), pp. 724-27.

Incorporation of Salem Grammar School. Trustees: Marston G. Clark, Benjamin Parke, John Kingsbury, Burr Bradley, Ebenezer Patrick, James Coffin. & Beebe Booth. *Laws*, 1823-24, pp. 75-78.

Incorporation of Walnut Ridge Library Company. Directors: Thomas & Samuel Denny, Samuel Brown. Stephen Akers, & George Hattabaugh. *Laws*, 1816-17, pp. 201-202.

Elisha Denny, agent, authorized to lease to Ruth McCleland the land on which she lives. *Laws*, 1822-23, pp. 132-33.

Wayne County

Formation of, effective Jan. 1, 1811. *Laws*, 1810 (Ewbank), pp. 108-11.

Regulation of town of Centreville. Trustees: Jeremiah Meek, James Jenkins, Thomas McCay, John Maxwell, & Job Huddleson. *Laws*, 1815 (Ewbank), pp. 682-84.

Regulation of town of Salisbury. Trustees: John Sutherland, George Hunt, David Harman, John C. Kibby, & David F. Sacket. *Laws*, pp. 666-70.

Relief of Thomas McCartney, David Harman, & Peter Weaver, sureties for John Turner, late sheriff. *Laws*, 1820-21, pp. 112-13.

BOARDS OF MEDICAL CENSORS TO REGULATE PRACTICE OF MEDICINE

1st district: Elias McNamee, Jacob Kuykendall, David M. Hale, Thomas Polke, Joel F. Casey. *2nd district:* Dr. Bradley of Salem, P. R. Allen, Andrew P. Hay, James B. Slaughter, Samuel Meriwether; *3rd district:* Jabez Percival, D. F. Sacket, D. Oliver, Jno. Howes, Ezra Ferris. *Laws*, 1816-17, pp. 161-65. *4th district:* William Trafton, Enoch Jones, Alva Pascho. *Laws*. 1819-20, pp. 66-67.

LAWS DISSOLVING MARRIAGES

David & Paulina Barker, formerly Paulina Moshier. 1813 (Ewbank), p. 431.

Benjamin V. and Sally Beckes, formerly Sally Harbin. 1811 (Ewbank), p. 237.

Lyman & Sally Beeman, formerly Sally Malott. 1821-22, p.81.

Henry S. & Marian Bornand, formerly Marian Galy. 1811 (Ewbank), pp. 223-24.

John & Mary Catt, formerly Mary B. Cooke. 1816-17, p. 235.

Josephus & Elizabeth Collett, formerly Elizabeth Tiffin. 1821-22, pp. 27-28.

John & Mary Daniels, formerly Mary Burge. 1815 (Ewbank), p. 655.

Peter & Sally Davidson. 1818-19, p. 133.

Daniel & Arrabella Davison. 1813 (Ewbank), pp. 458-59.

Ephraim & Elizabeth Green, formerly Elizabeth Purcell. 1813 (Ewbank), pp. 472-73.

Jonah & Elizabeth Green, formerly Elizabeth Purcell. 1813 (Ewbank), pp. 472-73.

Michael & Peggy Harnis. 1821-22, p. 15.

Josiah & Polly Jenkins, formerly Polly Hickey. 1821-22, p. 12. Lived Orange Co.

Willis & Dardania Kelly. 1823-24, pp. 11-12.

Green B. & Nancy League, formerly Nancy Dewees. 1823-24, p. 12.

Thomas P. & Elizabeth Lewis. 1823-24, pp. 12-13.

Crawford & Margaret McGee, formerly Margaret Thompson. 1820-21, p. 125. Lived Harrison Co.

John & Jane Reed, formerly Jane Knapper. 1819-20, pp. 62-63. Lived Fayette Co.

Issac & Elizabeth Richardson. 1811 (Ewbank), pp. 212-13. Lived Harrison Co.

Jacob & Jane Richardson. 1811 (Ewbank), pp. 211-12. Lived Harrison Co.

Charles & Hetty Sefret, formerly Hetty Mauzy. 1822-23, p. 135.

Nathan & Catharine Sellers, formerly Catharine Moffitt. 1821-22, p. 31.

Moses & Jane Spencer of Sullivan Co. 1823-24, p. 13.

Thomas & Maria H. Wardell, formerly Maria Pike. 1816-17, pp. 235-36.

Benjamin & Nancy Whitford & legalizing her marriage to Nehemiah Ives. 1814 (Ewbank), pp. 727-28.

Daniel & Anna Woodfell. 1816-17, p. 234.

RELIEF LAWS (NO COUNTY MENTIONED)

For James Besse & John Eastburn who pursued the late murderer John Dahman to Canada. *Laws*, 1821-22, pp. 3-4.

Adam Conrad, admr. of George Conrad, deceased, authorized to sell land. *Laws*, 1816-17, pp. 237-38.

Abigail Dickinson, admr. of Ebenezer Dickinson, deceased. *Laws*, 1817-18 (special), pp. 113-15. The law was repealed at the next session.

Payment authorized to Joseph W. Doke, inspector for 4th brigade. *Laws*, 1819-20, pp. 23-24.

William & Jane Fencher, admrs. of estate of John Fencher, required to purchase land for infant heirs. *Laws*, 1822-23, pp. 117-18.

For Daniel Fetter. *Laws*, 1810 (Ewbank), pp. 705-706.

For Salmon Fuller. *Ibid*.

Margaret Fulton, John Irvin, & John Anderson, guardians of infant heirs of Andrew Fulton, authorized to purchase real estate. *Laws*, 1819-20, pp. 28-29.

For James Garritt for damage caused by location of roads. *Laws*, 1823-24, p. 16.

James Maxwell & John G. Berry, guardians of infant heirs of Henry Heckey (?), authorized to expend a certain sum. *Laws*, 1821-22, pp. 42-43.

For James Hughes. *Laws*, 1810 (Ewbank), pp. 705-706.

For Jeremiah Lockwood, state seminary trustees authorized to pay. *Laws*, 1821-22, p. 13.

George Bentley & Elizabeth Barclay authorized to convey land to Ann Ludlow, she having paid Robert Barclay, deceased, for same. *Laws*, 1821-22, pp. 145-46.

For relief of Isaac Hudson & Amelia McMertry, admrs. of estate of John McMertry, deceased, & Tubby Bloyd. *Laws*, 1820-21, pp. 70-72.

For Daniel French for taking care of Robert Maffit of Pa. during his illness & death. *Laws*, 1815 (Ewbank), pp. 79, 655-56.

William Hurst, guardian of Andrew, Benjamin, James, Charles, John Josephus, & Evan Newton Morgan, heirs of John Morgan, authorized to purchase land. *Laws*, 1816-17, pp. 238-39.

The legislature of 1821-22 established a system of state roads, bringing together in one act provision made earlier for individual roads. See *Laws*, 1821-22, pp. 152-69. Commissioners appointed for each road were to mark and lay off the roads from the point of beginning to the point of termination, taking care to embrace the intermediate points mentioned in the law, and were to divide the roads into districts not exceeding five miles each. They then were to advertise in the respective counties through which each road passed that they would accept proposals or bids for opening and clearing the road and make contracts for same. After a contractor was designated, he had to give a bond for faithful performance and could then receive one third of the money contained in his proposal. The roads were to be cleared forty-eight feet in width, taking off all timber under eighteen inches in diameter even with the ground; that over eighteen inches could be cut at height of twelve inches. Gravel, stone, or timber could be taken from land adjoining the road, and used in marshy areas as a foundation. Commissioners were permitted to employ surveyors and chain men as needed.

Payments to contractors were made from the three percent fund, allocated by the Federal government from the net proceeds from the sale of land in the state. The numbering of the roads corresponds to the sections of the 1821-22 act, thus the provisions for No. 2 road are in Sec. 2 of the act; sec. 1 contained preliminary data. The names of the commissioners appointed to locate the roads are given in the act; the names of the contractors are taken from the *Senate Journal*, 1822-23, pp. 256-70. Contractors often for more than one section of road. No. 2 Evansville to Terre Haute. Comrs. John J. Neely of Gibson Co., Samuel Emmerson of Knox Co., & James Wason of Sullivan Co. Contractors receiving payments were:

John James	John Cody	Elijah Mays
John Owens	Arch'd M'Clure	Josiah L. Holmes
John Welsh	John M'Clure	Charles Mail
G.R.C. Sullivan	James Dunn	James Mail
James Welton	Elisha Moyes	David C. Nuckerson
Robert Stormont	David Nuckerson	John Hall
John Sids	David Niglay	Bazil Brown
Alex'r Johnson	Jno. M. Coleman	Henry French
Almarza D. Foster	John Osborn	Dan'l Vickery
Elias Wheeler	James Andre	

No. 3. Called the Petersburg Road, extending from the Wabash River to the "high banks" of White River. Comrs. James Robb of Gibson Co., Henry Hopkins and John Case of Pike Co. Contractors were:

James Joy	James M'Cune	Henry Brenton, Jr.
John Case	Peter Brenton	Dan'l M'Fetridge
Henry Beck		

No. 4. Called the Springfield Road, it ran from Mount Vernon to Princeton. Comrs.: William Casey & Dan Lynn of Posey Co. & Jesse Emmerson of Gibson Co. Contractors were:

James V. Drake	Jno. Schnee	Tho's Lovett
John Waller	William Nelson	Dan'l M. Garey
Henry Casey	Jesse Emmerson	James Smith
Elias Altigeir	Laban Day	Robert Downey
James Robb		

No. 5. Called the Boonville Road, it extended from Mt. Prospect to Petersburg. Comrs.: John M'Cord & George W. Zevault of Warrick Co. & Isaac Montgomery of Pike Co.: The following year comrs. Peter Brenton, Charles DeBruler, & Zachariah F. Selby of Pike Co. were appointed to relocate the road. *Laws*, 1822-23, pp. 75-76. Contractors for the road were:

Henry Brenton	Daniel Smith	Elijah Dedman
William Buckler	Adam Snyder	Kelly Johnson
William Barker	John Kilpatrick	William Hopkins
John Brownlee		

No. 6. Called the Washington Road, it extended from the Highlands on White River to Indianapolis. Comrs.: Elijah Hammon of Pike Co., Benjamin Stafford of Greene, & William M'Cormick of Daviess Co. Contractors were:

James Leaverton	Jacob Cutler	Philip Hedges
Chas. Sinks	John Dieson	Richard Osborn
John Andrews	John Andrews	Samuel Read
Sam'l Ventrees	Sam'l Dyer	Philip Shintaffer
Aaron Freeland	Peter Herrington	Aaron Freelow
Emanuel Ventrees	William M'Cormick	Seth Reddick
Elijah Chapman	David Johnston	Thomas Irons
Thomas Bull	Reuben McDaniel	John E. Clark
Thomas Read	J. W. Wines	John Johnson
Christopher Ladd		

No. 7. Called the Rockport Road, it ran from that town to Bloomington. Comrs.: Samuel Snyder of Spencer Co., Joseph D. Clements of Martin Co., & Michael Buskirk of Monroe Co. Contractors were:

Levi V. Lockheart	John Bausman	James Seals
John Henderson	Michael Buskirk	Zedekiah Wood
William Mattox	William Wright	Adam Jameison
John Mattox	Even Ross	Sam'l Moor
John Armstrong	John Fulfer	John Gray
Green & Pollard	James M'Elwain	Azel Dorsey
Nathan Fisher	Thomas Paygn	Zachariah Barnet
James Doke	Absalom Roby	James Prentiss
Joseph D. Clements	Andrew Denton	

No. 8. Called the Horse Shoe Bend Road, it extended from Fredonia in Crawford Co. to Indianapolis via Paoli, Palestine (now Bedford), and Bloomington. Comrs.: John Anderson of Lawrence Co., Samuel Chambers of Orange Co., & Thomas Posey of Harrison Co. Contractors were:

Isaac Sterns	Alex'r McDaniel	John Henderson
Joseph Hill	Isaac Anderson	Samuel Mitlock
Samuel Chambers	S.M. Leavenworth	David Mitlock
John Anderson	Joseph Johnson	William M'Cormick
Joseph Hill	Jonathan Braxton	John H. Farnham
Absolam Freeman	William Elrod	John R. Porter
Thomas I. Mattock	Thomas Irons	Thomas Lindley
Simpson Kilgore	William Irons	

No. 9. Called the Mauk's Ferry Road, it ran from the present Mauckport to Indianapolis via Corydon, Salem, and Brownstown. Comrs.: George Boon of Harrison Co., Jonathan Lyon of Washington Co., & John Craig of Jackson Co. A new set of comrs. were named by the following legislature to relocate the road. They were: Robert Weathers, Henry Boas, Thomas Kindell, all of Jackson Co. Still another set of comrs. were to change the road where it crossed the Muscatatuck River. They were: William Baird, George W. Boon, & Richard Beem. Jonathan Wright, Conrad Huddle, & Robert Baldwin of Harrison Co. were named as "reviewers." Contractors on this road were:

Jesse Stanley	John Tipton	Charles Crab
H. M'Callen	William Nicholson	John Craig
William Rodman	Richard Beam	Baird & Boon

No. 10. Called the Bono Road, it extended from New Albany to Bono in Lawrence County by way of Salem. Comrs.: Seth Woodruff of Floyd Co. & William Richards & Nathan Trueblood of Washington Co. Contractors were:

David H. Allison	Valentine Crafts	William Richards
Robert Evans	Geo. Holsapple	Hugh McPheters
Sam'l Marrs	William Jean	Jacob Bixler
John Prow	David Allison	Weth Woodruff
Robert Nuckols	Hugh Keyh	Sam'l B. Moor
Thomas Wilson	Fred'k Phillips	John Breedlove
William Penny	Jehoyida Swanson	John Dalton
Dan'l Shoemaker	Jno. B. Howard	John Milroy
Sam'l Martin	William Vest	William McNeely
Robert R. Stewart	Jacob Smith	Samuel Vest
Christian Pro	Lewis Brock	Joseph Akers
Robert Stewart	Jesse Hickman	

No. 11. The New Albany and Vincennes Road. Comrs.: Benjamin V. Beckes of Knox County, John G. Clendennin of Orange Co., & Maurice Morris of Floyd Co. Contractors were:

Thomas Lindley	John McDonald	William Fuller
James Harris	William Lindley	Maurice Morris
Isaac Lamb	Abraham Holliday	James Haynes
Morris Morris	Samuel Willson	Joel Scribner
Benj. Freeland	John D. Davis	J.G. Clendenin
George Newton	James Willson	John Brown
Abram Markle	Emanuel Ventrees	

No. 12. The Jeffersonville Road ran from that town to John Fleener's in Washington Co. Comrs.: Orlando Raymond of Clark Co. & William Lindley & Joel Combs of Washington Co. Contractors were:

Ebenezer Patrick	Elcazer Wheelock	Joel Combs
William P. Twilley	R.H. Murray	

No. 13. Called the McDonald's Ferry Road, it ran from the ferry near Charlestown to Brownstown. Comrs.: William Crenshaw of Jackson Co. & Evan Shelby & John M. Lemon of Clark Co. The road had been projected by the 1819-20 legislature with the following comrs.: Joseph Bartholomew & John Norris of Clark Co. & William Naylor & Jonas Crane of Jackson Co. A road from Jeffersonville to Brownstown was also projected with comrs. Nathaniel B. Palmer, Henry Ristine, & Alexander C. Craig. *Laws*, 1819-20, pp. 100, 102. Benjamin Carr & John Carr contracted to building the road from McDonald's Ferry to Brownstown.

No. 14. Called the Bethlehem Road, it ran from that town in Clark Co. to New Washington, Lexington, crossed the Muscatatuck at the State ford, thence to lower falls of the Driftwood where it met the road from Brownstown to Indianapolis. Comrs. were William Plasket of Clark Co., James Ward of Scott Co. & William Reddick of Jackson Co. Contractors were :

John W. Green	Daniel Gorman	John M'Caslin
John Hollinbeck	Joseph Ogden	Henry Brady
Solomon Reddick	Solomon Moffitt	James Ward
William Plasket.		

No. 15. The Madison to Indianapolis Road ran by way of Vernon and Columbus. Comrs. were: Joshua Wilkinson of Jefferson Co., William C. Bramwell of Jennings Co., & John Parker of Bartholomew Co. A portion of the road north of Columbus was relocated the following year by comrs. John Lewis of Bartholomew Co., Thomas Russel & Joseph Young of Johnson Co. who were to meet at house of William R. Hensley. Contractors on the Madison to Indianapolis Road were:

Sam'l Chapple	William C. Bramwell	John Vawter
William Brown	Jeremiah Grover	Lodge & Arion
William Sanford	William Milled	R. C. Talbott
Josiah Andrews	John Spann	Joshua Wilkinson
Orin Munson	Anthony Badgeley	Baird & Boon
J. Parker (payt to heirs)	Wash'n Ferguson	John Badgeley
Tho. Rosebery Jr.		

No. 16. The Vevay to Versailles Road was laid out by Simeon Slawson & Joseph Mailen of Switzerland Co. & A. W. Stewart of Ripley. It had been projected the year before with John Gilleland & Jonas Baldwin of Switzerland Co. & Joseph Bentley of Ripley Co. as comrs. (*Laws*, 1819-20, p. 104). Contractors were:

Joseph Bentley	Geo. W. Voiles	Montgomery Allen
Newton Hart	Thomas M'Intire	Simeon Slawson
John Gilleland	Leeman Andrews	Joseph Malin
Nathaniel Cotton	Huston Martin	John Parsons
Henry Banta	A. W. Stewart	Lawrence Nichol
Benjamin Cole	George Collins	Thomas Davis

No. 17. The Lawrenceburg to Indianapolis Road was laid out by Stephen Ludlow, Timothy Davis, & John Walker of Dearborn Co. It had been projected by the 1820-21 legislature with comrs. Stephen Ludlow, James Vaughn, & David Guard of Dearborn Co. & Amos Boardman of Ripley Co. (*Laws*, 1820-21, pp. 21-23). Contractors were Timothy Davis, Joseph Bentley, & Isaac Dunn.

No. 18. The Brookville Road ran from the Ohio state line east of Brookville to Indianapolis. Comrs. were David Mount, Samuel Shirk, & John Davis of Franklin. It had first been projected by the 1819-20 legislature with Matthew Sparks, Robert Luce, and Hezekiah Mount as commissioners. (*Laws*, 1819-20, pp. 98-99). Contractors were:

Sam'l Goudie	Sam'l Shirk	Peter B. Millspaw
Robert Brower	Henry Misner	Powel Hulick
William Gordon	Andrew Reed	H. Beakley & Graves
Thomas Winscot	Peter Vandyke	John Davis
Jonathan Eads	Robert Fossett	

No. 19. Called the Connersville Road, it ran from the Ohio state line through Connersville to Indianapolis. Comrs.: John Perrin & Stanhope Royster of Fayette Co. & Zachariah Ferguson of Union Co. Stanhope Royster was the only contractor listed.

No. 20. Known as the Centerville Road, ran from the house of Peter Fleming on the Ohio state line through Salisbury (formerly the county seat of Wayne County) to Centerville. Comrs.: James Peggs, Levi Jones, & John Scott of Wayne Co. When the road was first projected two years earlier the commissioners were Robert Morrison, David P. Fleming, and John McKee. The contractors were:

Elijah Lacy	John Shank	Elisha Long
Sam'l Stinson	William Scott	Elias Willits
James Scott	John Scott	D. J. P. Fleming
William Seward	Patrick Baird	L. M. Jones
Benjamin Parsons	John Smith	Thos. M'Cartney
William Cook	Philip Stiggleman	John Sutherland
William M'Lane		

No. 21. The Winchester Road began at the Ohio state line where the Greenville (Ohio) struck that line, through Winchester, and joined the Richmond road 20 miles from Indianapolis. Comrs.: Joshua Foster, John Way, & Ishem Puckett of Randolph Co. John Way was also the contractor.

No. 22. Indianapolis to Terre Haute Road. Contractors were:

James Blake, Indianapolis	John Hamilton, Vigo Co.	John Britton
John M. Coleman, Vigo Co.	Thomas H. Clarke	Robert Patterson
Benjamin Johnston,	Jesse Rollins	Abraham Lewis

No. 23. The Rising Sun Road ran from that town to Versailles. Comrs. were John Barricklow & James Lewis of Dearborn & John Hunter of Ripley Co. It had been projected two years earlier with comrs. Abel C. Pepper & John Watts of Dearborn Co. & Joseph Bentley of Ripley Co. Bentley was the contractor. (*Laws*, 1819-20, p. 101).

Other road legislation prior to that setting up a state system and later.

The roads are listed alphabetically according to the starting point.

Aurora to Napoleon. Comrs.: Jesse L. Holman, Abel C. Pepper of Dearborn Co., David Riggs of Ripley Co. *Laws*, 1822-23, pp. 57-58.

Bloomington to Columbus. Comrs.: Darles Griffith & Akina A. Wiles of Bartholomew Co. & William Jackson, of Monroe Co. *Laws*, 1922-23, pp. 60-61.

Cypresstown on Ohio River to Boonville. Comrs.: William Briscoe, Samuel Hindman, Silas Daviess of Warrick Co. *Laws*, 1823-24, p. 25.

Brookville to Harrison. Comrs.: Isaac Morgan & William Brundage of Dearborn Co. & James Johnson of Franklin. *Laws*, 1823-24, p. 21.

Brookville to Vernon via Versailles. Comrs.: John Quick of Franklin Co., William Wilson of Ripley Co., Samuel Campbell of Jennings. *Laws*, 1819-20, pp. 106-107.

Brookville to Versailles. Comrs.: Thomas Herndon and William Campbell of Franklin Co. & James Montgomery of Ripley. *Laws*, 1822-23, p. 61.

Brownstown to Bloomington. Comrs.: William A. Beatty, John Kindred of Jackson Co. & John Griffith of Monroe. *Laws*, 1819-20, pp. 101-102.

Charlestown to Corydon. Comrs.: John Harbison of Harrison Co., Absolom Little & John Lopp of Clark Co. Two years later the same road was projected with John Harrison of Harrison Co., John Flickner of Floyd Co., & Henry Bottorff of Clark Co. as commissioners. *Laws,* 1819-20, p. 106; 1822-23, pp. 69-70.

Charlestown to Madison. Comrs.: Walter Wheatly & John L. Pitman of Clark Co. & John Anderson of Jefferson Co. *Laws,* 1823-24, p. 38.

Corydon to Princeton via Mount Sterling. Comrs.: Nathaniel Holcroft, Amstrong Brandon, Harrison Co., Alexander B. McCray of Crawford Co., & Henry Hopkins of Pike Co. *Laws,* 1819-20, p. 103.

Corydon to Salem. Comrs.: James B. Slaughter & John Hurst, Jr. of Harrison Co. & Marston G. Clark of Washington Co. *Laws,* 1819-20, pp. 102-103.

Evansville to White River via Sandersville & Princeton. Comrs.: John M. Dunham of Vanderburgh Co., William Harrington & William Barker of Gibson Co. *Laws,* 1819-20, pp. 104-105.

Fort Wayne to the Piqua Road. Comrs.: Benjamin B. Kercheval, Alexander Ewing & Samuel Hanna. *Laws,* 1823-24, p. 25.

Half Moon Spring to Washington via French Lick. Comrs.: William D. Lynch of Orange Co., Cortland Seeley & John Rinehart of Martin Co., & James Alford of Daviess Co. *Laws,* 1823-24, p. 24.

French Lick to Hindostan. Comrs.: Jeremiah Jones & Isaac Smith of Martin Co. & Joel Charles of Orance Co. *Laws,* 1823-24, pp. 37-38.

Harmony to Poke Patch in Warrick Co. Comrs.: Benjamin Carter of Posey Co., Reuben Emmerson of Gibson Co., Zachariah Skelton of Warrick Co. *Laws,* 1825, pp. 83-84.

Hindostan to Carlisle. Comrs.: Julius Johnson & John Riley of Martin Co. & William Watson of Daviess Co. *Laws,* 1823-24, p. 24.

Indianapolis to Crawfordsville. Comrs.: Samuel M'George of Marion Co., Uriah Hults of Hendricks Co., & John M'Cullough of Montgomery Co. *Laws,* 1823-24, pp. 25-26.

Indianapolis to Fort Wayne & the State Line. Comrs.: James Blake of Marion Co., Alexander Ewing of Allen Co. & William Conner of Hamilton Co. *Laws,* 1823-24, p. 21.

Jacobs' Ford on Silver Creek to Slate Ford on Muscatatuck River via Pine Lick. Comrs.: Daniel P. Faulkner & Joseph Bell of Clark Co. & James Craig of Scott Co. *Laws,* 1823-24, p. 20.

Lawrenceburg to Fort Wayne via Brookville, Connersville, Centerville & Winchester. Comrs.: Henry M'Kinsey of Dearborn Co., Solomon Allen of Franklin Co., & Thomas McCoy of Wayne Co. *Laws,* 1822-23, pp. 43-45. The following year there was a new law regarding the road from Lawrenceburg to Brookville with comrs. John Dawson & David Guard of Dearborn & Samuel Rockafeller & Solomon Allen of Franklin. *Laws,* 1823-24, p. 22.

Lawrenceburg to Madison via Rising Sun & Vevay. Comrs.: Abel C. Pepper, Thomas Armstrong, & David McCoy. Another act by the same legislature appointed comrs. to lay out a road between the same two points by the nearest route. Comrs.: Richard Hopkins of Jefferson Co., William Ross of Ripley Co. & Samuel C. Vance of Dearborn. *Laws,* 1822-23, pp. 24-25, 58-59.

Lawrenceburg to Napoleon. Comrs.: Benjamin I. Blythe & Lemuel Moss of Dearborn Co., Wilson A. Stewart of Ripley. *Laws,* 1819-20, p. 99.

Lawrenceburg to Winchester. Comrs.: Jesse Hunt of Dearborn Co., Edward Toner of Franklin Co., James Craig of Fayette Co., Isaac Julian of Wayne Co., & John Wright of Randolph, to meet at home of Joseph H. Coburn in Lawrenceburg. *Laws,* 1819-20, pp. 97-99. The following legislature appointed to new set of commrs. for the same road: Thomas Palmer of Dearborn Co., William Templeton of Franklin Co., John Myers of Fayette Co., Jacob N. Booker of Wayne Co., & Charles Conway of Randolph Co. *Laws,* 1820-21, pp. 21-23.

Leavenworth to Terre Haute. Comrs.: John Benefield of Sullivan Co., Johnson Ferris, Sr. of Martin Co., John Pennick & Abram M'Clelland of Orange Co. *Laws,* 1821-22, pp. 124-27. The following legislature passed an act to revise the road. Comrs.: Andrew Kincaid of Crawford Co., Philip Conrad of Dubois Co., Julius Johnson & Caleb Rinehart of Martin Co., & William Harrod of Orange Co. *Laws,* 1822-23, pp. 131-32.

Leavenworth to Peter Stalcup's in Orange Co. & Stalcup's to Orleans. Comrs. Levi Nugent of Lawrence Co., Benjamin Bosley of Orange Co., Seth M. Leavenworth of Crawford Co. *Laws,* 1823-24, pp. 21, 25.

James McKay's on Ohio River to meet road from Vevay to Indianapolis. Comrs.: Abisha McKay, James Landsdale, Jacob Vanosdal. *Laws,* 1823-24, p. 25.

Madison to Fort Wayne via Versailles. Comrs.: Robert Branham of Jefferson Co., Merit S. Craig of Ripley Co., William B. Laughlin of Rush Co. *Laws,* 1822-23, pp. 59-60.

Madison to Greensburg. Comrs.: Thomas Wise of Jefferson Co., James M'Closky of Ripley Co., & John House of Decatur Co. *Laws,* 1823-24, p. 24.

Madison to Jeffersonville. Comrs.: Gerardus Ryker of Jefferson Co., William Plasket & Joseph Bartholomew of Clark Co. *Laws,* 1823-24, p. 24.

Madison to Lawrenceburg. Comrs.: Abraham M'Coy of Jefferson Co., Henry Banta of Switzerland Co., & Timothy Davis of Dearborn Co. *Laws,* 1823-24, p. 24.

Madison to Vernon. John Vawter & William C. Bramwell appointed to lay out. *Laws,* 1819-20, p. 97.

Madison to Versailles. Comrs.: Thomas Boicourt of Jefferson Co., Wilson Buchanan & John Richey of Ripley Co. *Laws,* 1819-20, pp. 103-104.

From Napoleon to meet the road from Greensburg to Columbus. Comrs.: Philip Riggs & William Wilson of Ripley Co. & Dudley Taylor of Decatur Co. *Laws,* 1823-24, p. 20.

New Albany to Bloomington via Palestine. Comrs.: David M. Hale, Floyd Co., James Gregory, Lawrence Co., & Roderick Rollins, Monroe Co. *Laws,* 1819-20, pp. 107-108.

New Albany to Princeton via Corydon. Comrs.: Anderson Long of Floyd Co., Samual Flanagan and James B. Slaughter of Harrison Co., Martin H. Tucker of Crawford Co., & Alexander Devin of Gibson Co.; they were to meet at house of David M. Hale in New Albany. *Laws,* 1820-21, pp. 21-23. Peter Kintner, Harrison Co., added to the commission the following year. 1821-22, pp. 45-46.

New Albany to Hindostan via Fredericksburg & Paoli. Comrs.: John Eastburn of Floyd Co., John G. Clendenen & Jonathan Lindley of Orange Co., Frederick Sholts of Martin Co. *Laws,* 1819-20, p. 108.

New Albany to Salem. Comrs.:Jonathan Lyon & Henry Dewalt of Washington Co., Charles Paxon & John K. Graham of Floyd Co., & James Packwood of Clark Co. *Laws,* 1819-20, pp. 99-100.

New Albany to Vernon via Charlestown & Lexington. Comrs.: Absolom Little of Floyd Co., Robert Robertson of Clark Co., Achilles Vawter of Jennings Co., & James Ward of Scott Co. *Laws,* 1819-20, p. 107.

New Castle to Indianapolis. Comrs.: Samuel Pickering of Henry Co., John Roberts of Madison Co., & Jeremiah Johnson of Marion Co. *Laws,* 1823-24, pp. 20-21.

New London (in Jefferson Co.) to Paoli via Lexington & Salem. Comrs.: Jonathan Carter & James Ward of Scott Co., James McKinney of Washington Co., & Joseph W. Doke of Orange Co. *Laws,* 1819-20, p. 109.

New York in Switzerland Co. meet road from Vevay to Versailles. Comrs. William Campbell, Joseph Kulp, Jerub Richmond. *Laws,* 1823-24, pp. 23-24.

Ohio State line to Connersville via Fairfield. Comrs.: Edgehill Burnside, Robert Swan, Morris McCray. *Laws,* 1819-20, pp. 108-109.

Ohio State line to Indianapolis via Liberty, Brownsville, Connersville, Rushville. Comrs.: John Perrin, Stanhope Royster, Zachariah Ferguson. *Laws,* 1822-23, pp. 70-72.

Paoli to Petersburg via French Lick & Portersville. Comrs.: James Ferris, William Edmonston, James Brenton. *Laws,* 1822-23, p. 59.

Petersburg to Washington. Comrs.: Peter Ammermand & William Ballard of Daviess Co. & Franklin Sawyer of Pike Co. *Laws,* 1823-24, pp. 44-46.

Poke Patch in Warrick Co. to Harmony. Comrs.: Zachariah Skelton & John Luce of Warrick Co. & Samuel Scott of Vanderburgh. *Laws,* 1819-20, p. 105.

Rockport to Vincennes. Comrs.: James Starke of Spencer Co., Zachariah Skelton of Warrick Co., & Isaac Montgomery of Pike Co. *Laws,* 1819-20, p. 102.

Rome to Paoli. Comrs.: John Riggs & John Cassedy of Perry Co. & Zachariah Lindley of Orange Co. *Laws,* 1823-24, p. 35.

Sand Run, Fairfield, & Somerset to Rushville. Comrs.: Jacob Bake, James Webster, & John Davis of Franklin Co. *Laws,* 1823-24, pp. 21-22.

Salem to Bono, review of road. Comrs.: James McKinney, Robert McIntire, & Absalom Sargeant of Washington Co. *Laws,* 1823-24, pp. 32-34.

Salem to Vernon. Comrs.: John Vawter of Jennings Co., David Fouts of Washington Co., & Harper Cochran of Scott Co. *Laws,* 1823-24, p. 25.

Terre Haute to Crawfordsville. Comrs.: Jacob Bell of Parke Co., James Smith of Montgomery Co., & Peter Allen of Vigo Co. *Laws,* 1823-24, pp. 18-20.

Terre Haute to Fort Wayne. Comrs.: John M. Coleman of Vigo, Josephus Collett of Parke Co., & Williamson Dunn of Montgomery Co. *Laws,* 1822-23, pp. 127-28.

Terre Haute to Illinois state line. Comrs.: John M. Coleman, Israel Harris, William Ray. *Laws,* 1825, pp. 82-83.

Tobacco Landing in Harrison Co. to Levenworth's Mill. Comrs.: James Pell, George Boon, & George Bentley of Harrison Co. *Laws,* 1823-24, p. 26.

Vernon to Fort Wayne. Comrs. William T. Stott of Jennings Co., Hiram Dayton of Decatur Co., & Adam Conde of Rush Co. *Laws,* 1823-24, p. 26.

Vernon to Stringtown in Jackson Co. Comrs.: William Ramsey & William Baker of Jennings Co. & John Stanfield of Jackson Co. *Laws,* 1823-24, p. 21.

Vernon to Versailles. Comrs.: John B. New & John Bonner of Jennings Co. & James Ray of Ripley Co. *Laws,* 1823-24, p. 25.

From "high banks" on White River in Pike Co. to meet road from Princeton to Boonville. Comrs.: John Crow, John R. Montgomery & Thomas Pride of Pike Co. *Laws,* 1823-24, p. 38.

Winchester to Indianapolis and Crawfordsville. Act to alter road to Indianapolis laid out by John Way, Joshua Foster, & Jesse Mooreman. *Laws,* 1822-23, p. 77. From Indianapolis to Crawfordsville. Comrs.: Alexis Jackson of Marion Co., William C. Blackmore & Curtis Mallery of Hamilton Co. *Laws,* 1823-24, p. 26.

Allen County

Papers regarding estate of Isaac Burnett transferred from Randolph to Allen County. *Laws*, 1830-31 (special), p. 106.

Bartholomew County

Election in 1821 of trustees Newton C. Jones, Nathan Thompson, Elias Bedford, John C. Hubbard, William Herod, David Deitz, Benjamin F. Wallace, and John Glanton confirmed and their proceedings legalized. *Laws*, 1825-26, pp. 39-40.

Boone County

Formation of, effective April 1, 1830. *Laws*, 1829-30, pp. 31-33.

Carroll County

Formation of, effective May 1, 1828. *Laws*, 1827-28, pp. 21-22.

Cass County

Formation of, effective April 13, 1829. *Laws*, 1828-29, pp. 26-27. Incorporation of Eel River Seminary. Trustees: John Tipton, Hugh B. McKeen, Gillis McBean, William Scott, Alexander Chamberlain, Joseph Barron, Hiram Todd, Chauncey Carter, John Smith, Sr. *Laws*, 1828-29, pp. 134-35.

Clark County

Relief for heirs of Benjamin Warner deceased for damage done by road from McDonald's Ferry to Brownstown. *Laws*, 1825-26, pp. 66-67.

Incorporation of town of Jeffersonville. Trustees: Athanasius Wathan, James Keigwin, William H. Hurst, Charles Sleade, John R. Winn. *Laws*, 1829-30, pp. 57-60.

Marriage of William Wright and Many (Mary ?) Inerd, solemnized by Rev. Leroy Smith on Nov. 5, 1807, legalized. *Laws*, 1825-26, p. 37.

Clinton County

Formation of, effective March 1, 1830. *Laws*, 1829-30, pp. 33-35.

Crawford County

Name of John Smith of Levenworth changed to John Lucius Smith. *Laws*, 1828-29, p. 78.

Incorporation of Levenworth Seminary: Trustees: John L. Smith, Elam Wiley, Andrew Beers, James B. Davidson, Seth M. Levenworth. *Laws*, 1830-31 (special), pp. 58-60.

Dearborn County

Incorporation of Cambridge Academy. Trustees: John Dawson, Andrew Ray, Samuel Goucher. *Laws*, 1825-26, pp. 21-22.

Act for benefit of persons likely to suffer from destruction of courthouse by fire on March 6, 1826. *Laws*, 1826-27, pp. 53-57.

Amos Bonestel & Elizabeth Wright, admrs. of estate of Peter B. Wright, authorized to sell land in sec. 25, T5, R3W. *Laws*, 1826-27, pp. 61-62.

Part of land purchased by Thomas & John Watts in sec. 29, T5, R3W to be sold. *Laws*, 1827-28, pp. 77-78.

Incorporation of Lawrenceburgh Bridge Co. to erect bridge over Tanners Creek. Comrs. to sell stock: Oliver Heustis, Mark McCracken, Jeremiah Phiney, William S. Durbin, Amos Lane, Jabez Percival, William Tate. *Laws*, 1830-31 (special), pp. 25-28.

School section 16 in T6, R1W, illegally leased to Robert Faulkner, Abraham Everson, Samuel Lawford, to be deeded to John J. Akin, Alexander Walker, & John J. Livingston. *Laws*, 1830-31 (special), p. 101.

Delaware County

Formation of, effective April 1, 1827. *Laws*, 1826-27, pp. 12-14.

Dubois County

Comrs. appted to relocate county seat now at Portersville. *Laws*, 1828-29, pp. 131-34; 1829-30, pp. 38-41.

Relief for James Faris, trustee of county seminary. *Laws*, 1830-31 (special), p. 104.

Elkhart County

Formation of, effective April 1, 1830. *Laws*, 1829-30, pp. 29-31.

Fayette County

Proceedings of trustees James Veatch, Elijah Corbin, & W. C. Jones, for school section in T13N, R13E, legalized. Same for trustees Aaron Houghman, Charles Hubbard, Aaron Delebar in T14N, R13E. *Laws*, 1825-26, pp. 40-41, 66.

Edmund I. Kidd, Theodore R. Lewis, & Meredith Helm appointed trustees to build bridge over West Fork of White-water at Connersville. *Laws*, 1830-31 (special), pp. 13-15.

Incorporation of First School Society. Trustees: James Kerr, Morgan W. Larimore, Thomas Logan. *Laws*, 1830-31 (special), p. 60.

Floyd County

Diana M. Bulleitt, admr. of Thomas Bulleitt, authorized to sell real estate for benefit of infant heirs. *Laws*, 1826-27, pp. 58-59.

Trustees of First Presbyterian Church, New Albany (Elias Ayers, Mason C. Fitch, James Shields, Charles Woodruff, Asahel Clapp) authorized to relocate. *Laws*, 1828-29, p. 128.

Fountain County

Formation of, effective April 1, 1826. *Laws*, 1825-26, p. 13.

Proceedings of Evan Hinton, supt. of school section in T21N, R7W, considered valid. *Laws*, 1826-27, p. 80.

Franklin County

Proceedings of school trustees legalized. James S. Coalscott, Andrew Reed, Amos Church in T9N, R2W; James Webb, Jacob Blacklidge, Joseph Price in T12N, R13E. *Laws*, 1826-27, pp. 80-81.

Incorporation of Franklin Cotton Mfg. Co. Comrs.: Nathan D. Gallion, Richard Tyner, Enoch McCarty, William C. Rogers, Samuel Goodwin, John Clingman. *Laws*, 1827-28, pp. 35-39.

Incorporation of county seminary. Trustees: Thomas W. Coalscott, William McCleery, Augustus Jocelyn, James A. Lowes, Abraham Lee, David Mount, Joseph Meeks, William R. Morris, John Davis, John Wynn, William Sims. *Laws*, 1829-30, pp. 155-156.

Gibson County

Former trustees of Princeton Academy, Alexander Devin, Robert Milburn, & Samuel Hall, authorized to deed lot to county seminary. *Laws*, 1826-27, p. 52.

Incorporation of Princeton Library Company. Trustees: John I. Neely, Charles Harrington, Charles D. Bourne, John Brownlee, Robert Stockwell, Samuel Hall. *Laws*, 1830-31 (special), p. 61.

Grant County

Formation of, effective April 1, 1831. Named for Samuel & Moses Grant of Kentucky who were killed in battle with Indians in 1789. *Laws*, 1830-31 (special), pp. 16-18.

Greene County

Alexander Craig authorized to erect mill dam across West Fork of White River in sec. 7, T8N, R5W. *Laws*, 1826-27, pp. 37-38.

Hancock County

Formation of, effective Jan. 26, 1827, date of passage. *Laws*, 1826-27, pp. 84-85. Organization of, effective March 1, 1828. 1827-28, pp. 19-20.

School section 16 in T15N, R7E to be leased to Othniel Sweem for mill site. *Laws*, 1827-28, p. 114.

Harrison County

Rebecca Heth, surviving admr. of Hervey Heth, authorized to sell real estate. *Laws*, 1825-26, p. 3.

Incorporation of county seminary. Trustees: Thomas Posey, Peter Kintner, Armstrong Brandon, Daniel C. Lane, David G. Mitchell. *Laws*, 1826-27, pp. 90-91.

Accounts of trustees Peter Charley, Elijah Hurst, & John Watkins of congressional T3S, R4E to be paid. *Laws*, 1827-28, p. 72.

Sum of $200 appropriated for bridge over Big Indian Creek on Mauck's Ferry Road. Walter Pennington did stone work on bridge. *Laws*, 1829-30, p. 116.

Hendricks County

Execr. of estate of William Ballard authorized to convey certain lands to Thomas J. Matlock. *Laws*, 1826-27, pp. 59-60.

Henry County

Conviction of Thomas Wyatt for rape of Telitha Foster to be erased. *Laws*, 1827-28, p. 75.

Jefferson County

Relief for William Reed for land sold to him in 1818 by Andrew Fulton, an alien, in sec. 30, T3N, R10E. *Laws*, 1825-26, pp. 64-65.

Polly Branham, admr. of Lindsfield Branham, authorized to sell land in sec. 21, T4N, R10E. *Laws*, 1826-27, p. 60.

Incorporation of Hanover Academy. Trustees: John Finley Crowe, James H. Johnson [Johnston], Williamson Dunn, George Logan, John M. Dickey, Samuel G. Lowry, Samuel Smock, William Reed, Samuel Gregg, Jeremiah Sullivan. *Laws*, 1828-29, pp. 136-37.

Incorporation of County Seminary Society. Trustees: Victor King, John Sheets, William Robinson, Gamaliel Taylor, John McIntire, Milton Stapp, Howard Watts, John P. Paul, James F. D. Lanier. *Laws*, 1829-30, pp. 157-59.

Incorporation of Madison Insurance Company. Comrs. to sell stock: John King, William Dutton, William J. Lodge, George W. Leonard, John Alling, Howard Watts, Robert Craig. *Laws*, 1830-31 (special), pp. 31-33.

Appropriation for Claudius G. Brown for his claim against Vincennes University. *Laws*, 1829-30, p. 107.

Proceedings of Isaac R. Finch, supt. of school section in T19N, R8E, legalized. *Laws*, 1829-30, p. 153.

Marion County

Incorporation of Indianapolis Steam Mill Co. Directors: Nicholas McCarty, James M. Ray, William Sanders, Noah Noble, Daniel Yandes. *Laws*, 1827-28, pp. 41-44.

Relief for John M. Coonfield for improvements made on school section 16 in T14N, R4E. *Laws*, 1830-31 (special), pp. 99-100.

Relief for David Buchanan, security for Joseph C. Reed, deceased. *Laws*, 1830-31 (special), p. 108.

Martin County

Comrs. appointed to relocate county seat then at Hindostan. *Laws*, 1827-28, pp. 16-18.

Knox County

Incorporation of Wabash Insurance Company. Board of directors: Samuel Smith, Samuel Judah, John Law, Homer Johnson, William Polke, William Burtch, Samuel Tomlinson, David S. Bonner, John C. Riley of Vincennes; John I. Neely of Princeton; James G. Read of Daviess Co.; James Galletly of Owen Co.; John R. Porter of Vermillion Co.; Lucius H. Scott & Demas Deming of Terre Haute. *Laws*, 1830-31 (special), pp. 33-37.

Jane Dubois, now Jane Shuler, to receive title to land purchased for her by her brother-in-law John Smith. *Laws*, 1830-31 (special), p. 104.

Lawrence County

John Hammersly authorized to erect wing dam at Indian ford on East Fork of White River near Bono. *Laws*, 1826-27, p. 38.

Sum of $249 appropriated to build bridge over Salt Creek where the road from Bedford to Indianapolis crosses said creek; bridge to be built high enough for Orleans boats to pass under it. *Laws*, 1829-30, pp. 10-11.

Incorporation of county seminary. Trustees: William McLane, Elbert Jeter, Winthrop Foot, John Vestal, Robert Mitchell. *Laws*, 1830-31 (special), pp. 53-56.

Madison County

Comrs. appointed to relocate seat of justice then at Pendleton; to meet at home of Moses Pearson. Another relocation act passed at following session. *Laws*, 1825-26, pp. 80-81; 1826-27, pp. 84-85.

Monroe County

Daniel Fetter & Louis Shryer authorized to occupy 5 acres in sec. 30 for purpose of building a steam mill. *Laws*, 1826-27, p. 58.

Toll rates established for bridge built by Joseph Campbell over Beanblossom Creek near Hartsock's mill. *Laws*, 1827-28, p. 74.

Comrs. of reserved township authorized to correct error in sale of sec. 6 to George Henry, James Borland, & Ellis Stone. *Laws*, 1828-29, p. 83.

Joel Ferguson appointed supt. of salt lick known as Jackson's lick. *Laws*, 1829-30, pp. 146-48. The following year Benjamin Rogers was appointed supt. *Revised Laws*, 1830-31, p. 456.

Asher Labertaw appointed to succeed John W. Lee as agent of reserved township. *Laws*, 1829-30, pp. 165-66.

Jacob Bales authorized to build bridge over Salt Creek. *Laws*, 1830-31 (special), pp. 9-11.

Montgomery County

Incorporation of Crawfordsville Seminary. Trustees: Nathaniel A. Dunn, Isaac C. Elston, William Nicholson, John McCullough, Jonathan W. Powers. *Laws*, 1829-30, pp. 162-63.

Morgan County

John W. Cox authorized to erect mill dam across West Fork of White River in sec. 20, T12N, R1E. *Laws*, 1825-26, pp. 41-42.

Names of John Peacock & wife Susan & children Louisa, Madison, & Betsey changed to Lamb. *Laws*, 1825-26, pp. 42-43.

Deeds executed by Moses & Phebe Alderson to John Carter & Joel Dixon for land in sec. 26, T14N, R1E considered valid. *Laws*, 1826-27, pp. 50-51.

Ohio County

Incorporation of Rising Sun Seminary Society. Trustees: Pinkney James, Matthias Haines, Abel C. Pepper, James Jones, Samuel Jelley, William Lanius, Basil James. *Laws*, 1829-30, pp. 163-65.

Orange County

Thomas F. Chapman authorized to contract for boring for salt water at French Lick. *Laws*, 1825-26, p. 79.

Thomas Coffin appointed to replace Thomas F. Chapman, deceased, supt. of salt springs. *Laws*, 1826-27, pp. 79-80.

Samuel Cobb appointed supt. of French Lick reserve. *Laws*, 1829-30, pp. 148-49.

Jonathan Gifford and securities Abraham Bosley & Stephen Elrod discharged from penalties for failure to comply with conditions of lease of French Lick reserve. *Laws*, 1825-26, p. 64.

Owen County

Robert R. Roberts of Lawrence Co. & Daniel Rawlins & Daniel Anderson of Monroe Co. authorized to keep public ferry on White River in Owen Co. at same place where Adam Brenton formerly kept a ferry. *Laws*, 1826-27, p. 27.

Thomas McCormick, Abner Alexander & David Lookingbill appointed comrs. to construct bridge over Mill Creek. *Laws*, 1830-31 (special), pp. 8-9.

Alexander Eson appointed comr. to superintend building bridge over Lick Creek. *Laws*, 1830-31 (special), pp. 11-12.

Proceedings of Jonathan Legg & Elizabeth Thacker, execrs. of David Thacker, deceased, legalized. *Laws*, 1830-31 (special), p. 105.

Perry County

Change of venue to Crawford Co. granted for trial of William H. Rothwell for murder of William Pitman. *Laws*, 1828-29, pp. 144-45.

Pike County

Franklin F. Sawyer, execr. of Daniel Sawyer, deceased, authorized to sell real estate. *Laws*, 1826-27, pp. 62-63.

Posey County

Indictment on charge of murder against Oliver P. Gram may be transferred to Gibson Co. *Laws*, 1830-31 (special), p. 169.

Putnam County

Incorporation of Greencastle Seminary Society. Trustees: John Cowgill, Alexander C. Stevenson, Enos Lowe, Lemon M. Knight, Isaac Ash. *Laws*, 1829-30, pp. 161-62.

Rush County

Robert Martin enters new lease for school section in T15N, R2E. *Laws*, 1827-28, p. 74.

Trustee of T14N, R9E authorized to pay Drury Holt & Vincent Cooper for improvements on sec. 16. The following year John Smith, John & Jacob Crowso paid for improvement on same land. *Laws*, 1829-30, p. 108; 1830-31 (special), p. 100.

Conrad Sailors, county agent, authorized to convey lot 26 in Rushville to Jesse O'Niel. *Laws*, 1830-31 (special), p. 103.

St. Joseph County

Formation of, effective April 1, 1830. *Laws*, 1829-30, pp. 28-29.

Scott County

John Kimberlin to be reimbursed for damages done to his property by volunteers in War of 1812. *Laws*, 1830-31 (special), pp. 185-86.

Shelby County

Arthur Major authorized to build bridge over Big Flat Rock River. *Laws*, 1826-27, p. 72.

Incorporation of county seminary. Trustees: Hiram Aldridge, Elisha Mayhew, William Fleming, Erasmus Powell, William Hawkins, John Hendricks, John B. Conover. *Laws*, 1830-31 (special), pp. 56-58.

Sullivan County

Comrs. appointed to relocate county seat now at Merom. *Laws*, 1829-30, pp. 35-37.

Switzerland County

Following trustees appointed for county seminary: Israel Whitehead, James Rouse, Simon Slawson, Aaron Chamberlain, William R. Wiley. *Laws*, 1827-28, pp. 124-27.

Sum of $300 appropriated to build bridge over Plumb Creek on road leading from Madison to Lawrenceburg. Newton H. Tapp, comr. *Laws*, 1829-30, pp. 11-12.

Tippecanoe County

Formation of, effective March 1, 1826. *Laws*, 1825-26, p. 14.

Town of Dayton established to take in town plats of Marquiss, Fairfield, & one at west end of Fairfield. *Laws*, 1830-31 (special), p. 168.

Union County

James Leviston, execr. of Amsey Ayers, deceased, authorized to execute deed for certain land to trustees of county seminary. *Laws*, 1829-30, p. 160.

William Youse authorized to build toll bridge across East Fork of White Water. *Laws*, 1828-29, pp. 142-43.

Vermillion County

Incorporation of Eugene Academy. Trustees: Samuel Baldridge, John M. Colman, James Groenendyke, William Clark, Josephus & Stephen S. Collett, John R. Porter, Richard Taylor, Asaph Hill. *Laws*, 1829-30, pp. 154-55.

Incorporation of town of Perrysville. Trustees: Thomas Dill, Simon Turman, Austin Bishop, Philip H. Lingle, John Brown. *Laws*, 1830-31 (special), pp. 51-53.

Vigo County

Will of William Markle, deceased, to be proved by execrs. Henry Markle, brother, and Abraham Markle, father. *Laws*, 1827-28, p. 73.

Uncompleted contract between agents of Shaker Society for sale of land to Westley Harrison abrogated & another tract deeded to his heirs, Madison C., Fenelon, Eusela, & Edith M. Harrison. *Laws*, 1828-29, pp. 86-87; 1830-31 (special), p. 103.

Warren County

Formation of, effective March 1, 1827. *Laws*, 1826-27, pp. 14-15.

Comrs. appointed to relocate county seat now at Warrenton. *Laws*, 1828-29, pp. 129-31.

Warrick County

Alpha Frisbie permitted to build dam across Little Pigeon Creek at his mill site. *Laws*, 1830-31 (special), p. 106.

Washington County

John E. Clark, supt. of Royce's Lick reserve, authorized to lease same. *Laws*, 1825-26, pp. 77-78.

Relief for Elizabeth Long for damages done by road from Mauck's ferry to Indianapolis. *Laws*, 1825-26, p. 67.

Proceedings of trustees of school section, T2N, R4E—John E. Clark, John Currey, Samuel Lindley—legalized. *Laws*, 1825-26, p. 41.

William Richards of Washington Co. authorized to act as guardian of minor heirs of Gabriel Richards, late of Jackson Co. *Laws*, 1828-29, p. 57.

Hugh D. Finley appointed supt. of Royce's Lick & Rock Lick reserves. *Laws*, 1829-30, pp. 145-46. Elisha Denney appointed to same office following year. *Revised Laws*, 1830-31, p. 456.

Wayne County

Jacob Caylor authorized to dig mill race thru school section in T16N, R12E. *Laws*, 1825-26, p. 42.

Henry Thornburgh & Henry Hoover, admrs. of estate of John Charles, authorized to convey certain water privileges. *Laws*, 1826-27, p. 57.

Ruth Thompson who was abandoned by her husband William, leaving unpaid debts, may acquire property in her own right. *Laws*, 1830-31 (special), p. 107.

Marriages and Divorces

Marriage of Daniel Bilderback & Abigail his wife dissolved & that of James Leonard & wife Abigail of Dearborn Co. legalized. *Laws*, 1830-31 (special), pp. 23-24.

Marriage of John C. Brown, now of Spencer Co., & wife Polly Brown, formerly of Jackson Co., dissolved. *Laws*, 1827-28, p. 26.

Marriage of Edward & Margaret Corbin [no residence given] dissolved. *Laws*, 1827-28, p. 26.

Marriage of Martha McBride of Dubois Co. & husband Daniel dissolved. *Laws*, 1829-30, p. 48.

Marriage of Nancy Maddox, formerly Nancy Leonard, & husband David T. [no residence given] dissolved; she appointed guardian of their infant children. *Laws*, 1827-28, p. 25.

Marriage of Sarah Pattengill, formerly Sarah Markle, & husband James [no residence given] dissolved; he appointed guardian of infant son Markle. *Laws*, 1827-28, p. 25.

Marriage of Benjamin Patterson & Abigail Hults, by Aaron Homan, justice of peace for Hendricks Co., on May 3, 1825, legalized. *Laws*, 1826-27, p. 34.

Marriage of Edward W. & Sally Rose [no residence given] dissolved; she appointed guardian of infant children. *Laws*, 1827-28, p. 26.

Marriage of Reuben Stout & wife Elizabeth, formerly Elizabeth Carr [no residence given] dissolved. *Laws*, 1827-28, p. 26.

Soldiers' Pensions

Memorial to Congress stating pension should be granted William Lindsey, Howard Putnam, Peter Houston, Francis Odler (or Outler), Culbrith Tisdell, William Ray, & William Owens even tho they cannot furnish all the proof necessary. *Laws*, 1830-31 (special), pp. 176-77; same for John Burk of Wayne Co. *Ibid.*, p. 195.

John Rodgers who was wounded at Battle of Tippecanoe should receive pension. *Laws*, 1830-31 (special), p. 179.

DUBOIS COUNTY MARRIAGES, 1839-1848

Compiled from microfilm copy of Book A of Dubois County Marriage Records in the Genealogy Division, Indiana State Library. The writing has been very difficult to read; when uncertain of the name, we have tried to check with census records and with the index to the county histories but many of the names were not found in these listings. The German names were sometimes written according to pronunciation, e.g. Maringer for Mehringer. The Marriage Records prior to 1839 were destroyed in a court house fire in August, 1839.

Abbartt, Morris - Mary Ward   lic.   4-22-1842
Abell, Eli - Nancy Cox   3-22-1846
Abell, James - Mary Cox   12- 4-1840
Adams, Edward S. - Martha Ann Harris
    lic.   12-16-1841
Adams, Ezra - Sarah Moseby   5-10-1842
Adams, John O. - Loetitia Harris   2-13-1840
Adler, Lawrance - Ann Margaret Harder (?)
    lic.   12-13-1845
Adye, Jason W. - Ellen Simons   9-14-1843
Ahirman, Joseph - Agnes Harwick lic. 1- 6-1845
Ahrens, Charles Henry - Mary Feldinger (?)
    3- 2-1847
Alexander, Asbary - Nancy C. Armstrong
    5- 8-1845
Allen, James G. - Amanda B. Cook
    lic.   9-21-1842
Allen, Louis W. - Irenia Curtis   6-27-1847
Alles, Jacob - Catherine Ward   7-31-1845
Alles, Jacob - Apalonia Smith lic. 2-12-1847
Anderson, David - Elizabeth W. McCausland
    9-16-1846
Anderson, John - Mary Ann Brown   1-20-1848
Anderson, William P. - Rachal M. Shandy
    9- 7-1843
Angerer, George - Barbary Laulner   11- 7-1847
Armstrong, George W. - Nancy S. Corn 5- 6-1841
Asby, Robert - Mary E. Powel   9-22-1844
Athens, Levi - Sarah C. Chambers   12-20-1846
Auffort, Lewis - Elizabeth Buchart   1-30-1847
Augg (or Amgg?), John - Anna Hepes
    lic.   12-22-1846
Baber, James B. - Mary Jane Harris 10-19-1845
Backman, William - Ruca (?) Raucher 1-27-1847
Baggerly, William M. - Mary Potts
    lic.   10- 3-1847
Baker, John - Elizabeth Battise   1-30-1845
Baker, William - Sarah S. Powers   2-27-1840
Ballard, William - Elizabeth Brown 11- 4-1847
Banty, Green - Caroline Hargrove
    lic.   3-23-1848
Barker, Henry W. - Eliza Jones   4-19-1842
Barker, Silas E. - Rodisa Hawkins   1- 9-1840
Batey, Walter - Emily Bury   12-25-1842
Baty, James C. - Mary A. Moore   6- 5-1846
Baty, Walter - Louisa Ventress   8-15-1844
Batz, Larance - Elizabeth Meninger
    lic.   2-18-1843
Batz, William - Sarah Wininger   11-17-1842
Baye, Anthony - Eve Hosfoden   5- 7-1844
Bayles, Robert M. - Elizabeth Morgan
    11- 3-1842
Beaker, Conrad - Mary Ann Freadman
    lic.   2- 4-1843
Beard, Dennis - Sarah Jane Beard   5-14-1846
Beard, Obedeant - Abegail Hargrave   8-10-1848
Beard, Sword - Catharine Walker   5-31-1848
Behrens, Peter - Geshe Henis   1-27-1848
Beihler, Joseph - Ursula Gitting
    lic.   6- -1848
Belew, Flemming - Ester McDonald
(of Daviess Co.)   5-11-1843

Benule (?), George - Rachel Beeler
    lic.   5-23-1843
Bernar, Frederick - Anna Mary Engle
    12-11-1847
Bichler, Adam - Teresy Miller lic. 4- 4-1842
Bixler, Simeon - Elvira Jane Blagrave
    8-10-1848
Black, William S. - Jane Ann Hurst 2-13-1840
Blessenger, John - Katharine Smith
    lic.   10-24-1845
Blomker, Jacob - Mary A. Donere (?)
    8- 4-1847
Bolin, Robert M. - Sarah Ann Woods
    10- 1-1844
Boling, John - Margaret Karing   no date
Boling, William - Massa Flat lic. 2-14-1846
Bolta, Harmon H. - Mary Catharina Weaver
    1-28-1845
Booker, Augustus F. - Tilitha C. Jewel
    10- 6-1841
Bowenditial, Gregory - Elizabeth Temple
    lic.   7-31-1843
Bradley, Elijah - Nancy Waddle   12-19-1841
Brament (or Beament?), Adam - Mary May
    lic.   4-29-1843
Brandle, Christopher - Margaret Rigle
    11- 8-1847
Bratz (Bretz?), Jacob - Elizabeth
    Partenheimer   lic.   8- 7-1847
Bredweaver, Peter - Catharine Heinsel
    8-24-1847
Brenton, William H. - Elizabeth Payne
    8- 8-1844
Bretz, Jacob - Eliza Weathers   4-26-1840
Bretz, William - Margaret Kebler   5-15-1842
Bridenbach, John - Dorothy Senner   7- 5-1844
Bridenbaw, George - Barbary Shoat   1- 1-1843
Brindley, John - Elizabeth Marker
    lic.   5- 2-1843
Brining, Bernard - Faney Ganning
    lic.   9-20-1847
Bristo, John - Eliza Jane Kinder   2-27-1848
Brown, John D. - Elizabeth Enlow   7-11-1840
Bruister, Benjamin - Mary Wheatly 7-14-1842
Bruner, Adam - Nancy Jane Wininger 3-12-1848
Buckhart, Michael - Amelia Dishinger
    6- 8-1847
Bugher, Jacob O. - Sarah Stone
    lic.   10- 9-1846
Burk, Jefferson H. - Missouri Barker
    lic.   12- 2-1841
Burk, William S. - Elizabeth Tislow
    6-28-1846
Burkhart, Michael - Susanna Rodletter
    lic.   9-20-1839
Burnet, Lorenzo - Matilda Ann Fisher
    2- 6-1848
Butler, John - Susan A. Hembra   2- 3-1840
Capehart, Thomas - Elizabeth Ann Moraz
    11- 5-1840
Carner, Conrad - Mackdalana Ashuary (?)
    lic.   2- 8-1847

Case (?), Charles - Susan Mary Kearby
                                    12-15-1842
Case, John - Axey(?) Anderson
        1- 2-1840 or   1- 9-1840
Case, John - Bretana Enlow   9- 6-1842
Casey, Robert - Matilda Kendall   6-20-1840
Casler, Conrad - Elizabeth Later
                    lic.   9-26-1844
Cato, Isaac - Nancy Taylor   2-15-1844
Cato, William - Elizabeth Taylor
                    lic.   10- 7-1846
Cave, James - Sarah Baggerly   4-12-1848
Cerper, Peter - Mary Magdaline Kerker
                    lic.   9- 7-1843
Chadd, Moses - Elizabeth Harbison 9-15-1842
Chambers, Arthur - Colista Kennoyer 3-11-1841
Chambers, Maxwell - Nancy Garland 3-11-1846
Chappell, Moses S. - Amand Melvena Susan
                    Twitty   6- 6-1842
Chew, James - Mary Stewart   9-12-1840
Collins, Finley - Polly Walker   7-11-1840
Colterbach, Bernard - Mary Smith
                    lic.   1- 6-1843
Combs, Lewis - Mary Haddock   1-10-1841
Combs, Milton - Sarah Davis   4-30-1843
Comstock, Norman - Rachel Harris 9- 4-1841
Conner, Alexander - Eliza Ann Casey 3-22-1840
Conner, Riley - Clarcy Bury   12- 7-1846
Conrad, Phillip, Sr. - Polly Hughlen
                                  4- 2-1840
Cook, Daniel J. - Louisa J. Sent (?)12-18-1846
Coonts, Joseph - Margaret Roletter 6- 1-1840
Cooper, John M. - Melvina Kinder 7-10-1844
Cooper, William - Margaret Kemp   7-29-1842
Cooper, William B. - America Brittain
                                  7- 5-1844
Corn (?), John W. - Margary Harris 8- 5-1846
Corn, William - Mary Payne   12-23-1841
Cox, Allen - Margaret Conley   7- 3-1848
Cox, Henry - Nancy Hall   12-18-1846
Cox, William - Eliza Abell   11-26-1841
Craft, John - Elizabeth Hamer lic. 12-20-1845
Craton, Solomon - Sarah Potts   10-17-1844
Crodle, John - Barbay Quackenbush 7- 9-1843
Daffren, John S. - Mary Evans   9-15-1842
Daniel, John - Mary Fraley lic. 7-16-1841
Dasheny, Paul - Catharine Kasper 11- 4-1843
Davidson, Thomas M. - Margaret Harbison
                                  3-15-1840
Davison, William - Laney (?) Anderson
                                  9-30-1846
Dawnhower, Simon - Mary M. Smyth 1-27-1846
Dawson, John - Jane H. Scott lic. 3- 1-1845
De Bruler, Lemuel Q. - Huldah A. Condict
                                  3- 7-1841
Debruler, Westly - Mary Spradling 12-15-1839
Deck, Peter - Elizabeth Shipman   1- 9-1844
Dedrick, John - Mary Peech   10-20-1844
Demott, John - Susanah T. Debruler 10- 3-1844
Demsey, Thomas M. G. - Margaret Kelso
                                  8-11-1842
Devine, James - Rachal Lenard lic. 11-12-1845
Devine, John V. - Polly Harbison
                    lic.   6-22-1840
Dickson, Robert B. - Sarah Woods 11- 5-1843
Dillen, Samuel - Martha Jane Adams 1- 1-1846
Dotson, Henry H. - Joannah Alexander
                                  2-17-1842
Dove, Henry - Elizabeth Ann Wininger 5- 6-1847
Drinkhaus, Jacob H. - Rebecca Sweltz
                    lic.   10-15-1842

Ebert, Marres - Mary Swemenevery (?)
                                  1-30-1845
Egenfelts, Mathew - Setseala Hurst
                    lic.   2-13-1843
Ehler, Joseph - Mary Courthouse   1-18-1848
Eicher, Francis - Catharine Jeil 6-17-1847
Eichler, Joseph - Mary A. Middleburgh
                                  6-22-1847
Ekerle, John George - Alavisa Oberst
                                  1-11-1848
Ellis, Marvin - Parmelia J. Roberts
                    lic.   10- 6-1841
Enlow, Henry - Rebecca Rust   2-25-1841
Enlow, William - Catharine Fisher 3-31-1843
Erney, Wendolin - Theressa Oberst 6-13-1848
Ewing, William - Malinda Taber   7- 3-1845
Famshoier, Harmon - Lot Neabaur
                    lic.   4- 3-1846
Farhabay, Littleton - Catharine Beard
                                  2-14-1845
Farris, Thomas - Elizabeth Hope 12-12-1844
Fenn, Conrad - Barbery Lawlis (or Sawlis?)
                    lic.   8-12-1847
Fisher, Alfred H. - Nancy Cox   9-23-1842
Fisher, John - Anna Margaretta Temple
                                  6-28-1841
Flick, Isaac - Elizabeth Baty   3-21-1844
Floyd, Matthew - Rachel A. E. McAlester
                                  7- 2-1840
Fogal, Conrod - Magdalena Meyeran 1-18-1842
Foster, Alexander H. - Mary J. Smithers
                                 11-13-1842
France(?), John - Mary Ann Dishinger
                    lic.   4-18-1846
Fratz, Christopher - Mary Agnes Falthouse
                                  8-10-1847
Freidman, Martin - Sophrona Gramelspacher
                    lic.   7-27-1846
Froman (?), John - Frances Gramelspacher
                    lic.   6- 4-1844
Gardner, Nicholas - Levinia Herter 5-11-1841
Garland, George W. - Alpha Amanda Powel
                                 11-27-1839
Garland, Joseph - Margaret Harris 12-14-1843
Garland, Joseph W. - Susan Powel 12-30-1839
Garland, Thompson - Ann Eliza Wood
                                 10-18-1845
Garrison, Acru - Sarah Cox   10-10-1841
Gates, Bazil - Christiana Barger 6- 1-1840
Gates, Mathias - Clarinda Buhler 5- 4-1847
Gaustrop, Thomas E. - Sarah Ann McLaughlin
                                 12- 1-1847
Geesler, Lawrance - Barbary Fraz
                    lic.   11-13-1845
Gerckin, John Henry - Mary Elizabeth Blomker
                                  1-27-1848
Gliesner, Gahart - Mary Stanen   1-19-1847
Goode, Harmon - Wilemina Batsha
                    lic.   12-25-1841
Goodman, George W. - Perlinda Powel
                                 10-22-1840
Goodman, McElyea - Lydia Taylor   9-17-1843
Graham, David - Nancy Wininger   12- 5-1843
Gramelspacher, Fredelin - Catharine Monday
                    lic.   2-18-1843
Gramelspacher, Helar - Franziska Knabel
                                 10- 3-1842
Grass, John Paul - Mary C. Shuck
                    lic.   8-21-1846
Grass, Virgil - Elizabeth Miller
                    lic.   12-30-1841

Grave, Joseph - Mary Ann Beemer lic. 8- 5-1843
Gray, James - Nancy Adams   6-13-1841
Green, Davis - Mary Ann R. Woods   12- 5-1847
Green, James - Nancy Lavina Strauther
                    Edmonston 10- 7-1847
Green, Robert - Melissa Miller   4-30-1844
Green, Willis - Elizabeth Garland   2- 8-1844
Grees, John - Dorothy Bratz   4-13-1846
Grosman, George - Avor Lottes lic. 3-14-1842
Guyle (Geil?), Lorance - Rosann Hahn
                        lic. 11- 6-1846
Gwin, David - Elizabeth Willson   12-10-1840
Haddock, White S. - Jane Harbison   1- 7-1844
Hall, Christopher - Melvina Cooper 10- 3-1846
Hall, Jackson - Nancy Kinder   10-17-1844
Halm, Dominzo J. - Sophah Kunkler   6-19-1844
Hamer, John - Barba Huffman lic.   6-24-1842
Hammons, John - Jane Stewart lic.   4-13-1843
Hankins, Abraham - Elizabeth Jane Wininger
                        lic. 6-29-1846
Hankins, David - Rebecca Pace   9- 8-1842
Hanks, James Anderson - Nancy Legrand
                        5-17-1845
Hann, Joseph - Mary Ann Forseiyh (?)
                        2-24-1845
Harbison, A. B. - Caroline Inman   11-14-1844
Harbison, John - Louisa Jane Wiese
                        lic. 12-15-1839
Harbison, John - Malinda Potts   8-30-1846
Harbison, John M. - Elizabeth Leonard
                        lic. 10-23-1844
Harbison, Richard - Bethiah Ledgerwood
                        11-22-1840
Hargrave, Richard H. - Eliza Palmer 10-16-1846
Harker, George - Margaret Rookcreekle
                        1-23-1842
Harker, John - Catharine Keffner   6-29-1843
Harker, John Ernst - Tressey Urick 1- 2-1842
Harmon, Jacob, Jr. - Leah Lindsey   7-14-1842
Harness, Joseph - Elizabeth A. Thompson
                        11- 4-1841
Harpst, John - Elizabeth Maringer
                        lic. 1-18-1842
Harris, Daniel - Elizabeth Farris
                        lic. 6-30-1847
Harris, Isaac - Eliza Ann Reed   1-14-1841
Harris, Isaac - Racheal Harnod   5- 7-1848
Harris, Peter B. - Susan Corn   10-22-1846
Harris, William - Hester Simons (?) 12- 5-1847
Harrison, George Washington - Sharlotty
                    Taylor   11-13-1845
Harse, John - Margaret Woolfert
                        lic. 6- 1-1844
Harsh, Valentine - Ludwinga Enger
                        lic. 10-19-1845
Hart, William - Isabela McElwain   2- 2-1846
Hatter, Charles - Mary Miller lic. 5- 8-1845
Hatter, John - Margaretta Arnold   11-20-1847
Hawkins, John Lewis - Mary Crinder 5- 7-1848
Hawkins, Robert R. - Eliza P. Carr 12-20-1846
Haxen, Michal - Malinda Shira lic. 2-25-1843
Hays, James P. - Sarah Hays lic.   10-12-1839
Hays, Nathaniel - Polly Simons   10- 7-1845
Helas, John Barney - Anna A. Tapel 6- 6-1848
Helsmear, Henry - Ann Mary Amiasman (?)
                        7-14-1847
Hemalem (?), Simon - Catharine Ahal
                        lic. 12- 6-1845
Hember, Richard - Margaret Ann Sanders
                        8-24-1845

Hembree, Jonathan - Dorcas Reed   6-26-1848
Hendreson, Reuben - Rhoda Morris
                        lic.   [1839]
Hendrickson, Lorenzo Dow - Leah Maris
                        11- 1-1842
Hill, William R. - Sarah Jane McDonald
                        4- 8-1841
Hill, William R. - Aceneth Rose   7-20-1848
Hobbs, Nathan - Barbary Newton   8-25-1846
Hobbs, Noah - Susan Hill   11- 2-1847
Hoggatt, Zimri H. - Jane Hawha
                        lic. 10-25-1839
Hohn, Preston - Treasey Ahler
                        lic. 11- 6-1846
Holland, Bartlet - Paulina Flick   1-26-1845
Hollender, John - Anna Mary Knepper
                        1-14-1847
Holler, Anthony - Catharine Sukus (or Lukus?)
                        lic. 3-20-1843
Hope, Adam - Mary Harris   9-29-1842
Hope, Adam - Magdaline G. McCausland
                        12-10-1845
Hoperjohn, John - Elizabeth Lambert
                        lic. 2- 2-1842
Hopkins, Thomas - Rachel Harris   12-10-1840
Horton, Isaac - Margaret Lemmon   8-19-1841
Horton, Raughley - Nancy Brown
                        lic. 1-17-1847
Houtch, Martin - Barbara Lifret   1-30-1842
Howard, John - Elizabeth Newton   1-19-1840
Huff, Henry - Sarah Ann Williams   9-20-1846
Huffman, John - Rachael Huffman
                        lic. 10-11-1845
Hurst, Harvey - Ann Davidson   3-31-1842
Hurst, Ira - Francis Jane McCausland
                        9- 8-1847
Hurst, Peter - Mary Ann Ell   1- 8-1844
Hurst, Peter - Mary Ann Boyer (?)
                        lic. 12-24-1844
Inman, Argyle H. - America Hope   2-15-1844
Ison, Francis S. - Josephine Dishinger
                        lic. 6-16-1844
Isonhood, John - _____(?) Cunett
                        lic. 11-26-1841
Jacobs, Elisha - Rency C. McCarty   8-27-1843
Jacobs, John W. - Malinda Weedman   10-31-1841
Jinkens, John - Susan Brown   9- -1848
Johnston, Benjamin - Jane Simonds (or Lemonds)
                        lic. 12-25-1839
Jones, Jackson - Eleaner Davis   2-14-1841
Keabler, Charles - Rosalea Free
                        lic. 6-20-1848
Keifer, Matthias - Wallburga Ell   6- 5-1848
Keifner, Wolfgang- Catharine Crodle
                        1- 1-1844
Keifner, Wolfgang - Catharine Suffett
                    (or Luffet?) 1-24-1847
Kellerman, Francis - Catharine Gerhart
                        9- 4-1845
Kelso, William J. - Nancy Ann McMahan
                        3-27-1845
Kemp, Greenberry - Eudnneld Patlow Meyers
                        4-13-1848
Kendell, William - Mary Newton   1-15-1846
Kerby, William H. - Virginia Wininger
                        4-30-1840
Kesterson, Jonathan - Mary Ann Painter
                        3-19-1840
Kimball, Samuel - Elender Enlow   1-15-1843
Kindle, William - Nancy Newton
                        lic. 9- 2-1844

King, James J. - Rachal Kindle   8-22-1844
King, John - Mary Kindle   7- 4-1844
Klea, Baltser - Francisca Ellenhogen   2-19-1846
Kleek, Balthasor - Catharine Schneider
                                        4-29-1845
Kliner (?), Larance - Rosannah Keifner
                                        7-19-1847
Knable, Mathias - Mary Burnett lic.   6-17-1843
Kramer, Peter - Catharine Lichner
                        lic.   4-30-1845
Krodel, see Crodle
Kunkler, Joseph - Dorothy Temple
                        lic.   9-23-1842
Langford, Walker - Catharine King   3-18-1848
Lashbrooks, Solomon - Carolin M. Kerby
                        lic.   3-26-1842
Laswell, Charnel - Anny Beardsley   7-11-1845
Lawmain (or Sawmain?), Henry - Meney Roetger
                                        11-23-1845
Leciner, Jacob - Elizabeth Hamer   2- 9-1846
Legrand, Jackson - Margaret Hanks   4-25-1845
Legrand, John - Sophiah Linch lic.   10- 4-1842
Legrand, Levi - Jane Sumner   4- 4-1840
Lemmon, Hiram - Nancy Beard   3-18-1844
Lemmon, Jacob - Elizabeth Corn   10-13-1842
Lemmonds, John - Eliza Green   11- 5-1844?
Lemmons, William D. - Martha Beatty
    of Orange Co.   6-26-1845
Lemond, John - Apsilia Miller   3-21-1841
Lemonds, Hiram - Phebe Williams   11- 7-1844
Lesle, John - Sarah Spradley lic.   2-16-1844
Lettis, Aaron R. - Elender Blair   5-29-1845
Lewis, John W. - Ann Proudfit   9- 8-1842
Lewis, Thomas H. - Sarah Wininger   2- 5-1840
Liener, Francis - Margaret Wagnerin   2- 7-1848
Limp, Simon - Emaline Bretz   11-15-1843
Lincus (or Sincus), Henry - Louisa Daffern
                        lic.   1- 3-1841
Lindsey, Lorenzo D. - Sarah Ann Harmon
                        lic.   12-13-1841
Lineback, Peter - Mary Eagler   11-15-1845
Lintner (?), Lawrence - Margaret Myer
                                        1-14-1844
Lotus, Everhart - Christina Hoffman
                        lic.   6-13-1841
Lotus, John - Katharine Shoal lic.   5- 2-1840
McAlister, Mathew - Martha Garland   1-16-1844
McCain, Hugh - Susan Case   7-15-1847
McCoy, Jesse - Elizabeth Griffey   10- 4-1840
McGrew, Washington - Susannah P. Archer
                        lic.   4- 6-1842
McMahan, Hugh - Elizabeth Hope   5- 1-1845
McMahan, Joseph A. - Nancy Armstrong   9-29-1842
McMahan, William R. - Mary Caroline Condict
                                        3-10-1842
McWood, Mountford - Lucy Ann Spradley
                                        9-14-1845
Machney, John - Margaret B. Price   6-10-1845
Mahana (or Mahrea?), John - Barbary Price
                                        2- 5-1844
Main, Franklin - Sophronia Gossman
                        lic.   10-21-1842
Main, Hiram - Rachal Floyd   9-20-1845
Malherdos, Jacob - Genariel (?) Mercher
                        lic.   6-16-1845
Maling, Christian - Barbary Walter
                        lic.   11-23-1844
Mann, Wolfgong - Margaret Harker
                        lic.   6- 8-1842
Maringer, Caspar - Elizabeth Ring
                        lic.   2- 5-1840

Maringer, Paul - Barba Goppner
                        lic.   3- 2-1840
Markel, Valentine - Henrietta Yeager
                                        3- 6-1848
Marker, Frederick J. - Elizabeth Monet (?)
                                        11-22-1842
Marker, John K.(?) - Odelia Trall   11-22-1842
Marker, Mathias - Rosanna Hites   11-23-1847
Martin, John S. - Jane Ann Kelso   12-11-1845
Mason, Marten B. - Sarah Haddock   8-29-1843
Mathews, John F. - Clarenda J. Hutchens
                                        8-13-1841
Mavety, Joel - Ailsay Wininger   10- 6-1842
Medcalf, Thomas P. - Martha Maine   5- -1844
Medcalf, William - Mary Ann Main   12-26-1844
Mehringer, Paul - Kenegund Steyer
                        lic.   4-24-1842
Mehringer, see also Maringer
Meinker, Henry - Catharine Newman
                        lic.   12-17-1841
Meyer, Adam - Elizabeth Houtch   1-21-1842
Meyer, Christopher - Ursula Meyer
                        lic.   3- 3-1843
Meyer, Frederick - Margarite Meyer   1-21-1842
Meyer, John - Barbery Crodle   8-17-1847
Meyer, John Michael - Margret Bak   1-13-1842
Mickler, James - Louisa Lincus   7- 4-1843
Mickler, John - Mary Ellen Simmons   2- 6-1848
Mickler, Martin - Lucy Ann Roberts
                        lic.   12- 7-1846
Milbern, David - July Ann Wininger   6-14-1843
Milburn, Robert - Rebecca Wininger   3-18-1842
Miller, Anthony - Clore Wards lic.   5-18-1843
Miller, Baltheser - Elizabeth Warner
                        lic.   9- 5-1843
Miller, Conrad - Martha E. Lore
                        lic.   5- 7-1846
Miller, Daniel - Margaret McMahan   6-29-1843
Miller, Francis - Mary Elizabeth Hine
                        lic.   2-14-1843
Miller, George - Elizabeth Shrader
                        lic.   9-19-1846
Miller, Huston - Mathilda Cumings
                        lic.   11-13-1843
Miller, James - Elender Lemmon   9-10-1843
Miller, John - Barbary More lic.   9-29-1846
Monkehaus, Herman Henry - Catharine Kempars
                                        8-18-1848
Monroe, William - Elizabeth M. Anderson
                                        1- 5-1848
Morgan, William - Margaret Robertson
                                        1-12-1844
Mosebay, Lewis L. - Mary Adams   1-21-1841
Moulder, Nicholas - Barbery Marker
                        lic.   1-28-1843
Nagle, Christopher - Angeline Hendrickson
                        lic.   7-21-1847
Nelson, Henry - Nancy Cane (or Cove?)
                                        9-17-1846
Newton, Peter - Nancy Margaret Hannon
                        lic.   3-21-1848
Nicum, George - Margaret Heapner   2- 8-1846
Niehaus, Benjamin - Elizabeth Miller
                                        3-29-1840
O'Neal, Frachour - Martha J. Maxey
                                        8-26-1845
Opil, John - Margaretta Crosman   3- 5-1840
Ornst, Francis - Mary E. Lineback
                        lic.   10-28-1843
Overbee, Joseph M. - Maria Jane Adkins
                                        12-22-1839

Pace, Wesley - May Wininger   5- 7-1846
Pake, John C. - Margaret Kalp   12-28-1845
Parmenter, Rufus - Elizabeth Harness
                                   lic.   6-18-1841
Parsons, George - Eloner Kesterson   7-14-1842
Pauling, Michael - Barbara Morganrode   6-22-1841
Payne, Hiram H. - Elizabeth McMahan   4- 2-1843
Penick, W. H. H. - Nancy McCune   7-14-1842
Penner, Hugh - Loucinda Resley   8-27-1847
Pennick, Calvin - Mary Jane T. Jackson
                                   lic.   3-11-1841
Pennick, Samuel C. - Patience McKune   11- 2-1840
Pilgrim, John - Elizabeth Wells   3-18-1840
Polson, Robert S. - Isabella J. Noble
                                          12-26-1843
Polson, Thomas W. - Nancy Jane Noble   9-29-1846
Postlethwait, Samuel W. - Sarah McElwain
                                           3-10-1844
Powell, James - Sarah Oxly lic.   11-23-1844
Powel, William C. - Emily A. Goodman   9-10-1845
Powers, Major T. - Malena Hawkins   11-14-1844
Preye, Henry - Elizabeth Sunerman   4- 1-1846
Price, John - Haner Whitenger   4-20-1845
Pride, Thomas - Marthy Palmer   11- 3-1846
Purkhiser, Henry - Maria McDonald   12-23-1841
Rahmann, Henry - Mary Breigemyer   6-15-1847
Ranker (or Rankin?), Henry - Mary Eversman
                                           5- 7-1844
Rankin, John P. - Elvira White   9-23-1840
Rausher, Jacob - Maria Shawley   1-17-1845
Reed, Wallis - Denicia Harris   9- 5-1844
Reichart, Elijah - Sarah Schlachter   1-12-1847
Reling, George - Manika Oberst lic.   5-12-1846
Richrigal, George - Margaretta Harker
                                   lic.   11-18-1841
Richy, Boyd F. - Elizabeth Corn   1-24-1847
Riepgrof, John - Kunegunda Gopner   9- 5-1848
Roberts, George Washington - Sarah Bradley
                                           4-16-1843
Roberts, Marcus L. - Frances Morgan   3-12-1848
Roberts, William - Sarah Ann Robertson
                                          11-30-1844
Rolinger, John - Barbara Rousher
                                   lic.   9- 1-1841
Rose, Henry - Mary Preyhoger   1-17-1844
Ruder, Simon Morgan - Catharine Abel   12-30-1847
Rush, Adam - Kunyola Boling   4-29-1840
Rust, Allbright - Coney H. Harker   1- 1-1844
Sanders, Nathaniel - Rebecca Edwards   4-20-1848
Schirter, Andrew - _____ Hurst
                                   lic.   11-21-1844
Scott, John - Alvyra Rubein lic.   10-12-1844
Scott, Thomas - Sintha Ann Sumerville
                                           7- 4-1844
Seger, Nicholas - Angaline Boyer lic.   1-23-1845
Seitz, John - Margaret Meyer   12-30-1847
Seker, Henry - Mary Bilter   lic.   1-28-1848
Sendlewick (?), Henry - Barbary Gaerl
                                   lic.   12-19-1845
Seylor, George - Susan Kable   10-29-1840
Shandy, John - Sarah Payne   4-16-1846
Sherritt, Samuel B. - Jane M. Cerwin
                                   lic.   2-15-1845
Shira, Peter - Elizabeth Kimmelshew   9-14-1840
Shivley, John W. - Mary Ann Shivley   1-25-1844
Shnitthoes, John - Mary M. Abart lic.   7- 9-1842
Shoemaker, William - Mary E. Cato   12-28-1843
Shuler, Bartley - Nancy Bowendetial
                                   lic.   6- 8-1843

Shutt, John - Margaretta Fogler   11- 4-1840
Silley (or Lilley?), Calvin - Elizabeth
                         Foster   5- 4-1843
Simmons, Jefferson - Elizabeth Kinder
                                    5-28-1842
Simmons, John - Mary Ann Dove   3- 3-1845
Simmons, John - Elizabeth Jackson   7-16-1846
Simmons, John - Martha Jane Dillen 4- 5-1845
Simmons, William D. - Martha Baty
(of Orange Co., Ind.)   6-26-1845
Smith, J. W. - Rebecca Archer   1-20-1844
Smith, Lawden C. - Adaline Smith   12-17-1845
Snyder, William - Harriet Dawson
                         lic.   12-18-1841
Speaks, Allen - Lucretia Williams   6-18-1846
Sperlock, William - Jane Baker   4- 7-1841
Staker, Adam - Barbary Groceman   2- 8-1846
Staker, Martin - Catharine Myer
                         lic.   9-15-1845
Stallman, Gerard - Catharine Wapkenburgh
                                    7-22-1845
Stampnail, Francis - Sauela Monday
                         lic.   7- 8-1848
Stark, John - Nancy Morris lic.   12- -1846
Steincamp, John F. - Mary Barkman 12-14-1846?
Stewart, John - Sarah Chew   2-26-1847
Stewart, Samuel - Elizabeth Stewart
                                    4-15-1841
Straeber, John - Ann Kerber   1- 1-1844
Strickfadden, Ignatius - Sophia Gasser
                                    1-26-1847
Suiar, Zacheriah - Susanah Beck   1-18-1848
Sumner, Jesse - Zerilda J. Walker   4-20-1845
Sumner, Phillip - Martha Goodman
                         lic.   10-13-1839
Sumner, Phillip - Rebecca Hanks   9-22-1844
Sumner, Thomas - Mary Walker   6-17-1842
Sumner, Thomas - Emari Oxly (?)   4-20-1843
Sunderman, Frederick - Elizabeth Kenipers
                                    2-22-1848
Swindle, John - Margaretha Swemling
                                    7- 5-1844
Swinger, Adam - Catharine Sawertice
                                    4-22-1844
Taber, Meret - Malenda Sanders   9-23-1847
Taylor, Hiram - Judith Willson   12-11-1840
Taylor, Hiram - Mahala Shirley   3-16-1845
Taylor, Riley - Permelia Ann Wethers
                                    1- 4-1845
Taylor, William H. - Rebeca Boyles(?)
                                    1-29-1846
Temple, John - Margaret Fen   7-26-1847
Theil, Joseph - Catharine Gleesner 2- 4-1847
Thompson, John - Ellen McCall lic. 1-22-1848
Timmerman, John P. - Margaretha Stacey
                         lic.   12- 8-1841
Tishinger, John - Margaret Crobarger
                                   11-13-1842
Tralor, John - Malinda Luce (?)   5- 2-1847
Traylor, Jesse - Jane McDonald   11-12-1840
Tuefel, George - Elizabeth Beck   5-28-1842
Van, Benjamin - Henrietta Harris   11- 9-1843
Waddle, George - Mary Boyles   1-30-1848
Wade, Harrison - Margaret Goodman   6-28-1840
Waggoner, Allen - Ann Harbison
                         lic.   12-15-1839
Wall, John - Mary Ann Mehling (or Mering?)
                                    9- 3-1844
Washam, John C. - Mary Payne   7- 5-1845
Watts, William - Sarah Peach lic.   4-17-1844
Weaver, John - Mary Kinem (?)   3-23-1848

Webb, Hiram - Rachel Judson lic. 8-20-1842
Whitacre, Henderson - Mary S. Beard 8- 3-1840
White, John - Mary Scott lic. 7-18-1846?
White, Samuel - Nancy Berker lic. 4- 7-1845
Wiant, Philip T. - Doratha Temple
                           lic. 9-12-1843
Wicker, John - Catharine Weigel lic. 5-16-1846
Wickel, John - Margaret Haxen 8-31-1847
Widenhamer, John - Barbara Crodle
                           lic. 1-27-1841
Wikle, Adam - Mary Magdalene Ison
                           lic. 9- 9-1843
Williams, Davis - Mary Williams
                           lic. 9-24-1842?
Williams, Horrace - Phebe Boolin 5-26-1842

Williams, James - Jane Fisher 10- 1-1839
Williams, James H. - Polly Main
                           lic. 2- 8-1842
Williams, Thomas - Obediance Mosbey
                          10-30-1842
Wilson, Hyram - Mariah Flatt 10-24-1844
Wininger, Alexander - Harriet McGranahan
                          5- 3-1840
Wininger, George W. - Nancy C. Milbern
                          6-14-1843
Wininger, Henry - Nancy Wininger
                        lic. 8- 1-1840
Wininger, Samuel - Angelin Quackinbush
                          4-17-1842
Wood, H. P. - Hulda Cummins 7- 7-1842
Wood, Robert - Jane Armstrong 12- 4-1845
Woolsey, Jeramiah - Mary Ann Burnett
                        11- 4-1847
Zurcher, John - Konaganda Beierlain
                        4-19-1848

DUBOIS COUNTY NATURALIZATIONS, 1852-1869

Compiled from a microfilm of the Declaration of Intention Record in Genealogy Division, Indiana State Library. The original record is in the Dubois County Courthouse, Jasper.

The many German names in the Dubois County Marriage Records created a desire to know more of these people who had migrated from their native land and settled in Dubois County. Noting that the Naturalization Records were available on microfilm we have transcribed the following list from the record kept of those men who appeared in the circuit court between the years 1852 and 1869 and indicated their intention of becoming American citizens. There is a later record for the years 1869-1906 and also records of those men who petitioned for and received their final naturalization papers. The records prior to 1852 are no doubt to be found in the circuit court order books but these were not available in the Genealogy Division. Except for the port of debarkation, all the information on the original record is given. Some of the names have been anglicized; others have not.

The following abbreviations have been used for the ports of entry: Balt. for Baltimore; Gr. Br. for Great Britain; Ire. for Ireland; N.O. for New Orleans; N.Y. for New York.

Name of Emigrant	Age	Country emigrating from	Place & date of arrival in U.S.	Date of Declaration of intent	Page
Alfers, John H.	36	Hanover	N.Y. 8-7-1843	2-21-1853	5
Allgeier, Anton	51	Baden	N.O. May 1854	3-19-1861	295
Altmann, John	31	Bavaria	N.Y. 6-18-1857	1-23-1866	335
Angerer, John	45	Bavaria	Balt. 10-25-1854	6-18-1855	92
Anstott, Thomas	30	France	N.O. 2-1-1857	10-8-1860	272
Appel, John Adam	52	Hessen	N.O. 1- -1855	1-18-1855	56
Arckenor(?), Charles	25	Prussia	N.Y. 11-19-1859	9-24-1860	258
Arnold, John	21	Bavaria	Buffalo 1847	10-9-1854	85
Aufterhar, Ernest	30	Prussia	N.O. 5-15-1852	4-23-1855	87
Bachar, Hiar	29	Baden	N.O. Jan. 1855	5-28-1855	89
Baer, Lorance	27	Bavaria	N.O. 6-1-1852	9-16-1854	31
Bahart, Anton	30	Baden	N.Y. 8-16-1854	8-12-1858	222
Baierleir, Titus(?)	41	Bavaria	N.O. 12-1-1858	10-8-1860	274

Baker, Francis	29	Prussia	N.Y. 8-24-1849	10-7-1854	40
Baltsmeier, H.F.	29	Hanover	Balt. 9-1-1839	1-17-1853	3
Banmert, Sylvester	62	Baden	N.Y. 1-22-1852	10-10-1856	145
Bannbein, John	30	Bavaria	N.Y. 6-29-1852	6-6-1853	14
Bar, John	43	Bavaria	N.O. 12-12-1854	2-12-1855	64
Bär, Thomas	24	Baden	Balt. 11-20-1854	10-13-1856	168
Barth, Joseph	28	Switzerland	N.Y. 3-15-1865	10-13-1868	409
Barth, Peter	31	Prussia	N.Y. 12-10-1857	3-30-1869	435
Bartholet, Jacob	40	Switzerland	N.Y. 1-31-1868	9-5-1868	377
Baudendistel, Anton	32	Baden	N.Y. 5-3-1859	9-24-1860	259
Bauer, John	33	Bavaria	N.O. 12-20-1858	11-2-1864	327
Bauermeister, William	36	Prussia	N.Y. 9-24-1849	5-2-1853	13
Baumert, Adam	50	Baden	n.p. June 1836	12-8-1856	193
Baumert, Peter	22	Baden	N.O. 12-19-1854	10-12-1858	224
Beatty, John	22	Ireland	N.Y. 12-26-1863	9-25-1868	385
Becher, Bernard	22	Baden	N.Y. 9-14-1852	8-1-1854	29
Beck, Conrad	24	Baden	N.O. 3-21-1856	10-8-1860	268
Beck, Francis J.	27	Baden	N.O. 5-30-1847	1-12-1854	18
Bencken, Gerhard C.	27	Hanover	Balt. 6-6-1864	11-2-1868	422
Böhmer, John Adam	54	Hanover	Balt. 8-20-1845	10-11-1856	149
Bonn, Carl	39	Prussia	N.Y. 9-23-1862	3-17-1864	316
Borger, Johann B.	26	Hanover	N.O. 6- -1855	10-31-1860	283
Bowemann, Loranz	24	Baden	Balt. 5-10-1852	10-10-1854	49
Brachtel, Thomas	39	Bavaria	N.Y. 1844	12-26-1853	17
Brames, Christopher	41	Hanover	Balt. 10-12-1861	4-5-1869	436
Brames, Peter	41	Hanover	Balt. 10-12-1864	4-5-1869	436
Braun, Conrad	29	Bavaria	N.O. 5-15-1861	10-5-1864	320
Brefort, Wilhelm F.	44	Hanover	N.Y. 9-15-1854	10-8-1867	363
Bresher, Henry	37	Hessen	N.Y. 10-1-1854	10-11-1864	326
Bretz, John Philipp	46	Hesse Darmstadt	N.Y. 8-1-1857	10-14-1861	303
Brockman, Henry	61	Hanover	N.O. 1-6-1846	11-1-1856	183
Broningez, Adolph	27	Prussia	Balt. May 1857	8-8-1859	236
Brormann, Lewis B.	31	Hanover	Balt. 11-30-1860	10-6-1868	398
Brosemer, Laurence	35	Baden	N.Y. Nov. 1839	7-25-1853	15
Brosmer, Christian	36	Baden	N.O. 3-22-1855	8-16-1856	117
Brucker, Leonhardt	46	Baden	N.O. 10-13-1852	9-27-1860	260
Bruening, Gerhart H.	41	Prussia	Balt. 1-5-1854	5-11-1856	110
Bruggamann, Theodore	26	Prussia	N.Y. 4-15-1854	11-20-1854	50
Brumlage, James	35	Prussia	N.Y. 9-26-1853	4-4-1855	81
Brust, Frederick	33	Prussia	Buffalo	11-1-1855	97
Buchart, John B.	56	Baden	N.O. 5-25-1855	11-4-1856	192
Bucher, Henry	31	Switzerland	N.Y. 6-14-1851	2-18-1855	53
Buess, Christian	32	France	N.Y. 2-13-1855	11-7-1859	238
Bullerman, Henry	21	Germany	N.O. 1-25-1854	2-15-1855	67
Büning, Bernard	27	Prussia	N.Y. 11-7-1861	7-29-1868	369
Burgdorf, Charles	32	Hanover	N.O. 6-12-1855	10-11-1856	150
Burgdorf, Frederick	35	Hanover	N.O. 6-10-1854	10-11-1856	152
Bürge, Friedolin	40	Switzerland	N. O. 11-28-1853	9-30-1862	309
Burget, Havier	30	Baden	N.O. 5-2-1853	9-16-1856	121
Burke, Johann B.	34	Hanover	Balt. Oct. 1857	2-21-1861	294
Burkkutter, Henry	28	Prussia	N.O. 1-1-1850	8-8-1853	16
Butz, Conrad		Page not filmed			360
Christmann, Louis	33	Hanover	N. Y. 4-20-1848	4-2-1866	340
Cullin, Barney	22	Ireland	N. Y. 7-2-1854	7-5-1859	235
Cutler, Kasper H.	29	Hanover	N.O. 10-25-1854 1853?	6-15-1854	27
Daschle, Leo	27	Baden	N.Y. 3-12-1866	10-12-1868	407

Debeur, M. John	30	France	N.Y. 8-5-1854	12-24-1856	194
Decker, Theodore	26	Prussia	N.Y. 2-28-1857	10-12-1858	225
Deickmann, Gerhard	24	Hanover	N.O. 10-28-1852	3-2-1855	72
Deinling, John	25	Bavaria	Balt. 10-21-1853	2-17-1855	69
Deuper, Henry	35	Prussia	Balt. 4-30-1858	2-25-1862	308
Dickänsper, John G.	37	Hanover	N.O. 12-24-1852	10-13-1856	154
Dieckmann, Henry	64	Prussia	N.O. 1-21-1853	9-14-1868	382
Dietz, Georg	59	Bavaria	N.O.	9-24-1860	257
Doernhoefer, Andrew	39	Prussia	N.O. 4-15-1860	2-24-1868	364?
Doll, Henry	48	Baden	N.O. 12-27-1854	10-7-1856	139
Dorkemeier, Johann H.	34	Hanover	Balt. 5-20-1858	10-8-1860	271
Dupps, Benedict	24	Baden	N.O. 5-1-1855	10-8-1856	141
Durlauf, Michael	39	Bavaria	Balt. 12-18-1857	10-9-1860	279
Eckerly, Mathew	38	Baden	N.Y. 6-16-1854	10-14-1856	161
Eckert, Charles	28	Baden	N.O. 4-12-1854	9-22-1856	124
Eckert, Dominic	25	Baden	N.O. 6-12-1847	5-12-1855	91
Eckert, Julius	23	Baden	N.Y. 12-6-1866	11-2-1868	423
Ehrmann, John Adam (Johann)	38	Baden	Balt. 10-18-1862	10-24-1868	411
Eifert, Conrad	43	Hessen	N.Y. 8-2-1849	10-30-1868	416
Ekstein, August	21	Baden	N.Y. 3-2-1856	10-9-1860	277
Ell, Adam	63	Baden	N.Y. 6-1-1842	10-13-1856	173
Enthofen, Bernard	32	Hanover	N.O.	8-27-1861	302
Enthofen, Henry	27	Hanover	N.O. 11-24-1851	10-9-1854	46
Ernst, Herman	32	Prussia	Balt. 12-17-1852	4-1-1857	202
Ewig, Conrad	22	Bavaria	N.Y. 6-1-1854	10-10-1856	143
Fangmeier, Johan H.	37	Hanover	Balt. 10-8-1854	8-21-1860	249
Farst, Adolph	45	Prussia	Balt. 10-15-1855	5-24-1856	54
Fehrenbach, Heinrich	24	Baden	N.Y. 9-4-1865	10-8-1866	345
Feldmeyer, Coonrad	53	Prussia	N.O. 11-4-1850	11-3-1854	50
Feller, Martin	38	Austria	N.Y. 7-28-1858	9-3-1860	256
Fiedler, Daniel	29	Hesse Cassel	N.Y. 10-18-1856	3-12-1860	240
Fincher, Andrew	39	France	N.Y. 7-4-1845	7-24-1854	28
Fischer, John U.	30	Bavaria	N.Y. 9-10-1867	10-13-1868	408
Fischer, Lewis	21	Hanover	Balt. 8-28-1866	9-14-1868	383
Fisher, John	21	France	N.Y. 6-20-1845	10-9-1854	48
Fix, Sebastian	49	Beyern	N.O. June 1852	3-20-1856	108
Fogler, John	23	Bavaria	N.O. 5-8-1843	10-9-1854	44
Foltz, Nicholas	49	Bavaria	Balt. Sept. 1839	4-14-1855	82
Foppa, John C.	25	Switzerland	N.Y. 5-27-1855	6-29-1855	96
Frank, Joseph	28	Prussia	N.Y. 9-30-1855	11-1-1856	186
Fraser, James	25	Great Britt.	N.Y. 10-9-1852	10-8-1860	67
Frechlage, Gerhard	54	Prussia	N.Y. 6-22-1842	12-4-1865	333
Freidle, John	39	Bavaria	Balt. 5-2-1845	8-12-1858	214
Friedel, Kaspar	41	Bavaria	N.O. 5-2-1858	8-26-1858	215
Frison, Joseph	32	France	N.O. 11- -1854	10-1-1860	263
Fuchs, Conrad	60	Hessen	N.Y. 8-15-1856	9-1-1856	120
Gabreal, _____	21	Baden	N.Y. 6- -1843	8-2-1854	30
Gasser, Marcus	35	Switzerland	N.O. 4- -1844	3-21-1861	296
Gerber, Andreas	24	Bavaria	N.O. 6-1-1854	10-13-1856	169
Gerber, Christian	24	Bavaria	N.O. 12-16-1856	10-12-1858	227
Gehle, Anton	27	Prussia	Balt. 10-28-1854	10-13-1856	165
Gessner, John	34	Bavaria	N.Y. 8-20-1854	2-9-1855	60
Ghlugert, George	24	Bavaria	N.Y. 7-5-1848	1-30-1854	19
Goth, Simon	26	Bavaria	N.O. 6-1-1854	9-17-1855	102
Goetz, Wendolin	47	Baden	N.Y. 7-1-1831	10-11-1864	322
Gottschalk, Anthony	31	Hessen	N.O. 1-13-1844	10-22-1856	176
Gottlieb, Leopold	20	Oldenburg	N.Y. 7-26-1866	9-29-1868	390
Grabber, Carl J.	21	Oldenburg	Phila. 9-17-1867	9-5-1868	375?

Grabber, Franz C.	53	Oldenburg	Balt. 9-25-1867	9-5-1868	373
Gresshof, George H.	25	Hanover	Balt. 10-15-1860	8-13-1868	370
Grinder, Anthony	28	Hessen	N.Y. 5-21-1854	1-17-1855	55
Grüner, Michael	31	Bavaria	N.O. 11-1-1858	8-24-1860	250
Gude, Bernard	81	Prussia	N.O. 12-29-1853	11-2-1868	424
Gutgesell, Andreas	36	Baden	N.O. 4-24-1854	10-13-1856	166
Haack, Christian	24	Prussia	N.Y. 9-1-1857	9-15-1859	237
Hacker, John	30	Bavaria	N.O. 5-15-1852	10-13-1856	155
Hackmann, Clement	45	Oldenburg	Balt. 10-15-1848	8-9-1866	341
Hackmann, Henry	33	Oldenburg	N.Y. 6-15-1865	8-9-1866	342
Hagen, John	25	Bavaria	N.O. 11-4-1851(?)	10-6-1856	131
Hagen, Martin	28	Bavaria	N.O. 12-25-1844	6-12-1856	112
Hanfer, Mathias	28	Baden	N.Y. 3-9-1853	10-12-1858	226
Hanka, Christian	45	Hanover	Balt. 10-7-1842	2-6-1854	20
Hennebutt, Heinrich	55	Hanover	N.O. 12-11-1866	6-29-1867	348
Harbick, Thomas	21	Hanover	N.Y. 1837	10-9-1854	47
Hanselmann, Heinrich	40	Switzerland	N.Y. 5-20-1865	10-6-1866	344
Hänze, John	37	Prussia	N.O. 11-2-1852	9-8-1863	312
Hauther, Frederick	30	Bavaria	N.Y. 8-17-1866	10-12-1868	405
Hauter, Jacob	25	Bavaria	N.Y. 5-5-1860	10-27-1868	412
Heckemann, John F.	60	Hanover	N.O. 3-15-1847(?)	2-2-1857	197
Heibner, John H.	28	Bavaria	N.O. 8-10-1847	4-4-1853	10
Hemmer, Gerhart H.W.	30	Prussia	Balt. 10-10-1855	2-8-1866	336
Henhoefer, John	31	Baden	N.Y. 11-29-1851	10-9-1854	41
Henninger, Andreas	34	Baden	N.O. 3- -1847	8-24-1860	251
Herman, Adam	39	Bavaria	Balt. 8-1-1853	9-1-1857	203
Hettrick, Mathias	25	Baden	N.O. 6-1-1854	10-12-1858	221
Hilmes, John Clemens	37	Hanover	N.Y. 11-2-1865	10-30-1868	415
Hob, Isidore	30	Switzerland	N.Y. 4-21-1857	4-9-1860	243
Hochgsang, Michael, Jr.	21	Bavaria	N.Y. 9-3-1848	10-9-1854	42
Hoelscher, Bernard	22	Hanover	N.Y. 8-5-1866	11-2-1868	427
Hoffman, Carl	21	Hanover	Balt. 4-8-1866	10-30-1868	414
Hoffman, John	24	Bavaria	N.Y. 9-15-1854	10-6-1856	130
Hoffman, John L.	26	Bavaria	N.O. 11-2-1845	11-3-1856	190
Hofling, Adam	36	Germany	N.Y.	12-29-1854	57
Hollenberg, Harman H.	24	Prussia	N.Y. 6-28-1866	3-24-1869	433
Holzbock, Charles	30	Hessen	N.Y. 10-14-1854	10-4-1856	136
Holzbock(?), Henry	21	Hessen	N.Y. 10-14-1854	10-4-1856	137
Höntrup, Franz	36	Prussia	Balt. 5-30-1857	10-12-1868	406
Hoppenjohn, Gerhard	28	Hanover	Balt. July 1846	3-31-1855	80
Horst, Edward	25	Baden	N.Y. 1841	10-9-1860	280
Houch, John G.	30	Bavaria	N.O. 11-12-1820	8-13-1855	94
Hratner, John U.	28	Bavaria	N.Y. 7-2-1866	9-24-1867	353
Huffschmidt, Ferdinand	38	Baden	N.O. 5-10-1854	10-13-1856	156
Humbert, Gerhard	40	Hanover	N.O. 5-8-1852	2-12-1855	61
Hurst, Edmond	47	Baden	N.Y. 10-21-1852	4-4-1853	11
Imhof, Joseph	25	Bavaria	N.Y. 5-2-1867	10-12-1868	404
Jaekle, Thomas	53	Wurtenberg	N.Y. 1-1-1861	10-4-1864	318
Jakle, Conrad	23	Wurtenberg	N.O. 12-16-1858	11-21-1861	305
Jochem, Jacob	32	Prussia	N.Y. 6-29-1847	3-28-1853	8
Jochum, Friederich	27	France	N.Y. 12-17-1855	3-10-1868	366
Jochum, George	51	France	N.Y. 12-24-1855	2-12-1864	314
Jogle, Valentine	78	Baden	N.Y. 5-22-1844	10-4-1856	135
Jordan, Johann A.	21	Bavaria	Balt. 5-5-1854	2-19-1858	210
Kaiser, Hermann	26	Prussia	N.O. 11-15-1865	3-24-1869	434
Kaiser, Peter	56	Bavaria	N.O. 6-7-1852	2-15-1869	430
Kartmann, Joseph	33	Prussia	Balt. 4-15-1833	11-1-1856	184
Kätter, Heinrich	31	Prussia	Balt. 9-30-1860	9-29-1868	387
Kaup(?), Stephan	29	Prussia	Balt. May 1851	11-4-1858	235

Keller, John	25	Prussia	N.Y. 6-22-1852	10-13-1856	158
Kemp, Michael	24	Bavaria	N.O. 12-26-1852	10-10-1856	146
Kemper, Anton	57	Hanover	N.O. 11-3-1856	11-2-1860	286
Kemper, Henry	22	Hanover	N.O. 11-3-1856	11-2-1860	285
Kennel, Sebastian	42	Bavaria	N.O.	11-30-1857	207
Kerkhoff, Johann F.	34	Oldenburg	N.O. 11-15-1860	2-28-1866	338
Kerner, Fred L.	24	Saxony	N.Y. 8-20-1854	8-13-1856	116
Ketlen, Henry	24	Prussia	N.O. 5-21-1849	3-28-1853	9
Ketter, Wilhelm	40	Prussia	Balt. 10-22-1860	4-7-1869	437
Kiefer, Anton	34	Baden	N.O. 5-2-1853	9-16-1856	122
Kilian, Henry	26	Hesse Cassel	Balt. 6-21-1852	9-27-1858	220
Kilian, Jonas	21	Hesse Cassel	N.Y. 9-4-1854	9-27-1858	219
Klamens, Peter	37	Prussia	N.Y. 6-1-1850	6-12-1855	90
Klausemeyer, John F.	26	Hanover	N.O. 10-27-1853	12-9-1858	232
Klein, Carl	23	Hessen	N.O. 12-28-1859	2-27-1865	332
Klein, Peter	68	Baden	N.Y. 8-13-1853	10-27-1856	181
Klein, Peter	36	Prussia	N.Y. 8-10-1854	11-3-1860	288
Kleinhelter, John B.	31	Hanover	N.O. 6-23-1848	2-14-1855	68
Kleinimann, Phillip C.	28	Prussia	N.Y. 8-10-1854	3-26-1855	79
Klostermann, Henry W.	21	Hanover	N.O. 11-19-1857	2-15-1859	233
Klümper, Anton	41	Prussia	Balt. 7-15-1864	10-11-1864	323
Knoepfly, Abraham	27	Switzerland	N.Y. 5-15-1852	10-9-1854	45
Koenig, Henry	34	Hanover	N.O. 12-25-1853	5-3-1864	317
Koessler (?), Augustin	47	France	N.Y. 1844	11-30-1860	290
Kometscher, John M.	25	Hanover	Balt. 4-15-1854	10=31-1868	417
Kraft, John Georg	60	Bavaria	N.O. 8-24-1850	2-12-1855	62
Kreiling, Franz	33	Hanover	N.O. 12-10-1854	3-27-1868	367
Kress, Balthasar	41	Hessen	N.Y. 11-2-1855	8-10-1858	213
Krodel, John	27	Bavaria	N.O. 11-7-1854	10-11-1856	148
Krodel, John	30	Bavaria	N.Y. 10-4-1861	10-5-1868	396
Krodel, Martin	26	Bavaria	N.Y. 6-17-1865	10-6-1868	401
Kroneberger, Peter	37	Prussia	N.Y. 9-24-1866	9-5-1868	378
Krüger, Frederick	56	Prussia	N.Y. 3-10-1846	10-13-1856	170
Krusenklaus, Henry	36	Prussia	Balt. 10-27-1855	11-23-1858	230
Kunkel, Adam	42	Bavaria	N.Y. 8-27-1845	11-3-1856	188
Kunkel, Lorenz	50	Bavaria	N.Y. 3-22-1864	10-5-1868	392
Kunkler, Fredrick	40	France	N.O. 5-4-1832	10-9-1854	43
Lackmann, Heinrich	24	Hanover	N.O. Dec. 1854	11-5-1860	289
Lackmann, Ferdinand	44	Hanover	N.O. 11-2-1854	10-11-1864	324
Lammers, Adolph H.	25	Prussia	Balt. 10-14-1860	2-8-1866	337
Landwehr, William	62	Hanover	Balt. 9-27-1842	2-12-1857	199
Lang, Peter	30	Prussia	N.O. 1-1-1847	11-1-1856	187
Lanbert (?), Joseph	54	Switzerland	N.Y. Jan. 1858	8-27-1860	252
Lau, Herman J.	23	Hanover	N.O. 1844	11-2-1860	284
Lechaner, Henry	42	Bavaria	N.O. 11-12-1853?	6-6-1854	25
Leggerman, August	21	Prussia	N.Y. 8-17-1857	10-6-1860	265
Lenin(?)gruber, Charles	30	Switzerland	N.Y. 5-17-1864	10-8-1868	402
Letsinhühter(?), Henry	21	Prussia	Balt. 10-25-1857	11-29-1858	231
Leykamp(?), Michael	25	Bavaria	N.O. 5-12-1854	10-14-1856	164
Libberd, Henry	25	Hanover	N.O. 10-27-1852	2-17-1855	70
Limberg, Francis	52	Prussia	N.Y. 11-7-1861	1-11-1864	313
Lisetzi, August	22	Baden	N.O. 11-20-1853	10-12-1858	222
Litschgi, Conrad	26	Baden	N.Y. 3-17-1866	4-1-1867	351
Lochner, John	33	Bavaria	Balt. 4-15-1852	10-13-1856	167
Loechte, Gerhardt	28	Prussia	N.Y. 5-16-1866	10-27-1868	413
Loew, Adam	28	Hesen	N.Y. 6-30-1854	1-1-1855	58
Lorai, Nicholas	32	Hasen(Duchy)	N.O. 6- -1854	9-23-1854	32
Loruy, Egide	46	Hessen	N.O. 11-2-1859	10-5-1867	359
Ludrauer, Erhardt	21	Bavaria	N.O. 11-10-1851	7-27-1860	248

Luese(?), George	45	Baden	N.O. 3-15-1853	9-10-1856	121
Luken, John H.	22	Hanover	N.Y. 9-19-1859	1-7-1861	293
Lutz, John	37	Bavaria	N.O. 12-12-1853	9-15-1855	101
Machenbaier, Lawrance	64	Bavaria	N.O. 12-25-1852	11-1-1856	185
Mader, Ferdinand	22	Baden	N.O. 3-19-1855	9-15-1855	97
Mahling, Peter	Page not filmed				35
Mankeld, Galone	46	Saxony	Balt. 8-9-1854	10-4-1856	133
Mann, Wolfgang	22	Bavaria	N.O. 1-16-1848	10-13-1856	160
Mathias, Adam	29	Prussia	N.O. 5-1-1849	7-19-1858	212
Mathias, Anthony	43	Germany	N.O. 6- -1848	2-12-1855	63
Mathias, Peter	37	Bavaria	N.O. 5-15-1850	10-3-1854	38
Mayer, Augustus	30	Baden	N.Y. 8-20-1856	11-7-1864	329
Mehling, George	23	Bavaria	Balt. 8-8-1848	10-25-1860	282
Mehling, Joseph	30	Bavaria	Balt. 8-8-1848	10-25-1860	281
Mehni, Conrad	33	Wurtemberg	N.O. 1-9-1846	10-10-1856	144
Merfer, Johannes	41	Waldek	N.O. May 1852	3-21-1861	297
Mersnam, Theodor	28	Prussia	N.Y. 5-7-1855	7-25-1856	114
Meyer, Frank R.	28	Hanover	N.O. 12-23-1856	1-5-1869	429
Meyer, George	48	Bavaria	N.O. 5-15-1852	10-13-1856	157
Meyer, Johann H.	23	Hanover	N.Y. 11-1-1865	9-17-1868	384
Meyer, Mathias	38	Hanover	N.O. 6-12-1856	10-20-1856	174
Mieszner, Joachim	26	Hanover	N.O. 11-29-1849	1-21-1856	107
Miller, Henry A.	21	Hanover	N.O. 12- -1853	6-5-1854	23
Miller, John	43	Bavaria	N.Y. 6-20-1853	10-14-1856	162
Miller, John H.	25	Prussia	Balt. 10-15-1860	1-7-1861	292
Miller, Peter	44	Prussia	Boston 5-8-1853	4-14-1855	83
Moeller, Bernard	28	Hanover	N.O. 6-15-1859	3-3-1864	315
Moerder, Herman	23	Baden	N.Y. Aug. 1856	10-8-1860	269
Moessner(?), Ignatz	42	Baden	N.O. 2-16-1855	3-1-1860	239
Mohr, John	Page not filmed				361
Monntel, Henry	22	Hanover	N.O. 10-26-1852	2-28-1853	6
Morgen, Mathias	28	Prussia	N.Y. 6-21-1857	10-12-1857	204
Motschman, Jacob	27	Bavaria	N.Y. 5-25-1853	2-23-1857	202
Müller, Henry	30	Hanover	N.O. 12-17-1857	11-28-1862	311
Müller, John	30	Baden	N.Y. 5-15-1857	6-7-1860	245
Müller, John A.	52	Bavaria	Balt. 10-21-1854	11-4-1864	328
Muller, Joseph A.	30	Hesse Darnstadt	N.O. 1-17-1854	9-7-1868	379
Nägeli, Hubert	35	Baden	N.Y. 10-16-1853	7-19-1856	113
Neuhäusel, Andreas	26	Hessen	N.Y. 3-16-1867	10-5-1868	394
Nickel, John	34	Bavaria	N.O. 12-14-1853	2-23-1857	200
Nohr, Peter	26	Bavaria	N.O. 3-20-1854	12-26-1861	306
Nüssmeier, Henry	38	Prussia	Balt. 10-1-1857	12-12-1865	334
Ochs, Allis	39	Wurtemberg	N.Y. 8-23-1853	10-14-1856	163
O'Conner, Bede	29	Gr. Br.	N.Y. 1-31-1853	6-29-1855	95
Oetinger, Karl	29	Baden	N.O. 1-1-1857	3-12-1860	241
Opel, Johann, Jr.	53	Bavaria	N.Y. 8- -1854	10-9-1860	278
Peters, Henry	35	Prussia	Balt. 10-13-1857	1-9-1862	307
Pfaffenbarger, John	41	Bavaria	N.O. 11-4-1852	4-8-1853	12
Pfister, Andreas	48	Baden	N.O. 11-28-1855	10-13-1868	410
Pieper, John	34	Prussia	Balt. 5-26-1857	3-17-1858	211
Preis, Michael	48	Bavaria	N.Y. 6-29-1860	10-1-1860	262
Prietsch, William	26	Prussia	N.O. 10-13-1867	3-23-1869	432
Propheter, John F.	51	Bavaria	N.Y. 6-25-1866	9-6-1868	380
Quante, Francis	22	Prussia	Balt. 10-15-1855	8-23-1856	118
Queste, Barnard	27	Prussia	N.O. 10-2-1853	10-3-1854	39
Rainer, Joseph A.	21	Hesse Cassel	N.Y. 9-1-1857	10-19-1857	205
Raley(?), Vincennes	27	Switzerland	N.Y. 5-30-1853	9-8-1855	98
Rau, Christian	24	Wurtemberg	N.Y. 12-3-1854	12-23-1854	73
Reichmann, Peter	28	Bavaria	N.Y. 7-4-1838	4-13-1861	298

Reinighaus, Ernie	26	Prussia	N.Y. 10-28-1865	9-29-1868	389
Reker, Joseph	55	Prussia	Phila. 8-4-1838	9-24-1860	255
Remke, Gerhard	28	Prussia	Balt. 10-15-1865	8-19-1867	349
Remke, Joseph A.	25	Prussia	Balt. 10-2-1865	10-3-1867	355
Renderer, John M.	26	Switzerland	N.Y. 1860	5-9-1861	300
Renderer, Justice	26	Switzerland	N.Y. 12-27-1860	5-9-1861	299
Reusz, Michael	26	Bavaria	N.Y. 8-2-1864	10-8-1866	346
Rickelman, Joseph	30	Hanover	N.O. 6-10-1848	10-27-1856	178
Riegelsberger, Charles	22	Baden	N.Y. 8-15-1862	10-1-1867	354
Riesenbeck, Moritz	37	Prussia	N.O. 11-4-1853	1-19-1857	196
Ringoh, Conrad	22	Hesse Cassel	N.Y. 9-4-1854	9-27-1858	218
Risse, Kaspar	42	Prussia	Balt. 5-29-1857	11-10-1857	206
Ritter, Christian	33	Switzerland	N.O. 12-25-1851	6-5-1854	24
Ritter, John	31	Switzerland	N.Y.	9-15-1855	100
Roesser, John	35	Bavaria	N.Y. 6-15-1854	3-24-1866	339
Rohrseheib, John J.	39	Bavaria	N.O. 10-25-1854	3-28-1859	234
Rowekamp, Gerhard H.	30	Hanover	N.O. 10- -1845	2-12-1855	65
Rudolph, John	22	Hesse Cassel	N.Y. June 1853	10-3-1860	264
Ruesche, Heinrich	44	Prussia	N.Y. 5-31-1857	10-5-1867	358
Ruidenspacher, Laurence	22	Baden	N.O. 3-20-1854	10-13-1856	171
Rutzer, Anton	43	Switzerland	N.Y. 6-20-1866	9-5-1868	376
Salat, Dominicus	41	Wurtemberg	N.Y. 10-3-1851	10-6-1856	126
Sallner, John	26	Bavaria	N.O. 5-18-1853	1-1-1855	59
Sandermann, Henry W.	42	Prussia	Balt. 11-1-1854	12-27-1855	105
Sandermann, John H.	48	Prussia	N.O. 10-15-1855	12-27-1855	106
Schafer, Henry	49	Hanover	N.O. 12-24-1852	6-5-1854	21
Scheidemann, Christoph	24	Bavaria	N.Y. 5-12-1867	10-10-1868	403
Schell, Clemens	42	Hessen	N.Y. 8-14-1851	10-27-1856	179
Schepman, Herman F.	25	Hanover	N.Y. 9-25-1855	10-28-1858	228
Schepmann, Ernst A.	23	Hanover	N.Y. 6-1-1867	3-3-1869	431
Scheuerman, Frederick	24	Hessen	N.Y. 8-15-1856	9-1-1856	119
Schiller, John	45	Germany	N.Y. 6-28-1852	2-12-1855	66
Schitter, Michael	23	France	N.Y. 6-1-1854	10-10-1856	142
Schlechter, Johann W.	65	Prussia	N.O. 3-29-1851	2-15-1865	331
Schlegel, Joseph	38	Baden	N.O. 5-22-1854	10-4-1856	134
Schmidt, Fredrick W.	25	Prussia	N.O. 11- -1854	7-20-1860	247
Schmidt, John H.	27	Hanover	Balt. Sept. 1852	12-27-1854	52
Schmidt, Mathias	21	Baden	N.O. 3-20-1854	10-11-1856	153
Schneider, Bernard	32	Baden	N.Y. 10-12-1866	10-6-1868	399
Schneider, Friedrich	32	Oldenburg	N.O. 11-15-1859	10-21-1862	310
Schneider, Joseph	25	Baden	N.Y. 1-12-1866	10-9-1866	347
Schneider, Laurence	46	Baden	N.Y. 7-4-1846	10-8-1856	140
Schnirefing, Bernard	22	Oldenburg	N.Y. 5-2-1858	11-3-1860	287
Schnorr, John	21	Hesse Cassel	N.O. Oct. 1852	10-8-1860	275
Schnorr, John	33	Hessen	N.O. 6-1-1852	10-6-1856	129
Schnorr, Peter	28	Hessen	N.O. 10-26-1852(?)	10-6-1856	127
Scholl, Christian	45	Wurtemberg	N.Y. 4-25-1856	11-26-1864	330
Schroerceeke(?), William A.	44	Prussia	N.O. 11-30-1852	2-2-1857	198
Schuble, Joseph	33	Baden	N.O. 11-18-1853	10-8-1860	276
Schwippe, Heinrich	55	Hanover	Balt. 11-2-1858	11-2-1868	425
Schumacher, Ferdinand	21	Wurtemberg	N.Y. Feb. 1852	10-3-1860	266
Schutte, Fredrick	32	Hanover	N.O. 12-25-1850	8-12-1861	301
Seibert, John	29	Bavaria	N.Y. 12-23-1856	8-27-1860	253
Seier, Jacob	55	Hungary	Balt. 5-4-1861	10-4-1864	319
Sellhaim(?), Conrod	19	Bavaria	N.O. 1-16-1850	5-10-1855	88

Name	Age	Origin	Arrival	Date	No.
Senninzer, Nicholas	21	Luxemburg	N.Y. Dec. 1849	10-1-1860	261
Sermersheim, Cornelius	23	Baden	N.O. 3-20-1846	10-4-1856	138
Sermersheim, Edward	22	Baden	N.O. 3-15-1846	11-3-1856	189
Siebe, William	21	Prussia	Balt. 6-2-1857	7-16-1860	246
Skezynacke, Martin	35	Prussia	Balt. 9-12-1867	10-1-1868	391
Smith, Altiser	38	Baden	N.O. 12-6-1853	2-24-1855	71
Smith, John	35	Bavaria	N.O. 1-1-1845	10-2-1856	132
Sonderman, Albert	22	Prussia	N.Y. 5-30-1857	10-8-1860	270
Sonderman, August	21	Prussia	N.Y. May 1854	1-19-1858	208
Stal, Francis	23	Prussia	N.Y. May 1854	1-19-1858	209
Stamm, Henrich J.	42	Prussia	N.Y. 12-22-1865	10-5-1867	356
Steffe, Timotheus	28	Baden	N.O. 5-2-1854	9-17-1856	123
Steffens, Herman	28	Hanover	N.O. 12-30-1848	10-27-1856	180
Stein, John G. Jr.	25	Hanover	N.O. 12-2-1845	6-5-1854	22
Steinhauser, Matheus	64	Wurtemberg	N.Y. 3-24-1866	10-6-1868	397
Steker, Conrad	32	Hessen	N.Y. 6-10-1854	10-11-1856	151
Stemle, Vincenz	28	Baden	N.Y. 9-15-1857	5-23-1860	244
Stendebeck, Joseph	31	Oldenburg	N.Y. 8-2-1866	9-5-1868	374
Sterringer, Phillip	34	Bavaria	N.Y. 8-15-1856	10-13-1856	172
Stirner, Carl	35	Baden	N.O. 12-20-1861	9-7-1867	352
Stirtkamp(?), William Sutkamp in Declar.	24	Prussia	N.O. 12-1-1839	1-17-1853	2
Stratmann, John	49	Prussia	N.Y. 4-19-1857	10-7-1867	362
Straub, Mathias	42	Baden	N.Y. 3-24-1867	9-26-1868	386
Straub, Stephan	32	Baden	N.Y. 10-2-1865	10-5-1868	393
Strotmann, Wilhelm	46	Prussia	N.Y. 10-21-1858	10-5-1867	357
Tebbin, Gerhard H. Sr.	63	Hanover	N.Y. 11-2-1865	11-2-1868	420
Tebbin, Gerhard J. Jr.	46	Hanover	N.Y. 11-2-1865	11-2-1868	421
Tieskoelter, Herman	24	Prussia	N.Y. 10-15-1867	11-2-1868	426
Tschapp, Alhanasius	52	Switzerland	N.Y. 5-27-1855	8-8-1855	93
Turner, Frederick	35	Hanover	N.Y. 1-1-1849	1-17-1853	1
Unger, John	29	Bavaria	N.Y. 6-27-1859	11-18-1861	304
Unliĕken, Bernard	40	Hanover	N.O. 12-4-1851	8-11-1856	115
Vogler, Andreas	41	Bavaria	N.Y. June 1841	4-9-1860	242
Volmer, Henry	42	Baden	N.O. 2-5-1853	11-1-1856	177
Vonderscheer, Charles	30	France	N.O. 11-11-1846	10-27-1856	182
Vonderschmidt, Beukart	28	Bavaria	N.O. 1-15-1854	4-19-1855	86
Vonzong, Christian	23	Hesse Cassel	N.Y. 5-1-1857	9-18-1858	217
Voss, Frederick	25	Prussia	N.Y. 7-21-1866	6-10-1868	368
Vost, Adolph	45	Prussia	Balt. 10-15-1855	5-24-1856	111
Waezearl, John	25	Bryn___	N.O. 10-15-1852	6-13-1854	26
Wagner, August	23	Wirtemberg	N.Y. 8-11-1867	9-14-1868	381
Walser, Joseph A.	35	Wirtemberg	N.Y. 5-26-1867	9-5-1868	372
Wandlehite, Henry	30	Hanover	N.O. 1-1-1851	4-7-1856	109
Warnsmann, Frederich	20	Hanover	N.Y. 11-1-1865	9-29-1868	388
Weber, John	36	Hessen	N.Y. 6-7-1852	10-6-1856	128
Weber, Leopold	28	Wurtemberg	N.Y. 9-9-1853	3-19-1855	78
Weber, Lewis	32	Hessen	Balt. 6-1-1856	10-13-1856	159
Wegemeier, Peter	51	Bavaria	N.Y. 10-15-1853	10-11-1864	325
Weglage, Johann H.	50	Hanover	Balt. 6-25-1841	1-10-1857	195
Wegnast, Henry	31	Prussia	N.O. Oct. 1853	4-16-1855	84
Weinerth, Lewis	25	Bavaria	N.Y. 5-4-1865	10-6-1868	395
Weischam, John F.	38	Hanover	Balt. 1848	3-7-1853	7
Weisel(?), George	35	Hessen	Balt. 6-24-1844	9-25-1854	37

Wendolin, Anthony	31	France	N.O. 8-1-1848	10-11-1855	103
Wenning, Wolfgang	32	Bavaria	N.O. 11-28-1854	10-10-1864	321
Werremeier, Ernst	24	Prussia	Balt. 10-14-1860	10-22-1867	364
Werremeier, Wilhelm	25	Prussia	Balt. 9-15-1860	10-1-1866	343
Wetz, Johann	34	Bavaria	N.Y. 11-28-1854	9-11-1860	254
Wiebking, Frederick	28	Hanover	N.Y. 10-2-1864	1-10-1867	350
Wiesel, Christophe	34	Bavaria	N.Y. 3-18-1866	9-5-1868	371
Winterhalter, Ludwick	21	Baden	N.O. 3-25-1853	10-17-1855	104
Wirsching, Bartholomew	40	Bavaria	N.O. 1-8-1854	10-1-1856	125
Wissing, John	36	Bavaria	N.O. 6-29-1856	11-3-1856	191
Wittle, John H.	27	Hanover	N.Y. 10-9-1842	2-17-1853	4
Wohlfahrt, Conrad	28	Wurtemberg	N.O. 2-28-1853	10-21-1856	175
Wüllers, Karl	25	Prussia	Balt. 10-15-1857	8-31-1858	216
Yochum, Jacob	62	Bavaria	N.O. 11-16-1865	10-6-1868	400
Zehr, Charles	25	Saxony	Balt. 8-14-1853	10-12-1856	147
Ziegler, Mathias	32	Bavaria	N.O. 11-29-1860	1-7-1861	291
Ziegler, Mathias	23	Bavaria	N.O. 11-20-1861	11-3-1868	428

NATURALIZATION RECORDS IN INDIANA COUNTIES AS LISTED IN WPA INVENTORIES

The inventories of county records made by the WPA in the early 1940s have proved very useful even though they are not always completely accurate. Two Indiana counties did not participate—Hancock and Wayne. New courthouses have replaced the 1940 buildings in many instances and in the removal of records some have no doubt been lost or discarded and some placed in other depositories. However, because of the great importance attached to the Naturalization Records, it is difficult to believe they would not have been carefully preserved. Although listed under varying titles, there seem to be two definite types of records kept: one, the Declaration of Intention, in which a person of foreign birth appeared before the circuit court and announced his intention of becoming a United States citizen. This declaration apparently could be made a few months after his arrival; two, after a longer residence he could petition the court for naturalization and at the end of five years if his petition was acted upon favorably he was granted citizenship upon his taking an oath of allegiance to the United States constitution, etc. Federal laws governing naturalization of aliens were changed from time to time; after 1929 citizenship was granted only by the Federal government.

In most instances the volumes in the county inventories were listed as Declarations of Intention; some were listed as Petition and Naturalization or Records of Naturalization, which we have taken to mean the second and final papers. The number of volumes given in the inventories has been included below as a help in identifying the series; since the volumes were of different sizes and pagination, the number is no indication of the number of names. The Order Books of the circuit courts should be checked for declarations of intention and records of naturalization prior to the date when separate records were kept.

It has been only since 1972 that the county clerks were allowed to furnish information from the Naturalization Records. From 1852 to 1911, the Indiana Supreme Court also granted citizenship; a card file of those who received their papers from this court is in the Archives Division, Indiana State Library.

ADAMS: Declaration of Intention, 1854-1929, 4 vols.

ALLEN: Declaration of Intention, 1844-1930, 23 vols.; Record of Naturalization, 1854-1929, 15 vols.

BARTHOLOMEW: Declaration of Intention, 1852-1935, 6 vols.

BENTON: Declaration of Intention, 1862-1929, 3 vols.

BLACKFORD: Declaration of Intention, 1854-1927, 4 vols. plus 1 file box;Record of Naturalization, 1906-1928, 1 vol.

BOONE: None listed.

BROWN: Declaration of Intention, 1860, 1 vol.

CARROLL: Declaration of Intention, 1852-1904, 2 vols.

CASS: Declaration of Intention, 1854-1929, 7 vols.; Record of petitions, 1848-1906, 1 vol.; Record of Naturalization, 1907-1929, 3 vols. plus 2 file boxes.

CLARK: Record of Naturalization, 1861 ff., 5 vols.

CLAY: Declaration of Intention, 1863 ff., 11 vols.; Record of Naturalization, 1904 ff., 5 vols.

CLINTON: Record of Naturlization, 1908-1929, 2 vols.

CRAWFORD: None listed.

DAVIESS: Declaration of Intention, 1856-1928, 2 vols.; Record of Naturalization, 1908-1929, 2 vols.

DEARBORN: Declaration those taking final oath, 1839 ff., 7 vols.

DECATUR: None listed.

DEKALB: Declaration of Intention, 1860-1905, 1 vol.; Record of Naturalization, 1909-1929, 3 vols. plus 1 file box labeled 1936.

DELAWARE: None listed.

DUBOIS: Declaration of Intention, 1912-1919, 1 file box. Those doing the inventory apparently missed the volumes mentioned above for which the Genealogy Division has a microfilm copy.

ELKHART: None listed.

FAYETTE: Declaration of Intention, 1858-1902, 1 vol.; Record of Naturalization, 1908-1926, 3 vols.

FLOYD: Declaration of Intention and Final Papers, 1904-1927, 4 vols.

FOUNTAIN: Declaration of Intention, 1854-1928; Record of Naturalization, 1894-1902, 1 vol.; 1913 ff. 5 vols. Separate index.

FRANKLIN: Declaration of Intention, 1836 ff., 2 vols.; Record of Naturalization, 1839-1904, 2 vols. Genealogy Division has microfilm of records, 1826-1929.

FULTON: None listed.

GIBSON: None listed.

GRANT: None listed.

GREENE: Declaration of Intention, 1854 ff., 7 vols. plus 11 file boxes; 1907-1929, 4 vols.; Record of Naturalization, 1856-1905, 1 vol.

HAMILTON: Declaration of Intention, 1855-1905, 1 vol.

HARRISON: Declaration of Intention and final papers, 1855-1920, 1 vol.; Record of Naturalization, 1913 ff., 1 vol.

HENDRICKS: Declaration of Intention, 1852-1924, 2 vols.; Record of Naturalization, 1856-1924, 2 vols.

HENRY: Declaration of Intention and final papers, 1854-1904, 1 vol.

HOWARD: Declaration of Intention and final papers, 1872-1931, 13 vols.

HUNTINGTON: Declaration of Intention, 1854-1929, 7 vols. Another series of 3 vols., 1896-1918, gives names and ages of children.

JACKSON: Record of Naturalization, 1852-1928, 4 vols.

JASPER: Record of Naturalization, 1870 ff., 10 vols.

JAY: Declaration of Intention, 1856-1906, 2 vols.; Naturalization Papers, 1909 ff.

JEFFERSON: Declaration of Intention, 1908-1926, 1 vol.; Record of Naturalization, 1834-1928, 3 vols.

JENNINGS: Declaration of Intention, 1908-1926, 1 vol.; Record of Naturalization, 1850-1928, 3 vols.

JOHNSON: Declaration of Intention, 1873-1908, 1 vol.

KNOX: Declaration of Intention, 1852 ff., 10 vols.; Record of Naturalization, 1855 ff., 7 vols.

KOSCIUSKO: Declaration of Intention, 1853 ff., 7 vols.

LA GRANGE: None listed.

LAKE: Declaration of Intention, 1854-1929, 17 vols. Separate index.

LA PORTE: Record of Naturalization, 1854 ff., 27 vols.

LAWRENCE: Record of Naturalization, 1881-1930, 4 vols.

MADISON: None listed.

MARION: Declaration of Intention, 1857 ff., 27 vols.; missing for 1866-79; Record of Naturalization, 1903-1928, 20 vols.; Naturalization papers, 1832-1906, 18 file boxes.

MARSHALL: Declaration of Intention, 1854 ff., 5 vols.

MARTIN: Declaration of Intention, 1867-1924, 2 vols.

MIAMI: Declaration of Intention, 1874-1928, 2 vols.

MONROE: Declaration of Intention, 1908 ff., 3 vols.; Record of Naturalization, 1904-1905, 1 vol.

MONTGOMERY: Declarations of Intent, 1855-1860; Record of Naturalization, 1855-1929, 4 vols.; plus 1 file box of petitions.

MORGAN: Declaration of Intention and final papers, 1876 ff., 2 vols.

NEWTON: Declaration of Intention and final papers, 1860-1917, 4 vols. plus 1 file drawer.

NOBLE: Declaration of Intention, 1859-1929, 4 vols.

OHIO: Declaration of Intention, 1914-1925, 1 vol.; Record of Naturalization, 1848 ff., 2 vols.

ORANGE: Naturalization papers, 1914 ff., 1 file box.

OWEN: Declaration of Intention, 1854 ff., 2 vols. (1921-27 missing); Record Naturalization, 1908 ff. 1 vol.

PARKE: Declaration of Intention, 1854 ff., 5 vols.; Record of Naturalization, 1888-1934, 5 vols.

PERRY: Record of Naturalization, 1852-1904, 3 vols. plus 1 file box.

PIKE: Declaration of Intention and final papers, 1867 ff., 4 vols.

PORTER: Declaration of Intention, 1872 ff., 4 file boxes.

POSEY: Declaration of Intention, 1854-1904, 2 vols. Also petitions, 1863-1917, 2 vols.

PULASKI: Declaration of Intention and final papers, 1856 ff., 8 vols.

PUTNAM: None listed.

RANDOLPH: Declaration of Intention and final record, 1854 ff., 16 vols.

RIPLEY: Declaration of Intention, 1851-1918, 3 vols.; R

RIPLEY: Declaration of Intention, 1851-1918, 3 vols.; Record of Naturalization, 1865-1930, 3 vols. Using these records and the Order Books of the Probate Court, Circuit Court, and Court of Common Pleas, Mrs. Ann

Gibbs of Holton has compiled Naturalization Record, Ripley County, 1837-1900, a typed copy of which is in the Genealogy Division.

RUSH: Declaration of Intention, 1851 ff., 4 vols.

ST. JOSEPH: None listed in Inventory.

SCOTT: Declaration of Intention, 1852-94. Using this record, the Federal censuses, and the Circuit Court Order Books, Carl R. Bogardus, Sr. and William R. Greear, have compiled and published *Persons of Foreign Birth in Scott County, 1817-1894.*

SHELBY: Declaration of Intention, 1868-1906, 2 vols.

SPENCER: Declaration of Intention, 1852-1884, 1 vol.

STARKE: Declaration of Intention, 1852 ff., 8 vols.

STEUBEN: Declaration of Intention, 1854-1929, 3 vols.

SULLIVAN: Declaration of Intention, 1864-1929, 7 vols.

SWITZERLAND: Declaration of Intention, 1841-1924, 2 vols.

TIPPECANOE: Naturalization Records, 1907-1926, 12 vols.

TIPTON: Declaration of Intention, 1856-1904, 1 vol.; Record of Naturalization, 1856-1906, 1 vol.

UNION: Declaration of Intention, 1918-1927, 1 vol.; Record of Naturalization, 1812 (?)-1898, 2 vols.

VANDERBURGH: Declaration of Intention and Record of Naturalization, 1857-1929, 2 vols.

VERMILLION: Declaration of Intention, 1897 ff., 15 vols.; Petitions and Record of Naturalization, 1900 ff., 11 vols.

VIGO: Declaration of Intention, 1858 ff., 30 vols.; Record of petitions for naturalization, 1906-30., 12 vols.

WABASH: Declaration of Intention, 1854-1928, 9 vols.

WARREN: Declaration of Intention, 1907 ff., 2 vols. Also petitions, 1856 ff. 2 vols.

WARRICK: Declaration of Intention, 1852-1900, 2 vols.

WASHINGTON: Record of petitions arranged alphabetically, 1892-1906, 1 vol.

WELLS: Declaration of Intention, 1856-1928, 2 vols.; also petitions, 1910-1929, 2 vols.

WHITE: Declaration of Intention, 1868-1928, 3 vols., plus 5 file boxes.

WHITLEY: Declaration of Intention, 1856-1905, 1 vol.; Record of Naturalization, 1856-1905, 1 vol.

Correction: In the list of courthouses having naturalization records (printed in December 1976 issue), Delaware County was omitted. They had both the petitions and naturalization records from 1851 to 1929, and these are now in the Bracken Library at Ball State University with other Delaware County archival material.

JENNINGS COUNTY MARRIAGES, 1818-1837

Compiled from microfilm of Book 1 and 2 of Jennings County Marriage Records in Genealogy Division, Indiana State Library.

Abbott, Lawson - Abigail Chace   8- 8-1834
Adams, David - Elizabeth Hall lic.   4- 9-1819
Adams, George W. - Margaret Keryea   9-21-1832
Allen, John - Nancy McCrory   1-27-1831
Alloway, John - Nancy Herring   6-16-1831
Amick, Abram - Sarah Griffith   1-12-1837
Anderson, Milton - Elizabeth Green
                                 lic.   1- 7-1830
Andrews, Alanson - Laura Hardin   1-23-1828
Applegate, Samuel - Polly J. Bridges   9- 2-1834
Arbuckle, James - Alice Owen   3-26-1834
Arbuckle, John - Elizabeth Phillips   9- 3-1835
Avery, Henry - Rachel Russell   7-12-1830
Bacon, Elijah - Almoda Ballard   2-10-1820
Baker, Anderson - Hannah Robbins   3-11-1835
Baker, David - Cythiana Glasgow
                                 lic.   4-30-1827
Baker, William - Sally Lewis   12-28-1820
Ballard, Aaron - Mary Dolph   1821
Bare, John - Eliza Riggs   6- 5-1823
Bare, John C. - Betsy Ann McKeehan   9-18-1833
Bare, Owen - Catherine Hoyt   4-14-1836
Barnes, John - Susannah Chandler   11-16-1820
Barnes, Robert - Cornelia Atchinson   4- 1-1830
Barnes, William - Elizabeth Smith   7-17-1831
Barnett, Ebenezer - Elonor Attcheson
                                       12-31-1829
Barnum, Timothy - Sarah Davis   2-21-1833
Baumgarner, George - Sarah Brooks   5-29-1836
Baxter, James - Patsy Stott   5-19-1829
Bayers(?), Augustus C. - Jane Merrell
                                       11- 6-1832
Beeman, Jesse - Nancy Pool   11-30-1824
Beeman, Jonathan - Polly Pool   5-13-1825
Bennett, Andrew - Kitty Osburn lic.   3-15-1828
Bennett, James - Katherine Moseley   12-13-1829
Bennett, Robert - Elizabeth Burk   12-18-1820
Bennett, William - Mary Hall lic.   4- 4-1821
Biggs, Robert Miller - Julia Ann Lindley
                                       11-20-1834
Bishop, Absalom - Zenah Barrett   3-26-1826
Blackburn, Thomas - Elizabeth Francis
                                 lic.   5-15-1824
Bland, Abraham - Maria Bland   5-21-1831
Bland, Isaac - Eliza Pendleton lic.   8-31-1833
Bland, Moses - Sarah Whitaker   10-13-1830
Bland, Osburn - Mary Clarkson   2- 4-1836
Bland, William - Polly Pennock   4- 7-1831
Blankenship, James - Maria Stark   8-11-1829
Blankenship, John - Mary McKeehan   5-27-1830
Blankenship, Perry - Matilda Boner   10- 9-1830
Boner, Elisha - Sally Meek   1-22-1829
Boyle, John - Maria Terrell lic.   1- 8-1822
Braddy, Henry - Nancy Dowell   8-15-1830
Bramwell, James H. - Julia Ann Vawter
                                       11-26-1833
Brandon, Moses - Betsey Chambers   11-11-1825
Branham, Danville - Alice McGannon   9- 3-1833
Branham, David - Eliza Sweet   3-10-1831
Branham, David C. - Cynthia Ann Watson
                                       10-19-1833
Branham, James - Nancy Owen   1-30-1834
Branham, Jesse - Polly Butler   12-16-1821
Branham, Simon - Jemima Chambers   12-14-1834
Branham, Uriah - Alsey Davis   12-27-1826

Branham, William - Narcissa Pogue 11-25-1835
Brickfield, Jeremiah - Sally Evans
                                       11-19-1822
Brougher, Valentine - Rachel Riggs 3-27-1827
Brown, Hiram - Elizabeth Ely   11-27-1824
Brown, Isaac W. - Deborah Pool   5-28-1818
Brown, John M. - Jane McGill   2-15-1827
Brown, William - Nancy Kennedy   6- 5-1836
Buchanan, Levi - Nancy Spaulding   4- 4-1833
Buckles, George W. - Ann Dawson Walker
                                        9-13-1832
Buckles, James - Martha Smith   6-29-1824
Buckles, James - Margaret Graham   9- 8-1836
Buckles, James H. - Maria Chambers
                                       10-20-1829
Buckles, John - Hetty Deputy   5-16-1828
Bullock, William A. - Lois Sanford 5-24-1821(?)
Bundy, Miles - Milley Pool   10-24-1819
Bunton, Alfred - Anna Haynes   9- 1-1831
Bunton, Anderson - Jane Woodson   12-19-1833
Bunton, William R. - Nancy Woodson
                                       11- 6-1834
Burton, David - Susannah Harness   3-15-1835
   David Woodson in return
Bush, John, Jr. - Sally Jane Robinson
                                       12- 2-1830
Bush, Lewis - Sarah B. Herring   1-26-1833
Busick, John C. - Nancy Sacrey   2-13-1836
   Mary Sacrey in return
Butler, Daniel - Elizabeth Francis 8- 6-1827
Butler, James T. - Jane Moncrief   1- 2-1833
Butler, John - Juliann Williams   2-24-1827
Butler, John L. - Julia Brooks   11- 1-1835
Butler, John M. - Thamer Pool   10-13-1831
Cain, Nathaniel - Mary Ellen Shields
                                        3-12-1835
Campbell, Allen - Emily Vawter   8- 6-1829
Campbell, Andrew W. - Lucinda Foster
                                        2-17-1822
Campbell, David - Ann Clinton   1-29-1818
Campbell, Francis - Rebecca Jeffers
                                        3-29-1826
Campbell, Harrison - Susan Minton 8-23-1834
Campbell, John - Esther Bagley
                                 lic.   6-30-1830
Campbell, Michael D. - Ruth Beltz
                                 lic.   7-18-1827
Campbell, William - Sarah Bagley 2-15-1822
Cantwell, Samuel - Frances Bush   3-18-1830
Carley, Bartholomew - Sally Dolph 9-22-1823
Carley, Bartholomew - Sally Dolph 9-22-1833
Carley, Richard - Eunice Dolph   8-27-1826
Carpenter, Jonathan W. - Lucinda Robinson
                                        4-22-1834
Carpenter, Orange I. - Sarah Jane Keith(?)
                                 lic.   9- 1-1836
Carpenter, Samuel B. - Jane Donnald
                                 lic. 10-12-1831
Carroll, Marvin - Ann King   12-16-1832
Carroll, William - Sarah Dwyer   2-10-1831
Carsey, Dennis - Ellen Goodwin   1-29-1835
Carsey, Shadrick - Nancy Tyler   1-18-1835
Carson, David C. - Delilah Sperry 3-10-1830
Carson, James P. - Elizabeth Bagley
                                 lic.   3-16-1822

Carson, Walter, Jr. - Jenny W. Graham
                                    2-22-1827
Catling, Silas - Nancy Gordon   3-17-1829
Chace, Seth M. - Phebe Wagner   [1829]
Chace, William - Ellen Johnson   6-19-1833
Chaille, William - Huldah Ann Neale 7-23-1835
Chamberlain, John - Elizabeth Johnson
                                    1-15-1835
Chambers, James - Barbary Clarkson 5-27-1832
Chambers, John - Polly Long   8-15-1830
Chambers, John G. - Lydia Hutchinson 7- 5-1833
Chandler, Alfred - Betsey Spaulding 11-19-1829
Cheever, Abner H. - Amy Wilson   5- 5-1822
Cheever, William F. - Amelia Jones 6-15-1834
Chitwood, James - Elizabeth Stott   11-23-1826
Church, Roswell - Catherine Magnum(?)
                        lic.   12-27-1823
Clapp, Daniel - Rachel May   12-22-1836
Clapp, Henry - Polly May   3-29-1829
Clark, George Fenton - Margaret Green
                                    7-26-1835
Clarkson, Lawson - Louisa Denton   9-19-1833
Clay, David W. - Beulah Carley   6- 2-1823
Clines, Elias - Phebe Ball   12- 8-1820
Clinkinbeard, Edward - Elizabeth Giddens
                        lic.   3-22-1822
Clinton, David - Jane Butler   12-22-1831
Clinton, Jacob - Margaret Hilton   2- 6-1834
Clinton, Samuel - Polly Adams   2-20-1832
Clinton, William - Ann Gaste   5-23-1833
Clover, Cornelius - Rebecca Persons 7-28-1818
Clover, Cornelius - Narcissa Billingsley
                                    11-18-1833
Cobb, Reuben - Almira Hopkins   3-13-1832
Cochran, William - Eliza Ann Padgett
                                    11-25-1826
Collins, Zachariah - Eunice Harrington
                                    3-22-1831
Compton, John L. - Isabella Shilliday
                                    7- 6-1834
Comstock, John C. - Ruth French   7-28-1820
Conner, Thomas - Catherine Dwyer
                        lic.   10-17-1836
Copple, John P. - Nancy Staley   5-29-1836
Cornell, David - Mary Harrington   11-13-1830
Corq, Wynal - Lucinda Frantz   10- 9-1824
Cowell, Chancy S. - Adaline Curtis 2- 2-1837
Cox, John - Martha Peoples   9-24-1834
Creel, Curtis B. - Eliza Clark   7-24-1836
Crockett, John - Nancy Smith   12-11-1834
Curry, George I. - Sarah Edminster
                        lic.   1- 7-1836
Curry, John C. - Elizabeth Bland   11- 6-1831
Curtice, Horatio N. - Betsey Hughes 10-22-1823
Cutler, Leonard - Elinor Blair lic. 2- 3-1825
Daugherty, David - Frances Bishop
                        lic.   4-30-1836
Daugherty, James - Polly Baar   9-27-1832
Davis, Addison - Milly Grinstead
                        lic.   7-14-1829
Davis, Charles - Sally Davis   12-19-1822
Davis, Daniel - Betsey Branham lic. 3-13-1827
Davis, Elisha - Dicey Hooker   lic. 7-30-1828
Davis, Hiram - Nancy Chiller   5-18-1832
Davis, John - Rebekah Shields lic. 10-15-1821
Davis, John - Ann Edwards   4- 4-1827
Davis, Jonathan - Susan Baker   12-20-1818
Davis, Joshua - Jane Glasgow   7-21-1825
Davis, Thomas - Esther Ann Hudson   4- 5-1832

Davis, Thomas - Nancy Rogers lic. 4-17-1837
Davis, William - Rachel Lewis   8-15-1822
Davis, William - Rosey Jones   7-14-1831
Davis, William - Sarah Ross   11-13-1832
Day, Charles - Rachel Robbins   8-30-1833
Day, Charles F. - Delila Robbins   2- 4-1834
Day, Cyrus - Harriet Kashow   1- 2-1833
Dean, Joseph - Ruth Brown lic.   3-19-1825
Denslow, John - Patsy Shepherd   9-30-1819
Denton, Henry - Margaret Jeffers   2-21-1833
Denton, Hiram - Margaret Green   4-26-1835
Deputy, Charles - Mary Rogers lic.
                                    12-23-1835
Deputy, Joshua - Polly Woodruff
                        lic.   5-15-1830
Deputy, Solomon - Susan Deputy   3- 2-1834
Deputy, Sylvester - Jane Fowler   1- 3-1825
Deputy, William - Cassandra Gasaway
                        lic.   11- 9-1827
Derringer, Joseph - Mahala Sayers
                        lic.   6-22-1836
Dinsmore, Thomas I. - Cheley Herring
                                    1-29-1837
Dixon, Ellison - Margaret Dinwiddie
                                    2-13-1834
Dixon, Henry - Rachel James   11-21-1833
Dixon, John - Margaret Wilson   9-30-1825
Dixon, Samuel - Margaret Shilliday
                        lic.   3-18-1824
Dixon, Williamson - Nancy Osburn   1-14-1836
Donica, Thomas - Elizabeth Davis   9-30-1830
Doty, Levi - Nancy Thorn lic.   1-25-1825
Doty, Thomas - Katherine Needham
                        lic.   8-25-1822
Dowdall, John - Elizabeth English
                        lic.   12-28-1820
Downs, James - Eliza Ann Byfield   5- 9-1833
Driver, John - Polly Grimes   4-18-1831
Dwyer, Edward - Nancy Lee   8-26-1830
Dwyer, William - Mary Minton   7-14-1836
Dyer, Samuel - Susan Johnson   2-12-1824
Eador, Solomon - Betsey Russell
                        lic.   4- 6-1825
Earl, Edward - Ann Rogers   12-13-1831
Earl, Jacob - Sarah Winscott   7-27-1834
Earl, Thomas - Nancy Bush   9-13-1827
Eastman, Buel - Elvira P. Childs
                        lic.   10- 6-1830
Edminster, Joseph - Delilah Chapman
                        lic.   7-20-1824
Edwards, James N. - Aurelia Hartwell
                                    9-24-1835
Elliott, David - Lucinda Spear   2- 7-1822
Elliott, John - Catherine Jeffers   8-25-1836
Elliott, Robert - Martha Miller   9-27-1836
Ely, Adam - Susannah Daugherty   3- 4-1830
Ely, John - Elizabeth Daugherty   10- 1-1829
Ely, Michael - Anna Bannister   4-12-1831
Falconbury, Jacob - Lavina Brown   1-29-1836
Farthing, Edward - Sally Higgins
                        lic.   11-15-1827
Farthing, Edward - Matilda Wells   1-27-1831
Farthing, Elijah - Betsey Ann Hill
                                    12-27-1834
Farthing, John - Polly Wells   6- 2-1835
Farthing, William - Sally Thomas   9-23-1829
Ferrell(?), David - Katharine Howk 3-31-1833
Ferris, Philip - Harriet Metcalf   3- 5-1835
Ferry, Azariah - Molly Hughes
                        lic.   5- 1-1822

302

Fish, James - Maria McMindes   2-27-1834
Fish, John - Elizabeth Wilson   4-10-1823
Fitzgerald, Nathan - Nancy Spencer   8- 8-1833
Fitzgerald, Thomas - Selina(?) Rice   2-16-1829
Fleming, Archer - Olive Ingalls   3-26-1820
Foster, Enoch - Esther Ely   12- 7-1826
Foster, James - Polly Branham   10-12-1823
Foster, Jared - Jane Branham   3-15-1836
Foster, Riley - Sarah Wallace   5- 6-1831
Foster, William - Jane Banister   11-18-1833
Fowler, James - Milly Stone lic.   12-20-1827
Francis, John - Jane Howk   7-14-1833
Francis, Joseph - Elizabeth Haynes   6-16-1831
Francis, Thomas - Eliza King lic.   12- 3-1829
Francis, William - Ann Patterson
                      lic.   9- 4-1833
Fredenburgh, Abraham - Dorothy Holford
                                       12-25-1834
French, Franklin R. - Virginia Irwin
                      lic.   8-30-1831
French, Horace - Mariane Eastman   [1821]
French, John L. - Polly Ross(?)   3-21-1824
Furguson, Alexander - Nancy Hamilton   5-19-1831
Gaddy, William T. - Bertha Prather   10-31-1833
Gageby(?), David - Malinda Wood
                      lic.   4- 5-1825
Gasaway, Richard - Polly Moore   8- 7-1834
Gillaspy, William - Rachel Tobias   4-10-1834
Gilpin, Barnet - Susan Sheets   6-16-1830
Gordon, Hugh - Jane Hicklin lic.   5-16-1827
Graham, Allen D. - Elizabeth Shepherd
                                       12-30-1823
Graham, Charles R. - Margaret P. McClelland
                                        2-17-1825
Graham, George S. - Elizabeth Wells   7-28-1831
Graham, James - Catada(?) Adams
                      lic.   11-20-1832
Graham, Lewis - Louisa A. Carson   12-21-1820
Graham, Robert - Martha Farthing   3- 5-1835
Graham, Robert W. - Mary Adams   9-22-1832
Graham, Samuel - Jane Watson   10-13-1818
Graham, Samuel C. - Elizabeth McGloughlin
                                        2- 8-1827
Graham, Thomas - Matilda Shilliday   2-11-1830
Graham, William W. - Sarah Shilliday   [1821]
Graves, Calvin - Christiana Banfield
                      lic.   1- 3-1824
Graves, Jedidiah - Mary Donnell   4- 3-1831
Green, Alvin - Philena Fitzgerald   12-28-1830
Green, Benjamin F. - Polly Barnes   10-30-1823
Green, Isaiah - Mary McKinney   5-15-1836
Green, John - Nancy Roberts lic.   8-30-1826
Green, John - Polly Marshall   4-14-1829
Green, Joseph - Elizabeth McCurry
                      lic.   8- 1-1831
Green, Joseph - Elizabeth Derringer   1- 1-1834
Green, Nathan - Nancy Carroll   7- 2-1834
Griffith, James - Iza Ann Dobbins
                      lic.   10- 7-1829
Grinstead, Jasper - Betsey Davis   2- 7-1825
Grinstead, Jesse - Polly Davis   1- 8-1833
Grinstead, John - Rachel Peacock   9-14-1824
Groce, Ephraim - Sarah Meek   11-20-1833
Hall, Abner - Marianne Degroms(?)
                      lic.   2-28-1822
Hall, Abner - Nancy Bennett lic.   2-25-1823
Hall, Evan - Maria Lett   12-22-1836
Hall, Isaac, Sr. - Esther Clines(?)   11-12-1820
Hall, Isaac - Polly Davis   1- 2-1835

Hall, John - Mary Ann Hufford lic.3-28-1837
Hall, Thomas - Elizabeth K. Eades(?)
                                       10- 4-1832
Hamant, David - Mary McConnell   10-29-1835
Hamilton, William - Mary Hays   8-25-1833
Harlan, Ephraim - Lucinda Denslow 4- 2-1835
Harrington, Isaac - Phebe Dolph
                      lic.   7-22-1824
Harrington, Joseph - Rachel Russell
                                        1-19-1826
Harris, Micajah - Polly Green lic. 6-18-1835
Harris, William - Sarah Chusco   3-26-1834
Hartwell, George - Mary Denslow
                      lic.   8- 2-1836
Hartwell, Phillip - Caroline Hartwell
                                        5- 5-1833
Henry, John - Margaret Dobbins
                      lic.   11-13-1829
Herring, Joel - Phebe Bowles   11-14-1833
Herring, Lewis - Susannah Alloway   9-28-1836
Hill, Allen - Betsy McCrory   3- 2-1821
Hilton, John - Sally Blankenship   8-27-1822
Hobbs, James - Sally Williams   11-13-1827
Hobbs, William - Maria Boyle   11-15-1826
Hollensaid, William - Margaret Thompson
                                        6- 5-1831
Holmes, George - Lucinda Knolton 12-28-1820
Holton, Jonathan W. - Charlotte B. Perry
                      lic.   12-27-1829
Hood, William - Sally Morris   10- 7-1819
  people of color
Hood, William - Judith Christie   1-30-1823
Hopkins, David - Polly Perry   8-28-1821
Hopkins, Thomas - Rebecca Lett
                      lic.   10-27-1823
Hopkins, William - Phebe Kyser   6-20-1829
Howk, Benjamin - Permelia Wilson   7-22-1832
Howk, Michael - Katharine Howk   3-15-1835
Howk, Samuel - Zelfey Oliver   3-31-1833
Howlett, Nelson - L. A. Taylor   4-28-1829
Hoyt, Rodney - Prudence Jones   4-17-1830
Huckleberry, Silas D. - Lettice Prather
                                        9- 4-1834
Hudson, Absalom W. - Mary Fowler
                      lic.   4-16-1825
Hudson, Boyd W. - Frances Stephens   [1826]
Hudson, Cutbird R. - Martha Elliott
                                        3-16-1836
Hudson, James - Angeline Skinner   9-25-1834
Hudson, Joshua - Tabitha Fowler   6- 3-1824
Hudson, Larkin - Sally Stevens   3-14-1832
Hudson, Patrick - Betsy Fitzgerald
                                       12-24-1822
Hudson, William - Elizabeth Davis   3-13-1829
Hughes, Dennison - Hannah Barnes   9-17-1820
Hughes, Evan - Mary Griffith lic. 8-10-1835
Hughes, Henry - Polly Barnes lic.10-22-1823
Hughs, Isaac - Jane Torbett   2-19-1833
Hughs, James - Jane Dunn lic.   9- 6-1831
Hull, Jonathan - Phebe Hoyt   10-23-1832
Hurlbutt, Lewis - Ann Woods   2-24-1822
Irwin, Presley - Artimetia French   2-13-1832
James, Cyrus - Susan Arbuckle   7-27-1835
James, Enoch - Emily Shepherd   4-21-1836
James, John - Nancy Hopkins   12-28-1820
James, John - Maria Turkeyhyser
                      lic.   10-14-1826
James, Daniel - Eve Fifer   3-15-1832
James, Joseph - Rebekah Hathaway   9- 4-1823

Jeffers, James - Martha Stott   4-17-1834
Jeffers, Robert - Nancy Stott   9-12-1827
Johnson, Barnett P. - Lucy Merrell   1- 1-1833
Johnson, Berry - Nancy Thompson   12-31-1834
Johnson, Berry - Mary Collins   1- 7-1836
Johnson, Bluford - Polly Ann Ruddle   7-29-1833
Johnson, Clement - Nancy Burk   6-30-1825
Johnson, Daniel - Lena Fifer   11-21-1836
Johnson, Daniel C. - Zerelda Stott   12- 5-1833
Johnson, Green - Mary Meek   10- 3-1833
Johnson, James - Phisina Smith   10- 7-1833
Johnson, James T. - Rachel Prather
          lic.   10- 7-1821
Johnston, Grenup - Maria Spencer   1- -1830
Jones, David Clark - Susan M. Prather
                                      12-19-1833
Jones, William A. - Sarah Ann Conner
                                       6-13-1834
Justice, David - Manerva Wilson   11-14-1830
Justice, Garrison L. - Nancy Noe   6- 3-1834
Justus (Justice?), Garrison L. -
    Martha McGee   8-22-1829
Keith, James - Lucy P. Wilson lic.   2-28-1821
Kellar, John - Nancy Riggs(?)   12-25-1834
Kelley, Daniel - Susan Kelley   10-10-1833
Kennedy, Lyman - Nancy Barrett   1- 2-1829
Kerry, Shadrick - Betsy Williams
          lic.   1-27-1825
Keryea, Phillip - Isabel Becourt of
    Decatur Co.   2-24-1833
Keyser(?), Solomon - Sally Stuckers   9-21-1824
Kieth, George R. - Sally Darnal   6- 5-1834
Kieth, Mason P. - Nancy Lewis   8-19-1831
Kinder, Peter - Eliza Roberts   [1819]
Kindrick, Major - Wealthy Hartwell   5-15-1823
King, John - Mahala Lively   9-19-1833
King, Peter - Lavina Blankenship   4-30-1833
King, Phineas - Susan Minton   10-10-1833
King, Spencer - Anna Henderson   10- 3-1822
Kirby, John B. - Elizabeth Johnson   6-23-1831
Kises, Frederic - Jane Cobb   8-22-1831
Knapp, Amos - Polly Butler lic.   9-18-1819
Knapp, Daniel - Sally Wilson   12- 9-1824
Knapp, John - Zilpha Chase(?) lic.   10-26-1822
Knapp, John W. - Mary Irwin   12- 8-1825
Knolton, Ephraim - Arena Butler lic. 11- 5-1827
Kulty, Whitfield - Maria Stott   8-12-1826
Kyser, Thomas - Rebecca Hopkins lic.   6-27-1829
Kyser, William - Sally Hopkins lic. 12-29-1829
Lakin, Daniel - Sally Johnston   3-27-1821
Lard(?), Charles R. - Jane Dinwiddie
          lic.   10-22-1834
Latimore, Daniel - Damon McGannon
          lic.   12-27-1823
Latimore, John - Hannah Stockton   2-29-1832
Latimore, John - Nancy Stites   4-10-1832
Latimore, Walter - Jane McGannon
          lic.   10- 3-1827
Leatey(?), Jacob - Polly Barrett   11-27-1829
Lee, Charles - Betsey Waggoner lic.   12- 9-1822
Lee, Charles - Betsey Williams   8-30-1833
Lee, John M. - Sally Lee   3-25-1835
Lee, Joseph - Malinda M. Lee   6-27-1832
Lee, Richard H. - Elizabeth Sage   3- 7-1833
Lee, Uriah - Betsey Lee   2- 7-1827
Leming(?), Hiram - Elizabeth Rogers   6-27-1836
Lett, Demarehus - Mary Hall   12-31-1836
Lewis, Daniel - Harriet R. Kieth   5- 3-1832
Lewis, Hiram - Ann Robinson   9- 4-1836
Lindley, James M. - Meletia Jane Biggs
                                       9-20-1832

Lindsey, Jacob - Dolly Link   7- 1-1833
Lockard, Thomas - Leah May   10-14-1834
Loughry, Joseph - Emily Brown   2- 8-1835
Love, James - Amanda Petty   1- 6-1831
Luallen, Wyatt - Fanny Ferguson   6- 3-1834
Lucas, Caleb - Polly Carley   1-19-1822
McCaslin, Newton - Martha Wilson   9-29-1825
McClelland, James - Minerva Miller
                                      12-26-1833
McCollister, James - Elizabeth Thompson
                                       6-13-1824
McCollister, William - Peggy Butler
                                       9- 5-1821
McConnett, George - Mary Amick   8-12-1830
McDowell, Mackleroy - Sally Sparks 1-17-1828
McGannon, Alexander - Sally Butler 1- 2-1834
McGannon, Hugh - [name blank] lic. 3-18-1835
McGannon, John - Polly Carney   10-14-1824
McGannon, Peter - Polly Collins   1-22-1828
McGill, Robert - Sarah E. Watson   11-15-1834
McKeehan, Benjamin - Nancy Williams
                                      12-16-1827
McKeehan, Benjamin - Rhoda Blankenship
                                       5-10-1830
McKeehan, George - Elizabeth Midcap
                                       8-24-1826
McKeehan, James - Ann Latimore
          lic.   8-15-1836
McKinzie, Cicero - Fanny Randall   5- 4-1834
McNew, George - Louisa Pickett   8- 6-1834
McWhorter, Amasa - Sarah Meek   12-29-1832
Maddox, Asa - Delila Butler lic.   4-27-1823
Maddox, Samuel - Betsy Pool   10-29-1829
Malcomb, Leven - Elizabeth Osburn 10-20-1833
Manson, James - Catharine Chumley
          lic.   9-16-1822
Martin, James - Mary Gordon   3-28-1825
Martin, William N. - Drusilla Midcap
                                      11-28-1819
May, Jonathan - Elizabeth Whitten(?)
                                       4-15-1833
May, Jonathan - Elizabeth Lewallen
                                      12-18-1836
May, Solomon - Polly Clapp   4-28-1831
May, Solomon - Eliza Brown lic.   7- 4-1836
Meek, David - Nancy Crockett   5-24-1832
Meek, John - Nancy Baker   4-10-1823
Meek, John - Ruth Boner lic.   5-11-1825
Meek, John - Rachel A. Day   2- 6-1829
Meek, Lewis - Abigail Ritchie   9-14-1824
Meek, Richard D. - Eleanor House
          lic.   5-15-1836
Meek, Samuel - Maria Baker   11-29-1822
Meek, Samuel - Sally Johnson   3- 9-1828
Meek, Samuel - Nancy McFarling   9- 1-1831
Meek, Samuel - Polly House   3-23-1832
Metcalf, Harrison - Eliza Harlan   10-10-1833
Midcap, Daniel R. - Matilda Earwood
                                       3- -1829
Midcap, John - Salley Sanford   5-11-1829
Mikesell, David - Mary Keryea lic. 11-10-1829
Miles, James D. - Tamar Pool   11- 1-1832
Miller, Alexander - Mary Owen   3-10-1836
Miller, John S. - Kitty M. Denslow
          lic.   3-19-1823
Miller, William S. - Rhoda Thomas
          lic.   11- 2-1831
Mitchell, Walter A. - Sarah McGannon
                                      12- 8-1836
Moncrief, Jackson - Lucy Price   12- 1-1836
Monroe, Campbell - Margaret Thorn 12-25-1832

Montgomery, Mathew - Nancy Bridges
                     lic.   10-30-1826
Moss, John - Hetty McGill   lic.   10- 4-1824
Moss, John - Jane Brooks   9-25-1833
Munrow, Nelson - Polly Russell   11-28-1820
Murry, John - Almira Smith   11-24-1831
Musselman, John M. - Maria Robinson 8-31-1823
Muster, Cornelius - Margaret McClelland
                            9-14-1834
Nation, John - Mahala Greene   9-27-1819
Neale, Davis - Nancy Jeffers   2-30-1834(?)
Neale, Davis - Emily Butler   5-12-1836
Neale, Doris - Eliza Butler   11-22-1831
Neale, Frederic - Margaret Heath   12- 4-1834
Needham, Enoch - Lucretia Spaulding 8-17-1823
Needham, Lewis - Frances Smith   3-14-1824
Needham, Nathan - Nancy Johnston
                     lic.   12-24-1828
Nelson, Jefferson - Mary Steinmets   3- 5-1835
    Sarah Steinmets in return
New, James - Elizabeth Torbet   5-19-1825
New, James D. - Huldah Stott   7-16-1835
Newkirk, Peter - Elizabeth Keryea   8- 7-1821
Newton, Daniel - Eliza Eastman   12-26-1819
Northway, James T. - Philinda Reed   7-30-1820
Oliver, Needham - Ann Brown   2- 6-1834
Pabody, Ezra F. - Mabel Butler   10-15-1820
Padgett, Reuben - Huldah O'Conner
                     lic.   2-18-1835
Page, Samuel - Polly Murphy   11-23-1831
Pagett, John - Polly Conner   9- 6-1832
Pagett, William Riley - Anna Dwyre   7-22-1830
Palmer, Joshua - Margaret Hollingsead
                     lic.   6-15-1835
Patrick, Solomon - Margaret Carney 10-23-1831
Patrick, William - Katharine Carney 6-12-1831
Paul, William W. - Cynthia Hartwell 2-26-1825
Pendleton, David B. - Catharine Smith
                            3-10-1822
Pennock, Alexander - Eliza Lindley
                     lic.   8-26-1833
Phillips, Thomas - Susan Wilson   3- 7-1833
Perry, William - Harriet Shepherd 11-17-1825
Persons, Abdial - Lucretia Burlinger 1- 9-1821
Phelps, Seth - Betsy Kassock lic.   4- 4-1821
Phillips, Jacob - Susan Brown   12- 7-1823
Plymate, Charles - Lydia Kelly lic. 6-27-1829
Plymate, Jarvis - Eliza Ann Edminster
                            7- 1-1832
Pollard, William - Mary Pool   4- 2-1835
Polley, Samuel - Jane Ann Thompson 10-22-1835
Pool, Isaac - Julian Price   9- 3-1829
Pool, Odom - Charlotte Temple McDonald
                            2-26-1834
Pool, Reuben - Polly King   8- 8-1833
Porter, John R. - Deadamia Miller   2- 3-1833
Prather, Hiram - Mary Ann Hucklebury 4-24-1834
Prather, John - Mary Johnson   1-24-1822
Prather, Lewis - Arpha Pool lic.   8- 1-1836
Prather, Thomas - Mary Prather   6- 7-1830
Pribble, Bernard - Elizabeth Maddox 4-19-1829
Price, Lewis - Maria Griffith   6- 5-1831
Pruett, David - Polly Wilkerson lic. 3- 9-1831
Pruit, Elijah - Sarah Banister lic.12-13-1836
Ragan, Joshua - Rachel Hood   10- 8-1826
Ramsay, William - Nancy McKeehan   9-22-1820
Randall, Benjamin - Margaret I. Hudson
                    lic.   6-10-1828
Randall, Daniel - Hetty Shepherd   12- 9-1832

Randall, Edward - Sarah Hudson lic.
                            12-29-1834
Randall, John - Cordelia Bennett 5-22-1836
Randall, Richard - Alice Conner   5-27-1835
Rano(?), John - Margaret M. Stagg 1-24-1833
Rayburn, William - Anna Fredenburgh
                            9-21-1831
Reed, John - Mary Rogers   12- 9-1822
Reeves, David - China Stillwell   [1821]
Reynolds, John A. - Mary A. Hutchinson
                            2-18-1832
Rhoods, Samuel - Agness Wykoff   2-28-1818
Rhodes, Sanford - Elizabeth Shields
                            7- 2-1824
Rice, William - Ann Stillwell   12-22-1822
Rich, Isaiah - Aurelia Carley   7- 6-1820
Rich, Justus - Elsy Wells   5-30-1819
Richardson, Isaac - Polly Banister 6-30-1831
Richey, Thomas, Jr. - Fanny Fitzgerald
                     lic.   12-23-1829
Ridlin, Abraham - Annis Ballard   5- 9-1822
Riggs, Henry - Cyntha Prather lic. 4- 1-1827
Riggs, Henry - Eraminta May   7-28-1835
Riley, Edward - Phebe Lafarg(?)
                     lic.   11-28-1836
Robb, Harvey - Maria Roby   12- 9-1830
Robbins, James - Polly Burton   5- 5-1834
Robbins, John - Margaret Woodson   4-10-1831
Robbins, Ransom - Polly Woodson   2-16-1832
Robbins, William - Polly Turner(?)10-27-1833
Robbins, William - Rebecca Hale   11-27-1834
Roberts, Sylvester - Charlotta Thomas
                          10- 8-1825
Robertson, Aquilla - Esther Deputy 9-30-1829
Robertson, Simon - Ann Welbourne   9- 2-1824
Robertson, Stephen - Cinda Sanford 1-30-1821
Robins, Andrew M. - Polly Hale
                     lic.   1- 9-1835
Robinson, Elisha - Louisa Thornton 9-10-1829
Robinson, Humphrey M. - Martha Brandon
                            11-28-1833
Robinson, Jesse - Nancy Scott   7-22-1823
Robinson, John L. - Abigail Whiteman
                            9- 9-1836
Robinson, Simeon M. - Elizabeth Malcomb
                            10- 5-1836
Roseberry, John - Polly Ritchey   7-25-1826
Ross, John - Derrizah Grinstead   3-20-1830
Russell, Robert - Nancy Lee   11-12-1824
Rutledge, William R. - Deantha Trindle
                     lic.   12-16-1836
Sage, George - Tamar Hollingsaid   5-25-1828
Sage, Wilkerson - Sarah Hollensead 4-11-1833
Sage, William L. - Nancy Randalls 5-12-1833
Sanford, Gideon - Christy Vanwert
                     lic.   7-10-1823
Sanford, William - Betsey Foster
                     lic.   8- -1819
Saum, Jacob - Eliza Hollensead   7-31-1831
Sawyer, Elisha - Lydia Campbell   5- 1-1837
Scott, Aaron - Louise Robertson   3-16-1826
Shepherd, Joshua - Nancy McClelland
                            6-22-1824
Shepherd, Miles - Levina Wykoff 11-14-1833
Shepherd, William - Julia Wilson 3-21-1830
Shields, James - Martha McCaslin
                     lic.   3-25-1835
Shields, Robert - Elizabeth Davis 3-30-1820
Shields, William I. - Hannah McLane
                            3-18-1823

Shilliday, Ephraim M. - Eliza Dougan(?)
                 lic.   8-17-1829
Shilliday, George - Isabella Graham
                 lic.   6-19-1820
Shilliday, Samuel G. - Sarah Jane Dungan
                       8- 2-1832
Shilliday, Stephen B. - Elizabeth Vance
                       6-15-1824
Short, Allen - Farby P. Edwards
                 lic.   11- 2-1829
Sibley, Albert G. - Harriett White   2- 5-1827
Skinner, Asa G. - Phebe Oinal (O'Neal?)
                       3-29-1832
Skinner, Daniel - Malinda Martin   12-17-1823
Skinner, Daniel I. - Polly House   1-13-1836
Skinner, Stephen P. - Clarissa Hartwell
                       1- 1-1830
Slocum, John - Nancy McGannon   12-28-1836
Smiley, David, of Ripley Co. -
         Rebecca Barnes(?)   12-29-1831
Smith, Irby - Nancy Jane Trindle
                 lic.   12-20-1834
Smith, James - Ann Wells   2-19-1824
Smith, Joseph - Alice Cox   7-19-1834
Smith, Robert M. - Harriet Denslow   5-15-1834
Snowden, David - Eliza Stokely   7- 5-1831
Snowden, James - Elizabeth Fear   11-12-1830
Snowden, James - Mary A. Hopkins
                 lic.   11- 6-1834
Spaulding, James - Celia Thompson   4- 4-1833
Spaulding, John - Jane Bland   1- 6-1830
Spaulding, Joseph - Sarah Needham   2- 9-1826
Spencer, Amasa - Pricilla Fitzgerald 1- 3-1835
Spencer, Amasa, Jr. - Nancy Meek   2- 7-1833
Spencer, William - Elizabeth Tate 12-17-1835
Stagg, John - Martha Phillips   2- 3-1833
Staley, Martin - Malinda Barr lic. 1-20-1828
Stanhope, Lucratus - Mary Whitcomb 9- 2-1833
Steadman, James - Eliza Earl   3- 2-1820
Stephenson, Lawson - Betsy Merrill
                 lic.   7-24-1828
Stevens, Charles - Lucinda Hudson   3-11-1831
Stevens, John - Polly Edwards   2-16-1832
Stillwell, John - Sarah Sellers   [1821]
Storey, Thomas - Jane Vawter   1-10-1826
Stott, John - Elizabeth Vawter   4- 7-1831
Stratton, John A. - Nancy Russell 10-12-1826
Stuart, Jacob - Sarah Lewis lic.   4-15-1834
Sullivan, Henry - Betsey Meek   4-10-1828
Sullivan, John - Elizabeth Meek   3- 4-1830
Sutton, Nicholas R. B. - Elizabeth Donica
                       5- 9-1834
Sweeney, James - Sarah Burton   10-23-1834
Sweet, George - Polly Magness   2-11-1822
Tanner, Simpson - Callagratta McGannon
                       9- 1-1835
Tate, Enos - Sarah Thomas   8- 4-1835
Tate, Jesse - Polly Sage   3- 3-1831
Terrell, Andrew - Elizabeth Jackson of
         Jefferson Co.   8-29-1831
Thelkeld, John - Polly A. Vawter   9-18-1835
Thixton, William - Nancy Paggett   1-15-1835
Thomas, Amos - Patience Chapman lic.12-30-1820
Thomas, Anderson - Polly Meek   9-22-1825
Thomas, Freeman - Mahala Lett   10- 1-1818
Thomas, Isaac - Sally Fitzgerald
                 lic.   4-15-1824
Thomas, John - Ellen Buckles   3-24-1831
Thompson, Abdallah - Melissa Miller 5- 5-1834
Thompson, Harrison - Delila Fenney(?)
                       4- 8-1834

Thompson, James - Lucinda Burk   [1825]
Thorn, Robert - Lucinda Spaulding 1- 7-1836
Thorp, Moses - Annis Shepherd
                 lic.   9-20-1831
Tindall, William - Diantha Eastman 2-14-1830
Tobias, John T. - Maria D. Jobes(?)3-24-1831
Tobias, John - Mary Kashow   8- 2-1831
Tobias, Tobias - Ann Jones lic. 10-11-1827
Tobias, William - Sally Kashow   10-22-1835
Toby, Nathaniel - Ruth West   12-18-1831
Todd, Levi W. - Demia Butler   2-28-1829
Torbet, John S. - Polly McGammon 7- 8-1830
Torbett, James M. - Isabella C. Latimore
                       3- 1-1832
Townsend, John - Betsy Winchil lic.3-30-1820
Tripp, Hagerman - Albina Stanhope Walker
                       11-17-1834
Tripp, John - Susanna Harrison   8- 7-1823
Truitt, David - Elizabeth Baker   4- 3-1823
Turkeyhizer, Jacob - Polly James
                 lic.   8-28-1827
Tweedy, Francis - Sarah Ann Simpson
                       11- 3-1836
Tweedy, Patrick - Pamela Zimmerman 2- 2-1827
Tweedy, Patrick - Jane Lindley
                 lic.   7-26-1827
Tweedy, Patrick - Betsy Carson   1-26-1837
Tweedy, Robert - Sally W. Mitchell
                       12-25-1834
Vance, William B. - Nancy Shilliday
                       1-23-1824
Vancleave, Jared - Mary Johnson   7-17-1834
Vancleave, Samuel - Nancy C. Johnson
                       1- 5-1837
Vandaren, Jabez - Polly Lee   [1819]
Vandusen, Martin - Sophia Fuller 5- 6-1830
Vawter, John - Jane Smith   11-21-1825
Vawter, John - Ruth Minton   10- 5-1826
Vawter, John Taylor - Permelia Dwyer
                       5- 9-1835
Vawter, Smith - Jane Terrell   4-21-1829
Vawter, Smith - Elizabeth Smith   1- 8-1835
Vest, Samuel - Polly Crocket lic. 8-29-1827
Waggoner, George W. - Ruth Bland 12-26-1833
Waggoner, Samuel - Polly Torbett 8- 4-1824
Waggoner, William - Ruth Bland   4-15-1834
Wagner, James - Sally Lowe lic. 8-26-1834
Wagner, Samuel - Tiletha Branham 9-10-1835
Walker, William R. - Penelope McGannon
                       9-18-1834
Wallis, Aran - Sally Booker   1- 8-1825
Walton, Andrew - Martha Smyth   [1819]
Walton, Daniel - Elizabeth Sprague
                       10-16-1826
Waltz, Thomas - Margaret Mead
                 lic.   2- 7-1836
Ward, James - Polly Ann Hill   9- 1-1836
Warner, Henry - Lucinda Hartwell 6-25-1824
Warner, Samuel - Louisa Williams 1-26-1823
Wells, John - Polly Hutton   4-10-1824
Whitaker, James - Lucinda Bland   8-18-1831
Whitcomb, Anson - Ann Child   2- 2-1837
Whitcomb, John - Esther Hedge   8- 6-1836
White, Edward - Sophronia Hinton 4-30-1818
White, William H. - Sarah Wills(Wells?)
                       10-19-1833
Whitesell, William - Nancy Hill   3- 9-1820
Whitesell, William - Rebecca Malcomb
                       10-23-1832
Whitsett, Samuel - Letta Jones   4- 5-1823
Wiley, George N. - Caroline Graves
                 lic.   3-24-1836

```
Wilkerson, Thomas - Louisa Tyler      9- 9-1832      Winchester, Lorin - Marrianne Miller
Wilkerson, William - Margaret Brown of                                            12- 8-1824
        Bartholomew Co.        12-11-1833    Winscot, Greenville - Elizabeth Peoples
Wilkinson, Joseph - Eunice Bailes                                                 10- 7-1835
                lic.           3- 8-1821    Winscot, Lewis S. - Nancy Earl   12- 8-1836
Wilkison, James - Margaret Ann Baker 1-28-1830  Winscott, Moses - Sally Earl     3- 4-1834
Wilkison, Joseph - Nancy Meek        7-27-1826  Weathers, Robert - Eliza Ann Blair
Williams, John - Leonor Tobias       4-14-1835                  lic.           8-19-1835
Wilson, James E. - Charlotte Boner   8- 7-1834  West, Jeremiah - Jemima Jackson
Wilson, Joseph - Eliza Brown   lic. 10-22-1826                  lic.           1-16-1827
Wilson, Moses - Orpha Chapman        1-21-1836  Woodson, William - Anna Burton    1-20-1835
Wilson, Samuel - Sarah Chapman lic. 4-30-1824  Woodson, William H. - Leannah Winscott
Wimple, John - Emily Powers         [1819]                                     11- 6-1834
                                                Woodward, Chesley - Elizabeth Blankenship
                                                                               3-30-1820
                                                Wray, James H. - Martha Spann(?)  5-15-1835
                                                Wykoff, James - Angeline McCaslon 3-15-1833
```

DEATHS RECORDED IN THE MINUTES OF THE WHITE RIVER ASSOCIATION OF THE PRIMITIVE BAPTIST CHURCH, 1857-1878

Copied from the original Minutes and sent in by Mrs. Charles S. Stein, Wilmette, Ill. The dates are from August to August. The persons listed were all adults and lived in the counties of Monroe, Greene, Lawrence, and Owen, Indiana.

Aug. 1857-Aug. 1858

Francis W. Hite	Elizabeth Minks	1861-1862
Elis Hall	Priscilla Sandifer	Levin Fisher
Jane Hughes	Sarah Colyer	Christina Gibson
Abigail Brassfield Combs		Stephen Fields
Andrew Burcham		Mary L Burch
Joshua Roach	1859-1860	Mary East
Wm. F. Sisco	Thomas Oliphant, Sr.	A. Storm
David Meredith	Wm. H. Burch	Jacob Tencher
Mahala Roberts	Jesse Wilson	Melinda Hays
Mary Roberts	Wm Touey	G.W. Gaine
Susan Owen	Juda McBride	Sarah Alexander
Martha Shorter	Tabitha Potter	Shelton Gentry
Nancy Inman	Agness Mitchell	Sarah Bennett
Elizabeth Secrest	Josephine Hannah	Lurand Hunter
Lucy Bray	Mary Clinton	Margaret Pressnall
	Eliza Jane Beasley	

1862-1863

Sarah White
Anna Woody
Hannah Pafford
Isaac Storm
Susannah Storm
Jane Carmichael
John Uland
Hiram Bingham
Lucy Hegwood
Sarah A. Uland
George Acuff
Charles Brown
Anna M. Christy
Elizabeth Laffoon
Hanson Humphrey
Jane Holiday
Wm Parks
George Wiseman
Nancy Bowlen
Frederick Richardson
Martha Richardson
Eliza Robertson

1863-1864

Susanna Smith
John M. Riddle
Verlinderbel Sears
Martha Carmichael
Elizabeth East
Abraham Hegwood
Elizabeth Walker
Thomas Martindale
Margaret Arther
John Richardson

1864-1865

Elizabeth Vawter
Rebecca McDonald
James Martindale
D. Acuff
Henry Murphy
Charlotte Hodges
Louisa Beasley
Mary Oliphant

Sarah Humphrey
Elizabeth Campbell
Wm Minks
Joel Richardson
Alexander Carmichael

1865-1866

James Harvey Oliphant
Jane Char
Elizabeth Thomas
Sarah Vooris
James Bennett
Hardy Sparks

1866-1867

Mary Stanbery
Elizabeth Baker

1867-1868

Sarah Baker
Lydia Thacker
Elizabeth Cooper
John Inman, Sr.

1868-1869

Rachel Wilson
Isaac Litton
Elizabeth Neal
Nancy Hodges

1869-1870

Mordecai Hatfield

1870-1871

Sarah Girdly
Melissa Kerns
S.S. Crabb
Catherine Layman
Rachel Arthur
Henry Arthur
Brazilla King
Richard Carmichael

1871-1872

Susan Kinder
Andrew Dodd
Zebulin Brinson
James Pedigo
Acha Sare

1872-1873

Naomi Turner
John Pennington
Sarah Wells
Elizabeth L. Parks
David Dunkin

1873-1874

Phebe Inman
Tabitha Pierce
Margaret Girdley
Moses Bray
Wm Graves

1874-1875

Augustine Carmichael
Sarah Brown
Charles Burch
Isabel Chambers
Zipporah Dodd
Andrew J. Chitwood

1875-1876

Abraham Rainwater
Anna Rainwater
Hughes East
Elizabeth Paton
Amos Presnal
David Neal

1877-1878

James Anders
Moses Hodges
Isaac Crum
Elizabeth Carmichael
Nancy Richey
J.C. Edwards
Rodah Henson

TIPTON COUNTY MARRIAGES, 1844-1856

Compiled from microfilm copy of Book I, Tipton County Marriage Records, 1844-52, and pages 1-147 of Book II, 1852-65. The latter volume is not an original record, but was compiled from the original by order of the court.

Acres, Finley - Nancy Jane Sanders   2-21-1856
Adams, Luallen - Emeline Herron   3- 4-1849
Aldredge, William F. - Nancy Jane Burns
                                      1-13-1854
Alexander, Jesse - Maria Kemp   9-27-1849
Alter, George - Harriet Danahoe   7-19-1852
Armfield, Wiseman - Nancy Groover   11-21-1850
Arrick, George W. - Louise Phifer   10-12-1855
Askren, David A. - Martha Jane Ramsey
                                      11-17-1853
Ault, James - Mary Ann Billhimer   11-16-1854
Austill, William D. - Lavina McKee   12- 1-1856
Axtill, Hiram - Nancy Thomas   10-25-1855
Ayers, Alfred - Edey Harlin   3-21-1855
  Edey Brown on return
Ayers, Ashley - Polly Ann Adams   3-16-1854
Baden, Samuel - Mary Jane Herron   9-12-1847
Badger, Jesse - Susanah Smith   10-27-1853
Bailey, Anderson - Amanda Reed   9-14-1851
Bailey, Joshua - Catharine Stephens   10-16-1847
Bailey, Mahlon - Malinda Reed   8- 3-1853
Bailey, Thomas M. - Lucetta M. Plummer
                                      5-22-1848
Ballard, Clark - Mary Elizabeth Redman
                                      1-23-1853
Barlow, John H. - Martha Jane Smith   2-23-1854
Barlow, Samuel Richard - Mary Smith   10- 8-1852
Barlow, William - Lavina McGee   10- 9-1856
Barnet, Albert - Rebecca Emehiser   9- 6-1849
Barnett, Albert - Lavina Emehizer   2-10-1854
Batterton, James W. - Lucinda Cooper 6-16-1853
Bebee, Enoch - Mary Jane Glenn   12-25-1851
Beeson, Peter - Rachael Hinton   12-29-1854
Belew, Allen P. - Angeline E. Rathburn
                                      9-11-1856
Belew, Smith Willis - Talitha Emily Plake
                                      1-11-1855
Berriman, Amzi - Mary Ann Wilson   2-15-1852
Berriman, Amzi C. - Louisa Gilleland 5-11-1854
Bess, Sebert - Elizabeth C. Cole   10-12-1855
Bickel, William - Sarah Ann Hopkins   3-22-1853
Bierley, William - Mahala Stephens   2-27-1851
Bilby, Sylvenis - Susan Basey   2-16-1851
Bird, Aaron - Caroline Goins   12-21-1850
Bishop, Charles - Martha Ellen Smith 8-19-1851
Bishop, Conde - Alice Green   5-12-1850
Bivens, Nathaniel - Amanda Mooney   11-27-1851
Boldon, Samuel - Elizabeth Sanders   1-27-1855
Bolden, Thomas L. - Mary Deer   6- 7-1849
Bolden, William - Pheby Ann Fouch   5-14-1851
Bolen, Christopher C. - Amanda Evans
                                      10-26-1853
Bolser, George W. - Elvira Shaw   9-15-1853
Bolser, George W. - Elizabeth Jane Beeson
                                      6- 6-1855
Bonham (or Banham), Elijah - Malissa Ann
                              Sparks 7-26-1853
Bourhard, James - Mariam Ann Sawyer
                              lic. 11- 9-1847
Bouse, Adam - Malinda Williams   2- 2-1855
Bouse, John - Jane M. Smith   3-10-1853
Boxley, Thomas P. - Elizabeth McCrain
                                      9-23-1852

Boyer, George - Rutha Buffington   4-15-1853
Boyer, Richard - Mary Paul   2-10-1856
Bozell, Stephen - Sarah Standridge   7-13-1855
Bracken, William - Jane Elizabeth Morris
                                      1-22-1852
Bradburn, Barnabas - Ann Henry   6-26-1851
Braddock, Ezra - Telitha Jane Decker
                                      5-11-1854
Bradley, Franklin - Susan Ressler   3- 9-1848
Brandon, Jesse - Serelda Fortner   5-22-1853
Bright, John - Margret Leavel   3- 3-1853
Bringman, John - Harriett Powers   10-20-1850
Brock, Heston - Sarah A. Nelson   4-11-1855
Brookbank, William - Nancy Jane Turner
                                      9-25-1850
Brown, George W. - Mary Jane Smith   5-14-1854
Brown, James - Mary M. Downhower
                              11 [12?] 6-1856
Brown, John - Philena Kaywood   2- 2-1845
Brown, Joseph G. - Dorinda Sharp   8- 8-1844
Buckles, John W. - Sarah J. Needham
                                      4-10-1856
Burkdoll, Stephen - Pheby Ann Richards
                                      8-27-1853
Burris, Allen - Mary Jane Mozingo   12-18-1851
Cain, John - Melinda Collins   4- 1-1846
Campbell, Andrew - Sarah Jane Bess   11-16-1854
Campbell, George - Mary Jane Ross   11-10-1853
Cantwell, Peter P. - Susannah Gilleland
                                      11- 3-1847
Carey, Jonathan - Susan Clark   3- 8-1854
Carter, Mason - Ann Eliza Keel   9-22-1853
Cash, Francis - Rebecca Berry   8-27-1852
Cashatt, John - Nancy Quakenbush   10- 5-1856
Casler, James - Margaret Mooney   3-23-1848
Casler, James B. - Mary Ellen Boyd   11- 8-1855
Casler, Milton - Malissa Young   9-10-1853
Caughman, John - Catharine Webbert   8-14-1851
Cleaveland, William - Mary Bailey   10-22-1848
Clossen, John C. - Ann Seward   2-24-1853
Cloud, Robert - Eliza Manning   10- 1-1855
Clouzer, Amos - Mary Ann Harris   6-24-1855
Coats, John - Sally Cooper   1- 1-1845
Cochran, Thomas - Leah Newkirk   3-20-1856
Coffman, Aaron - Emeline Gregory   8- 6-1848
Coffman, Morris M. - Elverah Gregory
                                      10-29-1850
Cole, Isaac - Mary Ellen Bess   9-14-1856
Cole, John, Jr. - Mary Mount   6-21-1849
Cole, Newton - Sarah Jane Orem   1-15-1853
Cole, Perry - Lucinda Wilkes   2- 9-1855
Cole, Samuel - Sarah Jane Jack   1-25-1845
Cole, William W. - Catharine Case   10-11-1855
Collens, Isaac - Mary Pitsenberger
                              lic. 4-29-1852
Collins, George M. - Lydia Ann Puckett
                                      8-27-1853
Collins, Thomas T. - Mary Ann Pucket
                                      6-19-1853
Colvin, William W. - Nancy A. Hunt   10-14-1856
Comer, Jesse - Margaret Jane Dunn   3- 8-1850
Conklin, James - Jane Stephens   9-10-1848
Conklin, William H. - Martha Jennings
                                      8-16-1856

Conner, Elias R. - Sarah Lilley   3-10-1845
Conner, Elias B. - Demande Ann Martin 8- 3-1854
Cook, Jefferson - Elizabeth Mooney   3-12-1846
Cook, John W. - Ibba L. Webb   2-10-1856
Coon, Abner - Rebecca Cameron   1- 7-1847
Coon, Daniel W. - Susanna Keel   9-27-1854
Cooper, John J. - Matilda Ressler   6- 1-1856
Cooper, Joseph - Catharine McGee   6-10-1855
Cooper, William - Sarah H. Smith   2-27-1848
Cooper, William - Silvania Purvis   12- 5-1852
Correll, Christian - Anne Lodick   10-17-1850
Cox, Harvey - Susan McGee   12-10-1851
Crull, Henry - Elizabeth Gregory   11-25-1849
Curran, Henry - Rebecca Ann Waldron   1-14-1847
Daily, John N. - Elizabeth Harden   2- 2-1851
Dale, James S.N. - Zarelda E. Lee   1-11-1853
Darrow, Simon A. - Isabella Ausborn   7- 2-1852
Darrow, Zadock - Cynthia Brown   4- 1-1847
Davenport, Austin - Mary Jane Coons   1-22-1854
Davis, Allan H. - Catharine Paul   8- 7-1854
Deal, Amos - Elizabeth Wright   9-23-1852
Deal, Henry - Annah Stroup   10-10-1850
Deck, Isaac - Agness Smith   5-16-1855
Decker, David - Elizabeth Barrow   8- 1-1856
Deen, George - Martha Jane Walker   5- 1-1853
DeLany, Josiah P. - Catharine Coston   2-26-1854
Denny, Harvey - Sophia Shaw   9-12-1844
Devers, Henry - Elizabeth Mundon   12-12-1852
Dickson, John - Catharine Fouch   1-21-1855
Dickson, Thomas - Ann Dickson   8- 9-1849
Diviney (?), Benjamin - Mary Jane Tucker
                                         11-30-1851
Dolby, John W. - Ruth A. Gooduck   9- 6-1855
Doolin, Bluford - Harriet N. Turpen   5- 6-1851
Duffy, Patrick - Eliza J. Brock   1-22-1856
Dunham, Amos - Margret Ellen Rees   8-11-1853
Dunham, Jacob M. - Eliza Stroup   7-21-1853
Dunham, Samuel - Eliza M. Reese   5- 3-1855
Dunn, William - Sevela Hire   2-12-1851
Dyer, Benjamin - Martha J. Tucker   5-14-1856
Dyson, Deluicous - Jane Bumgardner   4- 5-1851
Dyson, Delucius - Clarissa Hornbeck   10-17-1853
Eagan, William - Sarah (or Susan?) C. Black
                                         2-23-1856
Edwards, Alfred - Nancy Hobbs   2-19-1846
Ellis, Isaac H. - Sarah R. Pickering   5-15-1856
Emehizer, Ira - Margret Young   5-29-1853
Epard, John - Sarah Goar   8-21-1854
Eshleman, Henry - Elizabeth Webbert   9-28-1848
Evans, Henry - Jennett Boyer   7-12-1854
Evans, Jacob - Ursula High   2-11-1856
Evans, John - Lydia Decker   2-17-1853
Evans, Marion P. - Jane Smith   8- 3-1852
Evans, Oliver H.P.L. - Sarah Montgomery
                                         7-20-1850
Evans, William N. - Mary T. goodrich 10- 6-1855
Everling, Edward - Rebecca Hutto   12- 7-1854
Eytchison, Alfred - Lucretia Groover   3-27-1851
Eytcheson, Enoch - Susannah Starr   1-11-1852
Eytchison, Enoch - Sarah Stepp   10-17-1848
Eytchison, John R. - Rachel Thurman(?)
                                         2-12-1856
Farley, Jeremiah C. - Mary Barker   8-14-1853
Farley, Matt - Mary Stroup   4-17-1851
Farlow, Isaac James - Edith H. Wilburn
                                         8-15-1850
Fielding, Andrew - Margret J. Smith   5-26-1853
Fielding, William - Eurelia Little   10-23-1855
Fieldon, Robert B. - Nancy Ann Little 4-12-1855
Fish, Joseph - Harriet White   2-14-1856

Fouch, William H. - Elizabeth Ann Jack
                                         10- 7-1852
Freeman, Oliver - Nancy Mitchel   1- 7-1856
Freeman, Richard - Rheumela Ayers 9-11-1853
Fry, Jessie R. - Sarah Ann Crabtree
                                         12- 4-1856
Garner, Craven - Sarah Stephens   11- 7-1852
Garner, Enoch - Ann Elizabeth Osborn
                                         4-17-1853
Gasho, Henry - Ann Murray   2- 5-1854
Gentry, Cuthbert - Ruth J. Yeakley
                                    lic. 9-13-1856
Giles, James - Elizabeth Sparks   3-18-1852
Giles, James M. - Eliza Mooney   3-31-1852
Glenn, Joseph - Nancy C. Wiles   9-14-1854
Goar, Matt F. - Martha Ann Ross   12- 9-1851
Goin, Frederick - Hannah Wolford   2-22-1848
Goings, Allen - Adaline Goings   3-26-1846
Good, George - Amanda Redmon   2-23-1854
Graham, Ira - Lydia Grey   1-18-1855
Gray, Jacob - July Ann Hunt   3- 3-1853
Green, Milton - Caroline Gillmore 3- 9-1856
Grissom, James - Elizabeth Jessup 8-19-1847
Guge, James Y. - Margaret Jane Dickinson
                                   1-26-1854
Gwin, Wesley - Margaret Chapman   9-18-1854
Hall, Elias - Nancy R. Swope   4-27-1856
Halley, David M. - Elizabeth Fagg 8-15-1854
Hamilton, William - Emily Shepherd 1-11-1855
Harbet, Samuel - Elizabeth Headly 6-22-1851
Harden, William H. - Mary Hodgens 12- 2-1847
Hardin, Gideon - Lydia Brock   4-21-1850
Harding, Andrew - Nancy Dailey   10-22-1854
Harlan, Valentine - Martha M. Adams
                                   4- 5-1854
Harman, John - Quintilla Shirley   7-10-1856
Harper, Theodore - Lucinda Jones   5-24-1855
Harrison, John - Mary Horton   1-18-1854
Harting, John - Sarah Jane Wolford
                                   12-22-1852
Hartsoc, Marion - Sarah E. More   2-24-1856
Harvey, John - Nancy Goar   12-20-1849
Hawthorne, George W. - Elenor Armstrong
                                   1- 1-1854
Hay, James - Margret Umphres   5- 3-1853
Headley, Addison - Eliza Warner   11-27-1856
Headley, Arthur - Elizabeth Yohe   10-20-1850
Headley, Elijah - Caroline Yohe   6-22-1851
Heaton, William C. - Mary J. Beaty 9-22-1853
Hedrick, Solomon - Polly Jane Hennis
                                   7-28-1852
Helmick, Philip - Matilda Dison   12-21-1854
Helmuk, Solomon - Maranda Johnson 12- 8-1850
Hendren, John D. - Eliza Jane Giles
                                   9-26-1849
Henry, James M. - Mary J. Keel   6-29-1856
Herald, William L. - Nancy Garner 4- 4-1850
Heron, Joshua - Mary Jane Burris   8-12-1847
Herron, Isaac - Leticha Bevilhimer 1-12-1851
Herron, John - Nancy Herron   9-16-1854
Herron, John M. - Elizabeth Biggs 3-16-1856
Hickman, Jesse - Susan Phifer   9-29-1848
Hill, Ellis C. - Melissa Jane Sharp
                                   12-16-1856
Hill, Thomas N. - Elizabeth Deal   5-21-1846
Hinton, Robert - Mary Burch   3-12-1856
Hobbs, John M. - Mary Ann Green   8-18-1853
Hogan, Morton - Adaylin Goin   6-26-1855
Holloway, James - Chrystia Ann Alley
                                   9-28-1856

310

Hooker, Charlie - Eliza J. Spacy   2-17-1856
Horton, Jesse - Mary Craig   1-11-1851
Horton, Jesse - Mary Tucker   9-17-1853
Huff, Samuel - Hannah Redman   9-11-1856
Huser, Merrit - Mary Henry   4-17-1853
Huser, William F. - Mary J. Wright   7-16-1856
Hutto, Isaac N. - Mary J. Miller   3- 6-1856
Hyde, Peter - Catharine Swisher   8-13-1854
Innis, James A. - Jane L. Foster   10-19-1854
Innis, Nathaniel - Nancy Elenor Shank
                                      10- 2-1851
Innis, Thompson - Sarah Ann Askren   9-11-1849
Innis, William - Mary Ann McGill   6- 8-1848
Ishmael, Benjamin - Mary Louisa Little
                                      2-24-1848
Jack, James V. - Mary Rhoads   4-13-1854
Jack, John - Sarah Ann Foutch   8-19-1849
Jackson, Jesse - Sarah Mitchell   10-17-1850
Jackson, Samuel - Mary Jack   3- 8-1849
Jackson, William L. - Lydia Whitesel 5-14-1856
Johnson, Hugh - Mary High   12-14-1856
Johnson, Schuyler - Matilda Jane Whisler
                                      5-15-1855
Jones, John - Sarah S. Smith   12-18-1849
Jones, Pleasant - Mary Jane Plummer   8-29-1847
Jones, Thomas - Ellen Montgomery   7-12-1851
Jones, Thomas B. - Nancy Ann Stephens
                                      10-27-1850
Jourdan, Thomas - Sarah Jarret   9-11-1853
Jourdin, William - Louisa Turner   11-17-1856
Judy, David - Mary Houser   11-21-1856
Keel, Ira - Nancy Gray   6- 5-1851
Keel, Smith - Susan Orr   4-25-1852
Kemp, Abraham - Rebecca Ann Britain   1-13-1850
Kemp, David - Mary Ann Price   1- 6-1848
Kendall, Martin - Louisa Jane Walker 3- 2-1848
Kenworthy, David - Mary Dickinson   12- 1-1852
King, David - Susan Emehiser   7-14-1850
King, David - Hannah Vanbuskirk   3- 9-1856
Kinley, Samuel - Nancy Walker   6- 5-1849
Kirtley, Lemuel - Mary Jane Covert   7-15-1856
Kothe, William - Christina Meyer   4- 1-1854
Lambdin, William - Harriet N. Smith   10-16-1852
Lane, John T. - Drusila Sawyer   5-26-1849
Lane, Thomas - Sarah McCoun   4-16-1854
Lee, Stephen - Elizabeth S. Small   11- 2-1854
Leonard, Abner J.(?) - Mary Horton   5-17-1853
Lett, John O. - Elizabeth J. Mitchel 3-12-1856
Lilley, Nelson - Amanda Hobbs   1- 1-1854
Lilly, Green - Sarah Eliza Wright   12-14-1848
Lindsey, John M. - Sarah Ellen Shafer
                                      2- 6-1856
Link, Squire - Caroline J. Newman   11- 9-1851
Little, Hugh - Elizabeth Gilleland   4-26-1849
Little, Samuel J. - Harriet A. Molden
                                      10- 5-1854
Little, Thomas J. - Margaret Fielding
                                      9-11-1856
Little, Thomas M. - Rachel Decker   12-16-1856
Lockridge, Henry - Emily Jane Lane (or Law?).
                                      5- 5-1853
Long, Daniel - Elizabeth Cutsinger   3-11-1855
Loop, Henry - Hannah Stephens   1-24-1853
Lynch, Joseph P. - Martha Jane Robinson
                                      8-17-1851
Lyons, Andrew - Eliza Jane Adams   12-10-1848
McCoun, Elisha - Martha Jane Sparks   6-29-1854
McCoy, Patrick - Henrietta Philpot   7-16-1856
McDaniel, John - Mary J. Harry   5-22-1856

McIntire, Tuntis R. - Lavena Stroup
                                      9-19-1850
McNiel, William - Delila Chapman   1- 4-1856
McQuillan, Edward - Isidore Jane Ressler
                                      5- 7-1854
McReynolds, Ravin - Nancy Orem   2-19-1854
Mahaffey, Moses - Elizabeth Merrill
                                      10- 5-1853
Mains, William - Susan Letsinger   11- 3-1856
Marshall, Benjamin F. - Rebecca Level
                                      9-21-1854
Marshall, William - Lucy Ann Richardson
                                      11- 4-1852
Martin, David D. - Mary Ann Harbaugh
                                      3-18-1852
Martin, Fieldan - Nancy Jane Chase   6- 8-1854
Martin, Jarred Jackson - Elizabeth Susan Small
                                      6-14-1855
Massale, Daniel - Rebecca Kinley   3-16-1856
Mathews, Theodore - Nancy Leavell   8- 2-1856
Matze, Jeremiah - Dulsena Kaywood   12-25-1851
Maze, John A. - Mary Ann Umphries   10-25-1852
Mendenhall, John Milton - Nira Knight Hennis
                                      5-30-1849
Miller, Jonathan P. - Susan Ann Bolser
                                      6- 6-1852
Mills, Caleb - Susannah Haworth   3-13-1856
Mills, John - Louisa Horton   12-30-1849
Mitchell, Elias - Catharine Winters
                                      9-27-1849
Mitchell, Holcomb - Dorcas Ann Denny
                                      5-29-1853
Mitchell, James - Eliza Ann Plummer
                                      11-25-1852
Mitchell, William - Mary Margaret Rosier
                                      3-15-1849
Mittlen, Sampson G. - Christina J. Innis
                                      8- 2-1855
Molden, Thomas C. - Elector Short   12-19-1850
Montgomery, Isaac H. - Elizabeth Jane Evans
                                      7-10-1848
Montgomery, John - Sevilla Dunn   11- 3-1856
Mooney, Jacob - Catharine Giles   11-21-1853
Mooney, Joshua - Elizabeth Harris   2-13-1851
Moore, John - Sarah Ann Shaw   4-15-1849
Moore, William - Sophia Brown   11-12-1855
Mount, James - Aurella J. Nelson   4-27-1855
Mount, John S. - Mary Ann Buskirk   1-16-1853
Mozingo, Josiah - Elizabeth Fox   9- 4-1845
Murray, Daniel - Ann Webbert   3- 9-1848
Myers, John - Serelda Jane Martin   9-19-1852
Myers, Samuel - Malinda Goins   1- 5-1856
Neighbours, John - Susan McReynolds
                                      9- 1-1853
Newkirk, James - Melissa Haskett   3-19-1856
Nicholas, Anderson - Susanna Keep   10-29-1848
Norris, Aquila - Martha Jane Starkey
                                      5-29-1851
Nutter, John - Martha Ann Prichard   7-31-1845
Oldaker, Jesse - Sarah Levell   9-27-1855
Oldcraft, Robert - Charlotte Sharp
                                      10-12-1856
Page, George W. - Martha Ann Russel
                                      11- 1-1851
Parker, Isaac - Matilda Hall   3-16-1847
Parker, Moses J.H. - Ruth Ann Young
                                      4-30-1854
Parker, Noah - Deborah Williams   9- 9-1849
Parker, Peter C. - Rebecca Jane Hall
                                      10-27-1851

Parks, George B.W. - Cinthia Richardson
                                        7-26-1845
Passons, William - Susan Michael   4- 5-1849
Paulus, George - Elizabeth Deal   3-15-1855
Peters, William - Eliza Orr   11-20-1845
Peterson, John - Mary Day   8-31-1856
Phares, Jesse - Elizabeth Dunn   10-20-1853
Pharis, Solomon - Rebecca Jane Hamilton
                                        12-28-1853
Phifer, Henry - Rachel Sims   3- 8-1854
Phifer, John - Nancy Myers   4- 4-1850
Phifer, Joseph - Luvicy Welshons   1-27-1848
Pickard, Albert - Mary A. Reveal   9-25-1845
Pickens, Robert - Ann Campbell   6-19-1856
Pickering, David - Elizabeth M. Mitchel
                                        12-20-1854
Pickering, Milo - Cyrean Mitchell   3-19-1853
Pierce, William - Sarah E. Brown   10-16-1853
Ploughe, Abraham - Allivana Wineborough
                                        12-30-1852
Ploughe, Isaac N. - Sarah Ann Lett   5-18-1848
Plummer, Andrew - Sarah Deer   11-11-1852
Plummer, Andrew - Rachel Smith   11-10-1855
Plummer, Calvin F. - America Melvina Deer
                                        12-23-1849
Plummer, Ira J. - Caroline Bailey   3-21-1854
Plummer, Isaac - America Plummer   2-16-1854
Plummer, Martin V. - Frances E. Irish
                                        10-19-1856
Plummer, Salathiel V. - Martha Jane Gray
                                        1-18-1853
Poston, Abraham - Pertina Dement Mazingo
                                        8- 1-1855
Price, John - Margret Alexander   1-19-1851
Price, Joseph, Jr. - Eveline McElhaney
                                        9- 5-1854
Prichard, Daniel S. - Neoma Stroup   4-10-1856
Purvis, Andrew J. - Margaret Jane Bess
                                        4-19-1854
Rainey, Samuel - Mariah Vanhorn   3- 6-1853
Rains, Isaac - Charlotte Eads   1- 3-1850
Ray, John - Phebe Ann Bolser   4- 3-1856
Ressler, Abraham - Elizabeth Jane Letsinger
                                        12-25-1845
Ressler, Jacob - Mary Ann Cleveland 10-14-1854
Richards, Samuel - Rebecca Jane Hall 5-19-1850
Richardson, John - Malinda Maze   12-31-1851
Ridgeway, Alexander H. - Hannah E. Reed
                                        11- 4-1855
Roberts, Sterling - Caroline Lynes   8-24-1856
Robinson, Alexander - Eliza Custer   12-26-1850
Robison, Joseph H. - Nancy E. Bland 10- 6-1856
Roler, David - Margaret Ann Carr   10-17-1850
Roode, Thomas Harvey - Louisa Motz   4-15-1854
Ross, Andrew J. - Lydia E. Tuder   1-11-1854
Ross, James F. - Fanny Smiley   11-24-1847
Ruse, Thomas - Mila Suite   12-13-1849
Russell, Abraham - Martha Pratt   9-25-1856
Russell, George - Lyda Ann Hedgel   9-25-1856
Russell, John - Jane Peatt   8-28-1851
Sample, Elam A. - Mariah J. Alexander
                                        6-26-1853
Sawyer, James - Melinda Decker   6-16-1854
Sawyer, Stephen - Catharine Huffman   8-31-1851
Scott, Joseph M. - Louisa Jane Stephens
                                        7-27-1854
Scott, Uriah - Mary E. Brown   3- 8-1855
Shank, Caleb B. - Mary W. Askren   10- 2-1851
Shanon, Thomas B. - Nancy Dickey   8-22-1850

Sharp, Abraham - Martha Fester (?) 6-13-1856
Sharp, Samuel B. - Rebecca Emily Letsinger
                                        3- 4-1852
Shaw, Albin - Nancy Eytchison   11-13-1851
Shaw, Albin - Sarah Shaw   6-11-1852
Sheil, Thomas - Levicy Combs   8-26-1851
Sheppard, John - Margaret McElhaney
                                        12- 8-1853
Short, Andrew B. - Amanda Ressler   5-15-1852
Short, Lewis - Lisha Ann High   6-19-1851
Simmons, William - Sarah Ann Kinder
                                        3-26-1855
Simpson, Elisha - Nancy Byerley   11-10-1853
Singleton, Robert - Elizabeth Hall 3-30-1856
Small, James - Eliza Kelley   7- 3-1856
Smelser, Frederick - Margaret Beck
                                        12-30-1847
Smiley, Hickman - Elizabeth Mills   8- 8-1844
Smith, Dudley - Martha J. Purvis   11-30-1856
Smith, Enoch - Sarah Kirtley   10-17-1853
Smith, John, Jr. - Angelette Nelson
                                        12- 2-1852
Smith, William - Mary Ann Eytchison
                                        9- 4-1849
Smith, William - Mahala Kelley   8-10-1852
Smith, William - Sarah Barlow   10-11-1853
Smith, William R. - Rebecca Wallace
                                        11-13-1849
Sparks, Thomas - Mary Jane McCoun 12-21-1854
Stephens, Isaac - Mary Jane Williams
                                        2-20-1846
Stepp, Thomas - Evaline Cotton   4-16-1846
Stevens, Martin - Roxan Myerly   9- 9-1852
Stillwagon, John - Philepeone Wolf
                                        lic. 6-20-1855
Stites, Samuel I. (or J.) - Mary Ann
                            Alexander 10-11-1854
Stivers, Stanford S. - Elenor Hubble
                                        5-12-1853
Stivers, William - Matilda A. Young
                                        6-16-1851
Stroup, Reuben - Sarah Jane Wright 9-28-1848
Summers, John - Narcissus Ann McKay
                                        3-22-1854
Summervill, Landof M.W. - Nancy Bell Lee
                                        1- 6-1852
Sutton, Amos - Loiza Jane Lowder   8-18-1853
Swartz, Peter - Sarah J. Youngman
                                        lic. 10-20-1856
Swope, Andrew - Lavina McMurtry   8- 6-1854
Tansey, Calvin F. - Ellen Jane Hamilton
                                        9-27-1849
Taylor, Lucius - Nancy Conner   12-31-1845
Teter, Eli - Prunella Farley   5-27-1849
Teter, Eli - Margaret Palmer   4- 2-1856
Teter, Mahlon - Anne Dunn   5- 8-1851
Thomas, Abraham - Martha Ann Kenley
                                        3-18-1849
Thomas, George - Mary Jane Harden
                                        lic. 11-18-1847
Thomas, Uriah - Martha R. Lett   4- 3-1851
Thomas, William - Mary Frances Carr
                                        4-22-1855
Thompson, Henry L. - Mary Mitchell 1-30-1853
Thornburgh, Benjamine - Elizabeth Shofer
                                        9-29-1850
Thurman, Charles A. - Rachel Mount 3-18-1849
Tichenor, James R. - Mary Kindley 2-11-1856
Tollen (?), David - Martha Mitchell
                                        lic. 11- 4-1856

Tooley, George M. - Margret Jane Campbell 4- 2-1855

Townsend, Henry - Rose Ann Payton   1- 9-1853
Treadway, Amos K. - Mary E. Butler   4- 1-1852
Trout, Joseph - Catharine Green   10-27-1853
Tucker, Andrew - Elizabeth Conner
                          lic.   2-17-1845
Tucker, Charles - Harriet E. Manning 12-31-1856
Tucker, James - Martha Ann Norwood   3-19-1853
Tuder, David B. - Mary Dunham   4-17-1851
Tuder, George T. - Martha Batterton   9-25-1851
Tudor, Larkin P. - Hester Ann Fear   8- 7-1853
Turner, James - Rachel Hayworth   2-20-1851
Turpen, William - Elizabeth Murphey   6-18-1851
Turpin, Sylvester - Mary A. Molden   12- 3-1849
Tyler, James, Jr. - Lydia Eytchison   11- 7-1846
Umphres, William - Margret Maze   12-31-1851
Umphries, George W. - Burnetta Nelson 5-29-1854
Vanbuskirk, Joseph - Sarah Conaway   8-23-1853
Vanbuskirk, Joseph, Jr. - Mrs. Martha Clanton
                                  7-14-1850
Vandevender, Isaac - Sarah Foster   5-29-1851
Vanhorn, Moses - Eliza Ann Lemon   12-21-1851
Vicors, Elza - Nancy A. Letsinger   11-16-1845
Walker, James, Jr. - Sarah Jane Holiday
                          3-19-1846
Walker, John - Sarah Caroline Letsinger
                          3- 4-1852
Wallace, Samuel - Emily Kendall   5-26-1849
Wallace, William - Amanda Jane Hardin 7-26-1855
Wallace, William L. - Mary E. Ferguson
                          4- 8-1856
Wallen, Robert - Mary Morney (?)   4-24-1856
Walton, Samuel L. - Elsey Ann Headley 3- 7-1852
Waltz, George - Martha Ann Vanhorn   6-13-1852
Warden, William - Ellen Eads   10-21-1849
Warren, John - Jane E. Stroup   10-13-1853
Warren, Luke C. - Nancy Dyson   7-23-1850
Watts, Ede H. - Margret A. Sulivan   5-18-1851

Welchhonse, William - Sarah (or Sally) Farly
                          4- 5-1845
Welshhons, Daniel, Jr. - Tamer Jane Overman
                          3-14-1850
Whicker, James - Elizabeth Turpen 9-21-1852
Williams, William - Harriet Bolser
                          10-14-1853
Williamson, Rynal G. - Nancy Havens
                          11-17-1854
Winkle, Michael - Elizabeth Lawrence
                          5- 9-1852
Wise, George W. - Mary Genott LaFlesh
                          1- 4-1853
Wise, William W. - Nancy A. Owen 1- 6-1853
Wiseman, George P. - Catharine Michael
                          12-31-1848
Wisner, Vanransler C. - Martha E. Borlan
                  (or Barlow)   11- 4-1852
Wolford, Abraham - Matilda Goin   1-30-1848
Wolford, Simeon - Mary Teter   4-20-1856
Woolford, Valentine - Ann Mannan   7- 9-1854
Workman, Joseph P. - Permelia Guy 5- 4-1852
Workman, Samuel W. - Ede S. Workman
                          9- 1-1851
Wright, Ashlery P. - Mary M. Blunt
                          12-25-1852
Wright, Elmer - Mary Ann Brown   10-10-1850
Wright, James - Martha Eytcheson   3- 2-1848
Wright, Morgan - Celea Philpott   9-17-1855
Wright, Robert W. - Luiza I. Blunt
                          12-15-1850
Wymer, William - Julia Wolford   9-10-1846
Yohe, Alexander - Elizabeth Hagerty
                          10-25-1856
Young, Daniel G. - Mary Ann McElhaney
                          12-16-1849
Young, Jacob Israel - Maria Webbert
                          8-19-1855
Young, John - Katharine Kleyla   5- 7-1853

MONROE COUNTY MARRIAGES, 1818-1835

Compiled from microfilm of Monroe County Marriage Records, 1818-1852, in Genealogy Division, Indiana State Library. For many of the marriages there were no returns to show when the marriage was performed and in some instances when there was a return the person performing the marriage did not give the date he performed the ceremony. When the date used is the date of the license, it is so indicated.

Abel, Elias - Hannah Otwell	4-20-1828
Abram, Henry - Catharine Hendricks lic.	3-28-1831
Abrams, Charles B. - Lucy Hendricks	3-14-1833
Abrams, John - Martha Potts	4- 8-1830
Abrams, Joseph - Mary Taylor	6- 6-1823
Adams, John - Nancy Bell lic.	3- -1826
Adamson, John - Sarah Andrews lic.	5-22-1822
Adamson, Jonathan - Sarah Teague	1818
Adamson, Zedekiah - Sally Steward lic.	4-25-1824
Adamson, Zedekiah - Lucinda King lic.	4- 1-1835
Akin, Ransom - Sarah R. Sedwick	12- 9-1834
Alexander, Hiram - Patsy Brazier	11-12-1820
*Alexander, John - Nancy Cavins	3-16-1824
Allcorn, George - Elizabeth Rice	2-12-1833
Allen, John - Sally Cole	11-22-1832
Allen, John W. - Fanny Ione Clark	2-22-1829
Allen, William - Susan L. Burton	12- 1-1829
Allison, Noah - Polly J. Boswell	6-23-1820
Alsup, James - Elizabeth Poe	4- 7-1825
Alsup, Thomas - Susanna Newcomb	3- 7-1822
Alsup, Wesly - Lydia Cooper	4- 1-1832
Anderson, Cyrus - Abigail Wharton	2-21-1833
Anderson, George - Hannah Knighten	3- 4-1824
Anderson, Harvy - Nancy Ketcham lic.	3- 5-1828
Anderson, James - Mahala Burton	11- 3-1830
Anderson, James W. - Salena Marshall	8-25-1835
Anderson, John H. - Mary Ann Alexander lic.	10- 5-1825
Archer, Edward M. - Nancy J. Campbell	12-13-1834
Archer, John C. - Elizabeth Zink	7-20-1822
Archer, William - Statiras(?) Elkins	2-17-1824
Armstrong, John - Ruth Clendennin	3- 1-1827
Armstrong, William - Catharine Armstrong lic.	1-31-1822
Arnold, Samuel - Rebecca Armstrong	7-12-1823
Arnold, Wesly - Elizabeth Lebo	8- 1-1829
Arnold, William - Rachel Coffman	4-11-1822
Arter, John - Hannah Fry lic.	6- 4-1828
Arthur, Elias - Sarah Wright	4-23-1825
Arthur, Henry - Rachel Carmical lic.	4-23-1833
Arthur, John - Elizabeth James	6-30-1819
Ashby, Blaten - Francis Puett lic.	7-29-1833
Atwood, James B. - Elizabeth Glothling	5-18-1823
Bailey, Cherley D. - Polly Orrick	7-14-1821
Baily, Elijah - Massena(?) Followell	1- 3-1831
Baily, William - Nancy Adams	11-30-1826
Bails, James - Elizabeth Mitchel	8- 5-1818
Bails, James - Marinda Jane Neel	10- 2-1834
Bails, Thomas - Elizabeth King	3-15-1827
Baker, George - Sally Fulford	2- 5-1829
Baker, Henry - Betsy Adams lic.	12-16-1833
Baker, Jacob - Mary Anne Hite	3- 5-1835
Baker, Joseph - Mary Elliott lic.	8- 2-1830

Baker, Moses - Margaret Flora	12-17-1825
Barlow, Samuel - Susannah Lee	8- 6-1820
Barnes, John S. - Mary W. Owens	9-12-1828
Barney, Benjamin - Martha Davison lic.	9- 4-1834
Barns, David - Eliza Witham lic.	4-13-1825
Barrow, David - Elizabeth Rader	10-17-1832
Basket, Thomas - Margaret Copelin (or Copland)	2- 7-1832
Bastin, Henry - Eleanor Brisco	12-17-1835
Bates, Charles - Anna Rader lic.	10-11-1830
Batterton, George W. - Sarah Bagwell lic.	10-27-1831
Batterton, William - Sarah Archer	8-12-1824
Baugh, Peter - Elizabeth Curl	6-26-1829
Baxter, William - Polly Sea (or Lea?)	2-11-1833
Beaman, Alonzo - Adaline Deming	9-18-1832
Bell, Mathew - Jane Ralston	6-15-1831
Bell, Nathaniel - Celia Wright	4-26-1825
Bell, William - Patience Back lic.	3- 4-1835
Bennett, John - Susan D. Parks	12-20-1832
Bennington, James - Sarah Hartsock	12-21-1820
Benton, John E. - Lucinda Owens	5-29-1834
Berlingam, Clark - Lucinda Bennett	7-13-1825
Berry, Campbell - Salena Burton	9-22-1820
Berry, John - Gracy Treat	7-13-1819
Berry, John M. - Patsy Rand	6- 3-1830
Berry, Joseph - Eleanor Haines(?)	4-27-1825
Berry, William - Patsy Givens lic.	10-13-1825
Blain, John - Charity Turner	12-22-1831
Blakely, _____ - Anna Campbell lic.	5- -1830
Blessing, Christopher - Elizabeth Young	1- 4-1828
Boltenhouse, Isaac - Zelphia Williams	9- 1-1834
Boruff, William - Jane Dawar	3-15-1829
Bowland, John - Catherine Owens	4-30-1822
Bowlman, Lewis - Harriet Penwood(?) Stone	12-12-1833
Bowls, Augustus - Juliann Chambers	1-28-1834
Bowman, Septima - Polly Shuffield	2-15-1834
Boyd, Jonathan - Polly Dobbs lic.	3-26-1831
Brady, William - Sally Kirby	2-23-1825
Brannum, Jonathan - Elizabeth Griffith lic.	1-27-1831
Brazeal, Henry W. - Charlotte Matlock	4-22-1828
Bristoe, Moses - Peggy Arter	11-11-1830
Brooks, John - Mary Goodwin lic.	5-16-1822
Brown, Bryant - Manerva Carr	11-27-1826
Brown, Isaac - Susan Bennaugh	7-31-1829
Brown, Martin - Margaret Baugh lic.	7-28-1834

Brown, Thomas - Mary Kirkendall   12-30-1833
Browning, Nathaniel C. - Elizabeth Millikan
                                     12-14-1828
Brummet, Banner - Pheriba Young   6-18-1833
Brummet, Joab - Sally Brummet   3-24-1830
Brummet, James - Esther Brummet   9-16-1819
Brummet, Lankston - Sabry Brummet   4- 3-1828
Brummet, William - Jane Richerson   12-15-1831
Bruner, Henry - Elizabeth Phillips   2-17-1833
Bruner, John - Elizabeth Thrasher   3-27-1834
Bryant, James - Rebecca Dover lic.   11-18-1831
Bryant, William - Elizabeth Ooly
                        lic.   2- 8-1827
Bunger, David - Jaritha Berry   4-17-1833
Bunger, John - Eby Berry   1-29-1829
Burch, Achillas - Margaret Oliphant 1-20-1834
Burch, Achilles - Susannah Morgan   11-30-1835
Burch, Charles - Jane Oliphant lic.
                                     7-28-1834
Burch, George - Eliza Ann Christy   12-25-1834
Burch, James - Sarah Walden   2-14-1823
Burks, David - Nancy Burks   9-18-1832
Burks, Floyd - Helen E. Thompson
                        lic.   12-11-1835
Burks, Green D. - Elizabeth Bryant
                        lic.   9-20-1832
Burn, Philip - Catharine Mull   2- 8-1827
Burton, Jackson - Nancy May lic.   5-13-1834
Burton, Jesse M. - Molly Goans   1- 1-1833
Burton, Joseph - Nancy Hartsock   4- 4-1826
Busick, Kindrick - Nancy More lic.   6- 4-1833
Buskirk, James V. - Mariah Campbell
                        lic.   1-31-1826
Buskirk, John V. - Catherine Lebo   5-26-1822
Butcher, David - Sarah Flora lic.   4- -1832
Butcher, Leir - Mary Mosier lic.   5- 6-1834
Butcher, Levi - Ann Tatum   6-16-1834
Byers, David - Rachel Saunders   1-27-1831
Byers, Nathan - Sally A. Hamilton   2-21-1828
Cain, David - Malinda Baty   9-30-1832
Cain, Quinton N. - Polly Boles   2-25-1830
Caivens, Samuel - Priscilla Chandler
                        lic.   1-14-1822
Calfee, Reuben R. - Olive Cole   8- 5-1831
Campbell, Joseph - Mary Graham   1- 8-1821
Carmichael, James - Elizabeth Teague
                                     12- 9-1830
Carmichael, Thomas - Polly S. McBride
                                     9-10-1834
Carr (or Karr), William - Belinda Stipp
                                     2-27-1831
Carrol, Lewis - Mary Green   10-16-1827
Carson, Thomas H. - Mary Ann Hunter 7- 3-1831
Carter, John - Elizabeth Martingell 4-22-1832
Carter, Lewis - Martha Hall lic.   3-10-1835
Cartwright, Robert - Juriah Abrams   2-19-1824
Casey, David - Sally Collins   4-12-1822
Chambers, John - Nancy Parks   12-30-1830
Chambers, Zecheriah B. - Izabel Blair
                    (or Blain)   4- 8-1822
Chandler, Benjamin - Nancy Arthur
                        lic.   6- 2-1818
Chandler, James - Elizabeth Dover   4- 7-1831
Chesnut, Benjamin - Nancy Duffield
                        lic.   9-11-1824
Chesnut, James - Phebe Duffield   10-14-1827
Chesnut, John - Nancy Devore   5-12-1829

Chipman, Archibald B. - Sally Stewart
                                     4- 4-1833
Chipman, Samuel D. - Martha Smith
                        lic.   9- -1824
Clark, James W. - Esther Todd   3-10-1829
Clark, Joshua - Nancy Ryon   8- 2-1830
Clendennen, James - Iby Nuckels   2- -1832
Clendennin, Charles - Nancy Denny
                        lic.   3-31-1835
Cleveland, Alexander - Frances Botts
                        lic.   3-28-1835
Clutter, Israel - Rachel Leabo
                        lic.   10-13-1834
Coffey, Alfred - Susan K. Caivins   2-26-1830
Coffey, Alfred H. - Rachel Fullen
                                     11-12-1829
Coffey, Allen - Susan Basket   6-17-1830
Coffey, Albert - Sarah Goodnight   12- 5-1833
Coffey, Isom - Martha Smock   8-10-1832
Coffey, James W. - Malena Coffey
                        lic.   4-16-1833
Coffey, Martin - Jane Groves Coffey
                                     3-14-1833
Colder, William - Margaret Myers   3- 3-1831
Cole, Crawford - Eunice Allen   1- 9-1829
Cole, Crawford - Elizabeth Eller
                        lic.   7-31-1833
Coleman, Abraham - Elizabeth Manon
                                     5- 9-1831
Collins, Archibald - Nancy Taylor
                        lic.   2-13-1826
Collins, Washington - Catharine Carmichael
                                     11-31[sic]-1832
Combs, Martin - Mary Fodrill   11-22-1831
Cook, John - Sally Fitchpatrick   2-28-1830
Cooper, Samuel - Mary Wolfe lic.   8- 3-1833
Coplen, James A. - Elizabeth Tompkins
                                     2-15-1829
Cotron, Samuel - Betsy Mason(?)   8- -1819
Cox, Cornelius - Catharine Jackson
                                     4- 1-1824
Cox, George - Betsy Ann McGlochlin
                                     12- 1-1829
Cox, Nathan - Dorcas King   6- 7-1822
Cox, Stuart(?) - Delia Hoskins   3-14-1823
Cox, William - Elizabeth Jackson   11-23-1830
Crane, Richard - Rebecca Gardner
                        lic.   12-24-1824
Crocker, Orian - Olly Berry   6-18-1822
Curl, James - Anna Elliott   10- -1822
Curry, Samuel - Sarah Smith   8-21-1833
Daniel, Robert - Delitha Evans   1-23-1823
Davidson, Griffith - Tabitha Mosier
                                     11-15-1825
Davidson, Joseph - Matilda Wells   7- 1-1824
Davidson, William - Joann A. Jackson
                                     12-26-1828
Dawson, James - Rebecca Smith   8- 5-1830
Dawson, Joseph - Barbara Hinkle   11-17-1830
Day, James C. - Jane Legg   1-27-1825
Deal, Mareus L. - Nancy Morrison   10-22-1832
Dearman, George - Elizabeth Rogers
                                     2-24-1828
Dearman, James - Mary Ann Slown   6- 2-1831
Dearman, James - Leah Rader lic.   4-20-1835
Deckart, Adam - Sally Stewart   6- 5-1834
Deckert, Jesse - Sally Kinson   1-19-1832

Denney, John W. S. - Sally Gaskins
lic.   3-24-1835
Devon (or Devore?), Wilson -
Catharine Whisennand   [1831]
Dickins, Pemberton - Drucilla Turpent
8- 5-1819
Dickey, Ebenezer - Mary Esslinger   4- 1-1819
Dodd, William - Matilda Bratny   12-11-1834
Dole, Thomas B. - Catharine Burks   1-25-1831
Dollarhide, Evans - Hannah Lowe   2-22-1820
Doughty, Martin - Mary Fletcher   7-13-1824
Dover, Zephaniah - Jane Chandler
lic.   11-10-1830
Dowden, James - Rebecca Ketcham   11-12-1835
Dowden, William - Nancy Chambers   9-16-1830
Dubois, Jesse K. - Nancy Balterton 9-29-1831
Duffield, Robert - Patience Chesnut
10- -1822
Duffield, Thomas - Elizabeth Torr   8- 5-1828
Duke, Ephraim - Martha Swaney   6-11-1820
Duke, Robert - Nancy Goodwin   5-20-1819
Duncan, William - Minerva Myers
lic.   12-15-1834
Dunning, James - Harriet Litteral 12-20-1827
Dunning, John - Sally Wampler   9-11-1823
Dunning, Paris C. - Sarah M. Alexander
7- 6-1826
Durham, John - Anna Lamb   8-16-1820
Dyer, James S. - Sally S. Berry   1-31-1833
Dyer, John - Sarah Coonse   9-29-1819
Earls, Willis - Anne Long   8-21-1834
East, Jesse - Sarah Combs   9-22-1831
East, Joseph - Tobitha Howell   3-10-1831
East, Pinckney - Sarah Carmichael   3-12-1835
Eckels, Delana R. - Louisa K. Elliott
7-16-1827
Eddy, Audly - Thursa Campbell   12-27-1834
Eddy, Samuel - Elizabeth Rains   4-28-1825
Edwards, James - Susannah Fletcher
lic.   2-18-1823
Edwards, William - Belinda Davis   8-11-1826
Eller, John - Mahala Pauly   9-17-1835
Ellett, Dorsey O. - Elizabeth Bagwell
11-18-1835
Elliott, Richard H. - Isabel Smart
lic.   7-12-1823
Ellis, James N. - Rebecca Mariah Scott
12-24-1835
Empson, Perry - Margaret Chambers   5-22-1834
Enyart(?), Silas - Mary Sears lic. 5-22-1822
Eoff, John L. - Polly Roughton lic. 1-31-1833
Ervin, Charles - Jane Smith   12-21-1830
Etter, Jesse - Sophia Baugh lic.   12-28-1832
Evans, Abner - Mary Ashley   10-17-1830
Evans, Abner - Nancy Littlejohn   5- 6-1834
Evans, James - Nancy McCowen   9- 7-1834
Ewing, Robert - Anna Curry   3-30-1830
Fairly, James - Mary Linthicum   9-18-1834
Falkner, Emanuel F. - Rebecca Coffey
1- 1-1830
Farmer, Eli P. - Matilda Allison   10- -1832
Farmer, James H. - Emery Parks   10-21-1828
Farmer, Prier S. - Elizabeth Devore 2-17-1831
Fee, John - Nancy Gilbert   4-22-1834
Fine, Solomon - Enicy Sears   2-17-1823
Finly, Rufus - Nancy Mitchell lic. 11- 4-1835
Finly, William - Anna Miller lic.   1-18-1832

Fitchpatrick, Samuel - Ruth Walker
2-18-1830
Fleener, Aaron - Mary Ann Weddle 10- 8-1829
Fleenor, Michael - Elizabeth Robertson
6- 7-1829
Fleenor, Nicholas - Sarah Calor
lic.   12-20-1835
Flener, James - Louisa Rader lic. 6-23-1830
Fletcher, William - Abigail Morgan
9-21-1834
Florer, George - Mary Butcher
lic.   8-28-1835
Florer, John - Christina Fry   5- 1-1834
Followell, George - Anne Cox
lic.   11- 4-1824
Followell, Merideth - Catharine Earls
lic.   6-18-1833
Followell, William - Margaret Breedlove
lic.   12-15-1834
Fox, Hiram - Frances Kindrick   9-23-1832
Freeland, Benjamin - Mary A. Clark
2-15-1820
Freeland, Joseph - Mary Garrett   11-28-1819
Freeman, Micajah - Martha Brown   10-18-1831
Friend, John - Betsy Fullen   1- 6-1831
Frits, George - Hetty Davis   8-21-1833
Frost, William - Sally Irvin lic. 5- -1824
Fry, David - Dorothy Stewart lic. 5- -1823
Fullen, Jacob - Sarah Wampler   4- 1-1819
Fullen, John J. - Nancy Coffey   9- 3-1829
Fuller, Benjamin - Sally Hudson   8-19-1824
Fuller, James - Nancy Fuller   1-23-1823
Fullerton, John W. - Mary Roberts
11- 5-1835
Furgerson, Asa - Parthenia Anderson
10- 2-1828
Gainey, Meredith - Nancy Sadler   11-17-1825
Gainey, William - Elizabeth Sadler
1- 3-1826
Gardner, John - Jane Joy   4- -1820
Gardner, Joseph - July Ann Harmon 8-28-1834
Garner, James - Rachel Coffman   1-24-1822
Garrett, Ruben - Polly Bailey lic.3- 3-1834
Garrison, John - Eliza Alsop lic. 5- 1-1822
Garrison, John - Sarah Marshall   12-13-1830
Gibson, Elias - Elizabeth Garrett 6-14-1821
Giffing, Joshua S. - Sarah Ann Martin
lic.   12-22-1835
Gilam, Jesse - Celia Snowden   2-25-1821
Gilbert, James - Sally Wilson   3- 9-1827
Gilbert, John - Harriett Elliott   1-28-1830
Gilham, Enoch - Mary Combs lic.   1-25-1834
Gillan, James - Nancy Conder   9-25-1834
Girton, Jesse - Cressy Freeland   6-23-1831
Givans, Alexander M. - Mary Ann Crigger
2- 5-1835
Givans, Henry - Mary Ann Dyer   4-29-1830
Givens, Robert B. - Polly Bryant 11-30-1832
Givens, Samuel - Sarah Organ   1-29-1835
Goans, James B. - Elizabeth Burton
2-26-1830
Goble, Martin - Sarah Castner   6-24-1831
Goodin, Ammon - Susannah Leonard 2-28-1833
Goodwin, Abner - Nancy Hogan   1- 1-1826
Goodwin, John - Hannah Bails   6-14-1818
Goodwin, Josiah - Matilda Vandeventer
lic.   6-23-1831

Goodwin, Obadiah - Sarah Holly   12-23-1819
Gordon, James - Martha Marshall   12-13-1831
Gordon, Samuel - Margaret Curry   6-12-1832
Goss, Frederic - Cinthia Ann Cambell
                                      5- 1-1828
Goss, Joseph - Malinda Wilson: 3-10-1831
Goss, Peter - Mary Bell   5- 9-1825
Graham, James C. - Mary Wampler   11-17-1831
Gray, William - Nancy Ward lic.   4- -1824
Grayham, Enoch - Ann Wampler   3-24-1825
Green, Solomon - Resina Rhour(?)
                          lic.   6-24-1832
Greenwood, Joseph - Polly Wright   4- 2-1829
Grey, John - Mary Bennet   7- 5-1830
Griffin, Spencer - Cinthia Burch   3-13-1828
Griffith, John - Elizabeth Armstrong
                                      4-30-1826
Griffith, John L. - Esther Wampler   3- 7-1833
Griffith, Pryer - Elizabeth Hix   1-15-1832
Grose, Henry - Sarah Stines lic.   2-26-1831
Gross, David - Elizabeth Stines   8- 7-1828
Groves, Thomas P. - Anne Teague   6-12-1834
Gwinn, John - Lucinda Anderson   10-17-1835
Hall, Daniel - Hannah Treat   2-23-1818
Hall, John - Elizabeth McBride   8-19-1835
Hall, Warren - Cinthia H. Parks   9-22-1831
Hamilton, Robert - Hannah Berry   12-12-1826
Hampton, James - Eliza Followell   9- 4-1823
Handy, Thomas - Susanna Kirkendall   7-16-1835
Hardesty, Richard - Mary Armstrong   8-23-1821
Harrah, Osborn D. - Rebecca Reaves   2-28-1833
Harris, Persius E. - Manerva Stockwell
                                      1-25-1827
Hartsock, Samuel - Elizabeth Carter   3-16-1826
Harvey, William - Cassandra Jane Welsh
                          lic.   12- 7-1835
Hatfield, Armstead - Polly Richardson
                                      10-28-1828
Hatfield, Mordecai - Milly Richardson
                                      11-26-1835
Havens, Stephen - Esther Ooly   5- 2-1822
Hays, David - Sally Combs lic.   11- 3-1831
Hays, David - Rebecca King   8- 9-1832
Helms, John - Rachel Burns lic.   6-12-1821
Helton, Arnold - Sally Johnston   12-28-1825
Helton, Arnold - Elizabeth Robison
                          lic.   3-26-1833
Helton, William - Nancy Webb   10-15-1835
Hendricks, Samuel - Hannah Abrams   5-13-1832
Hendrickson, Joshua - Sarah Helton   1-21-1833
Hendrickson, Thomas - Catharine Wall
                          lic.   9-12-1833
Henry, George - Amanda Anderson
                          lic.   3- 4-1828
Henry, Philip - Catharine Yoder   1-22-1835
Henry, Thomas - Nancy Eddy   10-21-1834
Hensly, Joseph - Lucy Huff   5- 3-1827
Hensly, Nathan - Mary Mosier lic.   5- 8-1834
Marriage of Mary Mosier & Levi Butcher
   recorded   5- 6-1834
Henson, John - Rebecca Sheffield   2- -1820
Hewston, Alfred - Margaret Smith   10- 4-1827
Hewston, Richard - Rebecca Smith   9-20-1827
Hickman, Francis - Ann S. S. Blair   11-24-1823
Hill, Boswell - Charity Wright   9- 3-1820
Hill, Hugh - Sarah Wright   8-14-1831
Hill, Isaac - Elizabeth Call   12-15-1825

Hill, Mannon - Minerva Tatum lic.4- 6-1835
Hilton, John - Nancy Robison   3-28-1827
Hinkle, George - Barbara Yoder   4-22-1830
Hinkle, Jonathan - Catharine Lence
                                      11-30-1824
Hinkle, Jonathan - Catharine Lentz
                                      11-30-1830
Hinote, Ashael - Malinda Cooter   6- 6-1833
Hinson, William - Rebecca Sheffield
                                      2- -1821
Hite, Benjamin - Sarah Caivins   2- 2-1830
Hite, Felix G.(?) - Mary Wampler   8-17-1831
Hite, William - Diana Woodall
                          lic.   12-24-1834
Hix, Moses - Elizabeth Green   9-22-1818
Hodge, Philip - Mary Goss   5- 9-1819
Hogan, William - Rachel Boltinghouse
                                      12-19-1826
Holmes, Nelson - Julian Isiminger
                                      12-23-1832
Hopwood, Moses - Sally Ann James   7- 2-1835
House, James - Matilda Followell   3-29-1830
House, Michael - Polly Wiley   10-23-1832
Houston, Joseph - Lucinda Putman   3- 7-1827
Houston, Pernell - Mary Macumber   12-27-1832
Howard, Tilman A. - Martha A. Maxwell
                          lic.   4-29-1833
Howe, Samuel - Elizabeth Allison
                          lic.   3- -1822
Howell, James E. - Hetty Carrol   12-23-1830
Howell, Jonathan - Nancy Gillam   12-12-1830
Howell, Thomas - Anna Wilson   10- 7-1830
Hudson, Charles - Nancy Bagwell   11- 5-1827
Hudson, Lancaster - Elizabeth Fuller
                                      9-17-1823
Huff, James - Ally Brummett   8-24-1825
Huff, John - Polly Mathes   2-20-1834
Humphreys, David - Rebecca Fullen   2-18-1830
Hunter, Alexander - Angelina Goodwin
                          lic.   9-12-1831
Hunter, William B. - Sarah Cherry
                          lic.   6-10-1835
Huntington, Jonathan - Elizabeth Williams
                          lic.   1-19-1832
Irvin (or Ervin), John - Sarah Matlock
                                      7-11-1828
Iseminger, Jacob - Elizabeth Graybeal
                                      3- 6-1834
Isenhower, George - Sarah Calfey   7-21-1832
Isenhower, George A. - Elizabeth Calfie
                                      3-11-1834
Jackson, Edward - Agnes Rains   2-17-1832
Jackson, William - Britty Wilson   1-21-1820
James, Cairy - Sally James   5-24-1831
James, James - Hannah Arthur   6- 3-1819
James, James - Amelia Puett   6-14-1832
James, Jesse - Rebecca Givins   5- 4-1820
James, Jesse - Rebecca Gibson   1-10-1821
James, Joseph - Catharine Reeder
                          lic.   2-22-1831
James, Joseph - Catharine Reeder   6-27-1831
James, William - Sarah Frazer   6-12-1819
Jenkins, John M. - Aranna M. Freeland
                                      4-11-1819
Johnson, John - Rachel Kimberlin
                          lic.   4-14-1835
Johnston, Andrew - Lucinda Empson
                          lic.   3-10-1830

317

Johnston, Andrew - Eleanor Lamb
        lic.   9- 9-1834
Johnston, George - Mary M. Curry
        lic.   11-27-1835
Johnston, George H. - Susanna Boswell
              4-16-1822
Johnston, James - Lucinda Stepp   3-16-1829
Johnston, John - Elizabeth Young 9-24-1829
Johnston, John - Mary Swift   11-14-1831
Johnston, William - Sophronia Alexander
              1-29-1829
Jones, Wynn - Margaret Storm   5-25-1821
Joslin, Amasa - Mary Ann Allison
        lic.   9- -1824
Julian, John C. - Ann Philips   6- 8-1830
Keck, Phillip - Orpha Kootch   3-13-1834
Keith, Henry - Elizabeth McAlester 8- 2-1832
Keith, Michael - Mary Becket   1- 1-1834
Kelly, Isaac - Peggy Berry lic.   7-13-1833
Kenton, Benjamin H. - Martha McAlester
        lic.   3-14-1832
Kern, Coonrod - Polly Berry   7-20-1820
Kethcam, Daniel - Mary Worly   10- 8-1829
Killough, David - Sally Humphreys 12- 4-1823
Kindle, George - Lucinda Buskirk 2-25-1830
Kindle, William - Mary Marrs lic. 10-10-1832
Kindrick, Daniel B. - Jane Sullivan
        lic.   4-10-1835
Kindrick, William - Nancy Wilson 4-12-1829
King, Berry - Catharine Smith lic. 3-23-1830
King, Elisha - Sarah Batterton 8-13-1824
King, James H. - Margaret Iliff 7-25-1825
King, John B. - Sinny Hazlet lic. 12- 8-1832
Kinworthy, William - Perninah Rogers
              5- 5-1831
Kirby, Archibald H. - Mary Ann Sedwick
        lic.   6-30-1825
Kirkham, John - Lucretia South 12- 2-1832
Kizer, Samuel - Fanny Smith   12- 2-1824
Knighten, John - Elizabeth Moss 12- 1-1825
Koons (or Kirns?), William - Mary Shipman
              2-20-1834
Kootch, Ewing - Rachel Wright   [1831]
Kutchen, Bailey M. - Anna Bicler 6-25-1821
Lain, Solomon - Nancy Clendennin 8-10-1827
Lake, Joseph - Susan Lake   10-23-1831
Lake, Robert - Christian Lucas 10-12-1824
Lakes, John - Christian Lakes   9-12-1832
Laky, Jacob - Phoebe Bails lic. 2- 1-1821
Lane, Willis - Sarah Pennington 5- 3-1832
Larue, David - Nancy Cole   12-27-1832
Laurence, Randolph - Sally Bowles
        lic.   8-22-1834
Lebo, Jacob - Eliza Baily lic.   5-29-1824
Leabo, Josiah - Sally Buskirk lic. 5- -1824
Lee, Thomas - Patsy Cutter lic. 7-27-1821
Lemon, John A. M. - C. H. Taylor
        lic.   1-26-1832
Lemon, Joseph J. - Manerva Canning 11-20-1832
Lemon, Robert - Rebecca Smith   10-11-1832
Lentz, John - Betsy Kindricks   3-16-1830
Leonard, Elisha W. - Rachel Martin 3-26-1831
Leonard, Jacob - Elizabeth Armstrong
              3-22-1822
Letz (or Litz?), Leonard - Elizabeth Miller
        lic.   8-28-1834
Lewis, Joseph - Rosa Scott   9-24-1825

Litten, Lanford - Elizabeth A. Pachs
              5-27-1834
Litteral, Albert G. - Elizabeth Warner
              7-17-1830
Litton, Jacob - Delila Summett   2-18-1830
Lockwood, Oliver - Rebecca Buckner
              4- 3-1823
Londerman, Daniel - Jemima Stone 11-29-1832
Long, Christian - Charlotte Brummet
              9-12-1824
Loving, Lot E. - Arty Miney Lee 4-23-1831
Loving, Reuben - Hannah Devore   3- 4-1824
Loving, William - Elizabeth Lee 3- 3-1831
Lowe, Jacob B. - E. S. M. Blair 5- 3-1827
Lundia, Daniel - Rebecca Snodgrass
        lic.   10-18-1826
Lundy, Stockton - Nancy McHolland 4- 1-1827
Lytle, Francis - Martha Butler 10-30-1834
McBride, David - Mary Teague
        lic.   10- 3-1833
McBride, William - Elizabeth Sexon
              2-10-1833
McCarter, Moses - Sarah Ketcham 10-30-1834
McCullough, Johnston - Rebecca Campbell
             10-25-1832
McDurmed, Charles - Elizabeth Smith
        lic.   1-12-1823
McFarland, John - Sarah Todd   8- 6-1831
McGalen, Andrew - Lydia Gross   7-27-1832
McGee, Jackson J. - Phebe Carmichael
              5-10-1832
McHenry, William - Catharine Ashbaugh
              8- 2-1827
McPhetridge, Mathew - Amanda M. Seall
             11-13-1834
Maguire, Alfred - Anne Jackson 10-30-1832
Mahala, John - Sally Frazier   2- 5-1831
Mahaly, William - Lucinda Rise 12-10-1830
Maples, Dennis - Polly Woods   3- 5-1835
Marshall, Andrew - July Ann Williams
              3-13-1831
Marshall, James - Mary Griffith 3- 8-1828
Marshall, John - Anna Bell   3-13-1831
Marshall, Samuel - Lucinda Guthery
             10-15-1832
Martin, William - Mary Herd   3- 6-1828
Martindale, Ralph - Delila Devers(?)
        lic.   1-14-1834
Martindale, William - Diannah Wright
              8- 7-1833
Mathers, Robert - Celia Rains   6- 2-1829
Matlock, John - Sarah Hinkle   1-24-1830
Maxwell, Alfred - Mary Serjant   9-10-1831
Maxwell, Irwin B. - Deborah S. Owens
             10- 3-1832
May, Abraham - Elizabeth Moss   12-11-1828
May, Abraham - Nancy Burch   10- 6-1831
May, David - Sally May   3- 2-1826
May, Isaac - Elizabeth Sears lic. 1- 4-1825
May, Philip - Sophia Bilbo   3-11-1829
  Marriage license dated   3-11-1830
May, William - Elizabeth Shipman 4-15-1835
May, William - Clarissa Bennett 11- 8-1835
Mayfield, Leroy - Martha Basket 1-21-1830
Mays, Madison - Sally Stine   7-27-1835
Meadows, William - Sarah Ann Hunnel
             12-11-1834

Meriwether, George - Elizabeth Dodds
                              11- 8-1827
Milam, George - Mary Chipman   5-18-1826
Miller, Henry A. - Nancy Sears lic. 8- 5-1830
Minks, James - Martha Arthur   1- 6-1833
Mitchell, Pleasant S. D. - Mary Ann Ketcham
                              11- 7-1833
Mitchell, Thomas - Mary Waggaman 12-10-1835
Moore, Isaac - Marilla Mann   2-18-1830
Moore, John - Salina Smith   6-16-1831
Moore, Samuel - Mary Sears   12- -1821
More, Charles - Elizabeth Cupenbeaver
                         lic.   6-13-1835
More, Jonathan - Katharine Dyer   4-17-1834
Morgan, Absalom - Elizabeth May   5- 3-1825
Morgan, Prementer - Elizabeth Oliphant
                                  2- 5-1829
Morgan, Prementer - Dosha Burch   12-14-1833
Morgan, Solomon - Lydia Goodwin
                         lic.   10- -1825
Morris, John - Polly Givin lic. 12-24-1834
Moser, Jacob - Patsy Ashbaugh   12- 2-1830
Moser, Lewis - Nancy Hensly   9-15-1831
Mounts, David - Katharine Carroll 3-24-1833
Myers, Jacob - Patsy Huff   6-14-1828
Nail, Gilbreth - Minerva Coffey   9- 5-1833
* Nance(?), John - Susannah Isenhower
                         lic.   3-27-1835
Neal, John W. - Nancy Bails   6-19-1834
Neill, William Y. - Jane Snodgrass 7-24-1831
Nesbit, Thomas - Sarah Beck   11-11-1827
Newton, James - Louisa Young   5- 7-1829
Newton, Thomas - Margaret Moore   12-13-1827
Nicholson, Jesse - Esther C. Ketcham
                                  9- 5-1833
Nicholson, William - Matilda Pennington
                              10-24-1824
Noel, Matthew - Mary Pruett   3- 9-1821
Nuckels, David - Esther Chance   8-18-1819
Nuckels, James - Anna Boltinghouse
                         lic.   1-19-1825
Nuckels, James - Margaret Boltinghouse
                         lic.   11- 4-1831
Nuckels, John - Rachel Hartman   7- 8-1832
Oliphant, Thomas - Meeky Parker   6- 1-1834
Ooley, Thornton - Elizabeth Wharton 5-13-1830
Orchard, Samuel M. - Martha C. McPheeters
                                  5-27-1830
Osborn, Asa - Perilla Lockwood   4-14-1825
Owens, Clinton C. - Orpha Kirby   3- 8-1832
Owens, Ephraim - Mary H. Kern   1- 1-1824
Owens, John - Nancy Thornburg lic. 12-21-1820
Parish, Eli - Eliza Reaves   4-17-1834
Parker, Greenberry - Elizabeth Willoughby
                              12-11-1834
Parks, Albert - Elizabeth Dougherty 9-25-1832
Parks, Alfred - Martha Noel   4-11-1824
Parks, Ambrose - Martha Parks   1- 1-1829
Parks, Andrew - Jane Hensly   10-18-1832
Parks, Curtus - Amelia Sharp   5-20-1830
Parks, James - Frances Kindrick   8-27-1830
Parks, John - Milly Ann Guthrie   4- 4-1832
Parks, Meredith - Malinda Sharp   12-21-1820
Parks, Permenter - Lucinda Hite   12-23-1830
Patterson, James G. - Lydia Nicholson
                                  4- 7-1831
Patton, Henry - Rachel Adams   12-20-1835

Payne, John - Dionely Huff   6-28-1831
Peak, Josiah - Martha Lyon lic.   4- -1824
Pennington, Joseph - Mary G. Bennet
                         lic.   11- 1-1834
Perring, John O. - Matilda Dodds 2-19-1835
Peter, John - Milly Tatum   1-12-1832
Philips, John - Nancy King   2-10-1819
Philips, Joseph - Elizabeth King 2- 2-1821
Philips, Stephen - Susannah Hinkle
                         lic.   1-28-1831
Philips, William - Ann Davidson   1-14-1830
Phillips, Hiram - Nancy Smock   4- 4-1833
Piper, Jacob - Celia Rains lic.   2-26-1833
Pirtle, Henry - Alice Price   3- 3-1833
Poe, Fielding W. - Letty Nicholson
                              12-30-1830
Pollard, Absalom - Sally Loyd   5-31-1829
Pollard, Elijah - Catharine Fleener
                                  9- 4-1828
Pollard, William - Nancy Collins
                         lic.   3- -1824
Porter, John - Elizabeth Symms   3- 3-1825
Porter, William - Julian Symms   12- 1-1828
Posey, Benjamin - Orpha Springgate
                         lic.   5-31-1834
Posey, Hubbard - Elizabeth Reeder 5-14-1832

Prince, John - Anne Faris   12-16-1834
Proe, Phillip - Mahala Boltenhouse
                         lic.   3-25-1834
Puett, Armstead W. - Sally Millikan
                              12-15-1823
Puett, Austrian - Lucinda Puett   3-19-1823
Puett, Elisha - Pulina Noel   3-30-1824
Puett, Elisha - Harriet Lee   8-27-1829
Puett, William - Hannah Parks   10-14-1819
Purcifield, Thomas - Jemimah Breedlove
                         lic.   12-24-1834
Purcifield, William - Mahala Followell
                                  7- 7-1835
Purdin, Ira E. - Deborah Patterson
                              10-10-1826
Purdin, Ira P. - Deborah Patterson
                                  7-23-1826
Putman, William - Sarah Head   4- 5-1831
Rader, George - Emily Pollard   9-29-1830
Rains, Lewis - Mary Hensly   12-15-1831
Rains, Robert - Betty Pennington 8- 1-1823
Rains, Rolly - Eleanor Brummet
                         lic.   1-16-1833
Rains, Thomas - Sarah Polly   3-11-1827
Rainy, Squire - Sarah Murphy   11-23-1830
Rawlins, James - Cynthia Stout   7- -1822
Rawlins, William - Polly Sharp
                         lic.   7-20-1820
Razor, Michael - Susannah Jackson 3- 8-1832
Retherford, James - Sally Baty   12-18-1833
Rhea, Allen - Jane McGuire lic.   10-17-1824
Richardson, Alexander - Mahala Cox
                                  4- 1-1828
Richardson, John - Sally Cox   7-22-1828
Richardson, John - Elizabeth Duzan
                              12-29-1833
Richardson, Johnathan - Mary Young
                                  9- 7-1829
Riddle, William - Polly Parks   3-25-1830
Ridenour, James S. - July Ann Syms
                                  1- 6-1832

319

Rippee, Arthur - Belinda Young lic.11-21-1834	Six, Jacob - Mary Miller lic.	8-17-1830
Ritter, Lewis - Jemima Morgan 6- 3-1827	Skidmore, James - Julian Sims	11- 7-1833
Roberson, James D. - Mary Hardesty 10-26-1827	Slocomb, James - Mary Bagwell	5-18-1823
Roberts, Stephen - Mary Buckhannon	Slocomb, James - Matilda Flatford	

Rippee, Arthur - Belinda Young lic.11-21-1834
Ritter, Lewis - Jemima Morgan   6- 3-1827
Roberson, James D. - Mary Hardesty 10-26-1827
Roberts, Stephen - Mary Buckhannon
                    lic.   12- 1-1832
Robertson, Pleasant - Polly McCoy 6-26-1834
Robertson, Wesly - Nancy Lee   8-22-1832
Robertson, William - Margaret Robertson
                             9-20-1831
Robinson, Henry - Sarah Farmer   11-20-1827
Rogers, Aquilla - Phebe Powers   2-14-1830
Rogers, James - Mary Seall   8-30-1832
Rolla, John - Elizabeth Dukes   5- 3-1821
Roper, Wesly - Elizabeth Hendricks 5-31-1829
Roseberry, Alexander - Patsy A. Patterson
                             7-11-1828
Roseberry, Joseph - Nancy Chambers 2-20-1834
Roseberry, William - Eveline Hight
                    lic.   11-27-1834
Runnel, Jesse - Polly Putman   8-18-1830
Rup (or Russ?), Noble - Mahala Young
                             8-22-1834
Russel, James - Mary Helms   4- 5-1826
Russel, John - Malinda Helms   6-18-1826
Ryan, David - Polly Peyton   7- 5-1833
Sanders, Elisha - Patsy Simes   1-31-1833
Sanders, Isom W. - Elizabeth Elmore
                             10- 5-1835
Sanders, Joseph - Sarah Fritz   7-17-1831
Sanders, Thomas - Catharine May
                    lic.   11-23-1830
Sare, James - Virlinda Tatam   6-25-1835
  Married at home of Jonathan Tatum
Sares, John - Elizabeth Carmichael 8- 4-1831
Saunders, Joseph - Charlotte Ray   5- 3-1832
Savank(?), John - Lucy Ann Puett   1-24-1826
Scarlet, Robert - Nancy Newton lic.11-24-1824
Scoby, James - Rhoda Polly   10- 3-1826
Scott, Daniel - Susannah Faris   12-30-1824
Scott, James Uriah - Adaline Vails 3- 6-1834
Scott, John - Rebecca Johnston   7-21-1829
Scott, John - Nancy Ooley lic.   1- 6-1830
Scott, Thomas J. - Betsy Ann Vails 4- 5-1834
Seall, Stephen P. - Lydia Lowe   2- 6-1834
Secrets, George of Putnam Co. -
        Susan C. Shields   9- 1-1833
Sedurick, John J. - Matilda E. Archer
                             11-19-1833
See (or Lee?), William - Leah O'Neal
                       -     4-10-1834
Sexton, Joel - Abigail Davis   9- -1822
Shank, Jacob - Lucy Goddy   12-30-1828
Sharp, Hubbard - Mary Reeves   8-19-1824
Sharp, James S. - Celia Coffey   6-19-1827
Shelburn, Augustus - Lucy DeVore
                    lic.   8- 5-1833
Shipman, Nicholas - Winny Kirk   1- 1-1835
Shipman, Reason - Elizabeth Hight
                    lic.   7-15-1833
Shipman, Thomas P. - Susannah May   3-27-1834
Shirly, Richard - Surulda Buskirk   2- 7-1827
Shugart, Levi - Elizabeth Pickle   [1831]
        No lic. or return
Simpson, Luke - Ann Whisennand   4-27-1831
Simpson, Philip - Margaret Tincher 1-28-1821
Sipes, Claborn - Martha Buckhannon
                    lic.   6- 8-1833

Six, Jacob - Mary Miller lic.   8-17-1830
Skidmore, James - Julian Sims   11- 7-1833
Slocomb, James - Mary Bagwell   5-18-1823
Slocomb, James - Matilda Flatford
                             6- 8-1834
Sluss, William - Lucy Armstrong   8-16-1832
Smith, Dudley C. - Mariah Humphreys
                             7- -1821
Smith, Dudley C. - Isabella Parch
                             11-27-1834
Smith, George - Sally Eidson   4-13-1830
Smith, George W. - Louisa Mulkey 10- 7-1834
Smith, James M. C. - Jane G. Marchel
                             8-23-1827
Smith, John - Elizabeth Evans   1-27-1823
Smith, John C. - Olly Moore   8-16-1827
Smith, John L. - Mercy Elkins   7-31-1828
Smith, Richard G. - Martha C. Chambers
                             3- 4-1824
Smith, Samuel - Patsy Hensly   8-31-1826
Smith, Silas - Sophronia Davidson 2-17-1831
Smith, Wesly - Martha Sadler   6- 8-1830
Smith, William - Polly Sare   2- 2-1821
Smith, William - Lucy Fletcher   10-21-1828
Smith, William M. - Mary M. Johnson
                    lic.   11-28-1833
Smith, Zebulon C. - Patsy Finly   6-21-1831
Snowden, David - Malinda Moore   9-22-1820
Sowder, Caleb - Martha Blair   4-25-1822
Sowder, Joseph - Ruth Sare   2-26-1823
Sowder, Michael - Viny Eads lic.   5- 5-1832
Stansbury, Elisha - Louisa J. Coffey
                             1- 8-1832
Starts, Joseph - Perlina Baty   8-28-1825
Steel, James A. - Sally Philips   7-18-1827
Stein, Arthur - Elizabeth Basket 4-27-1831
Stevens, Adam - Catharine Hensly
                    lic.   9-16-1834
Stevens, John - Rachel Hensly   8-14-1828
Stevens, Jordan - Margaret McHenry
                             8-10-1828
Stewart, Dickson - Lucinda Roberts
                    lic.   1-24-1830
Stewart, William - Elizabeth Shook
                             6-24-1831
Stine, David - Rosinah White lic. 3-18-1832
Stine, Enoch - Barbara Shook lic. 2-16-1835
Stine, Frederick - Rachel Taylor
                    lic.   2- 6-1835
Stine, George - Rachel Teague   10-26-1827
Stine, Henry - Eleanor Turner   12-21-1832
Stine, Henry - Nancy Cooter lic. 5-31-1834
Stine, Noah - Lucinda Leabo lic.11-28-1834
Stine, Solomon - Barbara Gross   10-15-1829
Stites (or Stiles?), Johnston - Mary Grimes
                             9- 8-1825
Stockton, William - Maria Elkins 1-30-1834
Stoner, Daniel - Mary Earls   7-24-1834
Storm, Peter - Jane Burch   1-23-1823
Sullivan, James - Melinda Robison
                    lic.   8-13-1833
Summers, Jesse - Mary Hanson   4-21-1819
Summet, Daniel - Mary Taylor   11-19-1835
Summet, Jacob - Esther Kirby   3- 8-1832
Sutfin, James - Sarah Henderson   11- 9-1834
Sutherland, Alexander - Martha Koonts
                    lic.   10-20-1832

Swinford, William - Martha Johnston
                lic.   3-31-1830
Symms, Daniel - Rebecca Mason   2-25-1825
Tarkington, Eli P. - Martha Gay   10- 8-1835
Tarkington, Elsbury - Lucinda Legg 10-15-1831
Tate, Andrew L. - Nancy M. Daugherty
                        2-16-1832
Tatum, Nathaniel - Anne Ross   11-13-1834
Taylor, Joseph - Martha Kirkendall
                lic.   7-24-1833
Teague, Bryant - Susannah Bails
                lic.   6-24-1822
Teague, John - Malinda Smith   8-21-1833
Teague, William - Elizabeth Bales 6- 2-1819
Teel, James A. - Susannah Bly   4-13-1828
Thomas, Daniel - Sally Weddle   10-18-1830
Thornburg, William - Martha Armstrong
                        9- 4-1823
Throop, John W. - Lucinda Hunter
                lic.   2-16-1835
Tilford, Preston - Sarah Nesbit lic.
                      12-18-1826
Tincher, George - Sally Grimes   10-19-1823
Tincher, John - Mary Fullen   6-24-1824
Todd, John - Elizabeth Hays   8-25-1831
Todd, William B. - Elizabeth Newton
                lic.   2-25-1833
Townsend, Silas - Susan Murphy   10- 5-1825
Trosper, William - Elizabeth Cox 8-24-1828
Trotter, John - Esther Wilson   12-26-1827
   Esther Williams in return
Trotter, William - Nancy Fuller   5- 7-1823
Turpin, Zechariah - Ruth Buskirk 2-10-1831
Vest, Samuel - Rebecca Whisennand 3-24-1833
Vint, Henry William - Sally Stine 12-25-1833
Waggamon, Abraham - Mary Walden 5-25-1834
Wakefield, John - Helen Parsons
                lic.   9-24-1831
Walker, Daniel J. - Caroline M. Smith
                    12-18-1828
Walker, John W. - Mariah Woodall
                lic.   5-22-1830
Walker, Thomas - Cynthia Stewart Evans
                lic.   12-19-1835
Wall, Coonrod - Elizabeth Bays lic.12-15-1834
Wall, Scoffield - Elizabeth Johnston
                      3-31-1829
Wallace, David - Jenriett Summerville
                    12-29-1824
Walls, Moses - Polly Parks   10-12-1826
Wampler, Adam - Sarah Lee (or See?) 1-17-1833
Wampler, Andrew - Polly Parks   4-10-1829
Wampler, David - Jane Godsey   1-22-1834
Wampler, Henry - Polly Armstrong 9-29-1831
Wampler, Hezekiah - Sarah Godsey 4- 1-1832
Wampler, Jefferson - Nancy Ray   4-12-1827
Wampler, Joseph - Elizabeth Parks
                lic.   6- -1824
Wampler, Martin - Elizabeth Wampler 9-14-1825
Wampler, Peter - Rebecca Kirkham 7-23-1829
Wampler, Valentine - Angelina Rawlins
                lic.   4-22-1822
Ward, Addison - Margaret Reaves   3-13-1834
Ward, Austin - Elizabeth Buskirk
                lic.   5-13-1833
Ward, James - Catharine Nicholson 1-19-1826

Ward, Reuben - Lovina Otwell   12-11-1831
Warson, Daniel - Matilda P. Allen
                lic.   4- 2-1829
Waymon, E. G. - Nancy Sheters   5- 9-1829
                   [19]
Weatherman, John - Susan Livingston
                    10-13-1826
Weatherman, John - Mary Hudlen   1- 1-1835
Weathers, Daniel - Matty Matlock
                lic.   10- 7-1833
Weddle, Alfred - Mary Miles   1-24-1829
Weddle, James - Mary Davidson   1- 7-1830
Weddle, Stephen - Rachel Puett
                lic.   10-19-1830
Weddle, Thompson - Sally Miles
                lic.   6- 7-1828
Whaily, Joseph - Sophia Hall   4-23-1822
Whaley, John - Polly Tarkington
                lic.   5-26-1835
Whaley, John D.? - Polly R. Tarkington
                    5-28-1835
Wharton, Laurence - Sina Hinkle
                lic.   7- 4-1833
Wharton, Stanfield - Anne Berry   1- 9-1834
Whisennand, John - Lucinda Wright 1-19-1833
Whisennand, John K. - Mary Kirby 12- 6-1830
Whisennand, Nicholas - Nancy Wilson
                    3-19-1824
White, John - Matilda Johnston
                lic.   10- -1824
Whitesell, David - Martha Ann Devon
          (Devore?) lic. 4-19-1834
Whitson, Wesley - Jane Mitchell
                lic.   1- 1-1822
Whitson, Wesley - Sarah Back   2-25-1834
Widener, Emanuel - Thurza Condra
                lic.   3-27-1830
Wilcox, John - Martha Eslinger   3-30-1825
Wilkerson, Solomon - Polly Anderson
   Wilkeson in return   12-15-1833
Wilkinson, Henry - Happy Wilson
                lic.   2-23-1833
Williams, Alfred - Roda Hufstudler
                    1-24-1828
Williams, Henry - Susannah Stine 11-14-1833
Williams, Joseph - _____ Wright
                lic.   1-19-1824
Williams, McClure - Susannah Wright
                lic.   1-19-1825
Williams, Zachariah - Sarah Payne 1- 7-1820
Williamson, Isaac - Catharine Fry 1-27-1827
Willoughby, Benjamin J. - Catharine R.
             James   10-15-1829
Willoughby, Elijah - Sarah Young 5-31-1834
Wilson, Bird - Mary O. Weatherman 7-21-1830
Wilson, Christopher - Nancy Gilbert
                    3-15-1834
Wilson, Emsly - Perlina Murphy   1- 4-1827
Wilson, Jeremiah - Nancy Reese   5-24-1823
Wilson, John - Susanna White lic. 9-27-1821
Wilson, John - Rebecca Coffey   9-24-1828
Wilson, Lewis F. - Malinda Myers 8-17-1832
                lic.   1-17-1832
Wilson, Thomas - Judith Farmer 11-13-1828
Winkler, Peter - Rosina Cutright 12-26-1834
Winslow, Calvin - Mary Moudry(?) 7-11-1831

Winters, Larkin S. - Mary Evanson 2-12-1827
Wisely, Frederick - Elizabeth Woodard
                lic.   8-17-1831
Wisley, Peter - Patsy Woodard lic. 5-14-1830
Wood, Emsley - Elizabeth Wailey(?)
                lic.   5- -1824
Wood, John - Margaret Blair (or Blain?)
                lic.   7- 3-1821
Wood, William - Eleanor Davidson 3- 3-1831
Woodall, James - Nancy Adamson 6-17-1828
Woodall, Joel - Sarah Hight lic. 2- 4-1835
Woodall, Perry - Catharine Armstrong
                lic.   7-30-1835
Woodard, James - Malinda Goodwin
                lic.   8- 6-1832
Woodfork, Hillariah - Dicy Roads 11-15-1825
Woodin, Solomon - Eleanor Hill 6-30-1820
Woods, Andrew - Nancy Miles 9- 2-1832
Woodward, Silas - Sally Leonard 2-28-1833
Worly, Eli - Zarilda Pauly 8-20-1835
Worley, Hiram - Margaret Legg 9-16-1832
Worly, Zimri - Sarah Legg 4-30-1826
Wright, Aren - Catharine Cooter 2- 3-1829
Wright, David - Caroline M. Kootch 2- 3-1827
Wright, Elijah - Elizabeth Conder 4-17-1826

Wright, Emsley - Katharine Inyart
                lic.   1-21-1833
Wright, James - Polly Miller 10-22-1835
Wright, P. - Nancy Williams 4-26-1825
Wright, Peter - Elizabeth Fosset
                lic.   12-22-1832
Wright, Rolly - Elizabeth Cokner 7-19-1829
Wright, Wesly - Nancy Wright lic. 9-29-1824
Wright, William S. - Margaret S. Hite
                    3- 3-1825
Writter, George - Rebecca Stout
                lic.   6- 9-1830
Wyatt, Christopher - Margaret Ritter
                lic.   10-13-1830
                    [3]
Wyman, William - Lucinda Whitson 4-20-1820
Yoder, Henry - Ruth Ann Rader 5-23-1830
Yoder, Manuel - Rachel Shirly 9-23-1832
Young, Abraham - Susannah Whisenand
                    7-12-1827
Young, Harvy - Eleanor Weddle 2-17-1831
Young, Jacob - Martha Storm 12- 4-1818
Young, Jacob - Margaret Brown 1-30-1828
Young, Joseph - Barbara Whisenmand
                    2-16-1825
Young, Samuel - Lovina King 8-17-1831
Zink, Daniel - Jane Shields 5-27-1819
*Alexander, John - Margaret Clark 3-26-1833

Correction. Mrs. William E. Schofield of Anderson, Indiana, kindly supplied us with the correct name in one of the Monroe County Marriages published in the March, 1978, issue of Hoosier Genealogist. Instead of NANCE, JOHN the name should be NEACE, JOHN - Susannah Isenhower, lic. 3-27-1835. The German spelling is NEHS; anglicization of the name has produced various spellings-- NEASE, NEAS, NEACE, NEESE, etc.

Mrs. Schofield states that the family came from Germany on the ship Britannia, September 21, 1731, and lived in what is now Montgomery County, Pennsylvania, until 1755; then lived in Shenandoah Valley, Virginia, until 1802-1804 when they moved to Green County, Tennessee. In the early 1830s the Neaces came to Indiana, first to Monroe County and then to Boone. John Neace's brother William had married Mary Isenhower in Tennessee and when the Isenhowers came to Monroe County, Indiana, William and Mary also came. John Neace came later and married Susannah Isenhower.

WAYNE COUNTY MARRIAGES, 1811-1830

Reprinted from <u>Early Marriages of Wayne County, Indiana, 1811-1822</u>,compiled by Mrs. Irene Macy Strieby, and published by the Genealogy Section of the Indiana Historical Society in 1965, and compiled for the period 1822-1830 from the microfilm copy of Book A, Wayne County Marriages, in the Genealogy Division, Indiana State Library. <u>Wayne County Marriages, 1811-1860</u>, have been compiled by Mrs. Beverly Yount of Richmond, Indiana, and is available for purchase from her. Members of the Society of Friends were not required to obtain a marriage license; however, many of them did obtain a license and were married by; civil authorities; marriages of other members of the Society of Friends are listed in the records kept by the Society. The marriage records of Whitewater Monthly Meeting, the first one in Wayne County, and those of other Meetings in the county have been published by the Genealogy Section of the Indiana Historical Society.

Abbott, Nathan - Peggy Coy	7-16-1821
Abernathy, Thomas - Susannah Fall	12-24-1818
Abrams, Lot - Rosanna Miller	6-17-1821
Adams, David - Eleanor Dougan	12-27-1827
Adams, Henry - Agnes Chapman	6- 1-1830
Adams, John - Rebekah Hinkle	4- 9-1820
Adams, John - Mary Meek	1-24-1828
Adamson, Aaron - Sally Millman	2-12-1818
Adamson, Abel - Sarah Stout	2-12-1828
Adamson, Isaac - Nancy Gardner	4-12-1818
Adamson, Simon - Lydia Frazer	8- 7-1828
Adcock, Travis - Susanna Moorman	12- 7-1814
Addington, Bishop - Betsy Cain	4-19-1816
Addington, Charles - Elizabeth Hunt	2-10-1825
Addington, John - Lucretia Roberts	9-12-1822
Addington, Joseph, Jr. - Mary Barker	10-26-1825
Addington, Joshua - Rebecca Morgan	1-28-1814
Addington, Morgan - Jane Mendenhall	9-12-1822
Addington, Silas - Polly Davis	11-17-1828
Addington, William - Dorcas Mendenhall	9-28-1825
Addleman, Jacob - Mahala Starbuck	1-24-1828
Adel, Jacob - Rachel Teas	1- 1-1829
Aker, David - Elizabeth Aker	11-19-1827
Aker, Jacob - Elizabeth Shover	12-19-1816
Albach, Amos - Elizabeth Spicer	10-21-1829
Albertson, Charles - Maryan Deter	11- 7-1824
Albertson, Joshua - Catharine Deter lic.	1-21-1825
Alexander, Benjamin - Mary Hunt	4-29-1813
Alexander, Robert - Margaret Hawkins	1- 4-1815
Alexander, William - Mary Miller	11-24-1828
Allbaugh, Zachariah - Christiana Ulrich	12-25-1826
Allen, Ira - Marietta Weaver	1-17-1830
Allen, John - Francis Thompson	12-26-1816
Allen, Josiah - Sarah Harvey	12-26-1816
Allen, Thomas - Elender Walker	12-28-1820
Allen, William - Sally Prather	10-19-1826
Allison, Jesse - Isophena Reynolds	4-18-1822
Allred, James G. - Rebekah Walter	10-23-1828
Allred, William - Rebekah Spiva	9-11-1828
Alspaw, Jacob B. - Elizabeth Beeson	12- 3-1829
Anderson, John - Catharine Hiatt	12- 7-1823
Anderson, William - Lucinda Harlan	12-27-1827
Andrews, James - Sarah Whitehead	6- 2-1822
Andrews, William - Catharine Cook	6-15-1827
Antrim, Adin - Sarah Gray	9- 6-1827
Antrim, Benjamin - Fanny Gray	10-27-1825
Antrim, James - Polly Beard	8- 2-1827
Archer, Richard - Sina Curry	10-18-1827
Armstrong, Henry - Elizabeth Finch	3- 1-1827
Armstrong, William - Rachel Bright	9-19-1821

Arnold, Elijah - Rhoda Fife	9-30-1824
Ashby, Abraham - Mariah Jones lic.	8-28-1824
Ashby, Milton - Polly White	1-20-1811
Asher, Thomas - Polly Asher	11-28-1827
Atkins, Abijah - Joannah Newton	2-25-1825
Atkins, Jonathan - Phillaney Stafford	11- 2-1829
Austin, Ebenezer - Margaret Alexander	9-11-1828
Austin, William - Lavina Ashby lic.	2-14-1828
Bailey, Hugh - Mary Jordan	3- 8-1829
Bailey, John - Rebecca Ridge	12-29-1814
Bailey, John - Patsy Lamb	2-18-1817
Bails (or Bales), Parnelle - Elizabeth Koons	7-14-1822
Bain, John - Esther Horney	10-20-1824
Baldridge, John - Margret Fox	3-15-1821
Baldridge, Samuel - Betsy Rankin	1-19-1820
Baldridge, Samuel C. - Hannah Reid	5-20-1830
Baldridge, Thomas - Anna Morgan lic.	9- 4-1821
Baldwin, Asa - Polly Hoover	2-11-1830
Baldwin, Enos - Elizabeth Hoover	8- 8-1827
Baldwin, Isaiah - Elizabeth Bond	3-31-1825
Ball, Jonas - Rebecca Connell	3- 7-1820
Ballenger, Charles B. - Eliza Scovell	6- 3-1830
Ballenger, Edward - Margaret Thompson	10-20-1825
Ballinger, William - Polly Godfrey lic.	7- 1-1824
Baltimore, Benjamin - Eliza Parsons	1- 7-1830
Baltimore, Philip - Sarah West	7- 9-1823
Baltimore, William - Mary Scott	10- 2-1823
Banks, Thomas - Jane Moffett	11-13-1828
Banks, William Meek - Eleanor Bolin lic.	3-26-1828
Bannon, James - Lutas Ashby	6-24-1823
Barker, Abel - Margaret Cabe	12-24-1823
Barnard, George - Edith Baley (Bailey?) lic.	3-23-1819
Barnard, George - Nancy Harrington	8-15-1824
Barnet, William - Sally Williams	10-21-1827
Barton, Andrew - Celia Boswell	8- 3-1826
Barton, John - Rebecca Long	1-28-1816
Baxter, Joseph - Sarah Pegg	8-23-1829
Bayles, George B. - Anna Summey	12-16-1824
Beall, Nathaniel - Sarah Talbert lic.	1-11-1826
Beall, William - Susannah Cornelius	8-23-1825
Beals (or Bales, Seth - Susana Lewis lic.	3-13-1822
Beard, Alexander - Trulove Boswell lic.	1- 4-1825
Beard, John - Maria Burris	3- 4-1816
Beard, John - Charity Brady	6-26-1823
Beard, Thomas - Malinda Erwin	7-16-1818
Beauchamp, Mathew - Rebecca Mendinghall (?)	1- 9-1817

Beauchamp, Russ - Hannah Lamb   5-15-1815
Beck, Henry - Elizabeth Burroughs   3-20-1828
Beck, John - Judith Chinault   6-18-1818
Beck, William - Catharine Nethercutt
                                       6- 4-1830
Beck, Wilson - Pearsey Persons   1- 6-1825
Beck, Wright A - Margaret Meek   6-11-1829
Bedwell, James - Rachel Stanley   7- 6-1815
Beeler, Jacob - Esther Conn   3- 1-1812
Beeman, Jesse - Letty Crampton   8- 5-1822
Beesly, Thomas - Betsy White   2-18-1819
Beeson, Isaac - Eliza Rambo   9-19-1815
Beeson, Isaac - Polly Rambo   3-21-1824
Beeson, James - Sarah Little   6-19-1817
Beeson, Jesse - Nancy Williams   9- 6-1829
Beeson, Jesse G. - Anna Reniston   6- 5-1828
Beeson, Jonathan L. - Cynthia Wright
                                       1-14-1830
Beeson, Martin - Sarah Taylor   4- 9-1829
Beeson, William - Delila Harris   3-26-1827
Beeson, William - Lucinda Sincock   6- 9-1830
Bell, Nehemiah - Anna Beeman   1-27-1825
Benbow, Benjamin - Elizabeth Black   10-27-1827
Benbow, Edward - Mary Richardson   5-18-1821
Benefiel, John - Hannah Thomas   11- 7-1816
Benefiel, Robert - Mary Montgomery   9- 6-1814
Benefield, John - Rebecca Summers   8-30-1820
Benefield, John - Esther Benefield   4-28-1822
Benefield, John - Betsy Troxal   6- 1-1824
Benefield, William - Cynthia Kidwell
                                      11- 9-1826
Bennet, Francis - Martha Fleehart   11-22-1817
Bennet, William - Lydia Shelby   8-19-1819
Bentley, Reuben - Sarah Hill   8-14-1822
Berry, Benjamin - Nancy Renbarger   3- 2-1823
Berry, John - Jane McLenahan   6- 6-1830
Berry, Joseph - Sally Shaver   12-21-1815
Berry, William - Nancy Gray   2-14-1822
Bewise, Henry - Catharine Fincher   8-19-1824
Bidwell, Samuel - Eunice Stanley   1-16-1817
Biggs, Joel - Margaret Stout   7-25-1825
  Brigs on return
Biggs, John - Caroline Plummer   7- 7-1814
Bishop, Amos - Sally Richter   3-26-1829
Black, Alexander C.- Nancy Garrett   10- 3-1822
Black, Robert - Juliann Jackson   8-18-1825
Blair, James - Nancy Gay   2-19-1824
Bloomfield, Lot - Elizabeth Talbot   12-24-1823
Bloomfield, Robert - Mary Lewis   3-18-1819
Blount, Andrew - Sally Warren   3- 7-1816
Blount, John - Rachel Willis   3-29-1818
Blount, William - Jane Barnes   8- ?-1818
Bogue, Andrew W. - Jane Gay   4-15-1819
Bogue, Benjamin - Milly Hiatt   10- 2-1828
Bogue, Joseph - Nancy Asher   7-10-1823
Bogue, Newby - Hannah Palmer   7-25-1827
Boles, Ephraim - Rutha Hoggatt   3-21-1811
Bond, Benjamin - Anna Goldsmith   3-18-1828
Bond, Enos - Susanna Hoover   2-21-1830
Bond, Jesse - Mary Vore   lic.   4- 2-1822
Bonine, Isaac - Malinda Williams   2-25-1830
Bonine, Thomas - Patsey Talbot lic.   2- 6-1826
Bonine, William - Mary Druly   3-23-1828
Booker, Samuel P - Esther Guy   12-12-1822
Boon, Ovid - Ruth Baltimore   6-28-1821
Boon, Randall - Catharine Roddy   5-19-1827
Boroughs, Charles - Jane Harris   8-24-1826
Boroughs, John - Patsy Chambers
                            lic.   6- 4-1816
Boroughs, Thornton - Mary Spahr   12- 3-1829

Bowen, John - Nancy Morgan   4- 5-1829
Bowen, Squire - Elizabeth Dwiggins   8-13-1829
Bowen, William - Elizabeth Atkins   4- 7-1825
Bowman, Jacob - Elizabeth Leedes   2- 1-1829
Bowman, James - Betsey Watts   8-30-1821
Boyd, Adam - Elizabeth Hawkins lic.   6- 9-1818
Boyd, Hamilton D. - Rebekah Waltz   9-25-1828
Boyd, James - Hester Ruby   7-13-1824
Boyd, James - Milly Armstrong   10-19-1826
Boyd, John - Susanna Scott   7- 8-1819
Boyd, Robert - Narcissa Stinson   2-22-1821
Boyd, Samuel - Martha Lewis   4-10-1817
Boyd, Samuel - Barthenia Ladd   1-29-1829
Boyd, William - Polly Owens   10-10-1816
Boyd, William - Ruth Young   11- 6-1823
Boyles, John Susannah Dunn   7-20-1826
Bradbury, Abner - Mary Boyd   3- 8-1821
Bradbury, Daniel - May Elliott   8-24-1821
Bradbury, Ezekiel - Mary Tullis   6- 2-1825
Bradbury, John - Lydia Murphy lic.   1-16-1816
Bradbury, Thomas - Caty Hunt   2-23-1812
Braden, William - July Moorman   4- 2-1826
Brady, John - Mary Wright   3-16-1825
Branson, Benjamin - Molly (or Matty) Cotton
                                      12- 2-1821
Branson, Benjamin - Nancy Swope   3-23-1828
Branson, Nathan - Mary Wilkens lic.   12-17-1823
Bratten, William - Catherine Senn   11-25-1821
Brewer, Bryant - Eliza Briggs lic.   4-13-1820
Brewer, Nathan - Rhoda McChristy   3-12-1829
Brewer, Robert - Sarah Fife   1-31-1822
Brewer, Robert - Sarah Jackson   6-10-1828
Brewer, Stephen - Susanna Wright   8-29-1819
Brewer, William - Abigail Waymire   10- 8-1829
Bridget, James - Rebecca Allen   12-24-1815
Briggs, Alexander - Jane Stanley   10-26-1825
Briggs, John - Patsy Greenstreet   5-10-1822
Briggs, Richard - Jane Beard   8-25-1819
Bright, Joseph - Abigail Small   9-28-1822
Brightwell, Basil - Rhoda Wright   5-25-1824
Brittain, James - Sarah Martin   6- 1-1830
Brochus, James - Susanna Pike   7-19-1827
Brockus, William - Margaret Culvyhouse
                                       9- 6-1829
Brook, Elijah - Mary Way   9- 9-1812
Brothers, Henry - Sarah Gale   1-29-1824
Brower, Christopher - Judith Showalter
                                       1-15-1829
Brown, James - Peggy Smith   5-28-1811
Brown, James - Elizabeth Pope   11-20-1821
Brown, James - Susanna Parsons   4-19-1827
Brown, John - Ann Woodward   1-17-1821
Brown, John - Sabina Waymire lic.   1-22-1828
Brown, John - Rhoda Tomlinson   11-26-1829
Brown, Joseph - Ella Thomas lic.   9-14-1818
Brown, Joseph - Nancy Roney   11-21-1820
Brown, Richard - Barbary Caffil   6-22-1822
Brown, Samuel - Susan Stout   10-11-1821
Brown, Thomas - Nancy Dougherty   7-25-1816
Brown, Thomas - Mahala Chambers   12-11-1820
Brown, William - Sarah Martindale   2-23-1822
Broxson, William - Nancy Brady   1-16-1829
Bruce, Henry H. - Mary Wharton   2-17-1825
Brumfield, Thomas - Mary Crawford   11-12-1821
Brumfield, Thomas - Sarah Brumfield   7- 8-1822
Brunson, Sterne - Sarah Shank   4-27-1826
Bryant (or Bryan), Henry - Jane Crawford
     lic. 5-30-1816   4- 3-1817
Bryant, William - Elizabeth Key   6-10-1830
Bulla, Isaac - Mary Wade   12-27-1818

Bulla, William - Mary Edwards lic. 12-22-1827
Bunch, Richard - Ann Pearson lic.   2-10-1820
Bundy, Thomas - Mary Bogue   9- 9-1824
Bunker, Thomas - Rebekah Swain   3- 8-1827
Bunnell, David - Rachel Smith   12-26-1822
Bunnel, James - Sarah Ogan   12- 5-1829
Burckhalter, Cason - Jane Hill   6-22-1821
Burgess, James - Therissa Weaver   3-21-1822
Burk, Jesse - Betsy Watson   3-30-1817
Burk, Lewis - Mariah Moffett   11-27-1823
Burkley, William - Margrette Ham
  (or Henn)   1-31-1822
Burton, Elijah - Lean Williams   2-15-1830
Busbey, Isaac - Sarah Willits   10-14-1819
Butler, Burris H. - Jemimah Wilson   6-13-1826
Butler, Hiram - Peggy Woodkirk   7- 8-1812
Butler, Hiram - Hannah Jordan   1-17-1827
Butler, Jacob - Mary Fox lic.   1- ?-1818 ?
Butler, Levi - Betsey Carr   2-15-1823
Butler, Noble J. - Elizabeth Endsley
                                     12-14-1823
Butler, Samuel - Mary Davenport   2- 5-1818
Butler, Thomas - Sophia Thornburgh   10-21-1827
Buzan, Wills - Maria Kendall   3-10-1816
Byerly, Christian - Fanny Fox   3-28-1827
Cadwalader, Byram - Sally Hagen   7-25-1819
Cain, John - Hannah McCalla   6- 8-1815
Cain, John - Rebecca Veal   1-12-1826
Cain, Jonathan - Elizabeth Ballenger
                                      9-13-1827
Cain, Joseph - Patty Fielder   8-20-1811
Cain, Joseph - Polly Boon   8-16-1818
Cain, William - Delila Ballenger   4-19-1827
Calaway, James - Matilda Cooper   11-26-1820
Caldwell, Davies - Elizabeth Browne
                                     10-11-1820
Caldwell, Manlove - Esther Crane   5- 4-1815
Cammack, William - Adelaide Park   7- 1-1827
Campbell, Joseph - Sarah Walker lic.
                                      4- 7-1821
Campbell, Josiah - Mary Mason   2- 1-1820
Camron, John - Eleanor Hurst   2- 4-1830
Canaday, Hermon - Charity Mills   1-11-1827
Canaday, John - Hannah Perry   7-23-1820
Canaday, Lewis L. - Sarah Ring   12-18-1817
Canaday, Nathan - Nancy Leeson   4-23-1829
Canaday, Robert - Sarah Sumner   9-13-1827
Canaday, William - Rachel Sunderland
                                     12-28-1820
Cannaday (or Canada), David - Patsy Ring
                                     12-23-1815
Carey, John - Ruth Odell   8-27-1824
Carnes, David - Polly Gilliam lic.   11-25-1817
Carr, James - Susanna Hunt   1- 9-1822
Carroll, Hugh - Sarah Hobson lic.   2-19-1822
Carter, Isaac - Sally Foreman   2- 7-1822
Cartwright, John - Eve Shoemaker   11-23-1828
Cartwright, Jonathan - Ruth Hendricks
                                     11-18-1822
Case, John - Sarah Caldwell   6-11-1818
Case, William - Lavina Personett   4-14-1825
Caty, John B. - Sarah Harris   2-18-1827
Caty, Stacey B. - Sarah Ferguson   9-22-1829
Caylor, Obadiah - Magdalena Miller   11- 1-1828
Chadwick, William - Abigail Springer
                                      9- 3-1824
Chalfont, Evan - Anna Bulla   7-15-1819
Chambers, James - Mahala Chryst lic.
                                     12- 5-1814

Chambers, James - Mary Cunningham   8- 2-1824
                            lic.   1-24-1824
Chamness, William - Anna Reynolds   10-27-1825
Chapman, Thomas - Martha Delap   12-21-1826
Chappel, John - Polly Benge   7- 4-1824
Charles, Abraham - Jemima Pool lic.   5- 5-1828
Charles, John - Polly Smith   5- 8-1827
Chavers, Mathew - Rhoda Scott lic.   8-20-1829
Cheesman, Alexander - Nancy Russell   4-28-1830
Cheesman, Ebenezer - Jane Culbertson 2-14-1828
Cheesman, Nehemiah - Rebekah Cornelius
                                     11-20-1828
Chrisler, Allen - Jane Adams   5- 3-1825
  Cristler in lic.
Chryst, John - Catherine Hoover   6-15-1822
Clark, ---- - Elizabeth Moore lic.   10- 7-1829
Clark, Benjamin - Lavina Ralston   12- 4-1823
Clark, Francis - Rachel Marmon   2-18-1829
Clark, George - Theny Lewallen negroes
                            lic.   1- 5-1826
Clark, George - Betsy Mitchel   2-28-1829
Clark, George - Eliza Lee   12- 5-1829
Clark, James - Mary Longfellow   9-13-1827
Clark, Jesse - Everline Russel lic. 12- 9-1826
  On this blotted leaf
  I had need to be brief
  As I take up my pen in a hustle
  On Saturday last
  I made legally fast
  Jesse Clark to Miss Everline Russel
                    John Finley
Clark, John - Anna Staunton   5- 4-1820
Clark, John - Sarah Wright   3-15-1825
Clary, Squire - Anna Turner negroes
                            lic.   6- 4-1825
Clary, Squire - Ann Turner   10- 3-1826
Clawson, Abner - Betsy White   6- 6-1816
Clawson, Amos - Linna Davenport   10-21-1819
Clawson, Josiah - Sally McGraw   6-13-1820
Clawson, Mahlon - Polly Ann Brown   1- 1-1829
Clear, Henry - Mary Ann Welshons   10-30-1828
Clevison, John - Isabel Grewell lic. 1-31-1822
Cloyd, Joshua - Edy Sutherland   6-27-1822
Cobb, Dixon - Massey Shelby   2- 2-1820
Cobb, Thomas - Judith Railsback   10-22-1817
Cockerham, David - Elizabeth McVay   10-25-1825
Cockran, John - Rhoda Summers   6-17-1830
Coffel, Henry - Rebecca Williams lic.
                                      6-18-1827
Coffin, Greenberry - Ann Bond   7- 1-1827
Coffin, Hiram - Betsy Huffman   9-16-1819
Coffin, Nathaniel - Lydia Bunker   10-24-1822
Coggshall, Caleb - Mary Marine   12-30-1827
Coggshall, Job - Barsheba Harris   11-22-1818
Coggshall, Job - Judith Marine   2-22-1829
Coleman, Seth - Betsy Jacob   3- ?-1818
Combs, Michael - Polly Edwards   1- 1-1818
Comer, Amos - Polly Jessop   11-17-1828
Comer, John - Elizabeth Tingle lic.   1- 3-1823
Comer, Joseph - Sarah Dollerhide   4- 5-1820
Commons, Nathan - Martha Beard   10-28-1819
Commons, William - Sarah Brady   11-29-1815
Conner, Brittain - Lydia Lindley   2-20-1818
Conner, James - Mary McCoy   5-22-1817
Conner, John Mahala Brown lic.   1-22-1825
Conner, William - Sally Kelly   8- 4-1811
Conway, Charles - Louisa (or Laura) Roe
                                     12-20-1821
Conwell, George - Nancy Cragge   11-27-1822

Cook, Eli - Hannah Beard   1-27-1825
Cook, James - Sothy Ham   1-13-1820
Cook, James - Eunice Hunt   4- 7-1825
Cook, John Polly Beeson   9-28-1825
Cook, Thomas - Polly Burgess   9-28-1815
Cook, Thomas - Patsey Smith   12-14-1826
Cook, Zachariah - Anna Bundy   12-24-1829
Cooper, Joseph G. - Elizabeth Leonard
    8- 8-1822
Cooper, Samuel - Charity White   4-10-1818
Cooper, William - Elizabeth English 5- 7-1822
Copeland, Ephraim - Leah Copeland 11-28-1827
Cornthwait, John - Ann Barton   2-28-1828
Cory, Joseph - Matilda Greenstreet 12-24-1829
Cosand, Samuel - Mary Parsons   9-25-1827
Costlow (Coslow?), John - Malinda West
    lic.   2- 6-1819
Cotton, Isaac - Jane King   12-21-1829
Cotton, John - Nancy Voorhese   4- 2-1829
Cotton, William - Mariah Vorhis   8-15-1822
Cox, Harman - Martha Cox lic.   11-14-1818
Cox, Jeremiah - Rutha Andrew   7-10-1811
Cox, John Jr. - Martha Moffat   8- 3-1815
Cox, Moses - Sarah Hurst   12-31-1818
Cox, Solomon - Bier Jackson   1- 4-1829
Cox, Stephen - Polly Westcot   5-29-1825
Cox, William - Elizabeth Russel
    lic.   12-30-1825
Craft, Thomas - Hannah O'Harrow
    lic.   11- 6-1822
Craig, Barkley - Melissa Brotherton
    12- 8-1827
Craner, Joshua - Susanna Johnston   1- 5-1815
Crawford, James - Elizabeth Robbins
    11-22-1817
Crawford, John - Nancy McKoy   1-20-1825
Crawford, William - Sarah Merritt 10-30-1823
Creviston, Samuel - Harriett Willets
    3-28-1822
Crews, Isaac - Nancy Williams   10- ?-1818
Cripe, Abraham - Eliza Ervin   4- 5-1825
Crisher, Adam - Susannah Baldwin 10-30-1823
Crow, Abel - Mary Small   11- 6-1820
Crull, Benjamin - Elizabeth Custer 1-17-1830
Crull, John - Polly Worl   3-13-1828
Crull, Michael - Eliza Black   9-20-1827
Crum, Jacob - Martha Hanby   2-20-1828
Crum, Peter - Mary Nation   7-26-1821
Crumb, William - Sarah Jobe   12-16-1819
Cunningham, Andrew - Polly Fox   12- 3-1829
Cunningham, George - Catherine Peters
    lic.   8-31-1818
Cuppy, James - Laura McKinney   9- 5-1825
Cuppy, James - Sally Jones   11- 5-1826
Cuppy, John - Elizabeth Henderson 3-24-1825
Cuppy, Thomas - Jemimah Ward   9- 7-1820
Curtis, Saul H. - Frances Norton   5- 8-1828
Custer, Christopher - Elizabeth Clark
    6-12-1828
Custer, John - Rebecca Rippey   2-19-1824
Dale, Lydnor - Hetty Tyner lic.   10-19-1818
Davice, Mark - Rebecca Osburn   5-27-1822
Davice, William - Lucy Wilson   5- 1-1823
Davis, Aaron - Lydia Thatcher   5- 1-1828
Davis, Drury - Polly Bunworth   7-11-1822
Davis, Henry - Eunice Hays   2-24-1830
Davis, James - Rhoda Codington   10- 1-1818
Davis, Maxcey - Peggy Brown   4-27-1830

Davis, Willis - Ann Coggshall   6-29-1826
Dawson, Asa - Polly Hubbell   12-25-1817
Dawson, Eli - Rachel Summers   6-11-1820
Dawson, Isaac - Sarah Gamel (Gamble?)
    lic.   11-19-1818
Dawson, Mathias - Nancy Hardin   7-19-1817
Dawson, Samuel - Hannah Williams 3- 5-1818
Deardorff, Daniel - Elizabeth --- 8- 8-1824
Deardorff, David - Margaret Hendrix 12-18-1828
Dehaven, Jacob - Juliett Denny   5-12-1822
Dennis, Elisha - Elizabeth Wallace 6-15-1815
Develin, Henry - Malinda Stinson 11-24-1822
Dewy, William - Lucy Arvin   9-19-1829
Dial, Daniel - Anna Feckham negroes
    lic.   9- 8-1825
Dickey, Benjamin - Rebecca McColla 7-17-1823
Dickover, Jacob - Hannah Bannick 9-10-1829
Dicks, Ezekiel - Jane Woodward   1-13-1825
Dicks, Zachariah - Jemima Vestal 9-15-1814
Diggs, William - Charlotte Way   10- 6-1816
Dill, John - Rebekah Leonard   11-11-1824
Dill, Samuel - Rachel Cain   12-20-1821
Dillon, Frederick - Sally Wise   1- 6-1828
Dimit, Thomas - Rachel Elliott   1-20-1815
Dimmett, Miles - Sally Kinworthy
    lic.   9-17-1825
Dixon, James - Lylly McKinney   4- 5-1820
Doan, Nathan - Polly Jobs   2-25-1824
Doan, Nathaniel - Mary Coleman   4- 6-1823
Dobbins, Jesse - Elizabeth Chappell 6- 3-1821
Dollarhide, Hezekiah - Dice Brown 4-12-1827
Dougan, John - Rebekah Holmes   11- 8-1827
Dougherty, Zadock - Mary Willyard 5- 2-1822
Doughty, Thomas L. - Mary Jane Kibbey
    4- 2-1829
Doughty, William M. - Elizabeth Gay 12- 3-1818
Douglass, Joseph - Mary Steele   2-20-1828
Downey, Richard - Rebekah Baker   2-17-1830
Drake, John - Esther Elston   2-22-1816
Drake, Josiah - Martha Dickerson 4-18-1819
Drake, Moses - Rebekah Elston   6-13-1819
Draper, Jesse - Delphina Davenport 9- 5-1816
Draper, Jesse - Sarah Harlan   10-29-1829
Draper, John - Patsey Palmer   3-11-1822
Draper, Joseph - Biddy Jackson   2- 5-1819
Draper, Josiah - Catharine Pearson 11- 3-1822
Draper, Joshua - Huldah Pearson   5- 5-1825
Druly, Ransom - Anna Moore   7- 1-1830
Druly, William - Rachel Bonine   7-15-1830
Drury, Arnold - Sally Shortridge 6- 7-1816
Drury, Isaac - Hannah Rees   4-20-1821
Drury, James - Jane Moore   2-18-1819
Drury, Samuel - Violet Shortridge 2- 2-1819
Drury, Samuel - Polly Boswell lic. 9- 4-1821
Duhadway, Peter - Martha Reeves lic.
    10-31-1825
Dunham, Alanson F. - Hannah Cheesman
    4- 8-1830
Dunham, Jeremiah - Rachel Miller 10-16-1829
Dunham, John E. - Vashti Willets 9- 7-1826
Dunhem, William - Mary Miller   10-10-1816
Dunlavy, Anthony - Sarah Benefield 3-15-1830
Dunlop, William S. - Catharine Passage
    6- 4-1829
Dunman, Wm. - Susanna White   9-21-1815
Dunn, Silas - Jane Montgomery   1-23-1816
Duriala (?), John - Eliza A. Ward 7-14-1822
Durr, William - Dolly --- lic.   12-23-1817

326

Dutterow, Henry - Rebekah Harris lic.
2- 1-1825
Dwiggins, Elijah - Elizabeth Howard
11-28-1824
Dwyer, Jacob - Rhoda Smith   10[11]- 5-1818
Dyer, William - Margaret Hannah   9-28-1824
East, Joel - Sarah Bulla   9-13-1825
Eastridge, George - Elizabeth Jones
11-14-1828
Eaton, William - Phebe Gard   1- 4-1821
Edgerton, Daniel - Rachel Bundy   11- 8-1827
Edgerton, Samuel - Mary Sarjent   4-20-1826
Edmond (or Edmonds), Christian - Miriam
Caty   9- 8-1825
Edwards, Eli - Mary Crow   11- 7-1826
Edwards, John - Malinda Jacobs   10-18-1821
Edwards, William - Susanna Small   2-10-1825
Eggleston, Miles C. - Elizabeth Sutherland
3-10-1822
Eliason, Joshua - Phebe Smithson   5- 8-1821
Eliason, Joshua - Lucinda King   5-20-1830
Eliason, William - Harriet McCollister
6-19-1823
Elliott, Aaron - Polly Lindley   7-29-1814
Elliott, Ellwood - Sarah Gailbraith 6-14-1821
Elliott, Francis - Rachel Williams 10-11-1828
Elliott, Israel - Nancy Lamb   10- 4-1821
Elliott, Nathan - Rachel Bunch lic. 8-26-1816
Elliott, Seth - Rachel Addington   11- 3-1828
Elliott, Stephen - Anna Cook   9-23-1820
Elliott, William - Sarah Swope   12-30-1821
Elliott, William - Eliza E. Branson 6-19-1825
Ellis, Elihu - Elizabeth Alderson   2-28-1822
Ellzey, Gerrard - Susannah Vickary 10-16-1823
Elsbury, Jacob - Nancy Thornbrough   3- 5-1829
Elsbury, Thomas - Betsy Smith   12- 3-1828
Elsea, John D. - Sarah Fleehart   11-26-1829
Elwell, Eli - Elizabeth DeCamp   1-14-1823
Emil, Thomas - Huldah Little   2-19-1815
Emmerson, Edward - Jane McCoy   12-25-1823
Endsley, Andrew - Sally Williams   1-27-1818
Endsley, John - Rachel Butler   3-27-1823
Endsley, Peter - Mary Wright   4-27-1820
Esteb, James - Sally Ward   10- 7-1824
Esteb, John - Nancy Fisher lic.   8- 7-1826
Estridge, William - Cloe Black   5-27-1824
Evans, Charles - Marihah Haynes   12-27-1829
Eytcheson, Jesse - Polly Eytcheson 11- 5-1829
Fairbrother, Lewis L. - Polly Jones
12-11-1826
Faler, Samuel - Margaret Fruit   5- 8-1828
Farlow, John - Caty Miller   1-28-1813
Farlow, John - Hannah Little   8-16-1820
Farlow, Nathan - Martha Lewis   10- 6-1814
Farlow, Simeon - Mary Ritter   2-24-1819
Farlow, William - Betsey Miller   4- 4-1811
Felton, Robert - Eliza Felton   1-18-1821
Felton, Robert - Elizabeth Mason   9-10-1829
Felton, William - Sally Stonebraker
lic.   2-28-1825
Fender, Henry - Mary Long   12-22-1825
Fender, Jacob - Betsy Ann Holland 11- 3-1829
Fender, Jonathan - Nancy Black   4- 5-1821
Fenner, Jeremiah - Amelia Crane   5- 4-1830
Fennimore, Stephen - Jane McAllister
3-28-1830
Ferguson, Samuel - Nancy White   11-19-1818
Ferguson, William - Catharine Bakehorn
9-17-1828

Ferree, Israel - Judith Miller   11-28-1826
Fillinger, David - Catharine Miller 12-26-1823
Finch, Archibald - Margaret Clark lic.
2-15-1825
Finch, Cyrus - Theresa A. Booker   8-16-1821
Finch, James - Hannah Lauman   1-11-1827
Finch, John - Eliza C. Irvin   11-20-1823
Finch, Nathaniel - Kiziah Depew   12-25-1827
Fisher, Benjamin - Polly Resbuk   6-20-1812
Fisher, David - Polly Resbuck   11- ?-1811
Fisher, David - Betsy M. Hodges   10-12-1815
Fisher, Jacob R. - Amelia M. Lane   11- 5-1829
Fisher, Jacob W. - Sarah Grimes   10-15-1829
Fisher, John - Jane Starbuck   9-16-1819
Fisher, Thomas - Elizabeth Gardner 12-20-1827
Fleming, Andrew - Ann Mitchell   11-17-1825
Fleming, James - Elizabeth Roberts 12-28-1826
Fleming, Samuel - Margaret Finley lic.
1- 8-1823
Flick, Phillip - Miriam Small   4- 8-1820
Flint, William - Charity Little   11-25-1826
Foland, John - Jane Fincher   9-15-1826
Ford, Nathaniel - Sally Keen lic.   5-30-1829
Forehand, David - Rhoda Palmer   6- 1-1828
Foreman, Maurice - Mary Sanders   7- 4-1822
Foreman, Samuel - Elizabeth Sanders 5-29-1825
Forkner, James - Lydia Eliason   1-25-1828
Forkner, John - Mary Harrington   9-13-1828
Fosher, Matthias - Elizabeth Riffe 6-11-1829
Fosset (?), William - Rachel Hatfield
9- 9-1819
Foust, Daniel - Catharine Wolfe   12-18-1823
Fouts, David - Patsy Whitehead   4- 8-1824
Fouts, Levi - Sarah Small   1-29-1818
Fouts, Noah - Phebe Nelson   8-25-1814
Fouts, Samuel W. - Eliza Hunt   2-26-1828
Fowler, Filander - Mariam Luse   7- 4-1822
Fowler, William - Lucy Russel   10-22-1822
Fox, Uzel B. - Mahitibel Berry   8-27-1827
Frake, Conrad - Sarah Case   9- 2-1817
Fraly, Daniel - Polly Meek   4-25-1816
Frazer, John - Rachel Beard   4- 2-1818
Frazer, Nathan - Mary Turner   9-20-1827
Frazier, Simeon - Rebekah Valentine 11-19-1826
Frazier, William - Patsy McClelland 12-20-1816
Freeman, William H. - Susannah Hollingsworth
12-31-1829
Friend, Nicholas - Mary Hains   7-18-1822
Fry, Amos - Sarah Piggott   7-22-1824
Fryar, John - Sophia Russe   11-29-1828
Fudge, Adam - Barbary McDannal   9-20-1822
Fulton, Alexander - Ann Stump   8- 2-1826
Gaar, Fielding - Paulina Turner   11-18-1819
Gaar, Jonas - Sally Watson   11-12-1818
Gail, William - Penina Small   9-26-1820
Galbraith, James - Sarah Suttenfield 6- 2-1819
Galbraith, William - Patsy McLain   6- 5-1814
Gallien, Jacob - Polly Porter   9-29-1814
Gallien, Thomas - Tabitha Warren   11- 3-1814
Gallion, William - Mehuldah Lamb   1- 9-1817
Galyean, Daniel - Nancy Stanley   12-18-1823
Gapen, Otho - Amanda McClure lic.   3-21-1829
Gapen, Tindall - Therrisa Gray   2-20-1825
Garner, Laban - Jane Little   12- 6-1814
Garner, Vincent - Rachel Ratliff   11-15-1820
Garret, Nathan - Cassey Davis   3-30-1815
Garret, Thomas - Sophia Gray lic. 10-16(?)1820
Garrett, Joseph - Matee Scofield   12-18-1828
Gates, William - Elizabeth L. Boyd 2-21-1828

Gentis, Daniel - Marlina Heffley	11-22-1824
Gentry, John - Mary Webb	5-13-1824
Gentry, Samuel - Mary Foland	1- 3-1828
Gentry, Thomas - Pamela A. Fisher	9-30-1824
Gibson, John - Patsey Odell	12-15-1818
Gibson, Samuel - Anna Pollard	4-28-1824
Gifford, Ichabod - Betsy Addington	4-18-1822
Gilbert, Jonathan - Peggy Clark lic.	
	9- 3-1811
Gillaspie, Andrew - Maenerva Nichols	
	8-30-1821
Gillom, William - Phebe Cook	12-16-1815
Gilmore, Samuel - Nancy Roberts	12-16-1819
Gillum, Robert - Mary Smith lic.	3- 3-1818
Ginn, Job - Sally McKee	12-15-1814
Girton, John - Cyrena Johnson	2- 1-1827
Gist, Silas - Nancy Harlan	5-21-1829
Glancey, John - Susan Moore	4-27-1826
Glover, William - Catharine Walker	10-12-1826
Goldsmith, William - Mary Null	6-13-1824
Goodwin, James - Lavina Ward lic.	10-12-1817
Gordon, Anderson - Lydia James	12-28-1815
Gossett, John - Mary Petre	12-19-1816
Gossett, William - Charity Hageman	9-26-1815
Graham, Alexander - Parmela McHenry	1-19-1815
Grave, Nathan - Margaret Addleman	8-30-1825
Graves, James C. - Alice Addington	1-24-1830
Gray, Havens - Nepthaline Carter lic.	
	4-12-1821
Gray, James - Margaret Hunt	11-12-1819
Gray, John - Elizabeth Alberts	10-22-1818
Gray, William - Matilda Long	8- 9-1819
Gray, William - Caroline Albertson	12-25-1828
Griffith, Ethan - Ruth Harlan lic.	6- 7-1826
Grimes, Anderson - Susanna Beeson	9- 4-1828
Grimes, George - Mary Fouts	1-11-1827
Grinslade, Joseph - Betsy Smith	10-25-1821
Groenendike, Peter - Hannah Beard	6-28-1821
Guardner, John - Margaret Harris	9- 8-1825
Gruwell, Thomas - Letitia Gruwell	3-27-1828
Gunckel, David - Hannah Veal	10- 1-1829
Gunckel, John - Mary Daugherty	2-16-1830
Gustin, Elkanah - Nancy Troxel	1- 9-1829
Hague, John - Polly Cotton	4-10-1828
Hall, Benjamin - Nancy Roberts	2-21-1822
Hall, Benjamin - Esther Elsey	5-29-1830
Hall, Benjamin, Jr. - Priscilla Elsey	
	12-25-1828
Hall, Elisha - Eliza Burk	3- 4-1824
Hall, Joseph - Rebekah Hoover	10-12-1817
Hall, Samuel - Polly Small	9-22-1816
Hall, William - Jane Bell lic.	5- 4-1830
Hall, William G. - Pamela Mitchel	12-24-1828
Hall, William L. - Susanna Roper (or Raper?)	
	10-25-1821
Halstead, Leonard - Patsy Snodgrass	7-17-1830
Ham, Emsley - Pamela Talbott	5- 6-1830
Hamilton, Samuel - Nancy M. Stewart	8- 7-1828
Hammer, Austin - Nancy Elston	9- 7-1826
Hammond, Michael - Elizabeth Freestone lic.	
Rachel Freestone in return	5-14-1828
Hammond, William D. - Barsheba Owens	
	11-11-1824
Hancock, John - Elizabeth Pollard	5- 4-1826
Hannah, Abraham G. - Mary Hays	3- 5-1828
Harden, Daniel - Mary Williams	3-23-1818
Harden, Solomon - Catharine McCall	2-18-1818
Harden, Thomas - Selah Brewer	8- 7-1828
Harden, William - Prudence Walker	2-21-1828
Hardin, Isaac - Rebecca Jackson	3-17-1825

Hardwick, Pleasant G. - Elizabeth Trueblood	
	11-20-1828
Harlan, George - Emily Miller	10-28-1819
Harlan, George - Elizabeth Dunken	6-19-1823
Harlan, Nathan - Sarah Anderson lic.	5-27-1821
Harlan, Samuel - Melinda Owens	9-21-1820
Harlan, William - Sarah Johnson	10-17-1817
Harman, Andrew - Eliza Walker	4-27-1819
Harman, David - Rebecca Walker	1-12-1815
Harper, John - Sarah McClain	7-13-1820
Harrell, Byram - Martha Scott lic.	8-26-1824
Harris, Benjamin - Lydia Hiatt	12-27-1822
Harris, Jesse - Mary Tharp	6-23-1825
Harris, John - Nancy Harvey	6-19-1817
Harris, Obadiah - Sally Lewis	12-19-1811
Harris, Pleasant - Hannah Massay	10- 3-1811
Harris, Rowland - Polly Walters	1- 4-1827
Harris, William - Sophronia Branson	12-25-1828
Harris, William - Mary Hoover	9-11-1829
Harris, William T. - Jane Worril	1- 3-1821
Harrison, Gideon - Sally Wiley	11-18-1821
Harshfield, John - Elizabeth Shureigh (?)	
lic.	8-11-1820
Hart, Edward R. - Ann Maria T. Morton	
	8- 9-1827
Hart, John - Rachel Warren	3-15-1818
Harter, Jacob - Sarah Lawson	5- 2-1819
Hartup, James - Mary Fruits	2-25-1819
Harvey, Aaron - Esther Brumfield	2-19-1829
Harvey, Benjamin - Nancy Sellers	12-31-1829
Harvey, Francis - Elizabeth Snider	10-28-1813
Harvey, James - Margaret Canady	10-12-1820
Harvey, Robert - Abigail Summer	8-24-1815
Harvey, William - Sarah Charles lic.	5-18-1813
Harwood, Richard - Esther Tharp lic.	8-18-1821
Hasty, Peter - Jane Holmes	1- 2-1827
Hasty, Thomas - Ann Raper	3-20-1828
Hatfield, Jonas - Tabitha Neal	8-17-1821
Hatfield, Nathan - Emily Roe	4-26-1827
Hawk, John - Polly Moore	1- 1-1823
Hawkins, James - Rebekah Dale	9-24-1818
Hawkins, Jesse - Mary Jay	2- 5-1824
Hawkins, Jonathan - Mary Morrow	12-26-1827
Hawkins, Nathan - Sarah Wright	12-31-1829
Hawkins, William - Isabel Powel	3- 5-1818
Hawkins, Wm. - Sarah Zeek	1- 7-1830
Hayes, George - Elsey Little	10-23-1823
Hayes, William - Elizabeth Nugeon	5-29-1823
Hays, Elijah - Elizabeth Brown	3-15-1821
Hays, John - Jane Beeson	2- 6-1828
Haze, Lewis - Mary Beeson	2-10-1819
Hazer, Isaiah - Rebecca Hoover	10- 4-1823
Healey, Jesse - Sarah Bundy lic.	11-26-1818
Heath, Lambeth - Nancy Johnson	8-13-1818
Heathcock, Elijah - Anna Jones	3- 6-1828
Heathcock, Mark - Alice Jones	10-24-1826
Heaton, Eli - Mary Hurst	2-27-1819
Heiny, Samuel - Ana Schock	9-14-1826
Heman, William - Jane Bass	7-12-1829
Henderson, John - Hannah Moon	1-21-1824
Henderson, John - Mary Skidmer	3- 5-1828
Henderson, Richard - Margaret Hunt	1- 9-1822
Hendricks, William - Nancy Griffin	3- 2-1823
Hendricks, William - Harriet Miller	7- 3-1827
Hendrix Alpheus - Abigail Hendrix	12-17-1826
Hendrix, Henry D. - Theodosia Willits	
	3-19-1829
Henley, Samuel - Nancy Anderson	8- 5-1824
Henwood, John - Rebeca Spotha (Spahr?)	
	3-23-1820

Herington, Nathaniel - Nancy A McDonald
                    11-11-1821
Heritage, Samuel - Elizabeth Edwards
                    5-18-1826
Hiatt, David - Lavina Hiatt   9-17-1820
Hiatt, Enos - Sally Sullivan   9-26-1827
Hiatt, Jesse - Mahala Evans   2- 5-1824
Hiatt, Joel - Matilda Ferguson   11- 1-1829
Hiatt, Jonathan - Ruth Hiatt   12-29-1827
Hiatt, Josiah - Esther Hiatt   11- 3-1820
Hiers, William - Nancy Strong   7- 9-1818
Higgins, Daniel - Mary Howell   3-28-1822
Higgins, David - Sally Stevenson 4- 6-1826
Hill, Joel - Elizabeth Chryst   6-16-1814
Hillis, Symms - Mary Robbins   6-17-1817
Hindall, Christian - Eve Miller 2-13-1816
Hinkle, George - Sarah Stark   2- 6-1823
Hobart, Otis - Sophronia Holman 1-20-1825
Hobbs, Phillamon - Rachel Oliphant 2-15-1830
Hobbs, William - Sarah Cambling lic.
                    2-13-1824
Hockett, Zadoc - Katharine Blizzard
                   12-13-1827
Hodgen, Larkin - Jane Frazer   8-19-1823
Hodges, James - Margaret Galbreath 9-10-1828
Hodges, Jesse - Sally Boon   6-29-1817
Hoke, Michael - Mehala Smith (Smyth)
                  11- 3-1825
Holcomb, Mathew - Martha Shaw 11-30-1817
Holland, Elijah - Dicey Dollarhide 10-20-1814
Hollingsworth, Joseph - Rachel Vestal
                   1-17-1828
Holloway, Jesse - Sally Brockus 3-12-1828
Holloway, William - Betsy Fisher 4- 3-1828
Holman, Cornelius - Rachel Carson 4-26-1827
Holman, Edward - Miriam Rue   1813
Holman, George - Sarah McDonald 9-16-1824
Holman, Greenup - Leetha Druly 12-12-1824
Holman, James - Peggy Jordan   10-27-1811
Holman, Jesse H. - Nancy Galbreath 7-13-1826
Holsclaw, Samuel - Kisiah Ellsey 9-27-1823
Holtsclaw, David - Nancy Sanders 6-15-1827
Holtsclaw, James - Rhoda Asher lic. 8- 6-1816
Hook, David - Martha Sparks   4-20-1825
Hoover, Aaron - Charity Harris   9-21-1829
Hoover, Alexander - Frances Moore 10-12-1826
Hoover, Andrew - Matilda Worl   2-14-1828
Hoover, Emsley - Hannah Ridge   4-29-1819
Hoover, Jacob - Sally Waymire lic. 7-13-1822
Hoover, Joel - Lydia Thompson   1-25-1827
Hoover, John - Rachel Maudlin   10- 1-1829
Hoover, Joshua - Lydia Small   2-13-1829
Hoover, Levi - Margaret Harvey 10- 6-1827
Hoover, Martin - Sally Scott lic. 2-28-1825
Hopper, Wesley - Emily Drury   1-22-1829
Horner, Levi - Nancy Bray   1-23-1823
Horney, Stephen - Nancy Williams 12- 2-1824
Hornish, Jacob D. - Tamer Bently 4-15-1819
Hort (Hart?), John - Mary Clark 1-16-1823
Hosier, Henderson - Elizabeth Hoover
                   11-10-1825
Hosier, Henry - Ruth Hutson   11-26-1828
Howard, John - Rebekah Mundin   12- 6-1820
Howard, Joseph - Cynthia Hurst 12-30-1824
Howell, John - Lydia Lindley lic. 12-27-1817
Hubbard, Silas - Betsy Anderson 11- 8-1820
Huchison, John - Mary Thomas   3-20-1819
Huchison, Wilkison - Susan Allen lic.
                    8-26-1819
Hudlow, John - Ann Sheffer   12-25-1818

Huff, John, Jr. - Esther Boswell   11-25-1819
Hugh, Thomas - Margaret Byford   3-27-1815
Hughes, William - Jane Jamison   8- 6-1820
Hunt, Charles - Hannah Boon   3-12-1818
Hunt, Edward - Elizabeth Endsley   5- 3-1812
Hunt, Edward - Sarah Townsend   2-28-1828
Hunt, Elihu - Hannah Alburn   5-20-1825
Hunt, Henry - Elizabeth Roberts   9-16-1821
Hunt, Jesse - Catharine Pedrick 10-15-1825
Hunt, Jonas - Nancy Thomas   7-30-1816
Hunt, Joseph - Jenny Endsley   9- 3-1812
Hunt, Nathan - Hepsy Swaim   8-26-1821
Hunt, Peter - Rachel Wilkeson   10-19-1826
Hunt, Peter - Clarisa Sawyer   9- 3-1829
Hunt, Smith - Betsey Lamb   5-31-1812
Hunt, Stephen G. - Caty Lamb   8-22-1816
Hunt, Thompson - Polly Hardwick 12-27-1827
Hunt, William - Matilda Smith   9- 3-1815
Hunt, William - Mary Smith   10-21-1818
Hunt, William - Elizabeth Pedrick 10-12-1826
Hunt, William H. - Betsy Esteb   1-12-1813
Hunter, William - Miriam Moore n.d. [1815?]
Huntsinger, John - Elizabeth Waltz lic.
                   6-20-1828
Huntsinger, Joseph - Susanna Schoch 11-26-1826
Hurst, Bennet - Barbara Harris   10-17-1826
Hurst, Caswell - Catharine Jones 2-28-1830
Hurst, Meshack - Catharine Garret 2-19-1828
Hurst, Thomas - Nancy Montgomery 3- 4-1819
Hurst, Thomas - Sidney Haladay   2-26-1829
Hutchins, Benjamin - Martha Johnson 11-10-1817
Hutson, Chamberlain - Polly Noland lic.
                   6-21-1823
Hutton, Thomas - Isabel Hart   7- 4-1827
Imel, George - Betsey Derham   11-30-1814
Imel, Samuel - Susannah Black   12-23-1819
Ingle, Abraham - Rebekah Whitaker 12-23-1824
Ingle, John - Rosa Gaar   11-12-1818
Ireland, James - Polly Maxwell lic. 4-20-1812
Ireland, Silas - Zelpha Sibley   8-10-1826
Ireland, William - Annie Alexander 8- 3-1813
Ireland, William - Elizabeth Parsons
                  12-31-1827
Irvin, Hiram - Miriam Stalls   12- 3-1829
Ish, George - Mary Ann Wisehart 12-24-1816
Jackson, Isaiah - Fanny Shay lic. 2-23-1825
Jackson, John - Polly Walts   7- 1-1824
Jackson, Joshua - Ruth Hague   9-24-1829
Jackson, Thomas - Mary McKinney 6-23-1825
James, Daniel - Ursula Elliott   2-21-1822
James, Daniel - Mary Clark   3-15-1827
James, David - Jane Dwiggins   2-27-1817
James, Isaac - Naomi Stratton 12-28-1820
James, James - Mary Rambo   3-17-1822
James, John - Creasy Hunt lic. 10- 2-1821
James, William - Lucinda Russel 2-24-1820
Jarret, James - Peggy Blount   9- 4-1816
Jarvis, Thomas - Sarah Davenport 2- 6-1824
Jay, Evan - Hannah Way   11-15-1827
Jeffery, Joel - Hannah Case lic. 8-29-1821
Jeffries, Isaac - Elizabeth Stidham 6- 7-1826
Jennings, James A. - Nelly Thornbrough
                  10-31-1822
Jessop, Abraham - Hannah Wright 8- 3-1811
Jessop, Nathan - Alce Beauchamp 11-22-1822
Jessup, Jacob - Elizabeth Gray lic. 2-25-1815
Jobs, John - Polly Padgett lic. 3-30-1822
Johnson, Abel - Catharine Holloday 1-19-1820
Johnson, Daniel - Betsey Vincent 4-26-1827
Johnson, George - Marian Huff   5-17-1821

Johnson, Jediah - Delia Bullard   4- 3-1821
Johnson, Kinchen - Catharine Conway 7- 3-1823
Johnson, Mentor - Mahala Martin   5-19-1819
Johnson, Nathan - Sally Shaw   10-10-1818
Johnson, Philip - Martha Hubbard   7-22-1827
Johnson, Reuben - Susannah Samuels 11-19-1829
Johnson, Stephen - Abigail Macy   12-19-1822
Johnson, William - Rachel Smith   4- 8-1824
Johnston, John - Anna Way   3-14-1816
Jones, Amos - Patsy Hatfield   11-20-1813
Jones, Daniel - Lydia E. Baldwin   1-28-1827
Jones, David - Ruth Wade   4- 7-1827
Jones, Edmond, Jr. - Frances M. Brannon
                                      11- 4-1823
Jones, John - Sally Shortridge   3- 6-1816
Jones, John - Rachel Jordan   10-10-1818
Jones, Lewis - Caroline Leavell   3-26-1829
Jones, Richard - Hannah Thomas   4- 3-1820
Jones, Robert - Elizabeth Austin   12-31-1829
Jones, Samuel - Polly Pierson   1-27-1823
Jones, Stephen - Deborah Lewallen   10-28-1813
Jones, William - Nancy Connor   3- 2-1825
Jordan, Alexander - Rassey Streit   1-12-1826
Jordan, James - Nancy Jones   10- 8-1818
Jordan, Thomas N. - Mary Addington 12-11-1828
Jordan, William - Kezia Brannon   12-14-1820
Jorden, John - Rachel Roberts   5-13-1819
Julian, Jacob - Mary Harvey   6-13-1811
Julian, Renny - Charlotte Pearson   5-16-1816
Julian, Shubal - Biddy Hoover   9-18-1818
Justice, James - Elizabeth Williams
                              lic. 10-27-1820
Justice, Patrick - Catherine McGowin
                                       1-15-1818
Justice, William - Hannah Gray   12-30-1818
Keesling, Daniel - Catharine Zick   2- 5-1824
Keesling, George - Betsey Miller   2-17-1825
Keesling, John - Linna Bulla   8-25-1819
Keller, Lewis P. - Paulina E. B. Wheaton
                                      12-29-1829
Kelly, Austin - Rebecca Coffin   2- 1-1827
Kepler, John - Anna Foland   12-25-1828
Kessler, Daniel - Kizia Baltimore   3- 6-1828
Kessler, Joseph - Nancy Baltimore   4-12-1827
Kidwell, Sterling - Mary Benefield   1-11-1827
Kimel, Jacob - Matty Whitmore   6-21-1827
Kindal, Adam - Minty McKinny   10-28-1818
King, Daniel - Mariah McCollister   5-28-1822
King, Elisha - Belinda Rambo   6-13-1820
King, Lorenzo - Elizabeth Way   10-18-1827
Kirk, Timothy - Rebecca Kirk   8-14-1824
Kirkland, Jeremiah - Patsy Ballinger
                                       1- 9-1825
Kline, Jacob - Margaret Seller   2- 8-1821
Knight, Loyd - Catharine Stanley   12-27-1820
Knight, Solomon - Rebekah Hunt   2-16-1820
Knipe, John - Demima Smith   12-22-1826
Knott, Ephraim - Agness Hyers   4- 9-1818
Knutt, William - Jane Canaday   4-29-1819
Ladd, Isaac N. - Elizabeth Hutchins
                                      11-13-1828
Ladd, William - Isabella Boyd   12- 8-1825
Lakin, Joseph - Mary VanMeter lic. 9-24-1819
Lamb, Barnabas - Ruth Bentley   9-13-1820
Lamb, Esau - Elizabeth Moon   6-15-1826
Lamb, Ezekiel - Rachel Adamson   12-13-1829
Lamb, Hosea - Polly Cook   8-23-1818
Lamb, Miles - Elizabeth Gray   9-29-1826
Lamb, William - Frances Garr   12- 4-1817

Lambert, Jonathan - Betsy Wasson   12-10-1829
Lancaster, Ocky - Maria Weaver lic. 2-13-1821
Lancaster, William S. - Lucinda Meek
                                      11-19-1829
Landers, Samuel - Elizabeth Stretch lic.
                                       7-25-1820
Lane, (or Lain), James J. - Isabel Trueblood
                                      10-20-1825
Lane, John - Rosanna Crumb   9-16-1815
Langley, Curtis - Anna West lic.   8-14-1828
Lantz, Alexander - Sarah Stout   11-21-1821
Lawman, Alfred - Hannah McDonald   11-22-1821
Lawman, Daniel - Melinda Gay   1- 8-1818
Lawman, Daniel - Abey Vorhas (?)   12-13-1821
Lawrence, Benjamin - Sophia Hyde   12-10-1826
Leas, Thomas - Jane Walker   2- 9-1826
Leavell, James - Elizabeth Cooper   9-18-1823
Lee, James - Elizabeth Williams   7-12-1828
Lee, William - Polly Macy   10-11-1822
Legg, Amos - Amelia Burgess   3-23-1830
Legg, Walter - Barbary Burgess   7- 8-1819
Lennington, James - Elizabeth Pugh 11-29-1827
Lennington, William - Maria Powell   5- 1-1829
Leverton, Anderson - Phebe Starbuck lic.
                                       7-27-1819
Leverton, Thomas - Lydia Dwiggins   8-21-1821
Lewallen, Shadrach - Elizabeth Miller
                                      10- 9-1817
Lewis, Caleb - Polly Willets   10-21-1819
Lewis, James - Ann Dwiggins   7-27-1828
Lewis, John - Polly Bushong   11-29-1821
Lewis, Joseph - Patsy Boyd   3-22-1818
Lewis, Mathew - Rachel Scott   11-15-1829
Lewis, Stanford - Betsy Thompson   9-25-1828
Lewis, Thomas T. - Sally Meek   12-12-1816
Lewis, William - Emeline Herman   6-26-1829
Lighty, George - Nancy Cooper   4- 8-1830
Likens, Jonas - Ann Johnson   10-28-1824
Lindley, John - Mary McMullen   6-19-1828
Lindley, Tense - Martha Baltimore   3-19-1829
Lineback, Elijah - Betsy Little   3-23-1827
Little, Jacob - Sarah Adams   5-29-1823
Little, James - Susanna Seany   10-20-1814
Little, John - Barbary Porter   9-10-1818
Little, Joseph - Anne Bedwell   10- 7-1813
Livingston, Aaron - Margaret Personett
                                       8-11-1825
Lloyd, John - Hulah Izard   1-27-1827
Logan, Charles - Sarah Benna (?) lic.
                                       1-16-1822
Long, Gabriel - Peggy Jones   3- 5-1829
Long, Henry - Mary Rollins   4- 5-1821
Long, Henry - Agatha Weekley   8-26-1827
Long, Jesse - Eve Lybrook   5-13-1818
Long, John - Margaret Martindale   10-22-1829
Long, Poindexter - Catherine Lybrook 3-28-1818
Long, Samuel D. - Mary Fenimore   5-29-1828
Long, William Kinyon - Lucinda Holland
                                       2- 5-1827
Longacre, Anderson - Rebecca Pearson 4-23-1827
Longacre, Joseph - Nancy Pearson   4- 4-1822
Louthane, Samuel - Polly Williams   11-25-1819
Low, Helim - Mary Bowen lic.   12-12-1819
Low, Isaiah - Naoma Lamb   8-12-1821
Loyd, Humphrey - Rachel Clark   8-12-1824
Luce, Joseph - Electy Fowler   5[6]-12-1823
Luce, Mathias - Hanah Underhill   8- 3-1820
Lunard, George - Fanny Schoch   5-15-1827
Lyons, Daniel - Julia Knapp   9-10-1820

Lyst, John W. - Nancy Cohran   1- 6-1828
McAllister, James - Kitty Eliason   12-31-1829
McBrown, Edward - Peggy Cain   10-29-1821
McCain, Daniel - Mary Mitchell   5-28-1829
McCall, Montgomery - Charlotte McCain
                              lic.   5- 4-1824
McCann, Isaac - Polly Ann Longacre   11-13-1828
McCarty, William - Lucinda Pearson
                              lic.   2-16-1820
McCauly, Jacob - Nancy Shanks   2-19-1829
McClain, John - Caty Hoover   8-27-1815
McClain, William - Mariah Jones lic.
                                      10-28-1826
McClane, David - Polly Williams   12-25-1813
McClelland, Robert - Katharine Cripe
                                      3-26-1829
McCollister, John - Polly Daugherty
                                      12-12-1826
McCombs, Ellet - Sarah Gough   2-22-1824
McCombs, John - Sally Moore   7-30-1815
McCombs, John - Catherine Stroud   11-14-1823
McCormack, James - Patsy Perkins lic.
                                      6- 8-1818
McCormick, Robert - Elizabeth Job   8-30-1827
McCoy, George - Susan Stevens lic.   4- 2-1825
  negroes
McCoy, John - Peggy Longwell   1-10-1828
McDade, James - Polly McKinney   5- 6-1819
McDowd, William - Penninah Bundy   11-18-1824
McGraw, William - Martha Higgins   1-25-1816
McGrew, Noah - Elizabeth Thompson   4-16-1829
McGrew, Thomas - Polly Custer   3- 8-1824
McKee, John - Mary B. Dooley lic.   3-28-1825
McKee, Moses - Rachel Shank   4-12-1827
McKee, Tabor - Sarah Elliott   10-19-1820
McKeever, Isaac - Kesiah Baltimore lic.
                                      4- 1-1822
McKinney, James - Polly Little   3- 5-1819
McKinney, James - Susana Adamson   9-12-1822
McKinney, Nathaniel - Mary Milmon lic.
                                      9- 1-1821
McKinney, William - Anna Walters lic.
                                      11- 3-1828
McKinny, William - Mary Hodge   8-28-1819
McLane, George - Esther Garret   6-24-1819
McLane, George - Alice Longacre   2-22-1827
McLane, Thomas - Nancy Edwards   10- 5-1815
McLean, Henry - Rebekah Cain lic.   3-24-1812
McLelland, John - Matilda Asher   11-19-1829
McManus, Barney - Mary Bishop   3-23-1829
McMullen, Daniel - Rachel Lindley   1- 7-1830
McMullen, John - Sarah Russel   12-14-1826
McMullen, Samuel - Susannah Walters   3- 9-1824
McNeal, David - Sally Misor   12- 8-1816
McNeal, James - Elizabeth Garret   4-20-1819
McWhinney, Thomas J. - Nancy Alexander
                                      12- 1-1829
McWhiny, John - Pamelia Alexander   9- 2-1823
McWhiny, Samuel - Rachel Alexander   8-21-1824
Mabbet, William - Esther Lewis   6-10-1819
Mabbit (Mabit), Anthony - Sarah Doey
  (or Dewey)   9-25-1820
Mabbitt, Thornburg - Susannah Smith   6- 6-1822
Macy, Henry - Rachel Trotter   12-24-1829
Macy, Isaac - Eleanor Thornburgh   4- 5-1825
Macy, Joseph - Sarah Hobson lic.   3-14-1829
Macy, Seth - Rebecca Simmons   8-16-1829
Madden, Solomon - Ruth Robbins   3-11-1819
Malcomb, James - Priscilla Thomas   8- 7-1817

Manifold, Joseph - Susanna Butler   2-18-1819
Mannon, Aaron - Miriam Hill   6-20-1830
Marine, William R. - Abigail McCrey   11- 7-1827
Marine, Ziba - Anna Lane (or Lain)   12-15-1825
Markle, John - Sally Allen   10-26-1820
Marrow, Lewis - Catherine Bandy (Bundy?)
                                      3-11-1821
Marsh, Daniel - Morilla White   5-14-1825
Marshall, Aaron - Nancy Macy   12-24-1829
Marshall, John - Nancy Potter   3- 6-1817
Martin, James - Rachel Stevenson   5-16-1811
Martin, James - Polly Hendrix   5-18-1819
Martin, John - Lydia Noland   11- 6-1814
Martin, Samuel - Damaris Rambo   10-11-1814
Martindale, David - Priscilla Lewis   12-28-1820
Martindale, Elijah - Elizabeth Boyd   10-12-1815
Martindale, John - Polly Watson   11-29-1826
Martindale, John - Lydia Hatfield   10-15-1827
Martindale, Moses - Margaret Izard   10-27-1825
Martindale, Thomas - Rebecca Martindale
                                      2-18-1822
Martindale, William - Naomi Hancock   6-20-1816
Mason, Edgar - Hannah Vaughan   7-29-1830
Mason, James - Kesiah Sullivan   2-1(?)-1821
Mason, John - Flora McGuire   3- 4-1819
Mason, Thomas - Griselda Elliott lic.
                                      5-22-1816
Massey, Maberry - Lydia Pegg   8-14-1828
Massey, Mathew - Mary Ann Mills   10-13-1825
Massey Phineas - Betsey Mills   12-14-1826
Massey, Robert - Rebecca Bulla lic.   1- 6-1814
Massey, Robert - Rachel Wilkeson   4-22-1824
Massey, Tense - Elizabeth Ready   7- 4-1813
Matinlee, James - Elizabeth Harland   10-28-1821
Matthews, William - Jane Orr   10- 4-1827
Maxberry, Horatio - Mavor(?) Hill   10-28-1826
Maxwell, James - Sarah Clark   8-14-1828
Maxwell, James W. - Keziah Fleming   4- 8-1813
Meek, Isaac - Mary Davisson   2-19-1829
Meek, Jeptha - Margaret Nugen   4-20-1828
Meek, Jeremiah - Catherine Williams   10- 1-1820
Meek, John - Betty Gibson   4-23-1815
Meek, John - Sarah Cull   10-22-1826
Meek, Joseph - Julia Elmira Smith   3-24-1816
Meek, William - Patsy Holman   6- 6-1811
Mendenhall, Francis - Polly Albert   3-17-1816
Mendenhall, James R. - Lydia Wright   10-23-1824
Mendenhall, James R. - Sarah T. Williams
                                      11- 8-1827
Mendenhall, Samuel - Amy Stevens   1- 5-1826
Mendenhall, Stephen - Mary H. Spray   8-18-1822
Mendenhall, Stephen - Nancy Foland   1-14-1823
  Nancy Farland in return
Mercer, Aaron - Julian Skidmore   5- 1-1823
Merritt, John - Rebecca Sellars   4-21-1825
Michael, Daniel - Elizabeth Commons   9-15-1826
Miles, Elijah - Catharine Thompson   4-24-1824
Miles, William - Elizabeth Allen   5- 6-1825
Miller, Abraham - Polly Little lic.   12-31-1821
Miller, Abraham - Hannah Miller   4-12-1827
Miller, Daniel B. - Sarah Cravens   9-25-1823
Miller, David - Louisa Conner   1- 8-1829
Miller, Eli - Elizabeth Rector   ?-24-1829
Miller, Isaac - Martha Beard   10-28-1815
Miller, Isaac - Elizabeth Forkner   8-28-1829
Miller, Peter - Elizabeth Petre   6-16-1812
Miller, Samuel - Nancy Bowen   2-12-1824
Millman, Robert - Abigail Adamson   3-26-1818
Mills, Abijah - Sarah Moon   9- 2-1824

Mills, Eli - Elizabeth Gray	7- 3-1822	
Mills, Ransom - Jane Ritter	2-29-1827	
Mills, Stephen - Mary Miles	5-29-1825	
Milner, John - Nancy Case	12-17-1821	
Milton, John - Patsey Briggs	11-30-1826	
Miner, Benson - Sally Sutton lic.	7-24-1812	
Miner, James - Elizabeth Cartwright	4- 3-1820	
Mires, John - Sally Plummer	2-15-1816	
Misor, David - Eliza Beeson	7-31-1828	
Mitchell, William - Margaret Brown	7- 7-1821	
Mittan, William - Patience Rush	3-13(?)-1821	
Modlin, Enoch - Miriam Peacock	10- 7-1819	
Modlin, John - Rachel Palmer	3-11-1824	
Moffit, William - Mary Gunn	8- 8-1822	
Montgomery, James - Elizabeth Stephenson		
	4- 7-1812	
Montgomery, John - Sally Stephenson	4-16-1812	
Montgomery, Platt - Nancy Little	4-17-1817	
Montgomery, William - Polly Hays	3-18-1827	
Moore, Anderson - Lydia Price	12-18-1825	
Moore, Benajah - Susannah Jones	11- 6-1823	
Moore, Benjamin - Sally Hill	3- 2-1820	
Moore, George - Sarah Williams	1-11-1829	
Moore, Isaac - Belinda Willets	12-13-1825	
Moore, James - Esther Hiatt	8-24-1827	
Moore, James W. - Sarah Ann Cue	4-30-1830	
Moore, John Sarah Elston	9-24-1825	
Moore, John - Rebekah Wade	10-20-1825	
Moore, Jonathan - Margaret Nichols	12-11-1828	
Moore, Marshall - Rachel Antrim	4- 3-1828	
Moore, Robert - Jane Sullivan	9-14-1827	
Moore, Thomas - Harriett Willetts	3-30-1821	
Moore, Thomas - Elizabeth Stanley	11-22-1822	
lic 9-20-22		
Moore, William - Betsy Edwards	12-20-1821	
Moore, William - Matilda Jarvis	10- 6-1825	
Moorman, Eli - Molly Thomas	1- 5-1820	
Morgan, Charles - Susanna Moon	11- 9-1828	
Morgan, James - Nancy Mabbitt	12-27-1821	
Morgan, Silas - Margaret Vinage lic.		
	2-28-1825	
Morgan, William - Mary Harter	3- 9-1819	
Morris, Caleb - Mary Conner	9-19-1824	
Morris, Elisha - Elizabeth Showalter		
	11- 5-1829	
Morrow, Hugh - Elizabeth Holms	2-13-1823	
Morrow, Joseph - Latitia Smith	10-23-1828	
Morton, David - Ellen Stedum (Stedham?)		
	11-20-1821	
Moss, Abraham - Nancy Rife lic.	9-18-1825	
Moyer, George - Susannah Brower	9-18-1825	
Mundane (Mondon), Elijah - Jane Nixon		
lic.	8-17-1816	
Mundon, Burgess - Ruth Moore	10- 7-1824	
Murdick, Jesse - Rachel Jessop	3-21-1823	
Murlatt, Joseph - Elizabeth Perry	7-22-1826	
Murphey, William -Elizabeth Beecher	5-22-1823	
Murphy, Albert - Rosanna Whitinger	6- 7-1814	
Murphy, James - Anna Russel	11-14-1824	
Murphy, James Elizabeth Thompson	8-17-1826	
Murphy, John - Sarah Reeder	4-30-1829	
Murphy, Robert - Sally Burgess lic.	3- 6-1818	
Murray, Thomas - Sally Nicholson	11- 8-1827	
Myers, Alfred - Elizabeth McCray	5- 8-1828	
Myers, Gideon - Catharine Crull	7-25-1822	
Myers, Oliver - Drusilla Heathcock	3-15-1827	
Myers, see also Mires.		
Nail, Caleb - Anne Miller	3-28-1816	
Nation, Seth - Charlotte Nation	1-24-1822	

Neal, Thomas D. - Theny Steagall	12-10-1829	
Neel, Jesse - Rebecca Stratton	6- 7-1827	
Nelson, George - Aggy Williams	5-27-1830	
Negroes		
Nelson, Joel - Susan Cooper	2- 7-1828	
Nelson, John - Mary Mabbet	5- 3-1819	
Newby, Micah - Mary D. Coffin	12-17-1821	
Newlon, Benjamin - Joana Williams	3- 6-1823	
Newman, John S. - Eliza Jane Hannah	10- 1-1829	
Newman, Thomas - Amy R. Platt	3-17-1825	
Newman, Thomas - Milicent Albertson	11-15-1826	
Nicholas, John - Jemima Dye	2-16-1825	
Nichols, Elisha - Betsy Moore	9-14-1827	
Nichols, Joseph - Ann Mills	11-29-1829	
Nichols, Malecheck - Sarah Mann	12- 2-1824	
Nichols, Malicheah - Sarah Marine	12-20-1824	
Nicholson, Andrew - Sally Ann Lamb	7- 8-1830	
Nicholson, Joseph - Sally Murray	5-15-1828	
Nixon, Caleb - Betsy Jester	3-18-1819	
Nixon, John - Miriam Bundy	4-19-1816	
Noland, Brazelton - Nancy Russell	12-30-1824	
Noland, Daniel - Lena Noland	7-19-1817	
Noland, Stephen - Nancy Adams	9-12-1820	
Nordyke, Isaac - Mary Culbertson	12-16-1823	
Norris, Thomas - Sarah Brock	7-25-1816	
Norton, Elias - Sally Easterland	3-30-1825	
Odell, John - Jane Conway	12-25-1824	
Odell, Stephen - Rebekah Overman	11- 2-1826	
Odem, Demcy - Elizabeth Jones	12-13-1822	
Odom, David - Rebecca Sweany	1- 9-1827	
Odom, John - Peggy Gillam	11- 5-1818	
Ogan, Elias - Eliza Addleman	8- 5-1824	
Olaner, Elijah - Catharine Oeler	3- 9-1823	
Old, William P. - Elsey Ritter	9-21-1829	
Oler, John - Matilda Stanberry	5-23-1830	
Ogburn, Hartwell - Frances Fox	12- 3-1829	
Oliver, Turner - Nancy Hendrix	1-17-1828	
Olson, Jonathan - Rachel Small	2-24-1820	
Olvy, Thomas - Polly Brown	9-21-1827	
Osborn, Daniel - Mary Washington	10-28-1821	
Osborn, Jesse - Hannah Massey Lindley		
	1- 6-1824	
Osborn, John - Patsy Tyner	1-21-1818?	
Osborn, Jonathan - Mary Morris	11-18-1816	
Osborne (or Osborn), Allen - Nancy Ridge		
	7-30-1828	
Osborne, Elijah - Sally Elliott	6-10-1830	
Osborne, Jesse - Susanna Craigg	9-16-1819	
Outland, Benjamin - Catharine Terry	2-24-1826	
Outland, Edward - Lucinda Bell	8- 2-1829	
Outland, Samuel - Rachel Scott	3-10-1826	
Negroes		
Overman, Anthony - Polly Shaw	1- 5-1828	
Overman, Cornelius - Rebekah Ford	6-24-1819	
Overman, Ephraim - Miriam Draper	12-13-1817	
Overman, John - Mary Jane ---	5-19-1825	
Negroes		
Overman, Joseph - Huldah Hill	10- ?-1811	
Overman, Reuben - Jane Spencer	10-25-1815	
Overman, Terry - Tilly Purviance	8-11-1819	
Owen, Norman - Sarah Griffin	7-25-1824	
Owens, Thomas - Mary Ann Newgate	5- 7-1828	
Paddock, Reuben - Lydia Starbuck	1- 4-1827	
Pain, John - Sarah Wilson	11- 6-1828	
Palin, Henry - Huldah Hunt	8-26-1824	
Palin, Nixon - Pennina Asher lic.	5-17-1820	
Palmer, David - Sally Pearson	10-18-1818	
Parish, Woodson - Agnes Parish	11-20-1828	
Park, John - Harriet Jobs	11-15-1821	

Parkeson, Willis - Hariet Lawman   10-21-1818
Parnell, Nathan - Mary Ballenger lic.
                                    10- 3-1827
Paxson, John - Mary Cope   11-23-1820
Pearson, Barton - Nancy Pearson   3-26-1818
Pearson, Exum - Elizabeth Ratliff   6-10-1822
Pearson, Isaac B. - Elizabeth Stroud
                                    11- 9-1823
Pearson, James - Frances Denny   3- 4-1829
Pearson, John - Anna Small   6-23-1822
Pearson (or Pierson), Thomas - Frances Shank
                                     4- 1-1825
Pearson, William - Esther Cripe   11- 3-1822
Peck, Samuel - Susannah Welsh lic.   4- 7-1818
Peden, Silas - Sarah Gott   1-15-1828
Pegg, Jesse - Phebe Clark   9- 7-1819
Pegg, John - Lydia Cloud   2-12-1829
Pemberton, Joseph - Elenor Ashley   12- ?-1813
Pemberton, Thomas - Rebecca Shipley 1-21-1821
Penland, Andrew - Sarah Ashby   8- 2-1827
Perkins, George - Agnes Allen   2-24-1829
Perry, Lewis - Catharine Milman   12-23-1824
Personett, Isaac - Phebe Parsons   12-14-1826
Personett, Israel - Charlotte Ann Holman
                            lic.   10-27-1824
Personett, Rolley - Tamer Levingston
                                     4-18-1825
Persons, Solomon - --- Rambo lic.   6- 6-1826
Petty, Daniel - Betsy Murphy   7- 4-1819
Philips, John - Mary Thomas   2-24-1828
Philips, William - Polly Scanland   12-26-1816
Phillips, Joseph - Mary Carter   7- 1-1824
Piggott, Benjamin - Deborough D. Clark
                            lic.   11-29-1821
Pitman, Eli - Hannah Reed   4-12-1829
Pitsenbarger, Abraham - Lydia Feazle
                            lic.   11-17-1829
Platts, Jesse K. - Rachel Martindale
                                     7-23-1818
Plumer, Ira - Fanny Piercy   4- 9-1823
Plummer?, John - Isabella Harvey   8-13-1811
Poak, John - Mary Walker   2-26-1829
Polly, William of Darke Co. Ohio -
   Eda Harlin   7-30-1829
Pool, John - Elizabeth Fulton   1-28-1830
Porter, David - Penninah Overman   4- 8-1819
Powel, Harper - Margaret Jones   9-29-1827
Powel, John - Peggy Hoff   1-30-1816
Powel, Reder - Elizabeth Milman   3-15-1821
Powell, James - Sarah Jessup   1-30-1822
Powell, James - Emily Hancock   5- 2-1830
Powell, Simon - Anna Arment   4- 5-1819
Powell, Thomas - Mary Palmer   3- 5-1818
Powell, William - Sarah Reeder   4-12-1821
Powers, John - Rebekah Crews   5-11-1820
Prater, Isaac - Sarah Olvy   2-26-1829
Prater, Nathan - Jane Low   3-19-1829
Prather, Jonathan - Rebekah Griffin 4-22-1819
Prevo, Malachi - Nancy Conner   11-17-1825
Prevo, Samuel - Patty Addington   1-13-1820
Price, Alexander P. - Polly Alexander
                            lic.   1- 3-1823
Price, Rice - Susanna Keesling   12-13-1821
Price, William - Jane Massey   12- 1-1824
Prichard, Abel - Elizabeth Job lic. 7-21-1823
Prichett, John - Emily Talbott   3- 4-1830
Pritchard, Samuel - Patsey Davis   6- 8-1826
Puckett, Daniel - Rebekah Cook   1-17-1822
Pugh, William - Eliza Dunham   3-20-1822

Pumphrey, Levi M. R. - Leah Somers lic.
                                    10- 4-1827
Purviance, Levi - Sophia Woods   9-24-1811
Queen, Hampton - Hannah Williams   5-11-1820
Quinn, Hiram - Hannah Reed lic.   10-25-1828
Rader, Michael - Catherine Shelly   9- 2-1819
Ragan, John - Sydney Evans   4- 9-1826
Railsback, Enoch - Nancy Fouts   11- 8-1822
Railsback, Joel - Elizabeth Fouts   2- 4-1830
Railsback, William - Mary Rhodes   4-21-1825
Raines, George - Julia Drury   2- 9-1824
Rains, James - Elizabeth Wright   12-16-1823
Ralston, Andrew - Amelia D. Street   1- 1-1823
Ralston, Richard - Rachel Prevo lic. 1- 7-1823
Rambo, Adonijah - Phebe Beeson   4- ?-1818
Rambo, Adonijah - Nancy Montgomery 10- 4-1825
Rambo, Isaac - Ann Beck   1-29-1823
Ramsey, Thomas - Mary Beck   12-16-1824
Randall, John - Lydia Sawyer lic.   4- 6-1826
   Negroes
Ransford, Henry C. - Elenor Rue   11- ?-1820
Ransford, Richard - Hester Carson   7-12-1827
Ransford, Thomas - Priscilla Rambo 12-24-1829
Rash, William - Anne Eggers   8-26-1813
Ratcliff, Joel - Rachel Adamson   12-27-1825
Ratray, Mathew - Elizabeth F. Cheesman
                                    12-29-1825
Reagan (or Ragan), Thomas - Deborah Wilcox
                                     2- 3-1826
Rector, Landy - Lavina Chryst lic. 12-27-1821
Rector, Thornton - Nancy Little   11-16-1825
Reddy, William C. - Rhoda Mull   11-18-1828
Reed, Charles F. - Sarah Black   4-11-1822
Reed, Hornwell(?) - Betty Stevens   12-19-1822
Reed, Joel - Emeline Jobs   11-22-1827
Reed, John - Mary Stump   2-22-1818
Reeder, Jonathan - Synthia Hancock   5-16-1823
Reese, Jesse - Anna Osborne   11- 5-1829
Reese, William - Elizabeth Osborne 11-25-1818
Renbarger, Phillip - Ana Williams   2-24-1820
Rennington, Jacob - Sarah Smith   4-15-1825
Reynolds, Bartlet - Polly Pitt   2- 6-1823
   Negroes
Reynolds, Charles - Polly DeMoss lic.
                                     9-15-1819
Reynolds, Milton - Orpah Crum   3- 6-1828
Reynolds, Samuel - Anna Clevenger   12-13-1827
Rhodes, Sandford - Nancy Smith   8-29-1820
Rhyn, George - Nancy Miller   10-19-1826
Richardson, Aaron - Elizabeth Shaw lic.
                                    11-11-1817
Richter, John - Melinda Finch   2-14-1828
Richter, William - Lucinda Lewis   9-18-1828
Ridge, James Jr. - Nancy Hoover   1-12-1826
Rinard, George - Catherine Ready   12- 3-1813
Rinker, John - Jane Clevenger   9-15-1826
Rippey, David - Rebekah Ann Catey   11- 1-1827
Rippy, Mathew - Jane Montgomery   8- 3-1826
Ritter, Jacob - Elizabeth Miller   10-26-1826
Ritter, Michael - Rachel Parsons   2-11-1830
Robberds, William - Jane Walker   11-16-1828
Robbins, John - Sarah Fender   10- 1-1829
Robbins (or Robins), Walter - Rhoda Owen
                                     2- 1-1824
Roberts, Jesse - Amy Cox   9- 5-1814
Roberts, John - Hannah Coffman   3-26-1821
Roberts, Joseph - Youthy Cox   3-25-1828
Roberts, Stephen - Mary Brower   5- 4-1824
Roberts, Zachariah - Ann Knipe   4-17-1823

Rockafellow, Henry - Elinor Hurst lic.
                                    1-23-1818?
Roe, Charles - Katharine Runyon   2- 7-1828
Roe, Daniel - Martha Runnion   6- 9-1828
Roe, Eli - Margaret Martindale   1-23-1820
Roe, Watson - Elenor W. Platts   11-23-1820
Roe, William - Mary Martindale   12- 4-1818
Rolans, Harlan - Susana Fender lic. 4-22-1823
Rolston, James - Elizabeth Stover   8-23-1827
Rose, John - Patsey Huffman   7-12-1825
Roysdon, William - Harriet Wandle   1-26-1823
Royster, Robert - Seypheaney Johnson
                                       8-20-1817
Ruby, William - Selah Cain   12- 7-1826
Rue, Henry - Rebecca Talbert   11-18-1819
Rumley, John - Maria Willits   7-26-1829
Rupe, Henry - Patsy Mullendore   3-18-1830
Rush, Christopher - Liddy Bunch   10-25-1821
Russel, Samuel - Nancy Smith   8- 4-1823
Russel, Zadoc - Peggy Hays   11-23-1826
Russell, John - Polly Smith   8-30-1821
Russell, Price - Anna Hays lic.   1-25-1822
Ruth (or Routh), Joseph - Letty Burroughs
                                      12-18-1825
Rutledge, Benjamin - Elizabeth Odell
                                       9- 5-1816
Sailors, Thomas - Susanna Case   12-16-1815
Samms, Benjamin - Elizabeth Vottaw lic.
                                      10-24-1827
Saunders, Aaron - Abigail Osborne   7-24-1823
Saunders, Aron - Sarah Edwards   7- 8-1830
  Edmondson on lic.
Saville, Philip - Beulah Evans   7-17-1823
Scarce, David - Rebekah Edwards lic.
                                       9-25-1828
Scarce, Samuel - Elizabeth Vanaman   3- 6-1829
Scofield, Orr - Lydia Chamness   4-14-1816
Scott, Christian - Betsy Hunt   3-11-1830
Scott, James C. - Sally Willits   2-16-1826
Scott, John - Margaret Davis   4-20-1817
Scott, John - Elizabeth Levell   11-25-1819
Scott, Thomas - Sarah Manifold   11-20-1828
Scott, William - Mary Jane Woods   12- 3-1822
Seany, Bryan - Sally Little   4-20-1817
Seany, John - Polly Martin   9-10-1815
Seany, John - Martha Chambers   8-28-1817
Seany, Owen - Martha Grimes   3-24-1825
See, John - Polly Haze   lic.   7-28-1819
Segraves, Elam - Martha Moore   1-17-1828
Sellers, Nathan - Catherine Moffit 12- 4-1817
Shank, John - Mary Ann Brown   7-23-1829
Shanks, Stephen - Jane Baker   2- 3-1829
Sharp, Findly - Elizabeth Carpenter
                         lic.   1- 8-1822
Sharp, James - Anna Howard   5- 2-1827
Sharp, John - Cynthia W. Woods   11-16-1820
Shaw, Benjamin - Aley Moore   8-13-1820
Shaw, John - Nancy Jackson   12-24-1829
Sheets, Anthony - Esther Shock   4-10-1823
Sheets, Solomon - Abigail Perry   5- 6-1826
Sheffer, Ira - Hannah Jane Smiley   8-13-1829
Sheffer, Jacob - Melinda Frazier   9-11-1828
Shelby, John - Jane Gunn   lic.   8-10-1819
Shelley, Joseph - Elizabeth Williams
                                       8-18-1814
Shelly, William - Nice Stanley   10-11-1818
Shenefelt, William - Lydia Kepner   11-24-1827
Shepler, Herman - Mary Felker   8- 2-1824
Sherrick, Jacob - Catharine Shock   1-13-1825

Shipley, Thomas - Eliza Campbell   8-21-1829
Shoemaker, Daniel - Phebe Marine   9-24-1829
Shoemaker, Henry - Edith Elliott   2-21-1822
Shoemaker, Isarel - Elizabeth Davice   3- 6-1823
Shoemaker, John - Rosanna Bailey   11- 1-1827
Shortridge, Elisha - Hester Crumb   3-11-1819
Shortridge, George - Susanna Hoff(?)
                            lic.   1- 2-1815
Shortridge, Jesse - Caty Crumb lic. 9-13-1815
Shortridge, John - Ann Crum   5-10-1821
Shortridge, William - Jane Jarrett   7- 5-1827
Showalter, John - Elizabeth Personett
                                       7-22-1830
Shugart, Zachariah - Susanna Harris   1- 4-1827
Sibley, Nimrod - Nelly Mitchel   5-31-1827
  Negroes
Silvers, David - Anne Gibson   6-11-1824
Silvers, John - Frony Kruger   5-11-1818
Silvers, Nathan - Elizabeth Gibson   12-16-1824
Silvers, Thomas T. - Mary Millman   12-25-1827
Simmons, Samuel - Amy Bunch   1-19-1821
Simonson, Van - Abigail Gray   3-27-1823
Simpson, Amos - Olive Hethcock   11-26-1823
Simpson, Joshua - Betsy Martin   8- 5-1819
Sisk, Hugh - Mary Finch   7-22-1830
Skaggs, Zebulin - Sarah Sharp   12-28-1826
Skinner, John - Volinda Griffins   4- 9-1822
Skinner, Joseph - Diadema Elliott   10-29-1821
Slater, John - Sarah Olliver   6-26-1818
Sleeth, Robert - Mary Camplin   5-29-1821
Small, Amos - Rachel Hiatt   1- 1-1822
Small, Jesse - Mary Cory   11-21-1826
Small, John - Mary Lenington   11- 2-1826
Small, Nathan - Rachel Hawkins   12- 8-1825
Small, Samuel - Abigail Stafford   11-13-1819
Smelser, Adam - Sarah Banks   7-20-1823
Smith, Abraham - Rachel Stover lic.   1- 9-1829
Smith, Benjamin - Delighty Russell   2-18-1818
Smith, Charles - Letta Gillam lic.   9- 9-1818
Smith, Charles - Nancy Langley 11[12]-29-1824
Smith, Frederick - Nancy Freeman   2-18-1830
Smith, George - Nancy Conner lic.   8-10-1829
Smith, George - Clarissa Outland   5-22-1830
Smith, Henry - Polly Coble   lic.   10-18-1826
Smith, Jacob - Esther Hoover lic.   12-25-1824
Smith, James - Delilah Addington   4- 1-1819
Smith, James - Mary Massay lic.   12-15-1821
Smith, Joel - Catharine Wrightsman
                            lic.   5- 5-1825
Smith, John - Abigail Cowen   7-23-1812
Smith, John - Sally Meek   2-15-1816
Smith, Lewis - Sarah Garret   4-19-1825
Smith, Oliver H. - Mary Crumbfield   11- 6-1821
Smith, Solomon - Anna Haggarty   12-16-1827
Smith, Thomas - Esther Hiatt   2-10-1822
Smith, William - Martha Dewey lic.   6-16-1818
Smith, William C. - Phebe King   7-17-1828
Smithey (Smiley?), Eli - Mary Willis 5-12-1822
Snethen, Bela - Lydia Worl   7-25-1825
Snider, David - Evy Miller   10-22-1817
Snider, Michael - Nancy Summers   10-24-1816
Snider, Michael J. - Rachel Dawson   10- 8-1827
Spahr, John - Margaret Russell   6-29-1828
Spahr, Samuel - Jane Lamb   3-29-1827
Speakes, Charles - Mary Holloway   3-20-1829
Spencer, Joel - Elizabeth Hiare lic. 6-29-1822
Spencer, Joseph - Jinny Ring lic.   7-16-1813
Spencer, Michael - Elizabeth Miner   5-25-1815
Spencer, Rozzel - Mary Nelson   2- 2-1821
Spencer, William - Lydia McComus   1- 2-1817

Spiva, John - Losada Allred	3- 5-1829
Spray, Abner - Nayomy Lamb	9-28-1820
Spray, William - Dinah Mendenhall	6-23-1819
Spray, William - Elizabeth Lamb	10-17-1826
Springer, Barnabas - Maryann Foal	
lic.	1-20-1824
Springer, Ezekial - Betsy Thompson	
lic.	11- 5-1822
Springer, Matthew - Elizabeth Dobbs	
	2-20-1820
Springer, William - Sarah Buck	8- 6-1829
Stanley, Jeremiah - Dianna Esteb	5-27-1819
Stanley, Jonathan - Ann W. Perkins	4- 8-1830
Stanley, Thomas - Catherine Rinker	8-21-1819
Stanley, William - Nancy Brewer	5-11-1826
Starbuck, Andrew R. - Avis Garner	3- 2-1826
Starbuck, Edward - Judith Gardner	1-26-1823
Starbuck, John - Sally Pile	10- 6-1828
Starbuck, Paul - Lydia Wheeler	9- 8-1825
Starbuck, Robert - Hannah Addleman	2-12-1828
Starbuck, William - Nancy Cain	12-19-1821
Starlin, Thomas - Frances Porter	7-27-1822
Starr, Jesse - Mary Fall	12-11-1817
Starr, Jonathan - Elizabeth Moore	10-28-1824
Starrett, Robert - Margaret Montgomery	
	12-21-1820
Starrett, Samuel - Mary Russell	9-13-1825
Steagall, Jonathan - Mary Craner	11- 2-1826
Steagall, Lewis - Frances Case	3- 9-1826
Stephens, Robert C. - Caron Forkner	
	12- 6-1829
Stephenson, Joseph - Sally Martin	9-13-1811
Sterne, Ephraim - Anna Carver	11- 7-1827
Stevens, John - Martha Graham	7-23-1827
Stevens, Joseph - Anna Stevens	2-27-1821
Stevens, Spencer - Sarah Carter	
lic.	5- 7-1828
Stevens, William - Mary Fouts	5-20-1819
Stevenson, Lawrence M. - Lydia T. Evans	
	3-24-1825
Stidham, John P. - Terrese Hunt	8-12-1829
Stidham, Thomas - Amelia Alexander	8- 8-1825
Stiggleman, Philip - Susan Forkner	11-12-1823
Stillwell, Jeremiah - Candis West	12-28-1820
Stilwell, James - Mary Morgan	6-17-1820
Stinson, Frederick - Lydia Eastridge	
	11-29-1827
Stinson, George - Sally Waymire	3- 4-1829
Stinson, Samuel - Elizabeth Worl	3-31-1822
Stokes, John - Letitia Allen	1-31-1830
Stonebraker, George - Jane Brown	8- 4-1830
Stonebraker, John - Betsey Odom	
lic.	5- 2-1826
Stout, --- - --- Taylor	4- 1-1819
Stout, Isaac - Lydia Garner lic.	2- 9-1828
Strattan, Daniel - Eliza Jenkins	11-27-1826
Stratton, Levi - Ruth Crews	6-13-1822
Stratton, Zimri - Elizabeth Baker	10- 4-1827
Streit, James - Jane Jordan	3-23-1826
Stroud, Joshua - Lear Palmer	1-12-1823
Strouder, John - Martha Lasiter	
lic.	9- 8-1826
Stuart, Absalom - Betsy Bulla	11- 4-1818
Stubbs, Elisha - Elizabeth Townsend	
lic.	9- 4-1819
Study, David - Lydia Way	2-12-1824
Study, Henry - Sarah Lomax	4-15-1830
Study, Joseph - Hannah Way	2- 2-1826
Study, William - Harriet Steagall	8- 8-1826

Stump, Henry - Sarah Canada	1-31-1822
Stump, John - Anna Sutherland	3-14-1816
Stump, Joseph - Mary Reed	5-10-1819
Stump, Leonard - Nancy Louder	6-21-1816
Sulser, James - Nancy Weaver	4- 6-1824
Summers, Calvin - Sarah Kidwell	11- ?-1819
Summers, John - Nancy Harlan lic.	6-29-1814
Summers, John - Catherine Crumb lic.	8- 4-1818
Sumpter, Martin - Elizabeth Ridgeway	
	12-24-1826
Sutherland, Isaac - Lydia Woodward	9- 2-1819
Sutherland, Jacob - Martha Selgrove	6- 3-1824
Sutherland, John - Jane Brown	11-30-1814
Sutton, Henry - Eliza Freeman	5-17-1827
Sutton, Isaac - Alice Watts	7-26-1825
Swafford, Joseph - Margaret Knipe	3-17-1826
Swafford, William Jr. - Rachel Jackson	
	8-17-1826
Swain, Francis - Rachel Baker	11-25-1828
Mary Baker on lic.	
Swain, Obed - Mahala Boggs	11-12-1829
Swaney, Hugh - Maria Scott	2-25-1830
Swearingen, Burton - Polly Cox	6-18-1829
Swearingin, Zebedie - Lillus Owens (or Owen)	
	8- 6-1829
Swisher, John - Amelia Wright	8-30-1827
Swisher, William - Emily Wharton	6-18-1829
Swope, Asbury - Emily Roberts lic.	1-28-1829
Swope, George - Mary Ann Branson	9- 3-1828
Syms, Stephen - Betsy Sanders lic.	9-15-1825
Tatem, James - Becky Chambers	2-10-1814
Taylor, James - Charlotte McLean	3-27-1812
Taylor, James - Anna Alberts	1- 7-1818?
Taylor, James W. - Esther Fall	6-17-1813
Taylor, John H. - Nancy A. Tomlinson	
	12-10-1829
Taylor, Thomas - Sarah Alberts	9-18-1821
Teagle, Joseph - Ruth Bond	12- 8-1819
Teagle, Thomas P. - Rachel Bond	10-24-1817
Tharp, Alfred - Rebekah Moorman	4- 2-1819
Tharp, Jacob A. - Margaret Hendrix	12-20-1827
Tharp, Jeremiah - Sarah Marine	1-10-1828
Thomas, Jonathan - Mary Mendenhall	9- 7-1826
Tharp, William - Eleanor Bolin lic.	4-28-1830
Thomas, Henley - Polly Hunt	3-22-1827
Thomas, John - Peggy Whitinger	11-20-1817
Thomas, Phinehas - Anna Conn	3-12-1818
Thomas, Stephen - Margaret Clark	3-18-1819
Thompson, Daniel - Elenor Richardson	
	11-16-1819
Thompson, James - Mary Vinnedge	3-25-1824
Thompson, John - Hannah Braden	3-11-1821
Thompson, John - Mary Harrison	1-24-1828
Mary Thompson on return	
Thompson, John - Sarah Edwards	10-15-1829
Thompson, Mark - Jane Thomas	12- 3-1826
Thompson, William - Sarah Braden	2- 9-1822
Thompson, William - Calista Fox	2- 8-1827
Thompson, William - Nancy Vinnedge	2-18-1830
Thornbrough, Dempsey - Jane Mills	12-22-1822
Thornbrough, John - Eleanor Nordike	2- 3-1829
Thornbrough, Joseph - Polly Brockus	
lic.	2-16-1819
Thornbrough, Joseph - Mary Nordyke	1- 5-1824
Thornbrough, Walter - Rebekah Comer	9-17-1827
Thornburg, Absolum - Tacy Hague	1- 9-1823
Thornburgh, Jacob - Betsy Hoover	11-17-1825
Thornburgh, Jesse - Margrett Warren	5-13-1822
Thornton, Levi - Catharine Black	10-23-1818

Thornton, Thomas - Eleanor Brady
      lic.   10-15-1825
Thrale, Leonard - Elizabeth Fowler 9-25-1817
Tingler, John - Sarah L. Sacket 12- 8-1825
Tiry, Hiram - Nancy Moore   3- 2-1825
Toney, Isaac - Rose Jackson lic. 2- 1-1826
Toney, James - Sally Lybrook   10-26-1820
Townsend, Jonathan - Polly Clawson 9-28-1814
Trammel, William - Synthia Alexander
                6-20-1827
Treadway, John - Sally Vanbuskirk 12-23-1821
Trimble, Daniel - Sally Henson 3-13-1814
Trousdail, William - Mary Bishop 2-24-1825
Troxel, Daniel - Elizabeth Montgomery
      lic.   8-12-1818
Troxal, Daniel - Nancy Tiry   3- 2-1825
Troxell, George - Eliza Sterne 1- 1-1826
Trusty, Temple - Sarah Justice 2-10-1820
Tucker, George - Mary Conner   5- 2-1827
Tucker, James Jr. - Eliza Russell
      lic.   6-24-1823
Tucker, William - Eliza Kenneday 10-19-1823
Tullis, Arthur C. - Mary Silvers 4-21-1825
Turner, Jeptha - Martha Garr   1-14-1830
Turner, John - Katharine Pope 12-26-1828
Turner, Samuel - Lydia Starbuck 10-13-1825
Turner, William - Nancy McConnahay 1- 1-1830
Tweeday, Samuel - Nancy Skidmore 2-15-1821
Tyner, James - Zillah Reed   3-10-1817
Tyre, Elijah - Rebekah Miles   5- 8-1828
Ulrich, Samuel - Polly B. Irvin 3-28-1830
Underhill, John - Catharine Hedrick 2-20-1823
Underhall, Obadiah - Lucinda Biggs 8- 3-1826
Underhill, William - Ruth Mathers 4-23-1822
Underwood, Lewis - Kesiah Bond 10- 9-1817
Unthank, Jonathan - Rachel Williams 3-17-1830
Valentine, Jacob - Levina Lewis 11-13-1828
Valentine, James - Sarah Frazer 7-25-1828
Vanbuskirk, George - Sarah Helm 12-14-1826
Vanbuskirk, John - Dulsena Huff 6-13-1821
Vanbuskirk, John - Jane Powell 1-19-1822
VanBuskirk, Joseph - Polly Hoff 7-30-1816
VanBuskirk, William - Mary Reese 11-12-1828
Vannuise, Cornelius - Matilda Harrison
                2- 9-1827
VanNuys (Vanise), William - Salina Harrison
                4-23-1829
Vantreas, Jacob - Nancy Knox   12-16-1828
Veal, Andrew - Delia Kendle   6-27-1822
Veal, Enos - Sally Platts   4-20-1817
Veal, Enos, Jr. - Mary Davis   6- 2-1825
Verdemon, Morgan - Elizabeth V. Walker
                8-24-1813
Vicker, Abraham - Susana Holtsclaw 3-23-1822
Vinnedge, Alfred - Sarah Souders 2-21-1830
Vinson, Sullivan - Sarah Morris 4-28-1825
Virgil, Erastus - Sophia Hancock 6-20-1816
Waddell, Charles - Selah Nutter 8-22-1816
Waddell, James - Anne Cox   9-28-1814
Waddell, Robert - Lovina Nutter 11-16-1813
Wade, John - Dorca Prevo   1- 1-1818
Wade, Robert - Phebe Ann Kibbey 3- 2-1824
Waggoner, Bazaleel - Rachel Key 10- 4-1827
Waldron, Ebenezer - Eliza Jones 3-13-1830
Walker, James - Betsy Junken   1- 1-1828
Walker, Jess - Martha Roberts lic. 11- 8-1828
Walker, Samuel - Rebekah Dougan 10-30-1817
Wallace, James - Margaret Cooper 4- 3-1828
Wallace, James J. - Mary Mills 6-24-1830

Wallace, John - Mary Banks   3-16-1815
Walling, Samuel B. - Jane Lacey 9-21-1826
"Is there a wretch so cold, so rude
  So partial to a single life;
  Who would have felt no gratitude
  Had Heaven sent him such a wife?"
           John Finley
Walls, Matthew - Barbara Cain 5-18-1811
Waltz, Jacob - Elizabeth Luse   7- 2-1829
Ward, David - Rachel Martindale 11- 2-1820
Ward, Enos - Mary Esteb   5- 6-1826
Wardel, Benjamin L. - Sarah Smith 2-16-1827
Warman, Henry - Pheby Ginn   2- 1-1821
Warman, Henry - Nancy Parsons 4-30-1826
Warren, Azariah - Elizabeth Fruits 10-25-1827
Warren, David - Jane Hays   3- 1-1820
Warren, Henry - Margaret Lennington 5-13-1824
Warren, James - Sophia Gallien 11- 3-1814
Watkins, Diver - Jane Turner 11-19-1829
Watkins, William - Sarah Smith 3-19-1829
Watson, James - Milicent Albertson
      lic.   1-21-1825
Watson, William - Nancy Rue   4- 7-1811
Watts, John - Patsey Galbraith 6-15-1826
Watts, Richard - Sarah Edwards 10-11-1827
Way, Henry - Phebe Macy   2-11-1821
Way, Henry - Rachel Manlove 12-29-1816
Way, Joel - Eliza Schuyley 11-20-1828
Way, Jonathan - Sally Godfrey 4- 1-1830
Way, Thomas - Tamer Massey 10-30-1823
Way, William - Elizabeth Palmer 5-14-1822
Waymire, Noah - Mary Howard 10-15-1829
Weaver, Daniel - Magdalene Fryar 12- 3-1829
Weeks, James - Casandra Crampton 2-25-1830
Weeks, William - Mary Ann Freestone 2-21-1830
West, James - Elizabeth Underhill
      lic.   1- 4-1825
West, Jonathan - Sara Brock   4-24-1823
West, Thomas - Mary Benbow lic. 6- 9-1816
Wharton, Rice - Nancy McKee   7- 6-1820
Wharton, Samuel - Nancy McKee 12-23-1824
Wheeler, Michael - Maria Potts 6- 6-1824
Whitaker, James - Rebekah Starling 2- 1-1827
Whitaker, John - Nancy Williams 7-22-1830
Whitaker, Thomas - Elizabeth McGogan 9-28-1817
Whitchel(?), John - Catherine Hidy 3-25-1822
White, Aaron - Morning Lasiter lic. 11-25-1826
White, James - Jane Boswell   9-20-1814
White, John - Delilah Boswell 8-12-1816
White, Joseph - Alice Clawson 11-20-1821
White, Nathan - Betsey Cook   5-19-1825
White, William - Sarah Thornbrough 8-10-1815
Whitehead, John - Caty Brown   8- 4-1812
Whitehead, Lazarus - Levona Osborn 1-24-1822
Whiteman, William - Catherine Emert 11-20-1817
Whitinger, Jacob - Sarah Howell 7- 1-1830
Whitman, Jacob - Mary Farlow 12- 5-1816
Whitsinger, William - Mary Whitsinger
                4-12-1821
Wickard, John - Eliza Kratzer 7-22-1820
Wickersham, William - Idema Lloyd 12-28-1826
Widows, Joseph - Elizabeth Morris 9-30-1826
Widows, Uriah - Eleanor Hague 12-25-1828
Widup, Thomas - Elizabeth Lancaster 9-10-1819
Wilcox, James - Mahala Roe   6-19-1817
Wilcox, Joseph - Jane Brown   1-22-1824
Wiles, Aaron - Jane Scott   4-30-1829
Wiles, John - Jemima Pierce   1-21-1830
Wiles, Thomas - Lydia Williams 2- 3-1818

Wiley, Samuel - Kesiah Sullivan
                lic.   3- 3-1819
Willcoxen, John - Delilah Burges
                lic. 11-26-1823
Willcutt, David-Mary Marine   4-20-1826
Willets, Eli - Harriet Drury   4-13-1826
Willets, Elisha - Sally Huff   9-27-1818
Willets, Elisha - Mary Hannah   1-20-1820
Willets, Enos - Elizabeth Wright 5-22-1825
Willets, James - Lydia Jobe   1-18-1821
Willets, Robert - Sally Beard   2- 1-1820
Willets, William W. - Mary Fix 9- 8-1825
Williams, Benjamin - Margaret Bennet
                   12-20-1817
Williams, Charles - Emilia Lamb
                lic. 6-12-1824
Williams, Charles - Lydia Willitts 1-20-1826
Williams, James - Sarah Allen   1-13-1825
Williams, James C. - Margaret Pritchard
                   7- 2-1826
Williams, Jesse - Polly Hart   8-20-1820
Williams, Jesse - Elizabeth Crampton
                  12-28-1826
Williams, Jesse - Rosanna Newton 7- 1-1827
Williams, John - Polly Allen   3-23-1828
Williams, John P. - Sarah Hetherington
                   5-21-1822
Williams, Jonathan - Jane Lenington
                lic. 1-13-1826
Williams, Joseph - Martha Roberts 4- 7-1825
Williams, Josiah - Sarah Davenport 10-12-1826
Williams, Lemuel - Milcah Beauchamp
                  10-25-1818
Williams, Nathan - Margaret Adamson 2-15-1818
Williams, Samuel - Mary Ann Atkins 2-13-1825
Williams, William - Elizabeth Ralston
                   5-22-1820
Williams, William - Katharine Hoover
                  1- 1-1828
Williams, William - Lucretia Starbuck
                  2-28-1830
Williams, William - Rachel Speakes 6-20-1830
Williams, William R. - Rebekah Davison
  (or Davidson)   1-31-1828
Williams, Zadock - Anna Marine   4-10-1822
Willis, David - Lydia Coggshell 4-26-1829
Willis, Jesse - Amelia Stanford 7-16-1818
Willits, Cyrus - Mahala Mayes   3- 5-1829
Willits, Elias - Elisa Kibby   10-10-1822
Willits, Henry - Ann Brown   12-23-1829
Willits, Joshua - Eliza Willits 3- 8-1827

Willits, Lot - Sarah McMullen   6-15-1827
Willits, Nathan - Aseneth Schooly 7- 7-1830
Willits, William - Chariah Drury 4- 1-1830
Wilson, Griner - Ellenor Blair Walker
                   3-17-1814
Wilson, Jacob - Rachel Wilson   8-15-1816
Wilson, John - Ann Calloway   9- 7-1823
Wilson, Joshua - Susanna Cobble
                lic. 1-30-1818?
Wilson, Milow - Sarah Coy   3-22-1821
Wilson, Morgan - Elenor Meek   2- 6-1817
Wilson, Rheubun - Elizabeth Murffee 1-10-1823
Wilson, Robert - Nancy Deake (Drake?)
                  4-28-1812
Wilson, Robert - Nancy Briggs   3-28-1818
Wingfield, Bazel - Cynthia Burroughs
                  11-27-1825
Wood, Benjamin - Meca Boon   5- 5-1819
Wood, George W. - Agness Fall   1-14-1813
Wood, John - Polly Connoway   12-26-1813
Woodkirk, John - Rebecca Holman lic. 1- 1-1821
Woods, James - Susan Shelby   2- 2-1820
Woods, John P. - Peggy Alexander 2-27-1823
Woods, William M. - Maryan Horton 11- 7-1823
Woodward, Aaron - Sarah Cannaday 12-11-1823
Woodward, Asabel - Kitty Hollet 10- 1-1815
Woody, Joseph - Rebekah Dwiggins 3-29-1827
Woofter, John - Frances Bunch   4- 8-1824
Worl, Robert - Phebe Williams   2-19-1817
Worl, Robert - Elizabeth Dougherty 3-11-1830
Worrel, Milton - Elizabeth Hoover 2-28-1830
Wright, Aaron - Ruhamah Sellers 10-17-1827
Wright, Absalom - Susanna Baldwin 4-24-1828
Wright, Alfies - Elizabeth Williams 8-30-1821
Wright, Cyrus - Marian Cosand 10- 7-1824
Wright, Eli - Betsey Nelson   8-25-1814
Wright, James - Amelia Crouch   7-25-1820
Wright, James - Diana Wright   8- 2-1827
Wright, James H. - Rebekah Evans 11-11-1826
Wright, Jesse - Mary Brown   2-10-1825
Wright, Ralph - Usley White   4-27-1815
Wright, William - Nancy Malsbey 7- 6-1826
Wyatt, Barton - Sally Miller   7-12-1821
Wyatt, David T. - Nancy Hunt   8- 1-1816
Wyatt, Joseph - Nancy Esteb   9- 7-1819
Wymer, Henry - Synthia Scott   12- 6-1818
Young, Jacob - Rachel Pearcy   12-21-1826
Zeeck, Joseph M. - Mariah Street 12-20-1827
Zeek (Zeck), Adam - Elsey Williams 8-25-1825
Zeek, Daniel - Hannah Moore   11-16-1826
Zeek (Zick), John - Phebe Ann Bonine 6- 4-1829

CARROLL COUNTY OLD SETTLERS

     Prior to the organization of county historical societies, the old settlers' associations which were organized in some of the counties in Indiana played an important part in recording the early history and settlement of the state. Two of the earliest of these associations were those organized in Marion County in 1854 and in Carroll County in 1855. Unfortunately the registers of the Marion County association have not been found but the newspapers devoted considerable space to the meetings. The registers of the Carroll County Association and the reminiscences of those present are preserved in James H. Stewart, <u>Recollections of the Early Settlement of Carroll County, Indiana</u> (Cincinnati, 1872).

     Residents of Carroll County who had settled there prior to the year 1831 were invited to meet at the courthouse in Delphi on June 9, 1855, for the purpose of "spending a <u>social day</u> in reviewing the scenes of the olden time; and also with a view of forming a society to perpetuate the early history of the county." On the day appointed the following settlers gave the secretary their name, birthplace, age in 1855, and date of arrival in Carroll County:

Name	Birthplace	Age	Date	Name	Birthplace	Age	Date
Archer, John	Ohio	40	1831	Jackson, Isaac	Va.	40	1827
Barr, John	Ohio	47	1831	Little, John	N.C.	66	1826
Baum, David	Pa.	50	1825	McCain, Daniel	Ohio	55	1826
Burntrager, Andrew	Va.	55	1829	McCain, William	Ohio	52	1828
Conklin, Noble	Ohio	48	1830	McCord, William	Va.	59	1827
Cox, Joseph	Ky.	37	1829	McDowell, James	N.C.	69	1826
Ewing, John M.	Pa.	58	1827	Milroy, John P.	Ind.	35	1826
Givins, James F.	Ind.	28	1827	Odell, James	Ind.	44	1825
Givins, Wm. B.	Va.	37	1827	Porter, Adam	Va.	50	1829
Gresham, Sam. D.	Va.	49	1830	Robbins, Isaac	Ohio	39	1828
Gillam, John M.	Pa.	69	1829	Robinson, Abner	Ky.	54	1824
Gillam, John W.	Ind.	44	1829	Royster, George	Ind.	29	1830
Gillam, Thos. Sr.	Pa.	68	1829	Stansel, Enoch	Ohio	49	1830
Graham, Henry M.	Ind.	38	1829	Stewart, James H.	Ky.	46	1830
Gregg, Aaron	Ohio	53	1830	Stirlin, Thomas	Pa.	54	1825
Gresham, Sam. D.	Va.	49	1830	Wilson, Isaac	Ind.	24	--
Hughes, Wm.	Va.	68	1829	Wilson, John D.	Va.	26	1829

On June 14, 1856, the Old Settlers Association met again. In addition to many of those who were present the year before, the following persons enrolled as members giving their birthplace, age, an date of arrival in Carroll County:

Name	Birthplace	Age	Date	Name	Birthplace	Age	Date
Adkinson, Isam	Va.	77	1826	Kite, Michael	Tenn.	49	1831
Allen, William	Ohio	32	1829	Milroy, Martha	Pa.	70	1826
Baker, Daniel	Va.	76	1834	More, Samuel	Va.	56	1832
Ball, Amos	Ohio	31	1830	Royster, Phenia	Ky.	57	1830
Ball, Jacob	Ohio	36	1830	Royster, Robert D.	Va.	68	1830
Ball, James	Ohio	42	1830	Sandifur, Noah	S.C.	58	1832
Ball, Nancy Ann	Pa.	66	1830	Slane, Archibald	Va.	--	--
Baum, Daniel Jr.	Ohio	41	1825	Stirlin, Fanny	Ohio	52	1826
Beckner, John	Va.	63	1829	Thayer, Dan. V.	N.Y.	36	1831
Cox, Enoch	N.J.	72	1829	Thayer, Joshua	Ind.	31	--
Crooks, William	Ky.	--	--	Thompson, Hamilton	Ky.	48	1827
Elston, Jonas	Ky.	55	1832	Vandeventer, Danl. F.	N.Y.	59	1827
Hanna, John M. C.	S.C.	55	1832	Vandeventer, Christopher	N.Y.	51	1829
Hoffman, Solomon	Va.	38	1830	Williams, Cornelius	Va.	68	1830
Holmes, Samuel	Ireland	80	1833	Young, William M.	Ohio	38	1829
Holt, Vine	Ky.	42	1829				

In 1857 the following persons registered their name, birthplace, age, and date of arrival:

Name	Birthplace	Age	Date	Name	Birthplace	Age	Date
Angell, Charles	Ind.	35	1825	Hance, William	Ky.	62	1828
Armstrong, Franklin G.	Ind.	34	1829	Lenon, Daniel H.	Ohio	44	1829
Ballard, John B.	N.Y.	52	1825	Lenon, John	Ohio	36	1829
Barns, William A.	Ohio	46	1831	Merkle, George	Pa.	52	1832
Dewey, Joel H.	Ind.	32	1827	Milroy, Robert H.	Ind.	41	1826
Frazer, Martha G.	Ind.	26	--	Newman, Joseph H.	N.C.	60	1831

At the Old Settlers' fifth meeting on August 14, 1858, the following additional members were enrolled:

Name	Birthplace	Age	Date	Name	Birthplace	Age	Date
Brown, Aston L.	Tenn.	28	1833	Holt, Editha C.	N.Y.	33	1834
Brown, Cassandra	Va.	53	1833	Kuns, George	Ohio	--	1827
Brown, James	Tenn.	61	1833	Lenon, Samuel	Ohio	29	1829
Buford, William H.	Ky.	52	1832	McCain, Samuel	Carroll Co.	24	
Burns, Emeline	Ky.	--	1834	Milroy, James W.	Carroll Co.	30	
Carson, William C.	Tenn.	31	1834	Odell, Sarah	Ohio	49	1836
Curtner, John	Tenn.	37	1831	Patterson, Lemuel	Ala.	32	1832
Dale, Mary	Parke Co.		1832	Patterson, Malinda	Va.	32	1832
Dugan, Mirinda	Ohio	--	--	Phelps, Ambrose	N.Y.	58	1834
Dunkle, Mary	Ind.	30	--	Phelps, Charlotte	N.Y.	46	1827
Graham, Milton R.	Ind.	31	1829	Ramey, Nancy	Wash. Co.		1826
Graham, Sarah	Carroll Co.	33		Robinson, Sarah	E. Carroll Co.		--
Greenup, Henry H.	Ky.	40	1832	Robinson, Sarah	Ohio	60	1825
Greenup, John	Ky.	41	1832	Rohrbaugh, Israel	Va.	31	1828
Greenup, Louisa	Ky.	--	1832	Stauffer, Matilda	Ind.	35	1826
Greenup, Saml. G.	Ky.	39	1832	Williamson, Austin	Ohio	33	1830
Griffith, Jane	Ky.	63	1837				

In 1859 the following enrolled their names as members, giving age and birthplace:

Ballard, Susanna	Ohio	51	1825	M'Cully, Anna	Ohio	33	1835
Berkshire, Eliz.	Ohio	--	--	M'Cully, Hugh R.	Tenn	38	1833
Burntrager, Mary	N.J.	50	1829	Malcom, George	Va.	69	1831
Davidson, Margaret	Pa.	62	1835	Phelps, Rhoda	Conn.	59	1834
Davidson, Robert	Pa.	64	1835	Robinson, Ann C.	Carroll Co.	23	
Evans, John F.	Ohio	30	1834	Robinson, Lydia	Carroll Co.	20	
Fouts, George S.	Ohio	54	1834	Stansel, Elmira	Ohio	50	1832
Gregg, Elizabeth	Pa.	55	1830	Thompson, Thomas	Ky.	47	1831
M'Cain, Joseph	Ohio	62	1826	Williamson, Anna	Pa.	56	1830
M'Cain, Magdalena	Ohio	53	1826	Williamson, David	Pa.	57	1830
				Zook, George	Ohio	37	1828

The following persons were admitted as members at the meeting on August 25, 1860;

Armstrong, Mary J.	Ohio	29	--	M'Cain, Abigail	Pa.	53	1828
Barns, Edward M.	Carroll Co.	22		McDonald, Mary	Carroll Co.	24	
Barns, James H.	Carroll Co.	24		Martin, Mary E.	Carroll Co.	--	
Bragunier, Eliz.	Pa.	65	1836	Milroy, Matilda A.	Ohio	33	1830
Griffith, James	Carroll Co.	26		Sherfey, Lucretia	Vt.		1836
Grimes, Samuel	Md.	54	1835	Smith, Elizabeth	Pa.	--	1836
Hubbard, Nancy	Vt.	69	1833	Vandeventer, Geo.	Carroll Co.	--	
Kirkpatrick, Amanda	Ind.	--	--	Wharton, Ann	Pa.	40	1837
Kirkpatrick, James	Ind.		1836	Wharton, John W.	Pa.	48	1837
Lyon, Abigail	N.Y.	45	1833	Wilson, Harvey	Carroll Co.	25	
Lyon, Ann	Ohio	34	1829				

Additional names were added to the roll each year as the Association continued to meet.

DUBOIS COUNTY WILLS, 1841-1851

Compiled from microfilm of Dubois County Will Records, Book I, pp. 1-52, in Genealogy Division, Indiana State Library. The film was very difficult to read making the spelling of names uncertain.

ALLEN, BARNET. Will dated 11-17-1846; proved 12-5-1846. Heirs: sons, Barnet and Henry. Executor: Thomas Pride of Pike Co. Witnesses: Joel Strong, Steven M. Hopkins. Dubois County Will Records, Book I, pp. 18-19.

ALLEN, LARKEN S. Will dated 3-30-1846; proved 5-30-1846. Heirs: brother James Guelpin Allen. Executor: same. Witnesses: Andrew B. Spradly and Joseph Greenaway. pp. 17-18.

ARMSTRONG, GEORGE. Will dated 7-23-1844; proved 11-9-1844. Heirs: wife Elizabeth; sons, George W. and Madison; daughters, Nancy Armstrong, Elizabeth Anderson, Jane Niblack, Peggy Hopkins. Witnesses: John Armstrong and Abraham Card. p. 13.

BECKWERMENT, BERNARD WILLIAM. Will dated Feb. 1850; proved 5-2-1850. Heirs: wife Anna Maria; sons, Johann Bernard(eldest), Bernard Wilhelm. Witnesses: John C. Hoffman, John B. Beckerment. p. 33.

CORN, ADDISON. Will dated 9-6-1844; proved 10-1 or 7(?)-1844. Heirs: brother Joseph, and sister Susannah, plus other brothers and sisters not specifically names. Executors: Joseph and Jessey Corn. Witnesses: David Marchand and Isaac Harris. pp. 14-15.

CUMMINS, JACKSON. Will dated 9-24-1841; date of probate not given. Heirs: wife Mathelda, and 3 children, Patty, Thomas H. B., and Sinthean. Witnesses: Benjamin T. Goodman, Thomas Cummins, James C. Batz. pp. 6-7.

EDMONSTON, NANCY. Will dated 1-4-1844; proved 2-12-1844. Heirs: nieces, Rachel Hannah and Nancy Edmonston; brothers, Bazel B., Enoch, Benjamin R., William, James, Archibald, Ninian; sister, Dorothy Taylor. Executor: Benjamin R. Edmonston. Witnesses: John S. Martin, Harrison Blazman(?), Michal----not ligible. p. 10.

ENGERT, GEORGE ADAM. Will dated 4-10-1845; proved 5-19,1851(?). Heirs: wife Ludwina Engert formerly Hertz. Witnesses: Andrew Baudendistel, John J. Arkleder(?), Fredrich Gasser. Proved by George A. Lepper. p. 41

GERKIN, PAUL. Will dated 9-2-1843; proved 11-16-1847. Heirs: wife Margaret; sons, John Henry and Henry; daughter Anna Margaret. Witnesses: Herman Behrens, Henry Hastedt, W. G. Helfrich. pp. 21-22

GRAHAM, WILLIAM C. Will dated 3-4-1842; no record of probate. Heirs: wife Martha; daughter Helen, a minor; brother Robert M. Holds land in partnership with brother John A. Graham. Instructs that marker be erected at grave of father and mother in Warrick Co., near Boonville, and Methodist meeting house be erected where they are buried. pp. 4-5.

HACKER, JOHN E. Will dated 7-6-1850; proved 11-5-1851. Heirs: wife Therisa, and children (names not given). Executor: wife. Witnesses: William Batz, Stephen Geiger, John B. Melchior. pp. 42-43.

HAHN, ANDREW & MAGDALEN, his wife. Oral will dated 3-23-1846. No record of probate. Heirs: sons, Sebastian, Lewis, Martin (youngest), Florenz (been absent six years and bequeathed $5.00); daughters, Rosina, Catharine, Mary (youngest). Witnesses: Sebastian and Lewis Hahn (two sons who are of age), Bernard Merkel, Lorance Gail, Jacob Alles. Translated from German by Rev. Joseph Kundek 1-4-1848. pp. 24-25

HANGER, DAVID. Will dated 6-8-1851(?); proved 6-26-1851(?). Heir: wife Rebecca. Witnesses: Allen & Thomas Fleming, Eirson Pearson. p. 32.

HEMMER, FREDRICH. Will dated 12-7-1850; proved 2-4-1851. Heirs: wife Christina Fredrika; sons, Fredrich William, Herman Fredrich, & Fredrich Henry; daughters, Fredricka Elizabeth & Maria Elizabeth Hemmer. Witnesses: William Katterjohn & ----(not legible). pp. 36-37

HEMMER, JOHN WILLIAM. Will dated 7-25-1850; proved 8-26-1850. Heirs: wife Maria Elizabeth; sons, Henry and Fredrick W. Witnesses: Fredrick Stackhouse, Hermann H. Venneman, Gerard Rack(?). p. 31.

HOFFMAN, JOHN LORENZ. Will dated 7-13-1846; proved 7-1-1850. Heirs: wife Margaret; sons, George and Frederick. Proved by George Grossman and John Cradle. pp. 34-37.

HOPPENZAHUS, GERALD & ELIZABETH. Will dated 4-25-1844; no probate record. Elizabeth had received from her former husband George Lambert certain land which she wished her present husband Gerald to receive if living at time of her death; if he was not living it was to go to the first one of his brother Bernhard's sons that should come from Germany to claim it. Gerald wished his wife to receive his property if she was living at the time of his death; otherwise to go to the first one of his brother's children who should come to claim it. Executor: Gerhard Herman Gerstang. Witnesses: George A. Lepper & John Scofener. pp. 11-12.

HOWARD, LITLE. Will dated 5-18-1851; proved 10-11-1851. Heirs: wife (name not given); sons, Samuel, John, Isaac, Robert, Westley; daughters, Ann, Julia, Eliza, Maria, Alice. Witnesses: Francis F. Spencer and William H. Taylor. pp. 48-50.

HURST, ISSIDOR. Will dated 11-16-1843. Not legible.

HURST, JOSEPH. Will made on Steamer "Fashion" on Mississippi River, 7-10-1851; proved 8-6-1851. Heir: to brother, Bernard, of Dubois County, a leather purse said to contain $1,490 in gold; also $1,600 in bank in St. Louis; also note of James Lick of San Francisco for $9,310. Witnesses: J. B. Hatch of New Albany, Charles McCoffay, and Richard H-----, of Louisville. Proved Aug. 6,1851 by Stephen Jerger, who appeared in court and said the above witnesses were not residents of Indiana and were engaged in business on the river. At same time Joseph Sermersheim appeared and swore the will was in the handwriting of Hurst. pp. 28-29.

KELSO, THOMAS. Will dated 4-5-1821; proved 11-9-1840. Heirs: wife Jane; nephew, Moses Kelso, son of John. Executor: nephew, Joseph Kelso. Witnesses: Bazel B., Hannah, and Nancy Edmonston. pp. 2-3.

KRAMER, PETER. Will dated 5-5-1848; proved 2-4-1850. Heirs: wife Katherine, and any children that should be born to them. Witnesses: J. I. and Isabella H. Graham. Proved by Joseph Bramen and Phillip Decker, stating above witnesses were not residents of Indiana. p. 30.

KRAUSE, FREDRICH. Will dated 3-1-1850(?); proved 2-1-1851. Heirs: wife Catherine, b. Sehmiar; children, Christian, Catherine, Dorothy, Andrew. Witnesses: John Ernst Hacker, William Butz. Translated by Rev. Joseph Kundek and sworn to by him on Feb. 1, 1851. pp. 39-40.

MAIN, JOHNSTON C. Will dated 2-1-1841; proved 1-6-1843. Heirs: wife Sarah, and children (names not given). Witnesses: Lewis B. Wood, Hiram Webb. p. 9.

MEYER, GERHARD HENRY. Will dated 5-19-1847; no record of probate. Heirs: wife; son John Frederick; daughters, Mary, Engel, and Carolina, all minors. Witnesses: Henry Rodolph Afterhein and Powell Ghirkin. p. 27.

MIEULKOMAN(?), JOHN HENRY, of Ferdinand. Oral will dated 8-18-1847; recorded 8-28-1847; no record of probate. Heirs: Henry Schweghman, who "shall have all my real estate and personal property as a reward for service rendered me." Witnesses: John B. Pfoff, Gertrude and Mary Dorothy Schweghman. p. 20.

MILLER, JOSEPH. Will dated 3-27-1848; proved 7-19-1848. Heirs: wife Mary Ann; sons, Joseph, John, Nicholas, Conrad; daughter Mary Ann Fees. Executor: son Joseph. Witnesses: Henry Comingore, Dominick Erney. pp. 26-27.

NEWMAN, HENRY. Will dated 6-10-1841; proved 7-10-1841. Heirs: wife Catharine; son Charles; daughter Josephine. Guardians of children if wife should die: Herman Behrens, John L. (or T.) Dounce. Executor: wife. Witnesses: Gerhard Niehaus, Herman Behrens, Christopher Dufenduf. pp. 1-2.

NEWTON, JAMES. Will dated 7-28-1851; proved 10-2-1851. Heirs: sons, James C., William, Isaac; daughters Martha & Margaret Jain, $100 each; America Ann Anis(?), Elizabeth Howard, Mary Kendal, Barbary Hobbs, & Peter Newton, $1.00 each. Witnesses: Elijah Kendle, Job King, John B. King, Jr. Executor: John King, Sr. of Crawford Co. pp. 46-47.

PAND, FREDRICH, of Ferdinand Twp. Will dated 7-4-1850; proved 10-31-1850. Heir: wife Caroline. Witnesses: John Gerhard Hoffman, Bernard Heiler, p. 38.

PEWSEY, Thomas. Oral will dated 4-18-1842; proved 4-30-1842. Requests William Cavender attend to raising his children and Charles Pewsey be apprenticed to some trade at a suitable age. Administrator: William Cavender. Witnesses: Anson and Robert E. Cavender. p. 5.

SHNEIDER(?), JACOB. Will dated 12-7-1850; proved 2-1-1851. Heir: wife Elizabeth. Witnesses: Phillip Fetters(?), John Hoffman, Jasper Fetnay(?). Translated by Rev. Joseph Kundek. p. 35.

STEWART, JOHN. Will dated 9-13-1842; proved 11-8-1842. Heirs: wife Jane; sons, John, Robert, James; daughters, Jane and Betsey. Executors: James and John Stewart. Witnesses: Edward Woods, Jacob Shandy. pp. 8-9.

WAPKENBERG, JOHANN BERNARD, of Ferdinand Twp. Will dated 9-12-1851;
proved 10-30-1851. Heirs: wife Margaretha; son Johann Gerard; daughters,
Catherine and Elizabeth. Witnesses: Gerhard F. Derring, Johann G. Hoffman. pp. 51-52.

WOODS, EDWARD. Will dated 3-23-1847; proved 1-4-1848. Heirs: wife Sally;
if she should remarry land would revert to Ephraim E. Woods. Others(relationship not indicated), David W., Charles M., Mary Ann, and James G. Woods.
Executor: son Ephraim E. Witnesses: E. A. Glezen, David Green. pp. 22-23.

INDIANA MILITIA: BLACK HAWK WAR

Trouble that had been brewing between Black Hawk's band of Sauk and Potawatomi Indians and the Illinois militia reached a climax on May 14, 1832, when Black Hawk and a small band routed militia forces at a camp on Rock River in retaliation for the seizure of three Indians who had approached the camp under a flag of truce. Reports of the encounter spread rapidly and became exaggerated as they spread; some of the Illinois settlers living on the frontiers of that state fled south and east, causing alarm along the northwest frontier of Indiana. It was feared that the northern Indiana Indians would join the Illinois tribes and thus expose the Indiana frontier to Indian vengeance.

Upon receiving an express from Brigadier General Jacob Walker of the 20th Brigade, Indiana Militia, apprising him of the feelings of the settlers on the northwestern frontier of Indiana, Governor Noah Noble on May 27 ordered Major General Joseph Orr to "repair to the Wabash and in your discretion take such steps as circumstances may require, as relates to the procuring of arms, provisions, and the calling a sufficient force to the field, by entire companies, if increasing dangers demand it, or by requisition on each Regt. as pointed out by law if a stronger measure is not called for by the attitude and movements of the Indians. . . ."[1] The companies of Captains David H. Brown, Jesse Davidson, Samuel McGeorge, John W. Odell, John Roberts, and Daniel Sigler were mustered into service on May 26 and May 27 and attached to the 62nd Regiment under the command of Col. James Davis. After making an incursion into the Indian country and finding no hostile Indians they were disbanded on June 3.

The muster rolls of these regiments included the following names; those marked with an asterisk did not sign the payroll.[2]

FIELD AND STAFF OFFICERS AND MUSICIANS OF A DETACHMENT OF THE 62d REGIMENT

James Davis, Colonel
William M. Jenners, Lieut. Colonel
Hugh Milhollin, Major
James A. Groves, Adjutant
Aron Finch, Quartermaster
James H. Lyons, Issuing Commissary
John C. Mullay, Judge Advocate
John Sherry, Forage Master
Edward F. Richardson, Drum Major
Obadiah Campbell, Fife Major
Isaac Campbell, Assistant Fifer
Joseph Scudder, Drummer

DAVID H. BROWN'S COMPANY OF RIFLEMEN

David H. Brown, Capt.
William R. Kelsey, 1st Lieut.
Alban B. Slaughter, 2d Lieut.
James M. Bryant, Ensign
Sergts: Willis Brooks, E. C. Stephens, William Taylor, Jacob A. Franklin
Corpls: John H. Brown, Thomas Small, Mathew F. Logan, Nathaniel Bolin

Privates

James R. Dailey	Henry Robinson	Nelson R. Bell
James S. Pierce	Peter Burkhauleter*	James B. Trudall(?)
Andrew Miller	James Graham	J. M. Champ
James W. Ridgeway	Jonathan B. Tanner	John Eggleston
Robert Robinson	Thomas Collins	R. N. Stitt
Joseph Batesel*	Joseph Goldsberry	Isaac Cleaver
Francis D. Sunderland	Mark Jones	Joseph Cleaver
William Best	John Dolly	John G. McClelland
Jesse W. Murry	John Graham	John L. Piper
James Miller	George Tucker	Chockley Cleaver
Henry Bell	Daniel Pate	Thomas Leary(?)
Frederick M. Philips	George H. Piper	Servel C. Cleaver
Oliver Mahan*	Charles White	William P. Heath
James Shaw	David Jenners	
Marshall R. Parks*	Dudley Wilson	
William Creekpaum	John C. Riley	
William Stockton	John D. Johnson	

JESSE DAVIDSON'S COMPANY OF MOUNTED DRAGOONS

Jesse Davidson, Capt.
Henry Oilar, Lieut.
John McFarland, Ensign
Sergts: James Shriver, George Philips, Jacob Ferguson

Privates

James Cuppy	James Jones	John Murphy
Joseph Croy	Noah Jones	Robert Alexander
William Burk	David Hoover	Philip McCormack
James Chamberlin	George Stump	Samuel Knight
Newberry Stockton	John Philips	William Utt
William Anderson	John Smith	Peter Sunderland
A. Graham	Thomas Bilderback	Andrew Cortnay
James Graham	John Russell	Jesse Coleman
William Moore	James Barker	

SAMUEL McGEORGE'S COMPANY OF MOUNTED RANGERS

Samuel McGeorge, Capt.
Amos Allen, 1st Lieut.
A. W. Ingraham, 2d Lieut.
Sergts: Joseph Cox, Israel W. Cox, James McBroom

Privates

Joseph Crouch	John Bush	Benj. F. Brough
Absalom Ford	William Moore	Paul Cain
John Crouch	Chs. M. Page	Willm. Fox
Francis Ford	Demas Bard	P. H. Weaver
Joseph Tatman	Jno. Kennedy	Abraham Morgan
Matthew Killgore	Saml. Ford	David Patton
A. H. Cochran	Augustus Wylie	Mathew Orbison
Cornelius Conner	Simon P. Doyle	Thos. Reed
David Marsh	Morgan Shortridge	Jno. Fleming
Samuel Fullinwider	Jno. Bartholomew	Jno. J. Davidson
James R. King	George Nichol	Jno. Ross
Jonathan(?) Bartholomew	Saml. McCullough	Jos. R. Loveless
	D. F. Durkee	

JOHN W. ODELL'S COMPANY OF MOUNTED DRAGOONS

John W. Odell, Capt.
John Kennedy, Lieut.
Sergts: John Wilson, John Gilbert

Privates

	Paul Sherridan	David John
Samuel Rankin	Lewis Lickliter	James Parker
William Trimmer	William Robinson	William Coon
Thomas Moore	Samuel Moore	William Newell
Thornton Parker	Rufus Williams	William Hackney
		Benjamin Newell

JOHN ROBERTS' COMPANY OF RIFLEMEN

John Roberts, Capt.
John Murphy, Lieut.
Stephen Mendinhall, Ensign
Sergts: John Millhollin, John Huff, William Ivers, William M. Stretch

Privates

Levi Bringham
Joseph Rolls
Henry Stretch
John Gates
Daniel Wolf
Jesse Foust
Chas. Perenski
Peter Foust
Fielding Clevinger
Josiah Smith
Benjamin Childs
Henry Rookart
George Fleming

Robert Blue
George B. Cook
Anthony Foust
William Carden
Stephen Boyce
Samuel N Basey
Samuel Silvay
George W. Mott
John S. Forgey
William Geroe
William Morris
J. R. Moore
N. Robinson

William Foster
Alfred Thompson
William Henry
G. W. Howard
John Arnett
James Cox
James H. Doyle
Robert Williams
Samuel Seaton
Joseph Vanoy
Lewis S.(or L.) Whistler
George Barncutter(or Barnmiller)

DANIEL SIGLER'S COMPANY OF MOUNTED RIFLEMAN Putnam Co.

Daniel Sigler, Capt.
L. H. Sands, 1st Lieut.
J. W. Cunningham, 2d Lieut.
Sergts: T. W. Cowgill, George Pearcy, A. McGaughey, Charles Hanch

Privates

A. C. Stevenson
Henry Secrest
Ebenezer Smyth
W. D. Evans

Curran Smith*
George Haun*
Bentley Brown
B. S. Cunningham

W. Walls
Wm. Kitchen*
George Secrest

The above companies had just been discharged when Governor Noble received news of a new alarm from the citizens of Elkhart and St. Joseph counties caused by the reported murder of several men, women, and children at Fort Dearborn (Chicago) and the consequent mobilization of the Michigan militia. To meet this new threat, Governor Noble ordered Col. Alexander W. Russell of the 40th Regiment to organize a force of 150 riflemen from that regiment (in Marion County) to reconnoiter the northwest frontier. They were to rendezvous in Indianapolis on June 9 where they were to be joined by companies from Johnson and Hendricks counties. Letters were dispatched to John W. Wishard, colonel of the 57th Regiment (Johnson County) and to Thomas Nichols, colonel of the 61st Regiment (Hendricks County) to rendezvous on the ninth. The men from the three companies of the 40th Regiment and two companies attached to that regiment under command of Col. Alexander W. Russell met in Indianapolis as ordered and departed on the tenth for Chicago; from thence they went to South Bend and returned to Indianapolis on July 3 without having encountered any hostile Indians.

Among those who volunteered from Marion County was Stoughton Fletcher of Vermont who had just arrived in Indianapolis. His brother Calvin wrote: "He equipped himself with a rifle--two blankets, tom hawk, canteen--cap &c &c. His equipment & horse were appraised at $105. . . . He took 20 days provision consisting of parched corn, ground and mixed with sugar." 3

The muster rolls of the five companies under Colonel Russell included the following names. Those marked with an asterisk did not sign the payroll.

HENRY BRENTON'S COMPANY OF MOUNTED RIFLEMEN (40th Regt.)

Henry Brenton, Capt.
Israel Harding, 1st Lieut.
D. S. Vanblaricum, 2d Lieut.
James Porter, Ensign
Samuel Harding, 1st Sergt.
John Harrison, 2d Sergt.
Austin Davenport, 3d Sergt.
Thomas Shelton, 4th Sergt.

Laben Harding, 1st Corp.
David Small, 2d Corp.
Silvanes Shirtliff, 3d Corp.*
Lee Isaac, 4th Corp.

Privates

William Appleton
Henry James Brenton
Moses Barker
Evans Bristow
James Bristow
Lemuel Bryson
Henry Brewer (?)
Isaac Bassett
Henry Boles
John Brenton
N. Closser
Issac Coonfield
Francis Cossell
John Byrne
John Dawson
Noah Flood
Jonathan Glympse
Garret Garrison
James Furgeson
Joseph Howard
John Hooker

William Hull
Robert Hanna
John Hanes
Jacob D. Hudson
Henry Jackson
James Jones
Keney Jones
William Clark
Michael D. Kirkham
David Lough
William Lane
James Johnson
Nathan McLain
John McLain
James B. McLain
Sam G. Mitchell*
William Myers
Horatio McDowell
Larkin Monday
Samuel McIlvain
William McIlvain
James T. Marsh*

Thomas McDowell
Samuel Ray
James B. Ray
Samuel Seburn
Edward Sharpe
James Sharpe
Jona Stanley*
Joseph Smith
Samuel Smock
Elias Sympkins
John Tracy
John Thompson
Lewis Tyler
Michael Woods
James Walden
Asher Ward
Abraham Whitinger
James McIlvain
William Logan
Robert Robertson
William Troutman
Lorenzo D. Wright

JAMES P. DRAKE'S COMPANY OF MOUNTED RIFLEMEN (40th Regt.)

James P. Drake, Capt.
George W. L. White, 1st Lieut.
Bob McHatton, 2d Lieut.
Douglass Maguire, Ensign
A. F. Morrison, 1st Sergt.
Alexander Wiley, 2d Sergt.
Robt. McPherson, 3d Sergt.
Michael D. Faber, 4th Sergt.*
John D. Tharp, 1st Corp.
Andrew Wilson, 2d Corp.
Cornelius W. Van Houten, 3d. Corp.
William Hannaman, 4th Corp.
John C. Busic, Bugler

Privates

Charles Amos
Lewis G. Coy
Thomas C. Hill
Amos Dickerson
William Deford
Siias Drury
William Duncan
Miles Drury
Josiah Eaton
Eliott K. Foster
S. A. Fletcher
Peter Folsom
Gurden R. Gilmore
John A. Greer
Charles J. Hand

Elisha M. Huntington
Cuthbert Huntington*
Ezekiel Harper
Richd. M. Johnson Jr.*
John Jennison
John Livingston
James Morrison
William McPherson
J. L. Mothershead*
Amos D. McClure
William McFall
Anson Moore
Henry A. Milroy
S. V. B. Noel
Mathias S. Nowland

Samuel Richey
Thos. H. Sharpe
Arthur St. Clair
John Stephens
Wm. A. Sangster
John Steel
Harvey Wright
Benjn. L. Wilson*
Lazarus B. Wilson
Garrison Williams
Thos. D. Walpole
W. W. Wick
George Witham
John Jamison

JOHN W. REDING'S COMPANY OF MOUNTED RIFLEMEN (40th Regt.)

John W. Reding, Capt.
Harris Tyner, 1st Lieut.
Peter Winchell, 2d Lieut.
Joseph Johnson, Ensign
Joel Blacklidge, 1st Sergt.
David Fisher, 2d Sergt.
Milton White, 3d Sergt.
Thomas I (or J.) Head, 4th Sergt.
Stephen Yagar, 1st Corp.*
Andrew Morehouse, 2d Corp.
William Tucker, 3d Corp.
Henry Brady, 4th Corp.

Privates

Samuel Moore
Henry Cruse
Jasper Sellers
Alexander Brown
George Landrum
Francis Reed
John McLaughlin
Thomas B. Nelson
Robert M. Thompson
James J. Rooker
James Smock
James E. Eudaly
Thomas Gott

Thomas Brumfield
Samuel L. Smock
Henry Dougherty
Thomas McCollum
Johnston Reddick
John Cruse
John Emry
James Stapp
William Stuck
William Passley
James Passley
James M. Jones
Zebadee Miller

John Morrison (?)
Samuel Patten
George N. Plummer
William Plummer
Frederick Dysinger
Richard Howard
John Utter
Samuel McFarland
Samuel P. Letter (?)
James Wilson
Stephen Lane
A. Glazier

THOMAS NICHOLS' COMPANY (61st Regt. attached to 40th)

Thomas Nichols, Capt.
Willis C. Conduit, 1st Lieut.
John C. Julien, 2d Lieut.
William Faught, Ensign
John Nichols, 1st Sergt.
George Bailey, 2d Sergt.
Young L. Hughs, 3d Sergt.
Edie F. Johnson, 4th Sergt.
Lem Masten, 1st Corp.
Danl. C. Hultz, 2d Corp.
Thomas M. Moreland, 3d Corp.
Danl. W. Conduit, 4th Corp.

Privates

Thomas Butler*
Ozias B. Butler*
Preston Brown
Isaac Cassiday
Noah Crude
Clark Davis
Wm. H. Davis
John Downs
Martin Flinn
Sutherell Garret
Gabriel G. Gaylor
John Givins (or Gibbons)
William Glover

William Hamilton
Silas Hardwick
John Harris
Erasmus Hill
Samuel Hopkins
Lewis Jones
W. Kendall
William Carmichael
H. Lewis
Wm. D. McLain
Thos. D. McLain
Peter McRoberts
Alexander McVey
James Myers

George Nash
George Newel
Williamson Owens
Jonathan D. Parke
Isaac Pitts
William Shipley
John Stone
Abel Strickland
David Stutesman
Albert Thompson
Samuel Verbricke
Henry M. Voris
Bluford Wilson

JOHN WISHARD'S COMPANY OF MOUNTED RIFLEMEN (57th Regt. attached to 40th)

John Wishard, Capt.
Simon Covert, 1st Lieut.
Samuel Herriott, 2d Lieut.
Samuel Smiley, Ensign
David Allen, 1st Sergt.
George Titus, 2d Sergt.
Henry Drury, 3d Sergt.
Peter D. Banta, 4th Sergt.
Fielding D. Vorice, 1st Corp.
Simon Shaffer, 2d Corp.
Thos. D. Roberts, 3d Corp.
Timothy R. Thrailkill, 4th Corp.

Privates

Thomas Lewis
Joseph Tetrick
John M. Smiley
Squire Hendricks
Daniel Covert
William Jacobs
Samuel Lane
James R. Alexander*
John Henry
James H. Mitchell
Samuel McGill
Josiah Simpson
David Perry
Joseph Dorrel

Benjn. Mitchell
Perry Bailey
Jacob Patterson
John Q. Smock
David McAlpin
Garret Vandaver
Robert Farnsworth
John Brewer
William Perry
William Leach
Wm. M. P. Mitchell
George Bridge
Aaron Lagrange
James Sturgeon

John L. Dunn
William Norton
Jacob Walker
Isaac Vooril
John Banta
John Shaffer
Humes Sturgeon
Caleb Richardson
James Ware
Elsey Mathes
Powers Ritchey
William Williams
Simon Taylor
James Deetmore
Samuel Henry
John C. Jacobs

Meanwhile, Governor Noble had been in touch with Indiana's Congressmen and learned that Congress had passed an act on June 15 to raise six hundred mounted rangers; two hundred of these were expected to come from Indiana. Without waiting for additional word, Noble ordered General Orr on June 26 to organize a company of rangers to serve for three months, "keeping up an intercourse between our Wabash settlements and Chicago by selecting suitable stations, near the intermediate settlements, and keeping out parties of observation with daily communication." Orr reported on July 5 that he had recruited a number of men from the counties in his division and they had met at Attica on July 2 armed and accoutered for service and provided with provisions for ten days. "We took up the line of march from Attica on the 3d & arrived here (Iroquois, Ill.) on today all in good condition & good spirits.

"I shall make a small deposit of provisions here and leave a small corps of observation under the command of a lieutenant. From this place we will take up the line of march tomorrow for Kankakee River thence to some point on Hickory creek -where I shall select a suitable point to opperate our Range from.

I shall immediately inform the commandant at Chicago and such other posts near thereto and to the Commandant of the U. S. force in the N. W. of the object of our expedition and open a regular communication with our frontiers in the north part of the state and with the Wabash frontiers . . ."

The Governor's precautionary measures proved unnecessary; instead of moving toward Indiana, Black Hawk's band of Indians moved northwestward and were decisively defeated by the Illinois militia on August 2 in the battle of Bad Axe, Wisconsin. Noble wrote to Colonel Orr on August 6 to withdraw his troops and discharge them upon reaching a suitable point. "I regret exceedingly that the boys have not had an opportunity to achieve more, but as circumstances forbade it, you must all return, content with the reflection that you were ready to meet danger, have done your duty, and that your fellow citizens approve your conduct, so far as you have been permitted to act." The troops were mustered out of service on August 12 and marched to Parish's Grove where on the morning of the 16th, after being together 45 days,

MUSTER ROLL OF CAPT. JOSEPH ORR'S COMPANY OF MOUNTED RANGERS

Called into the Service of the United States, July 2 - August 12, 1832

County where from

Joseph Orr, Capt.	Putnam	
Eliakim Ashton, 1st Lieut.	Montgomery	Detached to post at Iroquois
Jesse Davison, 2d Lieut.	Tippecanoe	,, ,, ,,
Henry Slavins, 3d Lieut.	Parke	
James Gregory, Commissary	Warren	Furloughed for 10 days August 12
Nathan B. Stout, Surgeon	Fountain	
William T. Noel, 1st Sergt.	Parke	
Elisha B. Bell, 2d Sergt.	Tippecanoe	
Absalom Ketchum, 3d Sergt.	Montgomery	Appointed in place of Ristine
William Edmundson, 4th Sergt.	Putnam	Reduced to private by court martial
John Stephenson, 1st Corp.	Warren	
John Akins, 2d Corp.	Fountain	Promoted to 1st corp.
William Puett, 3d Corp.	Parke	Promoted to 2d corp.
Charles M. Watson, 4th Corp.	Tippecanoe	Promoted to 3d corp.

Privates

John G. Allen	Tippecanoe	
James Aston	,,	
Gabriel Bilderback	,, .	Detached to Iroquois post
Thomas Bilderback	,,	,, ,, ,,
William P. Bryant	Parke	On furlough
Thos. S. Barnes	,,	
Samuel Brady	Fountain	
Thomas Burge	Warren	Detached to Iroquois post
Eliott Boggs	,,	,, ,, ,,
Benj. S. Cunningham	Putnam	
John Cox	Tippecanoe	Detached to Iroquois post
Joseph Gray	,,	,, ,, ,,
John Caldwell	,,	
Stephen Cook	Warren	
James Collins	,,	
John B. Champaign	,,	Absent on extra duty
Joseph B. Cox	Tippecanoe	
Charnus P. Duffield	Putnam	
Eli Davis	Parke	Horse died in service
Lewis Depew	,,	
Benj. Davidson	Tippecanoe	Detached to Iroquois post
Newton Evans	Putnam	
Benj. Fancher	Fountain	
John Fisher	Parke	
Enoch Farmer	Warren	Detached to Iroquois post
Braselton M. Fugate	,,	
George Gates	Tippecanoe	
Lisles Gregory	Montgomery	
James Gilbert	Warren	
James Holland	Putnam	
George Hamm	,,	
Samuel B. Holcomb	Fountain	
Joel Hendricks	Parke	
Stephen D. C. Holcomb	Fountain	
Philip Hobaugh	Tippecanoe	
Jarvis Huntsman	Fountain	Detached to Iroquois post
John Huntly	Warren	
Anderson Johnson	Putnam	
David Jones	Fountain	
George Key	Montgomery	
Robert Lauderdale	Parke	
James W. Lacey	Fountain	Detached to Iroquois post

Edward W. McGaughey	Putnam	
John McCart	Tippecanoe	
James McDaniel	Parke	
Charles McMannus	Fountain	
John McCloskey	Montgomery	
Allen May	,,	
Jacob Martin	,,	
Jonathan King	,,	
Robert D. Norwood	Parke	
James Nicholson	Montgomery	
Jesse Nicholson	,,	
John Ristine	,,	Detached to Iroquois post
Joseph Rawls	Tippecanoe	,, ,, ,,
Elisha Rawls	,,	,, ,, ,,
James Rock	,,	,, ,, ,,
William Rodgers	Fountain	
Daniel Sigler	Putnam	
Henry Secrest	,,	
James Secrest	,,	
Thomas Starks	,,	
Moses Shelby	Tippecanoe	
William I. Span	Parke	
Joshua Stith	,,	
Jacob Staley	Warren	Detached to Iroquois post
Nimrod Stephenson	,,	
Adam Shriver	,,	,, ,, ,,
Jaconniah J. Semans	,,	
William Truatt	Montgomery	
Washington Walls	Putnam	
David White	Warren	Detached to Iroquois post
Jacob Wilkerson	,,	
H. H. Wilson	Fountain	
William Wilson	Montgomery	
Thomas Morris	Warren	Deserted July 3, 1832

Acts were passed by Congress on July 14, 1832, and February 19 and March 2, 1833, to pay the militia and reimburse them for horses and equipment lost. The pay was very small: $8.00 a month for sergeants; $7.33 for corporals; and $6.66 a month for privates. In addition some of the men were paid expenses for rations and forage, and eventually for horses lost.[4]

FOOTNOTES

1   See the *Messages and Papers of Noah Noble, 1831-1837* (Indiana Historical Bureau, 1958), pp. 105-108, 110-13, 114-15, 117-18, for correspondence relating to the Black Hawk War.

2   Photostatic copies of the Muster and Pay Rolls of the various Indiana companies that served in the Black Hawk War are in the Archives Division, Indiana State Library; the original documents are in the National Archives, Washington, D. C.

3   *Diary and Letters of Calvin Fletcher, Vol. I, 1817-1838* (Indiana Historical Society, 1972), pp. 180-81.

4   U. S. *Statutes at Large,* 4:533, 581, 613, 641. The Archives Division, Indiana State Library, also has the muster rolls of the men who joined the Mounted Rangers provided by Congress on June 16, 1832. The list includes men from Kentucky, Illinois, and Missouri as well as Indiana.